IN SEARCH OF THE
PERFECT
HOUSE

IN SEARCH OF THE
PERFECT
HOUSE

500 of the best buildings in Britain & Ireland

MARCUS BINNEY

WEIDENFELD & NICOLSON

Contents

Introduction 6

Bedfordshire
18

Berkshire
26

Buckinghamshire
42

Cambridgeshire
56

Cheshire
67

Cornwall
84

Cumbria
95

Derbyshire
102

Devon
111

Dorset
148

Durham
166

Essex
177

Gloucestershire
197

Hampshire
224

Herefordshire
249

Hertfordshire
256

Kent
264

Lancashire
294

Leicestershire & Rutland
303

Lincolnshire
315

Norfolk
328

Northamptonshire
354

Northumberland
382

Nottinghamshire
392

Oxfordshire
404

Shropshire
428

Somerset
454

Staffordshire
499

Suffolk
518

Surrey
550

Sussex
596

Warwickshire
618

Wiltshire
634

Worcestershire
667

Yorkshire &
Humberside
678

London
713

Scotland
734

Wales
796

Ireland
822

Jersey
840

Index of houses
and locations 854

Main index 857

INTRODUCTION

The search for the perfect house … I confess, I fall in love with them all, even if only fleetingly. But this is a game in which you can have many loves at once, losing your heart to houses of different periods in very different places. Above all it is a search for beauty. A perpetual quest for houses that are handsome or pretty, or have unusual, striking looks and unique features, or stand in a spectacular setting, or simply those that have been rescued from ruin and now stand proud again, ready for the next few centuries.

Over the past forty years I have seen many thousands of houses, of every shape, size and age. My travels began whilst at Cambridge in 1966, when I ambitiously embarked on a study of the architect Sir Robert Taylor, who, in the mid to late 18th century, had designed a series of brilliantly planned Palladian villas with rooms of unusual shape. Nothing prepared me for the state I found them in. Harleyford Manor, near Marlow, overlooks a lovely stretch of Thames, but was surrounded by rows of permanent caravans set several rows deep from the water's edge. Danson House was suffering from a severe outbreak of dry rot and about to be shut down by the council. Sharpham House in Devon alone remained unmolested and stood proudly on a grass sward sweeping down to a majestic wooded bend of the River Dart.

Heronden is Queen Anne perfection, with two tonnes of red brick and white trim.

The Old Manor Hall at Walton-on-Thames is an intact medieval timber-framed house just 15 miles from the centre of London.

Taylor's villas were also the subject of my first articles in *Country Life* in 1967. The next year I joined the magazine as architectural writer. I was now being paid to look at houses. I set off in search of buildings that would appeal to our readers and that had never appeared in the magazine before. My travels took me first to Palladian Constable Burton by John Carr of York, exquisitely faced in blemishless stone, and later to his equally elegant Norton Place in Lincolnshire. Early Georgian Barford House with its miniature crescent wings was one of my early favourites, followed by the Palladian casino at Ebberston Hall in Yorkshire, built as a summer retreat for a politician's mistress.

Soon after, I began a monthly 'Conservation in Action' page in *Country Life*, though, as one wag put it, the 'in' and the 'action' should have been joined together as most of the houses included were empty and decaying. The architect Clough Williams Ellis appeared in tweed suit and bow tie in our offices, despairing that the owners wanted to demolish Llangoed Hall, a glorious Cotswold-style mansion he had built fifty years before in the Wye Valley. Crowcombe Court languished after a fire with hardly any land. In Essex, Chelmsford Council had voted to demolish Hylands House, while later Highcliffe Castle had been surrounded by a barbed wire fence and left to rot in a public park.

All this interest culminated in the exhibition 'The Destruction of the Country House' at the Victoria & Albert Museum in London, which the architectural historian John Harris and I organised for the curator, Roy Strong. For the viewer a moment of high drama came in the Hall of Destruction where the 'stones' of tumbling columns were adorned with photographs of already lost houses. This brought home the sheer scale of destruction and caused a sensation. Before then photographs that had been taken of houses before their demolition had been mostly been tucked away in boxes in the National Monuments Records and never published. Both the exhibition and the accompanying book presented an alternative history of British architecture, including

Newton Surmaville in Somerset has a handsomely symmetrical gabled Jacobean front.

houses in many different styles, some sophisticated, some wonderfully old fashioned, but all either in a state of ruin or demolished.

The publicity generated by the exhibition prompted the foundation of SAVE Britain's Heritage, an organisation dedicated to highlighting threats to the nation's built heritage. I became the first chairman. It rapidly became clear that in addition to the immense toll of lost houses – which had reached over 1,600 by the time the exhibition closed – there were still more notable country houses standing empty or decaying.

When I started to visit these houses I thought I would find their setting compromised by a passing motorway, a nearby gravel works or a giant farm complex, but only on rare occasions this was true. For example, Stocken and Swinfen Halls were next to prisons or prison farms and a huge pylon stood beside Stayley Hall. But more often I found that they still stood in a good setting surrounded by parkland, pleasure grounds or gardens.

Some of the largest and most imposing country houses had only survived the lean years after the Second World War thanks to some kind of institutional use. Among them was Wentworth Woodhouse in Yorkshire, with the longest front in England, which was taken over as a teacher-training college. But after fifteen, twenty or thirty years, institutions tend to move on, leaving a grand mansion vulnerable again. Twenty-five years ago such houses looked condemned to decline as their settings were exploited for building plots. And the bigger the house, the more space it needs to sit comfortably in its surroundings. So often the house and its setting were designed as one. Divorce the house from its setting and it looks totally out of place.

I joined *The Times* in 1991 as Architecture Correspondent and soon after I was commissioned to write a column entitled 'Heap of the Week'. In time, this was succeeded by a 'House of the Week'. Estate agents recognised the publicity potential of the column and I recieved many invitations to go and look at houses of prime architectural quality as they came on the market. One of the first was Basil Spence's Gribloch in Stirlingshire, an immensely stylish and well-preserved 1930s house. Another was Ridgemead near Windsor, designed by Edwin Lutyen's son Robert.

I soon realised that the best stream of houses are those that are advertised week by week in *Country Life* – though in early days they would often be advertised on the back page of *The Times*. When I had worked at *Country Life* there was a well-established editorial policy of never writing country-house articles when the properties were for sale but I rapidly found that the great boon of visiting a house when it was for sale was that you saw the whole house, descending to the cellars and looking into every bedroom and bathroom, exploring the attics – sometimes filled with cobwebs and clutter, although elsewhere was smartly decorated to the very last corner. If you wanted to go out on the roof and survey the leads or the barley sugar chimneys you were welcome.

This was a very different story from the usual reception when visiting as an architectural historian, when owners tended to show only the principal rooms. Christopher Hussey, a 1920s predecessor on *Country Life*, drew a delightful cartoon of his predecessor, Avray Tippping, haring upstairs in order to catch a glimpse of upper floors. Hussey, both good mannered and shy, would rely on his wife to ask for the bathroom and be taken upstairs where she could report back on the interest of the bedrooms and the article-worthiness of the house.

* * * *

People often ask me what my favourite period is. My first love was the perfectly proportioned houses of the mid 18th century – classic Georgian. But the more you travel the more apparent it is that there are fascinating, finely built houses of every period. It is not just the architecture of the house that qualifies it but its setting. Every country house has a frame different to every other, whether the contours of the landscape, the parkland, gardens or the trees. They can steal on you by surprise, dramatically revealed in their full glory as

The Pavilion at Hampton Court Palace was built to stand on William III's bowling green.

you round a last bend, or stand out from afar. The appeal of this kind of house-hunting is that your dreams and realities can happily coincide. There is the utter perfection of a Georgian house like Culham Court with a mile and a half of Thames riverfront. Or the almost Parisian elegance of Eydon Hall in Northamptonshire, or Regency Maperton on the Dorset–Somerset border, voted by *Country Life* readers as their 'House of the Year' in 2005, with its verandas and conservatory surveying rolling lawns. Some of the houses in this book are set pieces of one period or another: timber framed clothiers' houses, grand mansions for Elizabethan courtiers, Jacobean halls built for newly rich lawyers, Charles II and William and Mary houses for city financiers, Queen Anne rectories, early Georgian farm houses with a certain old-fashioned baroque swagger, Palladian mansions built on the profits of sugar plantations or East India trade, Regency castles for newly created peers, Victorian piles for Manchester cottentots, Edwardian summer retreats and jazz-age Modern houses for engineers and manufacturers. Just as ravishing are the Brideshead, houses which have grown through the centuries to become an engaging medley of styles and materials, brick, stone, flint, half timbering and stucco.

As I travel around I am aware of the clear geographical distinctions in building styles and construction, rooted in local building materials, all of which have a part to play in the game of deciding on the perfect house. I am constantly amazed at the number of well-preserved 15th- and 16th-century timber-framed houses still to be found in Kent and Suffolk. Many of these were built for rich clothiers rather than yeoman farmers, reflecting the prosperity of the merchant class in the late Middle Ages. By contrast, Ellys Manor House in Lincolnshire was built of stone in the early 16th century for a merchant of the Calais staple where English wool exports were traded. Two counties stand out for their wealth of surviving Elizabethan houses. First, Devon, where quite plain-looking 16th-century manor houses built in the local stone often prove to have sensational ornamental plasterwork in halls, great chambers and even bedrooms with an impressive display of interlacing ribs, pendants, swirling foliage and portrait medallions. One of the finest examples can be seen in the barrel-vaulted great chamber at Knightstone

Winslow Hall in Buckinghamshire is Sir Christopher Wren's only surviving country house.

Manor. With these houses often comes handsome panelling and sometimes richly carved two-tier chimneypieces, as in the Job Room at Bradninch Manor.

Equally remarkable is the large group of Tudor and Elizabethan country houses in Norfolk, built of the local warm-red brick. These have their own vocabulary of stepped gables, tall chimneys and elaborate dormer windows. Much use is made of moulded brick ornament and, occasionally, terracotta. They boast some of the most romantic skylines in Britain and vary in size from modest manors like Little Hautbois to grand mansions like Breckles Hall.

Slightly later in period, Cromwellian houses form another distinct regional group and are found mainly in Surrey, in the style sometimes referred to as Artisan or Artisan Mannerist. They are mostly built of a homely, plum-coloured brick with the trim occasionally in stone but more often

Iver Grove in Buckinghamshire is a ravishing baroque villa of the 1720s.

in moulded brick. Typical features are horizontal bands of brickwork as found at Fulvens, or shaped gables as at Brook Place, built on an unusual cross plan with a central chimney.

There is another remarkable group of early 17th-century stone-built manor houses in Lancashire with a silhouette of close-set gables and fine mullion windows. Some of these, like Bispham Hall, have been rescued from parlous decay while others, like Clegg Hall and Stayley Hall, still await full repair.

Cheshire and Shropshire also have fine late 16th- and 17th-century framed houses, often retaining unusual features. One of these is the coffin drop at Churche's Mansion in Nantwich, where hinged floor boards fold back to reveal a view down to the hall below and a length of floor joist can be lifted out to make an opening large enough for a piece of furniture, or a coffin, to be lifted or lowered through.

For me, one of the most fascinating groups of houses are those built by 18th-century master builders such as the great Francis Smith of Warwick, whose houses, thanks to the research of Andor Gomme, are now recognised all over the Midlands. They, and those houses of other master builders such as Nathaniel Ireson and surveyors such as John Prince, are often distinctive compositions with lively baroque detail inspired by pattern books and engravings. There is a group of them in Kent, including Holliday Hall with its splendid shaped gable spanning the whole show front. In the Victorian period, Flintham Hall in Nottinghamshire has a wealth of inventive architectural detail as well as a grand and eccentric conservatory which is a not-so-distant echo of Paxton's Crystal Palace.

Heveningham Hall in Suffolk looks out across a Capability Brown park and lake.

Yet another still largely unexplored group is the large number of early 20th-century houses in Surrey, Hampshire and Berkshire, built by architects working in the Lutyens style. Long-derided as 'Stockbroker Tudor', many of them are well-built of good materials with a wealth of interesting features. Shielded in woodland behind banks of rhododendrons, they only come to notice when advertised for sale.

Some houses are attractive because they are untouched, providing glimpses into the history of past centuries. Others improve dramatically with attention and money lavished on them. When I first visited Ven House in Somerset, it was imposing but tired, and even a trifle dull. Now, thanks to the inspired work of Tommy Kyle and Effie Lecky, it offers a pitch of luxury and good taste, as well as astounding formal gardens. Moundsmere was built in the same baroque style two hundred years later, and has also benefited from restoration in the grand manner, with sunken garden, topiary and splendid vistas.

Setting provides another layer of attraction: an early Victorian house that comes close to perfection in every detail is Heath House near Stoke-on-Trent, commanding a glorious prospect of miles of hedgerow planted with noble Staffordshire oaks. And for breathtaking grandeur of setting, Encombe in Dorset is unsurpassed, nestling in a grand ring of rolling downs descending to the sea.

The use of water as a decorative element in both formal and romantic landscapes is a constantly attractive feature. Tennyson's moated grange is the very ideal of the romance of the past, a descendant of the defensive castle with its moat broadening out to into a lake as Caverswall Castle. There are formal baroque canals in the French style at Cransley Hall in Northamptonshire and Bradninch Manor in Devon, while at Blackland Park in Wiltshire the river is transformed into a broad canal as it passes through the garden.

Staunton Harold Hall in Leicestershire and Heveningham Hall in Suffolk stand on rising ground gloriously reflected in lakes below. At Ascot Place in Berkshire, lawns slope down to a large lake beside which is a remarkable grotto. Shrubland Park in Suffolk has magnificent Italianate fountains. Lutyens made exquisite use of mirror smooth sheets of water at Tyringham Hall in Buckinghamshire and Folly Farm in Berkshire. A recent creation of this kind is the large moonpond created by James Dyson at Dodington Park in Gloucestershire to mirror its noble portico.

The perception of beauty is made up of many elements. One characteristic which plays an important part in the look of a house are its windows, the eyes of a building, bringing it alive and giving it character. So often the multi-paned windows of early houses were replaced by single-paned, plate-glass sashes in Victorian times, giving the house a curiously blank look. Nevertheless, it is remarkable how much Elizabethan glass and leaded glazing survives, as at Churche's Mansion, Nantwich, where it forms perspective patterns of stepped cubes like those in contemporary marquetry. Sashes arrived in England from Holland in the late 17th century. First came sideways-sliding sashes – some still survive at Ledston Hall in Yorkshire. Next followed the more common vertically-hung sash. Queen Anne houses often retain sash boxes set flush with the window which, painted white, add greatly to the brightness of a facade. Before about 1750 sash windows had distinctive chunky glazing bars and although many were replaced by the slender glazing bars fashionable in the second half of the 18th century, many remain – or have been reinstated. Another appealing feature of these early sashes are number of panes of glass– sometimes set twelve over twelve or even sixteen over sixteen. Though usually painted, the slender astragals – as glazing bars are called – of the later 18th century are sometimes in oak or even mahogany, comparable in quality to the best cabinet making.

The staircase has a similar role to play in the 'feel' of a house. Early spiral stairs with worn stone treads are found in castles all over Europe but in Scottish tower houses they survive in a remarkable range of sizes and forms, rising not only from the ground but in corbelled

The magnificent portico at Thorndon Hall, Essex, was built by James Paine.

turrets springing out from the upper walls. At Breckles Hall in Norfolk a remarkable group of wooden spiral stairs survive, each tread solid oak. The typical Elizabethan stair is formed of short flights of five or six steps, rising round an open well or a square pillar. 17th-century wooden staircases often have extraordinary monumentality, as if carved in stone. The early 18th century saw a virtuoso display of elaborate corkscrew and spiral banisters. Their drama is often increased by cantilevering – flights which extend from the walls without support from below. Yet more elegant are the cantilevered stone flights fashionable in the late 18th century, often with the treads cut away in a scrolling curve. A fine early example is Wakefield Lodge in Northamptonshire, dating from about 1750.

Having considered the myriad different periods, building materials and details in different settings and counties I am torn between many competing claimants. Forced to narrow it down, my most covetable 15th-or 16th-century timber-framed house is Olden Manor in Suffolk. I do not think I have seen a more perfect Jacobean house than Anderson Manor in Dorset, or a more enchanting William and Mary house than Saddlewood Manor in Gloucestershire. Proudest and grandest of the houses of the age of Wren is Winslow Hall in Buckinghamshire by Wren himself, still virtually as he built it. For the early Georgian period, Chicheley, for me, is the loveliest house around. For the mid 18th century, I would choose Encombe in Dorset, a vision of heaven as Capability Brown might have imagined it. For the late 18th century, my choice is Eydon Hall in Northamptonshire, exquisite in every proportion and detail. For a ravishing house of

mainly Regency date it has to be Maperton in Somerset, while no early Victorian house has enchanted me more than Heath House in Staffordshire. For the Lutyens era, where one is spoilt for choice, my favourite is Folly Farm, in Berkshire. For 1930s International Modernism, it is Les Lumières in Jersey; for an ultra-modern house, Jacob's Ladder in Oxfordshire.

* * * *

The Manor House, Lindfield, has a pretty Georgian front to a 16th-century timber-framed house.

But to be able to play this game, to consider one's 'perfect house', other than as photographs in old books or distant memories, they must still stand. The big revelation that has come with writing this book is that dozens and dozens of houses which featured in my columns in *The Times* or appeared in successive SAVE reports on endangered country houses have found new owners and uses. It is easy to forget how desperate the plight of many of these houses was. Sometimes the owners would not sell or held out for an unrealistic price. Rarely could a district or county council be persuaded to serve a repairs notice. Sustained pressure and publicity has helped change this. Still more important has been the small but valiant growing bands of entrepreneurs willing to take on and restore these houses on a

Foxholm, Surrey is a delightful Victorian gingerbread house with stepped gables and latticed brickwork.

commercial basis. First came Christopher Buxton at Shillinglee in Sussex, followed by Kit Martin who from the late 1970s took on a steady number of ever bigger houses and adapted them as self-contained houses and cottages for ten, twenty or even more families to live in. In dividing the houses he followed the main structural divisions of the interior and made only minimal changes to the exterior. The gardens continued to be maintained as an entity, sometimes on a very grand scale, as at Tyninghame in Scotland. Martin also found that large, apparently awkward rooms such as the library at Cullen House, with shelving for 12,000 books, can quickly find a buyer wanting a highly unusual apartment and prepared in return to accept a much smaller kitchen and bedroom.

As Martin solved the problems of big, long empty or decaying houses, a growing challenge appeared in the form of major houses being vacated by government departments and institutions. The added problem here was that many of these very large houses had been surrounded by ugly additions which represented in themselves considerable size and value. At Wyfold Court in Oxfordshire, P.J. Livesey converted the vast French Flamboyant Gothic mansion into sumptuous apartments while the hideous cabin structures encroaching on the lawns were replaced by new buildings out of sight of the house. In Surrey and Sussex Michael Wilson, an architect turned developer, has given a new lease of life to large houses such as Snowdenham Hall and St Joseph's Abbey.

Two Americans have set up trusts to rescue and preserve remarkable houses, Fred Hauptfuhrer at Asgill House in Richmond-on-Thames and Dr Gerald Rolph at Allerton Park near Harrogate. The Spitalfields Trust, running short of 18th-century houses to restore in London, turned to Alt-y-Bela in Wales and now Shurland Hall in Kent.

Folly Farm in Berkshire is a Lutyens house surrounded by magnificent formal gardens.

A new, welcome band of of entrepreneurs is coming forward, interested in making large country houses that had mouldered in institutional use into grand family houses again. Anton Bilton has transformed Adderbury House in Oxfordshire, and Tyringham Hall in Buckinghamshire – where deer now roam in the park. His brother Laurence took on Capability Brown's vast and long empty mansion in Worcestershire, Croome Court, and restored it as a single house. James Perkins took on Dowdeswell Court near Cheltenham, a former nursing home, and transformed it into a version of Sir John Soane's Museum, filled with architectural and sculptural plaster casts. Perkins has also acquired Aynho in Northamptonshire, one of the large houses that came on the market when the Country Houses Association, set up to provide retirement flats in grand houses, collapsed.

In Nottinghamshire Chek Whyte has rescued a series of glorious houses from decay. First he took on Georgian Colwick Hall, languishing beside Nottingham racecourse, and restored it as a hotel. Then he tackled Clifton Hall, demolishing the rows of classrooms along the edge of the garden and restoring the main part of the mansion as a single house, despite its limited grounds. Remarkably the man who bought it one morning came back the very same afternoon to buy the rest of the house, which Whyte was about to transform into apartments, so he could return Clifton to a single grand residence for his extended family. Meanwhile Whyte acquired Bunny Hall south of Nottingham, then nearing collapse, for his own use. Now Bunny is restored, Whyte has acquired a still larger pile, Stanford Hall, complete with 1930s Art Deco cinema and sea lion pool.

In Cheshire, Georgian Lawton Hall, a house with excellent plasterwork, stood crumbling for years while the roof fell in and the external cornices collapsed, leaving the brickwork of the walls to dissolve in the rain. One day I arrived to find Georgian panelling on a bonfire in the entrance court. Remarkably the house was restored from the last stages of decay by Gleeson Homes and has been converted into apartments. Woodfold Park in Lancashire, an elegant classical mansion that stood a gutted shell for years, has been reconstructed as apartments by Reilly Developments. In Gloucestershire Gothic Revival Toddington Manor, boarded up for years, has been bought by Damien Hirst to become an art gallery. In Buckinghamshire long-empty Thame Park, used in the film *The Madness of King George* has been bought and restored by Paul Matthews. In Bath 1930s Kilowatt House, now known as Woodside House, is once again as white as a sugar cube, restored by local builder Mike Rosser. In Jersey Les Lumières, another stylish 1930s modern white house, has been immaculately restored by new owners.

The grant of licences for civil marriages has given a new lease of life to many major houses, including Vanburgh's King's Weston in Gloucestershire, Gibbs's vast Patshull Hall in Staffordshire and Salvin's Peckforton Castle in Cheshire, recently bought by a couple who were married there. These houses and others also function as hotels. Other, only slightly less large, country houses such as Somerset's Crowcombe Court, are family homes, but pay for their upkeep through regular summer weddings and parties.

To me the most romantic of all are the more modest houses where a young couple has rescued a long empty house from repair – Barge House in Herefordshire, for example, was without floors or ceilings when taken on by Sean Mason and his wife Sarah. My house of the year in 2005 was Gwerclas, magically revived by Steven West and Tina Shaw. 15th-century Maynards was lovingly repaired by New Zealand architect Quentin Roake while living there with his young family.

One of the purposes of this book is to show by so many examples that there is not just one perfect house but several hundreds. There are so many other beautiful houses which are not included, and many, many I have not yet discovered, despite forty years of looking. If any owner or reader wishes to tell me of their perfect house I will be glad to hear to hear their suggestions. Simply contact me at mbinney@msn.com. The search continues…

Les Lumières in Jersey is a brilliant restored example of the International Style.

BEDFORDSHIRE

CHICKSANDS PRIORY — Ampthill
Medieval monastery transformed in Strawberry Hill Gothick style

In 1988 Chicksands Priory was empty and crying out for a new use. Roger Freeman, Minister for the Armed Forces, had set up a working party to find solutions for disused or unwanted historic buildings on the Defence estates, and Chicksands was an obvious choice. But there was a hitch – the priory stood in the heart of one of the principal United States Air Force bases in Britain. However, there was no deafening roar of bombers lumbering up the runway, no Cruise missiles being manoeuvred through the gates, as Chicksands was the British headquarters of the USAF Security Service, a major listening centre announced for miles around by the 110-ft high Elephant Cage, a great ring of antennae, 400 yards across.

I found the Priory standing some distance from the operational buildings, amid spreading lawns with gardens stretching right down to the river. With the exception of the decidedly American patrol car that swept by at regular intervals, there was no obvious military presence.

Large hood-moulded windows have been set above a castellated porch.

Twin buttresses capped by obelisks frame the corners.

Chicksands was a house of the only medieval monastic order of English origin. This was the Gilbertine Order founded by Gilbert of Sempringham in Lincolnshire, born about 1083 and apparently living to the amazing age of 106. He was canonised in 1202, just thirteen years after his death. The Gilbertine Priory of Chicksands was founded as early as 1156 by Rose and Payn de Beauchamp with fifty-five canons and 120 nuns. Only about eleven such houses were founded and Chicksands ranked third in size.

The earliest parts of the Priory date from the 13th and 15th centuries. After the Dissolution of the Monasteries the Priory was acquired by the Osborne family. Sir John Osborne, who succeeded in 1699, wrote a delightful account of Chicksands for his son, which gives the lie to anyone who claims that preservation sentiments are a recent fad: 'Let no inducement whatsoever draw you to pull down one stone of the old building, being so antique as above 600 years, so strong and firm, so august and venerable … nothing of these new modern buildings are like it.'

Today it is significant principally as one of the earliest examples of the 18th-century Gothick Revival, spelt with a 'k' to indicate its engaging playfulness. It pre-dates both Horace Walpole's Strawberry Hill at Twickenham and Sir Roger Newdigate's fantastic interiors at Arbury Hall in Warwickshire. The architect was Isaac Ware, best known for Wrotham Park, which has appeared in numerous films such as *Gosford Park*. Ware removed the chimney stacks on the outside walls to create long even fronts with an impressive range of pointed arches on the first floor.

In 1813 the 4th baronet brought in the prolific architect James Wyatt, who built Fonthill Abbey for William Beckford. Wyatt was killed in a carriage collision that very year but nonetheless designed the entrance hall with richly ribbed vault and broad stair as well as a vaulted octagonal room. In about 1835 a tenant, the MP and collector Thomas Potter MacQueen, added a columned library in Pompeian style.

In 1975 the Friends of Chicksands Priory were founded, organising tours of the house as they continue to do today. The Americans left Chicksands in 1995 and the next year the base was taken over by British Intelligence and the Priory restored. The day when Chicksands is once again a house may still be far away but it is back in use and regularly open on Sundays in the summer.

THE HASELLS   Sandy
Mellow Georgian perfection rescued from years of neglect

I FIRST SAW THE HASELLS in 1980, standing empty and unloved on the edge of a large and beautiful Humphry Repton park. Yet the warm pink brick, the tall even rows of elegant sash windows and the crisp Portland stone balustrade around the roof were a perfect expression of the best Georgian craftsmanship. I had come to look at the new house just built by Francis Pym MP, but fell in love with the old.

At the outbreak of the Second World War, part of the estate was requisitioned for Tempsford Aerodrome, now famous as the departing point for secret agents parachuted into occupied France. Francis Pym inherited in 1945 aged 23, when he was still on active service in Italy. Soon after, the house was leased to the Government as a hospital. Conversion work was carried out cheaply and quickly and when the Hospital Board suddenly terminated the lease twenty-one years later it was in a wretched state, crudely partitioned, rubbish strewn through the outbuildings and dry rot spreading fast. Mr Pym, then Secretary of State for Defence, applied for consent to demolish.

Following a public inquiry, consent was refused by Pym's cabinet colleague Michael Heseltine, Secretary of State for the Environment. The next year the house was sold for a token sum to Kit Martin for repair and conversion as a series of self-contained houses, cottages and flats. His method was to restore his houses a wing at a time, selling the newly completed residences as they were finished and reinvesting the money. At The Hasells the residents had the bonus of a drive that led through the Repton park and an 18th-century terrace with a view over the Bedfordshire plain as well as an extensive Victorian woodland garden.

Even rows of tall sash windows give the garden front a suave elegance.

The Georgian entrance front with four-column portico became one single large house. The new houses in the south wing are entered from the courtyard behind, so the long south elevation with its gently projecting centre and ends was left unaltered. In the courtyard itself the only alterations were the removal of fire escapes and the creation of two additional doors. Every new house has a garden of its own, and the Summer House, which became a cottage, looks out over its own secluded garden of box hedges.

A 'Grange of Hasyseles' is listed in 1291 as belonging to Chicksands Priory. At the Dissolution of the Monasteries the manor was granted to Francis Pygott and after various transfers was acquired by Robert Britten, a yeoman, in 1634. His descendant, Baron Brittain, started a new house in about 1698. Debts forced him to sell to Heylock Kingsley, a prosperous haberdasher. One of Kingsley's daughter, Elizabeth, married William Pym in 1748. Their son Francis succeeded in 1788.

The Hasells appears in its present form in Repton's 1791 'Red Book'. A year earlier

Top: The entrance front as restored as a single house.
Below: The warm red brick front before restoration.

Lord Torrington, famous for his grudging remarks about country houses he visited, noted that Mr Pym had 'employed a large sum of money building a new house'. Insurance payments conveniently confirm this. In January 1789, The Hasells, with its contents and outbuildings, was insured for £3,200; by November the cover had increased to £8,000. Martin Cole, Pym's agent and surveyor in London, was responsible for the direction of the work and a later payment to Cole for a 'plan and drawing' of premises in Aldersgate suggests he was in effect the architect, evidence of the way skilled Georgian surveyors could produce houses of very high quality.

Francis Pym enjoyed his new house for more than forty years. It was he who first called his home The Hasells rather than Hasells Hall (the more phonetic spelling 'the Hazells' is also used). The house, and much of its furniture, was leased to the playing-card manufacturer Thomas de la Rue when Francis Pym II died in 1860 and his heir was tragically killed in a railway accident a few months later.

Seen across its large park, The Hasells still looks the grand family seat with no visible sign of the different houses within. The marks of its long years of neglect have vanished and, now that it is the home of several families rather than one, its future is more secure than it has been for a over a century.

HINWICK HOUSE   Harrold
Swagger baroque now back as a family home

HINWICK HOUSE HAS THE UNUSUAL DISTINCTION of looking almost exactly like Buckingham House, the handsome Queen Anne house that was remodelled to become Buckingham Palace. Both belong to a group of grand baroque houses in a distinctly English style, with rows of tall sash windows, flat parapets crowned by balustrades, and giant pilasters emphasising the corners and centre. These houses excel in superlative craftsmanship, the very finest brickwork, masonry and stone carving, as well as superb woodwork with grand panelled rooms and swagger staircases. Surprisingly, many were built not for grand aristocrats but for knights and squires. Hinwick House is the more remarkable as for well over three centuries the estate remained in the hands of the Orlebars, who built it, and was first sold in the mid 1990s.

It is best approached from the south-west, where, for nearly a mile, the country road takes the form of a grand avenue, flanked by closely packed lime trees so bushed out at the bottom that their formality is not immediately apparent. Just beyond the little village, Hinwick is gloriously displayed to the road in the manner of a French chateau.

Hinwick is built of local Weldon stone cut in blocks so thin that they look almost like brickwork. Beautiful Ketton stone (much favoured for Cambridge colleges) is used for the architectural trim. On the entrance front, which faces east, the Weldon stone has weathered to a warm gold, while round the corner to the south it remains palest oatmeal. The front door is surmounted by a fine swan-topped pediment. Unusually the house is entered on the level and the ground floor windows are set low so you see both in and out.

Part of the excitement is that each facade is completely different. The south front is dominated by a vast carving of Diana in her chariot drawn by stags and followed by hounds. Diana was the name of Richard Orlebar's wife, who tragically died in 1716, just two years after the house was completed. The carver was John Hunt of Northampton, who has been credited with the design of the house. He also carved and signed the splendid family monument in nearby Podington church on which Orlebar is memorably described as 'elegant, facetious and polite'. The west front is different again with a deep central recess and a second, fine hooded door flanked by a lead drain bearing the date 1710.

As the present owners had never lived here, the interior of Hinwick was bare, unfurnished and forlorn; but to anyone burning to restore a great house to its former glory this will be its main appeal. Hinwick is a sleeping beauty awaiting its prince or princess to bring it back to life. It has never been modernised, and there is only one bathroom in the old part of the house. The glory lies in its grand panelled rooms, complete with original folding shutters, brass door locks, stone mantles, stone flagging and oak floors.

There have been alterations – the large south-facing drawing room was made from two smaller rooms in the later 18th century and possibly even the stair was rearranged. It stands in the centre of the house rising to a large landing constructed of oak with turned balusters, though the sides are curiously of pine – perhaps they were once grained to match.

The proportions of the first-floor rooms are as grand as those below while on the second floor ceilings are lower. Here, unexpectedly, there is one very splendid panelled room, looking like a warm winter living room for the family. The roof has recently been relaid in lead and looks sound for a century. There is also a large Victorian wing to the east that was fitted out with tea room, bar and bedrooms by the Orlebars when the house was open to the public.

Hinwick offers fantastic potential for garden restoration. The large overgrown walled garden, entered through gate piers topped by stone balls, dips down to a stream. Beyond is a chain of ponds and little lakes. In front of the house are the remains of a ring of limes planted when it was built. To the south the park stretches to the village with a scattering of beeches and oaks. There are extensive outbuildings – including a dovecote and a 1600 cottage with a clock tower retaining its 1710 bell – approached up an ingenious horseshoe stair with built-in benches to enjoy the sun.

The original bills for the house survive, coming to the grand total of £3,848 4s 9d. Work began in 1709 and proceeded with amazing speed as the bill for glazing dates from May 1710, though fitting out was to continue for four years.

The house stands quite close to a country crossroads and one branch leads to the Santa Pod raceway, a flourishing drag-racing circuit three quarters of a mile away. Yet when I was there, the low-lying landscape was at peace, without a hint of the road noise found in so much of southern England.

Built of the local Weldon stone, Hinwick has an architectural trim of creamy Ketton stone.

LUTON HOO
Luton
Edwardian opulence awaiting revival as the Ritz of the 'shires

THE HISTORY OF LUTON HOO is that of both triumph and disaster. In 1767 the 3rd Earl of Bute began building an ambitious house to the designs of Robert Adam. Four years later work was halted by a fire but by the time another three years had passed, Bute had moved in and Samuel Johnson observed, 'This is one of the places I do not regret coming to see … magnificence is not sacrificed to convenience, nor convenience to magnificence.'

In 1830 Robert Smirke, architect of the British Museum, started to transform the house but in 1843 another savage fire destroyed much of the house and contents and Luton Hoo remained a burnt-out shell until sold in 1848 to John Leigh, a Liverpool solicitor and property investor. In 1903, on the death of his daughter-in-law, the estate was sold to the diamond magnate Sir Julius Wernher who employed Mewès and Davis, architects of the London Ritz and the palatial Royal Automobile Club in Pall Mall, to transform Luton Hoo into the most opulent Edwardian country house in Britain. Indeed Luton Hoo was more a palace than a house, designed in richest *fin de siècle* style. The marble dining room was hung with Beauvais tapestries and the supremely opulent circular stair housed Bergonzoli's statue *The Love of Angels*. Wernher's collection of masterpieces by Rubens, Titian, Hals, Hobbema and Fillipino Lippi rivalled those of the Rothschilds. When Werner's son Harold married Anastasia Romanov, the house was further enriched with Renaissance enamels and superb works of Fabergé.

The entrance front with the grand portico that formed the parting shot of Four Weddings and a Funeral.

For years, Luton Hoo ranked as one of the major stately homes of England, open to the public and still lived in by Wernher's descendants. All this came to an end when Nicholas Phillips, grandson of Anastasia, who still owned the estate, was caught badly by the sharp recession of the early 1990s; he committed suicide after an ambitious plan to build a business park on the edge of the grounds bordering fast-expanding Luton airport collapsed. Only the timing of the business park was unlucky – London's Canary Wharf fell victim to the same collapse of the property market – but the estate had to be sold to cover the debts.

The house as seen from the fountain garden.

I visited Luton Hoo after the sale when all its fabulous contents had either been removed (the Russian artefacts are now on permanent display at Ranger's House in London) or sold. Hotel use seemed to be the ideal solution as the public rooms were still almost as splendid as those at the Ritz, but for a long while no hotelier appeared with the resources for such a major project. It has now been taken on by Elite Hotels, who run Ashdown Park Hotel near Gatwick Airport – a former convent with a chequered history, which has become a flourishing 100-bedroom grand hotel. The throng that descends on Luton Hoo may not be as elegant as in Wernher's day but it is likely to be as numerous.

Opulent French interiors by Mewès and Davis: the stair with bronze balustrade (left) and a characteristic pier glass over a white marble fireplace (right).

BERKSHIRE

STANDING IN PERFECT SECLUSION just to the west of Windsor Great Park, Ascot Place is not just a villa for summer use but a full-blown country house with stables, walled gardens and lake. The house was brought to the pitch of luxurious comfort by Drew Heinz and her husband Jack, both great benefactors of the arts. It was bought next by Mick Flick, co-heir to the Mercedes Benz fortune, but sold the next year to a Middle Eastern owner for £19 million. The latest news is that this once immaculate house is suffering from leaks in the roof.

Ascot Place is a classic example of mid 18th-century Palladianism, extended by a pair of balancing wings. The architect was almost certainly Thomas Sandby, who was appointed Ranger of Windsor Park by the Duke of Cumberland. Ascot is not built of stone, as might be expected, but of strong yellow brick. A book by John Whitaker, *The Best* (1985), illustrates the work of H.H. Martyn Ltd, a company specialising in ironwork, woodwork and plasterwork, and provides the name of the architect A. Mitchell, who worked on the interiors at Ascot, probably in the 1920s.

J.C. Loudon, editor of *The Gardener's Magazine*, visited Ascot in 1829 and described the celebrated grotto, designed 'by the late proprietor Daniel Agace Esq' and executed under the direction of Turnbull & Scott. The interior may be due to the most dexterous grotto-builders of the day, Joseph and Josiah Lane. The mouth of the grotto was like a cave, and the small antechamber overhead had seats formed of rock. The main chamber, quatrefoil in plan, was lit by an octagonal lantern in the roof. All the walls were covered with clusters of glittering quartz crystals. Around the edges of the ceiling a double row of artificial stalactites descended, covered with more small white crystals.

The house and its spreading lawns as seen from across the lake.

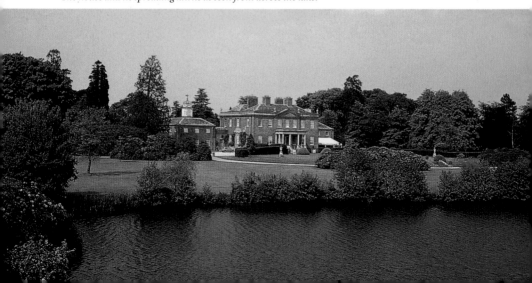

BEENHAM HATCH · Bucklebury
Farmhouse transformed with a Quaker-like simplicity as an architect's own home

To ADAPT AN ANCIENT EPITAPH, the architect Philip Jebb 'did the best of things in the worst of times'. Jebb was a true Palladian, born perhaps in the wrong century, who, from modest beginnings, built up an impressive list of discerning clients – all of whom combined a taste for Classical architecture with a passion for old buildings.

Not surprisingly Jebb's own house, Beenham Hatch near Bucklebury in Berkshire, is fascinating – not least for its almost Quaker modesty and simplicity. It stands towards the edge of the Berkshire Downs amid green fields and woods – one of a cluster of ancient yeoman farms and smallholdings which have existed for centuries between larger estates.

Known earlier as Hall's Farm, it was acquired by his grandfather, a canal engineer, on his retirement. Here his grown-up children lingered, becoming accomplished artists. Philip Jebb visited the house regularly, finally inheriting from an aged aunt in 1981. 'We decided at once to move from London,' said his widow, adding, 'Philip didn't approve of making houses huge.' As a result Beenham Hatch has no big rooms, only an intriguing cluster of square or almost square rooms leading one into another. Around the house, every outbuilding was brought into use so the whole place has the feel of a miniature village.

The oldest part of the house dates to about 1600. Jebb loved light so he replaced the tiny windows in the main front with an attractive three-part sash accompanied by a delightful bell-topped porch.

Philip Jebb kept the feeling of a modest farmhouse in his deft additions.

Jebb's alterations and additions suggest a house that has grown organically over the centuries, in painted stucco, pale pink brick and timber, all roofed in mellow handmade tiles. He had a penchant for playful Strawberry Hill Gothick and in the fanlight over the front door and the Venetian window above he used the characteristic interlacing glazing bars to form pointed arches.

When visiting his aunts as a young man, Jebb had always wanted to put in a 'proper stair' and he did this with panache by inserting a stylish Chinese Chippendale staircase in the centre of the house, opening on four sides into different rooms.

When a doorway was no longer needed, he didn't simply block it off but instead put in a small window on either side of the opening to form a unique and attractive double-sided display case.

The entrance hall doubles up as a library and dining room. At either end you walk through the centre of an entire wall of books – with windows punched through for good measure. Old fireplaces were carefully exposed – two are shallow brick arches with dagger-shaped bricks turning the corners. Log fires burn in all the grates and a wood-burning stove heats water for the radiators.

Upstairs 'the vanishing bathroom trick' awaits. Faced with the problem of introducing en-suite bathrooms in old houses, Jebb found there was usually an old cupboard that could be built into the wall, with one of the doors opening unexpectedly into the bathroom. Here *The Lion, the Witch and the Wardrobe* game is played neatly with the front of a Heals wardrobe.

A secondary stair leads up to the two attic bedrooms. Never one to waste anything, Jebb reused the spiral 'barleysugar' banisters of the old stair on the top landing. At the bottom, the balustrade can simply be unscrewed to make it easier to hump furniture to the top of the house.

Another tight spiral iron staircase up to the attic provides even more of a surprise. Finding that part of the roof space had simply been sealed off, Jebb decided to open it up as a tiny chapel, barely tall enough to stand in but just big enough for six people to attend mass.

Across the small farmyard stand a black weatherboarded barn and cartshed, and beside them an artist's studio which Jebb fitted up as his office with a desk in front of a large south-facing window.

Next door the potting shed has become a cosy two-bedroom cottage with its own stove – suitable for guests, grown-up children or elderly parents. The garage has been transformed into a studio.

The 13.5 acres form a country estate in miniature with vegetable beds, mount and lawn mown criss-cross fashion to create a downy quilt. At the end of the garden is a small plantation of ash and sweet chestnuts intended for coppicing for firewood. Mrs Jebb continued, 'I believe in the medieval system of pollarding. If you cut the tree higher up the deer can't reach up to nibble the new growth.'

With the Modernist credo triumphant on every side, Jebb used to say, 'I'm not a proper architect.' Seeing what he achieved in so small a compass at Beenham, it is tantalising to think what he could have done had he been given a commission for a magnificent mansion.

BENHAM PARK   Speen
Capability Brown mansion in Capability Brown park, lately restored

MAJESTIC BENHAM PARK WAS LEFT standing empty and gently decaying from 1946. This was an extraordinary situation given its prize position just off the old Great West Road outside Newbury. The vast estate with numerous gate lodges was a private Elysium with a large Capability Brown lake in the middle, fed by the River Kennet. The owners, the Sir Richard Sutton Settled Estates, would put it on the market occasionally, but only for short periods. Yet all suitors were rebuffed. At one time there was even an application to demolish it.

The large house was built in the early 1770s for the 6th Lord Craven to the designs of Henry Holland in collaboration with his father-in-law, Capability Brown. Lord Craven's heir then sold the house to his mother's second husband, the Margrave of Anspach in Germany. An attic storey was added in 1870. Finding the gates unexpectedly open at dusk one evening I drove into the vast park, growing increasingly excited as the great mansion with its noble Ionic portico swept into view. Then suddenly I noticed I was being tailed by a car with no lights. A gentle dash for the gates beckoned.

In 1983, soon after my excursion, Benham's long agony came to an end when it was sold and converted into offices. The price came in the form of large though reasonably discreet additions. The lake was dredged and the park restored showing the house to its best advantage. There is little hope now that Benham will be restored as one grand residence but its future as prestige offices looks secure.

The house was left for years while the grass grew long and visitors peered through the windows.

BOWDEN   Pangbourne

Richly detailed Arts and Crafts house on a balmy stretch of the Thames

THERE IS A SPECIAL CACHET in any house that is an autograph and little-touched work of a first-class architect, as Bowden is of Arnold Mitchell.

Among the most covetable of all English houses are the remarkable group of architect-designed homes built in the ten years before and after 1900. This was a golden age of good craftsmanship when houses were superbly built of first-class building materials. Above all, these houses are a *tout ensemble*, designed to be all of a piece, with every detail of the interior often designed by the architect. This applies whether the houses are avant-garde and Art Nouveau or more in the cottage-vernacular tradition.

They are associated above all with names like Voysey, Lutyens and Baillie-Scott but with these lions ranked a series of others, now rather forgotten. One of the ablest and most prolific was Arnold Mitchell. Mitchell's specialities were houses, schools and parish halls. He made a brilliant start as a young architect, establishing his own practice at the age of 22 after winning the coveted Soane Medallion and a Silver Medal at the Royal Academy Schools.

The excitement of Mitchell's house Bowden at Pangbourne is that it is an almost complete time-warp, barely touched since it was completed. Even the original chestnut-brown glazed tiles remain in the cloakrooms and bathrooms. Bowden stands in the grand rolling country immediately above Pangbourne on the River Thames – a stretch of river that still contains an Edwardian air of contentment worthy of *The Wind in the Willows*. From the upper windows are long glorious views across the river valley to Oxfordshire.

Externally it is a delightful and rather superior form of gingerbread house with tall chimneys and overhanging gables supported on sculpted brackets. The first floor is an extensive essay in tile-hanging – with scalloped tiles used to clad even the service wing at the north end.

Bay windows are everywhere, one an elaborate Elizabethan oriel built of golden honey-coloured stone. Unusually the windows are all set very close to the ground. 'It's as if it was built for a very small man who wanted to feel taller,' said my guide. He also had an intriguing theory that the house was built for a submariner (a very early one) as many of the doors are decidedly narrow and inset in shallow rounded arches such as you might find in a bulkhead.

The quality of detail in the house is apparent just from the letter box – as amusing as those of Art Nouveau houses in Brussels – with handle and doorbell inset.

The desire to create a homely feel is apparent at once as the staircase descends immediately in front, screened in by a forest of banisters to create a sense of enclosure and intimacy. These are grouped intriguingly in threes set first square on, then diamond-fashion. Around the top of the walls runs a frieze of swirling Art Nouveau flowers – a form of pressed paper retaining its lustrous copper and bronze tints.

The dining room has Elizabethan-style oak panelling as well as a highly elaborate brass lock and lock plate on a door that strangely leads nowhere.

The architect tried to echo the character of tile-hung cottages with mullioned windows.

Across the hall, the drawing room has a splendid inglenook fireplace with built in benches and a spyhole window on one side reflected in a globe mirror on the other, set in the panelling. The whole room has a cigar box feel, as if made entirely of wood – though the ceiling of the inglenook is lined with suitably darkened Spanish leather.

Beyond is a billiard room with a shallow wagon vault and the same cosy proportions. The built-in benches, usually raised up to provide a good view of the play, are here set barely 18 inches above the floor. Columns and panelling are in dark lustrous mahogany while the ornamental plasterwork has the engaging naivety of pie-crust ornaments, with thistles and roses for England and Scotland.

For many years Bowden was used as a junior house for Pangbourne College. Now the school has built a replacement on its main campus and Bowden is being transformed back into a private residence – the College is not keen to have another school on its doorstep.

Bowden cries out for the creation of a beautiful garden in its 4 acres of lawn which are fortunately well screened by trees as the road passing the house is a little too close for comfort. Against this you drive straight out to the open rolling hills of the north-west Downs, or downstream a mile to Pangbourne and one of the balmiest and best preserved stretches of the Thames.

THE MANOR HOUSE   Buckland
Elizabethan manor house to Georgian stable and back again

THE ENGLISH HAVE ALWAYS LOVED a good eccentric and the Manor House at Buckland is an eccentric in stone, an oddball house waiting for a new owner with energy, imagination and a huge reserve of determination to transform it into a magical place.

You get a glimpse of what the house could be from photographs in the *Country Life* article of May 12, 1915 when deep herbaceous borders overflowing with hollyhocks and lupins stretched from one end of the vast walled garden to the other. Kit Martin, the well-known transformer of large country houses, made a similar magical use of the walled garden at Tyninghame in East Lothian fifteen years ago.

The first thrill of Buckland is the rolling Oxfordshire country. Better still, for any lover of beauty and splendour in architecture, it has a most unusual and memorable approach. Turning off the A420 from Faringdon you are suddenly confronted by one of the most splendid Palladian country houses in Britain – Buckland House by the famous John Wood the Younger of Bath. Gloriously built of crisply cut limestone, it has a Classical centrepiece as tall as a palace on the Grand Canal, extended by low wings connecting to cupolaed pavilions. Better still, it stands perfectly displayed to every passer-by like a doll's house on a table – seen across a perfectly level lawn without a wall or a hedge to interrupt the view.

Your eyes are drawn from the house to an intriguing stable block half hidden in the trees beyond, built of golden stone that glows in the sun. This is your destination, the Elizabethan manor house of the Yates family transformed by the Throckmortons into a grand stable in the 18th century.

The tall arched entrance to the stables is through the large arch.

The turn to the Manor is at the small crossroads just beyond the Palladian house, along an almost private lane. First there is a group of former estate cottages then a splendid medieval parish church with the gates to the Manor immediately beside it. The glory of having the parish church on your doorstep is that inside it contains one of the grandest surprises in any English parish church, a sure way of astonishing your guests every time you take them for a walk. The nave is bare, even a little gaunt, and as a result the Victorian chapel in the south transept bursts on you like a firework. Here are glorious mosaics in ravishing pinks, blues and golds and a whole choir of angels, saints, prophets and martyrs with the verses of the *Te Deum* inscribed around them. It's the gift of William West, a famously bad-tempered director of the Great Western Railway evidently seeking to make amends for his sins on earth, and was designed by Henry Holiday working with James Powell & Sons.

The Manor looks out over the grass of the park towards the Palladian house. The delight is the absolute openness with barely a division between the properties, as well as a sweeping view down to the lake, balanced by the absolute privacy of the walled garden behind the Manor.

The character of the Manor House is that of an 18th-century castellated folly with the playful flourishes associated with Horace Walpole and the Strawberry Hill Gothick style. There are hexagonal turrets at the corners with quatrefoils and battlements. Indeed it looks like the work of Sanderson Miller, a gentleman architect who amusingly tweaked the houses of his friends in Oxfordshire and Warwickshire. The centrepiece is a Gothick version of a Roman triumphal arch. On either side, all the windows are pointed, while on the short south front 16th-century mullioned windows survive with hood moulds to catch the rain.

The long garden front has more pointed windows and Y-tracery but an Elizabethan-looking centrepiece with grand bay window and continuous bands of mullions. The old *Country Life* illustrations show the bay window originally had a rich balustraded cresting with widely spaced balusters and obelisks and flame finials on top. If these were put back the whole front would be transformed. The dormers, now rather suburban, were also much better then with diamond-leaded panes.

Inside a greater transformation still is needed. A long broad corridor runs down the centre of the house on both floors, almost as broad as an Elizabethan long gallery. Happily, the windows at the ends give enough light for this to be a splendid space if hung with pictures, tapestries or even carpets. At the south end the stables remain with large Edwardian-looking loose boxes set beneath cross vaults carried on stone columns. The original built-in water and straw bowls remain in the corners.

There are spiral stairs in the turrets and a room on the ground floor that can only be reached from the room above. The rooms upstairs, mainly square in shape, are well lit with good views over the park and the vale of the River Isis. In one room is a pretty Art Nouveau fireplace with cast-iron grate.

There is a need to banish the traces of institutional use surviving from the time when the Manor was an annexe to the school in Buckland Park. Now that the main house has a sympathetic new owner restoring its Palladian splendour, there is scope for a matching transformation of the Manor.

CULHAM COURT   Henley
All the compact elegance of a Georgian villa

FOR A HOUSE JUST 38 MILES from the centre of London, Culham Court enjoys as glorious and unspoilt a setting as can be imagined. Standing on a gentle slope above the river about two miles from Henley, it commands a 180-degree panorama of the Thames Valley in which barely a building is to be seen, a view that is as pristine now as when Culham was completed in the early 1770s.

Better still, Viscount Hambleden, grandson of the second W.H. Smith, who bought the Culham estate in 1895, gave protective covenants over land on both sides of the river to the National Trust, safeguarding the landscape in perpetuity.

Culham Court comes not only with a mile and a half of Thames frontage, with the towpath on the opposite bank, but an estate of 650 acres that has almost regained its 18th-century boundaries, thanks to judicious purchases by the last two owners.

From this sylvan paradise you are barely ten minutes to the A404 fast link to both the M4 and the M40 and a sprint to Mayfair.

For nearly half a century, from 1949 to 1996, Culham belonged to Felicity Behrens, wife of the banker Michael Behrens. They entertained writers and artists, including Edward Ardizzone, who did many sketches while staying here. They also employed Raymond Erith, the great post-war champion of traditional architectural values, to design garden terraces overlooking the river as well as a delightful flint-faced swimming pool pavilion with an exotic Pompeian-red mosaic interior.

More recent owners, Patrick and Annabel Nicoll, have carried out extensive but careful repairs, transforming the house into the epitome of smart, relaxed and comfortable country living. Like a number of mid 18th-century villas in the Palladian style, Culham is built into a slope. What appears to be an almost completely sunken basement on the entrance side opens at ground level towards the river. The service entrance at the side has been opened to make an attractive walled terrace for alfresco meals protected from the wind and for children to play in sight of kitchen windows.

Originally the floor of the kitchen was sunk several feet to allow smoke to rise and prevent servants looking out of windows onto the lawns. By the simple tactic of raising the floor, the Nicolls have created a large modern kitchen set cosily beneath the vaulted ceiling. At the same time the servants' rooms in the attics were transformed into a children's realm, complete with four-bed dormitory, which is hotly fought over whenever there are large family gatherings. Behind the central gable a spacious cinema has been installed. Standing in the doorway, you look out satisfyingly through bullseye windows on both main fronts.

Culham was built for Richard Michell, who bought the estate in 1760; he had married an heiress with extensive sugar estates in Antigua. He repaired the existing mansion, but after a fire caused by the 'carelessness of workmen' he decided to rebuild entirely on the present site. Recent research by John Martin Robinson in the Smith archives has produced a detailed specification for the new house by the architect Stiff Leadbetter, who designed Nuneham Courtenay, near Oxford. As Leadbetter died in 1766, Dr Robinson thinks that the job of rebuilding Culham was taken over by

Garden terraces descend from the house to the flint faced pool pavilion.

Sir William Chambers, designer of Somerset House, which is set equally splendidly on the Thames in London. Drawings by Chambers for 'Mr Michell's house' dated 1770 were sold at auction at Christie's in 1811 but cannot now be traced. I would like to introduce yet a third candidate for the position of architect, as there is a series of features in the house that point to Sir Robert Taylor, who designed nearby Harleyford Manor on the Thames outside Marlow.

Those characteristics include the elegant cross-vaulted entrance hall with a screen of columns at the back, the handsome hanging stone staircase with exquisite scrolled iron balusters, and the very distinctive domes and vaulted corridors similar to Harleyford's. The circular reliefs over the fireplaces in several rooms are also similar to those in other Taylor houses.

The recent repairs have been carried out by the architect Robin Moore Ede working with the interior designer Chester Jones, formerly of Colefax and Fowler. They have removed partitions to form a splendid central saloon overlooking the Thames,

Culham enjoys a mile and a half of Thames river frontage.

complete with a newly purchased marble chimney piece to a Chambers design. A delightful feature of the first-floor bedrooms are cupboards, or rather shelving, fronted by striped canvas curtains. The Chinese bedroom has a delightful pagoda-topped tented wardrobe.

The bathrooms, as is the fashion, are almost as large as the bedrooms. One has a very neat shower cabinet half set back into the reveal of a door to reduce its bulk, and teak-lined to give off a wonderful aroma. The other great game in smart bathroom design today is concealing the loo. Here it is done with a newly formed *chaise percée*, a variety of wooden chair similar to the commode with the seat adapted as a flap.

In 1771 Mrs Philip Lypp Powys, whose eldest son married Michell's daughter Louisa, found the house 'not finished' but with bedchambers 'exceedingly convenient' and kitchens 'all very clever'. In 1811 she described another visit by George III, his Queen, princesses, thirty-two horses and 'numbers of servants', noting the King 'always goes into every room'. When he startled a maid doing the flowers, the monarch put on a naughty-boy expression, saying: 'Don't be frightened – I won't steal any one thing.'

Early in the 20th century Culham was home to the collectors who founded the Barber Institute of Fine Art in Birmingham; and then to the newspaper magnate Cecil King, who tried to oust Harold Wilson as Prime Minister when the *Daily Mirror* trumpeted 'Enough is Enough' above a signed proprietorial denunciation, which led to King's own downfall rather than Wilson's.

When the Nicolls bought Culham ten years ago they were intrigued to find, beneath a vast thicket of brambles, an extensive rockery formed by huge Yorkshire boulders brought up the Thames by boat.

KINGSTON LISLE

Wantage

Baroque front concealing theatrical Regency staircase hall

THE ROAD PAST THE WHITE HORSE AT UFFINGTON is one of the most exhilarating drives in southern England, below the ancient Ridgeway along the grand smooth sweep of the Berkshire Downs. Kingston Lisle lies sheltered in rolling parkland barely a mile away. Country house parks are often thought of as 18th-century creations but here Alice de Lisle had license to empark 200 acres as early as 1336. The manor was sold to William Hyde in 1538 and one of his descendants, probably John, who died in 1745, built the baroque front of the present house with prominent keystones to the windows and raised centre with grand arched window over a rusticated front door.

In 1749 the estate was sold to Abraham Atkyns, one of the speculators who made a fortune (as opposed to losing one) in the South Sea Bubble. His son, also Abraham, left the house to his nephew Edward Martin who, in a very English way, took the name of Martin-Atkins, to acknowledge his good fortune. The wings added to the house by his son Edward are shown on a large and delightful trade card issued in 1830 by a Lechlade builder with pretensions to being an architect, Richard Pace. The card provides small engraved views of twenty-seven buildings that he and his son claimed to have built.

The house's most astonishing feature was almost certainly added by the next Edward Martin-Atkins (1808–59). He introduced an entrance hall and staircase grand

The emphatic baroque keystones to the arched windows stand out clearly.

enough for an opera house, which it is tempting to ascribe to a leading London architect such as C.R. Cockerell, though no evidence exists to support this.

The front door opens into a grand barrel-vaulted hall with inset coffering that is as deep and rich as that found in an ancient Roman temple. This in turn leads to a highly theatrical vestibule complete with columns carrying Classical figures in drapery rather in the manner of Robert Adam's anteroom at Syon. Above, fan vaults rise to support the central circle of the ceiling while a richly modelled grand arch frames the view of a flying staircase beyond, which appears at this point to hang suspended in space. It looks like pure showmanship but there is actually a practical element to it, as the hanging flights neatly connect the rooms at different levels on either side of the house.

Today Kingston Lisle remains a comfortable family home, let on occasion to businesses that are seeking an escape into glorious secluded countryside.

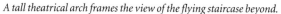

A tall theatrical arch frames the view of the flying staircase beyond.

LUCAS ALMSHOUSES — Woking

Charles II almshouses transformed into a delightful country house

IN APRIL 2001 ONE OF THE MOST BEAUTIFUL of all English almshouses was put up for sale with a guide price of £1.2 million – lower than many London terraced houses. It could have been converted into apartments by a developer, but not surprisingly the keenest interest came from private buyers.

The Henry Lucas Hospital stands in a secluded position looking out over the playing fields of Ludgrove School. Built of mellow red brick, it has the cottage-like proportions of many almshouses, lent grandeur by advancing wings and a giant triangular pediment inset with a coat of arms and topped by a cupola.

Externally the almshouses have remained virtually untouched since they were built in 1666. Leaded windows have never been changed to sashes, and large arch windows in the wings light a chapel and community room. At the back is a long range of single-storey outhouses providing a stable, workshop and stores for elderly residents.

The hospital was built and endowed with funds left by Henry Lucas, who also endowed a chair of mathematics at Cambridge University, which he had twice represented in Parliament. He died in 1663, a bachelor 'full of years and infirmityes', leaving his benefactions to be administered by the Drapers' Company. The almshouses were intended to house a master and sixteen poor brethren. The master

The long, low proportions of almshouses have a special appeal.

When the charity decided to move to modern premises, the building sold quickly as a private house.

was to read Divine Service every morning and evening and preach on Sundays and the brethren had to be single, aged fifty or over, 'of sober life and conversation … decayed in sickness or other misfortune and not by their own wicked courses, nor having of their own the clear value of £20'. Not all the masters were satisfactory, however, and in the late 17th century ten brethren petitioned the Drapers against the conduct of the master, forcing him to resign.

In recent years the Drapers' Company found the buildings increasingly expensive to maintain and ten years ago obtained permission, following a planning appeal, for a substantial extension in the walled garden. While the inspector accepted that this would damage the setting of the almshouses, he decided that it was justified as it would ensure their future. In the event, the extension was never built and the Drapers' Company instead obtained consent from the Charity Commissioners to sell the almshouses and rehouse the remaining residents.

This was not a building where the original interiors and layout remained unchanged. During the 1920s, when the almshouses were adapted for the use of married couples, they lost their original cellular arrangement and it was possible to walk the entire length of the building on both floors. Nowadays, only the handsome Charles II chapel retains its original fittings of simple pews, pulpit, large reredos and communion rails.

SHAW HOUSE
Newbury
Elizabethan clothier's house at last emerging from years of neglect

NOTHING IN ENGLISH DOMESTIC ARCHITECTURE exceeds the mellow splendour of a great Elizabethan country house. Shaw House on the edge of Newbury is an expression of the wealth and confidence of a rising merchant class, built in 1581 for a local clothier, Thomas Dolman. At the beginning of Queen Elizabeth I's reign, grand houses tended to be inward looking, built protectively round quadrangles, with few external windows, but Shaw House expresses a confidence in peace as well as prosperity, with almost as much window as wall, displayed for all to admire.

In the early 18th century the house was acquired by the Duke of Chandos, creator of the magnificent but long vanished baroque palace at Cannons in Middlesex. Shaw formed a staging post on his journeys west to his estates in Bridgwater in Somerset. The noble avenue leading to his handsome ornamental iron gates was crudely truncated by the link road from the M4 to Newbury; but this was nothing to the insult formed by a new school block erected barely 10 yards from the Elizabethan mansion.

Shaw House suffered the further indignity of being closed as 'unsafe'. First floorboards were lifted in virtually every room. Then the handsome panelling was removed for dry rot treatment to the walls behind. Worse, the former knot garden to the west of the house, still surrounded by a raised walk, had been filled with portacabin-style classrooms.

A dealer in antique books tried for years to persuade the council to let him buy the house, fill it with books and hold events there. Yet all the council was interested in was obtaining an impossibly optimistic sale price, unachievable because the house stood on a pocket handkerchief of land. In the end, however, perseverance paid off. In 2004 West Berkshire Council won a £4.1 million grant from the Heritage Lottery Fund to restore the house, open it to the public, use it for concerts and commercial events and make Shaw House a venue for civil weddings.

Large mullioned windows fill the interiors with light.

BUCKINGHAMSHIRE

CHICHELEY — Newport Pagnell

Built to the designs of Francis Smith of Warwick for Sir John Chester in 1719–25

CHICHELEY IS A HOUSE that looks as if it has always been loved. Its builder, Sir John Chester, gave all the craftsmen involved the opportunity to use the finest materials available, encouraging them to vie with one another in virtuoso displays of their art. Next came a long period of more than two centuries when it was left untouched by the latest fashions in decoration, furniture and gardening. And when finally in 1952 the Chesters decided to sell, Chicheley was fortunate enough to find in the late Admiral Lord Beatty a new owner with a sailor's concern for setting everything in perfect trim. Today, both inside and outside, the house has regained the radiant beauty it must have had when it was built.

When I visited in 1975, its future was uncertain. Admiral Beatty had died and a massive tax bill loomed but his young widow, now Lady Nutting, was determined to stay on. Chicheley now earns its keep through conferences and events, suavely arranged so they leave no visible mark on the interior or gardens.

Chicheley has long been as enigmatic as it is lovely. For many years a document dated 1701 referring to 'Ye new house on the hill' was taken as proof that Chicheley

The swept up-centre adds swagger to the front.

was built in about 1698–1703, even though the rainwater heads were dated 1721. As Castle Howard was only begun in 1699 and Blenheim in 1705, this put it in the vanguard of English Baroque. To some the excellence of the brickwork suggested Wren. Lutyens thought it was designed by a Dutchman.

Then in 1936 Arthur Oswald made a pretty convincing attribution to Thomas Archer, based on parallels with other Archer houses. However, building accounts showed the house was begun almost exactly twenty years later. The entries ran 'October 1719. Agreed with Mr

The wings have less stone trim but an abundance of fine brickwork detail.

Smith to pull down Chichley House, dig ye foundations for a new one' and 'Agreed with Mr Smith to build my house agreeable to ye model'. This was Francis Smith of Warwick, the Midland master builder, whose experience of working with leading figures like Thomas Archer, as well as a knowledge of the latest Continental Baroque, made him capable of producing as sophisticated a design as Chicheley.

The subtlety of the design lies in the ingenious build-up of architectural effects as one walks clockwise around the house. The north front is plain and not symmetrical and the cornice is moulded in brick. On the back elevation the cornice changes to stone and the windows acquire stone surrounds. On the garden front the giant pilasters turn from brick to stone and the windows have aprons beneath them.

The climax is reached on the entrance front where the Order changes from Doric to Corinthian and a full entablature emphasises the centre. Many of the most baroque details at Chicheley are taken, as was frequent at the time, from engravings, in particular the doorcases. The most unusual feature is the swept-up cornice, which suggests that the centre of the entrance front stands forward, though this is purely an illusion.

The Chester fortunes derived from Sir William Chester, Lord Mayor of London in 1650, who helped set up the first sugar refinery in England. Sir John created the three-sided canal at Chicheley in 1700 with the help of the famous gardener George London, who laid out the gardens at Hampton Court with his partner Henry Wise. Now that the canals have been dredged, the house is still more beautifully reflected in the still waters. Immaculate lawns, of breathtaking extent, form a perfect frame for both the house and matching wings.

The main staircase at Chicheley is a triumph of early Georgian craftsmanship with a trio of balusters to each step, one a corkscrew, one a spiral and the third a column, with extra flourishes such as an inlay of burr walnut on each tread and along the handrail. In Sir John Chester's library every panel and pilaster opens to reveal a cupboard. Add to this paint schemes by Felix Harboard and bedrooms by David Hicks and Chicheley is altogether the perfect house.

HARLEYFORD MANOR   Marlow
Delightful Thames-side villa saved from demolition

No COUNTRY HOUSE HAS EVER given me a greater shock than my first glimpse of Harleyford Manor. I had turned off the road out of Marlow and was looking forward to my first glimpse of the ingenious Palladian villa designed by Sir Robert Taylor. The house was there, perched on the edge of the Thames; but along all the banks of the river, shown in old *Country Life* photographs as velvet turf, was row upon row of caravans, not the travelling versions but giant cabins parked on hard stands. Harleyford belonged to a gravel extraction company. It had served for a while as a clubhouse for the caravanners but was now barely used.

The house was built in 1755 for Sir William Clayton. He was descended from Sir Robert Clayton who the diarist John Evelyn had described as 'a prodigious rich scrivener' or moneylender. The Claytons' many guests over the next 150 years included Emperor Napoleon III of France, Benjamin Disraeli and Kenneth Grahame, author of *The Wind in the Willows*, the classic tale of life on the banks of the Thames.

Mrs Lybbe Powis, who visited the house in 1767, noted that 'the whole of the offices are so contained in a pit as to be perfectly invisible – a great addition to the look of any place'. Entering the empty house I was fascinated to find that inside Taylor had made great play with niches, vaults and small domes in the entrance lobby and corridors. The main staircase had a pretty Chinese Chippendale balustrade and was surrounded at first floor level by an arcaded gallery leading to the bedrooms. In several rooms the doors and window shutters had octagonal panels to match the glazing of the windows, another Taylor signature. The tall wall panels of the saloon were still inset with lifelike plasterwork trophies of musical and gardening instruments, while in the library were mahogany bookcases set in niches, flanked by busts of great authors set on bracket. But the furniture had gone and the house stood forlorn and empty.

For years the grounds were filled with caravans.

The house has now had its unusual octagonal glazing restored.

Taylor liked to vary his plans with curved and three-sided or canted bays. Harleyford had a tall drum-shape bay towards the river and a canted bay on one side creating an unusual asymmetrical plan.

Several years after my first visit, the inevitable happened. The owners sought permission to demolish the house. They had no use for it. They were unwilling to sell as it stood in the centre of their estate. The case went to inquiry. It seemed incredible that SAVE had to fight prolonged battles to secure a reprieve for three of Taylor's most important Palladian villas – Harleyford, Barlaston in Staffordshire and Danson in Kent. But the long hard fight paid off.

When I next visited Harleyford the caravans had miraculously disappeared. Velvet-smooth lawns ran down from the house to the river extending several hundred yards downstream. A long line of pleasure boats was moored along the banks, and the house had been restored as a club house for the marina. Timber chalets from Scandinavia were hidden in the woods and available as holiday homes. Inside they were comfortably cosy and rather pretty. Still better was to visit the website and find Harleyford described as 'a splendid red brick Georgian, Grade I listed, Manor House … lovingly restored to an award-winning standard by the Folley family'.

HOLLY MOUNT   Beaconsfield
Built to the designs of leading Arts and Crafts architect Charles Voysey in 1905

HOLLY MOUNT IS AS PERFECT AND COMPLETE an example of a small Charles Voysey house as one can hope to find, quite astonishingly little altered since it was built. Even the tall oak garden gate in its freestanding frame remains – in a fragile state, it is true. The slate paving stones are exactly as Voysey laid them – set three wide on the main garden path leading from the road. Over the door is the exquisitely lettered slate name plaque carved with sprigs of ivy and the date 1907.

Voysey liked to give his houses a thick enduring coat of harling to ensure they remained cosy and warm in all weathers. Colour comes from the warm golden stone with which he dressed the windows. It is smooth and blemishless and without mouldings of any kind. The drip courses above the windows are formed of level rows of brick tiles with a little skirt of render above to throw the rain off. On the end of the gable there are three layers of these hood moulds, all ingeniously placed to prevent staining.

The front door is a delight – a large sixteen pane porthole or 'bullseye' under its own hooped drip mould with the original tiny letter box. A Voysey signature is the use of green-tinged Westmoreland roof slates and here they are carefully graded, becoming gradually larger as they descend the roof with a band of narrower slates just before the characteristic splay at the bottom. On the garden side is another delightful quirk – the rainwater gutter is carried across in front of the dormer windows supported on leggy iron brackets, like a miniature canal on an acqueduct.

The house was built for C.T. Burke, who had already commissioned one house from Voysey, and since then had had only four owners before it came on to the market in 2004.

The bands of mullioned windows contrast with the bull's eye window in the front door.

Voysey loved the simple domesticity of the English cottage, and hated the rattle of sash windows and the accompanying draughts. Here virtually every window is a Voysey original – formed in lead with a long latch that can be fixed in three positions – closed, wide open and just under half way. His bottle-green tiles survive on every inner sill. The blue-grey-tinged slate floors are dark but with a sheen that reflects the light. All the main rooms have Voysey fireplaces with brick tiled arches. In the kitchen is a built-in Welsh dresser with handles in the form of perfectly shaped dewdrops.

Voysey's characteristic harling and grey slates can be seen clearly.

In an article on 'The English Home' in 1911, Voysey set out his views. 'We must shake off the fashionable convention of obedience to style.' In place he set quality of 'repose, cheerfulness, simplicity, breadth, warmth, quietness in storm, economy of up-keep … harmony with surroundings, absence of dark passages or places, evenness of temperature'. Warm houses, he said, called for solid floors, avoiding the damp cold air beneath. Fireplaces must be fed with air through small flues direct from outside to avoid draughts under doors.

Voysey rooms have no cornices and only minimal skirtings. He railed against 'miles of inane moulding' but his particular abhorrence was for Italianate high ceilings. Rooms 'in good proportion to their size are easier to warm, to ventilate and to light.' If someone asked why in a room of 18 ft by 12 ft they could not have a ceiling of 10 ft or 12 ft high Voysey anwered, 'It would be wasteful and, therefore unfit and ugly. Such a room 8ft high would be just as healthy and more easy to clean, cheaper to build and to furnish, easier to warm and keep an even temperature and much more bright and cheerful, because the ceiling would reflect light into every part.' But don't tall Georgian sashes provide more light than shallow mullioned windows? No, said Voysey. Excessive height made rooms gloomy and also narrower. 'A predominance of horizontalism in any room is conducive to repose.'

Holly Mount has a typical Voysey stair with tall white painted banisters creating an effect like harpstrings. On the first floor landing the corner, or newel, posts are continued up as columns with his typical flattened capitals at the top. Here, as everywhere, the doors have latches and long blacksmith hinges running like arrows across the door. Another feature is the distinctive black cast-iron fireplaces, tall and narrow with tiny coal grates and inbuilt shelves. In every room the ornamental ventilation grilles survive. In some rooms are reproductions of Voysey wallpapers.

The one major alteration is that two extra bedrooms have been created in the attic with roof lights that sit awkwardly above Voysey's dormers. But the views over the garden to the country beyond are delightful. 'We have covenants ensuring nothing can ever be built here,' the owner told me.

MENTMORE TOWERS   Leighton Buzzard
Controversial sale of the contents of a great Victorian treasure house

IN JANUARY 1977 SOTHEBY'S ANNOUNCED it was to auction the contents of Mentmore Towers. A fortnight later SAVE published a lightning report *Mentmore for the Nation* with the first pictures of its remarkable interiors and contents. 'No proper description of it has ever been published – neither in *Country Life* nor *Apollo*, the *Architectural Review*, the *Burlington* or the *Connoisseur*,' I wrote.

John Harris evoked the treasures within: 'Some may prefer the fantasy of Nautilus shells in precious Augsburg silver gilt mounts, or others a knife-grinder in ivory studded with precious stones on a gold enamel stand … The fantasy, the richness is overwhelming. In the Limoges room walls and vitrines are crammed with choice 15th-, 16th- and 17th-century enamel plates and tazzas, ink stands and candlesticks, all by great enamellists such as Penicaud and Limousin, Reymond and Courtois. Layer upon layer; nothing cleaned or restored – all subdued by a dust that somehow accentuates the sense of what has been reposing here unseen for so long.'

Mentmore's architect was the great Sir Joseph Paxton and the foundation stone was laid on the last day of 1851, the year of the Great Exhibition made famous for ever by Paxton's Crystal Palace. The style, chosen by Paxton's client, Baron Meyer Amschel

Mentmore's rich, spiky silhouette was modelled closely on great Elizabethan houses.

The silhouette of the towers loom on the horizon from the valley below.

de Rothschild, was that of Jacobean Wollaton in Nottinghamshire with festive pinnacled towers at the corners, though the composition was more irregular and intentionally picturesque. The exterior, faced in pale Ancaster stone, was still in beautiful condition.

John Martin Robinson explained the advanced technology of Mentmore's fittings and equipment. 'The windows of plate glass in copper frames were provided by Alfred Garbett of Soho Square. Mr May, "an engineer of Dean St., Soho" provided hot water central heating for the whole house.'

An anonymous expert (in fact Simon Jervis of the V&A's Furniture and Woodwork Department) described 'the Entrance hall, lined with Caen stone and paved with Sicilian and Rouge Royal marbles ... the black and white marble fireplace designed by Rubens for his house in Antwerp'; the 'arcaded gallery at first floor level with a balustrade of alabaster and green marble'; the cornice elaborately carved with heads by Raffaele Monti, the well-known 19th-century sculptor, and the coved ceiling with walnut ribs.

Jervis described 'the Gobelins tapestries, a French Royal Savonnerie carpet, gilt Italian baroque furniture and gilt Venetian lanterns from the Bucintoro' (the golden barge of the Doges destroyed by the French in 1798). All this created 'a Baroque interior of quintessentially Rothschild magnificence'. The Green Drawing Room with curtains of Genoa velvet was filled with Boulle and ebony furniture and a collection of ivories. The White Drawing Room had curtains said to have been worked by Marie Antoinette and her ladies. The Dining Room was lined with dazzling white and gold rococo boiseries designed in 1731 for the Hotel de Villars in Paris with gilt Italian side tables and white marble candlesticks.

Rothschild's daughter Hannah had married the 5th Earl of Rosebery, strikingly handsome, immensely cultivated and very wealthy in his own right. Great things were predicted of him. Inheriting the title at twenty-one he became Foreign Secretary and then succeeded Gladstone as Prime Minister in 1894, partly thanks to his popularity with Queen Victoria. The same year he won his first Derby. Yet within two years his career was in ruins. Hannah had died in 1890, aged only 39, and in 1896, exhausted

The Great Hall has a balustrade of alabaster and green marble along the gallery.

by the divisions within his party, he resigned, never to hold office again. Instead he busied himself with his books and his racehorses, winning the Derby twice more and writing biographies of Pitt, Napoleon and Chatham.

Appropriately the superb furniture in Lord Rosebery's Sitting Room at Mentmore included renowned pieces such as the Augustus desk, the Royal safe and the Necker desk as well as bronzes of racehorses. The Du Barry Room, named for a bust of Louis XV's mistress, was filled with ormolu and Sèvres, the Amber Room with amber and enamel arranged in Boulle vitrines.

Our contention was that the Government should accept the present Lord Rosebery's offer of Mentmore and its contents for £3 million (a few months earlier it had been £2 million). Despite an immense national outcry we lost the battle, and instead the Government was forced to spend at least as much saving just a few choice pieces for museums. Fighting on, we won the war when the Government set up the National Heritage Memorial Fund which saved a string of great houses and their contents, including Kedleston Hall, Belton Hall, Calke Abbey and Fyvie Castle.

After the auction, which raised a record £6 million, Mentmore was sold to the Maharishi Mahesh Yogi and became the headquarters of the World Government of the Enlightenment. Now it is back in private hands, and was being used for filming when I last drove past, with plans approved for it to become a luxury hotel.

THAME PARK Thame
Left to rot by speculators, but now handsomely restored as a family house

'I'M LOOKING FOR A LARGE, INTERESTING, historic country house within 50 miles of London that needs some money spent on restoration.' How many times have I heard this? Well, in June 2000 Thame Park was that house, conveniently close to the M40 and Heathrow, yet utterly secluded in a vast ancient park.

The drive, then broad and pitted, was almost three quarters of a mile long and the house came suddenly into view on the right, shielded by handsome iron gates and ornamental balustrades. An even broader straight drive, flanked by spreading chestnuts, led up to a dream of a Palladian front, all in crisp-cut ashlar stone with a double staircase, almost hidden behind magnolias, ascending to a grand pedimented front door.

Thame Park is English history in stone. The Bishop of nearby Dorchester died in 971 AD 'in his mansion house at Thame' and the property was granted to the Cistercians in the 12th century. The abbey was 'in ruins' in the early 16th century but it was handsomely restored just years before the Dissolution of the Monasteries.

The Wenham family, who acquired the monastery, preserved the abbot's lodgings and a wing containing the abbey kitchens. A range with the new abbot's parlour survives complete with beautiful battlemented bay windows. In 1745 they added a grand west front, reputedly designed by the Smiths of Warwick, the greatest master builders of 18th-century England.

It was this wing that featured in the film *The Madness of King George*, when the King was brought here by force to endure a cure. The great hall looked half abandoned in the film and that was because Thame had been bought by a Japanese

The Georgian front as featured in the film The Madness of King George.

Late-medieval abbey buildings behind the main front were left standing empty and neglected.

couple who had been on a spending spree across Europe, picking up a string of fine country houses in Britain and France, including Glenapp Castle in Scotland and the Chateau de Rosny near Versailles. Money had run out, fine panelling had been stripped from chateaux and sold and the perpetrators put in prison as a result. Thame escaped unscathed in this respect and the original magnificent oak panelling – and some fine plasterwork – survives in some of the state rooms. These are mid 18th-century interiors on the grand scale with beautiful proportions and exceptionally fine carving.

The abbot's parlour retains 16th-century panelling with an exquisite early Renaissance acanthus frieze. The Wenhams, staunchly Roman Catholic, were under suspicion at the time of the Gunpowder Plot, and the 2nd Lord Wenham had his estate seized by the Cavaliers while Charles I was at Oxford.

The Lady Wenham who owned the estate until her death in 1870 established an intimate relationship with William IV, who made her a baroness. From her, the title descended to W. A. Wykeham-Musgrave, the owner of both Thame and Barnsley Park in Gloucestershire.

The house was last lived in by Sir Frank Bowden, of Raleigh bicycle fame. He kept a pet cheetah here, which he used to take on shopping excursions to Thame.

The lawns behind the house open onto a long 7-acre lake. There is a walled garden with large and once handsome hothouses, which in 2000 were begging for repair. The good news now is that Thame has found its prince and is once again a grand private house.

TYRINGHAM HALL   Newport Pagnell
Soane house embellished in an Austrian Baroque style

TYRINGHAM HALL IS THE FIRST MATURE WORK by Sir John Soane, held by many as England's most original and inspired architect, and was run for thirty-three years as a popular naturopathic clinic set up by Sir Maurice Laing, of the building firm. Faced with the need for major repairs, notably to the twin domed pavilions added by Sir Edwin Lutyens, the clinic placed the 35-acre property on the market.

The Soane house was built in 1792–7 for William Praed – MP, banker and first chairman of the Grand Junction Canal Company. The building of Tyringham, Soane wrote, 'engaged a large portion of six of the most happy years of my life'.

However, Tyringham's Edwardian owner, banker F.A. Konig, made several alterations not in keeping with Soane's original style. According to the new edition of Pevsner's *Buckinghamshire*, Austrian architect Ernst Eberhard von Ihne 'ruthlessly embellished' Tyringham 'in a Continental Baroque taste then fashionable in Berlin but entirely at odds with Soane's severe neoclassisicism.' He also added the flat-topped copper dome, which has a distinct resemblance to a Prussian military helmet.

The interiors – partly the work of Paris decorator Florian Kulikowski – are very much in the manner of Mewès & Davis at the Royal Automobile Club in Pall Mall, with each room handsomely treated in a different 18th-century style. Soane enthusiasts would like above all to see the entrance hall reinstated to Soane's design (von Ihne kept Soane's columns but cavalierly changed them from Doric to Ionic). A complete set of drawings and watercolours in the Soane Museum could also provide the basis for extensive reconstruction of Soane's lost interiors.

The building has now been brought back to life as a private house with deer in the park.

The house is reflected in the newly restored mirror ponds.

Yet the handsome imitation stonework, a technique known as stoneblocking is as good as that at the Ritz. The Louis XIV style dining room, overlooking the garden, has an elaborate frieze portraying hunting scenes, which proved too much for the clinic's vegetarian diners. 'Originally they were gilded but we had so many complaints that we painted them over in blue to match the walls,' I was told. Next door is a very pretty glazed library in French rococo style with built-in glass-fronted bookcases.

The architect Ptolemy Dean, author of a recent book on Soane, says, 'The further up you go, the more of Soane's work survives, including numerous fireplaces. The most important thing is to regain the top lit inner hall which has been floored over and filled in with tacky linen rooms.'

In 1924 König commissioned the famous Sir Edwin Lutyens to add a bathing pool more than 200 ft-long to the north of the house with twin domed pavilions, one a bathing pavilion, the other a temple of music but in reality a Theosophist chapel dedicated to the Supreme Spirit. Lutyens's work was recorded in its prime by *Country Life* but today the pool is empty, revealing unusual sloping sides. Until 1998 it was regularly used by patients but health and safety regulations then made it impossible, and the pool was drained.

The temple of music was suffering badly from the damp, and the surfaces of the malachite-green columns were turning to powder. Lutyens's striking vast mirror pools stood empty.

Tyringham's prospects changed completely when the house was bought by a man with a passion for architecture and an eye for fine house houses, the entrepreneur Anton Bilton who had earlier rescued Adderbury in Oxfordshire from years of institutional use. Here, as there, there are now deer in the park. The mirror ponds reflect the temples which are now rescued from decay. Hedges are smartly clipped and lawns mown in strips. Even ten years ago such a transformation would have been almost unthinkable.

WHITE GABLES   Gerrards Cross
Streamlined 1930s house built for a Cunard captain

THIS IS A CLASSIC AND STYLISH example of a white modern house built on a distinctive Y, or boomerang, plan, with the arms extending from a central rotunda tower. Dating from 1936 and sometimes known as Timbercombe, it was designed by the architects Mervyn White, Prentice and Partners. This is the streamlined look, long and relatively low when compared with Edwardian houses with their prominent roofs. Here horizontals dominate with a parapet ledge casting a crisp shadow. As with many 1930s houses, the fenestration is highly distinctive. There is a form of ladder window in the central drum and a window turning the corner in front of the secondary staircase in the wing. There are portholes too, a very Deco motif, but in this case highly appropriate as the house is said to have been commissioned by a Cunard Captain.

On the garden front the outer curve of the boomerang is emphasised by horizontal bands of windows with sills and ledges above the windows all adding to the streamlined look. Double doors lead into the staircase hall with the half landing just above the entrance to make maximum use of space. The stair rail is especially elegant – instead of using a traditional newel post to terminate the balustrade, the handrail turns down and 'dies' into the skirting, like a swan's neck plunged into water. Elegant too are the very slender iron balusters, which are alternately straight and twisted. Both the dining room and the master bedroom above it are elliptical in plan, rounded at the sides but with straight ends. The house has the additional luxury of an indoor pool, which has been amusingly frescoed to provide a panorama like that from the deck of an ocean liner, complete with barman bearing champagne in an ice bucket. A sunroom has been added with a continuous band of windows that are in keeping with the original architecture.

The entrance front with wings extending from a central stair rotunda.

CAMBRIDGESHIRE

THE PALE STONE WALLS AND WARM RED ROOF TILES of Sawston Hall are a perfect colour match. Some of the chimney stacks change to brick as they arrive at the level of the eaves, matching the tiles. The house is an unusually complete example of a Tudor courtyard plan with the start and completion marked by rainwater heads dated 1557 and 1584. These bear the initials of two members of the Huddleston family, Sir John and Sir Edmond, who were staunch Catholics and whose family continued to own the house until 1975. The earlier house, where Mary Tudor stayed a few days before she became Queen in 1553, was burnt down by the Duke of Northumberland, father-in-law of Lady Jane Grey. Mary made a gift of stone from Cambridge Castle to help with the rebuilding.

The main front is an almost symmetrical composition of five gables with large mullioned windows arranged in double bands – treble for the great hall and its oriel. There is no Renaissance detail – the Jacobean archway with coat of arms is a 19th-century introduction. The great hall is no longer open to the roof but entered at one end with the oriel at the other and a large, not quite central, fireplace. On the south side of the courtyard a spiral stair in a pentagonal tower leads to the first-floor Long Gallery, which runs the length of the south range. At the top of the stair is one of four well-concealed priest holes in the house. A private chapel in the south range was registered in 1791 – nearly thirty years ahead of the Catholic Emancipation Act. During the Second World War, Sawston was the operational headquarters of the 66th Fighter Wing of the 2nd and 8th Air Force. After serving as a language school it is now to be turned into a comfortable hotel, ensuring greatly increased appreciation of its architecture.

Built on a courtyard plan, the house was completed in 1584.

STIBBINGTON HALL · Peterborough
Delightful example of a modest Jacobean manor

IF STIBBINGTON HALL LOOKS LIKE THE PERFECT Cotswold manor house, the reason is that it stands in another corner of England that yields the very finest building stone. Just miles from the tiny hamlet of Stibbington are two of the finest quarries in England, Ketton and Collyweston, both of which are famous for their smooth creamy stone and noble stone roof slates.

Stibbington Hall can be found lying diagonally across a quiet lane from the delightful medieval parish church. The short drive to the hall leads to a forecourt with one of the most handsome 17th-century entrance archways in the country. Its charm largely derives from 'pierced' work at the top of the arch with a stone circle set in a flamed arch, similar to the windows of a gothic palace on the Grand Canal in Venice.

The entrance front, on a classic E-plan, is a richly ornate Jacobean composition, which has been subtly miniaturised to give it a more domestic feel. Though the first-floor rooms have mullioned windows that are just as large as those on the ground floor, two of them are set into the eaves like dormer windows in the manner later favoured by Arts and Crafts architect, such as Voysey. Four of the prominent gables are almost perfect equilateral triangles. This preoccupation with geometry is repeated in the circular lights that sit neatly in the centre of the gables. The main gable over the double-height porch is shaped in the Dutch fashion, while all the gables sport a trio of finials in the form of a single teardrop baluster with a stone ball balanced on top. A further flourish is added by the treatment of the double and triple chimneys, which are like square pillars.

The silhouette of the arched gateway echoes that of the entrance porch behind.

On the far side of the house formal gardens have been planted amid the spreading lawns, with a sunken garden with a pool in the Jekyll manner to the south and a box-hedged parterre with circular fountain to the east. While the entrance front is faced in smooth blemishless stone, the garden fronts are built of rougher squared blocks with a rainwater head dated 1835. It quickly becomes obvious that the Jacobean front was only one room deep, presumably added to an older house behind, which has in turn been rebuilt and extended at different dates. This impression is confirmed in the entrance hall, where the full-height panelling has been adapted to face a series of immensely stout pillars formed by cutting through an outside wall. The present owners have further enlivened the space behind the pillars with a colourful cycle of murals celebrating the house and its landscape.

As you walk through the house, each of the main rooms comes as a fresh surprise. The dining room has lustrous panelling in the William and Mary style; curiously, it is without a fireplace, although at one end there is an unusual recess where a chimney piece might once have stood. However, this omission is made up for in other rooms, many of which have impressive stone fireplaces, usually accompanied by a shallow Tudor arch suggestive of the Gothic Revival of the 1830s. There is also

The garden front is built of rougher stone with a rainwater head dated 1835.

a large L-shaped drawing room and a cosy library that looks over the forecourt. The staircase is said to have been brought from nearby Fotheringay Castle (where Mary Queen of Scots was executed) but its turned balusters, moulded handrail and swanky finials all fit the date of the house, so it is posssible that this is no more than a family myth.

The many clues to Stibbington's varied evolution, as with so many much-altered houses, lie in its changing owners, who in this instance include a long series of merry widows who quickly remarried.

There may have been an original Elizabethan house built by Sir Robert Beville who bought the manor in 1560. We know that the house in its present form was begun by Peter Edwards but he died in 1619, leaving the house to be completed by his wife Joan who was quickly remarried to the local rector, the Rev. John Hanger. All this history is proclaimed in the gable over the entrance by a shield carved with the arms of Edwards and his wife's family, the Knights. Below the shield are the initials 'IE' and 'IH', formed in lead and standing for Joan Edwards and John Hangar, as well as a tablet dated 1625 marking completion of the house.

After the death of their son Peter in 1667, Stibbington was bought by William Page, whose family owned the Barbican Estate in London. On his death in 1678, his widow Bridget then married William Wright, who is most probably responsible for the addition of the panelled dining room. On his death in 1708 the estate descended to Mrs Wright's daughter, also called Bridget, who lived here for nearly fifty years until her death in 1757, when the house was leased to a local farmer. A long period of gradual decline must have prompted the next occupant, Edward Steed Girdlestone, to carry out extensive repairs and improvements, and it is he who must have added the 1835 date on the rainwater head, though he did not move in until the next year – no doubt due to delays by his builders, just as common a problem then as it is today.

Edward enjoyed his new residence for only seven years, and his widow moved out just two years after his death in 1845 to enable her daughter to move in upon the latter's marriage to John Maylin Vipan. Their eldest son, Captain J.A.M. Vipan, brought new fame to the house with his creation of a natural history museum of treasures that he had gathered on his travels. In the same vein, he also built an aquarium, which *Country Life* said in 1904 contained 'the finest collection of freshwater fish in Europe'. Captain Vipan lived at Stibbington into grand old age. Upon his death in 1939 the house was sold to a Londoner, Philip Frere, whose unfortunate timing meant that he never actually lived at Stibbington as the house was promptly requisitioned as an RAF hospital. Following the war distinguished owners came and went at a breakneck pace – Sir Guy Thorold in 1945, Lord George Cholmondeley in 1949, Sir Peter Benton Jones in 1950 and Major Niall Campbell MacDiarmid in 1963.

Beside the house is a gabled coach house with a large flat above and an extensive walled kitchen garden, which has been well cultivated. For the modern-day tycoon Stibbington, being just half a mile from the A1, offers a sprint to London as fast as that which James Dyson commands from his majestic pile at Dodington beside the M4. And if this is not fast enough for you, there is also a helipad on the lawn.

48 STOREY'S WAY — Cambridge
Arts and Crafts gem by Baillie Scott

BAILLIE SCOTT WAS ONE OF THE MOST SUCCESSFUL Arts and Crafts architects, achieving renown with his house designs all over Europe. This house in Storey's Way is midway between a cottage and a small manor house, the perfect expression of the Edwardian idea of home. It is built in homely materials – limewashed pebble-dash-rendered brick with tile roofs and brick chimney stacks. All the windows are small-pane leaded lights set in timber frames.

The house was built for H.A. Roberts, secretary to the Cambridge University Appointments Board, in 1912–13. Inside it contains a wealth of Arts and Crafts detail. The doors leading into the principal rooms are of eight panels with iron or timber latches, while those going through to service areas are made of three vertical oak planks. The living room overlooking the garden has one of the large inglenook fireplaces that were in vogue at the time, complete with inset bench. The dining room has a plaster frieze and ceiling by J.C. Pocock and panelled doors with snakeshead hinges. Rooms have small brick fireplaces with slate hearths.

The large garden at the back of the house is laid out with a strong axis and divided into boxed compartments, a rare surviving example of a contemporary garden design for an Edwardian house. The house, which continues as a family home, has recently been restored by Diane Haigh, who was also the project architect for Allies & Morrison's restoration of Baillie Scott's Blackwell on Lake Windermere.

Baillie Scott began his practice unusually in the Isle of Man, moving to Bedford in 1901, by which time his articles had brought him international recognition. His charming gabled houses were praised in Germany for their liveability (*wohnlichkeit*) and influenced town planning in America and Scandinavia. Intriguingly a number of his designs are for buildings that remain unlocated though some were probably never built.

A formal topiary garden lies behind the house.

4 THE CRESCENT — Wisbech
Regency crescent built by a local bricklayer who made his fortune in London

THE ELEGANT, GENTLY CURVING GEORGIAN CRESCENT is Britain's greatest contribution to the beauty of towns. In Bath and Edinburgh they come in stone with full Classical trim. This plain-spun terrace in Wisbech, in the Fens to the north of Cambridge, is a reminder of the vanished brick crescents in South and East London, which long ago fell victim to the bulldozer.

So strong is its London character that the BBC chose The Crescent in Wisbech as the set for its production of *David Copperfield* in 2000. For three weeks the filming continued with freshly laid dirt hiding the modern road surface, while burglar alarms, wiring and street signs were carefully removed.

This strong resemblance to Victorian London is no mere coincidence, as The Crescent was built by a local bricklayer Joseph Medworth (*c.*1754–1827) who left his native town to become a builder in Bermondsey. By 1793 he had amassed a fortune sufficient to enable him to return to Cambridgeshire and buy the 17th-century house known as Wisbech Castle, which had been offered for sale by the Bishop of Ely for the princely sum of £2,305. The castle stood on the site of a Norman motte, or mound, built by William the Conqueror in 1087, and Medworth's crescent followed the circular line of that motte. In all, Medworth built nearly fifty houses in Wisbech, ranged around the castle gardens and along the roads he laid out, to the bridge, the market and the churchyard.

Mrs Medworth, however, had no desire to leave her comfortable home in Bermondsey and the amorous Mr Medworth gave two of the houses in The Crescent to his 'housekeepers'. His will details further bequests of houses to his children.

The Crescent was evidently one of the best addresses in 1909 when an aspiring young photographer named Lilian Ream bought No 4 and opened for business. Neighbours were horrified at the intrusion of trade in their select neighbourhood. Ream promptly built herself a studio in the garden and such was the landlord's concern that he demanded that if the business was not a success within six months every daisy in the lawn should be replaced.

Soon a stream of fashionable people was arriving at No 4 to sit for portrait photographs, including James de Rothschild, the local Liberal MP, members of the Peckover family (whose house in the town is now preserved by the National Trust) and the mayor, whose heavy chair was humped through the house each year to the studio for his official photograph.

In 1915 Lilian bought No 5 to move into while No 4 was taken over entirely by the studio. Here, she and her tailor husband (who had been apprenticed in Savile Row) lived until 1928 when Lilian was able to move to a still finer Georgian house.

In more recent years, No 4 has housed dentists, opticians and an antique shop, so it was a brave move when Robert and Carrie Norman decided to restore it as a single family house in 1993.

Carrie's mother, Jean Titmarsh, recalls, 'When they bought it, my husband just sat outside and held his head in his hands, it was in such a dreadful state.'

Deep white window cheeks brighten the façade.

Robert Norman is a builder by trade and Carrie is the headteacher of a local school. Now the work is finished only the 'before' photographs show the decayed state of floor, walls and ceilings.

Ream's studio has been flattened to make way for a lawn. The back of the house is now almost as handsome as the front, with a white wooden bay window and tall arched sash lighting the staircase.

The round arch over the front door has a distinct South London feel and opens into a pretty hall with a wooden stair rising in a curve at the end. The two ground-floor rooms, now knocked into one, have a Victorian atmosphere with ceiling roses and a marble fireplace with cast-iron coal grate.

From the street you would never know the house has a full basement, with newly fitted kitchen looking out onto the paving of the garden.

Wisbech, with handsome houses lining both sides of the River Nene, is one of the most atmospheric Georgian market towns in England. Yet with its location in a forgotten part of the Fens, one of the other houses in The Crescent was on offer in November 1999 for just a quarter of what would have been asked in London.

WOODCROFT CASTLE   Peterborough
Medieval castle reflected in a moat

A CASTLE REFLECTED IN THE STILL waters of an ancient moat is one of the most beautiful sights in all English architecture – so when one of the few still in private hands comes up for sale, a race is likely to be on. Woodcroft Castle is all the more intriguing as it is both unknown and hidden from view – closely screened by a belt of trees that might have been planted by the good fairy to hide the castle in *Sleeping Beauty* while it slept for a hundred years.

Though only the entrance range of the original castle survives, some of the windows have the distinctive 'shouldered' arches found at Caernarfon Castle, confirming the late 13th-century date traditionally given to it. With its walls of smooth Barnack stone and bold circular corner tower, it appears to have followed nearly the same plan as Edward I's mighty Harlech Castle built in the 1280s, though on a much more modest scale.

Today there are no evident traces of three other corner towers but the moat continues round a square plot, transformed at the back into a garden with box-edged beds overflowing with mint. To the south a slender bridge leads across the moat, while to the east a garden gate opens onto a path that allows you to walk round the outside of the tower. It is possible, too, that the castle was never finished – or that the ranges at the back were of timber and have long since disappeared.

There is no evidence of a drawbridge or portcullis and Woodcroft poses the question, long disputed by historians, of whether such castles were meaningful defences or simply built for chivalrous show. The moat today is all of 2 ft deep, beautifully clear but hardly a serious deterrent to a besieger. The original external windows all seem to have been narrow single 'lights', like those over the entrance, but old views of the castle show that the accommodation on either side was two storeys high rather than the present three.

The top storey is definitely a Victorian addition – there are survey drawings in existence that date to 1873 and so were made before the alterations. Early in the 20th century further additions were made at the back with long bands of mullioned windows – with the result that in one place a medieval window faces into the drawing room.

Tracing the history of the castle is even more confusing as historically it is part of the Soke of Peterborough, a kind of Andorra among English counties, which Sir Nikolaus Pevsner in his county series first included in the Northamptonshire volume and then transferred to Bedfordshire and Huntingdon. Today the castle is placed firmly in the county of Cambridgeshire.

The Manor of Woodcroft was held by the Woodcroft family from the 12th centurry to at least the 14th century for half a knight's fee from the Abbots of Peterborough, with the Preston family as sub-tenants for a quarter fee from about 1300. From the 15th century onwards the castle belonged to the Fitzwilliams, who held large estates nearby at Milton.

Like many English castles, Woodcroft's most dramatic moment in history came during the Civil War. Here Dr Michael Hudson, chaplain to Charles I, made a last

stand in true Alamo style against the Cromwellians. Hudson, a doctor of divinity at Oxford, was one of the king's loyalist servants, and had been imprisoned when the King himself was incarcerated on the Isle of Wight. Hudson managed to escape, but was caught and promptly sent to the Tower of London, from where he then managed to escape again. During the renewed fighting in 1648 he raised a large troop in Stamford, settling into Woodcroft where they were attacked by a large force of Parliamentary troops. According to the 17th-century Royalist historian Anthony Wood, Hudson and his men fought vigorously from the battlements but 'on promise of quarter, they yielded'. But no mercy was shown to Hudson, who was flung off the tower. Quick as Harrison Ford, he caught hold of 'a spout or outstone' as he dropped, but his hands were promptly chopped off by the merciless enemies and as he struggled out of the moat he was knocked dead with the butt end of a musket.

A century and a half later the castle appears in the autobiography of the pastoral poet John Clare. 'I was sent to drive the plough at Woodcroft Castle of Oliver Cromwell memory, tho Mrs Bellairs the mistress was a good kind woman & the place was a very good one for living.'

Woodcroft stands in the midst of the flat expanses of cornfield to the west of Peterborough, with the railway line only a few hundred yards to the north. Yet this is a place of profound peace sheltered from winter winds by the encircling trees. On the edge of the garden the former coach house has been recently restored as a self-contained house, suitable for holiday lets or for use by one of the family. Here the accommodation is all on one level but open to the roof timbers, giving every room an added sense of spaciousness.

Inside, the castle has a friendly Bohemian air and as it faces west many of the rooms are filled with afternoon sun. The stone-flagged hall is formed out of the entrance arch that led through to the original courtyard – the Northamptonshire county historian, Bridges, writes in the early 18th century of 'two large arches and seats of stone'. To the left is a large living room with hooded fireplace in the French medieval manner (presumably Victorian), which opens into the corner tower. Victorian ceilings in the rooms behind are of a rich rococo pattern that resembles lyncrusta, the stamped paper that was so popular at that time.

The former chapel over the entrance has a large eastern window and also retains a piscina, a shallow basin in a niche in the wall to the south of the altar that would have been used for washing the vessels for the Mass. Here the piscina has a pretty scalloped edge like an ancient flattened jelly mould and is provided, as was customary, with a drain.

The present owners, the O'Donaghues, have relished the wooden floors and bare stone walls. There are few fitted carpets and no fitted cupboards or fitted bathrooms. Instead they have scoured local salerooms to find unusual wardrobes, tables, settees and amusing baths and basins. The moat is filled with ducks and there have been swans, peacocks and poultry and even, at one time, a llama or two. As castles go, this is certainly one of the most homely.

The castle dates from the late 13th century but the top storey is a Victorian addition.

WOTHORPE GRANDSTAND　　Stamford
Grandstand built for the Marquess of Exeter

ONE OF BRITAIN'S MOST UNUSUAL small historic buildings, this 18th-century grandstand is the only one of its kind to survive in substantial condition. It was built for the Marquess of Exeter at Wothorpe on his estate near Stamford, with a first-floor room reserved for the gentry and for the display of the Stamford Gold Cup, now on show at Burghley House.

More recently, it provided a grandstand view of a rather different kind, for just three-quarters of a mile to the south is RAF Wittering, home of the Harrier Jump Jet. The good news was that the Harrier did not fly at weekends and the new double glazing was effective (indeed, if you opted for a third layer, it might be quiet enough for a recording studio).

The grandstand was saved from ruin by Jennifer Freeman, a former secretary of the Victorian Society. She cut her preservation teeth with the New York City Landmarks Preservation Commission, and set up her own small company to rescue historic buildings in extreme distress. The work at Wothorpe was aided by an English Heritage 'Buildings at Risk' grant.

When she bought Wothorpe Grandstand and just over an acre of surrounding lands from the Burghley estate, there was no roof, no floors, no ceilings, and just three external walls that rose only to eaves level. Even so, the extraordinary architecture of the two side walls made it clear that this could become a gem once again. Like a miniature Roman theatre, it was formed of arches – a full arcade on the ground floor and the semi-circular lunettes, known as Diocletian windows, above. There was also

a wealth of masonry detail – big bold quoins at the corners and emphatic keystones to every arch.

A detailed survey by Donald McKreth, a building archaeologist, revealed that there had been a kitchen and wine cellar in the basement, that the ground floor had been open and that the first-floor room used to have wooden shutters rather than windows. Originally there were two staircases, one for the servants and another for the gentry.

Photographs taken in the 1950s and 1960s show the collapsed arcade, and a small drawing by a local artist in 1820 showed a top storey. The architect, Brian Austin, has recreated this stylishly in a modern idiom, reusing some of the original stonework that was found on the ground nearby.

A glass belvedere has been added to the roof.

CHESHIRE

BRERETON HALL BELONGS TO THE SPECIAL GROUP of Elizabethan and Jacobean mansions known as 'prodigy houses', houses built for show, often in the hope of entertaining the sovereign, with a wealth of armorial detail and numerous apartments for courtiers to sleep in.

As it stands today, Brereton appears to be just the entrance range of an intended courtyard house with four grand fronts of equal length. Yet the royal heraldry is there with the arms of Elizabeth I over the entrance flanked by her personal 'supporters', a lion and a dragon, while on either side are a Tudor rose and Beaufort portcullis.

Sir William Brereton, who completed the work in 1585, was descended from a long male line in which Sir William succeeded Sir William with unfailing regularity. He was created 1st Lord Brereton, but the line was not to last. The 4th lord died without male heirs in 1722 and the house passed to the Bracebridges, from whom it was to derive new fame as Bracebridge Hall – also the title of a well-known novel by Washington Irving portraying life in an 18th century country house.

In 1817 an advertisement in *The Times* announced that the entire family estate (including Aston Hall, now one of the star museums of the City of Birmingham) was to be sold to pay creditors. Brereton never went to auction but was bought by a Manchester industrialist, John Howard, who transformed the house in fashionable Regency Gothic style.

His dynasty was not to last either. Brereton became a girls' boarding school, much patronised by families in the armed forces until Government financial cuts rendered it suddenly insolvent, like so many schools of this type. Now, after a spell in the hands of a pop star, who built a recording studio at the back, Brereton is back on the mend. Not, as you might expect, divided into apartments but as a single grand house waiting for a modern day Cheshire magnate or football king with price tag to match.

Brereton Hall stands in rich Cheshire farming country conveniently close to the M6 but with a great expanse of unspoilt country spreading eastwards all the way to the Peak District moors and Buxton Spa. The drive leads past the splendid medieval church to the house just beyond. The grand entrance range is built of dark plum-coloured Cheshire brick laid in English bond (with rows of 'headers' alternating with rows of 'stretchers' [bricks placed end-on and longways]). The carved stone detail of armorial shields is delicate and still surprisingly crisp.

Brereton is very much an outward-looking house with tall bay windows and an almost continuous band of large mullioned windows running across the centre and wrapping round the octagonal turrets. A nice story attaches to its design. Sir William succeeded to the title aged 9, and was brought up by his guardian Sir John Savage, who had a daughter of the same age. The two children watched while Sir John built himself a splendid new house, Rock Savage, also with twin octagonal turrets. When William duly married his guardian's daughter, he determined he would take her to a house as splendid as the one she left.

The present entrance is definitely the work of John Howard, with glazed gothic doors opening into a lower hall and a grand flight of steps leading ceremoniously to a long gallery running the length of the front. The ceiling takes the form of a handkerchief dome with crisply detailed gothic plasterwork.

The gallery leads to the drawing room, the most splendid room at Brereton, with a frieze emblazoned with the arms and names of nearly fifty ancient principalities around the Mediterranean including Bosnia, Cordova, Cyprus, Gallicia, Menorca and Slavonia. The chimney piece is carved with the Brereton family emblem, a muzzled bear. The story is that one of the medieval Breretons, possessed of a singularly vicious temper, was interrupted by his valet during dinner, chased the poor man upstairs and murdered him. He rushed to London to seek pardon from the king, who offered him one if he could devise a means of muzzling a bear within three days. Brought face to face with the bear in the Tower of London, he flung his rope net over its head, won his freedom and promptly adopted the muzzled bear as his crest.

The interior character of the house is now mainly Regency with plain plaster walls and one extraordinarily fine gothic chimney piece of this date in pale grey stone. Original late 16th-century work is found in two splendidly chunky grey stone

The gateway is flanked by twin towers connected by a bridge.

fireplaces taken from the book of the Italian Renaissance architect Sebastiano Serlio. These are carved in stone with scroll supports.

On the garden side, Brereton forms a characteristic Elizabethan E, though the central arm has been replaced by a Regency Gothic conservatory with the thin glazing bars typical of this date. Other intriguing rooms include the old kitchen with rows of servants' bells and a heavily moralising inscription: 'Do nothing this day which thou mayst repent of tomorrow'.

The small study of the 2nd Lord Brereton is a strong reflection of the fashion for learned men to withdraw to cabinets of curiosities, surrounded by their favourite books and objects of art. Here is an alabaster fireplace as richly carved and tinctured as a tomb in a church.

The room looks over an attractive cobbled yard behind service quarters with a colonnade providing shelter for servants on their way to larders, boot rooms and still rooms. Another unusual domestic feature on the upstairs landing is a pair of brass taps set just above the skirting over a lead-lined soakaway in the floor. These enabled servants to fill slip baths and basins without having to heave buckets up from below. In the basement is a Baxi Patent Ashbox – a small iron door at floor level for sweeping out ash, which dropped through a grille in the hearth above.

Brereton's pretty lead cupolas were taken down by Mr Howard and replaced by battlements. Curiously, just such a pair of lead cupolas stands on either side of the bridge across the moat at Elsing Hall in Norfolk. The lake in front of the main front is now silted up but there is planning permission to excavate it to create a handsome mirror reflection of the grand house.

BROCKHURST HALL   Birkenhead
Regency villa saved from demolition

JUST THREE WINDOWS WIDE, Brockhurst is a classical Regency villa beautifully faced in smooth blocks of the crisply cut stone known as ashlar. The portico has four slender Ionic columns in a miniature temple front and on either side are characteristic tripartite Regency windows with a central sash flanked by narrower ones.

It is hard to believe that a house so pretty and modestly scaled should have been threatened. Yet it was included in SAVE's Silent Mansions in 1981 because the owners (who lived in part of the house) had applied for listed building consent to demolish the house and erect six new dwellings on the site. Vale Royal District Council had commendably refused to grant this.

Meanwhile the dry rot in the servants' wing spread to the main house. The Georgian Group pointed out that the interior contained two fine rooms which together had once been a ballroom. In one there were marble Ionic columns with finely carved and gilt capitals and both rooms had good plasterwork ceilings and finely carved doors and doorcases, reflecting the prosperity of Cheshire towns in the early 19th century. In 1986 planning permission was granted for six new dwellings and garages in the grounds and two years later the battle continued when still more proposals for enabling development were submitted. In the end Brockhurst was converted into handsome apartments but at the price of an excess of new development. Today these properties bask in reflected glory, being advertised as 'well-presented family properties set in the grounds of Brockhurst Hall'.

The house was built of crisply cut stone with a Greek Ionic portico.

CHURCHE'S MANSION Nantwich

Built by the master carpenter Thomas Clease in 1577

ON MY WAY DOWN TO CHURCHE'S MANSION, I was concerned. According to the map downloaded from the internet, one of the most complete timber-framed houses in England appeared to stand on a roundabout with a filling station next door.

On arrival these problems melted away. No traffic noise intrudes within the house; there is a large walled garden behind with magnolia, mulberry, quince and walnut. This is a pleasant residential area with rows of traditional cottages lining the street opposite, a very handsome Georgian house next door and discreet sheltered housing behind. It's just a quick walk to the centre of Nantwich with its splendid medieval church and varied shops.

An inscription on the front of the building records that Rychard Churche and his wife Margerye 'made this work' with the master carpenter Thomas Clease in 1577. Churche was a merchant owning salt houses, tanning pits, a share in a corn mill and possibly also a glass works.

Just six years later the mansion escaped the dreadful fire that burnt for twenty days and destroyed most of the town centre. Ever since it has been most remarkable for the way it has escaped successive waves of changing taste. True, a few Georgian sashes were introduced, but by 1859 the house could only be let as a hay store. Ten years later it became a Young Ladies' Boarding School, a use that in those austere days involved no modern improvements of any kind.

The splendid oak timbers never underwent the blackening fashionable in Cheshire in the 19th century. The original carpenter's numbers can still be clearly seen on many

There is a dazzling display of 'wheels' and 'bullhorns' on the jettied upper storey.

of them. On the exterior the numbers are in Arabic, accompanied by capital letters indicating where they were to be placed. Inside Latin numerals were used.

The whole house was built as a kit of parts and could as easily be dismantled. This nearly happened in the late 1920s when it was advertised for sale in America – like Tudor Agecroft Hall in Lancashire, which is now standing in a suburb of Richmond, Virginia. The story of its

Armorial glass celebrates both the house's building and repair.

rescue is enchantingly told in a guidebook written by Irene Myott who, with her husband, took out a large mortgage to buy the house in 1931 and then had to snap up the associated farm to prevent encroachment. They reopened a long-hidden Elizabethan leaded window, removed modern grates and treated the fabric with infinite love and respect.

Rather than live in the house, they transformed it into a flourishing restaurant. In 1953, to mark the Queen's Coronation, they decided to replace the Georgian sashes with careful copies of the mullions that survived – adding an inscription so everyone should know what they had done. Their son and daughter-in-law took over, adding a stained-glass window to mark the house's 400th anniversary.

The picturesque appeal of the house lies in the 'jettied' or oversailing upper storeys and the large and small gables that jostle against each other on the main front. Here curved timber braces create a rich decorative pattern of wheels and bulls' horns while on the flank diagonal timbers form a herringbone motif.

Churche's Mansion is constructed on a typical Tudor H-plan. By this time, great halls open to the roof had gone out of fashion. Instead the off-centre front door opens into a ground-floor hall with a great chamber above. The puzzle is that neither of these rooms appears ever to have had a fireplace – a quite extraordinary omission in the two grandest rooms in the house. One possibility is that Churche used them for displaying valuable cloth and wished to avoid the risk of fire.

The glory of the interior is that almost every room had full-height panelling with intriguing drum-shaped bases to the doorways. After four centuries, the panelling has inevitably been made good with imported parts but the total effect is warm and harmonious. On the first floor the original long polished oak floorboards are 2 ft wide with fillets between. In the great chamber is an unusual 'coffin drop' which now serves for moving furniture up and down. Two 6-ft long floorboards fold upwards and the timber joist on which they rest can be lifted out to make an opening large enough for an oak chest or dresser. This is all the more important as the original stair, an ingenious wooden spiral set in a square tower, is very confined. Most of the leaded windows are careful restorations but in the tiny chapel over the front door, rare original 16th-century leading survives, an ingenious pattern of interlocking hexagons.

All these features give every visitor to Churche's Mansion an enthralling feeling of stepping back four centuries as soon as they cross the threshold.

DODDINGTON HALL   Nantwich
Built for a very rich clergyman to the designs of Samuel Wyatt

THE MONUMENT TO THE Rev. Sir Thomas Broughton, Bt, in Broughton church proudly records that the building of his house near Nantwich was paid for out of income and that the family estates were not encumbered by one penny in its erection. This explains why the house took twenty-two years to complete, despite the fact that the need for a larger house was pressing as Sir Thomas had thirteen children when he began work in 1777. This must rank as one of the very grandest houses built for a Georgian clergyman, with a Great Dining Room, 53 ft long. The architect was Samuel Wyatt, elder brother of the more famous James but also a major talent in his own right.

Only in the shallow relief of the long facades does the design show a distinct restraint. Around his house Broughton laid out a vast park and plantations, including a two-mile drive to the main house from the west lodge through the middle of grounds that previously had been 'a desperate waste'. And when Wyatt's plans were published in *New Vitruvius Britannicus*, the author made a mention of the fact that 'the offices and stables, hot house and green house now completing are on the same scale of magnitude as the house'.

The ground floor was occupied by the kitchen domain, with large comfortable rooms for the steward and housekeeper, a butler's pantry with inner bedroom and plateroom so the butler could guard the silver at night. There were two footmen's rooms each with three beds, as well as a china scullery and shoe room. The everyday entrance was through a lower hall opening into a large circular billiard room.

On formal occasions and in summer, Broughton and his guests would have ascended the grand outdoor flight of steps to the *piano nobile*, before entering a stone flagged hall with grand scagliola columns. When Gordon Nares wrote up the house in *Country Life* in 1953 he described the sensation of flinging open the double doors

The drive at the front of the house was used as a car park house while Doddington was still a school.

Top: The garden front with restoration under way.
Below: A three-part window has been set in a blind arch.

into the circular saloon: 'As in all the handsome mahogany doors of the piano nobile one has only to turn the handle of the right hand leaf for the left-hand one to open by some Sesame contraption of pulleys concealed in the soffit.'

By this time the house, although still retaining its original furniture and portraits, had been let to a girls' school. When I visited Broughton in the 1980s it was surrounded by a sea of cars. Soon after my visit the school closed and the building began to fall into a disastrous decline. The roof started to leak. Rot set in.

The contrast with James Wyatt's Dodington in Gloucestershire could not have

been greater. In 2002 that was on offer for £15 million and was snapped up by the entrepreneur James Dyson. By contrast the trust that stepped in to take over the Cheshire Doddington reported that the house was 'extremely hazardous' and could only be visited by appointment. The good news is that the long task of repairs has begun, of which the first phase – the refurbishment of the exterior – is now complete. Nearby Doddington Lake, overlooked by the Hall, has become a popular sailing venue run by a local sailing club, and the surrounding woods are home to a large variety of bird life. There is every chance that the house – which in the Second World War served briefly as the headquarters of the Supreme Allied Commander, General Eisenhower – may by degrees regain its splendour.

HASLINGTON HALL Crewe

A hall house with cross wings, dating from the late 15th century

THE BLACK AND WHITE HOUSES OF CHESHIRE are among the most distinctive in Britain. In 1819, Ormerod, the great county historian, recorded more than fifty of these houses. Today only about thirty remain. They are all stoutly built of the best oak as Cheshire was once a well-wooded county – the great forest of Macclesfield was a royal hunting preserve. As a result, brick building came late to Cheshire – only becoming dominant in the 17th century when the forests had been exhausted of good timber.

The origin of these distinctive houses is not yet established. The earliest is Baguley Hall, near Manchester, dating from the early 14th century and belonging to English Heritage; here, a Scandinavian influence can been seen in the wide timbers in the pattern of a St Andrew's Cross. The great age of Cheshire timber-frame building was the first half of the 16th century. Haslington is more interesting as the main part may be as early as 1480–1500.

This took the form of a hall house with cross wings at either end. The delight lies in the herringbone pattern of the timbers, the 'jettied' or oversailing upper storeys, the distinctive coving and the use of quatrefoils. These festive details were all part of early Tudor exuberance – later in the 16th century, timber-framing became steadily more sober.

The charm of these houses is their black and white livery but all the indications are that this is 19th-century romanticism. Peter de Figueiredo, co-author of the excellent *Cheshire Country Houses*, says, 'The timbers were treated with a pitch-like substance to preserve them, which it probably did, and this rapidly became a fashion.' Originally

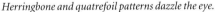

Herringbone and quatrefoil patterns dazzle the eye.

the timbers would have been left in their natural state. The infill was probably off-white rather than white – so far no trace has been found of the more varied colours, such as pinks and ochres, found on houses of similar date in Suffolk villages like Lavenham.

The Vernons, who owned Haslington in the 15th century, arrived in England with William the Conqueror and were granted fourteen manors in Cheshire. The present house was probably built for a Ralph or Richard Vernon. In 1588 Admiral Richard Vernon sailed with Drake against the Spanish Armada. Then in 1639, when Sir George Vernon died without a son, the property passed through his daughter Muriel to the Vernons of Sudbury, owners of one of the most splendid 17th-century houses in Derbyshire. From the end of the 18th century Haslington belonged to another great Cheshire family, the Delves-Broughtons.

Houses like Haslington were built not by architects but by master carpenters whose names remain unrecorded. The best detective work on Haslington has been done by Nicholas Cooper of the Royal Commission on Historical Monuments. By studying every wallpost, purlin and truss he has shown that the great hall in the centre of the house was not open to the roof timbers in the medieval manner but was single storey with a great chamber above. 'Haslington is an extremely early example of this form of gentry house,' he says. The collared roof with cusped windbraces can be seen hidden away in the attic above a flat ceiling.

One reason that fewer timber-framed houses remain in Cheshire than in Suffolk is that Cheshire did not suffer from the collapse of the wool trade like East Anglia and there was money to rebuild houses in the 18th and early 19th centuries in line with Georgian fashions. Haslington is intriguing because the house was only half rebuilt – perhaps due to both economy and an affection for the old hall. Instead it appears to have been turned round 180 degrees and given a new brick south entrance front with bay window, leaving the Tudor north front overlooking a farmyard at the back.

In 1923 another chapter opened when Haslington was purchased by Colonel Humphrey Watts. He was in the cotton business in Liverpool and owned a theatrical costumiers. His four daughters were all involved in the theatre. Among regular guests at Haslington were the author Agatha Christie and the actor Valentine Dyall, famous as 'the Man in Black' – narrator of a radio thriller series hugely popular in the 1940s.

Colonel Watts added a flourish of his own – a two-storey window bay to the left of the Georgian entrance, no deeper than an entrance porch but even richer than the rest of the house with wooden mullioned windows filling the walls on all three sides. Plans for these alterations dated September 1931 are signed by Jas Martin, architect Westminster Bank Chambers, Crewe.

The last owners, the Vernons (no relations of the original builders), moved into Haslington in 1972 after carrying out extensive renovations over two years. They re-roofed the house and renewed all the distinctive windows in oak, leaving it 'correctly' in its natural state.

Haslington stands in rich flat Cheshire farmland and part of its charm lies in the series of ponds that provide reflections of the house. The reed-edged big pond is thought to have been the clay pit used to make the Georgian bricks.

LAWTON HALL   Alsager
Proof that advanced decay need not mean demolition

NO HOUSE HAS ROUSED ME TO SUCH ANGER as Lawton Hall when I saw it in June 1992. Every pane of glass was broken, not by thuggish vandalism but by a decade of children idly throwing stones. Every one of the elegant Georgian sashes had been broken or rotted away. Yet the attraction remained clear. The house was built of a very pretty warm red brick with stone trim for the windows. Bold keystones to the window heads and brackets to the roof cornices provided lively flourishes.

Ten years earlier Lawton had been a school but soon after it was vacated water had begun to cascade through the roof, devastating the lovely rococo ceilings. Yet the house still stood in ample grounds overlooking a sizeable lake surrounded by rhododendrons. Next door was the parish church. The one drawback was that the entrance was by way of a scrappy bus repair garage – but given the land around the house, there was surely an alternative. The house had been built, presumably in the 1750s, for Robert Lawton, with wings added by his grandson Charles in the 1830s.

When I returned a few years later the house looked as if it had passed the point of no return. The big coping stones on the parapet had fallen or been pushed off and the rain was washing away the brickwork. In front of the house a bonfire had been made with the remains of panelling doors and skirtings. In despair SAVE asked Brian Morton, the engineer who has come to the rescue of many historic buildings, to inspect. He reported: 'Clearly there has been some further deterioration but the basic brick shell of the structure still exists and is in reasonable order and can certainly be restored.' Local people began to take an interest and in 2003 Lawton Hall was acquired by Gleeson Homes. The mansion has been repaired, missing sections of cornice reinstated and sash windows replaced with ones of the right proportions. Lawton is lived in again and no visible alterations have been made to the entrance front.

The Georgian front and matching wings were remarkable even when the house stood empty.

PECKFORTON CASTLE — Tarporley

Anthony Salvin's scholarly reconstruction of a major medieval castle

The strongly defensive gateway would have been intimidating to friend and foe alike.

THE GREAT SIR GEORGE GILBERT Scott described Peckforton as 'the very height of masquerading'. This has been both its downfall and its salvation. Scott accepted that Peckforton, a medieval-style castle built between 1844 and 1851, was not a sham like its Georgian forebears but a highly scholarly recreation of a medieval castle, correct not just in stylistic detail but in actual techniques of construction. But to him, that made it inappropriate as a habitable house. Or, as Mark Girouard put it, 'Small windows and bare stone walls tended to freeze out the owner in the end.'

Girouard describes Lord Tollemache, Peckforton's builder, as 'one of those tremendous rock-hewn Victorians who seem built on a larger scale than ordinary men.' He was a champion athlete, had twenty-four children and drove a four-in-hand in his eighties. He was a fervent evangelical and carried his feudalism well beyond the castle walls. 'The only real and lasting pleasure to be derived from the possession of a landed estate is to witness the improvement of the social condition of those residing on it,' he wrote. Each labourer on his 26,000-acre Cheshire estate was supplied with a substantial cottage and 3 acres – the origin, it is suggested, of the phrase 'three acres and a cow'.

The genius of Salvin's design is the way that the castle grows from the rock on which it stands, its irregular plan guided by the contours of the hill. Peckforton steps straight out of the pages of *Ivanhoe*. It would hardly be a surprise if knights on chargers with lances and plumed helmets rode through the gateway. Salvin's rugged stone walls and slit windows – complete with shutters painted with chevrons – are overpowering in their verticality. But while the walls are thick enough to endure a millennium or more, the roof has proved more of a problem. The flat ashphalt roofing, hidden behind the battlements, is prone to leak.

When Pevsner wrote his volume on Cheshire in 1971 he found the castle empty. 'What can its future be? Who could take it over? Some enlightened American university? Some luxury hotel?' In the event Peckforton passed from one would-be hotelier to another, attracted by the castle's romance but never able to raise the large sums needed to bring it into full repair with more than gimcrack furnishings.

Prospects changed with the advent of civil weddings – Peckforton offered a venue without rival in north-western England, though Gwrych Castle in North Wales rivals it for scenic splendour and theatricality. Yet when I looked at a website with comments on weddings, Peckforton had a series of entries describing weddings that had ended in tears and anguish – despite the cost – because the food, the service or even the supposed champagne had been a fiasco. Some, of course, were luckier and happier. Among them were Chris and Kate Naylor, who so enjoyed their wedding that, hearing the castle was for sale, immediately bought it for a reported £5 million in 2006 and are now investing £1 million in improvements. They bought it with Chris's parents, Tony and Gina Naylor, and have begun with the staterooms before moving on to the thirty-eight bedrooms. 'We want to create individual bedrooms, each with antique furniture,' added Chris. 'We will have new linen and upholstery throughout.' Soon there may be more luxury than Lord Tollemache ever imagined.

In his insistence on tiny windows Salvin made no concessions to comfort.

TABLEY HOUSE   Knutsford
Grand Palladian mansion by Carr of York

In 1987 I wrote, 'For several years Tabley House has stood empty while its owners, Manchester University, refused to take a decision on its future. But since the estate was placed on the market, eighteen serious offers have been received and three shortlisted for consideration by the University. Three vital questions must be answered. Will the paintings be shown in situ and be protected by some form of trust ownership? Will the great Turner of the Tabley lake remain in the house? And will the uses proposed for the rest of the house respect its character?'

Tabley's leading champion at the time was Selby Whitingham, art historian and veteran agitator on Turner issues. He frequently pointed out that this great ensemble had been twice offered to the nation and twice rejected. The first offer was made by the Regency owner of Tabley, Sir John Fleming Leicester, 5th Baronet. He had set out to make a collection of contemporary British paintings, which in 1823 he offered to the Prime Minister, Lord Liverpool, 'for fair remuneration' as the foundation of a National Gallery of British Art. The offer was not taken up but in 1826 Leicester was created the first Baron de Tabley in recognition of his public spirit as a collector – one wag suggested his title should be 'de Tableaux'.

One hundred and fifty years later, his descendant, Colonel John Leicester-Warren, who had inherited part of the collection along with the house, died in 1975 believing that Tabley House, its contents and estate would be preserved by the National Trust.

A horseshoe stair leads to the portico.

Tragically a tax liability prevented the Trust from accepting the gift and the executors decided that Manchester University would be a suitable alternative. The Colonel had set up a school in the house but this had closed in 1984 and the University appeared to regard Tabley simply as an agricultural investment and made no effort to use the buildings and paintings. SAVE and others pressed hard for the University to find a use for the empty building that would allow the collection of paintings to remain in the house. The result was that the house was sold as a nursing home, but with a lease of the main floor granted to a new trust that would display the paintings. So far this solution has worked well.

Tabley House is an impressive and elegant Palladian composition by John Carr of York, built between 1761 and 1767. The only 18th-century Palladian country house in Cheshire, the hall has a south-facing central block of soft red brick that is an almost perfect colour match for the pale red sandstone used for the portico and window surrounds. Instead of the more usual Ionic or Corinthian columns, Carr used the Doric order with a triglyph frieze, which is carried right round the house in slightly simplified form. Twin curving flights of steps up to the portico add grace to the composition. Inside, the main rooms remain largely unaltered with fine rococo chimney pieces and plasterwork in both the main house and the matching wings.

VALE ROYAL ABBEY   Northwich
Medieval foundation that became a seat of the Cholmondeley family

IN 1992 I WROTE IN *The Times*, 'Vale Royal Abbey needs a change of luck. More than fifty planning applications have been lodged in two decades but a solution appears as far away as ever.' The house was then a tragic site, the grounds had been trashed and a hideous security caravan was parked outside the front entrance. Such was the plight of great houses in England for the four decades after the Second World War.

The Abbey, founded by Edward I in the late 1270s, was at one time the largest Cistercian foundation in England. After the Dissolution it was for more than three centuries, from 1616 to 1947, one of the seats of the great Cholmondeley family.

The 19th-century work was carried out by Edward Blore and John Douglas of Chester.

The Abbey Church itself was 'plucked down' in 1543 by Thomas Holcroft, who formed a house in the south and west cloister ranges.

In the 19th century, work was carried out by two leading architects – Blore in the 1830s and John Douglas in the 1860s and 70s. Blore rebuilt the south-east wing for the first Lord Delamere and Douglas added a pretty porch and oriel dated 1877.

The entrance front stands proud after years of being left empty.

It was to take half a century for the Abbey to recover from wartime requisitioning. Sold to ICI in 1947 (when most of the heraldic glass was removed), it was taken over by a trust working with teenage children. One source of funds for repairs at this time was through the training programmes of the Manpower Services Commission but the work done here included hacking through the carved roof timbers of the south wing. Dendrochronology or tree-ring dating in the refectory range later showed the roof timbers there to date from *c*.1470.

In 1992 the development company BHC of Bradford put forward a new proposal for rescuing and restoring the estate. They wanted to create a golf club, using the abbey as a club house, all to be financed by the building of new houses in the grounds.

Their architect, Andrew Brown, told me, 'When I first saw the house two years ago it was in an abominable condition, wetter inside than out. The parapet gutters had failed and the structure was saturated.' Interior fittings were put into store while the roof was secured and the house dried out. The building work went ahead as planned, and now the Abbey is back in business and the clubhouse is thriving. The restored great hall with its impressive roof timbers frequently seats 130 at grand dinners and there is a King's apartment where James I is said to have stayed on his journey to be crowned in London. Mission Impossible has now been accomplished.

The great hall is now restored and back in everyday use.

WALMOOR HOUSE Chester

Superb stone mansion built by Victorian architect John Douglas for himself

SUCCESSFUL VICTORIAN ARCHITECTS could amass large fortunes. John Douglas, who settled in Chester in the 1850s, worked extensively for the 1st Duke of Westminster in and around Chester and also for Edmund Peel in North Wales. His work has a strong individuality and a splendid northern ruggedness. He was nearer 70 than 60 when he built himself a princely house on a bluff overlooking the River Dee in Chester. The house is built on local red sandstone with finely tooled surfaces and a grey-green slate roof. The plan of the house is an irregular L, with two storeys to the entrance courtyard, creating a welcoming domestic scale, but a full four storeys where the ground drops steeply down to the river.

Over the entrance porch is a private chapel lit by an oriel window. The windows are attractively grouped in threes with stone mullions, leaded lights and trefoil heads on the ground floor. To the left of the entrance is a three-storey tower with octagonal stair turret looking like a medieval keep. The massive oak stair is a symphony of dark polished woodwork with an arched screen on the landing supported on columns in the shape of ancient wine jars. The ceiling panels are richly stencilled. Douglas designed not only fireplaces but also doors, dado panelling, window seats and shutters. Like many large Victorian houses, Douglas's home was soon too large to continue as a family home, becoming first a girls' school, then headquarters of the county fire service. It is now lived in again, discreetly divided into three self-contained houses.

Though built in the late 19th century, Walmoor has a convincing medieval style.

CORNWALL

WITH MOST ABANDONED AND decaying country houses, the solution is to find a new owner. Boconnoc was different. The Fortescue family still ran the large estate with 14 miles of drives and the largest park in Cornwall, but in 1983 the house had not been occupied for fifteen years. There were no furnishings, water or electricity. Part of the house had been demolished in the early 1970s and dry rot was everywhere.

Now a new generation has risen to the challenge. Anthony Fortescue Enterprises have made Boconnoc one of the most beautiful estates in Cornwall. The house has been re-roofed and the stables are now in regular use for weddings and functions. There are holiday cottages, open days in spring and garden tours for groups – camellias, rhododendrons and azaleas are seen to magnificent effect on the spreading lawns around the house. There are opportunities to tour the restoration of the house and explore the 15th-century church immediately beside it. Mrs Fortescue runs a programme of events including lectures, a car rally and a steam fair. The estate supplies traditional park railings and tree guards and runs a tree-cutting service for turning fallen trees into full width planks and logs.

Both house and estate at Boconnoc were taxed in the Domesday Roll in 1087. In 1579 the Earl of Bedford sold the estate to Sir William Mohun, who rebuilt the house. Subsequently, Thomas Pitt purchased the estate with the proceeds of the famous Pitt diamond, which ended up in the hilt of Napoleon's sword a century later. The prominent 123-ft high obelisk was erected in 1771 by Thomas Pitt, 1st Lord Camelford, in memory of his wife's uncle and benefactor, Sir Richard Lyttleton.

The house makes a delightful group with the church and stables.

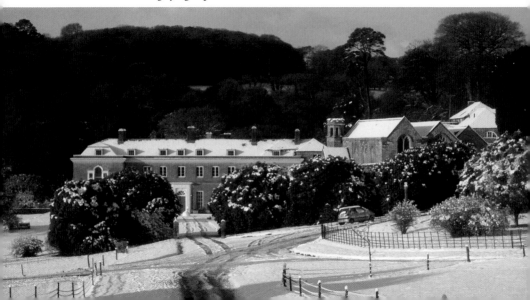

CATCHFRENCH MANOR   Liskeard

Georgian elegance with ruined Elizabethan manor in sheltered gardens

ENGLISH COUNTRY HOUSES ARE FULL OF surprises. Catchfrench Manor, set in the open rolling Cornwall landscape, is a sheltered world turned in on itself. The house, which was formerly occupied as flats, has been brought back into single family occupation, first by owners who lavished attention on the gardens and then by successors who worked on the house.

Like many other Cornish houses, Catchfrench is well sheltered by trees and plentiful shrubs. The entrance front is no more than a grand pavilion, slightly French, or even Belgian, in character but Edwardian in date, with a long view over parkland and fields.

The steep hipped roof dates from an Edwardian remodelling.

The extent of the house becomes apparent as you enter the garden and find a long front with Georgian gothic sashes and a central three-sided bay. As the lawn falls away dramatically, the basement gradually becomes a full ground floor with more arched sashes. The roof, however, is again distinctly Edwardian, rising steeply and inset with dormers that are full-sized sash windows. Over the bay a polygonal tile-hung gable has been introduced, rather like a Dutch bonnet. The circuit of the gardens descends through a grove of rhododendrons with wonderfully leggy branches, reminiscent of a mangrove forest. Beyond is a secret garden contrived in an old quarry but hard to find thanks to the Petra-like entrance through a crevice in the rock.

The big surprise of the circuit of the gardens is the discovery, tucked behind the house, of the ruined shell of the Elizabethan manor house of George Kekewyche, dating from 1580. In front is a pretty box-edged formal garden filled with roses. Though roofless, the Elizabethan house is in remarkably pristine condition with crisp cut stone mullioned windows and shallow Tudor-arch doorways contrasting with the narrow slatestone of the walls, now overgrown with ivy, climbing roses and clematis. One puzzle is the room over the entrance porch – now without floor or ceiling but containing a neat little fireplace above the door into the former great hall. The intrigue is that there is no sign of a door, so the only way in could have been by ladder.

Entering the main house I found a pretty stair with Chinese Chippendale style balustrade immediately inside the front door. Beyond, glazed doors lead to a broad corridor looking out on the Elizabethan house. The appeal of the interior lies in the numerous well-proportioned rooms and the Strawberry Hill Gothick windows which give immense character and charm to quite plainly treated rooms. None of this would have been apparent from a single photograph of the modest entrance front.

GREAT TREVERRAN — Fowey

Miniature baroque gem available for weekend and holiday lets

GREAT TREVERRAN IS AS ENCHANTING a small Queen Anne house as can be found in the length and breadth of Britain. I took the slow route to Cornwall – not the Okehampton bypass, which continues to within six miles of Great Treverran. As I drove west from Liskeard I found myself trailing behind overladen lorries crawling along winding roads. Turning south on the road to Fowey, I drove along a narrow and increasingly mud-splattered road up a hill crested by a none too pretty cluster of farm sheds with silo.

The lane off to Treverran – muddier still – plunged past another farm with a big open barn filled with farm vehicles and a stall for cattle. Then I turned the corner and there was the house, in full sun, even prettier than the photographs. I pulled over, parked and stood at the garden gate trying to find fault with this perfect scene. The front door was invitingly open, I was out of any wind, there was not a sound to be heard but the birds. A box-edged garden path led to a sundial which confirmed that the house faces almost directly south, enjoying the maximum sun.

I eyed the converted barns across the lane with their blue-painted shutters looking for signs of the neighbours from hell, but all was quiet.

Great Treverran is a doll's house, five windows wide and just one room deep. If the facade were on hinges, you would look into a central stair hall with bathroom above and two rooms on each floor, drawing room, dining room and two bedrooms above.

Built in a warm local granite, the house is given an extra flourish by giant Ionic columns.

The previous owner, Mr Turner, aptly described it as 'a small house with a touch of grandeur'. This is provided by the four giant columns – half columns to be precise – that rise the height of the house, each with its own slice of architrave, frieze and cornice. The columns are cut from a beige granite rich in fossils and evidently hard to carve as the Ionic scrolls have a blurred look, a little like a sandcastle after the first wave has washed over it. The facing stone behind is a pale pinky Luxulyan granite richly encrusted with lichens but clearly set to last for centuries in this clear air.

Five granite steps provide a dignified approach to the front door – though an extra one has been added at the bottom as the ground has fallen away. The seven eighteen-paned sashes are not the original but they are still set almost flush with the stone (a practice banned in London in 1709 to reduce the risk of fire spreading from one house to another).

The entrance hall is generously wide and the stair has a gentle ascent – indeed, at some stage the bottom step has sunk half into the floor. But there should be no worries here as the present owner is an engineer and he has carefully vetted every inch of the structure. When English Heritage refused him permission for a concrete floor above the cellar, he introduced steel to support the wooden beams instead. Now the cellar has just enough ceiling height to provide a utility room and workshop.

The panelled dining room has the character of 1700 weavers' houses in Spitalfields with bolection mouldings and elegant fluted pilasters on either side of the fireplace. One panel opens up to reveal a large hidden cupboard for storing china and glass and a granite arch that appears to be part of an earlier house. The bedrooms above are well lit with pleasant south-facing views – one has an engaging chunky cornice that fills one with ideas as to how to add interest to plain rooms.

For the rest, the accommodation is as ingeniously contrived as in a yacht – no space is wasted. There is a spare bedroom with ensuite bathroom opening off the half landing, and enough space under the sloping eaves of the attic for another bedroom and a study with two computer stations as well as walk-in closets at either end under the hips of the roof. Tucked into the roof beams the Turners found two shoes which the builder, a good old-fashioned Cornishman, insisted were put back immediately as they were good-luck charms.

The kitchen and adjoining breakfast room at the back are small but cosy, kept warm by underfloor heating beneath relaid granite slabs and new slate flagstones.

In such an isolated position the house naturally relied on a soakaway, but when Mr Turner asked Southern Water how the system could be updated, he was told that if he so much as flushed the lavatory he would be liable for a fine of up to £20,000, and promptly had to move out of his new house while a modern treatment tank was installed.

The house has been bought by an artist and an architect, Binny and Stuart Mathews, who have carried out careful renovations and now let Great Treverran for holidays. There are five bedrooms sleeping up to ten and a well-equipped kitchen as well as 'secret places for camping and camp fires, an orchard, a hammock and a barbecue'. The rooms are hung with paintings by contemporary artists, many of which are for sale.

NANSIDWELL   Falmouth
Edwardian summer retreat in glorious grounds on the Helford River

HOUSES WITH GLORIOUS VIEWS of the Cornish coast are in a class of their own. Along the north bank of the Helford river, with its deep moorings for large yachts, grand houses can sell for up to £6 million. Nansidwell, set back from the river, looks the other way across the magnificent sweep of Falmouth Bay, with a view down an emerald-green valley to the rocky shore half a mile away. This is National Trust land protected in perpetuity from development – a rolling patchwork of fields edged by high Cornish banks and woods in every hollow.

Nansidwell is an Edwardian summer retreat constructed on a lavish scale using the very best materials. It was built for a successful tax lawyer who made his name as junior counsel to the Inland Revenue at the critical moment when the South African wars had prompted a rise in income tax and estate duty was beginning to bite. Sir Sidney Rowlatt, as he became, rose to be a High Court judge praised for his common touch. His house was built between 1905 and 1908, and he came to Cornwall every summer with his six children. He kept *Black Bess*, a Cornish pilot cutter, in Falmouth harbour to enjoy the sailing; his passion for the sport is mentioned by John Buchan in his autobiography.

Born in Cairo in 1862, the son of a manager in the Bank of Egypt, Rowlatt showed acumen in his choice of architect, Leonard Stokes, whose finest work is the Art Nouveau Gothic college he built at London Colney, Hertfordshire.

Nansidwell is built of beautiful Killas stone from a quarry behind the house, with pink Cornish granite for the quoins and window mullions. The roofs are of classic Cornish Delabole slate, silvery in the sun. Inside, Stokes used a wealth of fine woodwork with dark mahogany doors and distinctive fireplaces. The best rooms are the large combined sitting room and dining room with twin bay windows and the large billiard room with deep oriel window.

Built of Killas stone from a quarry behind, the house has a roof of Cornish Delabole slate.

The large orangery fills the gap between house and coach house.

Judge Rowlatt sold the house in about 1928; ten years later it was bought by the Pilgrim family, who had just transformed it into an hotel when the Second World War broke out. In the war years it was used as a hospital, becoming an hotel again in 1945. In 1987 Nansidwell was acquired by Jamie and Felicity Robertson, who ran it as a non-stop house party. By 1999 they had exhausted themselves.

The Robertsons made the interior colourful and attractive, modernising kitchens and bathrooms. The present owners, who took over five years ago, have undertaken a new makeover to a very high specification. There are guest suites, a kitchen with twin Neff dishwashers, Aga and separate fan-assisted oven, walk-in kitchen freezer, as well as gym, sauna and spa baths. The Edwardian conservatory has long vanished but has been replaced in spades with a whole family of glasshouses. The large garden room catches the morning and evening sun without roasting at midday. It is filled with lush plants and cane chairs, though the beams are on the hefty side.

The cleverest part is the new orangery filling the gap between house and coach house, and combining Georgian window panes with shallow Victorian-style double-hipped glass roof and cresting on top. The picturesque effect is increased by a third conservatory serving the ground-floor apartment in the coach house.

Nansidwell looks to be in first-class structural order with no need for a major overhaul for the best part of a century. All the leaded windows have been replaced with double glazing that reproduces the original square-pattern leading.

There is a fine high-walled garden with an unusual number of wells all over the grounds. The best view is from the tennis court looking across Falmouth Bay to St Anthony's Head lighthouse. This part of Cornwall has a climate perfect for growing camellias and azaleas, tree ferns, gunnera and bamboos, and the garden is full of them. Close by is a series of celebrated gardens, including Penwarne and Trebah, as well as the spectacular coastal footpath.

PORT ELIOT St Germans
Claimed as the oldest continuously occupied ancestral seat in England

THE GROUNDS OF PORT ELIOT SURVEY a glorious river estuary with a view of Brunel's famous Saltash Bridge. There are early 19th-century summer houses, a large orangery, a battery of 18th-century cannons, ponds lakes and a maze. The late Earl of St Germans had an ambitious scheme to adorn his gardens with a fragment of every English cathedral, not such an impossible dream given the pace at which decaying stonework is being recarved and replaced. Above Port Eliot House towers the magnificent priory church, the cathedral of Cornwall in Anglo-Saxon times. The house, almost invisible behind it, surveys the spreading lawns where the annual LitFest is held.

Peregrine, the present Lord St Germans, points out that the discovery of the remains of a 4th- or 5th-century tiled floor within the curtilage of his house, dating from half a millennium before the foundation of the priory in AD may make Port Eliot the oldest continuously inhabited ancestral seat in England. A 13th-century undercroft survives as well as the refectory, transformed into the hall of the present house. Most of the house as seen today, including the long battlemented south front, is the work of Sir John Soane in 1804–6. Soane intended to keep the atmosphere of the place and, while picturesque, is gratifyingly low key. His interiors are in two ranges with a succession of saloons and drawing rooms.

Part of the charm of the house is that you step back in time. Some of the principal rooms were last redecorated in the 1890s with heavy French brocades. During the Second World War Lady St Germans made curtains from Irish linen tablecloths. This is a house where the accumulated bric-a-brac of the ages has rarely been thrown away and in the attics children's toys mingle with chaises longues and heavy bunches of keys. There is a 200-piece crested copper *batterie de cuisine*, a collection of hipbaths and seventy sets of fire irons wrapped in 1928 newspapers – the year electricity came

The priory church rises behind the house.

TREHANE
Truro
Two great gardeners created a ravishing setting for ruined Queen Anne mansion

ANYONE ABSORBED BY THE STORY *The Secret Garden* will find it hard to resist Trehane. Here is a forgotten Cornish garden with a wealth of glorious flowering trees and shrubs that rival those in the Lost Gardens of Heligan. Walking through these gardens in early spring you find a blaze of colour of ravishing beauty with dozens of camellias 10 and even 20 ft high and two large *Magnolia campbellii*, the type that flowers before the leaves appear, each with so many flowers you can barely see the branches. These are the progeny of a greater parent which bore 1,500 blooms and was one of the wonders of Cornwall.

Trehane has been home to two great gardeners. The first was Captain William Pinwill (1831–1926) who received a magnificent homily 'Ninety years a Gardener' in the *Royal Horticultural Society Journal* in 1950. Pinwill planted camellias, magnolias, rhododendrons and a wealth of exotics and was renowned for his generosity in helping others start their gardens. In season he would leave a daily plate of his special large dark strawberries out for the postman. His fruit included an enormous Royal George peach, which occupied 800 sq ft. So absorbed was he when planting that at meals times a bell would be rung from every window of the house.

During the Second World War the gardens were inevitably neglected – though Jewish refugees from Austria were housed in huts in the grounds (one remains). The house was then bought by a Mr Anthony Deakin who embarked on repairs only to see his future home go up in flames in 1946, the result of a blow lamp carelessly left burning in the roof.

Photographs dating from 1910 show a perfect Queen Anne house with steep hipped roof and four equal fronts, plain, handsomely proportioned and given warmth and character by wonderful early 12-pane sash windows. The house was built in 1700–03

The coach house incorporates a rainwater head and bell from the old house.

by John Williams. His wife bore him three children in quick succession before tragically dying in childbirth and leaving him to die broken-hearted just months later. The three orphans were bought up by their grandparents but soon after Trehane passed to the Stackhouses, for whom a splendid mid 18th-century zodiac ceiling with key pattern borders was added. There are also tantalising glimpses of handsome Palladian decorative panels on the stairs in the old photographs. Emily Stackhouse, the supremely talented Victorian botanical artist, grew up here.

Following the fire, Mr Deakin rebuilt the coach house from its foundations using old bricks from the ruin and incorporating an exquisite rainwater head with the initials of John Williams and his wife Catherine Courtenay, as well as the Sun Alliance plaque and a bell dated 1748. The wealth of shrubs and trees was increased by David Trehane, the great camellia grower, who moved here from his well-known Dorset nursery. His son Jeremy explains, 'Father bought Trehane about 1962. All six of us children would go with him every weekend. The gardens were a thicket of self-seeded ash and sycamore and bamboo. You could see flowering shrubs but not reach them. We worked dawn to dusk piling up a huge bonfire which would still be smouldering the next weekend. We would light a big fire in the coach house and stand the mattresses around it to dry them out.'

John Connell, who bought Trehane in about 2001 extended the coach house to provide extra bedrooms for his family, carefully matching the brickwork. With Truro

architect David Scott, he drew up detailed plans for restoration of the ruined shell. The Society for the Protection of Ancient Buildings urged him to build a 21st-century structure within the walls but he preferred a careful reconstruction. Sifting through the debris he found exciting evidence such as fragments of decorative plasterwork (much more remains to be found) as well as granite paving and Georgian floor tiles. The rebuilt Trehane will be a large house of 13,500 sq ft with four ranges of 72 ft laid out round a small central courtyard.

David Scott explained, 'The cost of a new roof and other structural repairs to make the house weathertight can probably be kept to £750,000. My view is that the house should be left to dry out for up to five years. The walls are damp and time is needed for the walls to adjust to their new loading.'

Costs of fitting out the interior could vary widely between £250,000 and £1 million depending on the specification. Of course you could simply live in the coach house, devote yourself to the garden, and preserve the shell as a romantic ruin. As you take visitors around you can point to the molten lead on the sills, which showered down during the fire.

Part of the thrill of Trehane is its intricate layout of informal garden rooms, which follow each other in unpredictable sequence with constant small changes in level so exclamations of delight await at every turn. There is also a splendid long walk running the length of the garden, bordered by magnificent shrubs for its whole length.

Above: The Queen Anne house gutted by fire during building work in 1946 is still a focal point at the end of a glorious spring garden filled with magnificent camellias and magnolias.
Left: There are glorious views across the rolling Cornish hills.

TREWARTHENICK Tregony
Georgian elegance at the hub of a 1736-acre estate

MANY HANDSOME COUNTRY HOUSES are today separated from their estates. When I arrived at Trewarthenick in 2004 it was on offer with 1,736 acres and without a footpath (except by the boundary) to disturb its seclusion. It looked out over a park of 200 acres, complete with one of Humphry Repton's 'red books' presenting his designs. There were five farms, thirteen houses and estate cottages as well as an extensive pheasant and wildfowl shoot with a couple of miles of frontage along the River Fal.

The Gregor family bought the estate in 1640, with a fortune made in trade. Francis Gregor, the first to sit in Parliament, was described by Boswell during his visit to Cornwall in 1792 as 'a most active sensible man'. To him must be due the handsome Palladian front with astonishingly large sash windows. Close to, the house looks for a moment to be built of brick, but in fact it is faced in local slate stone cut into slices almost as narrow as brick – though often longer – with matching Cornish Delabole slates on the roof. At the back is a red-brick Georgian wing. On the lawn, broad Irish yews until recently blocked the views from the bedroom windows but have been neatly cut back to look like giant coffee cups.

One of the glories of Cornish houses are the gardens, overflowing with spring-flowering camellias, rhododendrons and azaleas, often planted at an early date. Here extensive work was done on the gardens in the 1820s. In 1825, after a prolonged interregnum, the estate passed to Francis Gregor's niece Sarah and her husband Gordon. They commissioned the architect Henry Harrison to add matching wings, which were demolished in 1925. The house was a convalescent home in the Second World War and was finally sold by the Gregor family in the 1950s.

The south-facing front basks in the sun.

CUMBRIA

BLENCOWE HALL   Penrith

Two fortified Pele towers link to form a courtyard house

BLENCOWE HALL, ON THE OUTSIDE at least, has hardly changed in four centuries. The name goes back further still. Adam de Blencowe so distinguished himself serving the Black Prince, probably at the Battle of Poitiers, that he was granted his own coat of arms by the Lord of neighbouring Greystoke, whom he had accompanied to France.

Certainly the open farming country, measured out by straight stone walls, makes a good setting for the stout walls and battlements of this fortified house. Ullswater Fells and the Lake District are just a few miles to the west and on a clear day there are even longer views east to the highest range of the Pennines.

The thrill of Blencowe is the superb masonry with every stone telling the hall's history through variations in shape, size and texture with soft reds blending into dove greys. Over many of the windows there are conspicuous 'relieving' arches taking the weight off the straight stone window heads. Many of these are Tudor-style hood moulds with ball-shaped 'stops' at the corners carved with basketwork or lozenges.

The main south front gives the impression of being curiously slid open to reveal a lower, more domestic house within. The explanation is that Blencowe has not one, but two of the fortified Pele Towers common in these parts (pronounced hard as Peel, not as two syllables like the Brazilian footballer). The first south-east tower on the right is dated to *c.*1475. The intervening range has the date 1590 over the entrance door in the courtyard and the initials and coat of arms of Henry Blencowe.

The grandest parts of the house are still largely roofless.

Above are the words *vivere mori, mori vitae* (a cryptic Latin tag which can be roughly translated as 'live to die, dying is living'). This is held to relate to the words written by Lady Jane Grey to her sister on the night of her execution: 'Live still to die, that you may by death purchase eternal life.' It served as a subtle reminder that the Blencowes were related to Lady Jane Grey's husband, Lord Guildford Dudley. Henry Blencowe was a man of local standing. He had married Grace, the sister of Sir Richard Sandford of Howgill Castle across the border in Westmoreland. Serving twice as High Sheriff of Cumberland, he received a knighthood from James I. The south-west tower of *c.*1620 is also attributed to him.

Both towers are now little more than shells. The south-west tower has a savage gash running from top to bottom of the kind that Cromwell and Richelieu left when they 'slighted' castles held by their enemies, ensuring they could never be used again. There

is a strong possibility that this happened at Blencowe as Parliamentary forces under General Lambert took Penrith in 1648 and detachments were sent out to take Rose and Greystoke Castles, which were both burnt. As Blencowe was on the way from Greystoke to Rose, and traces of artillery platforms have been found in the fields nearby, there is every chance that Cromwellians savaged it.

Ruin certainly set in early, for as long ago as 1840 a local historian L.W. Jefferson observed a 'picturesque' and 'luxuriant plane tree which had its root under the tower wall'. Henry Prescot Blencowe, the last of the Blencowes, sold the property in 1802 to the 11th Duke of Norfolk, who had earlier remodelled nearby Greystoke Castle. For nearly two centuries it continued as a tenant farm.

The battlemented Pele tower commands long views to the south.

An archway leads through to a sheltered courtyard behind the battlemented front.

The challenge at Blencowe is to bring these towers back into use. They potentially contain the best and most interesting accommodation in the house. Even without floors or ceilings, fine stone doorways are visible, as well as several stone fireplaces suspended in mid-air, though in the south-east tower a wooden floor remains beneath a corrugated roof (with handsome fireplaces peeping out above). Here there is also a fine spiral stone stair set in the thickness of the wall, which could readily be connected to the rest of the house.

The entrance to Blencowe is through an archway in the west-facing gatehouse wing. It opens into a courtyard that was once enclosed by buildings on four sides. An interesting detail here is the two rows of sandstone tiles that sit along the lower edge of the roof with slates above. Only two ranges remain today, with the former chapel on the north side announced by a twin-pointed arch window. Today it is just a rough cattle shelter.

The front door opens onto a 19th-century stair with a large drawing room to the left and an old kitchen with characteristic large arch on the right. On the first floor are three modest bedrooms in the south range and three more large but bare bedrooms in the gatehouse range.

The farm is still tenanted and there are modern farm buildings to the north, which are partly shielded by a fine L-shaped range of stone barns with a date of 1703 and a duck pond in front. The barns have airing slits instead of windows (as well as clay drainpipes set into the masonry for further ventilation). Any alterations would need to be made very carefully. For anyone wanting outbuildings, whether as studios, workshops or for a collection of vintage cars, they have an immediate appeal. The present owners have kept horses. This is well-drained limestone country with quite an incline – ideal for gallops.

HAYTON HALL Brampton

Delectable Regency Gothic, restored and lived in again after years of institutional use

STANDING IN ROLLING COUNTRY east of Carlisle, Hayton Hall was designed by the architect of the British Museum, Sir Robert Smirke, and sensitively extended by his younger brother Sydney. Though Smirke is best known for grand Classical public buildings, here he designed a pioneer essay in Tudor, the style adopted a decade later for the Houses of Parliament. There are hood moulds to the windows, pretty shaped gables and a porch with a trio of slender Gothic arches topped by pinnacles, inspired by those on Henry VII's chapel at Westminster Abbey. But the gothic is only skin-deep and this is really a very spacious Regency house with tall sash windows and lofty ceilings.

The added appeal of Hayton is that it is built of a very pretty buff-coloured local sandstone with crisp carved detail. The entrance front is neatly symmetrical but picturesque elements are added with large bay windows on the west front and an ogee-domed look-out tower at the back.

Behind the house in the stable yard is a Pele Tower, one of the tall square fortified towers found all over Northumberland and Cumberland, which were built as a defence against marauding Scots.

The Regency sash windows are prettily combined with Tudor hood moulds.

Robert Smirke was employed by Thomas Henry Graham, whose family had owned the estate since the 17th century. He commissioned Smirke to build his new house in 1824, when he was just 30 years old.

Eric Graham, who inherited in 1937, had no children and obtained permission to break the 'entail' which bound the estate to be handed down from one generation to another. A consortium of local businessmen bought the house and 51,000 acres for £7,500. Fortunately they did not simply sell the timber and demolish the house ,as often happened in the depression of the 1930s but instead sold the hall to the Home Office in 1942 for use as an approved school for delinquent boys – after allowing Czech refugees to take shelter here in 1940.

When the school closed, Hayton was taken over as a country house hotel. The underbidder was Mr David Dyke, who instead bought a staff accommodation block and converted it into eight apartments. A year ago, Mr Dyke, thirty years after he first came to Hayton, fulfilled a dream by buying the rest of the estate. His metier is restoring and converting old buildings.

In tackling Hayton Hall he explains, 'I wanted to keep the main house intact. It's simply not suitable for horizontal division into apartments.' The Sydney Smirke wing set back on the east is intended as a separate house, though one potential purchaser expressed interest in combining the two. Further back the chapel will become another self-contained house with a conservatory on the exact site of the one Sydney Smirke designed. The stables will be converted into some fifteen smaller houses and cottages. The architects are leading London practice Casson Conder, where Mr Dyke's daughter Tina is a partner.

The long drive is shared but Hayton Hall has its own drive up to the house. The front door opens into a large entrance hall with Greek Doric columns framing the view through to a grand staircase, which has an impressive cast-iron balustrade lit by grand twin lancet windows on the half landing.

The main rooms on the ground floor are designed to provide a circuit for entertaining with one room leading to another. The double drawing room on the west is as brilliantly lit as a conservatory, with sashes and bay windows descending almost to the floor. In one bay, French windows lead into the garden, in the other the sash is so tall you can walk through it when it is open.

Smirke's cornices are as crisp as if they were chiselled in stone while the beams are adorned with *guilloches* (a circling rope motif). The dining room is a place for serious candlelit dinners. Upstairs the landing has a pretty rococo white marble fireplace. The seven bedrooms had bathrooms added when the house was an hotel; the temptation is to take down some of partitions and return subdivided rooms to their elegant Regency proportions.

One big surprise is the attic, adapted for a ballet dancer, with a large practice floor under the roof, but also suitable as a games room. It makes an unusual penthouse flat with separate stairs and bedrooms like tents under steeply sloping eaves.

Below the house is a delightful lake complete with small island and now restocked with fish. This will be shared between the residents, as will some 30 acres of beautiful woodland walks.

HIGH HEAD CASTLE   Ivegill
Majestic sandstone shell in the style of James Gibbs awaits restoration

HIGH HEAD CASTLE IS A NUMBINGLY BEAUTIFUL masonry shell begging to be lived in again. It belongs to Christopher Terry, who bought the house in 1986 to save it from imminent demolition. Many of the interiors had already been stripped and sold as architectural salvage following a fire in 1956. Mr Terry quickly stabilised the walls with the help of a £10,000 grant from the Georgian Group.

High Head is a fortified site set dramatically above the ravine of the river Ive. A licence to crenellate was granted in 1342 and the medieval castle was drawn by the Bucks in 1739. Five years later the castle was demolished, with the exception of a surviving Tudor wing, and replaced by a palatial new Classical house modelled on plates in James Gibbs's *Book of Architecture*.

The builder, Henry Richmond Brougham, a young man in his twenties, spent the staggering sum of £10,000 (much of it coming from his uncle John Brougham of Scales Hall nearby) on the house and steeply terraced gardens, which he barely lived to enjoy, dying aged 30. His masons came from Florence and the stonework has an almost Parthenon-like perfection, so closely set that the mortar joints are almost invisible. Much of the stone has hardly weathered in 250 years – though the east end partially collapsed in 1980 during a quake measuring 4.5 on the Richter scale.

Illustrations of the house in a 1921 edition of *Country Life* show a handsome marble-floored corridor with screens of Doric columns to the hall, reminiscent of Gibbs's Senate House in Cambridge, as well as a splendid Imperial stair in oak.

The shell is now stable, the lawns trimly mown, though nature grows in abundance all around. Mr Terry's wish is to rebuild the shell as eight substantial apartments – each with half of one of the four main floors (some 2,500 sq ft each). Until now this was not viable, but with property prices rising there is the prospect of selling the apartments for £550,000 each. He is looking for an investment partner with a passion for Georgian architecture.

Though the windows and roof have gone, the stonework remains beautifully crisp.

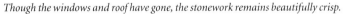

DERBYSHIRE

BRETBY HALL IS A GEORGIAN CASTLE on the grand scale, superbly built in stone, three storeys high with still taller round towers at the corners and dozens of sash windows suggesting comfortable, well-lit interiors. The estate is several miles in circumference with a series of drives leading to the mansion.

Bretby was the seat of the Earls of Chesterfield. The 1st Earl obtained Royal consent to enclose a park here in 1610 and proceeded to erect a magnificent house, today known only from early 18th-century engravings that show it surrounded by extensive walled formal gardens with fountains and statues set in ornamental *parterres* laid out by the Frenchman Grillet.

During the 18th century Bretby was little visited by its owners and the Earl was persuaded by his steward that the house was falling into ruin and should be demolished, a process that took four years and yielded the steward substantial sums from the sale of materials.

The best of both worlds: large Georgian sashes and imposing feudal battlements.

Designs for a new house were drawn up for the 5th Earl of Chesterfield by James Wyatt shortly before the architect's death. These were at least partly superseded by further designs made by Wyatt's nephew Jeffry. William Martin, an architect and builder living in Bretby, was probably involved in supervising construction and designed a series of estate buildings, including the home farm. The 6th Earl who succeeded as a minor in 1815, later laid out a racecourse.

In the mid 19th century the estate passed to the Earls of Carnarvon who resided at Highclere Castle in Hampshire. Bretby was assigned to the dowager Lady Chesterfield – a larger dower house would be hard to conceive. In 1915 Bretby and 1,200 acres of park were sold to a local businessman, J.D. Wragg MP, who called in William Barron to landscape the gardens but soon sold the house, which then became an orthopaedic hospital. Today it is divided into apartments still proudly surveying a vast park.

BRIZLINCOTE HALL   Bretby
Gloriously eccentric baroque, standing forgotten in a farmyard

BRIZLINCOTE HALL IS A GLORIOUS ECCENTRIC, dominated by huge curving gables on all four fronts. A square house with four virtually identical facades is intriguing – other baroque flourishes are the bullseye windows in the gables. The architect is unknown but the house could be linked to Bunny Hall in Nottinghamshire, the home of the 'wrestling baronet' Sir Thomas Parkyns, who designed equally wayward buildings.

Brizlingcote was built by the 2nd Earl of Chesterfield for his son Lord Stanhope. Doorways carry the date 1714 and strange Latin tags. The entrance doorcase has a mutilated monogram that once read 'PDS' for Philip Dormer Stanhope.

In about 1728, when the 3rd Earl died, the house was leased to a kinsman, Philip Barnes. Towards the end of the 18th century it was let as a tenanted farm, ensuring it escaped Victorian alterations. In 1923 the Lomas family, who were living there, were able to keep the farm when the Bretby estate was broken up.

Like many baroque houses, Brizlincote is monumentally constructed. The brick vaulted basement contained the service rooms including a large kitchen. The hall has a huge arched fireplace opening onto a staircase. The main rooms are on the first

Large segmental gables extend across each front.

floor, which is treated as a *piano nobile* with bolection moulded panelling. The attic contains four boxed-in lead cisterns, which drain off the water, and beside the hall is an early 18th-century range of outbuildings including a barn and former cottage. Though rundown, Brizlincote is an impressive survivor awaiting restoration with the swagger and panache that it deserves.

BUXTON CRESCENT   Buxton
Masterpiece of Georgian town planning, handsomely restored

THE CRESCENT IS ONE OF THE MOST ELEGANT, urbane and original of British contributions to town planning. Its inventor was John Wood the Younger of Bath, whose Royal Crescent at Bath remains the grandest and finest of them all. Next came The Crescent at Buxton, commissioned by the 5th Duke of Devonshire to provide lodgings for visitors to the Spa. 'I never saw another so magnificent as the Crescent tho it must half ruin me,' the Duchess wrote to her mother in 1783 when it was just one third complete. With its giant fluted pilasters, John Carr's Crescent has distinct echoes of Chatsworth itself, while the open arcade at ground level pays a nod to another classic of English town planning, Inigo Jones's Piazza in Covent Garden.

Among the final items needed to complete the facade were the ducal arms supported by life-size stags over the Devonshire's house in the centre. The bill from the carver Thomas Waterworth was paid in March 1785. The chandeliers for the magnificent ballroom in the Assembly Rooms at the east end arrived the next year and fitting out continued until 1789. The final account came to a princely £38,601. Carr deemed The Crescent his best work and when he came with his niece to Buxton in 1795 he found the town 'so full of company that we had a great difficulty to obtain a bed'.

When I visited The Crescent in 1989 it was in a pitiful state. The balustrades beneath the first-floor windows were spawling, the fluting of the pilasters was being washed away by the rain, while the glorious band of *guilloche* ornament, as finely chiselled as the carving on a Roman temple, had entirely crumbled away in several places. The crisis had begun when St Anne's Hotel, which occupied more than half The Crescent had been forced to close in June by the local council's hygiene officers. Worse was to come, when the town library, splendidly housed in the Assembly Rooms, was also forced to evacuate following a dry-rot scare.

Hope of salvation came when Kit Martin – saviour of Burley, Dingley and other houses illustrated in this book – drew up a detailed scheme for converting The Crescent into a series of houses and apartments for sale. As Carr had designed a large part of the Crescent as lodgings the necessary staircases were there, even though walls had been knocked through to make corridors for the hotel. Martin made an offer which was accepted but he was twice gazumped and the mortgage lender, the Bank of Egypt, sold the hotel to a newly formed company, Capitalrise, with the vaguest of plans for another hotel.

The Crescent declined into a still more disastrous state, until in September 1992 the national heritage minister Robert Key dramatically announced that he was giving Capitalrise ten days to produce a programme for repairs. Otherwise, he was prepared to serve a repairs order, followed by compulsory purchase. Government departments move slowly but by December the Department of National Heritage had drawn up a schedule for £900,000 of repairs and the next year High Peak Borough Council received a grant of £180,000 from the National Heritage Memorial Fund to cover the full cost of purchase.

Visiting Buxton in the summer of 2005, I found that The Crescent had been handsomely restored but was still empty. English Heritage, led by its chairman Jocelyn Stevens, had healed the wounds in the stonework, which was now crisp and radiant in the early morning sun. But the arcades were fenced off, debris was accumulating and nearly fifteen years had passed since Kit Martin had come close to acquiring it for conversion as not one but a series of perfect houses. Currently plans are being drawn up for a £23 million spa that will become what is being billed as the first genuine spa hotel in the UK. More public money is being invested and the teasing question at the end is whether a residential solution would not have been a great deal more economic. The Crescent looks out on a public garden resplendent with fine trees climbing a terraced hillside. What better view could one wish for from a bedroom window?

The Crescent was built by John Carr of York for the 5th Duke of Devonshire.

CALKE ABBEY · Ashby-de-la-Zouch
18th-century time capsule preserved with all its contents

PARKLAND SWEEPS DOWN to the great baroque front of Calke Abbey. No Repton or Barry ever came to introduce a more formal setting of terraces and *parterres*. Inside, the main glory of the house is that time has stood still here for more than a century. The hall is hung with antlers and the adjoining bird lobby is crowded with cases of stuffed animals from floor to ceiling. The colours in the drawing room are light and brilliant, fresh yellow and gold wallpaper, a warm pink carpet, a set of bright yellow damask sofas and chairs and others embroidered with pink and red flowers. All the ornaments are equally colourful – white biscuit statues, brightly tinted porcelain and glistening gilt picture frames.

Calke, with all its contents, park and enough land to endow it, was offered by the owner, Mr Henry Harpur-Crewe, to the nation in 1982 in settlement of some £8 million of capital transfer tax. His hope was that the Government would accept the package and hand it to the National Trust. The Treasury, however, did not accept the endowment, whether in the form of outlying land or capital raised from the land, and without this the Trust could not accept the house. The immediate need was to immobilise public opinion and we set out to do this through a SAVE leaflet: *This Magical House Must be Saved Intact. Now!*

We sent it to large numbers of MPs and peers as well as to SAVE supporters, encouraging them to write to the Chancellor of the Exchequer. Meanwhile Lord Gibson launched a correspondence in *The Times* in which he forcefully set out the National Trust's desire to preserve the house. But in the House of Commons, Neil MacFarlane, a junior minister, cast doubts, saying the Trustees of the National Heritage Memorial Fund 'did not consider Calke was of such high priority as other cases before them'. After this, *The Times* correspondence swung unanimously in

Calke is encircled by a vast park on all sides.

The baroque front has an imposing raised portico.

favour of Calke. James Lees-Milne was particularly fierce: 'I dare to guess that this most endearingly English of squires' houses would prove to be just as popular historically and artistically as the great masterpieces.' On December 9, 1983, *The Times* published a magnificent leader which concluded that 'even discounting the highest flights of enthusiasm, Calke Abbey is without question worth preserving intact'.

Then came a counter-attack by Lord Vaizey describing Calke as 'skiploads of junk … junk of two centuries never sorted out by a new wife, just piled up and rarely, if ever, cleaned'. The next Sunday a swift repost came from Sir Howard Colvin. Had Lord Vaizey looked more closely at these skiploads of junk , 'he might have written less disparagingly about a collection which included Bronze Age swords, silver by Paul Lamerie, 18th-century Chinese silk hangings in mint condition, an autograph musical score by Haydn, trophies of the Battle of Trafalgar, the library of a famous Egyptologist, and paintings not all "indifferent" by Landseer, Lawrence, Linnell, Ruysdael, Ferneley, Sartorius and Tilly Kettle.'

The news that Calke was to be saved came dramatically in the Chancellor's budget speech. A few months later Gervase Jackson-Stops rang me to say that the state bed that he had been hoping to borrow for the *Treasure Houses of Britain* exhibition at the National Gallery in Washington was too fragile to transport. 'Why not try the Calke bed?' I asked. He was dubious at first but when unpacked every single piece of Chinese silk embroidered with gold thread was there. The bed had been presented to Princess Anne, daughter of Queen Caroline, on her marriage to the Prince of Orange in 1734 but given as a perquisite to Sir Henry Harpur-Crewe when the couple left for Holland. It had never been used at Calke and emerged from its packing in pristine condition.

Calke has been preserved as a time-warp, dusted down (some say a little too much) but the clutter of centuries remains – antlers, birds' eggs, broken chairs, dolls' houses; but it is not mere chaos – the saloon remains an intriguing museum crammed with fossils, stuffed animals and Egyptian curiosities, while the school room overflows with vintage toys and children's books. You are not just looking at fine paintings and furniture but at every aspect of domestic and country life over more than three centuries.

EDNASTON MANOR — Ashbourne
Classic Lutyens house built for the founder of Imperial Tobacco

ANY HOUSE BY THE GREAT SIR EDWIN LUTYENS provokes a thrill of anticipation, putting one on the alert to spot every clever and amusing detail. At Ednaston the magic is immediate. Turning off the busy A52, you are in the deep shade and tranquillity of an avenue of chestnuts with the house visible at the end bathed in sun.

Lutyens was a Classicist who loved to be unpredictable. Here you approach the entrance front at an angle, through a half-moon court with three pairs of gate piers. Looking out, they form what the French call a *patte d'oie*, or goose's foot, with three radiating avenues.

The style of Ednaston is Queen Anne, with warm red brick and steep hipped roof. The great Christopher Hussey called it 'possibly Lutyens's best country house'. The bricks are the long thin reddy-brown Bedfordshires Lutyens loved, set in lashings of mortar the colour of marzipan. From the start it had that mellowness that elsewhere took years to achieve. The house is given a distinct character by the use of casements, not sashes. Even the front door takes the form of a pair of French windows with small glazed panes. Over them is a surging swan pediment inset with armorial shield, while the carved capitals at the top of the pillars are pure Lutyens, portraying the four seasons.

As at The Salutation in Sandwich, another famously ravishing Lutyens house, a wrought-iron gate in an archway tempts you to walk straight through to the garden where the south front opens out onto a terrace paved with herringbone brick. Here the view is framed by a pair of pavilions, each open on two sides so they are perfect for alfresco drinking and dining. The kitchen court, surrounded by steep-roofed outbuildings, is now one of the most attractive features of the house with twin Dutch gables in the shape of a letter M.

Ednaston was built for W.G. Player, son of the founder of Imperial Tobacco. Player was drawn to the spot, on the far side of Derby from the firm's Nottingham base, by the fine rolling country and the good fishing. He had seven children, whose interlaced initials are carved on more distinctive capitals on the garden front along with the unusual wartime date 1915, though the house was not fully fitted out until 1919.

Intriguingly the house already had a 1920s cosiness of scale, very different from the lofty proportions of Edwardian houses with their overtures of Empire. The front door opens into a small saucer-domed vestibule leading to a low entrance hall with black and white marble paving and a massive fireplace, the first of a series. But there is no long vista, no obvious way to go, so every door is a mystery.

Another curiosity is that, on the plan of the house as completed, there were just three reception rooms – drawing room, 'great' hall and dining room, while the service realm ran to an ample kitchen, pantry, scullery and servants' hall as well as larders – rather convenient, as it happens, for adapting to modern kitchen-oriented living.

The hall has the classic cigar-box feel with full oak panelling, wooden floor and imposing beams enclosing pretty *guilloche* plasterwork. Doors have richly carved, almost frilly egg-and-spoon surrounds, while in the centre is a massive marble fireplace with bolection moulding. At either end are glass-front bookcases with doors like those of the classic red telephone box. Drawing room and dining room are square in shape with windows on three sides and steep coved ceilings.

The staircase, as always with Lutyens, has both a grand flourish and an easy ascent. Unusually it is positioned in the corner of the house, glimpsed invitingly through a perspective of arches and steps. The short flights are formed of broad steps of local Hopton stone with a graceful wrought-iron balustrade. At the top a corridor leads zigzag fashion to the bedrooms with more deep arches at every turn, connecting with a second handsome oak stair which doubles as a service stair.

From the bedrooms – the main ones with more coved ceilings – you appreciate the glorious green rolling country around the house.

The attic is a world of its own with bedrooms attractively contrived under the sloping eaves and Lutyens chests of drawers built into the lower slopes so no space is wasted. Lutyens also cleverly avoided the problem of valley gutters by forming two delightful hidden roof patios. Each is surrounded by a continuous band of small pane windows with tile hanging beneath – like inside-out dormers.

Mrs Player did not take to her new house and her husband used it mainly as a fishing lodge. In 1948 he handed it to his son and after his death it was bought in 1979 by Mr Lionel Pickering. He replaced the crumbling bricks, the chimney stacks and all the roof tiles, using perfect matches from the Butterley works nearby.

The east front looks down over a terrace-garden where the lawn is mown in a criss-cross pattern. For some years Mr Pickering and his late wife ran a nursery here and high hedges form a series of garden rooms, from which the scent of roses wafts through the house.

The lawns have been artfully mown in a quilted pattern.

LONGFORD HALL   Ashbourne
Second seat of the Cokes of Norfolk, surveying fine formal gardens

LONGFORD HALL IS AN IMMENSELY grand yet strangely old-fashioned, looking house. It seems at first sight to consist of two long matching ranges on either side of a courtyard. This is partly an illusion created by the almost identical balustraded ends – the north range to the right is today shorter than the south range, which has a princely run of fifteen sash windows on all three floors overlooking the gardens. This unusual form dates back to the house built here by Sir Nicholas Longford in the 16th century, which was sold in 1622 to Clement, the sixth son of Lord Chief Justice Coke, whose descendants were created Earls of Leicester and built Holkham Hall in Norfolk.

In 1713 Longford was described as 'a very large ancient seat … which [Sir Edward Coke] has very much improved, particularly by gardens and watercourses.' When Sir Edward died in 1727, the house passed to the future 1st Earl, and when he died without children the Norfolk estates passed to his sister's son, Wenham Roberts, who was then living at Longford and assumed the name of Coke. Wenham employed the Derby architect Joseph Pickford to transform his house into a grand Georgian seat. Pickford introduced sash windows and added an extra storey in place of the Elizabethan gables. He capped this with a balustrade and urns in the manner of an Italian palace. The character of the long front comes from the four Elizabethan chimneystacks which Pickford retained. Old photographs show that to retain the level line of the balustrade, Pickford adopted an arrangement whereby the chimney flues were diverted up the slope of the roof in stovepipes to connect with chimneys on the roof ridge. Not surprisingly, this arrangement did not survive and trios of Tudor chimneys were reinstated in the 1930s. After a serious fire in 1942 the house was not fully restored until the 1960s but now the warm red-brick facades overlooking formal gardens, lake and park remain a glorious sight.

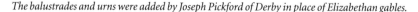

The balustrades and urns were added by Joseph Pickford of Derby in place of Elizabethan gables.

DEVON

THE ENGLISH DELIGHT IN ECCENTRICITY and A La Ronde is without doubt one of the most deliciously eccentric houses in Britain. Christopher Hussey, writing in *Country Life* in 1938, set it as a curiosity 'beside Strawberry Hill, Ickworth, Fonthill and the Royal Pavilion'. Yet in the early 1980s it was in serious danger. Mrs Tudor Perkins, who had inherited the house without any means of supporting it, was valiantly opening it to the public seven days a week for seven months a year, from 10 a.m. to 6 p.m., providing lunches and teas every day.

Four years earlier, she had sought to provide the house with an endowment by obtaining planning permission to build five one-storey houses in the field behind. The £180,000 that was raised might have sufficed but the taxman took £120,000 of it. Faced with such harsh realities, she was forced to put the house up for sale. The main problem was that because she inherited in 1974, Mrs Perkins was caught in a

Diamond windows turn the corners with matching diamond pattern sashes between.

tax trap that obliged her to pay a higher tax rate than applied before or after that date. Ironically 1974 was the very year when the *Destruction of the Country House* exhibition at the V&A drew attention to the impact of crippling taxes on historic houses and helped secure tax relief in return for public opening.

According to the sanguine financial advice, the only way of raising sufficient funds to preserve the house completely was to build thirty houses on an adjoining field – set behind so that at least they would not ruin the view from the house out over the estuary. I wrote in *Country Life*, 'This should not be allowed to happen. At present the house has an attractive rural setting. The whole atmosphere of the place would be changed if there were new houses within a hundred yards.'

The solution, I argued, was for the National Heritage Memorial Fund to provide the money for an independent trust or (better still) for the National Trust to take on the house. The case was strong. A La Ronde was more than a glorious architectural conceit on an unusual 16-sided plan. It was the best example of the amateur taste of the Regency period in existence. While many of the showpieces of the Regency – from Carlton House Terrace to the Blaise Hamlet – were created by professional architects and craftsmen, all the intricate interiors at A La Ronde were fashioned by the two Misses Parminter from 1798 onwards. They probably designed the house themselves and according to family tradition, their inspiration was the dome of the 6th-century church of San Vitale in Ravenna, which they had admired on a prolonged ten-year Grand Tour.

A model showed that originally the house was thatched. Their favourite trick was to use geometry, not to create order or harmony but to upset the established order of things. The diamond pane windows were set perversely across the angles. The octagonal chairs in the hall also had kinked not flat backs.

The Misses Parminter conceived and made with their own hands the hangings, the needlework and the panels of plumage, shells and mineral glitter. They made bird pictures and cornices of feathers, compositions in seaweed, sand and lichens, brilliantly intricate paper cut-outs and home-made versions of Florentine *intaglio* tables. At every turn there were flashes of ingenuity and humour, such as folding seats in the door reveals of the hall and a catflap in the wine cellar door to guard against mice nibbling corks. Of course it was all very fragile. As more and more visitors climbed the 20-in-wide steps to the shell gallery at the top of the house, they brushed against the fragile seaweed decoration, leaving a daily harvest of fallen shells which then had to be glued back into place.

No long campaign was needed to save A La Ronde. The National Trust stepped in, the National Heritage Memorial Fund provided a grant of £1 million to buy the property and all the contents, and A La Ronde is now open from the middle of March till early November, though now it has two days' rest a week.

It has been suggested that the Bath architect John Lowder, a relative of the Parminters, may have had a hand in the design of A La Ronde. In 1816 he designed the Bath and District National School, built on a circular plan with wedge-shaped classrooms, which, alas, was demolished in 1896. While visitors to A La Ronde can explore the house in detail, the shell-encrusted gallery is now considered so fragile that it has to be viewed on closed-circuit television.

AYSHFORD COURT   Sampford Peverell
Late 16th-century house with wagon-vaulted great chamber

THE FIRST VIEW OF AYSHFORD COURT comes as you cross the bridge over the still waters of the Great Western Canal and see the small 15th-century private chapel in the field in front. This isn't part of the house but is looked after by the Friends of Friendless Churches, who have carried out recent repairs, finishing the interior with a glorious salmon-pink limewash.

Ayshford dates from the late 16th century. The magnificent wagon-vaulted great chamber carries the date 1631. A substantial part of the house was demolished in 1755, and in about 1910 it was extended in all directions. As a result the outside walls are a mixture of plaster, stone and brick. To give Ayshford the air of romance it deserves, flowering plants need to be trained up the facades – roses, clematis or even the humble solanum.

Inside, a sitting room has been created in one of the fine rooms or the first floor. Downstairs you have a choice of long hall, drawing room, study or morning room as well as a spacious games room, also ideal as a home office, beyond the kitchen.

There is a substantial enclosed garden to the west and a paddock running down to the canal – which is no longer navigable but is teaming with wildlife.

The cottage-like proportions conceal the splendour within.

BORINGDON   Plymouth
Long-abandoned Elizabethan mansion which now welcomes guests

WHEN I FIRST VISITED BORINGDON in the mid-1970s I walked into a roofless ruin. The beautiful Elizabethan porch was surrounded by brambles. Internal walls were covered in ivy and flaking away. Yet the thicket of self-seeded saplings around the house helped to protect it. Interesting too was the fact that many of the Tudor windows were small, and there were towers rising four and five storeys high.

John Parker, who inherited in 1582, had remodelled a priory that was given by Henry VIII to his favourite, Thomas Wriothesley, Earl of Southampton. Work was complete in 1587 and Parker gave a banquet to celebrate the success of Drake's raid on Cadiz. The guests included Sir Walter Raleigh. The next year Queen Elizabeth stayed.

The great hall overmantle bears the date 1640 and is emblazoned with the arms of Charles I, flanked by figures of Peace and Plenty. Within a few years Cromwell's troops had burnt a large section of the house, which the family forfeited because of their loyalty to the Crown. In 1660 the Parkers were restored to their estates and in 1750 the family moved to Saltram House.

By 1920 Boringdon was a farmhouse but after the Second World War, it stood empty. Though bought in the 1960s by a company that organised medieval banquets, it was in too poor a state to be used. Decline continued until the City Council served a repairs order in the mid 1970s and in 1984 permission was given for restoration as a hotel. Today Boringdon offers forty-one bedrooms set in 14 tranquil acres.

The pretty Renaissance porch has unusual shell-headed niches on either side.

BRADNINCH MANOR   Bradninch

H-plan Tudor house with Georgian front and ornate great chamber

BRADNINCH OFFERS SPLENDOUR on a manageable scale. Set high above the passing road, it looks down on a sheet of water perfectly formed like a baroque mirror – too large to call a pond, too small to rank as a lake. The French would call it a *pièce d'eau* – a sheet of water. And this is the fun of Bradninch – high style set deep in the Devon countryside.

The house is built on a typical Tudor H-plan with three-storey gabled ends. It was begun in 1547 for a Devon lawyer, Peter Sainthill or Seynthill, and completed by 1553. A 1645 description mentions 'Peter's great and lofty hall'. Four of the hall roof trusses are visible in the attic.

Much of the charm of the entrance front comes from the Georgian doll's house sandwiched between the gables. The neat pedimented front door and sash windows with the original thick glazing bars suggest a date before 1750. The doll's-house air is increased by the smaller square windows on the first floor.

At the south end are more 16th-century mullioned windows including a central one with sawn-off timbers below suggesting it was once a bay window. The back of the house is more irregular with a large triple-height mullioned window lighting a splendid stair and next to it a charming three-light window with flamed top gothic arches – perhaps a later conceit.

The front door opens into a fine saloon, more like a grand Georgian dining room than an entrance hall, with a screen of fluted Ionic columns at one end, which may mark the position of the Tudor screens passage. When I visited seven years ago the room was painted a glowing canary yellow.

The staircase beyond is a scaled-down version of that at mighty Hatfield House, with a landing after every five steps in the best Elizabethan manner. The massive corner or newel posts are not squared but handsomely turned, like the balusters between, though on a more massive scale. Each newel sports a splendid heraldic beast, several of them evidently replacements but splendid nonetheless.

Tragically the decoration in several fine rooms, including panelling and chimney pieces, was illegally removed and sold by former occupants in 1980. The Job Room survives intact – a marvel to be set beside other fantastic Elizabethan rooms, which survive in larger numbers in Devon than anywhere else.

You enter the manor through a 'Whispering Porch', which has been diagonally set to keep out the draughts and is surmounted by openwork cresting. Rich Corinthian columns frame the entrance. The oak wainscot rises from floor to ceiling and the use of Classical mouldings and the absence of linenfold suggest a date of 1600 or a little later. Along the top of the wainscot runs a fretted wooden cornice of tiny half arches.

The centrepiece of the room is a two-tier Job fireplace with three panels of sculpted scenes – as rich as a triptych in a German church. On the left Abraham's hand is stayed by the angel as he brings the sword down on his son's head, in the centre are the trials of Job and on the right the prophet wrestles with the angel. Further naive but lively

The baroque mirror pool provides a clear reflection of the house.

figures flank the fireplace. and more rich carving adorns the pillars that punctuate the panelling. They are inset with military trophies and musical instruments in the manner that was so fashionable a hundred years later.

Formerly the drive swept round the park beneath the impressive ring of hills that protects the manor on the north and east. Today the entrance is through gates below the house. On the far side of the drive is a neat formal garden with hornbeams pleached to resemble a hedge held up on stilts.

THE GRANGE   Broadhembury
Jacobean house refashioned in an antiquarian spirit

ANCIENT AND PICTURESQUE manor houses are not usually associated with Swiss standards of comfort and efficiency. The Grange at Broadhembury, South Devon, was refurbished painstakingly for three years by a couple who intended to live there; however, in 2000, they found that their business commitments demanded that they move to Switzerland and so they put the house on the market.

Their new boiler room would have done credit to a five-star hotel, ensuring that hot water and heating reached every part of the house effortlessly, while the wiring was arranged so that computers, phones and other gizmos could be used all over the house. Yet the work throughout was done with respect for the historic features and ancient surfaces.

The Grange takes its name from the granary of the Abbey of Dunkeswell that stood on the site. During the Reformation it was bought by Edward Drewe. Like many builders of handsome Elizabethan and Jacobean houses, he had prospered as a law officer, serving as Recorder of London and Serjeant-at-Law. He died in 1622 and was succeeded by his son, who had been knighted at the coronation of James I.

The house bears the marks of later remodelling and the main entrance has occupied the east, south and west fronts successively. Inside survive several handsome panelled interiors dated at 1600. This is reassuring because the best room in the house, the drawing room, was sold to the Speed Art Museum in Louisville, Kentucky, in 1929.

John Harris, the leading expert on English rooms in American museums, says: 'This has always been accepted as one of the best Jacobean rooms moved out of

The entrance front has pretty white-painted glazing that matches the stone trim.

Large gardens and impressive hedges surround the house.

England … When you get behind the panelling there you see that it is made up of different woods.'

The Jacobean house was greatly reduced in size in the 1770s and the panelling redistributed around the rooms, an early example of antiquarianism. Not that The Grange is in any way small. It has eight reception rooms, seven bedrooms with bathrooms, and incorporates a guest suite with its own kitchen and provision to create a further small flat.

The main ground-floor rooms on the south range have distinctive octagon and diamond-pane sashes, on a smaller pattern than the usual six-pane late Georgian sashes. These were evidently intended to create a leaded-light look. Intriguingly, the sashes are formed without a crossbar in the middle, to avoid interrupting the intricate glazing pattern.

The main staircase is in oak and has the baroque flourish of swept-up handrails and three turned balusters for each step, while the landings are inlaid with the arms of the Drewes. Above, the swirling rococo plasterwork completes the effect.

The Grange had no undercroft or basement, so the wine cellar, with Georgian slate-shelved wine bins, was conveniently situated just behind the dining room.

To the east of the house is a formal garden with yew hedges concealing a tennis court and swimming pool. To the south the River Tale runs through the grounds, feeding recently restored medieval fish ponds. There are fine mature trees, including a magnificent copper beech, and a large walled garden.

The house is faced in a cream-painted render picked out in white. This gives the south front an attractive 'Strawberry Hill Gothick' look, although a 1904 edition of *Country Life* thought that overlaying the grey stone with stucco did 'mischief' to the house. Today The Grange is an enchanting sight, fresh and pretty and a house where you can instantly imagine moving in tomorrow.

CANONTEIGN MANOR   Christow
Wool merchants' house rescued from extreme neglect

CANONTEIGN MANOR IS SO PERFECT and blemishless that you could be forgiven for thinking it is some kind of a hologram projected onto a grand Devon lawn. Here is the archetypal Elizabethan E-plan house, symmetrical in every detail and without any of the changes that come with the age or any of the outbuildings usually found around a great building that is 400 years old.

The approach to the house is equally enthralling. Driving south from Exeter on the fast Plymouth road you take the turning for Canonteign Falls – claimed as the highest waterfall in England – and are soon bowling along a pleasant country road which, as you pass the entrance to the Falls, becomes a narrow lane. Almost immediately a giant octagonal chimney looms ahead. At its foot are the substantial ruins of the Exmouth lead mine. The entrance to the manor is just beyond, and before you see the front of the house you are overwhelmed by the glorious view.

When Nikolaus Pevsner came here in 1951, while writing the 5th volume of his *Buildings of England*, he found 'the old house neglected and divided into farmhouse and cottages … a splendid sight now, all covered with creepers'. The house, more often known as Canonteign Barton, was built for the Davy family, prosperous wool merchants of Crediton.

In 1812 the estate was bought by Sir Edward Pellew, a supremely gallant naval commander who was created baronet after he had personally come to the rescue of

The house is on a typical Tudor E-plan, with mullioned windows decreasing in size towards the top.

the East Indiaman *Dutton* which had run onto rocks off Plymouth Hoe during a storm in January 1796. Pellew fearlessly swam out to the wreck and helped rig a lifeline which saved almost all on board. Pellew was created Viscount Exmouth in 1816 and in 1828 his son commissioned the London architect Charles Robert Ayers to build Canonteign House, an exceedingly handsome Regency house, next to the old manor, which then became a farmhouse.

Rescue of the manor was undertaken by the widow of the 9th Viscount in 1972–5. She was the daughter of the Marques de Amurrio and held the Spanish title of Marquesa de Olias. Her work explains the perfectly even patina of the house on all four fronts. This is rubble stone with granite dressings, originally almost certainly covered with plaster or a regular shelter coat of lime to keep out the moisture, yet now rightly revealed because the stonework is a joy in itself, notably the 'relieving' arches over the windows.

A date of 1600 is suggested in the new volume of Pevsner and it is intriguing that, despite the symmetry, there are no Classical details of any kind, no columns, cornices or balusters. Instead there are just Tudor hood moulds and drip courses to keep the rain off the windows. These mullioned windows tell a story in themselves. Clearly there is no two-storey great hall marked by a tall oriel, yet at either end there is a great chamber or parlour with a 16-light window, very different from the earlier Tudor arrangement of master at one end and servants at the other.

Inside a still greater surprise awaits, a wealth of linenfold panelling lining not only the spacious hall but also the corridors, stairs, reception rooms and main bedrooms. The new panelling is but the latest in a series of works that have made Canonteign into a relay race in which each new owner picks up the restoration baton as soon as he arrives. Many of the smart bathrooms were installed by the previous owner, the businessman George Devlin, who also restored the still derelict upper floor.

The smart new pool is overlooked by the gabled end of the house.

The result is a house that is at once modern and ancient. In room after room the handsome stone-mullioned windows speak of the centuries, weathered inside as well as out presumably because the house was half ruinous. Otherwise the atmosphere is one of freshness and modernity with every room equipped for an on-line computer. The long gallery is a fully furnished gym with enough weights to bring a house down while the kitchen (supplied by Gainsborough Kitchens) is grandly neo-Elizabethan with woodwork supported on corkscrew columns like cider presses.

EGGESFORD HOUSE
Long-ruined shell rebuilt by an architect as his home

Eggesford

FOR YEARS EGGESFORD HOUSE STOOD an eerie ruined shell, telling a story of decline as tragic as any country house in Britain. Built in 1822, the house was designed by Thomas Lee, the architect of Arlington Court in North Devon, which belongs to the National Trust. Early photographs of Eggesford show a rich Tudor Gothic interior that is filled with tracery doors, pendant ceilings, crested wainscots and battlemented bookcases.

Lee, or his client, the Hon. Newton Fellowes, had chosen a new site above the River Taw. The vast estate then passed by marriage to the Earls of Portsmouth, who now had two spectacular country seats. The 6th Earl preferred to live at Hurstbourne Park in Hampshire, and Eggesford, with 3,277 acres, was sold to a new owner in 1913 by Knight Frank and Rutley.

The particulars describe a magnificently timbered park of 300 acres, two miles of carriage drives, an avenue of chestnuts, every variety of ornamental shrub, a long gallery and six state rooms, thirty bed and dressing rooms, stabling for forty horses and a 'stamp room' apparently decorated with postage stamps.

A contemporary newspaper cutting records 'Sold for £85,000 to a timber merchant, Mr Green of Chesterfield … the fifth large estate he has purchased in 12 month'. Less than a year later Eggesford was back on the market divided into eighty-three lots. Four years on, a 1917 cutting adds, 'the house was stripped of its fittings and the roof removed. The park was cut up and many of the magnificent trees felled'.

The architect Edward Howell, who finally bought the property in 1992, recalls: 'There were trees inside, trees on top, and the walls were dissolving.' Two years later he moved into the stables and after twelve years of painstaking repair reoccupied the house in 2006.

For years the house was a gaunt ruin standing in a field.

Expanses of glass announce the modern house now built within the walls.

The big attraction at Eggesford, evident right from the start, was the sequence of three grand rooms that overlook the Taw Valley – a drawing room, dining room and library. 'We had just completed a house in Greece for a client and this made me think it was possible to live in rooms of this size,' says Mr Howell. He is talking of 15-ft-high ceilings and rooms that are 35–40 ft long.

He continues, 'We put steel beams in place of the big oak timbers introducing metal decking floors overlaid with concrete.' The original library is now a large modern kitchen, while upstairs there are now five bedrooms and three bathrooms. The basement, until recently filled with rubble, now houses Mr Howell's office and a billiard room. The next project is to transform the large courtyard into a garden.

Tall spacious Georgian rooms allow the new library to have a gallery.

'Our one problem is that it never comes to an end,' he says with a cheerful laugh. One thing is certain, that without Mr Howell's initiative, Eggesford would soon have passed the point of no return.

ENDSLEIGH   Tavistock
Summer retreat in exquisitely restored Regency gardens

ENDSLEIGH IS ONE of the most
gloriously situated country houses in
England, a ducal retreat hidden from the
world in a secret valley on the borders of
Devon and Cornwall. It lies on the
16,000-acre estate that belonged to
Tavistock Abbey until granted at the
Dissolution of the Monasteries to the 1st
Earl of Bedford, at the same time that
Woburn Abbey was granted to his son.
The Bedfords did not build a house
here until 1810 when the 6th Duke
commissioned the architect Sir Jeffry
Wyatville, who had remodelled Windsor
Castle for George IV, to build him a
holiday retreat.

The grounds were laid out by the
famous landscape gardener Humphry
Repton, whose 'Red Book' survives,
showing his proposals for the garden. The

*The picturesque style of the house is set off by
intricate, colourful planting.*

Duke might have been expected to build a large house in fashionable Classical or
Gothic style, but according to Repton the spot was so picturesque that it was
'impossible' to build anything grander or more formal than the irregular farmhouse
that stood on the site.

Wyatville therefore built Endsleigh to look like a series of cottages, with low roofs,
numerous dormer windows and rustic verandahs supported on tree-trunk columns.
It is an English version of Marie Antoinette's famous farm at Versailles, designed for an
alfresco life with French windows opening directly on the gardens and a dairy, shell
grotto and Swiss cottage. The Duke and Duchess's twelve children had their own cottage
and garden complete with fountain and flower beds encircled by a runnel of fast-
flowing water. Inside the house was a strictly limited number of guest rooms, and as
much care was lavished on the salmon larders as on the ducal dining room.

The foundation stone records that it was the Duchess (the Duke's second wife)
who chose the spot in this 'sequestered valley for its natural and picturesque beauties'.
A darkly handsome woman with a passion for romantic beauty, the Duchess was later
adored by the painter Edwin Landseer, who became her constant companion in the
Highlands. She had acquired a taste for rustic living from her parents, the Duke and
Duchess of Gordon, who had cottages on their Scottish estates to which they retreated
in some comfort, with a French cook and a violin-playing footman.

Overleaf: The gabled and verandaed hous stands against a magnificent backcloth of trees.

The tree trunk verandah overlooks the former children's garden.

Though completely invisible from nearby public roads, Endsleigh enjoys spectacular views of rolling hills and the thickly wooded banks of the River Tamar with not a house in sight. It is described by Christopher Hussey as 'the outstanding and probably most nearly perfect surviving instance of a romantic *cottage orné*'.

The entrance is marked not by grand gates but by a pretty thatched lodge. The long drive plunges past rhododenrons and camellias growing beneath splendid oaks and rare conifers, the beginnings of an arboretum that extends above the river in both directions and boasts several British champions.

The 6th Duke of Bedford was a shy but extravagant man with a keen interest in botany and horticulture as well as a taste for Classical sculpture – it was he who acquired Canova's famous statue *The Three Graces* for Woburn Abbey. The entrance hall at Endsleigh spoke of an outdoor sporting life, with three long map cases mounted on the wall opposite the front door and a large fireplace inset with seats for wet walkers to dry out in. While the Regency period is usually associated with strong bright colour, the interiors at Endsleigh are comparative dark with an abundance of panelling and wood graining. In 2002, the furnishing of the main rooms had changed remarkably little since the 6th Duke's death in 1839. Furniture designed by Jeffry Wyatville included a table in the hall with ball and claw feet, the oak chairs in the dining room, a handsome set of painted bamboo chairs and a pretty octagonal gothic table in the book room. Plaster models of the Duke's favourite antique sculptures also remained.

For nearly half a century it was run as a charming but rather sleepy country house hotel by a fishing club set up to save the place when break-up threatened in the 1950s after the death of the 12th Duke of Bedford. It was a place so full of atmosphere that J.R. Hartley, the famous imaginary author of a book on fly fishing, might have walked through the door at any moment.

In 1987 the members of the Endsleigh Fishing Club launched an appeal and began repairs to the house, transferring house, gardens and arboretum two years later to a charitable trust which carried out extensive garden restoration, replanting Repton's magnificent borders and beds as he intended. But at the end of 2002 the hotel closed its doors and the club decided to sell. The furniture had to be sold to repay the grant given by the Heritage Lottery Fund for the restoration of the gardens.

Salvation came when Olga Polizzi stepped in in 2004 to buy the house and grounds and reopen it as a hotel. Daughter of the famous hotelier Sir Rocco Forte, she also runs the renowned hotel at Tresanton in Cornwall. Cream teas are served in front of log fires, the library is stocked with best-sellers, wellies stand ready for guests wanting to explore the garden, and fine linen and soft pillows ensure a blissful nights sleep.

FULFORD HALL   Great Fulford

Imposing semi-fortified house where Fulfords have resided for a thousand years

FULFORD HALL IS A RARE and impressive example of a semi-fortified Tudor manor. The house stands four-square and isolated in sweeping parkland descending to a lake. Instead of gables there is a continuous battlement parapet. Manor houses built in the first half of the 16th century were often semi-fortified, built round courtyards and with few windows on the outside, especially at ground level. All this changed after Queen Elizabeth I came to the throne in 1558 and houses were built with larger windows looking outwards over gardens.

Fulford is the home of Francis Fulford – when a house carries the same name as its owners, it is often a sign they have been there since Anglo-Saxon times. Fulford ownership was confirmed by a grant from Richard I in 1190.

The house has an unusually bright appearance thanks to the new lime render applied by Francis Fulford. The Fulford arms, with Saracen supporters, are set in the strapwork over the entrance with early Renaissance dolphins in the spandrels of the arch. Fulford has nursed the house back from decay without compromising its atmosphere. As you progress round the four wings you are left with an overpowering impression of cavernous halls and lofty saloons, some almost bare but speaking of the grand scale of life in past centuries. He explains, 'The house was restored in the 1680s after being occupied by both sides during the Civil War. They wanted grand rooms and forgot all about retaining walls and tie beams. It all fell in about 1810.'

The double-height great hall is paved in black and white marble with fine linenfold panelling and a Jacobean overmantel carved with scenes of Adam and Eve – restored by Fulford's grandfather in 1901, together with the early 18th-century grand staircase.

Like a number of houses not open to the public Fulford welcomes groups of visitors via the Historic Houses Association website.

The house glows with a new coat of render.

HILL   Christow
Boasting the smallest great hall in England

HILL CAN BE FOUND JUST 9 miles from the Devon coast, by way of a glorious drive through rolling green hills to the Teign Valley. The house stands just beyond the end of the village of Christow beside a quiet country lane. It is tiny but enchanting. The sloping grounds, nearly an acre in size, are full of pocket gardens formed of different types of plants, tiny ponds, pergolas and amusing features such as the stone steps from a spiral staircase in the Debtors' Prison. This is a medieval house with walls so thick that they take up almost as much space as the eight rooms. Here must be the smallest great hall in England, rising to a splendid trio of crucks and dominated by a vast hearth.

There are two ornamental ceilings with geometric patterns limited to the centre, as if the owners wanted the best quality but could not pay for it to go to the edge of the room. There are features such as the wig and bible cupboards (for the farmer's most prized possessions) and the hidden door that reveals medieval thatch perfectly preserved in the void beneath a later roof.

At present there is just one miniscule shower room on the ground floor of the house, but to create another bathroom you would have to sacrifice one of the three bedrooms. Outside there is a fine medieval barn.

The wonderful state of preservation is due in part to the previous owner, Essie Warren, who was here in the 1970s and called in the Society for the Protection of Ancient Buildings to carry out careful traditional repairs. Ancient doors and wooden screens have all been lovingly preserved and the latest view is that the house may be earlier than the date of 1300 previously given, as dendrochronology samples (tree-ring dating patterns) go back beyond what has been found elsewhere.

The very small windows are the clue to the house's great age.

HORN OF PLENTY   Gulworthy
The Victorian mine manager's house that inspired a chef

THIS PROSPEROUS-LOOKING VICTORIAN VILLA has an origin rather different from most country houses. It was built in the 1860s by a successful local mining company as a house for the manager of the mine. The plot near the hamlet of Gulworth was leased from the Duke of Bedfordshire's Devonshire estate and the new house was named Tamar View. Just up the valley Turner came to sketch and called the scenery 'altogether Italian'.

Tamar View is now a flourishing hotel, the Horn of Plenty, established by Paul Roston. Though only a few hundred yards from the main road from Tavistock to Cornwall, it enjoys complete tranquillity. In photographs it looks almost a doll's house, but the proportions are unexpectedly imposing and inside there are lofty ceilings and generously sized bedrooms. Further bedrooms are in the converted coach house. My room had a sanded wood floor, a large French-style armoire cleverly containing fridge and tv, and a sunken bath. The chef runs very popular cooking courses over the winter, both during the week and at weekends. These include three hours in the kitchen, followed by a three-course lunch, a glass of wine and petits fours.

Dartmoor and its vast panoramas of open moorland, sheep and deer are just ten minutes away, while Cornwall's glorious gardens beckon across the border.

The house enjoys a glorious setting above the Tamar Valley.

HOLYSTREET MANOR · Chagford

Tudor manor that was love at first sight for Edwardian heiress

HOLY STREET MANOR IS TUCKED AWAY amid narrow winding lanes and steep rolling hills, offering a degree of seclusion and tranquillity that most people can only dream of. The River Teign (you pronounce it Tin) tumbles down over mossy boulders in a great sweep round the house. Such is the force of water that a hydro-electric plant is established in an old thatched mill, providing free heating all the year round. 'It completely changes the way you live in the house. You can leave the doors open and it still stays warm as toast,' the owner, Mrs Sally Meadows, told me.

It was love at first sight for the 25-year-old Mary Ellis, a Howard de Walden heiress, who in 1913 chanced on the 'lovely old Tudor house which had everything for which I was looking. There were good outbuildings from which stables and a garage could be made, and though the house was in a ruinous state of repair, it only made matters more delightful as I felt it would be such a joy to repair it.'

A dashing young lady who had made a name as a racing motor cyclist, she then moved to Devon to farm and to hunt. She turned to Turner Powell, a Surrey architect who had built her mother's house 'Olde Ende' near Forest Row in Sussex – 'an expert on the Tudor period' and 'the very man for me'.

Powell's transformation of the old house was radical yet sensitive to place. Photographs taken by Miss Ellis before the work began show the old buildings where the present ones stand but most of the visible masonry is new – and of good quality.

Powell, whose dates are 1859–1937, had studied in Paris and designed a riding school at Zakoziel in Russia and, according to Alastair Service, an expert on Edwardian architects, he also designed Shovelstrode Manor at Ardmillan in Scotland,

The gables and tall chimneys lie secluded amid beautiful woods.

Great House Court at East Grinstead and a house in Hampstead Garden Suburb, 1 Turner Hill.

The house stands on the bend of a narrow country lane in the friendly and inviting fashion of medieval and Elizabethan houses. But it is a very quiet lane, leading only to a few other houses and to Gidleigh Park Hotel where, for a price, you are assured one of the best dinners in England.

The original entrance front, facing south, now looks out onto an enclosed walled garden. Beside it, Powell created a new entrance inside a new gateway leading to a large courtyard with stables opposite the house and a slate-hung coach house at the back, with chauffeur's flat and large workshop attached.

Heat is extracted from the stream running under the old mill to keep the house warm all winter.

The front door opens into a grand entrance hall cum staircase. Open stone arches lead off in different directions, creating a sense of open-plan living. The rooms are well-proportioned but also have an almost monastic simplicity, bearing comparison with Lutyens's famous Castle Drogo nearby. There are beautifully crafted oak doors with splendid hand-forged iron hinges and latches and sturdy lead-pane windows but little ornamental plasterwork. Virtually every room in the house has a fine fireplace. Those in the main rooms are hewn from large blocks of Dartmoor granite – one is overset with a beautiful panel of Renaissance carving. The study has a delightful inglenook – you sit under the hood and warm yourself in front of a much smaller fireplace set within it. 'They all draw very well,' says Mrs Meadows, and with an abundance of wood, there is every reason to use them. Upstairs the nursery has a fireplace with Delft tiles and a plate-warming cupboard inset above.

The main staircase is Elizabethan in style, rising in short flights to a wooden screen of shallow Tudor arches opening onto a long landing with impressive arched stone doorways. The roof of the stair hall is like two bays of a medieval great hall with large timber trusses, and overlooked by bands of both indoor and outdoor windows.

An outdoor staircase leads to a chapel created by Miss Ellis with special permission from the Catholic bishop. 'The walls, inside and out, were of granite, as was the altar, above which a proper east window was put in,' she wrote in her diary. Holy water stoops were cut into the walls. The outdoor stair allowed villagers from Chagford to attend mass without walking through the house.

The abiding thrill of Holy Street is the abundance of water. When the river is in spate the levels rise and fall dramatically. A mill race or leat feeds the old mill, clear and flat-bottomed so the trout are easily visible. 'The heat is extracted from the river water though a kilometre of narrow metal pipes – the opposite principle to a refrigerator,' says Mrs Meadows.

A leat also rushes past the stable, providing a ready source of fresh clean water to wash down the floor. With 21 acres, the thrill is to take a walk beside the river – in a wild state, with great boulders and fallen trees swept down by the current to emerge in a field where Mrs Meadows keeps a herd of white park cattle (relations of the famous herd at Chillingham). Here you climb the hill and emerge on a ridge over the house with a magnificent view of the Dartmoor hills.

When war broke out in 1914, restoration slowed but the older builders and carpenters stayed on to finish the house as the younger men were called up. When Miss Ellis's offer to serve as a dispatch rider was turned down by the War Office 'because ladies were not as yet employed in that capacity', she took over the local hounds and in 1916 married the badly wounded son of her neighbours, Dennis Critchley-Salmonson. Surprisingly they sold the house in 1925 but though it has changed hands several times it remains almost unchanged, waiting for new owners who will enjoy fishing their own stretch of river, pacing their own policies and extending the garden.

A story has it that Holy Street Manor was one of a number of very secluded houses on a shortlist for use by the Queen Mother during the Second World War. It is virtually invisible from the air but should you wish to arrive by helicopter there is an ancient barn near the house discreetly fitted out as a hangar. Otherwise it's a five minute drive to the A30 and dual carriageway all the way to London.

KELLY HOUSE   Launceston
Mid 18th-century house where time has stood still for 250 years

WARIN KELLY is the 31st squire in the male line to live at Kelly. They can be traced back to 1100, through fathers, grandfathers or brothers, with only one hiccup (as he puts it) when it passed to a first cousin, via an uncle. This puts Mr Kelly on a par with Francis Fulford of Fulford and that rare group of families who have the same name as their houses, the practice in pre-Conquest times, and the family are determined to stay there. Two rapid bouts of death duties, when Kelly's grandfather died followed swiftly by his father's elder brother, have left them with minimal funds. An exemption from inheritance taxes when his mother dies can only be secured if major repairs are carried out. And for these, alas, there are no funds.

Mr Kelly is an architect who believes in non-invasive care of old buildings. 'The death-watch beetle reappear every five years or so,' he says, looking up at the timbers over the kitchen, 'but they can't make much impact on oak of this age and density.' Periodic bouts of dry rot are also a problem but these are treated and kept at bay by controlling temperature and humidity.

Kelly House was built in 1743–5. The panelling is of glorious quality, robust yet superbly carved, whether a gadrooned chair rail, the finely carved Corinthian capitals to the hall doorcase or the chunky corkscrew balusters of the main stair. Original marble and stone fireplace surrounds remain.

The house was designed by Abraham Rundle, a joiner and architect who lived at Tavistock. His original estimate of December 29, 1742 survives, specifying a house measuring '68ft by 46ft in the out', a cellar of 7ft high, a principal storey 11 ft high 'in the clear' and a chamber story of 9 ft, the whole covered with a double roof and slated. The walls were to be built of common slate stone and 'wrought moorstone at the quoins', with a front doorcase of Portland stone. Sash windows were to be made in London and 'glaz'd with the best Crown Glass'. The great parlour and drawing room were to be panelled in deal while old wainscoting was to be used in the common parlour.

Time seemed to be standing still at Kelly when Samuel Laing of Papdale, a relation, came to stay in 1809. 'The family was extraordinary and old-fashioned in every way. Old Arthur Kelly … was the old English foxhunting squire of Fielding's novels, but whom in real life I never saw or heard of unless in this instance.' Laing describes 'wainscoted rooms, wood fires' and a 'profuse although somewhat rough style of housekeeping'.

When the Historic Buildings Councils were set up in the 1950s Kelly House would have been a candidate for grant aid, but recently Mr Kelly was told that English Heritage could not help because the increase in value of the restored property would be greater than the grant. In other words he could sell it, thereby bringing an end to 900 years of living history. But with English Heritage's own budget slashed year on year, the task of rescuing buildings as fine and important as these is becoming no easier.

The parish church stands behind the gently flaking Palladian front.

KNIGHTSTONE MANOR   Crediton
Tudor house given the perfect setting by gardening colonel

'OLD HOUSES LIE LOW,' runs the saying. And there are few more dreamy examples of a medieval and Tudor manor house than Knightstone in Devon. The house is sheltered by gently rising green hills and half hidden behind immaculate yew hedges. The first glimpse comes suddenly along a quiet lane, with an ornamental iron gate and garden path leading to the front door – the drive arrives discreetly in a courtyard to the south.

Much of the beauty of the building lies in the pale squared stone and large knapped flints, which vary in colour from pink to grey and onyx. Not a Georgian sash is to be seen – only large lead-pane windows that fill all the main rooms with abundant light.

This is a house that has grown through the centuries. A licence to build a chapel here was granted in 1381, and the H-plan layout dates from the late 14th- or early 15th-century. In 1554 it was bought by William Sherman, merchant, of nearby Ottery, whose son John married Margeret, daughter of Sir Bernard Drake, kinsman of the great Sir Francis. In 1803 Knightstone was acquired by the headmaster of Harrow School, the Rev. Dr Drury, and it is he who is responsible for the addition of the distinctive carved bargeboards on the gables.

Its modern reawakening is due to Colonel Reggie Cooper who acquired it in 1941. He was a significant restorer of old houses and had previously tackled Julian's near London and Cothay in Somerset. His importance as a gardener is evident in the entry in Harold Nicholson's Diaries for September 12, 1930: 'Go over to Sissinghurst with Reggie Cooper. We decide, on his advice, to make the bowling-green longer and to reach right down to the moat. Our general line is to keep the whole things as green and quiet and simple as we can.'

Cooper laid out the garden at Knightstone as a series of green rooms enclosed by distinctive yew hedges, which unusually do not rise straight up but have 'bombé' sides that bulge outwards towards the bottom.

The entrance porch, lined with benches like a church porch, shelters a 16th-century door that is in an amazing state of preservation. The outer arch has the shallowest of Tudor arches but the inner door has a straight top, as if the change from Gothic to Renaissance happened in the course of building it.

Inside is a typical medieval stone-flagged passage with a pair of doors to kitchen and scullery. Two steps lead up into a great hall with a splendid open timber roof with bold arch braces, which are clearly medieval too. The rough darkened timbers spring just a little uneasily from a delightful Jacobean frieze ornamented with jovial mermen and winged chimeras. The answer may be that a barrelled ceiling put in to conceal the medieval timbers later collapsed or was removed. Today, lit by two very large mullioned windows and warmed by a stone fireplace dated 1567, it is as light and comfortable as any great hall can be.

Thanks to the pale beige carpets and cream walls, the overwhelming impression throughout the whole house is one of harmony. Elegant but quite well-spaced furniture makes it easy to imagine moving in tomorrow.

Long yew hedges create a spacious series of garden rooms.

The whole house has been discreetly rewired and replumbed recently, and a borehole has been dug with a pressurised water system replacing the old tanks in the roof. There is a well-equipped but discreet modern offfice in the coal cellars. All the fittings in the kitchen, including the table, have been made from a single cedar of Lebanon, kiln-dried.

Upstairs, in the space occupied by a minstrel's gallery over the hall, a well-preserved wall painting of Adam and Eve, gaily painted in pinks and greys, has recently been uncovered and conserved.

Recently the garden has been planted with many old roses and tender perennials and Mediterranean plants, which have so far survived the winter in this well-protected spot. New ornamental iron gates have been added at the back to match those at the front. The house comes with 16 acres and a small herd of Ruby Red Devon cattle, which graze decoratively in the fields above the house.

LUPTON HOUSE — Brixham

Rebuilt after a fire, Lupton served as a wartime base for secret boat raids

SERENE THOUGH THEY LOOK, country houses have often led eventful lives. Lupton House was one of the eighty or more fine houses commandeered during the Second World War for use by Churchill's Special Operations Executive, set up to foster resistance in enemy territory. Lupton was Station 62b, used for naval operations, presumably including the Special Boat Service; however, it began life as a handsome Palladian villa built for Charles Hayne, the sheriff, in 1772 and then extended by the architect George Wightwick for Sir John Yarde-Buller.

In March 1926 Lupton, then owned by Lord Churston, was devastated by a fire. The house, it seems, was not on the telephone. According to a report in the local paper, the caretaker's wife ran half a mile in her nightgown to raise the alarm while her son cycled to Brixham to alert the fire brigade. The fire had started at 10.30 p.m. and by the morning Lupton was no more than a shell. The house was rebuilt without the upper storey as a handsome Italianate composition with a balustrade around the roof.

Today it is a school. In 2002, two teachers initiated an archaeological dig in which pupils took part, revealing an ashy layer containing much burnt wood (floor joists, parts of furniture etc), charred clothing, ceramic shards, electrical switches, light fittings and fuses. Finds of historic artefacts consumed in the fire include early 19th-century fine Chinese porcelain, early 18th-century delftware and Boer War militalia.

Despite the fire, the interior retains good features including plasterwork and chimney pieces, with screens of columns in the hall and library.

Balustrades beneath the windows and along the parapet provide a lively flourish.

MARISTOW HOUSE — Plymouth

The house's new residents now enjoy walks through 40 acres of pleasure grounds

MARISTOW STANDS IN A RAVISHING POSITION on the River Tavy, sheltered and infinitely peaceful, yet enjoying glorious long views down towards the Plymouth estuary. Not a building is in sight, only the distant silhouette of the bow truss bridge carrying a sleepy branch line across the River Tavy.

Yet for fifty years Maristow had as difficult and chequered a history as any country house in England. Three fires ravaged the mansion, which was last a family home in 1939. The Lopes family, despairing of finding a viable solution, sought permission to demolish.

Now Maristow is as pretty and fresh as any house on the Bay of Naples. Yet its Georgian appearance conceals many layers of history. Originally called Martinstowe, Maristow was the site of an ancient chapel of St Martin, which belonged to the canons of Plympton and after the Dissolution was granted in 1544 to the Champernownes, who in 1550 sold the property to John Slanning.

Today, only the unusually thick walls beside the entrance hall suggest a house of 1560 date. Maristow is essentially a mid 18th-century creation of the Heywood family,

The entrance front has Edwardian wings, added boy George and Yeates.

who inherited the estate by marriage. Peter Heywood served as Governor of Jamaica in 1716–18. His son James came to Maristow in 1733 to help run the estate and was succeeded by his son, James Modyford Heywood.

Lyson's *Magna Britannia* (1822) records that on August 22, 1789, George III, Queen Charlotte and 'three of the princesses … honoured Mr Heywood with a visit to Maristow, and were so much delighted with the romantic scenery of the grounds and woods, that they repeated their visit on the 24th'.

On Heywood's death his four surviving married daughters sold the estate to Sir Massey Manasseh Lopes, Bt, for the considerable sum of £65,000. The 1798 sales particulars describe 'a capital mansion elegantly fitted up, and fit for the immediate reception of a large and genteel family … standing in a beautiful lawn of about forty acres … a hall, floored with Portland stone'. On the first floor were three handsome bedchambers with dressing rooms and seven further bedrooms with attics above. There was a washhouse, brewhouse and dairy, excellent stabling for twenty-four horses and standing for four carriages as well as 'a very elegant chapel in the house'.

The Lopes family continued to embellish Maristow. In 1831 the famous stained glass artist Thomas Willement provided armorial bearings for the hall. The matching gate lodges at the entrance to the estate are by Charles Fowler, architect of the Covent Garden market buildings in London. The 3rd baronet, who succeeded in 1754, introduced an Italianate balustrade along the parapet and replaced the Georgian sashes with Victorian plate glass. In the 1870s he commissioned Piers St Aubyn (whose family resided at St Michael's Mount) to build a handsome gothic church behind the house. Of all St Aubyn's numerous churches, this is one of the most lavish, faced in sparrow-pecked Plymouth limestone laid in crazy coursing with a spire in Bath stone. The church contains an interesting series of roundels inset with mainly 16th-century Flemish and Italian glass. A splendid conservatory, built at about this time, appears in old photographs.

Sir Henry, the 4th baronet, succeeded in 1908, becoming 1st Lord Roborough in 1938. He invited Ernest George & Yeates (the original architects of Claridge's Hotel no less) to come down to Maristow; they gave the house a distinctly baroque flourish with the addition of a new three-storey porch complete with giant pilasters and a segmental pediment.

Requisitioned during the Second World War, ,Maristow was leased in 1950 by Lord Roborough to the Church of England Pensions Board as a home for retired clergy and their dependents. The first arrivals took up residence after £28,000 had been spent on repairs and furniture, as well as building a 25,000 gallon reservoir on the hill above the house.

Two years later the roof was badly damaged by a fire and the Pensions Board decided that restoration was impractical. Commendably, the county council took on the lease, carried out repairs and used Maristow as a special needs school for nearly twenty years from 1956. Left empty for another two years, it was taken over by a company that ran field-study and outward-bound courses. Tragically, a second fire ravaged the building in 1981, followed by a third three months later. Arson was strongly suspected.

The pretty south-facing front has bullseye windows and balustrades.

The Maristow trustees, wearied by these events, applied to demolish the now-derelict house. This was twice refused following successive public inquiries. A long stalemate ensued until finally in 1995 Kit Martin secured agreement to buy the freehold and to create twelve houses and cottages within the shell of the mansion, stables and outbuildings.

Though a large scaffold roof had been placed over the house to slow down decay, vandalism had continued and most of the upper floors had collapsed leaving a view of the gaping holes in the roof. Martin recalls, 'We were now faced with the theft of a large number of fireplaces, much of the 18th-century stair balustrading, the bookshelves in the library and all the Edwardian oak panelling in the dining room.' Working with the architects Peter Sutton and Mike Innes, Martin's solution has been to create twelve houses within the main house, dairy, laundry, stables and other outbuildings, ranging in size from two to five bedrooms and each following the pattern of structural walls.

The economics of restoring a house in such a desperate state without grants were problematic. The scheme was made viable by omitting the burnt-out attic storey but reinstating missing sections of parapet balustrade. The larger houses have glorious views across and down the river, looking out over spreading lawns. The new houses in the outbuildings have their own secluded gardens or courtyard. One of the most unusual is the garden created out of the former drying yard, which has rows of stone columns that once supported the washing. Maristow has become a community once again with residents paying for the upkeep of shared areas of grounds, which include walks through 40 acres of park and pleasure grounds.

POLTIMORE
Poltimore

Forfeit to the Crown, the house is at last undergoing an ambitious restoration

THERE IS A FINE VIEW of Poltimore from the motorway from Exeter to Taunton – a broad handsome Georgian front glimpsed through park trees. The house surveys a fine stretch of parkland with a large garden at the back protected by mature shrubs and trees. The architecture is Regency at the front and Elizabethan at the back.

Poltimore's decline began with requisitioning in the Second World War. Used as a convalescent home for American airmen, it became a nursing home and then a hospital annexe, closing in the 1970s. The property became forefeit to the Crown when the owners failed to send in an annual return. Though water was pouring through the roof, planners could not use their powers to serve a repairs order on the Grade II* listed building as such notices cannot be served on the Crown Commissioners.

For years planners watched helplessly as Tudor ceilings, early Georgian plasterwork and Adam-style decoration rotted. The saloon floor was ripped out by travellers for firewood. Finally, after the theft of the bannisters of the main staircase, fixtures such as Queen Anne fireplaces were removed for safe-keeping.

Though the Crown wanted to hand Poltimore over to a suitable restoring purchaser, of which there were plenty willing, stalemate arose because the Skipton Building Society was owed £1 million in interest on the mortgage. The chances of the money being recovered looked remote. In 1996 the Buildings at Risk Trust persuaded Skipton to relinquish its charge on the property in return for a payment of £60,000.

Today there is a Poltimore House Trust as well as the Friends of Poltimore, and there are ambitious plans for putting the house to a range of community uses with holiday apartments in the attics and the grounds. The difficult question is whether sufficient funds can be raised to meet costs of repair. But the scaffolding has gone up and a major restoration contract is underway.

The windows of the long, elegant Georgian front were boarded up for years before repairs began.

RASHLEIGH BARTON   Chumleigh
A simple H-plan manor containing a virtuoso display of Jacobean plasterwork

LOOKING AT COUNTRY HOUSES in Devon, it sometimes seems the county has more wonderful Elizabethan and Jacobean plasterwork than all the rest of England. Townhouses, yeoman farms, modest manors and grand country seats dazzle with a wealth of swirling strapwork, ornamental pendants, armorial flourishes and a menagerie of delightful animals. Rashleigh Barton is just such a house, wonderfully set amid the rolling hills of peaceful mid Devon. Here, however hot the summer, you will never be overwhelmed by tourists as on the north or south coasts.

The house is 20 miles from Exeter and 18 from Barnstaple and just two from the main road between them. But the approach is along narrow country roads and the drive is marked by nothing more than a fine spreading oak.

In recent years it has belonged to a succession of owners, all of whom have contributed to nursing the house back to life. This is a house for a family to put down roots and send children to local schools. For anyone with a small business of their own, or wanting to work from home, there is a large court of long, low farm buildings still untouched, consisting of a 17th-century barn and cart shed and 18th-century stables.

The ancient oak front door opens into a house that soaks up the sun. In essence, Rashleigh Barton is a late-medieval hall house remodelled in the early 17th century by the Clotworthys, to whom it had passed by marriage. The plasterwork bears the dates 1631 and 1633 and the initials 'I' (the Latin way of writing 'J') and MC, presumably for John and Mary Clotworthy. Originally the great hall was open to the roof, as can be seen by the arch-braced timbers in one of the bedrooms. But in the 17th century cold, draughty halls went out of fashion and there was a new emphasis on privacy and warmth. The entrance hall was given a low, beamed ceiling and a rich

The house has Jacobean mullioned windows on the left and Georgian sashes on the right.

The first-floor great chamber has a superb ceiling of interlacing ribs and pendants.

plasterwork frieze ornamented with shields. Just beyond is one of the prettiest rooms, the summer parlour, with an arched stone fireplace and a swirling ceiling, groaning with ripe pomegranates.

On the other side of the hall, where the rooms have Georgian sashes, there is a library paved with large, handsome flagstones. At the back, the house has been curiously extended, with the roof sweeping down rather like a giant lean-to.

A handsome oak stair at the end of a panelled passage leads ceremoniously to the upper floor, with a splendid dog-gate still in position. Hound-gate is probably the proper word in view of its splendour and size, nearly 5 ft high and with two rows of turned balusters. An added flourish at the top is provided by a small balustrade like that on the poop of a ship.

The first-floor great chamber, known as the Cromwell Room, has the finest plasterwork in the house with a shallow arch vault, lozenge-pattern strapwork and bold hanging pendants, one in the form of an upside-down sundial. There is an abundance of real and imagined animals: winged horses, sheep, swans, peacocks and pelicans with fish in their mouths. These shallow arch vaults are found in other rooms where the plasterwork is not on the ceilings but on the gable ends, with intricate strapwork threaded with fruit and coats of arms.

Behind the house is a secluded, paved herb garden from where you can appreciate the remarkable 'graded' roof slates that diminish in size row by row as they ascend. It is a feature found more usually with stone slate roofs, as in the Cotswolds. Here it has been done with a patience – and expense – that scarcely bears thinking about.

From 1682 Rashleigh Barton was tenanted for nearly three centuries. This explains the lack of later alterations, apart from a few Georgian sash windows. Although the estate has been sold, there is barely another building in sight.

ROUSDON HOUSE   Axminster
Victorian mansion on the grand scale peopled with new residents

I WENT TO ROUSDON HOUSE IN 2000, soon after the school that had been there for over sixty years had departed. Here was a Victorian house on the very grandest scale, secluded in the centre of a large estate and set on a hill high above the sea. The mansion was a romantic composition of gables, bay windows and tall chimneys, faced in half-timbering, hanging tiles and stone, and rising to a belvedere tower with views over the coast and gloriously unspoilt pastoral countryside.

It was built in the 1870s for Sir Henry Peek, a Tory MP, for £250,000. He commissioned plans for the house from Ernest George, the architect in whose office Lutyens worked.

The mansion, put on the market in 1999, had been sold to a group of three investors intent on a multiple development. One of them, Charles Burnett-Hitchcock, told me, 'Initially the planners wanted another institution or hotel, but we believed that residential was is the most sympathetic. All the ugly modern additions have gone.' Structural alterations were carried out to divide the main house and wings into self-contained houses and flats which were provided with services, leaving fitting out and decoration entirely to the new residents. 'We sold the units in phases at a series of auctions. It worked very well,' he says.

Below: A fine example of 1870s free style with grand bay-windowed front and half-timbering.
Right: The central cloister-like courtyard.

SHARPHAM HOUSE · Ashprington

Built by a naval captain who captured the richest prize of the Seven Years' War

SHARPHAM IS A BREATHTAKING marriage of architecture and landscape with the house standing on a promontory above a majestic S-bend of the River Dart. Beyond the ha-ha in front of the house, the contours plunge steeply down to the river. This is more than just the Capability Brown ideal of a house set in smooth green parkland.

The builder of Sharpham, Captain Philemon Pownoll, had captured the richest prize of the Seven Years' War, the *Hermione*, laden with 653 chests of treasure as well as quantities of tin, cocoa, saddlecloth and gold coin. His share, more than a quarter, came to £64,872 13s 6d. He bought the Sharpham estate with the proceeds, commissioning the architect Sir Robert Taylor to build him a handsome ashlar-faced Palladian villa which was completed in 1770.

Taylor liked to make play with rooms of unusual shape and Pownoll's octagonal entrance hall is inset with a ring of free-standing columns. Within the circle they inscribe the floor is paved to form a sixteen-point compass. A break in the wall, not a door, leads the eye through to one of the most dramatic staircase halls in England. It is as if Pownoll, yearning to be back at sea, was seeking to create the sense of vertigo you might feel on looking down from a mast top. The staircase hall is a cavernous oval, with the steps clinging to the walls. The flight from the first floor to the second is a continuous

The three sided 'canted' bay is a signature of the architect Sir Robert Taylor.

run of thirty-five steps, making you secretly wish for a handrail on both sides as on a rope bridge over a rocky gorge. The light floating effect of the flights of steps is increased by cutting away the underside of each tread in a delicate S-curve, to create a rippling effect. The unusual drama of the space is further emphasised by the dome, which rises directly from the walls with coffering diminishing towards a central oval lantern.

Taylor's villa has no basement and the services were placed in the older house which was retained behind the new villa. The grand rooms were on the first floor with ceilings nearly 15 ft high. The drawing room has a sculpted oval relief above the fireplace used by Taylor in other houses. Next door the octagonal saloon was embellished early in the 19th century. At the top of the house, within the three-sided bay, is another favourite Taylor motif – a pair of twin oval bedrooms linked by oval lobbies.

Far from retiring to lead a life of pleasure, Pownoll continued to seek action at sea and died in 1780, aged just 45, in a fierce action against a French cruiser, which his men finally drove ashore off Ostend. The estate passed to his 16-year-old daughter whose guardian, Lord Exmouth, quickly made her a ward of court. To no avail. In 1783, aged 19, she eloped to Gretna Green with 25-year-old Lieutenant Edmund Bastard, who had cunningly hired all the post horses in the district to baffle pursuit. Yet they lived long and happily at Sharpham, dying in the same year. Alas, their son appears to have gambled the estate away and it was put up for sale in 1841. The particulars claim the park was 'covered with rich velvet turf such as bordered the enchanted island of Calypso' and boasted 'a rhododendron walk which alone extends almost a quarter of a mile through the fields of Elysium'.

Sharpham today is a trust set up by its late owner, the economist and planner Maurice Ash and his wife Ruth, who filled the house and gardens with modern paintings and sculpture. The trust practises sustainable farming on the 550-acre estate as well as running Buddhist courses and environmental activities for schools and community groups.

The boathouse is on the River Dart with the house on the hill behind.

YOULSTON PARK   Barnstaple

Former seat of the Chichesters, medieval in origin but mainly 17th and 18th century

THE MOST LOVEABLE OF English country houses are often those that have grown through the centuries, with the taste of the family more evident than that of the architects; those where, as Evelyn Waugh wrote of Brideshead, 'time curbed the artist's pride and the Philistine's vulgarity and repaired the clumsiness of the dull workmen.'

Not to say that the craftsmen at Youlston were in any way pedestrian – the interior contains plasterwork of dizzying virtuosity as well as magnificent woodwork. This is a house with all the trappings of a grand stately home but on a manageable scale – just six bedrooms and five gloriously grand reception rooms. Better still, dare one say it, it belongs to that select group of places on which the Victorian age laid no trace.

Youlston (you pronounce it Yolston) is so tucked away that, but for the matching pair of pretty octagonal gate lodges, there would be no reason to suspect its very existence. A gently curving drive lined with chestnut trees, now growing to maturity, leads through the park. The house is in a hollow – lying low like so many old houses and providing shelter from strong west winds – with the grass sweeping down to the entrance front in best Capability Brown manner. For five centuries Youlston was the seat of the famous Chichester family. More than a dozen carefully tinctured Chichester coats of arms with innumerable quarterings emblazon the 17th-century panelling of the entrance hall.

The house is friendly and welcoming. No grand flight of steps leads up to the front door and the handsome sash windows of the main rooms are at ground level.

The entrance hall opens into a grand 18th-century saloon, practically a double cube, with a coved ceiling fitted cleverly beneath the arched trusses of the medieval great hall. Recent owners employed the decorative painter Alan Dodd to marble the upper walls and coffer the ceiling with truly Parisian sophistication. The turban-like door handles add a further flourish.

Beyond, the Morning Room has elegant 18th-century plasterwork looking as if it is concealing earlier open beams. Intriguingly the motifs change from one beam to

another – with oak leaves and acorns, a Greek key pattern and a *guilloche* motif of interlocking circles. Further on is the Venetian Staircase, so-called because of the grand Venetian or Palladian window on the half landing with central arch carried on fluted pillars. It comes with three turned balusters to each step and a swept-up baroque handrail at each corner.

By contrast to the lofty proportions of the main rooms, the dining room is low-ceilinged, making for intimacy and good conversation. The large traditional kitchen beyond retains vast open ranges with huge slanting stones hanging over the hearth in defiance of the laws of gravity.

Crossing to the west wing there is a still more splendid stair – this one of painted wood but with the monumental handrail and shaped balusters of a staircase built in stone. To increase the grand impression it continues on up to the attics, where the final landing is pressed so close to the eaves that the inside half of the balustrade has been shaved off to provide space to walk along it. Most eyes, however, will be diverted by the splendid series of mischievous satyrs' heads adorning the coved ceiling.

The climax of Youlston comes with the Chinese Room – papered from floor to ceiling with hand-painted scenes of Chinese life, full of humour and intriguing detail. I had been told to look out for the man with the fly on his head but never found him, and had to be content with admiring an endless variety of silk-robed figures in exotic slippers. Apart from a little staining where the squire's bath overflowed some years ago, these are in miraculous condition. Above them is a wonderful ornamental ceiling with garlands of flowers hanging free like Grinling Gibbons carvings. Next door these are trumped by the still more splendid plasterwork in the Red Sitting Room, inset with life-size herons holding serpents in their beaks – the Chichester emblem.

Youlston now needs someone to make something of the gardens. The potential is there – starting with two large walled gardens. Pleasure grounds sweep down to a beautiful lake surrounded by rhododendrons, which stretch out over the water to create the lushness of a mangrove swamp. At the far end of the gardens stands an unusual folly – the unroofed walls of the kennels for the Chichester's private pack of hounds is just asking to be turned into a secret garden.

Parkland sweeps down to the entrance front with the stable clock cupola visible behind the house.

Behind the house is a large 18th-century stable range with cupola and clock, laid out on three sides of a courtyard waiting to be used in any way you want. The park at Youlston is in effect two large fields on either side of the drive. But with sheep and cattle roaming free it is a splendid sight, the more thrilling for the spectacular views that open up as you crest the ridge, notably westwards towards the sea and across Exmoor.

DORSET

ANDERSON MANOR IS A BLISSFULLY pretty Jacobean manor perfect in every detail. The house is approached up a long avenue aligned on the front entrance. The gates into the courtyard are set on the far side of a stream which stands in for a moat. Rainwater heads provide a date of 1622 with the initials of John Tregonwell, who built the house. The great feature is the crisp geometry with a strongly projecting central bay in the form of a half-octagon contrasting with the steeply gabled wings. Behind the roof ridge groups of column chimneys reinforce the verticality. The warm red brick is interlaced with courses of burnt headers, while the plinth is of flint.

Anderson remained in the hands of Tregonwell's descendants until 1910 when it was rescued from years of decay by Mrs Gordon Gratrix, who revealed many original features hidden by later alterations and planted a topiary garden laid out with box and yew hedges.

Anderson is another comfortable country house that was used during the Second World War by Churchill's Special Operations Executive. In charge was the lean and handsome Gus March-Phillips. He wrote to his wife, 'I wish you were here. It's a really marvellous place, and the weather is perfect. Every morning I ride out through woods full of primroses and bluebells and violets with the dew still on them, and the sun shining through the early morning mist. I think when the war is over we must settle down here, perhaps in this house if we're very great people then. It's one of the most perfect gardens I've ever seen.'

A bridge across a fast-flowing stream leads to an entrance court with topiary and yew hedges.

BOWLING GREEN Milbourne Port
Comfortable 1920s house in the Cotswold style

BOWLING GREEN BELONGS TO THE DELIGHTFUL GROUP of newly built 'lesser' or smaller country houses that featured in *Country Life* after the First World War, designed for modern living by a large number of talented architects working in traditional styles.

It was designed by Sir Edward Guy Dawber, more usually known as Guy Dawber, whose houses are always thoughtfully conceived and finely built. Bowling Green had rather remarkably been empty for nearly twenty years when it came on the market in 2003. It is built in a Cotswold style of rough rubble stone with crisp ashlar trim to the mullioned windows.

The plan of the house is a simple H extended into an L by the addition of a large kitchen wing to the west. Part of its charm is that you can look through the doors and windows of the hall straight through to the lovely view beyond.

Over the entrance are the arms of the Montmorency family for whom the house was built, complete with a peacock crest. The main hall is a fine panelled room with a stone fireplace and another splendid coat of arms as the overmantel, all very atmospheric and romantic thanks to the bare scrubbed wooden floors.

The garden is full of good topiary in the form of clipped yew hedges and also gives fine views to the village. A pretty twin-gabled stone cottage is attached to a double garage and stables with tack room. On the south front is an unusually elongated dormer window – like the weavers' lights that can be found at the tops of houses in the West Riding of Yorkshire or Spitalfields in London.

The house is neatly symmetrical, except for the tall staircase window.

CHEDDINGTON COURT · Beaminster

1850s house doubled in size with new great hall by Sir James Dunbar-Naysmith

CHEDDINGTON COURT ASPIRES TO the Bill Gates league. Touch-screen terminals throughout the house offer a choice of analogue, digital, terrestrial, Sky or foreign-language films in different rooms. The temperature, or the music, in each room can be changed by touching an on-screen floor plan. Indeed the owner could do it from his car even before the main gates opened. The gardens alone have miles of cabling to serve the lights and pumps, allowing the hard-pressed company chairman to enjoy his gardens as much by night as by day.

The owners had turned to the doyen of Scottish architects, Sir James Dunbar-Nasmith. The Victorian house he found was not a portentous Gothic Revival mansion but a subtle evocation of the traditional Dorset manor house, Elizabethan in style, with every gable and mullioned window of a different shape and size. There were ball and obelisk finials, a belfry and a grand bay window all executed in the mellow local stone. Sir James matched the detail using the same Ham stone, 7,000 tons of it. His task was to double the house in size without striking a discordant note.

His clients wanted a great hall and so he used the ground that slopes away on the garden side and sunk the great hall by a whole storey, so that the floor is at the basement level of the 1850s house. You emerge in the hall on top of a minstrels' gallery, making a stately descent by a stair at one end. 'I also took the liberty of placing the large oriel window at the end of the hall, not the side as was usual in the Middle Ages, to frame the superb view to the west,' says Sir James.

The Victorian house on the left is designed like a traditional Dorset manor; the new great hall, to the right, is sunk into the slope.

The lake in front of the house has the regular form of a millpond.

The glory of the hall is the astonishing oak roof with flying ribs leaping across space. It's a British version of Hungarian organic architecture. 'A hammer-beam roof, which was my clients' first wish, works in two dimensions. I wanted a structure working in three,' Sir James explains.

Architects are used to trimming back adventurous schemes because of cost. Here the opposite happened. His clients demanded more and more elaboration, resulting in a tour de force of green oak construction with multiple king posts and pendants. Sir James's one regret is that building regulations meant that metal joints had to be used when he was sure that traditional timber ones were quite sufficient.

Sir James continues: 'The only proper way to light a great hall is with candles. I couldn't find a way of concealing an electric winch to raise and lower very large chandeliers to allow the candles to be changed. So it's done on a very clever system of counterweights, allowing you to pull down the chandeliers with an old-fashioned window pole.' The one thing that he did not allow for was that the massive candles would get lighter as they burnt down, so that during the course of the evening the chandeliers ascend very gently towards the roof.

The hall is dominated by a vast stone fireplace in crisply cut Bath stone and the rug there is so heavy that it had to be mechanically lifted to the entrance. The panelling, also Renaissance in style, is all in oak, polished to an antique finish.

In around 1900 the house was remodelled for Sir Henry Peto, in what Sir James considers an unsatisfactory Art Nouveau style. Later it became a low-key country-house hotel. During the recent alterations the roof was taken off and much of the interior remodelled. The new conservatory is a piece of architecture within as well as without, with pillars, frieze and cornice all of the same blemishless golden stone. Beyond is a pretty office with arched windows overlooking the garden. Cheddington also contains a private cinema and an exercise room concealed in the roof space.

The 17 acres of grounds are less than might be expected with a house of such pretensions, but the entrance front is attractively reflected in a stretch of water that has the feel of an ancient millpond, and on the garden side a new lake has been created, a full 13 ft deep.

CRANBORNE MANOR   Cranbourne
Hunting lodge built for King John, extended for Robert Cecil

CRANBORNE MANOR HAS OFTEN BEEN CALLED the loveliest manor house in Dorset, even in England. If it is more ravishing today than ever before, thanks are due to the dowager Lady Salisbury who has created one of the most romantic of all 20th-century gardens, with a formality that is softened by profusion and colour. Whichever way you view it, Cranborne has an exotic air. There are buttresses and battlements, pyramid-roofed towers and arcaded loggias. On the south front the tallest windows are on the ground floor, on the north they are at the top. The architecture is a delightful mixture of Norman, Jacobean and Caroline.

From the start this was a house intended for pleasure, first of kings then of ministers, a place where life could be enjoyed, if only fleetingly. Cranborne is the more appealing because it was allowed to sleep through the two centuries when it was most

The battlements, buttress and half-octagonal stair turret of the hunting lodge built for King John in 1208 are still clearly visible.

likely to come to harm, and was woken gently. Floors were scrubbed down, broken window panes replaced and the grass carefully pulled from the parapets and windowsills.

At the time of Domesday the Manor of Cranborne belonged to Queen Matilda, wife of William the Conqueror. Her son William Rufus granted it to Robert Fitzhamon, the conqueror of much of South Wales. In 1189 Cranborne came again into royal possession and was used by King John as a hunting lodge. A nimrod among kings, he accumulated the largest number of houses ever possessed by an English monarch, the majority of them in good hunting country. He is recorded as coming to Cranborne fourteen times and in 1207–8 there is a record of a payment for

The Jacobean stair has characteristic short flights and arches like cogs.

'building the King's house at Cranborne'. A plan and drawing of 1605 show in detail the lodge he built with a half-octagonal stair turret still visible on the south front. The house consisted of a hall and solar over a vaulted kitchen and cellar.

Shortly before the death of Queen Elizabeth I, Robert Cecil obtained possession of the house. Like other members of his family before him, he was an ardent builder. His father, Lord Burghley, had built Burghley and Theobalds as well as Cecil House in The Strand. Robert Cecil built Chelsea House and Salisbury House in London and by 1608 had begun work at both Hatfield and Cranborne. The mason at Cranborne was William Arnold, who supervised the building of Wadham College in Oxford. He retained battlements from the old house yet made the north and south fronts symmetrical with even rows of windows on both main floors, adding the loggias to both fronts.

Cecil was created Viscount Cranborne in 1604 and Earl of Salisbury the next year. He died in May 1612, a week before his 49th birthday, just as both houses were reaching completion. A vivid picture of him is provided by the Venetian Ambassador who describes him as 'short, crooked backed, but with a noble countenance … in matters of state he is of great weight. He has many enemies, but all have fallen … Of his wealth I will not speak for it passes the bounds of all belief.'

It is likely he remodelled Cranborne with the express purpose of entertaining the sovereign. James I's addiction to the hunt was such that it was the only sure way to his presence. When the 2nd Earl entertained the King at Cranborne in 1615, the menu included forty-eight muttons, twenty veals, twenty-two lambs, eleven dozen larks, pewits, herons, quails and curlews, great mullet, bass, congers, sea breams and twenty dozen lobsters, 1,000 opened oysters and 1,400 prawns, not to mention 870 pounds

The Renaissance loggias added by Cecil stand out clearly.

of butter. With this went three hogshead of claret, one of white wine and thirty gallons of Canarie or Good Old Sherry Sac and eight tons of beer.

At the outbreak of Civil War the 2nd Earl, after some hesitation, took the side of Parliament, and orders were given for the furnishings to be shipped for safety to Carisbrooke Castle on the Isle of Wight. In 1643 Salisbury's Steward wrote to him saying that five or six hundred Royalist soldiers had broken into the house, 'pulled out iron bars and casements, and carried away everything that was portable'. They even killed a hundred sheep, most of them in the house.

Repairs were soon under way and a design for a new wing on the west side of the house was prepared by Captain Richard Ryder, who was then working at Wilton under Inigo Jones. After two centuries of neglect, repairs were set in motion by the 2nd Marquess. The 3rd Marquess, the Prime Minister, had no particular feeling for the house and placed a limit of £400 on work when his wife wanted to make alterations, saying that if she overspent he would let it – both of which duly happened. The house came to life in 1929 when the 4th Marquess gave it to his son who installed heating and electricity and handed it to his son in 1954 as he in turn succeeded as Lord Salisbury. The work then undertaken included the paving of the south court and the remodelling of the library in Charles II style by T. Dalton Clifford. Today Cranborne's beauty remains undimmed and the garden is open every Wednesday in summer, while the garden centre and estate shop are open all the year round.

DOWNE HALL
Bridport
Adamesque mansion in secluded park 200 yards from the centre of a country town

HIDDEN AWAY ONLY 200 YARDS from the main street, Downe Hall was the archetypal secret garden depicted in children's stories, lived in by a reclusive old lady.

The handsome house was built in 1789 by Captain William Downe and reputedly modelled on his London house. Certainly the elegant Portland stone front with central pediment was good enough to be by a London architect – if not Adam, a figure like Thomas Leverton who worked of many on the houses in Bedford Square. In the late 19th century, the house and grounds were remodelled by E.S. Prior, the Arts and Crafts architect, who added terraces and a sunken rose garden.

The glory of Downe Hall was that it was a country house in a town, secluded by a belt of 200-year-old trees that encircled an enchanting miniature country house park of 14 acres ascending the hill behind the house with a smooth grass sward and noble park trees and woodland walks. The site was a haven for wildlife, and included numerous badger setts.

When its elderly owner Violet Snook went into a nursing home, local people gradually became aware of the treasure on their doorstep, a potential public park different from any other. Most public parks are 19th-century creations. Downe was 18th-century. It was as if the town had discovered its very own Hampstead Heath, offering wild nature within a few minutes' walk. Alas, English Heritage was unaware of the garden or its importance and permission was given to build eight substantial four-bedroom houses with double garages next to the Hall. When Jocelyn Stevens, the chairman of English Heritage, became aware of the significance of the landscape, he fought to reverse the decision. Locals pinned hopes on the fact that Downe Hall and its grounds were in a conservation area and an Area of Outstanding Natural Beauty. A local campaigner, Catherine Searle, valiantly took the case to the High Court, but sadly judgement went against her and the houses were built. Yet the saga serves as a spur to discover – and protect – other remarkable historic town gardens hidden behind walls and hedges, shrubs and trees.

Below: The handsome garden front is Adamesque in style.

Bottom: The house can clearly be seen from the park.

ENCOMBE

Kingston

Designed by John Pitt, cousin of the Prime Minister, for himself

THE 2,000-ACRE Encombe estate is a vision of Heaven as Capability Brown might have imagined it – huge rolling hills carpeted in smooth grass that is broken only by the occasional majestic shelter belt or clump of trees nestling in the fold of a valley. With it comes a two-and-a-half-mile frontage of breathtaking Dorset coastline, which has been designated as a World Heritage Site.

In more than a thousand years there have been only five significant changes of ownership at Encombe. In AD 948 the land was given by King Edred to the Abbess of Shaftesbury. Following the Dissolution of the Monasteries in the 1540s, Encombe was acquired by the Cullifords of Devon, who sold it in the mid 18th century to the Pitt family, cousins of William Pitt the Elder, the Prime Minister, who often wrote in anguish of the difficulties of finding time to visit 'dear, unknown, delightful, picturesque Encombe' and sent his

The house has monumental arches in the style of Sir John Vanbrugh.

'benedictions to the hills, rocks, pines, shores, seas' of the estate.

In 1807 the Pitts sold Encombe to the 1st Earl of Eldon, the longest-serving of all England's Lord Chancellors. He was one of the foremost reactionaries of his time, resolutely opposed to both the Great Reform Bill and Catholic emancipation.

The present house, while incorporating the shell of an Elizabethan mansion, also has flourishes that are typical of the work of Sir John Vanbrugh, the architect of Blenheim Palace. The most notable of these is a central chimney that takes the form of a triumphal arch. Almost certainly it was designed by Encombe's owner, the MP John Pitt, known as the 'great Commoner of the West', in humorous reference to his more famous cousin, the Prime Minister.

While many 18th-century country houses consist of a grand centre flanked by lower wings, Encombe is like five almost identical Classical cottages joined together. But though it looks Lilliputian from a distance, inside it contains a series of grand and lofty reception rooms, including a splendid double-height dining room.

Pitt, concerned that he could not glimpse the sea from his bedroom windows, laid out to the south of the house a large lake which winds out of view. Eighteenth-century engravings show he kept a small yacht on it, as if he could sail straight out to sea.

Encombe stands on the Isle of Purbeck, famous for its marble which was used in both Westminster Abbey and Salisbury Cathedral. The isle is a secret place that stands isolated from the rest of Dorset by the huge inlet of Poole Harbour on one side and military firing ranges on the other. The approach is past the ruins of Corfe Castle and the seclusion of the house is ensured by a mile-long drive.

With such an abundance of building stone, Pitt was able to pave the bottom of his lake, and also the streams descending from the hills, including one that doubles up as a ha-ha and neatly prevents the water from cascading straight through Encombe's front door.

Water to feed the lake is ingeniously brought along a half-mile tunnel through the hill to the east of the house. At 6 ft high, and lined in brick, it is said to have been much used by the smugglers who frequented this part of the Dorset coast, bringing in large quantities of brandy from France.

The 3rd Earl of Eldon created several scenic carriage drives around the estate, some of which are now overgrown. In the 19th century, a walk or ride to the sea would have been rewarded by a cream tea in the estate dairy and followed by a visit to the Cyclopean grotto formed of blocks of stone the size of tea chests.

For centuries the seclusion and beauty of Encombe have been guarded as jealously as if it were owned by the National Trust. Two public footpaths on the headlands that run out to the sea on either side command majestic views of the coastline and the Golden Bowl in which Encombe sits, but barely intrude on its privacy. The only small blemish in this paradise is the occasional noise from the nearby military firing range.

The long garden front looks out over a stone paved lake.

HIGHCLIFFE CASTLE   Christchurch
Gothic Revival house on a cliff above the sea, epitome of 19th-century romanticism

FOR YEARS HIGHCLIFFE CASTLE stood gently rotting on a cliff above the beach just four miles from Bournemouth. The house was built in the early 1830s by Lord Stuart de Rothesay, incorporating materials from the Hotel des Andelys near Rouen in Normandy, where Antoine de Bourbon, the father of King Henri IV, died in 1562.

Rothesay, returning to England on his retirement from the British Embassy in Paris in 1830, saw the hotel being demolished, bought it and had it shipped down the Seine and across the channel. This brought, somewhat unjustly, a stinging denunciation from Victor Hugo, who accused the Ambassador of the crime of 'Elginisme', repeating Lord Elgin's abduction of the Parthenon Marbles, a controversial topic even then.

Photographs taken in the 1950s show the house complete with its gardens, but creeping suburbia was already eating away its setting. The architect W.J. Donthorne, a pupil of Jeffry Wyatville, had an extensive practice, designing country houses and

Before restoration began, Highcliffe was gently rotting in a public park, surrounded by barbed wire.

parsonages especially in his native Norfolk. His great hall at Highcliffe is a not-so-scaled-down version of King's College Chapel in Cambridge, entered at the north end with a grand stair leading out at the other. When I first saw it in 1987 it was boarded up, derelict and roofless, its decay the more poignant because of the municipal flowers beds around it. Yet the exquisite oriel window survived as well as a wealth of ornamental carving and elaborate inscriptions.

After a spell as a monastery it was bought in 1967 by a group of local businessmen who applied for permission to build 150 beach huts in the grounds. They were refused and in 1977, after two fires had dangerously damaged the building, Christchurch District Council acquired the castle. Their prime purpose was not to restore the buildings but to

The oriel window was salvaged by Lord Stuart de Rothesay from Les Andelys on the Seine.

obtain a new access to the beach below the house and provide parking for a hundred cars in the pleasure grounds.

As the building decayed, councillors' thoughts turned to demolition. What changed their minds, I was told later by a local campaigner, was that some madman in London was sending a lorry round London with a large picture of the abandoned castle. The madman was me and the legend read, 'The council paid for the barbed wire.'

For years the only prospect of salvation lay in a series of totally unacceptable schemes for building blocks of flats in the grounds. Then, with the advent of English Heritage grants for buildings at risk and the Lottery, a phased programme of repairs began. First the conservatory was restored and opened as a visitor centre. Then followed restoration of the exquisite ornamental stonework and the gradual opening of the state rooms. The council has recruited an impressive loyal band of volunteers and the castle is once again the pride of the borough. Rothesay's superb collection of continental stained glass is being restored.

There is a continuing programme of exhibitions and concerts as well as weddings. The castle hosts up to three weddings a day – generally at 11 am, 1 pm and 3.30pm on any day of the week – with champagne, bucks' fizz andcanapes on offer. Understandably, confetti and rice are not allowed but wedding bubbles are available from the castle gift shop. Weddings can also be held in winter though as yet the castle has no heating or outdoor lighting. With fees for a civil ceremony set for £615 until April 1, 2008, this is clearly good business for the castle. The castle also provides a hundred carparking spaces on site – plenty of space for all your guests. After years of gloom Highcliffe is en fête.

KINGSTON MAURWARD · Dorchester

Grand four-square baroque house set in superbly maintained gardens

THE ABIDING APPEAL OF KINGSTON MAURWARD is the pale silvery stone of the facades. It is said this is due to George III. During one of the king's visits from Weymouth where he passed the summers with his family, the owner William Morton Pitt was enthusing about his house, hoping it would receive royal approval. All the king would say was, 'Brick, Mr Pitt, brick.' Between royal visits, and at vast expense, Mr Pitt had his house reclad.

For many years now the house has been an agricultural college and is a rare example of a good fit between an institution and a country house. I first arrived in 1978 while looking for unusual gardens to include in a conservation section for the V&A exhibition 'The Garden'. The paved terraces around the house were planted with large beds of pansies in dashing blue and yellow stripes. The grounds descended in an impressively smooth sweep of turf to the lake. Park and lake were formed by William Morton Pitt's father, John Pitt of Encombe, who succeeded to Kingston in 1774 on the death of his elder brother. A temple by the lake with an inset portico like the temples of Petra dates from this time.

The house was built in 1717–20 by George Pitt of Strathfieldsaye in Hampshire with a centrepiece of giant baroque pilasters. Arthur Oswald attributed the design to John James of Greenwich who listed among his patrons 'Mr Geo:Pitt of Hampshire'.

The house has a characteristic baroque centre of giant pilasters, raised cornice and 'skied' cornice.

KINGSTON RUSSELL
Kingston Russell
Bought in 1913 from the Duke of Bedford in advanced decay, now restored

A STRING OF BEAUTIFUL HOUSES bear the name of Kingston – in Dorset, Berkshire, Nottinghamshire as well as in Wiltshire. Kingston Russell was long in the ownership of the Earls of Bedford but was standing isolated in the fields, derelict and overgrown with ivy, when it was bought from the 11th Duke of Bedford in 1913 by George Gribble.

Gribble employed the accomplished architect Philip Tilden to restore it, building entrance gates, laying out lawns and planting an extensive formal garden, with low walls and bastions of clipped yew with tops as level as tables. Panelling that had been removed from the sitting room by the Duke of Bedford was traced and replaced.

Yet further alterations were carried out for Mr and Mrs William Vestey, who bought the house in 1939; they also redecorated the entrance hall in the manner of William Kent.

The present entrance front was added in about 1730 for John Michel. It has a Vanbrughian quality that echoes that of Eastbury, also in Dorset, or Adderbury in Oxfordshire. This is evident especially in the treatment of the windows, which are set back deep in the stone reveals – in contrast to the usual early 18th century practice of placing them flush with the walls. The windows in the centre are plain arches, those to the sides have emphatic

Baroque monumentality is combined with Palladian grace. Note the distinctive Vanbrughian sills under the windows, supported by brackets.

frames. Francis Cartwright, one of the masons working at Eastbury under Vanbrugh, has been suggested as the author of the design.

Michel's son, David Robert Michel, went to live in Dewlish and thereafter the house was let for long periods, which helped to preserve it through the rapid changes of fashion of the late 18th and 19th centuries.

The beauty of the house lies above all in the silvery hue of the Portland stone, cut with such superb precision.

STINSFORD HOUSE   Dorchester
Pavilion that stood abandoned in 1700 formal gardens

STINSFORD HOUSE FEATURED AS my Heap of the Week in *The Times* on April 4, 1992. That very morning I was told that there was a gathering of readers in front of the house, which looked like a Portuguese *quinta*, with a tall *piano nobile* set over a low basement and cosy attic bedrooms lit by dormers in the roof. Until six years before, Stinsford was a school. It had then been sold several times and was now in the hands of a bank. Planning permission had been granted both for an hotel and for seven residential units in the house, yet Stinsford cried out to be a single family home.

The garden front looked south over formal terraces secluded behind walls, presumably the original formal garden layout of around 1700. A garden door opened into the graveyard of the fine medieval church with a headstone to Dorset's most famous son, the author Thomas Hardy. The entrance front looked west along a fine avenue interrupted, it had to be said, by the new Dorchester bypass, but this went past in a cutting. Though the Chief Constable lived just 50 yards away, large areas of roof slates had been stripped and the floors were sodden with damp. Squatters had recently been in occupation. But the handsome panelling all looked characteristic of a 1700 date. The house had 6 acres and it was easy to imagine how it could be transformed with neat box hedges and cascades of rambler roses.

Alas, Stinsford went not to a private buyer but to a speculator who was able to claim that repair was uneconomical without enabling development. On this basis, those who wanted to buy Stinsford and restore it as a family house were outbid. Here is a cautionary tale emphasising that the best solution for empty historic houses is for them to be sold for a price reflecting their condition, not the planning permissions that may be granted. Stinsford has been saved, but compromised too.

Stinsford in 1992, six years after the school closed – crying out to be a family house again.

ST GILES HOUSE   Wimborne St Giles
Ancestral seat of the Earls of Shaftesbury with white and gold Palladian interiors

'THERE CANNOT BE A MAJOR aristocratic house in England that has fallen into a more agonisingly pitiful state in recent years,' I wrote in the *Sunday Telegraph* in February 1990. The rose-pink walls of the ancestral seat of the Earls of Shaftesbury were a gangrenous green. Blocked and broken drainpipes had started the rain running down the walls, washing away carved mouldings. Windows and shutters were firmly closed and the house was seized with dry rot. 'We are treating a major outbreak,' said the agent with remarkable candour, 'and I am not sure whether the house can be restored.'

St Giles was 'open for business only'. The Estate Office still operated from the back of the house but all around the lawns were overgrown and the terraced gardens running wild.

How this could happen in prosperous Dorset, where fine houses were as sought after and as difficult to come by as anywhere in Britain, was a mystery. St Giles had everything that people look for in a great house. It is secluded in the centre of a large estate, looking down over a large ornamental lake. Just across the park is a romantic gabled Jacobean stable block. Famous buildings nearby include Cranborne and Kingston Lacey.

St Giles had belonged to the Ashleys (later Ashley Coopers) since the 15th century. The present house was built for the 1st Earl of Shaftesbury, who was politically adept enough to be first a Royalist, then a Parliamentarian, then a supporter of the Restoration. St Giles was begun in 1651 – placing it among a remarkable group of Commonwealth houses including Coleshill (alas demolished), Thorpe Hall in Peterborough and Kingston Lacey nearby.

The house in 1990 with the gardens running wild.

The house is encircled by a large estate with parkland, lake and remarkable Georgian grotto.

Created Baron Ashley in 1661 by Charles II, and Earl in 1672, Shaftesbury had been the first A of the notorious CABAL Ministry, named after the initials of its members. In the 1680s he was forced to flee to Holland because of his hostility to James II.

The 3rd Earl was the famous philosopher of the early 1700s. The 4th Earl, in 1740–44, called in Henry Flitcroft, protégé of Lord Burlington, to create a sumptuous series of white and gold state rooms, with rich plaster ceilings and elaborate panelling. In about 1800 the 5th Earl rendered the sprawling house to give it a Classical unity. In 1854 the architect P.C. Hardwick added a pair of Italianate towers to enliven the composition for the 7th Earl, the great philanthropist.

All this was on display in a 10p postcard on sale in the village church. The shock was to find the towers gone and the wings truncated, leaving not an attractive manageable house, but an unshapely mass still bearing the hideous untreated scars of brutal demolition. An attempt to uncover the original brickwork by removing the render had simply exposed the house to damp as the facing bricks had lost their weatherproof surface when they were scored to take the render. St Giles was rapidly approaching the point of no return. Soon after, Lord Shaftesbury went to live in the South of France where his murder was reported prominently in the press.

Amid the decay there was one piece of good news, that the remarkable mid 18th-century grotto by the lake had been restored with help from English Heritage and the Georgian Group.

WRAXALL HOUSE · Maiden Newton

Jacobean house commandeered by Churchill's Special Operations Executive

THERE IS A WRAXALL IN WILTSHIRE and another in Somerset. I came to the Dorset Wraxall while tracking down the country houses requisitioned by SOE, Churchill's clandestine wartime Special Operations Executive, which sent secret agents to occupied Europe. Wraxall Manor House near Maiden Newton, like Anderson Manor nearby, was used by the small boats section of SOE. It is the perfect expression of a small manor house not secluded behind high walls but set besde a quiet country lane which opens up to form a green in front of the house. It has the welcoming feel of an overgrown cottage set a little way back behind a low wall. Mellow Dorset stone, one of the most beautiful of all building materials, is here used for walls, window mullions and chimneys to create a seamless whole. An unusual feature is the placing of the chimneys at the tops of the gables so the flues had to rise diagonally to avoid the windows, but this is not infrequent in Dorset and Somerset at this period.

The 17th-century owners were the Lawrences. It is thought the house was built by William Lawrence in about 1620 – he died in 1640. Another William Lawrence, born here in 1611, was a lawyer and wrote a tract *Mariage by the Morall Law of God*, said by a contemporary to have been written 'on a discontent arising from his wife (a red-haired buxom woman) whom he esteemed dishonest to him'.

The flues rise diagonally to chimneys placed above the windows in the gables.

COUNTY DURHAM

AXWELL PARK HAD BEEN STANDING EMPTY and decaying since 1978, until bought by the DARE Group in 2005. When I saw it in 1968 it was in use as a Borstal, efficiently run with plenty of fresh paint and still standing imposingly in its park, though the approach was compromised by the series of staff houses that had been built along the drive.

The house was built to the designs of James Paine for Sir Thomas Clavering, Bt, and when the Borstal closed, the authorities built a school, Clavering House, in the grounds, providing secure accommodation. When this closed in 2003, vandalism of the main house accelerated. The DARE Group initially bought Axwell with just 2 acres of land but when they negotiated the purchase of Clavering House they acquired a further 38 acres including park, lake, bridge and walled garden. The school has been demolished and is being replaced by eighteen very contemporary houses in the walled garden, clad in zinc, cedar, render and an abundance of glass.

Paine's house was in a desparate condition, without a roof and with only two sections of floors and ceiling remaining. The house is to be converted into twenty-one apartments, preserving the handsome vaulting in the basement, with work due to be completed in late 2008. This is a brave venture, giving hope for even the most decayed of country houses, transforming an eyesore into a noble landmark once more.

The purchase of 38 acres of grounds has helped make restoration viable.

BRANCEPETH CASTLE — Brancepeth
Major medieval castle extensively remodelled in the early 19th century

BRANCEPETH IS AN ARCHETYPAL creation of the Romantic movement, worthy of comparison with castles on the Rhine and the Danube. Yet when I saw it in the late 1970s it was standing empty, a colossus in urgent need of new owners and residents. For once they were not long in coming.

Thanks to its irregular layout around a polygonal courtyard, Brancepeth presents a wonderfully picturesque silhouette of battlements, towers and turrets with an array of arched and mullioned windows proclaiming its ancestry. Brancepeth began as a true fortified castle in the 14th century but major remodelling was initiated in 1818 by William Russell, whose father had bought the estate in 1796. Russell's architect was the Scot John Paterson who became the leading practitioner of the Castle style in succession to the Adam brothers.

William Russell died a bachelor and in 1828 Emma, daughter of Matthew Russell MP of Brancepeth Castle, married the 7th Viscount Boyne, who as an Irish peer was given the English title of Baron Brancepeth in 1866. Further alterations were carried out by Salvin in both 1829 and 1864–75.

During the First World War the castle became an active hospital treating over 4,000 casualties, then in 1924 Lord Boyne laid out a golf course in the deer park, which was sold to the members in 1961. The architects engaged to design and lay down the golf course were H.S. Colt and his partner Major J.S.F. Morrison. Brancepeth Castle was converted into flats in the early 1980s and the castle today looks down serenely on the golf course which laps the walls. It may not be the expected solution for a castle of this splendour but the place is alive and well-tended, and clearly appreciated by both golfers and residents.

The 19th-century additions have plentiful windows.

GIBSIDE
Rowlands Gill
Long-ruined Jacobean mansion surrounded by remarkable Georgian follies

TEMPLES AND FOLLIES WERE ONE OF THE GLORIES of the 18th-century country-house landscape, essays in architectural perfection or eccentricity that often exceeded the houses themselves in originality and sparkle. At Gibside there is a Column of British Liberty, a gothic banqueting house and an orangery. Best of all is the chapel, designed like a Roman temple with Ionic portico and dome. When I first visited in 1968 the chapel had already been restored by the National Trust and was standing beckoningly at the end of a noble avenue. All the other buildings were in an advanced state of decay or even ruin and took some finding.

Nearly twenty years later not much had changed except for the banqueting house. This had been immaculately restored by the Landmark Trust. A line of washing announced a young family was in residence. The gothic windows with sinuous arches were almost Mughal with pretty hexagonal panes in the sashes. Above, the gables were shaped like bishops' mitres and inset with crosses. Further exotic touches were added by the pierced quatrefoils in the battlements. The architect was Daniel Garrett, who also designed the Palladian stable block, as perfectly proportioned as a real Palladio villa in the Veneto. But the stables were going to rot and the sash windows were all open and without glass, blocked off with breeze blocks behind. Outside, an abandoned car stood rusting. The orangery added in the 1790s was roofless and windowless, the interior choked with saplings.

The shell of the Jacobean mansion is complete with stone mullioned windows.

The 18th-century gothic banqueting house has been restored by the Landmark Trust.

The biggest thrill was to find the main house an almost intact masonry shell with grand bay windows along the whole length of the south front. The glass had long gone but the stone mullions were still intact. At the back the house was perched dramatically above a ravine with potentially breathtaking views. Gibside Hall was built in 1603–20 for William Blakiston and enlarged in the 18th century for George Bowes MP, one of the richest of the Durham coal owners. His ornamental grounds once ranked with Painshill and Shugborough.

The landscape survived substantially intact until the 1930s when the Depression and death duties lead to the wholesale felling of the magnificent timber on the estate. But at least the grounds were not fragmented and in the 1950s more than 1,000 acres were let on a 999-year lease to the Forestry Commission. Part of the problem was that the sporting rights had recently been sold to a private buyer who was promised 'quiet enjoyment' of a large and good shoot. Gibside, I wrote, badly needs a plan.

Twenty years on, all has come right thanks to patient work by the National Trust, which has the ability to take a long view. Through the generosity of the Strathmore estates and the cooperation of the Forestry Commission, the Trust now has possession of all the parkland and has taken over the shell of the house, which will remain a romantic ruin like Sutton Scarsdale with grass growing inside the walls. The stables are to be repaired and to become a National Trust cottage available for holiday lets. The Trust has taken on the orangery too, and initial thoughts of it becoming a house have been replaced by the idea that this too should be a secured ruin. Gloriously, Gibside's magic and romance have been regained, with the secure future that the Trust alone can provide.

HAMSTERLEY HALL — Rowlands Gill

Georgian house enlarged in Tudor style for the Surtees family

THE MOST FAMOUS SQUIRE of Hamsterley Hall was R.S. Surtees, passionate huntsman and creator of Jorrocks. His father, grandfather and great-grandfather had all kept a pack of hounds. Surtees unexpectedly became heir to Hamsterley 1831, on the death of his elder brother, succeeding their father seven years later.

The early 18th-century house was enlarged for R.H. Swinburne and further alterations were made for Surtees's father Anthony in 1815. Another interesting chapter was added to the house's history in the 1930s by Standish Robert Vereker, who succeeded his brother as 7th Viscount Gort in 1946. Hamsterley had come by marriage to the 5th Viscount Gort, who had married the daughter of R.C. Surtees. The 6th Viscount was the famous field marshal.

S.R. Vereker's contribution was to incorporate numerous fragments of demolished historic buildings in and around the house, principally from the great Elizabethan house at Beaudesert in Staffordshire, demolished in the 1930s. Other items rescued were a 15th-century stone fireplace from Crosby Hall in London, 17th-century panelled interiors and a fireplace with Renaissance decoration and perspective scenes. A pinnacle from the Houses of Parliament became a garden ornament and a cupola from Beaudesert was transformed into a summerhouse.

S.R. Vereker also exercised his passion for architectural salvage (as it is now called) at Bessie Surtees' House in Newcastle. Bessie had eloped dramatically and he recreated a mansion on Sandhill as a memorial to her.

Below: Garden and house were filled in the 1930s with fragments from demolished buildings, including the domed cupola on the lawn.
Right: The 18th century-gothick staircase hall has been painted a fresh yellow.

LAMBTON CASTLE Chester-le-Street
Regency and Victorian castle building on the grand scale

LAMBTON CASTLE COMES UPON YOU SUDDENLY, powerfully set on a hillside. It was an eerie feeling in the late 1970s to drive up and find such a splendid place empty and boarded up. Here was the imposing seat of one of Britain's premier earls, written up in 1966 in *Country Life*, just a few miles south of Newcastle in a 2,000-acre park along both banks of the River Wear.

Lambton is a castle-style house built by the fashionable neoclassical architect Joseph Bonomi and then enlarged and castellated by his son Ignatius in the 1820s. Joseph Bonomi was working for W.H. Lambton, Ignatius for J.G. Lambton, later the 1st Earl of Durham. The house was severely damaged by subsidence (presumably caused by the family's own extensive coal mines) in 1854 and substantially rebuilt by Dobson of Newcastle and Sydney Smirke in 1857–62 and then partly demolished in the 1930s in an attempt to make it a more manageable size.

In recent years the castle has suffered a long slow decline. Lucy Lambton regaled me with stories of a spell as a theme park with plastic soldiers blowing trumpets on the ramparts. But parts of the castle are still lived in, and following the death of Lord Lambton, who had lived for many years in Italy, a new era may open. 'My brother has a tendresse for the castle,' she says.

Bastioned walls support the great terrace on which the castle stands.

SEAHAM
Seaham
1791 house where Byron wed reinvented as a chic spa

IN THE UPSTAIRS DRAWING ROOM at Seaham Hall, on January 2, 1815, Lord Byron married Anne Isabella Milbanke, daughter of Sir Ralph Milbanke, for whom the house was built in 1791–2. Here Byron wrote *The Siege of Corinth* and part of *The Hebrew Melodies*. Later additions were made in around 1830 by Lewis Vulliamy for Frances, Lady Londonderry.

Seaham stands in a clifftop position ideal for a romantic poet to be married in. The house has a Classical four-column Tuscan portico, but today it is the appeal of its reinvention as an ultra-chic spa hotel that brings in the visitors. There are paintings by Dale Atkinson, Ørnulf Opdahl and Paul Gallagher, part of an evolving collection of contemporary art fromNorway and north-east England.

There is sculpture by Nicolaus Widerberg, Andrew Burton and William Pye, who designed the water vortex at the front of the hotel. The stained-glass artist Bridget Jones has created a complete ceiling in the atrium, based on Byron's poetry.

Bedrooms offer intelligent lighting, surround-sound speakers, internet access, outside temperature indicators, master controls for adjustable mood lighting by the bed and the door and pinpoint reading lights, which come with sleep mode. Most rooms have sea views, there are candles in the bathrooms and insomniacs will note that this is a hotel that offers a choice of pillows. The modern spa built into the hillside and linked to the hotel by a tunnel provides Japanese facials, Chinese massage and Balinese Milk Ritual wraps. There is an aromatherapy shower, a 20-metre ozone-cleaned pool, sauna, steam room, ice fountain and hydrotherapy bath.

The even rows of sash windows and the shallow roof are typical of the 1790s.

WALWORTH CASTLE Darlington
Early 17th-century castle-style house rescued from decay

WITH ITS DISTINCTIVE ROUND CORNER TOWERS, Walworth has a strong family resemblance to the series of post-medieval castles that includes Lulworth Castle in Dorset and Ruperra Castle in South Wales. It dates from the early 1600s and was built for Thomas Jennison, one of whose sons was implicated in the Popish Plot of 1679. Walworth was bought by a Newcastle wine merchant in 1759 and in 1819 passed by marriage to General Arthur Aylmer, Lieutenant General in 1825 of the Durham Light Infantry, the regiment to which the castle was let during the Second World War. The castle contains 18th-century Palladian interiors and the west wing was refronted in 1864.

Walworth is one of numerous major country houses that owe their survival in the difficult years after 1945 to a county council. Durham County Council bought the castle in 1950 and used it as a girls' boarding school. After this closed, the council commendably kept it occupied as temporary offices (in contrast to most Government departments, which repeatedly leave houses empty in such circumstances).

Soon after this, Walworth attracted the first of a series of couples who have devoted plenty of time and energy to running it as an hotel. The castle was first opened for business by John and Jennifer Wayne, who later sold to the present owners, Rachel and Chris Swain. They have refurbished all the public areas and added a new conservatory roof to the courtyard. Rooms are now handsomely furnished with four-poster beds, and guests eat in the stylish Hansards restaurant, part of which is set in one of the round towers with curving bookcases ringing the walls.

The large windows show that the castle was built with no real defensive purpose.

WYNYARD PARK
Stockton-on-Tees

More palace than country house, built in the 1820s for 3rd Marquess of Londonderry

VICTORY AT WATERLOO BROUGHT a new scale to English architecture – witness the lofty ceilings and cavernous staircases of the houses in London's Carlton House Terrace. Among country houses, this new scale is nowhere more majestic than at Wynyard Park. The vast central saloon or sculpture gallery is 60 ft high and measures 120 by 80 ft – what the French call a *salle de pas perdus*, a room so large that footsteps die away.

The name Wynyard comes from the Anglo-Saxon words 'win' (meadow) and 'geard' (enclosure). There was a house on the site in the early 1200s that was the property of the crown, and subsequent owners included the de Chapell, de Lisle and de Langton families. The Davidsons lived here from 1633 to 1737, selling to Thomas Rudd, before the property went to the Londonderry family by marriage. John Tempest bought Wynyard in 1742 for £8,000. When his son John died in a riding accident aged 21, his nephew, Sir Henry Vane, inherited. A condition of the will was that he took the name of his uncle and he became Sir Henry Vane-Tempest. On his death the estate passed to his 13-year-old daughter Frances who married Charles William Stewart, son of the 1st Marquess of Londonderry, in 1819. The famous Foreign Secretary Lord Castlereagh became the 2nd Marquess and on his death, Charles became the 3rd Marquess.

The grand Corinthian portico is two columns deep and serves as a porte-cochère.

When Charles inherited Wynyards three years later, he began to transform the late 18th-century house, following an unexecuted design for a 'Waterloo Palace' at Stratfield Saye for the Duke of Wellington. The design had originally been drawn up by Benjamin Dean Wyatt, but here it was carried out by his brother Philip.

The house was largely complete by 1828 but in 1841 fire broke out at the west end, devastating more than half the interior. This was rebuilt following Philip Wyatt's drawings but with added flourishes in the even more opulent manner coming into fashion with extra marble and stained glass.

The entrance front has a giant Corinthian portico, two columns deep. The sculpture gallery is a tiered space almost like a wedding cake, rounded at the corners and with a spectacular clerestory with caryatids and balustrades

The barrel-vaulted chapel was restored in 1905 after a fire.

that are rich enough for an opera house. The rooms along the south front looking down to the lake are in the Wyatts' grand Louis Quatorze style that was used in their London houses of the 1820s.

The 6th Marquess succeeded in 1884. His wife, Lady Londonderry, was the model for the famous Lady Roehampton in Vita Sackville-West's *The Edwardians*.

The family continued to entertain on a grand scale under the 7th Marquess, whose guests included Winston Churchill, Harold Macmillan and the future Edward VIII. The present Queen stayed at Wynyard as Princess Elizabeth in 1947.

Wynyard is one of many large houses that, like Wentworth Woodhouse, only survived the austere post-war years through the use of much of the house as a teacher-training college. When the 8th Marquess died in 1955 he left an 18-year-old heir. With considerable courage the 9th Marquess renovated both house and park and tried to make the house earn its keep by letting it out for events. The family lived in one wing, with one of the rooms fitted out as a professional ballet rehearsal studio for Lady Londonderry, complete with a large practice mirror and a handrail running the length of one wall.

The estate was sold in 1987 to Sir John Hall, founder of Gateshead Metro shopping centre, with 5,000 acres. He employed Rupert Lord to oversee a £4 million restoration and later moved his company headquarters into the mansion, as well as his family. The estate was put on the market in July 2002 with 780 acres of parkland. With no suitable purchasers, Sir John decided to remain.

ESSEX

ALDHAMS IS A TRADITIONAL colour-washed Essex house that immediately poses a teasing question. How on earth did it come by such a magnificent pair of soaring Tudor-style red-brick chimney stacks, looking like the remains of a grand house built by one of Henry VIII's most flamboyant courtiers?

The house stands on the edge of Constable country, not far from beautiful Dedham and still closer to Manningtree and Mistley, with their many pretty houses, on the edge of the Stour estuary. A handsome double avenue of lime trees is exactly aligned on the front door and under-planted all the way with large strips of yellow and white daffodils. The entrance front is symmetrical with neat casement windows and a finely carved early 18th-century-style front doorcase, inset with a delightful carving which is a humorous play on the children's nursery rhyme, "'Won't you come into my parlour?' said the spider to the fly.' The spider's web and surrounding leaves are carved from a single piece of elm and are a pun on the name of Maurice Webb, the architect, who had the house built in 1933 as a country retreat.

Maurice Webb was the son and later the partner of Sir Aston Webb, the first winner of the gold medal of the American Institute of Architects, and best known for

The spider in the pediment over the entrance is a play on Webb's name.

Admiralty Arch in The Mall, the entrance front of Buckingham Palace and the Victoria and Albert Museum. Sir Aston had died in 1930, presumably leaving his son a substantial inheritance.

Maurice Webb's finest work is the Guildhall at Kingston upon Thames, a magnificent building of russet brick and Portland stone, complete with a 122 ft tower, a doorway surmounted by prancing horses and a council chamber with an Australian jarrah-wood floor, further evidence of the love of natural materials that can also be seen at Aldhams.

Old photographs show that Webb was transforming an earlier farmhouse, said to be of Queen Anne date. This was just three windows wide and forms the centre of the present front; its extent is marked by the chimneys on the roof ridge that originally stood at the gable end.

The roof of the new building was extended over the walls at both ends, forming impressive hoods to bold bay windows. The back of the house is also very different in style from the front and has three large interlocking gables, though their satisfying symmetry is somewhat confused by a brick-arched loggia that Webb put right in the centre of the lawn.

Webb's front door opens into the tiniest of vestibules, almost a spider's trap in itself as the way ahead is blocked and you must turn left into a panelled sitting room or right into a hall with the main staircase rising, unusually, behind the fireplace. The hand of a clever architect is evident throughout.

The doors are the first great feature of Aldhams. These are all cottage-style and formed of vertical boards with horizontal struts and flat-headed nails hammered in perfectly regular patterns (the nails are just as neatly placed on the elm floorboards). Every door has a wooden, not metal, latch and a pair of long blacksmith's hinges. The window latches are the second great feature, each specially made and incorporating a prominently silhouetted 'W'. The windows throughout are made of unpainted English elm, a wood that will never be available again, and all in excellent condition thanks to regular oiling.

This feeling that everything is shipshape, well-made and well-maintained, continues throughout the house into the kitchen realm, which is complete with larder, scullery and a large panel of servants' bells, still in working order.

The dining room opens from the hall through glazed doors and has a large Lutyens-style brick-and-tile fireplace with a raised hearth and deep recesses on either side. In one is a serving hatch to the scullery, which rises with such ease that it must have counterweights.

On the first floor the bedrooms open off a long corridor. The main bedroom connects to a dressing room via a gallery over the main staircase with a neat trellis balustrade. There is an abundance of cupboard space and the one odd feature is the placing of the secondary stair, which backs onto the entrance hall.

The garden extends to the side of the house with a brick-column pergola leading to a duck pond overhung with weeping willows. There are two black weatherboarded Essex barns, one with an outside stair to a separate loft above the garage, forming a perfect lair for children or teenagers.

BOWER HOUSE
Romford
Palladian villa by the architect Henry Flitcroft

BOWER HOUSE IS THE PRETTIEST of Palladian villas, built of a warm pinky-red brick with doorcase, windows and cornice all highlighted in crisp white paint. A visitor in 1771 observed that 'it commands the most delightful and extensive prospect into Kent … The river Thames is also seen very distinctly for many miles …'.

A Latin tablet over the fireplace in the hall reads: 'From the remains of Havering Bower, situated on the summit of the hill, this dwelling was founded by John Baynes, Serjeant-at-Law … AD 1729. H. Flitcroft was the architect. C. Bridgman the designer.'

The idea of a house built for retirement and pleasure was very much an 18th-century English concept. Baynes was emulating ancient Romans like Horace and Pliny, whose villas were built for retirement and leisure.

Flitcroft's villa has the typical Palladian form of a pedimented centre and a 1-3-1 arrangement of windows with an entrance hall leading to a great parlour. There are staircases on either side of the hall, the grand one leading to the first floor, the secondary one continuing to the second floor and descending to the basement. Flitcroft's interiors survive, with handsome panelling, doorcases and chimney pieces. The walls of the main staircase were painted with murals by Sir James Thornhill (best known for his painted hall at Greenwich) with scenes of the Judgement of Paris and the Drunkenness of Silenus preserved out of sight behind boarding. Two wings with arched windows were added about 1800.

After a battle against enabling development, the house has been acquired as a Bible school, currently with forty-six students doing a two year residential Bible course, more guests than even the hospitable Mr Baynes imagined.

A low parapet shields the hipped roof and dormer windows.

COPPED HALL   Epping
Ruined Georgian house being slowly nursed back to life

MANY PEOPLE FALL IN LOVE with country houses, perhaps especially those that are ruined and abandoned houses, which have a special romance of their own. I first went to see Copped Hall in the early 1970s when I was writing an article on road threats to country-house parks and the house was threatened by new motorways. Copped then stood in a large agricultural estate and I saw the agent in his office near Epping where he had a photograph of a South Pacific island basking in turquoise waters. 'I go there to escape every February,' he said. A good life, I thought. I went on to look at the house, an amazingly monumental brick shell which had stood roofless since a fire in 1911. Remarkably, all the stone trim had survived, including the balustrade along the parapet and stone sarcophagi on top of the chimneys, both enrichments that dated from 1895. The even bigger thrill came when I walked around to the back of the house and pushed my way through the undergrowth only to find the substantial remains of a very elaborate Edwardian formal garden, complete with stone bridges and a pair of fanciful stone pavilions. These were designed in an opulent French style, with big arched windows and gabled dormers.

Copped Hall was built in 1753–8 for John Conyers by the London architect John Sanderson, who was assisted by suggestions from Sir Roger Newdigate and Thomas Prowse. James Wyatt worked on the interiors in 1775–7 and also enlarged the house twenty years later. The estate was bought in 1869 by George Wythes, a railway magnate whose grandson Ernest built the stables and laid out the formal gardens. By 1900 there were thirty-one gardeners and twenty-seven indoor servants. Sadly, many of the

Fire gutted the house in 1917, but the monumental brick and stone shell remained largely intact.

The handsome bridges were part of the elaborate Edwardian formal garden.

contents were lost in a disastrous fire in 1917. Ernest Wythes never rebuilt the house, preferring instead to live in another house on the estate, Wood House, itself built shortly before 1900. The gardens of Copped, however, were maintained right up until the Second World War. Three years after Wythes's death in 1949 the estate was sold, and the staircases stripped out of the mansion, and railings and gates, garden balustrades, steps and statues were all also removed.

Today Copped Hall is witness to what a dedicated band of volunteers can achieve in the face of sustained pressure from development. The glimpse of Copped Hall from the passing M25 has prompted a great deal of commercial interest but all the proposals put forward, whether for an hotel or offices, always demanded a large amount of new building – so called enabling development – to pay for the restoration of the Hall. All the proposals were successfully fought off and in 1992 the Corporation of London, guardians of nearby Epping Forest, stepped in to protect the park from development. Three years later the specially formed Copped Hall Trust bought the mansion and gardens to secure their future.

Now temporary roofs are helping to dry out the walls and reinstated floors have made it possible for visitors to view parts of the interior. The racquets court is back in use as the trust's tearoom and gift shop. Lawns have been relaid and the ancient tree walk, cut down in the 1950s has been replanted. Extensive restoration has taken place in the Rock Garden and the Long Garden. The trust has bought the 4-acre walled garden, planted the beds around the walls and begun restoration of the orchid house. Freshly grown vegetables are on sale on open days. Copped Hall is an impressive example of how much voluntary groups can achieve even when they have no financial resources. By sheer simple perseverance Copped's friends have seen off damaging development, while the support that has been secured from the City Corporation is a major triumph.

One of the twin garden pavilions before restoration of the gardens began.

OLD GRAMMAR SCHOOL   Dedham
Baroque village school where Constable was a pupil, now a comfortable house

THE OLD GRAMMAR SCHOOL ENJOYS PRIME POSITION in one of the prettiest small towns in East Anglia. It stands on the diminutive Royal Square in Dedham and the main front looks across the small square to Dedham's princely church, while the north flank surveys the high street from the seclusion of an enclosed garden. Almost better still is the outlook at night when, owing to an almost complete lack of street lights, you might be deep in the country. The school closed in 1889 but has the distinction of being the alma mater of John Constable, some of whose most famous canvases such as *The Haywain* and *Flatford Mill* portray scenes within walking distance.

The Grammar School was founded in the 16th century by prosperous Dedham clothier William Littlebury but rebuilt in the early 18th century. It is matched by the equally handsome 1735 English School across the street which was the local primary school and now belongs to the National Trust. Both represent the apogee of the short-lived English Baroque style and are evidently the work of the same master bricklayer.

One of the delights of English Baroque is the use of fine 'rubbed' red brick for intricate architectural detail. Both schools have an abundance of it. On the Old Grammar School it is used for the gently arched window heads and the distinctive aprons beneath, and above all for the giant pilasters at the corners. These are a signature of Baroque and carry perfectly formed Greek 'triglyphs' in the frieze. The colouring is all the more distinctive as the main brick used is oatmeal in colour with the red brick used for the architectural trim.

The back part of the school, which is now a separate house, bears the date 1732 and name of Rev. Thomas Grimwood, who presided here for forty-eight years. He was

Fine 'rubbed' red brick was used to highlight the architectural trim.

followed by his son, who taught Constable. The Grammar School closed in 1889 and served briefly as an hotel from 1922–37 when it was bought by Mrs Stella Hamilton, who opened an antique shop here and was the mother of Elizabeth David, the cookery writer.

In 1949 Michael Ivan came to live here with the portrait photographer 'Bill' Avray Colebrook. Ivan arrived in England from Canada aged 19 as an actor and established himself working for Joan Littlewood, who took her travelling productions across Europe and was one of the finest directors of the day.

The handsome Doric front door opens into a broad welcoming hall with tiles laid on a diamond pattern and staircase framed by a baroque arch. On the left the headmaster's study has been transformed by Mr Ivan into a traditional kitchen with a large Belfast sink with scrubbed wooden draining boards and a cooker set beneath the imposing scrolled baroque mantle he has introduced. He has also commissioned a large wooden dresser from a local architect, Rodney Black, with a Doric frieze matching the front door. Other neat details are the Art Deco heads to doorways. The kitchen also retains one of two original 1730s sash windows with the chunky glazing bars of that date. The others have been replaced by sashes with thinner glazing bars over next century. Beside the massive chimney stack a brick arch leads through to a well-proportioned dining room with panelling on the fireplace wall.

On the other side of the hall is a complete panelled parlour original to the house. The pine woodwork has been carefully stripped to a gloriously warm tone and should be left as it is. Beyond is the drawing room with French windows onto the garden and a marble fireplace in Adamesque style.

The stair is a glorious example of early 18th-century carpentry, with broad handrail and two sturdy balusters to each tread, one a column, the other a corkscrew. The carved woodwork does not stop at the first floor but continues to the attic. On the first floor is one of the generous landings typical of 18th-century houses, broadening out at the far end into a full-size room overlooking Royal Square.

There are three handsome bedrooms on this floor and the huge depth of the chimney stacks leave room for closets on either side, which can serve as walk-in dressing rooms or small bathrooms – one has already been converted in this way.

The attics served as the boys' dormitories. There are lozenge-shaped peep holes in the doors (now blocked), which allowed the headmaster to peer in and ascertain if his charges were asleep. The whole attic floor could be used as a children's realm – either shut off to contain noise or left open so it is easy to call up or downstairs. Equally it can serve as a small flat or workspace – Colebrook had his darkroom here.

Mr Ivan carried out major repairs to the roof, complete with immaculate lead flashings to prevent leaks. It should keep the house dry for another 250 years.

The house also has an extensive cellar, largely paved and vaulted in brick. This is well aired and dry and serves to prevent damp riding into the house from below. 'On hot summer days,' says Mr Ivan, 'you simply open the cellar door and a cooling draught wafts through the whole house.'

He has planted the half-acre garden with yew hedges that form a series of secluded garden rooms. Along one side runs a lane containing what all Dedham houses most direly need in summer – a private garage.

GOSFIELD HALL   Halstead
Tudor house that grew through the centuries and escaped demolition in the 1950s

GOSFIELD HALL IS A STATELY HOME on the grandest scale, and comes with just 7 acres. A magnificent eighty-room house, generally in a very good state of repair, it looks out over former parkland to a mile-long lake. This is a Brideshead that has gathered romance over five centuries. Successive generations have made handsome additions but never swept everything away. Yet no famous architects appears to have been involved except (in the 1750s) the engaging Sanderson Miller who inherited a fortune aged 21 and amused himself by providing plans for his friends' houses.

Gosfield began as a grand Tudor house built of warm red brick round a large quadrangle. Like other early Tudor houses, it was constructed with an eye to civil unrest and there were no outside windows on the ground floor (the two visible today are later additions). All four fronts, though of different dates, are grandly symmetrical. The west front is faced in render, coloured to look like stone. The south front is built of a lovely warm plum brick. Almost all the bricks are headers – placed end-on. There are fine 'rubbed' bricks over the windows with thin joints, while the keystones have curious scrolls like the tops of Ionic columns.

Below: The Tudor house was designed protectively with the main windows facing inwards.
Bottom: The grand Georgian front.

A number of early 18th-century sashes survive with characteristic chunky glazing bars. The central windows are grand, with twenty panes to each sash. Above them Tudor Gothic mullions remain. Another house appears on the east front, with seven tall sash windows announcing the ballroom on the *piano nobile*.

The key to the house's history is supplied in a row of bells outside the butler's pantry. The names beneath read rather like clues for the Grail quest – the King's Room, the Queen's Room, the Wentworth Room, the Prophet's Room, the Nugent Room, the Priest's Room, the Queen's Gallery, the Painted Chamber and the Secret Gallery.

They unravel like this. Sir John Wentworth built the house in about 1545. The King was the exiled Louis XVIII of France, who lived here in 1807. The Queen was his consort Marie Josephine. The 106-ft long Queen's Gallery was named for Queen Elizabeth I of England (who stayed twice at Gosfield, in 1561 and 1569). The Prophet was local bricklayer William Juniper, who foresaw the future in his dreams. The rascally Earl Nugent inherited Gosfield through marriage.

The William and Mary work was carried out for Sir Thomas Millington, who bought Gosfield in 1691. His crest, a double-headed eagle, appears over doors in the courtyard. A founder member of the Royal Society, he was First Physician to both King and Queen. He employed Sir James Thornhill to do the ceiling in his Grand Salon or Painted Chamber. This rises one and a half storeys. Over it is the Secret Gallery, just 7 ft high, entered by a trap door in a room above. It is also a listening post as there is a trap in the chimney through which a fireside chat could be overheard – though this may have just been a convenient means of cleaning the chimney. The ornate marble fireplace is flanked by strange pairs of mermen with tails entwined.

The sparse furnishings in lofty Georgian rooms just before Gosfield was sold.

The Ballroom was added by John Knight, who bought the house in 1715. He was survived by his wife, who built him a grand tomb in the parish church and then went on to marry Robert, Earl Nugent, in 1737. Gosfield passed to Nugent's daughter by his third wife who married George Grenville, created 1st Marquess of Buckingham in 1784. The 2nd Marquess had little interest in Gosfield and in 1854 it was acquired by Samuel Courtauld, head of the famous textile company, who busied himself with repairs and estate improvements. His adopted daughter, Mrs Louise Lowe, lived here until her death in 1939.

Left empty after the Second World War, Gosfield was bought by Essex County Council to save it from being used to breed pedigree pigs. Demolition was only averted when the Wayfarers' Trust, a charity founded by the Women's Adjustment Board, took it on in 1954, still covered in wartime camouflage paint, to create residential homes for elderly people of slender means. A plaque in the hall lists 21 individuals and trusts contributing £1,000 or more, but even this was not enough and the home was sold on, almost as soon as it opened, to the newly formed Mutual Householders Association. The MHA's successor, the Country Houses Association, foundered in 2004 but Gosfield was acquired by James Perkins, saviour of Dowdeswell in Gloucestershire, who negotiated the acquisition of a further 43 acres. Institutional elements were removed, the full splendour of Gosfield's interiors became apparent, and it quickly sold as a wedding venue, ensuring its grand state rooms will once again be the scene of festivities and entertainments.

HATFIELD PRIORY   Chelmsford

1760s villa immaculately restored after half a century as a school

HATFIELD PRIORY IS NOT THE IVY-CLAD GOTHIC PILE you might expect from its name, but a trim 1760s Classical villa standing on a knoll. The drive is announced by a pair of octagonal stone gate piers, once at Orwell Park. Just beside them is the medieval parish church to which the remains of a Benedictine Priory were attached before they were demolished by the builder of the present house, John Wright, Master of the Guild of Coachmakers, whose descendants remained until 1927. Soon after, Hatfield was acquired by a Roman Catholic Mission and became a school, which closed some years before Mr and Mrs Cowell bought the property in 1979 and embarked on an impressively scholarly restoration of house and grounds.

Wright had employed the landscape gardener Richard Woods (on whom Mrs Cowell has completed her PhD) to draw up a plan for a *ferme orné* around the old priory with a chain of small lakes threading through the park. He laid out a perimeter walk and planted shelter belts as well as ornamental clumps of conifers at the corners of the arable fields. However, Wright evidently changed his mind about preserving the medieval remains, as the Chelmsford paper records that a carpenter was killed by a falling beam in 1769 as they were demolished. Three years later his newly complete villa is illustrated in Muilman's *History of Essex*.

It appears likely that Wright designed the house himself with the help of a first class master bricklayer. His tombstone in the church records that he had 'a more than ordinary knowledge of architecture, painting and the other liberal arts' and the house is very beautifully built of pale Essex brick made of the local Gault clay, not as white or grey as Norfolk or Suffolk bricks but a pale oatmeal with pink flecks where the red

Built for the Master of the Guild of Coachmakers, who appears to have been his own architect.

clay had not been fully separated out. In places you can clearly see the marks left by the drying racks on which they were placed after they came out of the kiln.

The brickwork of Georgian houses is often distinguished by 'penny-struck pointing', a crisp straight line about the width of an old penny drawn through the mortar while it is wet. Here Mrs Cowell points to the 'halfpenny pointing' – a still thinner line giving extra precision to each course of brickwork.

The twin flights up to the front door were rebuilt by the Cowells following the evidence of the 1772 print. They replace an awkward porch added by the prep school.

Wright's antiquarian interests are immediately apparent inside the entrance hall where a trio of reliefs of Alfred the Great, William III and George II face the entrance. Around the walls are a series of brackets on which stood portrait busts of Henry VII, Henry VIII and Cardinal Fisher. These were carved by no less a figure than Pietro Torrigiani, the Italian sculptor who carved Henry VII's tomb in Westminster Abbey and introduced the Renaissance to England. Wright's discernment is evident from the fact that they now adorn the V&A, the Getty and the Met in New York.

Today the focal point of the hall is a splendid stone fireplace over which is a large relief of the *Sacrifice of Diana* by the Flemish sculptor Laurent Delvaux. This is a variant of that at Houghton Hall in Norfolk, home of Prime Minister Sir Robert Walpole. Like the doorcases and some of the panelling, this appears to be 1730s in date, not 1760s. The explanation suggested is that these were features rescued from nearby Old Thorndon Hall, demolished at the time Hatfield Priory was built.

The hall opens into the drawing room with more splendid baroque surrounds to the windows and doors. A wealth of gold leaf has been used to highlight the decorative trim of doors, cornices, dados and skirting – the eggs in the frieze glow like Fabergé eggs. Here, as in all the main rooms, log fires burn in handsome grates.

The drawing room opens into a library ingeniously created by the Cowells by advancing the panelling forward to create the necessary depth for books. The false books on the doors are not the usual leather bindings as Mrs Cowell wanted spines that matched her own art books. Conveniently she was working at Thames & Hudson and was able to rescue a cache of books from pulping.

Hatfield has a largely untouched basement, handsomely paved in stone. At either end steps descend to a double-height kitchen and servants' hall. Further steps lead down to a second level of brick-vaulted cellars under the centre of the house, all ensuring the house is well-aired and dry.

The broad bedroom landing has a pretty trio of doorways rather in the manner of Strawberry Hill. Mr Cowell has designed a handsome dressing room with Doric cupboards, while another bedroom is hung with delightful Chinese silk wallpapers supplied by De Gournay.

Mrs Cowell has skilfully replanted Woods's pleasure grounds using evergreen oaks and laurels to provide colour in winter. She has also rescued fragments of his garden buildings from other properties and re-erected them as eye-catchers, making delightful excursions for picnics and drinks. Finding the neo-baroque swagger of the new church hall a trifle intrusive, the Cowells have masked it in style with a 70-yard-long hooped iron pergola suitable for roses, clematis and honeysuckle.

HILL HALL   Epping

Grand Elizabethan house completed in 1575 and now restored from ruin

HILL HALL HAD THE UNDIGNIFIED FATE of being burnt down by its own residents in 1969 while it was a women's prison. The shell survived but, even though it was Government property, no significant repairs were carried out until 1981 when the north range was re-roofed and detailed survey work began on the structure. In 1993 English Heritage, under Jocelyn Stevens, embarked on a £3 million restoration of the shell, stabilising the walls, replacing the roofs and the windows, carrying out delicate repairs to the ornamental plasterwork and conserving important wall paintings.

In 1998 the house was offered for sale on the open market 'in shell condition' and bought by the Manchester-based property company P.J. Livesey, which also restored Wyfold Court in Oxfordshire and Ingress Abbey near Dartford in Kent. Two years later apartments were on offer at £275,000 for 1,122 sq ft to £650,000 for 2,370 sq ft.

Hill Hall was built in 1569–75 for Sir Thomas Smith, probably largely to his own design, assisted by Richard Kirby, who he described as his 'cheefe architect, overseer and Master of my workes'. While the Elizabethan courtyard house, built in red brick, remains today, many of the windows were replaced with sashed ones in the 18th century when substantial alterations were carried out for Sir Edward Smith in about 1714. Humphry Repton also carried out substantial landscaping (his 'Red Book' is dated 1791). Extensive alterations were carried out by Reginald Blomfield in 1902–12 for the tenant Charles Hunter, while the gardens were transformed in 1927–8 by Philip Tilden for Sir Robert and Lady Hudson.

Sir Thomas Smith was a remarkable man, who lectured at Cambridge and took a degree at Padua, became interested in Greek pronunciation and served as Vice-Chancellor of Cambridge. He then served Protector Somerset, one of the key figures in introducing the Renaissance to England.

The burnt-out shell remained remarkably complete after a fire in 1969.

HORHAM HALL   Thaxted

A former Barnado's Home built to entertain the monarch now a private house

HORHAM HALL WAS MY INTRODUCTION to country house architecture. I arrived there in 1955 when my mother remarried after my father's death. My stepfather, George Binney, had bought the house from Barnado's Homes in 1947. Horham was an inspiring sight, with a majestic oriel window rising the full height of the house and a tower added for Queen Elizabeth I to watch the hunt when she visited in 1588. An old view showed that originally the house had been much larger, with a long-vanished wing running down to the moat.

Horham had a great hall large enough to swallow every other room in the house. To the south the early Tudor wing was of modest proportions, incorporating a timber-framed house of mid 15th-century date; to the north, the high-ceilinged Victorian rooms were without sun. My mother demanded central heating and one good Georgian room with a good southern aspect. As the long main front faces east, the only place to do this was the old kitchen. She had heard that the basements of the London County Council building were filled with panelling rescued from demolished London houses. When she arrived there, her guide was the architect Walter Ison, author of the classic volume on the Georgian buildings of Bath. He showed her the panelling of a very handsome early-Georgian room which fitted

The great hall has a magnificent full-height oriel and ornamental louvre in the roof.

perfectly the square dimensions of the old kitchen which had come from the Sunn Inn on the Strand, London, bombed in the Second World War. The floor had to be dug out to create the necessary ceiling height, allowing my mother to have French windows opening onto the garden, where Ison designed a very pretty fountain pool enclosed by a scalloped wall with niches and urns.

The beauty of Horham lies in the Tudor brick which, like all brickwork of that date, changes colour according to the time of the day and strength of the sun. In early morning or late evening it would be a deep reddy brown but in strong sun it would glow almost orange. Presented with long Tudor garden walls, my mother struggled with the unforgiving Essex clay to create wonderful colour-matched borders – reds and blues on the entrance side and yellow and white towards the garden.

My parents later moved to Jersey and Horham was bought by the writer Evelyn Anthony and her husband Michael Ward-Thomas. After a few years they moved to Ireland and Horham was bought by new owners who boldly took an important decision to remove the disfiguring Victorian gallery running the length of the great hall, installed to connect the two sides of the house at first-floor level. It was not only useful but for a child it was a great place for spying on what went on below. It was a formidable piece of carpentry but a brute too, dominating the hall and detracting the eye from the main features – the Tudor oriel and coved ceiling and the fine Tudor screen shielding the trio of archways that led to the kitchen, buttery and pantry.

HURST HOUSE — Woodford
1714 baroque villa still standing handsome on the outskirts of London

DATING FROM 1714, HURST HOUSE ENJOYS the unusual soubriquet 'Naked Beauty' taken from a statue by the Italian sculptor, Monti, that formerly stood in the garden. Though Woodford may not be fashionable London, Hurst House is a fine example of the numerous ambitious houses built in the environs of the capital for prosperous merchants who wanted to leave London at weekends or during the summer months.

The entrance front has baroque giant pilasters and urns on the parapet and the gently arched windows are typical of the period. The handsome baroque doorcase has a rounded pediment, open at the bottom.

This opens into an unusually broad entrance hall with black and white marble floor and a staircase that descends to a garden door as well as making the grand ascent to the first floor. The stair comes with all the flourishes, notably three different balusters on each step, a corkscrew, a column and a spiral or screw, all exquisitely slender. The broad oak handrail is given extra support by a stouter Corinthian column at each corner. The inner wall has a dado matching the stair, swooped to echo the stair rail. A large arched window, complete with oak window seat, fills the landings on both floors with light.

Some of the chimney pieces and decorative panels are said to have come from Bowood House in Wiltshire after it was demolished in 1955. These include the Painted Room with Adamesque fireplace, which has wall and ceiling panels in the style of

The giant pilaster s are topped by flamboyant urns.

Angelica Kauffmann. A rococo fireplace in the main drawing room, finely carved in white and Siena marble, is similar to designs for chimney pieces by Sir Robert Taylor, who also erected a column to 'his never failing friends' the Godfrey family of Woodford in the nearby churchyard.

Hurst House became a boys' school early in the 19th century and in November 1936 the top floor was gutted by fire. The brickwork was so conspicuous after it had been rebuilt that it was painted a camouflage green during the war. Remarkably, in recent years Hurst House has once again become, and remained, a private house. The main garden at the back was laid out by Percy Caine and is described in his book *The Earth is My Garden*. There are Coade stone balustrades and a pretty Doric temple in the garden and instead of the 'Naked Beauty' Italian statue, one of Winston Churchill stands on the green in honour of his forty years as the local MP.

The late 18th-century interiors are believed to have been brought from Bowood House in Wiltshire.

HYLANDS HOUSE Chelmsford

Grand stuccoed Regency house that fell into ruin in a public park

THIRTY YEARS AGO HYLANDS HOUSE was an archetypal example of how badly a local council could treat a fine country house. Today it is the very opposite – a model of enterprising use and painstaking restoration of almost vanished interiors. Hylands is open to visitors on Sundays and Mondays, and from Tuesdays to Thursdays it bustles with corporate events. On Fridays and Saturdays the house becomes a venue for civil marriages, and offers wedding breakfasts or banquets. Add to this a series of workshops and soirées, including Murder Mystery Evenings, a Masked Ball, a Dickensian Christmas Market and Christmas Soirées with the Chelmsford Theatre Workshop, and it is clear that this is the least stuffy of publicly owned country houses. The 550-acre landscaped park is also the setting for events, including the popular V Festival in August, which attracts 100,000 people over two days.

The Hylands House estate was bought by Chelmsford Borough Council in 1966 to create a public park outside the town. However, the house stood empty and decaying while Conservative councillors decided that it was a burden on the rates and should become a golf club, and Labour rejected any private use of public land.

The only proposal to attract a majority was one for demolition in 1975, which just happened to be European Architectural Heritage Year. Happily, after fierce opposition at a public inquiry from Essex County Council and preservation groups, demolition was rejected.

After the first phase of restoration was complete, the wings were reduced to their Regency proportions.

Hylands was shut off behind barbed wire while Chelmsford Council pressed for its demolition.

The baroque house built for Sir John Comyns, an MP and judge, was remodelled in 1810 for Cornelius Kortright, a Danish merchant with large estates in the West Indies. Kortright brought in Humphry Repton to make proposals for the park.

Hylands was then acquired in 1815 by Pierre Caesar Labouchere, a partner in the leading Amsterdam bank, Hope & Co. He was a Dutch-born Huguenot and a secret envoy for Napoleonic France. He was also a patron of Bertel Thorvaldsen, the Danish sculptor, and commissioned the architect William Atkinson to design new greenhouses and a large netted cage for a cherry garden. After Labouchere's death, Hylands was acquired by a Birmingham ironmaster, John Attwood, who had ambitions for a peerage and commissioned J.B. Papworth to add an extra storey for bedrooms and a nursery.

The last private owner of Hylands, Christine Hanbury (of the Truman Hanbury brewing family), wanted it to become the centre of the new University of Essex, but Chelmsford was deemed too near to London for the good of students, and Wivenhoe Park outside Colchester (famously painted by Constable) was chosen instead.

In the 1980s Esmond Abraham, the borough architect, removed the Victorian upper floors and restored the Regency appearance of the house. Yet, for all the gleaming stucco, the house remained empty, surrounded by a wire fence. It featured as 'Heap of the Week' in *The Times* in 1991.

Now the interior restoration is largely complete. Original hand-painted oak graining and gilding has been reinstated, with mirrors creating multiple reflections in all directions, to be enjoyed not just on guided tours but on festive occasions such as they were designed for.

LITTLE BARDFIELD HALL Great Bardfield
Elizabethan manor rescued from decay by impresario

I HAD LAST SEEN LITTLE BARDFIELD HALL in 1992 when I featured it as a 'Heap of the Week' in *The Times*. Every window was then boarded up and the bands of rich Essex plasterwork known as pargetting were falling off in large chunks. Even so, it was the idyllic small gabled manor sitting beside the medieval parish church. 'Surely there must be someone who will see the romance of this place and give it the love it needs,' I wrote despairingly.

Enter the engaging Mr Alan Goldsmith, who has made a career running airshows and pop festivals. He explains, 'When I was twelve years old I was dumped into a stately home, Elizabethan Hadham Hall in Hertfordshire. That was in 1952. It was a school for skivers. I learnt bugger all but I was put in a vat of medieval ambience which soaked into me.'

Mr Goldsmith first put his preservation energies into an extraordinary project – the total reconstruction of Mountfitchet Castle in Stansted Mountfitchet, a Norman castle that was no more than a few bumps in the ground. Today it's the only wooden motte-and-bailey castle in the country – straight out of a children's book. It was a major battle getting the consents but now more than a million schoolchildren have been to see it. Once through the pale of sharpened wooden stakes, you are in a film set, but one where real deer and goats graze the grass and plumes of smoke rise from the roofs of smithies and bakehouses, and the hushed voice of Mr Goldsmith welcomes you as you approach each little building.

Ever restless, he next proceeded to turn his nearby house into a toy museum (another hobby). 'After destroying my wife's home and her outlook I had to find somewhere new,' he jokes. When he saw Little Bardfield Hall, 'It took me straight back to the 1950s, when England was still beautiful and unspoiled.' This took imagination as the house was a pitiful wreck. 'People had helped themselves to plants from the garden. Thieves had stolen the slates from the roof. For months afterwards we were finding bags of rubbish buried under every tree.'

Yet after the Second World War Little Bardfield Hall had been a thriving country club where, he says, Dusty Springfield, Dionne Warwick and Alma Cogan came to perform to the American airmen then based at nearby Stansted. The house, refronted in Georgian times, had been cleverly returned to Tudor in 1919 by George Letts of Letts Diaries.

Goldsmith says modestly, 'I know nothing about restoring old buildings. I rely on other people to tell me what to do.' But he made an inspired choice of builder – Peter Sortwell, who lives in nearby Stebbing. Sortwell is a one-man band, an old-fashioned master carpenter. He says, 'I started aged eight or nine. My grandfather was a bricklayer and builder and his brother an architect. When I arrived at Little Bardfield there wasn't a door left in the house. They'd all been stolen.' He's put back traditional Elizabethan oak doors made of shaped vertical boards and restored the pargetting using silicon rubber moulds. All the leaded lights have been carefully repaired rather than renewed.

The result is a house that is as fresh and light-filled as the best Arts and Crafts or even Lutyens houses of a century ago. Simplicity reigns – light-coloured plaster walls, oak floors, impressive fireplaces and handsome ironwork to the windows.

On the ground floor there is a large sitting room, a 50-ft long drawing room, a snooker room overlooking the garden, a study conveniently beside the back entrance and a large kitchen with bay windows overlooking the garden in two directions. Upstairs there are seven bedrooms with still further bedrooms, or box rooms, on an upper floor with not a cobweb to be seen.

The coach house, although still waiting for modernisation, is large enough to form a separate house or a place for children and parties or perhaps a completely independent guest wing.

The 20 acres of gardens, lake and woodlands that make up the grounds had become a wilderness, but are now back in hand and maintained as a haven for wildlife. 'I won't let anything be killed on the property,' says Goldsmith.

In 2003, the one reminder of past abandonment was the attractive but roofless indoor octagonal swimming pool. Even without water it was a ready-made conservatory garden filled with climbing roses. The estate is now in frequent use for weddings, with the adjacent Norman church forming the perfect background. Film and photographic shoots also often take place in the grounds.

Note the band of characteristic Essex pargetting beneath the eaves.

THORNDON HALL   Brentwood
Gutted Palladian mansion that waited a century for restoration

BURNT OUT IN A CALAMITOUS FIRE of 1878, Thorndon Hall stood a gutted shell for a century before being bought by an enterprising firm of builders, Thomas Bates & Son. They created a total of eighty-four apartments, including six penthouses in the roof. Behind the tall windows of the *piano nobile* they inserted bedrooms on set back balconies. Beginning in the late 1970s the work continued for a decade. This was before the age of giant cranes, and all the steelwork had to be carried into the shell of the house by hand and winched into position. Lifts and fire-escape stairs were incorporated throughout, as well as panelled doors.

Thorndon was built for the 9th Lord Petre in 1764–70. His architect James Paine incorporated a magnificent portico designed by the Italian architect Giacomo Leoni for a house left uncompleted on the 8th Lord Petre's death in 1742. The portico has fluted Corinthian columns and was intended to have a carved coat of arms in the pediment – the uncut blocks stand out, still waiting to be carved. The 8th Lord Petre laid out geometric baroque plantations, importing many trees from North America. His successor turned to Capability Brown, who created a 1,000-acre park. In 1920 a golf course opened in 240 acres of the park, laid out by the renowned designer Harry Colt. The club house was installed in the east wing of the house, undamaged by fire.

The gutted shell was rebuilt as apartments with penthouses on the roof.

BIBURY COURT Bibury
Cotswold manor with an Art Deco flourish

THE ROMANCE THAT ATTACHES TO BIBURY COURT spans a full five centuries, reaching a climax with an Art Deco library of the 1920s intriguingly commissioned by a man who styled himself the former 'Legal adviser to the Ottoman Empire'. To the great William Morris, who lived nearby at Kelmscott, Bibury was the most beautiful village in England. Hundreds of thousands of visitors to the Cotswolds agree.

Yet Bibury Court stands in blissful seclusion. Though entered through gates off the handsome village square, the house only bursts into view for one glorious moment on the road from Lechlade, where it is seen as great country houses should be seen, across a glorious sweep of parkland backed by enfolding woods.

The house is built on a typical Elizabethan E-plan with projecting wings and central battlement porch. It bristles with gables, mullioned windows and tall chimneys. Yet the Tudor wing on the right of the entrance front is almost diminutive in scale compared to the rest. Englishmen had not suddenly grown taller, they had grander ideas and wanted to impress their guests with lofty rooms and large bay windows.

The Tudor wing was built for the Westwood, who acquired the manor, long owned by the Bishops of Worcester, at the Reformation. Robert Westwood died in Fleet prison and his son William sold the manor in 1625 to Thomas Sackville – whose family created the greatest of all early 17th-century houses, Knole in Kent. His initials and those of his wife Barbara, with the date 1633, surmount the richly carved coat of arms over the entrance.

When Sir Thomas's grandson Henry Sackville died in 1712, the estate passed to his daughter Elizabeth. Her grandson, Estcourt Cresswell, inherited in 1756 and set to work on a grand remodelling marked by rainwater heads bearing the date 1759. Tantalisingly, just one graceful rococo ceiling survives to give an idea of the interiors he created.

His main claim to fame was to snatch a Parliamentary seat from the Bathursts at Cirencester but the bribes he had to pay, as well as the expense of his house forced him to sell land to Lord Shelburne and then retire, on the orders of the Lord Chancellor, no less, to Bath. He left his heirs embroiled in a case in Chancery (one of the many said to be the model for Dickens's *Bleak House*) and his son was obliged to sell the rest of the estate to Lord Shelburne, who in 1829 commissioned Lewis Wyatt, one of the large Wyatt clan of architects, to remodel the house again. The Shelburnes were still there when *Country Life* illustrated the house in 1912 but in 1925 the estate was sold to Orme Clarke (the one-time legal adviser to the Ottoman Empire) who had married Elfrida Roosevelt, daughter of Alfred Roosevelt, cousin of the President Theodore Roosevelt, and was able to embark on yet another ambitious remodelling – though in 1931 Knight Frank and Rutley advertised it to let as 'Mr

The low, gabled Tudor wing is on the right with the grander 17th-century gabled extensions to the left.

Orme Clarke had gone abroad'. In the depth of the Depression the house appears to have found no tenant and perhaps because of this – or because in 1932 Clarke inherited a baronetcy from his uncle – he is still listed as resident in 1933. Sir Orme died in 1949 but Lady Clarke continued at Bibury until her death in 1963. The house was then sold to Jim Collier who transformed it into an elegant hotel, later run by his son-in-law Andrew Johnson, who put it up for sale in 2003.

Bibury still retains much of the handsome suite of furniture acquired by the Clarkes. They employed the architects Frederick Nightingale and George Kennedy for their remodelling, as well as Crowthers, the famous dealers in garden sculpture and interior fittings. Mr Johnson explains, 'Crowther used to come and stay for Cheltenham races, and behind the panelling in the drawing room I found a Crowther label saying "Panelling from the House of Commons".'

Sir Orme's most remarkable commission was the Art Deco Library, now the hotel bar, in place of a fine 17th-century wooden stair removed and sold by Crowthers. This was by Dominique, a very chic Parisian furniture and interior designer. The room has the éclat of the contemporary interiors for the Courtaulds at Eltham Palace with flush veneer panelling and black metal radiator covers with interlocking circle and sunburst motifs as well as Deco glass panels in the ceiling. The bedrooms retain many of the elegant 1920s bathrooms fittings.

Part of the appeal of Bibury Court is that as you ascend to the first and then second floors the views get better in every direction. The gardens are intriguingly laid out as a series of rooms with high hedge walls, the lawns stretch down to the smooth-flowing clear waters of the River Coln and there are splendid flowering trees.

Bibury Court also has extensive outbuildings, all built in beautiful stone with Cotswold slate roofs. Opportunities to buy such houses are rare in the Cotswolds and even rarer is the possibility of buying much of the rather handsome 1920s Georgian furniture – reproduction, it is true, but now with a period interest of its own.

CHURCH HOUSE · Bibury
Regency house with grandstand view of the parish church

ALTHOUGH CHURCH HOUSE IS IN THE CENTRE of the village, it is hard to suspect its existence, let alone the beauty and extent of its grounds. Once through the gates, the graceful curve of the drive ensures that the house is hidden until you are well inside. The stone front is seen across perfect lawns, surrounded by well-planted borders with carefully chosen flowering trees and shrubs. The drive then continues to the house, which is set behind a low wall with a short paved walk to the front door.

When the Clarke family sold Bibury Court in 1965, they retained Church House and a stretch of woodland on the far bank of the River Coln, protecting the property from any possible encroachment on the hill to the west.

Sir Tobias Clarke, who took over in 1973, brought the property to a pitch of perfection with help from the landscape gardener Lanning Roper and from Rosemary Verey, who lived nearby. Her husband David was a champion of Bibury's beauty and created a museum in the mill. Roper, American by birth, helped to make this an enchanted place by many subtle moves, most so natural that you barely notice them.

Immediately beside the house looms the magnificent west window of the parish church and to the right is a walled flower garden with a gateway leading to the churchyard. Beside it is a pump house, beautifully built in Cotswold stone.

A family of modest buildings lie across a small court. A billiard-room-cum-office is attached to a coach house with a large potting shed below and outdoor steps leading to a three-room loft, perfect as a studio or guest wing. The adjacent Pigeon House has garages below and an unusual one-bedroom flat above, with a sitting room surrounded by carefully restored nesting boxes with the occasional wood pigeon leaning cheekily out.

Church House also has a swimming pool and a tennis court with pavilion so engulfed by creeper that you can hardly tell it has walls. A bridge over the river is formed of two parallel tree trunks with a deck of railway sleepers leading to woodland walks. Beside the main entrance a group of cottages has been restored as a second five-bedroom house, standing in its own garden.

The house bears the date 1802 and the three-part windows on ground and first floor are typically Regency. Yet there is no cornice or parapet and the attic windows pop out through the Cotswold stone eaves.

Inside, Church House itself has a cosy feeling varied by small changes of level and direction. The front door opens into a staircase hall with the dining room and sitting room to either side, the latter with a window in line with the door looking into the garden. The main drawing room is down a step at the back with a large fireplace and bay window onto the garden. Many rooms are given colour by stylish Parisian wallpapers.

Church House is a paradise-in-waiting, with a garden so cleverly planned that the gardener keeps it in perfect trim working just three days a week.

Overleaf: The garden has been brought to a pitch of perfection with help from Lanning Roper.

DIXTON MANOR — Winchcombe

Gabled manor house with glorious views on the edge of the Cotswolds

DIXTON MANOR ENJOYS ONE OF the most breathtaking views in Gloucestershire, across the Severn Vale to the Monmouth hills. Its architecture is the quintessence of a gabled Cotswold-stone manor house.

In 1945, the estate was bought by Sir Charles Hambro, whose family seat had been Milton Abbey, the vast country house in Dorset, which in 1953 became the now famous public school. Among Sir Charles's many talents was a passion for gardening and it was he who laid out the box-edged rose garden below the south front and created a pear-tree walk running along a pergola in the large, still well-tended kitchen garden.

The drive up to the house opens off a quiet country lane from Winchcombe and is marked only by a vast and noble oak. The estate is listed in Domesday and remarkably never changed hands by sale until the end of the 18th century. The name of Johannes Huggeford (or Higford) is inscribed over the Tudor entrance porch with the date 1555. John Higford was knighted in 1592 by Queen Elizabeth I, who visited Dixton Manor while staying nearby at Sudeley Castle. Perhaps in anticipation of the Royal visit, he added the handsome west wing with its four steep gables.

The house, as it stood then, and the glorious landscape surrounding it, is recorded in a pair of delightful early 18th-century landscapes which are now in Cheltenham Museum. One shows scenes of haymaking, the other the house itself.

The early 18th-century sashes retain the original crown glass.

The entrance front then had three gables as well as the three-storey porch. The two gables on the left were destroyed following a fire in the early 19th century but the house remains an attractive composition, more so than photographs are sometimes able to convey.

Early in the 18th century the leaded Tudor windows were replaced with sashes either by James Higford or his parson brother who succeeded him. These sash windows have characteristically chunky early Georgian glazing bars with twenty-four or even forty panes to a window. Amazingly, they retain the original beautiful crown glass with panes that are signed and dated 1727 and 1760 by the ladies of the Higford household.

The original massive arched Tudor oak front door also survives with studs and strap hinges, opening into a stone-flagged hall. The green baize door leading out of the kitchen has matching pointed arches formed by a pattern of studs. The main Elizabethan features are the oak staircase with typical widely spaced balusters and a splendid full-height stone chimney piece in a small drawing room carved with a frieze of interlocking circles.

Dixton is a place where you instantly feel at home – the rooms are cosy and comfortable, yet the building is unusually full of light for a house that is solidly built of stone. Many of the rooms have windows looking out in two directions – some with windows descending to the floor so that you can enjoy the view whether in bed or the bath. The most amusing bathroom is installed over the front porch, with windows on three sides.

Matching the early Georgian sash windows are numerous handsomely panelled rooms on both main floors. A wing was added on the south by the Gist family in the early 19th century connecting with a surviving Elizabethan turret crowned with four gables. A further wing was added by the Hambros.

Lord Hambro, Sir Charles's son and a life peer, married twice – his first wife employed John Fowler to refurbish the interiors, and Fowler's fresh bold colour schemes and splendid curtains remain. The second Lady Hambro created a charming bathroom with murals of peacocks.

When I visited Dixton in 2006, the big opportunity was to create a much larger kitchen that extended, double-height, into the 1950s wing and could serve as a focus for family life. Eating out on summer days is already provided for on paved terraces which have a pretty verandah built on the curve, with a roof of Cotswold stone.

Dixton has a very attractive series of outbuildings including a coach house and stable yard where free-range chickens graze. There are walks and bridges along the Dingle, a stream running below the house, and further walks in woods above. Beside the drive are two pretty timber-framed cottages with red-brick infill, a reminder of how close Dixton is to the Worcestershire border.

Recently a new view has been opened through the beeches beyond the lawn. The Hambros were only leaving to move to another equally historic family estate situated nearby.

There is only one perceivable drawback to Dixton – a hill climb for six days a year on Preston Hill just across the valley. But then the cars *are* Bugattis.

DODINGTON PARK   Chipping Sodbury
Wyatt masterpiece bought by the entrepreneur James Dyson

IF YOU LOVE CLASSICAL ARCHITECTURE at its noblest, Dodington Park in Gloucestershire is the finest and grandest late-Georgian country house you will ever have the chance to see.

For many years after the Second World War it was regularly open to the public, welcoming thousands of visitors. Then in the 1980s it became too much for the Codrington family to maintain. House and contents were sold, the gates slammed shut and for the past twenty years virtually every request to see the house has met with a refusal. Those who stole down the back drive hoping at least for a glimpse of the church were met by large Alsatian dogs.

One American lady – a lifelong enthusiast for the architecture of James Wyatt – who gained entry was amazed to find large chunks of plasterwork laid out on the floor of the grand rooms, while the house was being rewired and minutely inspected for any trace of rot.

Dodington went back on the market after the death of one of the two reclusive gentlemen (said to be in the music business) who had owned it for a decade and put it in an immaculate state of decoration. The master bedroom (not exactly a Regency term) was as sumptuous as those found at Blake's Hotel in Kensington, with darkly decadent colours for walls, four-poster bed and curtains.

Below: The new pond reflecting the portico.
Bottom: The view from the park.

The scagliola-columned entrance hall had dark walls but the great James Wyatt interiors were as radiant and opulent as ever. Best of all is the vast imperial stair, grander than that in London's Carlton Club. It is a marvel seen through colonnades on three sides, and fills the whole centre of the house.

The almost breathtaking elegance of Dodington is trumpeted to every passing motorist by an exquisite gate lodge, ringed by a colonnade like Bramante's famous Tempietto in Rome.

Though bordered by the busy main road to Stroud, Dodington's 300 acres are secluded and completely pastoral. The estate stands on the very edge of a Cotswold escarpment hidden from view in a series of converging combes. Two enchanting lakes created by the wand of Capability Brown do not tame the character of the steep woods around.

Wyatt's magnificent stair is framed by pairs of Corinthian columns.

Dodington has show fronts so contrasting that they might belong to different houses. The south front has inset columns that overlook a formal garden, the east front a pair of Regency bows that survey a grass carpet sweeping down to the lake. Here the former dairy has been transformed into a dower house with its own delightful domed entrance porch.

Wyatt forsook the symmetry of the Palladian houses of the previous generation, and, instead of balancing wings, placed the offices and outbuildings on one side, screened by a curving colonnade fronting a conservatory with 18 ft-high windows.

Beyond is a domed Classical chapel, a stable block with clock tower, and a carriage house. Many of these buildings are in the same pale stone as the main house and seen from the back the composition is a cluster of strong, simple shapes like a village in a Poussin painting. The stables contain twenty-four stalls, three flats and workshops. There are a further eight houses and cottages as well as an indoor riding school.

Dodington has a swashbuckling history of adventurers, soldiers, sailors and plantation owners. Henry VIII's great chronicler John Leland recorded the medieval moated house of the Berkeleys, who had owned the land since the Norman Conquest. In 1796 Turner painted the immediate predecessor of the present house with the old parish church beside it.

Before 1600 the estate had been acquired by the Codringtons, one of whom had been Henry V's standard bearer. A century later it was sold to a kinsman – the great

Colonel Christopher Codrington, Governor of the Leeward Islands and conqueror of St Kitts and Guadeloupe.

A Fellow of the exclusive All Souls College, Oxford, he founded Codrington College in Barbados. On his death he left £10,000 and his books to establish the most magnificent of all college libraries at All Souls, which bears his name.

Sir William Codrington disinherited his only son and the estate passed to a great-nephew, Christopher, who commissioned Wyatt to rebuild in 1796. Building was funded from estate revenues and proceeded slowly – Wyatt was killed when Codrington's coach overturned near Marlborough seventeen years later as they sped back to London after inspecting the work.

Inside, Wyatt forsook the filigree ornament he had learnt from the Adam brothers, reverting to columns and rich marbles – a controlled Roman magnificence with a masculine rather than a feminine flavour.

Dodington was bought in 2003 by the entrepreneur James Dyson, who has brought new panache to the estate, beginning with a grand flourish in the form of an elegant circular pool reflecting Wyatt's magnificent portico.

DOWDESWELL COURT   Cheltenham
Regency house dramatically restored after years as a nursing home

DOWDESWELL COURT BELONGS TO THE GROWING LEAGUE of fine country houses that have been boldly rescued from years of institutional use and born again as spacious elegant family homes. James Perkins, who has brought about this magical and theatrical transformation, explains, 'When I bought the house four and a half years ago it was a 46 bedroom nursing home. Before that it was a Rolls Royce training college and before that an RAF training college during the war. The Queen Mother even came on a hush-hush visit.'

Today it is like stepping into the Soane Museum. 'You can see I'm a fan,' he says with a broad grin as we entered the hall, full of casts of antique statues and a whole lexicon of Classical architectural fragments. 'I was an antique dealer. I've been collecting casts for years. I have another 3,000 pieces in store.'

The transformation is all the more impressive when he shows you photographs of the interiors as they stood before he began work – false ceilings have been ripped out, and wires are dangling down. 'Only one original fireplace survived in the whole house,' he says.

But I am getting ahead of myself. Dowdeswell is entered through electric iron gates with arrow heads painted a rust red. 'There's been too much wind in the last few days to put on the gold leaf,' laughs Perkins.

The steep drive descends past handsome stone outbuildings before swinging round into a balustraded forecourt of Rothschild proportions. The house, faced in beautiful golden Cotswold stone, stands grandly at the end with a recessed centre and eight-column, single-storey Corinthian portico. It's the work of a Cheltenham architect Paul Rowland, built for Mrs Hester Rogers (the original merry widow, one suspects) in 1833–5.

Old photographs show that Dowdeswell was originally three storeys high with tall baroque pilasters at the corners. At some unspecified date in the 20th century, it was dexterously reduced to two storeys and today the pilasters, with exquisite Grecian capitals, are of perfect Classical proportions. The way a pair of capitals elide in the inside corners is specially sophisticated. Yet the windows are still baroque with 'flared' keystones and ears at the corners.

The deep portico opens into the hall in best Regency manner, without a step. The unusual asymmetrical layout dates from a remodelling in 1848 by Samuel Olney Junior, which created a spacious open-plan feel with light streaming down from a window at the top of the stairs flowing into the hall.

Nearly all grand Regency houses possess tall ceilings and so require a good eye for proportion. Mr Perkins continues, 'If you put in a normal sofa, table and chairs it looks, well, disjointed. You have to have a sense of scale.' This he certainly has. Dominating one end of the hall is the largest convex mirror that I have ever seen. 'It was made for me by Mike Aston,' he says. Mr Aston also made the impressive bookcase that fills the end wall of the dining room – resembling the front of a Classical temple, complete with the shallow pediment that was so favoured by the ancient Greeks.

The house stands on a terrace formed on a steep wooded slope with the church behind.

When Lord Hesketh sold his 'Hawksmoor' model of Easton Neston for £180,000 every smart country house owner started to want one. Mr Perkins was naturally ahead of the game and Mr Aston has already made one of Dowdeswell, flanked by two roaring pumas that definitely puts him top in the one-upmanship stakes.

What comes over most strongly is the immense fun Mr Perkins has had living in the house and doing it up. We walk into the drawing room where the new marble fireplace is a witty take on William Kent, with outsize dentils. From the kitchen next door comes the inviting sound of bubbling water – a fountain or a giant fish tank, I wonder. It turns out to be the soundtrack accompanying a film of tropical fish on a flatscreen TV. The kitchen is designed for modern living with a special circular table complete with revolving marble centre for circulating food.

The entrance hall is filled with architectural fragments and casts.

Upstairs the engaging surprises continue with every turn. 'My aim is the luxury of a hotel, the feel of home,' continues Mr Perkins. Visits to the latest boutique hotels provide a constant stream of new ideas. One four-poster bed is like a garden temple with columns at the corners, another has a pedimented mirror the size of a doorway at the back. All the baths are free-standing, the shape of ancient Roman baths cut from solid marble. Shower cabins are in frameless glass descending to the floor, so neatly detailed that Norman Foster would approve. One pair of basins stands on a bombé French rococo commode which, on closer inspection, turns out to have been an altar. From the upstairs windows there are ravishing views over miles of green rolling hills.

Of course there's still work to do. On the lower terrace, an octagonal Georgian gazebo needs restoring and a cheapskate conservatory from nursing-home days survives. Never mind, there's planning permission to replace it with an elegant orangery in stone matching the house, complete with indoor swimming pool.

The history of Dowdeswell Court deserves a full write-up. In a cellar beneath the raised forecourt I was shown an 8-ft tall stone mullion, presumably belonging to the 17th century house built by the Rogers family. The descendants of Mrs Rogers continued to live here – in the church that stands just outside the gate is a memorial to Trooper Richard Coxwell-Rogers of the Royal Gloucestershire Hussars, who was killed at Gallipoli in 1915 and whose parents Geoffrey and Aileen resided at Dowdeswell Court.

KING'S WESTON
Bristol
Vanbrugh mansion restored after years of disuse

WHEN I FIRST VISITED KING'S WESTON the house was immaculately maintained as a police college standing amid trim lawns with a thrilling staircase inside. The next visit presented a very different picture – the whole house was boarded up and suffering from vandalism. Yet this was a masterpiece by one of Britain's greatest architects, Sir John Vanbrugh, the designer of Blenheim Palace and Castle Howard.

Like all Vanbrugh buildings, King's Weston was monumentally constructed. The west front of the house gives the impression of being carved from solid rock. The triangular pediment does not stand out in silhouette but is set into a solid parapet as if chiselled from the natural stone. The chimneys are formed into a three-sided phalanx by interlinking arches. This is an early example of what the French call a *gloriette* – an eye-catcher designed to be seen silhouetted against the sky.

The house was built in 1710–19 for Edward Southwell, the Secretary of State for Ireland, and altered internally by Robert Mylne, who also designed the stables. It was sold in 1833 to Philip John Miles, a Bristol MP. When Miles died in 1845 his estate was worth more than a million pounds, making him Bristol's first recorded millionaire. He also financed the building of the railway and the docks at Avonmouth.

The last squire was Philip Napier Miles, a gifted musician and composer who entertained many young musicians at the house, including the young Malcolm Sargent. During the First World War King's Weston was converted into a hospital. To pay death duties, the King's Weston Estate was auctioned for £9,800 and bought by a school, which promptly began to erect dormitories in the garden, a process fortunately stopped by the war. Later the house served more appropriately as the Bath University School of Architecture.

Salvation for King's Weston, as for many houses taken over for institutional use, has come through weddings, functions and events and it is busy during the day as well as the evening with conferences, dinners and parties.

The chimneys linked by arches can be seen clearly when looking at the garden front.

NETHER SWELL MANOR   Stow-on-the-Wold
Cotswold-style manor house designed by Guy Dawber in 1902

FROM THE OUTSIDE NETHER SWELL OFFERS the illusion of a rambling gabled Cotswold manor with mullioned windows and moss-covered stone slates that are all of 400 years old. In fact, it is all the creation of the talented Edwardian architect Guy Dawber, built on a virgin site of stone quarried from the hill behind the house.

In an ideal world Nether Swell would now be an outstation of London's magnificent Wallace Collection, filled with gorgeous French furniture, paintings and tapestries. For Nether Swell was built for Walter Montagu Scott, the younger brother of Sir John Murray Scott, the capable private secretary of Sir Richard Wallace. Sir John Scott set up the Wallace Collection in Hertford House, but also inherited numerous works of art from Lady Wallace, many of which went to his brother's country house.

Walter Scott built Nether Swell in 1902–3 and greatly extended it five years later. Within, the Wallace links are very much in evidence – period French interiors by Marcel Boulanger, a decorator and supplier of furniture, stucco ornaments and panelling, a Louis XIV billiard room, a Louis XV rococo study and a Louis XVI dining room. By contrast the oak-panelled entrance hall and oak staircase are pure Cotswold in style.

The interiors are shown with French furniture in a *Country Life* article of 1910, and the Scotts remained till 1933, when the remarkable contents were dispersed in a two day sale, including statuary from the Chateau de Bagatelle in the Bois de Boulogne, which Wallace had also owned.

After the war Nether Swell became a prep school and was later taken over by Bedfordshire County Council, which ran residential courses here. The house's history was written by Stuart Fraser, the last principal.

But for the very substantial 'science block' type additions at the back, it might have been snapped up once more as a handsome private house. Standing just two miles from Stow-on-the-Wold, it is secluded at the end of a long drive, overlooking attractive meadows without a house in sight.

Instead it was acquired by Charles Church, the house builders, who converted the original house into four and replaced the science blocks with eight new houses. Too often such new-build schemes introduce a scattering of suburban-style houses on meandering drives, destroying the whole ambiance of the place, but here the Tetbury architect Christopher Kubale has laid out the new houses on a formal pattern that neatly picks out the geometry of the Edwardian garden layout. If the detailing and materials are as good as they appear in the plans, this scheme could be a model of its kind, helping solve the ubiquitous problem of how to replace the footprint of institutional enlargements in sensitive fashion.

Of the eight new houses, five are laid out around a formal cloister-like garden, each with their own private terrace or garden, while others overlook the newly restored cascade ponds. The houses range in size from a two-bedroom single-storey cottage to four-bedroom family houses.

In the main house, the developers have worked with the grain of the original Dawber design by creating one very large new house, occupying the main reception rooms, which is hardly overlooked by any of the other residents. This house also has exclusive use of the carriage sweep, main entrance porch and sunken garden ringed by statues.

Vertical division has meant that few alterations have been needed apart from the introduction of a new oak staircase to serve the second house. The fourth house has a handsome drawing room formed out of the old double-height kitchen lit by a clerestorey. Given the years of institutional use, the house itself remains remarkably unaltered with many of the original handsome fireplaces and almost all the beautiful ironmongery of the mullioned windows.

Estate agents sometimes say that Elizabethan houses are difficult to sell because of the small windows, but as Nether Swell is Edwardian all the reception room have large windows; and if the bedroom windows are mostly smaller, that will prove a positive advantage in chill Cotswold winters.

The picturesque gables complement the battlemented tower and two-storey Renaissance porch.

OWLPEN   Dursley
Medieval manor house in ravishing topiary garden

SET ON A STEEP WOODED HILLSIDE that basks in the sun, Owlpen is one of the most memorable of all English manor houses, still very much a private home but exceptionally welcoming to visitors who not only explore the house and gardens but can stay in no less than nine delightful cottages.

The garden has been described by Sir Geoffrey Jellicoe as possibly the earliest domestic garden in England to survive in something approaching completeness. There are garden rooms with walls, hanging terraces linked by gravel paths and steep steps, and always the hill looming heavily at its back.

The house dates from soon after 1464 when Thomas Daunt married an heiress, Margery Ollepen, and was built on a typical medieval plan of great hall with solar wing at one end and kitchens at the other. The house was put to sleep shortly after 1815, when the Stoughton family inherited, and a new mansion was built on the hills at the other end of the estate a mile away. But the gardens at the old manor were still kept up by a caretaker living in the east wing, who gave the topiary yews their annual tonsure and maintained the walled kitchen gardens for the Big House.

Owlpen was bought in 1925 by the architect Norman Jewson, a key figure in continuing the Arts and Crafts tradition in the Cotswolds between the two world wars, and his subtle introductions of panelling and plasterwork lend still further atmosphere to the house.

The current owners, Sir Nicholas and Lady Mander, acquired Owlpen in 1974 and have since bought back much of the old estate, including farmland, woodland and outbuildings. They have carefully repaired much of the manor and outbuildings and recreated an 'Old English' garden, complete with trim box-edged parterres.

When the family moved to a new house in 1815 the gardens were lovingly maintained.

PIERS COURT   Stinchcombe
Stucco front coloured to look like Bath stone

PIERS COURT IS RENOWNED ABOVE ALL as the home of the novelist Evelyn Waugh for over nineteen years, from 1937 to 1956. His son Auberon recalled, 'At Piers Court my father had a butler, housekeeper, page, cook, nanny, nurserymaid and two dailies, all supported by his earnings as a novelist.' Auberon Waugh described the house as 'an exceptionally pretty *gentilhommière* set in about forty acres', bought for his parents by Lady de Vesci before the war.

The main front is a beautiful essay in the villa style, in a stucco that looks like pale Bath stone. The style is Adamesque with fluting rather than dentils in the cornice – with the capitals of the pilasters treated in matching fashion. This new front was built by John Wallington, who bought the estate in 1793. Waugh added the coat of arms set in a rococo cartouche in the pediment in 1938. At the back, the house is a picturesque rambling composition with elements such as gables dating back to the 16th century when the house belonged to the Pinfold family.

Auberon Waugh described how the front of the house belonged strictly to his father, whose presence exuded from the library in a 'miasma compounded of Havana cigar smoke and gin'. The steps of the pretty cantilevered stair are undercut to create a rippling effect, and the handsome proportions of the library with handpainted Chinese wallpaper, drawing room and dining room are complemented by cosy rooms with lower ceilings in the old part of the house at the back.

Piers Court has an exceptionally attractive setting with long gravel drive flanked by beech hedges, a front garden with ornamental pond and fountain and a secret garden with high clipped yew hedges and gravel walks leading to a 'Gothic Edifice' created by Waugh. There is a croquet lawn sheltered by high beech hedging, avenues of fruit trees and a water garden in a walled enclosure. A mews was added in 1987 with five garages and two flats above.

The Adamesque front of the 1790s has a coat of arms added by Evelyn Waugh.

POULTON MANOR   Poulton
Handsomely restored small Cotswold manor house of 1710

POULTON MANOR IS AN EXAMPLE of the beauty and harmony that can grow from good proportions and fine masonry. It is built of Cotswold stone set in courses so narrow they can be mistaken for brickwork, with a roof of textured Cotswold slate. The entrance front is of smooth ashlar with quoins emphasising the corners.

Poulton marks the arrival of Classical architecture in the Cotswolds. Picturesque gables have given way to a straight roofline. The central front door is surmounted by a large segmental pediment. Yet the windows pre-date wooden sashes and still have leaded panes set within stone mullions and transomes. The roof has the added flourish of a splay or sprocket at the bottom, creating oversailing eaves. To maintain perfect symmetry all the chimney flues are gathered together in a single central stack.

The plan is simple, with the front door opening into a narrow hall with a staircase at the end. On either side are panelled rooms both front and back. This arrangement is repeated on the first floor, where a massive masonry arch supports the monumental chimney. The interiors retain original oak and elm floorboards and almost all have window seats with panelling in the reveals, which increases the sense of space. A pair of pilasters frame the fireplace in the main sitting room and in the dining room is a mid 18th-century fireplace from Clutton House, Kingston-upon-Thames. The staircase has a single sturdy turned baluster to each step and square corners posts.

The house is satisfyingly symmetrical with stone mullions and leaded windows.

In the middle ages there was a priory at Poulton and the manor was sold at the Dissolution to the Paget family, who built the present house in around 1700. In the 1930s, Poulton, by then in a sorry state, was bought by the Cartwright family, who renewed the roof and reinstated the ground-floor window mullions. After the Second World War the house was bought by Sir David Gamble, Bt, then by the architect Anthony Sanford, who continued the repairs, rebuilding the chimney in stone.

The house has only a single submerged cellar but the two floors above are of matching proportions, though the first-floor ceilings are a foot higher than those below – 9 ft 9 in as opposed to 8 ft 9 in.

Massive masonry arches above the stair support the central chimney stack.

Poulton stands handsome beside the village street, glimpsed through a splendid pair of ball-topped gate piers. The neatness of the design of the house has prompted an attribution to Peter Mills, one of the surveyors appointed to supervise the rebuilding of London after the Great Fire, but it is most probably the work of a leading local mason.

SADDLEWOOD MANOR · Leighterton
1690s Cotswold house on the edge of the Beaufort estate

IF YOU DREAM OF AN ENCHANTING William and Mary house, blissfully unaltered yet in apple-pie order, Saddlewood Manor is as close to perfection as can be. In 2004, the owners Sandy and Linda Scott had brought it to a peak of comfort and prettiness, while allowing every surviving element of the old building to speak for itself – the handsome stone fireplaces, the broad elm floorboards and the impressive collection of original doors (with brass locks).

The whole property was so perfectly shipshape that you'd think Sandy Scott must have been an admiral, but he said disarmingly that he started in the office of the architect Basil Spence, helping to make the model for Coventry Cathedral, before changing course and 'slipping into advertising'.

Saddlewood is a house that has escaped history – it receives no mention in Pevsner's Gloucestershire and on the 1953 Ordnance Survey is marked simply as a farm. The delight of the house is that the Georgians never touched it, while the Victorians made additions rather than alterations. The reason, I suspect, is that this was long a tenanted house. This is Beaufortshire, with the ducal polo ground just two miles up the road, and mighty Badminton itself just three miles to the south. The date given to Saddlewood is 1690, just as the 1st Duke of Beaufort was completing his great country palace and William III came to stay.

Throughout Saddlewood there is a correctness of detail, a standard of workmanship and a kind of seemliness that speaks more of a team of estate craftsmen more than of a local builder.

Saddlewood is approached up a long drive. Part of its charm is that there is no carriage sweep up to the front door. You park to the side and walk through a garden gate set in a beautiful low drystone, with a paved path up to the front door. There is a doll's-house perfection in the perfect symmetry of the main front, the more delightful because the stone mullions were never replaced by sashes. Above, neat 'relieving' arches take the weight of stonework off the tops of the windows. The proportions of the windows are nonetheless Classical and the front door is surrounded by a shapely bolection moulding wide enough to have housed a pair of double doors rather than the present single pine door.

The small hallway opens directly onto a wonderfully preserved oak stair with corkscrew balusters, square corner posts and broad handrail rising all the way to the attic – and the added flourish of shapely pendants hanging at the turns. The sitting room on the left of the front door is the neat square room expected at this date, but the drawing room on the right is larger and longer with the handsome stone fireplace set rather strangely to one corner, suggesting (with the inglenook fireplace in the dining room beyond) that the 1690 west front may have incorporated elements of an earlier south-facing house.

Relieving arches take the weight off the top of the windows.

Saddlewood is larger than it appears. To one side is a single-storey extension now containing a handsome library with impressively architectural Roman Doric bookcases – the work of Nick Coryndon, who worked for the Prince of Wales at Highgrove and St James's Palace. At the back is a handsome kitchen realm with large old-fashioned larder, perfect for keeping the Christmas turkey.

Upstairs there are six handsome bedrooms all with their own bathrooms. 'I can't bear to stay in houses and think "is it my turn in the bathroom?" ' laughed Mrs Scott. Indeed she has gone one better, for the main bedroom has two bathrooms. The bedrooms in the attic, where two new matching dormer windows have been introduced, all have an individual charm with roof timbers exposed.

A very pretty formal Italian garden has been created at the back of the house – the work of a young Italian designer, Luciano Giubelli – consisting of a series of garden rooms. The largest has smart diagonal stripes on the lawn, enclosed by beech hedges with tapering cones of yew – all brought quite mature from Holland five years ago – and another beech-hedged garden room has an inner horseshoe of beech in the middle.

Top: A main bathroom has more superb fitted woodwork by Coryndon, in rich orange wood with ebony-black trim.

Above: A mini baroque parterre is formed of cushions of clipped box set in raised stone beds.

Around the house is a series of fourteen outbuildings, all in first class order. There are two tithes barns, the larger with two sets of doors and splendid roof timbers. Half was converted into a secure garage by the previous owner for a collection of cars, the other remains untouched. There are two runs of looseboxes and a delightful dovecote complete with 1,000 nesting boxes. A farm cottage has been very smartly converted into a housekeeper's house – equally suitable for grandparents or grown-up children – while a bungalow tucked behind the house is now a very comfortable guest cottage with large 1950s panorama windows retained to take advantage of the best views on the property.

The big surprise is the party barn, extended by the previous owner in 1987. Inside is a warm and inviting turquoise pool with accompanying large bubbling jacuzzi.

The Scotts bought Saddlewood with 20 acres and expanded this to 172 acres – 22 are maintained as grounds and the rest are let to a farmer.

TODDINGTON MANOR   Winchcombe
Gothic Revival masterpiece saved by the artist Damien Hirst

TODDINGTON MANOR IS A LANDMARK in the Gothic Revival designed entirely by its owner, the gifted Charles Hanbury-Tracy, created Lord Sudeley in 1838, who was the all-persuasive chairman of the Commission to rebuild the Houses of Parliament after the fire of 1835. At Toddington, begun in 1819, Hanbury-Tracy adopted the Tudor Gothic style he was later to insist should be adopted for Parliament.

Today Toddington is all the more remarkable because it is unaltered externally and the golden Stanway stone is in almost pristine condition. Hanbury Tracy took his inspiration from Magdelen College and Christ Church Oxford. Though symmetrical on two fronts, the house is essentially a picturesque composition of breathtaking splendour presenting a romantic silhouette of pinnacles, battlements and turrets. The superb stone carving includes a wealth of ornamental window tracery, crocketed arches and carved bosses with heads of English kings.

Tim Mowl, an authority on houses and gardens in the region, was full of enthusiasm. 'The Gothic Revival is thought of as a Victorian phenomenon. The importance of Toddington has not been sufficiently recognised. The house forms the most spectacular ensemble with the grand 1870s church on the edge of the park containing Lord Sudeley's magnificent tomb.'

Following the bankruptcy of the 4th Lord Sudeley in 1893, Toddington passed in the 1930s to the National Union of Teachers and to Irish Christian Brothers, and more recently served as a language college for Middle Eastern students.

Placed on the market in 1997 with Jackson Stops & Staff with a guide price of £3.2 million, Toddington attracted interest from developers thinking of converting the house into apartments but an option was granted to Warner Hotels, the hotel group that has carried out a series of commercially successful but often controversial transformations of large country houses, greatly extending them in size. These include Elizabethan Littlecote in Berkshire, Georgian Cricket St Thomas in Somerset and Victorian Thoresby Hall in Nottinghamshire.

Following intensive negotiations with English Heritage and the local planning authority, Warner Hotels' architects, DTZ, modified their plans so that the large extension was connected by a glazed link to the stable courtyard and screened by new planting and trees. SAVE continued to maintain that this still severely compromised the architecture of the house, which is a completely free-standing composition.

English Heritage thought otherwise. A spokesman commented, 'There has been considerable opposition to this scheme but amendments have been secured, the extensions shifted and reduced and we are moving towards a scheme that is acceptable.'

The Georgian Group disagreed. 'A major development within the setting of a Grade I listed building is contrary to normal planning policy,' said a spokesman. The Garden History Society commented, 'The very large extensions made to three other houses run by Warner Hotels, namely Cricket St Thomas in Somerset, Thoresby Hall in Nottinghamshire and Holme Lacy in Herefordshire, have had a disastrous impact on the landscape around these houses, doubly so because of the extent of car parking.'

Sir Roy Strong, the Society's president, added 'Holme Lacy has been ruined. The granting of planning permission for such a very large extension at Toddington will also set a disturbing precedent.'

The present Lord Sudeley, who lists ancestor worship among his hobbies in *Who's Who*, said, 'We have had eighteen years of uncertainty. Warner Hotels are Toddington's only hope.'

Then in August 2005 the news broke that Toddington and 124 acres had been bought for a reported £3 million by the artist Damien Hirst. All the worries about extensions and enabling development fell away. As well as a farm in Devon and a houseboat in Chelsea, Hirst also owned a large studio in Gloucestershire. His plan for Toddington is to transform it into a gallery for his extensive collection, which includes not only his own work but also important pieces by Francis Bacon and Andy Warhol.

Adam Stanford, a local historian and archaeologist, commented, 'It's an eerie sort of place which I could imagine would chime with Hirst's imagination. It's the type of place which would lend itself well to the presentation of art, perhaps especially the sort produced by Damien Hirst.'

Though the house stood empty, the stonework remains in pristine condition.

UPTON HOUSE   Tetbury
Palladian elegance with baroque flourishes

As styles, Baroque and Palladian are opposites. Yet Upton House combines them to delightful effect. In 1973, writing in *Country Life*, I attributed the design to the engaging William Halfpenny, author of numerous architectural pattern books intended for use by Georgian builders. On the title page of several of his works he is described as 'architect and carpenter'. His known works include two of the prettiest 18th-century gothic houses, Stout's Hill near Uley and the Orangery at Frampton, which is large enough to serve as a dower house. Upton, though Classical, has the same light touch, a joie de vivre and a delight in constantly varied architectural motifs.

The archetypal Palladio villa has a pedimented centre with three windows. There is usually a raised main floor equivalent to the Italian *piano nobile*, with smaller bedroom windows above. Upton provides a perfectly judged contrast between the blocked masonry of the ground floor and the smooth ashlar above. There are Ionic pilasters with distinctive scroll capitals forming a temple motif in the centre. These carry the full Classical entablature of architrave, frieze and dentil cornice. Above, the roof is concealed behind a balustraded parapet where the balusters emerge from acorns – a Halfpenny motif. Other Halfpenny features are the 'quoins' emphasising the corners. In England these are usually alternately wide and narrow. Here, they form an even band in the French manner. Baroque touches include the oval bullseye (*oeil-de-boeuf*) windows in the centre and the hoop tops to those at the sides. Halfpenny was also fond of the 'aedicule' window – framed by pilasters and carrying a triangular pediment like a tabernacle.

Balustrades and bullseye windows add liveliness and dignity.

Giant pilasters and rich stucco ornament the baroque great hall.

Upton House incorporates a portion of a 17th-century house belonging to Nathaniel Cripps, a Quaker magistrate, in the 1650s. According to the *Victoria County History*, his house became a meeting place for the Friends and was visited several times by George Fox. Cripps and others were persecuted and imprisoned in 1660 but meetings continued in the 1670s. Cripps built up a considerable estate, which passed on his death to his son Henry, whose grandson Nathaniel had probably succeeded by 1752 when the new house was built.

Though Upton has the air of a handsome villa on the edge of Bath or Bristol, it comes with fair-sized grounds and a very well preserved ice house with a very architectural front covered in vermiculated or 'worm-eaten' rustication.

There is a sale notice for Upton dated 1820. In 1857 the house belonged to Maurice Maskelyne. Soon after it was sold to the Littles, who moved the entrance to the west side of the house. On the death of Major Cosmo Little in 1934, the house passed to his daughter Charlotte, who had married Major-General G.P. St Clair. The house was put up for sale but in the years of the Depression no buyer was forthcoming. Instead it was let to the famous art historian Kenneth Clark. The St Clairs returned in 1949 after the house had been requisitioned during the war. Recently the house has been extended for a new owner by the accomplished contemporary Classical architect Craig Hamilton.

WOOLSTAPLERS' HALL Chipping Campden
Fourteenth-century hall transformed by an Arts and Crafts pioneer

THE FRONT DOOR of WOOLSTAPLERS' HALL in Chipping Campden opens onto the finest high street in Britain. The houses that line the Cotswold street are the work of the best masons in the country, ranging from the 14th century to the 19th, and their glorious state of preservation is due to years of patient work by the Campden Trust, which was formed in 1929. The poet laureate John Masefield, who regularly visited Woolstaplers' Hall, wrote that there was 'beauty everywhere in that grey curving English street'.

The house is believed to be the oldest in the town, dating from 1340. Chipping Campden was then a major centre for the wool trade and one theory is that this was a merchants' hall and exchange. Another is that it was built for Robert Cals, a wool merchant with extensive links with Flanders and Florence, whose family certainly owned it in the 15th century.

Woolstaplers' Hall has an even greater claim to fame as the focus of one of the great romantic ventures of the English Arts and Crafts movement in the early 20th century – the exodus of talented artists and craftsmen that was led by C.R. Ashbee from the smoke of London to the pure air of the Cotswolds. Ashbee, an architect, designer and pioneer preservationist, had set up a Guild of Handicrafts in the East End of London, making furniture, silver and some of the finest and also most original Arts and Crafts jewellery.

When he arrived in Chipping Campden in 1901, Ashbee and his wife, Jane, acquired Woolstaplers' Hall with money from her father. By this time, says Ashbee's biographer Alan Crawford, 'the Guild numbered about thirty men and its life was

The neat symmetrical arrangement of windows is due to C.R. Ashbee.

not confined to workshop hours. Evenings and weekends would often be spent in communal singing, sports and amateur theatricals under Ashbee's educational eye.'

When the Guild was swallowed up by financial crisis because Ashbee could not bear to lay off the workers he had brought from London, the situation was resolved in front of an open log fire in Woolstaplers' Hall. Ashbee described the predicament to the soap manufacturer Joseph Fels – who said, 'I guess you'd better find some damned fool like me to put up the money.'

The neat symmetrical front of Woolstaplers' owes a lot to Ashbee. His work is seen in the central front door with massive keystone and matching windows on either side. Above is a bay window or oriel with a bottom that is shaped like a vase, though the mouldings have been shaved off rather than continuing along the front. A cottage-like touch is added by the mullioned window above.

An oriel window is a swanky feature for a modest town house. Technically it is an upper-storey overhanging or projecting window. Unlike a bow or bay window, it is carried on brackets or corbels – courses of brick or masonry built out beyond each other to support the window. The term 'oriel' is also used to describe large bay windows lighting medieval great halls. Oriel College Oxford took its name from a balcony or oriel window on a building that stood on the site. Oriel Chambers in Liverpool, dating from 1864, described in Pevsner's guide as 'one of the most remarkable buildings of its date in Europe', has an entire facade of projecting windows. *The Building News* said they looked as if they were 'trying to escape from the building'.

Ashbee wrote in 1902: 'Here we are once again, engaged in stripping walls and peeling plaster.' And he described the house as part of the 'inspired medievalism in which we live'.

Inside, 14th-century Woolstaplers' Hall consists of two long rooms. The front door opens into a dining hall with a huge fireplace begging for a roaring log fire.

Above is a great hall that is as impressive and delightful as any that can be found in a modest town house. It is open to the roof timbers, with two arched trusses and an end wall of timber framing. At the top Ashbee set a shield with a bee and ash boughs, proclaiming his name. The room is given added nobility by the carved stone surround to the bay window in full-blown Perpendicular style with openwork arch inset with pierced quatrefoils.

In a narrower wing at the back is a sitting room, study and kitchen with three bedrooms above. There's no denying that it's a little awkward to get around, but that's the price you pay for the charm and antiquity of the place. It has the advantage of a pretty back garden borrowed from the plot of the neighbouring house, with neat formal planting and miniature bay windows and porch painted in pretty green and white livery.

A lively social life awaits with excellent pubs and superb wine merchant nearby, and the final plus is a magnificent katsura tree just outside the house, which gives off a scent similar to caramel. Some say they cannot catch the smell, but once you do you will never miss it. On a dank November day when half the leaves had gone I could still smell it 50 yards away.

HAMPSHIRE

PARK, LAKE, MOAT, BATTLEMENTS … Beaurepaire has all the trimmings of a grand country estate on a manageable scale. Distinctive estate cottages with white diamond glazing stand along local roads.

From the pleasant Hampshire village of Bramley the main drive passes a gingerbread gate lodge up an avenue of tall limes. From the south another drive sweeps through the park providing a distant view of turrets across a small lake and medieval stew ponds.

For five centuries Beaurepaire was the domaine of the Brocas family from Aquitaine, who gave their name to the Brocas, the waterside meadow beside Eton College boathouse. In the 14th century the family were leading courtiers. Sir Bernard Brocas was master of the horse to Edward III, who gave him permission in 1369 to enclose the park at Beaurepaire. He was also a favourite knight of the Black Prince, fighting with him at the famous Battle of Poitiers.

He was a friend of William of Wykeham, founder of Winchester College, who appointed him 'chief surveyor and sovereign warden' of his parks. Later he became Captain of Calais, and steward of its buoyant customs revenues.

The Brocas crest of a 'Moor's head orientially crowned' was granted by Edward III and handsome Othello-like heads appear on gateposts and even on the parish church weathervane. Queen Elizabeth I visited 'Burraper' – an entry in the Bramley parish register records payments to the bell-ringers on the occasion.

The ancient moat at Beaurepaire survives, enclosing more than an acre of gardens and spreading lawns, but the castle-style house shown in old engravings and early photographs has largely vanished. This appears to have been a typical Georgian sham-castle of 1777 with tall sash windows, corner towers and battlements, but the architect is unknown.

Beside it stood a Tudor wing, with hood moulds to the windows. This is built in warm red brick with the trellis pattern of darker bricks known as diapering.

The Brocas family sold the property in 1873. Tragedy struck in 1942. The elderly owner, the financier Sir Strati Ralli, MC, was returning home when his chauffeur exclaimed, 'Sir, the house is on fire!'

'Take me back to the station,' came the reply. With post-war austerity there was no means of obtaining suitable building materials to repair let alone restore the house. The Tudor wing, which alone survived the fire, was faced in slates at one end to keep out the rain.

So it remained until Beaurepaire was acquired in 1959 by the diplomat Sir Roger Makins and his wife, who lived in a Georgian house, Sherfield Lodge, nearby (he was created Baron Sherfield in 1964.) They commissioned the architect Colonel Tom Bird, who made a speciality of elegantly downsizing county houses, to restore beauty and dignity to the remains.

Bird cleverly concealed the gash left by the fire, adding twin battlemented towers at the end of the Tudor wing with a pretty Regency style-veranda set between. The brickwork is inset with a diaper pattern matching the Tudor work.

Above the verandah, Bird set a large three-tier window filling the broad landings with light as well as providing a bathroom in one of the towers where the owner can recline in the bath looking out down the drive.

The drawing room created in the former kitchen has been amusingly frescoed by an Australian lady named Gill, who told her clients frankly, 'I'm a plagiarist. You can have Rousseau or Rubens.' Jungle animals and trees have delighted visitors ever since. There may be no mahogany doors but the handsome bread-oven door, with scroll hinge supplied by Messrs Wilder & Sons of Reading, is a good stand-in, not to mention the double-fronted safe on full view on the other side of the fireplace.

The spirit of caprice has been continued by the Makins' son Dwight, who has created a cloister garden with battlements, towers and stepped gables, approached through an archway flanked by an attractive white wooden colonnade. This is the work of the Henley architect Andrew Nichols.

The medieval moat encloses the house and a large extent of garden.

The battlemented towers were added to the Tudor wing by the architect Tom Bird.

The rooms around the courtyard are neatly designed to serve as either a self-contained children's wing or a unique place for summer and winter entertaining – alfresco in the central garden and indoors in a garden room that is complete with inbuilt gazebo.

In front of the house, the lawns, cleverly cross-mown in a trellis pattern to match the diaper brick, sweep down to the moat where engaging sentry-box-size tourelles stand at the corners. The lines of the vanished main house are marked out with formal planting.

Two footbridges cross the moat, one a miniature suspension bridge. The other leads to the stables and to an open two-stage pagoda, erected a century ago, apparently intended for drying fruit.

Basingstoke may not sound the best of addresses for an elegant country pad but Beaurepaire is in unspoilt country and marches with The Vyne, one of the National Trust's most beautiful Hampshire properties.

BRAMSHILL
Winchfield
Jacobean prodigy house on the grandest scale

BRAMSHILL'S NAME BELIES ITS SPLENDOUR. A magnificent example of a Jacobean 'prodigy' house, built for a courtier determined to show his stature, it was always more palace than home. The builder was Lord Zouche, patron of Ben Johnson and poets, who was sent as envoy-extraordinary to James VI of Scotland to warn him that Elizabeth would resist any landing of Spanish troops north of the border. While Bramshill was being built in 1605–12, he was president of Wales where he was described as playing 'rex' with the poor Welshmen. Zouche was made many grants of land by James I and invested heavily in the new colony of Virginia, becoming Lord Warden of the Cinque Ports in 1615. Like other grand Jacobean houses, Bramshill has a highly enriched and flamboyant centrepiece, set in now mellow facades. Zouche's exotic taste in architecture had been cultivated in extensive travels on the continent which took him to Heidelburg, Frankfurt and Vienna.

The Bramshill estate was owned by the Cope family from 1699 until 1935, when it was brought by Lord Brocket. Now the National Police Staff College, it has a ceremonial stature on what is a large and busy campus. The atmosphere of a great ancestral domain survives with immensely long drive, large park, lake and herd of rare white deer. The College was founded in 1947 with the mission of training the future leaders of the police. Every senior police officer has attended, as well as many from police forces overseas. Modern parlance has required a new name and from April 1, 2007 Bramshill became part of the National Police Improvement Agency. Meanwhile the European Police College has also made its base at Bramshill.

An intriguing copy of Bramshill is the Croker Mansion in New Jersey, built in 1902–7 and designed by the architect James Brite for George Crocker, the son of the builder of the Central Pacific Railroad.

The long battlemented garden front has bay windows and a twin-arched loggia at the end.

CHAWTON HOUSE  Chawton

Former home of Jane Austen's cousin restored as a library of women's writing

'SO MUCH RESTORED THAT IT IS NO LONGER A PLEASURE TO LOOK AT' was the somewhat damning verdict of the Knight family's ancestral seat in the Hampshire volume of Pevsner. All has now changed. Chawton House has emerged from a meticulously painstaking programme of repairs with its mellow good looks and charm refreshed. Here is a gloriously rambling late Elizabethan house in pink brick and clay roof tiles, all gables, chimneys and mullioned windows.

Salvation has come in an unusual fashion with the sale of the house on a 125-year lease to the Chawton House Library, founded by the American entrepreneur Sandy Lerner. The library is a collection focused on women's writing from 1660 to 1830. The new trust has also acquired the splendid stables of 1591, built of flint, as well as 275 acres.

Tree-ring dating has shown the panelling in the hall to date from the 1580s when the house was built, with some work from the 1620s. The hall is now used for events including evening lectures and conferences.

In 1781, when Thomas Knight and his wife Catherine showed no sign of having children of their own, they adopted a son of the Reverend George Austen, a cousin of Thomas Knight's. Edward Austen Knight took over management of the estate in 1797, and in 1809 he offered a house in the village to his mother and two sisters,

The gabled Elizabethan manor that has regained its mellow patina.

The staircase rises in short flights with balls on the newel posts and pendants hanging from above.

Cassandra and Jane. It was there that Jane Austen's career took off with the publication of *Sense and Sensibility* in 1811. This house is now a Jane Austen museum well complemented by the new library, which is open to the public by appointment. There are tours of Chawton House on Thursday afternoons; pre-booked tours of house, garden, parkland and estate can also be arranged throughout the year. Visitors can book light lunches and teas in the dining room or courtyard.

COLEBROOK HOUSE Winchester
Early Georgian facade fronting a timber-frame house

THE PRECINCTS OF WINCHESTER CATHEDRAL contain as many covetable houses as the Close at Salisbury. Colebrook House stands in a quiet street that once skirted a medieval nunnery. Yet few passers-by are aware of its existence, as the handsome front is at right angles to the street and well screened by trees. Even the entrance gateway, brought there in 1889 by George Ridding, a headmaster of Winchester College, has its show face towards the garden and so barely attracts a glance.

It opens onto a terrace and lawns brought alive by three medieval leats, or water channels, that race past the house on both sides. Those were turned to stunning advantage by Sir Peter Smithers, politician and plantsman extraordinary, who came to live there in 1951 after his mother's death. When Smithers left he sold the house to Sir David Calcutt, QC, then Master of Magdalene College, Cambridge, and retired to Switzerland, creating a still more spectacular garden on a hillside above Lugano.

At Colebrook Smithers made a place of enchantment. To protect his view he bought up three derelict cottages, creating a delightful Italian garden just across a lane leading to the inner close of the cathedral via the aptly named water close. This garden is on show to all passers-by. The wall opens to reveal a balustraded pool flanked by handsome hedges of clipped yew and a leafy bower sheltering a large Classical bust.

Medieval leats or water channels bubble through the garden.

In the main garden Smithers made equally clever play with the water, creating a keyhole-shaped bubbling fountain pool flanked by columns and flowing out along a brick channel that disappears under a miniature arched bridge by his new sunroom.

The garden front of the house is built of the warm red brick used in much of Winchester and sports a pair of splendid rainwater heads shaped like punch bowls and bearing the initials 'TB' and the date 1720. Strangely, though the names of many tenants and owners are known, there is a gap between 1664 and 1747.

The drawing room has linenfold panelling and a shallow Tudor-arched stone fireplace.

The front is not as symmetrical as it appears at a quick glance. The windows on the right are more widely spaced with shallow buttresses between. All becomes clear when you enter the hall. On the right the wall incorporates large structural posts and beams, making it evident that a complete 16th-century timber-framed house is enclosed within the brick building. This presumably is the 'new Frame' house that Simon Trippe was licensed to erect in the twenty-eighth year of Elizabeth's reign – 1586. Trippe was a local apothecary and physician.

At the back of the hall is a very handsome and typically early 18th-century oak stair rising round a spacious open well. Remarkably, the characteristic corkscrew balusters – three to a step, not the usual two – continue not just to the second floor but all the way to the attic.

The layout of Colebrook House, with a large room on either side of the hall, repeats itself on the upper storeys. The surprise is to find a succession of impressive stone fireplaces in all the main rooms. These have shallow stone Tudor arches and, because of their grandeur, one assumes they must be later introductions. The extensive linenfold panelling in the drawing room, all in mint condition, must also be a later import. Several rooms are still hung with loose fabrics introduced by Smithers rather in the manner of Old Master paintings. He also built the very elegant music room at the back of the house.

In autumn 2006 Colebrook House had all that could be desired of a large town house: seclusion, tranquillity and the peace of mind that comes from bordering cathedral precincts as well as nearby Wolvesey Palace, the bishops' residence. The upstairs bedrooms have lovely views of the cathedral's soaring east front. This is a house that would be ideal for those with many visitors. Smithers provided for alfresco living, with a sunroom opening off the main drawing room and large glazed arches opening to the garden. Colebrook House looked a candidate for another stylish makeover, but equally you could have moved in at once to enjoy as blissful surroundings as any English city can offer.

ONE OF THE MYSTERIES of English architecture is just how many pleasant secluded Lutyens-style houses are hidden in woodland settings in Sussex and Hampshire, lost from view by an abundance of rhododendrons and pine trees.

The cartoonist Osbert Lancaster wryly described them as 'stockbroker Tudor', only a notch above the 'bypass variegated' run up by the speculative builder in outer London suburbs.

Yet gates to grand houses such as Durford Court open up every 500 yards along the old Portsmouth Road as it approaches Petersfield from Liphook. The drive to Durford Court plunges into a thickly wooded dell, a haven shut away from the world and alive with birdsong.

Here are all the hallmarks of Lutyens's early domestic style, the deep spreading tiled roofs, the soaring chimneys, tile-hanging, bay windows and dormers with leaded lights, all on a rambling informal plan.

Adrian Bird, a local architect, who has researched these properties, said: 'Intriguingly it was built for a clergyman, the Rev Archibald, who bought the land from a Canon Mills. Construction by James Longley & Co was begun in 1912.' The owner, Rodney McMahon, had also heard that one of the Lyle family of Tate & Lyle lived here, employing nineteen full-time gardeners.

The architects associated with the house are the Unsworths, father and son. The elder, William Frederick, died in 1912 and could just have worked on Durford; the likelihood is that it is a joint work with his son, Gerald, who built up a flourishing practice in Petersfield. The Unsworths were in partnership at this time with H. Inigo Triggs, an accomplished designer of formal gardens. According to Michael Bullen, who is jointly revising Pevsner's guide to Hampshire, 'the sunken garden at Durford and the delightful dovecote are similar to those at Triggs's own nearby house at Little Boarhunt'.

Durford Court has delightful Arts and Crafts flourishes such as the splayed edges to the roof and a skirting at the bottom of the tile-hanging facades. The entrance from the front is in the form of an L with a square entrance court and stone gate piers, topped by obelisks, opening into the service court. In the corner of the L is a tall oriel lighting the staircase, which has the stepped windows that were sometimes used by Lutyens.

Much of the house's charm comes from the extensive use of dormer windows, not just in the attics but on the ground and first floors as well. The south-facing garden front is timber-framed with the vertical posts jointed with still-visible wooden pegs. The intriguing feature of the interior is that there is hardly a room that is a plain square or rectangle. The Unsworths had a penchant for L-shaped rooms with bay windows, oriels or fireplaces.

The wide front door has a gentle Tudor arch and massive blacksmith's hinges carried all the way across. The hall beyond has a hint of Chicago prairie-style open plan, with the wall of the corridor leading to the stair cut away to provide a view into the garden.

To the right, the former billiard room, one of five reception rooms, has a tall coved ceiling and corner fireplace with a tiled arch. The appeal of these rooms and many of the bedrooms, too, is that all are double aspect with windows in at least two walls flooding the house with light. Three of the main living rooms have doors leading to the garden, two of them into shaded loggias. The oak stair leads to a first-floor gallery with handsome square pillars and neat serpentine brackets supporting the beams.

In the whole house there can hardly be one window exactly like another; the shape, the size and the level of the sills is constantly varied to take advantage of views of the garden, and occasionally to provide privacy. Oak doors are beautifully made, sometimes with different panelling on each side. The treatment of the eight bedrooms is simple, their character coming from being built into the sloping eaves.

To the east the house looks out over the typically Edwardian sunken garden with a lily pond. To the south a broad avenue of copper beeches leads to a woodland garden with circular walks through 24 acres of grounds that go down to a broad clearing in the valley bottom, where you can walk the dog without ever leaving your own land and then climb back to the house via steps.

Durford looks back to the past with tile-hanging and sweeping roofs.

GRANGE PARK   Alresford
Majestic Greek Revival mansion rescued from demolition

THREE TIMES GRANGE PARK HAS BEEN BROUGHT BACK from the brink of destruction. On September 8, 1972, the *Sunday Times* reported that it was due to be dynamited within a week – on the eve of a magnificent exhibition on European Neo-Classicism at the Royal Academy. The Secretary General of the Council of Europe cabled the Prime Minister, Edward Heath, asking him to secure a reprieve.

Gathering at the house to see how far demolition had progressed, we found the slates stripped from the roof and even the marble treads removed from the grand staircase. But such was the volume of protest that the owner agreed that the Department of the Environment could take over the shell in guardianship and preserve it as a ruin.

Six years later nothing had happened. When I visited Grange Park, the Roman cement on the fluted columns was falling off in huge shards. The egg-and-dart moulding in the coffering of the portico was dissolving under the weight of water pouring through the roof.

Advised by Robert Carnwath, SAVE obtained a copy of the guardianship deed in which the Secretary of State undertook to carry out repairs and open the Grange to the public. We discovered that one senior civil servant, who had no taste for Regency architecture, was determined that not one penny of public money should be spent, and that the house should be left to rot until it was past the point of no return.

The Doric portico set high on a podium is faced in stucco imitating golden stone.

The Grecian frontages enclosed a 1670s brick house, just visible on the left.

Our solicitors drafted an affidavit seeking an act of *mandamus*, a judicial ruling requiring a minister to do what he is obliged to do by statute. For months the Department of the Environment prevaricated, but when we finally told them we would lodge the papers in the High Court the next day, they agreed to act.

The architect John Redmill, who had sent SAVE regular reports of the decay of the Grange, had shown that within the stucco Classical facades was a complete 17th-century redbrick country house. When repairs were carried out the Charles II brickwork was left exposed at one end, revealing a completely new chapter in the house's history.

Before work began there was a change of Government and Michael Heseltine, the new Environment Secretary, announced that he was reconsidering whether the Grange merited the considerable sum of money assigned for repairs. SAVE produced a lightning leaflet, *Ten Days to Save The Grange*, generating a massive salvo of support, and Michael Heseltine approved the repairs. Grange Park finally opened to the public on May 24, 1983, nearly eleven years after it had first been reprieved.

Since then Grange Park has sprung back to life as a venue for a summer opera festival. To Glyndebourne's princely 1,200 seat auditorium, the new theatre at Grange Park offers 530. Wasfi Kani opened the £2.5 million theatre in 2003, a season ahead of schedule, installing 400 red velvet stalls seats from the auditorium of the Royal Opera House in Covent Garden in the beautiful Ionic orangery, designed by C.R. Cockerell.

Dining tables are now elegantly set out in the preserved but unrestored interiors, given colour and atmosphere by watercolour scenes by Alexander Creswell.

MOUNDSMERE MANOR Preston Candover
Edwardian mansion in the style of Sir Christopher Wren

MOUNDSMERE IS AN IMPRESSIVE ESSAY in the Grand Manner with a formal garden extending the lines of the architecture across the landscape. Handsome lodges mark the entrance and a drive sweeps up through parkland to the house, which is protected by a number of fine mature trees.

The house was built in 1908–9 to the designs of Sir Reginald Blomfield for Wilfred Buckley, a successful businessman returning to England from America. He spent a long time looking for the perfect site for his new house and was well rewarded. Moundsmere Manor was monastic property, which at the Dissolution had become part of the dowry of two of Henry VIII's wives, first Anne of Cleves and then Catherine Howard. It was then granted to Winchester College and used for a while as a refuge for scholars during outbreaks of plague.

Blomfield provided a formal entrance court to the north of the house, which is built of a warm orangey-red brick in the Wrennish manner that Blomfield favoured. The grand garden front pays more than just a nod to Wren's work at Hampton Court Palace, with its handsome pilastered centrepiece topped by bullseye windows and a balustrade with urns. At a quick glance, it is convincing enough to be taken for work done in 1700. Other baroque details include the vertical linking of the windows.

In front, Blomfield designed a sunken garden with mirror pool reflecting the south front, now prettily edged with pincushions of box. Large irregular balls of yew flank the paths on either side of the sunken garden. The layout is extended by lawns and enclosed by long, neatly clipped walls of yew with scalloped buttresses on either side breaking the flower borders into compartments. On the main axis the ha-ha breaks forward in a half circle to provide a view across parkland and rolling Hampshire countryside. A smaller garden room is laid out to the west with pretty swimming pool and columned pavilion. To the east the garden continues on a grand scale with further yew hedges enclosing lawns scattered with splendid park trees.

One of the round windows looks out over the mirror pool and across the fields beyond.

The entrance porch opens into a spacious hall with a screen of Ionic columns framing the view of the staircase. Over the columns Blomfield dispensed with the usual architrave and frieze in favour of swagged garlands of flowers. The floor is laid with a French parquet of interlacing squares set in a larger diamond pattern. The late 17th-century-style ceiling is adorned with cartouches while the carved eagle over the fireplace used to preside over a portrait of George Washington – Buckley's homage to America. Swags of fruit hang from bows on either side.

Sir Reginald Blomfield's garden front is crowned by bullseye windows and urns.

The dining room is handsomely panelled in the early 18th-century manner with fluted giant pilasters on either side of the fireplace, which has a veined marble surround with Grinling-Gibbons-style swags above. The drawing room is a pretty coral pink and opens out through French windows onto the sunken garden. The library has tall sashed windows with folding panelled shutters as in all the other main rooms.

Moundsmere was brought to a pitch of glamour and perfect trim by Mark Andreae. When he was selling the house in 2005, one of the main delights was the discovery of a perfectly preserved set of Edwardian bathrooms complete with sturdy baths and basins and white glazed tiles on both the walls and floor. These bathrooms were exactly like the original bathrooms at the Ritz in London, which were stripped out in their entirety, making those at Moundsmere a rare and important survival.

On sale with 83 acres, Moundsmere came with all the trimmings of a traditional estate. These include a large walled garden with an imposing hothouse that runs more than half the length of the west wall, a delightful gardener's cottage with steep tiled roof and a central pair of chimneys linked by an arch in the Vanbrugh manner. Like all grand Edwardian houses, Moundsmere has a large service wing, here extending to the east of the house and designed to be discreetly out of view.

NUTLEY MANOR · Preston Candover
Regency farmhouse which comes with 856-acre estate

TEA AT NUTLEY MANOR WAS JUST LIKE being at the Ritz – egg and smoked salmon sandwiches in fluffy white bread, scones with strawberry jam and cream, and – well, I never got to the coffee cake. Tony and Sue Carter spent five years bringing their pretty Regency manor house to the pitch of smart perfection. It is not hard to see why.

Nutley is near Alton, in grand rolling Hampshire countryside where immaculate villages nestle between vast estates and the Sainsburys and Palmer-Tomkinsons are your neighbours.

Tony spent twenty years developing a prize partridge and pheasant shoot and the position of the eight guns on a dozen drives were all marked smartly in red on the plan at the back of the 2006 sales brochure. The whole 856-acre estate was as neat as a National Trust garden. Much of it was set aside, providing stubble for partridges or grass sward so smooth that, as Tony put it, his guns can go shooting in carpet slippers. One guest brought a set of boules to play during the mid-morning break.

The edge of every field was teeming with French partridges. 'There are also fallow and roe deer,' said Tony, pointing to the stalking hides in the trees, one a charming elevated seat halfway up a trunk with a ladder in front.

In one of the woods are towers for clay-pigeon shooting. Two 40 ft towers and one at 80 ft give guests a taste of high-flying birds such as they might find in Devon. The towers are all operated by hand-held remote controls with buttons for flight directions of the clays.

Shooting lunches are held in a delightful cricket pavilion with a veranda outside to enjoy any winter sun. The interior is lined with photographs of the guns at past shoots. The beaters eat nearby in their own smart tin shed.

The house is not much larger than a handsome estate farmhouse; it is built of attractive red brick with matching clay tiles and very pretty three-part sash windows. An oval plaque over the entrance carries the date 1814 *Anno Pacifico* (year of peace), just before Napoleon escaped from Elba to march on Waterloo, and the initials 'GPJ'. These stand for George Purefoy Jervoise, MP (1770–1847), of Herriard Park, some miles to the east. He owned estates at both Nutley and Preston Candover, where the pub is the Purefoy Arms, and also built numerous cottages on his extensive property.

The Manor of Nutley is mentioned in Domesday as belonging to Henry the Treasurer, who owned land around Winchester. His is the first name on the official HM Treasury website and, according to your view, was either one of the Conqueror's two most important financial officers or just the keeper of the King's 'treasure', which was kept at Winchester, not the Tower of London.

One intriguing feature of the house is the bowed glass in the windows, each pane billowing outwards like a sail. Charles Brooking, Britain's No. 1 window expert, identifies this as a 'faux' form of crown glass, most commonly used just before and after the Second World War.

Other improvements included a swimming pool pavilion with French windows on three sides, so that it is almost alfresco in summer. The single-storey brick pavilion is orientated to catch the sun all day. With it comes a multi-gym. 'All the usual bits of torture,' said Tony Carter happily. Ready and waiting were a running board, a StairMaster, an exercise bike, a punch bag – 'Think of the bank manager!' – and a collection of weights ready to strain every muscle in the body. Below is a cinema where films can be projected on a vast screen that materialises magically over the fireplace. Enveloping sound emerged discreetly from the ceiling. 'No ugly big speakers here,' said Tony.

When Sue Carter wanted to build a conservatory, she consulted a feng shui expert. He pointed to an empty site beside the house saying: 'This is your space.' Reeling at the thought of another battle with the planners, she replied: 'We'll never get permission.' 'I'll give you the date to apply,' said her expert and approval came in record time.

Nutley has all the toys for luxurious living. 'There's music available in every room, but don't ask me how it works,' said Sue.

The dining room had stunning murals of Chinese trees and flowers, with birds added by Simon Horn. 'I wanted an effect like a de Gournay wallpaper, but more open,' she said.

The new kitchen was all in oak with a burr oak frieze. Next door were chiller drawers and a wine cooler; a panel allows you to bring the Haut Brion to room temperature. Descending to the cellar I caught a quick glimpse of bottles of Richebourg, Romanée-Conti and La Tache. 'Could any of this stay with the house?' I asked innocently. 'No way!' said Tony.

The proportions may be engagingly cottage-like but the manor is mentioned in Domesday.

SHAWFORD PARK   Winchester
Charles II house made ever grander by city magnates

SHAWFORD PARK IS A TROPHY HOUSE with its own private polo ground and trout fishing in one of the country's best chalk streams, the River Itchen, which divides to flow along the property on both sides.

The house is a textbook example of the Charles II or 'Caroline' style and was built in 1685 for Henry Mildmay in typical doll's-house form with two even storeys and four steps up to a grand pedimented front door. What makes it unusual is the way the centre recedes on one side of the house and projects on the other. The facades are faced in smoothest ashlar with quoins at the corners – rather charmingly brick was used on the ends, economical but appropriate as the tall chimney stacks are also of brick.

In the mid 19th century the Mildmay descendants, who by this time also owned Dogmersfield Park in Hampshire, sold it to Major-General Edward Frederick. In 1911 the house was bought by Mabel Morrison, the widow of Alfred Morrison of Fonthill House in Wiltshire, the son of James Morrison who was reputed to be the richest commoner in England.

In 1912 she employed the architect Herbert Jewell to enlarge the front hall, bringing the entrance forward. He returned in 1920 to build a large ballroom beside the house, fronted by an elegant arcade. This is all in white stone to match the house, though the vault of the arcade is flawlessly executed in red brick.

Jewell extensively reworked the interior in a Lutyens manner with a quantity of sumptuous oak panelling and the very architectural lobbies which are such a feature of Lutyens houses. In 1934 Shawford was bought by Constantine Benson. His wife, the daughter of the 2nd Earl of Dudley, is remembered for the tremendous parties

The new swimming pool is disguised as a fountain pond.

she gave, including an annual party for the estate workers and local suppliers. During the war the house was requisitioned as a maternity hospital – polite strangers occasionally appear asking to see the house where they were born. In 1945, the Bensons sold the house to Sir Brian Mountain who was chairman of the Eagle Star Insurance Company. In 1975 a savage fire took hold in Lady Mountain's bedroom and the whole house would have been lost but for the gallantry of two local firemen who climbed onto the roof to douse the flames

The ballroom is now a living room.

till large fire engines arrived. Damaged rooms were made good with new oak panelling that carefully matches the Edwardian work.

As you enter the hall the double doors into the drawing room beyond provide a gorgeous view straight out into the garden. To the right of the hall is the oak library, likely to be everybody's favourite room. Bookcases line the side walls while at either end between the windows is a beautifully sculpted Classical niche.

The link corridor to the ballroom has both arch and cross vaults and a wooden flight of steps shaped like a bombé-fronted Dutch chest of drawers with a scalloped 'riser' to each step. The ballroom is perfect for modern-day grand living, a full 55 ft long, with a fireplace that is tall enough to stand in. The present owners have improved the outlook with a swimming pool that is shaped like a mirror, with a central splashing fountain.

The 1920s arcade on the entrance court.

Another architectural lobby, this time with lunettes, leads to twin sitting rooms for the master and mistress of the house. His is handsomely panelled in unpainted oak with figuring as delicate as watered silk. Hers is chastely painted in white in best Edwardian style. Steps lead down to the large dining room with stone-flagged floor, stone skirting and stone door surrounds with a distinct Deco flourish.

The kitchen is cleverly arranged for alfresco eating in either the garden or a courtyard patio. The tack room is the smartest place in the house, with rows of mallets hanging at a slant, while the 1920 squash court is now a seriously equipped gym – complete with instructions for honing your abdominal muscles.

Upstairs the main bedroom overlooks the garden with the added flourish of side windows in the cheeks of the projecting centre. There is a bathroom suite with comfortable armchair and twin oval basins in the outer sanctum and beyond, a strange conceit, 'his and hers' loos placed side by side as in a Georgian privy.

Spare bedrooms with glorious views over the garden are ranged above the dining room and kitchen – with bathrooms on the other side of the corridor. Remarkably, not a radiator is to be seen. 'The heating in the rooms below keeps them warm and most guests turn off the flame fires in the grates,' says the butler. Further bedrooms are in the attic, making eleven in all. The surprise is to find the floor on one side sloping sharply due to subsidence long ago – welcome proof that old timbers survive amid so many remodellings.

In recent years formal gardens have been laid out on an ambitious scale. You can't get close to the windows of the garden front thanks to the wealth of clipped box, yew and bay topiary, while on the entrance front a red flowering quince is neatly trained round the windows, providing winter colour.

The grounds are so extensive that a tour takes a good 20 minutes even in a buggy, perhaps because we took the occasional stop to admire the river. Grass paths meander between drifts of daffodils, leading to a balcony tree house in an ancient oak, perfectly placed for children to use as a fortress, or for the adults to have a peaceful evening drink by the river.

The sunken topiary garden is aligned on an axis with the garden door.

THE SOKE
Winchester
Town house of medieval origin rescued by an architect owner

TO THE STREET, THE SOKE PRESENTS a handsome three-storey Georgian front in the warm red brick typical of Winchester. The two rows of tall sash windows with smaller ones above suggest the 1770s or 1780s.

Yet the house is shown in the foreground of a magnificent panorama of Winchester, engraved in 1736 when it was already a century and a half old, with gables at the front, tall mullioned windows and a wealth of half timbering. The Soke stands next to medieval Chesil Church, with the River Itchen behind. Beyond lies Winchester's glorious cathedral in its large, leafy close.

The ancient word Soke or Soc indicates the right of holding a court. Until local government reform in the 1970s, England's most famous Soke, the Soke of Peterborough, stood proudly separate from either Northamptonshire or Cambridgeshire.

The principal builder of The Soke in Winchester was Sir Thomas Fleming, Queen Elizabeth I's Solicitor-General. He represented Winchester in two parliaments and was obviously a convivial host, for he died at a party he was giving for his servants in 1613. He has a niche in English history as one of the men who presided over the trial of Guy Fawkes and his fellow conspirators in the Gunpowder Plot.

The garden front has an impressive chimney stack added in the 1580s.

He bought The Soke in 1583. When the house was repaired painstakingly by John Browning, the Winchester architect, in the early 1990s, evidence appeared suggesting that parts of the building were much earlier still and pre-dated the 14th-century church next door. Browning explains: 'The 1580s house was built on an E-plan with a recessed centre forming a courtyard. In the entrance hall you can still see evidence showing that the upper storeys projected out over the lower ones.'

In the attic the original Elizabethan gable over the entrance, with its bargeboard and timber window, is preserved, hidden beneath a later gable added in front.

The house bears the marks of its many rebuilds. On the garden front there is a grand buttressed chimney stack built of chequered stone and flint dating from the 1580s, with paired red-brick chimneys set diamond-wise in characteristic Elizabethan fashion. The gabled end wall is tile-hung, inset with a handsome white-painted wooden bay window, suggesting a late Victorian date.

Inside, it is the same story – a glimpse of a gargoyle, a stone fireplace with a shallow Tudor arch, linenfold panelling of 1600 date, early Georgian bolection mouldings and Regency door frames with circular stops at the corners.

The Soke is a spacious house spread over four storeys. The front door opens into a panelled hall with a fireplace set in the corner in William and Mary style of about 1700. Both the dining room and drawing room retain complete Georgian window shutters, although the much thicker walls at the back indicate their earlier date.

The main staircase is in Elizabethan style and rises in short flights around an open well, with the corner posts continued up as columns. The main bedroom overlooking the garden has a gently sloping floor and a crooked wooden-mullioned window, suggesting settlement centuries ago. In the bathroom is a splendid mural painted on a wooden partition and dated 1609, clearly the work of Fleming. It consists of great sweeps of acanthus foliage painted dashingly in pink and grey, a giant version of a William Morris wallpaper. Curiously there is a gap in the mural, suggesting that it was painted around some long-vanished piece of furniture standing against the wall.

Browning says: 'When we bought the house it was suffering from extensive damp and rot. I realised it was largely a carpentry job and advertised for a carpenter, who virtually lived with us for two years stripping the roof and repairing it in oak.' Beneath the Georgian repairs to the staircase they found the original dimensions of the late 16th-century newel posts and were able to replace them .

The basement is straight out of the film *Gosford Park*, with glass-fronted cupboards in the pantry and internal glass partitions letting light into an inner hall, still paved in stone. The large kitchen opens directly onto a terrace sheltered by the medieval walls of Chesil Church. Thanks to garden lighting, the flintwork and fine, decorated tracery of the church are illuminated beautifully at night.

The garden is of a size unimaginable in Central London, wider than the house, with a Lutyens-like grass path flanked by paving stones leading down to a trellis arbour, glimpsed through a wall of grand yew topiary. Beyond, there are two charming small garden rooms, one containing a pretty pond set in the grass, the other a kitchen garden complete with asparagus beds. A water gate opens onto the river, looking across to the rose walk on the far side.

TWYFORD MOORS HOUSE   Twyford
Built for a sailor-artist by the gentleman-architect Henry Woodyer

THANKS TO HOGWARTS AND HARRY POTTER, the Gothic style is now back in fashion. Twyford Moors House is a rare architectural gem by one of the most original and accomplished Victorian Goths. The architect Henry Woodyer may not be as famous as George Gilbert Scott, Butterfield, Burges or Waterhouse, but all his buildings are sought out by the cognoscenti.

More recently Woodyer entered the limelight as one of the architects of Victorian Tyntesfield, which was saved by the National Trust from imminent break-up. There, Woodyer added some of the finest flourishes to the interior. Part of the appeal of Twyford Moors is that it is a kind of mini-Tyntesfield with an exotic spiky silhouette, delightful squirrels carved on the bay windows and a wealth of pointed arches, knotched woodwork and bursts of colourful decorative painting. Like Tyntesfield, it has some spectacular gothic fireplaces, including one inlaid with lapis lazuli and coloured marble.

The house was built for an intriguing sailor artist Conrad Mordaunt Shipley, who had entered the navy as a midshipman aged 14 and retired just sixteen years later at the agreeably early age of 31. Clearly a man who liked to do things in the right order he built his new house in 1861–2 and took a bride a year later.

When built, Shipley surveyed an estate of some 1,000 acres looking down to the River Itchen. Somewhat surprisingly to our ears today, the whole floodplain was compulsorily purchased by Southampton Corporation in the 1950s – in the days when county boroughs organised their own water supplies. The result is a landscape protected at someone else's expense – without a building to be seen all the way to the horizon.

Shipley wrote in his journal in February 1861 that Woodyer was 'a thorough gentleman' with 'good taste in furniture, decoration and the laying out of gardens'. The next day he relates that he 'drove over to Twyford to look at a site which we fixed upon' – evidently this was the first house to be built here.

The house is like a very substantial Victorian rectory, both picturesque and asymmetrical; it also makes use of the polychrome building materials that the Victorians were so fond of. The tower has a redbrick trim, and a pyramid-roofed superstructure complete with black and white woodwork, meaning that it looks almost as if it would be more at home in Normandy than in Hampshire. The great beauty is the extensive use of knapped flints, with

The house is built of knapped flints and golden stone with barely one window matching another.

A large bay window lights the drawing room with its chimney piece that rises to the ceiling.

golden stone for all the window surrounds, almost every one designed according to a different pattern. However, lest anyone should mistake the house for an earlier building, Shipley boldly stamped the date 1861 on numerous rainwater heads.

The entrance is sheltered by a porch that is as deep as those found on an ancient parish church. It opens directly into a characteristically large Victorian hall, with a handsome staircase that has been cleverly set back in a corner, and continues round as a gallery on two sides of the first floor. The tops of the huge newel, or corner, posts intriguingly serve as candlestands – useful for preventing a tumble down the stairs in the dark nights before electricity. The unusual balustrade has been designed in the form of a quatrefoil inset with a shield.

Instead of the rich intensely colourful Puginesque interiors that might be expected, there is almost an excess of white walls; but this serves to highlight the quality of the oak woodwork, the stencilled ceilings and the hooded gothic fireplace with bands of fish-scale ornament. The hood is carved with a Moor's head above an earl's coronet – suggesting the name Twyford Moors may allude to the saracen's head that was the crest of the Mordaunts, Earls of Peterborough. The Moor's head also appears above the staircase landing as a corbel, complete with gold earring.

The best Victorian country house dining rooms are appointed with built-in oak sideboards and Twyford Moors actually has two of them, as well as another hooded fireplace with a tent top and more coats of arms. The woodwork is of excellent quality with gothic oak doors and folding shutters and high skirtings that come up to the level of shallow window seats inset with iron heating grilles. At some point someone fond of giving parties has connected the bay windows of the drawing room and adjoining sitting room so its is possible to circulate from one room to another in the best French manner without doubling back and meeting the guests you have just been talking to.

Upstairs there are more pointed arches opening into spacious bedrooms, including an intriguing 'his and hers' of different heights. The doors have large ornamental black iron hinges spreading across the woodwork.

During the 1930s a cottage was sensitively added in matching flintwork on the far side of the paved kitchen courtyard, which retains the Victorian succession of boot room, flower room, and coal hole. Beyond, the garden forms an intriguing succession of garden rooms with a yew avenue and impressive boxes hedges which are as high as table tops.

THE VINEYARDS · Beaulieu

Designed by R.A. Briggs for a former physician to Queen Victoria

IN 1905 THE 2ND LORD MONTAGU suggested to a number of friends that they buy parcels of land on his Beaulieu estate on 99-year leases and build themselves country houses. The Vineyards was one of these houses, built in about 1906–7 by Sir James Kingston Fowler, a physician to Queen Victoria who became Warden of Beaulieu Abbey. His architect was R.A. Briggs.

The delight of the house is the garden front with a pair of slightly eccentric bell-shaped gables. Into these are set delightful bay windows, which have been designed like miniature pagodas, diminishing in size from one tier to the next. The ground-floor bay windows have a pretty curved tiled roof, the upper ones have a copper roof, which has again been splayed and capped by finials. From these upper-storey windows there are fine views across to the head of the Beaulieu River with the Isle of Wight in the distance.

The Vineyards was one of a dozen country houses on the Beaulieu estate taken over during the Second World War as the 'finishing school' of the SOE, the Special Operations Executive, where agents were prepared for the clandestine life they would have to lead when dropped in occupied Europe.

Commander Wallrock, who was living here when I visited The Vineyards in 2002, told me the agents would be put into a little hut on the edge of the lawn for three days to get used to looking after themselves. After the war the Gore-Browns came to live here on their return from South Africa and they planted the adjoining vineyard, which is now run by the Montagu family. They also commissioned an amusing series of wall paintings by John Hastings.

The shaped gables have pagoda-like bay windows.

HEREFORDSHIRE

IN THE MID 1990S BARGE HOUSE WAS a decrepit barn with an asbestos roof, standing in a wilderness. By 1999 it was worthy of a Civic Trust award for the sensitive rescue of an old building. It was all the work of a potato merchant at Ross-on-Wye – Sean Mason and his wife Sarah. 'I have this passion for being by water,' said Mason.

The Barge House stands right on the Wye with one of its tributaries running through the garden to join it. The house has the fishing rights over the Garron Brook but to fish in the Wye you need to join a club that thoughtfully allows owners of riverside properties to go to the head of the queue.

The Royal Commission on Historical Monuments suggested in 1931 that the building dates from the first half of the 17th century, with the roof carried down at the back later in the same century. It's also marked as The Old Forge on a series of Georgian maps. In 1725 the property, then 5 acres, was sold by the Duke of Kent, who owned ironworks here, for the substantial sum of £490 15s 4d to Thomas Fletcher of Goodrich.

From outside it's only the handsome stone archway around the front door that suggests this is more than a simple cottage. But as soon as you step through the door

The roof was carried down at the back later in the 17th century.

– either the front or the back – the charm of the place is apparent. So many old houses get clumsily bashed around – here, there is a sense that the Masons loved every minute of restoring it, enjoyed the feel of the brick and stone of which it is built, and took infinite pains over finishes, paints and papers.

When they began there were no floors or ceilings, only four vast elm and oak beams spanning from side to side, bearing notches for long-vanished joists. At the back was one internal wall, of brick not stone-inset with the narrow ventilation slits that are typical of Herefordshire barns.

The floor was raised, giving the space a cosier feel, and laid with large flagstones rescued from an old farmhouse. Behind is a new kitchen running the length of the building with worktops at one end and a breakfast table at the other. The floor is paved in Victorian tiles, some patterned but mostly plain brown, red and black, found in an old sheep shed. None of your imitation-Georgian kitchen cupboards here but salvaged window shutters sent off to the Cotswolds to be 'distressed' and set below a smart polished red granite top.

The kitchen opens through into one big room filling the rest of the ground floor, with sofas and armchairs on one side and a large dining table on the other. Dividing the two spaces is a free-standing fireplace open on both sides. 'Everyone said "don't do it" but it's never smoked,' said Mason. 'We burn peat,' added Sarah.

Otherwise the house is heated with good chunky vintage radiators. 'I was driving past the arts college in Hereford which was being demolished and saw them stacked outside. "You'll have to buy all forty" they said. So I did and had to find homes for the rest,' added Mason.

The most startling feature was the stair, which has a wild spaghetti balustrade of wire bent on the spot. It was by the Liverpool sculptor Paul Hilton, who received a start-up grant from the Prince's Trust.

Upstairs there's a broad landing and a large master bedroom. This is open to the roof with a gallery bridging across one half of the room. 'There's such a good view from the gable end window at the top that we had to put it in,' said Mason.

The walls are left as bare stone but curiously the house does not feel cold, only immaculately clean and fresh. The other bedrooms and bathroom all have very good colour schemes (paint from Farrow and Ball) and amusing wallpapers with matching blinds (papers from Lewis and Wood).

A lot of hard work was put in to making the garden. There are trios of mop head maples on the drive, while along the Garron a cluster of substantial trees has been planted, some 15 ft high. All have taken root. At the end there is a stone arched road bridge over the Garron which the men from the county council were repairing, endearingly referring to the bridge as 'He'.

The hoop railings enclosing the terrace around the house began as salvage with new ones made to match the old. The house is right above the river – there is no tow path on this side.

There's also a very neat new green oak garage, constructed like a barn but open at the front so you can see the roof timbers within and park the car under cover without having to bother with opening the doors.

EARDISLEY
Handsomely rebuilt after a savage fire

THE 6 AM CALL THAT WOKE Nigel and Jane Morris-Jones brought the news that their Queen Anne house in Herefordshire was on fire. By the time they had driven down from London, all that remained was the stone plinth, a chimney stack and fragments of outside walls. Roofs, ceilings, floors, even cast-iron baths, had completely vanished.

The officials who gathered wanted to demolish what little remained. But the Morris-Jones did not want a cleared site. They wanted their house back; looking and feeling much as it had before. They went first to the historian Dan Cruickshank and then to the specialist engineer Brian Morton. As a result, officials agreed that the fragmentary shell could remain if a 24-hour security watch was provided.

Before buying Eardisley the Morris-Jones had spent two years looking for the perfectly sited house. The main appeal of Eardisley was a 360-degree view looking out to the Malvern and Radnor Hills, the Black Mountains and the Wye Valley.

Though listed Grade II*, mainly due to a remarkable series of nine panelled rooms, the appearance of the house had not been improved by the addition of an attic storey at the end of the 18th century. At this time the whole exterior was rendered, probably to conceal the change in brickwork – before the fire, a small panel had been opened in the render of the main east wing, revealing pink brickwork with black headers creating the attractive chequer pattern found on so many Queen Anne buildings in the Home Counties.

The Queen Anne house was built by William Barnsley, a senior bencher of the Inner Temple, who had married an heiress, Jane, the daughter of a local landowner.

Enough bricks were salvaged to reface the whole house.

Following Barnsley's death in 1737 his will was disputed, a case so notorious that it is cited as the inspiration for Jarndyce v Jarndyce in Dickens's *Bleak House*. After years of litigation, the fraudulent lawyers were imprisoned and a memorial in the church to Elizabeth Barnsley and her husband has a triumphal ring: 'They were involved in tedious lawsuits for thirty five years to the great prejudice of their health and estates; at length they overcame and died conquerors.'

For architects the Morris-Jones turned to Donald Insall Asssociates, having heard them lecture on the restoration of Windsor Castle. The work was completed on time and the family moved back in August 2001, two and a half years after the fire.

While the massive 300-year-old timbers had been consumed by the fire, large numbers of bricks were salvaged. The soft lime mortar in which the bricks had been laid washed away easily and the bricks were patiently placed on palettes and counted. There was a worry that too many bricks would have been damaged when 'keyed' or scored to take the 1800 render. In the end, by turning some round and snapping others into halves, enough bricks were found not only to face the whole house, but to do the east front in the original chequer pattern.

For the roof, a large number of second-hand Cornish slates were acquired, giving the house a mellow feel, complemented by the painted woodwork of the windows, which in early 18th-century fashion were set flush with the walls, not recessed as they were later in the century. The one carefully hidden innovation is the incorporation of an ogee-shaped metal gutter as the top moulding of the new cornice.

NEWPORT HOUSE — Newport Almeley
Transformed back into a house after years of institutional use

NOT MANY PEOPLE WOULD consider restoring a country house with more than a hundred rooms as a single residence, but this was the task completed in 2004 by Richard Goode at Newport House in Herefordshire. Goode is a serial country-house restorer and has now moved on because the job is complete.

Newport House, 15 miles west of Hereford, could have suffered the fate of other houses that were demolished after the First World War, but the council bought the 4,000-acre estate and divided it into 50-acre farms for war veterans. They ran the house as a TB sanatorium until 1950. In 1953 it became a home for emigré Latvians.

Goode bought the house from two property developers who had been battling with the local council to convert the property into fourteen units, with further new houses in the grounds. Upon purchase, he discovered that they had chopped off the chimneys and dropped the bricks down the flues, which had then become wedged in and were causing damp. 'Though the house looked in fair condition, once we took the slates off the roof we found all the joists were rotten, and the whole house had to be rewired. There were only three bathrooms. Now we have made seven principal bedrooms, each with its own bathroom. The house is perfect for entertaining, with five large reception rooms all interlinked.'

To make the house more manageable, he has introduced four separate heating systems. 'With just one boiler it takes a long time for the heat to get anywhere. Now it operates on individual circuits for the separate areas in which we work, live, entertain and put our guests.'

Newport, sometimes Nieuport, has a long history. In the 14th century it was owned by the Lollard martyr Sir John Oldcastle, one of the models for Shakespeare's Falstaff. Early views show a long front with high gables, probably built in the 16th century by Devereux Pember. In 1717 Thomas Pember sold Newport to the first Lord Foley of Great Witley across the border in Worcestershire, who transferred Newport to his cousin Paul Foley. He rebuilt the house on an ambitious scale with grand Baroque terraces, traces of which remain.

In the mid 19th-century, the house was let briefly to Sir Benjamin Hall, Commissioner of Public Works, after whom Big Ben is named. Then in 1863 it was bought by James Watt Gibbs Watt, grandson and heir of James Watt, inventor of the modern steam engine. He introduced Victorian plate-glass windows and a new entrance in the form of a rustic loggia, flanked by colonnades. His many guests proceeded from entrance hall to main hall and a top-lit staircase hall with polished marble columns.

By contrast, the long garden front has retained its Georgian character. Seen across the extensive lawns, it has a distinctive doll's-house charm thanks to pale pink brick and almost naive Classical detail.

The two-storey Georgian clock house has been amusingly converted into a private pub, the Running Spaniel, with a self-contained flat above. The large stable block, also in a very pretty pink brick, is laid out round a quadrangle with overhanging awnings and entered under an archway; it contains a stable cottage with four bedrooms, two flats and garaging for eleven cars.

Cary Goode, who is a garden designer, worked extensively on the grounds, uncovering layer upon layer of history. Elements remain of the Victorian layout by W.A. Nesfield, who designed the Broad Walk in Regent's Park. The lawns stretch down to a sizeable lake with a stream running out through a wood at the far end.

The long garden front has retained its character, while the clock house was transformed into a private pub.

POSTON HOUSE — Vowchurch

Shooting lodge by Sir William Chambers rescued from oblivion

REMEMBER SHABBY GRAND, THE FASHIONABLE country-house style of the 1980s? Poston House is the opposite – immaculate baby grand, the suavest conceivable expression of the new taste for grandeur in miniature that is now in fashion among the seriously smart and wealthy.

It has all the attributes of a substantial country house but on a dimunitive scale – long drive, rare sheep in the park, colour-coded flower borders, Classical portico, domed rotunda and well proportioned Palladian rooms. Yet it's all contrived so you can relax in luxury without living-in staff. There are just three bedrooms in the house and a further three in a self-contained guest house across the lawn. It's a case of family 'by invitation only'.

Ten years ago Poston was on the way to oblivion. The rotunda was without a roof and the house was known only to a few country-house enthusiasts, who were drawn here knowing it was a shooting box designed in the 1780s by Sir William Chambers, architect of the pagoda at Kew.

The end pavilions were added by Philip Jebb to replace ill-fitting Victorian wings.

Its gentle rescue was placed in the hands of the late Philip Jebb, a brilliant but diffident architect with an unerring eye, superb taste and command of perfect Classical detail. Jebb rescued and sympathetically transformed many delightful temples and follies for the Landmark Trust.

The charm of Chambers's shooting box had been obscured by two ill fitting Victorian wings. They have been replaced by shallow pedimented end pavilions with bows and half domes.

Poston House claims to have 'some of the finest views in England' and, for once, this is no exaggeration. The south front commands a glorious 180-degree panorama over Golden Valley to the Black Mountains of South Wales, while to the north the grounds look across the Wye Valley. In the course of an hour I heard not a single intrusive sound, not the faintest murmur of road traffic, not the drone of a jet or the buzz of a light aircraft, a peace that has all but vanished from most of southern England today.

The house stands on an ancient hill fort, seeing but not seen. There was originally a fortified house here in 1227 and the medieval parkland has now been restored to its original boundaries. In 1635 the property was acquired by the Earl of Worcester, descending to Sir Edward Boughton, who commissioned Chambers to rebuild the house. Fine trees around the lawn date from around this time, including a prize Cedar of Lebanon.

For once Jebb was prevailed upon to design an indoor pool, something he actually considered inherently vulgar. At Poston, he placed it in a Classical pavilion that is like an 18th-century orangery with arched windows, which allow you to see the snow lying on the mountains when you swim in winter. Next door is another small pavilion in its own walled garden, as smartly fitted up as the main house, where you can curl up and read a book or log onto cyberspace.

The largest room in the house is the well fitted, spacious kitchen. On the other side of the hall is the choice of a cosy small library, with a single sofa opposite the fire, or a large drawing room, where Jebb placed one of his prize inventions – a sash window that also serves as a garden door. Jebb perfected this device by including the sash box as well as the lower sash, thereby providing the extra strength and solidity that a sash alone can never have.

Downstairs the stone-floored Georgian kitchen survives, as well as a cellar complete with traditional wine bins. The stone cantilever stair, painted a ravishing yellow, is one of the most compact I have ever seen, although a fraction too small to show off its own elegance, but leading to an ingenious octagonal landing that is shaped to resemble a birdcage.

The lodge has its own hall, cloakroom and comfortable sitting room, and a kitchen with its own Aga that doubles up as a breakfast room. Jebb died as the work was in progress and the garden cottage was entrusted to the surveyor William Bertram (who is probably best known for the pavilion that he designed at Highgrove for the Prince of Wales). The builders were Treasures of Ludlow, renowned for their careful treatment of old buildings, and at Poston it is clear to see that they have maintained their well-deserved reputation.

HERTFORDSHIRE

AYOT MOUNTFITCHET   Ayot St Peter
Much extended late-medieval hall house that retains its picturesque charm

ENGLISH COUNTRY HOUSES HAVE an infinite capacity to spring surprises. At Ayot Mountfitchet it is as if the owners wanted a Frank Lloyd Wright house in the prairie style, with one space flowing into another and wings thrusting out in different directions to take advantage of the views. Yet it is all done under the cloak of what seems to be a typical 16th-century Hertfordshire gabled and half-timbered house.

This is architectural *trompe l'oeil* in three dimensions, with so many layers that it is hard to see how its history can ever be fully deduced. A late-medieval hall house was ambitiously extended in the 15th and early 17th centuries only to become a tenanted farm, untouched until Edwardian times. Then a new owner, Lady Kesteven, gave it a new Tudor overcoat with a wealth of imported woodwork.

Finding a property that had been empty for two years, the owners employed the architect David Postins to provide a house that feels clean and light, with warm stone floors beneath the feet and the feeling that every cobweb has been brushed away. Panelling has been taken down temporarily, every last corner has been minutely inspected for decay.

Ayot Mountfitchet, until recently called Ayot Place, is just five minutes' drive from the A1 and a 40-minute sprint to Central London. Yet this is an enchanted country, a world of quiet rural lanes and village greens in which ugly development has not

The mellow patina of the house has emerged from painstaking restoration.

intruded. Today the drive sweeps round to the side of the noble avenue of trees leading to the entrance, past a pretty Tudor gazebo with a boat moored beneath an arch. The Dutch gabled entrance front is built of warm speckled brick with matching roof tiles, brick-mullioned windows and tall polygonal chimneys.

Despite the mellow quality, it is quickly apparent that much is the result of the painstaking work of the past ten years. Internally the house seems designed for a nomadic life with no single function for individual rooms, but giving guests the maximum freedom to circulate at receptions and parties. There are many doorways but seemingly far fewer doors. The main entrance opens into a modest hall with matching Classical archways on either side carved of blemishless white Portland stone.

Which way to go? Turn left and you are in a stone-flagged dining room with two more mighty Doric portals and an Italian Renaisssance marble fireplace that clearly did not begin life here. Turn right and you are in the staircase hall with a magnificent armorial, two-tier stone fireplace that must once have dominated a 17th-century great chamber but now faces a new stone stair a few feet away. Acquired after long years in storage, it is said to bear the arms of the Ducie family, owners of Charlton House in Greenwich.

From here steps lead to a gentlemen's cloakroom with thunderbox and Victorian blue and white washbowl cleverly plumbed in for modern use. Beyond is a traditional butler's pantry with lead sink and chef's desk looking out through a large mullioned window. The woodwork in the kitchens is of superb quality, done by a Leicestershire firm that was part of Balfour Beatty, with thick oak tops and plain sturdy drawers. More puzzling is the firewood stacked in the arch, which could betray the apparent reluctance of the current owner's chefs to use the Aga.

The showpieces are the reception hall and great hall beyond, both with an abundance of elaborately carved linenfold panelling, much of it dating from Lady Kesteven's time. Postins explains: 'It was heavily polished; we took it down and have tried to give it a thirsty look, stopping the polishers who longingly wanted to put a shine on it.' He has also added a triple archway to help screen the stair descending into the room.

The great hall beyond is open to the roof and timbers and retains the large Tudor stone fireplace. 'We dropped the hearth to avoid the pub feel,' Postins says. Above, a minstrels' gallery takes up almost half the room. Dated 1615, the once dark oak is now gaily painted in armorial colours with obelisks and openwork cresting rather than the usual solid balcony. Behind this is even more painted and gilded woodwork, which continues at the top of the staircase. Much of it is original, though rearranged, Postins says.

Upstairs the master bedroom suite is impressively large. The bathroom has a superb fan-pattern mosaic floor, inspired by the Art Deco bathrooms in maharajahs' palaces. Beyond, Postins has designed a dressing room inspired by the Austrian Biedermeier style. It is surrounded by cupboards on all four sides, like a 17th-century cabinet of curiosities, but here executed in Russian Karelian pine with ebonised columns. Drawers glide open on runners and cubbyhole shelves are designed for no more than two folded shirts.

The two other main bathrooms are even better than the accompanying bedrooms. One is Art Deco with yellow Siena marble trim and large sarcophagus bath. The other is long and narrow and open to the roof timbers. A pretty French neoclassical bath stands on a raised dais at one end. The washbasin is set in a beautiful length of solid oak with the wooden-seated thunderbox built in. To carry off pastiche requires great flair. One reason it works here is that the house is decorated in minimalist fashion with sparse but very elegant furniture.

The superb joinery continues in the second-floor children's realm. The vertical panel latch doors, with sturdy Z-pattern cross-bracing at the back, are all in oak. Ceilings and dormers rise into the eaves while other windows are set at floor level to maintain the external look of the house but presumably give small children a rare view of the world below. Good use has been made of old fittings, for example a large Edwardian bath with brass spout taps and plunge plug.

The gardens are formed into a series of green rooms. A fountain pool is enclosed by pleached limes while the swimming pool, with twin octagonal pavilions, is secluded behind walls of yew. The 1890s stable and garage court has a delightful Arts and Crafts dovecote standing in the centre with skirted walls – like a mini lighthouse. At Ayot Mountfitchet, such theatrical touches are never far away.

BRIDE HALL   Ayot St Lawrence
Tudor manor used for secret war work

DURING THE SECOND WORLD WAR, BRIDE HALL was Station VI of Churchill's Special Operations Executive, charged with building up resistance networks in enemy-occupied countries. Small arms, such as pistols and revolvers, were essential to this clandestine work and in July 1941 SOE's arms section moved to Bride Hall, where it was housed in the series of large timber barns that stand in front of the house. The barns walls were painted with black pitch, which continues to give them a distinctive appearance, and were lined internally with tarred brown paper to keep out draughts.

One barn became an armoury for repairing and servicing weapons, another was used for storing ammunition, bombs and machine guns, and yet a third became sleeping quarters for the non-officers, heated only by wood-burning stoves. The officers themselves dined and slept in the main house, while the other ranks came to eat in the servants' hall. A national pistol drive, aimed at encouraging owners of small arms to surrender them for the war effort, netted 7,000 hand guns in 1942 and 3,000 the next year. In all over 100,000 pistols and revolvers of varying types were sent to the field from Bride Hall.

Bride Hall is a handsome Elizabethan house that probably dates from the late 16th century, and has the special harmony that comes from being built entirely of one material, in this case a dark brownish-red brick, and from being without the stone trim that is often used in grand houses for windows and doorways. Here the original brick mullions survive, together with other brick details such as dog-tooth eaves and 'tumbled' brick gables. The west wing has a good example of a collar rafter

The brick walls and window mullions are perfect colour matches for the handmade clay tiles on the roof.

roof and in the staircase towers are late 17th-century newel stairs with simple turned balusters.

Bride's history can be traced back to the 12th century when Thurfleda, a pious matron, gave 'Bridela' to St Albans Abbey. 'Bridelle' was confirmed as belonging to the monastery by Kings Henry II and John. 'Brydylhide' afterwards came into the possession of William Veysey, from whom it passed at the end of the 15th or early in the 16th century to John Lawdy. From him it seems to have passed to Brian Roche and Elizabeth, his wife, and from them to the Botelers.

The house itself was probably built for Sir Philip Boteler. His ancestor, also Sir Philip, had been one of the Knights of the Body to King Henry VIII in 1516 and Sheriff of Hertfordshire four times – in 1524–6, 1530, 1532 and 1538–40. In 1530 Sir Philip was one of the commissioners for Hertfordshire charged with inquiring into the possessions of Cardinal Wolsey and in 1537 he was present at the christening of Prince Edward, afterwards Edward VI, and in 1539–40 was among the knights who were appointed to meet Anne of Cleves upon her arrival in England. In 1544 his name was listed as supplying men for the rearguard in the army against France, and later in the same year he was appointed to levy yet more recruits. He died in 1545.

Bride Hall is unusual in having its large array of barns laid out in front of the house. While it was common in the middle ages to have an outer court of farm buildings, from the 16th century onwards farms were usually separate from the house. Here, as in France, they are laid out in such a way that they make the house look grander; indeed, the barns are considerably larger than the manor. There are two long weatherboarded barns dating from the 17th century as well as a stables-cum-granary, with red-brick ground floor and weatherboarding above, which retains 18th-century stable bays within.

MACKERYE END — Wheathampstead
Dutch-gabled house which has kept its charm thanks to sensitive owners

MACKERYE END IS AS COVETABLE a modest manor house as can be found in all the Home Counties. It lies hidden amid narrow country lanes, little more than 30 miles north of Hyde Park Corner in the rolling arable country that gives its name to nearby Wheathampstead. As you stand outside the front door, the only building in sight is the spire of the parish church two miles away.

This is all the more miraculous as the M1 and the A1 are barely five miles away (though happily out of earshot), and Harpenden and St Albans are spreading outwards. Mackerye End nonetheless looks safe in its wedge of green, with the great estates of Luton Hoo, Brocket, Hatfield and Gorhambury standing guard nearby.

Charles Lamb, the famous essayist, loved this house, which he visited often to see his relations, even beginning a poem 'Hail, Mackeray End …' Under the ownership of the architect David Laing, the house reached a peak of perfection. In his hands and those of his wife, who is a keen horsewoman, the house became the ideal home for a large family, with numerous well-tended outbuildings containing stables, a well-equipped party room in a weatherboarded barn with kitchen and gallery, and an office to work from. Inside the house they have gone with the grain, inserting modern lighting and heating, but barely moving a wall, so the house remains a fascinating maze of cosy rooms full of character.

The danger is that someone would want to turn Mackerye End inside-out to fit their ideal of what a house should be, with en suite bathrooms (there is only one at present), indoor swimming pool, swank conservatory, gym and spa, and Bill Gates-style plasma screens in every room. Hopefully they will be put off by the severe evidence of subsidence over some of the ground-floor windows (sshh, it happened long ago).

I say this with passion because the Cory-Wrights, who had the house before the present owners, were great gardeners and over the length of the 20th century Mackerye End has achieved a faultless formal frame for its architecture. The short straight drive is flanked by walls and towers of yew, presumably Edwardian, which conceal a swimming pool and Classical temple behind. The walled garden has venerable espaliered pears and at the back is a sheltered paved garden to eat out during summer, shaded by a magnificent Ginkgo tree whose roots, it has to be said, are causing problems with the paving.

The oldest part of the house is a timber-framed wing, probably 16th-century, with infill panels of neat red brick rather than wattle and daub.

The Dutch gabled front that is the glory of Mackerye End today bears a date of 1665, and it belongs to a remarkable group of impressive brick country houses nearby. Several are of Cromwellian date in the style christened 'Artisan Mannerism', a homely successor to the dizzy excesses of Jacobean. The treatment of the windows here is very similar to Tyttenhanger of 1654, just to the south.

Here the bottoms of the windows were lowered for Georgian sashes while others were bricked up, not necessarily to avoid window tax but possibly because so many windows made corner rooms too cold. Over the door is the 18th-century fire insurance certificate of the Westminster insurance company, with the Prince of Wales feathers and the number 24520.

During the mid 17th century the house changed hands a confusing number of times and the likely builder is Thomas Hunsden, who was described as 'of Mackerye End' in 1665. Inside the front door, the narrow hall may mark the original position of a screen passage of a Tudor great hall. On the right is the drawing room which has a pretty rococo ceiling of mid 18th-century date, a fraction gummed up by too many coats of paint but done with a light touch. The dining room on the other side of the hall was reworked in the 19th century and now has an intricate repeating geometric ceiling. Beyond the dining room is a panelled library where traces of the original wooden fenestration, or more likely shutters, can be seen in front of a bricked-up window.

The 17th-century staircase, with magnificently beefy newel posts, is set curiously at the end of the house and may have been moved as the tall arched window is clearly mid 18th-century. Upstairs the bedrooms all have lovely views, the main ones facing east down the drive. Empty stone fireplaces have pretty colourful firebacks painted by Dione Verulam.

The low but spacious attic forms a chain of children's rooms. 'We made sure their sitting room wasn't above our bedroom,' said Mr Laing. Originally, as in many early 'single pile' (one room deep) houses, communication was from one room to another, but in the 19th century a corridor was added along the back on both floors, making the house work much better.

The Laings added many amusing flourishes – gates with animals supplied by Proper Gates and an armchair of clipped yew growing neatly in a frame on the front lawn. They also acquired nearly 100 acres in front of the house, protecting the view which is newly planted with a double avenue of chestnut and maple.

Chimney stacks and dormer windows are marshalled in perfect symmetry.

PIMLICO HOUSE — Hemel Hempstead
Early 20th-century house that became home to a powerboat racing countess

PIMLICO HOUSE IN HERTFORDSHIRE IS ALMOST the first country house you get to when you leave London, hidden amid narrow lanes in the gently rolling country just north of the M25.

For nearly half a century it was the home of Boofy, the amiable 8th Earl of Arran, who has a niche in history for introducing and piloting two highly controversial bills through Parliament. The first was the landmark Sexual Offences Bill, passed at the third attempt, legalising homosexuality. The second outlawed badger hunting.

Arran also wrote a pugnacious weekly column for the *Evening News* for nearly twenty years. A close friend of the 2nd Lord Rothermere, he was a director of the *Daily Mail* and General Trust.

He bought Pimlico House in 1937, the same year that he married Fiona, the daughter of Sir Iain Colquhoun, Bt. Though they led a hectic social life in London, they never had a town house. 'It was an easy 45-minute drive at night,' his son, the present Earl, told me.

The splayed window heads have the gentlest of arches.

The Countess of Arran also has a place in history as a powerboat racer. 'At one time she was the fastest person – not just woman – in the world in her class,' continues her son. Growing up beside Loch Lomond she had a unique understanding of water and waves and set a world speed record on Windermere. Her boats were built by her nephew Iain Colquhoun, a lighthouse keeper off Vancouver Island, and with them she repeatedly beat French and Italian racers in far fancier boats. According to her son, 'she only gave up powerboat racing after a last race from Cowes to Torquay when she came 8th out of 40 in a rubber boat after breaking two ribs. My father used to hover over her in a helicopter annoying her,' he says.

Pimlico House stands about 80 yards from the passing country lane and is approached down a broad avenue of limes, now in first maturity. The house was clearly modelled on the nearby Manor House at Chipperfield, an early 18th-century house with Edwardian wings.

It's a moot point if Pimlico House was built before or after the First World War. In some ways it is more Edwardian neo-baroque than polite 1920s Georgian. There is a chunky hooded front door and projecting 'quoins' at the corners, as well as gently arching heads to the windows.

Neither the architect nor his client have yet been traced, but in 1912 Abbot's Hill, the large neighbouring Victorian house built for the Dickensons of Basildon Bond fame, was leased as a school, just possibly prompting the building of a more modern country house for the family nearby.

A broad entrance hall leads to the domestic equivalent of the crossing in a church, neatly emphasised by a circular ceiling garland. Bold topiary arches just visible through the garden door tempt you to continue out onto the terrace. To the left, the eye is caught by a white painted 1700-style wooden staircase with turned balusters, lit by a Venetian window (the kind with the arch in the centre). At the end is a large drawing room with windows on three sides so it gets the evening as well as the morning and afternoon sun. Here Jacksons the plasterers, or one of their rivals, produced a whole array of Adamesque ornament – fan motifs in the ceiling and swags over the French windows (repeated on the outside).

All the main rooms on both ground and first floors face south and have two sash windows providing ample light even on a dull day. The doors have chunky baroque bolection mouldings and picture rails as well as neat little fireplaces, which are still Arts and Crafts in character.

The elegant dining room is to the right of the front door and beyond is cook's domain, where the two panel doors continue without the mouldings. Unusually the kitchen windows look out on the garden, though with higher sills than the rest of the house, suggesting the dawning of a post-Edwardian age in which slightly more concern was given to conditions for staff. The pantry retains its original cupboards. Beyond is a garage where the Earl kept the Lagondas and Bentleys that gave the Countess her taste for speed.

The garden at the back of the house sweeps down to an open valley. Pimlico House takes its name from the nearby hamlet of Pimlico, but the postal address is King's Langley, as smart as you could wish in these parts.

KENT

OLD MANOR HOUSE   Benenden
An intact Wealden house disguised by later additions

AT FIRST GLANCE, THE OLD MANOR HOUSE in Benenden looks like dozens of pretty Kentish village houses, picturesquely hung with warm russet-coloured tiles. Yet concealed behind these tiles is as well-preserved an example of a medieval 'Wealden' house as can be found.

Wealden houses are the glory of medieval Kent, satisfyingly symmetrical with a central great hall open to the roof timbers and a jettied (overhanging) first floor at either end, with a 'high' end for the family and a low end for kitchen activities, all concealed beneath a single steep roof.

Better still, the Old Manor House is a 'double Wealden' with the hall set back behind the eaves on both sides. All this becomes apparent within, where the timbers are still largely exposed to view, including the twin arch doorways that led from the great hall to kitchen and pantry. English Heritage, in their excellent volumes on Kentish houses, make it clear that this was grander than a yeoman's house, rather the house of a gent and landowner, probably the Benenden family or Sir William Brenchley who married the last of the Benendens and died in 1446. They date it with impressive precision to *c*.1390.

The house stands in the heart of Benenden village, not far from the large green with the parish church at the end. There are two good pubs, a school, a post office and a

The new entrance court was created after 1945.

family butcher, just what every village needs. The house is still surrounded by a moat on two sides and in 1923 was part of the 2,000 acre Hemsted estate put up for sale by Lord Rothermere.

The main house in the centre of the park is now the well-known Benenden School. Old Manor House appears to have been sold to a Mr Crossley, and later the Inghams, being acquired by an Italian lady, the Duchess of Laurino, in the war and then sold in 1945 to Sir George Wigham-Richardson, Bt, whose family ship-building business had merged with Swan Hunter.

The puzzle of the house is how to date the various extensions, which now form a very substantial house of 10,000 sq ft. Many houses in Kent, Surrey and Sussex were cleverly or not so cleverly altered in the early 20th century, sometimes using parts of other houses or elements that were aged to make them indistinguishable from the old.

One theory has it that the wing added to the original Wealden house to form an L-shape is no more than about a hundred years old. Yet it is there on the 1923 estate plan and Sir George's daughters Caroline Richardson and Jennifer Drayson are

Top: The minstrel's gallery was inserted in the 1930s.

Above: Twin arches open into the hall.

emphatic that it was there at least a hundred years before that, as Mr Crossley had converted the house back into one from a series of cottages.

At about the same time, formal gardens had been laid out with a paved path leading from a lychgate on the village street to the 1390 hall. After 1945, Sir George created a new entrance at the back with a carriage circle and a porch he acquired from Cranbrook Church when it was being restored.

This porch leads to a delightful stair of 1600 date, but possibly imported later, with short flights ascending on four sides of a central pillar with cupboards inset in a different face at each level. The 1390 house is such a text-book example that English Heritage used it to make drawings of the way these houses were first constructed and then remodelled.

Originally Wealden houses had open hearths from which smoke curled upwards, blackening the roof timbers. In the 16th century the desire for greater comfort and privacy led to the introduction of fireplaces and chimney stacks. Here, unusually, there are two, again putting the house at the top end of the scale. The first rises in the centre of the great hall with a hearth large enough to park a car. At the same time a ceiling was put in to make the hall cosier. The chimney breast, its red brick never plastered, rises through the room above (where a ceiling was put in a little later). Intriguingly the base of the king post is visible in this room, while the shaft and cap are in the attic. The second chimney stack, even more unusually, is of stone – the column-like external chimney shaft was taken down by Sir George.

The new first-floor room had to have doors connecting it to the rooms on either side and here (as often) this was done in cavalier fashion by cutting into the arched timber braces of the hall roof to get the necessary head height. Medieval wooden staircases have almost always disappeared or been enlarged. Here it is clear that the stair at the high end was in what is called an 'outshot' as the first-floor door arch is visible in the timber framing at the back of the house.

All through the 1390 house, moulded beams and door arches suggest what historians call 'high status'. The other remarkable survival is a very extensive series

of leaded windows. In many places such windows are Edwardian replacements of sashes, sometimes with decided Arts and Crafts flourishes such as the handles, others cleverly made to look old. Here, however, ancient subsidence and old mends suggest that some have considerable age, and that the misted old glass was not chosen simply for its prettiness.

Another surprise is a north wing (shown on the 1923 plan) which is open to the roof timbers, with a 'minstrels' gallery' added, it is said, in the 1930s.

Like many timber-framed houses in Kent, the Old Manor House was faced with vertically hung clay tiles in the late 18th or 19th century. These gave houses a more fashionable appearance, matching the tone of new Georgian brick buildings. They also provided much improved weatherproofing from both rain and driving wind. Tiles were made with two holes for square wooden pegs and set in a light mortar which improves insulation and prevents rattling.

The central hall and the jettied ends of the original Wealden house are enclosed by the sweeping roof.

BRIDGE PLACE   Bridge
Early 17th-century house kept alive by a spell as a nightclub

BRIDGE PLACE NEEDS TO RELIVE its age of glory. This came in 1660 as Charles II
knighted the owner Sir Arnold Braemes in Canterbury on his triumphant way to
London to reclaim his throne. Braemes, descended from a Flemish merchant who
had settled in Sandwich, was an ardent Royalist who funded the King in the Civil War,
joined Prince Rupert's fleet in 1648 with his own 30-gun ship, and as a Royalist agent
secured support for Charles II's return.

The next year Braemes was visited by the Dutch artist Willem Schellinks who
sketched his grand house and wrote that 'he keeps a princely table' and had 'an
extraordinary number of visits from knights and high-born gentlemen and their
ladies'. Braemes died in 1681 and shortly before or after his death another Dutch artist,
Jan Siberechts, painted a magnificent canvas of the house nearly 5 ft in width. This
shows a grand entrance front in warm red brick with steep roof and dormers.
Braemes had bought the estate in 1638 and the house he built then belongs to the
remarkable group of early Classical houses in Kent all in brick, which begins with
Chevening, now the country home of the Foreign Secretary.

Alas, Braemes overstretched himself and in 1704 his house was bought by a
neighbour, John Taylor of Bifrons, who demolished more than half of it. The
handsome wing that now remains is at once a challenge and a thrill.

It cries out for a new chatelaine with a passion for formal gardening who will
recreate the 'very fine and skilfully made pleasure gardens', orchards and vineyards
described by Schellinks, complete with 'dovecote like a chapel' and ever-running fresh
crystalline stream. He even left a sketch of the garden with wispy cypresses, scallop-
topped hedges and domed pergola that pre-dates those at Hampton Court Palace by
thirty years.

The brickwork, though weathered by time, is gloriously detailed with cut and
moulded brick for window heads, cornice and a double row of pilasters. Yet there are
puzzles too. The pilasters on the present entrance front are longer than those around
the corner where Georgian sashes have been inserted and the windows 'dropped' at
the same time.

Yet these are nothing to the puzzles that abound inside. For nearly forty years
Bridge Place has belonged to Peter Malkin, a compulsive rescuer of endangered
domains who bought the shell of Boringdon Hall outside Plymouth and restored it
as an hotel as well as long abandoned Jacobean Clegg Hall in Lancaster which he
handed on to the Pennine Heritage Trust. At Bridge Place he opened a night club and
today the interiors are filled with swords and gilt mirrors. But still earlier, probably
before or after the First World War, another owner with a craze for woodwork
evidently introduced quantities of antique panelling, including late 17th-century
panelling of high quality that is only given away by the occasional awkward fit.

I visited with Richard Garnier, Kent's No 1 house detective, who quickly spotted
that two of the fireplace surrounds were made of engraved Bethersden marble
comparable to that used about 1605 in the Ballroom at Knole, the greatest house in

The architectural trim is executed in moulded and cut brickwork.

Kent. These and other details, such as Tudor chamfers to wooden doorways, suggest there might be a still earlier house encased in Bridge Place.

The finest feature of the interior is a grand elm staircase with balustrades splendid enough to be altar rails for Archbishop Laud himself, complete with hanging ball drops at the corners. The flights are not short as in many Jacobean houses, but long like contemporary aristocratic houses in the Place des Vosges in Paris. Yet this stair has evidently been moved and reassembled as there are mortice holes in the corner posts made for handrails which once ascended and now descend. Presumably this was done after Taylor demolished half of Braemes's U-shaped house, leaving the present L.

Upstairs is what looks like a 1740s baroque ceiling by itinerant Italian plasterers complete with floating *putti*. Yet around it are Adam motifs that only came into use thirty years later. Another work, it seems, of early 20th-century antiquarianism.

Another clue lies in the carved stone entrance doorway, again early 20th-century in date. Gothic in style, this is carved with a portcullis suggesting an MP as owner and is now embellished with the name of Mr Malkin's son Oliver.

DANSON HOUSE   Bexleyheath
Left to rot by the Council, which has since supported an heroic restoration

AFTER FOUR DECADES OF BITTER STRUGGLE, one of the most elegant Palladian villas has been brought back spectacularly to life by English Heritage and a new trust formed by the London Borough of Bexley. This is ironic, as it was Bexley that originally neglected Danson House and sought to demolish it. Little more than a decade ago, three hundred pigeons were nesting in the house and there was a hole in the outside wall large enough to fly a Cessna through.

Danson was built in the early 1760s by the architect Sir Robert Taylor for the merchant Sir John Boyd, whose family had made a fortune from sugar plantations on St Kitts. Restoration has provided a set of interiors that can be enjoyed as originally intended. The three main rooms are licensed for civil weddings – the dining room, saloon and library. 'Danson will be open to the public on Wednesdays, Thursdays and Sundays, available for weddings and parties on Fridays and Saturdays and for business meetings on Mondays and Tuesdays,' I was told by Martin Purslow.

One key to the restoration was the discovery of an attractive series of watercolours of interiors by Sarah Jane Johnson, belonging to one of Boyd's descendants. These show furniture and a remarkable set of 1766 wall paintings set into the dining room panelling by the Aix artist Charles Pavillon, a delightful play on Boyd's imminent remarriage to a girl half his age. Bexley Museum had fortunately taken these into store before the house was left empty and began its savage decline.

Crisp new stucco shows off the elegant canted bays.

Though no original contents survived, the house has been given a furnished look by judicious loans and purchases, with an eye to what was available and practical rather than strictly correct in terms of date. A richly gilt set of Empire chairs and settees belonging to Napoleon's uncle Cardinal Fesche has been borrowed from Brighton Museum (at one time they were in Brighton Pavilion).

Pairs of elegant gilt neoclassical pier glasses in the dining room and saloon have been hand-carved in pine by specialist restorers Plowden & Smith following those shown in the watercolours and carefully matching the detail of surviving fragments. In the Library the delightful 1766 chamber organ supplied by the England family has been restored. The books now filling the shelves are a clever mix of false leather spines supplied by the Manor Bindery in Southampton, which did the faux books for the Frost Breakfast Show, and deft purchases of learned journals from Sweden where the tradition of leather binding carried on into the 20th century.

Two of the main beauties of the house are the solid mahogany doors (two strong men are needed to lift each one) and the marble fireplaces. Most of these were taken out for 'safekeeping' by a developer who had bought the house to restore it in the 1990s and were only discovered in the London docks thanks to a diligent Bexley official who set the police on the trail.

Scholarly research by English Heritage has helped to recreate the splendour of the interiors, which are colourful and lavishly ornate.

Helen Hughes of English Heritage has carried out sophisticated paint research, producing a Naples yellow in the hall and stair, a verdigris in the library and revealing the original painted *trompe l'oeil* panels in the dome over the stair.

The nearby stables had also fallen into a shocking state but have now been taken over and agreeably furnished as a pub, now run by Bass Taverns Ltd, opening the whole interior to the public. Twenty years ago the idea of allowing such commercial use of a building in a public park would have been viewed as sacrilege. Now it is evident that it will encourage many more people to enjoy both house and park.

FROGNAL HOUSE   Sidcup
1700 house once again filled with residents

HOUSES BUILT IN THE WARM RED BRICK of the age of Wren are always a delight to look at. Frognal stands surveying spreading lawns, a long front of eleven windows with the taller sashes unusually on the first floor. These have the gentle arched heads typical of a date around 1700 with chunky glazing bars and nine panes to each sash.

When I first saw it in 1980, Frognal reminded me of one of the Osbert Lancaster drawings that I had commissioned for the V&A exhibition 'The Destruction of the Country House'. These portrayed the likely fate of six of the great houses of English literature if they had had to endure the depradations of the 20th century. Lancaster portrayed Chesney Wold with the trees of the avenue cut down and a motorway whizzing past with a large lorry announcing 'Société Anonyme des Camions Énormes'. This indeed was Frognal's fate with the M20 rushing past towards the Channel ports.

Frognal was acquired in a very derelict state from the Department of Health by a developer. Lead had been stripped from the roof and all the fine plaster ceilings had collapsed under the weight of rainwater. In 1980 office use was widely thought to be the most lucrative form of country house conversion but Frognal had failed to find a tenant and five years later still stood empty. Salvation came with conversion to a nursing home offering a range of accommodation with independent apartments in the main house, assisted places in neighbouring buildings and special facilities for dementia.

Frognal once again demonstrates that the best solution for large historic houses is usually to have people living in them who will take pleasure from the architecture and enjoy the gardens.

Prior to restoration, the house stood boarded up and empty.

HOLLIDAY HALL   Bredgar
Swagger baroque house built for a London goldsmith

HOLLIDAY HALL, AS IT WAS NAMED a few years ago, is an enchanting example of England's most delightful home-grown style – country baroque. A signature of these charmingly eccentric houses is a swept-up cornice or boldly shaped gable, here with distinct alternating curves.

The keystone over the front door proclaims the house was completed in 1719 for Edward Holliday or Holaday, a noted goldsmith who in London lived near Handel in Brook Street. He bought the property, then 300 acres, in 1715, but sadly lived no more than a few months in his creation. Very soon after it became a tenanted farmhouse and this explains its remarkable state of preservation, complete with chunky early-Georgian glazing bars.

Swanton Farmhouse, as it used to be called, was distinct enough to earn an illustration in Kerry Downes's pioneering *English Baroque Architecture* but in the 1960s had to be rescued from demolition. Since then it has benefited from a series of owners who loved the place and carefully nursed it back to life.

When I visited in January 2007 it had been brought to a pitch of perfection by Paolo Guidi and Katherina Harlow, veteran house restorers. Appropriately Guidi is a jeweller and furniture maker and a highlight of the tour was an astonishing trio of cabinets, the Alchemist's Study, which deserve to go to the V&A as an example of modern craftsmanship.

The rich detailing is executed in extra fine 'rubbed' brick set in narrow putty joints.

One of the glories of English Baroque is the brickwork. Here, the plum-coloured brick of the walls is offset by red brick dressings to the windows and extra fine 'rubbed' brick window heads with putty joints. The keystones are capped by little ledges and there are cabinets for displaying blue and white Delft. Guidi imagined adding statues of the Four Seasons along the parapet, celebrating Holliday's friendship with Handel.

The whole building has the sense of a doll's house and if the facade folded back you would find pretty panelled rooms each furnished with a few choice pieces. The hall has a key-pattern frieze which is discontinued over the doors. To the left is a 24-ft-long drawing room running from front to back with characteristic window seats. Guidi found the early 18th century-panelling beneath dry walling. Behind the flush baroque fireplace is a larger hearth, suggesting that Holliday may have been incorporating parts of an earlier house. The dining room has a corner fireplace. Beyond, in the later coach house, the outside chimney stack has been retained with the fine red brick and burnt headers exposed to view as you ascend the stairs.

Top: An ingenious giant brick arch doubles the size of the kitchen.

Above: All the main rooms have built-in window seats and open fires still burn in the grates.

The kitchen at the back has been ingeniously extended to incorporate the farm lean-to by supporting the back wall of the house on a giant arch with the original bread oven sandwiched against it. The first-floor bedrooms are panelled with more pretty fireplaces. All this panelling has been painted in very pretty pastel colours, and the radiator covers alternate between Chinese Chippendale and Strawberry Hill Gothick. Every landing, half landing or alcove is a set piece with built-in bookshelves and a desk in front of the window, while a windowless attic is transformed by a French *lit-bateau*, or boat bed, framed by striped curtains. The house has a dry cellar with brick tiles on the floor and distinctive niches, presumably for candles in the walls. The basement windows at the level of the front doorstep retain the original leaded glazing.

Guidi believes there was formerly a screen of railings along the low wall fronting the road. He found a capping stone and a horizontal rail, and points out that the decorative panel in the garden gate (now upside down) was probably part of a grander wrought-iron gate set between piers.

INGRESS ABBEY   Greenhithe
Thames-side gothic villa left to collapse by the Greater London Council

INGRESS ABBEY IS A DELIGHTFUL EXAMPLE of Elizabethan revival, built at the very moment when Tudor was specified as the style for the new Houses of Parliament.

Edward III had granted the Manor to the Abbey of Dartford in 1363. In 1796 the estate was bought by William Havelock, a shipbuilder of Sutherland, and the father of General Sir Henry Havelock of Indian Mutiny fame. William Havelock drew up plans with the engineer John Rennie for converting Ingress into a Royal dockyard, but in the event Chatham and Sheerness were refurbished instead. Soon after, the estate was acquired by James Harmer, a leading City alderman and champion of Civil Law Reform, who had made his name defending those on trial after the Peterloo Massacre.

The new house he built at Ingress bears the date 1833. His architect was the otherwise unknown Charles Moreing, and the stone used was reportedly taken from Old London Bridge. On his death in 1853 Harmer left Ingress to his niece Emma, who had married Samuel Charles Umfreyville. Ten years later Greenhithe was en fête as the Queen arrived in the Royal Yacht *Victoria & Albert* and moored off Ingress Abbey.

This moment of glory was fleeting as Umfreyville's death in 1898 signalled the start of a long saga of decline. The house was sold in 1909 to cement manufacturers who denuded the grounds of their magnificent timber. Next it became a nautical college, which was taken over by the Greater London Council, who built large new premises alongside, leaving Harmer's house boarded up and a prey to vandals.

Salvation came at a price. The house and grounds were bought by Crest Nicolson, who received permission to build many houses on the site. The mansion, however was painstakingly restored by the P.J. Livesey Group, which rescued and transformed Wyfold Court. Ingress today is the classic lesson of the Prescott era during which ever-larger enabling permissions were granted to build in the grounds of country houses. The lawn down to the Thames has been preserved in front of the house but on either side a vast housing estate has sprung up, a harvest as alarming and sudden as that of the dragon's teeth in the Argonaut legend.

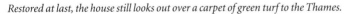

Restored at last, the house still looks out over a carpet of green turf to the Thames.

MAYNARDS   Tenterden

Decaying medieval yeoman's house spotted in a SAVE catalogue of buildings at risk

MONEY COULD NEVER BUY the love and care put into the repair of this enchanting Kentish yeoman's house. Over eight years, New Zealand architect Quentin Roake and his family have lived here, moving from one wing to another, gently nursing a 15th- and 16th-century house to an immaculate state of preservation.

The captivating charm of Maynards lies in its softness, the silvery oak, the light white walls and the warm red handmade tiles, with the patina that comes from decades of weathering. David Martin, the archaeologist who examined the house, says, 'It looks today very much as it did in 1590.' Maynards is one of a small cluster of handsome, venerable houses just outside the town of Tenterden. From the field behind the house is a magnificent panorama of the solitude of Romney Marshes.

Martin continues, 'The families that built these houses farmed the land but their prosperity came from other sources, as clothiers or merchants.' And for all its cottage-like proportions, Maynards proves to be unexpectedly spacious inside, with a floor space of 3,500 sq ft, including six bedrooms.

When Roake bought it, Maynards was a mess. Kentish tile-hanging, added about 1700, had been stripped off about forty years ago and the house given a crude black and white look – with some of the 'timbers' painted on for effect. The great hall chimney was on the point of collapse. Martin explains, 'If they had dug down another 18 inches they would have been building on bedrock. As it was they built on clay and the heat of the fire over centuries dried out and shrunk the clay beneath the hearth.'

His brilliance has been to create the sense of a seamless whole. Today there is an increasing trend to demand that new additions to old buildings should be in strong, even fierce contrast, to the old work. At Maynards everything is infinitely subtle.

Continuous bands of windows between close-set timbers create a distinctive livery.

The archaeologists found footings showing that the west front overlooking the pond originally had bay windows. Roake did not reconstruct them precisely – the evidence was insufficient – but put in new flat oriels which project just a few inches from the undulating facade.

The delight of this front is the almost continuous run of clerestory windows under the eaves. Martin explains, 'By the 1590s glass had become plentiful and affordable. Before that the last thing anyone wanted was a lot of windows letting in draughts.' This revolution coincided with the fashion for plaster ceilings in rooms that had previously been open to the roof. The white ceilings reflected light downwards and suddenly prosperous families had rooms glowing with natural light.

Roake has recreated all the timber mullions and leaded diamond-paned windows. The leadwork, by a firm that works on Canterbury Cathedral, is of a very high standard so the windows are sturdy, fit closely and open easily.

He has made two additions. First a new entrance with a projecting porch – both with scallop-shaped bargeboards and the date 1999 over the door, just in case anyone should be misled. And he has built a new kitchen block. But the trees were not all straight, and bent trees were selected for the tie beams in the upper storey, rising towards the centre of the room so you do not bump your head.

He says, 'We bought our own oak – 160 trees – and had it milled three miles up the road. To get value for money the key is to use green oak, as they did in the 16th century, not seasoned oak. We made our own lime putty, three tons of it with burnt lime from Derbyshire, a boiling vat of white yoghurt.'

Originally the infill between the wall timbers would have been wattle and daub but for better insulation Roake has used an Austrian wood wool fronted inside by plasterboard. The result is that the house is warm and easy to heat.

'I found the house in the annual SAVE Britain's Heritage catalogue of historic buildings in search of new owners and new uses in 1992,' he says.

Roake was concerned that the new oak spindles, or balusters, on the stairs would look mechanical. 'They gave the job to the least experienced man in the joinery workshop so there are slight variations from one to another,' he says. During repairs he found the remains of a boldly patterned, brightly coloured decorative wall painting. Vertical strips preserved behind later props have been exposed and covered with glass. The rest has been covered with protected boarding pending a time when a way has been found to remove the coat of emulsion on top.

The mellowness of Maynards is due largely to the use of whitewash. 'It's a very thin mix, the consistency of milk. The first coat simply makes the building look wet but after three or four skims the colour settles picking out the grain of the wood.'

The timber garage Roake has built comes with two handsome crown posts supporting the tiled roof. The pond in front of the house was dredged and given a 3-ft deep step on one side and all the hedges have been replanted with may, spindle, hazel and sweet briar rose – after eight years, these are so thick you can't even squeeze through. The orchards have been replanted with Bramleys, Grenadiers and Russets. All you need is a few Jacob sheep and you could be a yeoman living in the blissful heaven of the Garden of England.

PELLICANE HOUSE   Sandwich
Flint-faced town house of gloriously mellow character

STANDING ON THE EDGE OF THE PAVEMENT in the handsome historic town of Sandwich, the Pellicane House has a wonderfully weather-beaten air. Few houses carry the marks of successive alterations so well. The house is faced with flint with insets and mends of brick, Caen stone and Kentish Ragstone creating an extraordinary patina. There are battlements along the parapet, monastic-looking niches set into the first floor, Tudor hood moulds over Georgian sashes. The garden front might belong to a different house with white-painted walls, hipped roofs in warm handmade tiles amd eccentrically tall chimneys, presumably increased in height to cope with smoking fireplaces.

Thanks to the large sashes introduced in the 18th century, the interior is very light. There is one oak panelled room of 1600 date with characteristic small panels and a Chippendale style bookcase with octagonal glazed doors unusually built into the wall beside the door. Other rooms have tall rectangular panels of early 18th-century date rising from a dado or chair rail. There is a staircase with barley twist or spiral balusters and unexpected accommodation on a second floor.

Pellicane House is an example of the many unusual and interesting houses that survive in country towns, houses that have plenty of room for hospitality, both for parties and weekend guests. Here the large drawing room is said to have been the scene of the first performances by travelling players in the town. With its grassy lawn, walled garden and garage with four-fold doors, Pellicane has the essentials for elegant town life.

Georgian sashes have been introduced amidst mends of brick and Caen and Kentish stone.

THE GRANGE   Ramsgate
Pugin's house rescued and carefully restored by the Landmark Trust

I FIRST VISITED A.W.N. PUGIN'S HOUSE in Ramsgate in 1996 when the Landmark Trust had bought it to forestall subdivision into flats and were putting forward their initial proposals for restoration. It was both inspiring and depressing, full of fascinating detail but badly altered, and despite a magnificent clifftop position you had to avert your eyes from the container port below. Pugin built not just a house here in 1843–44 but a church next door, still in pristine condition, and St Edward's Presbytery across the road, still in use. The plans were to take the house back to its original state, removing not only the additions made by Pugin's son Edward, but some by A.W.N himself for his third wife.

A heated discussion ensued – surely this was a case of 'preserve as found', retaining successive alterations for additional interest. Landmark commissioned more studies of the building and agreed with the Victorian Society to set a cut-off date of 1875, marking the death of Edward Pugin and the end of the use of the house as a family home. The Society also agreed to the removal of a kitchen extension, cloakroom and bathroom, but the main gate, entrance courtyard and a bedroom designed by Edward for his mother have been retained and restored – a commendable example of English pragmatism.

Inside, the panelling is a reinstatement of the simple matchboarding used all through the house. The staircase is papered in the red and green version of the En Avant design based on his family motto 'Forward' which he designed for himself. On the floor are original tiles with his monogram AWP and the family emblem, the black martelet. In the Sitting Room the panelled ceiling has been restored and the fireplace repainted – the arch into the Library is closed with a curtain as Pugin hated slamming doors. The carpets are to Pugin's designs and the bookcases have been reconstructed from shadows left on the walls. In the dining room the pine panelling is stained in the shade chosen by Pugin and the walls are hung with a bright pink, red and white version of the En Avant paper. Here is the pristine dazzling colour of the Gothic Revival in all its original intensity restored with more attention to elaborate detail than any Landmark before.

Pugin's handsome church stands just across the garden wall.

THE SALUTATION
One of the most handsome of all Lutyens's houses

Sandwich

THE SALUTATION IS A MASTERPIECE by Sir Edwin Lutyens and the first 20th-century house given the accolade of a Grade I listing. Yet since the Second World War it has had an unsettled history, coming back on to the market and taking time to sell. The house has never been as fully or well photographed as it deserves. *Country Life* illustrated the interior in its great three-volume tribute to Lutyens, but no longer has those few photographs in its archives.

Sandwich is one of the loveliest of all English towns and The Salutation stands in a perfect position just inside the former town walls, beside the broad, grassy promenade along the river.

A long wall, much of it beautifully built in flint, gives complete seclusion to 3.5 acres of one of the most glorious town gardens in England. Further privacy from prying sightseers is provided by an almost medieval gateway inset with high double oak gates. This comes with distinctive Lutyens signatures: big chunky bolection mouldings and a pair of windows set like eyes on each side of the arch.

Inside the gate serenity reigns, with a large courtyard shaded by lofty lime trees and a glimpse through lace-like iron gates into the garden. It is the house that seizes the attention, with one of the most beautiful of all front-doorcases, swan-pedimented with carved cockleshells over the door. It is approached up what the French call a *perron* – a flute-shaped flight of steps with elegant S-scroll iron railings.

The steep roof and soaring chimney give an added flourish to Lutyens's design.

The Salutation is a Lutyens play on the most covetable of all English country houses, Ramsbury Manor in Wiltshire, a Charles II house that belonged to Lord Rootes (of motorcar fame) and was famously bought by Harry Hyams, the property developer who built Centre Point in London. The Salutation also has three show fronts, each slightly different and with similar groupings of windows and the same warm brick and tall hipped roof. The house shows Lutyens as a master in handling the best English building materials, a purpley brick with orange dressings to the windows and warm brown roof tiles perfectly matching the brick below.

For a moment, walking through the front door, I felt I had emerged inside the *baldacchino* beneath the dome of St Peter's in Rome, because the ceiling is low like a canopy and there are corkscrew columns on either side. The two corners on the opposite side of the hall are curiously taken up with glazed kiosks a little like the famous red telephone boxes, though painted white. The right one leads to a saucer-domed vestibule. 'Once painted with a night sky and stars,' I was told by the owner Mark Older. In each direction there are intriguing vistas through arches, but the vestibule is mainly a lobby to the staircase, a monumental construction in the manner of Italian Renaissance palaces rising between solid walls. Above you, balconies look out from hidden landings, waiting for guests to lean out, as in a Veronese fresco.

The house is named after a pub that once stood on the site and was completed in 1912 (the date over the front door) for the three Farrer brothers – one worked for Farrers, the leading firm of London solicitors. They were bachelors and had another wonderfully panelled house in St James's Square. They chose Sandwich for the sea air.

Their books were housed in a pine-panelled library off the hall with Chinese Chippendale grilles beneath the windows concealing the heating. There were more books on a book landing at the top of the staircase, where there is also a large linen cupboard in an archway. On the first floor were three large bedrooms for the three brothers, each with a bathroom.

The sunny drawing room and apsed dining room have French windows, designed to look like sashes, opening onto the garden. The drawing room looks out over a bowling green higher than the rest of the garden, enclosed by tall yews with another apse at the end. The dining room opens onto a terrace, stone paved with brick insets, which originally had no balustrade. 'A previous owner who was rather fond of his gin and tonics fell off one day and the builder arrived the next morning to put a balustrade on' continued Mr Older.

There is a pretty rose garden and numerous wooden pergolas for climbing roses. Along the perimeter wall is a narrow avenue of poplars planted by the French wife of a previous owner in the manner of Normandy gardens. Remarkably, no buildings can be seen from the garden. The house is embowered by trees – the only exception is the nearby Saxon church tower which looks wonderful when floodlit at night. With little sound from passing traffic, you listen to the cooing of wood pigeons.

So what are the drawbacks? A monumental and highly architectural interior is quite a challenge to furnish. It calls for Lutyens-style wheelback chairs and Chippendale desks and bookcases. Yet it comes with a series of cottages like a country estate, opening onto one of southern England's most enchanting towns.

SHURLAND HALL   Isle of Sheppey
Long-ruined early 16th-century courtyard house now being restored

GATEHOUSES WITH OCTAGONAL BATTLEMENTED TOWERS are one of the great motifs of Tudor architecture – witness St James's Palace, Eton College and Cowdray Park in Sussex. Shurland offers these on a modest domestic scale, the kind of house that many people could dream of living in. What survives is the front range of an important early 16th-century courtyard house built by Sir Thomas Cheyne who entertained Henry VIII and Anne Boleyn here on October 7, 1532. Yet for years it stood shockingly neglected in open fields on the Isle of Sheppey. Designation as both a Grade II* listed building and a Scheduled Ancient Monument appeared of little avail.

The house had first suffered when soldiers were billeted here during the First World War and much of the oak panelling and many of the fireplaces disappeared. In 1936 it became a farm store. When I first visited it the walls survived to parapet height. Since then they have steadily crumbled. The Landmark Trust tried to take it on without success. Finally the Spitalfields Trust, veteran rescuers of more than fifty early 18th century weavers' houses in Spitalfields, secured agreement with the Sillars family.

The Spitalfields Trust have recently saved a major 16th- and 17th-century manor house in Wales, Alt-y-Bela, and at the time of writing have completed repairs to more than two-thirds of the roof at Shurland Hall. English Heritage have offered a grant of £300,000. The key to success is the removal of a large and noisy grain-drying unit in the adjoining field. The trust has agreed to buy the farmyard for £260,000, enabling operations to be continued elsewhere. When repairs are complete in the summer of 2007, the Trust hopes to raise a figure in the region of £2 million from the sale allowing it to recover the large outlay.

With a new bridge completed in 2006, Sheppey is now within forty minutes' drive of Canary Wharf, an attraction to any romantic with a large City bonus to spend.

The twin octagonal towers of the gatehouse are built of brick with a stone trim.

SUNDRIDGE PARK   Bromley
John Nash villa in need of a private buyer after years of institutional use

SUNDRIDGE PARK IS ONE OF THE MOST original works of the accomplished John Nash, favourite architect of George IV. Nash gave London the great stucco terraces around Regent's Park as well as Buckingham Palace, which, without the staid Edwardian facade, would be the most beautiful in Europe. He also designed an enchanting series of country villas with handsome porticoes and corner domes. Sundridge is the most original of them all, laid out on a plan like that of a Delta-wing fighter.

The surpassing attraction of Sundridge is its situation. You are just 15 miles from central London, surveying a spectacular panorama over nearly 300 acres of well-wooded parkland rising to the crest of a hill nearly a mile away and not a building to be seen.

The park is a golf course but from the windows neither golfers nor greens are to be seen, let alone any pockmarking bunkers. Better still, the planes that relentlessly overfly south west London are gloriously absent.

This landscape is substantially the creation of the great landscape gardener Humphry Repton, whose proposals survive in the form of one of his trademark 'Red Books'. Here Repton told the the-owner of Sundridge that he must demolish his fine old house and rebuild on a new site nearby, so alarming his client that the poor man promptly sold the estate. The purchaser, in 1796, was Sir Claude Scott, banker and purveyor of corn to the armies of the Duke of Wellington. Not surprisingly, by the end of the Napoleonic Wars he was one of the richest men in England.

Nash exhibited the designs of the new house at the Royal Academy in 1799 but the task of designing the interiors was handed to his rival, Samuel Wyatt (sweet revenge for Wyatt, from whom Nash had just snatched a commission at Corsham Court in Wiltshire).

The interiors are a real teaser, for later in the 19th century every main room was enriched with further Adamesque or Wyatt-like detail. Yet the effect is dazzling with every inch of ceilings and walls enlivened with garlands of flowers and cameo medallions. Part of the fun is the succession of rooms of unusual shapes – ovals and rotundas as well as rooms with apsed ends and rounded corners. Nash was evidently paying tribute to his master, Sir Robert Taylor, whose London house was filled with rooms of exotic shape. The corridors have saucer domes and pretty cross vaults.

The circular staircase has a dome with plasterwork as exquisitely detailed as the best Wedgwood while the balustrade, which is later, looks both silver- and gold-plated, like the grandest Rolls Royce Phantom.

The ground-floor rooms are as white as wedding cakes but have a wealth of delicate ornament and some inset painted panels in the style of Angelica Kauffman the 18th century artist who dazzled with her looks as well as her talents. The climax comes with the King's Room in the first floor of the rotunda, named, I was told, for Edward VII, who came to shoot pheasants, though presumably while he was Prince of Wales. The shallow dome is a pattern of circles set in lozenges with pretty fan motifs in the corners

Overleaf: Nash's distinctive domed rotunda has a matching later wing on the right.

Left: The King's Room has filigree plasterwork by Samuel Wyatt.
Right: The domed circular stair has silvered and gilt balustrading.

and gilt arabesques. Subsequent generations added ever more rooms in similar styles as further wings were thrown out on both sides. There is an exceptionally graceful second stair ascending in a curve beneath a dome with slender brass balusters.

Upstairs I began to see the challenge that lay ahead, for almost all of the bedrooms with glorious views over the park had been subdivided. The story is this. In the 19th century the Scotts had grown steadily richer. Successive baronets built a grand conservatory, vast servants' wing and ballroom, and were even able to demand a special station, Sundridge Park, on the Bromley Line for their use.

When the 6th baronet, Sir Samuel Scott was left childless, he sold the park as a golf course – so grand that the club house was opened by the Prime Minister Arthur Balfour. After Nash's mansion failed to reach its reserve at auction in 1904 it was leased as an hotel. The 1929 Michelin Guide awarded it three roofs (comfortable, with modern improvements) but after the Second World War the hotel went into liquidation and the contents were sold.

Enter Ernest Butten, of PA Management Consultants, who tore down the conservatory and built a large redbrick training centre on handsome planted terraces, and used the house for conferences and weddings. In 2006 Sundridge's new owners, the Cathedral Group, demolished this and replaced it with three blocks of apartments, while converting Wyatt's half-moon stable block into a mews of seven houses.

They have commissioned John MacAslan, architect of the super suave makeover of Peter Jones in Sloane Square, to sort out the back of the house with an elegant, modern wing with spa and indoor pool. The spur has been their success with another nearby country house, Foxbury, where a buyer quickly appeared to make the sprawling house (which had also been a conference centre) into one grand residence.

WALDERSHARE
Eythorne
Talman house reconstructed by Sir Reginald Blomfield after a fire

WALDERSHARE STANDS SHELTERED from the world in an ample park in a part of Kent that has remained rural and largely unspoilt – an area placed, as one wag put it, behind the door opened by the channel tunnel. Waldershare has been the seat of the Earls of Guildford since 1766 and after the war was manifestly too large to live in. The solution has largely been a happy one. The houses have become apartments while the family maintain the park and estate and live nearby.

The house was built by Sir Henry Furnese in 1705–12 and has been attributed by John Harris to William Talman, the architect of two of Chatsworth's grand fronts. I arrived with John one Sunday morning to look around the house and quickly found ourselves looking at plans and drawings of the house and enjoying a convivial lunch with the Earl and his sister. One of the great features of Waldershare is the rich detailing in 'rubbed brick' – doorcases, triglyph frieze and cornice. Much of the interior was destroyed in a fire of 1913 and rebuilt by the architect Sir Reginald Blomfield on his usual grand scale, raising the roof in the process.

One challenge still remains at Waldershare – to devise a new use for the remarkable Palladian belvedere that stands abandoned nearby. Built by Sir Robert Furnese in 1725–7 at a cost of £1,703, it has had many suitors seeking to restore it either as a house or as a Landmark Trust-style holiday let but has so far defeated every effort to restore it. Fortunately it is so monumentally constructed it looks capable of enduring several centuries.

The house stands in a large peaceful landscaped park.

WILSLEY — Cranbrook
Medieval house and garden ravishingly extended by an Edwardian painter

WILSLEY IS AN ENTHRALLING HOUSE. The core is a splendid and well-preserved timber-framed hall house built for a rich Kent clothier at the end of the 15th century, and time has simply added new dimensions to its beauty and fascination.

Escaping Georgian and Victorian alterations, Wilsey was brought back to life at precisely the moment when early English architecture was most appreciated. In the later 19th century, when the clothiers had long departed, the pretty town of Cranbrook became a thriving artists' colony, with the architect Norman Shaw enlarging next-door Wilsley House for successful Royal Academician J.C. Horsley.

Wilsley's turn came in 1898 when the painter Herbert Alexander, friend of the poet Laurence Housman (brother of A.E.) came to live here with his artist wife Edith, a pupil of the great Sir William Orpin. They had been given the house as a wedding present by Colonel Boyd Alexander, who bought the property with the adjoining great Swifts Estate in 1862 and allowed the painter E.S. O'Neil to remain in residence. He respected the magic of the place, doing no more than adding a large oak front door and a delightful bay window in the parlour.

Herbert's explorations were mainly in France and Italy where, according to his granddaughter Ianthe, he would play the mandolin to pay for the evening meal. A photograph shows he was also a keen bodybuilder, known as 'the strong man of Kent'.

The original Kentish clothier's house has jettied ends and a central hall.

The east wing with pretty arched loggia carries a rainwater head with his initials and the date 1915. At the end of the First World War he set out back from India with a collection of carved woodwork intended for a second wing but only enough survived to make a gorgeous four-poster bed and matching cupboard.

His most important work was the extensive topiary garden forming a series of garden rooms with noble yew hedges terminating in boldly clipped peacocks. A large knot garden with lozenges of box hedging is flanked by lines of thin Italian cypresses. Beyond, across a bowling green, is a green outdoor theatre formed of clipped hedges with wings for actors to emerge unseen. Further on a mini-hippodrome is shaded by Mediterranean pines and a bog garden is set in a dramatically deep hollow.

The late-medieval house is unusual, consisting of two parallel ranges linked up around a charming small courtyard a century ago. The main west front now looks onto a secluded lawn but must have been built to make a grand show to the road. The great hall, complete with awesomely massive tie-beams and octagonal king post, appears originally to have had no fireplace. The roof rafters are without the slightest trace of smoke-blackening from an open hearth and the present fireplace and chimney stack look too small to be original. It is possible that the main hall was used primarily for the display of cloth and the reception of customers.

The east range, by contrast, contains a grand hearth running its full width and has clearly been a kitchen since Tudor times. Great halls open to the roof timbers went out of fashion in the 16th century and in about 1530, to judge by the massive beams, a ceiling was introduced to make a single-storey entrance hall with great chamber above. The original twin arch doorways to the buttery and pantry survive at the service end while at the upper, or dais, end the main beam is enriched with little battlements. The linenfold panelling here is highly unusual, consisting of a single crease in each panel rising from floor to ceiling. Around 1600 further panelling was added in both the parlour and the hall. By this time Wilsley was the property of the Sheafe family, leading Cranbrook clothiers. In 1639 Edmond Sheafe's widow departed with all but one of her children to live among the Indians in Connecticut. From Harmon Sheafe, who remained behind, Wilsley passed to another clothier, John Weston, who created two panelled rooms of 1680 date at the service end of the hall. The lower one is painted with an intriguing series of biblical scenes portraying the destruction of Sodom and Gomorrah, which are as menacingly depicted as Mordor in *The Lord of the Rings*. Below, Weston's harriers chase a large hare round the room while he himself, dapperly dressed in black, is portrayed beside the door.

Upstairs the silvered oak timbers of the great hall roof were re-exposed a hundred years ago, revealing the 'close studding' of the walls – a lavish display of vertical timbers proclaiming the wealth of the builders. On the west front the ranks of timbers are still largely hidden by pretty ochre render. But the overhanging jetties at both sides and ends are visible, supported by diagonal 'dragon' beams at the corners. With the projecting roof gables, these are details found only on the grandest timber-framed houses. The final flourish is added by the thatched studio complete with beehive-shaped dovecote built for Herbert Alexander's daughter Camilla, whose frescoes survive in several of the attics of the house.

YALDHAM MANOR   Wrotham
15th-century hall house encased in brick in the mid 17th century

ON MY VISIT TO YALDHAM MANOR, I followed the owner, Edward Lade, up a ladder, crawling through the roof space to inspect the smoke-blackened timbers above the ceiling of the medieval great hall – proof that originally there was an open hearth in the centre of the floor. He pointed out the neat holes in the rafters, where samples had been taken by Robert Howard, an expert in tree-ring dating. 'Every one was dated to 1412,' said Lade, with satisfaction.

Downstairs, he explained. 'My parents bought the house in 1951 … I was born after they came here.' Now he is married and, with two young children, he has decided it is time to move.

Lade is full of fascinating insights. When he rebuilt Yaldham's magnificent collection of seventeen soaring Victorian 'barley-sugar' chimneys, using much of the old brick, he discovered that the ornamental brick patterns had a purpose. 'The brick surveyor told us that strong winds could create a vortex, a suction effect that could bring down the chimneys. The patterned ribbing breaks up the force of the wind.' He also points out the typical Kentish galleting – small chips of stone or flint set into the mortar in decorative patterns. 'A heavy downpour can wash out lime mortar from the joints. Galleting helps throw the water off.'

Recently he has had dowsers – water diviners – to the property. 'They told me they were sure there had been a moat close to the house and, when I asked for a date, they said 1406 – virtually matching the date for the timbers.'

Between 1327 and 1713 Yaldham belonged to the Peckhams. James Peckham is held as the builder of the house, but the hall could be the work of his son, Reginald.

The medieval hall can be seen behind the 17th century gabled entrance front.

Above: Ribbing on the 'barley-sugar' chimneys breaks up the force of the wind; Right: To mark the end of the First World War, General Tuckfield Goldsworthy grew on the hedge to form the central crown.

The large mullioned window inset with heraldic glass appears to be early 16th-century, as does the fireplace.

Yaldham was inherited in 1837 by the Rev. Edmund Boscawen Evelyn. His alterations include the east wing to the left of the entrance. It was Evelyn who probably planted the magnificent yew topiary, which rises to 20 ft and is said to be the tallest in the south-east.

In 1890 Yaldham was advertised in *The Times* and sold to Major-General Walter Tuckfield Goldsworthy, MP for Hammersmith, who bred hunters and built the stable and carriage shed. Arthur Nye Peckham, who visited in 1911, noted the general had 're-opened the great hall, which had been cut into four rooms'. If this is so, it was probably the major-general who added the pretty painted floral pattern on the roof timbers.

A striking feature of the hall is the exposed timber wall at the west service end, probably dating from about 1600. Beyond it lies an unusual range with more smoke-blackened timbers, considered as a very late example of a medieval open kitchen.

In 1922 Yaldham was sold by the general's family to Herbert William Corry, managing director of the Port Line that sailed to Australia and New Zealand and was the first to provide single berths for every crew member. He built the garage and stone walls around the house. During the Second World War, his wife took in evacuee children from London.

A remarkable group of early photographs dating from 1850 and 1870 shows the house before the Victorian additions and without the glorious chimneys. They show that the present entrance front is a largely untouched example of the quirky 'Artisan mannerist' style of the mid 17th century, with diamond lead-pane windows and an unusual oval window over the entrance. The drive is lined with limes, with an unusual central island just inside the gate. The clock-pattern Victorian rose garden survives as well as a small village of outbuildings and cottages. Who could have guessed that all this survives just 30 miles from the centre of London?

YARDHURST — Ashford
Perfect example of a 1480 Wealden house with jettied ends and central hall

IF ANY BUILDING SPEAKS OF the essence of medieval England it is a well-preserved, well-tended Kentish yeoman's house. Today scholars prefer to talk of Wealden houses and a remarkable group of about 150 survives south-east of Maidstone, ranging in date from the mid 14th to the mid 16th century. Yardhurst is thought to date from about 1480 and stands a mile north-west of the village of Great Chart.

I found the garden at Yardhurst alive with the chatter of birds. No sound of the modern world intruded. Yet the house is only a ten-minute drive from Ashford International Station. The journey to Lille is quicker than London. You could shop and lunch regularly in Calais or use the weekly French farmers' market at Ashford.

Until half a century ago Yardhurst was still a typical medieval yeoman's holding of 80-odd acres divided into a dozen small fields. Such holdings were free of manorial duties, small enough to be worked by a family and rich enough to support the building of a good house, usually timber-framed. Today 15 acres remain.

It is tempting to think timber-framed buildings are all honest structure in the Ruskinian sense – with every post and beam doing a job of work and not there for show. Yardhurst is intriguing as its architecture was definitely designed to please the eye (or proclaim status, as modern parlance has it).

The main front was extravagantly constructed of 'close-studding' – vertical timbers set close together like columns, far more than are needed to support walls and roof. At the back of the house, which probably opened onto a farmyard, the posts are more widely and economically spaced with the arched braces exposed between. On the end,

The close-set timbers, known as close-studding, were for show more than strength.

by contrast, there is both close studding and exposed bracing, as if the master carpenter was determined to show off the whole lexicon of smart timber-frame construction.

The main front has the added attraction of being almost exactly symmetrical. Towards the ends the upper storey projects – the technique known as jettying. The centre, by contrast is flat, immediate evidence that there was an open hall within, rising to the roof timbers.

As in almost all medieval houses the front door is off-centre, leading into the lower end of the hall. The arch over the doorway is here formed by vertically splitting a tree with a branch conveniently at the height of the doorway. An added flourish is provided by a carved, gently arching beam which sits over the door like a crown.

It was usual to have a parlour at one end of a medieval hall, with a solar above, and the kitchen and pantry at the other end. However, Anthony Quiney in his excellent book on Kent Houses quotes examples of symmetrical houses like Yardhurst being built for two families with a shared hall between – a father and son or two brothers. This would explain the identical arrangement of windows on either side of the hall with ornate 'cusped' tops on the first floor.

It is clear from internal evidence that the house was always tiled not thatched, with the roof retaining its original hipped or sloping ends. The only change is the introduction of the chimneys. This was done at the lower end of the hall – perhaps when the house was united for single family use. With the introduction of a fireplace, the original open hearth was obsolete. The hall no longer needed to be open to the roof to allow smoke to rise and escape through the tiles. So, as in many of these houses, the hall was floored in – here creating two extra levels above.

In 2005 I found almost all the rooms with fitted carpets – apparently there were no ancient broad-boarded floors waiting to be exposed. Sturdy ranks of squared beams give character to the ground-floor rooms, with those supporting the jettied end at right angles to the others. In several places the door heads were carved with battlements, a distinctive chivalrous touch.

About fifty years before, a previous owner decided to create a more open-plan interior, turning the hall (now drawing room) and parlour into one and removing the infill panels from the inner wall of the dining room, leaving the timber posts as a skeletal screen. The temptation is to restore these rooms to their original proportions.

The bedrooms had attractive views over the garden and the climax came in the attic where the crown post stood in grand isolation in the middle of the floor with bulbous onion base, octagonal shaft and moulded top. The top of the supporting tie-beam emerged through the carpet like a surfboard.

Tom Eyton, the owner, was unhappy with cars parked in front of the house and has made a new entrance at the back, laying out a sheltered formal garden in front of the house. The entrance lobby, which retained the medieval embattled cresting over a door, has become rather forgotten as a closet.

Yardhurst has two handsome Kentish barns, neither converted to modern use. Interesting planting in the garden has been done by Tom and his wife Dorothy, creating ponds and pergolas and introducing a pretty iron bridge over the stream into the meadows.

LANCASHIRE

BANK HALL HAS BEEN EMPTY since the Second World War and after gently crumbling began to collapse dramatically. One corner of the tower fell away, leaving an open gash through which rain could pour in. When I visited in 1991, large numbers of pheasants were being reared in pens beside the decaying mansion. An application had just been lodged for consent to demolish most of the tower.

The appeal of the house is its playful Jacobean architecture with wavy gables and numerous finials and baubles crowning porch tower and gable tops. The silhouette is further enlivened by clusters of tall column-like chimneys. The house dates from 1608 but was enlarged in the early 1830s by the architect George Webster of Kendal who made a speciality of the Jacobean style. Two nearby houses of his at Eshton and Underley are also in this style, so the attribution of Bank is convincing.

The house was a family seat of the Lilfords who also owned Lilford Hall in Northamptonshire. Lord Lilford's agents had been granted permission to make the house into a country club in the early 1970s but this foundered when the council refused plans for an associated golf course. Yet some hope was held out by the agent, Thomas Bracewell, who told me. 'When Lord Lilford's heir comes of age in four years time we may have funds to restore the building. We are hoping he may reoccupy the house.'

Since then, hope has been kept alive by the Bank Hall Action Group which runs a lively website. With the Heritage Trust for the North West, they have approached enterprising developers Urban Splash hoping to draw up a viable scheme. A sum of £30,000 has been spent on repairs and scaffolding so there is hope yet.

Even in the midst of heavy decay, the silhouette retained all its romance.

BISPHAM HALL   Billinge
Gabled 1600 house now restored after a serious fire

BUILT IN ABOUT 1600, Bispham Hall is a play on the distinctive E-plan adopted for so many Elizabethan houses. The main front has five gables with two broad gables for the end wings. The centre is stepped back twice with the porch off-centre in the second gable on the right. The semi-circular arch of the porch appears to be a mid 17th-century introduction as the inner doorway has a shallow pointed Tudor arch. Otherwise the detail is entirely Tudor with hood moulds to the mullioned windows. Almost perfect symmetry reigns with no obvious difference between the high and low ends of the hall as there would have been in earlier centuries. There is also a telling hierarchy in the windows, which diminish in size towards the top.

Bispham was acquired in 1950 by the Boy Scouts Association. In September 1978 a serious fire gutted the interior leaving little more than a masonry shell. Demolition loomed and Bispham's plight looked hopeless, but the house has now been immaculately restored. The stone has emerged a warm beige after cleaning, the windows are all reglazed. Across the courtyard is a very pretty knot garden formed of clipped box. The Scouts now make intensive use of the grounds and the house itself is back in use for a whole range of events.

A gutted shell but with the mullions intact. Bispham at its lowest ebb.

CLEGG HALL   Rochdale

Splendid but long decaying 1618 house where restoration is at last under way

BETWEEN ROCHDALE AND OLDHAM the countryside is much built up but Clegg Hall stands in a near idyllic setting by a canal surrounded by fields. It forms a group with four weavers' cottages, a dye house and mill built by Joseph Fenton of Bamford in 1811. Clegg Hall is much older still, thought to have been built in 1617–18 for the splendidly named Theophilus Assheton of the Middleton family, though Nicholas Cooper, the expert on 'gentry' houses and author of the *Country Life* volume on Jacobean Houses, has suggested a date towards 1640.

When I first went to Clegg it was already a roofless ruin but one that, thanks to its sturdy walls, would have been relatively easy to repair. It was owned by a local farmer who had no use for it and as there were no takers the local authority was suggesting it should be taken into guardianship and preserved like a ruined castle or abbey.

I visited with SAVE's Northern secretary Ken Powell, champion of textile mills and nonconformist chapels, who was in close touch with Pennine Heritage, the first building preservation trust to take on historic textile mills, repair them and put them to use. Through persistence Pennine Heritage finally managed to acquire Clegg in 1986, opening the way to repair. The house is almost square, built to a satisfying design with three gables on each side, with the original stone-mullioned and transom windows still in place. There were taller, grander rooms at the front and lower ones at the back for the service quarters. The fireplaces were all set in a spine wall between the two, a pioneering arrangement, retaining heat within the building.

The latest person to take an interest is Jason Stead, who has completed an award-winning restoration at 17th-century Healey Hall near Rochdale complete with marble statuary from China, replacing seventy-eight windows to make it a home for his family.

The robust masonry allowed the shell to survive decades of neglect.

CRAWFORD MANOR   Crawford
Charmingly old-fashioned house of 1718 saved from long neglect

CRAWFORD MANOR WAS A PITIFUL sight when it appeared in SAVE's *Silent Mansions* in 1981. The garden was overgrown with brambles, the roof was rapidly collapsing, yet it was a small manor house of a size that could easily become a family house again. The house had the accolade of a Grade II* listing and was flanked by two barns, both listed. It had been used as a farmhouse until 1965 when the owner moved into a bungalow nearby and left it vacant, apprehensive that any new use could intrude on the seclusion of his new home. He had applied for consent to demolish in 1977 but no permission had been given. All credit therefore to West Lancashire District Council, as the house has now been saved. The price has been new housing in the grounds though the all-important vista up to the main front remains.

The stone front has emerged a pretty, speckled, almost pinky colour. For its date of 1718 the front is rather charmingly old-fashioned. Though sashes were in widespread use by this time, there are mullions and transoms though with an attempt at a Classical keystone. The corners are emphasised by vertical bands of quoins though these stop short of the central gable as if a cornice had been intended but dispensed with in favour of gables and dormers. The main rooms were at the front with two almost matching staircases across the corridor behind the hall. The grander one, for the family, has square newels and turned balusters.

Cleaning has removed centuries of soot to reveal the warmth of the original stone.

FORMBY HALL · Formby

16th-century house given a playful makeover in Strawberry Hill Gothick style

FORMBY HALL HAS FOUND ITS PRINCE. When I first saw the house, I found it pleasantly secluded in woodland. Though empty, it was still looked after and in good condition with pretty gothick windows.

The Formby family traced possession back to the 12th century. The core of the present house was built for William Formby in 1523. Battlements were added in the middle of the 18th century by John Formby, who lived here in 1721–1776. He was a close friend of John Chute, who was involved with Horace Walpole in promoting the Gothic revival, and also laid out the grounds, plantation and lake. In the later 19th century the hall was modernised by Colonel John Formby who added the west wing drawing room.

With the death of the last squire, Colonel John Frederic Lonsdale Formby, in 1958, the Formby line came to an end and the estate went to a nephew living in Australia. Much of the land was sold off for development, while the hall lay empty for many years and finally both it and the grounds became derelict. In the 1970s, John Moores Junior acquired a lease for the hall and the grounds and used them as a rest home for children from crowded areas of Liverpool, who were brought here and then looked after by members of the Brontë Society. During the 1980s he left and the hall once again fell into dereliction and was boarded up by the council. In the early 1990s Mike McComb and his wife Sharon bought the house, determined to save it, eschewing even a simple survey. Repairs are now triumphantly complete and Formby is once again one of the prettiest smaller country houses in the county.

The house standing empty before the present owners restored it.

OAK HILL   Accrington
Regency house which the local council wanted to demolish

IT IS HARD TO IMAGINE that such an elegant Regency house as Oak Hill should ever have come under threat, but in 1980 consent was being sought to demolish Oak Hill by its owners, the local council. The proposal was the more scandalous as the house had been given to the town in 1893 and until 1951 had housed the local museum.

Oak Hill was built about 1815 for Thomas Hargreaves, whose family were leading textile manufacturers and dominated the Accrington calico printing trade. The 1815 front was as neat as a doll's house, just five windows wide with a pretty fanlight over the front door. The one blemish was the wing added on the left, rather less refined in design and a little overwhelming in proportion thanks to the taller ceilings which came in with gaslighting.

When the house was acquired by the local council, the grounds had become a public park, complete with imposing First World War memorial. As happened so often with houses owned by local councils, economies led to lack of basic maintenance and the house was suddenly in need of major repairs. The obvious solution was to find a private or commercial buyer but many councils would not consider such an idea in a public park. Here, Michael Heseltine's new edict – that permission should not be given for demolition unless the house had been offered for sale on the open market at a price reflecting its condition – came into play. Soon the council was negotiating with three interested parties and Oak Hill was sold for £1 to the Abbeyfield Society as a home for the elderly. The house was repaired and is now a community once more, whose residents look out over a beautiful park.

The house stands in a public park and is now a home for the elderly.

STAYLEY HALL — Staleybridge

Long abandoned 16th-century house that has continued to decay

THIS SPLENDID HOUSE IS one of the longest-running scandals in heritage. The Grade II* listing runs: 'Seat of the De Staveley family from as early as the 14th century. One of Greater Manchester's most impressive halls which has been little altered since the early 18th century except through decay which is now well established'.

The main front is a wonderful example of gabled Elizabethan and there is no trace of foreign influence or imported fashions, just the tradition of first-class masonry. The plan is a continuation of the medieval one with central hall and projecting wings. But it also reflects the greater wish for comfort and privacy that developed in the 16th century. The hall has shrunk and is no longer open to the roof timbers, though the traditional entrance through a porch at one end remains. The wings now dominate the facade with bands of mullioned windows lighting rooms on both floors.

Intriguingly Stayley Hall (it is also spelt Staley) is a 16th-century timber-framed structure only clad in stone. The sophistication of the design lies in the alternating size and height of the gables.

When Stayley Hall was illustrated in SAVE's *Silent Mansions* it still had a roof, albeit with a few large holes. Today the roof has entirely gone and the crisp stonework is fraying as water gets in. Yet given the fact that the house has been standing empty since just before the First World War, it has survived well. The grounds are 5.5 acres with open land to the south, and the latest proposal is for a development of up to fifty dwellings, including apartments within the house. Stayley deserves a model solution and the house must be provided with a garden of sufficient size to show it off to best advantage without intrusive neighbours. Dozens of houses in this book show how it can be done. Stayley's turn must come.

A perfectly symmetrical arrangement of gables and windows with only the entrance off centre.

WOODFOLD PARK   Blackburn
Built for a Blackburn mill owner and now impressively restored as apartments

WOODFOLD PARK HAS A SPECIAL interest as the only known architectural work of Charles McNiven, who came with his brother Peter from Scotland, establishing themselves as 'surveyors and nurserymen' in Manchester. For years the house has stood as a noble but sorry shell overlooking a fine stretch of gently rising parkland and crying out to be restored. At last its time has come.

The house was built for a Blackburn mill owner, Henry Sudell, in 1796–9 on a virgin site that had a commanding view. Stone was quarried on nearby Abbot's Brow. The house itself, in the chaste neoclassical manner of the Wyatts, was

Woodfold stood a gutted shell for many years prior to its restoration.

on a grand scale around a central top lit staircase hall. Sudell stocked his grounds with deer and wildfowl, maintained his own hounds, and travelled into Blackburn in a coach-and-four with liveried postillions. He was a considerable philanthropist, founding St John's Church in Blackburn and roasting an ox in Blackburn's old marketplace at Christmas each year. When 6,000 handloom weavers marched upon Woodfold from Blakey Moor in 1818, Sudell acceded to their demand for a 5% rise; and even when his high living caught up with him nine years later, he left his butler with enough money to establish himself at the nearby Fox & Grapes pub.

The grand lifestyle was continued first by John Fowden Hindle and then by the Thwaites family who owned the estate until 1949, when the contents were dispersed in a three-day sale. Lancashire County Council refused permission for the house to be converted into a home for retired mill workers, saying it was too isolated – though it is only three miles from the centre of Blackburn. Woodfold Park was not listed until 1952 and the county planning officer was able to state damningly that 'it was not considered of sufficient architectural merit to take any action to preserve it'. Yet a year before *Murray's Lancashire Architectural Guide* had pronounced it 'a perfect example of late 18th-century design, probably the best and largest now surviving in Lancashire'. Worse was to come. In 1956 consent was granted to strip out mahogany doors, marble fireplaces and wrought-iron balustrades.

The house stood empty for nearly half a century until acquired by Reilly Developments of Chorley. Work began in 2000. The blackened stone emerged fresh and bright from cleaning and came alive when sash windows were reinstated. Four apartments have been created on the two main floors, all opening directly off the staircase hall. Further apartments have been created in wings at the back and in the coach house, with garages out of sight behind the house and screened by trees.

WOOLTON HALL
Robert Adam house at last on the mend
Liverpool

ROBERT ADAM WAS ONE OF the most original, creative and precocious of British architects, enlarging and embellishing numerous great houses. Yet in England much of his work consisted of interiors. A 1785 engraving of Woolton Hall sets the adrenalin running as it appears to be a free-standing composition that surveys extensive ornamental grounds. The entrance front has advancing ends with twin pediments balanced by central pediments in the flanks. Here Adam was re-fronting and extending an early 18th-century house that had belonged to Richard Molyneux, heir to Viscount Molyneux of Croxteth. This is evident from the centre, which has three floors compared to only two in the adjoining wings.

A large and impressive *porte-cochère* was added to Woolton in about 1865, and the Adam interiors contain fine plasterwork and an impressive suite formed of Saloon, Tapestry Room and Drawing Room as well as a delightful octagon room and cantilevered stair.

The house has a Grade I listing but in the 1970s the owners applied for permission to demolish, a forceful reminder of the repeated serious threats to even major buildings at that time. Woolton, it is true, had been compromised by additions made shortly before, when a convent and school were added only a few feet away. These were later described by Richard Pollard, secretary of SAVE, as 'contemptuous and contemptible … so close that there are only a few feet between the old and the new on two sides'.

In recent years the house has been used as an hotel and wedding venue.

The 1865 porte-cochère *juts out from the main front.*

LEICESTERSHIRE & RUTLAND

BRADGATE HOUSE WAS BUILT AS a hunting lodge for the 7th Earl of Stamford when he was Master of the Quorn Hunt. Sold for demolition in 1926, only his magnificent stables survive. Though just a few miles to the west of Leicester, the parlous state of the buildings has so far deterred all would-be restorers. Roofs long ago collapsed, demolishing everything beneath them.

The stables stand adjacent to large gravel workings, not a promising start, but elsewhere listed buildings beside gravel pits have been successfully rescued from decay, for example Middleton Hall in Warwickshire. And now gravel workings are used as landfill sites, generating money for environmental projects through the Land Fill tax, grants should be available for restoring splendid listed buildings like these.

The Bradgate stables stand against a backcloth of fields, trees and hedges, just what you would expect in prime hunting country, and are some way from the main road.

George Harry Grey, 7th Earl of Stamford, was Master of the Quorn in 1856–63. His new stables were complete in 1856, the year he took over, and were designed by M.J. Dain of 'Dain and Parsons'. Built in grand Jacobean style they are laid out round a large courtyard with accommodated kennels for the hounds as well as fifty horses. The most impressive feature is the series of very large, shaped Dutch gables built in red brick with white decorative banding with stone trim. The main front has a square entrance tower and the keystone to the arch sports a fox's head. Above is a large panel with the arms of the Earl.

The house still stands magnificent even while awaiting a knight in shining armour.

BURLEY-ON-THE-HILL
Oakham
Chequered history of a great baroque house triumphantly resolved

DANIEL DEFOE DESCRIBED BURLEY in his *Tour of Great Britain*: 'I do not know of a house in Britain, which excels all the rest in so many particulars, or that goes so near to excelling them all in everything.' The house was built between 1696 and 1700 by Daniel Finch, 2nd Earl of Nottingham, costing him a handsome £50,000 for the estate, and a further £30,657 6s 7½d building the house. He financed this partly by selling his London home – the future Kensington Palace – for £19,000 to William III in 1689.

Nottingham appears to have been his own architect, although before he started work he obtained advice from Sir Christopher Wren. He also drew up the agreements with his workmen, had a model made by Thomas Poulteney, the joiner employed on many City of London churches, and employed two able local surveyors, first Henry Dormer and from 1697 John Lumley to supervise the work.

Nottingham showed a sure eye for fine proportions. Although he used flat pilasters rather than columns, the design of the house has a noble grandeur. The one arguable flaw is that the colonnades form neither quarter circles (as with Palladio's villas) nor continuous arcs (as at St Peter's) but straighten out a little awkwardly towards the outer wings. The reason is that one wing was the stable block of an earlier house – shorn of its gables and given an even roof line to match the main house.

Nottingham was building in 'stone' country. Stamford is only 10 miles away and the masonry is virtually unblemished to this day. The Finches lost the Winchelsea and Nottingham titles in the 19th century but lived on at Burley. Nineteenth-century changes include J.L. Pearson's 1870 rebuilding of the adjacent church.

In the 20th century tragedy struck when a savage fire broke out in 1908 while the house was let. The fire began in the west wing and raged through the house,

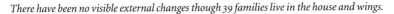

There have been no visible external changes though 39 families live in the house and wings.

The long colonnades linking the wings create the grandest forecourt in England.

destroying the Lanscroon frescoes in the Great Room, but stopping short of his painted staircase. The gutted west wing was fitted out by John Coleridge with new oak panelling and plasterwork, fine examples of Edwardian craftsmanship. By contrast a series of fully panelled late 17th-century rooms survive in the east wing. Yet Burley never regained its former splendour. Wilfred Finch died a bachelor in 1939 and the estate descended to a great-nephew, Colonel James Hanbury. During the Second World War, Burley was requisitioned as a hospital and not handed back for some time afterwards.

A two-day sale of furniture was held in 1948 by Knight, Frank and Rutley, while Colonel Hanbury was living in the vicarage and in 1955, when the hospital lease expired, the family moved back into the east end and opened the house to the public for a few years.

When Jos Hanbury inherited in 1971, much of the house was unused. He converted the wings at the far end of the colonnades into sixteen cottages and flats, selling Burley itself to Asil Nadir who had plans to convert the house into a luxury hotel with golf course and club house. Following Mr Nadir's bankruptcy the receiver continued to promote the hotel scheme, seeking permission for a four storey annexe at the south end of the garden terrace. This met strong opposition at a public inquiry and in 1992 Kit Martin acquired the house. He converted Burley and its outbuildings into twenty-three houses, all sold before they were finished. The main block was divided into five with a large house, like a rectory, at the east end looking out over a secluded garden enclosed by mature yew hedges. One big house is immediately to the east of the entrance hall, two to the west. Remarkably there were fine existing staircases to serve almost all the houses. As most houses have grand sash windows looking out over both fronts, the rooms are filled with light throughout the day.

The Great Room above the hall runs from front to back and has been retained as a shared space. Care was taken with the Lanscroon murals on the staircase – the paint had been flaking due to condensation but was carefully fixed, sealed and retouched on top so any new paint is separate from the old. Today thirty-nine families live at Burley.

DONINGTON HALL   Castle Donington

An exuberant example of Regency Tudor Gothic used for prisoners during the wars

THE ARCHITECT OF DONINGTON HALL was William Wilkins, who designed the National Gallery in London. Here he worked in a Tudor Gothic style, and the skyline is enriched with dozens of octagonal turrets. The house was built in 1793 by Francis Rawdon Hastings, the 2nd Earl of Moira, who was afterwards created Marquess of Hastings. His new house had two hundred rooms and a chapel in 14th-century style with collegiate pews and an elaborate hammer-beam roof.

In the 1920s it was recuperating from war wounds incurred while occupied by Prussian officers and in 1928 the estate was sold to an Exeter land speculator, but bought back by a member of the family, John Gillies Shields. A neighbour, Lord Howe of Gopsall, suggested the park would be ideal for a motor-racing circuit and in 1930 the now famous race track was opened.

During the Second World War Donington was again requisitioned for prisoners of war. The staff were given just five days to move out furniture, pictures, beds, linen, silver, china, curtains and carpets. The army left Donington in 1956, after seventeen years of occupation. The Hall, which had later been a billet for troops, was repaired and restored, though the chapel, eaten up by dry rot, was left a wreck. The house stood empty until an SOS came from the Hungarian Relief Committee at the time of the 1956 uprising and Donington became a hostel for refugees. Intriguingly Donington had played host to an earlier group of refugees following the French revolution of 1789, amongst whom were the future Charles X and his son; their portraits hung in the house until the sale of 1869 when 550 paintings were sold on the death of the 4th and last Marquess, who had lost his estates gambling on the turf.

Salvation for Donington came in an unexpected way as headquarters of British Midland Airways, for whom the location was conveniently near East Midlands airport.

The Georgian sash-windowed front was transformed by the extravagant use of pepperpot turrets.

GRACE DIEU MANOR   Ashby-de-la-Zouch
Gothic revival house built for patron of Catholicism

THE BUILDING OF GRACE DIEU MANOR in 1833–4 marked the start of a strong Catholic union. On July 25, 1833 Ambrose Lisle March-Phillips, a Catholic convert from an early age, married Laura Mary Clifford at St James's Spanish Place in London. Though his father never really approved of his conversion, Charles March-Phillipps nevertheless settled on Ambrose the manor of Grace Dieu and £1,200 a year.

The picturesque remains of the Priory, founded by Roesia de Verdun in about 1240, survived and the new manor attracted a constant stream of visitors, including the future Cardinal Newman and the 16th Earl of Shrewsbury, the greatest patron of Catholicism in 19th-century England. The March-Phillipps had sixteen children and Laura ran a school for the children of the tenants.

William Railton, the architect of Grace Dieu, designed the house in a Tudor Gothic style with a chapel containing the first rood screen to be erected in England since the Reformation. When A.W. Pugin saw it, it 'was so wonderfully to his taste' that he fell into Phillipps's arms. Pugin later embellished and furnished the chapel, building the Blessed Sacrament Chapel, but the rood screen, lateral altars, painted altar, pulpit and font all went during reordering in the 1960s. Pugin also built a wing in which to accommodate the March-Phillips children. Sir Banister Fletcher added a grand staircase to the house in about 1902 as part of the major conversion work that was executed for the Booth family, who rented Grace Dieu from about 1898 until 1932.

Grace Dieu Manor is today a flourishing Catholic school.

Pugin's chapel on the left adjoins a picturesque tower, complete with bell turret.

ISLAY WALTON MANOR   Castle Donington
Hansome 1700 house of square 'tea-caddy' proportions

THROUGHOUT THE 18TH AND 19TH CENTURIES this handsome house belonged to the London Guild of Bowyers. It had been left to them in 1625 by James Woods Esq, who is referred to in the company's papers as 'our great benefactor'.

Surveys suggest that the house may date from the 1690s and it has the distinctive look of a town house with three tall storeys and a pedimented front door with fanlight. Its chief delight is the very pretty pink brick scattered with occasional burnt headers which are used to form black diamonds, or diapers, between the top-storey windows. In the typical 1700 manner the sash boxes are set flush with the brickwork, not recessed. There is no adornment apart from a simple dentil cornice and a 'toothed' brick course between each floor. A double flight of steps flanked by minature obelisks leads to the door, adding a further flourish and increasing the character of the house.

Towards the end of the 19th century, the house was bought from the Bowyers' Company by Lord Hastings, whose seat, Donington Hall, was nearby. It served as a home for his agent, the colourful John Gilles Shields, who bought it from his employers in 1900 and started the important quarry at Breedon. Shields paid for numerous furnishings and repairs at the parish church and his family continued to live here until 1988.

The house has a three arched coach house and pretty walled garden with espaliered apples and box hedging and pleasant woodland walks.

With a grand flight of steps up to the front door, Islay Walton has the look of a town house.

NORTH LUFFENHAM HALL Oakham
Well-preserved stone house provided with every modern comfort

THE ROMANS HAD AN EXPRESSION FOR IT – *magnum in parvo* – grandeur in miniature. Not that North Luffenham Hall is exactly small but it has a doll's house perfection that makes it seem at once manageable and covetable. The blemishless white stone of the Queen Anne garden front will be love at first sight for almost everyone, but the gabled centrepiece of the entrance front, dating from a century earlier, is a beauty too.

Furthermore, the parkland in front of the house is safeguarded by a family trust so the reassuring distant baaing of sheep will continue to roll up from the meadow to complete the early-evening idyll.

North Luffenham steps straight out of one of those 18th-century bird's-eye views of gentlemen's country seats in which everything has a neat satisfying geometry – with the house surrounded by forecourt, stable court, *parterres*, walled gardens, avenues, impressive hedges, topiary and orchards – all laid out by rule. Yet interestingly, when you look closely neither main front is exactly symmetrical – the Jacobean shaped gable is off centre while the Queen Anne doorcase is to one side. The silhouette is further enlivened by numerous finials and impressively tall stone chimney stacks, single, double, quadruple and even a run of five crowning the whole composition.

The road into the village makes a sharp turn as if to avoid intruding on the privacy of the hall. The entrance is through a pretty arched gateway along a trim avenue of

The earlier gabled wing is visible on the left behind the handsome late 17th-century front.

maples with beautiful variegated leaves. The grass on either side is as closely mown as a golf green. Two greenhouses and a melon house peep over a wall on the right. Handsome gate piers topped by stone cannon balls stand guard at the entrances to the forecourt (stone balls were a sign the owner had a grant of a coat of arms). On one side is a noble buttressed stone barn bearing the date 1555 and on the other a clipped yew the size of a small cottage inset with an arch leading through to the rose garden.

The stable court to the north has more handsome buildings – loose boxes with stalls for hunters and a half-timbered upper storey that brings still more variety to the architecture.

North Luffenham is a house that has grown through the centuries, untouched only by the grandiosity of the Victorians. A house built in 1555 by James Harrington was bought by Simon Digby, who added the gabled front about 1616, while another Simon Digby or his son Kenelm added the doll's house front to the south. After this the house slept for a century and a half – the last Digby wife was left a widow and then the estate was sold to the Earl of Ancaster, who installed a tenant.

Revival came in 1894 when Guy Fenwick married Elsie Robarts and moved into the Hall. It took them some time to buy the freehold but when they did they commissioned the architect Sidney Gampier Parry to enlarge the house. This he did with commendable discretion, adding wings at both ends in banded stone which look as if they have always been there. *Country Life* in 1919 records that the splendid topiary was then just fifteen years old and the intricate sunken garden was also the creation of the Fenwicks: 'The pond was there but it was brought into shape and surrounded with narrow stepped terraces.'

The present owners have taken pride in bringing the house to a still greater degree of luxury – there is a handsome double-height kitchen open to the rafters, a whole wing to lose teenage children or guests in, with bar, barbecue room, billiard room and gym as well as indoor pool and sauna, all within thick stone walls built to contain the most vibrant sound.

The breakfast room beside the kitchen opens out onto the terrace so you can eat out in the sun, or with the door open into the garden, according to the weather. In winter you can retreat into the snuggery off the kitchen.

Part of the appeal of the house is its unpredictability. The large entrance hall has an indoor lobby to keep out the draught. One door opens into a library with large bay window, another leads down five steps into the loveliest room in the house – the panelled Jacobean dining room complete with carved double-decker fireplace. The large drawing room overlooking the garden is divided by a handsome baroque arch while the oak staircase has a handrail as broad as if it were in stone.

Upstairs the delight is to find that every bedroom has a gorgeous view. Several look over the topiary garden to open fields with a windmill on the horizon. Others have a spectacular view of the nearby parish church and its great east window or the leafy entrance court.

Of course, the cost of retaining so many fine Collyweston stone slated roofs may be daunting but this is a house where at every turn you can see a great deal of money has been spent on putting everything into perfect order.

STAUNTON HAROLD HALL Ashby-de-la-Zouch
For years a care home, now bought back by the family who own the estate

THIS COUNTRY HOUSE IS LONG CONSIDERED to be one of the most beautiful in all England. Even the great Sir Nikolaus Pevsner, not a man easily given to superlatives, conceded that 'for position, the house and the chapel are unsurpassed in the country – certainly as far as Englishness is concerned.'

Here is an exquisitely proportioned Georgian house with three show fronts, each more imposing than the last, set amid spreading lawns sloping gently down to a swan-filled lake, and a view out across a large ancient park scattered with noble oaks and limes. Inside, there are handsome, spacious rooms on two floors, all with a superb outlook through large sash windows, and none of the inconvenience of a raised main floor at the top of a grand flight of steps that turn fiendishly slippery in winter.

When I arrived in 2004, this vast mansion, all 32,000 sq ft of it, was generally in excellent condition, with lead-covered roofs that looked good for the next hundred years so long as you took the trouble to keep the gutters clean. Maintenance had been regular, the house was heated throughout, and I saw no sign or smell of damp. Only the odd sash windowsill needed attention, although all would require regular painting.

True, the house had been an institution for half a century, first a Cheshire Home, and since 1989 a Sue Ryder Palliative Care Home. Yet rarely has institutional use been introduced with such a light touch. The colours of rooms and corridors – pale blues, pinks and yellows – were pretty throughout. There was little scuffing of doors or walls, and where partitions had been inserted, obvious care was taken with proportions and mouldings.

The back of the house, though restrained, is impressively proportioned.

Looking down on the house from across the park, the view is long held as unsurpassed.

A glorious church stands on the lawn – at first sight perfectly medieval, all of one period, but in fact begun in 1653 – in the full grimness of the Puritan Commonwealth. The church was handed to the National Trust by Group Captain Leonard Cheshire VC – and remarkably remains the Trust's only historic building in Leicestershire. It is open most days and members of the Trust and the public at large have the right to walk down the front drive, through the splendid baroque gates with corkscrew columns (which also belong to the Trust) and up past the house to the church, which sits on the lawn just 25 yards from the front door.

The back drive runs past the thriving Ferrers Arts Centre established in the stables which last year attracted a staggering 175,000 visitors to its shops and cafes, a division dating back to 1954 when Staunton Harold was put up for auction. The mid-1950s were the years when country house demolitions reached their peak – one every five days in 1955. John Blunt, who runs the Ferrers Arts and Crafts Centre, recalls seeing surveyors pacing the mansion to see if it could be reduced in size and made more convenient for the Ferrers to move back into after the war (when it had been occupied by prisoners of war). Not many auction lots found buyers and in 1955 his father bought the three farms forming the core of the estate. The stables, with stabling for forty horses, two carriage houses, two granaries and a blacksmith's shop, were 'thrown in' – the courtyard was knee-high in weeds and saplings were pushing the slates off the roofs (Leonard Cheshire bought the Hall for £16,000 from the demolition contractors the same year).

The mansion could be sensitively divided into a number of large houses and apartments as the entrepreneur Kit Martin has done with great success at Burley-on-the-Hill and Dingley Hall nearby. There is, however, no prospect of any new building in the grounds – possibly not even of garages – as the National Trust holds covenants ensuring that the stand-alone setting of the house remains inviolate.

Another consideration is the sensitivity of local people. The Cheshire and Ryder Homes were significant local employers. Sue Ryder ran a gift shop and cafe in the magnificent Palladian Library, which gave still more people a reason to visit the house.

The house is listed Grade I and has fine internal features throughout – oak, not mahogany or pine doors in the main rooms, ornate doorcases, Classical cornices, dados and skirtings and all the Georgian shutters. This is emphatically a house where double or secondary glazing should not be allowed – shutters, all working, ensure equivalent heat retention during long winter evenings and some ventilation is clearly good for the house during the daytime.

Anyone on the M1 should consider a detour between junctions 22 and 24 and pause on the Melbourne road where house, chapel and lake stand in perfect harmony in the valley below.

STOCKEN HALL Stretton
Left empty for years while the grounds were used for a prison farm

ONE OF SAVE'S MORE BIZARRE BATTLES centred on Stocken Hall in Leicestershire, which John Harris ascribed to George Portwood, the most prominent of the master masons who had their yards in Stamford in the first half of the 18th century. The house had an exquisite early-Georgian front with giant pilasters, emphatic triple keystones to all the windows and matching Gibbs' surrounds with bracketed stone sills. On the right was a 19th-century Dutch-gabled wing with stone mullioned windows. Behind was a 17th-century wing, built by Samuel Browne, a gentleman of London origin.

In the early 18th century, the estate belonged to the Heathcotes, who lived at nearby Normanton. In 1862 Stocken's sole resident was a gamekeeper but it was let in 1877 to Lord Francis Cecil, second son of Lord Exeter. After his death in 1889, his widow, Edith, remained at Stocken with her second husband, Vice Admiral Tillard, until 1906. She described the May Day festivities on the sunny terrace in front of the old Manor House, with a throng of children carrying banners and long staves. Two well known architectural buffs were also brought up here, Peter and Roger Fleetwood-Hesketh, but the family left the house when it was requisitioned in the Second World War

In the 1950s, Stocken was bought by the Home Office, which turned the outbuildings into a prison farm. The house was repeatedly vandalised and every richly turned banister on the oak stair was stolen. In 1980 a public inquiry was held to consider the Home Office's application to demolish. Such was the opposition that Michael Heseltine and William Whitelaw, the two ministers involved, agreed the house should be put on the market for six months.

When Kit Martin and I met with officials to find out just what was on offer we quickly learnt that a new young-offender's establishment, surrounded by high wire fences, was to be built a few hundred yards away. Though the Home Office owned the whole estate of several hundred acres, officials would not consider the creation of a separate drive for the house or offer more than a pocket handkerchief of land.

They would, we were told, consider parting with 4 acres if the Department of the Environment would rebuild prison farm pigsties, but that would cost £900,000 by the time 20 per cent professional fees had been included. Kit Martin forcefully pointed out that modern pigsties were available directly from the manufacturers and obtained a figure for the best pigsties available in Britain. which came to precisely £57,750 including fitting out and builder's preliminaries.

Needless to say the Home Office stone-walled and offered the house for sale with a shared drive. Not surprisingly, another twenty years passed before restoration was under way with the house finally converted into apartments.

The work was done by a local company, John Smith & Co, and was financed partly by an enabling development of smaller mews houses, set quite discreetly to the rear of the building. The prison farm remains, but the residents otherwise live in grand isolation amid broad open fields, with a very long drive that leads to the A1 and from there to fast connections all over the Midlands.

Stone houses around Stamford are as handsome and well-built as those in the Cotswolds.

LINCOLNSHIRE

ONE DELIGHT OF LINCOLNSHIRE is that even quite modest country houses come with all the trimmings – grand gates, stretch of park, walled garden, stables and coach house. With its exquisite Grade II listed Regency front, Caythorpe Hall, near Grantham, would make a perfect film set for a George Eliot novel.

The house stands at the foot of the great limestone ridge that runs northwards through Lincolnshire, lined all the way with fine houses. In earlier times it was a seat of the great Hussey family, who owned several houses in the area and are commemorated in the nearby village church. Caythorpe Hall was built in 1824–7 for a Colonel G.H. Packe. He used an accomplished Leicester architect called William Parsons, who was active as a road builder and a railway architect. Caythorpe is his most important work, along with those archetypes of Georgian rectitude, the county jail and lunatic asylum.

The entrance front is faced in warm local Ancaster stone, more biscuity in colour than Portland. Parsons showed off his knowledge of Ancient Greek architecture, by then more fashionable than Roman, in the pretty entrance porch. Here the scrolls at

The entrance front has an Ionic portico built in the warm biscuity local Ancaster stone.

The garden front has the the shallowest of central bows.

the top of the Ionic columns at the corners bend outwards, following best archaeological precedent. By 1800 owners had become tired of negotiating grand flights of outside steps up to a front door – they could be treacherously icy in winter – and at Caythorpe there are just three shallow steps.

The east-facing garden front is also extremely refined, faced in the same blemishless stone with the shallowest of bows in the centre and long Regency windows descending to floor level. The sash in the bow is cleverly designed, so when it is raised you can walk straight into the garden without ducking your head. In place of the usual solid wall below the window, wooden shutters fold back to make a doorway. The trick was that it still looks like a window with the slender glazing bars typical of the age.

The paired front doors open into a slightly cramped entrance hall with a fireplace set oddly in the corner, but this is forgotten as you approach one of the finest staircases you can ever hope to see in a house of this size. The doors, unusually, are swing doors covered in faded baize, as if Colonel Packe, thirsty from a day's hunting, was damned if he was going to fiddle with any door handles as he strode in for a warming toddy by the fire.

The stone stair ascends elegantly in three flights with an iron balustrade as intricately detailed as the ornament on a Greek vase. Setting aside the fact that the smooth handrail is a near-irresistible temptation for children to slide down, this is a stair begging for young ladies in high-waisted Empire dresses and puffed sleeves to make the grand descent at a ball. Landing and arched galleries are perfectly placed to survey the throng below. A neat detail on the stair is the pretty chain slung below the handrail. Above, instead of the more usual dome, is a side lit roof light with bands of ornament so crisp that they might be porcelain.

To the right of the hall is a suite of three interlinking reception rooms – all with airy Regency proportions and Grecian detail around the ceilings, a frieze of the palmettes known as acroteria, and a band with a wave motif above. The fireplace in the drawing room is of flawless white Carrara marble, while that in the bowed morning room is in contrasting black-veined marble. The dining room still has the traditional arrangement of both large and small dining tables.

The bedrooms are equally well-proportioned, though I would perhaps be tempted to open a blank window in the main bedroom to give it fine views to the south as well as east.

This is a house for large family gatherings or house parties. Depending on how you count them, there are up to ten bedrooms on the first floor and a further ten in the attic. The attic rooms were originally for servants, although, unusually, every one has a neat little marble fireplace waiting to be brought back into use by a new chatelaine determined that every part of the house should look fresh and smart.

Beneath the house is a series of very well-built brick cellars with shallow Regency vaults that contain extensive wine bins. Two of those cellars have vaults supported on central pillars in an almost monastic manner and are ideal for parties or suppers. Here an interesting detail of domestic archaeology is the small stove that heated the hall above. The brass vent for hot air survives in the hall floor.

Another survivor is a traditional thunderbox with the loo concealed beneath a polished oak bench complete with inset plunge handle. And if you are into provisions, there is a larder on the north front with a full dozen hooks in the ceiling waiting for hams to be cured.

Below: The handsome staircase hall is top lit.
Bottom: The drawing room has tall sash windows.

ELLYS MANOR HOUSE   Ellys
Early Tudor manor left unaltered through years of gentle decline

The stepped gable end to the village street is the most richly treated of all.

ENGLAND ABOUNDS IN DELIGHTFUL, well-preserved timber-framed houses of the late 15th and early 16th centuries. Ellys Manor House is a rarer treat, a handsome early Tudor house beautifully built in white local stone and remarkably little altered in five hundred years.

It was built by Anthony Ellys, a merchant of the Calais Staple at a time when the Staple still retained the monopoly of all English wool exports to the Continent.

His house stands in the village of Great Ponton, and from the front door you have a splendid view of the tower that he added to the parish church, inscribing it with the words: 'Think and thank God of all.' Henry VIII's chronicler, John Leland, observes: 'Elis greatly risen bi merchandise' in his list of the Gentlemen of Kesteven, in the south-west of the county.

Clive Taylor, who works in films, bought the property in the 1980s with his partner, Violet Hamilton, curator of the Wilson Centre for Photography in London. 'We were looking for a Methodist chapel or village school to convert, anywhere within a 100-mile radius of London,' he says. 'When we saw the ad in *Country Life* we leapt straight into the car. It was perfect: the garden overgrown, no central heating.'

In true *Sleeping Beauty* style the house had entered a long decline through the 18th and 19th centuries. From 1923 until it was sold in the 1980s it was used as a rectory.

Taylor and Hamilton have done extensive research on the house and attribute it to Anthony Ellys's brother, Thomas, also a merchant of the Calais Staple. Either way the manor is powerful witness to the splendour of early Tudor England, when merchants as well as courtiers and landowners could live in splendidly decorated, impressively proportioned houses.

Intriguingly, the house presents four quite different faces to the world. The east front looking over the village street is the showpiece, with stepped gables reminiscent of Flanders, where so much English wool was sent. The windows are centrally placed with an emphatic double hood mould over the first-floor window and a charming two-light window at the top.

The north entrance front has tall, deep-set mullioned windows. There is a projecting stair of the type that frequently survives in Scotland and northern France. The elaborately carved corbel survives, although the stair turret has been reduced in height and given a sloping roof.

The front has a fine series of five deep-set mullioned windows with shallow Tudor arches, all with hood moulds to throw off the rain. Taylor quips that the house is really no more 'than a two-up, two-down with a lean-to and staircase' but, as he points out, you don't have to stoop in this medieval manor. The ceilings on both floors are 14 ft high and a sunken stone door in one wall suggests that the ground-floor level was originally even lower, so the ceilings in the hall and parlour could have been as high as 20 ft.

On the ground floor a corridor has been introduced along the north side, but the original ceiling beams continue straight across with traces of early paint. Both the hall and parlour have magnificent stone fireplaces that are set back-to-back in a single huge chimney stack. They have been restored and rebuilt by John Ford, who specialises in reconstructing old fireplaces using lime mortar and carefully chosen materials.

The stair to the first floor is not the stone spiral that might be expected but instead is made of wood, with generous steps that are presumably 17th-century. Taylor points to one step an inch higher than the others. 'A sword step designed to trip an assailant pursuing the occupant to the upper floor,' he says. But the marvel of the house is the extensive cycle of medieval wall paintings that were uncovered in the main bedroom in the 1930s and which rise from floor to ceiling.

It was not until the 1950s, however, that yet further removal of whitewash indicated the potential extent of the paintings. Because no funds were available, Dr Clive Rouse, an expert on wall paintings, suggested that the rector should do the work himself, gave him a lesson on how to do it, and now an almost complete scheme covering three walls has been revealed.

As a prosperous wool merchant, Ellys presumably could have chosen Flanders tapestries or painted wallcloths, but wall paintings were fashionable and considerably cheaper. As with contemporary tapestries, the paintings depict views out through columns into a verdant landscape filled with foliage, large flowers, fruit and seed heads, as well as a peacock and a deer.

Left: The staircase towers have corbelled corners.
Right: From the church spire you can see down into the circular drive.

HARRINGTON   Spilsby
Set in ravishing rose gardens, the house was restored after a savage fire in 1991

WARM PINK BRICK AND LONG rows of sash windows give Harrington an immediate and engaging sense of domesticity. On the ground floor the sills of the sashes almost touch the ground. Above, they press against the white-bracketed cornice. There is almost as much window as wall.

An engagingly eccentric touch is added by the narrow three-storey porch with Elizabethan diaper (trellis pattern) brickwork clearly visible on its cheeks. This too has sash windows inserted to match the long front.

When I wrote about Harrington in *Country Life* in 1974 it belonged to the Tory MP Sir John Maitland, whose wife had created a beautiful rose garden within a frame of low garden walls and high hedges and an enclosing backdrop of trees protecting the house from the wind.

After a fire in November 1991 destroyed much of the interior, the house was painstakingly restored over five years by the owner, David Price, who employed architect Guy Taylor to work alongside designer Christopher Nevile, adapting the

The long, late 17th-century ranges are entered through an Elizabethan porch.

house to modern requirements and at the same time reviving something of it's pre-fire atmosphere.

Harrington is mentioned in the Domesday Book and in the 13th and 14th centuries the manor was held by the de Harringtons. John de Harrington was a canon of Lincoln Cathedral and in 1346 obtained permission to found a chantry with two priests to say prayers in perpetuity for his soul. In the 14th century the manor passed by marriage to the de Copledykes with whom it remained until the death in 1585 of John Copledyke, 'the last and best of his race' according to the florid monument in the

The panelled baroque hall is divided by a broad elliptical arch.

church. It was probably his great grandfather who built the Tudor house if the tradition of a moulded jamb, dated 1535 but no longer visible, is correct.

In 1673 the estate was bought by Vincent Amcotts. He added a weathervane dated 1678 and the two-storey ranges on either side of the porch. Though carefully balanced, they are not symmetrical. Vertically sliding sash windows were first introduced in the late 1670s. A late 17th-century painting shows that Belton Hall in Lincolnshire, built in the mid 1680s, had them from the beginning – as opposed to the wooden mullion and transom in the form of a cross that were used with the earliest classically proportioned windows in England.

Sash boxes were initially set flush with the brickwork as they are here, giving the facade a much brighter look thanks to the prominent white paint. Here, as so often, thinner glazing bars were introduced in the second half of the 18th century. Rather odder are the tall flat pilasters on the porch in the so-called Artisan Mannerist style of the mid 17th century.

The splendid baroque hall offers clear evidence that the Amcotts retained more of the Tudor house than the porch as cross-pattern Tudor beams have clearly been concealed within Classical mouldings. Great halls open to the roof went out of fashion in the first half of the 16th century, replaced as here by a great chamber above. It is likely that the traditional screen remained at the entrance end as a dramatic baroque arch has been introduced in exactly the place where the screen would have stood. Such arches are a frequent feature of early 18th-century houses but this is unusually wide. The panelling is evidently the work of an accomplished master carpenter keen to show off his knowledge of correct Classical detail with a full Roman Doric triglyph frieze and little triangular 'guttae' above. This is supported by fluted pilasters on either side of the fireplace and quirky quarter columns in the corners.

Harrington has a splendid baroque stair richly carved in polished oak with three corkscrew balusters to each step and the added flourish of a swept-up handrail at the corners. The stairs ascend round three sides. On the fourth, the landing is visible through pairs of deep arches – with emphatic detail that is suggestive of the influence of Vanbrugh's work at Grimsthorpe in Lincolnshire. Intriguingly there is also work attributed to Vanbrugh at nearby Somersby Hall, which has a comparable elliptical arch.

On the death of Charles Amcotts in 1777 the estate passed to his niece who had married Sir John Ingilby of Ripley Castle. They appear to have let the house out. One of the tenants, Admiral Eden, had a ward named Rosa Baring, with whom the poet Tennyson fell in love. She is said to be the inspiration for his famous poem 'Come into the garden, Maud'.

Harrington was later the home of two masters of foxhounds, Edward Preston Rawnsley and then Major Thomas Jessop, who bought the property in 1919. At the start of the 20th century the east wing, the oldest part of the house, was demolished.

Lincolnshire is often thought of as flat fenland, but Harrington stands in the gentle hills of the Lincolnshire wolds, which remain gloriously remote and unspoiled.

NORTON PLACE · Market Rasen
Elegant 18th-century house by the prolific John Carr of York

FASHIONS MOVED FAST in the 18th century. First baroque stunned the eye. Then rococo delighted it. Next followed the Adam Brothers, who brought ravishing colour and a new delicacy in ornament. Norton Place is a perfect expression of this new refinement. Its beauty depends on simplicity and proportion, on crispness of detail and elegance of line. Baroque masonry was monumental and massive. Here the emphasis is on lightness. The cornice is slight, given just sufficient emphasis by the carefully chiselled dentils, while the parapet above is pierced by balustrades with the pediment rising gracefully through it. Instead of a grand portico rising full height,

The graceful entrance front has an unusually broad central pediment.

there is a modest porch with pretty Venetian window above. This porch was added by Lewis Vulliamy for Sir Montague Cholmeley, Bt, in 1830.

The *piano nobile* or raised main floor favoured by the first generation of 18th-century Palladians has been replaced by two even storeys of windows as found in Charles II houses a hundred years earlier and there are just four steps up to the door. Norton's architect was the prolific John Carr of York, who began designing pure Palladian villas but then quickly mastered the Adam style.

His patron was John Harrison MP, a noted agricultural improver. Arthur Young, the great agriculturalist, wrote, 'What is now Norton Place was twenty-three years ago an open field, under the barbarity of the commonfield system: there is now an excellent house, with offices complete, a large lawn, a water half a mile long, a very handsome bridge over it; a garden walled, with the appurtenaces, and shrubberies planted with taste, and kept in beautiful order, and the whole surrounded with flourishing plantations. There is on the whole, turn which way you will, a finished air, it is complete, and an extraordinary place for twenty-two years to have effected.'

Harrison, born in 1738, had inherited the estate from his father, John, and been educated at Eton and Trinity before being called to the Middle Temple in 1766. He married a local girl, Catherine, the daughter of the Rev. Robert Pinder of Owston Hall, also in Lincolnshire, and had three daughters. Succeeding his father in 1768, he rebuilt the house eight years later. Like many Georgian country-house owners, he had a seat in Parliament, being returned unopposed for Grimsby in 1780 and then for Thetford in 1796. The *English Chronicle* of 1781 describes him as 'a young man of genteel though not ample fortune' and 'the first of his family who ever aspired to the high honour of a British legislator'.

Inside, a modest entrance hall opens into an oval staircase hall of breath-stealing elegance. The stone steps rise in a continuous sweep to the first-floor landing, which continues the curve. The elegance is increased by the unbroken sweep of the mahogany handrail and the rippling effect of the slender wrought-iron balustrade, strengthened only at the very top and bottom by a vertical strut. These cantilever stairs are virtuoso pieces of construction. Each step is held in place by the weight of the walls bearing down on it but much of the load is carried down from one step to another to the stone floor of the hall. The treatment of the walls is strongly architectural with niches and arcades, with light descending from a dome resting directly on the walls. The floor is laid in stone with circles of black slate rather than the usual diamonds at the corners.

The plan of Norton is enlivened by canted or three-sided bays on the flanks of the house. Carr took advantage of these to create octagonal rooms on either side of the staircase. One of these is the dining room where bold architectural niches are set in the cross walls to provide space for side tables. The drawing room has an exquisite Adamesque ceiling with garlands forming pretty geometric patterns around a bold oval band of interlacing ornament.

Carr also designed a handsome pair of gate lodges which date from 1776, as well as a handsome three-arch Classical bridge over the lake, which for many years has been in poor repair, its balustrades crumbling and vandalised.

REVESBY ABBEY   Horncastle

Spirited essay in Jacobean revival style by the Scottish architect William Burn

REVESBY ABBEY WAS DESIGNED in 1844 by William Burn, the prolific Scottish country house architect, for James Banks Stanhope. By 1940, Burn, born in Edinburgh in 1789, had already designed or remodelled over ninety houses, as well as thirty churches and twenty-five public buildings. His success was due in considerable part to his skilful planning, particularly in accommodating large households of servants and guests.

Revesby is a delicious essay in Jacobethan style with shaped gables, oriels and spiralling chimneys all beautifully executed in crisp local stone. But in 1963, Mrs Lee, who had inherited the estate from her brother, built herself a neo-Georgian house barely 100 yards away. Revesby stood empty and unwanted for over ten years, and by 1976 the local council was considering an application to demolish.

SAVE and others vigorously opposed the application and it was refused following a public inquiry in 1977, but the house still remained empty. Four years later the local planning committee rejected a recommendation from their officers to serve a repairs order and instead resolved to invite the owner to apply again for permission to demolish.

Kit Martin and I then went to draw up alternative plans for our book *The Country House: To Be or Not To Be*. The proposal was to make nine apartments within the

Revesby has a lively Jacobethan front with richly-shaped gables and dormers, and a forest of chimneys.

The entrance porch has elaborately carved neo-Jacobean detail.

main body of the house, approached through the main entrance and using the grand stair hall. Two further houses, each consisting of three storeys, would be created in the wing, with their own separate entrance. The stable block would be converted into six cottages, each making use of existing entrances.

Stalemate continued, but in 1990 English Heritage served a repairs notice and sent in contractors to carry out extensive repairs to the roof to stop further deterioration. When these were complete, they sought to recover the cost by selling the property, but Revesby remained empty and the brand new lead on the roof was stolen, restarting the cycle of decay.

The house was then sold and resold at auction, invariably to speculators who had never seen the place and thought it looked a snip for fifty grand, only to realise the problems and move on. Alas, it was at this time that important interior features such as chimney pieces vanished from the house. The battle was kept alive by a building preservation trust set up by local people in 1997 to take on the house, energetically run by Jean Burton.

Revesby's luck changed dramatically a few years later when the house was bought by a builder from Derbyshire who is at last tackling the decay. Jean Burton told me, 'The house is now weathertight and they have been carrying out like-for-like repairs. Rotten floors are being replaced, all excellent work.' There is now the prospect, unthinkable for more than thirty years, that Revesby will be a family house once again. Meanwhile Jean Burton has diverted her energies to starting a new centre in nearby Horncastle exploring the intriguing links between Revesby, Australia and the famous Sir Joseph Banks.

The Revesby estate had been bought in 1714 by Banks's great grandfather. Banks himself, born in 1843, accompanied Captain Cook on his famous voyage to Australia, New Zealand and the Pacific, bringing back an extraordinary collection of plant specimens. At Revesby, Banks planted extensively in the grounds and woods.

Following his death without children in 1820, Revesby passed to the Stanhope family. James Banks Stanhope began rebuilding the house just two years after he inherited the estate in 1842. When Richard Stanhope was killed in 1916 on the Somme, the estate passed to his widow who remarried and had two children. When her son was killed while flying a Spitfire in 1942 the estate passed to his sister, Mrs Anne Lee.

THORPE TILNEY HALL   Thorpe Tilney
1718 house left almost roofless in 1945

COUNTRY HOUSE OPERA HAS BECOME a major feature of the summer season. It was born in the Pavilion at Thorpe Tilney, designed for Freddie Stockdale by the accomplished Yorkshire architect Francis Johnson. Freddie Stockdale's company takes its name, Pavilion Opera, from this delightful garden building and gave its first performances here – of Mozart's *Cosi Fan Tutte* produced by Christopher Newell – during the summer of 1981. Since then the company has travelled to country houses all over Britain and beyond. The pavilion is on a square plan designed for opera in the round with the audience on all sides giving performances an exceptional intimacy.

Thorpe Tilney Hall stands handsomely on a country road, set well back and seen across a broad stretch of lawn with the stable ranges on one side. Dating from 1740, it is built of an attractive brick, the colour of pomegranates. On both sides flourishes are provided by a few satisfying Palladian details – a Venetian door with a fanlight and half-glazed door, a Diocletian or semi-circular window in the pediment and twin Venetian windows on the entrance front. There are dormers behind the parapet with sashes and small segmental pediments. On the garden side, a splendid avenue strides out into the landscape, prolonging the main axis.

After being struck by lightning in 1718, the house is said to have been rebuilt by the Whichcotes of Aswardy as a dower house or a home for a younger son. It was bought in 1945 in an almost roofless state by a Mr Rothery, who had made large sums from building works in the London docks during the war. He had stopped here for a picnic during the village fete, decided to buy the house on an impulse and meticulously restored it, buying back additional land to improve its setting.

Thorpe is a delightful example of a modest Georgian house, with stables built in matching brick.

NORFOLK

BRECKLES HALL IS IN A miraculous
state of preservation. The mellow red
brick is perfectly matched by the clay roof
tiles, both of which have a sprinkling of
lighter and darker hues. The long garden
front has seven gables inset with three
floors of stone-mullioned windows. By
contrast the grand bay window at the
south end has much taller windows.

There is a series of large walled gardens,
with battlemented tops stepped up over
the archways. At the back of the house a
300-yard-long moat leads into a light
woodland with streams and snowdrops.

*The house is built of the mellow red brick typical of
Elizabethan houses in Norfolk.*

The house was built in 1583 by Francis
Wodehouse, whose ancestor acquired the property in 1469. The entrance front was
built on an Elizabethan E-plan and the perfectly matching two-storey porch was
added in about 1900 by the architect Detmar Blow. In 1909 Blow added an office
wing, whose brickwork and mullions also blend flawlessly with the old. In 1910
Breckles was sold to Edwin Montagu, who commissioned Lutyens to do alterations
and work on the gardens at Breckles in 1918.

The Second World War added further interesting touches – shell-pattern decorations
done by children evacuated from coastal areas and a remarkable mural of Bacchus in
the hall by the artist Rex Whistler, shortly before he was killed in Normandy.

The 72-ft long great hall runs the length of the entrance front and there are two
good south-facing living rooms with early 18th-century panelling. Between them
is a ravishing Elizabethan staircase, rising in long straight flights, not the short flights
common in the 16th century. The 7-ft long treads, each formed of a single piece of
oak, match the silvery woodwork on the walls. The spiral stairs threading through
the building are also all of wood, each a little marvel of ingenious construction.

Woodwork and panelling are everywhere. Broad ancient floorboards survive in
numerous rooms and, within the brick shell, much of the structure is timber-framed
with white plaster infill making the interiors unusually bright.

The attic has been partitioned for use by servants but all the windows are identical,
with original leadwork and matching handles suggesting that here there was once
one of the long galleries often found at the top of Elizabethan houses.

THE BROAD HOUSE   Wroxham
Early 18th-century house intriguingly extended in the 1950s

THE BROAD HOUSE STANDS on the large estate of Wroxham Hall, the seat of the Traffords. The handsome Queen Anne front is built entirely of brick, without the stone trim so often used to create emphasis at the corners and around the door and windows. This creates a simultaneous sense of harmony and warmth.

In the 1950s, when demolitions of country houses reached their post-war peak, the family decided to demolish Wroxham Hall and move to Broad House, so called because it sits on the edge of the Broad just a few miles east of Norwich. The remodelling of Broad House is an interesting example of a family scaling down but staying warm, comfortable and stylish. Extensive accommodation was provided by red-brick sash-windowed wings and a new entrance court was created to the west with space for cars to park. A flourish is provided by twin arches in the corridor leading to the study, drawing room and a little sitting room that enjoys the afternoon sun. In the process, the whole interior of the 1700 house was redone – only the timbers in the attic seem original. The marble fireplaces are all on the reduced scale of the 1950s but each room has its own handsome feature – a pair of glass-fronted cabinets set into arches on either side of the dining room fireplace, a glass-fronted bookcase above the desk in Mr Trafford's study.

The staircase has a typical Queen Anne swooped handrail but the neat compact proportions of the post war years. Upstairs is a very chic dressing room with swan tops over the window and mirror. Another amusing detail is a lattice panel door opening into shallow lockable medicine cupboard.

The servants' realm was clearly designed for a married couple as well as a daily or two. Curiously, the grand breakfast room is here, opening onto the garden through French windows. In the adjoining ballroom wing is a miniature but still imposing Imperial stair, whose swirls at the base are decidedly large but still a neat piece of work. They lead to an upstairs party room, complete with changing room, used for family theatricals.

Sold in 2006, Broad House is now being remodelled to become a chic boutique hotel.

The long low front looks down to the Broads.

BYLAUGH HALL   Foulsham
1850s house built to the designs of Charles Barry Junior

BYLAUGH, OR BEELA AS IT IS PRONOUNCED, was a victim of a strip job carried out not long after the house was derequisitioned in 1945. The lead was taken from the roof and all the saleable fittings removed. Not surprisingly the damp got in and the roof collapsed, taking the floors with it. Self-seeded saplings created a wood round the house, which could only be glimpsed through a tall set of railings. The shell remained remarkably poignant with the mullions silhouetted against the sky and the handsome pedimented dormer windows perched perilously on the parapet without any support from behind.

The hall had been built in 1850–52 to the designs of Charles Barry Junior and R.R. Banks for the trustees of Sir John Lombe. W.A. Nesfield laid out the grounds. When I visited the house in 1991 the owners, who lived in the stable courtyard, were seeking permission to build a new house at the end of the drive. This was refused and Bylaugh continued to rot until, remarkably, it was bought by Stephen Vince, who had plans to turn it into an hotel. He still remembers his first visit to Bylaugh Hall as a small boy in the early fifties. He came across it on a walk with his father, who farmed nearby. 'There was a builder peeling all the ornaments off the roof. We asked what he was doing, and he stared at us and said if we didn't leave, he might shoot our legs off.'

Bylaugh now stands gloriously restored with newly cleaned stonework showing off the richly carved Jacobethan ornament to dazzling effect. The handsome Classical orangery is in regular use for weddings and the house, like Lawton Hall in Cheshire, offers an inspiring example providing hope for even the most long-abandoned roofless shell.

Long a forlorn ruined shell, it has recently been fully restored.

DUNHAM LODGE
Little Dunham
Georgian box offering the ultimate in tranquillity and seclusion

WHEN I ARRIVED AT DUNHAM LODGE on a balmy summer day in 2006, almost nothing had changed since war hero Brigadier Peter Barclay went to live there in 1959, whether the apple green and pink walls of the drawing room or the octagonal pedestal basins in the bathrooms. In January 1940, as Captain Barclay of the Royal Norfolk Regiment, he won the first Military Cross of the Second World War, awarded to him on the spot after he took several German soldiers prisoner on a patrol near the Franco-German frontier.

From the roof of Dunham Lodge it is said you can see the spires of Norwich and Ely Cathedrals as well as the shipping in King's Lynn harbour. The views from the upper windows across the flat expanse of Norfolk fields and woods are like those in the film of L.P. Hartley's *The Go-Between*, filmed nearby at Melton Constable.

Twin curving flights lead to a front door at first-floor level, raised over a ground floor with low ceilings for winter warmth. Here there is a study and sitting room and large servants' hall used for shooting lunches.

Dunham is as neat as a tea caddy, with twin curving flights leading to an elevated front door'

The main front of Dunham is the archetypal Georgian doll's house. What makes it different is the low service wing at the back. Though built in the same warm red brick, it is less than half the height of the main block. At the back it opens into a delightful walled court perfect for *alfresco* meals in summer.

Inside, the world behind the proverbial green baize door was unchanged. There was a pantry and walk-in larder ('the dairy') which stays cool on the hottest day. Beyond, the household gathered for tea in the large laundry room. The wine cellar under the main stairs retained its Georgian white-painted brick wine bins.

The full-height Georgian bow on the north is a puzzle. It is clearly a later addition as there is a break in the brickwork and the courses do not line up. Yet the brick is otherwise a perfect match, suggesting it must have been added very soon after the house was built.

The front door opens into a hall with an inner fanlight over the stairs that is large enough to have come from a grand London house. It sits on scrolly, rather Victorian brackets, suggesting it is a later addition.

According to White's 1845 *Directory of Norfolk*, the Georgian house was erected in 1783 by Edward Parry Esquire, who had bought the manor and 680 acres for £11,500 the year before. Rainwater heads of 1785 marked its completion. Inside, the main rooms have lofty Georgian proportions with the original sash windows retaining their slender glazing bars. There are Adamesque fireplaces in white and coloured marbles and the main drawing room has a screen of the tall slender Ionic columns favoured by Adam, complete with little palm fronds below the capitals. The stone staircase is elegantly cantilevered from the walls with S-scrolls between the iron banisters and a pretty fan motif at the bottom rather than the more usual ivory stud.

Fine polished mahogany doors are a familiar feature in houses of this date but here they were not hung on the usual hinges but turned on iron pivots concealed within the rounded end, making a perfect snug fit. The Dining Room looked out through the arch-headed windows of the bow, and had the distinctive arrangement of large and small dining tables still found in very traditional houses.

With the craze for natural landscaping in the late 18th century, formal gardens were swept away and Dunham Lodge is one of those houses where the walled garden – for flowers, fruit and vegetables – is some way from the house, wholly concealed in a small wood. In shape it is a perfect half moon with the curved wall facing south to enjoy maximum sun. Only recently it was choked in undergrowth but it was possible to stand back and admire the pretty gothic garden lodge with pointed windows and quatrefoils – begging to be turned into a summer retreat. The 250-acre estate also contains an obelisk erected in 1814 to commemorate peace and Admiral Nelson, who was born at Burnham Thorpe to the north.

The stables are another period piece with seven arches each containing a semi-circular 'Diocletian' window. Inside there are loose boxes with spherical hayracks, shaped brackets for saddles, long wooden pegs for the collars of driving horses, shorter pegs for bridles, and hooks descending from the ceiling for putting tack on to clean. Nearby a woodland walk leads to a substantial stretch of medieval moat concealed among laurels.

ELSING HALL   Dereham
15th-century manor restored with flair by the young Thomas Jeckell

THE SPLENDOUR THAT IS ELSING is embodied above all in a famous brass commemorating the builder of the hall and the parish church. Both were built by Sir Hugh Hastings, who rose to fame and wealth in the early stages of the Hundred Years' War. When he died in his thirties, just before the fall of Calais, the church, which is claimed to have the widest nave of any parish church in England, was complete. His brass, set in the chancel floor, is enriched with gilding, enamelling and coloured glass. He is flanked by the three commanders under whom he served, Edward III and the Earls of Lancaster and Pembroke.

His original house, built in the 14th century, was encircled by a gatehouse, towers and precinct wall set in a D-shaped moat, which broadens out on the south side to form a small lake. This was long thought to be a 19th-century embellishment but Anthony Emery, an expert on medieval great houses, says, 'We are finding far too many of these medieval moats broadening out on one side for it to be coincidence.' The precinct walls have long gone, though there are remains of the gatehouse towers with 4 ft thick walls as well as a piece of curtain wall 5 ft thick.

Almost a hundred years later, the hall was rebuilt as a typical 15th-century manor house by John Hastings, who inherited in 1437 and died forty years later. The work was probably done soon after his marriage to Anne Morley as the arms of Hastings impaling Morley, are carved in the arch of the porch. The new house had a wide great hall open to the roof timbers with a tall oriel window at the dais end. The screens passage has long gone but a trio of arches leading to pantry, kitchen and scullery survive at the west end. At the east end was a solar, and beyond it a chapel, now entered only from outside.

Tudor cupolas frame the view of the entrance front.

Built of knapped flint, the house has a full complement of elaborate brick chimneys.

In 1540, Elsing passed to the Browne family, who continued here for four centuries. Early 19th-century watercolours in the Norwich Castle Museum show the hall retained its 15th-century character through Georgian times, though many windows were changed to sashes. The present enchanting appearance of the house stems from a remarkable restoration by the young Thomas Jeckell (he later changed into Jekyll). A folio volume specifying the works and including his colour drawings remained in the house.

Today, the entrance front and ends of the house are faced in beautifully squared and knapped flints, so pristine in condition that one is tempted to think they are all his work, but in his description he says he found the house already faced in flint. Quite different is the south front, with timber-framed wings infilled with pretty herringbone brickwork. Here the barge-boarded gables have crow-stepping below rather than above. They are Jeckell's work as much as the richly ornamented 'barley-sugar chimneys' supplied by the nearby Costessey brickworks.

The need in the 19th century was to provide a first-floor link between the rooms on either side of the great hall. Jeckell did this by building a new south front containing a gallery and a second oriel inset with a staircase, all beautifully executed externally in stone.

The charm of his work is that it has none of the high-minded seriousness of some mid 19th-century Gothic Revival. His craftsmanship is excellent, all done with the lightest touch, which makes Elsing one of the prettiest examples of 19th-century gothic.

Among many delicate features is the slender lead window tracery in the library, on a pattern of interlocking octagons. Since 1984, another layer of romantic beauty has been added by David and Shirley Cargill, who have embellished both house and garden with a careful artistic eye. The garden, at its best when the roses are out, is in

The stair in the great hall descends from the gallery above.

the Vita Sackville-West mould, gloriously abundant yet with good bones. The outside of the moat provides a new, ravishingly framed view of the hall every few yards. This is a plantswoman's garden in which even the honeysuckles are rare exotics and the bark of the silver birches and mahogany-barked maple are scrubbed with Fairy Liquid until they look like choice veneers. Brilliant, too, is the formal garden, with sixty-four squared and tapering yews set on a carpet of lavender and yellow pom-poms.

Jeckells' barge-boarded gables on the garden front can clearly be seen from across the moat.

Inside, much of the panelling has been painted by John Sutcliffe, one of the most sophisticated decorative painters at work today. Best of all is the painted floor in the dining room. Shirley Cargill says forcefully, 'The delight of this house is that nobody has ever had enough money to wreck it.'

It is evident nonetheless at every turn how much fun she and her husband have had in embellishing it, most recently the stable block where a second double-height great hall has been created with a large billiard table while the stalls for the horses have been retained, creating a perfectly secure place for children to be left to play. Lost in the winding lanes between East Dereham and Norwich, Elsing offers the deep peace of the Norfolk countryside, the perfect place for family life at its very best.

GILLINGHAM HALL   Beccles
Elizabethan house that has grown unselfconsciously through the ages

LOOK AT THE FOUR FRONTS of Gillingham Hall and you would hardly know they belong to the same building. This is a house that has grown through the centuries. The approach is quintessential old England, with the parish church standing prominently by the drive and a ruined church on the other. Beyond, the hall stands amid spreading lawns shaded by noble plane trees said to be the largest in England.

The entrance front has an easy welcoming domesticity with just two steps up to the front door and two even rows of Georgian sash windows. Yet with its tall projecting centre and ends this looks like a typical Elizabethan E-plan, complete with urns and finials on the gables. Yet when you look more closely at what appears to be pale Norfolk brick, it is evident that the whole house was once rendered to give it a unified and fashionable Regency look. This was so effective that Gillingham Hall is described as being of white brick in White's *Directory of Norfolk* in 1845. Today the render is flaking away to reveal strong orangey-red bricks but the window heads are set in narrow putty joints and it looks like a complete mid 18th-century refacing. Robin Bramley, the 17th member of his family to have owned Gillingham, who sold it five years ago and still owns the surrounding estate, says, 'I have old views that show the gabled ends as being slightly uneven.' This suggests a further reworking of the entrance front in the 1820s to make the ends matching in size.

The other intriguing feature is the tall tower with leaded dome and cupola, echoing those at nearby Stiffkey Old Hall, built by Sir Nathaniel Bacon in 1578. The south front looks out over a lake dotted with peninsulas and islands by Robin Bramley in 1985, with the tower of Beccles church in the distance. Here a bay window sits like an ugly duckling beneath a gable. Next to it is a trim brick block, three windows wide with very tall sashes

The house looks out over a lake dotted with islands and peninsulas.

The entrance front is filled by large sashes with the 1578 stair tower rising behind.

on the ground floor, the sign of a grand room within. All this is shown in a sketch in John Claudius Loudon's 1826 *Encyclopaedia of Gardening* complete with conservatories at both ends. Loudon also produced plans for the garden.

The east front is an engaging composition in which hardly one window matches another. There are two tall arched windows, one stepped above the other, which clearly light a grand early-Georgian stair, then a two-stage rocket-like tower with sash windows below and leaded lights above, while on the right are big arch-headed windows. These started life as lunettes lighting the kitchen, set high so the servants did not look into the garden, but have since been transformed into French windows. The north front is different again with black glazed pantiles.

The inside of the house is equally unpredictable. The stone-flagged hall has little squares of black marble used to create a diagonal pattern. This leads to the grand baroque stair with swept-up handrails, corkscrew balusters and carved ends to each tread and smart French parquet on the half landings. The stair was probably built for the 5th baronet, MP for Thetford ,who died in 1738 and was known as Gillingham Sir Edmund to distinguish him from his namesake at Garboldisham.

The stair opens into the lofty great room and the next-door morning room leads on to a library with a gents' lavatory which, unusually, has clear glass panels in the door reflecting the fact that it was until recently a writing room.

The rambling service wing beyond the proverbial green baize door – though here the door is faced in neatly studded leather – is full of pantries and laundry rooms with deep Belfast sinks, and is also home to a handsome fitted gunroom with mahogany cupboards and billiard room beyond.

Upstairs the main bedroom set high over the great room is reached by its own private flight of steps. Next to it is a chapel built by the Hon. Edward Kenyon. There are ample bedrooms with bathrooms in an early example of a bathroom extension of 1900 date. These retain original Edwardian white-glazed tiles on a brickwork pattern. In one, twin baths stand endearingly side by side. The stair tower retains its original woodwork with broad elm boards and a tight ascent towards the top, providing views of gutters and gullies.

THE MANOR HOUSE — Great Snoring
Tudor manor of c.1525 built for Sir John Shelton

TUDOR ARCHITECTURE IN NORFOLK has a vocabulary of its own, almost as rich as Scottish Baronial. This manor house, dating from *c*.1525, was built for Sir John Shelton in characteristic red brick with terracotta friezes on each storey with the monograms 'IHC' and 'MR'. The house's most engaging features are the polygonal corner turrets with blind gothic tracery. This is a wonderful example of the exuberant festive quality of early Tudor architecture. Terracotta ornament is normally associated with grand Tudor houses like Sutton Place in Surrey, but here elaborate enrichment is applied to quite a modest house with frieze bands over both ground- and first-floor windows.

The chimneys rising from the tops of the gables rise from stacks that are corbelled out of the wall and look almost like giant shields. Immediately below are perfect examples of Tudor windows with shallow arched heads and hood moulds to throw off rain water. A matching two-storey wing with a trio of chimney stacks was added in 1840. The manor was sold *c*.1611 by Sir John Shelton to Thomas Richardson (subsequently chief justice) and later served for a long period as a rectory. In 1978 it took on a new role as a rather grand bed and breakfast with six double bedrooms and sleeping up to 16 when booked for parties. In 2005 it came on the market and is now being elegantly transformed back into a delightfully unusual private house.

The house has been built with a wealth of intricate terracotta ornament.

GUNTON HALL   Hanworth

Vast decayed 18th- and 19th-century mansion beyond hope until acquired by Kit Martin

GUNTON IS A COUNTRY HOUSE on the grand scale. The main lodge is visible as soon as you turn off the road from Norwich, but after a straight run of a thousand yards the public highway sweeps deferentially to the right, never to glimpse the house. Once through the entrance arch and the belt of encircling woodland that shelters the whole estate from the outside world, the 1,800-acre park begins. A great expanse of lake opens up on the right, there is a glimpse of another still larger lake on the left, and the house itself, a Palladian villa of perfect proportions, is soon in view, looking down a long axial avenue and protected from the north by a looming mass of trees.

Gunton is built of the characteristic pale oatmeal Norfolk brick, which turns almost gold in strong sunlight. What is unusual is that the main front now looks out onto the garden, fronted by an elegant colonnade linking two pavilions.

Kit and Sally Martin first came here in 1979. They had just been to look at Melton Constable and had spotted Gunton and its huge expanse of park on

One Regency bow has been left in its gutted state while the rest of the building has been restored.

the one inch Ordnance Survey. Having just completed work at Dingley in Northamptonshire they were, says Martin, seeking a larger challenge, 'a really dramatic house in a completely unspoilt setting. No matter how derelict.'

Gunton was empty. Whole wings had evidently been shut off for years. Furniture had been left in place, whether the roof was leaking or not. In the stables the roofs had collapsed and the beds for the grooms were buried in the rubble. The owner, the Hon. Doris Harbord, who had retreated into the one habitable wing, had recently died, and no heirs had wanted to move in.

Martin wrote to the agents saying if they were ever interested in selling could they let him know. The reply came by return of post. 'What made it really attractive was this. We could buy the whole core of a major Georgian estate. House, stables, offices,

Overleaf: The Palladian centre is complete with colonnade and pavilions.

The kitchen pavilion looks out over the grounds to the lake.

huge walled gardens, pleasure grounds, shrubberies and woodland walks and rides, a small stretch of the park and estate buildings such as the lodges.'

The Palladian house, dating from 1742, was designed by Matthew Brettingham for Sir William Harbord. It had been gutted by fire in 1882 while let to a Mr Mundy of Shopley Hall, Derbyshire who each year paid a large sum for the shooting. Martin continues, 'As a result there were no really grand State Rooms. Instead we were able to make just four substantial houses in the mansion, each looking out in a different direction over its own private garden.'

Behind the Brettingham house, huge wings had been progressively thrown out. According to the memoirs of the 3rd Baron Suffield, 'The first Lord Suffield found Gunton one of the small gentleman's residences of the day and set apart £40,000 for the improvement of his residence. James Wyatt was employed, but the expenditure so far exceeded his estimate that when the offices only were finished the whole sum was gone!'

In the east wing, Martin made two large houses, each with a stretch of garden looking across to the church. In the walled garden, where most developers would have built a dozen new houses, Martin created a cottage in the old Bothy and Apple Store for his parents, restored the greenhouses, and just beyond built a prospect tower on the site of the derelict melon houses. Five new houses were created in the stables, one in each corner and one in the south wing. The detailing of new garage doors in the archways was taken from existing slatted gates. Wyatt's Audit House became a four-bedroom house with two bathrooms. The Brewery and Laundry made four little cottages and the Octagonal Game Larder became a house as well, the smallest of all with just two bedrooms, but with a living room that is 26 ft across.

Four other houses were made in the wing where kitchen, bakery, housekeeper's and butler's rooms were situated. Inside these retained contemporary fittings, fireplaces, grates, cupboards, doors and fanlights.

The scheme was completed with the restoration of Gunton Tower, the lodge at the north end of the park, where substantial sections of the parapets had crashed to the ground. No less than twenty-seven shapes and sizes of brick were involved in the restoration. As you ascend the spiral stair to the prospect room at the top, you gain an ever-widening panorama, first of the park and finally all the way to the sea at Cromer.

No sooner had the house been restored and reoccupied than a major battle began over the park. The Forestry Commission, which owned the shelter belt, decided to sell it, dividing the woodland into quarter-acre lots that might be suitable for a caravan. Then the farmers began to cut down the remaining park trees to create open fields for arable farming. After seventy fully mature park trees had been felled, protection orders were placed on the remaining trees. Next Martin, working with Ivor Bracka (who now owned Gunton Tower) and Edward Harbord-Harbord, bought up an increasing area of parkland, returning it to pasture and replanting trees. The biggest step was to recreate the deer park, now an area of 300 acres with herds of red, fallow and sika deer. The deer keeper at Gunton has now perfected a technique for herding deer into pens and then into a lorry so that an entire herd of eighty does (preceded by four stags) can be transported to another estate to start a new herd.

Today Gunton is the archetypal example of the rescue and rebirth not just of a derelict house but a vast estate, with park trees replanted, fisherman sitting contentedly around the two large lakes and the sawmill restored by volunteers.'

The sheep grazing in the park have now been joined by large herds of red and fallow deer.

HEDENHAM HALL
Bungay
Splendid early 18th-century refronting of an Elizabethan house

HEDENHAM HALL IS A STRIKINGLY handsome house and one that could only be in Norfolk. The stepped gables and soaring chimneys proclaim its Elizabethan origin and the even rows of sash windows and giant pilasters speak of an early 18th-century remodelling. Like many Elizabethan houses, Hedenham was built by a successful lawyer, John Richmond.

The remodelling is recorded and celebrated in a painting by Thomas Bardwell of *c*.1735 which hangs over the sitting room fireplace. This shows the entrance largely as it is today with white sash windows, set in pale oatmeal brick, with an almost salmon-pink brick used for the trim. Intriguingly the painting shows a shallow attic storey instead of the present trio of pedimented dormer windows.

Large external chimney stacks are typical of Elizabethan houses. Here the southern stack is inset with a sundial and coat of arms below the imposing row of six octagonal shafts, with moulded bases and linked tops providing greater stability. The entrance hall has characteristic baroque pilasters framing both the fireplace and the entrance. Beyond is a fine oak staircase in swagger style with three balusters to each step, column corner posts and swept-up handrails and matching dado. While the stair is baroque, the beautifully proportioned Venetian window lighting the stair is Palladian.

At the back Hedenham is a more rambling picturesque composition, mainly in a soft red brick with more stepped gables and tall chimneys. On the lawn is a pretty fountain pool enclosed at the sides by walls of clipped yew. The outbuildings all echo the architecture of the house with stepped gables and pantiled roofs, notably the Ostler's cottage set in a barn and the gardener's cottage.

The stepped gables and tall chimneys could only be in Norfolk.

LITTLE HAUTBOIS
Little Hautbois
Tall 1555 house with chimneys rising from the roof ridge

NORFOLK IS RICH IN TUDOR HOUSES, many taking a distinctive character from stepped gables and red brick. Little Hautbois (known to the locals as 'Little Hobbies'), by contrast, could be a late-medieval house in France thanks to its very tall dormer windows, which are topped with gables and finials.

The house is dated 1555 in a carving in the gable of a later porch. At this date it was still common to place the chimney stacks on the end gables outside the walls as a fire precaution. Here they are confidently set astride the roof ridge with two groups of three tall linked chimney shafts, an indication of the greater safety that came with brick construction. The sense of verticality is increased by the finials at the corners of both large and small gable. The house is built on a compact, narrow plan, just one room deep almost like a Scottish tower house, with three even storeys and an extra window in the end gable lighting the attic under the roof ridge. It stands in some 20 acres with a frontage to the River Bure.

Little Hautbois was probably built by William Baspole, who took a lease in 1553. There is a date of 1607 on a garden wall. The property was sold in 1671 by Richard Dey to Thomas Raven who, in 1667, sold on to the Rev. Edward Warnes. On his death Little Hautbois passed to a charitable trust. A spell as a tenanted house probably helped ensure it escaped alterations in the 18th and 19th centuries and when on the market a few years ago, it sold readily as a private house.

Little Hautbois is a hamlet of just eight houses. The church fell into ruin as long ago as the 15th century but a new church was built by Thomas Jekyll of Norwich in 1864. The hall, which is not so much a mansion as a large farmhouse, is set in grounds by the River Bure and may be seen from the track which runs beside the Bure Valley railway.

The windows reduce in size towards the top, though the dormers, like the gables, have spiky finials.

MELTON CONSTABLE HALL Melton Constable
One of the finest of all Charles II houses with handsome Edwardian extensions

THE ROMANCE OF MELTON CONSTABLE captured the imagination of millions in the film of *The Go-Between* starring Julie Christie and Alan Bates. Without doubt, it is one of the most beautiful houses in all England. Yet for years it has stood largely empty and decaying, and repeated effort to secure its future have foundered.

The house was built in 1664–70 for Sir Jacob Astley in warm red brick with stone trim and compares with Ramsbury Manor in Wiltshire in the perfection of its proportions. It has the steep hipped roof typical of Charles II houses, with a portico on the entrance side and a central pediment overlooking the gardens. Though the architect is not known, it is of a quality to compare with leading architects of the time such as Roger Pratt and Hugh May.

Early in the 20th century the house was extended with a low porticoed pavilion connecting to a wing built in the same smart brick and stone livery as the main block. Inside are plaster ceilings of superb quality – that dating to 1687 in the Red Drawing Room is richly modelled with game, fruit and flowers.

The house was sold in 1948 by Lord Hastings to the Grosvenor Estate, which let it to the Hon. A.M. Baillie. In 1959 house and park were acquired by a local farmer, Geoffrey Harrold, who never lived in the house but maintained the deer park. In 1983 Lord Hastings was considering moving back to Melton Constable, where he had spent part of his childhood. This was the moment when Kit Martin was nearing completion of nearby Gunton and a scheme was devised whereby Martin would take on the courtyards and outbuildings and restore them for sale as cottages on long leases, while Lord Hastings would move into the main house and take on the park.

Although part lived in, the rest of this glorious house stands empty.

This Classic composition has two even storeys of tall sash windows with dormers in a hipped roof.

But Harrold changed his mind and in December 1985 Norfolk County Council moved in to serve a comprehensive repairs order, not only on the house but on numerous decaying estate buildings, the 18th-century bathhouse, the 1840 dairy, the 17th-century dairy barn, the late 18th-century tea house, the 1820 stud farmhouse cottages and the 1810 Swanton gate lodge.

Nine months later Melton Constable was sold to Roger Gawn, a man with a keen interest in historic buildings, who owned the Custom House in King's Lynn and the Bethel Hospital in Norwich. At about this time the copper roof over the main house was ripped off in a storm. English Heritage paid for a first class new roof with leading ensuring that the house has remained watertight. But it has not been occupied and today it is a forlorn sight with numerous broken windows.

In June 2006 the *Eastern Daily Press* reported, 'Mr Gawn currently has associations with sixty-eight businesses registered at Companies House, several of which have gone into liquidation and many more of which have long since ceased trading ... Norwich Union forced him into bankruptcy in 1995 after the collapse of his property development empire and subsequently he was banned from being a company director.'

Currently the North Norfolk Building Preservation Trust is taking keen interest in the house. The good news is that when a survey was carried out a year ago, the condition was deemed not bad enough to serving a repairs order.

MORLEY OLD HALL
Morley St Peter
Traditional stepped gables mingle with Renaissance detail

THIS ENCHANTING EXAMPLE of a smaller manor house stands within a moat. Dating from *c.*1600 it has the distinctive crow stepped gables often found in Norfolk, fashioned in brick. The two gables are precisely symmetrical with four tiers of windows diminishing markedly in size from one storey to the next. By contrast there are distinct asymmetries in the recessed centre with the front door set to one side, a holdover from the medieval great hall which was always entered at one end through a screens passage.

The house was built by the Sidley family who acquired the manor in 1545 and owned it until *c.*1790. After the Second World War it belonged for a period to Field Marshal the 1st Lord Ironside but in the early 1960s lay empty and derelict, attracting visitors in search of ghosts. Country house ghosts have their own large following and in 1964, Anglia TV filmed a documentary at Morley Old Hall, in which Anthony Cornell demonstrated how a ghost hunter worked. After a night's investigation, he was interviewed in the room where the ghost was said to have appeared. He concluded there was little evidence for the haunting, though five people contacted the TV company to say they had seen a 'hooded monk' between Cornell and the interviewer, Michael Robson. Although Robson could see nothing when he re-ran the film, he decided to broadcast it again. This time a further twenty-seven wrote in, fifteen saying they could see a monk or priest.

The classical pediments over the windows diminish in size towards the top.

NARBOROUGH HALL　　　Narborough
Georgian house and park now hosting contemporary art exhibitions

NARBOROUGH IS A WONDERFULLY RAMBLING Georgian house built in pretty pink brick that has been mellowed by passing centuries. One front is battlemented with slightly projecting towers at the ends and a central three-sided bay window, according with a date of *c.*1770. Though Norfolk is famously flat, Narborough provides an example of the fine parkland found around many houses in the country with the greensward descending gently to the edge of a lake in which the house is beautifully reflected.

The Tudor house here was built by the Spelman family. In 1773 it was acquired by the Tyssen family and bought in 1875 by William Jardine, who resold in 1878 to Joseph Critchley Martin, from whom it passed to the Ash family in 1927.

Today Narborough belongs to Robert Sandelson, an art dealer in London's Cork Street. Each summer there is a special exhibition at Narborough devoted to a contemporary artist. Visitors are free to explore the Victorian kitchen garden and woodland walks – one of which leads through a henge dating from 3000 BC.

In recent years the grounds have been the venue for a fair organised by the Fairyland Trust. Several thousand visitors congregate to admire and make an array of miniature homes, using natural materials from the estate. There is fairy jewellery and cooking for trolls – a large event involving 190 volunteers and staff over a three-week period. At The Perfect Spot Café, which is open during exhibitions, visitors can enjoy home-grown and organic food for which there is no charge but donations to the Fairyland Trust are welcome.

The Georgian sashes and brick battlements are matched by handmade roof tiles.

THORPE HALL   Norwich
Built by the Pastons on the site of the Bishop of Norwich's summer residence

THORPE HALL IS SET ON AN IMPRESSIVE sweep of the River Yare, little more than a mile from Norwich station. Rescued from extreme decay, it combines the beauty of mellow Tudor brick with the local flint that gives character to many Norfolk buildings.

In the Middle Ages Thorpe Hall was a summer palace of the Bishop of Norwich, probably built by Henry Despenser in the form of a defensive quadrangle. At the Reformation, Henry VIII tricked the Bishops out of their Norwich revenues, taking over the manor of Thorpe in 1536. He then granted it to Thomas Howard, Duke of Norfolk, but seized it back when Howard was attainted.

In 1547 Edward VI granted Thorpe to Sir William Paston. His son Edward, a staunch Catholic, largely demolished the palace and in 1590 began rebuilding not only Thorpe but Appleton Hall near Sandringham, where he erected a house ordained for the reception of priests hidden in a wood. Thorpe's riverside position was ideal for smuggling in priests by night and there is a plausible priest hole at the top of the stairs.

In 1670 the Pastons sold Thorpe to Rowland Dee and in 1838 the hall came to a naval commander, Thomas Blakiston, who carried out a Victorian remodelling. Thorpe then passed by marriage to Major Frank Astley Cubitt who lived to his nineties, refusing to modernise the Hall. When his son inherited in 1929 it was without bathrooms or electricity and so dilapidated that he had to sell to an unscrupulous antique dealer, who removed at least one carved stone fireplace before selling on to a boatbuilder who promptly demolished the chapel to make room for an engine repair shop.

During wartime requisitioning Thorpe received a direct hit from an incendiary bomb. Worse was to come as a boat-letting firm in the 1960s turned the lawns into a car park and felled a magnificent cedar. By the 1970s vandals had smashed not only

The new bay window masks a gash in the gable end.

The restored Tudor mullioned windows have broad triangular pediments

the glass of the windows but the distinctive mullions. The dining-room panelling and the stone fireplaces were stolen by dealers.

Two public inquiries were fought to prevent demolition before a saviour appeared, Henry Burke, a Norwich businessman with a passion for the arts. He bought the house for £1 and asked the architect Anthony Rossi to draw up plans for repair.

The exterior had been covered in a hard modern render. When this was removed, brick and flint proved to have a wonderful patina. While not historically correct, the decision to leave the walls exposed has given the house an extraordinarily mellow beauty and charm. The interior takes a matching warmth from the survival of Tudor timber-framed partitions and ceilings with the large mullioned windows ensuring the main rooms are remarkably light with an impressive staircase built in chestnut.

Rossi's restoration of the large 1590 mullions has given back to Thorpe its touch of grandeur. Not only are they immensely broad but they have the splendid Renaissance flourish of a large triangular pediment. Originally they were of moulded brick covered in render. Rossi confides that the replacement bricks he ordered were so long in coming that they threatened to halt the project. He redid the mullions in concrete, though as they are rendered you would never know. 'We were able to use the bricks elsewhere when they finally arrived,' he says.

One problem was how to treat the huge gash in the end wall of the south gable. The historic buildings inspector wanted Rossi to put in mullioned windows to match the others. He refused, saying there was no evidence, and eventually won his way, introducing a double-height bay in timber in a distinctly Arts and Crafts manner. His too are the dormers, unusually large and making the second-floor rooms a delight. He also rebuilt the chimneys in a diamond fashion in carefully matched brick.

WALLINGTON HALL   Downham Market
Tudor house with handsome 18th-century additions

WALLINGTON HALL BELONGS TO THE lovable group of houses that have grown through the centuries in rambling unselfconscious fashion, sitting peacefully in broad acres far from the troubles of the world. For nearly a century it has been the home of the Luddingtons, but now Andrew Luddington, who took over from his father in 1996, has decided to emigrate with his family to New Zealand.

Yet his enthusiasm for the place is undimmed. The house, he says, 'hums to the tune of nature and mortar bees'. The recently rebuilt pond in front of the house is where he and his siblings sank models of the *Bismarck* and the *Tirpitz* with air rifles from the attic windows. On the lawn to the north he points out his one-hole golf course, jokingly called the Royal Wallington and West Norfolk, with the fairway leading down to a lake. 'Ten is par and on the green you chip into a hole in an ancient oak tree.'

His grandfather planted woods for shooting and his father created a chain of four willow-fringed lakes, each with its own island fed by a small tributary to the Ouse. His mother was a keen horsewoman, hunting and breeding horses, then adapting her stables for Riding for the Disabled, which now operates an indoor riding school.

He has adapted one of the barns, which he lets as a forge, and opened a 'five-room, five-star B&B' in part of the hall to help with its keep. Returning from a lime-mortar course run by the Society for the Protection of Ancient Buildings, he set the whole family to work on repairing another barn.

Wallington Hall is mentioned in the Domesday Book, but the present house dates mainly from 1525 and belongs to the group of early Tudor red-brick Norfolk manor houses, a flourish of stepped gables, moulded battlements, ornamental terracotta detail

The ball-topped gate piers open into a sunken garden.

and soaring chimney stacks. The west gable end has unusual blind battlements and a chequerwork of alternating brick and stone panels and the large X-patterns in the brickwork known as diapering. The two-storey porch on the north front has octagonal corner turrets capped with bristling obelisks. Over the entrance archway are terracotta flared arches and Tudor roses set in a band of latticework. Inside the arch the original tile floor laid in herringbone fashion survives.

The Tudor house was built for William Coningsby, a lawyer. Large beams survive in the smoke room and dining room. Coningsby's granddaughter married

The impressive Tudor beams loom above panelling that was installed c.1920.

Francis Gawdy, who became Lord Chief Justice, sitting in judgement on Mary, Queen of Scots, the Earl of Essex and Sir Walter Raleigh. Remembered locally as a monster, he drove the villagers off his estate and pulled down the parish church but left the tower. On his death he was, not surprisingly, refused burial in the churchyard.

Happier times came forty years later with the Bells, who were kinsmen of Henry Bell, architect of the 1683 Custom House at King's Lynn. In around 1700 Philip Bell must have laid out the walled sunken garden below what is now a Georgian front with three rows of sash windows. This is a wonderful survival of the formal early 18th-century garden, many of which were swept away in the naturalistic landscape craze.

At that time gentlemen's houses were often approached on foot through a formal flower garden, announced by a pair of gate piers, at which guests dismounted. These survive here, built of fine red brick with narrow joints, and topped with large stone balls. A later Bell created the Palladian drawing room with pretty plasterwork over the fireplace. Changes in the brickwork on the gable ends suggest further alterations.

What was probably the Tudor hall was made into a dining room by James Luddington who acquired the property in 1916 and introduced Jacobean-style oak panelling with embossed pilasters and a stone fireplace with carved overmantel and corner door. The tall mullioned window lighting the room is presumably of this date.

The old system of servant bells still works in most rooms: a red button lights up on the bell board to announce which room is calling. Intriguing, too, are the 1930s-style windows on the right of the Georgian front. They look like Crittall metal windows but are actually in oak. Another item for preservation is a notice on the spiral stair to the attic. Dating from wartime military occupation and addressed to 'All Ranks', it states: 'The person discovering an outbreak of fire will shout Fire! Fire! Fire! Until help arrives.' Alas, the church tower, after surviving four centuries, finally collapsed into a heap of stones ten years ago.

Today the estate of 590 acres is surrounded by woods and invisible to the world. Broad headlands and verges around the fields encourage wildlife.

NORTHAMPTONSHIRE

APETHORPE HALL   Oundle
Magnificent seat of the Fanes enlarged for James I and the Duke of Buckingham

APETHORPE HALL IS LIKE AN Oxford or Cambridge college laid out around two quadrangles where Elizabethan, Jacobean and Palladian architecture blend together. House and village are just 12 miles from Stamford, home to generations of stone masons. Yet its recent history has been tragic.

The house was begun in the late 15th century by Sir Guy Woolston, passing in 1550 to Sir Walter Mildmay and in 1617 to Sir Francis Fane, later Earl of Westmorland. He was a favourite of James I, who came regularly to hunt. There were at least thirteen royal visits between 1566 and 1636 and at the express order of James I, Sir Francis Fane built a new suite of state rooms in 1622–4 for the King's 'more commodious entertainment … and princely recreation there'. Francis Fane also added the 110ft Long Gallery and the roof above, with walkways to enjoy the spectacular views of the Northamptonshire countryside and the perfect spectator platform from which to watch the King hunting.

The 7th Earl of Westmorland began another remodelling in the 1740s and more alterations were carried out in the mid 19th century. In 1904 the estate was sold to Leonard Brassey, later Baron Brassey, grandson of the railway contractor Thomas Brassey, who engaged Sir Reginald Blomfield as architect.

After the Second World War came years of use as an approved school – a Borstal run by the Roman Catholic Diocese of Northampton. A series of substantial staff houses were built along the drive, giving a grim institutional air to the approach. Worse, the original approach through grand gates near the church was cut off by a new house built within the grounds. As a result the front courtyard now looked out onto a thicket of conifers planted to keep the two houses out of sight of each other. Today Apethorpe desperately needs a new drive across the fields.

In 1983 Apethorpe and 43 acres was sold for £750,000, to a Libyan Wanis Bewela, who planned to use it as a college for Libyan and Arab students. His plans did not proceed, perhaps because, after the shooting of W.P.C. Yvonne Fletcher

An heraldic supporter by the front door exemplifies the superb craftsmanship both outside and in.

The house was gradually strangled in creeper while an absentee owner allowed it to fall into decay.

outside the Libyan Embassy, many Libyans were unable to renew their visas. Mr Bewela visited Apethorpe, but never lived there.

In the 1990s SAVE was approached by a surveyor who had drawn up plans for creating three very large houses around the main courtyard and several smaller ones round the rear courtyard. These would all follow the main structural lines of the building and at avoid damage to important interiors. He had, for the first time, established contact with Mr Bewela and was near persuading him to sell. However, the local council remained adamant that it would only allow Apethorpe to be a single large house.

By 2000 there were holes in the roof, hastily patched to keep out the rain and prevent the collapse of the house's magnificent Elizabethan and Jacobean ceilings. In June 2002 compulsory purchase proceedings were served on Mr Bewela by London solicitors acting for Tessa Jowell, the Secretary of State for Culture, Media and Sport.

English Heritage is currently undertaking a £4 million programme of repairs, due for completion in spring 2008, with the aim of finding a buyer who will complete the restoration of Apethorpe as a 'single-owner private country house'. English Heritage has taken the bold step of demolishing a series of decaying warden's houses which blighted the approach, and if Apethorpe can once again be given a setting worthy of its glorious architecture, the vision of Simon Thurely, its chief executive, will become reality.

AYNHO

Aynho

Twice plunged into crisis in fifty years, now being restored as a family house

MANY ENGLISH COUNTRY HOUSES are set deep in landscape parks. Aynho is like a French chateau, displayed in all its splendour to the passing road. The house was the seat of the Cartwright family from 1616 and was rebuilt and enlarged on successive occasions, after the Restoration by the leading London master mason Edward Marshall, then by Thomas Archer in 1707 and by Sir John Soane in 1799–1804.

In 1954, just after *Country Life* had published three articles on the house, two generations of the Cartwright family were killed in a car accident, incurring double death duties. Aynhoe became one of the growing number of country houses taken over by the Mutual Householders Association, which seemed the new salvation for grand country houses. Here people could come and live in retirement in apartments created within the mansion. A central kitchen provided meals taken in the dining room, while the grounds were maintained. The MHA, renamed the Country Houses Association, opened its properties to the public but in 2005 was plunged into financial crisis. All its houses had to be sold. Ayhno was acquired by James Perkins who had recently completed a courageous and highly stylish rescue of Dowdeswell near Cheltenham.

He has undertaken a major restoration of the interior, furnishing it, as at Dowdeswell, with his remarkable collection of plaster casts. He describes his approach as 'classical with a contemporary twist'. Soane's staircase and the lantern above are handsomely restored and the paints chosen for the main interiors match the colours found as scrapes were taken. Perkins has established his plaster restoration workshops in the old coach house and leased the wings to an IT company.

The entrance front, flanked by matching wings, opens onto the village street.

BROCKHALL MANOR   Brockhall
Untouched by Georgian and Victorian alterations thanks to years as a tenanted farm

FOR SHEER BEAUTY THE IRONSTONE VILLAGES OF Northamptonshire vie with the best of the Cotswolds. The landscape may be flatter, but there is a compelling sense of secrecy and peace about many of these villages, increased by the great estates that have girded them for centuries.

Brockhall is as perfect a small estate village as can be imagined. Every building in the hamlet is listed. The noble Elizabethan seat of the Thorntons, Brockhall Hall, has recently been converted into apartments, as have the stables.

Brockhall Manor, or Brockhall Manor Farm as it was known until recently, stands on the other side of the lane through the village. It is as delicious a sight as any small manor house in England. The Brodies were tenants here from 1900 and bought the house and 414 acres when the Thorntons sold nearly forty years ago.

Like many long-tenanted houses, it remains remarkably unaltered. No fashionable Georgian sash windows ever intruded and the stone mullions and leaded windows remain, one engraved with the date 1781 to prove it. 'Square leads for gentry, diamond for cottages and servants,' says James Brodie, pointing to the one diamond lattice window in a gable at the back.

As the village is effectively a cul-de-sac (the road to the north is gated), the fact that the manor stands close to the quiet lane through the village only adds to its charm. It makes a ravishing group with the lodge and a long barn all in matching stone. A large group of nesting boxes for doves is set in the walls on either side of the central archway. Intriguing, too, are the triangular ventilation slits and the four-step mounting block, inset with a dog kennel entered through a shallow Tudor arch.

The front garden opens onto a quiet country lane through the village.

The Jacobean stair has solid wooden bannisters and rises all the way up to the attic.

The house bears the date 1677 and is laid out on a compact U-shaped plan with the massive chimney breasts that were often found at this date. Almost all the rooms are square, cosy in feel and with a double outlook. Interesting features are the upward sliding shutters beneath the windows. 'I thought they were unique, but they are found all over the Althorp estate,' Brodie says. The staircase opens from the back of the hall, but the upper half appears a later addition, as notches for joists show that there was once a floor beneath the upper window. There are many 17th-century cupboards which make use of every possible recess, all of which retain their original splayed hinges.

The manor's 414 acres form a miniature estate with a stretch of the parkland that extends (in various ownerships) all round the village, as well as fields, woods and a well-established shoot.

Though Brockhall is less than a mile from the busy M1 and only 5 miles from Northampton, it remains a gloriously remote place where nearby roads are narrow lanes with little traffic. This is a well-wooded landscape, with large rolling fields and few houses outside the villages and hamlets.

CASTLE ASHBY   Denton
Elizabethan and Jacobean house that welcomes visitors but is not open to the public

WHEN I VISITED CASTLE ASHBY IN 2002, The Marquess of Northampton had set a unique mission statement for his ancestral seat in Northamptonshire: 'Castle Ashby, the second stately home of the Compton family, was built in 1574 expressly for entertaining. Still owned by the family, this magnificent castle together with its famous furniture, paintings, and collections is used exclusively for prestigious and important events. It is the only great castle in England that is not open to the public, not lived in by its owners and can be booked in its entirety for a wedding, a banquet, conference or a range of other events.'

Among many good marketing lines were surprise parties. 'Imagine. She believes you are off to the restaurant round the corner and instead you carry on driving and turn under the grand entrance archway to come up the 2-mile Avenue towards a fairytale castle that emerges from the landscape. Flaming torches frame your path and you are ushered into the warmth and splendour of Castle Ashby and a magnificent room filled with friends all gathered to enjoy the evening of a lifetime.'

No longer. Castle Ashby has now joined that intriguing and growing number of country houses which are coming out of institutional or commercial use and becoming family homes again. The website now announces: 'Because the house is now going to be utilised solely by the Compton family, we are no longer able to take bookings for Corporate, Private, or Wedding functions inside the actual house.' Events can still be held in marquees in the castle courtyard, the garden behind the house and the 16th century walled garden. There are also plans for opening a teashop in the walled garden.

One part of Castle Ashby, however, is still there for all to enjoy. This is the two mile long avenue leading to the house, with the broadest grass verges in the land, grand enough for a royal palace. I enjoyed the full monty at Castle Ashby in January 2002 when the principal preservation societies in England gathered together at the invitation of a benefactor to find ways of pooling their resources. The result later that year was the birth of Heritage Link of which I was the first convenor – whose mission is to give hundreds of independent heritage organisations a collective voice.

Castle Ashby was begun by Henry, 1st Lord Compton, in 1574 and was continued by his son, William, later created Earl of Northampton. Around the house dated 1624 is an inscription from the 127th Psalm which translates 'Except the Lord build the house they labour but in vain they who build it; Except the Lord keep the house the watchman waketh but in vain'.

When Queen Elizabeth visited the house in 1600 there were eighty-three household servants and in 2002, there seemed almost as many. Catering was on a grand scale and all twenty-six bedrooms were ready for use, many with four-poster beds. The state of upkeep was immaculate. Now that the house is back in sole family usage, let us hope it remains that way.

The pure Renaissance frontispiece sits sandwiched between Jacobean wings.

CRANSLEY HALL — Kettering
18th-century gem bought by the milkman

CRANSLEY HALL LIES IN A PLEASANT village, on the quietest of cul-de-sacs, with the medieval church, walled garden and old rectory beyond. Outbuildings have been converted into cottages, roses spill over walls and all is peaceful.

The Hall springs into view at the end of a short drive and is built of the rich golden ironstone that is the glory of the county. Originally it was the perfect Queen Anne doll's house, just five windows wide, with tall white sash windows and the centre breaking forward in best baroque manner with the squire's shield of arms over the door. This was harmoniously extended around 1900 with matching windows and a billiard room and bow on the right. It's asymmetric but not disturbing.

The south garden front is built of the same stone with a mid 18th-century canted bay, looking down onto baroque terraces. On these stand a series of Cedars of Lebanon, just beginning to shed limbs, but still awesome in size. The lawns run down to a vast mirror of water, filled with waterlilies and home to Canada geese. 'There's a date of 1697 in the tunnel under the dam,' Bryan Perkins, the owner, told me.

On the far side is a delightful boathouse and we walk up to the garden to the west of the house where the church, with its glorious spire, is in full view just the other side of the garden wall. The stone stables opposite the west front have been sold and the new houses have a generous chunk of garden in front. But thanks to formal hedges you hardly notice.

The perfect Queen Anne front has the squire's coat of arms over the entrance.

Mr Perkins continued, 'I was the milkman. The house had been bought by a shoe manufacturer in Kettering in 1942 and was in a very run down state. I sold out at the right moment and bought the place twenty years ago.'

The deep plan of the house makes you think it must have gloomy backstairs rooms but it transpires to be laid out around an enchanting small courtyard with bands of windows on every side. The house is a bit of a muddle in the way of all quintessentially English family houses that have grown through the centuries, with a room or a wing thrown up when a son has inherited or married an heiress.

The mid 18th-century bay window matches the Queen Anne work.

Cransley is mentioned in Domesday as Cranefleg, and in 1585 was acquired by Sir Thomas Cecil, heir of Lord Burghley. The house we see was built by the Robinsons, merchants from Yorkshire who settled into the life of country squires. Henry Robinson, who died in 1727, seems the best candidate for the Queen Anne work but he was declared a lunatic in 1701 so perhaps his son John had taken over. In 1708 Sir Justinian Isham of Lamport rode over and wrote in his diary that 'they were building a new front of five windows to the old part of the house'.

The next question is whether John, who died in 1745, built the fabulous dining room, or his son, also John, who could have built it to entertain the county when he was sheriff in 1754. This has the sumptuous plasterwork more often found in Yorkshire houses of this date, usually by Italian craftsmen. The room at Cransley is at the top end of the scale, with mirrors set in the walls, grand Palladian plaster picture frames with eagles on top, garlands of fruit and flowers over the doors, trellis work on the ceiling and a riot of swirling curves around the central rose – all on the stylistic cusp between French Regency with its ribbonwork and full blown rococo.

In 1904 Cransley was sold to Major A.H. Thurburn from Oxfordshire, a keen member of the Pytchley Hunt. It looks as if he added the splendid oak-panelled billiard room with full Ionic columns and the panelling in adjoining rooms. With so many sash windows, the main rooms all have a splendid outlook – to the south, over the lake up to the hill on the horizon. There is also a pretty oval cantilevered staircase and a wealth of rooms on both main floors to choose from for any purpose.

Cransley has a wonderful roof of graded stone slates covered in moss but in places it leaked. Patches of plaster had crashed to the floor exposing timber as well as a certain amount of wet rot. But Mr Perkins insisted the leaks were only occasional, the buckets did very well and the water never came through to the first-floor bedrooms. He also explained how simple it is to access the valley gutters and sweep out the leaves. For anyone willing to tend the blemishes, this is middle England at its most enticing.

DINGLEY HALL — Market Harborough
Elizabethan and Charles II house rescued from imminent collapse

IN 1958, THE SALES PARTICULARS for Dingley Hall announced that the house was 'in an exceptional state of repair and has been consistently well maintained'. Fifteen years later Dingley was a wreck. Panelling, doors, doorcases, chimney pieces had been stripped out, the stone slabs of the main ground-floor rooms had gone, roof slates had been stolen, and almost all internal walls, floors and ceilings removed. Chimney stacks were collapsing as a result, bringing down further sections of roof as they fell.

In 1975 Kit Martin saw the house and bought it a year later, calculating he could hardly be refused permission for restoration. His plan was to reconstruct the house internally to form fourteen self-contained houses (later reduced to ten). Failing to secure a Historic Buildings Council grant he decided to tackle the project in five stages. Capital could be recycled and the various trades could be continuously employed.

Work began first on the early-Elizabethan wing. The gatehouse carries an inscription 'God Save the King 1560', an unexpected sentiment as Queen Elizabeth I had come to the throne in 1558. The work was carried out for Sir Edward Griffin, a noted papist, and has been attributed to the mason John Thorpe. The Griffin house was built around a courtyard with few windows in the outer wall but a graceful arcade within supported on clustered columns. There was more exquisite early-Renaissance detail in the delightful series of gables along the parapet, carved with shells and surmounted by finials.

Dingley was next remodelled by another Sir Edward, a fervent Jacobite who joined James II in exile when he fled in 1688. In 1684 he added a Charles II front beside the gatehouse with tall Classical windows and steep-hipped roof.

The Charles II wing shows no visible marks of its transformation into three houses.

The distinctive grouping of the windows on the 1680s garden front is close to that at Combe Abbey in Warwickshire and Belton Hall in Lincolnshire, both designed by Captain William Winde. At the same time two sides of the courtyard were rebuilt in what here appears a rather French manner, as at nearby Boughton Hall.

Later in the 18th century Dingley passed to the Hungerford family, who made extensions at the back, while in 1883 the house was acquired by Viscount Downe; he sold it to Earl Beatty, hero of the Battle of Jutland, who laid out the terraced gardens to the south of the house.

In the 1680s wings, both floors and ceilings had vanished and Martin was able to raise the floors and lower the ceilings to provide complete sound insulation between the apartments. Instead of sash windows he introduced wooden mullions with casements (inward opening windows) based on the French model. Residents were allowed, indeed encouraged, to choose their own finishes and decoration, and organise their own kitchens and bathrooms. The sizes of the houses varied from two bedrooms to six.

Dingley was the first of Martin's heroic rescues of great houses. It showed that a very derelict house could be restored without historic buildings grants. Once the first three houses were completed, there was strong interest from people wishing to buy all the remaining units. Almost all the houses were sold before they were completed and some even before they were begun.

ECTON HALL — Northampton

Delightful example of mid 18th-century Gothick that narrowly escaped demolition

ECTON HALL PROVIDES A VIVID EXAMPLE OF the epic battles that have had to be fought to save hundreds of delightful country houses from decay and actual demolition. With its pretty shaped gables and battlemented oriels Ecton is a delightful – and early – example of Strawberry Hill Gothick. Better still it is built in beautiful golden stone which still remains crisp in every detail.

In the 1920s Ecton Hall was owned by Colonel Sotheby who married Marjorie McCorquodale in 1923. Her brother Alex later married the novelist Barbara Cartland who was a frequent visitor to the house. Their daughter Raine later became Countess Spencer, mother of Princess Diana. During the Second World War, Ecton was occupied by Canadian troops. Colonel Sotheby died in 1950 and his widow moved to London and the contents of Ecton were sold. Amusing details of life below stairs are provided in a memoir (to be found on the village website) by Betty Cunningham. Frequent shooting parties were held at Ecton with a 'big shoot' just before Christmas when beaters were given steak and kidney puddings and a ball held in the evening.

SAVE first illustrated Ecton in *Tomorrow's Ruins* in 1978 when it had been empty for twenty years and was deteriorating badly. Things went from bad to worse and we had to fight off an application to demolish. The land agents remained convinced that restoration and conversion was not viable and that it would interfere with farming activities on the estate.

Faced in the warm local stone, the Georgian sashes contrast with the flame-headed arches of the windows.

Yet the house stood in an attractive village just to the east of Northampton, close to the parish church, with good views to the south over fields. In 1981 Kit Martin had joined the battle, putting proposals to Wellingborough Council for converting the house and outbuildings into eleven dwellings that would vary 'from a two bedroom flat to a five bedroom house'.

The key to success was to persuade the agents and trustees of the estate that the outbuildings should be included with a small stretch of park in front of the house. Kit Martin continued, 'I understand from the agents that none of the buildings are necessary for or used by the farm. The only loss to the farm would be the 5.69 acres of grazing land which forms the park setting and view to the south of the house.'

Martin estimated that building costs would amount to £595,000 and was ready to step in if the council would use its compulsory purchase powers for acquiring neglected listed buildings. The offer was refused on the grounds of 'excessive land take'. Robert Carnwath QC provided us with an opinion, confirming that it was reasonable to seek to include the outbuildings to make the scheme viable; but the council received another opinion suggesting such an order would fail as the buildings were physically separate from the hall.

It looked an impossible stalemate but we kept the pressure up on the agents who replied tetchily, 'the points you make are noted, although we would say that few of them are agreed by the Trustees' but at last adding 'the Trustees are doing all in their power to sort out a difficult situation'.

Shortly after, in 1986, Ecton was sold – with its outbuildings and parkland – to Period Property Investments, who created twelve apartments in the main house, made two houses in the laundry and game larder and built nine stone cottages around a new courtyard. After standing empty for half a century, Ecton is now full of happy residents.

EDGCOTE HOUSE   Chipping Warden
Handsome example of 1740s Palladianism with matching wings set to the side

EDGCOTE HOUSE VIES WITH WOLVERTON HALL in Norfolk for the title of the most comfortable country house in England. It is not by a leading architect, it has no grand portico and is built in homely brick rather than stone. Yet it is a perfect Palladian composition with grand flights of outdoor steps up to a first-floor entrance, bay windows on the side elevations and a garden front that mirrors the grand entrance front.

The Palladian practice was to build matching wings on the flanks of the house to create a grander effect. At Edgcote they are set to one side, forming an enclosed courtyard. In 2005 Edgcote was offered for sale with an unusually large estate of 1,700 acres. *The Times* reported 'No photographs were taken, and no glossy brochures were printed. Only a handful of select buyers were invited for a tour of the hidden Regency splendour of Edgcote House and its 1,700 acres of park and farmland. And it sold within a fortnight.' The final offer was well over the guide price of £25 million.

Unusually the stables were built first, in 1745–7, designed by William Smith, eldest son of Francis Smith of Warwick, the leading master builder in the Midlands. There is a payment to William Smith of £40 6s for 'surveying the building' which may have been for the house itself, but this was largely built under the direction of William Jones who took over after Smith's death in 1748. Jones may have simply been carrying out Smith's design, but there is a distinct stylistic change between stables and house, from baroque to Palladian. Jones was the designer of one of London's major pleasure domes, the imposing Rotunda in Ranelagh Gardens, Chelsea.

The interiors are of added interest as they are the work of Abraham Swan, a carpenter and joiner who published several books, one of which, *The British Architect*, was the first architectural book to be published in America in 1750.

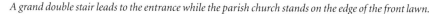

A grand double stair leads to the entrance while the parish church stands on the edge of the front lawn.

EYDON HALL — Eydon

Exquisite villa of the 1790s spotted by Nancy Lancaster while hunting

WHEN I FIRST SAW EYDON HALL in Northamptonshire over thirty years ago, I thought it the most desirable house I had ever seen. Visiting it again, it was still pure perfection, with glorious views over gently rolling country without a pylon, a mast or an ugly farm building in sight.

So it struck the famous Nancy Lancaster, out hunting with the Pytchley in 1927. She was looking for a house for her aunt Phyllis – younger sister of the celebrated Nancy Viscountess Astor, who became Britain's first woman MP. The hounds had lost the scent, Nancy Lancaster rode up to the house to ask if she could make a telephone call, learnt from the butler it was for sale and promptly rang her aunt to tell her it was just like Bremo – the most perfect Palladian house in Virginia.

Phyllis's husband, the economist Lord Brand, was equally enchanted and within months they were living there. Eydon was built in the early 1790s by the Rev. Francis Annesley, a typical 18th-century 'squarson' (parson squire), who established himself in good hunting and shooting country miles away from his 'living' in Somerset. His architect was James Lewis, the author of two volumes of designs for villas and town houses, *Original Designs in Architecture*. The subscribers to the second volume of 1797 included Catherine the Great of Russia and her architect Giacomo Quarengi.

The slender, widely spaced columns and sweeping stair give the portico exceptional elegance.

Villas, wrote Lewis, were exposed to view from every angle and at Eydon he made a virtue of this, giving each front a distinctive treatment. The entrance front looks like a Robert Adam town house, the west side has a graceful bow rising its full height, while the garden front has a portico like a pre-Civil War mansion in the Southern States with tall, widely spaced columns and balustraded top.

A special beauty of the house is that it is entirely built of the richly coloured local ironstone quarried on the estate – warm brown with a touch of orange. The walls are formed of perfectly cut blocks like a Roman Temple. Almost the whole village is built

of the same rich stone. The gates to the house stand at the top of one of the most perfect high streets of any English village. They open into a country house Elysium with the ancient church looking out over a low stone wall into the park and a walled garden beyond. The park in front of the house is not grazed by sheep or cattle but treated as ornamental grounds, with spring bulbs growing amid the long grass and specimen trees.

The garden front by contrast looks out across a large spread of perfectly mown lawn continued by a vast sweep of pasture beyond the ha-ha. To the left, low walls

Designed as a free-standing composition, the graceful bow window is just visible on the left.

enclose a sunken garden overlooked by a grand orangery perfect for summer parties. Across the lawn the house is sheltered by the stateliest of cedars with nearly a dozen bows spreading from a colossal trunk. Hidden in the pleasure ground beyond is a grand oval *bosquet* formed of perfectly level tall clipped beech hedges looking like an open air theatre at Versailles.

Inside, Eydon has four levels of well-lit rooms rather like a London house, allowing you to live in any way you want. The 'basement' is almost a full ground floor with windows looking out into the gardens. Here the late Gerald Leigh made an everyday entrance opening into the office from which he ran his thoroughbred empire while Mrs Leigh has made an attractive dining room in the vaults of the old kitchen.

The rooms on the main floor have ceilings nearly 20 ft high and tall sash windows filling the house with light and fresh air. The principal rooms open off a central top-lit stair with elegant cantilevered flights unsupported from below. Unusually these are made of of oak not stone, with each tread cut away beneath in a graceful S-curve to lighten the effect.

Thanks to a sash invisibly adapted as a French window, you look straight out of the house from the main entrance to the garden beyond through a perfectly aligned set of doors. The best room is the dining room that was prettily painted by Lord Brand's daughter Virginia, who inherited the house on his death and lived here in great elegance with her husband Sir Edward Ford, Assistant Private Secretary to the Queen.

Lewis also ingeniously provided intimate small rooms in the French manner. The front corner rooms looking out in two directions are particularly appealing with one window descending to the floor, perfect places to doze on a sofa in front of a blazing fire, while the bow room is a perfect oval with pretty curving windows. The drawing room has a bookcase by Sir Herbert Baker, an architect whom Lord Brand presumably knew from his rebuilding of the Bank of England.

Eydon has an unusually spacious and elegant back stair with graceful sweeping handrail that rises the full height of the house. The Leighs have taken out the lift that filled the stairwell, exposing a winch at the top used to haul up buckets to fill a slate-lined water tank that provided running water to at least the main bedroom and presumably a water closet, luxuries that many country houses were not to have for a century.

Much of the 600-acre estate is laid out with large paddocks with rounded sides to avoid foals becoming trapped in the corners and wide rides for exercising horses. The Regency stable block has been ingeniously adapted by Quinlan Terry to provide larger stalls for thoroughbreds with a curving Tuscan colonnade and new roof replacing Baker's parapet. Terry has also designed a handsome stud manager's house, Annesley House, as well as a house in the High Street, both in early 17th-century style with mullioned windows, all in the local stone.

For at least eighty years, and maybe much longer, the chatelaines of Eydon have all been ravishing beauties, caring for its *bella figura* as effortlessly as their own. May this long continue.

FINEDON HALL — Finedon
Playful early-Victorian house that fell into extreme decay

Neglect affected a richly carved Victorian entrance doorway.

WHEN I FIRST SAW FINEDON in 1982 it looked the ultimate lost cause. The house was surrounded by a sea of new housing on all sides with new kerbed roads criss-crossing the grounds. The house was an utter wreck with huge gashes in the masonry. Yet the rich ochre of the local stone and the sheer playfulness of its architecture continued to give it immense appeal.

William Mackworth-Dolben, who built the house, was evidently an impish figure and, like Frank Crisp at Friar Park outside Henley, fond of architectural quirks and with no shortage of money to indulge his tastes. He had added the name of Dolben to Mackworth in 1835 after his marriage to Frances, the granddaughter of the 4th baronet of Finedon, Sir John English Dolben. Both Mackworths and Dolbens had Welsh blood and the gables of the entrance front were emblazoned with the words *Gwell Angua na Cywikydd* – 'Rather Death than Shame', an all too apt motto for its decay. Mackworth-Dolben's engaging eccentricity was apparent at every turn – in the Bell Inn, the Almshouses and the Ice Tower and numerous curiously named cottages –

Seen here when restoration had just begun, Finedon is a picturesque composition where each shaped gable is different from its neighbour.

Thingdon Cottage, Ice Brook Cottage and Windmill Cottage. The latter was an earlier building to which he had added a battlemented top so that it looked like a castle on a chessboard. Looking at the dates on all these buildings, it was clear the Mackworth-Dolbens had been at work continuously for nearly four decades, beginning in 1835.

An article on Finedon Hall in *Country Life* in 1901 concluded, 'Northamptonshire has more famous houses, but few more satisfactorily and none better cared for than Finedon Hall.' The black and white photographs show neat Victorian *parterres*, raised flowerbeds and heliotropes growing proudly above circles of bedding-out plants. 'A noble avenue of stately limes' led to the house. There was a fine arboretum and a 'large sheet of water, which in the winter is the resort of large numbers of wildfowl'. The finest feature was a magnificent triple avenue of limes and chestnuts, enclosed in an ancient holly hedge.

Forming a courtyard with Finedon Hall are a remarkable range of outbuildings all in the same strongly coloured ironstone, including a museum and winter garden (formerly the Old Chapel), probably designed for Mackworth-Dolben by E.F. Law.

Yet salvation was at hand. A local surveyor with a limitless amount of courage and resourcefulness has gradually repaired the house and the outbuildings, recarving the lost masonry, and the whole place is full of new residents living in self-contained houses and flats.

THE MENAGERIE   Horton

Long-abandoned 1750s eye-catcher restored as a house set in enchanted garden

BUILT IN THE 1750S AS A BANQUETING SUITE for the 2nd Earl of Halifax and designed by Thomas Wright, with a saloon decorated with elaborate medallions showing the signs of the zodiac and bedrooms furnished in gothic fashion, The Menagerie is without doubt one of the most enchanting follies in England. Here is a garden that for sheer *jeu d'esprit* vies with Highgrove in invention if not size.

All this is due to the ultimate enthusiast for country houses and gardens, the late Gervase Jackson-Stops, architectural adviser to the National Trust, who was awarded the OBE for mounting the *Treasure Houses of Britain* exhibition at the National Gallery in Washington in 1985. Aspiring to architectural glory, but without the means to build lavishly, Gervase bought a crumbling ruin in a field without so much as a track leading to it.

Horton House itself had been ignominiously demolished in 1936 and the once-vast park shorn of trees. The Menagerie appealed to Gervase's imagination. He quickly discovered it was the work of the so-called Wizard of Durham, the astronomer turned architect Thomas Wright, and even before planning a kitchen or bathroom, Gervase was working out how the large medallions of the zodiac had been placed around the saloon, with the winter months near the fireplace and summer around the bay window.

All the splendid ornamental plasterwork was pieced together by the designer artist Christopher Hobbs over three years, using fragments that remained. Just so future generations could never be deceived by their artifice, they left a clue in a plasterwork sheet of music inscribed with Shirley Temple's 'Animal Crackers in My Soup'. Hobbs also did the magnificent bronzed urns in the saloon, representing the continents,

The long vanished animal pens have been replaced by luxuriant borders.

which he adapted from a drawing by Rex Whistler. They are adorned with a dromedary for Asia and an alligator for America. 'The Menagerie pre-dates the American eagle,' says Hobbs.

Wright was born in County Durham and by the age of 14, he was, in his own words, 'much in love with mathematics' and 'very much given to the amusements of drawing ... and buildings'. As architect and landscape gardener he worked for a series of noble patrons, including the 4th Duke of Beaufort, the 4th Earl of Berkeley and the Ansons of Shugborough.

Many of Wright's buildings were mock castles, gothic follies and grottoes, often designed to be built of rustic materials such as stone, roots, unhewn timber and thatch, and covered with ivy, moss and honeysuckle.

The initial challenge was that The Menagerie had just one show front. At the back the enclosures for the animals had long vanished. A young tiger, a bear, warthogs,

One of the two thatched pavilions that were built as guest rooms in the 1990s.

storks and raccoons were noted by Horace Walpole in 1763.

Then in about 1990 the family sold their interest in Jackson-Stops & Staff, and Gervase, without any hesitation, decided to lavish his share on The Menagerie. A new garden was laid out by his friend Ian Kirby, a landscape gardener trained at Kew. He created a 'Wicked Garden' full of spiky and thorny plants approached by a winding yellow brick road.

The main part of the new garden was laid out like a goose's foot with three radiating walks. Between these, Gervase commissioned Charles Morris to build two enchanting thatched pavilions, with roofs descending to the ground almost like tea cosies. These were inspired by Thomas Wright's designs for 'Arbours and Grottoes' and represent the Classical and Gothic. Gervase, being an 18th-century man at heart, chose Strawberry Hill Gothick, not the serious 19th-century version.

The Classical Arbour has two porticoes, one Doric, the other Primitive with tree trunks for columns. Inside, the Gothic Arbour has gothic furniture made by a local craftsman after designs by Hobbs.

When it came to introducing a shell grotto beneath the house, hedonism knew no bounds. Shell grottoes are now the fashion but most owners build them as garden rooms. Gervase built his with a sauna, shower and octagonal whirlpool. The faces of friends appear on stones over archways beneath a ceiling encrusted with shells and minerals.

As The Menagerie grew, so did the standard of comfort. It comes with elegant book room, bathrooms more like map rooms, a kitchen garden, complete with its own workroom, and, at last, a proper drive.

LILFORD CASTLE   Lilford
Grand 17th-century house with shaped gables and soaring chimneys

A REVEALING GLIMPSE OF the English country house in wartime is provided on the website of the 303rd Bomb Group Association 'Hell's Angels'. This shows an aerial view of the park at Lilford Hall in May 1944, then an American Air Force hospital, filled with row after row of Nissen huts. As well as smiling pictures of officers who married nurses, there is a photograph of the garden front showing the grass of the garden terraces growing long, many of the windows shrouded by rampant creeper, but the crisp masonry of gables, balustrades and dozens of tall column chimneys all intact.

Lilford carries a date of 1635 and is Jacobean on the grand scale, finely built of smooth ashlar masonry which was much, though well, restored in the 19th century. In the 1740s a staircase, entrance hall and stables were added for Thomas Powys by Henry Flitcroft, endearingly known as Burlington Harry thanks to the patronage of the architect Earl of Burlington, who became Flitcroft's protector after the young man fell from the scaffolding while working at Burlington House.

Powys's grandson was created Baron Lilford. The 4th Lord Lilford, born in 1833, was a leading ornithologist and travelled widely, especially around the Mediterranean and established a large aviary at Lilford. This included rheas, kiwis, pink-headed ducks and a pair of free-flying Lammergeiers. He was responsible for the introduction of the little owl into England in the 1880s.

In the 1940s the family was forced to sell the house to pay death duties but the 7th Lord Lilford bought it and reopened the aviaries to the public. Many visitors came but the house remained closed, a tantalising sleeping beauty, and finally the estate was sold again about 1990. Recently it has been bought by a trademark attorney.

A rich silhouette of groups of tall chimneys are link to form open arcades.

MEARS ASHBY HALL
Mears Ashby
1637 Jacobean manor extended by Anthony Salvin

SMALLER JACOBEAN MANORS ARE AMONG the most distinctive and enchanting country houses in England. Part of the charm of these houses is the way the masons concentrated the architectural motifs at the top to create a festive silhouette. At Mears Ashby the central ogee gable is as exotic as the onion dome of a central European church spire. There are spiky finials on the end gables and in the centre an obelisk and ball over an open oculus.

The main front is exactly symmetrical. In place of the hood moulds that were used in Tudor times to throw off rainwater from the windows there is a continuous drip course. The principal Classical flourish is the porch with its pair of fluted columns on pedestals – a motif much used in 17th-century France. The arch over the entrance is inset with the initials 'TC' for Thomas Clenden, who built the house in 1637.

Much of its charm comes from the pale golden stone matched by the stone roof tiles which are laid in diminishing courses. The chimneys, clusters of four square piers, stand symmetrically on the roof ridge. There is a strict hierarchy in the windows which diminish in size towards the top

A Victorian wing was added in 1858 for the Stockdale family by the architect Anthony Salvin. His new rooms have much higher ceilings – two floors being equivalent to three in the old house, but he handled the transition skilfully, placing a tower between so the change of scale does not jar. His drawing room has a neo-Jacobean ceiling with crossed ribs and scrolly pendants as well as a Victorian rococo fireplace. In the grounds a Georgian tea house provides a view over the formal garden.

The Victorian tower and wing lie to the right of the five-gabled Jacobean front.

78 DERNGATE   Northampton
Triumphant restoration of the last work of Charles Rennie Mackintosh

At the back the town house was given a bedroom verandah with guest balcony above.

IN JANUARY 2004 THE LONG-SUSTAINED campaign to do honour to the memory of Charles Rennie Mackintosh, Britain's greatest pioneer Modernist, was finally crowned with the restoration of his last work. This is a Georgian terraced house in Northampton, just 15 ft wide, that was dramatically transformed for W.J. Bassett-Lowke, the famous maker of model locomotives and boats. The 39-year-old Bassett-Lowke commissioned Mackintosh in 1916, at the height of the First World War, to prepare the house for his bride. Thanks to the war work he was doing, Bassett-Lowke was able to fit out the house in style with bathroom fittings brought from America and furniture that was made to Mackintosh's designs.

Mackintosh's luminous interiors in Glasgow have long mesmerised visitors. This £1.5 million restoration was a triumph for the Derngate Trust, set up by Keith Barwell, the owner of the Northampton Saints rugby team, and his wife Maggie. The architects for the restoration, modernists John McAslan & Partners, carefully combined fastidious restoration with elegant new additions behind the scenes. A remarkable series of photographs of the house taken by Bassett-Lowke himself provided vital evidence, aided by two highly detailed articles in *Ideal Home* in August 1920, in which No 78 is described as a 'house of the future'.

Bold as always, Mackintosh took out the internal cross wall and turned the staircase through 90 degrees. This allowed him to create a front lounge-hall as nocturnally dark as some Freemasons' lodges, jet black and full of Aztec Egyptian motifs which are more Art Deco than Art Nouveau. Mackintosh himself wrote of a 'velvety blackness', but the sepulchral feel is alleviated by a 3-ft-deep frieze, stencilled with a cascade of golden arrowheads like some extraordinary shimmering necklace.

The handsome Mackintosh settee is a replica of the original, now in the V&A, made by Professor Jake Kaner of the University of the Chilterns. McAslan has stylishly reconstructed the central circular light with electric candles. Above is Mackintosh's highly geometric take on the traditional ceiling rose, a form of giant waffle made of balsa-wood blocks and ply and copied from the original, which still belongs to the family. At the back of the room the staircase rises behind a trellis screen.

The first-floor front room, unusually, is the bathroom, equipped with a free-standing bath and decorated with a clever pale grey mosaic wallpaper. Frosted glass keeps out prying eyes from across the street, while a clerestory brings extra light onto the stairs.

The tour de force is the guest room on the second floor, where bold black and white striped fabric is carried up behind the beds and across the ceiling to form a canopy as memorable as that of a great baroque state bed. The ensemble is completed by matching curtains and bedspreads, inset with iridescent blue silk and emerald-green satin. It is a foretaste of the famous Ascot set in the film *My Fair Lady*. On the walls, no picture interrupts the pure geometry. George Bernard Shaw slept here twice, and when his host expressed concern that such busy decoration might keep him awake, laconically replied, 'I always sleep with my eyes shut.'

Mackintosh's ingenious back extension cleverly enlarged the house, providing a bay window to the ground-floor dining room, a covered veranda to the Bassett-Lowkes' bedroom and a balcony to the guest bedroom above.

Such a small house is obviously difficult to show, but the trustees have taken their cue from Sir John Soane's Museum in London and bought up two adjoining houses. No 80, as narrow as No 78, has been transformed into a gallery that connects to the basement and second-floor levels, so that visitors do not have to retrace their steps. It also contains a lift. The glass sides of McAslan's crisp modern staircase double as showcases for Mackintoshiana (including the original front door, brought protectively in from the street) and Bassett-Lowke models.

The Bassett-Lowkes stayed in the house for just nine years before moving to a new country house designed by the German Modernist Peter Behrens. They took the Mackintosh furniture with them. After the Second World War, No 78 and other houses in Derngate were acquired by Northampton High School for Girls, which commendably left the Mackintosh bathroom intact when the house was listed Grade II*.

The end house, No 82, serves as an office for the trust. This scheme is a beacon in a town that for half a century has been bedevilled by ring roads and cloddish redevelopment. Happily there survive around Derngate several well-preserved streets of early 19th-century terraced houses in very pretty pink brick. No 78 Derngate is regularly open to the public.

The zebra stripes in the guest bedroom did not disturb George Bernard Shaw.

RUSHTON
Kettering
Palatial Tudor house of the Treshams extended in the early 17th century

RUSHTON IS A HYMN to the survival of the English country house. It has been an ancestral seat over six centuries, changing hands repeatedly and emerging from the 20th century remarkably unscathed. Dating from the early 16th century, it has been aggrandized with gables dated 1595, 1626, 1627 and 1630. These dates mark the purchase of the house from the Tresham family in 1614 by Sir William Cockayne, a successful London merchant and financier. His son was created Viscount Cullen in 1626 and after the last Viscount died the estate was sold to William Williams Hope. On his death in 1854 the estate was sold to Clara Thornhill and after she died it was leased to a succession of tenants.

During the Second World War Rushton became an army officers' training establishment and the scene of parties and dances, according to one of the Land Girls who attended.

After the war, Rushton was one of a select group of houses saved through the National Land Fund set up in 1946 as a national war memorial. Rushton was bought for a bargain £19,487 and restored by the Ministry of Works for £73,747 as there was 'no other way of securing preservation' before being presented to the Royal National Institute for the Blind. As a school for the blind, Rushton resonated with music and song – considered a vital way for pupils to express themselves. The house took both day pupils and boarders as well as offering 52-week care. When the school departed in 2003 Rushton was acquired as a luxurious country house hotel, catering for weddings and corporate events, offering antique four-posters and now a spa and gymnasium.

Massed topiary surrounds a house on which each century has left its own mark.

STOKE PARK

Stoke Bruerne

Twin pavilions and curving colonnades attributed to Inigo Jones

IS IT BY INIGO JONES OR NOT? The question continues to tease historians. An equal question is whether this is one of the most beautiful compositions in all English architecture. Certainly it is among the most photogenic thanks to the subtly varying shades of tan and rust-coloured stone which glow even in a watery sun. Contrast this with the dark waters of the reflective lily pond, with a stone coping as well judged as the frame of an old master, and you have a composition to rival any Palladian villa in the environs of Vicenza. To this is added a subtle but distinct vein of melancholy, in the best romantic sense, enhanced by the heavy foliage of the trees that close in behind the building.

This is partly because the central block has disappeared, destroyed by fire in 1886, leaving only the two wings and quadrant (quarter circle) colonnades which are themselves without roofs. The source for the attribution to Inigo Jones is Colen Campbell, author of *Vitruvius Britannicus*, who says that 'this building was begun by Inigo Jones: the wings and colonnades, and all the fountains were made by him: but the front of the house was designed by another architect, the Civil wars having interrupted this work.' Giles Worsley in his new book, *Inigo Jones and the European Tradition*, points out that Sir Francis Crane, for whom the house was built, was 'an intimate' of Charles I. He had been appointed his auditor general in 1617, the same year he was made a baronet and a member of the Prince of Wales's council, and in 1626 he was made lay chancellor of the Order of the Garter. All this suggests he had the best possible entrée to Charles I's court architect, Inigo Jones.

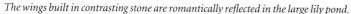

The wings built in contrasting stone are romantically reflected in the large lily pond.

WAKEFIELD LODGE
Potterspury
1750s hunting lodge built for the 2nd Duke of Grafton

FOR A HOUSE THAT ONCE STOOD in the centre of a forest, Wakefield Lodge has as commanding a view as can be imagined. It stands at the top of a gentle slope, looking across a long ornamental lake, now a sanctuary for migrating birds, to a vast sweep of parkland, some 250 acres in extent, known as Wakefield Lawn.

In the middle ages Whittlewood, or Whittlebury, was one of three royal forests in the county and entries in the Pipe Rolls show a hunting lodge was built or rebuilt here early in the reign of Henry II. Henry III failed to keep it up, neglecting it in favour of the neighbouring lodge of Silverston, and nothing further is known of its history.

In 1541 it was made part of the Honour of Grafton and it continued as a royal demesne under the first two Stuarts. In 1673 Charles II granted the property to Henry Fitzroy, then Earl of Euston, the second of his three natural sons by Barbara Villiers. Fitzroy, who was created Duke of Grafton in 1675, came into the estates at Wakefield and Euston ten years later, the same year as he distinguished himself in the defeat of the rebellion by his half-brother Monmouth. Renowned for his reckless heroism, he was mortally wounded at the battle of Cork.

His only son and heir, the 2nd Duke, who was to be the builder of Wakefield Lodge, inherited before his seventh birthday. He held the post of Lord Chamberlain for over thirty years serving both George I and George II. Waldegrave wrote that, 'He was a few days older than the king [George II] and had a particular manner of talking to his master on all subjects, and of touching on the most tender points, which no other person ever ventured to imitate.'

The 2nd Duke was also passionately devoted to hunting and when he travelled from Wakefield to Euston would take his hounds with him. He also used to hunt

Above: William Kent used distinctive eyebrow arches over the windows.
Right: The elegant spiral stair has had the undersides of the treads cut away to create a rippling effect.

south of the river at Croydon and the delays of the Thames ferrymen led him to promote the bill for the construction of Westminster Bridge to speed the passage of his hounds across the river (not the most obvious reason for the second crossing of the Thames in London).

In 1751 Horace Walpole wrote to his friend George Montagu, 'I saw a pretty lodge just built by the Duke of Grafton in Whittlebury Forest; the design is Kent's but, as was his manner, too heavy.'

William Kent had already worked for the Duke at Euston, where he landscaped the park and built the temple. Kent's design at Wakefield Lodge was a variant on the classic Palladian front, with twin towers at the ends, but the distinctive massing has been blurred by the addition of a second storey between the towers. Pevsner aptly called the design 'cyclopean' – appropriate as the central lunette peers over the porch like the central eye in the Cyclops's forehead. The windows in the towers are also set under flattened arches. The house is also distinctly high-waisted thanks to the strongly modelled cornice above the windows of the main floor, stronger than that at eaves level.

Inside Kent pays a handsome tribute to Inigo Jones, father of Palladian architecture in England. The great hall, almost a perfect cube with monumental first floor balcony is modelled on the hall of the Queen's House at Greenwich with a coffered ceiling here containing the Duke's Garter star. Wakefield's circular hanging stair, with steps rising round the walls is also inspired by the exquisite Tulip Stair at Greenwich.

THE OLD RECTORY — Yardley Hastings
Doll's-house perfection of a Queen Anne rectory

IN THE VILLAGE OF YARDLEY HASTINGS, hard by the Marquess of Northampton's vast Castle Ashby estate, is one of the most delightful of all Queen Anne rectories, though as it is dated 1701 we should more correctly call it William and Mary. It is a masterpiece of the bricklayer's art, built in a very pale pink brick subtly varied by a chequer pattern of burnt 'headers' (bricks laid end-on).

The mellowness is increased by the simplicity of the design. The only features are the segmental pediment over the front door in moulded brick and the scalloped tops to the first-floor windows. The brightness of the facade comes from the white-painted sashes and sash boxes, which are set flush with the brickwork – a practice banned in London in 1708 to reduce the risk of fire spreading. Other distinctive features are the blank panels, the pedimented dormers and the swooping gable ends.

Inside, the house is exceptionally well lit, a result of it mostly being just one room deep. The front door opens into a sumptuously oak-panelled entrance hall with a staircase leading out of one corner. This matches the house in date, but is said to have been removed from the baroque Streatlam Castle in County Durham, which was demolished in 1933.

The adjoining drawing room, with fluted Ionic pilasters flanking the fireplace, comes from Felling Hall, south of Newcastle. This work may have been carried out after the diocese sold the rectory in 1935 or done by the architect Sir Albert

Richardson, champion traditionalist, who lived little more than 20 miles away at Ampthill and made alterations for Mr and Mrs Peter Richardson, who came to live here in 1949. Later it was the home of Major D.W.A. Swannell, chief handicapper for the Jockey Club.

The Old Rectory also has pretty panelled bedrooms and an unusual attic that runs for almost the entire length of the 1701 house, making a spacious self-contained flat. The lower ground floor is also a realm unto itself, low-ceilinged for winter warmth with study and sitting room opening onto extensive gardens.

To the east a series of garden rooms enclosed by yew hedges has been created with vistas cleverly framing well-placed urns. The front door is approached along a paved path through a delightful front garden, so no cars will ever sully the best view of the house. When you arrive laden with shopping, you can park conveniently by the kitchen door at the side.

This masterpiece of the bricklayer's craft has subtle variations from its chequer pattern of burnt 'headers'.

BELFORD HALL
Belford
Built to the designs of James Paine with wings added by John Dobson of Newcastle

IN THE SUMMER OF 1968 I obtained permission to visit Belford Hall from the firm of gravel extractors that owned it. Inside I discovered room after room of filigree 18th-century plasterwork. The house faced south with a view over parkland and it was tragic to see it languishing unused. Twelve years later the whole building was boarded up, with elders growing from the parapet and holes in the roof letting the rain in.

A year later, all the internal joinery had been removed except the window shutters. Collapsed floors made it impossible to enter the rooms. A pipe taking rain from the valley gutter had been removed so 12,000 gallons of water a year were discharging onto the landing at the head of the stairs.

Salvation came when the Northern Heritage Trust acquired Belford in 1983. Backed by Simon Sainsbury's Monument Trust, Belford was restored and converted into sixteen self-contained houses and flats. The project was put in the hands of Hugh Cantlie, the surveyor who had worked successfully with SAVE to avert the demolition of Billingsgate Fish Market in London. Cantlie explains, 'The entrance and staircase were kept as communal space. The public can look in and also descend to the unusual apse-ended wine cellar which is stocked with empty bottles drunk over a lifetime.' Building costs, by the time the project was completed in 1987, amounted to £1.5 million, assisted by a £450,000 English Heritage grant. The net loss in rescuing the house from extreme decay was £90,000. 'Just £10,000 more than the figure I gave Simon Sainsbury at the beginning,' says Cantlie with understandable satisfaction.

The handsome stone-faced south front was restored after years of abandonment.

BELSAY HALL
Morpeth
Neo-classical masterpiece built by Sir Charles Monck largely to his own design

AT THE TIME THAT SAVE PUBLISHED *Tomorrow's Ruins* in 1978, Belsay Hall had stood empty for twenty years. When I visited the house, every single window was boarded up, ensuring it was thankfully secure. The grounds, magnificently planted for spring colour, were well kept up. This was when The Grange in Hampshire still stood rotting in the hands of the Department of the Environment and not long after Stratton Hall, another great neoclassical house in Hampshire, had been demolished.

Belsay was built in 1807–17 by Sir Charles Monck, largely to his own design. While The Grange was faced in stucco, Belsay was beautifully built of stone that remained in pristine condition. Inside the rooms were forlorn and bare of furniture but light still flooded into the central hall, which had been conceived along the lines of the atrium of an ancient Greek house. It was surrounded on all four sides by tall slender Ionic columns, with yet more columns on the landing above. Monck also developed the remarkable Quarry Garden, created where stone was cut for the building of the Hall and full of ravines, steep rock faces and pinnacles.

To ensure that houses like Belsay were not forgotten or allowed to decay, SAVE wrote a steady stream of letters urging councils to inspect houses and require repairs. At Belsay the county architect for Northumberland supervised the vital repairs. Finally, in 1984 Belsay was taken into guardianship and has since become one of English Heritage's flagship properties. This is a house of such strong character that the lack of furnishings does not disappoint visitors and English Heritage each year brings the property alive with imaginative installations and exhibitions.

Built in honey-coloured stone, Bywell is a perfect expression of the simplicity of the Greek revival.

BYWELL HALL

Bywell

Handsome Palladian house in park along the bank of the River Tyn

IN 1968 I SET OFF TO Yorkshire and Northumberland in search of the villas of the 18th-century architect James Paine for a series of articles I was writing for *Country Life*. I had found Belford Hall abandoned, Axwell Park a busy Borstal, and Gosforth House behind Newcastle racecourse a seedy restaurant smelling of cabbage. At Bywell Hall, I was suddenly in a different world. The house stands in a park on a bend of the north bank of the River Tyn. Bywell is an attractive village and Bywell Hall was still a family home belonging to the Allendales.

Paine had remodelled an existing house here for William Fenwick in 1670 and, like several of Paine's houses, it was distinctly high-waisted, with the temple front of columns and pediment set over a high ground floor. Like all Paine's northern houses, it was beautifully faced in stone. The Fenwicks evidently had money, for only seventeen years later James Fenwick commissioned designs for extensive additions by the mason John Carter.

At the beginning of the 19th century the estate was purchased by the Beaumont family whose descendants were created first barons and then Viscounts Allendale in 1911. The Beaumonts had extensive lead and coal mines and a still more splendid seat at Bretton in Yorkshire, which they sold in 1948 to the West Riding County Council.

Thomas Richard Beaumont died in 1829 leaving his son, Thomas Wentworth Beaumont, as the heir and the 'richest commoner in England'. He set up home at Bywell Hall and sold off the contents of Bretton at a grand auction in 1832.

The triple pediments of James Paine's front make it fairly unusual.

CALLALY CASTLE   Rothbury
Medieval Pele tower which grew into large 17th and 18th century mansion

FOR MOST OF THE 20TH CENTURY, Callaly had just one owner, the venerable and much-loved Major A.S.C. Browne, who took over from his father in 1925 and died aged 91 in 1988. Many owners faced with a house of this size would have severely truncated it after the Second World War, but Major Browne, continued to live in his ancestral home, changing little but retreating little by little into the kitchen wing and opening the house to the public every summer. By 1985 it was obvious that a painful decision had to be made to sell either some land, the house or the contents. The Trustees decided to disperse the contents and Kit Martin was invited to look at Callaly, producing a scheme that allowed Major Browne to keep the main wing and the principal family portraits.

As you drive up Whittingham Vale towards the house, there are wonderful views of rolling hills on either side, with the heather of the moors visible on the top. The estate is announced by a long park wall and encircling belt of trees, which date from 1704. The drive plunges down steeply to the house. Great lawns roll down to the south front but the drive continues on past the house, signalling the existence of estate buildings out of sight beyond.

The core of Callaly is a 14th-, or early 15th-century pele tower, now hidden behind Georgian refacing. This was built for the Claverings, whose descendants owned the estate until sold to the first Major Alexander Browne in 1877. Robert Clavering's will of 1582 mentions a manor house and the *History of Northumberland* states his son Sir John 'modernised the castle in the same style in which Chillingham was also being altered'.

The earliest work visible today is the south front, attributed to the Newcastle mason Robert Trollope. The broken pediments are a signature of his, as is the carved ornament with a tremendous armorial trophy over the front door and a sundial dated 1676. The wing on the right bears the date 1707 together with the initials of John Clavering and

Few external changes were needed to divide the large rambling composition into self-contained houses.

The grey stone is set off by the lush green of lawns and rolling parkland.

his wife Anne. The Claverings were Catholics and deeply involved in the 1715 Rebellion. Ralph, who succeeded his father in 1748, registered as a papist and promptly set about building a new chapel, conspicuously attached to the house. The foundation stone is dated 1750, seventy-nine years before the first Catholic Emancipation Act.

A vivid picture of life on a great estate is provided in D.P. Dixon's *Whittingham Vale* (1895). In the new stable block 'the men have their apartments, their dining rooms, sleeping rooms and comfortable reading rooms, well supplied with current literature, newspapers sporting and otherwise, as well as chess and draughtboards, cards and all kinds of games.'

'House, stables and several cottages,' he continued, 'were all lit by electric light.' Power here was provided by a pair of 9 horsepower engines supplied by Marshall of Gainsborough, and a pair of dynamos by Kepp. In the castle itself there were over 700 lamps varying from 8 candle power to 100. In the 1890s a remarkable music room was created by roofing over an internal courtyard. This is hung with trophies of big-game hunting expeditions. The star piece is a Kodiak bear from Alaska. Next to it is a python draped round a tree. Nearby are the heads of two of the wild white cattle at Chillingham, shot by the wife of the first Major Browne as part of a rehearsal for the Prince and Princess of Wales, who went to shoot two bulls in October 1872. Groups of native spears add overtones of Empire and Africa. Most dramatic of all is the cast-iron spiral staircase providing access to the roof ascending in three full circles to a roof-level gallery.

Kit Martin created twenty houses, cottages and flats. Major Browne's house was the size of a village rectory with eight bedrooms. The next-door house included the 1890s ballroom, built on the site of the Catholic chapel. In the walled garden a series of cottages was created from the crumbling bothies and potting sheds. By opening up small windows in the wall, these were provided with stunning views over the gardens to the castle while enjoying complete seclusion within the walled garden itself.

CHILLINGHAM CASTLE   Chillingham

Major 14th-century castle awoken from a century of slumber

OF ALL THE GRAND HOUSES that stood empty and slowly decaying in the 1970s Chillingham Castle was the most poignant. Imposing and four-square, it stood amid terraces where the grass was still mown, with a Renaissance frontispiece showing off the Classical orders similar to that at the Bodleian Library. In the medieval park, enclosed in the 13th century, the wild white cattle of Chillingham continued to graze.

The castle dates from 1344 when Sir Thomas Heton was granted a licence to strengthen his house with a stone wall, crenellate it, and convert it into a castle. Work must have proceeded quickly, as in 1348 he granted the vicar of Chillingham quarters over the castle gateway with stabling for two horses in the west hall.

In the 1980s Chillingham was fortunate enough to find a new chatelain with a burning passion for the beauty and history of the place, bringing every tower, attic and dungeon back into active use. Sir Humphrey Wakefield is both antique dealer and collector, with an eye for flamboyant, unusual and intriguing furnishings. 'Heritage would not approve of this' is his constant refrain as he dashes from one wing to another.

Far from being a museum, the castle is in constant use for events of every kind, for filming, antique auctions and banquets. Sir Humphrey knows many visitors are fascinated by ghosts and dungeons and he caters for them in spades. In October 2000, Fox Family Channel dared an average family from Illinois to spend the night in the most haunted castle in England. It had to be Chillingham and it resulted, says Sir Humphrey, in the highest-ever ratings. His dungeons include a stretching rack, a bed of nails, a spiked chair, a hinged metal casing for a live body, leg irons, cages, mantraps and branding irons.

The massive medieval masonry contrasts with the refined elegance of the columned Renaissance entrance.

CRAGSIDE   Rothbury
Mountain eyrie of Victorian arms manufacturer

CRAGSIDE TODAY IS IMMACULATELY looked after by the National Trust. When I first went there in 1974 its prospects were very different. Two years earlier Lord Armstrong had inherited both Cragside and Bamburgh Castle and was faced with massive death duties – and this was two years before the Government introduced tax exemptions for houses that were open to the public. Lord Armstrong's ancestor, the builder of Cragside, and a leading armaments manufacturer, had been a great entrepreneur and the first to light his country house with electricity. The new Lord Armstrong was determined to show similar spirit and had decided the way to meet his massive tax bill was by building new houses on Cragside's extensive estate. To this end he formed a joint company with Bellway Holdings, vested with 900 acres of pleasure grounds. The plan was to build up to 150 substantial houses on three sites, one of which was around Tumbleton Lake, part of the original landscaping of the grounds. Other houses would have intruded on the famous first glimpse of the house on the approach.

Locally there was some support but there was also strong opposition waiting to be voiced. I wrote up the issue in *Country Life*'s 'Conservation in Action' page, describing the 'immense Gothic landscape full of the mysterious darkened drama of hidden lakes, thickly wooded chasms, cliffs, waterfalls, and splashing burns; with banks of rhododendrons and azaleas contrasting sharply with vast outcrops of barren rock,

Norman Shaw's freestyle at its zenith, creating a soaring silhouette of gables and clustered chimneys.

The herringbone pattern half-timbering contrasts with the smooth stone.

and mile upon mile of scenic carriage drives and walks. At the centre of it all is the house, floating dreamlike above the valley below, a Neuschwanstein of the north, growing out of the rock on which it stood.'

More than that, Cragside's interiors were virtually untouched and complete with furniture that had been both made and bought for the house, carpets, wallpapers, tiles, stained glass, even curtains and covers, stuffed birds and framed photographs. Cragside, I argued, was 'a house of the quality that the National Trust's country house scheme was set up to preserve and should be bought complete with its contents and grounds and transferred to the Trust like Dyrham.' The planning objections, in a designated area of 'Great Landscape Value', were so strong that it was hard to see how the application for new houses could be approved.

A week later Lord Armstrong appeared in the *County Life* office with a suitably enormous stick determined to remonstrate with me. Lady Armstrong protested with even greater verve when I spoke to her on the telephone. But honour was satisfied in the end when the National Land Fund was used to compensate the Treasury for the loss in tax and Cragside and its surrounding estate were transferred to the National Trust at a cost of £562,668. Lord Armstrong generously gave part of the endowment and was able to continue living at Bamburgh Castle.

Today Cragside's lakes remained unsullied by development and visitors enjoy one of the largest rock gardens in Europe, as well as dramatic cascades, a rhododendron maze and the first prototype steel bridge. It is also home to some of the last red squirrels in Britain.

GOVERNOR'S HOUSE Berwick-upon-Tweed
Monumental baroque house in the style of Vanbrugh and Hawksmoor

BERWICK-UPON-TWEED IS ONE OF
the most impressive fortified towns in
Europe. The Elizabethan ramparts,
begun in 1558, are among the best-
preserved early artillery defences that
exist anywhere. Cloaked in smooth grass,
they merge with the golf links along the
sea to form a landscape as invigorating as
the finest 18th-century parkland.

I went to Berwick in 2003 in response to
a threat to build forty-two flats in the
grounds of the 1719 Governor's House,
attributed to both Vanbrugh and
Hawksmoor, and built in the baroque
ordnance style associated with them. Three
storeys high, the Governor's House
dominates both the Palace Green and the
Avenue, a delightful run of Georgian
houses looking over the Governor's garden.

The house from the ramparts. The garden needs to be freed of later buildings.

The Grade II* listing spoke of the 'outstanding historic and architectural
significance of the site' and 'the importance of [the] Governor's residence and gardens
within the hierarchy of the early 18th-century garrison'.

With the help of strong opposition from local people and the local authority, the
development proposals were defeated at a public inquiry. My model for the revival
of the Governor's House is the 18th-century William Paca House in Annapolis in
Maryland, home of the US Naval Academy. There the town's bus station had been
built over the grounds but local people set up a trust, bought the house and recreated
the historic garden, and it became a focal point for the town's cultural life.

The importance of trees and gardens to Berwick's ramparts is immediately evident
if you stand at their northern end and look down into the beautiful graveyard around
the Cromwellian church, where trees have grown to a maturity that is hard to believe
on this windswept coast. Remarkably, the succession of fine trees continues all the way
along the coastal ramparts and in the splendid series of town gardens that are on view
behind the larger houses. The walk goes past the early 18th-century barracks and the
buttressed powder magazines, all beautifully restored by English Heritage. Towards the
south end the Elizabethan defences give way to medieval town walls strengthened in
the 18th century but still covered with a carpet of emerald grass and shaded by good
trees. It is here that the Governor's House and its garden provided the perfect
counterparts to the canopied churchyard. The Governor's House and garden must
be restored, as a museum, an hotel, or why not a family home, as all would enjoy the
sight of lawns and flower beds from the ramparts.

HOWICK HALL
Alnwick

Georgian house rebuilt by Sir Herbert Baker after a fire in 1926

THE GREAT BEAUTY OF HOWICK HALL lies in the gardens planted and improved over a period of nearly eighty years by the 5th Earl Grey, who inherited in 1917, and his wife Mabel, and continued by their daughter Lady Mary Howick. Lord Grey's uncle was George Holford of Westonbirt in Gloucestershire (now the National Arboretum) while Mabel's brother was Lewis Palmer, a noted plant breeder.

Lord Howick planted an extensive woodland garden in stands of hardwood and Scots pine 200 yards from the house where the lime-free greensand soil was perfect for rhododendrons. Lady Howick planted thousands of daffodils and Howick now has a ravishing collection of 1920s and 1930s daffodil cultivars. When I visited in the late 1970s the noble stone house stood mostly empty with a large question mark over its future.

The late 18th-century house had been rebuilt by Sir Herbert Baker after a savage fire in 1926 and to reduce the size of the house Baker, in his cavalier way, had introduced a portico with an open well behind. 'Disciples of Georgian architecture are not amused,' says the present Lord Howick.

As the gardens lapped the house the family did not want to sell, and the solution has been to place the gardens in a charitable trust, which now has a team of five gardeners. Since 1985 the present Lord Howick has been on annual expeditions to collect wild seed in different parts of the temperate world – including ten expeditions to Sichuan. The gardens at Howick are open daily from April 1 to October 31. The long-term plans for the house are to open it with an exhibition on the family, including the Great Reform Bill introduced by Lord Grey in 1832.

The stone is so crisp that even shallow mouldings create strong shadows.

BUNNY HALL — Bunny
Baroque folly designed by the 'Wrestling Baronet'

BUNNY HALL IS ONE OF the most eccentric and engaging houses in Middle England. Dated 1723, it was built by Sir Thomas Parkyns, the wrestling baronet, whose splendid life-size monument, designed by himself, in the parish church across the road shows him poised for a bout of wrestling. The inscription relates that he had a competent knowledge of architecture 'contriving and drawing all his plans without an architect'.

Parkyns recommended wrestling as a means of preparing for war against the French. He called on Parliament to 'establish a stage in every market-town at which gentlemen wearing swords can settle their affronts'. Notwithstanding this, Parkyns would wrestle with his servants (and on occasion be the loser) at the annual wrestling matches held at Bunny which began in 1712 and continued to 1810.

Born in 1662, Parkyns had gone first to Westminster School and then to Trinity

Although it looks like a church tower, it was designed for watching the hunt.

College, Cambridge, where Sir Isaac Newton had noted Parkyns's liking for mathematics. Succeeding his father in 1684, Sir Thomas rebuilt farmhouses, re-roofed the church and erected the adjacent school in an intriguing primitive style. As well as rebuilding Bunny Hall at a cost of £12,000, he spent £5,000 on constructing a wall around the park, built unusually on arches.

The main feature of Parkyns's house is a 60-ft tower that was built to provide a magnificent panorama of the hunting country all around. Seen from the village it looks like the tower of a baroque church with a giant segmental gable sheltering a splendid carved coat of arms bursting with spears and guns. The arms are those of Parkyns impaling Cressy – his mother being the daughter and sole heiress of Thomas Cressy. From close to, the composition is stranger still, with a pair of massive stepped buttresses supporting the tower, inset with blind arches and shallow niches. The brickwork of the tower is very fine, laid to form a chequer pattern of burnt headers.

In the gable there is Tudor-style diapering (a criss-cross pattern) showing Parkyns's disregard for fashion. On the south flank there is more crazy detailing – the giant pilasters marking the ends are both Ionic but one is in stone and the other in brick. On the east side is an immense sundial, with an upside-down clock face tracking the movement of the sun.

Thomas Boothby Parkyns was created Baron Rancliffe in 1795. His son, the 2nd Baron, succeeded in 1800 and extensively remodelled the hall in 1826–35. The contents of the house were sold up in 1910, in a five-day sale that included an amazing collection of dated silver.

In 1910 Bunny was bought by the Mayor of Nottingham and then sold on to Dr R. H. Cordeux. During the Second World War, the house was used briefly by a girls' school, but it had been empty for more than forty years when it was bought by the entrepreneur Chek Whyte in 2000. He told me, 'One more winter and the roof would have fallen in and pushed the walls out. I bought it without going inside. The deal was completed in 24 hours.'

The vaulted hall opens into a grand trio of reception rooms linked by quadruple folding doors that open up for grand parties. The cornices have crisp Grecian detail with grand fireplaces below. On the ground floor of the 17th-century wing Whyte installed a columned Roman swimming pool, while preserving the massive Victorian ovens immediately beside. Wherever he has found an interesting feature, be it a meat hook hanging from a ceiling or a leaded kitchen sink, he has preserved it.

CLIFTON HALL   Nottingham
Back as one grand house after decades of institutional use

THE BRIDESHEADS OF ENGLISH ARCHITECTURE – country houses that have grown through the centuries – always have a special fascination. The most fortunate have remained with ancient families for generations. Others have survived only through decades of institutional use.

One such is Clifton Hall, south of Nottingham, which had, until half a century ago, the rare distinction of being in the hands of Cliftons since the Norman Conquest. A poignant memorial in the churchyard by the house records the death in 1944 of Colonel Percy Robert Clifton CMG DSO, the last Lord of the Manor to live here. After the war Clifton Hall became a girls' school and then a teacher training college which was absorbed into Nottingham Trent University.

When institutions occupy country houses, it is almost an iron law that first they demand major extensions for expansion and then, after fifteen to twenty years, decide the property is no longer suitable for their needs. Exactly this happened at Clifton Hall.

Leaving the M1 for Nottingham, you are quickly confronted with a huge power station which on a grim grey day looks like the entrance to Hell itself. So the turning to Clifton village restores faith in the English landscape, with almshouses and a grand dovecote (2,300 nesting places no less) set on a village green that opens onto a long winding village street. Clifton Hall stands at the very end, past the stables that are now in City Council ownership.

The bow was added by the architect John Carr of York in the 1780s.

The Hall is sited on a bluff above the River Trent, though the majestic view has been all but planted out – perhaps to shield the sprawl of factories below. The long entrance front is impressive, built of a pleasant pink Georgian brick with an indented centre uncannily like that of Nottingham Castle.

The generations of Cliftons who have lived at the Hall are a study in themselves. Sir Gervase the Gentle is credited with starting the building of the present house in the 1560s. His grandson, another Gervase, married no less than seven times, burying six wives and being followed quickly to the grave by the seventh. Yet another Clifton is praised for 'port and hospitality' exceeding the nobility, and for a 'cheerful facetious spirit.'

Inside the state rooms, layer upon layer of history unfolds in confusing order. The present entrance lobby has dividing arches on stout Corinthian columns, and leads through to an elegant 18th-century stone stair. But this is not how you should see the house.

Instead, the double doors behind the colonnade should be thrown open so you enter directly into one of grandest of all Georgian halls, which was just possibly designed by the great apostle of English Palladianism, the Earl of Burlington, who designed a temple in the garden that was sadly demolished in the 1960s. His hall is a soaring octagon rising the full height of the house – it was built for Sir Robert

Clifton in about 1750 and has niches inset with casts of Classical statues and a dome with gloriously rich acanthus decoration.

The octagonal hall opens into another imposing stair, which leads up to a Jacobean Great Chamber with a colossal fireplace that rivals those at Hatfield House. It is attributed to John Smythson, son of the greatest of Elizabethan architects, Robert Smythson.

In the 1780s another Sir Gervase Clifton brought in John Carr of York, the architect who, it often seems, had a hand in almost every house of significance in the North of England in the later 18th century. Carr added a prominent bow to the end of the house as well as a wealth of fine plasterwork.

The greatest thrill is the so-called Page's Room that dates from the 1630s, with over fifty deftly painted panels of soldiers in armour taken from a Dutch manual demonstrating the use of pike, halberd and musket. Almost next door is a Charles II bedroom with an ornamental plaster ceiling that is as thick with fruit and flowers as any Lucullan banquet.

Clifton Hall was bought by the enterprising Chek Whyte who has rescued a series of houses in the county. He restored the east wing as a single house, planning to divide the west wing into three apartments. Remarkably, the Malaysian gentleman who had visited the east wing one morning and agreed to buy it, returned the same afternoon to buy all three apartments and unite the hall as one big house for his extended family.

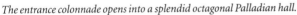

The entrance colonnade opens into a splendid octagonal Palladian hall.

COLWICK HALL   Nottingham
Elegant Georgian house by Nottingham racecourse rescued from years of decay

A SUDDEN FLASH OF SUN IS RARELY BETTER seen than on the garden front at Colwick. The brick turns to pink and the stone trim glows gold. Handsome Ionic columns and an elegant roof balustrade provide a touch of grandeur, yet the house sits comfortably on the ground with garden doors opening onto the lawns. It is hard to see how such a covetable house should ever have been left empty and decaying.

Colwick was designed in 1776 for John Musters by John Carr of York, architect of dozens of Palladian country houses all over northern England. Dramatic events took place during the Chartist riots of 1831. when a mob assembled in Nottingham after the Great Reform Bill had been rejected. One group proceeded to Colwick and entered the house, smashing furniture, slashing pictures and then setting fire to the building. Mrs Musters and a guest escaped to a shrubbery and hid beneath spreading laurels.

In 1892 a racecourse opened in the grounds of Colwick Park and surrounding land was steadily built on. Colwick Hall served on and off as a public house for racegoers but was eventually shut up and left to decay. When the brewers Scottish and Newcastle took over in 1987, Nottingham Council demanded reinstatement of missing doors and fireplaces. The brewery appealed and squatters and vandals moved in. In 2002 Chek Whyte stepped in to restore Colwick as an hotel. He sold it in 2004 to two Malaysian brothers, Selva and Kumar Muthalagappan, who had restaurants in Kenilworth, London and Leeds.

Today the hotel is a flourishing wedding venue with a restaurant offering Colonial Malaysian menus. Singapore Slings are on offer in the champagne bar and you can sleep in the King George II or Lord Byron Signature Suites. Grand Italianate fountains play on both sides of the hotel and a large marquee has taken up permanent residence.

The garden front with elegant roof balustrades is set off by Italianate fountains.

FLINTHAM   Newark
Rare Victorian mansion remaining in the hands of the family that built it

MANY VICTORIAN HOUSES ARE ON such a grandiose scale that it is hard to see them ever becoming family homes again. When institutional use ends, the best options tend to be hotel use or sensitive division into apartments, houses and cottages. Flintham is the glorious exception, remaining the home of the Hildyard family who built it, rescued from wartime decay and splendidly maintained for nearly forty years by Myles Hildyard.

Flintham is a brilliant essay in the Italianate style pioneered by Sir Charles Barry. The architect was T.C. Hine of Nottingham, best known for his work on handsome warehouses in Nottingham's Lace Quarter. At Flintham he was reincasing an earlier Georgian house but he so varies this, with a tower and projecting bays, that from the park it looks a wholly Victorian building. He created a lively, almost baroque silhouette with spiky urns along the roof balustrade, which is itself given exaggerated height by an unusually tall plinth.

The *porte cochère*, or carriage drop off, is incorporated beneath the tower and fronted by paired columns and more urns. Hine made the windows on the entrance front into

This is Victorian Italianate at its liveliest, with a silhouette crowded with urns.

The imposing conservatory has a hooped roof like Paxton's Crystal Palace.

linked compositions. They are an intriguing blend between the swan-top Georgian bookcase and the Palladian window with a central arch. Most exotic of all are the porthole windows with butterfly-shaped panes below. Inside, Hine's distinctive windows rise almost from floor to ceiling, maximising the amount of daylight.

The north front further showed off his knowledge of Italian architecture with a stair window modelled on 15th-century Venetian gothic palaces with flared or ogee arches surmounted by roundels. Below this is a delightful Romanesque arcade with distinctive cushion-like capitals.

The magnificent conservatory has a hooped glass roof like that of the 1851 Crystal Palace – the wall-lights inside were trophies from the Great Exhibition. The conservatory is integrated into the house by plate-glass windows that look out from the library onto the luxuriant vegetation, and above a bedroom opens charmingly onto a Juliet-style balcony. The walled garden is no longer simply a kitchen garden, but a romantic flower garden with box-edged beds and yew arches and well-placed statuary.

Flintham has recently been taken over by Myles Hildyard's nephew Robert Hildyard. I went there to look at the effects of dualling the busy A46 running along the edge of the park. What was proposed was an assault on an Elysium, cutting down fine mature oaks to create a lay-by, introducing intrusive lighting and a raised roundabout. One of the most damaging proposals was for a footbridge arching high over the road and visible across the park. One alternative was a tunnel. Reading Myles's delightful wartime memoirs, I found he had suggested just this to his parents half a century before.

SHIREOAKS
Worksop
Robert Smythson house and baroque water garden saved from decay

LEO GODLEWSKI DISCOVERED SHIREOAKS when he set off as an architectural student in search of Elizabethan buildings by the Smythsons. Robert Smythson was Bess of Hardwick's 'Surveyour' at Hardwick Hall in Derbyshire while his son John was the architect of nearby Bolsover Castle.

Shireoaks was built in about 1600 for Henry Hewett, almost certainly to the designs of Robert Smythson, and remodelled for Sir Thomas Hewett in 1719–26. The house had been gutted by fire in 1811 but restored the next year. When Godlewski arrived it was once again decaying and the remarkable garden going to ruin. By dint of extraordinary energy and enthusiasm, Godlewski persuaded the owner to sell the house and 45 acres – at the same time inveigling his parents to be the buyers.

The most remarkable feature of Shireoaks today is the extraordinary baroque water garden. This begins as a canal in front of the garden facade of the house, 250 yards in length and originally flanked by clipped yews. Water was supplied by a great circular basin half a mile away. Between the canal and the basin is a series of fourteen oval and circular pools, lined with stone and fed by some thirty-four cascades. As early as 1825 the *History of Worksop* by John Holland reported that the lake was stagnant and the 'glittering cascade gone to ruins'. By the 1970s the whole water garden was choked with mud and weeds. Leo bought a second-hand bulldozer and started to remove silt. Soon the water was flowing down the original channels and each water basin was full to the brim – a rare example of a formal baroque garden that survived the great craze for natural landscaping in the later 18th century.

The early 18th-century canal aligned with the house is a rare survival of formal garden layout.

STANFORD HALL   Stanford-upon-Soare
Georgian house extended for manufacturer Sir Julian Cahn

SEEING THE GATES OF STANFORD HALL OPEN in 2005, I drove in. The house had a red-brick centre with tall Ionic pilasters but the curving wings added an institutional air not helped by the plate-glass windows. I found the south-facing garden front bathed in sun, looking out over magnificent parkland. In front was a large terrace enclosed by balustrades and laid out with formal gardens and on the upper lawn was a Romanesque cloister, with columns supporting semicircular arches capped by a neat hat of roof tiles.

Walking on, I found a caretaker who pointed to a pond below the house built for a colony of sea lions for the Nottingham manufacturer Sir Julian Cahn in the 1930s. Next I was shown into the remarkable 352-seat Art Deco cinema-theatre designed for Cahn by Cecil Aubrey Massey, with murals by the artist Beatrice MacDermott. A coved ceiling concealed the lights while glass panels were etched with signs of the zodiac. The 1930s alterations were carried out for Cahn by Messrs Allom. They redecorated the interiors of the house in a variety of period and modern styles. Lady Cahn's boudoir had a mirrored ceiling, while a concealed doorway was reputed to lead to a lavish marble bathroom. Alloms also designed a rock-faced garden pavilion with fish-scale roof, a swimming pool with streamlined curved concrete diving boards and slide and a game house with octagonal wooden louvre.

The Georgian house was built for Charles Vere Dashwood in 1771–4 by the Loughborough architect William Henderson, and extended in the 1890s by W.H. Fletcher for the Ratcliffe family.

A year after my visit I heard that Chek Whyte, who had rescued three other Nottinghamshire houses, had bought Stanford Hall and he was going to live there. The whole family had already decided which rooms were going to be theirs.

The Georgian cetnre block is flanked by Victorian wings with plate glass windows.

THORESBY HALL — Ollerton
Salvin set out to make the house the grandest of the Nottinghamshire Dukeries

FIFTEEN YEARS AGO THORESBY HALL was the only one of the stupendous Nottinghamshire Dukeries, the grandest houses in Britain, to remain intact. The National Coal Board had bought the house in 1980, when intended mining operations threatened it with subsidence. Calculating that it would be cheaper to shore up the house in advance, the acquisition was a safeguard against heavy subsidence claims from the family. As the whole future of the house was uncertain, the family retained ownership of all fixtures, fittings and moveable contents – everything that could be stripped out if Thoresby was ever threatened with demolition.

The mining never took place, but the Coal Board opened the house to the public for eight years until in 1988 they decided to sell. Contracts were exchanged with an Australian company intending to convert the house into a luxury hotel, but requiring the clearance of the spectacular furnishings of Thoresby's state rooms to allow intensive use of the space. Despite strong protest the sale proceeded, but though the furniture was lost to the house, the grand interiors remained intact with all their splendid fittings, panelling, plasterwork and even stained glass.

Thoresby then descended into a desperate state with leaking roofs prompting outbreaks of dry rot. Salvation came when Warner Holidays acquired the house. The price has been a major extension to the house containing over 200 bedrooms and

This is Victorian baronial with a feast of architectural detail that is almost impossible to digest.

The elaborately enriched clock tower and cupola are positioned over the entrance.

completely changing its character. Today the approach to the house is via a car park as large and regimented as that of a supermarket, with an unattractive glazed modern reception block at the back of the house, a large new coffee bar and numerous corridor links. But the state rooms are now back in use. The drawing room has a bar complete with fruit machine, but the dining room is elegantly furnished, and the great stone-walled hall is resplendent in all its cavernous grandeur.

Thoresby was designed by Anthony Salvin and built in 1864–75 for the 3rd Earl Manvers. This is England's answer to Scottish baronial, with a skyline that is as rich and exuberant as contemporary buildings by David Bryce, north of the border. The entrance front is a full five storeys like a grand hotel rather than a country house, and dominated by a stupendous three-tier tower that rises to an open bellcote. The long garden front has three splendid bay windows, each to a different, more elaborate design. Above there are massed ranks of dormers and spiky gables, clusters of chimneys with emphatic stonework, and domed corner belvederes with ironwork finials. The composition is at once awesome and a little indigestible, impressive more than loveable. It takes time to realise that the whole design is an exercise in studied asymmetry – though each front is carefully balanced, one half is very the match of the other. Be sure to walk out of the original main entrance, through the walled courtyard into the park towards the lake, or to turn up to the extensive *parterres* where the fountains once again play.

Built of fire proof construction, the house appears originally to have been without bathrooms – the large indoor staff not only lighting fires throughout the house but filling portable baths and wash stands in the bedrooms. The elaborate service quarters occupied all four wings of the basement and one wing of the main floor. A mezzanine over the serving rooms was exclusively for the use of female staff with individual bedrooms for the housekeeper and cook and shared bedrooms for maids and visitors' ladies' maids . In the basement were the steward's room and another for the groom of the chambers, a brushing room, a luggage room, store rooms, a place for washing vegetables, a still room (for beer), wash house, laundry and bakehouse, all very similar to the hierarchy and divion of labour in a contemporary grand hotel.

MANOR LODGE   Worksop
Towering five-storey Elizabethan Lodge that was once taller still

HOUSES BUILT IN THE COUNTRY TODAY are usually of two storeys, rarely three. Manor Lodge at Worksop is a full five storeys and John Holland's *History of Worksop* (1826) says it once had a further two. The plain masonry and rows of mullioned windows have distinct resemblance to the first multi-storey textile mills built in the West Riding in the early 18th century. Yet here we have a date of 1595 when 'Mr Portyngton's newe lodge in worsopp' is described as nearing completion. Mark Girouard explored the history of the house in his book *Robert Smythson and the Elizabethan Country House*.

Smythson was the greatest of the Elizabethan mason-architects and Manor Lodge was built for the 7th Earl of Shrewsbury, whose great mansion Worksop Manor stood nearby until burnt down in 1761. Manor Lodge compares to Wothorpe Lodge near Burghley, which the 1st Lord Exeter built to go to 'when his house of Burleigh was sweeping'. A literary counterpart is provided in *Arcadia* where King Basilius built himself a star-shaped lodge as a retreat from the cares of government.

The centre of Manor Lodge projects forward on both sides and contains two great rooms, one above the other, equating to four storeys on either side. This arrangement is akin to the Venetian *portego* – the grand saloon that runs from front to back in Venetian palaces with windows at both ends. The interiors are plainly detailed. A typical Elizabethan stair rises in short flights around a solid masonry pier. Here is one of the most unusual of 16th-century houses, which changed hands as recently as 2006.

The projecting centre contains two double-height saloons running from front to back.

OXFORDSHIRE

ADDERBURY HOUSE   Adderbury
Baroque splendour returns after years of institutional use

FOR THOSE IN SEARCH OF GRANDEUR, nothing in English architecture approaches the work of Sir John Vanbrugh, the architect of Blenheim Palace. Adderbury House is a stately essay in the Vanbrugh manner, which the historian Richard Hewlings has shown was mainly the work of the master mason William Townesend, who worked with Vanbrugh's partner, Nicholas Hawksmoor, on the Clarendon Building in Oxford.

The house stands in the village of Adderbury, south of Banbury, and has a noble entrance arch almost tall enough to admit a double-decker bus. Like the house beyond, it is built in the rich local ironstone that glows gold in the sun. The west front of the house, enticingly glimpsed through the arch, is taller than it is wide, with the elliptical and arch-headed windows typical of English Baroque.

On the left is an arcaded wing with square piers similar to that at Vanbrugh's Seaton Delaval in Northumberland. The entrance front has the same noble simplicity, with not a trace of ornament apart from the lead rainwater heads dated 1722. The windows have the simplest of sills, and instead of the usual cornice there are only plain masonry bands – demonstrating that Baroque architects could be minimalists too. Intriguingly, the facade is not quite symmetrical, probably because earlier work is incorporated within.

The task of making Adderbury into a modern trophy house was begun a dozen years ago by Anton Bilton, who then transformed Sir John Soane's Tyringham Hall, across the Buckinghamshire border. When he bought Adderbury, it had been empty for ten years after the closure of the old people's home that was established here after the Second World War.

A new formal garden has been laid out by the side of the house.

Although it came with a limited amount of land and Bilton gave the ice house and two lakes to the village, the garden now has tall yew hedges that form a series of large garden rooms, although more work is needed to make it an equal match for The Ven in Somerset.

Since then the most surprising visitor has been Johnny Depp, who came over from Blenheim Palace, where he was filming *The Libertine*, playing the 2nd Earl of Rochester, who lived here at Adderbury. The earl was a lover of wine, women and

The entrance front was remodelled by a Derby winner c.1900.

the theatre, a patron of Dryden and other Stuart playwrights. He was too grand to be seen on stage himself, but would appear in disguise, doing outrageous impersonations which, at least once, landed him in a duel.

The estate passed in 1717 to the 2nd Duke of Argyll and it was he who employed Townesend. In 1801 Adderbury was acquired by a Mr Field who greatly reduced the size of the house and introduced Regency balconies.

More change came with Major James Larnach, whose horse, Jeddah, won the Derby at 100–1 in 1898. He restored the house to its baroque grandeur, adding the projecting centre of the entrance front and the matching east and west facades. The stone is a brilliant match and the only giveaway is in the awkwardly large Ionic capitals of the porch.

The front door opens into a staircase hall with a broad baroque arch framing a view of a monumental stair with twisted wooden banisters. This is continued in stone in an elegant cantilever to the second floor and lit by a graceful oval dome.

It is tantalising to find so few survivals of the 1722 house (one report is that a fire officer ordered panelling to be stripped out when the house became an old people's home), but many rooms retain their generous baroque proportions. A sale catalogue of 1774 states that the house had fifty-six rooms; today there seem to be at least as many. Mr Bilton has created two self-contained houses in the back range, each of three storeys with its own stair. Adderbury needs an enterprising owner interested in using the wealth of drawings by architects such as James Gibbs, Roger Morris and Sir William Chambers to create some truly stunning interiors.

ASHBURY MANOR
Ashbury
Late 15th-century manor little changed thanks to centuries as a tenanted farmhouse

BUY ASHBURY MANOR AND ELEVEN CENTURIES of English history will be yours, I wrote in 2005. According to nothing less than the great chartulary of Glastonbury Abbey, the manor of 'Asshebury' was given to St Dunstan, the 10th-century abbot, by a Count Edric who received it from King Edred. A 13th-century survey shows that the abbot's desmesne here comprised 667 acres of arable land and 129 acres of meadow.

In the later Middle Ages Ashbury served as a hostelry for monastic scholars on their way to and from Gloucester College, the Benedictines' place of study in Oxford.

A house has probably stood here for more than a thousand years, but the present manor, all of one build, dates from the late 15th century, the first years of Henry VII's reign. Solidly built of squared white chalk and a creamy oolitic limestone, it consists of a ground-floor great hall with two grand chambers above, one a dormitory for the students and the other the abbot's own chamber. The service end of the main block has a lower roof and contained a steward's room on the first floor.

The glory of Ashbury is the extent to which all this is unchanged. The medieval sloping buttresses survive, and the richly carved mullioned windows have flat tops inset with shallow cusped arches; similar windows are found at the George Inn at Glastonbury, built for pilgrims by Abbot John Selwood, a great builder whose initials appear on several Somerset churches. Ashbury can confidently be attributed to him. Only the top of the porch has been rebuilt, in red brick with darkened or burnt 'header' bricks, creating a chequer pattern typical of Berkshire and bearing the date 1697.

Today, thanks to a 1974 boundary change, Ashbury is in Oxfordshire, close to the Wiltshire border, and reflecting the border between Mercia and Wessex. The approach from London is an exhilarating drive along the Berkshire Downs, through

Stepped corner buttresses and cusped window heads proclaim the house's age.

the Lambournes and 'the valley of the racehorse' and past the National Trust's Ashdown House. The road crosses the ancient Ridgeway at 668 ft before descending to Ashbury, a delightful village on the edge of the Downs.

The manor opens off the centre of the village. Its survival intact has a simple explanation: even before it came to the Craven estate in the 1620s it was a tenanted farm, reasonably well maintained but neither altered nor improved. Robert Spence came here in 1927 and bought the farm from the Craven estate in 1956. 'Father rer-oofed the house – it was an eighteen month job. The stone slates we saved were supplemented by others from a barn of my uncle's on the other side of Lechlade. They were all stacked, sorted and graded and placed on the roof in diminishing rows,' says his son James.

Ashbury is still very much a working farm. The approach is through the farmyard, with large modern barns on the left. On the right is a splendid aisled barn, ideal for events, and nearer the house a yard surrounded by lower byres, easily adapted as offices and garages.

The porch opens into a screens passage, with a vista through stone arches at either end. In the 16th century the ground-floor hall was divided into two rooms, probably for Sir William Essex, who was granted the manor in 1543 after the Dissolution of the Monasteries. This was done with a sturdy oak partition placed so the central south window gives life to both rooms. The partition consists of tall, narrow panels with a single horizontal division, plainer than the usual linenfold panelling of this date but rather grand and gloriously mellow in colour. It is also pristine in condition, apart from a few scorch marks from candles. Richly carved ceiling bosses survive in both rooms, one with vine leaves and another with a Tudor rose.

A tight, well-worn stone stair, beginning on the curve, leads to the first floor. On the left is the 15th-century garderobe, where the original lavatory seat, made of a thick, hollowed-out plank of elm, was discovered boarded over when a bathroom was inserted in the 1950s.

The two upper chambers have later plaster ceilings but were originally open to the roof. In the attic the splendid arched timbers with arch-braced collar beams and cusped wind braces can still be seen, silvered in one half, blackened in the other, perhaps by smoke from the abbot's fire. The rooms are divided by a sturdy 15th-century wooden partition of vertical planks with chamfered edges – a simple treatment using timbers of a size that now seems breathtaking.

In the abbot's chamber a dark wooden frieze runs round the room carved with Flamboyant-style tracery of an almost French richness. No less remarkable a survival is the late 15th-century screen opening into the chamber over the porch. The openwork upper panels suggest that this was the abbot's private chapel or oratory.

Throughout the house a satisfying simplicity reigns – there are five bedrooms and two bathrooms with three rooms in the mid-Victorian cottage annexe. The office, with large internal glass partition, looks a pleasant place to work, while a kitchen in a Victorian north wing looks out over the garden. From the 2-acre garden are fine views over the vale below, as well as a glimpse down to cress beds fed by a spring, asking to be turned into an exotic water garden. All around is unspoilt country, and though Swindon is only seven miles away it seems another world.

JACOB'S LADDER   Chinnor
Glass box floating in the landscape

THE CLASSIC MIESIAN GLASS BOX has a temple-like perfection but it is one that depends for its success on a very well-thought-out relationship with the landscape around. Jacob's Ladder takes its inspiration not only from Mies but from the famous Case Study houses in California. There is a touch of Frank Lloyd Wright, too, in the way the pool pavilion breaks out dramatically from the box to create a play on horizontal planes. The best modern architecture, like the best Palladian or Classical design, takes much of its beauty from good proportions. Though the house is built on a modernist grid, it is not a grid of squares or cubes but of carefully judged rectangles, both vertical and horizontal.

The beauty comes too from the way the architect Niall McLaughlin has used minimal structural elements, creating the maximum sense of openness and transparency. The columns taper to a point at the top. The beams they carry appear equally slight. The roof shading that sails out over the glass walls also looks paper thin, as does the decking, thanks to the simple device of a projecting lip.

The house is approached by a glass side bridge with a view through to the landscape beyond. Though Jacob's Ladder is welcoming, privacy is paramount and the glass wrapping the stair is opaque. Once inside, an entire wall of glass in the double-height living room provides an amazing view. The house's other most remarkable feature is the infinity swimming pool, long and narrow but with glass coming down to the level of the water, creating reflections that suggest the pool is glass-sided too. The roof above has also been designed as a shallow pool, floating over the landscape.

Needle-thin columns and slender structure create maximum openness and transparency.

COTE HOUSE

Bampton

Gabled Cotswold manor with pyramid-roofed stone tower

GABLED COTSWOLD MANORS STAND HIGH among the most covetable houses in England. Built of pale local stone, they are often roofed as well as walled in stone. Though often described as stone slate, they have nothing to do with slate, but then neither are they manufactured like tiles. The local masons gave them Hobbit-like names according to their size – muffities and wivetts, tants and cussems (or cussomes).

At Cote House all were relaid in about 2000 ago, preserving the feel of a building that has grown entirely from the landscape in which it stands. The house is set in tranquil seclusion on a country road lined with village houses. Turning off the road from Stanton Harcourt to Bampton, your eye is caught by the soaring 17th century gable of Cote Baptist Chapel, proclaiming country where Dissenters walked tall and now carefully preserved by the Historic Chapels Trust.

Five hundred yards further on, set back behind a broad grass verge, are the high walls of Cote House, with a central pair of gate piers allowing a brief glimpse of a garden path leading straight to the front door. The whole scene steps straight out of an early 18th-century engraving – that age when old manors were still secluded amid walled gardens and ha-has had still to be invented.

Today, as probably three hundred years ago, the drive comes up along the side of the walled front garden, lined by a stately row of large lime trees. A second pair of gate piers, close by the house and topped by stone balls, leads to the front door and is matched by a third pair, perfectly on axis, leading through to the north garden. A fourth pair, with the scrolliest baroque ironwork of all, completes the set, conveniently carrying the date 1704, celebrating Marlborough's great victory at Blenheim.

The walled garden was planted with sentinel yews in the 1950s by the landscape architect John St Bodfan Gruffyed, who was working for the then-owner Thomas I.M. Walker-Munro. These are noble but a little austere, signalling to me that Cote's owner needs now to be a passionate gardener who loves roses and clematis in rambling profusion and will introduce colour with well-massed borders.

The entrance front has the charm of being almost but not quite symmetrical, with the Cotswold characteristic of gables that elide and overlap. The front door, the one feature with Classical detail and proportions, is exactly central, engagingly sandwiched between two large mullioned windows.

Part of the appeal of Cote is that each front offers a very different aspect. The west or garden front is dominated by a four-square staircase tower with a shallow pyramid roof giving it the look of a chateau in the Dordogne. To the north is a large sunken fountain basin and beside it a topiary garden where hedges are now sprouting clipped animals – a fox pursued by hounds. Here the gardens are formed into a series of green rooms bounded by hedges and walls, one concealing a swimming pool.

From late Anglo-Saxon times there was a large royal estate here, granted in 1238 by Henry III to the Pogges family. In the 16th century the new rich arrived from London and the estate was bought by the mercer and alderman Sir Roland Hill, who in 1553 sold it to a lawyer Alan Horde, a bencher of the Middle Temple. Initially it

The baroque walled garden was replanted with topiary in the 1950s.

appears simply to have been an investment until Sir Thomas Horde bought the house at Cote, which was an independent freehold, and settled here about 1630.

A little earlier, in 1614, Cote House was bought by Sir Lawrence Tanfield, an Oxford judge and MP. He did not live here but let it until in 1627 he was forced to take it back as his daughter had become a Catholic and been thrown out by her husband, who had forcibly taken custody of the children. Following legal proceedings she received a settlement that allowed her to live at 'the mansion house called Cote' with her husband providing meat, drink and other necessities befitting her quality, including nine servants, furniture, clothes and £100 a year.

Horde remained at Cote until his death in 1662. His son Thomas was another outspoken anti-papist, and was committed to Oxford Gaol accused of supporting the Duke of Monmouth's rebellion against the Catholic James II. This experience prompted him to establish a charity on behalf of poor prisoners, providing coats and stockings for ten men and ten women every year, continuing to the 20th century.

Cote was taxed in 1662 on eleven hearths – by far the most in the hamlet. From the mid-18th century it was let to tenants, largely escaping the Georgian and Victorian improvements usually carried out by resident owners. Substantial renovations were carried out in 1949–50 by the architect Thomas Rayson.

The central hall, with a Tudor-looking stone fireplace, has a ceiling consisting of three parallel shallow arched vaults. Beyond lies a drawing room with tall early 18th-century-style bolection moulded panelling, again with a Tudor arched stone fireplace. There are eight bedrooms, three on the second floor of the low-ceilinged south wing, while in the large attic over the centre of the house there is a 60-ft-long space waiting for use.

FAWLEY HOUSE · Henley-on-Thames

18th-century rectory grandly remodelled by Quinlan Terry

LUTYENS USED TO CALL IT THE GREAT GAME: the art of playing with the Classical orders of architecture – Doric, Ionic and Corinthian – and adapting them to modern life. Quinlan Terry plays it with superb finesse at Fawley House, near Henley-on-Thames.

This is a part of the Chilterns where houses are lost amid trees and woods. Fawley House has no grand gates – just a gap in a hedge that leads into a cobbled court enclosed by a tall, circular beech hedge. Terry's highly theatrical front is a delight, sophisticated enough to stand in Oxford or Cambridge amid buildings by Wren and Gibbs.

Yet, for all the fanfare, the house is engagingly domestic, just one step up to the front door and a modest three windows wide – ennobled on each storey by four blind arches. This is not mere artifice but Terry's way of concealing the fact that he was remodelling an 18th-century rectory that had been bodged by alterations over the years.

Lord McAlpine, the former Tory party treasurer, at once saw the house's potential when he bought it in the mid-1960s. A passionate collector and transformer of houses and gardens, Lord McAlpine says: 'The house was 'Mary Anne' in front and Queen Anne behind, the best facade at the back.' He duly put on a new entrance front in brick 'to iron out an ugly kink left by the Victorians'.

Beside the house he also built a large gallery for a collection of early Staffordshire pottery, in the form of an orangery fronted by a colonnade with a pretty gothic cornice inside. Then he sold the house and moved on, first to London and then to West Green in Hampshire.

With all its pillars, keystones, arches, urns and a double pediment, Fawley House could be in the Veneto.

In the 1980s his younger brother, David McAlpine, bought back Fawley House and immediately called in Terry, whom he had used earlier to alter his house at Little Roydon in Kent. Terry's eye was taken by the grandly rustic 18th- century arch around the garden door in rough flint. This was his cue for transforming the facade – to which he added a third layer. 'It gives you the deep windows that look so good on Classical buildings,' he says. Terry used flint and creamy portland stone to create a front like the backdrop of a Roman theatre, with a rounded pediment set within a triangular one.

The sitting room has panelling in an early 18th-century style.

Inside he transformed a rather narrow, slightly gloomy corridor with yet more architecture, creating a perspective of columns and arches intended to recall Palladio's Teatro Olimpico in Vicenza.

An arch on the right opens into a staircase hall paved in highly polished slabs of grey and green marble. Other rooms he transformed with handsome full-height panelling of the kind found in so many houses in New England. There are marble-framed fireplaces inset with blue and white tiles, doorcases with broken tops into which porcelain can be set and, in the green sitting room, fluted Ionic pilasters and arches over the doors. In the dining room there are no electric lights – only candles set in chandeliers and wall sconces – with the walls painted deep purple and looking like brushed velvet.

The long drawing room is slightly on the narrow side – though Terry advised against broadening it. It has the nice conceit of a sash window in the curving bow, which rises from the floor so you can step out, barely needing to duck your head.

Upstairs there are more surprises. The master bedroom occupies all three windows along the garden front and the bathroom is approached through a concealed door in the panelling. It turns out to be a whole suite, ingeniously devoted to bathing and dressing with walk-in wardrobes and a circular bath big enough for two, with taps on both sides so there need never be an argument over the hot water.

The main garden walk leads down to a narrow Edwardian-looking pond that is surrounded by paving. At one end is a pretty *tempietto*, which transpires to be the grandest of garden sheds, while at the other is a trellised and domed gazebo.

When visiting Fawley in 2003, I thought that if I were to buy the house my first move would be to create a ha-ha, remove the fence between the lawn and the paddock, and open up views through the belt of trees that marks the boundary of the property. This would create a grand impression of parkland akin to the illusions Terry has created indoors.

The Queen Anne garden front is just three windows wide, like the entrance front.

FRIAR PARK — Henley-on-Thames
French Gothic fantasy built for an authority on medieval gardens

THE BUILDER OF FRIAR PARK WAS Sir Frank Crisp, best known as the author of two volumes on medieval gardens published in 1924. His gardens consisted of a series of lakes stepped one above the other, so that from the top it looked like a continuous sheet of water. Stepping stones were concealed beneath each cascade and anyone crossing looked as if they were walking on water.

From here begins the first great adventure of Friar Park, the entrance to the underground caverns, large enough to row a boat around. Crisp called these the Blue Caves of Capri. They had two main caves with long connecting passages containing 'owls, bats, frogs, toadstools, gnomes, waterfalls, fossil trees, petrified birds nests'. According to the 1910 guide, the middle cave was 'beautifully illuminated by day, especially on sunny mornings, by blue glass skylights'. In the large cave was a waterfall lit by coloured lights. Limited numbers of visitors could go by boat while a footpath along the edge of the water served larger groups.

The second great feature of Friar Park was the scaled-down version of the Matterhorn, created out of huge blocks of millstone grit, 7,000 tons in all, transported by sea from Yorkshire and brought up the Thames by barge. The Matterhorn was reputed to have secret tunnels running to both the house and the caves.

The house is a spiky composition in French Flamboyant Gothic style. The sale catalogue described it as 'of highly diversified Gothic detail borrowed from the Pays Bas'. Inside Crisp made continuous play on the 'Friar' theme. Moveable noses of friars served as light switches and figures of friars held electric lamps.

The lake and cascades were designed to complement the house.

HEYTHROP PARK Chipping Norton
Baroque palace begun in 1706 and restored after a fire

HEYTHROP PARK IS A ROMAN BAROQUE PALACE in the English campagna. The long drive ascends through woodland, passing a series of ambitious modern buildings smart enough to belong to a university even if not quite what is expected on the approach to a great country house. They mark the house's period as a staff training college for the National Westminster Bank and before that a spell from 1922 to 1969 as a Jesuit College. In its latest incarnation, as hotel, golf and country club, Heythrop once again brims with guests.

The house was begun in 1706 for the 12th Earl and 1st and only Duke of Shrewsbury, who had just returned to England after five years in Rome, bringing with him an Italian wife. His architect was Thomas Archer, the only English architect who had studied in Italy, and Heythrop boasts inventive baroque detail such as 'ears' to the windows. The builder was Francis Smith of Warwick, who was to carry this new vocabulary of details all across the Midlands.

The Shrewsburys rarely visited the house and in 1831 it was tragically gutted by fire. It was rebuilt forty years later for Alfred Brassey, son of the railway magnate. His architect was Alfred Waterhouse, designer of London's Natural History Museum but not such an inveterate Goth that he wouldn't turn his hand to other styles. Waterhouse's interior is overwhelmingly opulent, even florid, but with distinctive Vanbrughian elements, especially in the double arcade of the hall.

The vast entrance court was not improved by the rebuilding of the wings in 1923 and for this reason it is important to persevere on through until you emerge on the garden front where the terraces, lawns and fountains are maintained in the Grand Manner.

The formal garden terraces are separated from the house by balustrades and grand flights of steps.

KIRTLINGTON PARK   Kirtlington
Palladian house whose magnificent dining room was sold to the Met

FINE 18TH-CENTURY HOUSES in Oxfordshire are now prizes beyond compare. Yet thirty years ago many seemed beyond the reach of family use, too large to heat, and too impractical to live in. With its attached portico of giant Ionic columns and matching wings each with cupola, Kirtlington is an extraordinarily handsome Palladian composition beautifully faced in stone. Here I learnt that ascending outdoor flights of stone steps in frosty weather can be dangerous, one reason that many houses like Kirtlington have entrances at the bottom of the steps that open into a lower hall.

The house was built for Sir James Dashwood, 2nd baronet, who had made the Grand Tour and married an heiress. In 1741 he paid both James Gibbs and Daniel Garrett for designs but the house was built by William Smith of Warwick and completed by John Sanderson.

It is a measure of the plight of great houses that in 1932 Hubert Budget sold the sumptuous dining room interior to the Metropolitan Museum in New York (it was not installed there until 1954). The price was an impressive $78,353. Most rooms exported in this way had wooden panelling. Here, the walls as well as the ceiling were made of plaster – a major challenge for the removal company.

Kirtlington's saviour Christopher Buxton was the first to stand up and say that great country houses no longer needed to be demolished if they were too large to live in, and that instead they could be adapted for several families to live in self-contained houses and apartments. At Kirtlington he has nonetheless contrived to retain the whole of the main house as one, though the wings have become very desirable houses. The polo ground in the park attracts large numbers of spectators.

The entrance front is approached by matching flights of stone steps.

MIDDLETON PARK   Middleton Stoney
Last of the great Lutyens country houses

COMPLETED IN 1938, MIDDLETON PARK marked the end of an era, the last great country house completed before the outbreak of war and barely lived in by its builder, the 1st Earl of Jersey. I arrived at Middleton in 1999 to visit an SOE veteran who had been SOE's head of security in Italy during the war. As I left, I exited through the Lutyens hall, a brilliant perspective of arches with a playful geometric black and white marble floor.

Lord Jersey, a handsome and delightful man, had first married an Australian beauty, Patricia Kenneth Richards, from whom he was divorced in 1937, promptly marrying the film actress Virginia Cherrill (former wife of Cary Grant). The new Lady Jersey did not take to the new Middleton, refusing to live there.

The old Middleton Park was a Georgian house where the family kept their racehorses (an enthusiasm Lord Jersey did not share). Lutyens undertook the commission with his son Robert but the design bears all the hallmarks of the great man. As with many French chateaux, the main front only comes into view with a last-minute change of axis. The grand entrance court is preceded by four pyramid-roofed lodges (housing servants both resident and visiting) which flank the eagle-topped gate piers. The entrance front to the left unusually has no windows on the ground floor – like the screen wall of an aristocratic hotel privée in Paris. Round the corner, Lutyens reverses the treatment in typical puckish mode. Alas, it was too clever for the new countess, who divorced Lord Jersey in 1946, by which time he was already thinking of settling in the island whose name he bore. Middleton's conversion as apartments was nearly flawless, with virtually no external change and retention of all the handsome Lutyens interiors.

The south front has external shutters and false bottoms to the upper windows.

SARSDEN HOUSE   Chipping Norton
Ravishing Regency house and garden by Humphry Repton and his son

SARSDEN IS ONE OF THE FIRST HOUSES I visited for *Country Life*. It was of relative few houses of the size and interest which had never appeared in the magazine. Built of pale golden stone, its architecture was inviting not grand, surrounded by beautiful lawns and lush borders. Though it was all kept up on a splendid scale there was no ceremony, no sign of servants just mother and grown-up daughter coming in for tea after an afternoon's gardening. This seemed truly the perfect place to live, as comfortable as the legendary embassy built for our man in Kabul, who was felt to need a really decent and handsome residence to compensate for the tribulations he had to endure.

Sarsden was rebuilt after a fire in 1689 but the house today is substantially a creation of the Reptons, both Humphry and his son George Stanley. It is witness to their still under-sung genius in the creation of architecture as well as gardens and landscape and a perfect marriage between the three.

Sarsden is faced in warm smooth ashlar stone with a stone slate roof. The house's most beautiful features are the porte-cochere and loggia, both with paired Ionic columns and balustrades above. The loggia cleverly incorporates a bay window at one end and a conservatory at the other. These additions were made for James Langston in *c.*1823–25, to whom Repton submitted one of his Famous 'Red Books' showing 'before' and 'after' views of his landscape proposals. Langston was a major patron of the arts, rebuilding nearby All Saints Churchill with a tower copied from Madgelen College Oxford and Chipping Norton town hall

When the MP Shaun Woodward acquired the house in 1994, a major programme of work began. Sold again for a reported £25 million in 2006, Sarsden remains the perfect Regency house, secluded in a world of its own, with handsome outbuildings and surrounded by gently rolling pasture with long views and abundant trees.

The garden colonnades is prettily married with a bay window and the orangery beyond.

SHIRBURN CASTLE   Watlington
14th-century moated castle which reached its nadir in 2004

THE MOST SECRET MOATED CASTLE IN England stood empty and forlorn, its future unknown and undecided after over seven centuries of occupation. Ancestral portraits had been stripped from the walls, books emptied in their thousands from the shelves and Georgian furniture removed by the lorry-load.

Yet the castle remained as romantic as ever, reflected in the waters of the moat that laps the walls. Shirburn, at the foot of the Chiltern Hills, is like Bodiam in Kent, square and symmetrical with circular towers at the corners and built when French invasion threatened in the 1370s and 80s. It can only be entered by means of a drawbridge. One leads to the stone entrance tower, another, a narrow footbridge, crosses to the kitchen.

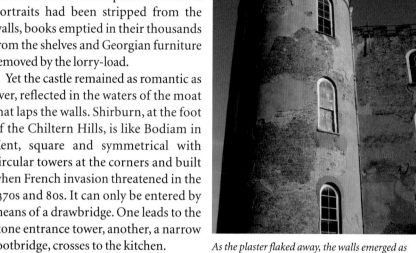

As the plaster flaked away, the walls emerged as pink brick.

The Earl of Macclesfield, the 9th of his line to live here, was evicted in 2005 as a result of a court order secured by his relatives. With him has gone one of the finest private libraries in England. His ancestor, the 1st Earl, who acquired Shirburn in the early 18th century, was Lord Chancellor of England and a pall bearer at Sir Isaac Newton's funeral. The 2nd Earl was President of the Royal Society and formed an important collection of 17th-century English mathematical manuscripts. Aided by the future Astronomer Royal James Bradley, the 2nd Earl built the best equipped observatory in the country and made important observations on the great comet of 1743.

Both the 1st and 2nd Earls were pupils of the mathematician William Jones who lived in the castle as one of the family and assembled a superb scientific library, which he bequeathed to Shirburn. This was added to by the 3rd Earl, who detected the horrific 1755 Lisbon earthquake in strange movements in the waters of the moat.

The cause of the break-up is the will made by the present earl's grandfather, the 7th Earl. To avoid death duties that would have precipitated the break-up of the 2,250-acre estate, the 7th Earl placed it in a company, dividing the shares among various members of the family. The present earl holds only a minority of shares and for thirty years he had been at odds with his uncle, his uncle's son and latterly his brother. Meanwhile the castle had fallen into decrepitude. The moat was all but drained and the walls were shedding their protective plaster, though repairs were under way to stop the leaks in the roof.

A still greater tragedy is that, thanks to the intense privacy of successive earls, no proper photographic record of the atmospheric interiors was ever made. The castle's

The castle rises sheer from the moat with sash windows showing the extent of Georgian remodelling.

history over seven centuries has only recently begun to be studied. Thirty years ago one architectural historian who crept across the park and into the garden to gain a glimpse of the hidden castle was marched off at the point of a shotgun.

A royal licence to crenellate or embattle Shirburn was granted in 1377 – seven years earlier than Bodiam. In the Civil War the castle was held for the king and besieged and shelled by Parliamentary troops.

Soon after Lord Chancellor Macclesfield bought the estate in 1716, he took advice from the Surveyor-General of the King's Works, Sir Thomas Hewett, and reconstructed the castle for the then large sum of £7,000. Now that the 19th-century plaster has fallen from the walls, much of it proves to be of pretty pink early 18th-century brick with the arch-headed windows and thick window glazing bars typical of this date. Inside the castle are many baroque flourishes – a grand wooden staircase with three carved balusters on each step, an imposing pillared library and veined white baroque marble fireplaces. George IV's favourite architect, John Nash, later remodelled the entrance hall beside the medieval gate as a gothic-style armoury. Only the entrance tower and adjoining walls are of clearly medieval date, built of large blocks of stone with arrow slits.

A series of Sotheby's book sales are raised more than £20 million for the Earl. In one cupboard was a cache of letters from Sir Isaac Newton and a collection of Newtoniana sold to Cambridge University for £6.37 million. The Art Fund led a campaign to save the Macclesfield Psalter from export to America.

Yet none of this money will be spent on the castle. Today the handsome orangery stands roofless and the dome of the elegant *tempietto* nearby has collapsed. As he departed, the present Lord Macclesfield said scornfully of his relations, 'They haven't a clue what they are going to do with the place. They should sell it.' The other side of the family retains a staunch and discreet silence so I hope that this ancient castle is heading for better times.

THE MANOR HOUSE   Sutton Courtenay
Pretty medieval manor with fine 16th- and 17th-century additions

WITH ITS MANY GABLES, PINK-PLASTERED WALLS and pale silver half timbering, Sutton Courtenay Manor speaks of peaceful Suffolk more than Oxfordshire. The house stands in a village that has prospered for a thousand years, opposite a Norman parish church and village green. Yet it is perfectly secluded, with extensive grounds running down to a quiet sweep of the River Thames, a perfect Elysium to escape the frenetic pace of life in southern England.

In 1945 the property was bought by David Astor, legendary editor of *The Observer* who died in 2001. In 2004 the house still had a touch of post-war simplicity with the simplest of white bathroom fittings and a feeling of a place that had been gently falling to sleep – still bright and clean and fresh, yet untouched by modern gadgetry and tastes.

This is a very ancient place. In the 8th century the Abbot of Abingdon gave it to Kenulf, or Cynewulf, king of the West Saxons. The Witan, the supreme council of the Anglo-Saxons, met here in 1042. After the Norman Conquest King Henry II gave it to Reginald Courtenay, whose descendants lost it in the Wars of the Roses.

In the mid 17th century the manor came to the remarkable 1st Earl of Craven, a lifelong friend and supporter of the Winter Queen, James I's daughter Elizabeth of Bohemia. The Earl, a passionate builder in Berkshire, is best known for the National Trust's Ashdown House, but he also built a grandiose palace for himself at Hampstead Marshall outside Newbury – of which little more survives than a series of stupendous gateways. At Sutton Courtenay he also left a glorious pair of tall ball-topped gate piers but his main legacy is the two enchanting arcades on either side of the north wing.

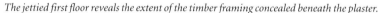

The jettied first floor reveals the extent of the timber framing concealed beneath the plaster.

The wide arches have pineapple pendants – this was the moment when the first pineapple grown in England was presented to Charles II. Above these arcades is a grand run of fashionable 'Ipswich' windows, nine in all. Named after those on the town house of the Suffolk merchant John Sparrow, these windows consist of a central arch set within a large rectangular wooden-mullioned window.

The house is built on a deep U-plan facing the river and the arcades and inner courtyard give the feel of an old coaching inn. The patina extends to the red-tiled roofs, gently undulating and with a rich carpet of venerable moss. Handsome lead downpipes complete the picture with the best castellated rainwater gutter I have seen running the length of the west flank with a continuous cresting of little battlements.

The heavy oak front door swings open into a comfortable sitting room dominated by a splendid fireplace of 1700-type with bold bolection moulding. On the near wall the panelling looks 1600 in date, inset with a pretty landscaped scene said to be Dutch, but to me looking like an early picture of the Thames with swans and church spires.

Old photographs reveal that this room was formerly open to the dining room on the right. The screen of columns and low wooden balustrade between the two rooms are still there, hidden by hangings introduced to cut out draughts. Remove them and you will be standing in a Renaissance interior with a perspective of columns multiplied by further columns supporting the dining-room ceiling.

The shallow Elizabethan staircase leading out of the room has almost cottage-like proportions with carved newel posts extended as columns to support the landing above. The upper flights leading to the attic have a still more monumental handrail and balusters, suggesting they were added a century later.

On the landing you get a first glimpse of the huge roof timbers that are one of the wonders of the house, with a massive arched brace disappearing into a cross wall. Nearby, a low oak door with ancient H-hinges leads into an attic where I found myself crouching beneath the timbers of a splendid medieval hall roof with four grand trusses and finely shaped arch braces. The challenge is to imagine how the bedrooms below could be opened up into this space to form a first-floor solar.

Curiously this is not the splendid medieval great hall shown in *Country Life* photographs of 1904 and 1931 – that has entirely disappeared. It had a minstrels' gallery, a great fireplace, extensive Tudor panelling and rather rough roof timbers. Though hailed in Hampton's splendid 1920 sales particulars as 'presenting a perfect specimen of mediaeval architecture', this may have been a recent confection. Christopher Hussey, writing in 1931, was positively elliptical in his diplomacy: 'At Sutton Courtenay Colonel and Mrs Lindsay have created something exquisite, in which colour and atmosphere and romance blurr the lines of objective truth.'

The great hall nonetheless pre-dates the Lindsays and it may be that their final contribution was to spirit it away to make further rooms for their many guests.

The gardens are formed into a series of long parallel rooms by walls and hornbeam hedges with box edging and geometric topiary. Towards the Thames are more informal grass walks. The river bank, quite thickly lined with trees, provides glimpses rather than panoramas of the still water. A boathouse is set back in an inlet and bridges carry paths across streams gurgling towards the Thames.

TUSMORE HOUSE   Bicester
Palladian house of the grand scale completed in 2003

As REBUILT IN 2004, TUSMORE HOUSE is a design of spell-binding beauty with one of the most majestic of all country house porticoes. It takes the form of a temple front with six giant Ionic columns. The whole building is faced in blemishless white limestone imported from Dijon in Burgundy, which perfectly matches the chalky white stone of surviving outbuildings.

All this is very different from the previous house that stood here, designed by the architect Claud Philimore. The almost orange stone was a painful contrast to the outbuildings, The house was almost puny in terms of its setting, the interior disappointing and nobody objected to its loss. The first proposal was to rebuild the magnificent Palladian house on the site, ignobly demolished as recently as 1961. This was the domestic masterpiece of the architect Robert Mylne, whose greatest work, also demolished, was Georgian Blackfriars Bridge.

The reconstruction of Mylne's house would have been a fascinating project, not least because the proposal was put forward by the architect Philip Jebb, the most

Both centre and ends break forward from the garden front.

The staircase hall has a magnificent domed rotunda with twin flights rising to a columned gallery.

resourceful and accomplished Classical architect of his generation. But such a proposal, alas, was not in tune with the times, even among traditionalists.

Instead, Wafic Said, the owner of the estate, decided to commission a new Classical design. A proposal was drawn up by Quinlan Terry, another by Julian Bicknell. The design adopted is by Sir William Whitfield, best known for more contemporary variants of traditional styles. Here Whitfield set out to show that he could step back two centuries and design with mastery and assurance a grand country house that was convincing in proportions and detail .

Today it is fashionable again to have a basement or lower ground floor with games rooms, cinemas, gymnasia and swimming pools. Whitfield conceals this by creating a grand grass verged ramp leading up an axis to the portico. The result is that for all its imposing height, the portico is not overbearing and the proportion of the entrance front is strongly horizontal rather than vertical.

On the garden front Whitfield adopts a different rhythm with an emphasised cente and ends. The end pavilions have Venetian windows on the *piano nobile* – above are the three part windows often found on Regency houses. The centre breaks forward as a three-sided or canted bay with entrance porch.

The deep square plan of the house demands a central top-lit staircase and Whitfield has designed this in the form of a domed rotunda with staircase rising in twin flights hugging the walls. The columns, in fluted Siena-coloured marble, ring the landing with a rich wrought iron balustrade between. The frieze above is picked out in matching hue above, rather strongly for some tastes. But this is Classical design in the grand manner and the staircase compares in splendour with that at Wardour Castle in Wiltshire on which it is modelled.

Tusmore stands in a large well-maintained estate surrounded by park walls. The scale of the new house is appropriate to the landscape around it and sits well with other estate buildings. This is a big contrast to Eaton Hall, as rebuilt in the 1950s, which, like the Phillimore house at Tusmore, was too small for its surroundings. Sir William and Wafic Said have set a new benchmark for Classical building on the grand scale and it will be fascinating to see what progeny is produced.

WYFOLD COURT   Henley-on-Thames
Opulent French mansion built for Manchester's richest cotton manufacturer

WHEN I FIRST SAW WYFOLD COURT in the early 1990s it was a sight that made the blood boil. Here was one of the grandest of all Victorian houses, a stupendous essay in French Flamboyant Gothic built for the richest of the Manchester 'Cottentots'. Yet all around the lawn were grotesque modern extensions, which only a government department would have been allowed to build, utterly disfiguring the totally glorious setting to provide extra space for a psychiatric hospital. 'Now that the hospital has departed,' I asked myself, 'is there still worse to come?'

The house at least had been well maintained. The silhouette was of dizzying richness, with square *donjon* tower, *tourelles*, crocketed gables, ornamental lead roof cresting, pierced balustrades, carved heraldic beasts and finials, and a host of sculpted dormers. Wyfold, first discovered and written up by a chairman of the Victorian Society, Peter Howell, was far and away the grandest creation of its architect, George Somers Clarke, a pupil of Sir Charles Barry, who had helped prepare the drawings for the Houses of Parliament.

Clarke's client was Edward Hermon MP, a Lancashire cotton magnate who in just one generation made and spent a substantial amount of one of the great textile fortunes of Victorian England. In 1865 Hermon became sole controller of the largest of the mid-century cotton spinning and manufacturing firms, with ten factories, 2,775 looms and 3,300 operatives. He built his house in 1874–6, surveying a

There is a wealth of French Flamboyant Gothic detail on the entrance front.

magnificent panorama of the Thames Valley, with fields, houses, and even Reading itself, lost amid a profusion of trees. The pleasure grounds were designed by a 'Mr Milner', presumably Edward Milner, and consisted of lawns, terraces and slopes, a rosary, an ornamental fountain and an ashphalted tennis court.

The beautifully moulded and panelled chimney shafts, as well as part of the open traceried parapets, were executed in Cossey brickware from Gunton's Fields, near Norwich. The carving was done by L.T. Carter and his assistants – Carter was sent to France by Somers Clarke to obtain casts and make studies of the best medieval Flamboyant work.

Many grand Victorian houses were built with an internal flight of steps leading to a *piano nobile*. Wyfold is entered at the level. A vaulted carriage porch and vestibule leads into a large entrance hall and then into a spectacular 42 ft high Grand Staircase with a full-height oriel window filled with stained glass adorned with the arms of every English monarch from William the Conqueror to Queen Victoria. The stair, constructed in teak, is surmounted by a ceiling of moulded and carved English oak.

The entire east flank was occupied with a 100-ft long picture gallery with bay windows at the ends and a central lantern providing top lighting for the pictures. The reception rooms along the south front have 18-ft high ceilings and consisted of drawing room, ante drawing room, morning room, dining room, 'Mr Hermon's Room', billiard room and – at the very end – a smoking room.

The fit-out of the main rooms is just as grand as the House of Commons itself, with parquet floors and robust gothic doors and doorcases in walnut. The main rooms open off a long stone vaulted corridor with windows along one side creating the feel of a monastic cloister. The brass supports of the gas lamps are emblazoned with fishes, tortoises, wine and cheese.

Behind the service door came the butler's domain with pantry, plate room (guarded by under butler) and then the housekeeper's corridor with the upper servants' dining room, still room and stores all under her eagle eye. Beyond these lay the large kitchen.

Hermon's picture collection was sold by Christie's in 1882, three years after his death, including the famous Babelonian Marriage Market he had commissioned from Edwin Long. The 1,700-acre estate was put on the market at the same time but it was not sold and his daughter Frances Caroline continued to live there. She had married Robert Hodge, a

The bay window is richly carved with heraldic beasts on the finials and a coat of arms below.

Conservative MP who was created Baron Wyfold of Accrington, in 1919. Three years after her death in 1929, the house became the psychiatric hospital which it remained until the early 1990s, the time of my first visit.

When I returned in the late 1990s, Wyfold had been taken over by the P.J. Livesey Group and was being converted into apartments following the grain of the house. The ugly huts had vanished, replaced by an underground car park that was topped by a lawn with a tunnel, allowing residents to walk into the house without getting wet. Livesey's were aiming to avoid cramming in too many units and were making just eleven apartments in the mansion. Two were 5,500 sq ft each, and even the smallest units were 2,500 sq ft, about three times the size of a two-bedroom flat.

The unwieldly space of the picture gallery had been made into two split-level apartments, one with a roof terrace, and a modern hospital window had been neatly replaced with a new bay window matching the Clarke originals on either side.

The ground floor corridor was designed like a monastic cloister.

Livesey's in-house architect, Ralph Brocklehurst, coped with the problem of flights of stairs that effectively have to rise two storeys to reach first-floor level by inserting generous mezzanine landings, large enough for a couple of armchairs or a work table. 'We've tried to make a master bedroom on the ground floor, so you don't have to rush up two flights if you find you've left your wallet behind,' he said.

The first apartment was sold to the Danish Count Schimmelman. 'The large windows fill the rooms with sun and we can enjoy the garden without having to work in it,' he told me.

Apartment 4 was like a gothic rectory, where you were barely conscious of the rest of the building. For someone not worried by stairs, the big attraction was the Tower House, an apartment that begins at second-floor level and rises to a sixth-floor belvedere room with a stupendous panorama.

The large footprint of the hospital buildings made it inevitable that the health authority would seek planning permission for an equivalent volume of new housing. Most of this has been placed just off the long drive, half a mile from the house. Wyfold has regained its majesty.

SHROPSHIRE

APLEY PARK — Bridgnorth
Vast Regency Gothic house lived in again after years as a school

WHAT COUNTRY HOUSE ENTHUSIAST has not dreamed of discovering some vast romantic mansion, unknown and shut away from the world in a vast encircling park. Apley in Shropshire is such a place, almost a palace in fact, in which you wander in amazement from one astonishing room to another, marvelling at panelled rooms, vast fireplaces and ornamental ceilings.

More exciting still, this is a house with a better claim than any other to be the inspiration of P.G. Wodehouse's Blandings Castle, the country seat of Lord Emsworth, his eccentric family and his prize pig, the Empress of Blandings. Driving out of Bridgnorth you pass a gate lodge and continue for a long way. Finally you turn off down a second long drive, bowling through mature parkland until the house emerges with stables and outbuildings strung out behind to overwhelm you with the grandeur of it all.

A licence to crenellate or 'embattle' a castle was granted here in 1308 but no trace of this remains and the modern history of Apley begins with Sir William Whitmore, who purchased the estate soon after 1600. The Whitmores had the record of holding a Parliamentary seat at Bridgnorth from 1660–1870, with a single break from 1710–13, and for 41 of those years they held both borough seats. But the

Apley was finished in 1820, complete with turrets, battlements and cast-iron window tracery.

voters in Bridgnorth did not come cheap and though in 1795 Thomas Whitmore inherited an annual income of £20,000 a year (well over £2 million today), the combined expenses of politics and building forced him to sell £100,000 of land and saddled his heir with a mortgage of £180,000.

Though this heir lived 'very quietly', the whole vast estate had to be sold in 1867 – for a staggering £550,000. The buyer was William Orme Foster, a vastly rich Coalbrookdale ironmaster who had inherited his uncle's £700,000 fortune in 1853 and his father's in 1860. Not surprisingly he progressed steadily up the country-house ladder, going from red brick Himley Hall to Stourton Castle in 1853 and then to Apley in 1867.

The house stands in a vast park with the stables behind.

Even so he was taken to task by the Victoria County History for buying Apley at an inflated price. So rich was he that, though he received not a single penny of profit from any of his industrial enterprises for twenty years from 1874 (partly because he was reluctant to shed labour), his personal fortune, independent of his business, rose to £3 million on his death.

The Fosters continued to live here in style, though evidently coming to regret the appearance of what *Country Life* in 1917 refers to as 'an unfortunate example of the Gothick taste'. In the 1930s they were at the forefront of fashion, building a grand indoor pool in the conservatory. Then during the Second World War Apley became a convalescent home. Faced with post-war austerity, the family retreated into a wing until the house was taken on a twenty-one-year lease by a school, which moved here from Millichope Hall 15 miles to the west.

The school moved out in the 1980s (though old boys keep alive its memory on the internet) and the house then remained empty until it was acquired in the late 1990s by Neil Avery, a man with a remarkable passion for troubled houses, who also took on James Gibbs's magnificent Patshull Hall in Staffordshire. He obtained permission for conversion of the house into nineteen dwellings and following its sale, the conversion has begun. Ten mews houses have been sold in the courtyard and the first two houses in the main block have also been sold.

The entrance front is not quite as symmetrical as it first appears.

This is a house that Queen Victoria and Prince Albert are rumoured to have looked at buying for the Prince and Princess of Wales before they decided upon Sandringham – it offers a similar level of seclusion and privacy and the park is well managed and looked after by the Apley estate. However, the scene has changed considerably since 1867 when Thomas Shirley wrote in his *English Deer Parks* that Apley was 'celebrated for the great beauty of its sylvan scenery'.

Begun in 1811, Apley already had the triumphant scale of houses that were built after the final defeat of Bonaparte at Waterloo. The architect was the intriguing John Webb – not the disciple of Inigo Jones, but a landscape gardener who, like Capability Brown himself, turned his hand to the design of the occasional great house.

Apley is a typical example of 'frothy' Regency Gothic (as opposed to the serious Victorian kind). The entrance front is as neatly symmetrical as a toy fort with corner turrets, mock battlements, bay windows and a turreted *porte-cochère*. The strange part is the traceried window at one end of what appears to be a grand family chapel. Upon closer inspection, this transpires to be a complete sham, as immediately to the side are three rows of sash windows of an earlier wing.

The grandest feature is the monumental staircase in the centre of the house, lit by an octagonal lantern supported on fan vaulting. An imperial stair (one flight dividing into two) takes you to the first floor, while the upper flight clings perilously to the wall as you mount to the second floor, reassured by the stoutest of gothic cast-iron railings nearby Coalbrookdale could produce.

BLETCHLEY MANOR — Market Drayton

Late-Elizabethan house that has regained its ancient patina

BLETCHLEY MANOR STANDS PROUDLY displayed to the road from Whitchurch to Newport. When the designer Nigel Daly and his partner Brian Vowles first came to look at it, it appeared to be entirely Victorian, tricked out with black beams that had merely been painted on.

In the attic they were amazed to find massive 400-year-old timbers. Tree-ring dating proved these to be from trees that were felled in the spring or summer of 1594. 'It's one of the closest datings yet, with two rafters and one purlin identified as coming from the same tree,' said Nigel.

With infinite care they have exposed the original external silvered timber framing with pretty pink brick infill. In 2006 I found the house full of character with the beginnings of a very attractive small formal garden. The rendered west wing contained a 'great room' with very handsome Classical twin marble fireplaces that were designed by Daly. His fine sense for the detail of mouldings is also shown to good effect in the handsome new staircase in blond oak and a library where bookshelves conceal a hidden door.

One tricky task was to move the downstairs loo from its bizarre position inside the large hall fireplace – 'You had to duck,' laughed Daly. The house had been given atmosphere by stone-flagged floors and ancient early wooden doors and archways. There is a very handsome early 17th-century panelled parlour, underfloor heating and smart bathrooms. The attics, with pale timbers that have also been carefully cleaned, make charming small bedrooms.

Pink brink and silvered timbers were revealed beneath a coating of black paint.

BROGYNTYN

Oswestry

Grand but run-down Regency house sold in 2006

OWAIN BROGYNTYN, A DIRECT DESCENDANT OF the King of Powys, established Castell Brogyntyn as a fortified settlement in about 1140. In the 15th century the property was called Constable Hall, but by the end of the following century it had become Porkington and was the residence of Sir John Owen, secretary to Sir Francis Walsingham, Queen Elizabeth I's secretary of state.

Porkington perfectly expresses the Blandings-like character of the estate. As at Apley, it is easy to imagine a contented Lord Emsworth enjoying these broad acres and entertaining fellow Drones Club members. It was renamed Brogyntyn in 1870 by the 1st Baron Harlech, J.R. Ormsby-Gore, whose family owned the estate until they sold in 2001 to a local builder and developer, Roland Pickstock, who five years later resold it to concentrate on his business interests.

The present house was built for William Owen by Francis Smith of Warwick, the Midlands master mason who became one of the most prolific country-house builders of his age. In 1814–15 the house was remodelled in fashionable Greek Revival style for Mary Jane Ormsby and her husband William Gore. They employed a local architect, Benjamin Gummow, who practised at Ruabon in Denbighshire; he was a pupil of the accomplished London architect S.P. Cockerell and worked extensively for Lord Grosvenor and Sir William Watkyns-Wynn at Wynnstay. He added the noble Ionic portico, rendering the brickwork so it looked like smooth ashlar stone and adding a balustrade above the cornice to shield the roof from view. The Harlech coat of arms fills the pediment over the portico.

The east front has dated rainwater heads of 1814. Service ranges to the north dated 1870 were added by Benjamin Ferrey for Ormsby-Gore, matching the early 19th-

The Greek Ionic portico fronts an early-Georgian house.

The entrance arch to the stables is topped by a cupola.

century work. Coming from nearby Oswestry the splendid park was approached through an entrance arch and lodges with quadrant sweeps of railings and stone gateways for those on foot. Another later lodge, in round-arched style, stands on a country road.

The entrance hall contains a carved wooden Jacobean fireplace dated 1617, presumably from an earlier house on the site. The oak staircase beyond is at the top end of the scale with three turned balusters to each step, with column newel posts in the corners accompanied by swoops in the handrail. There is a matching dado on the inner wall and the banisters are continued across the first-floor landing. The stair is by a 19th-century octagonal lantern.

A corridor with pretty saucer domes supported on Classical arches leads to the library and drawing room, which has a bay window overlooking the garden. A large part of the delight of Brogyntyn lies in the varied estate buildings. These include a stable entered through a Classical arch topped by a cupola and a pretty Swiss cottage with tree-trunk loggia. Inside, the octagonal saloon has a star-pattern gothic vault and richly flared arches to the windows. The grandeur of the room is explained by its use for shooting lunches.

In addition there are several estate cottages giving a flourish by banded brickwork, a home farm, kennels, two lakes and a waterfall. From Swiss Cottage, a path runs round the lake, across a bridge, towards the site of the old castle, disappearing into a 213-ft-long tunnel built under the old castle mound.

BUNTINGSDALE HALL Market Drayton

Baroque house of c.1720 bought back by a descendant of the builder and restored

IN 1986 BUNTINGSDALE'S LAST HOPE EXPIRED. Or so it seemed. The house was built to the designs of John Prince for Bulkeley Mackworth between 1719 and 1724. It was faced with giant pilasters, some fluted, some plain, and had numerous intriguing baroque details taken from engravings of Roman palaces.

The RAF acquired the estate in 1936 and maintained the house in reasonable condition, although two fine panelled rooms disappeared at this time. The mile-long drive was flanked by row upon row of service housing, but at least the immediate grounds remained intact. Then in about 1980 the MoD sold the house and a small patch of land to a company called Ready Grange, which began conversion into apartments. Superb early 18th-century brickwork was gouged out to make doorways and windows. The elaborate cornice in the Saloon was hacked off to make way for a new corner staircase to the rooms above.

Suddenly work stopped. The banks and building societies entered a desperate scramble to claim various parts of the property. For three years the Monument Trust struggled to combine the various parts in one ownership. When they withdrew, North Shropshire District Council took up the fight with financial backing from English Heritage.

Three repairs orders were served. The roof was repaired, timbers treated and dry rot eliminated. Meanwhile Richard Mackworth, a descendant of the family that built the house, started buying back the property wing by wing. In 1991 he at last secured the central block. Mr Mackworth began repairs using direct labour and stone from the Grinshill Quarry used by Francis Smith. Today Buntingsdale is fully furnished and back in use.

The baroque flourishes include emphatic keystones, giant pilasters and a split pediment over the door.

COTON HALL
Bridgnorth
Regency perfection with an Italianate tower of c.1860

COTON HALL IS ONE OF THOSE RARE places that has luckily escaped the attention of a century of country-house hunting by architectural historians. Beautifully faced in pale grey stone, it stands on a gentle eminence with rolling Shropshire hills in every direction.

The house was built soon after 1800 for Harry Lancelot Lee who had married the daughter of an Oxford vicar. The Lees owned the estate from the 13th century and one of their descendants, Thomas Lee, built Stratford Hall in Virginia, one of the grandest Colonial houses in America and the birthplace of the great Confederate general Robert E. Lee.

Harry Lancelot died at his house in Bath, having let Coton to a local curate. When Coton was sold after his death in 1821, the estate ran to 5,000 acres. Today just 6.5 acres are left but the setting

The ruined chapel on the lawn is no antiquity and was designed by the architect Thomas Pritchard.

remains inviolate and from the upper windows there are views down to the lake.

The entrance off a quiet country road is modest – there is no lodge but simply a pair of low gate piers topped by large stone balls. The house is hidden until the last moment and it is the ruined chapel on the grass circle in front that first comes into view. Local historians have claimed that this is the chapel of ancient Saxon kings, but it is a simple Palladian box with a pretty Strawberry Hill Gothick window in the east end. It is attributed to the talented Shrewsbury architect Thomas Farnolls Pritchard. Alas, the roof collapsed in 1878 and the Lee monuments were moved to nearby Alveley church.

The elegant simplicity of the house is pure Regency but to Victorian tastes it was a little too plain and a picturesque Italianate tower and wing was added about 1860, all in finely carved stone.

The unexpected quality of the interior is evident as soon as you step through the front door. At the end of the narrow hall is a stately screen of tall fluted Greek Ionic columns with the scrolls delicately picked out in gold leaf. The doors are in the manner of Sir John Soane with reeded frames and rosettes in the corners – a clever detail that eliminated the need for mitred joints.

Oddly, the front door does not line up with the screen of columns. Indeed, all through the house there is a slight awkwardness at odds with the exquisite finishes. It is as if a local builder had just worked with a leading architect and was using the same fashionable detail and skilled craftsmen but not equipped with a proper set of plans.

The lofty dining room has an intricate key-pattern cornice and a giant sunflower in the ceiling rosette.

Tall sash windows fill every room with light. The expanse of glass evidently proved excessive as windows facing the east have been blocked off, while the Victorians put in heating pipes beneath the windows with deliciously ornamental iron grilles. More importantly, the house has a full complement of original panelled shutters, all in working order, giving insulation as good as double glazing.

The elegant drawing room has long windows descending to the floor on one side which look like a Victorian alteration, particularly as they are filled with plate glass. Nonetheless, 'sash windows to the floor' are mentioned in the 1821 sales particulars. In the library next door is a magnificent Regency oak bookcase running the length of the long wall with break-fronted centre and raised attic built into the wall. The dining room has an intricate key-pattern cornice and a fine central ceiling rosette, still perfectly crisp, and consisting of a giant sunflower with a perfect ring of petals surrounded by long fronds of acanthus.

Beyond, the Victorian wing contains a large music room entered through a lobby with a chunky archway. Interestingly, the pillars supporting the arch are inset with grilles and open up to reveal the original Victorian ladder-like hot-water radiators.

The house is built on top of a full set of brick-arched cellars, with the original brick and stone paving still largely intact and a wine cellar half a level lower complete with characteristic Georgian slate-shelved wine bins. These cellars have kept the house well aired but as a double precaution against rising damp Coton is surrounded by an invisible dry ditch lined with brick and wide enough to walk round. Under the entrance porch is an opening into a tunnel leading to the chapel.

The bedrooms are approached up a splendid oak staircase, in character more like a baroque stair of 1720 than 1800, with wooden treads and three balusters to each step. The ends of the treads are each carved with a different floral pattern.

A half landing spins out the ascent so the balustrade runs in a continuous sweep around all four sides of the stair hall. At the top the landing is given an added flourish by imposing arched doorcases, each with a tiny cross-vaulted vestibule behind. Bed- and dressing rooms all have attractive decorative cornices, and several have pretty Regency fireplaces in grey-blue fossil marble. Many of the original oak sash windows still exist, never painted, with glazing bars as slender and finely moulded as on a Chippendale bookcase. In the back staircase a full complement of servants' bells also survives, with their wires and pulleys, still jingling happily.

COUND HALL   Shrewsbury
Splendid example of Queen Anne Baroque that stood empty for years

THIS GRAND BAROQUE HOUSE STOOD EMPTY for years surveying a fine stretch of park just a few miles from Shrewsbury. It was built in 1703–4 by John Prince, who appears to have been a bricklayer by trade, for Edward Cressett. H.A. Tipping, *Country Life*'s early architectural writer, saw and illustrated a drawing for the main front, now no longer traceable, signed John Prince *Inv et Delineavit*, portraying the house with a rare clarity of detail and a few extra flourishes such as urns and statues on the parapet. Both north and south fronts of Cound have grand fluted pilasters with rich Corinthian capitals. An added sense of verticality is created by the narrow, tall sections of architrave and frieze perched on top, with only the bold dentil cornice carried across the façade. Thanks to the very tall windows on the first floor there is almost more glass than brick. The original chunky glazing bars survive to the left of the front door, the rest of the windows have characteristic late-Georgian sashes with slender astragals or glazing bars. One theory is that the windows were replaced after an earthquake in about 1840. Interestingly the early 18th-century interiors appear to have survived best in the parts of the house where the sashes have not been replaced.

The great feature of the interior is the large floating staircase rising the full height of the house. The flights at the back of the hall do not hang from the wall but ascend across space supported by columns from below. The drama is baroque but details such as the ends of the treads are Adamesque and the quatrefoil decoration under the flights is Jacobethan. The best guess is that it was done by Mrs Thursby who inherited in 1838 and died in 1852, but it may yet prove to be Edwardian.

Many of the original early sashes remain. The more slender glazing bars were introduced after a fire.

THE READER'S HOUSE — Ludlow
Handsome town house of the 1550s

THIS NOBLE ELIZABETHAN TOWN HOUSE stands overlooking the churchyard in the centre of the fashionable market town of Ludlow. It is a large house, on three storeys (with medieval cellar), with oak floors, panelling, ornamental plasterwork, mullioned windows – all the very features that make houses of this date so special.

For many of the people likely to fall in love with the Grade I listed building, its unmodernised state in 2003 was likely to be an added bonus. David Lloyd, Ludlow's historian, said, 'The Council has a very good conservation advisory group and there will be a lot of help for anyone who is sensitive in their approach. We want these to be living buildings. The Reader's House has tremendous potential.'

Large timber-framed houses are one of the glories of England and Ludlow carpenters evolved a style distinct from Shrewsbury, with S-shaped braces, diamond struts, cusped quatrefoils and lots of barley-sugar mouldings. The most famous example is the Feathers Inn, but the magnificent gables and oversailing porch of the Reader's House have long been sought out by visitors.

The main constraint is access. You can't park outside as the front door opens off a footpath beside the church. But think of the bliss of not having the noise of passing

The three-storey porch was added in 1616 by Thomas Kaye, Chaplain to the Council in the Marches.

traffic. Houses in Bradford-on-Avon where the sole access is by foot are much in demand – why not here?

There was also the question of the Bull Hotel which backs onto the small garden – but again it was only the rear wall of the pub – without windows.

The peaceful garden had a camomile lawn. Lloyd continued, 'The back elevation is one of the best examples of timber-framing we have in the town. People just don't know how imposing it is since it can't be seen from any public place.'

The Reader's House is a physical expression of the age when Ludlow stepped on the national stage. Ludlow was already a thriving cloth town in the Middle Ages, prospering further from the manufacture of gloves and arrows. Then in 1536 the Lord President of the Marches and his Council, the effective government of Wales, established themselves in Ludlow Castle. Landowners, lawyers, officials and merchants built or leased handsome houses in the town.

The timber-framed east front dates to c.1550 though the herringbone gable may be part of the 1616 work.

The Reader's House was built by the town's bookseller John Dalton in the 1550s – a two-storey house adorned inside with Tudor roses, pomegranates and fleurs-de-lys. Sixty years later, the new tenant, Thomas Kay, chaplain to the Council of the Marches, added an elaborate upper storey and the fine three-storey timber-framed porch which bears his initials and the date 1616 on its bargeboards. The vines carved round his front door were described by Alec Clifton-Taylor, champion of English country towns, as 'a masterpiece of Ludlow carpentry'.

Early in the 18th century the Ludlow Corporation decided the house should be the official residence of the parish Reader – the first to live here was Rev. Page Newborough, nephew of the headmaster of Eton. The Reader, with the Preacher, assisted the Rector, taking prayers during services. Later Readers were often to live elsewhere, letting the house to supplement their income. As a result the house remained unaltered, retaining lead windows when fashionable Georgian sashes were introduced in other buildings. Later, in 1909, the house became a private museum of furniture and works of art, with a one-shilling entrance charge.

David Lloyd continues, 'The house has an unusually spacious oak staircase for its date, with a fine series of carpenters' marks, extending into the bay window over the porch. Here you can sit looking out over the churchyard and get a glimpse of Long Mynd – Shropshire's longest mountain – and Wenlock Edge.'

MINSTERLEY HALL · Minsterley

Timber-framed house built for Sir Henry Thynne to replace Caus Castle c.1653

MINSTERLEY HALL IS A TIMBER-FRAMED HOUSE of enormous charm, set in a pretty village between Shrewsbury and the Welsh border. For nearly three centuries it belonged to the Thynnes of Longleat who came here to inspect their lead mines.

The house presents three grand gables to the visitor, each with a ball finial at the top, with a fourth distinctly lower gable to the left. This is the original house, built in about 1581 for Robert Clough. His house has delicious diamond- and lozenge-pattern woodwork on both fronts. When it was extended the original half timbering on the flank wall was left intact and is now seen exposed and in perfect condition beside a staircase in the house.

Sir Thomas Thynne of Longleat bought Minsterley in 1634. At that time the family seat in Shropshire was Caus Castle on top of nearby Aston Hill. Caus was garrisoned for the King in 1645, but quickly taken and demolished by Parliamentary forces. Minsterley was then enlarged in 1653 for Sir Henry Frederick Thynne, but for much of the next two centuries the house appears to have been lived in by sisters and younger sons. Sir Thomas, who was created Viscount Weymouth in 1682, built the delightfully eccentric baroque church in the village in 1689 but the fine communion plate, now kept in the bank, was 'the gift of the ladies Thynne' in 1692.

Created Marquesses of Bath in 1789, the family continued to visit at regular intervals to collect their rents. The 4th Marquess evidently had his own grand bedroom suite where he installed a handsome Renaissance-style marble chimney

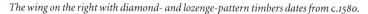

The wing on the right with diamond- and lozenge-pattern timbers dates from c.1580.

piece, carved by Italian craftsmen and dated 1878. This relates closely to a series of white marble door surrounds introduced by the leading Victorian decorator John Dibblee Crace at Longleat in a suite of ground-floor rooms running from the Ante Library to the Lower Dining Room, and also to the chimney piece in the Breakfast Room in this suite. Kate Harris, the curator at Longleat, suggested to me that the Minsterley chimney piece might have been one deemed superfluous at Longleat. The dates fit as Crace began working on these ground-floor rooms in Easter 1879.

Presumably for safety reasons, the four soaring brick chimney stacks were placed in pairs at the ends of the house with just one internal stack serving the hall. John Newman, in his excellent new edition of Pevsner's *Shropshire* points out that building 'in timber on such a scale was becoming old-fashioned' by 1600 but a house on a double-pile plan (two rooms deep) was 'right up-to-date even in London'.

The timber-frame structure is exposed in many parts of the house, including the large living room (top) and imposing stairway (above).

The 1600 hall opens onto the present garden front and retains a screen with a single large central arch which may have come from Caus Castle, though much of the panelling was replaced in the 19th century. The adjoining dining room has very splendid 17th-century oak panelling, the panels being unusually large and finely figured with a diamond pattern frieze along the top. The house has very handsome 17th-century oak staircases, one with corner posts topped with pierced pyramids.

Two 1830 watercolours show the house has been rendered. In the 1870s brick replaced rotten timbers on the ground floor of the garden front and large dormers were added. When the Thynnes were forced to sell the estate to pay death duties in 1927, a poignant *graffito* was left by a servant in the attic, running: 'I hope dear Peter will be happy in our old home.'

Minsterley was bought by the Barratt family from Cheshire, paint manufacturers. Mr Barratt, ('dear Peter'), posted in Shropshire in the First World War, married a local girl, bought the estate and half the village and was survived by his second wife. More recently the house was bought by Robert Sutherland. Finding Minsterley's fine timbers covered in black bitumen, he engaged the historic house architect David Morris (who restored Shrewsbury Abbey) to reveal the silvery oak beneath. Today the house has regained a glorious patina of age, matched by the wealth of splendid roof timbers exposed to view in the attics.

NETLEY HALL   Shrewsbury
Victorian mansion which is a family home again after years of neglect

MANY LARGE COUNTRY houses have been given a new and secure lease of life through conversion into apartments, or earn their keep through weddings, parties and events, as did Colin and Michele Poole, who bought Netley in a forlorn state in 2000. A grand Victorian mansion, dating from the 1850s but still almost Georgian in feeling, it was designed by the Shrewsbury architect Edward Hackcock for Thomas Henry Hope-Edwardes, descended from an Amsterdam banking

Though built in the 1850s, it is still Georgian in feel.

family. Grand reception rooms open off a central hall with a staircase that Pevsner observed was as grand as a London club. Light streams in from above through coloured glass panels set in the ceilings.

For ten years until 1954, Lady More, the heiress to the Hope-Edwardes lived at Netley before moving to her husband's house, Linley Hall. More recently a commercial fishery has been created with lakes in the grounds. This provided the cue for the Pooles, who turned Netley into a sporting estate centred on fishing holidays, with guests staying in cottages in the grounds. Netley was sold again in 2007, but the holiday cottages remain and the house has become a family home again.

PITCHFORD HALL   Pitchford
Widely held to be one of the most beautiful timber-framed houses in England

I FIRST WROTE ABOUT PITCHFORD HALL in *The Times* in 1992 when little more than thirty days remained to save it for the nation. The house was on the market, and on August 1, instructions were due to be given for all its contents, representing five hundred years of family history, to be auctioned by Christie's on the premises on September 28–30.

The National Trust was eager to take it on and was bidding for a £12m grant from the National Heritage Memorial Fund. Hope rested with the flamboyant new chairman of English Heritage, Jocelyn Stevens, who had dashingly offered to take on the house and contents while a long-term solution was found.

The immediate cause of the sale was losses on Lloyd's insurance syndicates by the Colthurst family, the more poignant because Oliver and Caroline Colthurst were the latest of three generations to put heart and soul into keeping Pitchford together.

Pitchford was one of the most beautiful and romantic of all timber-framed houses, equal to Little Moreton and Speke. Passing centuries had added mellowness and patina, admirably respected in the latest repairs carried out with English Heritage grants. Tragically, break-up loomed just as the house was due to be opened to the public.

The approach to Pitchford is along narrow by-roads, with a distant view of the Welsh hills, and it is easy to understand why, in 1940, it was one of three country houses that were chosen as potential safe retreats for the royal family in the event of a German invasion.

Horace Walpole observed that 'old houses lie low', and Pitchford and its gardens sheltered idyllically beneath the lee of a hill. A medieval hall stood there when Thomas Ottley, a Shrewsbury wool merchant, bought the estate in 1473.

His grandson added two wings to form a south-facing courtyard. This work was evidently started in 1549, when John Sandford, the leading Shrewsbury carpenter of the time, took up residence nearby to supervise the work. The difference was easy to spot. The original west range was built of closely set vertical timbers; Sandford's wings are a dazzling display of diamond and herringbone work as boldly abstract as a piece of 1960s kinetic art.

The 15th and 16th centuries were high points of domestic architecture, producing buildings that were more truly English than almost any that came after them. Pitchford was tangible evidence that black and white buildings were not simply quaint, but examples of craftsmanship of the highest order.

The romance of the place was well understood by the architects who worked here in later centuries. The first was Thomas Farnolls Pritchard, who introduced Georgian sliding sash windows but made no attempt to conceal the half timbering. He also built a black and white tree house with rococo gothic plasterwork, believed to be the oldest surviving tree house in Europe, and perhaps in the world, unless there is an older one somewhere in China.

The dazzling 1550s herringbone work contrasts with the plainer timbers of the 15th-century wing on the left.

The listed treehouse at Pitchford dates from 1692 and has 18th-century plasterwork inside, including gothick corner colonettes with stiff-leaf capitals.

In the 1880s George Devey carried out a remodelling as subtle and sensitive as his work at Melbury House, Dorset. Devey turned the house round, making the north front the entrance front and remodelling the 17th- and 18th-century service wings so that they resembled the Elizabethan work.

He created a seamless whole, and the recent repairs under the architect Andrew Arroll continued in the same spirit. Nowhere have I seen an old stone roof that has been more beautifully relaid. There was no didactic attempt to make the new timbers stand out sharply from the old. Because of the leaded lights reintroduced by Devey, the panelled interior was strongly atmospheric and undisturbed by later intrusions.

Inside, the contents spanned the centuries and included a fine series of family portraits, good furniture and a mass of porcelain, all enriched first by descent from the Liverpools and then by marriage to the Roseberys.

The Colthursts offered Pitchford and 76 acres to the nation as a gift if £1.8 million could be found for the contents, which would have been topped up by the tax rebate that is given on sales to the nation. Tragically the bid came in a year when the National Heritage Memorial Fund had depleted its resources in saving another important house for the Trust, Chastleton in Oxfordshire. Hopes rose when Jocelyn Stevens offered to 'garage' the house (as he put it), paying the running costs and finding a tenant, leaving only the purchase of the contents to be financed by the NHMF. For this Stevens needed approval from David Mellor, the new Secretary of State for National Heritage.

Fortuitously, I was at Pitchford on September 2, the day that Mr Mellor was due to make his announcement. The champagne was in the fridge. Then came the call that Mr Mellor had rejected the plan, saying: 'While the object is desirable on its own terms, the calls on the resources of English Heritage are already great and support for Pitchford can only take place to the detriment of other activities.'

The contents of Pitchford were dispersed in the three-day sale by Christie's at the house at the end of the month. The house was sold to an Egyptian buyer and today, to the dismay of all who look at Pitchford from over the wall of the adjacent churchyard, the house appears forlorn, empty and decaying.

For the new owner there was no obligation to open the house to the public, a condition attached to historic buildings repair grants, and Pitchford's beauty is now lost to view.

PLAISH HALL
Church Stretton
Elizabethan house of the 1570s, built for a lawyer

PLAISH HALL IS AS COVETABLE an Elizabethan manor house as can be found, built in warm pink brick with stone trim. It was built, like so many houses of this type, for a lawyer, William Leighton, who rose to be Chief Justice of North Wales. He was a minor when he inherited in 1533 and lived until 1607. The house has been variously dated to 1540 and 1580.

Leighton received licence to enclose a deer park shortly before 1577 and the 1570s appear the likely date. Plaish was acquired in the early 1880s by Edward Sayer who employed his son C.E. Sayer to carry out alterations.

The house is on the traditional H-plan with identical end or cross wings, the north for the family rooms and the south for the service rooms. Until the 1930s, the great hall filled both storeys, with a ceiling supported on hammer-beam trusses.

There is an intriguing hierarchy of chimneys, all set externally with the tallest to the north. Another trio sits behind the hall and there are rather lower chimneys for the service wing. As often happens at this date, the form of the house is carefully symmetrical but the placing of the windows in the central range is irregular, reflecting the layout of rooms within.

In the early 1980s the future of the house was a matter of some concern, with the gardens running wild and the house apparently standing empty. Since then the house has been sold and is again what it should be – a very comfortable home.

The house is built on a traditional H-plan with chimney stacks attached to the outside walls.

THE ALMSHOUSES Preston-on-the-Weald Moors

One of the most princely of Georgian almshouses built in 1721–5

THE ALMSHOUSES IN THE SMALL SHROPSHIRE village of Preston-on-the-Weald Moors are as noble as contemporary Oxbridge colleges. Built in the 1720s with money bequeathed by Lady Catherine Herbert, daughter of the 1st Earl of Bradford, they consist of a grand central hall, flanked by arcaded wings, open to display through a magnificent set of wrought-iron gates and railings. Warm red brick and pale grey stone are set off by a run of tall sash windows, mostly retaining their chunky early 18th-century glazing bars and crown glass.

The architect is unknown, but one obvious candidate is Francis Smith of Warwick, just conceivably with some help from the great James Gibbs, as the central hall has tall, arched 'Gibbs' windows with prominent quoins, just like those seen at Gibbs's St Martin-in-the-Fields, which was built at the same time – between 1721 and 1726.

The almshouses were unusual in providing a home for both twelve elderly women and for twelve girls between the ages of 7 and 16 who were trained 'in whatsoever could make them useful as servants'. For nearly three centuries they were looked after by the Bradford Estate, and were restored and modernised with the help of Historic Buildings Council grants in the late 1950s. But with further work needed to meet the latest regulations, the costs were too great and in 1999 the trustees decided to sell.

When the almshouses were put on the market there was much interest from developers, some of whom had highly unsuitable proposals. The scheme that won support of both planners and the Bradford Estate was put forward by Tim Jackson-Stops, former partner in the estate agents, and Douglas Blane, for years the prime mover behind the Spitalfields Trust, which has rescued and found solutions for more than sixty early-18th-century terraced houses in London.

The residents of the new apartments enter through grand wrought-iron gates.

Their offer removed the pressure for over-intensive conversion of the almshouses by proposing six new houses in the grounds designed by the architect Francis Machin in the manner of estate buildings, with a symmetry and gentle formality that matched the original layout. One, the Bothy, is a delightful play on Palladio's frequent motif of a gable within a gable.

Machin proposed converting the almshouses into a mix of houses and single-storey flats, with two cottages in the entrance lodges and the exteriors left

The central hall also served as a schoolroom.

almost completely unaltered. He explains: 'In a scheme like this garages have to be provided for all new residents and these can be intrusive. Instead of building lines of garages in isolation we have placed them between the new houses so they have the feeling of a stable block or row of potting sheds.' Machin has also made a clever play on the diamond-pattern pierced brickwork found on Shropshire barns, using blue bricks set back in the facades.

The conversion work on the almshouses was done by Shropshire Homes, the company that had tackled the 19th-century Ear, Nose and Throat Hospital in Shrewsbury. Howard Thorne, the managing director, told me: 'We sold 11 of the units before the show house opened last week. The new houses are going to families, the units in the almshouses to a wide mix of people, including first-time buyers and locals who spend time abroad.'

The biggest challenge has been the former hall, 28 ft high and designed to serve as both chapel and schoolroom. This is a magnificent oak-panelled interior with two grand fireplaces and high windows. The purchaser, Ross Lister, commissioned a young architect, Martin Markcrow, to devise an imaginative way of using the space.

Working with the structural engineers Atelier One, he proposed the introduction of a highly sculptural aluminium balcony, set back from the windows so that it is not visible from outside. The full height of the room remains open at either end. 'The structure uses technology more associated with Formula One cars or stealth fighters,' he said. To ensure that all building work was carried out to the highest standards, the almshouses were released to the builders in phases. The result is a model conversion where at first glance nothing appears to have changed.

ROWTON CASTLE
Georgian castle that lay derelict for fifteen years

Rowton

ROWTON CASTLE LAY DERELICT for fifteen years before restoration as an hotel. Before that it was a school surrounded by modern classroom blocks and other humdrum extensions that could have stepped straight from an Osbert Lancaster cartoon wryly portraying the fate of great houses. When I arrived in the early 1980s it looked as if things could only get worse. This was agonising as the castle was a charming composition of towers and battlements, all stepping picturesquely up a hill.

The original house was a Queen Anne box of 1700ish date that was then castellated in two stages. First Colonel Richard Lyster employed one of the Wyatt clan, George Wyatt, to add a big three-storey north block. Then in the 1820s a more romantic approach was adopted by Henry and Lady Charlotte Lyster, who added the tall circular tower.

The hotel opened in 1989 and embellishments have continued under Jacques de Sousa, who took over the property in 1997. Rowton now stands in well-tended grounds, with manicured lawns, clipped topiary and luxuriant borders. De Sousa has employed decorative artists to paint a series of monkey pictures, in the manner of the playful *singeries* popular in 18th-century France. The main rooms are traditionally furnished with bold accents of colour. There are nineteen comfortable bedrooms in the castle, which is now a very popular venue for weddings. Against all the odds Rowton has found its prince and wonders have been worked on both the castle and its setting.

Smartly planted borders replace the makeshift huts that once disfigured the lawns.

STOKESAY COURT
Stokesay

Late-Victorian time capsule that survived complete with all its contents

STOKESAY WAS BUILT IN 1889–91 for John Derby Allcroft, a rich glove manufacturer. His architect, Thomas Harris, also built a major country house for Titus Salt II. The contents of Stokesay were exceptionally complete. The bulk of the furniture was purchased from leading manufacturers such as Howards and Shulbrede, representing the wide range of furniture available at the period, all exactly documented, graphically showing the hierarchy of the household, not only between the owners and their servants, but the gradations of comfort in different guest rooms.

When the house was requisitioned in 1939 the bulk of the contents were carefully packed into the roof space and lay there untouched for fifty years. The textiles included summer and winter curtains, original case covers, both decorative and for storage, and sun curtains. The carpets came with matching hearth rugs. Metalwork included the fire irons and fire dogs and the early electric light fittings. There were also extensive collections of marble sculpture, silver and ceramics and a large collection of paintings by Thomas Sidney Cooper, R.A. An album of snapshots showed the house in various stages of construction, complemented by account books, diaries, invoices and other photographs showing the newly furnished interiors and the park and estate.

In 1994 the house was valued at £500,000, and the contents at £3.5 million, but the tax bill was likely to be some £2 million so the total cost of acquisition by a public body was likely to be no more than £2 million, though further sums would be required for repairs.

The National Trust had said that it could not take the house without an endowment, but English Heritage asked Kit Martin and I to look at the house with a view to suggesting a viable way by which they could take it on and find uses for parts

The long gabled flank looks over formal terraces.

The grand gabled front overlooks balustraded garden terraces.

of the building that would not be open to the public. We reported that 'this is a wonderful house, all the more exciting and surprising as it is virtually unknown. As a piece of architecture it has been seriously underrated in the past. The entrance court is a powerful and original composition and the spectacular central hall and staircase are the Jacobethan counterpart of the hall and stair of the Reform Club half a century earlier, the richest and most evocative of their age.'

We suggested that 'visitors must see all the main family rooms on the ground floor and walk along the west wing as far as the billiard room. They should also be able to explore the service wing, though the kitchen was probably the ideal place for the tea room as little of the kitchen equipment appeared to survive. Upstairs, visitors should see the main family rooms and one or two rooms in the ladies and bachelors rooms, though not every room as this would have been repetitive and require a disproportionate number of watchers.'

The rest of the house, we proposed, could be converted into a series of self-contained houses and apartments which could be sold on long leases, reducing the running costs and generating funds for repair. There was also the possibility of the family retaining one of the apartments, probably the west wing, for their own use. At this moment we received strong support from Gervase Jackson-Stops, then very ill, who for years had been the National Trust's Historic Buildings Advisor. He had been the main force behind the rescue of Canons Ashby and Calke Abbey for the National Trust, and felt very strongly that Stokesay was the Victorian counterpart. English Heritage, alas, decided they could not proceed and Christie's sold the contents early in the summer of 1994. One member of the family remained, showing the house and gardens to pre-booked parties, catering for lunches, dinners and other events.

STYCHE HALL
Market Drayton
House and stables built for Clive of India in 1762–6

DRIVING ROUND SHROPSHIRE, I HAVE ALWAYS BEEN struck by the number of handsome stable blocks which often survive even when country houses have been demolished. At Styche Hall the stables were built, like the house, to the designs of the great Sir William Chambers. Chambers, who was architectural tutor to George III, was a master of Classical composition, and his buildings always have intuitively good, satisfying proportions.

The extent of the stables at Styche reflects the fact that Chambers's client was the great Clive of India. House and stables were built in 1762–6, begun just two years after Clive had returned a hero from India and been elected MP for Shrewsbury. Clive was the eldest son of an impoverished Shropshire squire, born and brought up in the parish of Moreton Saye in which Styche is situated. Both house and stables are of brick, though the house is now whitewashed. Following the conversion of the house to apartments, it was the turn of the stables. Reflected in the still waters of a large rectangular pond, these are a handsome sight. Yet the architectural detail is sparing – with brick quoins at the corners but no cornice beneath the eaves of the hipped roofs. The layout consists of a rectangular coach house and an L-plan stable block which has readily divided into self-contained houses. The transformation was carried out by Alexandra Countryside Developments. The only external alterations have been the lengthening of two windows to become doors with an arched doorcase overlooking the pond.

The stable block is beautifully reflected in the calm waters of the pond.

YEATON PEVERY   Shrewsbury
Handsome 1890s Arts and Crafts house that stood empty for years

THE ARCHITECT ASTON WEBB was one of the giants of the Edwardian age, designing Admiralty Arch and the main front of Buckingham Palace, as well as the grand entrance range of the Victoria and Albert Museum, complete with its white Venetian domes and *campanile*. And before he rose to full Imperial grandeur he was a talented, even inspired, Arts and Crafts designer, his masterpiece being the magistrates' courts in Birmingham.

Yeaton Pevery is his only country house, built in 1889–92 for Sir Offley Wakeman, Bt. It featured in SAVE's first report on endangered country houses, *Tomorrow's Ruins*, in 1978 as it had been standing empty for at least six years, since the girls' school that was there had closed down. It remained empty for many more years and the owner bellowed down the phone to me, 'It is the ugliest house in the kingdom and every time anybody writes about it people come along wanting to do something about it. I will keep it wind- and watertight but otherwise I just want it left alone.'

In 1981 SAVE successfully applied for the house to be upgraded to a II* listing. When the house appeared again in SAVE's *Endangered Domains* in 1985, it was the

The fine craftsmanship was left to gently moulder for years.

Fortunately the panelled interior remained wonderfully complete.

chief planning officer at Shrewsbury and Atcham who complained this time about the number of enquiries that he received about the house.

Yeaton Pevery is a large house but very well built of good materials. It provides an example of the Free-style that was so popular in the late 19th century, when smooth red stone and half timbering was mixed with carefully graded Westmoreland roof slates. The one discordant note is the hard red Midlands brick that was used for the chimneys, durable but still without any kind of patina a century later.

The house forms a long, spreading composition and opposite the main front are attractive domed pavilions with sun seats. A frieze along the front of the house bears the words from Psalm 127 'Unless the Lord Build the house…'. Garden terraces were designed by H.H. Milner, who also worked at Apley in Shropshire.

Though empty and forlorn in 1985, the interiors had the sense of home that is familiar in Arts and Crafts houses – fireplaces with inglenook seats, wainscoting in abundance, heraldic glass. In all there had been thirty bedrooms grouped, according to an article in *The Builder*, for 'the convenient accommodation of guests, the family and nurseries, the men servants, maid servants, and stranger servants'.

The most remarkable of the interiors was the characteristic Victorian combined hall and staircase, with every element executed in wood – floor, panelling, ceiling with flying ribs and pendants and balustraded gallery. There are pierced finials on the newel posts and barleysugar balusters.

Twenty years on all is changed. The house is lived in and repaired and three smart apartments have been created, immaculately equipped for renting to local people wanting to live in the country and commute to Shrewsbury.

SOMERSET

ASHTON COURT IS LARGELY EMPTY and superb interiors are stripped out or collapsing from years of neglect. Weddings and events are held in parts of the house but the most beautiful interior, the Long Gallery, once of almost Inigo Jones quality, is now no more than bare walls. The Strawberry Hill Gothick dining room retains pretty blind arcading inspired by Venetian palaces and filigree ceiling decoration but all pockmarked by damp, peeling paint and graffiti, not to mention holes that allow you to see the roof.

This is the greater scandal as the house belongs to the City Council and stands in extensive grounds that are well maintained as a public park. For four centuries, from 1545 to 1946, Ashton was owned by one of the great merchant families of Bristol, the Smyths. Now, following agitation by the Bristol Civic Society, there is a glimmer of hope that the City may address the problem. The main issue concerns access. The drives are long and run through a public park, and uses such as conference centre or hotel could generate a great deal of traffic and require a large amount of car parking nearby. Recently Lottery money has been spent on the gardens south of the house, making it difficult to restrict public access close to the building and to provide privacy for users of the building. The best solution may be a mixed scheme, with public access to the most interesting interiors but office suites and apartments in other areas. Both of these are uses that, if well-managed, would generate relatively little traffic and provide capital or income for repairs and upkeep.

Ashford is collegiate in its grandeur but large parts are disused.

BARFORD HOUSE
Bridgwater
Enchanting early-Georgian house rescued from advanced decay

BARFORD LIES ON THE LOWER SLOPES of the Quantocks in rolling country, commanding marvellous views towards the Severn estuary. Bridgwater is only five miles away but the narrow sleepy lanes hear nothing of the endless stream of traffic that goes to and from the coast. A more puissant landowner would have moved the road beyond the park boundary in the 18th century, but the view of the house from the passing road lends immense charm to the scene – the hedges disappear and for a brief moment the public road seems like a private drive.

The tombs in the local church at Enmore give the names of the families who have lived here. James Jeanes of Barford House died in 1759. His nephew Andrew Guy, also of Barford, died in 1798, having served as Deputy Lieutenant and High Sherriff of Somerset. His daughter Anne married John Evered who died in 1848. But by 1837 his son Robert Guy Evered was living in the house and in turn, he handed Barford to his second son, Captain John Guy Courtenay Everard, who served in the Crimean and Second China wars. He lived to be a hundred, reputedly drinking the waters from the garden spring.

Like all naval men, he kept his house in perfect order, but on his death in 1937 Barford passed to a son and daughter who lived here during the Second World War. By the time they died in the 1950s the house was almost derelict, and suffering from extensive dry rot.

The main front is delightfully extended by curving wings that end in pavilions.

The soft red brick of the house can be seen from across the park.

Barford was lucky enough to be rescued by Michael Stancomb, who bought the house from the executors in 1958, and instigated a series of repairs that have brought it back to life.

The architect was almost certainly a local master mason or bricklayer. One candidate is Nathaniel Ireson, who built Crowcombe Court on the other side of the Quantocks in about 1734. More probably it was a man from Bridgwater, as the brackets beneath the windowsills resemble those on houses built for the 1st Duke of Chandos in Castle Street, Bridgwater. Some of these were built by Benjamin Holloway, a local carpenter, whom Chandos thought 'A very great Knave' but employed 'being a good workman and the only one thereabouts'.

The appeal of Barford lies in the colour of its brickwork, reds as rich as the local soil, mixed with others of deep orange. The colour of the wings is a harder and more even red, but the two set each other off brilliantly. The abiding charm of the composition lies in finding Palladian matching wings on a house of modest size. Here the 'quadrant', or curving, links to the wings are combined, rather than being treated as hyphens, with a continuous entablature uniting both.

Behind the house is a large walled garden with unusual rounded corners. A little further away is a Victorian pleasure ground, probably laid out in the 1860s. There is an archery glade lined with noble beeches that opens into a woodland garden divided by laurel hedges.

BARROW COURT
Barrow Gurney
Rescued from decay in the 1890s and surrounded by Edwardian formal gardens

BARROW COURT STANDS IN A THRILLING architectural garden of a quality that you might expect to find at the villas around Vicenza. The best part is that though the house is now divided among several owners, the gardens remain an entity. They were illustrated when newly complete in *Country Life* in 1902 when the house was the seat of Mr H.M. Gibbs, who had recently rescued it from advanced decay. The gardens are substantially the creation of Francis Inigo Thomas, who was also responsible for the well-known gardens at Athelhampton House in Dorset. Thomas led the revival of formal gardens at the turn of the last century with Sir Reginald Blomfield, author of the seminal work *The Formal Garden in England*. Published in 1892, this was illustrated by Thomas himself.

Thomas designed the grand hemicycle around the entrance court with twelve busts representing the months of the year. These are superbly carved by Alfred Drury and echo those around the Sheldonian Theatre in Oxford. The garden is laid out with long terraces and impressive yew hedges. There are walled courts with obelisks at the corners, a sundial court, garden pavilions with arched and columned loggias and gently curving rooflines. Thomas was a master in the use of stairs, steps and balustrades. There are twin curving flights leading to one pavilion, and convex and concave steps in front of another forming concentric circles around a half landing.

Barrow Court was originally a Benedictine Nunnery sold to become a house following the Dissolution of the Monasteries. The nunnery was rebuilt in about 1545 on a Tudor E-plan and extended with an L-shaped range to the west in 1602.

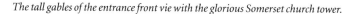

The tall gables of the entrance front vie with the glorious Somerset church tower.

BASSETT HOUSE · Bath

1836 Bath villa on the cusp between Grecian and Italianate

Dramatically set over a steep ravine, 7 acres of grounds extend along the canal.

AMONG THE MOST DELIGHTFUL OF all English country houses are the Picturesque villas built around prosperous cities and towns in the later 18th and early 19th centuries. Villas ideally were built to enjoy a ravishing view and stood in ample grounds surrounded by lofty trees with gardens overflowing with shrubs. They were manageable in size and did not bring the responsibilities of farms and estates. They were designed to enjoy what the French call *la douceur de la vie*, the sweetness of life, for gentle retirement, good conversation, a hospitable way of life and the enjoyment of balmy summer air.

In the early 19th century, villas came in all styles, gothic, rustic, Italianate, and some of the finest were built in the sylvan surroundings of Bath, placed to enjoy views of rolling hills and green valleys – with names like Montebello and Fiesole.

Bassett House, to the east of Bath, may have a more prosaic name, but in every other respect it is the epitome of the Picturesque. It is set in a plunging ravine with views across the Avon Valley to a steeply rising green hillside with upper slopes cloaked in leafy woods. At the bottom of the garden is the Kennet & Avon Canal, with longboats gliding quietly by.

Dating from 1836, the villa is built in warm golden Bath stone and perfectly oriented to enjoy the view, with terraces and balconies on three levels. The style is an enchanting mix of Regency Grecian and the then newly fashionable Italianate. Among the Italianate features are the arched windows (some grouped in threes as in Venetian houses) and the oversailing eaves. The squared colonnades and x-pattern balustrades are Grecian.

The house was so deliciously attractive that it was recorded in a print as soon as it was completed and the view confirms that it is unchanged in virtually every respect – whether the stone balconies or the semi-circular 'Diocletian' arch at the lower level.

Houses built on hillsides can present problems but this appears immensely sturdy and the present owners have re-roofed and rewired it and tanked the cellars against the hill. Some time ago, extensive structural work was unexpectedly done on the terrace by Wandsworth Borough Council, which briefly used Bassett as a retreat for wayward London boys.

The challenge for the next owner is to decorate the house in best Regency style. I would love to see the drawing room, dining room and bedrooms painted in strong Regency blues, reds and greens, with dashing striped wallpapers and dark lustrous mahogany furniture. If you wish to be exact, there is a ready model nearby in William Beckford's Lansdown Tower, recently immaculately restored by the Landmark Trust with deep heavy crimsons, rich curtains and carpets, and fabrics on the walls.

Here the rooms on the main floor open out onto the colonnaded verandas – offering a perfect form of indoor-outdoor living, ideal for both intimate lunches and large parties. The verandas are deep enough to eat out in even if it starts to rain, with twin external flights leading to the lower level.

The house was built for George Vivian. He also owned Claverton Manor, now the American Museum in Britain, which his father had commissioned from Sir Jeffry Wyatville who transformed Windsor Castle for George IV. Who then was the architect of Bassett House? One candidate is Henry Edmund Goodridge, who built a series of villas around Bath, including Montebello (for himself), Casa Bianca, La Cassetta and Fiesole as well as Beckford's Lansdown Tower, but Christopher Woodward of Bath's Holburne Museum is more inclined to James Wilson, better known for his churches.

The lower level of Bassett House is equipped as a self-contained summer house with living room, kitchen, bedroom and bathroom, where the owners can descend to enjoy the cool in summer, or let as a self-contained flat with a separate side entrance. Here there is also a spacious soundproof workshop as well as a cellar with the original Georgian wine bins.

The main drawing room now has French windows but the glass in the arch suggests it may have once had triple hung sashes (the type favoured by Thomas Jefferson) – a system by which both lower sashes slid up to the top, creating a full-height opening like a doorway.

The ample accommodation in this compact villa is evident from a 'To Let' advertisement in *The Times* on May 10, 1858, which lists four reception rooms, five bedrooms and no less than nine servants' rooms. Some of these are in the attic, approaching by charming twin branch staircases rising under the eaves.

There are seven acres of grounds extending along the canal with tennis court and newly reclaimed wall garden. Below the house, steps lead down to a grotto with impressive stone arched vault. Nearby is a secret door onto the canal, where it is a short walk to the mighty Classical arch of the Dundas aqueduct which carries the canal over river and railway and is now being restored. From here you can walk all the way to Bath along the towpath or climb the hill on the far side of the valley and take a circular walk of over an hour enjoying snowdrops, daffodils and bluebells as spring arrives.

Even though the adjacent coach house is now in separate ownership, Bassett House retains complete privacy extending through woods along several hundreds of yards of canal. The one drawback is the busy road that passes close above the house. You will no doubt become adept at turning in or out of the fast-moving traffic but the noise is more insistent and windows have been double glazed on the road side. But if you can come to terms with this, you will be living in Elysium.

8 THE CIRCUS — Bath

The house chosen by William Pitt, the Prime Minister, as his Bath residence

BUILT OF GLOWING GOLDEN Bath stone, No 8 The Circus offers the opportunity to live in prime position in one of the grandest compositions in all English architecture. The architect, John Wood the Elder, originally dreamed his smart town mansions would look out on a 'Grand Circus for the Exhibition of Sports'. Instead the central grass sward is today filled with a noble grove of six lofty plane trees, allowing every house an open view of this matchless reincarnation of Ancient Roman splendour.

The Circus was begun in 1754, the year John Wood died. The work was taken forward by his son, John Wood the Younger, who offered William Pitt, the Prime Minister, a choice of house to set the development off to a good start. Pitt was MP for Bath for eleven years until created Earl of Chatham in 1766. He chose two houses, No 7 as his office and No 8 as his residence. The reasons for his choice are obvious. The front of the house enjoys morning sun, while the back looks south-west with a sylvan view over Victoria Park and the green in front of the Royal Crescent.

For nearly half a century the two houses have been a nursing home. Five years ago they were acquired by Nigel Slydell, an entrepreneur who cut his teeth developing land at Emsworth harbour near Chichester.

The basement areas in The Circus are exceptionally large, giving each house a grand approach between cast-iron railings. The front of No 8 has been newly cleaned, revealing the exquisitely crisp detail of the three ascending Orders of columns – Doric, Ionic and Corinthian. The Doric frieze over the ground floor is the richest with a constantly varied run of classical motifs – including sword and buckler, Mercury caduceus (baton entwined with a snake), cornucopias and laurel crowns.

The interiors of the house are superbly proportioned if a little on the plain side. To give them éclat Mr Slydell commissioned the designer Johnny Gray to create kitchen ranges, cupboards and dressers that are as much pieces of sculpture as furniture. The two ground-floor rooms open into each other. At the front is the dining room where the deep drawers of the sideboard-cum-dresser pull out to reveal three washing-up machines so you can put plates and glasses in without even getting up from the table. Ingenious, yet a trifle odd for the super-smart dinner parties the house appears designed for.

Designed on a curve, The Crescent has, in ascending order, Doric, Ionic and Corinthian columns.

The kitchen has a central slender oval island with the hob, while oven and large American fridge swing out in a matching curving from the wall with the larder tucked in a cupboard behind. The long slow curves perfectly match the graceful bay window at the end. The use of woods is exquisite with walnut, ash, burr walnut and burr sycamore. Worktops are in French limestone and Jerusalem Gold stone. 'The men love it, the wives are less sure,' says my guide. One strange detail is that the fireplace wall opposite is completely bare apart from the marble mantle – a dead space.

A new glass sided bridge leads over the basement area to the garden.

The houses around The Circus are wedge-shaped but this is hardly evident here except in the stair which is set at a slight angle to the entrance hall, lit by a gently curving double sash on the half landing. To make the grandest exit into the large back garden, Mr Slydell has deftly made the central sash window into a door opening on to a sleek all-glass bridge across the back basement area. It's a glorious flourish but will require very regular cleaning if it is to remain spotless. At night, with lights in the room below, the stainless steel rails glow enticingly.

On the first floor is a double drawing room with sliding doors that glide smoothly into the dividing wall. Here, as everywhere else in the house, the original floorboards have been exposed and polished, creating a minimalist contrast with the pale plaster walls and whitened cornices.

The second floor, with the master bedroom suite, brings more surprises. There is an egg-shaped bath by the window, a large walk-in clothes closet and a 'wet room' up half a flight of stairs overlooking the garden. Here floor and walls are all clad in buff mosaic and carefully textured black slate, a welcome change from the ubiquitous use of marble in bathrooms. At the front is a second bedroom with its own bathroom and window onto The Circus. On the third floor are three more bedrooms, one with its own shower room, the others sharing.

The lower ground floor is well-lit thanks to the large basement areas. There is a games room in the splendid vaulted front kitchen, with a further bedroom and bathroom at the back where the glass bridge allows light to stream in through the windows. The final surprise of the house is that even without double glazing the cars in The Circus are virtually inaudible, though a little more evident at the top of the house.

Bath's former conservation officer James Elliot told me, 'After the Second World War, people thought they would never be able to find servants again, and the idea of flats had not yet started. So many of these glorious town houses were taken over for institutional use.' They are now becoming town houses again – 18th-century elegance is evidently a sound investment.

BATHEALTON COURT
Bathealton
Classic Georgian house with all the trimmings

THE MAIN APPEAL OF BATHEALTON COURT is that it comes with all the trimmings – a pretty Gothic Revival gate lodge, a drive up an avenue underplanted with daffodils, a stretch of park, walled garden and stables. An early 19th-century print shows a lake below the house.

With its steep hipped roof and two even rows of tall sash windows, it looks late 17th-century, though it is said to date principally from the 1760s with further remodelling in the 1850s. Inside the rooms are panelled in 1700 fashion as well as the pretty short flight of steps connecting library and drawing room. The Grinling Gibbons-style carvings in the dining room include delightful songbirds over the niches. There is a spacious stair rising round an open well with pretty spiral balusters – often referred to as barley twists.

An intriguing feature is an ornamental plaster ceiling on the first floor, said to be Adam, but done in a very freehand manner with repeating bands of a scroll or wave motif alternating with acanthus and palmettes. It is as if the traditional vocabulary was being varied by a craftsman from the Cotswolds working with the Chipping Campden group. The fan motif in the centre is certainly very Adamesque but there is a looseness to it all that suggests a fascinating reinterpretation. When I visited in 2005, the service quarters were still wonderfully unchanged with cobbled floors and built-in dressers.

In April 1923 Bathealton was advertised for sale as 'a Gentleman's well-built residence (fifteen bed and dressing, lounge hall and three reception rooms)' with two excellent farms and well-placed coverts for game.

A gentle curve gives the roof an extra flourish.

BISHOP'S HOUSE — Bristol
1711 house attributed to John Strahan

BRISTOL HAS MORE HANDSOME 18th- and 19th- century stone-built houses than any city in England, Bath included, and possibly more than Edinburgh. The Bishop's House in Clifton is even more special owing to its majestic position – right at the top of Clifton, facing two other wonderful houses – Palladian Clifton Hill House of 1747 and Goldney House, belonging to the University, with its large garden and exquisitely restored shell grotto.

Until 2003 this was the residence of the Bishop of Bristol but it was built as plain Church House, beside the ancient parish church which was bombed in 1940. The churchyard survives, filled with noble trees providing sheltered views for the bedrooms in the east wing. Next to it is a large but tranquil public garden.

Naturally the views from Church House improve as you rise up the building and are best of all from the balustraded roof, where you look out to the green slopes across the Avon Gorge and down to the noble spire of St Mary Redcliffe, the docks and more rolling hills.

A mature yew hedge shelters the front garden. You drive in at the side through gates that shut off the large back garden from the world, but one of the pleasures of living here would be to walk out straight into Clifton's fine streets and nearby shops.

The house has been well maintained by the Church Commissioners, with a good roof and even newly restored urns along the parapet. Of course it is a little institutional within, but only in a way that sets the imagination rolling. A bookcase,

By 2004 the house was considered too grand for a bishop and sold as a private house.

installed for weighty theological tomes, can be removed to open up front and back rooms on the ground floor. Upstairs partitions can be taken out to make more spacious bedrooms and bathrooms – perhaps six en suites rather than the present eleven. On one side there are three flats with a separate entrance off the street which, if smartened up, could be let to be a big help with the mortgage.

Church House was built on the church close, which was bought by John Hodges who commissioned the present house, dated 1711 over the entrance. There is a strong probability the house was designed by the leading Bristol architect John Strahan who is the author of some of the best baroque houses around Bristol. According to Shiercliff's *Bristol and Hotwell Guide* of 1789, Strahan 'built Redland-Court House and many other capital mansions in and near Bristol'. He was also smart enough to have his bust carved by the great sculptor Rysbrack.

Church House has the baroque flourishes expected of Strahan – arched windows with keystones, a handsome front-doorcase with fluted Ionic columns. Inside, the hall is imposingly broad, opening through a baroque elliptical arch to the grandest of mahogany stairs with three balusters to a tread and a landing with a curved balustrade.

George Townsend has also been suggested as the architect. A brother of the well-known master mason William Townesend of Oxford, he had established himself in Bristol and was made a freeman of the city in 1706, upon his marriage to Margaret Harford, daughter of a former burgess. In 1710 he was paid £12 for the frontispiece at the council house. He was probably also the mason who worked for Vanbrugh at King's Weston, near Bristol.

Most of the rooms retain fine Georgian sashes and often shutters in working order. The best panelled rooms are the bishop's study and former secretary's office.

In 1766 the house passed to a famous Bristolian, Samuel Worrall, a rich lawyer and clerk to the Merchant Venturers. The Worrall family remained here till 1902 when the house was acquired by Sir George Oatley, a leading local architect who is commemorated on a plaque outside. He was the author of Bristol landmarks including the grandiloquent Wills Tower, the thrusting centrepiece of Bristol University. The garden and the summer house owe much to him including, presumably, the serpentine balustrade that encloses the rose garden at the back. Today one half of the garden – nearly 80 yards long in all – is a lawn flanked by borders and the other is a neatly planted fruit and vegetable garden providing all the benefits of a country garden.

Even though some of the rooms have rather less in the way of features, such as fine cornices, ceiling plasterwork and handsome fireplaces, than one might hope for in a house of this class and size, the rooms are well-proportioned and well-lit, there is a handsome secondary stair continuing on to the upper floor, good vaulted cellars and of course private parking, which in populous Clifton is a very big asset indeed. Here you can be at once a recluse and entertain in fine style.

The earlier Bishop's Palace was burnt on October 29–31, 1831, during the fierce rioting in Bristol over parliamentary reform. The militia was ineffective and during extensive looting, Queen's Square, three prisons and the Bishop's Palace were burned.

BRYMPTON D'EVERCY   Yeovil
Chequered history of one of the most lovely of all English houses

FOR AT LEAST A CENTURY HISTORIANS and writers have written of Brympton d'Evercy in rapturous terms. Sir Nikolaus Pevsner in his guide to Somerset describes the ensemble of house and church as 'of exquisite beauty' adding that the golden colour of the Ham Hill stone 'can nowhere be seen to better advantage'. Christopher Hussey of *Country Life*, who knew English country houses better than anyone before or after him, declared that 'there are greater, more historic, more architecturally impressive buildings in grander scenery; but I know of none where the whole impression is so lovely. None which summarises so exquisitely English country life.'

Brympton's surpassing beauty derives from mellow golden stone. The first view of the house only comes as you turn into the forecourt with medieval church, priest's house and manor forming the perfect picturesque group. An attempt has been made at symmetry in the grand mullioned windows on either side of the castellated porch, but jammed up against it to the left is one of the most delightful survivals of all early-Tudor architecture. An octagonal stair turret with paired arched windows jostles with an exquisitely carved oriel, banded with fretwork and crested with battlements.

All this exuberance is balanced on the right side by a single beautifully proportioned Georgian window set high in the wall. When you turn the corner to

The garden front in golden Ham Hill stone is given rhythm by the alternating window pediments.

the south front you see why. The mason has achieved perfect harmony by repeating a single window design on two floors, varied only by the alternating triangular and segmental heads to the windows. Amazingly no Georgian sashes were ever inserted here, leaving us with the delightful and now rare sight of stone mullions that are set in classically proportioned windows. At times it has been suggested that Inigo Jones was the architect of this front, but no architect as steeped in Classical grammar as he was would have designed a run of windows with a rounded pediment and ended with a triangular one, thus offending a sense of balance and symmetry, though barely noticeable unless pointed out.

The entrance porch is delightfully glazed and castellated.

For 250 years Brympton D'Evercy was the home of the Fane family. The last of them to live in the house, the splendidly triple-barrelled Charles Clive-Ponsonby-Fane, heroically undertook the task of turning Brympton back from a school into a family home. He threw his energies into opening Brympton to the public. His problem was that Elizabethan Montacute, one of the most famous and perfect properties of the National Trust, was just two miles away, and of course free to all Trust members.

When Mr Clive-Ponsonby-Fane put Brympton up for sale in 1991, it was described as 'a house without hope' but the Weeks family who bought it have cared for it beautifully. The church is open to visitors and the main house is regularly used for weddings and other events.

By 2004 it was in danger again, soon to be engulfed by factories following a vote by South Somerset Councillors to assign 60 acres of unspoilt agricultural land for development. Brympton's predicament stemmed from its position just two miles from the centre of the expanding Somerset town of Yeovil. Until then the ring road had provided a clear boundary to the west of the town – industrial development had been kept within it. Beyond were green fields, ensuring that Brympton remained isolated and safe within the country lanes that surround it.

This was a test case. Brympton now stood in just 25 acres. If permission were given to build on 60 adjoining acres (or more) towards Yeovil, further applications would almost certainly follow, probably all but encircling the house within decades. If this could happen to the most beautiful house in England, I reasoned, what hope was there for the rest? The application went to public inquiry. The inspector agreed to new development west of the ring road but ruled that it should be to the north, where it would intrude less on Brympton. This was a victory and now we must hope that it proves a long lasting one.

THE ABBEY
Charlton Adam
Fragment of a former abbey that has the feel of an Elizabethan hunting lodge

THE ABBEY AT CHARLTON ADAM in Somerset sits waiting to be chosen as the setting for a film in the mould of *Four Weddings and a Funeral*. It has a garden gate that opens directly into the churchyard of one of the most enchanting small parish churches in England, seating no more than one hundred and kept in perfect trim. The choir has four neat rows of handsome choir stalls, while the 17th-century monuments in the side chapel are like miniature temple fronts.

The Abbey incorporates a chantry chapel founded in 1237 for masses to be sung for the souls of the dead. It was a dependence of the abbey of nearby Bruton. After closure at the Dissolution of the Monasteries in 1536, it served briefly as a rectory before coming into the hands of the Hodges family, who held it till 1636.

Inside, the house has more the feel of a late-Elizabethan hunting lodge, four-square and tall, as if built to command views of the hunt charging across neighbouring fields. The layout on each floor is of four interlinking rooms around a massive central chimney stack.

Outside, the charm of the house lies in the greeny-grey local stone known as 'lias', which is cut into rough squares and laid in courses that, towards the top, are almost as narrow as brickwork. Both stone and mortar are so mellowed as to be barely distinguishable. The lias is set off by the golden Ham stone, also local, used for the windows and other details such as the caps of the buttresses.

Each of the four fronts is strikingly different with barely one window matching another and not a sash window in sight. The plain clay roof tiles are a warm brown and there is a fine array of tall chimney stacks, some of them octagonal and built of smooth-cut 'ashlar' stone.

The Abbey is the epitome of the picturesque with windows set where they were needed.

Two early windows, perhaps of the 15th century, have cusped heads, other have Tudor hood moulds. Stepped buttresses are found on south and west fronts, while the east front has a delightful trio of gables, each set behind the other.

The house is of two storeys in part and three storeys in others. Various theories have been advanced about its evolution but the most convincing is that the main part is the upper wing of a late 16th-century H-plan house which has subsequently lost both hall and lower service wing.

Though much altered in later centuries, the Abbey has largely slept through the 20th century and was carefully repaired after partial damage in a fire in 1960. The last major works were carried out three generations ago, immediately after the Abbey had been bought by Claude Neville in 1905. The bill for £1,787 11s 6d survives. Neville's architect was probably C.E. Ponting, who was fresh from a careful restoration of nearby Lytes Cary Manor, which now belongs to the National Trust.

Here he created a delightful miniature great hall inside a new entrance on the west front. It is open to the rafters, and lit by windows at two levels, though the upper ones are of wendy-house size. A flash of grandeur is provided by a large and splendid stone fireplace filling the end wall.

The further half of the 1905 hall contains the stairs with Jacobean-style newel posts and finials added by Ponting. At the top is an original run of oak balustrade with balusters intriguingly numbered from I to XI and a round-arched wooden doorcase formed of two vertical timbers.

The main room on the ground floor is a splendid oak-panelled drawing room of early 17th-century date with a lozenge motif carved along the top, echoing the carving on the imposing two-tier oak fireplace complete with paired Ionic columns and scrolls at the sides. The huge oak beams were probably once concealed by a rich plaster ceiling. Next door the dining room has another of Ponting's large stone fireplaces with massive lintel across the top.

The spacious kitchen is fitted out with dignified traditional wooden cupboards – one cleverly concealing a large fridge. This in turn opens into a pleasant morning room with French windows opening into the garden.

The main bedroom on the first floor is a good 15 or 16 ft high and so approaches a perfect cube in proportions. The tall mullioned window with its high sill suggests that this was once a first-floor great chamber. It probably ran the width of the house as there is a matching tall window on the north and the present internal walls are no more than partitions.

As in many ancient houses, unexpected features are found in many rooms. Everywhere there are handsome stone-mullioned windows but also more early stone fireplaces, one almost pink in colour in a bathroom, another in Ham stone charmingly set between two windows in the attic. Two upstairs bedrooms have arched or barrel ceilings. Two others have capacious Edwardian baths.

The biggest opportunity lies in making a garden. The bones are there, a large walled garden to the east and a sunken garden to the south. The Abbey stands in what has the feel of a large private village green. There are roads on four sides but these are far enough away for you to look out across pasture. Village life is yours as well as seclusion.

CROWCOMBE COURT
Crowcombe
Lovely Baroque house that stood empty and decaying in the Quantock Hills

CROWCOMBE IS A CLASSIC EXAMPLE OF THE TIME and dedication it can take to nurse an abandoned country house back to life. When I first saw it in the 1970s it was a poignant sight, a grand early-Georgian house in the lush steeply rolling pasture of the Quantock Hills. Yet it had become a virtual untouchable as it had been sold with only a small parcel of land and in poor condition.

The house is built of a glowing warm orangey-red brick with baroque giant pilasters emphasising the centre and the corners. The surprise was the pair of massive wings at the side forming a courtyard linked by quadrant wings to the main block. Inside there were still early-Georgian interiors of the highest quality with grand pediment doorcases, chimney pieces with rich overmantels and superb ceiling plasterwork.

The house was damaged by fire in 1963 and left empty, descending to a desperate state. The service wings were sold for residential conversion in the 1980s and the main house became a care home. Salvation came in 1999 when the house was bought by Pat Smith and Richard Anderson, who began careful repairs. Crowcombe is now a family home again, with the main rooms and vaulted cellars available for weddings and receptions.

Crowcombe was built from 1723 to 1738 by Thomas Carew, who began work as soon as he came into his inheritance. Thomas Parker, the joiner from Devon contracted to build the house, was dismissed for financial irregularities and it later emerged that he had stolen old coins worth a princely £900, which he had chanced on while demolishing the old house. In 1734 work was recommenced under Nathaniel Ireson, a leading master builder from Warwickshire. Of the hall, Pat Smith says, 'Everything is profuse, from the great eagles that preside over the pedimented doors, to big theatrical swags over the Venetian arch, from the daintiest of shells and flowers to grinning lions' masks'. There are two 1730s staircases, while on the first floor a grand gallery spans the house.

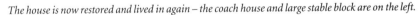

The house is now restored and lived in again – the coach house and large stable block are on the left.

HADSPEN
The home of Hobhouses since 1785

Castle Cary

FROM THE PASSING ROAD, HADSPEN IS as ravishing a sight as any house of its size in England. Built in the warm local stone, it is of perfect Palladian proportions set off by a hipped roof rising behind the parapet and stands in a park judiciously scattered with fine trees. There is no park wall, no thickly planted shelter belt, simply a house placed to take advantage of the sun and the views and as a result on show to every passer-by. This is the beau-ideal of the English country house, handsome but not too large or grand, speaking of tranquillity and retirement.

The house, dating from 1767, has belonged to the Hobhouses since 1785. Penelope Hobhouse, the well-known gardener and garden writer, added to the beauty of the gardens, planting with romantic profusion and a glorious sense of colour. Her son Niall is seeking to add a very new contemporary element to the landscape. This began with the commissioning of a 17-metre obelisk designed by Peter Smythson, architect of London's *Economist* building in St James's. Now he has launched a competition for the walled garden – The Hadspen Parabola – with a brief prepared by Foreign Office Architects. The garden had been open to the public since 1970, developed first by Penelope Hobhouse and then by Nori and Sandra Pope. When the Popes retired, the walled garden was first allowed to run wild, then cleared completely to ensure that the product of the competition would be a completely new creation.

The house has a low parapet and alternating triangular and segmental pediments to the windows.

HALSWELL
Goathurst
1680s house brought slowly back from disaster

EVER SINCE I FIRST SAW IT in the 1970s Halswell has been both dream and nightmare. Here, amid remote Somerset farms below the Quantock Hills, is a wonderful baroque house with plasterwork approaching the quality of that in Wren's City churches. A fast stream through the gardens feeds a fountain and stately canal, while all around the landscape is studded with follies and temples.

The nightmare is that for years, ever since the contents were sold in 1948 and the estate auctioned off two years later, all has seemingly been in irreversible decay. The park has been ploughed and every single tree on the approach cut down, while the interior had become an impossible muddle of makeshift flats.

Miraculously, over the last fifteen years, the place has been slowly on the mend. The enterprising Somerset Building Preservation Trust has restored the shell of Robin Hood's Hut on the hill behind, originally built in 1767, as well as the Temple of Harmony in the field below – based on the 1st-century Temple of Fortuna Virilis in Rome. Stone repairs have been completed on the rotunda on the far side of the canal, though the dome still needs to be put back.

The grand north front is an important and early example of English Baroque with an Italianate balustrade around the parapet. Barely visible Latin numbers, above a tinctured coat of arms with enough quarterings for an Austrian duke, announce a date of 1689.

If the recessed arch around the front door is strangely like that in the tower of Wren's St Mary-le-Bow in London, it is because the architect of Halswell is now known to have been a London man, William Taylor, a City surveyor who made a

The 1689 north front has baroque arched windows and a coat of arms above the entrance.

design for the Pewterers' Hall in Lime Street. A letter of his states he must be at 'Sir Halswell's before I come to London'. This was Sir Halswell Tynte, 1st baronet. His martial interests are signalled by a burst of military trophies above the front door – drums, pikes, axes and swords.

The stone is wonderfully mellow, part golden, part softest russet red. Sheltered behind is a Tudor wing, the first part of lofty proportions with two tiers of tall, noble, stone-mullioned windows, the second gabled with three storeys.

Inside, the excitement is that this is a house of constant surprises – it is impossible to predict what lies beyond any door. The large baroque hall, panelled to shoulder height, opens into a dining room, with a deeply coved ornamental ceiling. The central motif is an elegant ring of Prince of Wales feathers surrounded by a hymn to fertility and abundance, with vines and grapes, oaks and acorns, and pomegranates.

The adjoining door opens into a magnificent oak stair with balustrades and handrail so broad they seem designed to be built in stone rather than wood. Globe lamps stand on the corner posts. The condition is so good that this must be a faithful restoration after the fire of October 27, 1923 (recorded on a plaque outside), like the plasterwork ceiling groaning with fruit and flowers.

On the first floor the Chintz Room is continuously hung with a colourful set of imported Chinese wallpapers, where the game is to spot the gloriously plumed birds amid foliage bristling with flowers and fruits. As the papers have not been hung on batons but pasted onto the wall, damp has affected parts but their freshness remains

The Temple of Harmony is one of several delightful follies in the grounds.

remarkable. Across the staircase is the Alcove Room with a broad arched recess and raised step on which a state bed must once have stood.

On the other side of the house is an untouched late 17th-century second stair rising three storeys with massive oak balls at the corners. At the bottom is a hound-gate with S-pattern flat balusters and one of the 1900 fire hydrants with canvas hoses that abound through the house.

Just beyond is a double library with floor-to-ceiling bookcases round every wall but no floor – stripped to treat the dry rot that was attacking this end of the house. The Bow Room across the corridor has an oval mirror inset in the wall surrounded by trailing vines and a ceiling cove lined with elegant water reeds blowing in the wind.

The Great Room on the first floor was evidently designed for grand parties, or routs, as they would have been called in the 18th century. The arched windows are tall enough for a college dining hall. Each lower sash has sixteen panes and unusually they descend to the floor.

The second floor is not a cramped attic but also has good ceiling heights with rooms opening off a broad well-lit corridor. In the Tudor wing the old kitchen survives, with vast hearth and pointed arch door; nearby is an intriguing, rather primitive plasterwork panel of Daniel in the Lion's den which could be as early as the mid 16th century.

The interiors of Robin Hood's Hut have been restored by the Landmark Trust.

Halswell is now back in the business it was designed for, as the scene of memorable parties. Wedding ceremonies are performed in the morning room or the ball room and up to 160 guests can be seated for a wedding breakfast in the dining room, morning room and bow room. Your venue, they say, should not shrink into the background but play major role at your party. For those who wish to stay overnight there are seven bedrooms with further accommodation in the tudor wings and cottages.

HAPSFORD HOUSE   Frome
Idyllic summer retreat of a Frome cloth manufacturer

A MORE PLEASANT PLACE FOR DAY excursions, summer picnics and languorous suppers is hard to imagine than Hapsford House, a delightful Regency villa outside Frome, Somerset. Once through the entrance by way of a semicircular carriage court, with stables to one side, you are in a private Elysium shut away from the world.

The house was bought fifteen years ago in a derelict state by Angela Enthoven, who has coaxed both house and garden back to a vision of delight. She explains: 'We think it was built as a day house [one used for day trips where the owners rarely slept]. The attic rooms are low-ceilinged compared with the lofty ground-floor rooms and do not appear originally intended for permanent residence.'

An impressive gothic porch stands on the edge of a country lane. Grand balustraded steps edged with banks of white-flowered viburnum lead to the sloping lawn, where the house is placed to perfect advantage at the top. A wisteria-draped Regency veranda with black ironwork and glass roof runs the length of the garden front. All the rooms have French windows, as does the conservatory at the end.

The house was built for George George, a Frome woollen cloth manufacturer, in about 1820 and is marked on Greenwood's Map of Somersetshire based on a survey of 1820–1. A talented local architect, probably from Bath, must have provided the design. The house was built on a virgin site; a map made six years earlier shows only a paddock, mill buildings, cottage and millstream.

Cast-iron verandas and gothic sash windows make this one of the prettiest of Regency cottages ornées.

George purchased additional land, which now forms part of the wilderness garden, from Sir Henry Strachey, the lord of the manor, in 1834. His widow remarried, to Captain Henry Morish of the Royal Marines. In the mid 19th century the house was known variously as Vallis House, Vallis Cottage, and Vallis Villa, from the picturesque valley above which it stands. Captain Morish died in 1864, but his widow lived on at Hapsford House until her death in 1876. Hapsford Mill continued to produce woollen cloth, becoming a sawmill in the late 19th century; intriguingly, in about 1900 a quarry tramway was constructed on the eastern boundary of the property.

Part of the charm of the house is the mix of gothic and classic detail. Tudor hood moulds and sash windows with interlacing pointed arches mingle with Grecian scrolls and Roman urns.

Inside, the thrill of the house is the extent of fine detail, with elaborate and inventive gothic cornices still perfectly crisp, and a wealth of cusped arches and quatrefoils. The Regency glazed door opens into a hall with a staircase at the end. On the right is a Chinese cabinet painted the colour of red lacquer. Mrs Enthoven says: 'I could not find the Chinese wallpapers I wanted so I employed a decorative painter, Danny West, who worked for me for five years, happily mounting the scaffolding aged eighty-five.'

West, who liked to say he was born fifty years too late, was a master of decorative effects. Here the walls are painted in bamboo patterns. Across the entrance hallway, the pretty vaulted saloon has gothic *colonettes*, or slender columns, and ceiling ribs now picked out in gold leaf. In the dining room beyond West stencilled the walls with fleurs-de-lys on a speckled background and picked out the cornice of trailing vines in strong Regency red and pale blue.

The stair rising in a graceful half circle has a delightful pointed-arch iron balustrade with an ebony-black strip on the handrail. Bedrooms have low-silled windows providing delightful views of the gardens, while bathrooms are ingeniously contrived beneath the eaves.

The gardens are sufficient reason for buying the house. So much gardening today is formal and geometric. This is a revival of picturesque gardening in a subtle and sophisticated way – with a palette of blues and purples worthy of Rosemary Verey. The circuit begins with a sweep of York paviours set in the lawn, continuing along a laburnum walk of such impressive length that you feel there must be a mirror at the back. This was designed by the garden writer Penelope Hobhouse, who lived at nearby Hadspen. It leads to a wild garden with walks cut through long grass continuing down to a bridge over the mill-stream to an island, once a croquet lawn, complete with grotto that has been left in a tumbledown state.

Amid the long grass is a wealth of wild flowers. Mrs Enthoven says: 'We start with snowdrops in February followed by fritillaries and then geraniums – a continuous programme until November when we cut. I was very keen to bring the land back to its state before people started farming. In some places we have used only seeds from the local area. We've also brought in a lot of chalk, which wild flowers love.' Her inspiration, she says, is Pam Lewis's garden at Sticky Wicket in Dorset.

Here is a house and garden restored with phenomenal taste and care, but don't underestimate the learning curve involved in maintaining such a place.

Left: The colonettes and ceiling ribs are picked out in gold in the Gothic Saloon.
Right: The dining room is stencilled with fleurs-de-lys.

LEIGH COURT — Abbots Leigh

Noble Greek Revival house by Thomas Hopper for Bristol's first millionaire

WHEN HUNTING FOR COUNTRY HOUSES there is always a thrill in finding a house you never knew existed. So it was when I was driving along the south side of the Avon towards Brunel's Suspension Bridge, passing Leigh Court. The first sight of this imposing mansion is almost as impressive as Belsay in Northumberland. Here is Greek Revival architecture on the grand scale, all beautifully built in stone.

Alarmingly, Leigh Court was empty, recently vacated as a hospital and clearly a major challenge. By good fortune I found a caretaker willing to show me inside. The interiors are on a stupendous scale ranged around a gargantuan staircase hall with a pair of long cantilevered flights rising on either side and meeting on the first floor. One room after another has superbly crisp Grecian detail with brass gasoliers and an 1814 organ by Flight and Robson.

The Tudor house on the site was demolished after the 250-acre estate was sold in 1811 to Sir Philip Miles, a Bristol ship owner, sugar baron and banker and Bristol's first recorded millionaire. Miles commissioned the architect Thomas Hopper to rebuild the house in 1814. Hopper had recently completed alterations to Carlton House for the Prince Regent that included a cast-iron gothic conservatory modelled on Henry VII's Chapel at Westminster Abbey.

Externally the architectural style of Leigh Court is Palladian and built of Bath stone. The interior style is Greek Revival and decorated in impressive 19th-century decor, with many of the original features still intact.

In 1988 Leigh Court was sold for use as offices and has now developed into a successful conference venue run since 2004 by Business West, the former Bristol Chamber of Commerce. The 2-acre walled garden is used for growing organic fruit and vegetables, which are on sale at Bristol's Farmers' Market.

Below: Hopper designed both a projecting portico and a recessed colonnade.
Right: The joints in the stonework are so thin that the columns look like monoliths.

MAPERTON
Maperton

Covetable Regency house in warm golden stone

THE WOODED ROLLING HILLS where North Dorset spills into Somerset contain as many covetable houses as any corner of England. Beautifully built in stone, secluded in pastoral countryside, they often open directly off pretty, unspoilt villages, a sure mark of an ancient manor house. Maperton, not to be confused with enchanting Elizabethan Mapperton further south, offers just such an idyll.

Indeed it lives up to Henry James's famous paean that 'of all the great things the English have invented the most perfect, the most characteristic, the only one they have mastered completely in all its details is the well-appointed, well-run, well-filled country house'. As much as any middling-size house on the market in the last few years Maperton offers all that is best in comfortable, relaxing country-house living brought recently to an absolute pitch of smart good taste.

The drive sweeps in through eagle-headed gate piers past an attractive cupolaed stable block to an unusual entrance front that seems almost the prototype for the Sainsbury wing of the National Gallery in the ingenious, playful way it sweeps round a corner. The columned front porch is artfully set beneath a bay window which is quickly followed by a second. To the left two older gabled wings with quirky, tweaked pediments at the top speak of a late 17th-century date.

The show front looks out over a splendid expanse of lawns, backed by a wooded rise that shelters the house from north winds. Here one can tick all the boxes for

The garden front surveys a perfect English lawn echoed in the gentle curve of the Victorian conservatory.

The entrance porch is set unusually at an angle creating a picturesque grouping of gables and bay windows.

features that lend charm to elegant country houses, a pretty Regency veranda, the parish church tower peeping through the trees, a graceful Victorian conservatory leading off on a curve from the house. At the far end of the lawn, hidden in a walled garden, is a columned pavilion with Cotswold stone slate roof; nearby a discreetly sheltered swimming pool, with changing room embowered in clematis; a gently curving laburnum arbour and well-trimmed young *allée* of pleached limes.

Though the architect appears unknown, the garden front is a sophisticated essay in Greek Revival style with the shallowest of pilasters and raised central attic.

While mid 18th-century houses are often approached up flights of steps, Regency houses are more often on the level with French windows opening, as here, directly onto the garden.

The modest entrance lobby, festooned with antlers, leads into a comfortable hall furnished with sofas and chairs and padded leather fire seat. Drinks stand invitingly on a large hall table. Vistas open up under the stairs and along a broad inviting perspective of arches on the left.

The handsome staircase has pairs of corkscrew balusters to each step, and leads to a dome-lit half-landing broad enough for a grand piano. Of similar early-Georgian date is a pretty panelled sitting room with an egg-and-spoon overmantel with characteristic 'ears' at the corners, eight-panel doors and handsome brass lockcases.

The main run of ground-floor rooms consists of a drawing room with Regency white marble fireplace, a bowed end and windows over the garden, then a library with a wall of handsome glazed bookcases and garden doors cleverly contrived in the four-part window opposite. The dining room beyond leads into the lushly planted conservatory with octagon patterned tile floor. At the end is a delightful circular fountain pool ringed by shell-headed niches.

The kitchen is another set piece with splendid white built-in dresser along one wall filled with china and ranks of pretty mugs. There is, in fact, not a corner of this house that has not been decorated or furnished in some smart, amusing or unusual way. Better still, the upstairs layout is perfect both for country-house weekends and a large family with children. Four large bedrooms all with stylish en suite bathrooms lead off the large first-floor landing and the eye is cleverly drawn to the main bedroom suite by a shallow flight at the end with an upper landing lit invisibly from the side like an altarpiece in a Roman baroque church. To the right a corridor opens off into a children's wing, with more large airy rooms and a handsome secondary stair leading up to a spacious attic. This is a world of its own with a grand vista along a games room running the length of the roof, and more, spacious, bedrooms opening up invitingly under side gables.

In the early 18th century Maperton belonged to the Bennet family who also owned one of the finest houses in Bath, Widcombe Manor. Philip Bennet, MP first for Shaftesbury and then Bath, rebuilt Widcombe in 1727 and was closely associated with Ralph Allen, builder of next-door Prior Park. Bennet was a fortunate man, inheriting Widcombe through his mother Jane, who was the daughter and heiress of Scarborough Chapman, scion of one of Bath's leading families. After standing down as an MP in 1747, he embarked on a 'career of wild dissipation, squandering his fortune with reckless prodigality'.

In 1728 Maperton was sold to Sir Thomas Lockyer. He, in contrast with his predecessor, was a man on the way up. His obituary in *The Gentleman's Magazine* in 1785 notes that he was a Dissenter from Ilchester who 'from small beginnings as a broker, a banker, an East India trader, and a dealer in the funds, acquired a great fortune.' Following his election in 1747 he sat for Ilchester for fourteen years but retained control of the borough until his death in 1785. Lockyer could equally have been responsible for the early-Georgian work at Maperton.

In 1800 the house was sold to Thomas Southwood and either he or, more probably, Colonel Thomas Fitzgerald, who owned the house in 1821, were responsible for the Regency extensions. Further extensive additions, mainly at the back of the house, were carried out for Todd Walton in the 1870s – one set of surviving plans was provided by Foster & Worth, architects in Bristol, in 1875. In around 1900 the Ridley family added the front porch and bay window. By 1945 the house was reportedly almost derelict, with cattle in the drawing room.

One of the gabled Victorian wings has since been demolished and the stable yards reconfigured to make a pleasant back courtyard with convenient family entrance through the kitchen.

With just 7.8 acres Maperton is short of land but, that said, it gives every appearance of being well-protected and safe in its exquisite, peaceful setting.

THE COURT HOUSE · Martock
Dating from the late 15th century and now a house after years as a school

IN FRANCE, HANDSOME STONE-BUILT medieval town houses can be numbered in thousands. In England they are amazingly rare. The Court House at Martock, though not built as a house, is as fine and delightful a building of the late Middle Ages as one can hope to find. It has a noble pedigree as it was built for Margaret Beaufort, mother of Henry VII, who devoted herself to good works after her son came to the throne in 1485 and is held as the foundress of both Christ's College and St John's College in Cambridge. As the owner of vast estates spread across England, she was also businesslike in collecting her rents, holding a great court at her Somerset manor of Martock in 1467 and building a council chamber and lock-up at her large house at Collyweston in Northamptonshire and a prison in Kendal.

The Beauforts also paid for the rebuilding of the nave and tower of the parish church that rises behind the Court House. Nearby are other fine houses, one baroque, another Regency, with the Treasurer's House, belonging to the National Trust and dating from the 13th century, immediately beyond. The surpassing beauty of this delightful group derives from the blemishless Ham stone, more golden even than Bath stone. It has a mellow warmth on a dull day while in strong sun it is almost blinding in its intensity.

The town used to be called Martock inter Aquas and a stream flows past the Court House to the south. Prosperity came from wool and the church is lined with monuments of rich clothiers. At first glance the Court looks like a row of cottages or former almshouses, long and low and without ostentation. The courtroom occupied the whole length of the first floor, lit by an evenly spaced row of mullioned windows

and approached by an outside stair at the north end which now descends into the garden at the back.

The street front is built of large blocks of stone laid in regular courses of varying size, rapidly narrowing towards the top. None of the front windows have the hood moulds found on many Tudor houses – the arches are set back and delicately cut away at the top to emphasise their shape.

In 1661 William Strode of nearby Barrington endowed a grammar school here, introducing a new central door with his coat of arms above and the word 'God' carved in Hebrew, Greek and Latin with the exhortation 'Martock neglect not thine opportunities'. Daniel Defoe visited in 1705 to see his friend the schoolmaster while writing his *Tour Through the Whole Island of Great Britain.*

A row of windows marks the first floor court room.

The school continued until 1872 when the local vicar bought the house for church purposes. Even today many people in Martock remember playing snooker in the hall on the first floor. By the time it was sold in 1976, the Court House was in a run-down state. The new owners, seeking funds for repairs, obtained consent to transform the first-floor court room into five bedsits but then decided to sell.

Salvation came when the film-music composer Paul Lewis and his wife Geneviève saw the sale board as they drove through the town in 1983. Over fourteen years they awoke the genius of the place with imagination, charm and sensitivity, work that was carried on in the same spirit by the next owners, Mr and Mrs Moxham.

Genevieve explains, 'We had a lifelong fascination with medieval art which we had studied all over England and France, collecting medieval woodwork as we went. We tried to bring the house back to life in the fashion of a 15th-century Flemish painting.' They reopened fireplaces, researched the colours, using the same pigments, and releaded all the windows, introducing occasional panes of coloured medieval glass. Above all they took great care over the woodwork, doors, panelling, shutters – some of it old, some incorporating salvaged materials, and some made to their own designs.

A succession of blacksmiths and no less than nine carpenters were involved. Tony Williams was responsible for the first-floor bedroom, which they based on the bedroom of Louis XI in the Chateau of Plessis-lez-Tours in the Loire Valley. This has a wealth of linenfold panelling with a rich cresting along the top. The bed, originally built into one corner, has been moved by the present owners but is all part of the listed fittings of the house.

Genevieve continues, 'In medieval times the linenfold was sometimes painted to look like real fabric, on the back of the door we had it carved as if hanging from hooks to add to the illusion.' The stars on the ceiling were cast in lead and then gilded.

Next door, the bathroom has carved cusped arches around the numerous mirrors and a linen cupboard that is like the whispering door (or internal porch) of an Elizabethan great chamber.

Though ceiling heights are low, accommodation is surprisingly spacious. On the ground floor is a kitchen cum sitting room. Original stone paving survives in the narrow entrance hall and corridor, off which opens a ground-floor bedroom and cloakroom, while at the end is the parlour with magnificent shaped beams intersecting to form a series of giant coffers. This is now painted a rich ochre, following traces of the original. The fireplace was set to one corner so the flue did not stand in the way of the door at the top of the outside stair. The tiled floor is Victorian, revealed beneath later covering.

The first-floor court room, over 36 ft long, is generously lit by windows on both sides and provides a large room for entertaining, unexpected in so modest a house. Though the ceiling is quite low, the proportions are very satisfying and the window looks out on the church and the stocks by the gate. In the attic, open to the roof timbers, are two further bedrooms and a bathroom.

The one drawback of this delightful house is that it is beside quite a busy road (though there is talk of a bypass) but inside I was hardly conscious of traffic. This is due to the thick glass which cuts out noise well. With church bells chiming on the quarter hour, this is the village equivalent of living in the beauty of a cathedral close.

ORCHARDLEIGH Frome
Victorian time capsule rescued from sad abandon

THE GLORY OF THE ENGLISH COUNTRY HOUSE has long lain not just in grand aristocratic seats but many more middling houses. Orchardleigh, set apart from the world by a vast encircling park, is a classic example of a house that should have been saved intact with all its contacts and family associations. The house was built by the Duckworths, Lancashire ironmasters who moved here from Beechwood House in the New Forest in 1855. Their architect, Thomas Henry Wyatt, built Orchardleigh in Elizabethan style on a site overlooking the lake a short distance from its 17th-century predecessor.

A substantial amount of furniture had been made for the house, the best supplied by the firm of Morant, Boyd and Morant, documented by accounts preserved at Orchardleigh. Other pieces came from Gillows of Lancaster. The most interesting item was an amboyna side cabinet, made by Morant, Boyd and Morant and inset with a triptych of Venice by Edward William Cooke RA. Cooke wrote to William Duckworth declaring 'it is considered my *capo d'opera* … I never executed a more difficult or laborious work'. He was given a blank cheque and thought 250 guineas would meet with Duckworth's approval. Morant, Boyd and Morant also supplied 'handsome carved French polished walnut tree bookcases', Ottoman seats in amboyna for the library and a chimney glass 'with handsome ornamental frame, with branches for lights, richly gilt in burnished and matt gold for the chimney of the drawing room'. As well as furniture they provided upholstery, including 'figured net curtains lined with pink calico and trimmed with Daisy fringe'. There was an intriguing collection of nursery furniture including a mid-Victorian see-saw.

The house is gingerbread on the grand scale with a wealth of frilly and spiky detail.

The large servants' wing extending from one corner was almost as big as the house.

The contents were auctioned by Christie's on September 21 and 22, 1988 and the estate house was sold to become a golf course. This was the moment when the Royal and Ancient Golf Club of St Andrews had called for the creation of a thousand new golf courses in Britain, creating a rash of speculative proposals in country house parks. With the onset of the recession in the early 1990s many of these developments collapsed before they were completed and the park at Orchardleigh was one of these. Left for nearly a decade, it resembled the battlefield of the Somme, its smooth turf replaced by huge mounds of earth intended to become the future tees and greens. Rescue finally came with the conversion of the house as a smart country house hotel ten years later, now with a complete 18-hole golf course.

PARISH'S HOUSE — Timsbury
Regency villa built for a retired naval captain

PARISH'S HOUSE NEAR TIMSBURY IS A GEM of Regency architecture with a wealth of superb decorative detail all in pristine condition – cornices, ceiling roses, marble chimney pieces and doorcases. Set just 7 miles south of Bath, it looks out across rolling hills to the Mendips.

The house, known as Honeylands in the 18th century, takes its unusual name from a naval captain, John Parish, who had married a local heiress. Parish had a share in a captured Spanish frigate laden with spice and merchandise, the *Pomona*, taken off Havana in 1806. Failing to make port against a strong current, the *Pomona* was trapped by two British frigates, the *Arethusa* and the *Anson*, and though the Spanish out rushed out gunboats all of them were blown up, sunk or driven ashore. A few months later Parish was promoted to Commander for 'an unparalleled morning's work' when the *Arethusa* took part in the lightning capture of the Dutch island of Curacao.

Both Parish and his house are quintessential Jane Austen. He retired here to live an idyllic life, dining weekly with two other naval captains who had built houses in the same valley. 'After breakfast I accompanied Captain Parish to his new house and found it in every respect most completely finished,' runs an entry for November 11, 1816, among the Egerton manuscripts in the British Museum.

Parish kept the existing house on the site as a service wing, adding, like Lord Burlington at Chiswick House, a perfectly proportioned, ingeniously planned villa to entertain his neighbours with an upper storey containing the main bedrooms. Like all Bath houses, it is built of the blemishless, smooth local stone and has the 1-3-1 arrangement of windows that is the hallmark of the Palladian villa. The garden front has a shallow central bow and the tall three-part windows fashionable in Regency times. The design has been attributed to Thomas Baldwin, a former City Architect and Surveyor of Bath.

The showpiece is the drum-shaped Doric porch, not open to the elements but filled in with windows and handsome bracketed doorcase. Inside it contains a smart circular hall with cornice that carries round into the window recesses. Both windows and doorcases are stylishly on the curve. Parish loved his architectural trim. The rich detail usually reserved for two or three reception rooms here continues in every bedroom and even closet.

The handsome staircase hall is an almost perfect cube with hanging flights gracefully ascending round three sides. Each step is undercut to create a rippling effect. The exquisite wrought-iron balustrade has a mahogany handrail ending in a sweep with an ivory button inset.

Light flows down from a side-lit rotunda in the ceiling, inset with a superb acanthus motif swirling like a Catherine wheel. On the right is a double drawing room with folding doors in the cross wall and a grand niche at the end. Here and all through the house the windows have elegant frames matching the doorcases, standing slightly proud of the wall to contain the curtains. The frames are prettily reeded with palmettes at the corners. The sash windows are as finely made as Sheraton cabinets with the slenderest of glazing bars. As is usual in Regency houses, the main windows descend to the floor, filling the rooms with light.

The drum-shaped porch contains a circular entrance vestibule.

In the small bowed drawing room, pretty French windows open into the garden. The dining room has a ceiling rose so crisp that it might be a Roman antiquity carved in stone. The doors have ebony handles inset with ivory studs. Mrs Parish lived to the age of 90 after which the house was bought in 1877 by a Mr Phelps who, continuing the tradition of unusual names, christened it Pendoggett. In 1938 a sensitive restoration was carried out by the architect Lord Gerald Wellesley (later Duke of Wellington), who must have added the columned loggia overlooking the garden. The work appears to have been done for the Dowager Lady Sysonby, who was visited here by Queen Mary on April 29, 1940.

Soon after, Lady Mount Temple moved in. Her elder daughter Edwina had married Lord Mountbatten and Lady Mount Temple had resolved she would only live in a house as beautiful as the Mountbatten home at Broadlands.

Immediately after the war Parish's House was bought by the shipping magnate Major Bernard Cayzer ,who later donated one of Bath's finest houses, No 1 Royal Crescent, to the Bath Preservation Trust. A man of taste who built an impressive neo-Georgian house on a bomb site in Eaton Terrace, Belgravia, he commissioned the interior decorator Jean Monro to smarten up the interior of Parish's House. This she did with style, introducing pretty radiator boxes with trellis ironwork and pairs of shallow cupboards in the bedrooms containing wardrobes and basins matching the doorcases. Now approaching her ninetieth birthday, she says, 'I met Bernard in Jamaica. He was bored of the beach and asked me to do his house in London. At Parish's I also did the swimming pool.' Her business continues at 70 Cadogan Place.

The house comes with a pretty stone coach house, waiting to be restored as a cottage, and a gingerbread Victorian lodge. There is a large walled garden and two large copper beeches stand nobly on the lawn. The front forecourt is enclosed by a balustrade while an avenue of clipped yews forms a vista from the front door. Were an ancient Roman to return to Bath, he would recognise Parish's House as the perfect place to lead a carefree country idyll.

Tall Regency sashes descend almost to the floor of the ground-floor rooms.

REDLYNCH HOUSE   Redlynch
Matching wings handsomely remodelled by Lutyens

THERE IS A SPECIAL BEAUTY IN HOUSES that consist of two identical wings like the famous Villa Lante, or Stoke Bruerne in Northamptonshire. Here it is the result of the demolition of the main house following a fire started by suffragettes in 1914. The house, built for the 1st Earl of Ilchester in the 1740s by Nathaniel Ireson and Henry Flitcroft, was a sad loss. However, parts of the building had fallen into disuse as early as the 1830s, and in 1851 it had been partly occupied as a farmhouse.

In 1901, the 5th Earl, who had succeeded in 1865, commissioned Lutyens to convert the stable block for his use. Lutyens's hand can be seen in the splendid rustic gateways in the garden walls. In 1912 the 6th Earl sold the estate to speculators and it was then that the fire started. In 1935 Redlynch was bought by Margeret Countess of Suffolk, who lived here till her death in 1967, after which the house served as a school for over a decade.

The charm of the two wings comes from the handsome handling of the local stone, carefully squared, with Doulting stone used for the trim such as the window surrounds and the steepish hipped Welsh slate roofs rising behind the parapet. The wings, which originally contained stables, coach house and servants' wing, are unusually long. The two wings are separated by a central carriage court. Each block is constructed in stone with a hipped slate roof and attics lit by dormer windows. They are designed on a U-plan with open courts to the north. Like the main house they were built by Nathaniel Ireson for Lord Ilchester, although the main house has vanished as completely as its predecessor, which was designed by Thomas Fort for Sir Stephen Fox in 1708, and was built next to the 16th century house on the site.

When I went to Redlynch in about 1980, one of the wings was standing empty but the property was soon after bought by a developer and converted into apartments, ensuring this delightful composition continues to stand in well-mown lawns, surveying gently terraced gardens.

Dormer windows on the near wing contrast with the cupolaed stable block beyond.

SOUTH WRAXALL MANOR Bradford-on-Avon
Late-medieval manor that took years to find a buyer

ONE OF THE MOST BEAUTIFUL medieval manor houses in England, historians consider South Wraxall Manor to be one of the finest and most important country houses of the 15th and 16th centuries. Mark Girouard, England's leading country-house historian, says, 'It is a remarkable medieval house with extremely high quality embellishments of 1600 date. The combination of the two make it one of the great houses of England.'

Close to Bath and Bradford-on-Avon, South Wraxall Manor stands in peaceful farming country lost among winding country lanes. It has the mellow colour of houses in the Cotswolds with walls, roof tiles and chimneys all built of the same oatmeal-colour local stone.

For centuries the house belonged to the Long family, one of the many families of rich clothiers who flourished in these parts. Robert Long, the first known to have owned land in the parish, represented Salisbury in the Parliament in 1433 and at one time eleven members of the family reputedly sat simultaneously in one Parliament. Sir Henry Long attended the Field of the Cloth of Gold in the train of Henry VIII's Earl Marshal. The Longs, according to the historian John Aubrey, were 'great knights'. When Sara Morrison, the last member of the family to live here, sold the house in 1966, she had to prove ownership as no sale had taken place in recorded history.

The house preserves its early character to a remarkable extent. There is a lofty 15th century great hall and elaborate timber roof with collar beams, arched braces, raking queen posts and cusped panels. At one end is a richly carved Renaissance screen and minstrels' gallery above and at the other a 25-ft-long oak table, which has been in the room since it was built.

The large mullioned window of the great chamber is to the left of the arched entrance porch to the great hall.

The climax of the house comes with the first-floor great chamber with its arched 'wagon' roof ceiling with pendants and interlacing ribs. The room is dominated by a massive double-decker carved stone fireplace with figures of Geometry and Arithmetic.

Mark Girouard continues, 'South Wraxall has the grandest series of sculpted chimney pieces in England of 1600, date which can now be attributed to the Friend family of stone masons in Bristol.'

While many medieval houses were inward-looking, built for security around enclosed courtyards, South Wraxall has evolved into an outward-looking house with numerous large bay windows and mullioned windows with

The medieval masonry is beautifully set off by cascades of wisteria.

views over terraces full of stately clipped topiary. To the south of the house a neat avenue of pleached plane trees leads to a rare Elizabethan gazebo built on an octagon plan with a stone dome.

In the 20th century the manor had a chequered history. The male members of the family who lived there were killed in the two world wars. The previous owner omitted to obtain listed building consent for alterations to a Grade I listed building when they closed in the arches of an Elizabethan *loggia* to enlarge the kitchen.

Also attached to the house is a barn, various farm buildings, a chapel split into two, a couple of 1960s farm labourer's cottages and a farm managers house.

Stone roof tiles perfectly match the mellow stone of the walls and mullioned windows. The handsome two-storey gatehouse has a perpendicular oriel with trefoil window heads. Later windows, almost all leaded, have both arched and straight tops. Tudor, Elizabethan and Stuart owners progressively added wings and grand apartments with one of the finest series of large carved Renaissance fireplaces in all England.

When I saw the house, it needed the warmth of tapestries and it would also have gained much from the removal of fitted carpets. On the first floor, ceiling tiles cry out to be lifted to reveal ancient roof timbers. The main staircase has also been curiously reconfigured. Most disturbing of all is a large bucolic mural filling one end of the great hall, attractive in itself maybe but jarringly out of place in this noble medieval space.

Then there is the water garden, ravishing in photographs but set oddly in a large, strangely curved former swimming pool built in full sight of the house. But these quirks are nothing to the delights of the house – the stately topiary, the walls overflowing with wisteria, honeysuckle and roses, the peaceful setting, and a delicious domed octagonal gazebo approached along a miniature avenue of pleached limes.

TYNTESFIELD
Wraxall
Built for an ardent churchman who demanded everything in the gothic style

'THIS WONDERFUL HOUSE CRAMMED with treasures is almost as unknown to the world as Tutankhamun's tomb was when Howard Carter first broke the seal in 1922.' I wrote this in early April 2002 in *The Tyntesfield Emergency* published by SAVE. It was not mere hyperbole. Mark Girouard, doyen of English country house writers and author of *The Victorian Country House*, said, 'I feel quite confident in saying there is now no other Victorian country house which so richly represents its age as Tyntesfield.'

That week Savills had announced the sale of the house and 1,870 acres with an asking price of £14.5 million. Fiona Reynolds, the National Trust's new director-general, had taken a lead ,saying, 'This is the most important country house sale in twenty-five years. The Trust cannot stand by and let such an important and extraordinary survival be broken up.'

The property had been put on the market because the late Lord Wraxall, breaking with the long-standing English tradition of leaving country houses to the eldest male heir, had divided his estate between nineteen members of his family. Unless the Trust could make a serious offer by early June, Christie's were to be instructed to proceed with a major sale of the contents, which were forecast to fetch some £15 million.

Tyntesfield is largely the creation of William Gibbs, who made an immense fortune importing guano and nitrates from Peru for use as agricultural fertiliser. An ardent High Churchman, he demanded everything in the gothic style, down to the balustrades and stone seats in the garden.

The bay window, porch and corner turret have beautiful filigree carving.

Spiky gables, pierced balustrades and crested parapets enrich the garden front.

Victorian black and white photographs give no idea of the extraordinary colourfulness of the interior. The original deep-pile patterned carpets made especially for the house survived in many rooms, as did curtains and coloured stencilling on walls. Fireplaces were inlaid with so much coloured marble that they looked like cakes.

Everyone who visited Tyntesfield came away enchanted by its intensely evocative atmosphere. While many large Victorian houses seem impossibly cold and draughty, Tyntesfield, for all its 43 bedrooms, exuded an aura of comfort.

There were well-upholstered chairs and sofas, some still covered in the original red and gold silk, numerous four-poster beds and large Victorian baths. The Gibbs family liked to be warm. Virtually every room had a fireplace and many rooms also had hot-water radiators concealed beneath window seats – and hot-air ducts.

Most astonishing was the sheer wealth of delicate ornament. In places it was as if one night, after the builders had left, the ornament had begun to grow of its own accord, spreading across doorways, ceilings and walls.

The romantic turreted and pinnacled exterior also has a wealth of exquisite stone carving, not just the usual Gothic 'stiff leaf' but beautifully crisp ferns, flowers and seed pods as well as hedgehogs, owls, mice and squirrels.

The central stair hall was like the courtyard of a medieval Venetian palace with stone flights and iron railings and a landing that continued round to form a balcony over the bottom flight. The underside of each stone step was intricately carved. Generous top lighting cast a lustrous sheen on the gold frames around the huge family portraits.

One great showpiece of the house was the billiard room. Black and white buttons along each side of the vast billiard table allowed players to mark up their score wherever they stood on electronic scoring dials on the wall. The undersides of the table were inset with carved panels showing different British sports, such as real tennis. Tyntesfield also contained a great deal of sporting equipment – bowls, croquet, tennis, cricket, as well as early skis and skates – reflecting the numerous sports that the British were the first to take up.

Large quantities of household equipment survived – numerous sets of breakfast, tea, dinner and dessert china, glassware, including heavily cut decanters, carafes, finger bowls and bonbonniers, not to mention antimacassars (to protect chairs from hair oil), tray cloths and doilies.

Male and female servants at Tyntesfield were carefully separated. The footmen slept over the servants' hall, in rooms accessible only from outside, while female staff had rooms on the second floor of the housekeeper's wing.

Soaring directly behind the house is the family chapel, with an abundance of rich Purbeck marble, inlaid floors, superb metalwork, enormous stained-glass windows and blue and gold mosaics around the apse behind the altar. The iron grilles designed to keep out birds when the heavy oak doors are opened are like filigree lace.

The vigorous campaign for Tyntesfield was a triumphant success. On March 19, 2003, the National Heritage Memorial Fund announced a donation of £17.4 million towards the purchase of the house, contents and 540 acres of parkland. The National Trust raised £8.2 million in just 70 days, including donations from over 70,000 of its members.

VEN HOUSE · Milbourne Port
Baroque mansion brought to the pitch of smart perfection by recent owners

VEN HOUSE HAS AN INTOXICATING GRANDEUR that overwhelms as soon as you turn through the gates. If the sun is out, the warm orangey-red brick – like that at Hampton Court Palace – positively glows. There are tall sash windows, giant pilasters, an attic storey crowned by a balustrade and urns, all the hallmarks of baroque swagger. Like a French château, it steals the breath by insistent symmetry. An axial drive leads straight to the main entrance, there are matching wings in the form of Roman triumphal arches and a pair of magnificent cedars of Lebanon stand in smooth expanses of lawn mown in perfect stripes.

The great Avray Tipping who wrote the most lavish series of books ever published on the English country house did not mince words on Ven House. It ranked, he said, with Chatsworth and Belton 'in fully representing, in its own manner and scale, and in singularly perfect condition, the ideal of a country house, complete in all its parts and accessories.'

Ven House was built in about 1725 for James Medlycott, a lawyer who in 1706 secured the coveted position of a master in Chancery, thus assuring prodigious fees. The Ven estate had the added attraction that it brought with it a seat in Parliament in the neighbouring pocket borough of Milborne Port. Even so, wooing voters was an expensive matter and, combined with the stupendous cost of his new house, brought Medlycott onto the bankruptcy list in April 1731, the month before his death.

But the family rallied and stayed on for over two centuries until 1957, though in 1918 the Rev. Sir Hubert Medlycott held a major sale of farms and cottages.

The architect of Ven was Nathaniel Ireson, a master builder who ranks with the Smiths of Warwick and the Bastards of Blandford for the splendour of his country houses. The wings and conservatory were added a century later in 1836 by Decimus Burton, architect of the Athenaeum Club in London.

It is instructive to compare recent colour photographs with the marvellous black and white photographs taken for *Country Life* early in the 20th century. The great avenues of elms striding out across the landscape to north and south have gone but the gardens have been ravishingly replanted in the grand manner.

More surprising, perhaps, is the removal during the 1970s or 1980s of fixtures and furniture that had been sold with the house by the Medlycotts in 1957, including a Chippendale overmantel mirror from the drawing room, as well as the migration of chimney pieces, sad evidence of lax listed-building controls.

Recent owners have brought it to a pitch of opulence and suave grandeur reaching to every attic and corner of the garden. 'It's magnificent but not so vast that it's impossible to live in,' Effie Lecky, told me in 2004.

In 1991 the house and 35 acres were bought by the American Tommy Kyle, who, beginning in France, has made a speciality of finding crumbling mansions and

The parterre *has been recently planted with yew hedges, with Decimus Burton's conservatory on the left.*

A new box-edged rose garden lies to the west of the house.

throwing his all into reviving, decorating and furnishing them, with a sale of both house and contents as the grand finale. 'I am a gypsy – I move on after five years,' he says. Mrs Lecky had equally terrific taste, though in place of gilt, ormolu and marble the interiors were transformed with vibrant colour – every bedroom had a distinctive schemes with paint, papers, carpets and fabrics perfectly matched.

Inside, the rooms are all of noble proportions and thanks to the large sash windows, filled with light. And all have a wonderful outlook over the formal gardens and landscape beyond – the side views are more intimate, looking down over a delightful box-edged rose garden to the west and extensive walled gardens to the east.

The main sunken south *parterre* is planted with cones, obelisks and giant pincushions of yew. To the west is a picturesque lake with beautiful grass verges and a Chinese bridge, matched to the east by woodland walks along paths mown through tall grass which in spring is ablaze with daffodils.

The entrance lobby opens into a grand double-height hall with curving oak gallery. The original baroque staircase must have stood here but this was removed by Decimus Burton and replaced by a cantilevered stair to the side with elegant stone steps projecting from the walls, unsupported from below, with a pretty drum-pattern iron balustrade. Burton added a further flourish with an arched orangery leading columned glasshouse in the form of a giant jewel casket, planted inside with exotic tree ferns.

This is a house perfect for entertaining, with one reception room opening into another, making a circuit that leads out of the hall on one side and returns on the other – allowing easy circulation for guests.

Introducing bathrooms in houses where bedrooms are very large has long presented a problem. Mrs Lecky resolved it by making bedrooms into capacious bathrooms creating a feeling of extraordinary luxury. The result is that on the first floor there are just two bedroom suites, with a further five bedrooms – all with bathrooms – on the second floor. The baths are not tucked against the wall but placed like beds, often projecting into the room. In one of the wings Mrs Lecky had recently created an attractive studio under the eaves.

The one drawback is that the road running past the house into Milborne Port is heavily used. Mr Kyle firmly screened it from view with a tall yew hedge and on the garden side you forget the road altogether. Ven is a house that can provoke love at first sight. 'The road is dreadful but as soon as I saw it I knew I just had to buy it,' says Kyle.

WEACOMBE West Quantoxhead
Doll's-house perfection on the edge of the Quantocks

WEACOMBE STANDS IN A GLORIOUS POSITION at the western end of the Quantock Hills in as ravishing a site as one could hope to find a middle-sized country house in southern England. Every mile of the drive from Taunton is exhilarating. On one side the road is followed by the snaking line of the West Somerset Railway, with steam engines pulling coaches in brown and cream GWR livery. On the other is a majestic sweep of steep, smooth, rolling hills topped with a cresting of woods.

This is an enchanting small estate of 289 acres, providing enough land to protect you in every direction with views across a broad fertile valley to the Brendon Hills and Exmoor beyond. The house is set with its back to the hill and a short walk up the hillside provides a magnificent panorama of one of the grandest sweeps of the Bristol Channel. With the sea so close, winter brings no severe frosts and spiky echiums from the Canaries flourish in the gardens.

To the south of the house is a crescent-shaped canal, large enough to call a lake, stretching out in a gentle curve with the end intriguingly hidden from view. Garden walks on either side take you through a magnificent display of rhododendrons, 160 varieties in all, many grown from seedlings by John and Marian Greswell and providing continuous colour for seven months a year.

The main front is a delightful specimen of mid-Georgian architecture with a doll's-house pediment to the centre, a handsome four-columned porch and 'Gibbs' windows – the emphatic stone surrounds favoured by the architect James Gibbs, whose designs for country houses were widely used in North America.

The likelihood is that the house is the work of a good local master builder but one who had worked with an accomplished local architect such as John Strahan of Bristol, picking up fashionable detail and correct Classical proportions.

The manor of Weacombe is listed in the Domesday Book when it belonged to Roger de Cursell. From 1534 till 1789 it alternated between the Harrison family and the owners of nearby Dunster Castle when the manor was bought by the St Aubyn family. In 1870 Mr Greswell's great grandfather, the Rev. Ottiwell Sadler, bought the estate. His eldest son lived here until his death, when the house passed to Mr Greswell's mother, who was married to the famous Somerset cricketer W.T. Greswell.

The glazed – Victorian – front doors open into a handsome hall painted a pretty coral pink, with rounded corners adding a baroque flourish. The six-panel pine doors, now stripped, open on the left into a lofty, beautifully proportioned dining room and a matching drawing room on the right. Both have finely carved wooden chimney pieces, a little later in date than the house, brought from another house by the Rev. Sadler. Both rooms have windows at the ends as well as the front, filling them with light. Beyond the hall is an elegant wooden stair cantilevered out from the walls. It is constructed without half landings, with steps fanning out to create a curve on each corner, though the single baluster on the corner steps just slightly weakens the effect. Above, the first-floor bedrooms at the front again have a double outlook with views across to the hills.

Part of the appeal of the house to anyone who likes rambling, informal layouts are the very extensive domestic quarters at the back – old kitchen, larder and scullery and wine cellar with studded door, stone paving and neat brick channel for washing the floor down. These provide extensive space for an office, study, studio and flower room as well as a self-contained attached cottage. Upstairs there are seven bedrooms in total with potential for more in the attic, where there is a very pretty Chinese Chippendale fretwork balustrade at the top of the stair.

The main windows at the sides of the house also have Gibbs surrounds and all retain the original, satisfyingly chunky mid 18th-century glazing bars that were so often replaced by thinner glazing bars in later Georgian times. Though it is tempting to think this is all of one period there is a break in the west flank, and a roof slope concealed within another, suggesting that the house may have been extended soon after the main front was completed.

The first-floor games room retains panels of Regency coloured glass that are painted in shades of grey and gold with Napoleonic motifs, spears entwined with snakes, and scrolls of acanthus.

Behind the house is a stable yard with a pretty stable block that is lit by lunette windows, and a large walled garden that has been cleverly planted to form a series

The cantilevered wooden stair in the hall and the drawing room are richly decorated.

of informal garden rooms with interconnecting vistas. The land behind the house rises to the top of the hill where the estate marches with National Trust land. Here, a large punchbowl is a swirling mass of wild rhododendrons.

Weacombe also has a delightful polygonal Regency gate lodge with a wooden veranda. This stands guard along the lane approaching the house. The drive up to the house was once closed briefly when the lake began to leak but this has now been attended to and there is the opportunity for a gloriously picturesque approach to the house.

The entrance front is reflected in a lake that winds out of view.

WOODSIDE HOUSE   Bath
Bath's only Modern Movement house, newly restored

WOODSIDE IS BATH'S ONLY MODERN MOVEMENT house, sleekly designed with wrap-around Crittall windows and trademark flat roofs which could be flooded for summer cooling. The architect was Mollie Taylor (her married name was Gerrard) who was then working in her father's practice, Alfred J Taylor and Partners. It is said that a condition of the building permit was that it should be painted the colour of Bath stone but today it is pure Mediterranean white with black trim for the windows, doors and balconies. Other characteristic details are the projecting ledge below the parapet and the oval stair tower at the back with curving ladder window.

The house was built on a quarry site for an electrical engineer, Anthony Greenhill, who was much preoccupied with acoustics. The house contained no less than three recording studios. The present double-height drawing room was the largest – 16 ft high and measuring 45 by 23 ft. The sitting room served as Studio Number Two and the main bedroom upstairs as Studio Number Three, with a shallow dome and concealed lighting. A tank room on the roof acted as an echo chamber for mixing the sound output of the studio apparatus. He also produced colour music that illuminated a 'cascade of glass' with each note producing a different colour. The light became brighter as the volume increased. All these gadgets used 150 kilowatts of power, giving Woodside its first name, Kilowatt House – complete with transformer chamber.

The white marble chippings on the drive match the bright white walls of the house itself.

STAFFORDSHIRE

BARLASTON HALL   Barlaston
1750s Palladian villa bought for £1 to save it from demolition

SIR ROBERT TAYLOR'S VILLAS WERE THE SUBJECT of my first articles in *Country Life* in 1967. Fourteen years later I was involved in buying one of them for £1. Two public inquiries were fought over Barlaston when the Wedgwood company – which had moved its factory to the estate in the 1930s and had no use for the house, which was suffering from severe coal mining subsidence – applied for permission to demolish.

At the first inquiry in 1975, Christopher Buxton and John Harris appeared for SAVE Britain's Heritage and won the day; at the second, the National Coal Board appeared to give evidence, painting the gloomiest picture of the house's prospects. Wedgwood's QC, Leo Price, poured scorn on what he termed 'the United Aesthetes' trying to save the house, but we had powerful champions too – our advocate, the fiery solicitor David Cooper, backed by precise plans and calculations by our architect Bob Weighton (then a partner of Kit Martin) and the engineers Peter Dann and Partners. After three days of heated exchange, Price offered to sell SAVE the hall for £1. If we failed to restore it in five years they would have it back – for £1. Sophie Andreae, SAVE's secretary, accepted the challenge and the inquiry inspector gracefully offered the 10p deposit,

The distinctive octagon-pattern sashes survived and were repaired. One of the stone balls on the roof was rescued from the lake.

Just one flight of the Chinese Chippendale stair had survived, dangling in space.

thereby absolving himself from the need to write a report. This proved unfortunate as the Coal Board soon after claimed they were not obliged to pay the compensation they had offered if the decision was to preserve the house, as the inquiry had no formal outcome.

The builder of Barlaston was Thomas Mills, an attorney of the Staffordshire town of Leek and land agent to Lord Harrowby at nearby Sandon. The date was fixed by an entry in the parish register recording the marriage in December 1756 of Thomas Sutton, a young bricklayer from Northwich 'who had worked at his trade in the parish of Barlaston, at the building of Mr Mills' house, several months'.

When we bought the house it had been boarded up for years. We walked in the front door to find ourselves looking out through the roof. Ceilings and floors had crashed to the ground one after another as rain gushing down the walls had rotted the ends of the joists. High overhead we could see 18th-century doors flapping in the wind, as well as the occasional remnant of a rococo fireplace set in a wall. But the main marble chimney pieces had disappeared, leaving no more than an exotic rococo outline. One remaining flight of the Chinese Chippendale staircase dangled from the wall, as did the doors of the handsome mahogany bookcase fronts in the library.

Sophie Andreae took charge of the repairs. As our builders, Swan and Partner began to sift through the debris, here (as later at Uppark) a remarkable amount of original craftsmanship appeared – both woodcarving and plasterwork. Best of all was the survival in situ of all but one of Taylor's remarkable octagon-pattern sash windows. These festive windows are the signature of English rococo and no other house has them in such numbers. Amazingly it was possible to repair all but one, in most cases reusing the original lead sash weights.

It took a lawsuit to persuade British Coal (as it had become) to pay compensation for subsidence and more importantly to provide the concrete raft that was to protect the house from future subsidence. As originally proposed the raft would fill the whole lower-ground floor. Our engineer, Brian Morton, showed it could in fact be set below ground. It consists of a concrete slab inserted under the whole house with a grid of steel beams supporting the walls above. Between is a series of jacking points allowing unequal settlement to be corrected as required. All went well till the contractors, Pynfords, one of the largest in the business, went bankrupt in the recession, leaving problems it took nearly two years to solve.

By now all the structural repairs had been done, thanks to help from English Heritage, the National Heritage Memorial Fund, and above all from Sir John Smith of the Manifold Trust, who told us he supported 'burning decks not bandwagons'.

But it was clear that the Barlaston Hall Trust could not marshal the resources to complete the restoration of the interior. An advertisement in *Country Life* secured the two people in England who would respond with relish to Drake's memorable challenge that the true glory in any great matter lies in 'continuing to the end until it be thoroughly finished'. James Hall had acquired a taste for fine architecture from his parents – his father was director of the Scottish National Gallery of Modern Art. Carol Hall's father ran a successful building firm in Rotherham.

English Heritage, before giving a grant for restoration of the main rooms, wanted to know the evidence was there. The archaeologist Kirsty Rodwell reported, 'I looked at what survived in the rooms, as well as the fragments in store, and compared them with old photographs. I studied skirtings, chair rails, panelling, cornices, doors and shutters and found the evidence needed for the reconstruction in each room.'

The Halls' most important decision was to move into the house within weeks. They made a large comfortable kitchen-cum-dining room below the library looking onto the garden and established bedrooms on the second floor. Between lay what James Hall described as the war zone. They chose as their architect Peter Ware. The builders were G.W. Construction and Hayes and Howe, a Bristol firm, did all the specialist plasterwork and joinery. About a quarter of the stone floor of the entrance hall survived and could be reused; Peter Ware found stone from the original Derbyshire quarry to match it.

The most delicate task was the restoration of the rococo ornament on the dining room walls. The new work was done by Maggie Kite, a sculptor turned stuccador. She 'pounced' (pricked) the design onto the wall with tracing paper then applied coarse sand, lime, gypsum and glue-water before adding a topcoat. On the back of some of the salvaged fragments she found traces of the charcoal drawing of the original stuccadors.

The final coup was the reconstruction of the staircase. Elegant cantilevered staircases, projecting from the wall without support from below, are another trademark of Sir Robert Taylor. Usually they are in stone, with each tread deeply undercut. Barlaston belongs to a small group of Taylor's early cantilevers that are in wood. The stair rises in one short and three long flights with the landings supported mainly on a diagonal joist going back into the wall. Each flight was supported on stepped cast-iron 'carriages' into which treads and risers were screwed before an oak balustrade was fitted.

In the library, the mahogany-fronted bookcases have been repaired, mainly with fragments found in the debris. Only one of the original portrait heads of poets survived – the Halls have commissioned a head of Betjeman to sit opposite that of Shakespeare.

Restored rococo plasterwork in the dining room frames the portrait of the builder Thomas Mills.

BIDDULPH GRANGE
Biddulph
Romantic garden rescued from decay

IN THE EARLY 1970S BIDDULPH GRANGE was the most romantic lost garden in England. The house was an orthopaedic hospital which no longer had funds to maintain the extraordinary fantasy garden created by James Bateman from 1845 onwards. Parts were wired off to prevent vandalism but it was possible in the late afternoon or at weekends to have the garden to oneself. The Chinese Garden, with temple and bridge as perfect as a scene on a willow-pattern plate, was hidden, surrounded by trees and entered through a narrow cleft in the rock. You could walk into the Swiss Cottage and emerge through an Egyptian temple front fashioned in yew. We included the 1900 *Country Life* photographs of the garden in the 'Destruction of the Country House' exhibition in 1974 and then more photographs of Biddulph's decaying state in the V&A's 'Garden' exhibition in 1979. This steady pressure paved the way for the National Trust to take over the gardens and restore them to their Victorian splendour.

The future of the large Victorian house used by the hospital remained in doubt. Bateman's house of 1848–60 had incorporated the earlier farmhouse on the site but was rebuilt in 1897 in a portentous baroque style, handsomely faced in sandstone by the architect John Bower. If the health authorities tried to demolish it and replace it with new housing it would have been disastrous, but equally there was no way the house was a candidate for preservation and opening by the National Trust. The solution, conversion as apartments, involves no changes to the outside, maintaining the house as a focal point of the rock garden and providing the new residents with fine views over the grounds.

Above: The Chinese temple was gorgeously painted during restoration.
Right: Prior to conversion, the house stood empty and in need of a new use.

CAVERSWALL CASTLE   Stoke-on-Trent
Moated 13th-century castle transformed in the 16th century

CAVERSWALL CASTLE HITS THE HIGH NOTES in the grand symphony of English architecture. Here is a moated medieval castle, dating from the 13th century, that was transformed into a grand Jacobean hunting lodge by the famous Smythson family of architects, and then in the 19th century enriched with strange, dark woodwork almost as overwhelming as that at Victor Hugo's extraordinary house in St Peter Port, Guernsey.

The outskirts of Stoke-on-Trent may not be most people's idea of a stalking ground for country houses but to the east of the city the posher suburbs, with their immaculate front gardens, suddenly give way to traditional countryside and pretty villages. The village of Caverswall is a discovery in itself, wonderfully unspoilt with two churches standing guard at the entrance to the castle.

One is the splendid medieval parish church set in a dignified churchyard filled with the exquisitely lettered headstones found in these parts. The other is a sizeable Victorian Catholic church, also built in stone. Between, the drive to the castle runs past a handsome stone gate lodge, now in separate ownership.

The broad moat reflecting the castle is a medieval feature, not a product of the Romantic Movement.

The large, square castle precinct is entered dramatically by way of a masonry bridge across the deep moat, which is now dry on this side. The entrance arch is framed by a pair of half-octagonal towers with further octagonal towers at the four corners of the castle ward. Though the stonework is imposing, it does not look a serious defensive fortification, more a splendid chivalrous display.

A licence to crenellate was granted by the king in 1275, making Caverswall earlier than nearby Eccleshall Castle of 1300, which also has octagonal towers, or beautiful moated Maxstoke Castle of 1345, which has a gatehouse on a similar plan.

Anthony Emery, England's leading expert on greater medieval houses, says, 'Caverswall is an early example of medieval landscaping with the moat broadening out on the west to provide a romantic reflection of the castle, as at Bodiam and Leeds Castles.' This is even more impressive when you think that this happened at Caverswall nearly five centuries before Capability Brown began to create lakes in front of grand Classical houses.

Henry VIII's antiquary, John Leland, on his famous tour of England, found Caverswall to be a 'pretty pile' in the 1540s but by about 1600, Erdeswick, in his *Survey of Staffordshire*, sadly describes it as 'now quite let to decay by one Browne, farmer of the demesnes'.

In about 1614 the mayor of Stafford, Matthew Cradock, commissioned one of the Smythsons to transform the castle as a modern residence, demolishing the main medieval range which presumably stood on the west of the quadrangle facing the gatehouse. Mark Girouard, author of *Robert Smythson and the Elizabethan Country House*, says, 'The Jacobean house is clearly based on an early Smythson design for Slingsby Castle in Yorkshire. Caverswall must be by John Smythson not his father Robert who was dead at this time.'

John Smythson's best-known work is Bolsover Castle in Nottinghamshire, a grand and nostalgic display of medieval chivalry. At Caverswall he gave the castle a distinctive Renaissance air by placing Classical balustrades on the tops of the corner towers, as well as the house, though here they were replaced by battlements in the 19th century.

Among the hallmarks of Smythson houses are shallow three-sided bay windows and almost continuous bands of mullioned windows, more window than wall it sometimes seems. Here the leaded lights shown in a *Country Life* article of 1911 have gone, but otherwise the house is externally little altered.

This is thanks partly to two colonies of nuns who were here first at the time of the French Revolution and then again in the early 20th century. One reminder of their

The Renaissance balustrades on Smythson's Jacobean range have been replaced by battlements.

The ornate panelling, roundly condemned by Country Life *in 1911, was then a recent import.*

presence is a series of crosses around the outside of the moat, presumably forming the Stations of the Cross found in Catholic churches. A lift was installed for the nuns, with the motor hidden in a stone blockhouse on the roof, standing incongruously among the Smythson chimneys.

In the later 19th century the Jacobean house was transformed internally by a Mr Homes of Liverpool, whose 'improvements' met with violent disapproval when *Country Life* visited the house in 1911. 'The old woodwork was evidently thought too plain and meagre. Much of an ornamental character was added, and the whole dealt with in the dark and juicy manner dear to the Wardour Street of the last generation.' The dining room was condemned for the 'furious chimney piece' destroying the effect of the plain panelling.

Today these enrichments have a renewed interest, comparable with the extraordinary interiors that Victor Hugo created in his house in St Peter Port during his long exile there. Both show the same taste for highly worked, even grotesque, Jacobean carving, all baubles and finials. At Caverswall there is a staircase with carved heraldic beasts and emblems on every corner post, and also superb Victorian ornamental tiles on the hearths and cheeks of the fireplaces (this is the Potteries after all). In the dining room is a Victorian sideboard grand enough to have been exhibited in the Great Exhibition of 1851.

Under its last owners, Ron and Yvonne Sargent, Caverswall enjoyed a new revival as a rather splendid upmarket bed and breakfast. Three of the corner towers were converted in simple but charming fashion to self-catering holiday accommodation with living room, small kitchen and double bedroom above. There are also rooms with grand four-poster beds in the house.

The north-east corner of the castle is in separate ownership with its own access. There is a temptation to open up the west drive to the house, past a lodge and along a handsome avenue which provides the best view of the castle across the moat.

GREAT BARR HALL   Great Barr

1770s Gothic Revival villa where the Lunar Society used to meet

THIS DELIGHTFUL GOTHIC REVIVAL house has a place in history thanks to meetings held here by the Lunar Society of Birmingham, attended by Matthew Boulton, James Watt, Joseph Priestley, Erasmus Darwin and Josiah Wedgwood.

The Scott family who owned the estate was settled here by the 1500s. John Scott (1685–1755) created ash and oak nurseries, a walled garden, a pool, a cascade, and a botanic garden, in the manner of a *ferme orné*, a fusion of farm and garden.

In 1777, Joseph Scott began rebuilding in the gothic style. The obvious parallel is with Horace Walpole's Strawberry Hill at Twickenham. He was obliged to mortgage the property in 1786 to Samuel Galton Jnr., a prominent Birmingham banker and gunmaker who invited the Lunar Society to meet at the Hall.

Further work was undertaken the in mid 19th-century for Sir Francis Scott, the third baronet, by Sir George Gilbert Scott (unrelated to the Great Barr Scotts). In the late 1950s clock tower, stable and coach block and servants' wing were demolished, followed in the late 1960s by the twin oriel windows, which were replaced by metal windows.

The last of the administrative staff moved out in 1978 but no attempt was made to secure the building against vandals or the elements.

Despite many previous reports of intruders, this vulnerable building remained unsecured and on New Year's Day 1981 the chapel attached to the Hall was totally gutted by arsonists. A wealth of old records dating back to Poor Law days were destroyed. Eighteen months later a large section of banisters and handrail were removed from the famous flying staircase by vandals. Four years after being vacated the Hall was finally boarded up. It still awaits its saviour.

The perfect Classical symmetry has been concealed in Gothic Revival dress.

HEATH HOUSE
Lower Tean

Inventive Gothic Revival house of the 1830s

HEATH HOUSE IS A PERFECT and enchanting example of the picturesque, Britain's one unassailably original contribution to the arts of Europe. Begun in 1836, a year before Victoria came to the throne, and completed four years later, it is on the cusp between Regency and Victorian. The gardens are good enough to be by the great Humphry Repton himself and its architect might be the prolific and talented William Burn. In fact, it is entirely the work of local architects from Lichfield.

When I saw it in the summer of 2006 it had survived almost magically untouched. *Country Life* gave it the full treatment in 1963 but black and white photographs could not convey the glint of finely polished gilt picture frames, the freshness of original wallpapers and colour schemes, the light flooding through the large windows, the lush green of the park grass and hundreds of fine Staffordshire oaks (England's best), or the abundance of pretty roses in the sunken garden. It's true that the local Hollington stone is rather grey, but like all English building stone it glows in the sun.

Heath House is a gentleman's residence with all the trimmings. There are three entrance lodges, one presumably by John Shaw, who exhibited a design for a lodge here at the Royal Academy in 1816. The style of the house is Jacobethan, almost gingerbread in its exuberance, with bay windows, a tower and turrets, gables and gablets, spiky finials and a forest of soaring octagonal chimneys, all in the same well-preserved local Hollington stone.

The architect of the house, Thomas Johnson, had a highly inventive line in battlements. They are sharp and pointed over the double-height bay windows, while the miniature gables on the parapet are like upside-down valances or pelmets.

As with much Picturesque architecture there is symmetry and asymmetry. In the best Repton manner the house is bedded in the landscape by formal terraces.

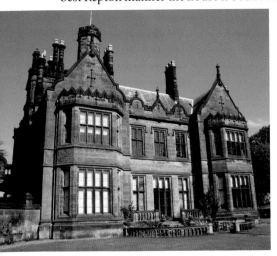

The arch of the porte cochère *is just visible on the left of the garden front.*

The conservatory, by Thomas Trubshaw, is a delight – with arched French windows and hipped glass roof. It overlooks a formal rose garden with edgings of box surrounded by elevated balustrades. The iron and glass roof of the conservatory had just been restored with the help of an English Heritage grant and the roof vents were ingeniously opened by wire pulleys.

One of the comforts insisted on by 19th-century country-house owners was a covered porch where carriages could drop off visitors. At Heath, the underside reveals the stone in its original pale barley colour. A short flight of steps lends ceremony to the arrival through the

Heath has clusters of soaring chimneys and frilly gables, with a service wing to the right.

welcoming glazed doors favoured by the Victorians. Further glazed doors provide a view through to a grand and lofty staircase hall. The staircase is an imperial one with a single flight branching into two and continuing to form a first-floor gallery with newel posts as massive as ships' cannon.

All through the main ground-floor rooms there are pretty plaster ceilings with interlacing ribs, ornate pierced friezes and splendid gothic fireplaces. A charming feature is the linking of library and drawing room through broad folding doors, with facing mirrors over the fireplaces providing an infinite reflection.

The gilt wallpaper in the drawing room is stunning. The tall mullioned windows descend from the cornice to a low dado rail, with cushioned seats filling each bay.

As in many early-Victorian houses, the service wing is huge. Intriguingly there are three generations of kitchens and sculleries. The quality of construction is consistent throughout, with brick-arched ceilings, massive masonry walls, stout oak-grained doorways and extensive cellars.

The appeal of the bedrooms is that there are exceptional views on all four sides. Heath House has 127 acres of parkland and a long vista across pristine pastoral country to the south.

The estate had been in the Philips family for four centuries. It remained a time warp partly because Mrs Philips lived here to the grand age of 93. Her son made heroic efforts to continue, opening the house and gardens to the public in the summer and making a big effort to generate the capital needed for repairs. A carefully prepared scheme of enabling development was rejected by Staffordshire Moorlands District Council, so the house was put up for sale. It should have been preserved intact.

HIMLEY HALL   Himley
Baroque house with imposing Regency additions

IT WAS AN EERIE SIGHT in the mid 1980s to drive up to a house as grand as Himley Hall and find it standing empty, with lawns growing rough and garden terrace walls crumbling. Like so many houses at the time, it had come to the end of a spell of institutional use when houses such as these were seen as cheap floor space. It had been a hospital during the Second World War and was later used by Wolverhampton Polytechnic School of Art and Design. At Himley there was the added frisson that the house had for some while been occupied by the National Coal Board, against whom SAVE was pitted in a life and death struggle over Barlaston Hall to the north.

The west front had a grand baroque centre in the manner of the great Midlands master builders like Francis Smith of Warwick, tall with three even rows of sash windows, giant pilasters and a balustraded parapet like that at Stoneleigh Abbey. Regency wings with paired Doric pilasters had been added in the 1820s by William Atkinson, severe in their treatment and 'correcting' the playful baroque interruption of the frieze. The equally long south front had a grand four-column Ionic portico built by Atkinson, who was then working for the 4th Viscount Dudley.

After failing to find a buyer, Dudley Council decided to run Himley itself and the house is now abuzz with exhibitions of arts and crafts and is open regularly from April to September, with the main rooms in demand for conferences, receptions and civil weddings.

In 1934 the Duke and Duchess of Kent spent the first two weeks of their honeymoon at Himley and Edward VIII (later the Duke of Windsor) spent his last weekend there before his abdication.

The giant pilasters and tall sash windows with keystones are typical of Midlands baroque.

INGESTRE PAVILION   Ingestre
Georgian temple front with comfortable modern quarters concealed behind

INGESTRE IS AN EXAMPLE of the magic the Landmark Trust can work on the most unlikely buildings and places. For over a century and a half the Pavilion was no more than a facade, a noble eye-catcher at the end of a long forest ride. It had been built in 1752 for the 2nd Viscount Chetwynd by a local mason, Charles Trubshaw, who on occasion practised as an architect.

The Pavilion has such assurance and grandeur that it looks the work of a leading neoclassical architect acquainted with the most advanced French design. Instead of the usual temple-front portico, the pediment here sails across the whole facade with a semi circular barrel vault set above the colonnade. The facade is in crisp-cut blocked masonry, while the vault is executed in beautifully coffered plasterwork.

The genius of the Landmark Trust's architect, Philip Jebb, was to create a new house behind the facade that is wholly invisible as you approach. Yet on the other side it is a complete Palladian villa of the kind pioneered by Sir Robert Taylor at Asgill House in Richmond, with a three-sided or canted bay containing an octagonal saloon. The internal design is perfect for the needs of the Trust's visitors. There are three double bedrooms and a very well equipped kitchen. The two upstairs bedrooms and bathroom are connected by a gallery running across the double-height saloon.

Jebb needed to place a door in the bow to provide access to the lawn at the back. If the glazing of the door is different from that of the adjoining sash windows it always strikes a jarring note, so Jebb invented a brilliant device – the Jebb jib door – to avoid this. Part of the sash box is merged with the sash, giving it added strength as it opens.

Ingestre Hall, the imposing former home of the Earls of Shrewsbury, is a rose brick mansion now in intensive use for residential arts courses.

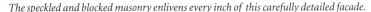

The speckled and blocked masonry enlivens every inch of this carefully detailed facade.

PATSHULL HALL   Burnhill Green
Massive Midlands mansion rescued from years of steady decline

PATSHULL HALL, THE MIGHTY PILE by the great architect James Gibbs et al, lies to the east of Wolverhampton, on the Shropshire-Staffordshire border, overlooking a glorious Capability Brown lake. Built of dark red sandstone, it is in some ways more like a vast chateau than a typical English country house. The drive approaches on steadily rising ground exactly aligned on the main entrance, first through an outer court with a screen of railings and gate piers, then through an archway into a *cour d'honneur*. On the garden front there is a massive bastion terrace of the kind so often found in France, with dramatic flying staircases leading to lower side terraces. Yet all this mighty garden terracing, it transpires, is the work of the 19th century, of the prolific Scots architect William Burn and his nephew and partner J. McVicar Anderson.

Gibbs had been called in to design a new house for Sir John Astley in the 1730s and the work was supervised by Francis Smith, often said to be the finest master builder in the Midlands. In 1765 Sir John sold Patshull to Sir George Pigot, Bt, a nabob and owner of the Pigot diamond. In 1848 the Pigots in turn sold the property to the 4th Earl of Dartmouth, with whose descendants it remained until the 1960s, although much of the surrounding estate had to be handed over in payment of death duties in 1958.

Next it was taken over by the local health authority as a rehabilitation centre and was well looked after until closure in 1990 when it was left empty for twelve years.

In 2004 it was remarkable how much had survived such long neglect – a baroque entrance hall and vast saloon with rich plasterwork, a library, panelled bedrooms and corridors framed by impressive arches, and a mezzanine of low-ceilinged rooms for winter use, such as are often found in Venetian palaces.

James Gibbs' Georgian house is set on a terrace with William Burn's additions behind.

An aerial view shows the axial approach to the house and Capability Brown's naturalistic lakes.

As the ground falls away so steeply to the south, there is an extensive lower floor of service quarters, with rows of bells to exotic rooms such as the Rustic Parlour and Chinese Dressing Room (the bell in the butler's room still rings). Below this is a further sub-basement complete with original Georgian wine bins. Outbuildings there are aplenty – and thanks to the courtyard arrangement, most of them communicate internally. My guide said he had counted 150 rooms.

Grandiose though all the additions are, they have by degrees robbed Gibbs's original Palladian villa of some of its charm. Yet there is little chance of obtaining permission to strip them away, as most contain impressive rooms with fine fireplaces and fittings. Today Patshull is one of the growing group of large houses which has leapt back to life through use for events. There are weddings, dinner dances and house parties, conferences and seminars, shows and fairs, and self-catering accommodation is also available. The house is furnished and the gardens are maintained – 50 acres in all, including a well-stocked arboretum The lake is in separate ownership, as is the parkland in front, which has become a golf course. But even from the top windows of the house there is hardly a building to be seen, just farmland, woods and Brown's mile-long lake.

SINAI PARK — Burton-on-Trent

Thought to be a summer retreat of the monks of Burton Abbey

FOR YEARS SINAI PARK stood forlorn on a windswept hill, to all appearances beyond hope. The photograph in SAVE's *Endangered Domains* published in 1985 showed an impressive timber-framed house of the 15th to 17th century, laid out around an open courtyard and grimly covered in render and patched up with corrugated iron sheeting. There was no glass in the windows and those on the ground floor were not even boarded up.

The unusual name indicated monastic origins and the house possibly served as a hunting lodge or summer residence for the abbots of Burton-on Trent. The north-east wing contained 14th-century masonry as well as timbers dated to 1494–1534 by dendrochronology (tree-ring dating). At the Dissolution the property was acquired by Sir William Paget.

When I saw the house it was in a still more parlous state. The render had been removed, exposing the timber frame and the lath infill but many of the vertical posts had rotted away through damp so that in places the building barely seemed to touch the ground. But in 1994 Sinai found a very determined saviour in Kate Newton, who lives here with a large menagerie of dogs, cats and other animals. She has carried out careful, scholarly repairs, welcoming groups arriving for guided tours. The timber framing is now a beautiful silvery colour with no trace of creosote, the handsome external brick and stone chimney stacks are stabilised and the mullions have been reglazed. The major part of the house is now occupied. This is an heroic rescue showing that timber houses can be brought back from a state of extreme fragility.

While the house awaited rescue, the timber frame was laid bare for all to see.

SWINFEN HALL   Lichfield

Long blighted by the next-door prison, now lavishly restored

SWINFEN HALL IS A HANDSOME red-brick house in the manner of Francis Smith of Warwick, the great Midlands master builder of the early 18th century but puzzlingly was built in the 1750s rather than the 1720s or 1730s, to the designs of Benjamin Wyatt, whose sons Samuel and James became the great rivals of the Adam brothers. Then, as a letter on the SAVE files from Andor Gomme points out, 'Very large additions were made in 1912, in style with the old house, of great sumptuousness and again excellent craftsmanship – making the smallest possible disturbance to the old house and extremely interesting in their own right.'

When I visited Swinfen in 1981 it was shattering to find a fearsome 20-ft high prison security fence running along the edge of the garden. The house was in good condition but no longer used and one side of the drive was lined with warders' houses. I wrote at once to Michael Heseltine, the Secretary of State for the Environment, the one minister who would respond quickly and practically to letters about listed buildings, as the obvious danger was that the building would fail to sell and that the Home Office would use this as a pretext for demolition. Heseltine wrote back saying he appreciated our concern for 'this fine building' and copying the correspondence to the Home Secretary. Though there was little initial interest, this warning shot to the Home Office proved the saving of Swinfen and in January 1987 the house was bought by Helen and Victor Wiser, who restored the house and opened it as an hotel in December that year. In 2003, they bought a further 95 acres of surrounding farmland to create a deer park. This opened the next year with the arrival of two stags and twelve hinds. It extends from the hotel to the lake, encompassing woodland to give the deer natural shelter. Plans are currently under way to repair a derelict wing and outbuildings to create additional bedrooms.

Built for Samuel Swynfen in 1755–8, the house is of a warm red brick with stone trim.

WESTON HALL · Weston
Gabled dower house built for the Earls of Shrewsbury in the 1660s

WHEN I ARRIVED AT WESTON HALL in 1992 the local agent Ray Fuller had placed a poignant notice on every door. 'Weston is an important Grade II* property. There are no items or materials of any value in the house. Causing damage to this structure would be pointless and could be compared to the mugging of an old-age pensioner or the robbing of your grandmother.'

At the back of the house a forest of TV aerials and numerous letter boxes proclaimed that until recently the house had been divided into eleven flats, though some of these could have been little larger than one-room bedsits. Grey corrugated-iron garages added to the grimness of the scene, as well as hard stands for Nissen huts on the terrace that seemed to date back to wartime requisitioning.

Yet Weston stood in an acre of steeply rising grounds with commanding views across the Trent Valley. Though most of the glass in the mullioned windows had been broken, the stonework was in good condition. In past centuries it had been a dower house for the great seat of the Earls of Shrewsbury at Ingestre nearby.

There is a continuous band of mullioned windows on the first floor, and two types of bay window.

The impressive front with three gables and grand bay windows dated from 1660. A further, slightly larger gable had been added on the right in about 1900, as well as a grandiose external stair, but so carefully matched that this was barely noticeable. The architecture was dignified and austere and without a trace of Renaissance ornament.

In 1992 Roy Fuller was inviting offers of £100,000 and over, and many viewers had come to assess whether it could viably be made into a family house again. The one drawback was that it was quite close to the road, though for some uses that could be seen as an asset.

Definitive rescue was not long in coming, with purchase by a local businessman, Paul Reynolds, who has transformed the house into a restaurant with eight comfortable bedrooms. Work was completed in 2001 and Weston is now surrounded by trim lawns, with the major part of the house in use once again.

WROTTESLEY HALL — Tettenhall
Handsome 1920s pavilion replacing a grand 1700 house after a fire

THIS DELIGHTFUL HOUSE HAS the appealing proportions of a pavilion but its Georgian appearance is misleading. The 1700 house that stood here was a much larger affair, designed by Francis Smith of Warwick. It was a building of three full storeys with projecting wings on either side of the pedimented centre. Built for Sir Walter Wrottesley, Bt, by Francis Smith of Warwick, it was demolished after a fire in 1897. Some twenty years later a phoenix rose from the ashes, incorporating a carved coat of arms and swags of fruit in a pediment similar to the one that crowned the old house. The new house was completed in 1923 with lower wings projecting at either end. The whole composition has the modest proportions of an almshouse, and resembles many of 1700 date built in the same warm red brick. During the 1980s the house was divided into three, the centrepiece forming a neat four-bedroom house with two bathrooms and a hall with a screen of columns.

Sir John Wrottesley was given a peerage in 1838 and married as his second wife Julia Conyers of Copped Hall in Essex. His son, also named John, was a founding member of The Royal Astronomical Society and was elected President of the Royal Society in 1854. He succeeded the Prince Consort as President of the British Association for the Advancement of Science for the Oxford meeting of 1860 when Bishop Wilberforce famously clashed with T.H. Huxley over the theory of evolution. He was visited at Wrottesley Hall by the leading American sailor and scientist Commander Matthew Fontaine Maury. The Wrottesley crater on the moon is named after him. General George Wrottesley, a younger son of the 2nd Baron Wrottesley, was the founder of the Staffordshire Record Society.

The central gabled pavilion is extended by lower matching wings.

SUFFOLK

ASHMAN'S HALL — Beccles
Elegant Regency villa linked to handsome stable block

NEVER, NEVER GIVE UP the battle is the lesson to be learnt from Ashman's Hall. When I first saw the house in the 1970s it was an almost perfect Regency villa on the outskirts of Beccles, attributed to a leading local architect Francis Sandys. Born in Northern Ireland, Sandys had settled in Bury St Edmunds where he designed the handsome Assembly Rooms (now the Athenaeum), as well as serving as the 4th Earl of Bristol's architect at Ickworth and designing Worlingham Hall.

At Ashman's, Sandys designed a staircase in the form of a domed rotunda with the steps ascending in elegantly curving arms to the first-floor landing. He used screens of Ionic columns to frame the cross vista, with light streaming in through a circular dome.

In October 1982 Jennifer Freeman reported to SAVE that the house was 'open to the skies … the roof and floors have in part disappeared, but the staircase is still there and although the handrail sports a good growth of moss it is firm and hard (mahogany)'. Two months later we were fighting off an application to demolish, submitted not by the owner but by a potential purchaser who wanted to erect a new house on the site. The owner, we pointed out, had been offered a repair grant the year before but turned it down as too small.

The next photographs I saw showed that the elegant wrought-iron stair railings had mostly vanished and a large portion of the dome had collapsed. Yet perseverance paid and finally in 2004 Ashman's was removed from the Buildings at Risk list as a new owner had rebuilt the house without a penny of grant aid.

The Regency entrance front has a domed rotunda on the right and a stable block on the left.

BENTLEY HALL   Bentley
15th-century hall house with jettied end wings

THIS IS THE EPITOME OF the ancient rambling English manor house, altered and extended many times, but with the mellowness that comes of using traditional materials, whether timber-framing with herringbone brick infill, plaster render, soft red brick or hand made roof tiles. The original form of the house seems clear, with a broad central hall and jettied end wings. These project to the south to form a small three-sided courtyard looking across to a noble barn that dates from 1458 and is now known as the Court House.

This house was built either by John Tollemache in about 1469 or possibly his son, also John, following his second marriage to an heiress, Elizabeth, widow of William Joyce of Helmingham.

In the 16th century Lyonell Tollemache introduced a floor across the medieval great hall, creating a singl- storey hall below with a great chamber above. At this time fireplaces were served by a massive brick chimneystack built outside the south wall. Before that the medieval great hall would have had an open fire. An elaborate bressumer beam, carved with the Tollemache crest and several mythical beasts, may have been introduced about 1585 by another Lyonell.

In about 1749 John Gosnall, the new owner of Bentley, created two Georgian bedrooms within the great chamber. In 1827, another John Gosnall replaced the timber-framed east wing of the medieval house with a brick structure. More recently Bentley was considerably restored in the 1970s when the Regency staircase was removed. The Court House at the back is also timber-framed with brick infill making a very attractive group with the house.

Half-timbering, painted render and ancient brickwork create a wonderful patina.

ABBEY HOUSES
Bury St Edmunds
Georgian and Victorian houses in the ruins of the Confessor's Abbey

AMONG THE MOST UNUSUAL Georgian and Victorian houses in England are those built in the ruins of the west front of Edward the Confessor's Abbey at Bury St Edmunds – the greatest abbey in all England until the Reformation.

For years the Ministry of Works was determined to pull these structures down to expose the remains of the great entrance front. The fiery medievalist John Harvey wrote: 'In most continental countries there is little doubt that the occupiers of the intrusive houses would have been expropriated.' But thanks to the Society for the Protection of Ancient Buildings, as well as Sir John Betjeman and archaeologist Sir Mortimer Wheeler, the houses were reprieved. They have remained one of the most picturesque sights in any English churchyard.

Despite these champions, the houses deteriorated and the tenants left. The owners, St Edmundsbury Borough Council, commendably restored the house at the north end (as well as two smaller houses behind). The work was done by the borough architect David Penistone. He introduced a two-stage staircase that brilliantly exploits the yawning void that he found within. He also exposed one of the great abbey arches, partly rebuilding it when it began to collapse during the conversion. The result is a delightful, cosy house in which you are conscious of the fabric of the abbey all around.

A long tussle then ensued over the approach to the restoration of the remaining houses – whether the original medieval features, concealed when the houses were first created, should be exposed, and whether plaster and lath could be replaced by modern plasterboard. At one time it looked as if more would be spent on scaffolding than on the restoration of the houses. Now repairs are largely complete and the houses are being sold. For the new residents it is almost as good as living in Salisbury Cathedral Close.

Though the remaining medieval masonry is highly eroded, the whole composition has great charm.

COCKFIELD HALL — Yoxford
Tudor house extended to entertain Henry VIII and James I

For generations, successive owners of Cockfield Hall have had one aim – to be pavilioned in splendour. This is no ordinary Tudor and Jacobean manor but what the great historian Sir John Summerson called a prodigy house – a mansion designed to entertain the monarch.

Sir Arthur Hopton, who built the original large Tudor house here, was knighted for valour at the battle of the Spurs in 1513, attended the Field of the Cloth of Gold and was present at the reception of the Holy Roman Emperor Charles V in 1522, the coronation of Anne Boleyn in 1533 and the christening of Prince Edward in 1537. As the heir also to vast estates in Yorkshire, he was called to play a major role in suppressing the Catholic rebellion in the north in 1536. Two years later the king granted him the dissolved Priory of Blythburgh. He entertained Henry VIII at Cockfield at least once.

His son Sir Owen, as Lieutenant of the Tower of London, had a rather different 'Royal' visitor, Lady Katherine Grey, sister of Lady Jane Grey, who was briefly proclaimed queen in 1552 but executed by Mary Tudor. Katherine was imprisoned first in the Tower and then at Cockfield, where she died within a year.

Sir Owen sold Cockfield and a few years later, in 1597, it was bought by Robert Brooke, an alderman of London, whose son, succeeding in 1600, had even loftier ideas and remodelled the house in grandest Jacobean style to receive James I. From the Brookes, Cockfield passed to the Blois family (pronounced Bloyss) in the 1690s, owners of extensive estates in both Norfolk and Suffolk.

Today a thatched lodge marks the entrance to the drive off the busy Lowestoft road but beyond all is serenity – a grand expanse of park dominated by the romantic silhouette of the Tudor house. The drive does not sweep up to the main front in 18th-century fashion but peels off to enter by way of the service court. Or I should say the

The top storey was added to the Tudor range in the 19th century.

outer great court, for immediately you are locked on to an arrow-straight drive that passes through two gloriously ornate stepped and finialed Jacobean gateways in perfect line. The outer court is of vast extent with an octagonal dovecote (still complete with four hundred nesting boxes) standing in the centre of an expanse of emerald green lawn.

The intense beauty of the place is due to the perfect mellow match of red brick walls and tile roofs. It has a domestic air, too, with a long almshouse-like block on one side (containing stable, hayloft and cottage). In front of the main house stands the pretty Tudor gatehouse with panelled 'lodging' above – all untouched by the restorer's hand.

Opposite is a grand 100-ft-long coach house and barn and beside this another step-gabled barn with bell tower and clock dated 1821.

The house itself is so busy with battlements, gables and spiralling 'barley-sugar' chimneys that it is at first hard to comprehend. To the right is an enchanting Tudor wing with large windows yet modest proportions, a house in itself. In front stands the Victorian great hall added by Sir Ralph Blois in 1896 (to the designs of E.F. Bishopp) while on the left is another grand Tudor range, heightened in the 19th century, with corner buttresses soaring vertically like mini-Cape Canaveral rockets.

Inside, the great hall is of stupendous proportions with a grand arcaded gallery running across one side and coved ceiling inset with three shallow octagonal cupolas. The wood carving is full of delicate and absorbing detail. Over the fireplace the acanthus leaves are formed into a miniature band playing cymbals and lyres. The grand staircase has the longest run of corkscrew banisters I have ever seen. The rich French parquet has black edging in the border, while the doors have diagonal trellis on the bottom half and square panels above.

Cockfield would never have survived as a private house after 1945 had the Germans not secured a direct hit on the south wing, destroying forty-two rooms and making the house a more manageable size. The Blois family returned but when Owen and Anne Roberts came in the 1990s, decline had set in and the house had been empty for two years.

By 2005, the whole main house was in first-class decorative order. The early Tudor wing is comfortably self-contained for winter use with large kitchen. Upstairs there is still a wealth of delightful Tudor detail – carved stone fireplaces the shape of Holbein headdresses and intriguing carved wooden arches to the doors. One room has an unusual ceiling with no beam running the whole way across; instead they form a grid rather like a 'seat' made from four interlocking human arms.

The house is also licensed for weddings. Rather than convert the outbuildings, Mrs Roberts has commissioned a large marquee which stands on the back lawn for fourteen weeks during summer. Instead of the usual pseudo-Georgian cartwheel-topped windows it has amusing Gothick pointed arches as well as an extra metre in height, creating much better proportions inside.

There are 36 acres of grounds with enclosed privy garden, extensive walled gardens and a stretch of moat. Peaceful Suffolk stretches out to the west while Aldeburgh and its glorious coast is barely fifteen minutes away.

The oak stair in the 1896 great hall rises to an arcaded gallery.

EARL SOHAM LODGE   Woodbridge
Medieval hunting lodge embellished and remodelled by a series of illustrious owners

A HOUSE ISLANDED IN A BROAD MOAT is always a romantic sight. The charm of Earl Soham Lodge is that of a modest Georgian rectory built of pink brick with white sash windows. Yet it is a larger house than it first appears and the back ,intriguingly, might belong to a different house altogether, painted pale cream with gables and leaded windows.

It comes with one thousand years of history. The 'Earl' speaks of a link to the Earls (later Dukes) of Norfolk, Ham means beside the lake or water, and Lodge indicates a hunting lodge, one of several moated hunting lodges used by the Earls of Norfolk, including Kettleburgh nearby.

These medieval hunting lodges were evidently grand affairs, even if little remains above ground to testify. At Earl Soham there was a deer park. At Domesday, in 1086, the demesne was held by Earl Alan of Brittany and was sold in the mid 12th century to Hugh Bigod, 1st Earl of Norfolk. In the 14th and 15th centuries it was held in dower of the widows of successive earls and dukes. Then in 1547 it was granted to the widow of Henry Howard, Earl of Surrey, who has been credited with introducing the sonnet from Italy to England. Forty of his sonnets, including 'Description and Praise of his love Geraldine' were published in 1557, seven years before Shakespeare was born.

After fighting valiantly in France he was condemned and executed on wild, trumped-up charges of treasonably quartering royal arms and advising his sister to become the king's mistress.

The one obvious survival from this time is the low two-arched Tudor brick bridge leading across the moat with an unusual trefoil top to the wall just beyond. In 1655

The entrance range was rebuilt in 1789.

The arches were added to the Tudor hall in the 1920s.

Soham Lodge is described as 'fayrely builded, being a large timber house' with bridge and 'gate to enter in', three barns, three stables, a mill house, a malthouse and a large dovecote. In 1789 it is recorded that 'a handsome brick house was built this summer by John Ayton, Esq.'.

The list of early 20th-century owners is impressively distinguished including Sir Auckland Colvin, author of *The Making of Modern Egypt* and Lieutenant-Governor of the North-West Provinces of India, followed by Lady Grant Duff, widow of Sir Mountstuart Grant Duff.

In the 1920s the property was acquired by Major William Edgar Mann DSO, younger brother of the Manns of Thelveton in South Norfolk. He carried out major repairs and improvements and was almost certainly responsible for the Tudor hall its present form, cleverly reworking 17th-century oak panelling so it is hard to tell what changes were made. The ceiling is quartered by four massive chamfered beams supported at one end by a free-standing post and arches. The door to the adjoining dining room looks 16th-century until you realise it had been sandwiched onto a Georgian six-panel door that must date from the 1789 rebuild. At the far end of the Tudor hall, another impressive Tudor-looking door leads out onto an enclosed terrace overlooking the moat and enjoying the afternoon and evening sun.

The entrance hall is modest but the stair divides intriguingly on the half landing, with one short flight leading on to the rooms at the back of the house and the other returning to those at the front. To the right of the entrance is a library with French windows opening onto the garden at the front, while behind is a morning room with another pair of French windows – this is a house with a sitting room for every time of day and all weathers.

Upstairs, Earl Soham Lodge offers an impressive thirteen bedrooms but six of these are in the attics and in 2004 did not appear to have been in use for some time. But if

A broad moat surrounds the house.

your family or for those who do not mind sleeping under the eaves there is a kingdom of its own up here with dormer windows enjoying lovely views over unspoilt country. The views are equally good from the well-proportioned bedrooms on the first floor.

One intriguing feature of the house is an almost complete set of brass electric light switches – still in working order, with a few bakelite ones too. The owner, Bruce Hinton, told me, 'The house still has much of Major Mann's light wiring, which has survived thanks to heavy duty insulation set within steel tubes, all still well earthed.' Preserving these rare fittings is a challenge that needs advice from someone who is expert in 20th-century domestic technology. The same is true of the impressive pre-war Esse stove in the kitchen – a company that once had a quarter share of the market and went head-to-head with Aga in the battle for country-house kitchens.

Earl Soham has 7.5 acres and a series of heavily overgrown medieval fishponds. The charm of the Lodge is to be close to village life yet at the same time remain secluded from it.

HENGRAVE HALL
Bury St Edmunds

One of the finest early-Tudor houses in England, sold in 2006 after years as a school

HENGRAVE IS ONE OF THE PRIZES of early Tudor architecture, a house that is 'in all the books'. It is as ravishing as a small Oxford college, with arched gateway leading into a handsome stone-faced quad, a great hall and a chapel filled with exquisite stained glass, all set in a broad expanse of pretty Suffolk countryside. The house not only has a small village of attractive outbuildings but has been very well looked after, with not a cobweb to be seen in its hundred-odd rooms. There is an elegant monastic simplicity to the whole place, reflecting the fact that for half a century its occupants have been Sisters who ran the house first as a girls' school and latterly as a Christian retreat.

Remarkably, the building accounts for Hengrave survive. In 1525 Sir John Kytson, a rich cloth merchant, contracted with John Eastawe to 'make a house of all manor [manner] of mason's worck and bricklaying' according to a 'frame' – evidently an early architectural plan. This was the contract for the carcass of the house. Another is an agreement with Thomas Neker for 'seelyng' Hengrave, a reference to fitting out the interior.

The oriel window over the entrance was commissioned separately, like a piece of sculpture, from John Sparke. Dated 1538, is is a series of billowing curves as richly treated as the windows of Henry VII's chapel at Westminster Abbey. It bursts exuberantly from the wall, gothic above with fish-scale crowns, while below are shields with the Kytson trout supported by pairs of Italian putti, two in Roman armour.

The whole vocabulary of Tudor architecture is on display on the long south-facing entrance front – octagonal turrets bristling with crockets, battlements, gables and hood moulds to the windows. It is all so busy that it takes a moment to notice the front is not quite symmetrical, lacking a tall bay window on the right to match the chapel window on the left. In 18th-century engravings it is there, but it disappeared in remodelling in

The tall chapel window is on the left of the long entrance front.

the 1770s. This was the work of the Gage
family, to whom Hengrave passed in the
17th century. Another slight surprise is
that only the 'trim' is in stone. The rest is in
brick. This is not the usual warm Tudor
red brick but pale oatmeal Suffolk brick.
By contrast the numerous barley-sugar
chimneys are red brick.

I walked round the outside first.
Anticipation had already been heightened
by the long park wall, the splendid pair of
gazebo lodges and lake inside the entrance,
the grand expanse of park and the noble
avenue aligned on the entrance front. The
east front has another surprise – an
enchanting former parish church built in
flint and complete with Saxon round

*The richly sculptural oriel window has newly
tinctured heraldry.*

tower, acquired by the Sisters and now an adjunct to the house. Inside are breathtaking
family tombs set in columned tabernacles. A knight lies in state between his two wives.

Projecting from this front is a gabled wing and a modern addition by the Sisters. At
the back of house is an attractive 1890s pavilion and a vast walled garden. Stretching out
from the west front is a Victorian sunken garden with fountain and several matching
flights of steps as well as a half-timbered garden pavilion with herringbone brickwork.

Entering through the Tudor arch, it is obvious that Hengrave is built to a regular plan
with lofty passages looking out over the courtyard on both floors. From the courtyard
the perfect harmony of stone walls and stone paving, with grand oriel window complete
with heraldic beasts, is evident. The masonry details are exquisite, a continuous band
of quatrefoils, shallow arches to all the windows and intriguing boxed-out windows on
the first floor, as well as an Italian well head in the centre.

The tour of the house begins with the chapel (fine fan vault above the window),
continuing on the east front with a gallery or great chamber now divided but with a
lovely strapwork plaster ceiling. The great hall has a splendid open timber roof and
much Victorian panelling, the work of Sir John Wood, who acquired the house in
1896. There is a minstrels' gallery complete with inscription 'Drede god and honor
the King'. The rooms of the first floor are as lofty in proportions as those below, with
splendid ceilings that balloon up into the roof space in trefoil fashion. One corner
room has an intriguing handkerchief vault.

Many of the rooms are white-walled and plain, but throughout there are splendid
timber doorways and doors (including some faced in leather with brass trim) as well as
numerous handsome fireplaces. At the back there are further cosy rooms in the attics.

Hengrave comes with 46 acres – the parkland is separately owned but intact. The
simplicity of the rooms means that good modern furnishing could work as well as fine
antiques. A transformation could be achieved with splashes of brilliantly coloured
fabrics, though equally the present Shaker-like white has a beauty of its own.

HEVENINGHAM HALL   Halesworth

Palatial composition built in the 1770s for one of the richest merchants in Europe

HEVENINGHAM HALL SHOULD BE, and perhaps now is, one of the great trophy houses of England, sought after by the world's richest. Yet for nearly thirty years it suffered a fate that no house of this importance should ever endure.

The view of Heveningham from the passing country road is one of the most breathtaking of any house in England. The grand palace front, Roman in its magnificence, is seen across a Capability Brown park and lake. Inside, the neoclassical interiors by James Wyatt are the equal of Robert Adam's at Syon and in 1970 were complete with their Wyatt furniture. The exquisite colour schemes were Wyatt's originals, never retouched. The house was built in the late 1770s to the designs of Sir Robert Taylor for Gerard Vanneck, whose father had been described in the *Gentleman's Magazine* as 'one of the richest merchants in Europe'.

Though scarcely comfortable, the house had been lovingly maintained by Andrew Vanneck who had placed it in a trust in the hope of keeping Heveningham intact – something he would have been allowed, even encouraged, to do when new tax measures in 1975 prompted the opening of almost all of Britain's great houses. But he died in 1965, and new tax rules on trusts were set to force the break-up of the house. Desperate for a solution, the owners threatened to sell all the Wyatt rooms, and a reluctant government stepped in to buy Heveningham, 300 acres and the Wyatt furniture for what now looks the bargain price of £300,000.

For nearly a decade the house was very well run by the National Trust, which also replanted the gardens. Then in 1981 the new Environment Secretary Michael

Sir Robert Taylor's garden front glows in the sun after re-rendering.

James Wyatt's entrance hall is the equal of Adam's hall at Syon.

Heseltine decided it should be sold. The Iraqi buyer, Abdul Amir Al-Ghazzi, undertook to open the house for thirty days a year and the furniture was loaned back. Alas the doors remained closed while an epic struggle took place over an application to move the public footpath along the lake for security reasons. Next a savage fire destroyed the Wyatt Library and adjoining drawing room. Thieves then drove across the park and smashed a hole in the dining-room wall, tearing out Wyatt's superb white marble fireplace. By this time the Government had taken fright over the furniture. When officials arrived to collect it, they found a scene straight out of a Roald Dahl short story. To make the side tables more transportable the legs had reportedly been snapped off by the guards. Certainly little of the fine furniture has been exhibited again.

When the estate was put on sale by the receivers, Cork Gulley, in 1991, the Government declined to exercise its option to buy back the house. Instead it was sold to the owner of the Foxton's group of estate agents. A major programme of restoration and replanting has taken place in the park and the interiors are now said to be in good condition, but Heveningham remains a very private place. Yet even though its doors have remain closed for many years, it now appears immaculate enough to ensure it will sell immediately if it comes on the market.

NETHERGATE HOUSE · Clare
Tudor clothier's house of 1500 sensitively restored four hundred years later

THERE ARE HOUSES SO STRONG in atmosphere and character that you can immediately picture the idyllic life you will lead there. Nethergate House in Clare is one, a house of noble architectural quality, yet not so large that the responsibility need wear you down.

Clare is a delightful country town surrounded by pretty villages. A splendid Suffolk wool church floats on the skyline and several bookshops speak of civilised interesting people. Remarkably, Clare boasts three town houses listed Grade I, witness to the wealth of the wool trade from the late Middle Ages through to the 17th century.

Built for a rich clothier in around 1500, Nethergate House has had a more eventful history than its serene appearance suggests. Like a town house in a Dickens novel it was successively a boys' school, a plumber's shop, and again a school. It was then acquired by Miss Jefferies – afterwards Lady St John Hope – who carried out a restoration so subtle it deserves a special study in itself. She did the work with the architect H. Munro Cautley, later the author of the classic book *Suffolk Churches and their Treasures*.

The work they did is marked by a great feeling for history, a love of old materials and their patina. From the street it is immediately clear that the centre of the original Tudor clothier's house was refronted in the later 17th century. The sides are of black and white timber construction with oversailing upper floors, while the centre has taller, classically proportioned windows with the cross-pattern mullion and transom typical of the late 17th century.

The game at Nethergate is to decide which features are original, and which were introduced by Miss Jefferies and her architect, knowing that they often incorporated

The centre was refronted in the late 17th century, leaving the timber framing on either side.

fragments rescued from fine buildings being demolished. They introduced the oriel or bay window in the right-hand wing, copying it from one at the back of the house, but the oak beam immediately above, carved with a trail of leaves, is supposedly original, complete with carved drops at the ends. The magnificent cluster of four soaring chimneys was rebuilt by Miss Jeffries using darker and lighter bricks, giving it the weathered look of centuries.

The first fixed date, 1644, is inscribed on a beam at the back with the initials 'FCE' for the clothier Francis Crosse and his wife Elizabeth. A rainwater head at the back is inscribed 'DM 1760', while Miss Jeffries's work is marked with the initials 'MJ 1906'. Inside there are also the initials 'CPS PHJ' for the great academic C.P. Snow and his novelist wife Pamela Hansford Johnson, who lived here in the 1950s. Further clues are to be found in a well illustrated article in *The Queen* magazine on June 2, 1926.

Despite its massive roof, the main part of the house is only one room deep and much of the accommodation is in a long wing running down the side of the garden, with long bands of windows. The garden itself is secluded, ending on the tree-lined bank of the River Stour, where the present owners have a little dingy which can be used throughout the year except when the river is in spate.

About twenty years ago Nethergate was bought by two families – a local brewer, who clearly loved the place, and friends who made the left wing into a self-contained house. Cleverly, the first floor at the back was retained as part of the main house – a form of flying freehold – ensuring the back garden is not overlooked.

Anyone tall will need to bend their head as they pass beams and go through doors. The stone-flagged hall is dominated by a large deep fireplace demanding a roaring log fire. Intriguingly, two staircases open off the back of the room as if this part of the house was also once adapted for two families to live in. The smaller stair is Jacobean in character (though perhaps as late as 1644), rising in short flights with large acorns on the newel posts and pendants hanging from the beams. The larger staircase must be half a century or more later – with Classical 'tear drop' balusters and a broad handrail. A tall, gently bowed sash allows light to flood in from the garden.

This is a house where you walk through one room to another, though a delightful first-floor galleried landing gives privacy to guest rooms. The dining room leads through to a generous kitchen, well equipped with worktops and its own dining table. The main bedroom above is open to the rafters with all the main timbers exposed and light coming in from both sides. If you are averse to early-morning light in the summer, you will need to be extremely ingenious in the use of curtains and blinds. The bathroom, just across a back stair down to the kitchen, is a clever combination of ancient and modern. Once again all the timbers are exposed and you will have to duck deeply to get into the bath. More intriguing is that the brick chimney has been exposed from behind the wattle walling that once shielded it. Square basins have been cleverly set on a table top.

There is one Georgian pine-panelled bedroom at the front with Dutch tiles in the fireplace and a pretty bedroom overlooking the garden, again open to the rafters. At the top of the house is a large workroom beneath the roof with dormers on one side and a skylight on the other.

OLDEN MANOR   Higham
Well-preserved late 15th-century timber-framed hall house

OLDEN MANOR IS A QUINTESSENTIAL H-plan Tudor house with a great hall in the centre and balancing gabled cross wings. Standing in the pleasant Suffolk village of Higham, just over the border from Colchester, and surrounded by Dedham Vale, this is English domestic architecture at its best. There are diamond-pane mullioned windows and ornately carved 'bargeboards' to the wing gables. A great oriel window lights the hall. The black and white timber framing is inset with both white plaster and pretty pink bricks laid diagonally 'herringbone' style. At the front the first-floor rooms are 'jettied-out' over the ground floor, supported on ornately carved 'bressumer' beams.

There is a tendency to assume that houses like these were heavily restored in the early 20th century when sash windows were replaced by diamond panes, and painted plaster stripped off to reveal timbers which were then blackened to give a sense of great age. Leigh Alston, a local architectural historian explains, 'Large numbers of fine timber-framed buildings were demolished a hundred years ago and numerous features were rescued and incorporated in houses nearby.' But while Olden Manor was certainly worked on at this time – the porch, like a little lychgate, is typically Edwardian – it was done with extraordinary sensitivity.

Many of these timber houses in south Suffolk have never been studied. Olden was listed Grade II in 1955 on the basis of a cursory look at the exterior. Philip Aitkens, another expert on Suffolk architecture, says, 'A great number of good buildings in this area have never been looked at by the present generation of architectural historians.'

The jettied end wings and the large oriel lighting a full-height great hall suggest a date of 1500 or earlier.

The great hall is open to the roof timbers.

After the middle of the 16th century it was unusual to build a great hall open to the roof timbers – many were floored in to create comfortable rooms easier to heat – so this house could be early 16th- or even late 15th-century.

The ancient oak front door opens to reveal a great hall of soaring proportions filling the width of the house. A huge wooden overmantel rises to the eaves. It is carved in three tiers, with linenfold below, niches above and a frieze at the top with curved brackets. The fireplace is of stone with a typical shallow Tudor arch.

The hall opens at the west end into a large withdrawing chamber running from front to back. The delight of this room lies in the long runs of mullioned windows on all three outer walls. These are set high but at either end drop down to form pretty bay windows and contain much ancient woodwork. The walls are handsomely panelled and at one end Archdeacon Kirkduncan, a previous owner, made a neat little room for serving drinks, with a door out to the garden terrace.

Over the deep brick-lined fireplace is a sculpted overmantel with the coat of arms of the Worshipful Company of Tallow Chandlers – presumably set here for a master of the Company. Heavy swags of fruit rest on ornate scrolls, over which a pair of long-eared hares peep out.

At the other end of the great hall there are the usual twin-arched doorways that led to kitchen and scullery – grander houses had a third doorway leading to a pantry as well. One now leads into a panelled study, with unusually tall panels of linenfold. The proportions are exactly those of the modern snug for watching television in front of the fire. The other arch leads to a large, well-equipped kitchen and cloakroom.

A stair with widely spaced tapering balusters and chunky newel posts leads up from one corner to a convenient corridor running along the back of the hall and looking down on the floor below through an open screen. Here there is rich plaster decoration with a large Tudor rose, fleurs-de-lys and thistles. These may celebrate the Union of the Crowns of England and Scotland in 1603.

The bedrooms have more black and white timbers and in the main bedroom there are twin Royal Crowns ('closed' or covered as at a coronation), one surmounting a richly petalled Tudor rose, the other a quartered coat of arms with fleurs-de-lys and cub-like lions. All through the house are high ancient doors of tall vertical panels.

The real delight of the house is that the character and quality are consistent throughout. Most people will want to introduce more modern bathrooms but generally the house has been exceptionally conscientiously maintained.

The garden front is more irregular than the entrance front but has a delightful colonnaded loggia with stout Doric columns, each a single shaft of wood. This is the Renaissance arriving in Suffolk, after 1550, perhaps even early 17th-century. Confusing but part of the thrill of the house is its complex architectural history.

SHRUBLAND PARK · Ipswich

Grand country seat of the de Saumarez family put on the market in 2006

SHRUBLAND PARK HAS ALL THE ATTRIBUTES of a major stately home including 1,300 acres and forty-two cottages and farmhouses. Indeed, in almost every other European country it would be called a palace. The closest comparison is with Osborne on the Isle of Wight. Like Prince Albert's creation, it is a grand Italianate composition with belvedere tower, breathtaking terraced gardens, Swiss cottage (a Russian one too) and five drives, three of which are still in use.

Shrubland is a fusion of three classic moments in English architecture, Palladian, Greek Revival and Italianate. The Palladian house was designed by the talented James Paine, whose best-known works are mighty Keddleston Hall in Derbyshire and Brocket Hall in Hertfordshire. His client at Shrubland was a clergyman, the Rev. John Bacon, not the impoverished stipendiary of Jane Austen's books but a scion of the Bacon family of Norfolk, a 'squarson' who lived like a nobleman.

On his death Shrubland passed to his brother Nicholas, also a clergyman. In 1796 the estate was acquired by William Middleton, whose father had returned to Suffolk from South Carolina after inheriting Crowfield Hall near Stowmarket. At Middleton Place, near Charleston, the Middletons had created what remain one of the grandest houses and gardens on the eastern seaboard of America. Evidently they were determined to rival it in Suffolk and in 1801 Middleton's brother Henry gave him £30,000 (a good £6 million today) which he had just won on the Lottery to spend on improvements at Shrubland.

A little puzzlingly, the work only began in 1830 when Sir W.F. Middleton, Bt, called in the architect J.P. Gandy Deering, who had accompanied Lord Elgin to Greece to transform Paine's brick villa into a Grecian mansion. If carried out in full, Shrubland

The mid-Georgian garden front was remodelled by Barry with balustrades, urns and belvedere tower.

18th-century interiors were enriched in the mid 19th century with inlaid 'boulle' door.

would be on a par with The Grange in Hampshire or Belsay Hall in Northumberland. As it is, fine Gandy Deering interiors survive as well as his handsome conservatory. Twenty years later the baronet brought in Sir Charles Barry, the architect who invented the Italianate style with the Travellers' and Reform Clubs in Pall Mall.

As a result Shrubland boasts one of the grandest entrances to any English country house. The front doors open into a domed vestibule like a Renaissance chapel, with columned gallery on either side. Ahead is a grand staircase, a single straight flight inspired by the Scala Regia in the Vatican, with a shallow Grecian vault as exquisite as work by Sir John Soane in the Bank of England.

The main rooms have decorative plaster ceilings with a delicacy and crispness rivalling those by Robert Adam. Paine took pride in employing Yorkshire plasterers whom he said equalled 'the performances of the best Italians that ever worked in this kingdom'. The drawing room has an overmantel carved with game and fish as delicate as the work of Grinling Gibbons, though later. The doorway into the Library is an extraordinary creation in French boulle work – all inlaid brass and tortoiseshell with matching ebony black bookcases. The library ceiling is full-blooded Victorian with scrolls of foliage modelled in three dimensions.

The thrill of the house is the ascent to the belvedere, where a further spiral stair leads to an upper balustraded terrace that has breathtaking views over the park and formal gardens. These are one of Barry's very best creations and turn a plain Suffolk hillside into a version of the Villa d'Este at Tivoli outside Rome. Here he formed one of the most breathtaking vistas in all English gardening – through a carved portal down a stately stone stair across a fountain to an exquisite open-arched pavilion. The cost of making and maintaining this stair practically bankrupted the Middletons, one of whom – tempting fate – was called Broke Middleton. The ascent rivals the extraordinary hillside staircases of northern Portuguese monasteries.

The formal gardens are breathtaking in their extent with numerous balustraded terraces and urns, splendid yew topiary and a second fountain garden enclosed by curving walls topped by stone balls. The Swiss cottage is complete with knotched woodwork, overhanging roofs, painted inscriptions and balcony. Grazing sheep fill the park and there is a newly enclosed deer park.

Shrubland passed in 1882 by marriage to the de Saumarez family, famous for its admirals. The 6th Baron started a health clinic in 1965, building a modern retreat – 'The Vista' – that looks down dramatically across the gardens along an equally grand cross avenue. The Old Hall, where the present Lord de Saumarez lives, is also an intriguing house with important Elizabethan features.

There is a Georgian Gothic tower, heightened in 1857, surveying the park and two enchanting ponds set in woodland glades. The Palladian stable block needs restoring to its original handsome proportions. The gatehouses are as grand as the best early-Victorian stationmasters' houses.

Barry's Italianate style was the inspiration for formal gardens on the French Riviera that were created a hundred years ago and are now being snapped up by the new Russian plutocracy. The estate was sold in 2006.

The domed vestibule inside the main entrance is breathtakingly grand.

THURSTON END HALL   Hawkedon
Late Elizabethan E-plan manor house

MELLOW RED BRICK and silvered oak framing are two of the most beautiful of all English building materials. Thurston End Hall combines them to form one of the most enchanting Elizabethan houses in East Anglia. You are ready to fall in love with the place before you see it, warmed first by the peaceful expanse of Hawkedon Green and its dignified medieval church, then by the long winding lane leading to the hall, crossing a ford on a tight corner. After nearly a mile Thurston bursts upon you, seen to full advantage head-on up a short drive.

This is 16th-century architecture at its most exquisitely picturesque, with no attempt at precise symmetry and gables of varying size. Both first and second floors are jettied and so are most of the windows, although the brickwork beneath the three ground-floor bay windows has been built out to provide extra support.

The timbers are close-set – a sign of wealth – and the bricks between are laid herringbone fashion with intriguing variations at some of the corners. Like all Tudor bricks they change magically in colour during the day from a warm orange in bright morning sun to a deeper red in the afternoon. Above, the attractively weathered roof tiles are a perfect colour match.

It is usually suggested that the house was built in 1560 with additions in 1607 (the date over the entrance porch) but the architecture is consistent enough to suggest that it is all of one date, probably between 1570 and 1590. The scalloped bargeboards on the end of the gables appear later, probably introduced during restoration in the 1920s. Around this time the richly carved porch may also have been embellished, possibly with elements from the family pew in the church. Another surprise survival is a trio of Georgian Sun, Phoenix and Norwich insurance plaques with the numbers of the policies beneath.

Numerous close-set timbers were a sign of affluence, here with delightful herringbone brick infill.

The likely builder is Ambrose Everard, after his marriage in 1576 to Martha Ray of nearby Denston. The house passed through a daughter to the Maltywards of Rougham and by 1736 was owned by Pamplin Richardson. He was followed by John Gotts of Timworth and John Wiseman, who passed it to Orbell Ray Oakes. The 1920s restoration appears to be the work of Bernard Gaussen, whose wife was a descendant of Napoleon's brother, Joseph, King of Naples. Tim Orbell, who was selling the house in 2005, had inherited it from Captain and Mrs Basil Williams, who bought the Hall in 1936.

The well-preserved barns have remained farm buildings, kept in good repair although never modernised. One barn, with untouched 16th-century timbers, was used for occasional concerts and seats up to 140 with a stage at the end. 'The thatch is all Norfolk reed, which lasts much longer than straw,' said Mr Orbell. The neighbouring weatherboarded barn has an aisle inside, which forms a pleasantly enclosed court with the low byres opposite.

The south end of the house looks out onto an arena garden enclosed by noble 20 ft-high yew hedges. Here the Orbells have held operas in the open air and in a marquee. Behind are the remains of the moat, as well as a pond probably excavated to provide clay for the bricks. Just beyond is the fast-flowing stream of the River Glem and a rustic 1930s timber-clad cottage that also belongs to the estate.

The 31 acres that come with the house stretch for nearly a mile along the river, providing a most pleasant walk for anyone with a dog to exercise, all on your own land with discreetly placed swimming pool and tennis court providing further opportunities for exercise.

At the back of the house are two magnificent chimney stacks almost the size of cathedral buttresses, built in good English bond (alternating layers of bricks laid end-on) and just above the eaves an intriguing set of blind battlements. At the top of one stack is a quartet of delicious ornamental Tudor chimneys, each with a different moulded brick pattern. The great hall, as with most 16th-century halls, does not rise to the timbers but is roofed over with massive chambered beams and cross timbers. The beam ends rest on pillars with Classical bases and capitals, although these are shaved off at the sides, suggesting that the local carpenter had no clear idea of correct Classical detail.

The north drawing room has a fireplace with Salamonic (corkscrew) columns wound round with oak twigs. Unusually, Thurston has two good timber staircases, with the short flights typical of Elizabethan date. The larger one has the newel or corner post carried up as columns supporting the upper flights and the added flourish of matching banisters.

The main bedroom has a handsome early-Georgian wooden fireplace and is well lit by the large timber mullions, as are other bedrooms. The attics are also full of character with ancient broad floorboards and a long run of laundry cupboards. The second staircase is also unusually handsome, although it is probably a later 17th-century addition with delightful cut-out flat balusters. Everywhere you look there is a glorious sense that time has stood still. Even the garage is a pre-war period piece, complete with trio of double doors on long hinges.

WESTGATE HOUSE   Long Melford
Regency refronting of an earlier timber-framed house

JOHN TANNER, WHO SOLD WESTGATE HOUSE in the autumn of 2004, is a breathlessly energetic man who has only to look at a garden, a house or a room to see it has 'capabilities'. Over twenty years, as antiques dealer and interior decorator, he had brought his handsome town house in Long Melford to the point where there was nothing left for him to do.

For the purchaser it was like buying the super-deluxe model of a very expensive car and finding every conceivable extra thrown in free. 'At a pinch I'd sell the house with all the furniture too,' he told me. He bought the property when, as he put it jokingly, it was 'a council house'. The county council had just published four options for a Long Melford bypass and one of them went past the back of Westgate House. As the property had just gone on the market, the then owner served a notice on the council, forcing it to buy the place.

Having dinner with a 'Suffolk lass' one weekend, Mr Tanner heard she had just seen a wonderful house with 'a drawing room as big as a ballroom'. Brimming with enthusiasm, he arrived the next morning at the empty house, found his way in through the cellar and decided at once that it was for him.

Long Melford, with its mile-long high street, has as many historic houses as any village in England. Westgate House is on the road to Haverhill and looks out over green fields on every side. The Regency entrance front speaks of an architect abreast of the latest fashions. Mr Tanner thought it must be the architect of the town hall at nearby Sudbury and the Court House at Clare. The house is faced in white Suffolk brick with 'rubbed' brick over the windows and a baroque front-doorcase. The roof has Tuscan eaves with the cornice omitted from the gable to give it a rustic Italianate look.

Like many houses in the area, this was a re-fronting of an earlier timber-framed house. The re-fronting was not just a brick skin applied to the timber front, as often happened, but a whole new front range with elegantly proportioned Regency rooms.

The front door opens into a broad hall with a staircase at the end seen through a screen of columns, as in federal houses of this date in America. Inside, a dust door is covered in smoothest suede with neat brass buttons. The mahogany letter box is original, while the splendid brass-edged mahogany lock comes from Ireland. The hall is paved with generous flags of limestone, set in a diamond pattern, and the columns are ragged to look like marble.

The capacious drawing room's broad pine floors continue through the main rooms. All the decorative detail, the toothing of the cornices and the key-patterned dado rail, is carved in wood with crisp egg-and-dart mouldings on the shutters, and the walls are hung in white slub silk from India, padded out on a backing of Dacron.

'Every room has a way in and out,' joked Mr Tanner. Double doors open into the library, and have boldly projecting hinges, allowing the doors to be folded back 180 degrees. When he bought the house the library walls were planked oak covered in cloth with a thin layer of plaster. Now they are a smart apricot with a quadruple-glazed door opening onto the garden.

The dining room opposite has emerald-green baize walls and black woodwork. The butler's pantry had been transformed into a miniature gallery for displaying glass. The kitchen retains a handsome pine dresser, matched by a range of drawers from an old haberdasher's in Hatfield. The boiler room has been fitted out as a laundry with deep airing shelves. The boot room has built-in kennels for the dogs and a delightful snug has a coved ceiling, fireplace and French windows opening on to the garden. 'The heating is organised so it can warm two, four or seven bedrooms,' I learnt.

The main stair has a generous half-landing and continues up to the master bedroom, where extra height is gained from the steeply coved ceilings under the eaves. The pine cupboards are recycled Georgian window shutters, and the king-size bath is placed grandly on an axis with a pair of sash windows. On the sills stand neatly clipped box topiary, providing a little modesty as you emerge from the bath.

Here, and in every other bathroom, is a large glazed cabin with a power shower, another of Mr Tanner's trademarks. The bedrooms are all handsomely decorated, one with a superb double swan bed, another with Georgian sashes descending to the floor and little guard balconies outside, while a third is set beneath the gables of the old house with the arch-braced roof timbers exposed to grand effect.

At the top of the house is a self-contained apartment approached across a 'bridge' where the hatch doors that opened onto the roof valley are now replaced by gothic windows. Behind the house is a large walled garden, yielding views of Long Melford's ancient parish church.

Like many houses in the village, Westgate has a large garden behind.

WINGFIELD CASTLE
Wingfield

Moated late 14th-century castle built for the Earls of Suffolk

ROMANTICALLY REFLECTED IN its broad moat, Wingfield looks the perfect compact medieval castle. The entrance range, nearly but not quite symmetrical, has battlements, corner towers and a tall gatehouse. Here is a castle built of local Suffolk flint, with stone for the architectural trim. There is a portcullis and the original doors remain with a smaller wicket door in the west leaf for those on foot. These defensive trimmings make it look like a fortification but the windows in the curtain wall make it clear that the castle was never intended nor capable of sitting out a siege.

Though the original moated quadrangle remains, much of the castle was taken down for building materials in 1525 and by degrees the castle descended to a farmhouse. Rescue was initiated by G. Baron Ash who bought Wingfield in 1943 and spent nearly thirty years carefully nursing the castle back to life.

The license to crenellate was granted in 1385 to Sir Michael de la Pole who was granted the Earldom of Suffolk just three months later. In 1361, aged 30, he had married the 12-year-old daughter and heiress of Sir John Wingfield. Sir Michael spent a considerable time in France campaigning with John of Gaunt and the Black Prince and negotiated Richard II's marriage to Anne, the daughter of King Wenceslas of Bohemia. He became Lord Chancellor in 1383 but his closeness to an unpopular king made him a target for the barons and in 1386, when his castle can have barely been complete, he was impeached and heavily fined. He fled the country, was found guilty

The castle is built of local Suffolk flint with timber-framed domestic buildings behind.

of treason in his absence, and died two years later in Paris. His son Michael, who was restored to the earldom in 1398, appears by then to have completed the castle.

The building of Wingfield marks the transfer of the family's centre of operations from Hull to East Anglia. William de la Pole became a favourite of King Henry VI, effecting the king's marriage to Margaret of Anjou and three years later becoming Lord Chamberlain for life, and then in 1448 Lord High Admiral for England and Duke of Suffolk. Such favour brought him enemies and he was murdered at sea in 1450 while fleeing to Flanders. An inventory of the castle taken in 1467 lists tapestries of hawking and boar hunting, cushions, bed linen, books and clothing underlining the importance and value of fine and colourful fabrics in late-medieval houses.

William de la Pole's son John supported the house of York and married Elizabeth, the sister of Edward IV and Richard III. Richard III's declaration that John's son was the heir apparent to the throne marked the final disaster in the family fortunes as Henry VII imprisoned the young earl and Henry VIII beheaded him and confiscated all his estates.

The domestic buildings appear to have been timber-framed and the living accommodation at Wingfield is in a west range extending along the moat from the octagonal south-west tower at the end of the entrance range. The main residential apartments would almost certainly have been in a hall range on the north side opposite the entrance tower and Anthony Emery in his three-volume study, *Greater Medieval Houses*, suggests the courtyard house on the west contained the private apartments of the de la Poles. Seen from across the moat, its white plastered walls make a delightful contrast with the flintwork of the entrance range and towers.

WINGFIELD COLLEGE   Wingfield
Founded in 1362 and retaining a wealth of ancient fabric

Tucked away down narrow Suffolk lanes, Wingfield College is a place of pure enchantment with the glorious medieval church immediately beside it. Yet it is far from what it sounds or even seems in photographs. Though 'College' suggests a school, it has been a house since 1542 when Henry VIII disbanded the priests who said masses for the founder and educated local boys.

The long main front looks like an English country cousin of George Washington's Mount Vernon. In fact this is a pure illusion and the grand Venetian windows are little more than dummies inserted for show by the 18th-century owner, Squire Buck.

The College was founded in 1362 on the death of Sir John de Wingfield who had fought with the Black Prince and captured and ransomed a rich Frenchman. Today just one range of the original quadrangle survives with the great hall projecting into the garden behind.

The present owners, artists Ian and Hilary Chance, have nursed the house back to life and health. Every element of old structure, every ancient plaster surface or floor tile,has been lovingly exposed though they have not hesitated to introduce an abundance of modern artistic furnishings. Their approach is to use the house for a social purpose, holding concerts and exhibitions and sharing it with visitors.

The long Georgian front disguises a remarkably intact timber-framed house behind.

Today Wingfield College rates three stars in Simon Jenkins's *England's Thousand Best Houses*. Yet there is no obligation to continue opening the house to the public and a new owner can opt for a life of seclusion and retirement, leaving the artistic mission of Wingfield to be continued by the Arts Trust established out of sight in a group of barns next door.

I doubt if there is a level floor, plumb wall or straight beam in the place. This perhaps is a slight exaggeration as there are new tiled floors in some rooms but the well-worn brick-tiled corridors undulate continuously and the broad elm floor boards in the bedrooms – up to 18 inches wide – look as old as the house.

The hall is of impressive height, open to the roof timbers. When Ian Chance began it was divided into five rooms. 'Initially we thought it part of an early manor house which pre-dated the college but dendrochronology has shown the timbers date from 1377,' he says.

Originally it was an aisled hall but in the 16th century the aisle posts were cut out and the weight of the roof truss supported by a massive oak tie beam. At some stage this cracked alarmingly but it is now well secured by discreetly placed steel plates. The Chances have remade the elegant bay window with two rows of beautiful moulded timber mullions, while on the north is a simpler 14th-century form of window with diamond-shaped posts – at that date there was probably no glass. At one end is an exquisite section of linenfold panelling carved with the heads of Charles Brandon, Duke of Suffolk, and his wife Mary Tudor, widow of the King of France and sister of Henry VIII, who came to live here in the 16th century.

The one puzzle is that there is no place for a blazing log fire. Instead the house is heated by warm-air ducts beneath the floor and fed through the roof space into the bedrooms above – cleverly eliminating the need for radiators. A bigger modern boiler

might even end the need to don several extra layers of woolly jumpers in winter. Nor are you living entirely in the Middle Ages for to the right of the front door is a lovely Georgian panelled room dating from the 1750s but in character similar to the highly sought-after 1720s houses in Spitalfields.

The modern topiary garden is full of pyramids and cones of clipped yew and box.

At the back of the house is a highly original modern topiary garden where, Mrs Chance explains, 'The clipped cones are in box and the clipped boxes of yew.' There are rhomboids, prisms and a nearly mature yew version of the icon of Russian Constructivism – Vladimir's Tatlin's angled, spiralling monument to the Third International. Just beyond is a large duck pond brimming with waterlilies, ideal for the increasing band of brave souls who like swimming in fresh, unchlorinated spring water. Mrs Chance says, 'It's 12 to 13 ft deep in the middle now we have had it dredged. I go in also to thin out the bulrushes, they're thugs.'

The walled garden has been imaginatively transformed into an artistic Millennium Garden with modern minimalist planting showing off the shapes of individual plants set in rectangles of slates and stones – very good also at keeping the weeds down. 'There are six 'stations', including an amphitheatre for poetry readings, stones from the beach at Sheringham where I grew up, and a musical garden where clipped balls and their shadows look like notes on a score,' explains Chance.

And if you see a coach and four driving by you will not need to pinch yourself. It's John Parker, the world-record carriage driver, going past in the Royal Norfolk Mail Coach.

The gallery looks down over the great hall, with its oriel window.

WORLINGHAM HALL   Beccles
Regency villa of 1810 designed for a local magistrate

WORLINGHAM IS A PRETTY REGENCY HOUSE in white Suffolk brick, seen to advantage from the road out of Beccles towards Lowestoft. It was built for a local magistrate, Robert Sparrow, about 1800. He was not, it seems, a loveable character, and was described by a neighbour as haughty, imperious and selfish. But Henry Davy, in his *Views of Suffolk Seats* (1827), says that Sparrow was a keen gardener and 'showed much taste in the arrangement of the plantations and the general disposition of the grounds'.

Sparrow's father had bought the estate in 1755 for £3,850. Sparrow does not seem to have thought of remodelling his house until some twenty years after his father's death. In 1785 he commissioned plans from the young John Soane, but failed to pay for them. Soane complained to a local rector, saying that he had made the plans 'with a great deal of care and consideration, consisting of eighteen fair drawings' and requiring 'two journeys myself and one my clerk's for which the charge is £26 and five shillings'. Sparrow had offered a mere 10 guineas, saying he had never asked for so many drawings in the first place. He paid in his own time, eleven years after he received the drawings.

The architect of Worlingham as it stands today was Francis Sandys, best known as the builder of Ickworth. In 1800 Sandys exhibited a drawing of Worlingham at the Royal Academy. The similarity of the main front to his Athenaeum in Bury St Edmunds confirms the attribution. In typical Regency style the house consists of two

The house is designed with a raised centre in the manner of a Roman triumphal arch.

almost even storeys with the ground-floor sashes descending almost to the ground and only a couple of steps up to the front door. The central portion of the front has a raised parapet in the manner of a Roman triumphal arch.

The great beauty of Worlingham is the unexpectedly grand octagonal staircase hall. The stair begins with a short flight leading up to a grand pedimented doorcase and then branches into two, with the steps dramatically cantilevered from the walls. The elegant iron railing, pinched at the top in the manner of hairpins, has a continuous mahogany handrail that sweeps down in an uninterrupted curve. Curiously the pedimented doorcase opens into nothing more than a cupboard. The dome above, rising directly from the walls, has pretty latticework coffering diminishing in scale towards the centre.

The interior contains a considerable amount of distinctive architectural detail, screens of columns in the Drawing Room and the bedrooms, pretty cross-vaulted corridors and arcades overlooking the stair. The entrance hall is entirely filled with large doorcases. Those on the side are like miniature temple fronts with large triangular pediments over two pairs of double doors. The doors at the end, leading through to the staircase hall, are grouped under an arch with a pair of blind doors on the left and the real doors on the right neatly concealing a slight change of axis.

Top: A screen of columns has delicate Classical detail.

Above: The octagonal staircase is top-lit.

The house was rescued in the 1960s from a state of considerable dilapidation by Viscount Colville. The park abounded with secluded walks, rustic cottages and copses, and there was even a farm 'in the Norman style of architecture'. According to Davy, Sparrow was 'a great admirer and promoter of the fine arts' and commissioned Sir Francis Chantrey to sculpt a family monument in the church. After Sparrow's death in 1822 the house passed to his daughter, Mary, and her husband, the 2nd Earl of Gosford.

YEW TREE HOUSE — Earl Stonham

Little altered 15th-century hall house rescued from decay

MANY DREAM OF RESCUING an ancient house from decay. Oliver Leigh-Wood has done it. In the heart of east Suffolk, he found a 15th-century hall house that had been unoccupied since 1970. Sitting in a secluded garden of two thirds of an acre, it had tin and tarpaulin on its roof, boarded-up windows and dirt-stained walls. Yet as early as 1955, it had been given a Grade II* listing as 'a good and exceptionally little altered example of a rural 15th century house'.

Since 1802 Yew Tree House had been in the Runeckles family, well-known local organists. Here they had run a blacksmith's forge, repaired shoes, assembled bicycles, traded in sheet music, given piano lessons and run a sub-post office from the kitchen. Arthur Runeckles and his sister had a great affection for the house, even if their ideas of maintenance were minimal. It took Leigh-Wood months of patient negotiation to secure the property. When asked what he would do with it, he gave the right answer: 'Nothing. I'll just clean it.'

He adopted the principles of William Morris's Society for the Protection of Ancient Buildings – retain rather than renew, repair rather than replace. As architect he took on Jim Boutwood, a former chairman of SPAB. He began by sifting through the clutter and debris that filled every room and the garden. This yielded vital historical detail and building materials for repair. The whole process has been a model of sustainability that has taken over two years.

He explains, 'When built, this was a typical late-medieval hall house, with a central hall and smoke rising from an open fire to the roof and escaping through smoke hoods. The hall was entered by a cross passage with wet and dry larders on one side and a chamber above. At the other end was a family room or solar, with another chamber under the eaves.'

About 1600, a chimney was introduced and the upper part of the hall was floored over to make an extra room. At about the same time a wing was added at right angles to the west end. Intriguingly, this was largely built of second-hand materials including timbers with 13th- and 14th-century knotched lap joints.

The whole house has now been rethatched using older varieties of corn grown by the Suffolk Thatchers' Association which are much longer than modern straw. The biggest change has come from the reinstatement of the smoke hoods in the ends of the roof. The 1600 wing (and the whole of the west or garden front) has the characteristic local parget – panels of geometric patterns drawn on wet plaster. The new work is shallower than the old, done with a three-, not four-, prong fork so the difference will be apparent in the future. It needs to be covered regularly with a fresh coat of limewash. The windows are 19th-century casements painted in sugar-bag light blue from Farrow & Ball.

The lime plaster ceilings in the service rooms had largely collapsed but were mixed with new goats' hair and reapplied to the original oak laths. Rising damp had partially dissolved the wattle and daub walls but again the daub was scooped up, broken down with a spade, and more straw added. Old wattles were reused supplemented by new ones from the garden and the recycled medieval daub laid on with a trowel.

In the kitchen, a hatch door survives with the post-office counter on the lower half. An old Aga has been installed and new kitchen cupboards made following the Georgian moulding over the hearth. The old copper, the size of a beer barrel, for boiling up clothes, has been kept, as well as the bread oven. On the walls are old greetings cards from post office days and a series of old bills with splendid copperplate headings. One of 1933 is from Reginald Chaplin, 'Corn, Cake, Offal and Manure Merchant'.

In the small dining room beyond is a framed display of thatching irons found in the roof, as well as a bunch of pre-1600 straw, blackened from the open fire.

The parlour in the wing has a deep inglenook inset with a later fireplace. A paint conservator, Andrea Kirkham, is painstaking exposing the faux brickwork above – imitating the local white bricks rather than the more usual red.

The showpiece is the upstairs bathroom, largely panelled in cedar planks found lying in the garden. Leigh-Wood taps the panelling opposite the bath and the whole wall springs forward to reveal an astonishing sight – a section of medieval roof complete with half blocked dormer that was hidden when the 1600 wing was added. If it were a collage by a contemporary artist it would hang in the Tate Modern.

At a glance, the handsome wooden floors in the house look new – in fact, the wide planks are sawn from old joists which dealers are now cutting up for floors.

Amid the painstaking process of repair, Leigh-Wood has allowed himself a few conceits. There are no less than ten specially contrived hidey holes – such as a drawer in the skirting beneath the kitchen cupboard.

The best conceit of all is the dormer window that lights the early 17th-century room over the hall. For extra light this now has glass in the triangle over the window, which is beautifully engraved with reminders of things that have happened in the house over the last two hundred years – bicycles, sheet music, a washing mangle, a radio, stamps of successive reigns and the masonry bees that were found in the chimney.

When Yew Tree House was restored in 1999, it was given a fresh coat of limewash and a new thatch.

SURREY

ALBURY PARK HAS HAD AN EVENTFUL history. The late 17th-century gardens were laid out by John Evelyn for the Duke of Norfolk, complete with *pausilippe* – the Italian name for a tunnel through a hillside. The entrance, no longer accessible, is at the centre of a series of impressively long garden terraces.

Fire severely damaged the house in 1697 but in 1763 George III held his Coronation Ball in the Great Room, now the site of the library. Sir John Soane was called in to extend the house in 1800 and his staircase, library and drawing room survive. In 1819 Albury was bought by the banker Henry Drummond, who, between 1846 and 1852, commissioned Augustus Pugin to remodel the house in Tudor Gothic style, adorning Albury with sixty-three chimneys, each with its own individual design.

His daughter married into the family of the Duke of Northumberland, to whom the estate passed on her death in 1890. After standing empty in the 1960s, Albury was sold in 1969 with 5 acres to the Mutual Householders Association, later the Country Houses Association, and converted into retirement apartments. The MHA philosophy was to use the principal rooms for residents to eat and relax in and furnishing them as far as possible in a traditional manner with portraits on the walls. When a financial crisis hit the organisation in 2003 and all its properties were threatened with closure, the residents at Albury held together and in May 2004 the house and grounds were bought by the Whalley family, who have three generations' worth of experience in care and retirement properties.

There are now thirty-seven one- and two-bedroom apartments sold on a lifetime licence which offers a saving in stamp duty. They vary from a modest 600 sq ft to over 2,000 sq ft with prices ranging from £180,000 to £750,000 for the Licence.

The house has been handsomely remodelled in Tudor Gothic style, with stepped battlements, finials and buttresses.

ASGILL HOUSE Richmond-on-Thames
Enchanting 1760s villa on the Thames

ASGILL IS A BRILLIANT AND INGENIOUS variant of one of Andrea Palladio's most inspired designs – the pediment within a pediment, used in his two famous churches in Venice, the Redentore and San Giorgio Maggiore. Sadly, in the 1840s the owner added a new entrance hall and utility wing and raised the roof, almost completely destroying the unusual proportions of the house on both main elevations. The side roofs were raised between 1832 and 1841.

Asgill was built in 1761–62 on the site of the brewhouse and kitchen garden of the long-vanished Richmond Palac , and is named after its builder Sir Charles Asgill, a successful merchant banker who

After disfiguring alterations were removed in 1970, the exquisitely crisp stonework was revealed.

began as a clerk and rose to be Lord Mayor of London. His architect was Sir Robert Taylor, whose houses are always cleverly planned with rooms of unusual shape. At Asgill, there are two fine octagon rooms within the three-sided bay. Asgill is the smallest and most ingeniously planned of Taylor's villas, which are all 'astylar' – adhering to Classical grammar and proportions but eschewing the use of columns.

The house was one of numerous 18th-century houses, built on and near the Thames between Chelsea and Hampton Court as retreats for London merchants. They rarely had farms or estates like country seats further from London, though many had gardens and ornamental grounds.

Asgill was designed with the overhanging 'Tuscan' eaves that Inigo Jones used on St Paul's, Covent Garden. The ground floor is faced with Taylor's favourite rusticated stonework with smooth-faced ashlar stone above. Another Taylor signature is the 'vermiculated' stonework around the doorways on both sides of the house.

Fred Hauptfuhrer sensitively restored Asgill in 1969–70, removing the Victorian additions and restoring the roofs to their original proportions to recreate one of the most distinctive villa designs in English Palladian architecture.

Internally the hall and staircase are neatly contrived in matching ovals. The staircase does not rise directly to the second floor but continues at right angles, ascending under the sloping eaves. The change in direction comes by way of an elegant serpentine curve in the landing with a beautiful cross vista between two Venetian arches.

Past residents include the MP James Whitshed Keene, Mrs Elizabeth Palmer and Benjamin Cohen. James Bracebridge Hilditch, son of the painter George Hilditch, lived here from 1882 until his death in 1920, and his widow lived on after him until at least the start of the Second World War.

Built to command fine views, the house is faced in smooth ashlar stone.

BOTLEYS IS A FINE PALLADIAN VILLA beautifully faced in blond stone from Headington in Oxfordshire. During the 18th century, numerous delightful and pretty houses were built on or near the bank of the Thames for summer use. 'I find two thousand houses which in other places would pass for palaces ... west of London only,' wrote Daniel Defoe as early as 1726. 'Never built a Charming house for yourself between London and Hampton Court,' Horace Walpole cautioned a friend in 1763. 'Everyone will live in it but you.' Botleys, near Chertsey, is further west and was built for Sir Joseph Mawbey, Bt, who at the age of seventeen became a partner in the vinegar distillery of his uncle Joseph Pratt at Vauxhall.

In 1763 he bought Botleys to take part in county affairs while serving as an MP for thirty years. Walpole described him as 'vain, noisy and foolish' and Wraxall as 'a man, who from some unfortunate circumstances in his private life, never could obtain a patient or a candid hearing in Parliament [but] nevertheless spoke with great good sense.' Contemporaries were amused by his keeping pigs fed on the husks of barley used in distilling, bringing him frequent taunts in the House.

Kenton Couse, his architect, completed the house in 1765 and in *Vitruvius Britannicus* it is described as standing on a hill commanding 'very extensive views over a great part of Surrey into the counties of Middlesex, Bucks, Herts, Berks and Southampton.' The columns and decorative elements were carved in stone from another Oxfordshire quarry near Barrington.

Unusually the grand columned front was not on the entrance side but looked out over the garden and instead of the usual square Palladian plan a bite was taken out of one flank to form a small courtyard

Like so many grand houses, Botleys became an institution, acquired by Surrey County Council in 1929 for use in 'caring for backward children and adults'. A new wing was added as well as accommodation blocks in the grounds to house patients.

After a fire in 1994 Botleys' plight looked dire. But an electronic data company stepped in to restore the house, attracting interest from a former state architect of California, Sim Van Der Ryan. As home to the data company, Botleys is in its third incarnation and receives a very modern accolade as an 'intelligent building' capable of adapting to different users.

BROOK PLACE
West End
Dutch-gabled Cromwellian house built on an unusual cross plan

BROOK PLACE IS A CHARMING Dutch-gabled Surrey house of exceptional interest to the history of architecture and taste. The main gable is dated 1656 with the initials 'WB', announcing that it belongs to the intriguing group of country houses built under Oliver Cromwell. These are in a style quaintly known as Artisan Mannerist, announcing they were usually the work of master bricklayers rather than architects. The grander ones are fronted with pilasters; lesser ones, like Brook Place, simply have scrolly gables in the Dutch manner. The grandest ones were built by men in high office, or high favour, under the Protector.

At first Brook Place looks an engaging muddle, with twin gables on two sides and odd extensions on different fronts, all rather carefully matched in with the original plum-coloured brick which has a liberal speckling of blacker 'glazed' bricks.

Look a little more closely and it suddenly becomes apparent that the house was originally designed on a perfect Greek cross plan, like idealised Renaissance churches in Italy, with four equal arms. This is evident from both the untouched intersecting roof ridges and the brickwork – despite clever matching when the secondary gables were added.

The cross plan is given a further flourish by the impressive central chimney, a cluster of four square stacks. The builder of Brook Place was brave to use papist symbolism in Puritan England. It could be that he himself added the secondary gables to disguise the imagery from passers-by on their way to Bagshot.

Built with a liberal sprinkling of black header bricks, the chimneys are grouped in a single central cluster.

The initials 'WB' could stand for William Bray, whose family arrived in the village in the 16th century, but Ronald Schueller's *History of Chobham* notes that the Brays had by this time sold the estate to William Beauchamp.

Inside, the house retains a 17th-century charm with low ceilings and large impressive brick hearths in the main rooms on the ground and first floors. Hidden beside one of these, a priest hole is said to survive. Hampton's sales particulars also boast of the unique panelling of a dining room known as The Breda Room and the principal bedroom, The Rubens Room, brought to England from Holland in the 1820s and placed at Goodrich Court in Herefordshire.

When I mentioned this to John Harris, who is just completing a masterpiece of detective work on period rooms stripped out from historic houses, he exclaimed, 'You've found it. The Breda Room that disappeared in the sale of fittings from Goodrich Court in 1947 shortly before it was demolished.' Goodrich Court was built for Sir Samuel Rush Meyrick in 1828–31 by the prolific country-house architect Edward Blore. In it he incorporated fittings and panelling from the Breda Government House, including a fantastic 1690s ceiling.

The panelling at Brook Place is earlier in date, probably nearer 1600, with vases and exotic birds inspired by Raphael's famous Grotesques in the Vatican as well as more old-fashioned linenfold. Mr Harris suggests it may have come to Goodrich via the 'Wardour Street trade', a group of dealers specialising in panelling who supplied the German Room to Chatsworth.

Further intriguing details are provided by Patricia Gavigan, a writer who since 1987 has run the charitable trust that has used Brook Place as a retreat. 'We bought the house from John Bolton, author of the classic 1971 Bolton report on small businesses. Before he had even bought Brook Place he set off to the sale at Goodrich to buy antique furniture. He arrived a day late when the fittings were being sold and ended up bringing back a trailer full of panelling.'

She continues, 'It had all been painted a deep black when the family were in mourning and was carefully restored over two years by Keeble & Son of Kingston who adapted it to fit the dining room and main bedroom at Brook Place which he had by then bought.' There is also an intriguing built-in panelled cupboard in one of the bedrooms in both light and dark wood with diamond studding and butterfly hinges.

Remarkably there are no Georgian sashes, only wooden mullions appropriate to the date of the house. This may be due to the Surrey architect J.D. Coleridge, a Lutyens pupil who restored the house well in 1927, according to Ian Nairn's *Surrey*.

Bolton adapted the charming granary behind the house as his office. The trust use it as a chapel. Other outbuildings include a splendid timber-framed barn with splendid roof trusses and gallery. It's tempting to think this is an early 16th-century tithe barn – Chertsey Abbey once owned the estate – but it is probably nearer 1600 in date. It could generate a handsome income if used for weddings, concerts and events as, unusually for these parts, Brook Place has a 'C' class designation, allowing commercial use.

There is a pretty formal garden at the back with walks into the valley and a columned temple adding charm to the view.

BURLES LODGE — Farnham

Secret house built in defiance of the planners with salvaged materials

BURLES LODGE IS LIVING TESTIMONY to one man's war against the 20th century – not only the flat roofs and metal windows of Modernism but to planners and their meddling and controls. In 1937, in a secret valley south of Farnham in Surrey, the brilliant maverick architect Harold Falkner bought a patch of land hidden from view of surrounding roads and began two houses beside a chalk quarry. The upper one, Burles, is built from two Gloucestershire barns and an old granary. Burles Lodge, illustrated here, is a rustic English version of the delightful *pavillons de plaisir* built around Paris in the 18th century.

In photographs it can look no more than a single storey with dormer windows above but in fact it has an extensive bedroom storey and a full lower-basement floor tucked away behind – a perfect place for parties to continue late into the night without troubling neighbours.

Burles took Falkner thirty years to build and he had not finished it at his death. Fortunately, subsequent owners have loved it for its wayward qualities and its character remains almost pristine. If this is what some describe as pastiche then it is proof there can be very good pastiche as well as bad. Burles is really a piece of film-set building. More than that, it is glorious evidence of the forgotten but vital art of making remarkable, unusual things from the driftwood of architecture, from old bricks, fanlights, salvaged columns and panelling rescued from the builder's skip.

It is said that Falkner used gipsies as builders and that they would trick him by putting up a wall and taking it down overnight, charging him again and again for the same work. To me it speaks of his direct involvement in the detail with numerous ingenious and unusual flourishes.

Though it looks like a simple pavilion, the house has three full storeys.

Inside, the architect Harold Falkner mixed old and new elements to create handsome Palladian interiors.

The lovely weathered orangey-red bricks – infinitely precious to Falkner – are set in thick mortar to make them go further. When the front door proved too wide to open into the corridor, he simply scooped a curve out of the wall behind so it could swing back with less than an inch to spare. He planned his house in terms of vistas and there is always something to look at. To the right of the front door, tall fluted columns frame a view of the staircase rising from the end of the drawing room; to the left, a floral iron grille, almost Indian in its voluptuousness, is set over the door into the sitting room.

The grey-blue dining room is like a panelled room in an early 18th-century house in Spitalfields. The wood never seems to have been repainted so the grain shows through in places. In the ceiling is another piece of salvage, a painting, possibly an overdoor, here placed to look like a *tondo* floating above you. Another clever detail is the near-perfect colour match of the marble facings of the pretty mid 18th-century fireplace with the walls. The niches on either side contain pretty serpentine-shaped shelves.

The door leads out onto a terrace with a grand columned porch. Here Falkner neatly solves the problem of designing a door that is indistinguishable from the sash window on either side. The trick is that the sash frame swings out as well as the sash, giving the door added strength. This was originally intended to be the main entrance but Falkner never got around to building the steps up to it.

The bold white-painted porch has handsome Roman Doric columns curiously set forward to allow light in at the sides. The balustrade around the terrace is given an added flourish by a coping of specially moulded hump-back bricks.

Behind the house is a sheltered terraced garden with a shallow arch bridge crossing to a little island, and beyond a delightful folly which purports to be the surviving fragment of an ancient ruin. The lower part incorporates an Ionic column from the porch of a blitzed house in London, while the upper part is a gazebo in the garden of Burles, the house above.

The stair to the bedrooms has a pair of corkscrew banisters to each step with a charming bay-window seat on the half landing. It leads to an arched passage with roughened cave-like walls lit by a deep-set bullseye window. The bedrooms themselves have exposed wooden rafters, cottage style.

While the garden is small, it enjoys a ravishing view across the narrow valley to open woods formed of tall slender saplings interspersed by a cluster of small meadows ascending the hill, all on the same Lilliputian scale as the house.

The story of Harold Falkner's life and work has been told in a brilliantly researched book by Sam Osmond, *Harold Falkner: More than an Arts and Crafts Architect.* Falkner was responsible for more than 115 buildings in Farnham, removing Victorian buildings he thought out of scale and introducing new retro buildings so convincing that it is hard to tell if they are Queen Anne, Georgian or Tudor. Sir Nikolaus Pevsner, the champion of Modernism, even wrote an obituary acknowledging his 'eccentric genius'.

Burles is a house made for giving memorable parties. There is a barbecue in a tile-roofed garden pavilion that is open on three sides but complete with fireplace for blazing log fires in the evening. The present owners have put a hot tub rather incongruously on the little island in front, though it is clearly a supremely hedonistic way of relaxing on a summer evening. The deep-set vaulted basement is the ideal place to play loud music deep into the night without disturbing neighbours, while the current owner has adapted the garage as a music studio. It's all designed for an alternative lifestyle. Falkner would have approved.

CEDAR COTTAGE Chobham
Lutyens' cottage built to demonstrate the appeal of wooden houses

RARE IS THE OPPORTUNITY to buy a small house by a great architect. Yet the hand of Sir Edwin Lutyens, whom some believe to be the greatest British architect of the 20th century (or any century), is apparent everywhere in Cedar Cottage.

The house is set, like so many Surrey houses built in the early 20th century, along a winding leafy country road, secluded behind high hedges. It stands plum centre in half an acre of garden, with a small paddock beyond and a larger stretch of water meadow on the other side of the road running down to the sleepy River Bourne – filled with reeds and all of 6 ft wide.

The beauty of this Lilliputian domain, which is so peaceful and balmy that it might step from the pages of *The Wind in the Willows,* is that there is really only one other house, the immediate next-door neighbour, to be seen.

Lutyens designed many cottages as adjuncts to larger houses but this one was built for the timber merchant

The roof is made of 2-ft-long cedar shingles with unusual sideways sliding shutters.

C.B. Gabriel of the well-established firm of Gabriel Wade & English to demonstrate the appeal of wooden houses. The builders were W.H. Colt, of Bethersden near Ashford in Kent, founded in 1919 and still well-known suppliers of timber houses.

Gabriel's son Ralph, who lives nearby, says, 'My father owned a field here and decided to build a row of high class wooden houses. He got Lutyens to design the first but had great trouble in selling it so no more were built.' Whether this was because of an English hesitation over wooden houses, or the uncertainties caused by looming war, is not clear.

For previous owners, Nick and Louise Rowntree, there was no such worry – they came here from a 1796 wooden house in upstate New York and immediately felt at home. Cedar House is wood all the way – built, clad and roofed in wood, with wooden floors and panelling within. It is also wonderfully unaltered apart from a 1950s wing at the back, carefully matched in materials and proportions to the original cottage. Within, the extension provides what the original cottage lacked – a large and spacious master bedroom – with a lovely view over fields merging into trees. Below is a utility room and extra living room, currently a music room, but previously a garden room opening onto a veranda.

Mr Rowntree knew how to treat the cedar cladding every five to six years but was none too happy at the way the sawtooth gables had been picked out in gloss paint. 'It looked like Snow White's cottage,' he said, and he stained them to blend harmoniously with the rest of the cladding.

Some of the cedar shingles on the roof have a pronounced curl, but apparently there is a supply of spares in the garage. Each one is over 2-ft long and splinter shaped, thickening from a sharp point to an inch at the other end. An advertisement for Colt houses in *The Countryman* in July 1935 illustrates Cedar House and talks of 'incombustible red cedar tiling' that 'will last a hundred years without preservatives or paint', adding 'it weathers like oak or elm and gets more beautiful with age'.

Cedar houses, promised Colt, 'are permanently dry, safe from condensation', while British Columbian red cedar (Empire red cedar it was then) ensured 'guaranteed immunity from dry-rot'. Timber houses, it added, had stood the test of time in Sussex, Scandinavia and Switzerland, wherever climate called for snug housing. Better still, they were fifteen to twenty-five per cent cheaper than any other.

Lutyens's windows are unusual – horizontal sashes that slide sideways on rails, a form that figured briefly in the late 17th century before the characteristic vertical sashes took over. Even the original metal catches survive. Outside the windows have been painted at a later date but inside the handsome joinery remains untouched and in perfect condition.

The recessed entrance porch shelters an outdoor wooden letter box. The front opens into a central hall with the pièce de résistance, a very handsome Chinese Chippendale stair, with criss-cross balustrade that continues around the landing upstairs.

The hall and adjoining rooms are faced in broad, beautifully smooth vertical cedar boards. The internal dividing walls are thin – in the manner of simple 18th-century artisans' cottages – but the bold, alternating convex and concave mouldings are altogether grander.

Though the house was built in 1935, it is very much in the Arts and Crafts tradition with rooms centred on the hearth. The fireplaces have charming hoods formed of bookshelves. The dining room retains the bell for the maid as well as a hatch through to the kitchen.

The house now has central heating as well as an Aga, and not only warms up quickly but retains the heat. The upstairs bedrooms are under the eaves in the best Surrey style with extra cupboard space under the lower slope of the roof. Cupboards and doors retain large hinges that speak of the blacksmith's forge. Even the wooden latches are original and appropriately well-worn.

Lutyens also designed the free-standing garage that matches the house and would make a handsome studio or workspace.

There's even a miniature Lutyens water feature – a rectangular pool set in sunken paving, which in turn fills to the brim when it rains, doubling the size of the pool, but not encroaching on the surrounding rose beds.

One reason that there has been no recent building nearby is that the meadows opposite are part of the Thames Valley flood plain. Cedar House happily is just 3 ft above the road and has never suffered from flooding.

Lutyens apart, the real virtue of this house is that it is in as perfect a stretch of green belt as could be wished. Both the M25 and the M3 are just minutes away but on the still and sunny day I arrived there was no drone of traffic at all.

The only drawbacks are that, come rush hour, there is a surge of traffic on the road past the house, and there is occasional noise from private planes taking off from nearby Fairoaks airfield. These are mainly little tiddlers, but can make an intrusive buzz as they fly across the meadows opposite. That said, this is still an idyllic spot.

Lutyen's wrap-around corner windows anticipated the modern houses of the 1930s.

CHILWORTH MANOR   Chilworth

Hidden in a secret valley just 30 miles from Hyde Park Corner

CHILWORTH MANOR IS THE FILM LOCATION expert's dream, a secret Elysium set in ravishing gardens just 30 miles from Hyde Park Corner, in a Surrey valley secluded by encircling hills. Nearly two centuries ago, William Cobbett in his *Rural Rides* described the valley as a Garden of Eden, 'one of the choicest retreats of man ... formed for a scene of innocence and happiness' but desecrated by nothing less than the devil's own 'grand manufactory', a gunpowder mill powered by the River Tillingbourne.

Today Chilworth has the impression of a place where the clock stopped ticking when it was bought by Sir Lionel and Lady Heald in 1945 after their house in Regent's Park was bombed. Not many people were looking for large houses at the time, but Sir Lionel, MP for Chertsey, was a brilliantly successful lawyer, later serving as Churchill's Attorney General, while Lady Heald, long-time chairman of the National Gardens Scheme, had ambitions to create a beautiful garden to her own design. Wrapped up in London life, they came only at weekends, leaving their children to a *Swallows and Amazons* existence.

To this day the house remains as Lady Heald first decorated it – all white paint and Regency stripes in the manner of Syrie Maugham. But with it comes more than a thousand years of history. According to Domesday, Chilworth was held by one Alwin during the reign of Edward the Confessor then, after the Conquest, by Odo, Bishop of Bayeux, William the Conqueror's half-brother. There was a monastery here in the Middle Ages but by 1580 the manor had passed by inheritance to William Morgan, whose son John was knighted when Drake 'singed the King of Spain's beard' at Cadiz in 1596. Through his daughter Anne the house passed to the Randylls, who took over the powder mills during the Commonwealth.

The house has grown over three centuries, each wing of distinctive design, materials and proportions.

At this time Vincent Randyll probably built the entrance range in dark plum brick in the style known as 'Artisan Mannerist', with a prominent, shaped Dutch gable. The front door is framed by both stone and brick pillars, an awkward but charming detail typical of the way Classical motifs were interpreted by bricklayers and masons.

Morgan Randyll, ruined by his largesse to the electorate of Guildford, was forced to sell the house to a Richard Houlditch, wool-draper. His tenure was short as he was a director of the South Sea Company at the time of its collapse in 1721. He sold the estate for £30,000 to Sarah, the hot-tempered 1st Duchess of Marlborough. She is best known for brutally berating the great Sir John Vanbrugh, architect of Blenheim Palace, and denying him even a glimpse of his great masterpiece, for what she considered his baroque excesses. Yet – what a hypocrite – here she appears to have built a grand and splendid baroque walled garden with banded Vanbrughian gate piers and a corner pillar as tall as a mill chimney. It is tempting to think her architect was Henry Joynes, the Comptroller of the Works at Blenheim who was employed at Carshalton House in Surrey.

But whether designed for the Duchess, for Houlditch or for the Randylls, the walled garden is a remarkable survival with three stepped terraces within, not simply a kitchen garden but designed for a magnificent display of flowers and potted shrubs, as Lady Heald immediately recognised.

The 'Marlborough' wing at the back of the house is also attributed to Sarah. To the north, where it overlooks the garden, it has Ionic pilasters arranged in curious groups of three and rendered over at a later date. The neighbouring front to the west, in warm pink brick, looks later with broad Regency-style three-part windows. A delightful detail is the 'penny-struck' pointing – mortar joints that look as if a penny has been dragged along them to give them extra crispness. Intriguingly this takes up from the 'galletting' in the side of the Cromwellian wing – mortar inset with runs of tiny pebbles.

On her death in 1744 the Duchess left the house to her grandson, the 2nd Earl Spencer, but he so overspent on Althorp that he was forced to sell Chilworth to the Tinklers, the very gunpowder makers Cobbett railed against. They sold it to Henry Drummond who lived at nearby Albury, later one of the many seats of the Dukes of Northumberland.

In the 1930s the Dukes sold Chilworth to Alfred Mildmay who remodelled the house stylishly, creating a grand gallery-corridor linking the Randyll and Marlborough wings and rebuilding the centre of the house around a courtyard opening onto the lawn.

Lady Heald's great contribution is to the gardens below the house, laid out around the remains of medieval fish ponds and planted with the choicest specimens of her favourite shrubs and ornamental trees. There are glorious view west over parkland and, behind the house, to the grand sweep of St Martha's Hill, crowned with trees. With the property comes a well-preserved Second World War pillbox isolated in a field.

While the setting is perfection, the rambling layout of the house is a challenge, requiring you to retrace your steps as you explore one sitting room after another, ending in Sir Lionel's attractive library looking into the walled garden. Upstairs the bedrooms have ravishing views over the grounds.

The back of the house, including the extensive kitchen quarters, looks like a small village, with a mix of brick, stone and tile-hanging. Latterly Lady Heald peopled these nether realms with law students from Guildford College.

FULVENS
Shere
Farmhouse of Cromwellian date, sensitively restored in the 1920s

FULVENS HOUSE STANDS ON an idyllic site in the Surrey Hills, beside the road going south out of the village of Abinger Hammer. Until 1918 a farm of 130 acres, it is one of a group Artisan Mannerist houses, which have interesting Classical details but appear to be the work of master bricklayers rather than architects.

Dated to the middle of the 17th century, the beauty of the house lies in its almost flawless pink brickwork, a textbook example of Flemish bond. The two-storey porch could be a later addition, but the brickwork matches and narrow central porches are a frequent feature of this date, a leftover from the Elizabethan E-plan. All the windows have distinctive splayed brick heads that fan out to the side. The archway to the porch has a hood mould of round bricks – worn but never restored. Above is a triangular pediment made with more shaped bricks, embellished with dentils formed of bricks the size of a matchbox. An extra flourish is provided by an S-shaped iron tie over an upstairs window. The windows retain leaded panes in the original stout wooden mullions. The venerable front door is formed of broad planks with blacksmith's hinges and bolts and a splendid wooden lock box more than a foot long.

Inside the fashionable brick walls the builders reverted to timber-frame construction, and the preservation of the interior seems to be thanks to a respectful repair apparently carried out by the Edwardian architect Basil Procter, working in the 1920s for the county cricketer Alexander Webbe. It must have been Procter who exposed the timbers in virtually every room. They form big 3-ft squares, presumably infilled with lath and plaster, or possibly brick, behind the plaster.

There is a very pretty tile-hung barn to the south, given style by a large oriel window in the tall barn door, with mullions echoing those of Fulvens.

The decorative details of the porch are executed in moulded brick.

GODDARDS   Abinger Common
Superb example of Lutyens working in traditional Surrey vernacular style

SHOULD A BUILDING SPEAK of its time or its place? Today's fashion is for every building, addition and alteration to be in a contemporary, contrasting, even clashing mode, recoiling in horror from anything that might be labelled fake, copy or pastiche. At Goddards, Lutyens was in the mood for designing traditional country buildings. His generation discovered the vernacular in the same way as Italian Renaissance architects turned their eyes to the ruins of Ancient Rome, finding a whole new vocabulary of forms and details. Traditional Surrey houses nestled beneath steep roofs and tall chimneys – at Goddards, Lutyens offers a picturesque composition of gables, dormers and square chimneys set diamond-wise on the stacks.

Intriguingly it was not conceived as a family home, but built between 1898 and 1900 as a Home of Rest where ladies of small means might repair to for a holiday. This involved a common room with bedrooms above and in the wings. Here, in 1901, Lutyens played a game of skittles with three nurses and two governesses who were staying there.

Lutyens's client was Sir Frederick Mirrielees, an Aberdonian who had resided in Russia and Persia, settling in Dorking to become the head of Currie & Co, merchant bankers. After being used for invalid soldiers during the Boer War it was adapted as a house for Mrs D. Mirrielees, with a new wing. The house was generously given to the newly formed Lutyens Trust in 1991 by Mr and Mrs M.W. Hall, who had owned Goddards since 1953. The Lutyens Trust have leased Goddards to the Landmark Trust and it now sleeps up to twelve people who have the enjoyment of the large Jekyll garden. The Lutyens Trust retains the use of the library.

Goddards is highly picturesque, yet symmetrical in nearly every detail.

GREEN LANE FARM   Shamley Green

Traditional Surrey farmhouse seamlessly extended during the last twenty-five years

AT FIRST SIGHT GREEN LANE FARM looks like a typical 17th-century Surrey farm house built on a shallow H-plan with a hall in the centre and 'high' and 'low' ends containing solar and kitchens. The timber frame has weathered to silver and the infill panels are of pretty soft-pink brick. As you look at the main front, there is a large chimney stack at the right end of the house where the solar would be and the entrance porch is towards the low end of the hall. A plaque over the porch with a date of 1661 confirms the impression of a house mainly of one build.

Yet all is not what it seems, for Green Lane Farm is substantially a creation of the last quarter century. It was bought by Heather Martin Dye who built up a flourishing livery business in the stables behind the house. With her second husband and the builder Adam Clements, she set about enlarging the house in a seamless manner using salvaged materials. She explained, 'Adam was our guide on every bit of building work. He did it with his father and two labourers. He had done his own house with such integrity that we snapped him up.' Tiles came from a terrace of cottages being demolished in Southampton. Cleverly, the bricks in the panels are not laid in level courses but dip as if the building settled centuries ago.

In populous Surrey, part of the appeal of Green Lane Farm is that it stands at the end of a very long lane in complete seclusion. There is a large barn with fine timbers inside on the forecourt to the left of the house and behind lies a granary and other traditional outbuildings. This is a little paradise for horses as well as people.

The silvered timbers with brick infill are actually more modern than they appear.

GREYFRIARS — Wanborough
Voysey masterpiece built in 1896 for the novelist Julian Sturgis

WITH 47 ACRES AND A GLORIOUS VIEW all the way to the South Downs, this major house designed in 1896 by the great Arts and Crafts architect Charles Voysey is one of the best in the Home Counties. There is just one drawback, the roar of the traffic along the Hog's Back above the house and, to make it worse, the traffic on the A3 across the valley to the south, though this is all but invisible amid the magnificent panorama of trees and woods and hills.

Voysey is a household name, internationally acclaimed when he was still in his thirties for the finest of new English domestic architecture – houses built of natural materials set harmoniously in the landscape, comfortable within and full of exquisitely crafted detail. The delicious paradox of Voysey is that he abandoned historical styles yet, in his own words, made 'no claim to anything new', seeking inspiration in the simple tradition of country building.

Greyfriars, first known as Merlshanger and then as Wancote, is a house on an impressive scale, a full 156 ft long, low and narrow, that brings to mind the words of Bossiney, the young architect in Galsworthy's *Forsyte Saga*, 'Hang the cost … look at the view.'

Ducking out of the fast traffic on the A31, you dive through an arched Voyseyesque gatehouse and then turn along a level stately drive lined with magnificent beeches. The house is approached end on, not frankly its best aspect and not improved by a rather ungainly squash court. Voysey's distinctive gables and overhanging roofs only come fully into view as you park in the spacious forecourt to the north.

Voysey's characteristic steep slate roofs sit above long bands of mullioned windows.

Generations of art history students know Greyfriars from Voysey's own glorious watercolour perspective of the south front, showing white harled walls and glowing golden Bath stone. Curiously, for an architect renowned for his honest building, the stone is actually pale grey, though the wonderful green slates are as Voysey depicted, carefully graded so they grow progressively smaller towards the top.

The great features of Voysey's splendid south front were the long bands of mullioned windows and the powerful gable at the west end. Alas for Voysey, along came Sir Herbert Baker, a fine architect with zero sensibility for anyone else's work, who pushed out an extension, rudely interrupting the long downward sweep of Voysey's roof.

Inside, Baker also had no hesitation in 'improving' on Voysey by introducing a conventional stair with turned balusters and transforming the living room, behind Voysey's great double-height bay window, in baroque style with a coved ceiling and matching Georgian fireplaces set in expanses of stone wall at either end.

It's imposing but the real sense of excitement begins as you walk around the house and more and more Voysey detail appears, continuing all the way into the attics.

Service quarters in Victorian houses tend to be pushed out of sight; here they are a continuation of the main range with good views and well-proportioned rooms. Nor was there a very strict division on either side of the proverbial green baize door. The Snooker Room (which Voysey's plans show as a kitchen) lies beyond it, while the telephone cabin is in the back yard beside the coal cellar and meat larder. All these doors have ventilation holes in the form of characteristic Voysey hearts.

The house was built to take advantage of the glorious view from the Hog's Back.

The drive and paths were straight, in contrast with the picturesque compostion of the house.

Indeed, throughout the house there is the charming but slightly cloying feeling of living in a Valentine card. Hearts are everywhere – engraved on the door hinges and door latches, with the front-door letter box set in the largest heart of all. The local blacksmith must have been inundated with work – there are huge pairs of heart-ended black iron hinges on many doors. Upstairs, delicate heart-shaped keys survive in heart-shaped lock plates.

The present owners, who arrived twenty years ago, chose pale ivory and white interiors in keeping with the simplicity of Voysey. For a Voysey lover there is potentially enormous amounts of fun to be had in researching original decorative schemes – for the house was illustrated in numerous magazines, both in Britain and abroad. Voysey produced no less than twenty sheets of plans and drawings for the house.

As well as the natural wood doors, the great features are the iron windows, robustly designed and largely untouched with their latches, pop-up flaps, and ingenious arms with an S-curl at the end and a double 'eye' that allows them to be fixed firmly in both the open and the closed position.

Other Voysey details to be relished include the numerous internal windows along corridors that provide borrowed light and the characteristic flat ledges over the doors. There is a typical Voysey stair rail that goes from the columned first-floor landing to the attic with close-set wooden banisters and a typical oversailing flat top to the end post. In the attics there is a series of diminutive fireplaces with coal grates that are barely 12 inches wide, but capable of providing a warm glow in the evening on a meagre coal ration.

Voysey's client was the widely travelled novelist Julian Sturgis, who had earlier lived in a Voysey house in Hans Road in Knightsbridge. Sturgis wrote the lyrics for Arthur Sulivan's *Ivanhoe.*

Though pictures of Greyfriars are regularly accessed around the world on the internet, curiously the house is not even listed, an omission that presumably cannot last for long. The gardens were terraced by Baker and the most attractive walks are to be had by descending one hundred steps to the valley below, where a gamekeeper's cottage stands picturesquely crushed by a fallen tree, and long disused stables are waiting to be restored while looking out over the fields.

Period reconstruction is not exactly fashionable at the moment, but if this was America, a Voysey enthusiast would buy Greyfriars and spend a decade or more researching, redecorating and refurnishing it (and having a great deal of fun in the process), finally leaving the house to a grateful nation.

HOLMDALE
Holmbury St Mary
The architect G.E. Street, 'the most Gothic of all Goths', built this for himself in 1876

An essay in Old English style, there is stone, half-timbering and a host of soaring brick chimneys.

LIKE ARTISTS' SELF-PORTRAITS, the houses that architects design for themselves can be intensely revealing. Holmdale in Surrey was built by G.E. Street, architect of the gloriously spiky Royal Courts of Justice in the Strand. When Street died, burial in the local churchyard was not enough, even though he had designed the impressively stately parish church nearby. Lord Leighton, President of the Royal Academy, secured a funeral in Westminster Abbey, where Street is buried beside two other giants of Victorian architecture, Sir George Gilbert Scott and Sir Charles Barry.

His fellow architect, Sir Arthur Blomfield, wrote that Street was 'universally acknowledged to be the first architect of his day', and his obituary in *The Architect* described him as 'the perfect embodiment of the romanticism militant of his generation. In a Gothic Age he was wholly Gothic, the most Gothic of all Goths.'

As might be expected, Street's country house is no modest affair but embellished with so many soaring chimneys and gables that, at first distant glance atop its hill, it looks like a rural version of Wolsey's Hampton Court.

For Street's first wife, Maraquita, Holmdale's glorious position had been love at first sight. In 1872 they were on their way to visit the landscape painter H.T. Wells. As the breathtaking panorama of the Sussex Weald came into view, she exclaimed: 'It is heaven's gate.' To their delight they found the land was on the market.

Street began by employing gangs of men to create smooth sweeping contours and a carriageway from the other end of the estate. The next year he wrote: 'I have made a charming arrangement of terraced gardens and lawns in a deep dip between two steep hills, on top of which my chateau is some day to rise.'

It was not long in coming. By the summer of 1876 building work was finished and two years later Street gave a bibulous midsummer party for his fellow academicians.

Holmdale is not High Victorian Gothic triumphalism but rather an essay in the Old English style pioneered by Street's pupil, Richard Norman Shaw. The composition is centred on a tall Norman-looking stone staircase tower with a glorious view from the battlements over red clay-tiled roofs and octagonal brick chimneys. Street mixed stone with half-timbering and tile-hung gables on the entrance and long garden fronts overlooking the valley. Pattern and colour are important elements, with warm, red brick 'nogging', or infilling, between the black timbers, laid in varying patterns.

The large medieval-looking front door opens into a vestibule with a glazed screen and swing doors leading into a grand double-height staircase hall panelled in oak, with a rich pierced balustrade to the stair and gallery. Beyond, the large L-shaped drawing room is divided into two by a shallow archway with grand fireplaces in both halves of the room and a traceried door opening into the garden through a bay window. The panelled ceiling is inset with prettily interlacing ribs with the floral detail picked out in gold leaf. Holmdale's most stunning feature (which continues all through the house) are the leaded windows glazed in constantly varying diamond, octagonal and circular patterns.

The west wing with library and games room was completed only after Street's death to a subtly adapted design by Sir Aston Webb, architect of Admiralty Arch. His work is in a playful mix of Tudor and Art Nouveau with the date of AD 1900 over the fireplace in the library.

Street died in 1881 after suffering a stroke on the three-mile walk home from Gomshall station. His son Arthur first let the house to the munitions manufacturer Lord Rendel (who moved on to nearby Hatchlands Park) and then sold to the diamond millionaire Henry Barlow Webb. It was he who employed Aston Webb (no relation), who also designed the shallow-domed pavilions at either end of the garden terrace.

The third self-made man to occupy Holmdale was Lord Catto, who in 1944 became Governor of the Bank of England. The son of a shipwright, he was made a baronet for his work in supplying food and munitions in the First World War. After the death of his widow the house was bought in 1999 by John Witney, an entrepreneur in his own right, and his wife, Sue.

At this point most houses of this size and date would have been bought by a developer to be divided into apartments. The Witneys have kept it all as a single residence. He explains: 'We employed W.S. Atkins to renovate the house to a standard that would ensure it will last another 130 years.' Interior decoration was carried out by White House Interiors. The views from the first-floor windows are sensational; Street's specimen trees are now mature, and beyond the vista stretches to the distant South Downs.

Street's handsome half-timbered coach house remains, now an office and flat with the original loose boxes. He and his wife would be pleased by how well 'heaven's gate' has survived. The mansions around were owned by heads of Castle Shipping, Brooke Bond Tea, Guinness, Stephen's Inks, Doulton's Lambeth and Wedgwood Potteries, and Edwin Waterhouse, founder of Price Waterhouse. Glorious Joldwynds, designed by Philip Webb, has gone, Hopedene by Norman Shaw and Moxley by Basil Champneys remain.

The library was completed after Street's death to a subtly adapted design by Aston Webb.

HOMEWOOD Esher
Modern Movement house designed by Patrick Gwynne for his parents

WHEN I FIRST VISITED HOMEWOOD in 1991 it was still lived in by the architect Patrick Gwynne, who had designed it when he was aged only twenty-four. He built it for his parents in International Modern Style.

Mr Gwynne wanted to leave the house to the National Trust. The question was whether it was considered a fine enough example of Modernism to be accepted. Much of the appeal of the property came from its 6 acres of woodland gardens. 'It is very much the modernist idea of taking an existing wood, thinning it out and creating vistas,' said the Trust's Edward Diestelkamp.

Patrick Gwynne had been working with the pioneer modernists Wells Coates and the design of Homewood was also clearly influenced by Le Corbusier's Villa Savoie near Paris. Huge 11-ft-wide panoramic windows wound down to create the feeling of an outdoor room.

Gwynne explained, 'The Victorian house we lived in had so many rooms you never knew which one to be in – drawing room, morning room or hall. So I made one big room. In the late 1930s everyone was crazy about dancing. The radiogram had just been invented and cheek to cheek was the rage. I gave the whole room a sprung maple floor like a squash court.'

The 11-ft-wide panoramic windows look out over the Surrey woodland.

The circular stair has a streamlined chrome handrail.

Following Le Corbusier's exhortation, the house was designed on a grid, here of 4-ft squares. 'Eight foot is a reasonable width for a single room and twelve foot for a double,' he continued.

The dining room was divided from the main living room by a marble wall, inspired by Mies van der Rohe's famous Barcelona pavilion. The circular dining table he designed had a concealed panel under the edge allowing him to change the colour of the light in the centre.

Flowers could also be set in a sunken vase so they did not block guests talking to each other across the table. The bedrooms retained many original fittings. 'A lot of washing was done in bedrooms those days, a hangover from the time when maids brought hot water up to every room.'

Windows glided open and shut at the turn of a handle. 'I introduced this device to cope with the problem of Venetian blinds. It is very hard to get at windows at night when the blinds are down,' explained Gwynne. The house was originally designed without central heating. 'In those days 65 degrees F was considered the optimum temperature and we just used electric heaters as electricity was very cheap then.'

Though Mr Gwynne's offer of Homewood and six valuable acres was a generous one, the problem for the National Trust was that it would come without an endowment. Martin Drury, then the Trust's Deputy Director, had the idea that it should be let to a tenant. Following Mr Gwynne's death in 1999, this happy arrangement has been put into place and you can now simpy telephone the tenant to make an appointment for a visit.

HORSLEY TOWERS East Horsley

Exotic creation of the Earl of Lovelace who married Byron's daughter

HORSLEY TOWERS INDULGES the English love of eccentricity on a grand scale. The village of East Horsley is dotted with delightful quirky buildings erected by the owners of Horsley Towers. What is even more remarkable is that the house has found a use that ensures it flourishes throughout the year and generates the healthy income needed to keep such an extraordinary place in good repair.

The architect Sir Charles Barry built a Tudor Gothic house here for William Currie in 1834 – the very moment when the Palace of Westminster was destroyed by fire and Barry went on to win the competition for rebuilding the Houses of Parliament in Tudor Gothic style.

The exuberant exotic appearance of Horsley today is principally due to the 1st Earl of Lovelace, scientist and Fellow of the Royal Society, who married Byron's only legitimate daughter, Ada. Her mother had left Byron one month after Ada was born and Byron signed a deed of separation three months later, leaving England for ever and never seeing either again.

Ada was a genius in her own right and is credited with devising the world's first computer programme some seven years after she married the future Earl of Lovelace. Tragically she died at the age of 36, bled to death like her father by her doctors.

Horsley was greatly extended by the Earl in a picturesque combination of flint and polychrome brick. A rocket-shaped tower is built out into a large lake, there are curving courtyards, Albanian cloisters and hammer-beam roofs. Today Horsley is run by Devere Hotels as a conference venue aimed at management training with 170 bedrooms, complete with four-poster beds, set in 70 acres of parkland, and available for weddings. The whole vast mansion is in intensive use and there is plenty more to explore in the grounds, including lodges and bridges.

The tower, as tall as a campanile, has an external stair turret.

HUF HAUS   Weybridge
Stylish and spacious prefabricated house from Germany

A NEW VISION OF MODERN LIVING is offered by the Huf Haus, winner of the National HomeBuilder Design Awards in 2000. Huge panels of glass bring the garden indoors and allow light to flood into the house throughout the day. Most importantly, it was affordable, with smaller houses in 2000 starting at £180,000 (you provide the site), and a guaranteed fixed price.

For much of the 20th century, modern houses were built wigh spelt flat roofs that sooner or later started to leak. Here pitched roofs not only provide traditional weather protection but valuable extra height, giving even small bedrooms and bathrooms a sense of spaciousness. The post-and-beam construction with bold overhangs and balconies also give the house something of the elegance of Japanese temple architecture.

The Huf Haus is the product of a well-established family company that has built 6,000 houses in Germany. Now, Peter Huf, the architect member of the family, is living in one of the firm's houses in St George's Hill, Weybridge, Surrey, in the hope of bringing the business to Britain.

He explains, 'Our company is 85 years old. My grandfather started as a carpenter in Westerwald near Frankfurt where the company still has its base. In Germany a carpenter starts by constructing roofs before building complete houses. The big break came when my father was invited to build the German Pavilion at the Brussels World Expo of 1958.'

Prefabrication greatly shortens and simplifies the construction process on site. A Huf Haus is built on a concrete foundation slab or over a basement enclosed in precast concrete slabs,mwhich serves for a plant room and utility room.

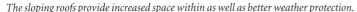

The sloping roofs provide increased space within as well as better weather protection.

The double garage has overhanging roofs to match the house.

'The house comes on a truck from Germany. The walls go up the first day, the roof is on within a week. After that the heavy construction is over – a great benefit for neighbours too. Landscaping around the house can continue at the same time as fitting out inside,' continues Huf. Completion is in just ten weeks. 'That's with wiring, painting, plumbing, bathrooms and kitchen,' he says.

He continues, 'People don't like unreliable builders. We bring our own team from Germany.' And because they all stay in a nearby hotel ('comfortably, for they will be working very hard'), there's an added incentive for the company to finish on time.

He continues, 'The timber we use is Scandinavian spruce. The big difference is that it is all laminated [multi-layered]. This way we avoid felling old trees, using first generation timber. There is also no waste on site while waste in the factory can be recycled.'

The timber is stained to create a smart palette of black and white. It can also be painted brown, white or grey, though Huf is less happy about brighter colours. 'Black or white allow you complete freedom in introducing colourful furniture and furnishings,' he says.

He is insistent that his magnificent double-glazed windows are durable. 'They come with a ten year warranty and if you want to check, I'll happily give you 6,000 phone numbers of Huf clients. A family company like ours is dependent on its name and we cannot afford unsatisfied customers.'

One happy customer is William Dalrymple, whose Huf Haus 25 miles south of Glasgow was completed in October 1998. 'Watching it go up was like poetry in motion. You can specify what you want at the factory. They make it very easy for you. Usually building a house is a horror story but I'd go back to these people tomorrow.'

With any house in the country, you want to throw open the windows and hear the sounds of nature on a warm day – this is done with precision-manufactured sliding glass panels that perfectly match the windows.

As the houses are designed for the longer, harder winters in Germany, they are well-insulated and energy-efficient. 'Atmospheric comfort is very important – you need to feel warm in winter and cool in summer,' he says. In smaller rooms vertical radiators are neatly placed behind doors (where they waste no space) and good insulation ensures that they never need be scalding to the touch. In summer, 'clerestory' windows in every room can be left open when you are out to allow a breeze through the house.

But will it feel like a goldfish bowl? 'I guarantee that after four days you will like it so much you will never think about it again,' says Huf with a disarming smile. He also points out that the houses are more transparent looking out than looking in.

But what about burglars – can't they just look through the windows and see your prize possessions on display inside? 'Thieves do not like houses where anyone who approaches is in full view,' he says. And with so many kinds of garden light available today, it is possible to illuminate the garden (without resort to crude floodlighting) so that you can see outside in the evening.

Privacy (and shade) can also be provided by external Venetian blinds. These are motorised and descend on rails. As they are made of quite stiff aluminium they provide an extra degree of security if you are away. Lighter internal Venetian blinds fit neatly into glazed gables to ensure you don't wake up too early in summer. And solid wall panels can be substituted for glass at any point.

Ceilings consist of a timber panel 7 cm thick, with 9 cm of insulation above and a 6 cm concrete screed laid directly on top. 'You wouldn't expect to hear a rattle in a Mercedes. When your kids are running around and dancing upstairs you won't hear a thing,' says Huf, though he concedes that wooden floors are not advisable upstairs.

Huf is an architect and draws up plans to suit individual needs. 'First I visit the site, assess the sun, the view, the wind. The best orientation is usually south-west,' he says. Then he does freehand sketches, meeting the clients as many times as necessary until they are happy with the plans. At a certain moment all clients are taken to Germany to see the seven show houses beside the factory.

With a strong pound, a Huf Haus can be exceptionally good value. Prices exclude land, of course, but a four bedroom house of 2,400 sq ft could be had for £210,000. The large house illustrated here was 4,900 sq ft and cost, said Huf, £490,000 including kitchen and bathrooms.

The Huf brochure has simple diagrams showing how the basic unit can be expanded to a house of five times the size. This means extensions are also easily done – you simply take out a prefabricated wall panel or window and bolt them on.

The houses are available in three modules – 2.30 m, 2.50 m and 3.00 m. The house in St George's Hill is built on the 2.50 module and provides spaces of very elegant proportions.

A garden loggia is cleverly created opposite the kitchen simply by extending the garage roof at the back – suitable for children to play outdoors even during a shower and for eating out in summer.

Huf is convinced that an abundance of daylight is life-enhancing. 'I have been hearing of doctors diagnosing SAD syndrome, resulting from a deficiency of light.' That's one thing you should never have in a Huf Haus.

MILFORD HOUSE   Milford
Queen Anne house that was gutted by fire

THIS SPLENDID EARLY-GEORGIAN HOUSE stands proudly displayed to the road through the village of Milford near Godalming. I wrote about it as a 'Heap of the Week' in *The Times* in May 1992. The house had been a matter of grave concern since a fire in 1983 left it a gutted shell and the owners collected the insurance money and sold it in a derelict state. At the time of the fire, Milford was an hotel and restaurant and in 1992 Merivale Moore had just obtained planning permission to convert the house into offices and add an extra 29,000 sq ft at the back to pay for restoration. An earlier application to delist the house, opening the way to demolition, had been successfully resisted. Finally Milford was converted instead into apartments, ensuring its architecture is appreciated to the full by people who live in the building rather than work there. Highly sought after, they rarely come up for sale, and do not remain on the market for very long.

The newly cleaned pink brick is very pretty and, facing west, the house enjoys the sun for much of the day. Milford was built for a prosperous merchant, Thomas Smith, who evidently wanted to show off his success. Though it looks like a Queen Anne house, it is in fact early-Georgian, built in 1730. The entrance front is a fine marriage of Palladian and baroque styles. From Palladio comes the 1-3-1 arrangement of windows and the central pediment. Baroque features are the stone quoins emphasising the corners and the attic with level parapet largely concealing the steep hipped roof. There are emphatic keystones to the windows and a boldly modelled front-doorcase.

The windows are given an added flourish by the rubbed brick 'aprons' below.

MUNSTEAD GRANGE · Godalming

Lutyens-like house designed by Edward Mountford, architect of the Old Bailey

THE YEARS AROUND 1900 WERE a golden age in English domestic architecture and though houses by Lutyens and Voysey are well-known, there are hundreds of other delightful and intriguing architect-designed houses lost among thick rhododendrons and lush Surrey woodland that only ever come to notice – briefly – when placed on the market.

The hunt to identify these houses is now led by a splendid group, 'The Arts and Crafts Movement in Surrey', and of course there is no better place to start than Munstead near Godalming, where the famous Gertrude Jekyll laid out her famous garden at Munstead Wood and Lutyens designed her house. Another accomplished Edwardian architect who worked here was Edward Mountford, the designer of the Old Bailey with its handsome dome paying homage to Wren's St Paul's.

Mountford was not only the architect of portentous Classical public buildings – another is the lively 'Wrenaissance' Battersea Polytechnic in Battersea Park Road. He was also working in Arts and Crafts style, designing the enchanting cottage-style library on Lavender Hill, Battersea with gables, bay windows and stained glass.

Mountford's three Munstead houses included a house for himself, Munstead Grange, which was proudly illustrated in *The Architect* on September 1, 1905, with characteristic sweeping tiled roofs and tall chimneys. Mountford worked out every detail of the house with his wife, who tragically died in 1901, but he remarried and lived here until he himself died in 1908, while some of his best work was being built.

Here, there is firm evidence that Gertrude Jekyll made designs for the gardens as her drawings dated 1902 are among the collection of her papers at Berkeley University

The half-timbered gables project picturesquely over the bay windows.

The large spacious rooms have low ceilings for warmth and cosiness.

in California. Happily there are also copies of these available in the admirable Godalming Museum.

A second set of Jekyll drawings, dated 1910, are those that were presumably done for the new owner of the house, the magnificently named Sir Edward Farquhar Buzzard, Bt, physician to both George V and George VI.

Munstead Grange stands off a quiet country lane east of Godalming, secluded from the world in thickly planted grounds – so much so that one's first thought is to make cuts to open up the undoubtedly beautiful views across surrounding hills; but this may not be easy, for crucial trees stand just outside the perimeter and hereabouts are likely to be closely protected.

Munstead Grange is in Mountford's Arts and Crafts manner with overhanging gables and parchment-coloured render trowelled over in great swirls, creating an effect akin to palm fronds. The front door opens into an arch-roofed entrance vestibule with delightful plasterwork on the ceiling – tall-stemmed graceful Pre-Raphaelite flowers and an explosion of wild life – butterflies, dragonflies, lizards and snails. The brass doorplates have tall door handles in the form of stylised tulips.

Beyond is a large hall, or 'hall-parlour' to use the Edwardian expression, overlooking the garden. The fashion in 1900 was for the hall to be the focus of life. A bottle of sherry placed on a table by the present owners makes this very point. Hermann Muthesius the German author of the classic book *The English House* (1905), wrote that halls were 'one of the most attractive assets of the English house … the comfortable all-purpose room in which each member of the family can follow their favourite pursuit and spend time as they like.' To create a sense of cosiness, halls, he said, were often panelled, as here, in wood. They were usually equipped with a fireplace and carpeted – though all-over carpeting was to be avoided because of wet clothes from outside. Deep-piled warm rugs were preferred, especially in front of the fire.

The original bell panel still in the kitchen names the reception rooms around – drawing room, dining room and billiard room. A Voyseyesque caged stair leads up to a long, well-lit corridor. The whole house has recently been renovated to a very high standard. Original fireplaces remain in most rooms as well as oak doors, while the sturdy lead windows are in excellent working order, with protective child bars added in upstairs rooms.

The hall opens into the garden through an open-roofed porch held up on stout oak columns – one dramatically entwined by a wisteria of serpentile strength and proportions. At this point the planting is so lush that not a stretch of lawn is to be seen, but as you explore the grounds a series of garden rooms unfolds, one containing a well-gated swimming pool.

For a dedicated garden lover intent on following Jekyll's designs there is abundant material waiting to help you in your research, including not only plans but lists of plants and shrubs. Jekyll wrote, 'the big west bank wants Permattya and other green shrubs, tree ivy, Skimmia, fifty Gaultheria, Rhodo Myrtifolium.'

The original sizeable property was divided into four freeholds in 1968 when the house itself was divided into two. But two years ago the present owners were able to buy both parts of the house and reunite them.

The one drawback to the house at present is that the approach to the former coach house, the Lodge, goes right past the front door of Mountford's house. As a result the entrance that is usually used is now the side porch, added when the house was divided. This has the added advantage that there is ample space for parking beside it. Mountford's low-walled front garden remains attractively planted and, with an outlook over a lawn, has been cleverly contrived to look like the beginning of yet further well-planted grounds.

NORTH BREACHE MANOR — Ewhurst
Early work of Sir Aston Webb dating from 1881

AS A BOY PETER NUTTING, THE FORMER OWNER of North Breache Manor, lay on the lawn watching the Battle of Britain overhead through a pair of binoculars. He was able to do this as the house had not been requisitioned for war use like many others nearby, though he says 'there was a fuel depot in the wood and lorries were parked under the trees for most of the war'. Was it purely coincidence that at the time his father was military assistant to Field Marshal Sir John Dill, Chief of the Imperial General Staff after Dunkirk, whom Churchill cruelly called Dilly Dally, until Alanbrooke took over eighteen months later?

Today the 270-acre estate at Ewhurst, Surrey, remains a secret place. The ordnance survey map shows it bounded by roads with buildings on all sides, but these are long-established small farms, not recent suburban development, and they are invisible from the house amid a mass of trees.

The drive is a handsome avenue of chestnut and lime. The surprise is to turn into the gravel sweep in front of the house and be confronted with a view of smooth rolling parkland worthy of Capability Brown himself.

Mr Nutting explains engagingly: 'It was all small fields and paddocks. We dragged out the hedges and piped the ditches to create large enclosures, but the land proved useless for arable, so we gave up and put it back to grass.' Today there are thick woods along the ridges – perfect for high-flying pheasants.

The house is of interest as an early work of the architect Sir Aston Webb, who built Admiralty Arch and the main front of Buckingham Palace. Webb's early work was

not all imperial pomp and includes the delightful 1877 Arts and Crafts almshouses of the Royal Grammar School at Worcester. His design for North Breache, entitled 'House at Ewhust about to be Erected', was published in *Building News* on December 30, 1881. Mr Nutting has a theory that the house may have been built or owned by Cuthbert 'C.E.' Heath, who sent the famous cable after the 1906 San Francisco earthquake saying, 'Pay all our policyholders in full irrespective of the terms of their policies', ushering in a golden age for Lloyd's underwriters.

Near the house is an early 18th-century cottage with Horsham stone slates, a massive chimney stack and a 17th-century timber-frame Surrey barn. Both are listed Grade II, though Webb's house has yet to receive the accolade. It is built of pale Leith Hill stone (the quarry is now closed) in a free gothic style with battlements, gables and soaring brick chimneys. There is an abundance of high-quality decorative carving – armorial emblems and foliage – in the frieze.

The house was advertised on the first page of *Country Life* on April 15, 1933, as the property of the late Dr M. J. Rowlands. The charm of the interior lies in spirited Arts

Carefully considered details such as the inglenook window beside the chimney breast add to the charm.

and Crafts detail and very good craftsmanship. The staircase hall has a trio of arches held aloft on decidedly quirky square columns on tall pedestals. The oak woodwork of the stair is of exceptional quality, as is the chimney piece with stylised leaves.

The first floor is compact and easy to warm, with bedrooms opening off the top-lit landing. En suite bathrooms are cleverly contrived for all four bedrooms and the lofty billiard room is now an office. There are two further bedrooms in the attic, where the large skylight over the stair sits like an upturned boat on the landing.

The climax of the tour is the ascent of the tower emerging under Webb's cupola. Here the 360-degree panorama includes the wooded flanks of Holmbury Hill, Pitch Hill and Leith Hill – its tower on top taking it over 1,000 ft to qualify for mountain status. In the distance the North and South Downs are visible. All this just 33 miles from Hyde Park Corner. Here the Nuttings held an outdoor concert on the last night of the Proms, attracting 7,000. 'The acoustic was superb,' he says.

ORCHARDS Godalming

Lutyens was awarded the commission after Gertrude Jekyll extolled his talents

ORCHARDS IS A WONDERFUL EXAMPLE of Lutyens's fertile genius, full of inventive and amusing detail. I went there at a magical moment in 1978 on a tour of Lutyens and Jekyll houses and gardens with the county conservation officer. The house, divided into flats after 1945, was empty and the garden beginning to run wild in a romantic way, with cascades of roses tumbling over garden archways and grass growing through the paving stones.

Inside, the house was still in excellent condition with sunlight flooding through the plentiful windows in the corridors. Lutyens kept the house looking long and low by placing the first-floor windows immediately below the eaves with vertical accents provided by clusters of soaring brick chimneys. The assurance with which Lutyens handled materials as a young architect is phenomenal, whether the beautifully laid courses of stone or the huge sweeps of roof tiles lightened by a splay at the bottom, with the angles emphasised almost in the manner of braiding. Over one of the fireplaces was an elaborate plan of the house and gardens painted on blue and white tiles and inscribed 'Built by Thomas Underwood for William Chance, Edwin Lutyens Architect'. Chance was a banker and the tiles were designed by his artistic wife Julia (nee Strachey). The Chances already had a site for their new house and an architect, Halsey Ricardo, an old friend. Mrs Chance later recalled, 'Passing through a sandy lane we saw a house nearing completion, and on top of a ladder a portly figure giving directions to some workmen. The house was a revelation of unimagined beauty and charm, we stood entranced…' The portly figure was Gertrude Jekyll, inspecting her new house at Munstead Wood, and she so extolled Lutyens's talents that he took over the design of the Chance's house. Orchards has now cast its spell on another Lutyens enthusiast and collector, Geoffrey Robinson, who also restored Lutyens's Marsh Court in Hampshire.

In best Surrey tradition, the roofs descend snugly over the first-floor windows.

PARK CLOSE   Englefield Green
1900 house near Windsor Park designed by the architect Herbert Huntly-Gordon

ONE OF THE THRILLS OF THE COUNTRY HOUSE chase is to find an unknown marvel by an architect of talent. On the edge of Windsor Great Park I found my perfect quarry. Driving through the immaculate green meadows of Runnymede, dazzled as always by the exquisite Lutyens pavilions at either end, I turned up through the beautiful fields and woods close to the National Air Force Memorial and then into secluded lanes where lavish houses are hidden behind gated drives, high walls and hedges.

Park Close is glimpsed along a lane that leads to an enchanting pub with Regency veranda and the Savill Gardens just beyond. All that can be seen down the closely planted drive is a tower gateway. The flavour is Art Nouveau Tudor Gothic. But the tower is a feint and leads not to the house but to the kitchen and garage courtyard. A spur leads off to the house proper with a large gravel circle around a Renaissance-style fountain, hemmed in with topiary.

The entrance front is in the manner of Voysey with bands of stone-mullioned windows with leaded lights and the long, slightly curious flat-topped gables he liked. The main entrance is another tower, rather like a double-height Suffolk church porch, with black flint chequerwork.

Rainwater heads carry the date 1900, while more tantalising is a finely carved royal coat of arms over a door at the end of a wing with the date 1902 and the initials 'ER' for Edward VII. Could the builder be one of the cluster of Edwardian courtiers and financiers who lived nearby, like the Droghedas and the Schroders?

The house is faced in a pretty sand-coloured pebbledash, which is a perfect match for the crisp stone trim of the mullioned windows. The towers have the extra flourish

Grandeur is imparted here by length not height, with the house merging with the coach house.

of squared and knapped flintwork set in shiny black chequers and the double stepped battlements have Art Nouveau carving.

To the left of the house a long pergola stretches out, smothered in ancient wisteria, with a canopy towards the end evidently intended for the family to continue taking tea during a shower. Behind the house, spreading lawns lead down to a canal planted with yellow irises and waterlilies. The garden front is an impressive composition with the centre and ends breaking forward and long runs of mullioned windows framed by raking buttresses.

Inside the arched front doorway is a pair of glass-paned doors, swept up in baroque manner towards the centre. The large reception rooms overlooking the garden, generous in size and each lit by broad bay windows, cry out for imaginative redecoration.

The first clue as to who lived here comes in the kitchen corridor where the bell panel announces Lord Fairhaven, Lady Fairhaven and the Hon. Captain Henry Broughton. Here had lived the Fairhavens who created the glorious National Trust gardens at Anglesey Abbey.

Park Close, it transpires, was bought by the 1st Lord Fairhaven's father, Urban Hanlon Broughton, in 1918. After studying engineering in London, he went to America to build railways and married Cara Rogers, daughter of the builder of the Virginia Railway, taking over as President of the Company on his father-in-law's death in 1909. Three years later

The subtle asymmetry only becomes apparent when you count the windows.

he returned to England, was elected MP for Preston and was on the honours list for a barony when he died suddenly in January 1929. In such favour was he held that the peerage was given to his eldest son, Huttleston, with Cara taking the title of the Lady Fairhaven. Provision was made for the title to go to Urban's second son Henry, if Huttleston had no heir.

To commemorate Urban's name the family decided to give Runnymede, famous in both Britain and America as the place where King John signed Magna Carta, with 182 acres to the National Trust for perpetual preservation. Neglected and overgrown, the meadows were in danger of being built over. Today, thanks to the Fairhavens, they are a piece of scenery unmatched along the whole length of the River Thames. Since the Fairhavens left in 1939, the house has changed hands several times but its domestic character has largely remained the same.

The Dower House, with its own battlemented tower, was originally built as a laundry (the largest country-house laundry ever built) with the extensive

The chequerwork porch blends Art Nouveau with Tudor Gothic.

ground floor entirely faced to shoulder height in white faience tiles with pretty trim, surviving intact through recent use as an engineering workshop

The question still remains as to who built Park Close. Clues are provided by the heraldic crest by the clock which has unusual supporters, an owl and a cockerel, and the motto *virtute non verbis* – deed not words, or by valour not by boasting. Above the clock (still keeping perfect time) is the inscription 'Days and Moments Quickly Flying'.

The one sure fact is that the architect was the little-known Herbert Huntly-Gordon. Educated at Harrow and articled to Sir Aston Webb, the author of the main front of Buckingham Palace, he designed a series of buildings in the City, including 90–94 Fleet Street and 123–127 Cannon Street. His interests soon turned to property development, beginning with the building of his own offices in Cannon Street and continuing with City properties in Cheapside. He acted as his own builder, employing his own men – a process by which an architect, if he is successful, can make a great deal of money. According to his obituary of 1929, 'he designed, and in the same way built a charming house at Englefield Green for his own occupation'. Could this be Park Close? Certainly he sold it and went on to build another house in Bishop's Avenue, Finchley, a second Millionaire's Row to Kensington Palace Gardens.

PUTTENHAM PRIORY   Puttenham
The ultimate home office which once belonged to the proprietor of Picture Post

PUTTENHAM PRIORY TAKES THE CONCEPT of working from home into a new era. The shipbroker who bought the house in 1993 decided to move his whole operation from the City to Surrey. With the help of architect Neil Morton, he transformed the garage block into an office suite that looks out through Georgian sash windows over leafy grounds to an ornamental tea house. Even the fire escape is a hump-arched Chinese bridge. A pillared doorcase opens into an elegant stone-floored lobby with walls of floor-to-ceiling glass. Upstairs, the main open-plan office is as slick as a yacht, laid out on three split levels with navy blue stairs and galleries and gleaming stainless steel balustrades.

When the scheme was submitted, local planners insisted that the main part of the house remain in residential use, hoping that in this way the character of the place would be maintained. So far the policy has held, the offices are invisible and, apart from the provision of a parking area behind the house, the ambience of a country house remains, with sweeping lawns descending to an attractive colonnaded swimming pool, stately hedges of yew and holly and a stretch of parkland bristling with young clumps of trees.

Puttenham has had a surfeit of tender loving care. The 1970s owners modernised the house, putting in false ceilings with downlighters into many of the rooms. Their successors promptly set about unpicking the interior and were lauded by the magazine *Period Living* for 'ten years of hard work', making the house structurally sound and treating floorboards and joists for dry rot.

Over the last nine years the house has been worked over again. Plaster has been stripped from walls inside and out, floors lifted, ceilings opened up to ensure not a mischievous trace of rot or decay remains, while the basement has been tanked to eliminate any prospect of damp. The roof has been re-leaded and slated and the whole house painted in a soft, radiant yellow. Every room has been wired for computers and ceilings prepared for discreet low-voltage picture spotlights.

The result is a house where all is not quite what it may seem. The handsome stone spiral stair in the turret is a new introduction, while its cast-iron predecessor has been moved to the ice house in the garden, which has ingeniously been transformed into a wine cellar with racks ringing the walls. The basement boiler room is equipped like a ship's engine room with eye-level gauges and an abundance of gleaming brass and chrome. The kitchen doorstep is a circle of bulletproof glass over the manorial well. Heavily knotched 17th-century roof timbers have been exposed to create a lofty Jacobean bedroom.

All this continues a history that was equally eventful in earlier centuries. In 1744 the house was purchased by General James Oglethorpe, who, touched by the death of a friend in a debtors' prison, had persuaded the Government to let him carve a new colony out of South Carolina, to be called Georgia, for the settlement of poor people. With 120 men, women and children he sailed in 1732, remaining for ten years as Governor.

He sold in 1761 to Thomas Parker, a member of the Inner Temple, who added the handsome Palladian front with Adamesque capitals. This must have been done by 1775 when sales particulars describe the columns 'finished by a pediment' and a stone staircase and gallery inside. The estate was bought in 1775 by Samuel Cornish, who five years earlier had inherited a fortune from his uncle, Admiral Samuel Cornish. Serving under his uncle, the young Cornish captured Manila in the Philippines for the British and inherited his uncle's share of one of the richest prizes of the Seven Years' War, the Spanish galleon, *Santissima Trinidad*. In 1782 Cornish fought at the Battle of the Saints under Admiral Rodney off St Lucia in the Caribbean.

Cornish's widow sold the Priory to a relative, Richard Sumner, who diverted the road, the Pilgrim's Way, which ran uncomfortably close to the house, to the far side of the parish church. This now sits handsomely on the edge of the garden. Situated discreetly beside the churchyard is a garage for eight cars, amusingly divided into three pavilions complete with clock tower and steel security ramp to ensure nobody can make off with the Lamborghini.

In 1919 the famous Gertrude Jekyll prepared a plan for the garden; in 1931 the property was bought by the Dowager Viscountess Harcourt, a great friend of Queen Mary who often visited the Priory. In 1946 Puttenham was acquired by Edward Hulton, proprietor of *The Picture Post,* only to be sold four years later to the Ministry of Health as a nursing home.

Surrey is often thought of as wall-to-wall suburbia, but Puttenham enjoys a panorama of open meadows and woodland all the way to the South Downs which is almost as spectacular as that from the ridge of the Hog's Back just above the village.

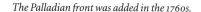

The Palladian front was added in the 1760s.

RIDGEMEAD   Englefield Green
Completed in 1938 to designs by Robert, son of the famous Edwin Lutyens

RIDGEMEAD WAS BUILT FOR Captain Woolf Barnato, considered by W.O. Bentley as 'the best driver we ever had'. Barnato won at Le Mans in 1928, 1929 and 1930 and famously raced the Blue Train overnight from Cannes back to England, parking neatly in St James's four minutes before the train reached Calais. The Barnatos were diamond millionaires from South Africa. In her memoirs, Marie Louise Ritz, wife of the great hotelier, refers waspishly to 'poor Barney Barnato and his habit of carrying round a pocketful of diamonds to play with'.

Ridgemead is a monument to a vanished way of life. It stands just a few hundred yards from Windsor Great Park, with views across Runnymede and of the towers of Windsor Castle. It was completed in 1938, months before the Second World War broke out, and its life as a private house came to an abrupt end in 1950. Crippling taxes, austerity, the lack of servants and problems with heating made large houses unsustainable. Ridgemead became a nursing home.

By 1999, when it was for sale for £2 million, it looked set to become a house again. Certainly infinite satisfaction was to be gained from the none-too-difficult task of unpicking the dismal signs of institutional use – removing plastic gutters, ugly downpipes, metal treads on the stairs and partition walls.

Ridgemead is the most important work of the son of Sir Edwin Lutyens. The house is signed proudly 'Robert Lutyens Architectus 1938' by the right of the front door.

The house is in the California Mission style – what Osbert Lancaster preferred to call 'Spanish Super-Colonial' in deference to Florida real-estate speculators. In England it was a fashion that provided us with Curzon Street baroque and wrought-iron window grilles and, above all, the blue-and-green glazed tile roof.

The golden stone archways were designed in the California Mission style.

Ridgemead comes with white-painted brick, golden stone archways, small leaded windows, a low-slung first floor and the shallowest of roof slopes. Best of all are the broad stone carriage arches into the front courtyard and the handsome portal flanked by raked stone walls and suggestive of a fort on the Spanish Main. Over the front door is a carved escutcheon worthy of a conquistador.

Still more intricate are the keystones above the adjoining windows, one carved with the sterns of two galleons set amid Grinling Gibbons-style fruit and foliage, the other with a dagger, pearls, a fan and a long Spanish hair comb.

The twin oval ponds provide a beautiful mirror reflection of the garden front.

Country Life in 1940 saw Ridgemead as part of a 'gradual reassertion of traditional values in country house design since 1930'. What the Barnatos received from Robert Lutyens was a house with all the Lutyens trim – delicious gate lodges (three in this case), a charmingly enclosed entrance courtyard and beautiful formal gardens wedded to the house. But the details are always better than the whole.

On the entrance front, Robert Lutyens introduced a delightful series of large stone amphora beneath the eaves. Beside the bay windows overlooking the garden are huge stone planters the size of fountain basins. Above are more planters, this time in metal, intriguingly set into the balconies so flowers fill the views from the bedroom windows. Between the French windows below are beautifully carved stone roundels.

The twin oval ponds, set in an expanse of York paving, are worthy of Lutyens père. Pergolas are artfully constructed from layer on layer of flat red tiles. Beneath is a deeply sunken garden approached by sweeping flights of steps on three sides, begging in 1999 to be planted with old-fashioned roses. On the other side was a sizeable, but long-empty, swimming pool, with a shallow fountain bowl over which water once bubbled.

Inside the house, Robert Lutyens set out to create a sunny, almost *alfresco* feel by continuing the white walls and golden Clipsham stone trim along the vestibule corridors and landing. The best feature is the woodwork, notably a bookcase like a Palladian window with glazed doors and a central arch, and the handsomely panelled chapel, originally a small breakfast room. On the upstairs landing is a remarkable wind vane indicating no fewer than thirty-two compass points.

Ridgemead is a house where the blacksmith received the commission of a lifetime. Every metal window appears to have been handmade, with ornamental handles and neat locking devices allowing the window to be held open at different angles.

Many of the bedrooms are under sloping eaves, and the main one has a broad-arched roof. A well-preserved Art Deco bathroom is clad in marble with a hoop ceiling, while another has the original American-style diagonal tub, designed to fit into spaces where English baths do not go.

SNOWDENHAM HALL   Bramley
Designed by J.F. Bentley, architect of Westminster Cathedral, in 1885

MICHAEL WILSON BELONGS TO the select band of entrepreneurs who bring back grand country houses from years of institutional use and make them appealing homes once again. His prime stalking ground has been Surrey and Sussex; more recently he has begun to look west to Somerset.

The question with country-house conversions is whether they go with the grain of the architecture, making the most of a building's intrinsic qualities, or simply cram in the maximum number of living units.

His most impressive conversion is Snowdenham Hall, near Godalming, Surrey, built for the Courage family in 1885. The architect was J.F. Bentley, designer of the glorious Roman Catholic cathedral at Westminster. Here Bentley shows himself a master of large-scale composition, with ebullient bay windows, black-and-white and tile-hung gables and clusters of soaring chimneys. Arts and Crafts architecture was never more muscular and self-confident.

The conversion works well. Wilson has tackled the great height of the building by creating duplexes, the lower ones occupying the ground floor with bedroom windows opening to a buttressed garden arcade below. The upper ones have bedrooms beneath the eaves with fine views.

The flats share the splendid great hall which, unusually, is entered from the end rather than the side. A soaring oriel window fills the far end, with row on row of heraldic stained glass. While working on the interior, Wilson discovered William Morris-style wall paintings with a swirling pattern of pomegranates.

Boldly projecting buttresses and bay windows create a powerfully dramatic composition.

STOCKETTS MANOR   Oxted
Late-medieval hall house with a wealth of 17th-century glass

STOCKETTS MANOR IS THE ARCHITECTURE OF England, written not just in stone but in brick, tile-hanging, medieval oak and 17th-century lead and glass. Even more so, it is the epitome of Surrey Picturesque, with the weathered mellowness and soft colour that only age can bring. Oak has turned to silver, clay roof tiles are a perfect match for the brick and the carefully graded Horsham slate roofing slabs along the front have a venerable coating of lichens and moss.

The chimney stacks that were added on the outside of the walls nearly four centuries ago are as large as medieval church buttresses with tiled slopes and diagonal bands of brickwork diving into the straight courses. The charm of the place is doubled by the adjoining oast house with twin pyramid and conical roofs. Oast houses were drying houses for hops which were spread on wooden floors with fires beneath. The steam and hot air produced escaped through the distinctive cowls on top.

Attached to the oast house is a large timber-framed barn, the whole group linked to the house by a low cloister with pretty tiled roof. Beyond the barn is an ancient stone-edged millpond, while lining the drive is a remarkable set of ancient staddle stones. These are the mushroom-like supports that are used to prevent mice climbing into granaries.

Chimney stacks shaped like church buttresses were added to the outside walls.

The outdoor swimming pool is claimed as the earliest in England.

This is a house on which the Georgians and the Victorians left none of the usual traces of sash and bay windows. Here every window is a mullion, framed in either stone or timber.

Stocketts lies near the pretty village of Oxted. As you leave Old Oxted, suburbia vanishes and you are in open rolling country with no more than a scattering of farms. The feeling is that of blissfully rural parts of Kent and this is what opens out before you as you drive across the county border towards Edenbridge.

As in many Surrey houses, the ceilings are low but huge beams at the top of the staircase give a hint that the 15th-century house may have had a great hall that was once open to the roof timbers. Another clue comes with the discovery of twin wooden door arches of the kind that habitually would have led from great hall to kitchen and scullery.

All this was confirmed in the most exciting way as I climbed into the darkened roof space and, with the help of a camera flash, found the medieval king post of the great hall roof. This is a short octagonal pillar with shaped capital and base half hidden in a wattle and daub wall. Smoke-darkening suggests there may once have been an open fire in the middle of the floor. What a temptation to open up the full height of the medieval hall! There can be no chance that this would ever be allowed as the insertion of floors and ceilings dated back to the 16th century. In almost all the rooms created are fine stone fireplaces with characteristic shallow Tudor 'four-centre' arches.

At the same time the house was given a new entrance front of warm brown brick laid in distinctive English bond (alternate courses of header and stretcher bricks) with stone mullions to the long bands of new windows on both floors. Still more remarkable are the leaded windows inset within the stone. Often these are 1900 replacements. Here it is quickly evident from the misted state of the glass that the windows must be the originals.

As if to confirm no Georgian windows were ever introduced, there is a touch that is pure Jane Austen. Inscribed on one original pane of glass in a fine copperplate are the names of Robert and Sophia Young, the names of their ten children and the date 1827.

The leads in which this ancient glass is set are more elaborate than the usual diamond lattice and if you look closely form a clever Renaissance perspective of stepped cubes. This makes them an infinitely rare and precious survival.

Other strange features are the wooden box downpipes and wooden gutters lined in copper. These are not old but an improvisation of Richard Fenton, who bought the house in the 1970s. The pipes needed replacing but he did not want the modern ones to be left showing. However, on the south side two carefully preserved rainwater 'hoppers' or heads peep out, one with the date 1801, the other with a scallop shell and laurel leaves.

Stocketts has many surprises. One is an outdoor swimming pool claimed as the earliest in England. This may be an exaggeration but it shows in an aerial view taken in the 1930s and the broad single-plank oak diving board is silver with age. There's also an indoor pool built about 1990 by the Fentons, cleverly sunken and approached by a corridor in the manner of swimming pools in Alpine resorts. It looks out over a fountain basin brimming with koi carp and a Zen garden of rocks and stones.

Though the original great hall has disappeared, a substitute has been created in the barn. This is a magnificent space that is open to the roof timbers with a minstrels' gallery at one end and a billiard room with scoreboard and cue rack in the round tower, though it is a mystery how the billiard table arrived and left.

Other features at Stocketts include a large number of ancient timber doors with latches operated by leather thongs and large blacksmith's hinges. Many rooms retain neat paired brass electric switches and servants' bells connected to the original bell board.

A previous owner was the theatre lover Edward Sutro, possibly a relation of the playwright Alfred Sutro, who lived on the other side of Surrey at Witley. Sutro lived here in Bohemian chaos but for every first night in London would don a black cape and set out in a white Rolls Royce. Like the car, Stocketts is always going to be in need of a careful owner.

The ancient timber doors have large blacksmith's hinges and latches with leather thongs.

WOTTON HOUSE · Dorking

Where John Evelyn had a hand in laying out gardens for his brother George

FOR COUNTRY-HOUSE WATCHERS, there is a never-ending fascination in the stream of large forgotten mansions that suddenly come on the market after years in institutional use. These vast piles were often taken over after wartime requisitioning simply because they offered large amounts of cheap floor space. The golden rule is that however much the house has been extended and adapted to meet the requirements of the new occupants, suddenly after twenty or thirty years the institution decides to leave.

Precisely this happened at Wotton House, near Dorking, the historic seat of the Evelyn family, where the great John Evelyn had a hand in laying out the gardens his brother George. After the war it was taken over as a Fire Service training college and extended with classrooms and lecture halls, none of them things of beauty, until it was suddenly sold on to British Telecom, which used the house for just five years.

When I first went there on a summer's evening in the 1990s, the only inhabitants were a brigade of rabbits keeping the lawn as short-cropped as a golf green and a very startled fox sunning itself on the garden terrace.

Wotton is an intensely romantic place. The north entrance front is almost a country cousin of Hampton Court Palace, built from a warm orange brick and resplendent with shaped gables, tall barley-sugar chimneys, octagonal turrets and heraldic stone griffins. By contrast, the garden front is more like a series of houses on Kew or Richmond Green, with Georgian red brick, Victorian terracotta, bargeboarding and tile-hanging, and a range of windows that tell the complete story

The house is ornamented with tall barley sugar chimneys, octagonal turrets and heraldic stone griffins.

of the English house, beginning with diamond-leaded panes, and continuing with sashes and bay windows and pointed and cusped arches.

John Evelyn wrote admiringly in his diary of Wotton: 'It has rising grounds, meadows, woods and water in abundance … the gardens, fountains and groves [are] the most magnificent that England afforded, and gave one of the first examples of that elegancy so much in vogue … in the managing of waters and other ornaments.'

The remains of Evelyn's terraces and mount, rising in three grand stages, deserved the most careful unpicking. Fortunately, rescue came from a

The saloon has wallpaintings by the Belgian artist Jean Deneux.

sympathetic privately owned group, Hayley Conference Centres, a fast-growing operation running six other substantial country houses. The company was set up by Alan English, a man with a vision who saw a gap in the market and decided to fill it. This was between country-house hotels that were trying to attract conference business but did not have the facilities of civic conference centres, and conference centres that did not offer the luxury and ambience provided by historic country-house hotels.

After taking a 125-year lease from the Evelyn Estate for £1.75 million, the group spent a prodigious £20 million on the house. It opened in the 1990s with 107 bedrooms, a full complement of chefs, 60 staff and 40 conference rooms equipped to seat any number from two to two hundred.

A smart newly laid brown gravel drive leads down the long avenue off the Guildford–Dorking road to lawns in front of the house, where magnificent trees screen a new car park to the right. Two new bridges have been added to the existing delightful series of five little brick bridges that cross the neatly channelled River Tillingbourne as it passes in front of the house.

The bedrooms, new dining room and conference rooms are housed in large discreet wings at either end, replacing the hotch-potch of previous additions. Inside, remarkable interiors of three centuries survive, beginning with an 18th-century wagon-roofed vestibule and continuing with an arcaded gothic hall with two large hooded alabaster fireplaces. At the other end of the house, the splendid Palladian saloon has delightful wall paintings of Chinese scenes by the Belgian artist Jean Deneux.

Joan Littlewood, the sales manager, told me: 'Our business plan looks to open up five more establishments in the next eight years.' This brings new hope to the rescue of large problem houses, particularly those that until recently have looked irreversibly engulfed in hideous, disfiguring extensions.

SUSSEX

BALCOMBE PLACE Balcombe

Built in 1856 by the architect Henry Clutton for J.A. Hankey JP

BALCOMBE PLACE IS A SPIRITED VICTORIAN COMPOSITION of soaring gables and thrusting chimneys designed by the accomplished architect Henry Clutton in 1856. The house was built for J.A. Hankey JP, and stands on a hill commanding fine views. In Saxon, 'Bal' was a hill and 'Comb' a hollow or dell. Bay windows and battlements add variety to the facades and the extensive service buildings attached at one corner have the same steep roofs and clusters of tall chimneys. Though the scale is lower than that of the house, the two combine to provide an exceptionally lively silhouette.

Like many large Victorian country houses, Balcombe had become a school in 1954 but when SAVE included it in *Tomorrow's Ruins* in 1978 it had been empty for several years. 'The owner, Mrs P.A. Greenwood, wants to demolish the house and erect a bungalow on the site,' we wrote. Her first application had been refused the year before but resubmitted on the basis that no purchaser had been found. We took the view that the house had not been sufficiently marketed or advertised. Balcombe thus

Pale grey local stone and handmade clay roof tiles create the sense of an ancient house.

received another reprieve and has survived, well looked-after as a luxurious care home. The grand rooms – music room, library and dining hall – are shared by the residents. Nowadays, houses like these have staffs almost as numerous as in Edwardian days. There are chefs ready to meet individual dietary requirements. Hairdressing, physiotherapy and chiropody are all on offer and rooms have bathrooms, television, telephone and nurse call-bell system.

During the Second World War, Balcombe Place became the headquarters of the Land Army set up by the formidable Lady Denman, who continued to live here. The Women's Land Army filled many of the jobs that had been left vacant when men went to fight and by 1943 there were some 90,000 Land Girls working on farms. Britain imported about 60 per cent of its food before the war; thanks largely to the efforts of the Land Girls, the amount of land used for growing crops, especially wheat and potatoes, increased by 50 per cent during the war, mainly by using pastureland and marshland.

Today, the beauty of Balcombe is its sense of belonging in the landscape around it, sheltered by the trees, yet enjoying splendid views.

FIFE HOUSE — Brighton
Built in 1827–30 for the bachelor Duke of Devonshire

FEW GRAND TOWN HOUSES, even in London, boast such a history as Fife House in Brighton. It occupies a prime place in one of the grandest compositions in all British architecture with terraces, crescent and central square all forming one continuous run of splendid stucco houses looking out over gardens and seaside promenade to the magnificent expanse of the English Channel.

Fife House takes its name from the Duke of Fife, husband of Princess Louise, Princess Royal and daughter of Edward VII. They bought the house in 1896 and the King came to stay while convalescing after an illness in 1908.

The house was built in 1827–30 by the famous bachelor Duke of Devonshire, patron of Sir Joseph Paxton of Crystal Palace fame, who was a frequent visitor. Palmerston dined here in 1851, Thackeray in 1855. Two years earlier, the Duke lent his house for a month to the painter Sir Edwin Landseer.

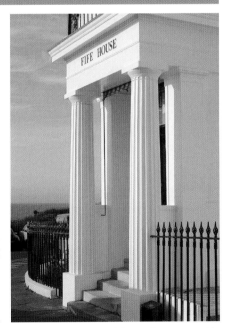

The snow-white stucco of the porch contrasts with the smart black 'tasselled' railings.

Fife House, or No 1 Lewes Crescent, is one of three adjoining houses which the Duke opened into one another, turning the corner from the Crescent into Chichester

Terrace. The houses were subsequently separated and eight years ago Fife House was acquired by Todd Cooper and Guiseppe Sironi in a sorry state of neglect.

It has been restored with astonishing éclat with a wonderful eye to detail, colour and materials. Thomas Kemp, who built these stupendous terraces, planned every third house with grand Corinthian pillars and an imposing columned porch. Here, at the top of the steps, the original pair of boot scrapers survive on either side of the front door with decorative ends in the form of Greek *acroteria* or palmettes. The large polished brass door bell on the left is inscribed 'servants' in dignified capital letters. The bell on the right, for visitors, has been so zealously polished that the letters have completely worn away. The panels on the front door are magnificently studied. In front are rods down which a Regency-striped awning descends.

The characteristic spear-headed basement railings have the added flourish of tassels with an eight-pointed star over each spearhead, which I thought must be the Duke's Order of the Bath until I saw it continuing up the crescent. The front door opens into a broad stair hall with walls painted to look like large blocks of yellow Siena marble, with black marbled trim for the dado rail and skirting.

On the right is the dining room, ducal in size, with a splendid built-in sideboard attributed to Gillows and surmounted by a mirror clearly of the very largest proportions that glass could be manufactured at the time. At the back of the hall, a passage leads to a private lavatory installed for the king with a specially large wooden seat to carry his immense weight.

A cantilevered, or 'hanging', stone staircase rises in three unbroken sweeps to the third floor. Each Portland stone step tapers to a point at the back so the underside of the stair is completely smooth. Yet however hard you tread, there is not a tremor in

The Duke linked three houses that wrapped round the corner of the parade.

the mahogany stair rail, which is held firmly in place by a continuous run of smart bronzed metal banisters with leaf capitals.

On the first floor the conservatory over the porch is arranged with low divans in Turkish style, a perfect place to sit and enjoy a brilliant sunny winter's day looking out onto a sparkling blue sea.

Opening off the landing is the drawing room, formerly the Duke's ballroom. When Anthony Dale wrote *Fashionable Brighton* in 1947, he lamented that the ceiling had been covered by thick Lincrusta paper. During restoration, the original decorative painting has been revealed – all fresh pinks and blues. It is the work of Crace and Son, who the Duke employed at Chatsworth.

As the staircase rises to the second floor, a hidden jib door opens into an ingenious circular stair for the servants, contrived round the narrowest of open wells and rising from the basement to the top of the house. On the second floor, a very smart master bedroom suite has been created. The bath stands grandly in

The drawing room was decorated by the Crace Brothers, who also worked at Chatsworth.

the centre of the floor with a sentry-box glass shower at the end. On the third floor is another comfortable bedroom suite with a built-in double chest of drawers painted to simulate sycamore, with smart ebony black trim.

The fourth floor, in the attic, is contrived beneath the slope of the roof. The bathroom arrangements are especially ingenious. It is only possible to stand at the basin thanks to the extra headroom provided by a roof light, which gives a sensational view over the Crescent; the shaving mirror installed just below is barely six inches from your chin.

By this point it has dawned that the odd thing about Fife House is that it is really only one room deep – the Duke himself observed that the plan is like a fan without a handle – but the basement, which is 60 per cent of the house, is still to come.

Brighton houses are one of the best places to explore the intriguing world of upstairs-downstairs. Here the kitchen quarters were scarcely touched by the 20th century. There are stone-flagged floors, sturdy built-in cupboards with rounded corners that don't get chipped by servants hurrying by, and large internal sash windows looking into inner courtyards now glazed over to make extra rooms. The coal hole under the pavement is a sizeable wine cellar, while the housekeeper's room at the front is a cosy office. The showpiece is the kitchen, rising 30 ft with a roof light as large and as elaborate as many of the conservatories at Chelsea Flower Show. Now there are gleaming modern stainless-steel ranges suitable for professional caterers on one side, while opposite is the restored cast-iron Victorian oven, The Brighton, supplied by a local iron founder, E.G. Brown.

Beyond is a scullery equipped as a second kitchen serving the unusual three-storey butler's cottage at the end occupied by Baker, who was the Duke's butler for twenty-five years and, according to gay rumour, more than just a servant.

The one catch is that with all this glorious sea air, a film of sand quickly collects on the windows, which need to be cleaned regularly if you are to enjoy the view. Fortunately they are casements, not sashes, which open inwards so window cleaners and ladders are not a prerequisite.

BUXTED PARK — Buxted
Ambitiously rebuilt immediately after a fire in 1940

FROM THE MOMENT you sweep through the gates, Buxted Park Hotel puzzles and intrigues you. A grand, well-tended medieval parish church stands in proud isolation in the park, a large forecourt ringed by statuary frames a strangely narrow temple-front entrance. In one room after another are stupendous, positively ducal marble fireplaces. The handsome white-painted Palladian stair has vertical proportions more suited to a very grand town house. And there is a telltale gap between the tops of the columns and the entablature above, as if it had been imported from elsewhere and did not quite fit.

My curiosity increased *Country Life* articles of 1934 showed a strikingly different house to the one I was standing in, of three storeys not two and red brick rather than

The house was handsomely faced in stucco after the top storey was destroyed.

stucco. In 1934 it was the home of the legendary Basil Ionides, the architect who between the wars transformed Claridges and the Savoy and designed the Art Deco Savoy Theatre, ablaze with silver and gold leaf.

On February 23, 1940 a devastating fire gutted the house. With Britain at war with Germany, most people would have abandoned hope but Ionides persuaded Sir George Chrystal, the civil servant in charge, that he would be doing a service in rebuilding the house as many local builders were unemployed.

As the hotel guide puts it, Basil 'visited bombed out buildings salvaging covings, cornices, chandeliers and beautiful show doors. So good was the quality of the items he salvaged that some scurrilous people have actually suggested he was paying the Germans to bomb particular houses.' Further notes suggest that many of Ionides's choicest pieces came from houses demolished before the war. These include Adam mahogany doors from 23–25 Portland Place, the staircase from 30 Old Burlington Street and a fireplace from Clumber Park in the Dukeries.

The house was next bought by Kenneth Shipman, the owner of Twickenham Studios, who 'used it to entertain his stars such as Marlon Brando, Dudley Moore and Gregory Peck', while Mrs Shipman added a large new wing to serve a luxurious spa. When the Shipmans divorced, the 'young staff of over a hundred beautiful girls' stood around in tears at being given notice.

Buxted was then acquired by the Ambassador of the United Arab Emirates for use by the ruler of Abu Dhabi. The spa wing was adapted for the women of the Sheikh's household, guarded by a eunuch and every window boarded up except for six inches at the top.

Left 'to fall into a terrible state of dilapidation', the house was bought in 1986 by the Amalgamated Engineering Union and then recently by Julia Hands, energetic chairman of Hand Picked Hotels who in the last few years has spent over £35 million in restoring a selection of mainly country-house hotels where 'you have our permission to be outrageously self-indulgent'.

Top: Ionides filled the house with features salvaged from houses that were demolished in the 1930s.

Above: The garden front was given handsome Regency proportions after a wartime fire.

Work is under way on bringing the large garden into order – we saw a flourishing group of wild orchids outside the walled garden. Fallow deer are still to be seen. Curiously the village was removed from the park as late as the 1840s when the Earl of Liverpool, finding his tenants reluctant to move, simply let their cottages fall down (though he did build them new homes in the village).

CHARLESTON MANOR   Lewes

A rare 12th-century upper hall house emerged during repairs

THE WOODED COOMBES ON THE EDGE of the Sussex Downs provide the setting for some of the most covetable of all English houses. Charleston Manor lies in the cleft made in the hills by the River Cuckmere as it approaches the sea. There is no view of the house from the road and on first sight at the end of the drive it appears an overgrown cottage more than a manor house.

Yet when the architect Walter Godfrey carried out repairs for Sir Oswald and Lady Birley he found that the older part of the house, described vaguely as a medieval chapel, was the almost intact shell of a late 12th-century upper hall house. While Norman churches and castles survive in abundance, smaller houses of Norman date are extremely rare in England by contrast to France. Godfrey revealed a deep-set twin-arched Norman window with five exquisite column shafts.

The walls were faced in flint with window dressings in Caen stone. In plan the house was an almost perfect double cube and presumably consisted of an upper hall set above an undercroft. In the 13th century a large canopied fireplace was introduced, of the type so often found in France. Early in the 16th century, a new wing was built out at right angles – some linenfold panelling of this date remains. The sash-windowed range was added in the 18th century, still in scale with the house, making a delightfully picturesque composition.

When Oswald and Rhoda Birley bought the house it stood baldly in a farmyard. The bones of the beautiful garden they created were also laid out by Walter Godfrey, extending the lines of existing walls. Godfrey had trained in the office of George Devey, whose architecture was born of an intense love for the traditional cottages of Kent and Sussex countryside. Godfrey's ideas on gardening were set out in a brilliant book *Gardens in the Making* published in 1914.

The circular dovecote sits a short distance from the house and stables.

The architect, he wrote, should lay out walls and hedges, terraces and walks, lawns, pools, avenues and glades. He wholly rejected the 18th-century idea of opening house and grounds for all to see as they approached. 'The result is the complete absence of shelter, the wind sweeps round the house and everyone who walks in the garden is visible, willingly or unwillingly, to the chance visitor.' Gardens, he counselled, should be screened from the road or drive. At Charleston a wall runs almost the entire length of the drive. The beauties of a garden, continued Godfrey, should be revealed by degrees, a garden should be many gardens.

Lady Birley's interests in the theatre, the arts and gardens never waned after her husband's death. Following her own death in 1980, the Charleston Festival has continued to flourish with its own dedicated website.

Each year the leading British cellist Robert Cohen invites outstanding musicians to join him for the festival. The audience gathers to enjoy chamber music beneath the venerable timbers of the 16th century tithe barn, which seats three hundred people. Afterwards, there are candlelit dinners in the coach house and picnics on the lawns.

COOKE'S HOUSE West Burton
Medieval and 17th-century manor sensitively restored by Major J.S. Courtauld

I HAD BEEn AT COOKE'S HOUSE for an hour before I thought, 'Where on earth do they park the cars?' So completely had we stepped back in time that for a while the world seemed to consist only of panelled rooms, venerable wooden floors and diamond-pane windows looking out over resplendent topiary.

The excitement is greater as the entrance is so mysterious. We left the car in a quiet country lane and ascended a gentle paved ramp to a stone doorway set in a long high wall. Stone balls on top of the gate posts announced an ancient armigerous family. Grey-green lichens spread across the rust-coloured stone and a magnificent cedar of Lebanon loomed over the wall.

The sundial is set in the middle of geometrically-planted box edging.

The gate opens to a perfect example of the smaller English manor house. Here there was never a carriage sweep – simply a straight paved path leading up to a gabled porch carrying three further stone balls. Though the porch is carved with the dates 1610 and 1634, it is quickly evident that the house is earlier still. Within the porch there is a brick Tudor arch with a hood mould, showing this was once an outside door.

The luxuriant formal gardens are bounded by yew hedges.

Set above the large stone mullioned windows there are further brick mouldings (drip moulds they are sometimes called), though curiously these are longer than the windows. Closer scrutiny shows the windows were originally wider as there are clear signs of infilled stone down the sides.

How, one asks, does this delightful small manor have such a strange name – Cooke's or Coke's House. A map of the village shows half a dozen houses with similar names. All are evidence of the Cooke family who lived here till 1683.

When *Country Life* first wrote about the house in 1909 it was tenanted, as houses often were at the time, and had deadening plate glass in the windows. In the 1920s it was bought by the Courtauld family and very sensitive alterations were carried out by Major J.S. Courtauld, whose initials are on a gabled wing he built at the back with the date 1928. The major was an architect and lived nearby at Burton Park near Petworth – he made the alterations for his brother-in-law, Wilfrid Holland.

When Burton Park was requisitioned in the Second World War and used by the Royal Marines, Mrs Courtauld came to live here, not taking too kindly to what she thought of as a dreary tenanted house. But she and her daughter Jeanne remained. It is to Jeanne, a talented painter and Royal Academician, to whom the continuing magic of the house is due. She became a passionate gardener and was the county organiser of the National Gardens Scheme, regularly opening the garden in the spring when the daffodils are out. Every summer, mother and daughter set off to the Mediterranean where Jeanne would paint, occasionally returning to stay by the sea in the Isle of Wight at Bembridge.

Inside the house there is not a fitted carpet, only fine lustrous broad-planked floors scattered with rugs. The main rooms are not low or dark as in some Tudor houses but have lofty ceilings and are lit from two sides by large stone mullions – wood in the 1928 addition at the back. The diamond-pattern windows put in by Major Courtauld are of superb quality with bold, scrolled handles like those of Georgian teapots.

The large hall opens into a marvellous panelled room with a rich deep Jacobean plaster frieze filled with the fruits and flowers of summer. The panelling below is adze cleft, perfectly showing off the grain and feather of the oak.

As in many old houses the stair ascends in short gentle flights of five steps, here around a central pillar rather than an open well. Into this is set, on each successive face, a neat oak-fronted storage cupboard. At every corner dangles a rope, so you can pull yourself up or steady your descent, but even more popular with small children who can swing out into space Tarzan-style.

The house has six or seven bedrooms, all well lit. Above are a pair of lofty attic rooms with large windows in the gable ends. The kitchen wing has butler's pantry, scullery and walk-in larder that is colder than the fridge in summer. It opens out onto a sheltered courtyard paved in a circular pattern in brick, stone and pebbles. Across the yard is a low barn with an upper room that would make a perfect home office.

The climax comes with the succession of garden rooms enclosed in walls of yew or beech. The name of Gertrude Jekyll is frequently mentioned and Leonard Borwick, the tenant a century ago, visited her at Munstead Wood. Nonetheless the garden rooms are really the creation of Wilfrid Holland. From the walled garden in front of the house you ascend past a holly bower at least 20 ft tall with a niche hollowed out for a seat. The next green room contains four yews, intended to be perfect cubes set on low pedestals but as they have grown higher, they have become more difficult for the gardener to clip, and intriguing undulations and asymmetries have crept in. In a third garden room the yew is clipped in the form of stately peacocks. Beyond, beech hedges planted by Jeanne Courtauld lead down to informal lawns that merge into fields with a magnificent backdrop of the smooth, rounded South Downs beyond.

There are broad oak floors throughout and not a fitted carpet to be seen.

EASTWOOD FARM · Herstmonceux
Delightful 1990s folly built for the pioneer of country-house opera

EASTWOOD FARM REPRESENTS A TRIUMPH for new architecture in the countryside. Freddie Stockdale, who built it, has a passion for country houses and an encyclopaedic knowledge of their architects. He sketched the design himself, a miniature version of Osterley Park with portico and ogee domes, and then asked Robert Adam, the well-known classicist, 'to make it buildable'.

Here is an ingenious example of what is sometimes termed 'bungalow eating'. It was an opportunity to build in a gloriously secluded site, sheltered by mature hedges, in an Area of Outstanding Natural Beauty. Stockdale describes it as a wrap-around of an existing farmhouse. Permission had already been given for a substantial ten-bedroom house on the site but the planners did not take to Stockdale's delicious folly. He was told there was no tradition of red brick in the Weald. What about 15th-century Herstmonceux Castle just a few miles away, the largest brick building in Britain when it was built, he asked? Robert Adam had the ingenious idea of placing a model in the council offices where all the councillors would see it. When it came before the committee, the proposal was approved. 'Then the officers appealed on the basis that the scheme was contrary to the structure plan. I had no idea they could do that,' says Stockdale. Finally approval came through from the environment minister John Gummer.

The bricks came from the Brick Factary [sic] in Winchester, where a huge range of bricks of all colours and textures were on display. 'The handmade bricks were very expensive but we found a very pretty machine-made pink brick from Devon,' he continues. The portico was built in wood after timber proved to cost a third of the cheapest quote for stone. The leadwork on the ogee domes was done by local firemen. An unexpected bonus is the minimal cost of heating. 'It's the first time I've lived in a house without draughts,' says Stockdale.

The onion domes and colonnade were inspired by Osterley Park.

ISFIELD PLACE   Uckfield
Mid 16th-century house built for a family of courtiers

ISFIELD PLACE RESONATES WITH A HISTORY that stretches back two millennia. The Romans established a staging post here by a ford across the River Ouse – the stretch of Ermine Street that led from Newhaven on the coast to London. King Harold, slain nearby at what is now Battle, held lands in the parish.

The medieval church, isolated since the Black Death, stands in the fields south of the house. Beside it are the remains of a motte-and-bailey castle that belonged to the De La Warr family. In the 16th century, Isfield Place was acquired by the Shurley family, court officials whose increasing royal favour is recorded in a splendid series of monuments in the church.

John Shurley was chief clerk to the kitchen of Henry VII, becoming 'cofferer' or treasurer in 1520 to Henry VIII, a post also held by his son, Edward. His grandson, John, rose to be deputy lieutenant of the county, and is said to have been a man of 'exemplary industry' and 'stout in good causes'.

Towards the middle of the 16th century, the Shurleys began to build an imposing mansion built of local brick. Its size and splendour is evident from a vast enclosing rectangular wall with octagonal towers at the corners, one of which survives largely complete as a gazebo. The wall along the south of the garden is inset with a series of bastions so distinct that they might be the bases of Elizabethan bay windows, in which case the house would have been very grand indeed, perhaps built around two courtyards.

The shaped gable was built in a mellow brick to blend with the earlier work.

More archaeological study is needed. The surviving brickwork of the walls is 16th-century, built in English bond (rather than the Flemish bond used in the 17th century) with bricks laid in alternate rows of 'headers' and 'stretchers'. Much diapering – bricks laid in a diamond pattern – is evident.

Early in the 18th century, perhaps after the estate had been inherited by two orphaned Shurley daughters, the house was radically downsized and transformed into a pretty Queen Anne box with hipped roof. Tudor arch windows were confusingly moved from one place to another, as indeed the splendid two-storey stone porch may have been. With Doric columns below and Ionic above and a family inscription 'abstain and sustain', this is a prize piece of Renaissance architecture.

The house slept for a century and a half. It was let until about 1870, when its new owner, Henry King, added a kitchen wing with bay window and exotically shaped gable. However, these alterations did not meet with the approval of *Vogue* magazine, which complained of the deadening effect of plate-glass windows and the outrage of plate glass in the front door. Fortunately these were soon to be replaced by leaded lights introduced by a sensitive restoration architect, Basil Oliver.

More recently, Andrew and Sarah-Jane Tillard have undone clumsy 1950s additions on the entrance front, which they have effected by introducing a shaped gable and slender arched windows over the entrance. The front door opens into a hall-cum-dining room filled with light that allows you to look out of the house in two directions, down through the long kitchen and ahead through windows into the garden. The panelled drawing room has an impressive carved fireplace, rising the height of the room, painted to suggest stone. Out of sight of the hall is a large billiard room and well-equipped rod room designed to take advantage of the excellent trout fishing on the Ouse.

On the first floor the whole of the 17th-century south front is occupied by a spacious master bedroom suite with palatial carpeted bathroom, as well as a second bathroom and dressing room designed to enable a husband to slip away early to work without disturbing the family.

By making use of the attics the Tillards have cleverly contrived nine further bedrooms with bathrooms nearby, all with interesting views.

Today the grounds are the making of the house, filled with stately topiary and formed into a series of attractive garden rooms, providing a choice of sheltered places to sit out and eat, as well as concealing an inviting swimming pool close to the house.

Opposite the entrance, a small stretch of moat survives with a fountain pond beyond. There is also a 16th-century gatehouse and chapel that have been converted into a cottage and a flat respectively. Other outbuildings make the house appear like a picturesque small village with coach house and stables and a pair of oast houses serving as a garage.

The swimming pool is overlooked by a Tudor gazebo.

The climax comes with the so-called party barn, a large traditional aisled barn open to the roof timbers and splendidly preserved as a single open space, and now equipped with kitchens and loos serving for every kind of event. It has also proved popular for hire by singers rehearsing for performances at nearby Glyndebourne.

Isfield stands secluded at the centre of 300 acres with an ancient lime avenue leading north from the house. The estate is unusually well watered, with the Ouse meeting the Uck and a splendidly broad six-stepped weir where you can watch the fish leaping.

Stately topiary forms a series of garden rooms on the grand scale.

LITTLE THAKEHAM — Thakeham

1903 Lutyens house that became a popular hotel and is now a house again

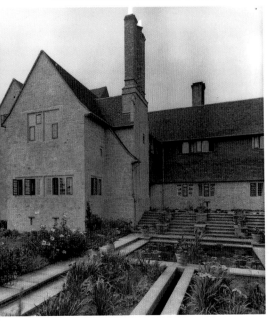

Lutyens loved to place fountain pools and lily ponds in front of his houses.

THE BEST HOUSES OF Sir Edwin Lutyens rank among the most covetable buildings in English architecture. Little Thakeham was one of Lutyens's own favourites – he describes it as 'the best of the bunch' in a letter to the architect Herbert Baker.

Built in 1902–3, the house is delightful, looking like a perfect gabled Elizabethan manor that has been transformed within by a leading early-Georgian architect. Lutyens's client was a Kent schoolmaster who two years earlier had inherited a fortune from his father. It stands far down a longish drive, secluded in its own forecourt paved in the Lutyens manner and inset with flower beds. The plan is an 'H' with wings wrapping round to create a sense of enclosure. Lichened stone blends with mellow roof tiles.

Inside, Lutyens set out to surprise and delight. He loved big halls, imposing corridors and intriguing staircases. Hall, stair and passages take half the volume of the two main floors. The hall is full of Lutyens conceits and jokes. What might be a medieval screens passage is inset chunky Classical stone doorways. Over the central fireplace is a small minstrels' gallery – exactly where the smoke should rise up the chimney. There is a magnificent oriel window that is the full height of the room.

There is no deceit in the quality of materials used throughout the house – floors of stone and wood that will last for centuries, smooth stone window surrounds and brick sills. Solid oak doors and small-pane iron windows all remain intact. Cosy low-ceilinged living rooms and bedrooms contrast with the great height of the hall.

The staircase rises in short straight flights onto successive landings that are in effect balconies overlooking the hall – the perfect place to look down onto a party.

When Lutyens visited the house in 1904 on a lovely July evening he found 'the great Downs bathed in reflected light and the garden wonderfully good'. From this letter it is also evident that Ernest Blackburn was his own gardener – not Gertrude Jekyll, whose name is always conjured up as soon as Lutyens is mentioned.

Lutyens continued, 'He has made the pergola delightful in a way quite his own – with hollyhocks … his attitude is so unlike the general run of people: like leaving a picture unfinished to enjoy the initial stages.' Blackburn's stone walls, yew hedges and sunken lily pool remain.

The building of Little Thakeham was accompanied by a furious row in the architectural press. Blackburn turned to Lutyens after he had begun a new house to the designs of another architect, Hatchard Smith. Smith saw Lutyens's acceptance of the commission as an appalling breach of professional etiquette. The magazine *Building News* took his side, abusing vacillating clients and intriguing architects.

Blackburn replied, vigorously attacking the view that 'houses are built in order to display the skill of the architect ... Houses are built for men to live in, and those who live in them are entitled to have them built to suit their fancy and convenience.'

Blackburn's daughter recalled, 'My father had meant to build a country cottage; instead he had twelve bedrooms, and – more significant at this period – three bathrooms... '

In 1979, Tim Ratcliff, a third-generation hotelier, moved to Little Thakeham to open a country-house hotel. Unlike many country-house hotels, it has not been enlarged with new annexes and bedroom wings and has prospered modestly with just nine bedrooms. 'I tell my chef that we don't want a Michelin star, people coming down from London want country food,' he says.

The house is listed Grade I and as there is little hope of gaining planning permission to build the extra bedrooms most hoteliers would want, it is more than possible that Little Thakeham will become a family house once again. The drawbacks are minor ones. The house has relatively little land, just 5 acres, and the stables (a discreet distance away) are in separate ownership. That said, this is an undoubted masterpiece in an idyllic spot.

The garden front is dominated by Lutyens' polygonal oriel window.

MONKTON   West Dean
Surrealist creation of Edward James

MONKTON IS THE EXTRAORDINARY surrealist creation of Edward James, millionaire eccentric and patron of Salvador Dali, who died in self-imposed exile in the Mexico jungle in 1984. Two years later, faced with news of the impending sale of the house and the dispersal of its contents, SAVE and the Thirties Society published *Monkton: a Vanishing Surrealist Dream*, in an attempt to preserve the house for the nation.

Monkton is approached by a long rising drive through Sussex beechwoods. Designed by Sir Edwin Lutyens in the style of a Sussex farmhouse, it had been sensationally transformed by James in the 1920s. Clive Aslet wrote, 'When you reach the house today – oh brother! Palm trees sprout under the eaves; the walls are in violet; the tiles on the roof (specially imported) are in stripes of green and black: a weird sort of clock tells you what day of the week it is, but not the time.'

Dali, who often stayed in James's London house, advised on Monkton. One of his ideas was for a drawing room with walls that swelled in and out like the inside of a dog's stomach. Much of the surrealism at Monkton, however, was James's own. He took on the designer Norris Wakefield, who went down to Monkton every Tuesday for four years. The pink front door opened onto a staircase hall with a jazzy, wavy wallpaper that jumped before your eyes, a forerunner of the kinetic art of the 1960s. The sweeping stair had a solid balustrade that was covered on both sides with the wave wallpaper, increasing the overwhelming effect. Half way up, a porthole window looked into a fish tank in the form of a glass column, once filled with anemones and tropical fish, which rose beside a 'Fish' bathroom with fishy paper, and wall and ceiling lights brought from Paris.

A high point of the house was the two bright red sofas in the dining room, designed by Dali, modelled on the lips of Mae West. When the tops of the sofas showed signs of

Palm tree-columns were added to the existing Lutyens house, while the interior was sensationally transformed by the decorator Norris Wakefield.

moth, James had them patched with little caterpillars of green baize to match the carpet. The deep-buttoned upholstery of the alcove seats was continued across the wall to create the impression of a luxurious padded cell.

When it came to the study James told Wakefield, 'I want a blue and yellow room. Blue like my suit.' The upholsterer's fabric sent down was rejected. James wanted serge, which had to come from a tailor. The colour of the yellow sofas was taken from the cowslip James wore in his buttonhole. Beside them stood a standard lamp made from a stuffed snake shot by James's father.

James's four-poster bed was derived from an illustration of Napoleon's hearse with palms at the corners. The greeny-black silk hangings were fringed with gold. The walls were hung with a fine silvery net while the radiator skulked behind chainmail. The next-door bathroom was lined with peach-coloured alabaster while the globe shaving mirror was etched with lines of longitude and latitude. In the map room James wanted a bed to 'lie in and look at the sky – just as though it was there'. Wakefield covered the ceiling in dark blue glass, back-lit and studded with stars.

Gavin Stamp described the house as a 'Twentieth century monument of the greatest importance and interest' and 'quite enchanting and wonderful'. Lord Montagu, then chairman of English Heritage, lent his strong support, emphasising that what 'now seems odd and eccentric will be increasingly appreciated for its brilliance'. Alas the sale went ahead, and the doors of Monkton never opened. Yet a house it remains, hopefully with some of its extraordinary interior intact.

PAXHILL — Haywards Heath
Elizabethan E-plan mansion that became a home after years of institutional use

IT IS A RARE TREAT TO FIND a stately home that is virtually unknown. At Paxhill it is the more surprising as the house stands just outside bustling Haywards Heath in Sussex. Mrs Persaud, who has nursed it back to health, says, 'I lived in the town for eight years without knowing the house existed.'

One explanation is that, over four centuries, Paxhill's owners were always plain esquires, never baronets, noble lords or even MPs. Though the house has clearly been Victorianised, the core is a grand Elizabethan E-plan with gables, mullions and lively bay windows, all built of the greenish stone typical of the county. There is a 1780s drawing by S.H. Grimm in the British Library showing it in unaltered state without a single sash window – quite remarkable at that date. Over the porch is the date 1595 and then the initials 'NB' standing for Ninian Boord (spelt also as Boorde and later Board).

Paxhill's moment of fame came when General Montgomery stayed here early in 1944 and on May 22 George VI came to review the troops as they prepared for D-Day. Hard times came when Paxhill, like so many larger houses, descended to institutional use as a nursing home.

Today a sense of splendour has returned. A long drive flanked by parkland ascends to the house, which stands on a knoll with grand gates and a huge balustrade-enclosed gravel courtyard. To the south the large garden terrace has a commanding view down to a lake, over the tops of newly clipped Irish yews.

The smaller 16th-century mullioned windows contrast with the larger Victorian ones on the left.

Inside, Paxhill is one surprise after another. The great hall is not Elizabethan but early Georgian with bolection moulded panelling and twin fireplaces set curiously at the ends of the long wall. To the left a lobby leads into a large dining room richly panelled in Jacobean style. The plaster ceiling is on an intricate pattern of squares and quatrefoils inset with portrait medallions and with all the signs of being done by hand around 1600. It is also very close to a series of these late-Elizabethan ceilings in houses such as Mapledurham in Oxfordshire and the old palace at Bromley-by-Bow, now in the V & A Museum.

Ron and Kay Persaud bought Paxhill in 2001 and rapidly made it into a family home once more. 'My husband's work is in property and our initial plan was to make apartments but very quickly we decided this was wrong for the house.'

Behind the dining room is a large modern kitchen opening onto the garden. On the other side of the hall, puzzlingly, is a second hall with a grand screen of columns. This transpires to have been the main staircase, stripped out just before the house was listed (rather late) in 1973. Beyond lie the finest rooms in the house, a panelled sitting room where the beautifully figured oak looks like watered silk. Neo-Jacobean may be rather heavy to the modern eye, but the woodwork here is exceptional in quality, superb joinery using oak of the finest quality, all still in pristine condition. The panelling in the drawing room is an intricate pattern of squares within squares, Renaissance arches are set in the double doors, and there is a massive two-tier chimneypiece and a plaster frieze coloured to look like Spanish leather. In the Library beyond is real Spanish leather, darkened by years of smoke but all the more atmospheric for it.

Upstairs there is a large run of spacious bedrooms, well-lit by large mullioned windows, while the attic makes a home office suite on the most generous scale. The north wing is a separate realm where teenagers can play music or even drums at maximum volume without disturbance.

For anyone wanting to run a business from home or supplement their income by organising events and weddings, Paxhill has impressive possibilities. The drawing room opens onto an elegant arched loggia facing south, with more than an echo of the most exquisite of all Renaissance loggias, at Cranborne in Dorset.

The Boords, whose tombs are in the church at Lindfield, continued at Paxhill until 1790 when the estate passed by a daughter's marriage to Gibbs Crawfurd. The north wing was added for Northall Laurie in 1865, and a south wing for William Sturdy, who bought the estate in 1877. His rainwater pipes are dated 1889. Augustus Hare, who came in 1894, thought the house 'much spoilt by modern additions'. Today we can see them as belonging to a series of opulent Victorian rebuilding and remodelling of major Sussex houses, including Worth Abbey, Wakehurst and Warningleigh.

Behind the house the garden is laid out as a series of enclosed terraces, with a very pretty gazebo or garden pavilion of 1600 date. A walk leads up to an informal pleasure ground with two ancient limes of such enormous girth that they look a full four hundred years old. The Persauds have increased the land that goes with the house from 5 acres to over 60 and it now has a sense of seclusion and peace.

The coach house beside the house is in separate ownership but in the magnificent sweeping views from the house even nearby Haywards Heath is barely visible.

The Elizabethan ceiling is inset with portrait medallions.

SHILLINGLEE   Haslemere
Georgian house that stood a gutted shell until restored as apartments

HANDSOME GEORGIAN HOUSES BUILT OF deep red brick are one of the glories of Sussex. In 1936 Shillinglee Park was awarded the accolade of a full article in Country Life by Arthur Oswald. Seven years later it was gutted by fire. It stood a ruin until 1976, when it was the first house taken on and converted into apartments by Christopher Buxton, pioneer of country-house conversions, who now lives at Kirtlington Park in Oxfordshire.

Shillinglee's graceful proportions and fine detail appear to be the work of Thomas Steel of Chichester, a carpenter who on October 18, 1734 agreed 'to survey or carry on a Building or Dwelling house at Shillinglee Park According to a Draught'. Beneath the central pediment is a panel with the initials 'ET' and the date 1735. 'ET' stands for Edward Turnour. A south wing was added in the 1770s for Edward Turnour Garth (who took the name of Turnour in 1744) and was created 1st Earl of Winterton (an Irish peerage) in 1766. Turnour had applied in 1756 to the Duke of Newcastle, the great political fixer, for a peerage and received one for voting consistently against Bute and Grenville, though like many 18th-century MPs he never spoke in the House. The 6th Earl achieved the rare distinction of serving as both 'Baby' and 'Father' of the House of Commons, winning a by-election at Horsham at the age of 21 and still being an MP forty-seven years later.

The house now looks out once again over a noble stretch of park.

ST JOSEPH'S ABBEY   Storrington
Many-gabled house with the South Downs in the background

ENGLISH COUNTRY HOUSES OFTEN OWE their survival to their adaptability. St Joseph's Abbey was formerly a religious retreat just by the church in Storrington, West Sussex. It began as a 17th-century rectory and was bought in 1911 by an antiques collector by the name of Bethell, who introduced a Queen Anne-style oak staircase. Most rooms are panelled. In the 1920s a new owner added a ballroom and music room. 'The house splits very neatly into periods, each becoming a separate house,' says Michael Wilson, the entrepreneur who has bought and converted it. In one new home, the former chapel with wagon-shaped plaster ceiling has been converted into a kitchen and dining room.

The only external change has been the insertion of a new front door, leading to a rooftop penthouse that he has created over the ballroom. All the main rooms retain original lead glazing, each to a different ornamental pattern. The new houses overlook lawns, and the more formal parts of the garden by the house are assigned to individual residents, so that no one walks in front of a neighbour's window.

One big challenge with conversions, Wilson explains, lies in introducing new plumbing without damaging historic interiors or being heard through the new party walls. He used cast-iron pipes at St Joseph's to ensure that the plumbing was silent. He says: 'There is strong demand for these conversions, but problems arise when people can't sell the houses they're moving out of. So now we look at their houses and weigh up the potential for improvement, or for selling off a small plot of land. If it works, we take on the house, enabling our purchasers to complete.'

The additions of each period have become separate houses.

WARWICKSHIRE

BRAMCOTE HALL — Polesworth
Swagger baroque house left rotting in a cornfield

BRAMCOTE STANDS IN OPEN ROLLING farmland, well placed to see and be seen for miles around. Most substantial country houses are sheltered by trees. Bramcote is different, largely because the modern farm buildings nearby announce the highly commercial approach to large-scale farming employed, in which trees are an obstacle. But for this, Bramcote would be a prize country house in immaculate order, commanding a seven-figure sum. Instead it is a text-book example of what happens when those with the powers to protect listed buildings fail to use them.

Alternate windows appear to have been blank from the start.

Bramcote's commanding presence is due to its splendid swept up gables, a baroque gesture suggesting a date in the second quarter of the 18th century. The large number of windows – nine along the front and six along the sides on both main floors– seem designed to take advantage of its position. Some, it is true, appear to have been blank from the beginning – it is more likely that this was due to the internal arrangements of the rooms than to the tax on glass introduced in 1745. Without the blank windows, some of the corner rooms would have been very cold indeed in winter.

When I visited the house in the late 1980s it had already stood empty for years. The steps up to the front door were choked with weeds. But in March 1990 I received an encouraging reply from the solicitors acting for the Trustees of John Gilmour's Marriage Settlement, owners of the Hall, saying a grant was being sought. I wrote to the Chief Executive of English Heritage asking whether Bramcote was eligible for one of the new emergency 'buildings at risk' grants introduced by Jocelyn Stevens, the chairman. The reply I received was equivocatory, if frank. 'An application was made and we are now in the process of refusing it,' I was told. 'We shall therefore rely on market forces, on listed building controls and if necessary – on support for the local authority on the service of statutory notices'. The result? Bramcote has stood rotting ever since. Yet with its warm red brick and handsome proportions, the house would be stunning if restored.

CASTLE BROMWICH HALL · Castle Bromwich
Late-Elizabethan house in urgent need of a caring owner

AS THE STRONG WINTER SUN STREAMED IN through the magnificent Elizabethan mullions of Castle Bromwich Hall early in 2007, I gazed out over the gloriously replanted formal gardens, fervently praying that this great house could once again find an owner who would lavish on it the love and money it deserved. Here, Elizabethan architecture is married with superb James II interiors of the very finest quality, all surviving remarkably unaltered, with not a Georgian sash in sight. The Victorians added a tower and re-panelled the entrance hall, but otherwise house and gardens have changed little in nearly three hundred years.

The Hall's last resident, Ida, Countess of Bradford, died in 1936. Even then Birmingham suburbia was engulfing the estate. Yet the Hall remains the centre of an attractive historic enclave. The box garden to the north has gilded gates leading to the still thriving 1726 baroque church. The handsome coach house to the east is now smart offices. The grand vista looking south is still green, framed by trees and carpeted by turf. Best of all, walled gardens on every side provide the seclusion and the protected setting that the Hall needs to survive with dignity.

The Elizabethan house was built in about 1599 by Sir Edward Devereux and sold in 1657 to Sir John Bridgeman, whose coat of arms and monogram were carved on his imposing new porch. To carry out his ambitious plans for both house and gardens, Bridgeman turned to the soldier-architect Captain William Winde, whose country houses are as fine as those by Hugh May and Roger Pratt.

Winde regularly employed the very finest craftsmen, notably the sculptor Edward Pierce, who supplied statues and chimney pieces for Castle Bromwich Hall, and Edward Goudge, the plasterer whose ceilings, groaning with flowers, fruit and foliage, rank with carving by Grinling Gibbons in virtuosity.

A Charles II porch was added to the designs of Captain William Winde.

A large section of the baroque terraced gardens have been superbly restored by a trust.

On the entrance front the stone of the Elizabethan mullions has so mellowed that it barely stands out from the soft red brick. By contrast Winde's two-storey baroque porch adds a strong classical note with Salamonic or twisted columns and niches inset with statues of peace and prosperity.

The Hall, last occupied by Bovis as offices, belonged to a Dubai investor. With a guide price of £2.75 million, and a floor area of some 21,000 sq ft, it had potential appeal to the new breed of entrepreneurial owners who like to put great houses to work to earn their keep. The opportunity was to create a magical synergy with the trust that has so beautifully restored the gardens with help from the Heritage Lottery Fund.

The baroque terraces step down the hillside with beautifully replanted *parterres*, bowers, kitchen garden, orchards and wilderness. Cross vistas are handsomely terminated by Classical pavilions and trellis archways. There is an archery ground and a maze – so many garden rooms and axial walks that it needs a full hour to explore them all. The restoration has been done to the most exacting standards, with hundreds of yards of trim holly hedges tapering to a point like obelisks.

The big challenge was the work needed inside the house. The legacy of the last commercial occupants included (in the finest rooms) trunking for electric cabling run across superb oak panelling in front of fireplaces, hot water pipes that cut straight through door frames, and hideous griddle lights (even suspended from Goudge's peerless ceilings) in virtually every room. But some of the unpicking could be fun. Beneath the carpet tiles in the hall, an elaborate stone and marble floor was immediately visible. Over one fireplace, a mural of scrolled foliage on a crimson ground has recently emerged beneath wallpaper. If restoration of the house could match the standard that has already been set in the garden, Castle Bromwich Hall could once again be one of marvels of middle England.

COMPTON VERNEY   Kineton
Set in a vast Capability Brown park, the house stood empty for forty years

SET IN A VAST PARK SLOPING DOWN to the still waters of two extensive lakes, Compton Verney is the epitome of the 18th-century idea of natural beauty. Yet on repeated visits during the 1970s and 1980s there was also an extraordinary tristesse. The house was shut up, though fortunately not vandalised, and only came partly to life with the occasional gymkhana. Harry Ellard, the night club owner who had bought the estate in 1958, would not respond to any approaches about restoring or selling the house. In SAVE's 1984 book *The Country House:to be or not to be*, Kit Martin illustrated an outline scheme for converting the house into eight houses and apartment without a single external alteration, simply be using five existing doors which opened off the courtyard.

The house was rebuilt by Francis Smith of Warwick for the 12th Baron Willoughby de Broke, soon after he inherited in 1711. George Vertue, who came in 1737, describes Compton Verney as 'a well built house of 1714'. A dignified stable block was added by James Gibbs in about 1735. Robert Adam was commissioned to remodel the house in 1760, which he did externally in a style echoing the baroque work.

The 19th Baron Willoughby de Broke sold the house in 1921 to Joseph Watson, a soap manufacturer who the next year became Baron Manton of Compton Verney. During the Second World War the park was taken over by the Army School of Smoke Camouflage, where boffins dreamt up schemes to baffle the Luftwaffe with vast clouds of smoke over British cities. Then on VE Day, the Pioneer Corps stationed

The monumental arched windows are in the style of Vanbrugh.

The colonnaded entrance court has now been transformed into an art gallery.

there jubilantly tipped the balustrades of the Adam bridge into the lake – one piece of vandalism the War Office actually agreed to pay for after James Lees-Milne had questions asked in the Commons.

After that the house was never to be lived in again. In the mid 1980s it was bought by Christopher Buxton, the demon country-house rescuer who had also bought Croome Court and Kirtlington Park. Buxton thought first of a residential solution, selling off the walled garden with permission for new executive houses.

His ideas then turned to the idea of a Glyndebourne of the Midlands – the house is close to Stratford and the M40. Thanks to substantial sponsorship, consultants were dispatched to look at the very latest opera houses and facilities. The outcome was an ambitious proposal for a 1,200-seat opera house with a stage that would be large enough to take travelling productions from major city opera houses such as the Met in New York, with some seven side and back stages (equal in size to the main stage). Alas, with recession biting at the end of the 1980s, it all became too difficult to fund and though the winning design by the Danish architect Henning Larsen was approved, Compton Verney and its park were sold in 1993 to the Peter Moores Foundation.

Moores told me, 'Every great house must have something going on inside.' To him Compton Verney was the perfect place to display a major art collection. 'We could afford it and half the population of England was within an hour and a half's drive.'

The restoration of the house was carried out by Rodney Melville & Partners, the new work by Stanton Williams. Their new wing is invisible on the lake approach and only comes into view on the garden front, where bare stone walls and flat roofs are a complete counterpoint to the arched windows and shallow gables of the old house. It is a shock, but a gentle one and the blemishless, beautifully grooved new stone highlights the weathering, colour and texture of the old stone on the mansion. Old and new are joined only by glass.

COOMBE ABBEY — Coventry
Left decaying as the council would not serve a repairs order on itself

'Water, water everywhere … and not just in the moat' ran the caption to my article on Coombe Abbey in *The Times* on April 11, 1992. The ladies who ran the medieval banquets in the ground-floor rooms told me, 'We cross our fingers and hope the rain does not pour through the ceiling.' As an economy measure, the council had decided to stop all maintenance work seven years earlier. 'It's the hidden gutters which are choked with dead pigeons,' I learnt.

As Coventry District Council was unlikely to serve a repairs order on itself, the best solution seemed the National Audit Office, which at that time had condemned a Government Department for allowing Teddington Hall in south-west London to fall down. Hope, however, arrived in the form of an hotel proposal drawn up with Lumley Castle Ltd and the promised employment of leading consultants such as the archaeologist Warwick Rodwell, the conservation architect Martin Ashley and the landscape architect Hal Moggeridge.

The Abbey, founded in 1150, had become the richest in Warwickshire, but after the Dissolution was sold in 1622 to the Cravens, remaining in the family till 1923. The cloister walks date from the 15th century. The pediment west range, built to the designs of the soldier-architect Captain William Winde, is one of the most handsome Charles II fronts in the country. A vast east wing was added in the 1860s by the gifted architect W. Eden Nesfield, whose father, W.A. Nesfield, laid out the formal gardens. In the 1920s Coombe Abbey was sold to a local builder who stripped out fireplaces, panelling and even ceilings. Fortunately, during a three-day sale in 1925 many items remained.

In February 1995 Coombe Abbey opened as an hotel opened with sixty-three bedrooms, cloister restaurant and chapter house bar. This is no minimalist hip hotel – bedrooms brim with antiques and one bedroom has a voluptuous silk-lined tent-topped canopy, surrounded by balustrades.

The graceful Charles II front looks out over the extensive formal gardens.

GRIMSHAW HALL — Knowle
1600 E-plan house rescued by a pen manufacturer

GRIMSHAW HALL TAKES YOU BACK FOUR HUNDRED YEARS in an instant. It looks, so it seems, exactly as it did in 1600, with leaded windows, soaring chimneys and overhanging upper storeys. Here is the full dazzling virtuosity of English half-timbering with herringbone and lozenge patterns almost as intricate as the markings of a leopard.

The front is a perfect example of the E-plan in honour of Queen Elizabeth I, with projecting ends and central porch. Better still, the sides and the back are every inch as picturesque. Then the thought dawns – how can the house have survived so miraculously intact through the centuries without a Georgian sash or Victorian servants' wing?

The answer is that, yes, the clock has been put back, on two occasions, but so cleverly and sensitively that it is hard to tell the old work from the new. This is not pastiche but Victorian Arts and Crafts and the Edwardian love affair with the past.

The amount of herringbone- and lozenge-pattern timbering is almost overwhelming.

On both occasions exceptional architects were involved – adopting an approach that English Heritage and too many local authorities might summarily reject today – that of blending the old with the new to create a seamless whole.

The house was built by the Grimshaw family in the second half of the 16th century. By the 19th century it had become three cottages. It was then acquired by Joseph Gillot, a prosperous pen manufacturer known as 'his nibs'. He brought in the architect J.A. Chatwin, who had been given the delicate task of restoring and extending what is now Birmingham Cathedral. Then, just before the First World War, the family called in W. Alexander Harvey, the architect who had laid out the famous Bournville Estate for the Cadburys.

The result is a composition that is richer and grander than most half-timbered houses in Sussex or Suffolk and as exuberant as almost any in Cheshire. For those who live or work in the vast bustling megalopolis that is Birmingham, this is a prime site indeed. Though

The first-floor bay windows are built on bracketed supports set beneath projecting gables.

just three miles from Solihull, Knowle retains the feel of a country village, with a few too many modern buildings on the high street perhaps, but a ravishing medieval church at the end. Grimshaw Hall is secluded in the centre of its 17 acres of grounds – with extensive lawns flanking the drive, trim yew hedges enclosing a modest formal garden to the side, and further lawns sloping down to a small lake.

When I visited the house in 2003, there were are white doves on the roof of the dovecote, ducks on the water and Canada geese. Part of the substantial coach house block had been converted into an indoor swimming pool with dance floor next door. The wall of sliding glass was fairly horrendous from the outside but fortunately not visible from the house itself.

Inside, Grimshaw Hall lacked the great chamber with rich plasterwork one hopes to find at this date but the exposed timbers gave every room great character – timber posts in the walls, timber beams and, at the top of the house, the roof trusses were exposed to dramatic effect. There were just two discreetly placed bathrooms for seven bedrooms – and more would not be easy to achieve, even by converting bedrooms.

Though in good condition, the house gives the impression that its last owner, businessman and motorcycle enthusiast Keith Moore, who bought it in 2001, barely occupied it. In 2002, Solihull Council fired a warning shot that may have deterred developers seeking to break up the Grade I listed property – officers recommended the refusal of an application to turn the outbuildings into ten dwellings and build twelve garages and it was withdrawn. This is one of the best surviving country houses in the Birmingham area, not too large for family use, and should remain in one ownership.

MAXSTOKE CASTLE   Coleshill
A licence to crenellate was granted in 1345

MAXSTOKE IS ONE OF THE BEST-PRESERVED medieval castles in England. In form, it is like a child's toy castle – an almost perfect square complete with battlemented walls, twin-towered gatehouse and octagonal towers at the four corners. It is surrounded on all sides by a moat, though the pink sandstone walls do not rise straight up from the water but are softened by a narrow stretch of turf.

Like many medieval castles, Maxstoke can be dated precisely by a licence to crenellate that was granted here in 1345 by Edward III to William de Clinton, Earl of Huntingdon. The wording describes Maxstoke as 'a dwelling place for the use of John de Clynton', Huntingdon's nephew and heir. Huntingdon had been created an earl, then virtually the highest honour in the land, in 1337. The first marquessate was only created in 1385, as was the first non-royal dukedom, that of Duke of Ireland, granted to Robert de Vere, a favourite of Richard II.

Born in about 1304, Clinton rose rapidly. In 1327 he was one of the small band of the King's followers who entered Nottingham Castle by an underground passage, seized Mortimer and rushed him to the Tower of London. Immediately after, he was made Constable of Dover Castle and warden of the Cinque Ports. Maxstoke was clearly not intended as an impregnable defence like the great Welsh castles. There are no chain holes for a drawbridge; however, there is a slit for a portcullis over the

Set four-square in its moat, Maxstoke Castle is dazzlingly reflected in the still water.

The timber-framed residential range contrasts with the stonework of the battlements.

entrance as well as a group of 'murder holes' through which rods could be thrust at attackers or water poured to douse a fire started against the gates.

Doors on either side of the first-floor chamber of the gatehouse open onto a wall walk behind the battlements. Interestingly, there is no access to three of the towers at this level, only a short linking passage to the next section of wall walk. By contrast there is access to the larger Lady Tower, presumably for the use of the castle's keeper. Though there are no arrow loops in the battlements, the grooves in the sides of each battlement (or merlons, as they are correctly called) show they were designed to hold protective wooden shutters which could be propped open to allow defenders to fire without revealing themselves.

The first known test of the defences took place in 1357 when the Patent Rolls record a complaint by John de Clinton that Henry de Arden and others 'broke the walls of his castle and houses at Maxstoke, carried away his goods and assaulted his men and servants'. Two years later a pardon granted to one of the accused mentions the theft of vessels of silver to the value of £40 and a hundred shillings of silver money. John de Clinton was probably in France at the time – he fought at the battle of Poitiers in 1356. Henry IV was a visitor in 1404 when he signed letters patent here. In 1438 Maxstoke came into the hands of the great Humphrey Stafford, who was created Duke of Buckingham six years later. He spent long periods at the castle which was conveniently placed at the centre of his vast estates and the castle doors were covered with iron sheeting embossed with the Stafford knot. Fragments of the iron remain. Maxstoke was also close to Coventry where Henry VI often held court and Buckingham was the King's most loyal supporter, joining the monarch at nearby Kenilworth Castle with a strong guard at the time of Jack Cade's rebellion in 1450. During the minority of the 3rd Duke, custody of the Stafford estates was granted to

Lady Margaret Beaufort, mother of Henry VII. For her the main apartment was furnished 'thoroughly with glazing'. By 1582 the hall and great chamber were 'moche in decaye' and during the Civil War the castle was garrisoned by Lord Brooke. As a result Maxstoke stood in danger of being 'slighted' like Kenilworth to render it indefensible. Instead William Dilke, whose family had acquired the castle in 1599, was allowed by Cromwell's Council of State to give £2,000 in security that his house 'shall not be made use of or possessed by our enemies'.

Large gothic windows looking out over the moat on the west side of the castle indicate the position of the great hall and chapel of the medieval castle, though the original buildings around the courtyard have largely disappeared or been lost to view in remodelling. The great chamber or banqueting hall has been handsomely restored and the timber roof, hidden by Victorian alterations, has been reopened to view. The cellar in the Lady Tower remains, with a shallow vault supported by impressively massive ribs. Today, the Fetherston-Dilkes family remain in residence and the castle is open occasionally for charity.

The timber roof to the banqueting hall was long hidden.

STONELEIGH
Kenilworth

Vast Midland seat of the Leigh family, where Jane Austen came to stay

STONELEIGH IS APPROACHED BY A LIME AVENUE that is nearly half a mile long, crossing the Avon on an elegant Classical bridge. Founded in the 12th century, the abbey was acquired after the Reformation by a Lord Mayor of London, Sir Thomas Leigh. The great west front by, Francis Smith of Warwick, is a stupendous sight, almost palace-like in its proportions with three tiers of tall windows set in a noble sandstone facade. Grand castellated stables laid out on a half moon plan were added by Charles Samuel Smith, a pupil of Sir Jeffry Wyatville, in 1815–19, as well as a conservatory by the precocious William Burn in 1851. Inside the Smith wing, there is superb early 18th century plasterwork and panelling. The medieval gatehouse was built in 1346 and is one of only a few in Britain still standing complete.

Yet for half a century Stoneleigh had a chequered existence. A large part of the grounds had been sold off as the National Agricultural Showground. By 1997 the house had been closed to the public for eight years as debts had forced the trustees to sell furniture and to halt even the most basic maintenance. Pieces of stone

The palatial front was added by the master mason Francis Smith of Warwick.

cornice had crashed to the ground and dry rot had taken hold. The roof of the vast Regency stable block had collapsed from end to end.

The only way to prevent the break-up of Stoneleigh appeared to be by the creation of a new charitable trust that would take on both the abbey and its contents, reopening the state rooms and finding self-sustaining uses for other parts of the buildings.

With financial help from the Lottery and the European Regional Development Fund, Stoneleigh has now been rescued and restored and the main staterooms, park and woodland opened to the public. Kit Martin has created nearly thirty houses in other parts of the house and nearby estate buildings. Luckily, virtually no external alterations were needed on the buildings around the former abbey cloister. The stables have been restored from end to end and let as offices, while two sections with the Regency stalls for the horses have been faithfully restored. The former riding school is now let for receptions and events.

Stoneleigh plays its own part in literary history as Jane Austen came to stay here in 1806, accompanying the Rev.

Top: A courtyard lies behind the gabled monastic buildings.

Above: Scagliola columns imitate Siena marble.

Thomas Leigh who, in the manner of one of her novels, had unexpectedly had the good fortune to inherit the house and estate. She found 'long avenues, dark rookeries and twenty-six bedchambers in the new part of the house and a great many (some very good ones) in the old'. Her description of Sotherton in *Mansfield Park*, almost certainly recalls her stay at Stoneleigh eight years earlier. She describes 'old-fashioned rooms, amply furnished in the taste of fifty years back', walled gardens and chapel with a profusion of mahogany and 'crimson cushions disappearing over the ledge of the family gallery above'. Charles II and Queen Victoria and Prince Albert have also stayed at Stoneleigh.

The main saloon has rich scagliola columns and a striking frieze depicting lions and unicorns, the crest of the Leighs. Beyond, further staterooms retain their magnificent oak panelling. The Stoneleigh chapel is one of the finest family chapels in England with woodwork by George Eboral and Benjamin King and stucco by Benjamin Wright.

TYSOE MANOR   Upper Tysoe
1340s house that has grown through the centuries

IF YOU DREAM OF A TRADITIONAL CHRISTMAS in the Cotswolds, Tysoe Manor could hardly be bettered. Never have I seen such quantities of brilliant red berries in a garden – plentiful sprigs of holly, soaring pyracantha and low-branching cotoneaster weighed down with scarlet berries growing as profusely as grapes on a vine.

Adrian Wield, who bought the house in 1987, has made the garden a perfect frame for the house, choosing shrubs that take fifteen or more years to start flowering and are now in their first maturity. For a while he was a financial adviser to Ambrose Congreve, creator of the legendary gardens at Mount Congreve near Waterford, and many of the plants came direct from the nursery there.

Better still, the garden has been ingeniously planned for the longest possible flowering season, with early and late plants such as blue-flowered ceanothus and honey-scented philadelphus. To contain it all, Irish yews are pinned together from inside and shrubs wired up to stop them spreading. The beauty of the house is the warm butterscotch stone that glows as soon as the sun comes out. Tysoe has the special charm of houses that have grown through the centuries. Each section of roof neatly indicates a different construction period but succeeding generations have sought to blend, not contrast, with the earlier work, carefully matching both stone and roof tiles.

In the 14th century Tysoe belonged to the de Staffords, who had crossed to England with William the Conqueror. Theirs is the earliest block at the west of the long south-facing front. It is thought to date from the 1340s, just before the Black Death, and it retains a pretty gothic window with twin pointed arches on the first floor. Excited professors

The gardens have been planted for colour through the seasons.

from Norwich have pointed out that the house was once moated – following the line of the present ha-ha around the garden. Tysoe passed to the 3rd Duke of Buckingham, builder of Thornbury Castle, who met the familiar fate of those who surpass their king in the magnificence of their building and was beheaded. The manor was granted to the Compton family, who soon after built the glorious Elizabethan country house, Compton Wynyates, in the next valley.

The monumental oak staircase was added in the 1920s.

Tysoe became a secondary house but was important enough to be extended shortly after the Restoration of the monarchy in 1660. A new entrance was added in the 1720s.

Scandal hit the family when the 6th Marquess of Northampton had a romance with the actress Daisy Markham, who bore him twins. In a famous 1913 court case he was held to have broken his word to marry her and had to pay out £50,000, then the largest sum awarded for breach of promise. Tysoe was one of several farms sold – in this case to the tenant farmer – to pay the debt.

In about 1928 the farmer sold the house to General Horace Sewell, a veteran of the First World War. He called in architects from Warwick to build a long new wing, cleverly linking with the haybarn to make Tysoe into the grand extended composition it is today. During the Second World War the Sewells went to Jamaica, though the General played a key role in the British Information Service in New York, while the manor housed refugee children from Coventry.

The long wings mean that Tysoe is the perfect place for different generations of a family to do what they like. The house could be a nightmare to heat but the Wields know that traditional wooden shutters are one of the best forms of insulation and these are in good working order throughout the house, with ingenious concertina shutters folding out across the long mullioned windows.

General Sewell's large handsome dining room has windows on three sides and massive doors formed of a sandwich of three planks of oak. The equally large room above with another wrap-around corner window has superb views over the garden and is furnished with impressively large desks so that the Wields can enjoy the sun while they work. Unusually the house has two imposing staircases with handsome turned balusters, one of the 1840s (though in the manner of the 1720s), the other of 1928.

Major elements of the 14th century exist inside the house. At the top of the stairs a duo of stone-pointed arches stand in a corner, while ascending to the attic you emerge beneath a splendid medieval great hall roof with five massive trusses – though unusually there are wind braces only on one side. 'The carpenters knew the winds here come from the south-west,' says Benedicta Wield.

WILTSHIRE

BELCOMBE COURT   Bradford-on-Avon
Miniature Arcadia created by John Wood the Elder

Top: The pavilion wing is built from golden stone.
Above: A small tempietto looks out across
Yerbury's grotto.

IN 1734, FRANCIS YERBURY CREATED AN enchanting Palladian house at Belcombe Court, accompanied by a garden that is a miniature Arcadia, a Lilliputian rival to Stourhead, with Classical temple, *cottage ornée*, cavernous grotto and sheet of water. His architect was John Wood the Elder, creator of the Circus in Bath. Wood in his 1765 *Essay on Bath* describes Yerbury as the provider of a 'thin Superfine Cloth made by him, and only him' supplied to the Ottoman Court for 'Robes of State'.

The majority of Classical country-house architecture is symmetrical; here, Wood created an irregular composition of great charm. The entrance arch, surmounted by what looks like a circular dovecote with dome and cupola, leads to a small courtyard open to the garden on the fourth side. The entrance wing has a pedimented gable with chimney emerging from the top. Curiously it abuts a much grander temple front overlooking the garden with Ionic pilasters and urns. The windows here have pediments and balustrades – Wood loved to elaborate the detail. On either side, Classical balustrades slope down to the garden, framing the composition enchantingly. The finest interior is the what Wood called the 'octangular Study, of twelve Feet Diameter' with scrolled sides to the windows and an ornamental plaster ceiling with garlands of flowers and fruit.

Yerbury's garden developed over time. His grotto dates from the 1740s, a decade later than those at Wanstead and Chiswick, but it is an elaborate design with ammonites in the floor and mock-stalactites descending from the roof. It is built in the usual way, of tufa. The Yerburys remained at Belcombe until the early 20th century, and the house is now in the caring hands of Tim and Caroline Weiland.

BLACKLAND PARK Calne
Georgian house rescued from decay by John Betjeman's daughter

CLOSE YOUR EYES AND DREAM OF the perfect Georgian house, gracefully proportioned yet manageable in size, and you have Blackland Park in Wiltshire. It stands in perfect seclusion enfolded in a large park with lawns descending to a broad expanse of water. The ancient parish church stands just across the gravel sweep in front of the house; beyond there is a stone-built coach house with an immense dovecote complete with hundreds of nesting boxes. Numerous trees have achieved mature splendour and well-protected walled gardens luxuriantly planted for colour stand close to the house.

The puzzle is that the two main fronts might belong to two quite different houses – the garden side looking like an Irish Georgian house, without columns or central emphasis, while the entrance front is more in the English Palladian tradition, with a delightful Venetian window in the centre topped by a Diocletian lunette and small triangular pediment. Only the projecting bays on the ground floor give away that this is a chaste Victorian remodelling with none of the flourishes one would expect.

Though the architects are unknown and the house has never been written up in *Country Life,* it has a niche in country-house history as the home of Candida Lycett Green, John Betjeman's daughter, and her husband Rupert. They bought it in 1973, when a local farmer was living in the downstairs rooms following a fire at the beginning of the war. The insurance money had paid for a new roof but the upper storey was still in a blackened state.

They introduced a screen of columns to break up the long thin entrance hall and had the missing overdoors repeated in plaster. They also cleverly altered the upper flight of the staircase which had cut across the windows overlooking the garden,

The River Marden forms a broad canal as it passes the house.

The doorway at the foot of the staircase gives just a glimpse of lawn and water.

resetting it to great advantage at the other end where the Venetian window and lunette are now to be seen together, one above the other, to theatrical effect.

The present house was built by Thomas Maudrell, grandson of Henry, the 17th-century oriental traveller. Early in the 19th century it was sold to John Merewether who planted a magnificent cedar to commemorate the Battle of Waterloo – it is now over 100 ft high, .

Thus began a pattern continued ever since whereby the property changed hands every twenty years or so (and recently more frequently). It was bought at auction in 1848 by Christopher Beaven who sold it to Marshall Hall in 1859. Then came Henry Brown, JP, followed by Commander Robert Murray Rumsey, RN, who served as a District Commissioner on the Gold Coast, followed by a pretty 32-year-old widow, Mrs Margery Wingfield-Digby.

The large expanse of water at the bottom of the garden is not a lake but the River Marden formed into a broad canal by a dam in the form of a large tumbling cascade. In former times the force of the water could support fifteen mills along the valley.

Beyond stands a roofless shell house begging to be restored – faced with large rustic stonework in the manner of Thomas Wright, the famous grotto designer known as the Wizard of Durham, though it may again be 19th-century. A 1903 *History of Calne* mentions 'thousands of shells, all beautifully arranged, and of an infinite variety of size and form, interspersed with many fine specimens of coral and polished stone.'

Extending from the house is a conservatory that is a miniature version of the famous glass house at Bicton in Devon. Here, rather as at Bicton, the sheets of glass are not set into frames but held together by clips.

A spacious new kitchen, complete with splendid big arching timbers, has been added on the other side, with French windows opening onto the garden and ingenious roof lights with flats operated by screw handles, providing a cooling through-draught in summer – the mind boggles at the intricacy and expense.

Upstairs the house is ideal for a large family of several children, with main bedrooms on the first floor and children's rooms above. If you heat the ground-floor rooms the warmth will rise through the rest of the house. For the pampered husband there is a splendid built-in wardrobe fitted out generously with shoe racks and different drawers for every type of clothing.

The Lycett Greens even found the old-fashioned soakaway all lined in porcelain leading from the house to a copse nearby.

In former times the A4 ran along the edge of the park, but now that most of the traffic has gone to the M4 the road is much quieter and well screened by a belt of trees; and though Blackland is on the edge of Calne, it remains a secret place.

BRAYBROOKE HOUSE

Salisbury

Schoolmaster's house in Salisbury Cathedral Close

BRAYBROOKE HOUSE IS A FEW TANTALISING STEPS short of utter perfection. It stands in a ravishing position in Salisbury Cathedral Close, arguably the most beautiful place to live in all England. There are no less than sixty-six houses in the Close, many of exceptional architectural appeal, and this stands in a prize position in the loveliest part of the Close, Choristers Green. There are delighrful houses all round the green, almosst all with views of the cathedral. The houses, it is true, are not as grand as those further along West Walk but they make a wonderful ensemble, set close together in the friendliest fashion. A more peaceful and beautiful place in a city is hard to imagine. The National Trust's Mompesson House stands on the north-side.

Braybrooke is the old Schoolmaster's house next to the handsome red-brick Wren School of 1714. It is named after William de Braybrooke (1298–1319), executor and beneficiary of the will of Bishop Nicholas Longspee. A William Osgodby lived here in the late 15th century entertaining (too frequently for the divines living nearby) Mistress Alicia Hoskyns, an immodest lady of the city.

In 1559 the Dean and Chapter gave the house to Christopher Bennet, the first recorded headmaster of the Cathedral School. It has the trimmest of front gardens – with a lantern arch over the gate and tile-edged rose beds flanking the path up to the front door. The best moment comes when you turn round under the hooded entrance and look back to the view of the cathedral with the spire soaring above, surely as breathtaking a view as can be had from a front garden in England.

Built of pale red brick with stone trim, this is an archetypal Queen Anne doll's house. The bright-white-painted sash windows are set flush with the facade – a practice outlawed in London in 1707 to reduce the risk of fire spreading from one

The perfect Queen Anne proportions are set off by a generous front garden.

house to another. The dormers still have leaded panes rather than sashes or casements – another hangover from the 17th century.

One special attraction of houses on the west side of the close are the long gardens running down to the River Avon. Braybrooke's consists of a wide stretch of immaculate lawn flanked by a deep border set against a long and noble garden wall built of flint and stone, with its own attractive tiled top. Towards the far end is a pretty red-brick summer house. A trim hedge encloses a fruit garden with neatly clipped ornamental apple trees. Beyond, cleverly placed clumps of bamboo shield the garden from the view of the public park across the river.

The one problem with the garden is that it is not behind Braybrooke House but behind the Wren school next door. However, the back of the school is extremely handsome and fortunately the windows are set so high that no one can look out of them and disturb your privacy.

What appears to have happened is that before or after the First World War, the headmaster forsook his own garden to provide some building plots so the back windows of Braybrooke House look out at a series of tile-hung cottages.

The result is that buying this delightful house presents a challenge – can you find a way of living in it that overcomes the awkwardness of the offset garden and the rather odd configurations of rooms that have resulted within? What survives of the early 18th-century house is mainly just one room deep. On the ground floor are two handsome panelled rooms looking out to the Close – a perfect, almost square dining room and a larger sitting room with a rather out-of-place oak neo-Jacobean fireplace.

On the first floor are two well-proportioned bedrooms, one with baroque niche for the bed, again with lovely views over the Close, and in the attic are two more, a little on the small side but with views that more than make up for it. For here you look out over the rooftops right across the centre of the city. Astonishingly there is not one blemish to be seen – not one ugly roof extension, or nasty office block poking above the old houses.

While enjoying these matchless views you have to accept awkwardly placed bathrooms, either up or down steps. Part of the problem lies in a back stair that does not connect from the ground floor to the first.

The spacious back kitchen has a tall bay window looking out over the garden – though you have to be in it before you can fully enjoy the view. Above the kitchen is the one grand room in the house, a large drawing room measuring 26 by 20 ft with a lofty ceiling. From here steps lead down to a sunny terrace that has been paved with large flagstones.

While one window looks out over the garden, the other looks out over the rather dark gardens of the houses behind – dark partly because of the Leylandii hedge planted along one side of the Braybrooke garden to keep them out of view.

Though it is listed Grade I, some judicious alterations could be made, though they would have to be of a very high quality. But an owner with a flair for making the best of space and an eye for colour could make this house an enchanting place to live.

THE IVY   Chippenham
Lively baroque town house built in 1728 for a lawyer

CASTLE HOWARD AND BLENHEIM ARE TOO VAST for most of us even to dream of living in but The Ivy is swagger baroque on an inviting scale. I first saw it in about 1970 when Miss Susan Rooke was living there, passionately concerned and worried for the house's future. The entrance front is faced in a warm, almost golden Bath stone and inside there are splendid panelled rooms and a staircase with parquetry in the half landings formed in a compass pattern.

Yet for eight years this Grade I masterpiece stood empty and was systematically vandalised while 280 new homes were built nearby and the council built an inner ring road in front of the gates. Then in 1981 the young Julian Bannerman, who has since become a leading garden designer, architect and builder of arbours and grottoes, bought the house and boldly embarked on its rescue.

Just by looking through the gates you have an immediate sense of how stylish the transformation has been. Lawns, gravel drive and lines of trees are satisfyingly aligned on the house and screen the long service wing, which otherwise would detract just a little from the éclat of the main front. To help with the costs of the restoration this service wing and the west end of the entrance front have been sold as three separate houses but, ingeniously, this is not at all apparent from outside.

The house was built by a lawyer, John Norris, and the rainwater heads bear the date 1728. Norris was married to Elizabeth Thresher, daughter of a wealthy clothier who lived just outside Bath. Gervase Jackson-Stops concluded in *Country Life* that the architect of The Ivy was a Bath man, probably Thomas Greenway of Widcombe, the outstanding Bath-stone carver of the era.

Although boarded and neglected in the late 1970s, the house is now as smart as a Normandy chateau.

CHUTE LODGE   Ludgershall
Free-standing Palladian villa of c.1768 with large school extension

SENSITIVE DIVISION OF COUNTRY HOUSES into self-contained houses and apartments has been the salvation of many houses. Chute Lodge was the first such house I visited and presented a scene like Bedlam. The essence of a good conversion is that the grounds are maintained as an entity so the architecture of the house is still seen in its designed setting. Chute Lodge had only recently been a school and the signs of institutional use remained – fire escapes, new doorways, parking spaces – and it was hard at the moment to see how it could regain its dignity.

I came in search of villas by the architect Sir Robert Taylor, on whom I was writing my dissertation at Cambridge. Taylor's documented works at that time were relatively few but his houses in particular followed distinctive plans using three-sided or canted bays, on the sides as well as the garden front. Another signature was vermiculated or 'worm-eaten' rustication. His Palladian villas were usually 'astylar', that is of Classical proportions but without columns or grand porticoes. Inside Chute had a domed oval stair almost identical to the one Taylor had designed at Danson in Kent.

Like many houses of this date, it had been built on the fortunes of the West India sugar trade. John Freeman was the younger son of John Cooke, an East India merchant who had taken the name of Freeman on succeeding to the estates of his uncle, William Freeman of St Kitts and Fawley. Other Taylor patrons with strong West Indies links were his namesake Sir John Taylor, who had extensive estates in Jamaica and lived in a Robert Taylor house at 9 Grafton Street, and Sir John Boyd of Danson who had inherited property through his mother, daughter of Judge Peters, on the island of St Kitts. In Taylor's house at 8 Grafton Street lived Sir Ralph Payne, who was Governor of the Leeward Islands and whose father had been Chief Justice of St Kitts.

Chute has a Tuscan eaved roof and canted bays on three sides.

LANHILL HOUSE
Yatton Keynell
Built in the 19th century for Joseph Neeld as consolation after a disastrous marriage

The delightful estate farmhouse has an unusual looking four-stage tower.

THIS ENCHANTING EXAMPLE OF THE Picturesque style was built *c.*1845 by James Thompson, a villa architect who designed terraces around Ladbroke Grove in London. His client, Joseph Neeld of Grittelton House, was the MP for Chippenham and the fortunate heir of the silversmith Philip Rundell (of Rundell & Bridge), who died in 1828 and left nearly £1 million to his great-nephew, then aged 39. After a disastrous marriage to the daughter of Lord Shaftesbury, Neeld had consoled himself with architecture, rebuilding and remodelling Grittleton to display his collection of sculpture and paintings. Grittleton House is now a school and a venue for weddings.

Neeld also embellished his estate with several other delightful buildings by Thompson and one characteristic of these, as with his house, is their very large scale. Lanhill House was built as a farmhouse in about 1845. The dominating feature is the splendid four-stage tower containing the porch, with sundial, bellcote and ornamental wind vane on top of the pyramid roof. The half-hipped roofs (sloping in two directions) are carried forward on either side over white-painted Tuscan eaves.

The house is beautifully built of squared stone with stone-tiled roofs, and the windows are all designed with great attention to detail. The arched window over the entrance has a hood mould and corbelled window box, while those on either side are miniature bay windows supported on stone brackets. At the back are clusters of tall octagonal chimneys.

Though the small casement windows on the front convey a cottage feeling, the rooms within are well-proportioned with good ceiling heights and the farmhouse has effortlessly transformed into a full-blown country house with extensive gardens and outbuildings including a long stable range – now garages – and a two-storey addition to the north-east with rendered walls and a matching stone-tiled roof, containing a snooker room.

Nearby are estate farm buildings and stables built by Thompson around the same time. Neeld was one of Chippenham's great benefactors and built the town hall with an open-arched cheese market below, later adding the Neeld Hall. On Neeld's death in 1856, Grittleton passed to his brother John and then to Sir Audley Dallas Neeld.

LATIMER MANOR · West Kington

E-plan manor house of principally 1600 date, restored to prime condition

LATIMER HAS ALL THE HALLMARKS of a perfect small Cotswold manor: an engaging sense of domesticity, a perfect match between the oatmeal-coloured stone and the weathered stone slates on the roofs, crisp masonry details to the windows and gentle undulations in the roof slopes. The ancient walls are without blemish and, although it shows the marks of changes and additions, it is all of a piece without a Georgian sash window to be seen.

The house stands peacefully in the stretch of still-remote country west of Chippenham, between the M4 and the old Great West Road, near one of the best-preserved (and least known) small country towns in southern England, Marshfield.

Latimer Manor is two miles away on the edge of the little village of West Kington. Most of the village is tucked away in the valley below, seen prettily from the garden at the back of the house. On the lane where the manor stands there are no more than a few houses and Latimer has that special charm of old houses that show off all their beauty beside a quiet country lane.

West Kington has an heroic niche in English history. In January 1531 the influence of Anne Boleyn brought a fiery young rector to the living, Hugh Latimer, who shortly before had provoked uproar at Cambridge with a demand that the Bible should be translated into English. It is the story told in Foxe's *Book of Martyrs* that earned Latimer a place in the first rank of English heroes with his steely words to his companion as they were burnt at the stake by Queen Mary: 'Be of good comfort, Master Ridley, and play the man: we shall this day light such a candle by God's Grace in England as I trust shall never be put out.'

Though the house is symmetrical in plan, the fenestration is irregular.

The owner, Michael Dolan, likes to think that Latimer lived here. The house is at the other end of the village from the church, but there is an early Tudor window on the west front. The major part of the house dates from about 1600, with an entrance front forming a characteristic 'E' and a projecting two-storey porch between gabled wings. A stone carved with the date 1617 survives in an upstairs room.

The porch opens into a single-storey great hall – halls rising to the roof went out of fashion in the early 16th century. A splendid grid of chamfered oak beams divides the ceiling into six large panels and the mouldings are Classical, not gothic. When this work was done the early Tudor window was preserved, or possibly even moved to its current location.

Mr Dolan wanted to take out a later partition, which cut clumsily across the main mullioned window, to open the hall to its original proportions. As there was evidence that there had once been a screens passage for servants, English Heritage suggested that this should be marked by a thinner row of flagstones in the floor.

The original stair was presumably spiral: an octagonal centre-post remains with the first flight wrapping round it.

The modernisation of Latimer Manor has been very respectful, with the clean, smooth, painted walls and restored wooden floors serving as a foil to old features that have been carefully preserved, such as the handsome stone window mullions. The most remarkable

An extensive group of vintage farm buildings lies on the other side of the farm pond.

feature of the interior is a splendid collection of monumental stone fireplaces. Some of them combine shallow Tudor arches, still Gothic but with Classical details such as a moulded egg and spoon. The fireplaces also appear in upstairs bedrooms and bathrooms, suggesting that the house could be kept very warm even as far back as four centuries ago.

Latimer Manor also has an exceptional series of barns and other buildings dating from the 17th century onwards, variously built as hay barns, cart sheds and cow byres and making the property ideal for anyone who wants to keep horses, run a business or hold events. One of the barns has consent for residential use. At present they are organised as studio, stables, tack room and coach house.

Behind the house is a sheltered courtyard garden planted with squares of box. Otherwise an almost Japanese atmosphere of perfect manicuring pervades, with trimly cut grass and climbing roses. There is a major opportunity to create an extensive garden in a series of walled and sheltered enclosures. Low drystone walls, beautifully laid with slender squared stones, enclose the pretty garden along the lane. There is a walled farm pond planted with waterlilies and a sunny outdoor swimming pool.

THE MANOR HOUSE   Milton Lilbourne
Mellow warmth of a Queen Anne manor in a village street

MILTON LILBOURNE IS A CLASSIC EXAMPLE OF the infinite subtle variations that make Queen Anne houses such a delight. At a quick glance it is no more than an enchanting doll's house built of mellow red brick with stone trim softened by lichens. The main flourish is the rounded segmental gable over the projecting centre. The curve is picked up in all the windows below, contrasting with the straight-topped windows at the sides. Every detail is satisfyingly considered – the plain stone band between first and second floor, the more emphatic cornice above, the quoins at the corners and the stone surrounds to the windows emphasised by roll mouldings.

The house is a classic example of the double-pile plan, two rooms deep with the fireplaces and chimney stacks in the end walls. The hipped roof is partly concealed by a parapet, which also ensures the servants in the attics are unseen. Grand stone gate piers capped by massive balls frame the vista from the village street to the main front, jostled by a pair of giant yews clipped into cones.

The garden front is equally pretty, if more conventional, with a broader centrepiece looking out over spreading lawns enclosed by extensive walls. The broken pediment over the front door contains the arms of the Dukes of Somerset. Last sold in 2005, the house now contains the antique shop Gently Rupert.

There are characteristic baroque arched windows in the projecting centre.

NUNTON HOUSE   Nunton
Queen Anne house complete with rare surviving brewhouse

NUNTON HOUSE RANKS IN THE TOP FLIGHT of enchanting village houses. It stands in a quiet hamlet of two hundred souls populated by doctors and professionals working in nearby Salisbury, though when Hugh Colvin came to live here in 1955 it still seemed feudal – in thrall to the nearby Longford estate, ancestral seat of the Earls of Radnor.

Nunton faces south, enjoying full sun throughout the day. Attached to the back is an older farmhouse and Harry Joynt, Mr Colvin's son-in-law, says, 'The story is that the farmer's daughter was courted by a young wool merchant from Salisbury. She said she would marry him if he built a nice house and her father would provide the land.'

The two houses have been separate for nearly three centuries. The warm red brick and hipped roof of Nunton House may still be Queen Anne but there are distinct baroque flourishes, such as the giant pilasters that frame the end and centre.

The main front gives the strong impression of being the work of an accomplished master builder keen to show off his skills, rather than an architect. The front is entirely built of 'header bond' (end-on bricks) with great care taken over the mortar joints. These are all penny-struck – looking as if a penny has been drawn through the mortar while it is still wet giving an added crispness to the slightly crumbly handmade bricks. No less intriguing are the numerous tiny holes in the mortar, and occasionally in the bricks themselves. These, says Mr Joynt, are the work of mortar bees.

The stone trim looks to be a Portland stone but the keystones over the windows are yellow, perhaps the local Chilmark or Ham. The original sashes would have had chunky early 18th century glazing bars but the present ones are Georgian replacements with thinner bars and casement (inward folding) windows in the basement.

Despite its doll's-house appearance, Nunton has extensive accommodation on four floors. The front door opens into a pleasantly wide staircase hall. The stair is handsomely

Giant pilaster and keystones add a baroque flourish.

The window seats beneath the sash windows are in keeping with early 18th-century fashion.

carved in oak with three turned balusters to each tread, columns at the corners and a good 'swirl' at the bottom. At each corner, and on the matching panelling on the dado, the handrail sweeps up with a baroque flourish.

The delight of the interior is that all the main rooms are fully panelled with tall panels above the chair rail and lower ones below, all raised and fielded in the best early-Georgian manner. In the drawing room the main panels have baroque 'ears' at the corners and on either side of the windows end in a delightful S-scroll, suggesting the joiner was equipped with pattern books or engravings showing the latest baroque details. The fireplaces in the drawing room and dining room are Regency in style but in one of the upstairs bedrooms a baroque white marble surround survives with keystone. The generous sash windows ensure the house is wonderfully light inside and there is further accommodation in the attic where the parapet has been cut away to allow a view out of the windows.

The slightly sunken basement is unexpectedly large, at present arranged as a self-contained flat. There is a temptation to recreate a large kitchen here and move the present dining room (to the right of the front door) to the back room where the kitchen now is. This would give you two sitting rooms at the front, though if you like entertaining at lunch rather than dinner you may wish to continue with the present arrangement, which offers maximum sun.

Outside, Nunton offers a wealth of unexpected treats. Across the lawn is an elegant low-branching Scarlet oak. To the east is a pretty arena garden laid out by the great landscape gardener Brenda Colvin, sister of Mrs Joynt's father who bought Nunton in 1955. At the end a garden seat is enclosed by a massive back and arms shaped in yew. The garden is divided by a long Georgian brick wall with steps half way, leading to an enchanting baroque orangery looking over a small formal water garden and fountain. Further on there is a tennis court and beyond a woodland garden with a great splash of rhododendrons – growing in a tiny pocket of acid soil discovered by Brenda Colvin in the middle of the chalk.

The final surprise is an intact brewery, tracked down by Pamela Sambrook in her cleverly researched *Country House Brewing in England 1500–1900*. Because water was suspect, beer or small beer were the staple drinks of both children and adults until the late 18th century or later. Brew houses had to be high inside to let the steam out. Dr Sambrook explains, 'Here there was probably a copper on either side of the chimney. The usual equipment also comprised a fermenting tun and a working tun, both coopered barrels, with a long flat wooden tray for cooling the beer.'

THE MANOR HOUSE Ogbourne St George
Ancient manor that helped deceive the Germans about Allied invasion plans

THIS ANCIENT WILTSHIRE DOMAIN HAS A PERPETUAL niche in the romance of English history, for it was the headed writing paper of The Manor House, Ogbourne St George, that was used for a love letter written to convince the Germans that *The Man Who Never Was*, whose body was washed up on the Spanish coast early in 1943, was a Royal Marines officer carrying word of the Allied plan to invade Greece rather than Sicily. The ruse worked – Hitler sent troops to the Balkans that could have been used to defend Sicily when the Allies landed in July.

No German, the plotters surmised, could resist the Englishness of a name like this. Indeed, had the hard and thorough men of the Abwehr (German military intelligence) had access to a wartime supply of *Country Life* (via a spy in Gibraltar perhaps?), they could have studied the photographs of the house in the issue of December 25, 1942, showing that the home of Mr and Mrs Oliver Frost was one of relatively few country houses which had not been taken over by the military, and where the sweetheart of the dead man might indeed have been staying.

Instead, the papers had come from the War Office branch that was requisitioning the land across the road, on which a large army camp was constructed. In 2003, the owner, Tim Frost, remembered, 'Before the Suez campaign the tanks would go in green and come out in yellow desert camouflage.'

Today the military has gone. Yet as I drove north from Marlborough towards the grand sweep of the Ridgeway, I had a shock. Turning off to the village you can see the

Symmetry governs the placing of the windows but not the doors.

main road curling round immediately above the roofs of the houses, more like urban Genoa than rural Wiltshire. Fortunately the village is long and winding and the manor is the very last house at the far end, looking out across glorious rolling country. When you gaze out of the windows you cannot see the village at all.

'My parents had their bedroom on the east as they thought their guests might not like looking over a graveyard,' says Mr Frost. Considerate certainly, but who could really object to waking to a view of a churchyard fine enough for Gray to have written his Elegy there?

For five centuries the manor belonged to King's College Cambridge until Maynard Keynes, the great economist, unfeelingly sold it in 1927. It was one of the original endowments granted by Henry VI to his new College in 1441 and before that had belonged to the Abbey of Bec Herlouin whose records take the history of fields and tenants back to 1246. Before that the manor (and that of neighbouring Ogbourne St Andrew) had belonged to Maud of Wallingford, the heiress of a prominent Norman family in Oxfordshire who gave the manors to Bec Abbey.

The names of all the tenants are meticulously recorded but nothing is known about the various periods of building – though precise tallies were kept of the number of sheep that had to be driven each year to Cambridge for the Fellow's table and of their weight on arrival.

The best clue to its age is a date of 1619 on a chimney stack that was recorded in an early article in *Country Life* but the chimney stack was later taken down. The large stone-mullioned windows correspond with this date. There is an approximate symmetry in the placing of windows, though not doors. With its steep end gables, the house looks as if it was originally 'single pile' – one room deep, but puzzlingly there is a parallel south range with large tripartite Georgian sash windows, which is built of the same brick with no apparent break between the two ranges. The low plinth containing the cellar also runs evenly the entire way around the house, built neatly in stone and flint.

The tower of the village church looms over the entrance court.

Ogbourne St George is a perfect place to admire the best of English brickwork. It is built in English bond – alternate rows of headers and stretchers (bricks placed end-on and longways). Shallow 'relieving' arches take the weight off the wide window heads. Intriguingly, on the extension to the west English garden-wall bond is used – three rows of stretchers to one of headers – known as American bond across the Atlantic. Originally all of this brick would have been concealed, covered by a regular coat of protective limewash.

The heavy oak front door opens into a staircase facing away from you – suggesting the entrance may originally have been from the south. The stair, built massively in oak, is a splendid thing with scissors-style intersections of balustrade at each 180-degree turn.

The dining room is panelled from floor to ceiling in oak, while the 17th-century panelling in the large drawing room beyond consists of alternating tall and square panels. The large south-facing library has another weighty door inset with a row of knotched arches at the top – said to be the original front door.

English houses abound in legends of tunnels that often supposedly provide links to the parish church. Here, however, a well built shallow-arched brick tunnel is still visible from the cellar, running for about 20 yards before a turn, although it is now only about 3-ft high as the floor level has risen.

Previous tenants added the early 18th-century-looking hooded front door on the south front – the scrolls are probably authentic. Their architects were Pakington and Enthoven. Several rooms have Tudor-style stone fireplaces.

An intriguing feature is the boxed-in rainwater gutter beside the top of the staircase, which drains the hidden valley in the centre of the roof. Don't store a roll of carpet here, as one previous owner did, promptly causing a flood. The house has extensive, well-lit attics and twin doors opening into the hidden roof valleys offer a wonderful means of sucking a cooling draught of air through the house on a stifling summer day.

A heavy studded door leads to the library (below), where copies of many editions of The Man who Never Was *fill the shelves (above).*

PHILIPPS HOUSE   Dinton
Classical house by Sir Jeffry Wyatville leased by the National Trust

AT FIRST SIGHT PHILIPPS HOUSE has it all, a breathstealingly beautiful Classical exterior surveying a rolling park descending to a large ornamental lake. From the park the spire of Salisbury Cathedral is visible in the distance. The village of Dinton is quiet and pleasant with a handsome medieval church containing monuments to generations of Wyndhams who lived at the hall.

The estate belongs to the National Trust, which in the dark days of the Second World War acquired four historic houses in the village. Depending on how you count there are eighteen bedrooms, plus a further six in a wing which has been prepared as granny flats. Even now there are maids' rooms in the attic still waiting to be modernised.

One obvious boon of living in a National Trust house is that the structure is in good order. The roof has been magnificently re-leaded and is fit to last at least a century without a major overhaul. Better still, the house is entirely faced in crisp pale stone from the nearby village of Chilmark – also used for Salisbury Cathedral. The large sash windows all have the exquisitely thin 'astragals' or glazing bars which are the hallmark of the best Regency architecture. 'Buy a shipload of mahogany to make all ye sashes & doors & skirting boards,' an uncle advised William Wyndham when he was planning the house.

The new hall, then called Dinton House, was designed by Sir Jeffry Wyatville who, as James Lees-Milne cryptically remarked, was best known for cardboard castle creations (George IV employed him at Windsor Castle). Wyatville's first designs date from 1813 and the house was completed five years later at a cost of £10,869. William Wyndham had married Laetitia, the daughter of a master of Chancery (a sure road to riches in Georgian times) and they lived in Jane Austen-like contentment raising a family of six boys and six girls. One of them, George, went to Australia and founded

The house is faced in the blond local Chilmark stone that was also used to build Salisbury Cathedral.

the Wyndham Vineyard in Hunter Valley. Four generations of Wyndhams lived here until 1917, when the mortgage foreclosed and they were forced to move.

Dinton was then acquired by Bertram Philipps. Until then, carriages had driven up in a grand sweep through the park to the four columned portico and continued on to the stable yard at the back of the house. In the new age of the motor car, Mr Philipps did not want parking in front of his main view and so created a new entrance on the east.

During the Second World War, American forces took over the property and filled the park in best Brideshead style with roads, huts and parade grounds. In despair perhaps, Mr Philipps gave the house and 200 acres of park to the National Trust in 1943 on condition it was renamed Philipps House. With it came fine furniture, paintings and books, which remain in the principal rooms. Two years later it was leased to the Young Women's Christian Association as a holiday home. When they left in 1995, the Trust set about restoring the main rooms, returning Wyatville's bookcases (and the Wyndham books) to the library and removing every last vestige of wartime concrete from the park.

In winter the Georges, the current owners, live principally in the library with a blazing log fire. In summer they move across to the former ladies' drawing room where you walk out into the west garden through a sash window with little shutter doors beneath, which fold back into the panelling.

The centre of the house is filled by a magnificent Imperial stair, overlooked by balconies on both sides where musicians can play and children watch the assembly below. Thanks to the large round central lantern in the roof, it is at its most beautiful by moonlight, says Mrs George. And it's not even impossible to heat – in 1830 Laetitia Wyndham wrote to her son, 'We have made the house delightfully warm and comfortable by a judicious alteration in the hot air stove in the cellar … it is like living in the south of France.'

The front of the house is filled by a suite of three grand rooms connected by pairs of mahogany doors. First is the drawing room, which comes with a fine group of Venetian landscape paintings, then the central hall dutifully painted in authentic, if boring, stone colour by the Trust, with a delicious frieze of cornucopias and scallop shells. Beyond, the dining room retains a Regency dining table perfect for family celebrations, seating eighteen in comfort.

The house rests on an extensive vaulted cellar which in the past has been prone to flooding, though the problem is solved, I was assured. When the Georges arrived, many of the first-floor rooms were still partitioned from YWCA days. They have restored Georgian proportions and furnished them with attractive simplicity. En suite bathrooms can only be created by using bedrooms – luxuriantly large but just the fashion. In the attic are still more spacious rooms, though suffering from parapets built to stop servants looking into the garden.

The carriage houses at the back are very suitable for anyone wanting to run a business from home and the agreement with the National Trust is that the house is open two half-days a week. There are also public footpaths across the park. However, neither house nor park are ever overwhelmed with visitors.

POULTON HOUSE   Marlborough

Pretty Queen Anne house dated 1706 on the rainwater heads

POULTON HOUSE IS A SCALED-DOWN VERSION of what many consider the most perfect house in all England, Ramsbury Manor in Wiltshire. This is no mere coincidence, as Poulton is just six miles from Ramsbury. It stands just on the edge of the handsome historic town of Marlborough and is a country estate in miniature with 50 acres of well-groomed, attractively planted grounds. There are five cottages and a stable block approached by a back drive. The main drive is edged with trim beech hedges and verges ablaze with daffodils in spring and continues through ornamental lawns, providing pretty views of the entrance front.

The house is Queen Anne at its most delightful, with the date 1706 and the initials of its builder on the rainwater heads. Here are all the typical features of the style. A sweep of five steps leading up to a handsomely carved stone doorcase. Rows of white-painted sash windows stand out brightly as the sash boxes are set flush with the brickwork. Stone 'quoins' emphasise the corners and the central triangular pediment is set against a hipped roof with dormers.

The pretty pink brick is enriched with burnt headers (kiln-blackened end-on bricks) and finer 'rubbed' brick over the windows. As in other Wiltshire houses, mortar bees have made tiny holes in the pointing. The basement kitchen to the right of the entrance still has stone-mullioned windows with leaded glass. The sides and back of the house are plainer but retain the early form of windows with wooden mullions and lead panes. On the east end is a pretty ogee-topped bay window to the drawing room.

The facade is enlivened by kiln-blackened 'header' bricks and stone quoins at the corners.

Poulton was built for William Liddiard. His handsome stone tomb slab is set in the parish church at Mildenhall, a favourite excursion for Betjeman when he was at Marlborough School. The slab is incised not with a coat of arms but a large Classical capital, suggesting Liddiard's interest in architecture may have been enough for him to have designed his own house with the help of a first-class local master bricklayer.

Liddiard first married in 1672 or 3 but did not build his house until several years after his second marriage, dying only six years after it was finished. It passed to a son and then a daughter, who let it to a stepbrother. In 1790 it was bought by the Ailesbury estate, who let it to tenant farmers. As a result Poulton largely escaped alterations. The Victorian wing was done in a very conservative manner, carefully matching the early 18th century materials and detail – just what you might expect from a well-run traditional estate office. It was sold in 1926 when the Ailesbury estate sold a large group of farms and villages to raise cash, and since then has had no more than half a dozen owners.

The front door opens in a spacious square entrance hall from which rises a superb oak staircase with a pair of corkscrew balusters to each tread. Unusually, the stair is off-centre but this is cleverly disguised by two splendid baroque archways on either side. These are of stripped pine and just a little cramped, suggesting they may be slightly later imports. The stair is lit by two tiers of windows and as you ascend you suddenly glimpse the glory of the interior, a sumptuous plaster ceiling with a cove inset with vine leaves and luscious bunches of grapes. It's all in a Charles II manner a little earlier than the house with a circular wreath of flowers and fruit.

The layout is not the typical two-room-deep Queen Anne box but a more unusual L-shape, which offers a more practical arrangement today. On the left of the hall the dining room has original panelling – the drawing room on the other side has a later 18th century feel. The window sills in both these rooms have been lowered (this is evident in the brickwork outside), providing pretty views out even when you are comfortably seated.

Behind the dining room is a library with a plaster ceiling adorned with a trail of flowers, which quickly reveals itself as a clever insertion of the present owners, done by Caspar Taylor who worked on the restoration of Uppark. Beyond there is a spacious kitchen with French windows looking along a garden terrace – cleverly planted with spheres of box and drum-shaped holm oaks, providing a handsome vista to an ornamental glass house. This has been rebuilt reusing the festive Victorian trim. Beyond the kitchen is a well-organised utility realm with a pantry-cum-ironing room and a back door opening into a courtyard where cars are parked out of sight to one side of the house. An amusing note is provided by the pretty striped canopy top to the bantam house.

The main bedroom has windows on two sides catching the early-morning sun and providing views over the gardens. Two other main bedrooms face south, while there are two more in a west wing and a further four in the attic. Handsome brick cellars ensure the house is dry.

There is a pond with an island nest for swans, and a pretty winding walk through trees where I was shown one of three bottle wells, brick-lined and flask-shaped, fed by rainwater from the roof.

ROWDEN MANOR   Chippenham
Stone-built manor house containing splendid arched trusses in the attic

STANDING JUST TO THE WEST OF CHIPPENHAM, this looks a typical 17th-century stone gabled farmhouse. The clue to something grander comes in the blocked up windows in the left gable. Originally there were three tall sashes on each floor, but those at the side had been blocked. The stone doorcase, largely smothered in ivy, is also unexpectedly broad with a baroque 'bolection' or roll moulding. Inside, the stone-flagged entrance hall leads to a pretty staircase rising in short flights around an open well in typical Elizabethan fashion. Beyond is the first big surprise, an oak-panelled drawing room of the highest quality, as good as you would find in a grand Queen Anne country house or the vestry of a Wren City of London church. It is constructed of large pieces of seasoned oak with the panels 'raised and fielded' in the best 1700 manner. In one corner there is a glazed cupboard with a pretty shell-headed niche, while stately Corinthian pillars flank the fireplace. All this is presumably the work of Thomas Long, who acquired Rowden in 1698. But not all is quite as it seems, for in one corner both floor and ceiling slope sharply, suggesting settlement. Yet the panelling has not cracked or warped. Suddenly it becomes clear that the corner sank before the panelling was installed three hundred years ago. The carpenters cleverly tailored the panels towards the sloping corners, doing the same with the pretty acanthus-leaf frieze over the doors, which tapers to one end.

Above is another fine panelled room, this time painted white. Here again both floor and ceiling take a dive towards one corner. This time the individual panels step down

The homely gabled facade gives few clues to the wealth of interesting features inside.

Inside is an unexpectedly fine oak-panelled saloon of 1700 date.

in size like a staircase, while the door, though a perfect fit, has neither a straight top nor bottom. On either side of the window there are cupboards with early H-hinges. Opening these, I found window seats exactly matching the one beneath the central window. Ascending to the second floor I emerged in a different, much earlier-looking house. Here the internal walls are timber-framed, a chequer of posts and beams with white plaster infill, suggesting a date nearer 1600 than 1700. The doorways have shallow Tudor arches, each formed of a single piece of wood. Walking into the bedroom behind the southern gable, it is immediately clear that the gable has been built out from the earlier transverse roof. The horizontal purlin has been cut away so you can get to the window without stepping over it – the slots in the rafters show where it was.

A still bigger surprise came in the attic above the panelled rooms. Here I was confronted with a large, gently arching roof truss with wooden pegs fixing it to equally large rafters. Between were diagonal wind braces. In all there were three of these trusses, suggesting a large space such as a hall open to the roof timbers. There was none of the smoke blackening from open fires found in late-medieval halls but the straight wind braces suggest a date after 1550. Could this be one of the earliest-ever barn conversions? I put this to Edward Roberts, an expert on dating timber buildings. He said no, but possibly a grand stable for 'showing off gentlemen's horses' – Rowden at the time was the property of Sir Edward Hungerford MP, a leading Cromwellian. The 17th-century Wiltshire historian John Aubrey described Rowden as 'a large well built gothic house, square with a moat about it' but this had been pulled down after a siege, prompting rebuilding on a more modest scale as the Hungerfords had several other seats.

STANTON HOUSE   Highworth
1930s Cotswold-style house complete with indoor pool and squash court

BUILT IN 1935 STANTON HOUSE IS A CONVINCING essay in traditional Cotswold style, complete with the latest luxuries including squash court and indoor swimming pool with 'sliding glass roof worked by an electric motor', according to *Country Life* in 1942. It was designed by Henry W. Binns for the American Robert Ducas and built on the foundations of an earlier house, though no visible trace of this remains. Modern soilpipes for the bathrooms were concealed within the walls and some of the vents ingeniously disguised as nesting holes for doves.

The house is built on an informal rambling plan and the hub of it, curiously, is not the grand bay-windowed Lounge (as it is called on Binns's plan) but a small panelled snuggery overlooking the lake. This 'extensive piece of water' was laid out by the Rev. John Ashfordby-Trenchard, one of a series of Georgian 'squarsons' (parson-squires) who had lived at Stanton.

Until his death in the 1970s Stanton House was run in fine style by my godfather, Sir Geoffrey Tritton, with a pedigree Jersey herd in the Home Farm, luxuriant herbaceous borders and glass houses supplying fruit and flowers for the house. Two magnificent cedars of Lebanon stood guard on the lawn. There was only one problem. The address might have been Stanton Fitzwarren near Highworth but the centre of Swindon was only five miles away and giant factories were closing in. I went back in 2000, intrigued yet nervous as to what I would find. The house had become a country-house hotel, catering for Japanese executives working for local corporations. A large bedroom extension had been added, fortunately out of view of the garden front. Yet as I walked down the long herbaceous border to the walled garden, the years rolled back. Borders, clipped yew buttresses, the door into the kitchen garden and the glass houses were all exactly as I remembered them thirty years before.

Magnificent cedars stand on the lawn alongside the ha-ha that kept cattle out of the garden.

STOCKTON   Heytesbury
Gabled Jacobean manor built of stone and knapped flint

THE GREATEST BEAUTY OF STOCKTON IS its colour. Even in a watery winter sun it seems almost silver thanks to the colonies of lichens that cover the stonework, freckled with tints of green and orange from the mosses. The stone alternates with bands of knapped flints that diminish in size towards the gables. The house has a wonderful geometry to it. The rows of gables, four on the main front, three on the flanks, are perfectly even, with roof ridges all in line. Large mullioned windows speak of spacious rooms on both ground and first floors with well-lit attics above.

At the Dissolution of the Monasteries the manor was granted to Sir William Herbert, who was created Earl of Pembroke in 1551. His son sold it in 1585 to John Topp, a rich clothier and merchant tailor of London. It was clearly his son, also John, who rebuilt the house. The probable date is 1600-1610 and it appears to have been designed by the mason William Arnold, who worked at both Wadham College in Oxford and Cranborne Manor in Dorset, and was described as 'the honestest workman in England'. Further embellishments were carried out for Edward Topp, who succeeded in 1675 and laid out a formal garden.

In 1772 the property was acquired by Henry Biggs, whose long-lived son Harry commissioned an elegant new Regency staircase in 1802 by Jeffry Wyatville, which rises in two arms, uniting to leap across space. Biggs also built the range of stables in a traditional style cleverly blending with the house, using flint chequerwork and a

The banded stonework of the entrance front contrasts delightfully with the chequerwork of the stables.

hooped gable. These were designed for him by a Wiltshire neighbour, the MP John Bennett, who rebuilt his family seat Pythouse, near Tisbury, to his own designs. The Biggs family pew in the parish church was panelled in deal and lined with green baize with brass nails. There was a stove and coalbox in the pew and Harry Biggs used to replenish the fire noisily when the sermon was too long.

The interior of Stockton retains a remarkable series of early 17th-century rooms that have magnificent fireplaces. Only in the hall has the once elaborate plasterwork now vanished. The great chamber has a gorgeously rich ornamental

A Venetian well head makes an unusual feature in the centre of the lawn.

ceiling adorned with flowers and animals and a large chimney piece with coupled columns on both tiers. In one corner is a fine example of a 'whispering chamber' or wooden lobby to exclude draughts, richly carved with figures. The Shadrach room has another two-tier chimney piece, carved with a relief of the three Israelites who refused to worship Nebuchadnezzar, were put into a fiery furnace and, to everyone's astonishment, failed to burn. The chimney piece is of stone below and plaster above. Around the room runs a beautifully detailed frieze with pairs of winged horses. The ceiling, an intricate pattern of diamond and heart shaped panels, is decorated with roses and thistles symbolising the union of England and Scotland. That in the white drawing room, also panelled, bears the initials 'IMT', for John Topp and his wife Mary, who died in 1617. The design and detail of some of these chimney pieces bears a close resemblance to a series of drawings in the Devon Record Office, dated 1665 and inscribed 'John Abbott His Booke', though the drawings appear earlier. The Abbotts were a family of west-country craftsmen who appear to have worked at Stockton.

The house was restored and extended by Benjamin Ferrey in 1877–82 for Major Yeatman-Biggs. Rainwater heads bear the date 1879 – the new service wing has banded masonry matching the house. The house was acquired in 1921 by the Hon Violet Skeffington Smyth who removed the Spanish leather from the Elizabethan bedroom. In 1926 the house was let to Lord Plunket and the Duke and Duchess of York came to stay while in the neighbourhood for a dance at nearby Longleat. In 1935 the estate was sold to the Hon Mrs Michael Scott, who added a swimming pool and squash court.

During the Second World War, Stockton was requisitioned and in 1943 Princess Elizabeth, then aged 17, reviewed the Grenadier Guards in the park, the first public ceremony she attended unaccompanied. When peace came the War Office would not give it up and the family was not able to return home. In 1950 the estate was sold to a man who immediately tried to sell off the panelling but was prevented from doing so by the Society for the Protection of Ancient Buildings. In 1970 the house was acquired by Captain and Mrs Derek O'Reilly, who put it in excellent order.

STURFORD MEAD — Warminster
Regency house by the Bath architect John Pinch

EVELYN WAUGH, LORD BEAVERBROOK AND REX WHISTLER were frequent guests at Sturford Mead in the 1930s when the Marquess of Bath (then Lord Weymouth) entertained here before he moved to Longleat and introduced the lions. With his first wife Daphne he commissioned Russell Page, the landscape gardener, to create a ravishing white garden enclosed by yew hedges, with a statue set in a recess at the end. Page edged his borders with smart stone copings following bold baroque curves. His masterstroke is the cross vista through narrow gaps in the yew hedges framing a tantalising glimpse of an Italian pool guarded by tall sentinel cypresses.

The pool is prettily edged by low clipped box forming a zigzag. Mrs Joan Bradshaw, who has restored Page's work, says, 'There used also to be two knot gardens on either side. You can see the outline when it snows.' Page next lures you along a gently curving walk flanked by beech hedges.

The main south-facing lawn has a ravishing view through a cleft in the low hills to a glorious green vale stretching to the horizon. In the foreground rises a grass knoll, picturesquely grazed by sheep. On the far side of the lawn an alley of neatly pleached limes leads diagonally from the house to a column prettily topped by an urn. This was planted by the diplomat Lees Mayall, who bought the house after the Second World War.

The garden walk continues through a sheltered walled garden where a traditional long narrow potting shed survives. Beyond is a remarkable water garden where a series of fast-flowing serpentine rills feed a small lake to the north of the house, across which the golden Bath stone of the entrance front is seen to perfect advantage.

Sturford is picturesque informality at its most inviting.

Sturford Mead is a Regency gem, attributed convincingly to the Bath architect John Pinch. Two other houses nearby, Corsley Manor and Bishopstrow House (now an hotel), share a number of features with Sturford Mead and are clearly also by Pinch.

The delight of the interior is the sophistication of the architectural fit-out. The entrance hall is paved in large flags of stone lit by windows on either side of the double front door, which retains a fine polished brass lock case. A broad doorway leads on to the stair hall surmounted by a large and graceful fanlight. Rounded slots in the frame suggest there were originally swing doors.

The stone staircase is cantilevered from the wall with a perfectly smooth underside formed by cutting away the treads. The iron railings are alternately straight and cleverly kinked to form a Greek key pattern motif. Mr and Mrs Bradshaw found the original 'stoneblocking' – murals imitating masonry – beneath the wallpaper. No less than seven doors open onto the staircase hall , all with handsome pilastered door surrounds.

The formal garden by Russell Page has a vista framed by tall cypress trees.

The library on the left has been fitted out in Strawberry Hill Gothick style for the Bradshaws by the designer John Bannenberg, with overdoors like bishop's mitres and bookcases with colonettes and fretting. Next door, the drawing room retains a sumptuous double flock paper which has faded to beautiful ochre. Mrs Bradshaw decided to retain it after learning that to replace it (available from Coles) would cost £800 a roll and that was ten years ago.

Sturford Mead has an unusually complete 'downstairs' realm where sash windows look out onto a dry walk that circles the Regency house, ensuring damp does not penetrate. Here Robert Bradshaw has a workshop where he invented and perfected a chemical sniffer no bigger than an early mobile telephone for use by British troops in detecting chemical weapons.

Servants' bell boards list ten bedrooms. Nearby is the untouched servants' bathroom with three wash basins in a row and a bath on the other side of the room.

The Bradshaws have made a spacious kitchen lit by a splendidly long run of windows. Cupboards were commissioned from Smallbone at nearby Devises with a large pair of Belfast sinks set in a 16-ft long draining board made from a single plank of wood.

Sturford Mead was built in 1817–21 for Henry Austin Fussell, whose family were toolmakers with six ironworks around Mells. Fussell, as the second son, had entered the cloth trade in Frome and in 1808 married Margeret Carpenter. The Fussells had twelve children, ten of whom survived to adulthood. The house was bought in 1853 by the then Marquess of Bath to protect his great estate but sold after the war to help pay death duties. Woods and fields around still belong to Longleat, hopefully ensuring the views will long remain inviolate.

TOTTENHAM PARK   Marlborough
Imposing Regency house built for the 1st Marquess of Ailesbury

TOTTENHAM HOUSE IN SAVERNAKE FOREST near Marlborough stands in a Capability Brown landscape that is on a scale comparable to Stowe Gardens. A century ago the deer park was sixteen miles in circumference, larger even than Windsor Great Park. Now plans to transform the house into a £70 million resort hotel, a 'Gleneagles of the South', have been submitted.

Tottenham was devastated at the end of the Second World War when American troops who were billeted there decided to dispose of a large quantity of explosives in the park. Making a giant miscalculation, they blew out every pane of glass in the building and wrecked the grand Classical conservatory – which has stood as a rusting iron skeleton ever since.

The family, daunted by the cost of restoring the house to reoccupy it, leased it to Hawtrey's, a boys' boarding school, which suddenly closed ten years ago. It is now let as a drug rehabilitation clinic run by the Amber Foundation. Major repairs are needed, and since 1998 the Grade I listed house has been on the English Heritage register of outstanding historic buildings at risk.

Tottenham as it stands today is largely the work of the 1st Marquess of Ailesbury, who was ennobled in the coronation honours of George IV. His architects, Thomas Cundy and his son, also Thomas, had both held the important post of surveyor to the Grosvenor Estate when the London suburb of Belgravia was laid out. Cundy the younger transformed Moor Park in Hertfordshire and added a great picture gallery to Grosvenor House in London.

Tottenham's glorious Regency interiors contain sumptuous plaster ceilings that look like crisply cut marble, a circular domed music room and a cavernous staircase hall surrounded by galleries. The ballroom, which was inlaid with marble, was

All the glass was blown out of the conservatory when a cache of explosives was let off.

The ceiling has plasterwork of surpassing crispness.

executed by Italian craftsmen who would down tools if they thought any Englishman, including the Marquess, was watching and learning their methods.

The Marquess entertained on a lavish scale. His second wife, Maria Tollemache, 'the evergreen marchioness', was a famed hostess and one of the great beauties of the 19th century. Guests at the proposed hotel may have use of the bath carved from solid Carrara marble for the Prince of Wales, who visited the house.

The Earl of Cardigan, son of the 8th Marquess, owns the house and is warden of Savernake Forest. He says: 'I have spent more than ten years looking for a hotel company which will restore the place without ruining it with unsuitable alterations and additions.' He has offered a 150-year lease to the Buena Vista Hospitality Group, a company running large resort hotels in Florida. Planning permission was granted and they are now creating a golf resort and conference centre with 148 guest suites.

Very large hotel additions to country houses have recently become extremely contentious. Here, eighteen of the guest suites will be in the main house. The remainder will be out of sight in the 4-acre walled kitchen garden hidden in woodland some 200 yards from the house. Lord Cardigan says emphatically: 'Not a brick of the new additions will be visible from the main house or the park.'

Ronnie Nathan, the British partner in the hotel consortium, says: 'Guests at a resort like the freedom of moving between buildings and will be able to drive about in buggies. If on a cold winter night a lady wishes to dine in the main house it will be a case of "Madam, your carriage awaits".'

The Cundys faced Tottenham in golden Bath stone, enclosing an earlier house by Lord Burlington, the architect earl whose best-known work is Chiswick House in West

London. Just one Classical room by Burlington survives. Nathan says: 'This will be on a much larger scale than existing luxurious country house hotels such as Cliveden, with a planned average daily room rate of £185–200. Our research shows it will be in demand from local companies, as well as parents visiting their children at Marlborough College.'

A conference centre will be built, hidden in the kitchen court to the left of the house, which conveniently has its own grand entrance through an arch with the family heraldic lion added by the 2nd Marquess soon after he was made a Knight of the Garter. The fine Empire furniture bought in Paris in the 1820s by the 1st Marquess was sold at auction at the end of the Second World War, but all the family portraits will be loaned back for display in the hotel.

The 18-hole golf course, designed by Peter Alliss, will be laid out in former parkland to the south of the house. Robin Pope, of the architects Tripe & Wakeham, says: 'Avenues and clumps will be replanted in precise historical positions.'

Sandy golf bunkers notoriously look like blisters in the smooth greensward for which Brown was famous. Here, the developers promise that any that could appear in a photograph looking towards the house will be grassy, not sandy, hollows.

If carried out to the high standards promised, the conversion offers new hope for many grand houses that have been taken over as institutions. Construction began in January 2007 and completion is scheduled for late 2009.

TRAFALGAR HOUSE   Salisbury
Granted to the family of Admiral Nelson after his death at Trafalgar

WITH ITS WARM RED BRICK GLOWING IN THE SUN, Trafalgar House is a classic example of Georgian well-being. It is impressive yet not overbearing, with grand central block and balancing wings standing in satisfying harmony. The house is named for England's greatest naval hero, Admiral Nelson. After his death in battle in 1805 there could be no call to build a great palace like Blenheim. Instead a grateful Parliament bought a country estate for his family.

Nelson's immediate heir was his elder brother the Rev. William Nelson, who succeeded him as Duke of Bronte and was created Earl Nelson of Trafalgar. In 1814 he was given Trafalgar, then known as Standlynch House, which stands high above the River Avon, south of Salisbury. According to *Country Life* in 1945, 'No lovelier situation could have been chosen.' The house looks west towards the slopes of Cranborne Chase and is approached through a grandly landscape park.

Trafalgar was built in 1731–3 for Sir John Vandeput by John James, the architect of St George's, Hanover Square. His ambition was to show 'that the Beautys of Architecture may consist with the greatest plainness of the structure'. At Trafalgar he relies on the texture of materials, fine brickwork and stone trim to provide finesse. The strongest treatment is reserved for the windows, with emphatic triple keystones in the baroque fashion and more blocked stonework at the sides. By contrast the attic windows have plainer surrounds, indicating it was added later.

Vandeput, whose ancestors had come from Antwerp in 1568, bought the estate in 1726. Forty years later it was acquired by Henry Dawkins, MP for Southampton, a wealthy man who owned 20,000 acres of sugar plantations in Jamaica where he lived in the 1750s. Southampton was a borough with strong West Indian connections and Dawkins returned there in 1760 on the death of another West Indian plantation owner.

Dawkins's elder brother James was a pioneer traveller who helped Robert Wood prepare his two great books on the ruins of Baalbec and Palmyra. Later he assisted James Stuart and Nicholas Revett with the famous volumes on the Antiquities of Athens. So it was only natural that his brother Henry should commission Revett to design a Greek Doric portico at Trafalgar based on the Temple of Apollo at Delos – one of the first examples of pure Greek Revival architecture in England. Henry Dawkins also added the wings connected to the house by long corridors at basement and ground floor only.

Internally, the glory of Trafalgar is the sumptuous baroque hall rising almost the full height of the house. The treatment is richly sculptural. The magnificent two-tier fireplace has scrolls, herms, medallion and bust. There are decorative panels of foliage over the doors, floral garlands above the niches and a continuous band of acanthus linking the Corinthian capitals. Still richer are the swirling palm fronds and shell work of the coved ceiling. This is in fullest rococo style and cannot date from before 1745 when, presumably, the attic storey was added. To complete this lexicon of virtuoso plasterwork there are exquisite Classical ceilings by Revett.

After the Nelson family sold Trafalgar in 1948, the house was separated from the surrounding estate and left with only 7 acres of land. The north wing was badly affected by dry rot and developers were seeking permission to build in the grounds. Happily, Trafalgar was saved by the opera impresario Michael Wade, who has brought the house back to life with concerts and musical events. Nothing could be more appropriate, as in the 18th century Trafalgar had its own music room with murals of romantic landscapes by G.B. Cipriani. Trafalgar House has now resumed its 18th-century role of a home that is a centre of hospitality for the whole county and beyond.

The wings and corridor links are neatly replicated on either side of the house.

WARDOUR CASTLE   Tisbury
1770s masterpiece of the architect James Paine

EXTRAORDINARY AS IT SEEMS, mighty Wardour Castle failed to sell at auction in December 1991 with a reserve believed to be just £800,000 for the house and 52 acres. This was partly a reflection of the severity of the recession in the property market. Some potential purchasers, looking for the privacy of broad acres, were also deterred by the fact that three years earlier the magnificent chapel attached to the house had been vested in a trust, becoming the local Catholic parish church.

New Wardour Castle, as it is properly called, was built in 1770–76 for one of the leading Catholic peers in England, the 8th Lord Arundell, to the designs of the architect James Paine. Wardour Chapel is the most magnificent Cathoic church built in 18th century England, a full fifty years before the Catholic Emancipation Act. There were, it was said, more Catholics around Wardour than anywhere else in England and more than a hundred were supported by work on the park and estate.

In its dimensions the castle is more palace than house, requiring conversion as apartments rather than self-contained houses with their own front doors, which is more practical when a house has grown over time and has many entrances. Wardour was fortunate in finding a purchaser, Nigel Tuersley, who saw how the house could be sympathetically adapted as a series of very splendid apartments, both for sale and for let. As a result the house retains its full Augustan splendour, dominating the park, and residents use Paine's breathtaking domed and columned staircase hall to approach their apartments.

This is the best possible solution to a great house that was for years in institutional use, first with the Society of Jesus, which had links with the Arundells dating back to the 18th century, followed by Cheshire homes and then Cranborne Chase Girls' School from 1960 to 1990.

Curving quadrants link the centre to the matching wings.

WORCESTERSHIRE

THIS DELIGHTFUL HOUSE IS AS PLAYFUL an example of the style known as Strawberry Hill Gothick as can be found. Every window is a little masterpiece. The architect is unknown but the mix of rococo and gothick is close to that used by the builder-architect Thomas Farnolls Pritchard of Shrewsbury. The exotic detail, however, was largely taken from one of the most popular pattern books of the time, Batty Langley's *Ancient Architecture*, published in 1742.

The Pool House at Astley looks down to a brick-edged pond. The front, dating from 1760, is faced in smooth red sandstone and is inset with four Venetian windows, transformed from Classic to gothick by the use of ogee (flame-headed) arches. The window in the centre is in matching style, as is the front door, though this has a stepped-up hood mould to throw off the rain. The attic is different again, less refined in its treatment but bolder, with three large ogee gables. These are inset with quatrefoils, with pretty petal-pattern glazing. When the owners wanted a conservatory, they went to the architect Francis Machin, whose ogee glass houses have a silhouette matching the gables.

The earliest part of the house is believed to date from 1660 and the house has a substantial complement of ten bedrooms and an extensive set of outbuildings. The gothick detail continues inside – the showpiece is the drawing room with clustered colonettes and a matching fireplace with blind tracery. The staircase in polished oak ascends in a graceful curve with straight-sided balusters and a sweeping handrail. A pretty 18th-century sketch shows the garden terrace had latticework balustrades.

Built in local red sandstone, the house has gothick Venetian windows and shaped gables.

THE GREAT HOUSE — Brockamin

Eye-catching early 18th-century house with a tall parapet concealing attic windows

IN 18TH-CENTURY FRANCE, LEADING ARCHITECTS did not consider brick a noble material like stone. In the English Midlands it was very different. Tall, well-proportioned brick houses are a dominating feature of the landscape, the work of accomplished master bricklayers who produced buildings of lasting quality, more enduring indeed than stone. These houses were built for local industrialists and entrepreneurs as much as for the local gentry and are often surrounded by attractive groups of outbuildings and walled gardens.

The Great House is an expression used in the Caribbean, especially Jamaica, to describe a house with an estate. The Great House at Brockamin is given added presence by the unusually tall blind parapet above the first-floor windows. Believed to date from 1732 it is, like many baroque houses, engagingly quirky. The window over the front door is decidedly larger than those to the sides with a distinctive 'apron' below the sill. The glazing bars in the arch interlace at the top forming a series of pointed arches – a Strawberry Hill Gothick motif that is likely to date twenty or thirty years after the house was built. There is similar pretty glazing in the doorcase.

The architectural trim is kept simple, possibly for reasons of economy. Instead of the usual giant columns or pilasters, there are vertical strips of quoins. These are of two kinds – alternately broad and narrow quoins at the corners (typically English) and the straight-sided bands of quoins in the centre (favoured by the French).

The gothicky detail continues inside. The early 19th-century staircase rises in a pretty curve to the first floor where the corkscrew balusters are continued round the landing. The house looks out over an extensive Japanese water garden.

The limestone trim provides an interesting contrast to the warm orangey-red brickwork.

CROOME COURT Croome D'Abitot
Designed by Capability Brown for the 6th Earl of Coventry and completed in 1752

TEN YEARS AGO NO ONE WOULD HAVE BELIEVED that Croome Court could ever be a private house again. It had stood empty for fifteen years. Before that, Hare Krishnas had camped in its great staterooms, picking out the fruit and flowers on one of the 18th-century ceilings in tutti-frutti colours for their marriage ceremonies.

The great collections of the Earls of Coventry departed from the house soon after the Second World War. The sumptuous tapestry room was sold, complete with all its plasterwork, to the Metropolitan Museum in New York. Croome became a school.

Yet its beauty survived almost unblemished. The golden Bath stone has remained crisp, yet mellowed to perfection. The rich plasterwork inside, much of it by Robert Adam, remained – and the Met even thoughtfully left a replica of the ceiling they had taken. Then the National Trust stepped in to save the 670-acre Capability Brown park, helped by a £4.9 million grant from the Heritage Lottery Fund.

But the magnificent Grade I listed house, also attributed to Brown, remained empty. The irony was that the National Trust could have had it for £1. In 2004 Croome Court and 33 acres of grounds were for sale at £3.5 million.

Better still, every room was freshly painted, from the basements to the attics. The roof was not just watertight but had been re-leaded and re-slated, using many of the original handsome blue-green Westmoreland slates.

The man behind it was Laurence Bilton, an entrepreneur who, with his brother Anton, has made a speciality of rescuing decaying old buildings. He said cheerily:

The garden front and grand Ionic portico are built of warm, almost buttery limestone.

Corner towers project boldly above the balustraded parapets.

'We had to do a vast amount of cleaning, washing, de-fungusing. In the hall, awful carpets had been glued to the stone floor but were able to turn the stone over and wax it. The main staircase was worst, water pouring in, three inches deep on the floor, mushrooms everywhere. Now we live in the whole house. We have seventeen bedrooms. Before we drew up the particulars, I had always imagined that I had 24,000 sq ft.'

The measurements, however, showed that he had 36,500 sq ft – an increase equivalent to six good-sized, four-bedroomed houses. There are two staff flats in the basement and a further flat – and a gym – in the attic.

So which were his favourite rooms? 'First, the salon in the centre of the garden front overlooking the park. We sit and have drinks on the portico. Then the family room, where we hang out in summer and winter. The fire picks out the gold on the ceiling. The long gallery at the end of the house is one gigantic playroom with sun in it all day long where we spend a lot of time with the kids.'

Upstairs, the main bedroom and dressing room occupied an area the size of a large dockland apartment with stunning views of the park. On this floor were a further ten bedrooms, including four turret rooms at the corners – all made possible by an impressive row of four strapping boilers in the vaulted cellars. 'That's a million BTU [British thermal units] capacity, what's needed to heat a fifty-room house,' he told me.

'I've got the main running expenses, heating, electricity and insurance down to £20,000 a year. I employ two people to look after the grounds, though you could do it in a contract. Overall running costs are now roughly similar to those of a large manor house.'

But with the National Trust all around, isn't it like living in a goldfish bowl?

'It makes you think twice,' Laurence Bilton said. 'But the Trust has dredged the lake, greatly improving the views, and now they're embarking on a major tree-planting programme.

'Our front lawn is nine acres – 300 yards to the boundary. When people come to look at the church on the hill they're dots on the horizon.'

On the south side the ha-ha has been rebuilt. 'The way I look at it is that the landscape around is secure in perpetuity. None of it can ever be built on,' he says.

Croome has long been famous for its Classical temples and follies, but one of the most beautiful, the domed rotunda, remains with the house on the nearby hill surrounded by noble cedars. From here there is a breathtaking panorama across the fertile Worcestershire plain, a perfect place for picnics or drinks in the evening.

One reason that Croome Court stayed empty for so long was the extent of decaying stables and outbuildings. After converting and selling a first group, including the coach house, Bilton sold the stables to another developer, who has created another ten houses. These had a separate access from the main house and hardly impinged on it. Earlier plans for a large suburban-looking development in the 7-acre walled garden were fought off.

In 2007 came the news that a Croome conservation trust, backed by the National Trust, had agreed the purchase of the house and grounds, with a view to opening Croome to the public. House and park will be reunited and visitors will be able to see the splendidly restored interiors, hoepfully alongside portraits and other items on loan from the family. This is a fairy-tale ending to a long and often desperate saga.

The domed temple is built in Bath stone and attributed to Robert Adam.

ROUS LENCH COURT   Rous Lench
16th-century black and white house extended in the 19th century for a clergyman

GREAT TOPIARY GARDENS ARE ONE OF THE WONDERS of England. Most famous is Levens in Cumbria, but many of the most impressive topiary gardens are in Worcestershire, Gloucestershire and Herefordshire. I waited for years to visit Rous Lench, where the long yew hedges marching up the hills were compared to 'the walls of Troy' in an early *Country Life* article.

The village of Rous Lench stands on the last spur of the Clent Hills before the Vale of Evesham, looking out over a park rolling down to the ancient parish church. Like many houses in these parts, Rous Lench Court is a delightful black and white house with chequer-pattern timbers, and is in part a creation of Victorian romancing. It stands like an ancient manor, hard by the country lane that runs past it. There is a glimpse into the courtyard through a coaching arch inscribed 'Welcome ye coming speed ye parting guest'.

If you approach from the east, a mighty brick water tower at the top of the hill will have awakened your interest but otherwise the long walls of yew hedge shut out any glimpse of the extraordinary place within. But once through the modern gate piers you see it all. The black and white house is grandly set at the top of two impressive flights of steps, linking grand stretches of lawn.

The drive carries straight on past a group of stables and outbuildings in pale red brick now formed into cottages, and climbs to a formal courtyard in front of the house.

Grand flights of stone garden steps contrast with delicate diamond- and herringbone-pattern woodwork.

By this time you will have been spellbound by the magnificent cedars of Lebanon at the peak of their splendour. The first wave of cedars, planted in English gardens towards the middle of the 18th century, have largely vanished, or been painfully lopped to eke out a last few years of life. The cedars of Rous Lench, planted little more than a century ago, have plenty of life ahead, like the splendid Wellingtonias and pines around them.

This is an ancient estate, known before the Conquest as Biscopelenz or Bishop's Lench because it belonged to the see of Worcester. It is said that Oliver Cromwell slept here before the Battle of Worcester. After the death of Sir Thomas Rous without heirs in 1721, it passed through the female line until in 1876 Sir Henry Rouse-Broughton, Bt, sold the estate to the Rev. W.K.W. Chafy, who not long after raised himself to the dignity of Chafy-Chafy. Dr Chafy, a Doctor of Divinity, extended the garden with the astonishing series of yew hedges looking like fortified walls and laid out around a series of terraces ascending the hill so they loom above you. Behind the house is a giant *bosquet*, a circle of yews, inset with windows and doors with the yew arching inwards to form a roof.

Everywhere there are steps, flanked by stone balls, the longest series making a dramatic ascent the whole length of the garden beside the road, hemmed in by yew hedges on either side.

The house is a romantic sight, though what architectural historians impolitely call 'boiled'. Some timbers are of great age, others clearly 19th-century, but the Victorian reworking was done with panache, with ornate bargeboarded gables and clusters of ornate terracotta chimney pots.

Inside a greater surprise awaits, for Rous Lench has recently been done over in showman style that is pure Midlands. In some ways it is more like a country hotel, with large bar and high stools, and large conservatory beyond. Behind the bar is an extraordinary wine library set in a cellar with glistening vault in glazed white tiles and lined with massive library bookcases, stepped out at the bottom as if for large folio volumes, but fitted out with racks for wine, not shelves for books.

The main rooms are panelled, some with robustly carved linenfold, as well as a massive Italian Renaissance-style hooded stone fireplace. Specially painted Cromwellian history pictures hang on the walls and everywhere the initials of the house 'RLC' are emblazoned on hangings and even picture frames.

Upstairs the bathrooms will leave you open-mouthed. In the master bathroom the bath is set in the centre of the room like a four-poster bed with canopy and columns, not to mention a marble pillow at the end. The glass-fronted shower cabinet is like the 'whispering door' in an Elizabethan great chamber, designed to keep draughts out and set across the corner. Further bathrooms are only marginally less opulent, and I am not talking of the gold taps, but of the swan-tops to shower cabinets, washstands and dressing tables – nowhere are there less than two. Your taste may not accord with that of the owners but there's no question of the gusto with which they've tackled it.

I had been told before I went that Rous Lench is haunted, but it is hard to think of a house that looks less spooked. Almost every inch of the house, all through into the attics, is carpeted and every awkward space is turned into a feature of some kind – including the central valley in the roof where a little glass house has been contrived to enjoy views over the park to the Malvern Hills.

WOLVERTON HALL   Pershore
Early 18th-century house that played an unusual role in the Second World War

THE VALE OF EVESHAM BRIMS WITH PEACE, fertility and contentment. Standing almost at its heart is Wolverton Hall, a handsome Queen Anne house surrounded by a cluster of delightful buildings, a pretty coach house bearing the date 1714, a black and white Worcestershire barn and matching bothy, and a walled garden and stream opening out into a pond. There are 18 acres in total, comprising woodland and paddock.

Some of the feeling of being shut away from the world may come from the fact that Wolverton was long the home of recusants – Catholics who held to the old religion and paid the penalty in taxes and forfeiture of any role in public life. In 1581 William Cooksey bequeathed the manor and house at Little Wolverton to the male heirs of his sister Alice, wife of Humphrey Acton. His descendant, Thomas Acton, was an ardent Royalist whose estates were sequestered, but they were restored and for nearly two centuries generations of Actons, all called William, lived here. The William who married a Margaret Perkins from Bath is the likely builder – a keystone bears the date 1715.

The house is like a tea caddy, tall and square with a parapet screening a shallow pyramid roof. On the two garden fronts there are so many sash windows there is almost more glass than wall, promising lovely light rooms within.

The windows on the entrance front are fewer and more widely spaced with a fine, crisply carved columned porch, all suggesting a remodelling in the mid 18th century to conform with fashionable Palladian proportions.

The deep plan of the house suggests that lurking within must be a secret room. In fact Wolverton has more than this, for there are 18th-century tunnels beneath the lawn – presumably to keep servants out of sight. It must have been these that gave Wolverton its own very special war, recorded in intriguing detail in *The Mercian Maquis: the Secret Resistance Organisation in Herefordshire and Worcestershire during World War II* by Bernard Lowry and Mick Wilks.

Wolverton Hall provided a refuge for the van Moppes brothers, who brought a large stock of industrial diamonds out of Amsterdam just before German forces arrived in May 1940. Churchill, then First Sea Lord, was determined to secure the diamonds for use by the armaments industry. With fears of an imminent German invasion, they were stored in the strong room at Wolverton, conveniently accessible to Birmingham and its metal industries.

The Hall also became the local headquarters of the Auxiliaries, the secret army that was to be left behind to harry the Germans as and when they invaded. The idea was proposed in a top-secret paper headed 'Pessimism' and given to Captain Peter Fleming, brother of Ian, to develop. Colin Gubbins, who took charge (and was later head of SOE), wrote, 'There would be no question of coordinating these forces into large units or grouping them for battle; they must be very small units, locally raised able to melt away after battle. The highest possible degree of secrecy must be maintained … for the personal security of those left behind.'

It was all rather like the Lost Boys subterranean home in *Peter Pan* with hideouts in woods, farm buildings, cellars, even deserted badger setts. Peers and poachers were to serve together, trained in grenade throwing and the use of plastic explosives.

The front door opens into a pine-panelled hall with carved fireplace and pretty niche. The strong room with massive steel door is hidden in the archway leading to the staircase. This has a trio of pretty turned and carved balusters to each step, swept round at the bottom with a baroque flourish. The elegant dining room, drawing room and morning room all retain 18th-century folding window shutters in working order.

The bedrooms, eight in all, are on two levels. On the second floor the sheer number of windows would have been overwhelming and this, rather than the window tax, probably explains a number of false windows on the top floor. These upper rooms are reached by a pretty, secondary stair which retains the original flat S-pattern balusters. The views also get better and better as you ascend – with Bredon Hill, the last spur of the Cotswolds, to the south and the Malvern hills to the west.

The spacious kitchen is in a single-storey wing overlooking the garden. To the left of the entrance court is a two-storey wing containing a well-appointed billiard room. With two external doors, this wing could serve either as two cottages or partly or wholly as an office. The coach house provides another spacious self-contained cottage; the barn, though retaining its original timbers, needs substantial repair but the bothy is perfect as a well-equipped garden shed or workshop.

Just beside the house, the former estate farm remains very much a working operation while in a field beyond is a large pheasant-rearing operation.

The entrance front of warm red brick, now clad in ivy, opens onto a courtyard.

10 COLLEGE YARD — Worcester

Handsome Charles II house with glorious views over the River Severn

Choral evensong in a great medieval cathedral has to be one of the most uplifting ways to end the day. No 10 College Yard stands just 20 metres from the north door of Worcester Cathedral. From the upper windows, the magnificently decorated crossing tower fills the view. There can hardly be a better bedroom in any English town to wake up in. And now the house has another claim to fame, for just as Roberta Edgar and John Houseman were putting the property on the market, it appeared on the new £20 note celebrating Edward Elgar's association with Worcester and its cathedral.

On the garden side, the house stands above a glorious bend in the River Severn, where the sun sets beside a graceful stone-arch bridge. The riverbanks are thick with trees, while a colony of at least a hundred swans congregates on the water beneath.

The lower stone walls of the house date back to the 13th century and set the square form of the house that was built here in the 1680s by Chancellor Price, the author of a manuscript that is preserved in the Bishop's Registry and records changes following the Reformation.

Unusually for a town house, it has windows in the flanks filling the rooms with light from all sides and providing new bathrooms with unexpected views over the cathedral and the garden of the old bishop's palace next door.

The house stands in a secluded position in the cathedral precinct.

The entrance front, raised up on a small terrace enclosed by railings, is dignified rather than truly handsome and needs a voluminous wisteria to bring it to life (*Solanum* would do the job quicker). The river front has engaging tea-caddy proportions, with a bright brick that bears the marks of many puzzling alterations, as well as a trim white-bracketed cornice.

Inside, the delight of the house is an altogether unexpected sense of openness and space, almost that of an open plan, which Ms Edgar has cleverly played up by painting the interior from top to bottom in a pale parchment colour, with woodwork in a slightly darker tone.

The spaciousness is increased by the size and number of handsome sash windows. Thrown open on every side of the house, they fill the rooms with air that is as fresh and balmy as that you might find in the Loire Valley on a spring day. On the front entrance these windows have the chunky glazing bars that are typical of the years around 1700. On the river front they are exquisitely slender, matching the trellis-pattern Regency balconies on the outside. One sash ingeniously slides up into the wall above, allowing you to step out onto the veranda and walk down to the garden.

Edgar explained: 'When I embark on a house, I like to do as little as possible. It has to be comfortable, with a new kitchen and bathrooms, but I keep all the old plasterwork throughout.'

All the handsome broad elm floorboards have been left exposed and the house now has eight open fireplaces, four of which have been in regular use already.

There is also efficient central heating, though it has had the unexpected effect of causing glass panes to pop in the windows as the wood dries out.

The stone-flagged entrance hall, furnished as a drawing room, opens through an Edwardian arch into a morning room with a grand piano. Beyond, the new kitchen has pride of place, resplendent with a smart black Aga. The basement comes with a Georgian wine cellar with a full complement of slate-shelved wine bins.

Rising from the bottom to the top of the house is a magnificent oak staircase of a size and grandeur that you would expect in a substantial country house – spot-on for a house of the 1680s. Like many Charles II staircases, although carved in wood its balustrades have the monumentality of stone and it is all the more imposing for being lit by large three-part Georgian windows.

The signatures of Ms Edgar's interiors are a vast oval bath in the master bedroom that might have been chosen by César Ritz, plenty of walk-in cupboards and showers and loos fitted in closets.

The top-floor rooms have been opened up to the eaves, leaving beams exposed and Velux windows hidden in the valleys to provide extra top light for the bathrooms.

The garden steps down to a high wall over the towpath. Better still, No 10 is set back in its own little close, so the sound of traffic is faint from the inner ring road, even when the windows are open.

You can gripe about the trio of high-rise flats the city fathers decided to build some way back across the river, but your eye will be quickly deflected to the distant view of the Malvern Hills.

YORKSHIRE & THE HUMBER

WHEN ALLERTON WAS OFFERED for sale, it was described as 'ideal for institutional purposes', but to everyone's surprise it was bought by an American, Dr Gerald Rolph, with a passion for Gothic architecture and an ambition to refurnish a stately home in High Victorian style. Recently retired, his plan was to vest Allerton (pronounced Ollerton) in a charitable trust and use it for educational purposes.

Built in 1852 for Lord Stourton by the architect James Firth, Allerton is the House of Lords transported to the Yorkshire countryside. The scale, the opulence and the overwhelming grandeur rival Barry and Pugin at the Palace of Westminster. When I visited in 1983 the task looked almost impossible. Paper was peeling from the walls and water was dripping into every corridor. Four years later, the glazed double doors in the entrance opened to reveal a brand new red carpet ascending the steps up to the great hall. At the top two huge china dalmations announced the new owner in residence.

Below: The drawing room is richly patterned.

Bottom: The great hall has a hammer-beam roof.

The doors into the hall were at least 15 ft high, swinging smoothly and silently on huge brilliantly polished brass hinges. The hall was panelled with richly cusped blind arcading. Flame-headed doorways with spiky finials soared above a massive gallery soared. All this was crowned by a hammer-beam roof recalling Hampton Court. A great ballroom stair swept down through an arch at one end. Michael Farr, the curator, told me the woodwork had been treated with a mixture of linseed oil, white spirit, malt vinegar and sugar to give it lustre.

The house lost most of its furnishings in a 1965 sale, but the architectural

The clerestory of the great hall rises above the roofs.

elements such as brass light fittings bookcases and sideboards remain. Dr Rolph had been buying on a major scale, snapping up massive pieces of furniture, sideboards, desks, beds and cupboards that no other private buyer could accommodate. The library had been re-hung with a Pugin paper made from the original blocks at Coles, the same design as used in the House of Lords, with the background changed from white to gold to blend better with the woodwork. The carpet, with a lily and rose motif, was woven by Mercier, weavers of Leeds. In the dining room the original table remained with a new set of twenty Victorian armchairs, recently acquired from a Scottish estate and reupholstered. By contrast the drawing room struck a feminine note. The walls were hung with huge 19th-century gilt rococo mirrors.

The service quarters below the house were on an equally grand scale with a railway track in the floor for bringing trolleys of supplies from the courtyard to the various stores and the kitchen. The early electrical fittings were still in place.

In January 2005 a savage fire broke out in a disused service wing, devastating the interior. Dr Rolph told me, 'We have lost the dining room and part of the library with its gothic bookcases but the great hall with its hammer-beam roof, the grand staircase and the ballroom are virtually intact.'

Emergency works were carried out with impressive speed. A month later the fire officer gave permission for the house to reopen for business. Dr Rolph explained his approach. 'I was determined Allerton should not be like a National Trust or English Heritage property with a ticket booth and gift shop. I like people to come to the house for a party and enjoy it as its creators intended. We have weddings every Friday and Saturday with most dates taken all through this year and next.'

BARKISLAND HALL — Barkisland
1638 house built for a Pennine clothier

BARKISLAND BELONGS TO A WONDERFUL GROUP of handsome Pennine country houses that speak of the fierce pride, rugged independence and entrepreneurial drive of the Yorkshire clothiers of the 16th and 17th centuries.

Like many of these houses, it wore a startling mantle of soot from the mill chimneys that grandsons and great-grandsons erected in the valleys. Built of local stone, these houses are dignified by coats of arms and family emblems over the entrances and have thick walls and numerous chimneys, ensuring that they were always warm and welcoming.

Their distinguishing features are massed ranks of stone-mullioned windows and projecting porches, often with the flourish of a rose window above. At Barkisland, the mullions are six, eight and even twelve 'lights' wide, the counterpart of the walls of glass at great Elizabethan houses such as Hardwick Hall in Derbyshire.

Barkisland has all the more appeal because it surveys a largely unchanged landscape of steep rolling hills and stone-walled fields, with the inspiring solitude of the Pennine moors opening immediately to the west.

Huddersfield, which Frederick Engels described as the 'fairest of the English industrial towns', has kept its distance, not crossing the M62, whose steady roar is the one intrusion in this splendid scene.

The valley from Ripponden down to Stainland has been little spoilt by recent development and the grand 19th-century stone-built mills still stand in rural isolation. The one immediately below Barkisland is to be transformed into smart apartments by Michael Wilson, the specialist developer who has successfully converted many country houses in the south.

Barkisland has a further unusual claim to fame. It was for fifteen years home to Lord Kagan, the maker of the Gannex raincoat and a confidant of Harold Wilson,

Traditional in design, the hood moulds above the large mullioned windows will throw off the rain.

who frequently came here while Prime Minister and who used to sneak across the field at the back to go to the local pub.

Externally the house is almost perfectly preserved. Georgian sash windows were never introduced and the small windows at the back, lighting the original staircase and the servants' quarters, remain unchanged, as well as a door on the second floor that opens into space. Its purpose is explained by a timber roller above, used for hoisting and lowering bales of wool and cotton. The end slopes of the roof are still laid with the stone slabs characteristic of the West Riding.

The entrance is through a two-storey porch with Doric columns below and Ionic above and a date of 1638 with the initials I and SG for John and Sarah Gledhill.

One reason that the house is so little changed is that it was divided into six tenements in the 19th century. Evidently it had fallen into parlous decay when it was bought in the 1920s by Tom Casson, a mill owner. Though he took infinite care to leave the exterior unchanged, he was compelled to rebuild the interior, inserting new concrete floors and retaining no more than a number of stone-arched fireplaces.

Barkisland therefore lacks the glorious Jacobean panelling and rich ceiling plasterwork groaning with fruit and foliage found in other contemporary manor houses. In its place, Casson introduced a wealth of solid oak panelling with individually carved panels.

David and Joan Rhodes, who bought the house in 1988, carpeted over the parquet floors because they used the house for local charity events and found that stiletto heels were digging into them. The main drawing room has fine-figured mahogany veneer doors in Queen Mary ocean-liner style. Beyond is a cosy dining room with old panelling. 'You can see it's imported as the wall behind is plastered, which it wouldn't have been if the panelling was there originally,' said Mr Rhodes.

Opening off the main bedroom is an Art Deco bathroom with glazed sea-green Vitrolite tiles and a mosaic floor (also found in the downstairs cloakroom). At the back of the house is Lord Kagan's sauna with massage room next door. 'They had a psychiatrist's chair – he was into kinky things,' laughed Mrs Rhodes.

The attic rooms are lofty and well-lit and form a self-contained apartment complete with built-in kitchen dining table with seats made from church pews. In the Black Room, at the back, an original 17th-century diamond-lattice-paned window survives.

A few pieces of furniture, including an elaborately carved dresser in the hall and stone-slab tables in the cellar, had evidently been in the house since it was built and appeared impossible to remove. Another interesting survival was a bedroom suite made by Gillows in the style of Louis Seize, with kidney-shaped dressing table, large armoire and cane-ended bed with round corners.

Mr Rhodes was a local builder who retired to play golf in Spain after building about five hundred houses in the area. However, he soon found he was bored and returned home. Barkisland had been empty for six years when he bought it, signing the contract in the House of Lords in front of Wilson's friend Lord Houghton, after whom he named a bedroom. The Rhodeses still had Lord Kagan's visitors' book – the first guest was Wilson's flamboyant colleague, red-headed Barbara Castle. Barkisland is now the home of Lady Eve Williamson.

BLACKBURN HALL   Grinton
Part-medieval manor house enlarged in 1635

AN ANCIENT MANOR HOUSE STANDING in a sheltered garden beside a village church is part of the English dream. Blackburn Hall in the Yorkshire Dales dates from the mid 12th century ,when the monks of Bridlington Priory chose this site to build a priest's house to serve the Dale.

The durable weatherworn stone used in Swaledale does not lend itself to precise dating but historians point to some tooling on the inner stone of a doorway that could be 12th-century, while the leading medievalist Pamela Tudor-Craig noted a carving of a bear's head on a first-floor fireplace which she considered to be 12th-century carving.

The implication is that the main block of the house is medieval and that the north wing was added in the early 17th century. Here there is a stone fireplace with shallow Tudor arch carved with the initials EHB and the date 1635, marking the marriage of Elizabeth Hutton of Marske-in-Swaledale into the Blackburn family.

The house stands in a prominent position in the centre of the pretty little village of Grinton between the River Swale and St Andrew's Church. The drive to the Hall is the end of the Corpse Way, an ancient road running the length of Swaledale along which the dead were brought for burial in the consecrated ground of the churchyard. The Blackburns had extensive lead-mining interests in the Dale and Elizabeth Hutton's mother was a god-daughter of Queen Elizabeth I.

Blackburn Hall has an enchanting formal garden with box hedges forming geometric patterns and a delightful pair of spirally clipped yews. Inside the house the atmosphere of an ancient manor is wonderfully preserved with oak panelling, exposed ceiling beams and stone flagged floors. There are leaded windows and stone mullions, while excavations by the Bowes Museum in the 1960s revealed traces of a medieval kitchen beneath the beech hedge in the garden.

The hood moulds over the windows are tweaked in the manner of Classical pediments.

BRODSWORTH HALL
Doncaster
Built in 1861–3 to the designs of Chevalier Casentini of Lucca for Charles Thelusson

'PLEASE DON'T CALL BRODSWORTH A TIME CAPSULE,' begged Caroline Whitworth when I visited the house in 1994. Four years of cataloguing and conserving 17,000 objects had left her with the overpowering sense that the house was not simply a set piece of the 1860s but witness to a hundred years of country-house life, beginning with Rothschild-style opulence and ending in remorseless decay that was worthy of Brideshead.

The builders of Brodsworth Hall, the Thelussons, were one of several continental banking families attracted to England by the openness of its society and the opportunity to make money. They had established a finance house in Geneva after fleeing from religious persecution in France. Isaac served as Geneva's ambassador to Louis XV; his son Peter established a bank in London and bought a mansion at Plaistow in Kent and extensive estates at Brodsworth in Yorkshire.

Peter Thelusson's fortune at his death in 1797 has been estimated at between £600,000 and £700,000, making him one of the wealthiest commoners in England. After leaving £100,000 in bequest to his family, he left the rest to accumulate at compound interest during the lives of his sons, grandsons and great-grandsons. After lengthy litigation the House of Lords pronounced in 1859 that the estate was to go to two great grandsons, Lord Rendlesham and Charles Sabine Thelusson, whose share included Brodsworth. Charled Thelusson had been born in Florence and spent part of his youth in Paris and Belgium. He set about replacing the large Georgian house at Brodsworth with a new house that would have been as much in place on the shores of Lake Como as in the middle of an English landscape park. Its design was commissioned from an otherwise little known Italian, Chevalier Giovanni Casentini, architect and sculptor of Lucca.

The columned porte cochère *stands to the right of the garden front, which descends to terraced gardens.*

The survival of Brodsworth was due to Sylvia Grant Dalton, who lived there for seventy-two years. She wed the heir to Brodsworth, Charles Grant Dalton, in 1916, and following his death married his cousin. She died in 1988 and was determined to the end that it should be preserved with its furniture and collections intact.

The trumpet for Brodsworth was first blown by Mark Girouard in *Country Life* in 1963. 'I know of no house that embodies the feel of a particular decade with such intensity as Brodsworth – the 1860s have been miraculously preserved in the amber richness of its rooms,' he wrote.

After Mrs Grant Dalton's death, it was found that atmospheric pollution had eaten huge holes in the stonework and the whole building was tilting at one end due to mining subsidence. Just as compensation had been agreed with the National Coal Board and a repair grant offered by the Historic Buildings Council, the trustees of her estate decided to halt all work. Brodsworth looked doomed to collapse and its contents destined for the salesrooms.

Hope came with Lord Montagu, first chairman of English Heritage, who decided that his newly founded organisation could provide a cheap alternative to the National Trust, taking on major country houses and maintaining them out of its annual budget. Brodsworth became the test case. After lengthy negotiations, Mrs Grant Dalton's daughter and heir, Mrs Pamela Williams, gave the house and gardens to English Heritage and the National Heritage Memorial Fund bought the contents for £3.6 million.

'We want people to see Brodsworth as we found it,' Caroline Whitworth explained. 'We'll show the old kitchen as an abandoned kitchen. It's part of the history of the 20th century that places like this cease to function. People may think it's not looking terribly smart. We accept that.'

Brodsworth differs in one significant way from most other Classical country houses in Britain: you enter not through the centre of the main front but at the narrow end. There is artifice in this. The architect Casentini had a strong theatrical sense and conceived his interiors as carefully as stage sets. Each room has elaborate inlaid floors, marbled walls, gorgeous picture frames, furniture, and domes casting shafts of light on to carefully placed white marble statuary.

In the hall, bands of Minton tiles alternate with smoky blue Parian cement paving. On top of the cornice English Heritage found the signatures of thirteen painters who decorated the room in 1866. To the left is the morning room, which for English Heritage was a classic exercise in freeze-framing a moment of decay. The richly patterned Victorian wallpaper, a convincing imitation of Spanish leather, had almost entirely perished at the bottom because of rising damp, but cleaning had restored the blues, reds and golds in the rest of the paper to their original lustre.

All these ground-floor rooms have French windows supplied with steel roller blinds. The mechanisms are concealed behind the shutters. Lead weights the size of church kneelers dangle on leather straps and the weights are so carefully balanced that the blinds can be pulled up with ease.

The large staircase hall is sumptuously marbled – all *verde antico*, yellow sienna and red porphyry. In fact all the 'marble', complete with fissures, is brilliantly convincing paintwork. Some areas are painted with brushstrokes that are almost like cross-hatching. It is an effect designed to be seen at a distance.

Special pride was taken in the rare survival of sixteen *portières*, heavy anti-draught curtains that hung across doorways. Soot-black, they emerged from the conservation studio at Blickling a crimson wool, like a fireman's uniform.

Most remarkable of all were the frayed but still beautiful silk wall hangings. Of late, the restoration trend in such cases has been towards having the silks rewoven to match the original, but at Brodsworth the silk had been hung by fixing it directly on the wall, not on the usual batons, and it had also been badly frayed by light. English Heritage has not replaced it but backed it with cotton and ingeniously hung it in a sandwich of fine nylon net, painting the wall to match where it has perished entirely.

Should rooms like this be as fresh and inviting as they would have been when the house was still flourishing or is the original fabric interesting to see even in a damaged state? English Heritage was determined we should think about it. On this occasion I go for the shock of the old. And it's rather beautiful too.

BROUGH HALL   Richmond
From the late 16th century the home of the Lawson family, Catholic recusants

THE PLANE BOUND FOR THE CARIBBEAN had just taken off from Heathrow on Christmas Eve when Lady Birk, the minister entrusted with listed buildings, saw the item on Brough Hall on the Court page of *The Times*. Beneath a beautiful *Country Life* photograph of Brough standing serenely in its park, she found herself roundly condemned. This was 1975, European Architectural Heritage Year, and SAVE had awarded her boss Anthony Crosland, Secretary of State for the Environment, a special loss-of-heritage award for giving permission to demolish two-thirds of Brough to

Built of the local stone, there are numerous Venetian windows as well as 16th-century mullions.

The Palladian centre and matching wings are handsomely set in parkland.

make it more 'preservable'. The decision had been Lady Birk's – Crosland was an enlightened minister who had recently reprieved the City of London Club. Bizarrely only a small portion of the central block at Brough was to remain. I heard from Lady Birk's husband later that, incensed by our cheek, she had all but demanded that the plane turn back immediately so she could deal with the matter.

The central block of Brough Hall, we pointed out, was Elizabethan, concealed behind a Classical front of 1730 and extended by handsome balancing wings added by Thomas Atkinson in the 1770s. Some very fine interiors were due to be demolished, including the panelled Elizabethan hall with a very good plaster ceiling, a handsome George II saloon running the length of the first floor and some Elizabethan plaster friezes in second-floor bedrooms.

The decision was all the more surprising as the house had received a big write-up in *Country Life* in two articles by John Cornforth as recently as 1967. Sanity fortunately prevailed. Demolition did not proceed and instead Brough Hall was converted into ten apartments without alteration to the handsome exterior. This was an early example of the sensitive division of a country house, and a successful one.

The Lawsons, owners of Brough from c.1575, were recusants and, in addition to their private chapel, built the catholic church of St Paulinus in 1834–7 in the grounds of the Brough Hall at their own expense. A stone shrine contains the relics of St. Innocent, found in the catacombs of Rome, and presented to Sir William Lawson by Pope Gregory XVI.

CLIFTON CASTLE   Hambleton
Elegant Regency house built for Timothy Hutton

THE NAME CLIFTON CASTLE IS BORN OF the Romantic movement. The handsome Classical house built by Timothy Hutton in 1802–10 is a Palladian villa without castellar features of any kind, though Leland in the 16th century describes a 'house caullid Clifton, like a pele or castelet'. By 1789 this was a ruin, part inhabited by a gentleman farmer, Mr T. Beckwith.

Hutton rebuilt the house on the old foundations, taking advantage of a glorious site above a bend in the River Ure, with long views across to Wensleydale. This is a wonderful example of a 'borrowed' landscape with the pasture beyond the river planted to look like a continuation of the park when in fact it is part of the adjoining Swinton estate. In the woods is an intriguing set of rustic summer houses in the form of thatched conical huts with columns made from bunches of poles.

The Huttons were a long-established Yorkshire family who had supplied two archbishops of York. The principal family seat was at Marske in Swaledale. Timothy Hutton was a fortunate fourth son, inheriting Clifton after his second and third brothers had been passed over. As his architect he chose a local man, John Foss, whose stepfather, a mason, had taken Foss into his business, where he acquired the trades of both mason and carver, going on to become a self-taught architect and Mayor of Richmond. He worked principally as a country-house architect in the North Riding and Clifton Castle is his most accomplished work, elegantly proportioned and finely finished both inside and out. Though compact, the house is given grandeur by the full-height Ionic columns and pediment containing richly carved coat of arms.

The style of the house recalls that of John Carr of York, architect of Constable Burton, but the internal detail is fashionably Regency and abreast of fashion. Tall sash windows descend to the floor, while the doors of the main rooms are made of solid mahogany. The decorative detail of ceiling plasterwork is exquisitely crisp, all reflecting very good craftsmen working in Yorkshire at the time.

The grandest feature is the staircase which begins in a single set of stairs and then branches into two separate flights. The hanging flights, which are boldly cantilevered from the walls, ascend in graceful curves around the walls. Added grandeur is provided by the tall Ionic columns that support the first-floor gallery and frame the imposing tripartite sash window which floods the stair hall with light from above.

In 1963 Clifton was acquired by the heir to the Marquess of Downshire, Robin Hill. His son Nicholas Hillsborough now runs the estate and house and gardens are opened to the public by appointment only.

Tall Regency sashes provide abundant light for the main ground-floor rooms.

CONSTABLE BURTON — Leyburn
Palladian villa of the 1760s built to the designs of John Carr of York

WYVILLS HAVE OWNED CONSTABLE BURTON for over four and a half centuries since the estate came to them by marriage during the reign of Edward VI. The unusual name of their house stems from their position as constables of Richmond Castle. The Elizabethan house that stood on the site is recorded in an early 18th-century engraving by Kip, which shows it built on an H-plan with a raised centre. Sir Marmaduke Wyvill, 6th baronet and son of another Marmaduke, was described as 'a great man for sheep in Yorkshire' and was genially appointed Postmaster General of Ireland by his brother-in-law Thomas Coke, later Lord Leicester, the English Postmaster General.

After his death in 1754, his nephew, also Sir Marmaduke, rebuilt the house *c.*1762–8 to the designs of John Carr of York. Farington in his diary tells the story that Carr mistakenly pulled down the house, forcing Sir Marmaduke to lay out '£10,000 to build another house'. It's equally possible that Carr was actually rebuilding on the foundations of the Elizabethan house and perhaps incorporating the walls, as the footprint of the new house is similar to the old and Carr's distinctive *portico-in-antis* could be an infilling of the recess of the H.

Either way, Carr's design is a perfect mid-Georgian villa, of exquisite proportions, idyllically set in a large park. It is entirely faced in smooth blemishless ashlar stone. The architectural trim is paired to the minimum without being so

The recessed Ionic portico is approached by a grand flight of stone steps.

The house looks out across a large, gently rolling park with a central vista framed by fine mature trees.

sparse that it could seem dull. The main front has the typical 1-3-1 window grouping of Palladio's villas with a tall *piano nobile* and lower basement and attic. There are emphatic Gibbs surrounds to the lower windows and a staircase up to the portico that makes a dashing leap across space, like a bridge. The longer flank, following that of the Elizabethan house, has seven windows with a bow window on the east front.

Carr concentrated on crisp detail that would cast strong shadows. The bold dentil cornice is carried round the whole house, while the entrance portico has a plain frieze but the architrave is omitted. Like other Palladian villas in England, Constable Burton has a central stair lit not by a dome but by the large semi-circular lunettes known as Diocletian windows. The stone flights are cantilevered from the walls with a delicate wrought-iron railing with scrolly balusters. In the large basement area, Carr set the cellars and larders under the central hall with kitchens and office quarters around the outside.

Queen Elizabeth I was entertained here shortly after the original house was built and in 1611 the Wyvills were among the first baronets created by James I. When I wrote about the house in *Country Life* in 1968, it was let to a tenant, Mrs V. Burdon, who lived here quietly but in some style, planting extensively in the gardens. Since then Charles Wyvill has reclaimed his inheritance and the family now live in the house and open the gardens to the public from the middle of March to the middle of October.

EBBERSTON HALL   Pickering
Summer pavilion of 1718 by the Scottish architect Colen Campbell

EBBERSTON HALL IS AN ENCHANTING small house, built in 1718 as a summer pavilion. Here is the perfect country estate on a Lilliputian scale, with parkland, encircling woods and a cascade garden terminating in a grand mirror pool reflecting the house.

On the entrance front a flight of a dozen steps flanked by miniature obelisks ascends to a terrace with a further half dozen steps to the front door, all giving the little building a sense of presence. With just one window on either side of the front door, it looks no more than a cottage but columns dripping with bands of rustic work impart grandeur.

The doorcase inside the front door is as grand as that outside with a full Doric frieze of triglyphs and a segment-shaped pediment. The drawing room has fluted pilasters framing fireplace and door. The loggia overlooking the cascade has Ionic columns with an intricate frieze and sturdy niches.

The house was built in 1718 by William Thompson, MP for Scarborough and Warden of the Mint, for his mistress. His architect was Colen Campbell, the pioneer of the Palladian Revival in England. The original design for the house included a square cupola with a lead roof built on the roof of the Hall; this was demolished in 1905.

William Thompson died in 1744, and the estate passed to the Hotham family in 1771, remaining with them until 1814, when it was sold to George Osbaldestone, the sporting 'Squire of England', who could outride, outshoot and outbox any man of his weight in the country. In 1848, when the Squire had run through his fortune, Ebberston became a farmhouse. In 1941, Sir Kenelm Cayley sold the property to Major de Wend Fenton, whose son is the present owner. A long programme of repairs has been completed, dry rot eliminated and all three waterfalls are once more in working order.

The colonnaded loggia on the garden front was glazed during the 18th century.

FORT HORNE
Thornton Seward
Regency castellated folly named after its builder

SOMEWHERE, THERE SHOULD BE A PERFECT HOUSE for us all. Sarah Pirie found hers in a village in the Yorkshire Dales. It is a pretty castellated folly raised up on a terrace above the lane through the village. Fort Horne is named after its builder Captain Horne, a man well known for his eccentricity. He lived at Old Hall nearby, and held a commission in the Loyal Dales Volunteers, a regiment raised during the Napoleonic wars. The Fort was built, like others in various counties, to house the militia if the French invaded.

Like all follies and eye-catchers there is a delightful playfulness in the design – a tall three-storey centre with battlements and single-storey flanking wings with Venetian windows with pretty intersecting glazing bars. The front had suffered from some crude alterations and the little building had been divided into two. But inside there were well-proportioned rooms, a pretty stair and on each floor the views improve dramatically as you begin to look over the trees. Repaired and modernised, it makes a delightful and unusual house, opening out onto a large stretch of lawn that would make a perfect playground for a family.

The Fort appears to be early 19th-century in date. In *Bulmer's Directory* of 1890 it is listed as being occupied by Mrs Mary Ann Waddington.

Built of the attractive local rubblestone, the house retains the original Venetian windows.

THE RUIN, HACKFALL · Ripon

Former banqueting house restored by the Landmark Trust as a holiday cottage

THE EXTRAORDINARY DINGLES AT HACKFALL – steep wooded valleys descending to the River Ure – are neither a park nor a garden, but more a secret woodland Elysium representing one of the earliest examples of the Picturesque in the country. When I first explored them in 1986 they were almost impenetrable and the follies on the verge of collapse. Hackfall was the creation of William Aislabie, whose father John was Chancellor of the Exchequer when the South Sea Bubble burst. Deeply implicated in suspect share dealings, he was first imprisoned, and then forced to pay more than £2 million in forfeitures.

John Aislabie sought solace in the creation of the superb water gardens at Studley Royal, which his son William completed with the purchase of the nearby ruins of Fountains Abbey. While Studley Royal is formal and geometric, with shaven lawns, canals and moon ponds, Hackfall is woods, cliffs and raging torrents – the first stirrings of the Romantic movement. Turner painted here in 1816. Arthur Young, the great agriculturalist, was enraptured on a visit in 1777. 'Nothing can exceed the beauty of this landscape,' he wrote. Gilpin, the great apostle of the Picturesque, exclaimed 'You are struck with one of the grandest and most beautiful bursts of country that the imagination can form.'

During the 19th and early 20th century Hackfall was freely open to visitors, with a tea room in the banqueting house selling postcards. It was especially popular with courting couples, who came to admire the distant views of York Minster – 30 miles away – and the jagged peaks of Roseberry Topping. In the 1930s Hackfall was sold to a Ripon timber merchant, who promptly felled all the noble trees. Such was the state of ruin of one of the follies, Mowbray Castle, that the local hunt used to jump in and out of the windows. This is a stocky medieval-looking tower of the kind intended, in Horace Walpole's phrase, to conjure up 'the true rust of the barons' wars'.

Salvation came with the formation of the Hackfall Trust by James Ramsden and others living nearby. First £30,000 was raised to enable the Woodland Trust to take on a 999-year lease of the property. The Hackfall Trust next raised funds to restore Fisher's Hall, an octagonal belvedere by the river named after Aislabie's head gardener complete with tablet inscribed WA 1750. Nearby was a circular pond complete with miniature island. The Woodland Trust opened up the paths and cut back undergrowth to reveal cascades and rivulets tumbling down over numerous artfully placed boulders. Among the sites to be seen are the Forty Foot Fall, the Weeping Rock, the Alum Spring and the Rustic Temple.

Next the Landmark Trust took on the shell of Mowbray Point, Aislabie's banqueting house, to restore it as a holiday cottage, like numerous other follies in its care. It took a full fifteen years to negotiate purchase and to stabilise the shell, precariously perched over the ravine. The terrace on which The Ruin, as it is now known, stands had suffered a severe collapse and had been shored up thanks to a welcome initiative by English Heritage. Despite emergency scaffolding the central dome collapsed in December 2001 and to avoid further disastrous decline, the

The doorway is flanked by pretty Strawberry Hill Gothick windows.

Landmark Trust set an experienced stonemason, John Maloney, to work on repairs. He rebuilt extensive areas of collapsed masonry with hidden underpinning and grouting using salvaged stone. He also rebuilt the flues and the roof under the direction of the architect Andrew Thomas. Water and electricity were brought from the main road in buried cables and a small sewage treatment system installed to safeguard the natural habitat below. The internal walls were replastered with lime mortar on sawn laths and painted a blue-green verditer found through paint samples which was a popular colour in the 1760s.

The entrance leads through to a rugged triple-domed ruin in the manner of Piranesi, with a terrace overlooking the torrent below. The archaeologist noted a resemblance to a watercolour by Robert Adam entitled *Capriccio on Ruins*, suggesting the great architect had a hand in the design. The Ruin sleeps two people. The living room-cum-kitchen is surrounded by pretty gothic niches and doorways and flanked by a bedroom on one side and a bathroom on the other. You flit between the two across a moonlit terrace overlooking the ravine.

HELLABY HALL
Hellaby
Baroque house built c.1690 for Ralph Fretwell

Old fashioned mullioned windows survived in the large gable contrasting with sash windows below.

THE FIGHT TO SAVE THIS DELIGHTFUL baroque house lasted for many years. It was built in about 1690 for Ralph Fretwell, who had made his fortune planting sugar in Barbados, and some have seen the influence of houses from the Dutch West Indies in the design of Hellaby Hall. The delight is to find such a full blown essay in baroque, with huge scrolls sprouting acanthus-leaf ornament continuing as a curvilinear gable containing a generous attic. The originality of the house was recognised by a Grade II* listing but the country road on which it stood had become a busy highway that intersected with a new motorway that lies just a few hundred yards away.

In 1976 SAVE issued a press release strongly opposing an application to demolish submitted by Euroway Estates. The architects, Sir John Burnet Tait Powell (early in the 20th century they were among the most distinguished in the land), claimed that not only was the house in a serious structural state, but that the cost of reinstatement would greatly exceed the subsequent market value. We pointed out that the Hall had been occupied until early in the year and that Rotherham Civic Society strongly disputed all claims that it was beyond repair.

Rotherham District Council commendably rejected the application and, when the case went to public inquiry the next year, argued that simple repairs would be all it took to make the building habitable. The Council won, but Hellaby continued to rot and the environs deteriorated with a huge lorry and bus park next door. Finally Hellaby was taken over as an hotel.

A massive ninety-bedroom annexe has been added behind, not exactly an award-winning stylistic match but the baroque house has been carefully restored and panelled rooms retained. A swimming pool, gym and health spa are on offer and the restaurant serves local produce. The hotel is popular for weddings, with the baroque house making an attractive backdrop for photographs. As *The Times* wryly put it in 2005, 'It doesn't get more romantic than this in Rotherham.'

KILDWICK HALL   Skipton

1640s house of the Currer family from whom Charlotte Bronte took her nom de plume

KILDWICK HALL, WHICH BEGAN LIFE IN THE CIVIL WAR, has been refurbished with a love of high-tech gadgetry and fine fittings that one might find on the most luxurious of yachts.

Kildwick Hall is for ever assured its own small niche in English literature. Six miles south, the Brontës lived at Haworth; Kildwick belonged then to the Currers and when Charlotte Brontë sought a *nom de plume* so that she might pass for a man, she chose the pseudonym of Currer Bell. The arms of the squires of Haworth are impaled by those of Currer over the front door at Kildwick and, as at Heathcliff's house in Emily Brontë's *Wuthering Heights*, one step brings you into the family sitting room, an old-fashioned great hall.

Not many people could have been building grand country houses in 1642 as civil war loomed between Charles I and Parliament, but this is the year that John Coates completed Kildwick. Not for him the court fashions of Inigo Jones, the King's architect. Kildwick is a house in the Elizabethan or even late-medieval master mason tradition, all gables and stone-mullioned windows, massively built of the local millstone grit with heavy stone flags on the roof.

For three centuries the house passed by inheritance until finally, becoming too large to live in, it was sold as an hotel. Now it is a private house again, immaculately

The off-centre front door opens into one end of the great hall.

The house and the garden walls were built out of the same local stone.

refurbished with an attention to detail and a wealth of high-tech gadgetry and fine fittings. It lies in Airedale, beyond Keighley and its mills on the way to Skipton. Moorland opens up behind the house and all around are lush green fields.

The road into the village crosses the River Aire and the handsomely restored Leeds to Liverpool canal with its brightly painted narrowboats, then winds up past a magnificent medieval church set in a churchyard filled with huge Pennine tomb slabs and table tombs. Kildwick Hall stands at the top of a steep stretch of ancient-looking parkland scattered with trees. As squire you can walk down across it and enter the churchyard through your own lychgate.

Like many old houses, Kildwick stands close to a quiet country lane. The entrance gates, topped by a splendidly lithe pair of lions, are of William III era, as are the grand baroque urns on either side. These were added by Henry Currer, who also built the imposing temple-like courthouse on one side, presumably after he married a rich widow following the death of his first wife in 1697. His tombstone relates that he was 'a great proficient in the study of the law' but, allured by the charms of a private life, returned to the place of his birth where he chose to become a magistrate rather than 'improve his fortune' at the Bar in London.

The 1640 entrance front is gabled and almost symmetrical, but the entrance is set to the side as if the owner was not going to have windows where he did not want them and demanded the porch should open into the great hall in the traditional manner, not in the middle. The ground and first floors have impressively long runs of mullioned windows while the second floor, pressed under the gables, has two ogee or flame-topped windows still medieval in feel.

Inside, the hall has a huge stone-arch fireplace large enough to park a Mini. The beautiful full-height panelling is original, although a *Country Life* photograph of 1911 shows that the carved herm figures on two of the walls are a later introduction. But the frieze with the Currer lions and the wolves of the Wilsons, who had inherited the house, are visible on one side.

In every room at Kildwick the stone of the mullioned windows remains exposed on the inside and it does not take long to realise that the leads framing the glass are unusually slender: these are recent replacements, superbly crafted in minimalist style yet traditional in pattern.

Today the centre of life is the kitchen at the back, which has another large-arch fireplace, dated 1673, and is equipped not only with an Aga but also an in-built flame grill as well as the usual breakfast bar. This is not a place to burn the oil on the stove, as there are no doors between kitchen and dining room. Perhaps that is why there is a second, more traditional dining room opening off the entrance hall, far from any kitchen dramas.

The family dining room opens into a bar with a smart Art Deco theme and a very handsome door with modern marquetry attached to the older door behind. Beyond, the drawing room extends into a Victorian wing and has a handsome Italianate ceiling and deep maroon walls. An extreme neatness extends to every corner with even the remote controls set carefully in line on the carpet by the sofa.

The first floor is laid out on lavish lines with a large master bedroom suite of four rooms. There are steps up to the large bedroom, a spacious bathroom lined with mirrors and a walk-in dressing room where clothes and shoes are set in cupboards without doors, so that your entire wardrobe is visible at a glance.

The staircase, and there is only one, ascends in short flights in the Jacobean manner around a solid pier rather than an open well. The steps are stone and bare on the underside. The upper floor is a teenage realm where the ceilings have been opened to the eaves, revealing massive roof timbers and creating the opportunity for raised galleries in both bedrooms. In one, a staircase leads up to a bunk bed behind a wooden balustrade. In the other, a free-standing spiral stair rises to a workstation floating under the roof timbers.

The bathroom here is the smartest in the house, with a sculpted basin made of a single sheet of moulded glass that flattens out as a table top, and a transparent shower cabin with a door on 12-in hinges that closes like that of a jetliner. The heater is a full-height ceramic panel against which you can toast yourself.

The house stands looking south across the valley, protected by the rising hillside to the north and sheltered by tall trees all around, including a magnificent monkey puzzle. Below the house is another, more formal garden, with arched wooden pergolas on brick piers, which descends to a lower level with a greenhouse as elaborate as most modern conservatories.

Recent owners have acquired the adjoining house, The Mullions, and also transformed the old courthouse into a spacious modern office. Old houses inevitably prompt concerns about repairs and maintenance costs, but at Kildwick the house is of such massive construction it looks set to last a thousand years.

LEDSTON HALL · Pontefract
17th-century house with a grand array of Dutch or 'Holborn' gables

LEDSTON HALL HAS A FESTIVE AIR thanks to its unusual onion-shaped gables which are repeated to grand effect on the flanks and ends of the projecting wings. With its tall thin corner towers, the whole composition has a distinct resemblance to Blickling Hall in Norfolk.

In the 13th century Ledston was a grange belonging to Pontefract Priory. The monks built a chapel here and the undercroft of this still remains. In 1629 the estate was bought by Thomas Wentworth, the famous Earl of Stafford, who was impeached and executed for treason in 1641. It was then acquired in 1653 by Sir John Lewis, who is credited with introducing the so-called Holborn gables.

Sir John's granddaughter inserted the sash windows in about 1730 as well as adding the monumental doorcase approached by steps. The windows have retained the early form of glazing with twelve panes over twelve on the *piano nobile* and, still more unusual, a number of sideways-sliding sashes on the upper floor. These were first introduced in the 1680s but were rapidly superseded by vertically sliding sashes and rarely survive.

On September 29, 1806, the Prince of Wales and the Duke of Clarence paid a visit to Michael Angelo Taylor, son of the architect Sir Robert Taylor who was then resident here. Another, earlier, visitor was the Methodist preacher Benjamin Ingham, who had travelled to Georgia in 1732 and composed an Indian grammar.

When SAVE published *Endangered Domains* in 1985, part of the house had been converted into five flats but the north wing was empty. Some of the windows were boarded up, others had been broken. Yet the house commanded extensive views and had the remains of a very extensive formal garden layout, with terraces that descended the hill. Today the house is restored and converted into apartments.

There are 24 pane sash windows on the main floor and a rare form of early sideways sliding sash above.

LEYBURN HALL
Leyburn
Mid 18th-century house built with the help of architectural pattern books

MANY SMALLER 18TH-CENTURY COUNTRY HOUSES were built without resort to an architect. Instead the owner or his builder took features or copied plans from architectural pattern books. At Leyburn Hall, Venetian windows, doorcases and overmantels were taken directly from James Gibbs's widely used *Book of Architecture*.

The house was built by John Yarker and a rainwater head, now vanished, carried the initials 'AIY'. These stood for Alice and John Yarker and suggest the house was completed soon after their marriage in 1752. A Yarker genealogy, privately printed in 1882, traces the family's unusual surname to the early Norman habit of adding characteristics to names such as 'the Bastard' or 'the Fat' and relates that 'the North Yorkshire branch of the Yarkers were generally men of Herculean proportions and used the word "Yarker" as a provincialism signifying great size or strength'. According to Atkinson's *Cleveland Dialect*, Yarker meant 'a large or particularly fine specimen'.

Luke Yarker (1699–1746) was a JP with extensive estates in Yorkshire. His property narrowly escaped confiscation after Bonnie Prince Charlie's rebellion in 1745, suggesting he was a covert Catholic. Intriguingly, several features at Leyburn echo those in houses of known Catholic or recusant families. On the garden front, the windows with emphatic quoins, are taken from Gilling Castle, while the plasterwork of the staircase ceiling is similar to that at Brough Hall – both owned by Catholic families.

John Yarker had the rare good fortune to live in his new house for half a century. Succeeding generations lived the comfortable life of 'squarsons' – at once squires and parsons. John's son Luke was rector of Fingall in Yorkshire. His son, also Luke, was rector of Chillingham in Northumberland and had five daughters, four of whom married into the clergy. The husband of the second daughter eventually succeeded to the Leyburn estate and adopted the name of Dunn-Yarker. For much of the 20th century the house was let and was sensitively renovated by Jeremy Pearce.

The west pavilion contains a full-height music room which may once have been a Catholic chapel.

NUN MONKTON HALL — Nun Monkton
Built c.1660 for George Payler in a quiet village by the River Ouse

COLOUR AND TEXTURE ARE OFTEN THE REAL BEAUTY of many English houses. Nun Monkton, with its warm red brick and stone trim, is an excellent example. The brickwork is unusually in neither English nor Flemish bond, but in garden wall bond with one row of headers to two or more rows of stretchers. The stone trim is a trifle quirky too, with a band on the giant pilasters and stone 'ears' to the ground floor windows.

Warmth comes too from the steep hipped roof, tall enough to contain a full storey lit by substantial dormers. Further vertical accents are provided by the tall chimneys designed as clusters of square pillars with pedestal base, shaft and capital. The roof oversails the brick walls supported on prominent pairs of brackets over the pillars.

Traditionally the house was said to have been built about 1690 for Nathaniel Paylor but many of these details relate to the group of so-called Artisan Mannerist houses built in Cromwellian times from *c*.1640 to 1660. There is a notable group of these houses in Kent, with similar pilasters, notably Lees Court and Syndale Court, both dating from the 1650s.

A sketch by Samuel Buck, who drew and engraved hundreds of country houses , dates from 1723 and provides interesting clues about the windows. Today the sashes have slender glazing bars in the late 18th-century manner but the sash boxes are set almost flush with the brickwork as was the custom half a century earlier. Buck's drawing shows that the upper windows have mullions and transoms (and leaded

The house has giant brick pilasters and a steep hipped roof.

The mid 17th-century staircase has a swooping handrail and shapely balusters.

panes), which were what was commonly used before sashes came into widespread use during the 1690s.

All these elements suggest the house was built for George Paylor or Paler who acquired the estate in 1650, some time before 1672 when the Hearth tax returns suggest a substantial house was by then standing on the site, with twenty-one hearths. George Paylor died on October 31, 1678 and the house passed to Nathaniel, who was succeeded by his son, also Nathaniel, on whose death in 1748 the house passed to Samuel Tufnell of Langleys in Essex. The second Nathaniel's tomb proclaims him 'the last male heir of an ancient family in this county ... with a mind truly contented and superior to ambition'. The rococo frieze on the first floor carries the Tufnell arms, neatly coinciding with the fashion for rococo ornament in the 1750s.

Nun Monkton has a splendid chunky staircase corresponding with other mid 17th-century staircases in houses in York. Standing on the newel or corner posts are carved figures of Faith, portrayed as the virgin with a burning lamp, Hope with an anchor, and Charity by the Mother and Child. The bold balusters are bulbous enough to be carved in stone, not wood, with a dashing swoop in the broad handrail on the little half landings.

In 1928 the house was acquired by Captain C. Whitworth, who carefully restored it. His architect is said to have been Colonel R.B. Armistead, later the chairman of the Bradford Wool Exchange, who had built up a considerable practice in Yorkshire between the First and Second World Wars. He probably added the swan-pedimented doorcase over the entrance.

Nun Monkton has a very pretty garden running down to the River Ouse with an early 18th-century gazebo. Though barely 8 miles from York, the former priory stands secluded at the end of a cul-de-sac by the church. 'Monechetone' is mentioned in Domesday and a priory was established here soon after. In 1394 the archdeacon of Richmond accused the Prioress and her fifteen nuns of 'wearing and permitting to be worn in the Convent divers precious furs, garments of silk, valuable rings, tunics fastened with broaches' and of 'attending the offices of the Church attired in these Fripperies'. Amid heavy competition at the Dissolution, the Priory was acquired in 1538 by John, Lord Latimer. When his son John died without children, Nun Monkton descended to the Percys.

OULTON HALL
Leeds
Designed by Sir Robert Smirke c.1822 and rebuilt after a fire in 1850

IF ANY COUNTRY HOUSE SHOULD HAVE BEEN SAFE from vandalism it was Oulton Hall near Leeds. Yet in the ten years it belonged to the West Yorkshire Police Authority, Oulton was systematically wrecked. Every window was smashed and the house left largely gutted and roofless. Tipping stones from the parapet became a favourite local sport. Inside, the glass dome over the stair collapsed and all the chimney pieces vanished. Thankfully a surprising amount of ornamental plasterwork detail remained.

Finally, in 1984, public outcry prompted Leeds City Council to buy the house in the hope of finding a new owner. For all its dreadful state Oulton was excellently situated, standing in extensive grounds close to the M62. The councillors began by creating a new 18-hole golf course, leaving just 9 acres with the house. They did not accept the advice of *Country Life* and sell the house for a nominal sum reflecting the amount of money that was needed to restore it.

When De Vere Hotels appeared on the scene, the price for a 125-year lease was £125,000, paid over for the construction of a new golf clubhouse. Not surprisingly, restoration of the mansion was only 'viable' with a 99-bedroom extension, soon expanded by another thirty-six. De Vere's invested some £20 million in Oulton and looking at the handsome house over lawns and fountains no one would guess today how close it came to destruction.

Oulton is one of an interesting series of suburban villas erected by prosperous Leeds merchants. John Blayds, who bought the old farmhouse on the site, was deputy receiver of the land tax for the West Riding of Yorkshire. By 1777 he had become a partner of Becketts, the dominant Leeds bank, leaving his property to one of his partners, John Calverley, on condition he changed his name to Blayds. The new Mr Blayds called in Humphry Repton as well as the architect Robert Smirke. Following a major fire in 1850 the present house was built to the designs of local architects Perkin & Backhouse in an opulent Italianate style, with lofty ceilings well suited to luxurious bedrooms.

The house was handsome even in decay, before restoration began.

PAPER HALL — Bradford
Mid 17th-century hall rescued from 150 years of extreme decay

PAPER HALL IS HELD TO BE THE OLDEST BUILDING in central Bradford after the cathedral, yet it stood for decades on death row. As long ago as 1841, John James wrote in his history of Bradford of its 'miserable state of dilapidation and neglect'. In the 1960s Paper Hall was threatened with demolition for a road-widening scheme, and though there was a reprieve the ring road was built straight in front of it.

The house was built in the 1640s for William Rookes – there is a date of 1643 over the doorway. In plan it was a typical H with three storeys and broad gabled ends. The mullioned windows varied in size but still had traditional hood moulds to throw off the rain. The upper gable windows were stepped to admit the maximum light, a feature known as a West Riding gable, here with four lower lights and two upper ones.

On the right of the entrance front, the gabled wing had been remodelled and taller cross-mullioned windows introduced. Above these the hood moulds were tweaked to form Classical pediments. The lower part of the front had been damaged when a parade of shops was built out in front. When these were stripped away they left dreadful scars. The interior retained large arched stone fireplaces and roof trusses supporting short king posts.

With the help of English Heritage, the Clothworkers' Foundation and the John Paul Getty Foundation, all this was progressively put to rights and Paper Hall reopened for business as suites of offices. Well-designed railings have restored dignity to the setting and the Hall is subtly illuminated at night. Across the road the early-Victorian pub has just reopened. This is a victory against overwhelming odds, showing fine old buildings can be rescued from the most desperate state.

Though abandoned and derelict, the stone mullions of the windows survived.

SCOUT HALL
Halifax

Grand three-storey house built in 1681 for local clothier John Mitchell

THE HILLS AND MOORS AROUND HALIFAX have an architecture that is all their own, whether mill or chapel, weaver's cottage, farmhouse or manor. The distinctive local stone, millstone grit, remained in use for centuries ,creating an extraordinary sense of harmony and continuity.

Scout Hall, built in 1681 for John Mitchell, is a building of considerable pretensions with tall, classically proportioned windows rather than the long bands of mullions found in early and mid 17th-century houses in the area. The 1680s was the decade in which the use of sash windows became widespread and it is remarkable here that the earlier form of window, with a stone mullion and transom forming a cross, has remained in place.

Whenever I visited Scout Hall it seemed enveloped in a swirling Heathcliffian mist. It was a tragic yet still proud sight. There was not a pane of glass left but this at least ensured it was well ventilated and prevented rampant dry rot.

Scout Hall was in what the late Sir John Smith, founder of the Landmark Trust, called legal trouble – the drive was only a right of way and there was very little land. Yet it was a biggish house with three almost even storeys. It was on a deep plan with three large mullions in a row on one gable. On the main front, small elliptical openings broke up the long runs of windows, forming them into uneven groups of two, four and three, a subtlety it is easy to miss. Numerous masons' marks still survive, carved into the stone.

For almost two decades, Scout passed through a succession of owners who could not, or would not, restore it but eventually, in the 1980s, repairs were carried out by a local businessman, Peter Mellor.

The carved frieze over the front door contains scenes of a fox hunt.

SWINSTY HALL   Little Timble

Stone-built gabled hall dating from 1575 and remodelled in the early 17th century

MASSIVELY BUILT IN LOCAL STONE, the Elizabethan and Jacobean halls of Yorkshire are as impressive and distinct as those of Norfolk. Swinsty has characteristic long bands of lead-paned mullioned windows set in walls that are more glass than stone in places, with pretty stepped windows set in the gables. Built in 1570 by the Wood family to replace a 14th-century hall, Swinsty was described by the 19th-century historian William Grainge as 'the best, most substantial and majestic of the old halls which grace the valley of the Washburn, many-chimneyed, mini-gabled, grey and grand'.

The house passed to the Robinson family to whom it belonged till the late 19th century, when it was bought by Leeds Corporation as part of the land acquisition for the Swinsty and Fewston Reservoirs. For nearly a century Swinsty was barely occupied, until the house returned to private ownership in the 1980s. In 1992 it was taken on by the Taylor family who carried out a remarkable restoration. A beautiful box-edged knot garden has been laid out in front of the house with a butts lawn (as used for archery practice), a rose garden and woodland walks. New work has been dated and initialled for posterity. The handsome new oak doors have joints fastened with wooden pegs in the traditional fashion. There is a stone-flagged entrance hall, an oak panelled ceiling with massed ranks of sturdy ceiling beams and, at the top of the house, a gallery, like the upper part of a great hall, set beneath gently arching trusses and cusped wind braces.

Work by the Robinsons is recorded in a series of inscriptions, including a window with 'R 1672' and doors inscribed 'IR 1639' and 'WR 1745'.

Characteristic Yorkshire stepped windows in the gables and continuous bands of mullions light the hall.

THORPE SALVIN HALL   Worksop

1570s courtyard house with circle towers surviving as fragmentary shell

THORPE SALVIN HALL IS ONE OF AN interesting group of Midlands 'high houses' that are as sophisticated as the work of the great Elizabethan architect Robert Smythson, but not necessarily by him. It was probably built in the 1570s for Henry Sandford, who died in 1582. Already a roofless shell when SAVE included it in Tomorrow's Ruins in 1978, a great gash in the main front made it look like a castle 'slighted' by Cromwell so it could never be used as a defence again.

The surviving circular corner tower still has intact stone fireplaces on the upper floors.

Thorpe Salvin is an example of the way Elizabethan architecture looked backwards as well as forwards. The round towers at the corners give it a castle air but the large outward-looking windows proclaim an age when England is at last at peace and no longer in fear of marauders. The plan is symmetrical, with a square tower over the entrance porch and tall chimney stacks on either side with chimneys rising above the parapets.

In 1978 the situation was desperate – the Hallamshire Historic Buildings Society and the local branch of the CPRE had launched an appeal but had raised just £900 – well short of the £5,000 needed before the Department of the Environment would contribute the other half. But these efforts were not in vain – the ruins are now stable and looked after by English Heritage. It is an interesting question, nonetheless, whether ruined shells like this could – or should – be restored and lived in again.

Massive chimney breasts form a major feature between the windows.

TONG HALL   Bradford
Unusual design by a local lawyer who dabbled in architecture

TONG HALL IS ONE OF HUNDREDS OF handsome houses in the West Riding that have only survived through office or institutional use and it is an interesting question whether here, as elsewhere, some of these houses may in due course become fine homes again. Tong Hall is a rare example of a substantial brick house in an area where stone was ubiquitous. Its good looks derive from bold massing – a raised centre with gently stepped forward wings. It is one of the always interesting group of country houses designed by gentleman amateur architects. Tong's designer, Theophilus Shelton, was 'the

The house is approached by a short formal drive that terminates in a carriage sweep.

son of a clergyman in one of the eastern counties' who established himself at Wakefield. He appears to have been a lawyer by profession, serving as clerk of the peace for the West Riding. At Tong his contribution is recorded in a portentous Latin inscription describing him as engineer and true architect. A drawing of the main front, thought to be in Shelton's hand, survives in the muniment room at Nostell Priory. Shelton also designed the market cross at Beverley

The house was built in 1700–2 for Sir George Tempest. A rare feature is the stained-glass sundial of 1709 by Henry Syles, depicting the sun and the four seasons, set in the fanlight. The short flight of steps with delicate iron balustrade is likely to date from 1773 when the house was enlarged, probably by the architect John Platt. The interior retains much of the 1702 panelling with the redecorations of 1773. The large entrance hall is lined to three-quarter height with 'fielded' or raised panelling, topped by a cornice that sweeps up to a richly carved overmantel carved with a pair of stags, flowers and a grotesque head. This is matched by carvings over the doorways all evidently inspired by continental engravings by artists such as Daniel Marot which were much used in England at the time as a source for ornamental details. Another ground-floor room is handsomely panelled in elm, again 'fielded' with an inlaid overmantel. There is another fully panelled room on the first floor with a coved ceiling and more grotesques in the French manner. The elm staircase has carved balusters rising from sprouting leaves and a swept-up handrail.

Tong Hall was restored as a museum of local history in 1975 but this closed five years later. In 1981 it was sold to a local entrepreneur and developer, Paul Finn, who has transformed the house into a business centre. 'The roof had gone and cost £56,000 then to repair. Now we have accountants working here, debt collectors and insolvency practitioners who turn businesses around. There are never less than fifty people working here.' Next he's turning his attention to the 12 acres of grounds.

WENTWORTH WOODHOUSE   Wentworth
The grandest mansion in England is a private house once more

'IF YOU LAY OUT YOUR MONEY IN improving your seat, lands, garden etc., you beautify the country and do the work ordered by God himself.' So wrote the first Marquess of Rockingham in the letter of advice he left for his son, the future Prime Minister, shortly before his death in 1750. According to his own reckoning he had, over the previous quarter of a century, spent £82,500 improving his house and grounds at Wentworth (more than the £78,250 spent on Castle Howard), providing it with the longest front of any country house in England, looking out over an immense park.

The family fortunes came from coal mines but the Fitzwilliams, descended from the Rockinghams, were enlightened proprietors concerned with the welfare of their workers. When George V stayed at Wentworth Woodhouse in 1912 he woke to the news of a pit disaster at a nearby mine, which created sixty-one widows and left 132 children fatherless. The explosions should not have happened and had been predicted by Earl Fitzwilliam whose mines were much safer.

Yet when war ended in 1945, Manny Shinwell, minister of fuel and power, told Peter Fitzwilliam, 'I'm going to mine right up to your bloody front door.' He was as good as his word. The whole park was turned over to open-cast mining which aerial photographs show came right up to the house. Wentworth Woodhouse was saved by the West Riding County Council, which acquired the house as a teacher training college and used the magnificent Palladian hall as a gymnasium, fully equipped with climbing ropes, vaulting horses and balancing beams, with a wooden floor laid over the elaborately patterned marble.

The baroque west front is built in warm red brick.

Matching flights of monumental stone steps ascend to a giant portico.

Few people realise that behind the great 600-ft-long Palladian front is a second house with a grand baroque front, built of red brick with stone trim. Though completely contrasting in style, the two fronts are part of a single building programme which continued from 1724 to 1749. It was as if the First Marquess had been forced into a stylistic about-turn under pressure from Lord Burlington and other apostles of Palladianism in Yorkshire, such as Sir Thomas Robinson. When the teacher training college moved in, the family retained the baroque west wing in its entirety, simply locking the doors between the two sides – though only visiting the house intermittently. There was a completely separate drive and complete privacy as the west front was invisible from the park. In the extensive gardens was a large camellia house – one of the earliest in England.

The great Palladian rooms in the east front were as grand as many contemporary royal palaces in Europe. The lower hall was a forest of a dozen stout stone columns opening into a lofty top-lit staircase hall. Statues of Roman gladiators, the remnants of the great collection of antiquities, remained. The staterooms were an essay in ancient Roman magnificence with richly sculpted friezes and ceiling beams. The magnificent plaster frame designed to house Stubbs's famous portrait of a stallion stood empty but was still a showpiece, with grand swan top and garlands of stucco flowers hanging down the frame. In the bachelors' wing, rooms open off long corridors and though they looked plain beside the state rooms they had decent cornices, doors and shutters and anywhere else would have been instantly covetable.

In 1988 Sheffield University surrendered its lease and the mansion was put up for sale. I took Kit Martin to visit and he devised a plan by which the central portion of the Palladian front with the staterooms could be shown to the public, while the bachelors' wing and extensive service quarters, as well as the huge stable block, could be transformed into self-contained houses. Unquestionably these would have sold

The marble hall has Classical statues in the niches and a gallery linking the upper rooms.

well as the village of Wentworth is one of the nicest places to live within the vicinity of Sheffield and Rotherham.

However, the next year it was bought by Wensley Haydon-Baillie, whose London house stood at the end of Millionaire's Row next to Kensington Palace. Said to be worth £80 million he had invested in a cure for herpes which never materialised and in 1998 he admitted to debts of £13 million and the property was repossessed by a bank. After a year it was bought for the asking price of £1.5 million, no more than the cost of a house in Hampstead. One London property developer, I later discovered, had written to a series of major museums saying he would give a £1 million donation if they lent some of the many pictures in their basements for display at Wentworth Woodhouse.

This came to nothing and the new owner is Clifford Newbold, an architect from Highgate. He lives there in complete seclusion and privacy with his family – hardly enough to people such a palace – but those who have been there report that the house is being well looked after. Though the mansion is never open, it is possible to walk in the restored park, which is vested in an Amenity Trust that owns many of the houses in the village, thus ensuring that housing is available for local people at affordable rents.

The Amenity Trust also looks after the series of garden follies, including the Needle's Eye. It is said to have been built following a wager between Lord Rockingham and one of his guests that he could drive a coach and horses through the proverbial Needle's Eye. The folly was built in the form of a gatehouse with a carriage arch large enough for him to drive through at full gallop. The magnificent Rockingham mausoleum has also been restored and is open to the public on summer Sunday afternoons.

WOMERSLEY HALL

Womersley

Georgian house rescued from decay by Lord Snowdon's mother

WOMERSLEY IS A CLASSIC EXAMPLE OF A HOUSE that has grown through the centuries – a large rambling manor house on a confusing plan with rooms sometimes three or four deep. Here the young Tony Armstrong-Jones, now Lord Snowdon, was brought during the Second World War as a boy, while the army service corps occupied most of the house. His mother Anne, a beautiful woman who gently cast a spell on everyone she met, persuaded the young soldiers to lay out a formal box garden. Nor was it planted with cabbages in deference to the war effort-like the *parterres* at Blenheim Palace, but with quantities of roses.

Lord Snowdon's mother was the sister of the talented Oliver Messel, designer of stage sets and numerous houses in the West Indies, and by this time she had married a second time – to Michael, the 6th Earl of Rosse. Together they shared a passion for gardens, furniture, paintings and preserving old buildings of many dates. They had settled on Womersley as the safest place to bring her children by both marriages as war broke out, while Michael joined the Irish Guards.

Their second son, Martin Parsons, who has lived at Womersley since 1976, explains, 'The house was then in a dreadful state. It had been empty from 1920 to 1935.' Many of the farms had been sold, as well as the furniture – as the house would have been, if it had found a buyer. There was not even a floor in the drawing room – it had been ripped up and auctioned too. Anne Rosse was astutely able to buy back a few pieces she found in antique shops in Pontefract.

After the war the Rosses lived principally at the family seat in Ireland, Birr Castle. The rest of their time was divided mostly between London and Nymans in Sussex, which her father had given to the National Trust, and where the Rosses lived in a wing, lavishing infinite care on the glorious gardens.

The 18th-century entrance front has been rendered to look like warm buff-coloured stone.

Left: The early 18th-century stairs end with a swirl on both sides.
Right: The drawing room contains elegant late 18th-century plasterwork, particularly on the ceiling.

Anne had received no formal education but she had a mastery of the domestic arts and organised the interiors of her houses herself until at Womersley in 1958, when she asked the famous decorator John Fowler (who she had first met when he was working at Peter Jones) to paint the drawing room.

The room, with a grand screen of Corinthian columns at one end, has been attributed to both James Paine and John Carr of York. Fowler, who at this time was causing huge controversy with his startlingly bright colour schemes in grand 18th-century rooms, adopted very subtle shades here so the room would not be out of harmony with the mellow feel of the rest of the house.

For at least four centuries Womersley had passed by descent or marriage, never by sale. Martin Parsons explains, 'The Elizabethan house, built of local limestone, is visible in the basement where the original small windows remain.'

The house, built by Tobias Harvey in the early 18th century, passed by descent until Frances Harvey, the heiress, married the 3rd Lord Hawke in 1805 – taking the name of Harvey-Hawke. More than half a century later Cassandra Harvey-Hawke married the 4th Earl of Rosse.

This does not explain one of the mysteries of the house – the great coloured-glass window in the grand staircase hall which carries the arms of the Fairfaxes. 'Lost in a bet but they couldn't be bothered to take it out,' continues Martin Parsons.

The mahogany stair descends in grand style, standing just a little proud of the wall and so showing off the extra flourish of a full balustrade on both sides.

The entrance front is long and low, without steps up to the front door, and a first floor with windows slightly longer than those below suggests pleasant well-proportioned rooms in every part of the house. Martin Parsons, who sold Womersley Hall and 45 acres of park in 2004, continues to operate a very successful business from the walled garden. 'Here we produce the best condiments in Britain. We grow herbs in the walled garden and blend them with fruit,' he says. His products include vinegars, balsamics, dressings, infused oils and herb jellies.

LONDON

4 CUMBERLAND PLACE · Regent's Park
One of four houses designed as a large villa with Corinthian portico

THE GREAT NASH TERRACES AROUND Regent's Park are one of the glories of English architecture. Here is Classical splendour on a scale to compare with Paris and St Petersburg and a view to rival Central Park in New York.

No 4 Cumberland Place has the added advantage of looking west across the Park, enjoying full uninterrupted sun from the late morning till dusk. It is also one of a select group of four houses designed to look like a small palace with delightful Regency bows windows on the flanks as well as the ends. From No 4 you look out along the incomparable splendour of Cumberland Terrace, the noblest of all Nash's compositions. Approaching from the south, you pass through the grand triumphal arches of Chester Terrace.

The end house of the terrace has the advantage of having windows on three sides.

The basement area outside the bow has been glazed over.

The great palace-terraces around Regent's Park were virtually all completed between 1820 and 1828, ranking among the most successful pieces of speculative development in the history of London. The downside, inevitably, was that some of the houses were jerry-built and too many of the designs were rushed off in Nash's office by assistants. Certainly Cumberland Terrace gives the odd impression of a row of houses that were turned around after they were designed but before they were built. From their elevations, you would expect the front doors to face the Park, like those of the adjoining terraces. Instead, they are at the back, where the facades are made of plain brick not stucco, with pimple-like porches that appear to have been hastily added to give a touch of dignity. A further telltale sign of this reversal is that at No 4 the staircase strangely faces away from you as you enter.

As this is an end-of-terrace house, it has windows along the flank that give glorious views of grass and trees and flood the house with light. By contrast, all the windows at the back of the building are blank, looking as if the Crown Commissioners (who were probably exempt from window tax anyway) had nightmares that it might be reintroduced.

The Crown Commissioners say that this is one of the very last terraced houses to come available in a long programme of rehabilitation that has continued for more than fifty years. After wartime bombing and neglect, their condition was so bad that the Gorell Committee, set up to advise on the future of Nash's masterpiece, observed there was 'not a single Terrace, with the partial exception of Hanover Terrace ... which does not give the impression of hopeless dereliction'. Happily the Committee, urged on by the Georgian Group and the London County Council, recommended preservation – though it is said the plan was only approved by Cabinet on the casting vote of Attlee himself.

No 4 and its neighbours were divided horizontally into flats. When the leases ran out the Crown Commissioners decided to return them to houses and Octagon, fresh from success in creating terraced houses in the extravagant gothic asylum at Virginia Water, took on the project.

Thanks to the most thorough of structural makeovers the house is now in markedly better condition than it was when it was built. Its shallow foundations have been underpinned – one problem they found on doing this was a plane-tree root that extended for 19 metres under the house. The roof has been relaid in finest milled lead. Original stucco has been carefully retained, achieving a commendably harmonious tone.

Nash's lofty sash windows have been beautifully repaired (and occasionally renewed) and, with the help of special Meaker pull cords, now glide up and down with glorious ease. All the glass is crown glass with a gentle ripple that brings extra life to the elevations.

The house has all the smart kit, a convection system that instantly provides cool or warm air, with heaters below the large windows to eliminate any condensation. Rooms are wired for every gismo. Lights can be programmed in any way you want. There are fire detectors in the upper storeys sensitive enough, I was told, to distinguish between a cigarette and a cigar. To ensure the gutters are easily swept of the large number of leaves that blow in from the Park, there are hooks for abseiling window cleaners (plentiful around here, apparently).

My quarrel is with the layout of the rooms. As completed, the house is more like an hotel than a home, though perhaps this is what the birds of passage who come to live in these parts actually want. Nash's house planning was never as sophisticated as the best in Edinburgh or Bath, let alone Paris. The ground floor is basically identical to the first floor – perhaps that was why there is no photograph of it in the very sumptuous brochure.

On both floors dividing walls have been put back between front and back rooms. These cleverly contain all the vertical services but the double doors linking the rooms are too narrow to create the necessary grand sense of parade. Inset in the partition is a motorised dumb waiter but this begins not in the large and lavish basement kitchen but across the corridor. Beneath the garden a 38-ft long entertainment room has been created but the bow window eats into the centre just where you might want to place a billiard table. Surely this was the space for a swimming pool which could have been designed to conceal the odd shape.

The garden above is also somewhat lacking in privacy – though surrounded by an expensive new Portland stone balustrade – and urgently needs shrubs and hedges.

The entire second floor is grandly fitted out as a master bedroom suite with his-and-hers bath and shower rooms and walk-in closets. A whole wall of the bedroom has been taken up with fitted cupboards.

By making use of the mansard and reintroducing dormer windows, two more floors of bedrooms have been contrived with a charmingly ingenious S-form staircase. Under the eaves is a splendid top-lit studio room. Measured by floor space this is a big house, but the impression I was left with was that there had been a desire to play safe and to create something that would be pleasing to everyone. Personally I would have much preferred an interior that was either much more adventurously modern, or that passionately recreated the splendour of the Regency in brilliant blue, red and gold.

EAGLE HOUSE   Mitcham
Queen Anne house that waited years for restoration

THE LAND ON WHICH EAGLE HOUSE STANDS once belonged to Sir Walter Raleigh. The rainwater heads bear the date 1705, with initials that are thought to stand for Fernando Mendes, a Portuguese physician brought to England by Charles II's wife, Queen Catherine of Braganza.

Soon after 1705, the house was bought by James and Mary Dolliffe, whose initials appear on the wrought iron-screen fronting the road flanked by pillars bearing eagles. Every room in the building retains its original panelling, and none was remodelled in Georgian or Victorian times. In 1825 the house became a boarding academy of the type familiar to readers of Dickens.

In the early 1980s, the London Borough of Merton closed down the teachers' centre that had occupied Eagle House for many years, and local surveyor John Hearsum offered to convert the Grade I building to offices on a joint venture with the council. 'We completed the work in 1991 at the depth of the recession and for the next four years I fought a running battle against vandals and thieves,' Mr Hearsum said. He has spent £900,000, half on Eagle House and half on a new free-standing 'stable' block, built in plum brick with characteristic early 18th-century red-brick trim to English Heritage specifications. Finally in 1995 he found a tenant.

The latest incarnation of Eagle House is as a special school for autistic children, which opened in 2004 as a primary and now also a secondary school. Eagle House today is as handsome a sight as at any time in its history with roof balustrade and cupola beautifully restored. This is as perfect a Queen Anne house as can be found, blighted for years by road proposals, but now back in use as a school as it was before.

The house is complete with a cupola and roof terrace and has a decorative shell-headed entrance.

GROVELANDS   Southgate

Designed by Nash, the most handsome neoclassical villa in the northern suburbs

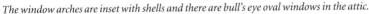

AS LONDON HAS CREPT OUT INTO THE COUNTRYSIDE, engulfing the villages that surround it, large country houses have been acquired with their grounds to become public parks. The perennial problem is that the local councils that own them cannot afford to maintain the houses, yet are unwilling to agree private uses in a public park.

Grovelands, originally known as Southgate Grove, was built in 1797 to the designs of John Nash for the brandy merchant Walker Gray, with grounds laid out by Humphry Repton. It is one of Nash's best villa designs with three show fronts each with a different giant portico. Inside there is a grand Imperial staircase and an exceedingly pretty 'birdcage' room – an octagonal breakfast room painted in imitation of a bamboo cage with lifelike flowers growing along the dado. The house was designed for entertaining with double doors leading from one room to the next, aligned on the windows to provide a vista.

The house served as a hospital from 1916 until 1977 but then was left to stand empty and decaying while Enfield Borough Council explored plans for using it as an arts centre. In 1985 Grovelands reopened as a private psychiatric hospital, now part of the well-known Priory Group. The restoration was supervised by Donald Insall & Partners and new buildings, added at the back after prolonged exchanges by SAVE and others to ensure they did not intrude on views of this the most handsome of Nash's villas. General Pinochet was held under house arrest here when prevented from leaving England.

The window arches are inset with shells and there are bull's eye oval windows in the attic.

HANGER HILL GARDEN ESTATE   Acton
Half-timbered houses and flats of 1928–36 by Douglas Smith & Barley

THE HANGER HILL Garden Estate, built in the 1930s, is best likened to a herd of zebras grazing on freshly mown suburban grass. The great Nikolaus Pevsner, author of the classic *Pioneers of Modern Design*, described Hanger Hill as 'the beau idéal of romantic rural Metroland. Immaculate half-timbered houses and flats … unusually well-landscaped: the large blocks of flats stand in spacious lawns and the houses are set off by attractive planting.'

In the late 19th century, Acton's main claim to fame lay in its 180 laundries, bringing it the soubriquet 'the washtub of London'. Change came with the opening of the Central Line in 1923. The prescient developer of the Hanger Hill Estate was a 'Mr Cooper' of Buckinghamshire. From the start the whole enterprise was an engaging, paternalistic affair in the best sense. The estate consists of 361 houses and 258 flats in three-storey blocks, built to the designs of the architects Douglas Smith and Barley between 1928 and 1936. Initially they were all strictly for rent, and the estate office, larger than the other houses, is still to be seen opposite the West Acton tube station.

The Coopers and their staff took pains to ensure the estate was immaculately looked after. They maintained the hedges and ornamental planting. Painters, decorators and cleaners were employed as well as an electrician and a plumber. Lawns were mown in front of the flats as they are today.

The apartment blocks are three-storeyed with shared entrance.

All the houses as well as many of the flats had garages, though not many tenants actually owned cars when the estate was first built. Tradesmen were not allowed to call at the front doors, but had to use the back doors on the mews-type service roads that still survive, providing access to the garages (and useful extra car-parking for house guests).

House tenants were allowed to hang out their washing only on Mondays and Tuesdays. Flat tenants were not permitted to hang out washing at all.

Pairs of houses perfectly express the romantic rural ideal of Metroland, beloved of Betjeman.

Since the war, many of the tenants have been able to buy their own properties, a case not so much of gentrification as upward mobility, and it remains a complete model village, almost a West London version of Hampstead Garden Suburb. Much of this atmosphere can be attributed to the fact that just as the estate regulations were melting away, in came conservation-area control.

Today, Ealing Borough Council will not even allow residents to enlarge the garage at the bottom of the garden for a 4x4, and the council exerts strict control over the backs of houses, refusing rear extensions. It may seem Draconian, but it ensures the estate retains a rare harmony and consistency.

Margaret Quinn, who put 18 Tudor Gardens on the market in 1999 for £329,950, told me: 'When I bought the house in 1982 it had been rented out for ten years and was very neglected. An artist had evidently been living in the garage. The walls were covered in paintings and the rafters were packed with newspaper for insulation.'

The main appeal of the house was that it retained much of its interior trim. A wide staircase hall has a vista that leads through the sitting room and kitchen to the back garden beyond.

A feature of many of these houses – a hangover from the Arts and Crafts movement – are the plate racks, surviving all round the hall and the sitting room. With them come distinctive original doors with three panels at the bottom and a square panel at the top, sometimes inset with leaded glass.

Pointing to the original fireplace, a period piece of red brick and thin red tile, Mrs Quinn said, 'I spent days and days scraping off coats of thick white gloss paint.'

Now it burns with a gas fire, though the original coal sheds survive next to the garages in many of the gardens. The appeal of the living room is that it is almost open-plan, with new false beams in the front half to match those at the back. Like many 1930s suburban houses, it had a very neat staircase ascending in short flights, contrived to give the impression of an open stairwell.

Unusually, it continued all the way to the attic with square newel posts at the corners, straight balusters and broad handrails, all fashioned in the best Arts and Crafts tradition.

THE HILL · Hampstead
Lord Leverhulme's astonishing garden rescued by the City Corporation

THE HILL WAS CREATED BY LORD LEVERHULME, the soap manufacturer, between 1906 and 1925, to provide a grandstand view over Hampstead Heath. The most remarkable feature was the pergola running a total length of 800 ft, and supported on a forest of 332 stone columns, as long as the Canary Wharf Tower in Docklands is high.

Leverhulme created the massive terraces on which the pergola stands with the help of 17,000 wagonloads of spoil from the excavations for the tunnels of the Northern line, which surfaces nearby at Golders Green. He was fond of lavish garden parties and the raised terraces ensured that his guests were out of sight from the heath, while providing a vista all the way to Harrow-on-the-Hill.

Not content with the large garden laid out for him by Thomas Mawson, the leading landscape architect of the Edwardian era, Leverhulme bought up the houses on either side. When the council refused to sell him a right of way between the properties, Leverhulme built a bridge over it, and extended his colonnades on the other side.

This part of the garden was later taken over as Golders Green Park, but its future came into question when the Greater London Council was abolished in 1989. At the same time, Lord Leverhulme's imposing house, long used as a trade union nursing home,

was put up for sale. Though it was a focal point of the garden, the house was not listed and was advertised as ripe for redevelopment. Salvation came when Hampstead Heath was taken over by the City Corporation. By this time, the colonnades had been damaged in the 1987 and 1990 storms and the timbers had largely rotted. Wisteria was strangling the columns, and the trellis domes, beautifully built in seasoned oak, were in various stages of collapse. The Corporation brought the whole length of the pergola under one ownership and embarked on systematic restoration.

The domes and tent-shaped roofs were repaired using French oak, seasoned for three years and brought from the border near Switzerland. English green oak was used for the larger timbers. The borders beneath the pergolas have been planted using Lord Leverhulme's original plant lists, with wisteria, jasmine, clematis, honeysuckle, ivy and rambler roses.

The colonnaded pergolas, set on terraces above Hampstead Heath, have now been restored.

HOLLAND HOUSE   Mayfair
First occupied by Edward Shepherd, who helped develop the Grosvenor estate

MAYFAIR BOASTS THE BEST COLLECTION of grand town houses in London, all too easily forgotten as so many of them have been converted into offices. Now a magical transformation is taking place. Houses turned over to commercial use sixty years ago, when wartime bombing created a shortage of London offices are now being made back into supremely opulent single houses.

Peter Wetherell, who has made a speciality of Mayfair property, observed astutely, 'For years it was said there was no demand but that was because there was no supply'. With Westminster Council pressing for an end to the wartime licences, Wetherell produced for the Grosvenor estate a handsome booklet entitled 'Quintessential Mayfair: a portfolio of ten elegant Georgian properties'. The idea was that the houses might sell to a single developer, but at the last moment the Duke of Westminster decided to retain 68 Brook Street (next to the Grosvenor Estate Offices) and as a result other houses were snapped up for individual restoration.

No 72 was acquired by the elegant Tiggy Butler, who previously has transformed the Lyons demesne in Ireland and a broodingly beautiful house in Kentucky. She brought in her own thorough team of restorers led by Aldi, a firm of Polish builders. The lift went. There is no swimming pool in the basement. Instead the effort went into creating interiors as comfortably and richly furnished as a freshly decorated suite at nearby Claridges.

Now known by the rather grander name of Holland House, after Sir Henry Holland who lived here in 1822–4 and 1827–73, No 72 is one of the earliest houses in Mayfair. Its interest is all the greater as it was built as a show house by Edward Shepherd, after whom Shepherd's Market is named. Shepherd deserves to be a legend among London's architects and developers as, unlike so many, he appears never to have overstretched himself or been caught by a slump in the market.

Shepherd's baroque front survives with upper stories that were added later.

In 1730 the *Daily Post* described him as 'that ingenious architect Edward Shepherd who built the Duke of Kent's fine house in St James's Square, the Earl of Thanet's and Albemarle's in Grosvenor Square, and many other magnificent Buildings for his Grace the Duke of Chandos and Other Persons of Quality and Distinction'.

Left: A lavish bathroom has been installed on the first floor.
Right: Shepherd's original cross-vaulted entrance hall still survives.

Shepherd is named in the rate books as being the occupant between 1726 and 1729. At his death in 1747 he was living in a small house in Curzon Street on the site of princely Crewe House and was stated to be the owner of 'many other buildings about Mayfair'.

No 72 is one of a series of houses thst Shepherd built as pairs – others are 11 and 12 South Audley Street and 74 and 75 South Audley Street. This one is paired with No 74. His trick was to introduce a kink or zigzag in the party wall so the staircases in both houses could be set to the side of the main rooms and not eat up space.

Here the house is narrower at the front and wider at the back, with one splendid grand room on each main floor occupying the width on the garden front. And what a garden. In most of Mayfair, back extensions and enlarged basements have consumed gardens, leaving little more than patios. Here the gardens of a dozen houses seem like a private London square, running the full extent of the block and shaded by noble mature plane trees.

The front door opens into a strikingly architectural hall with cross vaults and a bold arch inset with fine Classical coffering. To the left is the dining room, the best 1720s interior in the house, with fine deal panelling, arch-headed alcoves and a plaster ceiling full of baroque swagger with fruit, flowers and Juno masks.

The main ground-floor drawing room, looking out over the garden, has the proportions of a drawing room in a grand 18th-century country house with the windows on the long wall. Richly swagged curtains hide the fluted columns of the Venetian window behind. The ceiling is Adamesque and Vincent Carmody has added extra ornamental plaster flourishes on the walls.

The butter-yellow paintwork with white trim is the work of Alastair Erskine. Indeed the whole room is an overwhelming symphony in shades of the same colour, in silks, satins and velvet. The vibrant yellow continues in the bedroom above with four-poster bed with ribbon twined *colonettes* and more specially made English silk curtains. Floors of pale Polish oak complete the all-blond effect.

Above the first-floor bedroom suite are no less than three further floors, two floors of bedrooms and a studio or gym complete with shower at the top. The basement offers a complete alternative lifestyle with large family room opening straight out into a paved terrace through three pairs of French windows.

The one puzzling note is the street front. The red-brick arches and quoins look Edwardian by comparison to the darkened London stock brick of other 18th-century houses in Mayfair. Yet this is red brick of the age of Wren, with baroque touches like the fine group of houses in the Vanbrugh style in nearby Hanover Street. If Edward Shepherd were to return, he would be mightily impressed.

HOME HOUSE — Portman Square
Built to the designs of Robert Adam for Elizabeth, Countess of Home, in 1773–6

ROBERT ADAM'S FINEST LONDON HOUSE was built in 1773–6 for Elizabeth, Countess of Home (pronounced Hume), heiress of a fabulously rich West Indian merchant. She was in her seventies when the house was completed, and according to William Beckford, who attended one of her parties, was 'known by all the riff-raff of the Metropolis as the Queen of Hell'. Never, he said, had he beheld 'so splendidly heterogeneous a repast as the dinner nor ever heard such a confounded jumble of good and bad music'.

With typical English understatement, the facade tells little of the splendours within.

Born in Jamaica in 1704, she had become the original merry widow in her twenties, remarrying the 8th Earl of Home, a distinguished soldier, in 1742. He, however, deserted her within a year. She was nearly 70 and without children when she embarked on her splendid new house, moving into it in the summer of 1776.

For once Adam had had free rein to exercise his originality as both planner and decorator. With his great country houses he was usually remodelling already existing mansions. Home House was the opportunity of a lifetime. On the two main floors there is not one room that is a plain rectangle. Everywhere the walls are curved or inset with niches and apses, or broken up with columns.

This was a house designed for entertaining. Each room opens into the next so you never need to retrace your steps. The staircase is breathtaking, a tall domed cylinder, rising four storeys high, with curving flights hugging the walls. For many years the house was the home of the Courtauld Institute of Art, presided over by the spy Sir Anthony Blunt. John Harris, Curator of the RIBA Drawings Collection next door, never knew why the burglar alarm in his building rang so frequently in the night, until much later he learnt that secret agents were entering to check listening devices in the attic connected to Blunt's study.

The portico has Adam's distinctive capitals.

The Courtauld carried out an exemplary repainting scheme under the direction of Ian Bristow on the evidence of paint scrapes and the Adam drawings at the Soane Museum. Some rooms were painted in subtle variations of the same colour, blues, greens or pinks. In others mauves, creams and greens were mixed with richly gilded wall panels. The Music Room, the finest of them all, overlooking Portman Square, has circle after circle of exquisitely modelled floral ornament bursting across the ceiling. The walls are so crowded with pilasters, apses and doors that there was hardly space to hang a picture. Of equal quality was the Etruscan Room with characteristic terracotta and black Greek vases.

The leafy garden behind the house had never been built over while Adam's stable survived intact, used as a restoration studio. The basement, with stone-paved floors, retained many of its kitchens and pantries and many of its fittings. There were calls for the National Trust to take on the house and open it to the public, on the model of the Georgian houses in Edinburgh and Bath. But the Portman Estate was determined to find a tenant who would pay a commercial rate and the lease was sold to a private club. The Home House Club has eighteen suites named after Anthony Blunt, the Duke of Newcastle and others, deliciously decorated by Edward Bulmer, who has an artist's eye for bringing comfort and colour to historic interiors.

Adam's dramatic staircase is inset with statues and reliefs painted in grisaille.

4 MAIDS OF HONOUR ROW   Richmond
1720 terrace built as lodgings for the entourage of the Princess of Wales

WHEN MAIDS OF HONOUR ROW was built, Richmond upon Thames was considered the most beautiful and enchanting place to live in all England. No 4 has hardly changed in 250 years. It still looks out over the broad expanse of Richmond Green, surrounded by as many covetable houses as Salisbury Cathedral Close.

Remarkably for London, the last major change to the house took place in the 1740s, when the fashionable Italian painter Antonio Joli filled the entrance hall with a series of murals painted for the director of the Haymarket Opera House, John James Heidegger. Over the door to the stairs is an aria from the opera *L'Inconstanza Delusa*, which was performed in the little theatre at the Haymarket in 1745, the larger one being closed that year due to Bonnie Prince Charlie's rebellion. The opera was written by the mysterious Comte de St-Germain, who had arrived in London after a stay at the court of the Shah of Persia, used many aliases, was said to be a secret agent of Louis XV and, according to Horace Walpole, 'sings and plays on the violin wonderfully'.

We know all this and much more thanks to the fact that one of the most spirited museum curators in England, Edward Croft-Murray, of the British Museum, lived here for half a century. The author of the definitive two-volume catalogue on English Decorative Painting, he was a keen musician, party-giver and man of taste. As a result the house, though delightfully decorated and furnished, has escaped the successive makeovers that have eroded the character of so many older London houses.

The front of the Green has distinctive pink 'rubbed' (finely moulded) brick dressings to the windows, set off by white-painted sash windows, keystones and cornices. Maids of Honour Row is a group of four imposing houses, each five windows wide with a parapet hiding the roof. The *British Journal* for April 1724 reports that the Prince of Wales (the future George II) 'hath given directions for erecting a new

The houses retain wrought-iron railings and entrance gates.

building … to serve as Lodgings for the Maids of Honour attending the Princess of Wales'. They were built on the site of Henry VII's palace at Richmond, just beside the entrance gate.

Heidegger, sometimes known as the Swiss Count, was a controversial character who acted as Director of the King's Balls. He was caricatured by Hogarth as a promoter of licentiousness and debauchery. When Heidegger died in 1749 a Miss Pappet was living in the house. Two years later she married her naval admirer, Peter Denis, who rose to be a vice-admiral. By 1754 a wealthy Jewish lady, Judith Levy, was in residence, living here for nearly half a century until her death in 1802.

The hall has landscape scenes by Antonio Joli, painted for the director of the Haymarket Opera.

All four houses in Maids of Honour Row have large, paved front gardens entered through ornate wrought-iron gates. No 4 has a similar gate to the porch, allowing the front door to be left open in summer and a breeze to flow through. The house also has an almost perfect orientation, the front facing north east and the back south west, so it catches the early-morning sun and then basks in sun at the back for the rest of the day.

The special appeal of early Georgian houses lies in intimate proportions and handsomely panelled rooms. Here the wooden panelling continues through the house with tall panels and wooden cornices above a dado. Joli's landscapes in the hall are set in frothy *trompe-l'oeil* baroque cartouches (Croft-Murray calls them Bolognese rococo). Thanks to his researches, the subjects and sources are largely known: a view of Basle with bridge across the Rhine, the famous waterfalls at Schaffhausen, Vesuvius and Tivoli.

A distinctive feature of the house is that all the fireplaces are in the corners of the rooms. The drawing room behind the hall has a large later bay window looking out over the garden and red marble fireplace. The stair, as in many houses in Spitalfields in East London, has pretty carved ends to the treads and two turned balusters to each step – a design subtly simplified in the flight up to the second floor.

One problem with the late 17th- and early 18th-century houses can be the lack of a large room for entertaining. Here the Long Room on the first floor occupies the full width of the house with five windows and two matching fireplaces. The window shutters are all in working order with window seats in each recess.

Bedrooms are cosy, well-lit and overlook the garden on the upper floors; there is the opportunity to make a big front bedroom by removing a second floor-partition.

The basement hardly feels sunken at all. There is a spacious kitchen with huge original fireplace, as well as utility room, wine cellar and storage vault.

London offers no more delightful early 18th-century terraced house.

50 OXFORD GARDENS   Ladbroke Grove

Handsome 1870s detached villa by Henry Currey on the St Quintin estate

ONE OF THE MYSTERIES OF LONDON ARCHITECTURE is just how many fine Victorian interiors remain in large Italianate houses in Kensington and Notting Hill. Hundreds were stripped out in the 1960s and now the skips are back again as a second wave of makeovers gathers momentum.

This is why 50 Oxford Gardens is a minor marvel, a Victorian house complete with all its trim, not just cornices and ceiling roses but spectacular ironwork and encaustic floor tiles. The house stands on the estate laid out by the St Quintin family beside the 1864 extension to the Metropolitan Railway from Paddington to Hammersmith via Ladbroke Grove.

Along Oxford and Cambridge Gardens and Bassett Road an impressive group of double-fronted and paired houses survives. Their elegance and consistency suggests they were built by St Quintins' architect Henry Currey, architect of St Thomas's Hospital and many buildings in Eastbourne and Buxton for the 6th Duke of Devonshire.

As was usual in London, a dozen different builders were involved, but some built large runs of houses – John Gimbrett built 74 in Oxford and Cambridge Gardens in 1871–86 and John Bennett 69 in the same streets over a similar period. The fortunate

A grand flight of steps leads to a broad front door flanked by bay windows.

owner at this time was Matthew Chitty Downes St Quintin, a former colonel of the 12th Lancers, who inherited the estate from his brother in 1859.

During the Second World War the houses lost the iron railings that enclosed the large front gardens but here there are modern replacements. Currey added a real touch of grandeur with the broad flights of a dozen steps leading up to the front door. The lacy black stair railings were almost certainly supplied by Macfarlanes of Glasgow, the leading manufacturers of architectural cast iron.

The splendour of these houses comes from their double fronts with matching bay windows on either side of the columned entrances. The bay windows are topped by chunky Victorian balustrades and the first-floor windows have charming little shields instead of keystones. In the north Kensington air, the almost white London stock brick has remained pale and not been blackened by smoke as in much of the capital.

Currey's front door is solid, with studded panels, opening into a hall which

Top: The master bedroom has windows on both sides of the house.

Above: The dining room has its original fireplace.

retains a full complement of colourful Victorian tiles laid in a bold lattice pattern. Typically these were supplied by Minton or the Jackdaw Works at Ironbridge.

London houses tend to be long and narrow – here the double fronts allowed Currey to build on a shallower plan, with a garden window filling the end of the hall with light. Instead of the usual front and back rooms with twin fireplaces, linked by double doors, Currey created grand saloons with windows at both ends and a single central fireplace. In true High Victorian style these are arched not square, allowing a larger area of ornamental carving.

The windows at both ends descend almost to the floor, filling the rooms with light. They are of plate glass with distinctive S-shaped sash 'horns' found on sash windows from 1840 onwards. The dining room across the hall also has a fine ceiling rose and a fireplace cleverly simulated to look like black marble.

The staircase, at right angles to the hall, has more cast iron-railings set not on the steps but attached to them – each baluster is in the shape of a giant paper clip, cleverly designed to create an open airy look while ensuring there is not enough space for a child to fall through. The handsome mahogany rail swoops down to a corkscrew column on the bottom step with a base as elaborate as an altar candlestick.

REGENT'S PARK VILLAS   Regent's Park
New houses by Quinlan Terry taking up Nash's original plan for fifty villas

RANGED ALONG THE OUTER CIRCLE in Regent's Park is a series of six remarkable new Palladian villas designed by Quinlan Terry, who was instructed by an enterprising former official at the Crown Commissioners, Michael Tree, to 'step into Nash's shoes and go on walking'.

The first of Mr Terry's houses, the Ionic Villa, is occupied by Lord Bagri, whose family crest of twin Indian elephants on their hind legs is now flamboyantly displayed in the gable on the front of the house. Another villa belongs to the Sultan of Brunei.

Following the severe property recession in the early 1990s the Crown Commissioners decided they would not build the last three houses themselves and sold the land on a 150-year lease with the proviso that the houses had to be built to Terry's designs. The three plots were bought by two brothers who sold the first house, the Regency Villa in Greek Revival style, for an estimated £7 million, and completed the two remaining houses for themselves.

The most exotic of the three is the Corinthian Villa, with a baroque serpentine front and false perspective to the windows.

Next door is the Tuscan Villa with bold overhanging eaves like a barn in Tuscany, but closely modelled on 18th-century Asgill House on the Thames near Richmond.

All the villas have balustraded terraces and steps on the garden side where the land falls away sharply to the canal. Here Terry had the problem that the traditional pear-shaped Classical baluster no longer conforms to modern building regulations as the gap at the top is wide enough for a child's head to become stuck. To resolve this he copied baroque balustrades from the Pesaro Palace on the Grand Canal, where every alternate baluster is upside down – cleverly narrowing the now illegal gap.

The backs of the Corinthian and gothic villas overlook the Regent's Canal.

VALENTINES   Ilford
Long-forgotten but splendid Georgian house in a public park

ON FIRST ENCOUNTER, VALENTINE'S IS AN EXTRAORDINARY SIGHT, a large and imposing Georgian mansion standing amid well-maintained gardens. Yet for more than twenty-five years it has been empty or barely used. The good news is that it is reasonably well looked after and secured and now, with a surge of interest everywhere in historic houses, there is a large group of local supporters. The Friends of Valentines Mansion hold events and collect historical material. They have completed restoration of the Victorian kitchen range in the dairy wing. Valentines Park Conservationists, formed in 1999, carry out practical projects in the park and the aim of Redbridge Council is to vest the mansion in a charitable trust.

The earliest part of the house appears to date from 1696–7, built probably by James Chadwick, son-in-law of John Tillotson, Archbishop of Canterbury, whose widow Elizabeth owned the estate. Valentine's was next enlarged by Robert Surman, deputy cashier at the South Sea Company. Rainwater heads bearing the crest of Charles Raymond and the date 1769 mark further building work. Raymond had made money as a captain with the East India Company and was a founder of Williams Deacons Bank. By his death the estate had grown to 40 acres. Early in the 19th century Charles Welstead added a *porte cochère* and built stables, a granary and a brewhouse.

In 1899 47 acres of grounds were opened as a public park and by 1912 the council had acquired the mansion and the remaining grounds. Valentine's prospects are now encouraging, with a growing programme of annual events. The question is whether the costs of looking after so large a house might not be recouped by having some residents, leaving parts available for the local community and events but bringing in capital by the sale of long leases.

The garden front of c.1769 has a central pedimented window disguised by a Regency awning.

WALPOLE HOUSE · Chiswick
Named after a nephew of England's first Prime Minister

WALPOLE HOUSE MUST STAND HIGH on any shortlist of the finest and most covetable terraced houses in London. The street front looks almost like three separate houses with a run of eight windows on first and second floors commanding a stupendous panorama of the Thames. Between house and river is no more than the pleasant lane known as Chiswick Mall and across it a narrow strip of gardens on the water's edge. Sun bouncing off the river gives the impression of almost doubling the amount of daylight in every room, not least because light is reflected up on ceilings.

Walpole House takes its name from the Hon. Thomas Walpole, nephew of England's first Prime Minister, who lived here from 1798 till 1803. He was a cousin of Horace Walpole, who lived at famous Strawberry Hill in Twickenham.

The house began to take its present form when acquired in 1700 by Barbara Villiers, Duchess of Cleveland and a former mistress of Charles II. To her must be due the three-storey garden front, as handsome as any 1700 house in fashionable Cheyne Row on Chelsea Embankment. Here the windows have thick early glazing bars and red-brick surrounds with unusual flared tops, a brick version of a stepped keystone.

On the right is a trio of octagonal chimney stacks, rebuilt at the top but clearly part of a Tudor house on this site. Plentiful panelling of 16th-century date is to be found inside. The house appears to have had another major reworking between 1710 and 1720, when the river front largely took on its present form, more restrained than the garden front and with larger sashes. This date fits the imposing entrance porch, which is two arches deep and with rich Corinthian capitals. Inside there is an

The garden front of c.1700 has distinctive red brick surrounds to the windows.

abundance of fine 1720s-style panelling with tall panels rising from the chair rail to the cornice. The grand oak staircase rising round an open well is of the same date with a trio of balusters to each tread, two fluted and one corkscrew. The ends of each tread are carved with scrolls and the handrail ends in best baroque style with full circular sweep.

Grand houses in the 18th century had a great room for routs. Walpole House has a high-ceilinged banqueting room on the ground floor and an equally large and lofty drawing room above, both with tall sash windows providing glorious views of the Thames. The banqueting room has a baroque mantel, the drawing room a fine columned black and white marble chimney piece and giant Adamesque

Baroque cresting surmounts the handsome wrought-iron entrance gate.

bookcase. The main bedroom occupies the centre of the first floor, and opens into a sitting room that delights every visitor, with a corner window looking along the river, the perfect place to enjoy maximum sunlight and balmy air.

All the bedrooms have wonderful outlooks, thanks not only to the river but the size of the garden which extends round the back of the neighbouring house as well running several dozen yards to the road at the back. Here a pair of gate piers stand ready for a carriage entrance to be opened. There are also two garages nearby. The garden terraces and paths are beautifully paved in York stone as is the Edwardian fountain.

The immaculate order of Walpole House is due to the architect Jeremy Benson who lived (and worked) here for half a century and carried out exemplary restorations of great Georgian country houses such as Honington in Warwickshire and Sezincote in Gloucestershire. I have rarely seen a roof where the tiles and flats look in better trim, evidently fit to last a lifetime.

The internal layout is highly flexible with an attic floor with some rooms attractively open to the rafters where young, or grown-up, children could lead a semi-independent existence. Even the basement is worth a sixpenny tour, with fine dressers in the old kitchen as well as a vintage scrubbed kitchen table. There are ample cellars – one entirely clad in glazed tiles, like a dairy.

When Chiswick fell out of fashion in the early 19th century, Walpole House served for a while as the Royal Victoria Asylum for Girls – the young Queen paid a visit in 1838 describing it as 'a most interesting and delightful establishment … for poor vagrant girls'. In 1840 it became a boys' school. Thackeray studied here and used it as the model for Miss Pinkerton's Academy in *Vanity Fair*. By 1885 the house was in bad repair and it was rescued by Sir John Thornycroft, whose family owned the prestigious boatyard that built the first launches for the Boat Race, as well as early torpedo boats.

SCOTLAND

ACHNACARRY — Spean Bridge
Castle-style house by James Gillespie Graham completed by William Burn

THIS IS A PLACE OF ABSOLUTE enchantment. There cannot be a cosier or more domestic-looking castle in the land, certainly not one set in such scenic splendour. From the tall Regency bow windows you look out across the fast-flowing waters of the River Arkaig, which flows for just two miles from Loch Arkaig to Loch Lochy. Yet this is the ancestral seat of Lochiel, head of the Cameron clan.

The gothic windows in the centre are framed by angle turrets and parapets pierced by quatrefoils.

The gently winding bank to the east of the house is planted with a long line of closely planted beech trees. Here in 1745 'Gentle Lochiel' was about to plant an avenue of beech trees leading to Fort Augustus when, hearing that Bonnie Prince Charlie had landed, he placed them in a hastily cut trench and hurried to persuade the Prince of the futility of his enterprise. The Prince's eloquence won him over, and following defeat at Culloden Lochiel was never able to return. The trees remain close packed, just as he left them.

Achnacarry was begun in 1802 for Donald Cameron, the 22nd chieftain, and is the first country house designed by the prolific and talented architect James Gillespie Graham. Work halted in 1805 when money ran out and the house was only completed by William Burn in the late 1830s. An engineer who came in 1837 found 'the plaster ornaments of the ceilings lay all that time ready to be fixed, and the doors of the rooms, of beautiful Highland pine, grown brown with age, leaned against the wall ready to be screwed on'.

I first visited Achnacarry to find out how the house had been used for commando training during the war. Lochiel and his wife showed me photographs of the nearby loch being used for rehearsals of the D-Day landings. Landing craft were powering through the water surrounded by huge bursts of spray as shells appeared to land all around them. Alas, towards the end of the war the house was accidentally set on fire and much of the upper floor destroyed. It was restored by Ian Lindsay, one of the great post-war champions of Scotland's architectural heritage, and redecorated in the 1950s with advice from Walter Schomberg Scott, the National Trust for Scotland's architect and curator.

ARCHERFIELD   Dirleton
18th-century house with matching wings smartly restored after falling into ruin

ARCHERFIELD WAS BUILT FOR WILLIAM NESBIT in the late 17th century, remodelled by the architect John Douglas in the 1740s and by Robert Adam in 1790. *The Morning Post* of October 31, 1805, described a 'most magnificent colonnade' being installed by 'Mr Wyatt', with columns of porphyry and *verde antico* all dug up from the ruins of Herculaneum and selected by the Earl of Elgin, who was married to Mr Nesbit's only daughter.

The house was butchered– this is not too strong a word – in 1962, when the farmer who had acquired the estate punched a huge hole in the main front, stripped out the Robert Adam interior and installed a grain dryer. Poetic justice followed when he was forced to sell, having exhausted his finances trying to grow vegetables on the impossibly sandy soil beside the Firth of Forth. This was allowed to happen as until 1968 most historic buildings were only 'provisionally' listed and without effective protection.

Soon after, the property was acquired by the Duke of Hamilton, remaining a forlorn shell surveying a treeless park. Hopes rose when Kit Martin, nearing completion of his transformation of nearby Tyninghame, sought to take on Archerfield. Others came forward with more ambitious plans, gambling that planning permission would be forthcoming for development in the open country only 15 miles east of Edinburgh. Enter Pavilion Leisure, who had plans to build two huge wings that would dwarf the house and also put up between two hundred and four hundred 'Fairway Homes'. Fierce opposition prompted a public inquiry and Archerfield was soon in the hands of the receiver.

Yet the Archerfield saga has an impressively happy ending. Following five years of work the house has reopened as an hotel where all fifteen bedrooms can be booked for parties, while nearby there are twelve 'sumptuous Golf Pavilions' instead of 200 houses. The warm speckled stonework shows no signs of former scars and tall sash windows light handsomely furnished rooms.

The house stood battered and decayed for decades before restoration began.

ARISAIG HOUSE — Mallaig

Rebuilt in Cotswold style in the 1930s and now a private house again

ARISAIG HOUSE STANDS IN A GLORIOUS POSITION with grand terraced gardens that descend right down to the sea shore. When I arrived in the autumn of 2002 it was a luxurious Relais-Chateau hotel that was smartly furnished and decorated with ten extremely comfortable bedrooms. But the very next week it was due to close as the owner decided to live here in retirememt while his son started a new business renting five comfortable self-catering estate cottages 'on the romantic road to the isles'.

Arisaig has a place in history as a wartime Highlands base of Churchill's Special Operations Executive, which carried out commando-style training of secret agents who were accommodated in a series of nearby deer-stalking lodges. Arisaig housed the officers who were training the agents. They were lucky enough to have all the comforts of living in a virtually new house, as the original Arisaig had been ambitiously rebuilt following a fire in 1935.

The first house dated to 1864 and was built to the designs of Philip Webb, the English architect who was the apostle of the Arts and Crafts movement. Here he chose to work in a vicarage style – his gothic windows still survive on the entrance front. Webb's client was Francis Dukinfield Palmer-Astley. The owner of the hotel, Mr Smither, told me, 'the remarkable thing about this house is that it has always belonged to English families apart from a brief two-year spell'.

After the fire the house was rebuilt by I.B.M. Hamilton & Orphoot, Whiting & Lindsay in a Cotswold style with tall gables and chimneys, but in grey rather than golden stone. The new interiors have a touch of the stripped-down classicism of the 1930s with simple groin vaulting in the drawing room, widely spaced, chunky balusters on the stairs and a hint of Art Deco in the dining room, which has smooth cigar-box-style panelling.

Sweeping lawns and banks of shrubs match the grandeur of the rugged setting.

AUCHINLECK   Ochiltree

Lord Auchinleck himself may have had a hand in the sophisticated design

IF THE APPLE HAD TO BE AWARDED, Auchinleck would be on the shortlist for the most handsome Palladian house not just in Scotland but in the British Isles. Its beauty stems not just from the crisp blemishless masonry but from the very subtle proportions. Set on a shallow basement with a short flight of steps leading to the entrance, it has engaging domesticity rather than aristocratic grandeur.

When SAVE published *Houses at Risk in Ayrshire* in 1983, Auchinleck was in a desperate state, empty, vandalised and suffering from dry rot. 'The parapet urns have been pushed off the roof, most of the windows have been broken, whole window frames have been pushed in, guttering has been removed and continual break-ins have resulted in the stripping of the interior,' ran the commentary.

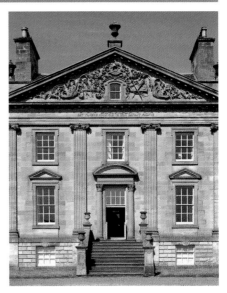

The temple front centrepiece has Ionic columns and rich carving disguises the tiny attic window.

Auchinleck was the home of the renowned biographer James Boswell. The house was built in 1759–61 by his father, Lord Auchinleck, who himself appears to have had a hand in the design. Boswell's friend and mentor, Dr Samuel Johnson, famously argued about politics with Lord Auchinleck in the library at Auchinleck, which Boswell and Johnson visited at the end of their tour of the Hebrides in 1773. When Boswell inherited, he recorded his guests in a book of Company and Licquors.

Today almost all the marks of the house's former plight have vanished. The hero of the piece is the architect James Brown of Simpson & Brown, who first repaired the shell of the house for the Scotttish Historic Buildings Trust and then completed restoration for the Landmark Trust. Even before work began they employed the master carpenter Tom McFadyen of Addyman and Kay to 'decode' the panelling which had been hastily placed in store to avert further vandalism. More than half has since been reinstated.

Plate glass windows have been replaced with sashes following the original glazing pattern and greatly improving the look of the house. The richly carved pediment has been cleaned and repaired. Auchinleck unusually has just a single staircase for family and servants. The ceiling mouldings here were made of papier mache not plaster, a common practice in the 18th century. The ornamental bird flying over the stair had lost its head has been given a hawk's head modelled on the family crest. The magnificent library looks across to the Isle of Arran.

In the grounds are two pavilions, obelisks and a bridge across the Dippol Burn, on the banks of which are an ice house and grotto. The house itself sleeps up to thirteen.

BALBIRNIE   Fife
Ambitiously remodelled in Greek Revival style in 1815–19 for General Robert Balfour

HANDSOMELY PROPORTIONED GREEK REVIVAL houses are among the noblest in Britain – witness The Grange in Hampshire, Belsay Hall in Northumberland and Leigh Court near Bristol. Balbirnie House is their Scottish counterpart, one of the largest and earliest Grecian–style houses north of the border. The entrance front has a four column Ionic portico with delicately detailed capitals contrasting with the smooth column shafts.

While the entrance front has the compact form of a villa, the long garden front has a recessed portico like that at Leigh Court. Its length is explained by the fact that it incorporates a house of 1777–82, where the family continued to live while the house was extended. This was built to the designs of James Nisbet who as a young man supervised work for the Adam brothers.

The Regency extensions were carried out for General Robert Balfour who owned extensive coal mines. His architect was Richard Crichton, who would be better known if he had not died at the relatively early age of 46. He too had worked for the Adams, as a draughtsman.

Too many Regency houses in Scotland were demolished in the 1950s and 1960s. Balbirnie was bought by the Glenrothes Development Corporation, which established a craft centre in the stables but had no use for the house. Balbirnie thus escaped the institutional use and has sprung back to life as a comfortable and stylish privately owned hotel set on a 416-acre park and estate. The park, originally landscaped by Thomas White, is now a golf course but the immediate grounds have changed little.

Houses like Balbirnie were originally run by a quantity of servants so it is interesting that the house in its latest incarnation, catering for weddings and events, now boasts a 'brigade' of helpers that is a hundred strong.

The entrance portico is just visible on the right of the long garden front.

BALLENCRIEFF CASTLE　　Aberlady

Long-ruined seat of Lord Elibank saved from imminent demolition

MANY DREAM OF OWNING A CASTLE. In Scotland tower houses are plentiful, offering all the romance of a fortified castle, and comfort and warmth as well. Ballencrieff Castle comes with the full array of gun loops beneath the windows and Scottish features such as crow-stepped gables, circular stair towers and a drum-shaped bartizan growing from the parapet.

More than this, it has the excitement of being a house brought back from death by the present owner, the engineer Peter Gillies, who bravely agreed to buy it in 1989 when a demolition order had been served and was due to be carried out in five days. The SOS came from the prolific Scottish writer Nigel Tranter, author of 130 novels as well as books on fortalices and castles. He had been alerted by the local farmer, best known for his tasty Ballencrieff porkers reared nearby, and suddenly faced with a large bill for demolition and removal of rubble. Photographs of 1966 show the castle a battered shell, burnt out in 1868 by a spark from the laundry.

Though Ballencrieff comes with just an acre and a half of land, its appeal is that it is just 17 miles to the east of Edinburgh and, using the ring road, forty minutes from the airport. While some tower houses contain rather cramped spaces within their massive walls, Ballencrief has extensive accommodation over four floors, or five if you include the mezzanine at one end. Peter Gillies and his partner Lin Dalgleish keep fit by migrating from the vaulted kitchen to a bedroom beneath the eaves at the other end of the house, an ascent of sixty-eight steps. But if the thought leaves you breathless, the best bedroom in the castle, the laird's chamber, is directly above the drawing room off the great hall and there are a full seven bedrooms to choose from.

The windows tell of a house with rooms on six levels.

A special feature of Scottish tower houses are the spiral stone staircases known in Scotland as turnpike stairs. At Ballencrieff a broad stair sweeps up to the great hall while another spiral stair provides a private link between the laird's chamber and his lady's immediately above, and a third allows Mr Gillies to descend directly from the top floor and let the dog out, without waking guests by walking past their bedrooms.

Today the house again bears the date 1507, marking its original completion by James Murray. This was burnt down in the 'rough wooing' when Henry VIII was using force to press the suit of his son Edward for the hand of the infant Mary Queen of Scots. Ballencrieff was rebuilt in 1586 by John Murray and the heraldic ceiling in the great hall added by Sir Gideon Murray, whose son, a keen Royalist was created 1st Lord Elibank by Charles I in 1643.

A new north front and east end were added in about 1730. Mr Gillies decided the Georgian work was too far gone to restore. 'We took the remaining walls apart stone by stone and found numerous carved stones from the earlier buildings,' he says. The work was done with a Glasgow restoration architect, John Brown, and was completed in 1996.

He continues, 'Very little is conjecture. When we arrived the great hall was roofless, just rubble and self-seeded trees.' By careful sifting he found numerous fragments of the plaster ceiling, the ribs, and the initials and emblems of the builders. To these he added his own, as well as providing a small box at the corners for the plasterers James Black and Hugh Harris to insert their initials. The floor has been laid in splendid large dark Caithness slabs.

'We found the fireplace smashed into hundreds of tiny pieces. It must have exploded with the heat of the fire. I glued them together and assembled half of one of the pillars at the side.' From this he started drawing, determining the precise curve by which it descended to the surviving base. Inside the huge hearth he has placed a metal shutter to prevent warmth being sucked up the chimney when the fire is not lit. 'You'd just be heating the birds and the draught would suck your hat off,' he quips.

A recess in the long wall, he deduced, must have contained a built-in buffet and he has constructed a new one in English oak with his initials.

A number of garderobes and closets that survive, opening off the various chambers and proof that en-suite facilities were valued in the Middle Ages too.

For the lady's bedchamber no fragments of heraldic plaster ceiling survived. 'Instead we bought timbers from a Leith warehouse which was being demolished. When I asked the local sawmill to cut them up they said they would only do it if I guaranteed the Tungsten blade against damage from nails embedded in the wood. So we set up a jig on site and ruined a couple of chain saws in the process, a much more economic solution.'

He wanted simple traditional doors formed of vertical and horizontal planks nailed back to back. 'I found the appropriate handmade nails in Glasgow which are hammered through and bent over on the far side,' he adds.

While Ballencrieff retains numerous small windows appropriate to a castle, it also has the advantage of tall sash windows in the hall and other rooms above so the interiors are light. The views improve as you ascend. The third floor is 50 ft up and his daughter chose the very highest room under the eaves – with a roof as steep as a tent.

BELHAVEN HILL HOUSE — Belhaven
Handsome 1760 sandstone house with Edwardian wing

To MAINTAIN CONTACT WITH ITS NUMEROUS AGENTS and resistance circuits all over Europe, Churchill's Special Operations Executive had a series of houses used for wireless training and transmission. In Scotland SOE had a wireless training establishment at Belhaven School, outside Dunbar near Edinburgh. I had always wondered why SOE had departed from its normal practice of taking on comfortable country houses until in 2002 I drove up to find a large, handsome, late-Georgian house which had become a boarding school in the 1920s and remains so today.

As there are very strict rules forbidding photography of children at schools I went in, showed a copy of my book on SOE agents, *The Women who Lived for Danger*, to a teacher, explained about my research and was told yes, I could take a photograph. No sooner had I done so than an imperious figure, obviously the Headmaster, strode down the steps and cried, 'What on earth do you think you are doing?'

'I'm Marcus Binney…' I started to explain. 'I know who you are,' he stormed before suddenly relaxing. 'We last met at a bus stop on the island of Crete in 1966, the year we both came down from Cambridge. I'm Michael Osborne,' he said. A moment later I was having a full tour of the handsome interior and being shown wartime photographs of SOE wireless operators undergoing training at Belhaven. Trainees would tap out coded messages to the SOE school at Fawley Hall just outside Henley-on-Thames 300 miles away so they gained first-hand experience in the interference and irregularities that came with live transmissions.

Today Belhaven Hill School is a flourishing co-ed prep school with a hundred boarding and day pupils between the ages of 8 and 13 and continues to stand in large well-maintained grounds.

The handsome dormer windows were added c.1900 by the architect George Washington Browne.

BLANERNE HOUSE   Duns
Border seat of the Lumsdaine family for four centuries

REBUILT IN 1895 AFTER A FIRE, Blanerne House dates from the golden age of British building when good building materials and craftsmen were in plentiful supply. The entrance hall is all of 35 ft long, the drawing room a stately 20 by 30 ft, and the dining room of the same proportions. There is a large billiard room and library and upstairs are ten large bedrooms.

The country around is a little bleak – big open expanses of farming country and wood, impressive but a bit featureless.

Blanerne comes with full clannish credentials. It belonged to the Lumsdens for many centuries until sold as a school in 1929. The manor of Lumsden in Berwick is first mentioned in 1098 and Adam de Lumisden paid forced homage to Edward I of England in 1296. His descendent Gilbert married the heiress of Blanerne in 1329 adopting her crest of a *blanc erne*, or white-tailed eagle, preying on a salmon.

Impressive masonry fragments survive of Blanerne Castle, which dates back to the 16th century. A new house was built in 1830 to the designs of the prolific Scots country-house architect William Burn, but this was rebuilt after a fire. The style is a stripped-down version of Scots baronial with the very Scots feature of chimneys at the top of each gable. Until the sun comes out, like many Scottish houses it is a little dour.

The numerous tall sash windows make the interior seem much lighter, brighter and airier than many baronial houses. Three of the rooms have vast triple sash windows rising from the floor and as panoramic as any modern house. Some of the bedroom windows are dormers opening through sloping eaves as in Arts and Crafts houses in southern England. For good measure there is a full basement under the house, in rudimentary state but with workshop, fishing-tackle room and ample space for storage. There are extensive lawns and a commanding view down to the river, which has 560 yards of double bank fishing. Recently, the new owners have created a three-bedroom apartment which is available for holiday rentals.

Tall windows announce grand rooms on the first floor, with lower ceilings above and below for greater warmth.

BRANTWOODE Helensburgh

Designed by William Leiper and named after Ruskin's house in the Lake District

MANY DREAM OF LIVING IN an Arts and Crafts house by Voysey or Lutyens. Brantwoode is a Scottish counterpart, full of the inventive, intriguing flourishes that proclaim a first-class architect has planned it to the last detail.

Renowned for balmy summers and clement winters, Helensburgh became a fashionable resort on the north bank of the Clyde when a paddle-steamer service to Glasgow began in 1812. With the arrival of the railway in 1857 it became possible to commute. And when the West Highland Line came through in 1894 another burst of activity began further up the hill. Brantwoode is a two-minute walk to the night sleeper, which leaves at 11.15 and arrives at Euston at 8.00 the next morning.

The roads in upper Helensburgh are laid out on a grid plan with broad grass verges, giving the roads or drives, as some are called, a distinctly American feel. Brantwoode still has the full original *feu*, or plot. Here, on the upper slopes where the views are most inspiring, stands a splendid group of signature houses by William Leiper, Baillie Scott and others, while a little further up the hill is Charles Rennie Mackintosh's world-renowned masterpiece, Hill House, now immaculately looked after by the National Trust for Scotland.

Brantwoode takes its name from Ruskin's Brantwood overlooking Coniston Water in the Lake District. It was built in 1895 for James Alexander, who had made a fortune with the Jameson Oil Refining Company and was a passionate admirer of Ruskin.

William Leiper, the architect of Brantwoode, is a name to conjure with. While studying in London he had moved in the brilliant artistic circle around William Burges and E.W. Godwin. His best-known work is Templeton's Carpet Factory in Glasgow, modelled on the Doge's Palace in Venice and another tribute to Ruskin. He designed some of the best Aesthetic Movement houses in Scotland, including nearby

The house is built in an English style with half-timbering and mullioned windows.

Cairndhu of 1881 with Anglo Japanese decoration, and did the interiors of the Russian Imperial Yacht *Livadia* then the largest steam yacht ever constructed.

The walls of Brantwoode are constructed principally of a warm, almost purple sandstone. Unusually, Leiper designed it in the old-English domestic style of Norman Shaw with bargeboarded gables and tile-hanging on the upper floor.

To take full advantage of the sunny south-facing slope, Leiper set the entrance on the north side behind the house. His large gabled entrance, like a church porch, is placed at one end, opening into a broad hallway leading to the stair.

Brantwoode is designed for entertaining and for elegant soirées – with the three main rooms interconnecting. The panelled doors off the hall are exceptionally broad, made of Kuari pine from New Zealand which now has a wonderful mellow glow thanks to two years of work removing treacly stain. They are made in traditional manner, fixed with wooden pegs not nails.

Leiper makes great play with his fireplaces. Immediately inside the entrance there is one with a characteristic Arts and Crafts inscription carved in stone: 'In the world a home – in the home my world.' In the drawing room the fireplace is set in a large inglenook with a coved top rather like a cathedral choir stall, while in the living room the chimney breast retains the original brightly gilded William Morris wallpaper. Lead windows are on different delicate patterns in each room with gold and emerald mosaics over one of the drawing-room windows.

In the bay windows Leiper leaves the crisply cut sandstone exposed on the inside. The living room has a French window, beautifully executed in lead, cleverly set into the side cheek of the bay so you can walk out into the garden.

Strangely, there is no obvious dining room on Leiper's plans. The kitchen opens into the parlour at the east end but the living room in the centre has a serving hatch with folding shutters and flamboyant brass hinges.

Part of the charm of Brantwoode is that the back-stairs area is so complete, with built-in glass-fronted dressers and a scullery containing three deep Belfast sinks supported on porcelain columns. The cupboard under the back stairs was devised to contain a tin bath for the use of the maids. This folded down onto the floor where the water gurgled out through a central drain. The bath survives, stored in the garage.

The main staircase, lit by a large stepped window, leads up to a broad landing lined with cupboard doors in Kauri pine. Further storage cupboards cleverly make use of the space under the sloping eaves.

In the main bedroom the windows retain the original wooden secondary glazing complete with hinges and bolts. The adjoining bathroom is an Art Deco set piece, entirely faced in Vitralite tiles, soft lemon yellow above, pale tangerine below. Over the wash basin the matching mirror (an irregular diamond-like hexagon) survives in a broad, shiny black Vitralite frame. In the corner is a patent shower with its original chrome fittings and horizontal jets that spray you from head to toe.

The garden has been terraced using 70 tons of Penrith sandstone formed into dry-stone walls, which fan out to form a central ascent of tulip-shaped steps. In the garden a pair of century-old, large-leaf rhododendrons was found, along with what is known as 'The Story Tree', a many-bowed cypress where children can sit while being read to.

CASTLE OF PARK · Cornhill

Characteristic white harled Scottish tower house that now welcomes house parties

CASTLE OF PARK STANDS IN THE GENTLY ROLLING landscape that extends from Aberdeen to the Bannffshire coast where each smooth hill looks like an island that once rose in a long-vanished sea. It's an easy hour's drive from Aberdeen airport and just ten minutes from the charming fishing village of Portsoy.

Here you are at peace with nature – the only sounds are the cawing of the rooks at dusk, the hoot of an occasional owl and perhaps the odd explosive roar of a low-flying RAF jet, but then it is rare to find a beauty spot in Britain that is exempt from that nowadays.

The artist James Duncan bought the castle in the late 1980s and ran it as a low-key guest house. 'We don't advertise – most of our visitors have found us on the internet. Look under "Castle",' Mr Duncan told me in 1999.

They began in a more earnest way but now serve meals to guests or prebooked parties. That's with the possible exception of Christmas Day when, in a really cold spell, neighbours faced with burst pipes and electricity cuts ring up in desperation. This is because they know the Duncans are sitting there as warm as toast within 3-ft thick walls. 'Once the castle is warm it holds the heat through the winter,' says Mr Duncan.

Castle of Park has a stirring history. It was granted to a Norman knight in 1242 by King Alexander II, passing to the Lords Saltoun who gave the castle its typically Scots

The Georgian bow and battlemented tower are later additions.

Z-plan with a tower set diagonally at either end – the canny Scots quickly realised just two towers rather than four were needed to provide flanking fire along a castle's walls.

The white-harled castle bears the mark of succeeding centuries. Each generation made a new entrance. There is a 16th-century archway over one, a marriage stone of 1723 over another. Georgian bows were followed by a battlemented tower in the style of Sir Walter Scott at Abbotsford.

The Gordons, who acquired the estate in 1604, and their successors the Gordon-Duffs were made of stern stuff. Sir William Gordon raised the standard at Glenfinnan for Bonnie Prince Charlie and when the Prince reached Derby he was all for marching on to London when other counsel prevailed, ending with the disastrous defeat at Culloden.

For the next few years Sir William, like Hereward the Wake, avoided capture by the redcoats, living in the hills around his estate and riding into the bogs where no one would follow. Though the castle was ransacked, he had already spirited away all the family valuables. Never to be pardoned, Sir William escaped to Douai, joining Lord Ogilvy's regiment in the French service, where he died, but his brother, Captain John Gordon of the Marines, was a fierce anti-Jacobite and gained possession of the estates.

Lachlan Duff Gordon, who succeeded to Park in 1855 and then to the larger estate of Drummuir, had been shipwrecked in the Red Sea, thrown himself on the mercy of Mehmet Ali, and then, after innumerable quarantines in successive ports (for fear he might be carrying the plague), arrived in London just as he was about to be posted lost, in time to carry his regimental colours at Queen Victoria's coronation.

Mrs Pat Heathcote, the last of the family to live in the castle, says, 'It was one of those houses with the most lovely warm family atmosphere. We would go every summer and fish on the Deveron nearby. The house is extremely old. In earlier centuries they drove the cattle in downstairs to provide central heating. I remember it with all the hooks on the ceiling.'

After 1945, said the Duncans, Castle of Park nearly joined the large number of Scottish country houses blown up by the army (who liked a little explosives practice). Even so, the dry rot was so bad in the handsome Classical entrance front of the 1750s that it was demolished.

You won't find plastic windows here – the beautiful Georgian sashes remain, including the curved sashes in the bows and one room with a rare set of bronze sashes, ironically painted in white to match the rest. Instead of the small mullioned windows you expect in a castle, one bedroom after another has long windows providing a panorama of the grounds.

From the medieval undercrofts to the third-floor rooms in the 1820s tower, the castle was freshly painted. Thanks to a new roof that was put on by the previous owner there was not a sniff of damp – every room seemed as fresh and well-aired as a farmhouse in Provence.

Castle of Park is now run by Lois and Bill Brecon, who hold a lively series of painting, photography and creative writing courses as well as hosting weddings, birthday and anniversary celebrations and getaway weekends for groups of friends, who stay in seven double bedrooms.

CAROLINE PARK — Edinburgh
Long blighted by industry, Caroline Park is handsomely restored and lived in again

CAROLINE PARK OWES ITS UNUSUAL NAME to the 2nd Duke of Argyll who bought the house in 1739 and renamed it in honour of his daughter, the Countess of Dalkeith. The date of 1696 carved on the dormer window over the entrance records the completion of the high-browed main front that was added by George and Anne, Viscount and Viscountess Tarbat. Here the massive ballooning roof has a distinctly French character, as do the banded pillars on either side of the entrance. Over the columned entrance porch is an intricate wrought-iron balustrade with the intertwined initials of the Viscount and his wife surmounted by a coronet.

The house was at once a country villa outside Edinburgh and a power base for political entertaining – the family's main estates were in Ross-shire. A Latin inscription on the north front records 'Riches amassed are useless, but spent produce much good', engagingly describing the house as a 'shepherd's cottage'. Inside it contains rich Charles II plasterwork with swirling acanthus foliage and a matching acanthus wrought-iron balustrade on the state stair.

Lawrence Weaver memorably portrayed the house's romantic melancholy in *Country Life* in 1911, carefully disguising the fact that it had become offices for A.B. Fleming & Co whose nearby printing-ink works were the largest in the world, supplying ink to every London paper. When I wrote about Caroline Park in the early 1980s it was one of a series of grand houses around Edinburgh standing empty and without a use. With its remarkable balloon roof it had the air of a splendid 17th-century French chateau. Its plight was explained by the soaring octagonal gasholder beside it – not the type that telescopes into the ground as the gas is used up. Soon after, Caroline Park was acquired by the Dukes of Buccleuch, who in an improving market have been able to modernise the house so that it is lived in again by a series of tenants who all reside in magnificently stylish apartments.

The 1696 garden front, with distinctive bell-shaped roofs to the towers, has a Baroque grandeur.

CRAIGENGILLAN   Dalmellington
Home of the inventors of tarmacadam with 1900 Parisian interiors

SOME PEOPLE DREAM OF RESCUING an ancient house from decay. In Ayrshire the surveyor Mark Gibson turned his energies to the revival of an entire 3,000-acre estate. 'It was all barbed wire and keep out notices. Every house was damp, cold and rotten, the fences and dykes were no longer stock proof,' he says.

Craigengillan was the home of the MacAdams from 1580 and had never been sold before 2000. The most famous of the family was John MacAdam, the great engineer and inventor of tarmacadam, who succeeded to the estate in 1724. He redesigned the old house and added the Palladian stables with handsome clock tower capped by an octagonal dome.

Early in the 20th century the McAdams commissioned Maison Jansen, the leading Paris interior decorators, to create a grand suite of rooms on the ground floor for entertaining with panelling, plasterwork and ironwork almost as opulent as the Paris Ritz. Over the last five years Gibson, working with a local master builder Tommy Hiddleton, has patiently repaired roofs, dormer windows and chimneys and installed new heating using massive 1900 German radiators.

The stables have been restored as a thriving livery offering riding lessons and are now operating at full capacity with forty-five horses. 'Children join in eagerly to muck out, groom, wash and feed,' says Gibson.

Fifteen miles of new hedgerows have been planted, weeded by hand until established. Several miles of stone dykes have been repaired and three new lochs created. Ness Glen, described in 19th-century guidebooks as the best example of a true rock gorge in Britain, is again accessible to walkers – with a new path along the River Doon taking visitors past rapids, waterfalls and cliffs as steep as the wall of a house, rising nearly 300 ft.

Paired chimneys top the gables with a glazed loggia between.

CULLEN HOUSE   Cullen

Magnificent baronial seat of the Earls of Seafield restored as a series of large houses

I FIRST ARRIVED AT CULLEN HOUSE AT 9.30 on a grey April morning in 1981. Kit Martin and I were being shown around by the Factor of the Seafield Estates, Mr Lang. He had had his fill of architects, antiquarians and aesthetes telling him this was a marvellous historic place. None of them had any practical solution to the problem. The house was empty. Decay was setting in and it was about to become a massive liability on the estate.

We embarked on a tour of the house designed to baffle and dismay – up one tower staircase, down another, back up a third, all at a furious pace through processions of empty rooms and long corridors to glimpse every peeling attic. Cold, bare staterooms alternated with newly papered bedrooms and bathrooms that had never been used.

As with so many problem country houses, the setting of Cullen remained superb. The south range stood on an outcrop of rock overlooking a dramatic woodland bowl planted with hundreds of rhododendrons. To the west a great arched bridge spanned a gorge cut by the burn.

After little more than two hours, Kit Martin proceeded to outline a scheme for adapting the house for up to two dozen families to live in. Hardly an hour afterwards we were amazed to see Mr Lang and Lord Seafield pacing the boundaries of the land they might sell with the house.

At first glance the sheer scale of Cullen, with its silhouette of gables and turrets, suggests a predominantly Victorian house. Close inspection shows that much of the building and its enriching detail are earlier. The windows offer immediate clues. The large plate glass bay windows are clearly mid 19th-century introductions: small windows with thick glazing bars suggest the 17th century and big sash widows speak of the 18th.

The west courtyard, where existing doors serve as the entrances to the new houses created within.

The medieval house on the site forms the core of the present building. By tradition this was extended westward in 1543 by a range of vaulted cells for the monks of the Collegiate Church of Cullen. The funds for the work were provided by Alexander Ogilvy whose monument, still gothic in style, stands in the church.

By 1578 the estates passed to Sir Walter Ogilvy and the town records state that on March 20, 1600 the Laird's house at Cullen was begun. The family gallery in the church dates from 1602 and bears the arms of Sir Walter and his second wife Dame Mary Douglas. A new range was added to the east. In a corner of the west courtyard stood the main entrance of the house, now blocked, with the knobbly columns associated with furniture of 1600 date. The turret above bears the initials of Sir Walter and his wife, 'SBO' and 'DMD'. The other main features to survive from this date are a series of highly elaborate dormers, some carved with armorial emblems, others sculpted with winged fishtailed horses.

Sir Walter's additions reflect his rising political ambitions. In 1599 he joined the council of the Duke of Lennox, the King's Lieutenant in the north. He was created Lord Ogilvy of Deskford in 1615. His son James succeeded in 1625 and was created Earl of Findlater in 1638. Any further thoughts of building were brought to an end by the Civil War and the Commonwealth; the next additions were carried out for the 3rd Earl who succeeded in 1659. There is a date of 1668 on a tower in the East range.

His son, the 4th Earl, a strong supporter of union with England, was created Earl of Seafield in 1701 and the next year became Lord High Chancellor. The 7th Earl of Seafield, who succeeded in 1853, called in David Bryce, the great exponent of Scottish Baronial. In 1882 the whole house was harled but this was removed in 1945.

Kit Martin's fundamental decision was to create very large houses. Five of the seven principal houses are on four floors and each has at least one of the staterooms. The general principal was to put kitchens and dining rooms on the ground floor with living rooms above. The 65-ft long library in the south wing with shelving for over 12,000 books became the living room of a highly unusual one bedroom apartment with kitchen and dining room in vaulted undercrofts on the ground floor. The buildings around the service court were turned into pleasant two-storey cottages. Local architect Douglas Forrest created a very attractive studio apartment in the cavernous double-height 18th-century kitchen, introducing a gallery carried on four Tuscan columns turned into Venetian bargepoles with the help of red ribbons.

Sadly on the morning of June 17, 1987, just two years after restoration was complete a savage fire started in a house that had recently been resold and was being refitted for its new owner. For three hours sixty-three firemen with eight fire engines fought to halt the spread of the flames. Virtually half the house was gutted but the division into separate houses slowed the spread of the fire thanks to blocked-off doorways and firebreaks in the roof. Within twenty-four hours Douglas Forrest had secured the agreement of the four owners affected to proceed with restoration. Bryce's library had been 90 per cent destroyed. Fortunately a snapshot of a box of nails on a shelf enabled him to deduce the exact measurements of the bookcases. From the Bryce drawing room, Forrest salvaged examples of each part of the ornate ceiling – ribs, pendants, cornices and heraldic emblems, enabling an exact reconstruction.

DUDDINGSTON HOUSE   Edinburgh

Elegant neoclassical villa of 1763–8 by Sir William Chambers

Grass is now growing through the steps of the beautifully carved Corinthian portico.

JOHN HARRIS, AUTHOR OF THE definitive volume on Sir William Chambers, describes Duddingston as Chambers's 'ultimate villa' with a noble portico that 'almost converted the house into a temple'. It was built for the 8th Earl of Abercorn, who had bought the Barony of Duddingston from the Duke of Argyll in 1745. It was designed in the summer of 1762, begun the next year and completed in 1768.

The main road into Edinburgh from the east deflects respectfully as it passes the house. When I first visited the house in 1976, I found it languishing as a rather seedy hotel, with pints of beer being pulled in the hall.

Returning in 1990, I hoped to find that the house had been handsomely restored as apartments. Sadly, that was not what lay in wait for me. 'Imagine,' I wrote in *The Times* weekend section, 'a block of twenty-eight new flats on one side of Stourhead, the Hoare family's famous house in Wiltshire, with planning permission granted for another twenty-six units on the other side. Unthinkable, of course. Yet this is precisely what has happened at Duddingston, on the edge of Edinburgh, probably one of the finest Palladian villas in Britain.'

A new back drive, flanked by a security fence that would be more suited to the perimeter of an airport, led to a huge new development that was barely a dozen yards from Chambers's stables. Worse still, the asphalt road, municipal in character and complete with concrete kerbs, continued right past the north front to await Phase II. 'The new residential block offends first by its size several times that of Chambers's house and still more by its character … It might be an office block in a business park,' I wrote.

The plan was that Phase I of the development would pay for the restoration of the villa itself but that had not happened. It took time but now the villa has been restored as the Edinburgh offices of one of Britain's largest architectural practices, Percy Johnson-Marshall and Partners. Most of the park that was laid out by James Robertson in *c*.1735–41 survives as a golf course.

DUFF HOUSE

Banff

Built to the designs of William Adam for Lord Braco, later 1st Earl of Fife, in 1735–41

SCOTTISH ARCHITECTURE OF MANY PERIODS has a flair and originality of its own, remaining distinct from the main stream of European building. Duff House is proof that this can apply to Classical architecture too. The architect was William Adam, whose buildings can be at least as fine as those of his more famous son Robert.

The appeal of Duff lies in its exuberance, a delight in covering every inch of surface with interesting, rich and lively detail. With this comes the perennial Scottish love of a rich and romantic silhouette. The crowning balustrade is topped by a flurry of urns and domed pavilions at the corners, capped by pepper-pot finials.

Duff House was built for William Duff, later Lord Braco and Earl of Fife, who on his father's death had inherited the largest fortune in the north of Scotland. Building costs spiralled and Duff's correspondence is full of references to 'that villain Adams' – such was his anger that he is said never to have occupied the house. Adam's quadrant colonnades and pavilions were omitted, leaving the house a ravishing free-standing composition with all four fronts handsomely dressed and richly carved.

When I first saw Duff House in the early 1980s it was firmly boarded up and empty but surrounded by well-mown grass. The crisp masonry sparkled in the sun and one could walk round admiring it and taking photographs.

Now, Duff House has been fortunate in finding an excellent use, reopening in 1995 as a country-house gallery under an enterprising partnership between Historic Scotland, the National Galleries of Scotland and Aberdeenshire Council.

The house stood nobly but empty before restoration as a gallery.

DUMFRIES HOUSE
Cumnock

Built in 1754–9 to designs by John and Robert Adam for the 4th Earl of Dumfries

As I write, Dumfries House remains an almost miraculous survival – a complete and undisturbed work of the Adam brothers, John and Robert, exquisitely built, perfectly symmetrical in plan, with delicate ornamental plasterwork and fine marble fireplaces. It contains, intact, Chippendale's first important commission – consisting of an extensive set of mahogany chairs, sofas, giltwood overmantels, girandoles and pier glasses, exotically crested rococo four-poster beds, as well as towel rails, chamber pot cupboards and trays. Dumfries House also contains furniture by the best Scottish makers, notably Francis Brodie, William Mathie and Alexander Peter.

The house was commissioned by the 4th Earl of Dumfries, and Robert Adam stayed for three months at old Leifnorris Castle in 1754 as the guest of the Earl, laying out the foundations.

Dumfries House is built of a most attractive buff sandstone with a tinge of red. The stone is still in superb condition, with the original diagonal tooling or chiselling. The house stands in an Arcadian park with a handsome three-arch bridge over the River Lugar straight out of a landscape painting.

Dumfries House passed by marriage to the Butes, who in the 19th century built two of the most astonishing houses in Britain, Cardiff Castle and Mount Stuart on the Isle of Bute. Dumfries House became a dower house, left untouched until the 3rd Marquess commissioned Robert Weir Schultz to extend it. With great subtlety, Schultz doubled the depth of the wings, introducing domed corridors and a gallery.

When the present Marquess – better known as the racing driver Johnny Dumfries – inherited, he was faced with a financial challenge. Thanks to his imagination and energy, the Mount Stuart Trust is now endowed and open to the public. The question is, can a way now be found for the nation to preserve Dumfries House too?

Dumfries is a perfectly balanced composition of centre and balancing wings.

DUNMORE PARK · Dunmore
Tudor Gothic house built for the 5th Earl of Dunmore to the designs of William Wilkins

WILLIAM WILKINS, ARCHITECT OF THE National Gallery in London, had a light touch. This is the enduring appeal of many of his buildings, whether the delicious gothic screen fronting the quad at King's College, Cambridge or the elegant porticoes of Downing College. Of course lightness can be taken for weakness and the dome of the National Gallery is a touch slight. Wilkins's country houses in Scotland manifest both lightness and grace, both Dalmeny House for the 4th Earl of Rosebery and Dunmore, built for the 5th Earl of Dunmore in 1820–25.

Dunmore Park has stood empty and seriously decaying since 1972, the more sorry a sight as the parkland around it has been neglected too. The house nonetheless is an excellent candidate for restoration as self-contained houses and apartments. It is handsomely faced in smooth ashlar stone with a pretty two-storey *porte cochère* and hood moulds to the mullioned windows. It is laid out around a central courtyard with entrance hall and business room on one side, dining room, drawing room and library on another, family rooms on a third side and kitchen and servants' offices on the fourth.

One reason for keeping hope alive is the glorious restoration of the nearby folly in the form of a giant pineapple, begun in 1761 but only given its spiky dome after 1777 when Lord Dunmore was forced to step down as the Governor of Virginia. The folly was saved by the enterprising Landmark Trust and is an enchanting place to stay with accommodation in twin pavilions and a small saloon beneath the giant festive beehive dome of the pineapple.

Now Dunmore itself looks set to be restored by the Manor Kingdom group, which has built a number of smart developments around Edinburgh. Though the initial plans were rejected because fifty-four houses were proposed in the group rather too close to the mansion, the scheme is being modified.

With its romantic silhouette and crisp restoration, Dunmore has begged for rescue for thirty-five years.

ERSKINE HOUSE   Bishopton
Regency Gothic Revival house transformed into grand hotel

ERSKINE HOUSE SITS IN A MAGNIFICENT position above the River Clyde looking across to the Kilpatrick Hills and expresses the phenomenal confidence and wealth of Britain in the reign of George IV. The house was designed in 1828 by Sir Robert Smirke, the architect of the British Museum in London. Erskine House is evidence that Smirke could work equally successfully in gothic style, particularly in creating dazzling interiors. The 110-ft grand hall has a glorious fan vault picked out in gold and opens into a series of reception rooms overlooking the river, with more grand chimney pieces and ornamental ceilings. Smart modern furnishings sit well with the Gothic Revival decoration which is sufficiently strong not to be diminished by the contrast.

Smirke's client was the 11th Lord Blantyre, who succeeded to the title aged 6. A soldier who rose to the rank of Major-General, he was killed aged 53 by a chance shot during the insurrection in Brussels in 1830.

A quarry on the estate provided the stone but the oak plentifully used in construction came from Quebec. The cost on completion was £50,000. In 1916 the house became the Princess Louise Scottish Hospital for Limbless Sailors and Soldiers, who were trained in skills such as basketmaking.

A £15-million refurbishment begun in 2002 has transformed the house into a fifty-three bedroom hotel, renamed Mar Hall. It is heartening that a Gothic Revival building long in institutional use can attract funds for such a lavish and comprehensive programme of restoration.

The garden front has Regency stone-mullioned windows and Tudor-style angle buttresses.

FASQUE CASTLE   Fettercairn
Designed by John Paterson for Sir Alexander Ramsay, Bt, and his son, built in 1807–11

FASQUE STANDS IN A FINE POSITION on the first slopes of the Grampians with views across undulating parkland. The pastoral landscape of fields, hedges and woods could be mistaken for a scene several hundred miles south. Yet conditions in the Mearns, as Kincardineshire is traditionally known, can be hard and snow can lie on the ground for many weeks.

The present house was begun in about 1809 by Sir Alexander Ramsay, Bt, and is attributed to the Edinburgh architect John Patterson. A year later Ramsay was dead but the project was completed by his 25-year-old son and heir.

The main front is a delightful stepped composition rising from two storeys to four in the centre. Perfect symmetry and smooth-faced ashlar stone give the house a lightness and liveliness that is lacking in many later castles with more correct medieval detail. The proportions of the sash windows are very carefully considered with a low ground floor surmounted by a *piano nobile* and smaller bedroom windows above.

In the centre, taller windows take maximum advantage of views across the park. The octagonal corner turrets have narrower windows, practical Georgian versions of medieval slit windows. Old prints show the fourth storey was a slightly later but happily matching addition. The columned *porte cochère* was added *c*.1845–50.

The glory of the interior is the oval staircase hall. The stair begins with a short flight which branches into two cantilevered flights hugging the walls. The undersides of the treads are cut away to create a flowing effect increased by the continuous run of the handrail and the slender iron balusters, the Regency counterpart of fashionable minimalism. The plasterwork of the dome is equally delicate with a pretty gothic

Designed as a summer palace, Fasque enjoys marvellous views and long hours of summer daylight.

The Imperial stair has handrails that descend in a continuous unbroken sweep.

frieze marking the point at which the vault begins. The exquisitely crisp floral motif in the centre of the ceiling is surrounded by ears and husks of corn, ringed with plasterwork as delicate as lace.

In the early 1970s Fasque lay closed while Sir William Gladstone devoted his energy to establishing the family seat in Flintshire as a residential library centred on the Prime Minister's papers. The house was rescued by his younger brother Peter and his wife who set about the repair and redecoration of the house with breathtaking energy – Peter painting all the main rooms himself in the course of one season. As at Erddig and Calke Abbey, this was a house where nothing had ever been thrown away. Servants' carrying sticks, carriage foot-warmers, hot bricks for the hot cupboard, home-made beetle traps and patent sponge-holders have all been identified and neatly displayed. Among the curiosities discovered are a bathmat made of old wine bottle corks and a combination gentleman's garden tool supplied by the Army & Navy stores.

Fasque welcomes parties of visitors by appointment as well as hosting weddings, lunches and dinners, and other events. The estate maintains a network of paths for hillwalkers and offers fishing, deer-stalking and shooting.

FLICHITY HOUSE   Farr
Handsome example of Edwardian baronial built for Glasgow industrialist

FLICHITY IS BUILT OF WARM PALE-BROWN GRANITE with sandstone trim in a lively baronial style with a distinctly light touch. There are no grand flights of steps. The windows of the main rooms look out over the gardens on the level. The whole rich vocabulary of Scottish Baronial is here, stepped gables, bay windows with armorial cresting, richly carved dormer windows and a keep tower with gargoyles and battlements and a corner turret that is first round, then square and capped by a gabled roof.

The original house probably dated from the early 1800s but was altered in the mid 1850s for John Congreve and sold in 1872 to Alexander Guthrie who died the next year. In 1906 the estate was bought from trustees by Sir William Beardmore, a rich Glasgow industrialist who owned Parkhead forge and the Naval Works at Dalamuir on the Clyde.

At one point Sir William's shipyard at Govan was the largest industrial concern in Scotland, employing more than 40,000. He sponsored Shackleton's 1907 Antarctic expedition and as a result one of the world's largest glaciers was named after him. He was also responsible for the R-34 airship built at Inchinnan which flew the first double-crossing of the Atlantic. Beardmore was created Lord Invernairn in 1921.

On purchasing Flichity, Beardmore instructed the Inverness architects Ross and MacBeth to convert the house into 'a spacious and highly modern highland residence'. Beardmore spent a great deal of time here after the First World War. He died in 1936 without children and the estate passed from his widow to her relatives the Ballentines, who sold the estate in 1989.

Richly Scottish baronial, there are stepped gables, gargoyles and a turret house at the corner.

The estate is entered through wrought iron gates and stone gate piers carved with stone eagles. In best Scottish fashion the drive continues past the Mains of Flichity and the Kennels. The great hall rises to the roof while the billiard room walls are faced with exotic Moroccan tiles complemented by Moorish honeycomb cornice. Spreading lawns drop sharply to a wooded gorge with a burn at the bottom.

There is a walled rose garden terraced and a walled kitchen garden divided into square beds with box edging and gravel paths in the traditional manner. The 640-acre estate includes scenic woodland walks planted with rhododendrons, Scots pine and Wellingtonias and there is salmon- and trout-fishing on the River Nairn.

FLOORS CASTLE   Kelso
Built for the 1st Duke of Roxburghe in 1721–6 and remodelled in 1837–43

THE FIRST DISTANT VIEW OF FLOORS, set proudly on a natural terrace above a majestic sweep of the River Tweed, never fails to inspire. What strikes first is the sheer grandeur – the vast extent of house and wings, the velvet carpet of turf that rolls down to the river, and above all, the forest of lead-clad turrets glinting in the sun like the helmets of some fearsome oriental horde. 'The modern mansion of Fleurs,' wrote Sir Walter Scott, 'with its terrace, its woods, its extensive lawn, forms altogether a kingdom for Oberon or Titania to dwell in.'

Here are all the hallmarks of a great aristocratic estate, beautiful parkland, massive plantations, extensive walled gardens and hothouses, model farm buildings and cottages and above all superb sport – today falconry, hawking and archery as well as shooting and unsurpassed salmon-fishing. It was in the shot pool on the Floors Upper Water that the record Tweed salmon was caught in 1886, weighing 57½ pounds, length 4ft 4½ in, girth 2ft 4½ in.

Just across the Tweed stood Roxburgh Castle, one of the great strongholds of medieval Scotland, taken by Edward III in 1346. It was still in English hands when James II of Scotland laid siege with two new cannons he had recently acquired from the Duke of Burgundy. One of these exploded, killing the king.

In 1488 James IV granted the lands at Roxburgh to the Kers. Robert Ker was held in high favour by James VI and accompanied him on his journey to be crowned as James I of England in London. In 1616 he was created Earl of Roxburghe. The 5th

The architect W.H. Playfair dramatically enriched the skyline of the early 18th-century house and wings.

Earl was instrumental in the passing of the Act of Union between England and Scotland in 1707 and was created Duke of Roxburghe, the last creation of the Scottish peerage. For him William Adam, father of the famous Robert, designed a new house in 1707 on a ducal scale, though austere in the extreme, with a large central block flanked by advancing wings.

The house was given its present grandly romantic form by the 6th Duke. Inheriting Floors when still a boy, he commissioned William Henry Playfair immediately after his marriage aged 20 in 1836. Playfair is best known for the National Gallery in Edinburgh and the glorious silhouette of Donaldson's Hospital. He concentrated all of the architectural effect on the skyline, and was very much influenced by what he

Playfair's dining room was designed with twin fireplaces for extra warmth.

termed the 'old English style' houses, such as Blickling and Audley End, which have square corner towers with leaded ogee roofs.

Eighteenth-century architects working in the Castle style, such as Robert Adam, had used battlements, corbels, arrow slits and occasionally bartizans – circular turrets at the corners of the towers. At Floors, Playfair introduced a whole new vocabulary to the castle style, reviving forms of Scottish Baronial buildings such as Heriots' Hospital. There are stepped battlements, soaring chimneys, an extraordinary number of corner turrets and rows of gargoyles in the form of cannons with twisted, fluted and spiralled barrels. In creating such a romantic silhouette he was consciously competing with the Houses of Parliament and wrote to a friend in London asking 'if my work looks much inferior to Barry's'.

In 1760 Bishop Pococke had found it 'strange that so large a house should not afford one grand room' and though Playfair created some elegant Jacobean-style interiors, the interiors were not grandly fitted out until the 6th Duke married a New York heiress, May Goelet, who brought with her fine 18th-century furniture from the Goelet Mansion on Long Island. The main rooms were remodelled in French and English 18th-century style to provide a suitable setting for these treasures. The ballroom was transformed to display a superb set of Gobelins tapestries.

More recently the present Duchess has brought warmth to the interiors with her use of bright varied colours and Floors has finally achieved a sense of being a much-loved family home.

Floors has one of the most exotic roofscapes of any house in Britain.

MILLER'S TOWER   Formakin
Edwardian country house by Robert Lorimer, left unfinished

MILLER'S TOWER IS PURE ENCHANTMENT. Here is a Scottish tower house with all the trimmings – stepped gables, stone dormers, 'rolling pin' mouldings to windows – yet steeped in domesticity, a house you could settle into the very day you arrive.

Though it looks centuries old, it is one of the most remarkable of all examples of the Edwardian love affair with the past, associated with Lutyens in England and Sir Robert Lorimer in Scotland. Lorimer's client was a successful Glasgow stockbroker, John Augustus Holms, who wanted to build a romantic country seat to house his collections of furniture and textiles. In leisurely style, he laid out the formal gardens and outbuildings before he began the main house. Then catastrophe struck. Holms suffered massive losses and the house was left an empty shell and never lived in. The estate was sold after his death in 1938 to an eccentric Glasgow cinema owner A.E. Pickard (one of whose tricks was to pay very large bills in pennies) who lived here refusing entry to all. Finally losing interest he decided to sell the 150-acre estate for housing development but was confounded by the location of a large ammunitions factory a mile away at Dargavel, which made the land too dangerous to build on.

Instead, in 1984, the enlightened planning officer of Renfrew District Council, John Dunbar, formed a trust to take on Formakin and, with a grant from the National Heritage Memorial Fund, opened the estate to the public. But there was a steady annual deficit and once again the estate was faced with break-up, until Kit Martin stepped in with a scheme to restore Formakin's remarkable buildings for seventeen families to live in, drawn up with a local architect, Fiona Sinclair.

Intriguingly the Miller's Tower was the last to sell, but its purchaser was a landscape painter, Robert Innes, who had first studied architecture and saw at once how to make it an idyllic home for a young family. The tower stands on one side of the entrance arch to the stable and coach yard. The ground floor was used for washing down horses, above was the laundry and accommodation for the maids. The tower makes a delightful composition with the Miller's House on the other side of the entrance arch. On the roofs

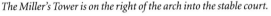

The Miller's Tower is on the right of the arch into the stable court.

Left: Lorimer's twin gate lodges flank the entrance.
Right: A shell-headed dormer window stands out against the grey stone.

of both are playful monkeys carved in stone (recalling the live monkeys that walk the parapets of Agra Fort) while the arch is carved with the date 1694 and the initials 'DL'.

The tower is built of stones individually chosen for their shape and patina – 'with black volcanic stone as well as several shades of sandstone'. Miller's Tower has its own well-protected garden surrounded by a beech hedge that keeps its leaves in winter. Three delightful buildings face onto the paved yard at the back. First is the cartshed, now adapted as a studio with folding glazed doors designed by Innes to let in abundant light and air. The sturdy stone piggeries, complete with diminutive arches, are used for storing wood while the bothy serves as a store (the further half serving as shed for the gardener who looks after the Formakin park and gardens).

The entrance hall opens into a large liveable kitchen with handsome exposed sandstone arches. Across the hall is a cosy dining room. A single flight of stairs beside the kitchen leads directly up to the main living room above, making it easy to call up and down to children. The way the stair rises into the room cleverly disguises the rather low ceiling. At the back Innes's office still contains the copper vat used by the maids. The upper floors are reached by the handsome spiral stone stair. As the lower steps are worn new wooden treads have been built, painted to look like marble. The large main bedroom on the second floor has windows on three sides and Innes demonstrates the clever Scottish device that allows the lower half of a sash window to open out on hinges making the glass much easier to clean. The top floor is a children's realm with bedrooms beneath the eaves and an ingenious light shaft providing good light to the windowless bathroom. Use is made of every single space so it is a very friendly house to live and also, thanks to modern insulation, very warm.

A well-paved path, lined with clipped hedges, leads from the garden into Formakin's extensive park, emerging just behind the gate lodges. The park is filled with large drifts of snowdrops, daffodils and bluebells and is shared by all the residents. But, Innes says, 'I feel as if it's my own private park – I almost never meet anyone else.'

FYVIE CASTLE   Turriff
Saved by public outcry complete with its contents, including the Raeburn portraits

WHO COULD HAVE FORETOLD at the start of 1982 that the three great castles bought or built by American millionaires at the turn of the 19th century would all be on the market within a matter of months? First came the news that Hever Castle in Kent, remodelled by William Waldorf Astor in 1903–9, was on offer with all its contents. Soon after, Andrew Carnegie's Skibo Castle in Sunderland, built in 1899–1903, was for sale. This was followed in September by the shock announcement of the sale of Fyvie Castle, spectacularly remodelled in the early 17th century and bought by Alexander Leith.

Of the three, Lord Leith (as he became) was the least known. The whole course of his life had been sparked by a chance meeting at a San Francisco ball. Margaret Forbes, his mother, was considered the belle of all Aberdeen, but she was widowed when Alexander was only 8 years old, and took her children to Berlin. Alexander was sent to sea. 'The navy,' his mother told him, 'is said to be the cheapest profession for one of extravagant tastes. On fifty pounds a year a midshipman can live handsomely.'

In 1870 Alexander's ship, HMS *Zealous*, the flagship of the Pacific Squadron, was posted to San Francisco at the outbreak of the Franco-Prussian War to await orders from the Admiralty. There he met the pretty Miss Louise January, visiting from St Louis with her parents. It was love at first sight. They married in Paris the next year. Alexander left the Navy to work with the Missouri Furnace Company in St Louis. When one of their companies was in difficulty, he was appointed receiver. In fifteen years he rebuilt it as an immensely successful corporation, moving to Chicago and then New York. In 1901 with J. Pierpont Morgan he was one of the prime movers in the creation of the United States Steel Corporation.

The great entrance tower of Fyvie has been ranked as 'the crowning achievement of Scottish Baronial architecture'. It is the one great house in Scotland to rival the extravagance of prodigy houses like Audley End or Wollaton south of the border though it is wholly Scottish in character with hardly a trace of Renaissance influence. The enrichment is concentrated on the skyline. Angle turrets have conical hats. Dormer windows burst through the parapets. Finials take the form of fearsome diminutive warriors.

The great south and west ranges are the work of Alexander Seton, who was created Earl of Dumfermline in 1606. According to a family history, he was 'a great humanist in prose and poetrie … well versed in the mathematick, and had great skill in architecture and herauldrie'. Seton was remodelling an earlier castle dating from 1400.

Fyvie was acquired by the Gordons in 1733 and in the 1770s General Gordon added the Gordon tower, matching the early 17th-century work. In the 19th century Fyvie fell into disrepair, and in 1889 Leith received the news that the estate was for sale for £175,000: he immediately bought it (by coincidence, this was the asking price for the house and five acres in 1982). He called in the architect John Bryce, the nephew of David Bryce, the great apostle of the Scottish Baronial revival. John Bryce added a new tower at the north end of the west range with large oriel windows at the upper levels.

Internally the main surviving feature of the 1600 castle is the imposing wheel stair with sixty-three steps rising the full height of the house and broad enough for young Gordons to ride their hunters up for a wager. At the top an inscription carved in oak is dated 1603. John Bryce followed the 17th-century practice of placing the principal rooms on the upper floor with a handsome barrel-vaulted gallery in the new wing.

When Leith bought Fyvie, a number of fine paintings had come with the castle, including a fine Pompeo Batoni of General Gordon in Highland dress. Leith was an exceptionally discerning collector. He acquired some fifty-five paintings from Agnews in London including several Raeburns and paintings by Gainsborough, Lawrence, Linnell, Millais, Opie Reynolds, Romney and Wilkie.

Such was the public concern when Fyvie was put up for sale that Sir Andrew Forbes-Leith agreed to postpone the auction for six months, giving the National Trust for Scotland six months to find a means of keeping the house intact. Within a year the castle and its contents had been saved for the nation with the help of a substantial sum from the National Heritage Memorial Fund.

The grand baronial entrance front was remodelled c.1600 with warrior statues as finials.

HOUSE OF GRAY   Dundee
Built in 1716 and attributed to the architect Alexander McGill

ONE OF THE PRETTIEST GEORGIAN COUNTRY houses in Scotland, the special charm of the House of Gray lies in its romantic silhouette with four delightful bell-topped towers containing beautiful stone spiral stairs. With its raised centre and neat matching wings, it is French chateau and Palladian villa all in one.

Today its white facades glow in the sun, unimaginably different from the sight that greeted me twenty-five years ago. Then the house had not been lived in since 1938. The slates had been torn from the roof. Floors and ceilings had disappeared. The gutters had gone and rain was cascading down the stone facades, washing away the fine carved detail of swags and coats of arms. Yet inside 18th-century wood panelling miraculously clung to the walls, with the added flourish of baroque giant pillars on either side of the main fireplace.

Now the House of Gray has an immaculate new roof in West Highland slate with pretty scallop-edged leadwork over the corners of the towers. Every window has been renewed in oak with chunky early-Georgian glazing bars and spun glass.

Though little more than a mile from the edge of Dundee, the setting is remarkably unspoilt with a view from the bedroom windows across the grand expanse of the Firth of Tay to the rolling hills beyond. Thanks to the local farmer who owns the land all around (in Scotland known as 'the policies'), the landscape remains undisturbed, even though only 2.7 acres come with the property. The mansion stands with a splendid sense of geometric precision at the centre of a large rectangular block of farmland, partly edged by low stone walls and bisected by a grand avenue that runs past the house to the farm beyond and on again.

Inside this grand sweep of open farmland, the house is secluded by small sections of park to the north and south, which any new owner will clearly hope to acquire in due course. A good number of the 'uncommonly large trees' noted in a late 19th-

The house and balancing wings are bright white after the stonework was re-harled.

century description survive, including an oak of enormous girth behind the house.

The Grays came from Normandy at the time of the Conquest. James II of Scotland created Sir Andrew Gray the 1st Lord Gray in the 1430s. The 2nd Lord Gray built Castle Huntly, the 3rd built Broughty Castle. The House of Gray, built in 1716, is said to be the work of the 12th Lord Gray and the architect of the house was almost certainly Alexander McGill. McGill was associated with two other houses with distinctive bell-topped towers, the original Mount Stuart on the Isle of Bute, and the House of Nairne, which was demolished in the 1860s.

The south-facing entrance front also looks fresh and clean after repainting and re-roofing.

In 1822 the Grays moved to a magnificent new seat in gothic style, Kinfauns Castle by Sir Robert Smirke. The House of Gray became a dower house and was later let to tenants. Acquired by the Ogilvy family in the early 20th century, it was briefly used for evacuee children in 1940 and after the war was bought by the Smedley family, who used in for storing fruit for their canning business.

The house was bought by a group of investors in about 1995. One of them, Conrad Aldridge, says, 'We saw it in a national newspaper article saying there were 300 houses like this in Scotland in need of honest developers to restore them.' Unfortunately, one of the previous developer-owners had stripped all the panelling out of the main rooms and sold it. When LASSCO, the London Architectural Salvage and Supply Company, learned that it had been illegally removed, they readily agreed to return it.

Mr Aldridge and his partners initially drew up plans to restore the House of Gray as a country-house hotel. James Simpson, the architect in charge of the work, said, 'The house was built of a sandstone which looks very good when new but when wet sheds successive layers of its surface.' He found an early 19th-century painting suggesting the house was once covered in a coat of white lime plaster and gave it a new coat of lime plaster painted over with limewash. On top of this, Mr Aldridge has added a coat of paint to make the house still brighter.

The beauty of the House of Gray is that both north and south facades are equally grand compositions. The eastern wing is suitable for use as a self-contained cottage, while the main room in the west wing begs to become a large sunny kitchen. The rooms on the main floor are arranged as an enfilade with all the doors in line. With the 18th-century panelling put back, they would make a wonderful series of reception rooms.

As well as repairing the main house, Mr Aldridge and his colleagues rebuilt the lodge with an indoor swimming pool, the idea being that it could be used as a spa for the hotel. To stop any further building on the site, Historic Scotland should register the whole of the original policies as a protected landscape, also ensuring that Dundee cannot creep an inch further into this remarkable landscape.

GREYWALLS   Gullane
Lutyens house of 1901 extended by Sir Robert Lorimer

FEW, IF ANY, LUTYENS COUNTRY HOUSES still survive in the hands of the families that built them. Giles Weaver, who now owns Greywalls, is the third generation of his family to live here. The house was designed as a holiday home for the Hon. Alfred Lyttleton, sportsman, statesman and valued friend of Lutyens until his death in 1913. Lyttleton was the first man to play both cricket and football for England. As a keen golfer, he insisted his house should be built 'within a mashie niblick shot of the eighteenth green at Muirfield'.

Completed in 1901, the house had been under discussion since 1896 when it was to be called High Walls and took the form of a lofty Norman keep with towers at the corners. Lutyens changed tack, acknowledging 'Mrs Lyttleton can't have a fortress and large windows too', and turned, as he often did, to the local vernacular, building a low spreading house of warm honey-coloured stone from the local Rattlebags Quarry with pantiles from Holland (some say Denmark).

In 1905 Greywalls was bought by William James, who commissioned Lutyens to add the gate lodges in 1908 and then asked Sir Robert Lorimer to build a 'Nursery' wing to the west in 1911. The lodges served as footmens' bothies – partitioned to sleep eight manservants in each. This might seem excessive but Lord Derby, who rented the house after the First World War, would have a footman stationed behind every chair at dinner.

During the Second World War, Greywalls was requisitioned as accommodation for fighter pilots at nearby Drem airfield. In 1948 Colonel Weaver and his family restored Greywalls as one of the first country house hotels in the British Isles. Giles Weaver took over in 1977 and his wife Roz commissioned Laura McKenzie to replant the gardens in Jekyll style.

Greywalls overlooks the championship golf course at Muirhead, and offers twenty-three bedrooms, croquet, grass and hard tennis courts, with a panelled library and menus that are strong on local produce.

Lutyens's distinctive curved entrance front has a pair of matching chimneys.

GRIBLOCH
Stirling
Designed by Basil Spence for the Glasgow steel magnate John Colville in 1938

GRIBLOCH IS ONE OF THE MOST STYLISH and comfortable of 1930s houses. The house was built for the Scottish steel magnate John Colville and his Californian wife Helen in 1938–9 and was bought from the Colville family by James MacGregor in 1984.

MacGregor's daughter, Caroline, wrote a remarkable history of the house in 1994, using original letters for research and showing how the Colvilles took ideas from articles in American magazines such as *House Beautiful*, which were all preserved in the library. The house commands a magnificent panorama of the Grampians and was built on a virgin site where Colville picnicked as a boy.

In photographs, Gribloch can look quite modest, but the first glimpse of the long white front from the road below sets the adrenalin racing. The house is approached up a steep, curving drive (Mr Colville complained to Rolls-Royce that his car wouldn't take it in third gear) and delivers visitors onto a manicured gravel sweep perched on the crest of a hill and surrounded by the shortest of mossy grass.

Colville gave his architect, the young Basil Spence (later the architect of Coventry Cathedral), firm instructions about combining both 'the view and the sun' in all the main rooms. Once the front door is opened you look straight out of the house on the other side, through a giant oriel window to a swimming pool immediately beyond. When the sun bursts through the clouds the whole staircase, painted a luminous powder blue, is filled with rippling reflections.

Cascading down across the window is a flying staircase that might have been designed for Ginger Rogers, in which, amazingly, the great Sir Nikolaus Pevsner had a hand. Mr Spence rose to his brief in the conception of the house but unfortunately became so busy with clients that he called in Perry Duncan, an American architect, to move the plans forward.

The house was built on an unusual Y-plan with a gently convex entrance front.

He handed the interior decoration over to John Hill, who responded perfectly to the Colvilles' desire for elegant understatement, achieving impact by brilliant use of fresh, mainly pale colours and superb decorative details. The hall has a wonderfully original shell-and-rope cornice and bold matching rope mouldings around the doors and archways. His carpet, in shades of mulberry, blue, white and beige, was rewoven to the original design in Donegal and still lay on the floor.

The living room has wrap-around windows with the original bullion-fringed pelmet. In 1998 the silk satin curtains in shades of oyster, purple and turquoise were neatly folded away in the linen-room cupboards. Restored, they would have made the room as smart as the penthouse in Claridge's.

Mr Colville's desk in Australian walnut remained, designed by Betty Joel with solid wood drawers that clicked shut on ball bearings. Beside the fire was a shining chrome coal box. Or was it stainless steel? 'Bright metal,' said Mr MacGregor diplomatically.

The dining-room doors are veneered in mahogany with *guilloche* mouldings copied from the Colvilles' sideboard. The door handles are cut glass, the top end of a hierarchy that descends through chromium plate to Bakelite in the servants' rooms. Even the original glass panels survive in some places – the glass allowed the wall paint beneath to show through, making the switches all but invisible.

The Colvilles had a 1,400-acre sporting estate and so the house haa its own gun room and adjoining cloakroom with cupboards containing hot pipes on which to hang clothes to dry.

Upstairs, the master bedroom haa a handsome deep fireplace entirely faced in lustrous copper, with massive copper firedogs and copper pelmet rings gathering the curtains over the windows.

In a letter written in 1937, Spence talked of designing a house 'of the 16-bedroom variety'. In fact, there are twelve on his plan, including servants' bedrooms and the night nursery. Each pair of main bedrooms shared a bathroom and Colville had special electric locks installed that close both doors at the push of a button. The bedrooms are named after mountains that fill the views from the windows. There are serpentine-headed twin beds, matching dressing table and stool, mirror-fronted fireplace and mirrored waste-paper basket.

The house is not affected by the wind – Mr MacGregor pointed out that the trees around the house are not bent or bowed like some in the valley below. Fast-moving clouds mean the sun is constantly breaking through, illuminating distant hills and the valley below. Sunsets are spectacular, and if there is mist, it often hovers on the valley floor, turning it into a vast loch.

Gribloch has three self-contained cottages – a gate lodge and staff houses on either side of a capacious thirteen-car garage made out in a half-circle like a Victorian steam engine shed, complete with inspection pit. There is also a sandstone walled garden and a peach house complete with peaches, nectarines and camellias. Scented azaleas and huge rhododendrons abound.

Beside the swimming pool is a terracotta seal balancing a revolving copper ball on its nose. This needed attention, but the Tivoli-style wall of water jets spurting across the pool still worked at the press of a button.

INVERLOCHY CASTLE   Fort William
Victorian baronial house which is now the last word in pampering

'I NEVER SAW A LOVELIER OR MORE ROMANTIC SPOT,' Queen Victoria recorded in her journal when she stayed at Inverlochy Castle in 1873. The castle stands in a breathtaking position reflected in the still waters of Loch Na Marag near Fort William with purple mountains rising behind. It is a bravura example of hotel use, bringing style and sparkle to a house described (a little harshly) in *The Buildings of Scotland* as a 'large but not very exciting castellated-manorial house built of bull-nosed rubble'.

The special interest for me was that early in the Second World War the castle housed the Polish Independent Company. By July 1940 remnants of the Polish Army were assembled and reorganised in the Glasgow area as the 1st Polish Army Corps. Their duties included building coastal defences along the coast between Fife and Angus. Inverlochy Castle was made available to the Poles for Special Forces training.

The castle was built in two stages for the 3rd Lord Abinger, first in 1863 to a design by the London architect Robert Hesketh (his is the *porte cochère* topped by carved angels, the Abinger supporters) and extended in 1889–92 by the accomplished J. MacVicar Anderson.

The interiors now dazzle with a palette of brilliant pinks and yellows, with silk upholstered chairs in the drawing room and colourful fabrics in the seventeen bedrooms – armchairs, curtains, and four-poster beds and bedspreads. Today Inverlochy offers pampering and superb food. Twenty or thirty years ago institutional use often seemed the only solution for such houses. Now the gardens are immaculately maintained and visitors arrive on transcontinental flights.

Inverlochy is gloriously reflected in the loch, with heather-clad mountains rising behind.

KEITH HALL   Inverurie
16th-century tower house grandly remodelled in the 1680s

PERMISSION HAD BEEN GRANTED TO DEMOLISH a substantial part of Keith Hall when the Earl of Kintore, hoping to find a less radical way of making his crumbling mansion more manageable, arrived at Cullen House. He had come to view Kit Martin's rescue of the vast mansion and he brought with him a copy of the letter Charles II had written from Cullen to his ancestor John Keith, the 1st Earl, thanking him for his courage in rescuing the Scottish royal regalia at the siege of Dunottar Castle in 1651.

At the Restoration Charles II created Keith Knight Mareschal and in 1662 Keith married an heiress, Margaret, daughter of the Earl of Haddington, who brought him a £10,000 dowry. The following year he bought Caskieben, a 16th-century Z-plan tower house that remains the core of Keith Hall. However it was the high office that he attained towards the end of his life, and the Earldom of Kintore which he received in 1677, that prompted him to remodel the house on a grand scale renaming it Keith Hall. All this is commemorated in a grand armorial display above the front door with an earl's coronet placed above his initials joined with his wife's, flanked by the thistles of Scotland proclaiming his gratitude to his king.

The house stands in glorious seclusion set in an extensive park.

The Earl added an imposing new south range to the old house with ogee-capped corner towers linked by a lower balustraded range. Further remodelling was carried out for his descendants by a series of leading architects including William Adam, John Paterson, John Smith, David Bryce and Sidney Mitchell. Finally the 10th Earl, succeeding in 1930, married Helena, Duchess of Marlborough, formerly Miss Zimmerman of Cincinnati, and reworked the interior, introducing panelling and fine 18th-century fireplaces.

When Kit Martin bought the house in 1984, Lord Inverurie, the son of the 10th Earl, moved to a comfortable house in the handsome Regency stables by John Smith, allowing Martin to create eight apartments that were approached through the main entrance hall and stairs. The former estate offices were divided into four cottages with their own entrances from the north and the original tower house became two further houses. All this reflects Kit Martin's philosophy of creating a range of different sized houses in each property he tackles, each with a distinct character. To protect the setting of the house, covenants were granted over the parkland that immediately surrounds it and a garden management company run by the residents looks after the grounds. Upon completion of the conversion, all the apartments sold quickly, despite a slump in Aberdonian house prices, and Keith's future, which looked so bleak, is now secure.

LOCHTON HOUSE — Abernyte
Regency country villa with an Edinburgh-like sophistication

EARLY 19TH-CENTURY CLASSICAL HOUSES in Scotland are often exquisitely planned and built. Lochton House is an example of this sophistication. Though quite modest as a composition, it is beautifully faced in pinkish stone and sits in attractive grounds. It was built for the Kinnear family but let on a lease when a new house, Lochton Castle, was constructed on the estate half a mile away. This was burnt in 1920 and rebuilt in a reduced form. By this time Lochton House was known as Old Lochton and descended into a rather sad state. No longer. When the house came on the market in 2006, it was very smartly decorated.

The great feature of the interior is the circular domed staircase hall, with a flight of cantilevered stone steps rising in an unbroken sweep to the first floor. Circular spaces can, of course, create awkward corners in rectangular plans. Here the problem is deftly minimised by the apsed ends of the drawing room and sitting room on either side of the entrance hall, which neatly abut the curving walls of the stair hall. The entrance hall has elegant cross-vaults springing from wall pillars, with stone floor and inner fanlight.

All this is very accomplished and suggests an architect of considerable skill. The house has been attributed to James Black, the town architect of Dundee, but it may be the work of an Edinburgh architect where numerous Regency town houses were planned with similar aplomb. The broad glazed fanlight over the front door has a town house look. Another candidate is William Macdonald Mackenzie of Perth who, according to his obituary in *The Builder*, designed 'forty to fifty churches', most of

Neoclassical reserve shows in the subtle advances of the centre and ends and the gentle rise in the parapet.

which wait to be identified. All the joinery is of exceptional quality, and it is not only the six-panel pine doors that are polished rather than painted but also the sash windows, shutters and window reveals.

As in many compact Palladian villas, good use is made of the basement, which is effectively a full ground floor with lower ceilings and therefore easily kept warm in winter. The large kitchen looks out in two directions over the gardens. The circular walls supporting the staircase hall above serve as a wine cellar.

MANDERSTON HOUSE   Duns
The swansong of the great Classical country house, remodelled in 1901–5

EDWARDIAN COUNTRY HOUSES EXUDE suave opulence. The interiors at Luton Hoo are by Mewès & Davis, architects of the London Ritz. Manderston was built to emulate Robert Adam's glorious interiors at Kedleston, actually excelling them in lavish display. Sir James Miller, who inherited Manderston in 1887, had proposed to his future wife, the Hon Eveline Curzon, at Kedleston and the fireplace in the hall is an almost exact copy of that in the hall of the great Curzon seat in Derbyshire.

Miller had inherited a house with bombastic French Renaissance roofs. He commissioned John Kinross, an architect of great sophistication and finesse, to remodel the house in a restrained but graceful Classical manner. Kinross disguised the roofs with an elegant balustrade capped by urns and added a bachelors' wing (essential for large house parties) with its own marble entrance hall with glass-fronted gun cabinets.

The warm, evenly coloured Swinton sandstone continues round the house to the late 18th-century garden front enlivened by rounded bows and overlooking richly planted *parterres* on impressively long terraces.

Work on the house was completed in 1905 at the prodigious cost of £221,000. Though the portico has only four steps, a further touch of grandeur is added by the short semi-circular flight of steps progressing from the oval vestibule to the columned hall. The main reception rooms form a grand suite for entertaining, each opening into the next and returning to the hall with enticing vistas along marble floored corridors. The oval morning room leads to the anteroom, drawing room, ballroom and library. The Louis XVI decoration is probably by Charles Mellier & Co, who fitted out Miller's London house in Grosvenor Square. The delicate Adamesque ceiling in the ballroom is based on that in the dining room at Kedleston. The climax of the tour is the top-lit Silver Staircase, rivalling and even excelling the silver- and gold-plated staircase at Sundridge Park in Kent.

The 109 rooms at Manderston are put to good use. Today you can arrange to have lunch in the dining room, complete with butler in attendance, sleep in a choice of nine comfortable bedrooms, enjoy full Scottish breakfast, tea and dinner. Sir James's descendant Lord Palmer, has taken on the challenge of opening and running this vast pile – well before Edwardian houses had become fashionable – with immense energy and verve, making it an enormously enjoyable place to visit. The house also starred in the Channel 4 series, *The Edwardian Country House.*

The Edwardian bachelors' wing stands beyond the long, late 18th-century garden front.

MAVISBANK HOUSE   Loanhead
Built in 1723–7 for Sir John Clerk to the designs of William Adam

THE BURNT-OUT SHELL OF WILLIAM ADAM'S Mavisbank, surrounded by abandoned cars and caravans, was one of the most poignant images in the V&A exhibition *The Destruction of the Country House* in 1974. Mavisbank's owner, Archie Stevenson, was a notoriously difficult man and when John Harris and I visited in 1979. Mr Stevenson appeared, red with rage. John spun the line that he was an antique dealer from Stockport and that he had a picture of the house and wanted to see it. Mr Stevenson's rage subsided and we were able to pick our way through the debris to admire the shell.

Adam's design was a Palladian villa with all the trimmings. A long flight of steps led up to the front door. The carved foliage in the pediment was still pristine but the balusters in the parapet were falling down and only two shapely finials remained. The lintels over the windows were almost all fractured or approaching collapse. Year after year SAVE had pressed for action. Midlothian District Council, to its credit, initiated a series of legal actions forcing the clearance of the cars and the caravans.

Mavisbank stood above a coal mine and its plight was complicated by subsidence problems. Engineers decided the shell was stable, but on March 26, 1987 the district council declared it dangerous and hired contractors to begin demolition in two days. The courts were the only hope and, at the last minute, the Lothian Buildings Preservation Trust, backed by £500 from SAVE, won an order staying demolition.

Finally, in 1991, Ian Lang, the Secretary of State for Scotland, initiated compulsory purchase proceedings. By this time the house had been bequeathed to three untraceable people living in America but purchase went ahead and the shell was stabilised. A Mavisbank Trust was set up in 2003 but the question remains – when will the house be rescued as others in this book have been?

Exquisite even in decay – the house before restoration began.

MELVILLE CASTLE   Lasswade
Built in 1786–91 to the designs of James Playfair for the 1st Viscount Melville

IN THE SUMMER OF 1992 I DROVE TO Melville Castle to find a sign announcing 'Major development opportunity'. The particulars contained an artist's impression of a proposed six-storey fifty-bedroom extension in the form of a Scottish tower house, larger than the castle itself. I wrote attacking the proposal in *The Times*, highlighting the one piece of good news – that Midlothian Council had served a repairs order.

The castle was built in 1786–91 for Henry Dundas, later created Viscount Melville. He held high office for over twenty years, acting as virtual minister for Scotland and then taking responsibility for the war with revolutionary France. He acquired the estate through his marriage to a 14-year-old heiress, Elizabeth, daughter of Sir David Rannie, who had built up a vast fortune through the East India Company. Dundas commissioned the talented James Playfair to build him a castle-style house – a toy fort with round turrets at the corners and lower wings. The main rooms were lit by large tripartite sash windows with pointed windows in the turrets. The interior showed off Playfair's considerable talents for designing elegant neoclassical interiors in a Soanian manner. However, Dundas's preoccupation with state affairs led him to lose his wife's fortune in the crash of the Ayrshire Bank, after which she left him.

Both George IV and Queen Victoria visited the castle but after the Seccond World War the 9th Lord Melville moved to a smaller house and leased the castle. After a spell as an hotel, it was left suffering badly from dry rot. In 1993, with floors collapsing and the roof open to the rain, the castle was acquired by the Hay Trust, which has painstakingly restored it. It reopened as a four-star hotel in June 2003, smartly decorated and furnished, with luxurious bedrooms and no ugly additions. The setting, just eight miles from the centre of Edinburgh, is magical, secluded in a hidden wooded valley.

The miserable state of the castle in 1992 before the Hay Trust began the work of rescue.

NEWHAILES   Musselburgh
Designed by the leading Edinburgh architect for himself in 1686

RARELY HAS THE PHILOSOPHY of 'conserve as found' been carried through with such ardour as by the National Trust for Scotland at Newhailes, the early 18th century house just east of Edinburgh opened to the public in 2002. Designed in the 1680s by the architect James Smith, now recognised as the 17th-century pioneer of 18th-century Palladianism, the house was first embellished and then lovingly preserved by generations of the Dalrymple family.

The previous curator of the National Trust, the engaging David Learmont, liked the interiors of their houses to look smart and attractive. Newhailes was always going to be different. The point of saving the house was that it was a time capsule, showing the decorative art of the first half of the 18th century 'untouched by the hand of the "restorer"', as *Country Life* put it as early as 1917.

The thrill for a new generation of conservators and curators, led by Ian Gow, was to find so much interior detail – upholstery, wallpapers and fabrics – intact. Gow said: 'Newhailes is all about surface textures. There was no way we were going to make the interior look like a million dollars. I would not let the conservators take the wallpaper off for remounting – I wanted the original linings left. There is a tapestry still hung on 1730s tacks – I was not going to sacrifice these to the goddess of Velcro.'

The most impressive room is the magnificent library completed in 1720 and described by Samuel Johnson as 'the most learned room in Europe'. The discoveries continue in the adjoining porcelain cabinet where dozens of exquisite Japanese, Chinese and Meissen pots are arranged on 18th-century ornamental brackets.

Gow observed that 'so many country houses have boring bedrooms'. At Newhailes, no Dalrymple could sleep except in a miniature version of a Classical temple. It is as if all the architectural motifs they omitted from the outside of the house were brought inside where they could be seen better – fluted pilasters, pediments, full entablatures.

The library wing on the right was added c.1720 for Sir David Dalrymple and matched twenty years later.

On the outside of the house I found the policy of doing 'as much as is necessary, as little as possible' becoming questionable and perhaps a justification for avoiding decisions that should be taken. External elements are subject to nature and the weather and cannot be frozen in the same way as an interior. More than that, I felt that the beauty of the place was not well served by preserving it at the bottom of the cycle of decay.

The garden to the north of the house, looking towards the Firth of Forth, was an expanse of neglected grass full of flattened molehills, while the parkland or 'policies' beyond was choked with weeds, without a grazing animal in sight. Twee stainless-steel open books told the visitor what he or she might have seen 250 years ago when statues and sphinxes enlivened the lawns. With the National Lottery supporting the project, a scholarly garden restoration was a possibility and I wanted to see it. The evidence was there for a restoration or reconstruction of features that would add greatly to a visit – ponds, an unusual ladies' walk, a shell grotto and cascade.

Twin flights of steps lead to the main entrance. The ironwork has been preserved in its decayed state, announcing the time capsule within.

The exterior of the house is harled – rendered – with channelling to suggest masonry. For two centuries, at least, it must have received a regular coat of limewash, giving it a warm buff stone colour. In 2003 much of the render had discoloured to an ugly grey or even black splotches. This was far from the romantic faded and peeling ochre of Rome palaces. Missing patches have been replaced, with channelling to match the original, but this only increases the piebald effect. A new coat of limewash was urgently needed.

The flat ends of the central gable or pediment also looked weak; they were designed for urns to add a flourish to the silhouette. Evidence could surely be found to provide appropriate replacements. There was one crowning the centre of the gable which, if put back, would conceal an attic chimney that was clearly heightened at a later date and now looks awkward, even silly. The once-graceful perron of steps ascending to the front door had been frozen at the moment of most extreme neglect with carefully conserved blistered black paint and naked rust.

Angrily I wrote in *The Times* that 'sensitive, practical conservation requires individual decisions to be based on both needs and appearances. All those who look after historic buildings have to make aesthetic decisions – and they should not use philosophy or science as a means of ducking them.'

PITMAIN LODGE

Kingussie

Stylish modern hunting lodge with breathtaking views

HIGHLAND SHOOTING AND STALKING lodges may appear to be architecturally modest but they are often intriguing and unusual buildings with interiors of great charm and indeed style. Pitmain Lodge is near Kingussie, a planned village laid out by the Duke of Gordon in 1799. The old castle on the opposite bank of the Spey at Ruthven had been burnt down in 1689 during the Jacobite rising and Ruthven barracks had been on its site. There was a redcoat watchpost on top of the highest hill at Pitmain.

The original lodge at Pitmain was built by an industrialist, James Douglas Fletcher ,in the late 19th century for deer- and grouse-shooting. This was demolished after being used as a hospital during the Second World War, reportedly because many of the structural timbers had been cut up as firewood. The present lodge was built in 1983 with further additions twelve years later. It is sheltered by mature woodland behind with a breathtaking view down to Loch Gyrack. The estate offers grouse-shooting and roe-stalking and is designed to cater for house parties of up to sixteen.

There are two entrance halls in the two wings, one opening into a large drawing room with two bay windows, the other designed as a sporting entrance with a handsome stone fireplace and a stair ascending to a first-floor gallery. The walls are hung in the best Highlands manner with pairs of antlers hung at alternating centres to create a snaking pattern up the walls. The two halls are connected by a library with bookcases cleverly concealing the cloakroom. Pitmain Lodge comes with a well-equipped laundry and large linen cupboard – essential on wet days – with eight bedrooms on the two upper floors. It may be in rugged country but the comfort rivals the most chic modern skiing chalet.

Like many Highlands hunting lodges, Pitmain has few architectural pretensions.

RAMSAY GARDEN — Edinburgh

Apartments designed by S. Henbest Capper in 1892 and extended in 1893–4

RAMSAY GARDEN IS HALF SCOTTISH BARONIAL, half English country cottage, with an extraordinary silhouette of pyramid and bell-topped turrets, gables and soaring chimneys. Red half-timbering contrasts with the white harling and rich local sandstone. It is the most eye-catching group of buildings on the heights beside the castle and the creation of Sir Patrick Geddes, whose ideas on town planning were taken up all over the world. He believed architects and planners should study local character, writing that 'each place has a true personality … a personality too much asleep it may be, but which it is the task of the planner, as master-artist, to awaken'.

Geddes initially conceived Ramsay Garden as a hall of residence (with rooms for forty-five students) and cooperative block of twenty-three apartments. In 1894 his new residents produced a Christmas book enthusing about the friendliness between neighbours, the constant exchange of news, 'corporate courtesies and private feasts', a way of life that still exists in the buildings today.

Geddes purchased the property in 1890 and spent the next few years extending and embellishing the cluster of houses to emphasise their clifftop position. His aim was nothing less than to attract back the professional and middle classes who had deserted to Edinburgh's elegant New Town a hundred years before. From the start, it was a place where people would live close to their work and move around the city on foot.

In the late 1990s the Burrell Company created a group of new apartments in a section of Ramsay Garden previously used by a bank as a training centre. On the landings, Burrell has retained the Arts and Crafts plasterwork on the lower walls emblazoned with crests – thistles, doves and lamps of wisdom.

The views are captivating, across the valley to Princes Street and beyond over the rooftops to the Firth of Forth and the mountains of Fife. Residents all have access to the shared garden beneath the houses – consisting of a level stretch of lawn protected by a thick bank of shrubs.

The breathtakingly picturesque composition of gables and bay windows look out from the clifftop.

SETON HOUSE — Prestonpans

Designed by Robert Adam for the lawyer Alexander Mackenzie in 1790

SETON HOUSE IS ONE OF THE FINEST Robert Adam castle-style houses. Adam is, of course, famous above all for his fabulous interiors, full of dazzling colour and delicate ornament, but his other life longlove affair was with the castle. Adam loved both the perfect symmetry of Classicism and the rugged unpredictability of the Picturesque. At Seton House he provided both. Seton, near Edinburgh, was the more romantic, as like Adam's Culzean Castle, now belonging to the National Trust for Scotland, it was a castle set against the backdrop of the sea.

According to Alistair Rowan, author of a book on Adam's castles, Seton was built for a client in his early twenties. This was a dashing young Lieutenant-Colonel in the 21st Dragoons, Alexander Mackenzie, for whom Adam provided one of the most delightful of all sham castles – the kind of building that the Victorians were to abhor as 'frivolous'. Yet Seton is a true *jeu d'esprit* – an enchanted castle as perfectly symmetrical as a villa by Palladio with matching wings that contained both stables and kitchens.

The wings are perfect *beau-geste* forts in themselves with square corner turrets and flat parapets. The house in the centre is fancier, with both square and rounded turrets and the usual Adam flourish of a central round tower on the garden side in place of a Georgian bow. What incensed the Victorians even more was that Adam used standard sash-windows, both square- and round- headed, and not true pointed arches. Adam nonetheless played with slits and even cross slits, all part of what some had called the 'true rust of the barons' wars'.

The courtyard in front of the house, complete with gravel turning circle, is entered through an archway and beautifully secluded – like the courtyard of a grand

The main building is flanked by matching castle-style wings with square corner towers.

aristocratic mansion in Paris. By contrast, the front door, with a vast lunette, is more like an opulent Adam house in Edinburgh's Charlotte Square.

Sadly, the setting is part beauty, part beast. The new A1 trunk road has been pushed out of hearing but a stretch of dual carriageway runs in front of the house, so when out-of-doors you hear traffic. A threat of open-cast coal mining to the south has been resisted, but on the shore of the Firth of Forth to the north there is a power station on one side and a caravan park on the other, masked by trees but too close for real comfort. The town of Port Seton on the shore looks unlikely to spread closer to the house but it is critical that the glimpse of the sea from the end of the long stretch of garden is never interrupted by development.

Adam, in his drawings of ruins, as well as his designs for castles, loved nothing more than an approach across a bridge over a ravine. Here he achieved the effect in a surprising way, by preserving one range of the ruined palace of Seton that runs over a gulley behind the house. Adam capped the ancient walls to create the effect of a bridge with grass beneath the feet where you can lean over a low wall to admire the view.

The banks are enshrouded in cascading vegetation – this is a marvellous site for a wild garden. The romance of the place is further heightened by the remains of a collegiate church that stands amid manicured lawns to the east of the house, in the care of Historic Scotland. Like a Romanesque church in southern Burgundy, it is empty of furniture and completely serene – just bare stone walls, floors and vaults, inset with handsome family monuments.

The stone from the old Renaissance palace of the Setons was plundered for the new house. Its availability explains the speed at which Adam built. The building contract is dated November 12, 1789, and Adam dined with his client in the completed house on June 11, 1791.

Adam's castles tend to be much plainer inside than his grand town and country houses. This is no exception. Mackenzie died aged 29 and for much of its 200-year history the house has been tenanted. As a result, the house remains remarkably untouched – retaining all its rooms of unusual shape. The entrance hall has a cornice with Mackenzie stag heads in place of the more usual Roman ox skulls. In the 1950s the house was leased to the director of the National Trust for Scotland, who put in curious rococo ornament – it was 'queerly embellished', says *The Buildings of Scotland*. Tenants don't spend money on improvements and most new purchasers would therefore want to install new plumbing, wiring, kitchens and bathrooms.

In 2004, the house needed fresh bright colours and perhaps quite simple bold furnishing. Instead of fancy draped curtains, a modern minimalist approach might be more sympathetic, closing the shutters at night and providing a splash of luxury with colourful paintings or fabrics on sofas and chairs. There are four floors of accommodation, with cosier, low ceilings on the top floor and the basement on the garden side.

There is much exploring to be done – turret stairs in the stables that no one appears to have climbed for years, as well as the original wooden stalls for the horses and tack room with fireplace.

TAYMOUTH CASTLE · Aberfeldy

Huge castle-style house built for the 1st and 2nd Marquesses of Breadalbane c.1810–42

IT SEEMS INCREDIBLE TODAY THAT a castle the size of Taymouth should be built during a major war, the Napoleonic wars no less, in 1806–10. Nor was it the only one, for Loudoun Castle and Stobo Castle were rising on an almost equally grand scale at the same time. All three were designed by the architect Archibald Elliot, working here with his brother James. Loudoun and Taymouth were both built for branches of the Campbell family and modelled on, and intended to eclipse, the great Campbell seat at Inveraray. Taymouth, like Inveraray, is symmetrically designed but with a tower intended to rival Fonthill Abbey.

The castle stands in a majestic position at the top of Loch Tay. It was built for the 4th Earl (and 1st Marquess) of Breadalbane and his son, who represented the senior cadet branch of Clan Campbell after the Dukes of Argyll at Inveraray. Taymouth's tower was complete in 1807 but it was two years before the Earl decided to commission the London plasterer and sculptor Francesco Bernasconi to work on its interior. One stage is piled on another, first an immensely grand stair, then a lofty arcaded gallery, next a tier of filigree blind arcading, followed by a double-height clerestory capped by a fan vault that looks like the star bursts in a firework display.

The Breadalbane estates were broken up shortly after the First World War and the castle eventually sold to become a hotel. Taken over as a convalescent home in the Second World War it later briefly became a school. Recently, one developer after another has put forward ambitious schemes for restoring the long-empty and decaying castle. One attraction is the golf course in the grounds of the castle. The latest plans are for an hotel, promoted as six stars not five, scheduled to open in spring 2008 but already the subject of delays and controversy. When its doors reopen, all Scotland will throng there.

The castle stands beside a well-known golf course but its sheer size had defeated most rescue proposals.

THIRLESTANE CASTLE   Lauder

Grand Scottish baronial architecture built for the Earls and Dukes of Lauderdale

THIRLESTANE IS A SPECTACULAR EXAMPLE OF Scottish Baronial dating principally from the 1590s, the 1670s and the early 1840s. There was a motte-and-bailey castle here in the 12th century, followed by an artillery fort of Italian design erected by the English in 1548 but dismantled by the Scots two years later. In 1587 the property was bought by Sir John Maitland, Chancellor of Scotland and the minister who played a crucial role in establishing James VI's power over the nobility. He built the tall central keep, with a circular tower at each corner and five pairs of semicircular turrets along the flanks. There were wall walks and gun loops but the baronial architecture was mainly for display. The principal apartments were at the top of the castle and on the second floor is a remarkable early 17th-century ceiling on a pattern of quatrefoils and crosses inset with portrait medallions of Alexander, David, Hector and Joshua.

Thirlestane began to take on its present appearance in 1670–79 with a great remodelling by the 1st Duke of Lauderdale. Following his second marriage to the Countess of Dysart, the Duke set about improvements to three of his northern houses Thirlestane, Letherington (the modern Lennolove) and Brunstane, while also carrying out great works at Ham House on the Thames near Richmond. The Duke, like his grandfather, was a dominant figure in Scottish politics. A contemporary, the Earl of Ailesford, described him as 'endowed with a great memory, as disagreeable in his conversation as his person, his head was … a Saracen fiery red … his pronunciations high Scotch'. The Duke's architect was Sir William Bruce, surveyor-general and 'overseer of the King's Buildings in Scotland', with Robert Mylne as master mason.

Seven tiers of windows are set in the massive stone walls.

The late 17th-century swan -pedimented doorcase is flanked by Ionic columns.

The keen interest the Duke took in houses is evident in a letter written in 1671 to his brother about Thirlestane. 'Let all the house high and low be plaine with a handsome moulding above the hangings. Only let the 2nd storie be as fine work as is possible.' He goes on to describe a typical state apartment of the period with upper vestibule, great chamber, great drawing room, bedchamber and closet. All these rooms have sumptuous Charles II plasterwork heavy with foliage flowers and fruit but extremely lifelike, thanks to perfect crispness and almost three-dimensional modelling.

The 9th Earl, succeeding in 1839, found Thirlestane in disrepair and commissioned the prolific William Burn to remodel and enlarge the house with balancing wings. The south wing contained his own suite and the north numerous room for guests. Burn was almost certainly assisted by his brilliant assistant David Bryce.

In the 1970s the future of great Scottish houses looked grim. The historic buildings grants that had stimulated major programmes of repairs in England had not taken off in Scotland. Captain Gerald Maitland-Carew, who inherited Thirlestane in 1972 aged 30, was faced with carrying out repairs on a colossal scale with no fewer than forty major outbreaks of dry rot. Undaunted by such an overwhelming task, he determined to make a start, aided by an initial grant of £50,000 intended simply to halt deterioration. Over the next four years major repairs at last proceeded, aided by £250,000 of repair grants, and Thirlestane is now vested in a charitable trust. With state rooms splendidly hung with ancestral portraits and four-poster beds in prettily decorated bedrooms beneath gorgeous plasterwork, Thirlestane is an inspiring example of the commitment of families to the upkeep of immense houses and extensive gardens and grounds, here in regular use for weddings and outdoor events.

TOWIE BARCLAY Turriff
This 16th century tower house was the first of many to be restored from ruin

TOWIE BARCLAY CASTLE HAD NOT BEEN lived in for two hundred years when bought by the American musician Marc Ellington in 1970. 'It was marked on all the maps as a ruin,' he says. From the beginning of the 12th century to 1733 the estate belonged to the Barclays, one of whose descendants became the celebrated Russian general Prince Michael Barclay de Tolly.

The castle is a classic example of a Scottish tower house. It was certainly completed by 1593, as shown by a date stone, but a castle is already mentioned in 1558. In 1792 the turrets and embrasures were removed, two storeys taken off and the protective ditch around the castle filled in. It is massively built with walls that are 12 ft thick at ground level, complete with arrow slits and gun loops. Ellington explains 'People ask why fortified castles were constructed at such a late date. I found letters from the Barclays living here in the early 17th century saying they can't come to Edinburgh because of "the persistence of Egyptians in the area".' He continues, 'Egyptians was a term for vagabonds or gypsies. At that time the main punishment handed out by the fortnightly courts held at manors such as Towie Barclay was banishment. Upwards of twelve people a month were being banished at each session here and forty-five to fifty in Aberdeen. As a result there was a large body of travelling tinkers who were a threat to property.'

The front door opens in to a groin-vaulted vestibule with the Barclay coat of arms. At the end of a passage a spiral staircase rises to the top of the house. The great hall on the first floor has rib-and-groin vaulting and there is a pre-Reformation chapel with the four evangelists carved on the corbels.

The pink colour of the harling derives from the local sandstone.

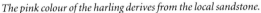

TRAIGH HOUSE Arisaig

1784 highland lodge with Edwardian front in cottage ornée *style*

TRAIGH HOUSE IS ONE OF A DELIGHTFUL GROUP of deer-stalking lodges on the beautiful coast road to Mallaig; another is Garramor, which has antlers over the entrance. Set back from the road, Traigh has an attractive Edwardian gabled front. This conceals a late 18th-century core that was built by Major Simon Macdonald and remodelled in 1867 for the land-improving lawyer, Aeneas Ranald Macdonell. The house has a spectacular view across the water to the islands of Eigg and Rhum. On a clear day, with blue sky and sea and distant mountains, the majesty of the panorama is intoxicating.

Today, Traigh is a comfortable home but in the war it was used by Churchill's Special Operations Executive as a base for commando training for secret agents. The different nationalities were kept separate so that they could give away no names if captured. Traigh was used mainly by the Czechs and French. Agents who trained there recalled the hard one-hour exercise session every morning on the grass in front of the house. To Camusdarach next door, came the first Czechoslovakian group of eight men, brought by lorry from Morar Station. Gabcik, who played a decisive role in the assassination of Heydrich, was among them.

Further Czech groups came to Traigh House from June 1942 until May 1943. They were organised in groups of twenty, with two British in each party. In all, 160 future Czech parachutists were trained at Traigh. Though they returned home briefly as liberators in 1945, three years later, with the communist takeover, they were imprisoned for 'training with the Imperialists'.

A pretty veranda looks out over a stretch of lawn to the islands of Eigg and Rhum.

TYNINGHAME HOUSE East Linton
Remodelled in the baronial style by William Burn for the Earls of Haddington

A WALK THROUGH TYNINGHAME'S MAGNIFICENT gardens reveals hardly a sign that the house and adjacent estate buildings have been transformed into seventeen self-contained houses and cottages. The luxuriant borders and beds created by the Dowager Lady Haddington after the Second World War are maintained in all their splendour.

Tyninghame's future came into question when in 1986 the present Earl of Haddington inherited the house, five miles west of Dunbar, from his father. While his parents lived at Tyninghame, Lord Binning, as he then was, had taken over the family's other great seat at Mellerstain, the great house by Robert Adam near Melrose.

The new Earl began exploring the possibility of handing Tyninghame to the National Trust for Scotland, or setting up a private charitable trust as at Thirlestane Castle. But this depended on obtaining a suitable endowment from the National Heritage Memorial Fund and the Fund's trustees decided they could not use scarce resources to support a family with two great houses. So in September 1987 the major part of Tyninghame's contents were sold at auction by Sotheby's. The family nevertheless wanted to retain the estate. A chance meeting with Kit Martin led to a solution whereby Martin took over the house and 60 acres. He undertook to maintain the grounds around the house and also to leave the exterior and all the principal rooms unchanged. Lord Haddington gave covenants that the parkland would be left as pasture and the trees and avenues maintained, thus ensuring that Tyninghame's setting and its magnificent views down the Scottish Tyne and the Firth of Forth would remain unspoilt.

The rose pink sandstone house is framed by gloriously luxuriant gardens.

The stepped gables and candle-snuffer turrets create a romantic silhouette.

At first glance Tyninghame looks an entirely 19th-century house, but William Burn's masterly remodelling of 1829–33 was a reworking of an existing house of almost the same size. The first mention of Tyninghame concerns St Baldred, who by tradition lived here as an Anchorite, dying in 756 or 757. The monastery, which existed here in the 9th century, owned lands covering much of East Lothian. In 941 the village and church at Tyninghame were sacked by Aulaf, the Danish King of Northumbria. Surviving today, marooned on the lawn, is the shell of the 12th-century parish church which continued in use until the village was cleared in 1761.

In the 13th century Tyninghame was a country residence of the Bishop of St Andrews. The Haddingtons acquired the property in 1628 after Sir Thomas Hamilton had taken the title of Earl of Haddington. The present house incorporates a 16th-century tower with very thick walls. A document of 1617 records that masons were 'bigging the lady's house' and were called to answer the charge of playing golf on Sundays (as strangers, they were spared punishment).

The estate owes its present appearance largely to the precocious 6th Earl, born in 1680, who was only five when his father died. Like a number of peers who played an active part in promoting the union with England, he created extensive plantations, consisting principally of avenues and shelter belts, intended to yield commercial timber. He wrote, 'When I came to live in this place in 1700 there were not above fourteene acres set with trees … It was a received notion that no trees could grow here because of the sea air and the north-east winds.'

According to Small's *Castles and Mansions of the Lothians* (1883), the house in the early 19th century was 'A plain old Scottish mansion of large size'.

Burn's earlier houses had been principally Tudor or Gothic and then Jacobean, but at Tyninghame the Scottish Baronial vocabulary of turrets, bartizans, crow-stepped gables and dormers emerges. Here Burn shows an exceptional lightness of touch using almost pencilsthin towers with gently tapering candle snuffer tops. Burn largely refaced the house in a very pretty pink sandstone, though some of the older, more random, masonry is visible in the courtyard on the south front.

Burn's entrance hall and staircase have become one very substantial house, including Burn's library, which overlooks the rose garden. Next door Sir Timothy Clifford, Director of the National Galleries of Scotland, took on the west wing – a very grand house on four storeys. It is hard to imagine there will ever be a better example of a large Victorian stateroom transformed into a comfortable living room with such panache. There is furniture of the right scale for the house, the original flock wallpaper has been retained and the pictures have been double-banked to splendid effect. Faced with the success of the Cliffords, other new residents might have despaired and preferred to gaze at white walls. Not so the engaging Elaine Kale from Chicago, whose carpets were so deep you felt constrained to remove your shoes on entering. There was a double rail of hand towels beside every basin, one for use and the other emblazoned with the crest of Bloomingdale's department store, purely to impress. Who could have envisaged five years before that Tyninghame would have so many proud owners?

The long west front has become two very grand houses.

VELLORE HOUSE — Linlithgow
Late 18th-century summer villa built by a returning hero of the Siege of Vellore

VELLORE HOUSE COMES WITH AN INTRIGUING STORY. It takes its name from the Siege of Vellore in India, where British officers withstood a fierce two-year encirclement by Hyder Ali, the Sultan of Mysore, and a formidable opponent of British rule in Hindustan. Desperate efforts by the Madras Government and Sir Eyre Coote kept the fort supplied with rice and the siege was only lifted on Hyder Ali's death in 1782. To commemorate the victory, one of the officers, Major Duncan, returned to Scotland and changed the name of an old farmhouse to Vellore Castle, onto which he built a castle-style villa for his retirement with towers intended to recall those of the 17th-century fort at Vellore. Very probably these were built to his own design, like the long earth mound, suggesting a continuous rampart, that he built around the perimeter of the property.

The house was rescued from virtual ruin by Edinburgh stockbroker John Henderson. He explains, 'The roof was falling to bits. You could stand on the earth and look up at the sky. In the garden there was not one flower or plant, just some lovely old mature trees.' His architect, Marcus Dean, adds, 'Previous owners had embarked on the most horrendous attempted conversion I've seen, stripping out fireplaces and partitioning every main room.' Now this modest villa offers thirty-five rooms, including nine bedrooms and six bathrooms.

The house stands on elevated ground with views towards Linlithgow and its magnificent ruined royal palace. In the late 18th century this was considered country steeped in romance – where Walter Scott's publishers, the Cadells, lived. Vellore was one of a series of delightful villas built here in the late 18th century, often by amateur architects, more substantial than the summer villas in the immediate environs of Edinburgh, but still close enough to take part in the social life of the Scottish capital. Another, Almondell, was ignominiously blown up in the 1950s.

As West Lothian became industrialised in the 19th century, much of the country here was robbed of its charm but now that the industry is defunct the rural character of the landscape is returning, and pressures are relenting just as they are increasing on the other side of Edinburgh in East Lothian.

The approach is along country lanes past a nearby farm. The drive sweeps past the old curling pond. 'We have made it into a water meadow, raising the level with fertile silt dredged out of the nearby Edinburgh to Falkirk canal,' says Henderson.

Tall trees seclude the house from the road. The 1780s entrance front is well-proportioned Georgian box with graceful sash windows, pretty battlements and a gothic porch with a 'flamed' ogee arch. The towers have arrow slit windows in the form of crosses. In the 1850s, the then owners, the Urquharts, added single-storey links to the towers, with triple lancet windows inset with stained glass. Then in 1905–12 twin pavilions were added by the architect James Strang for William and Mary Brown, containing a billiard room and schoolroom.

The Hendersons set up their own building company and had three workmen living in the house for four years, with Mrs Henderson acting as clerk of the works.

The iron deadline finally fixed was that the builders would be out before their baby was due. Henderson recalls, 'The carpenter left finally at 5 and my wife went into labour at midnight.'

Doing much of the work themselves, always to a limited budget, meant a constant search for economies. '"Don't throw away that floorboard", I'd say to the workmen,' laughs Henderson. The delight of the house internally is the use of strong fresh lustrous colour, giving the interior a bold contemporary feel. These are lovely light interiors lit by large sashes with slender glazing bars – with the special Scottish touch of handles on the bottom of the lower sashes to make them easier to open.

When a house has so many rooms, some tiny, it is a challenge to find uses for them all, let alone furnish every last corner. The Hendersons have done it with flair. The schoolroom is a spacious office, beyond is a more secluded study and beyond that is a circular library in the turret, where a curving stair ascends to the perfect reading room with space for just one chair.

There is an elegant dining room and a smaller breakfast room, where parents and children can hold rival parties. Cut off from his favourite bar in Edinburgh, John Henderson has built his own amusing replica, with a handsomely fitted-out wine cellar beyond, suitable for the occasional tasting with a few friends. Opposite the

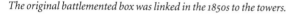

The original battlemented box was linked in the 1850s to the towers.

Inside, Vellore is a comfortable well-lit family house retaining original trims such as the folding window shutters, with rooms painted in bold colours.

dining room is a pantry, brilliantly placed for whisking plates out between courses, and beyond a kitchen with a gothic touch, fitted out by Mrs Henderson herself. Beyond this is a small granny/nanny flat with its own outside entrance.

Upstairs the bathrooms are as spacious as bedrooms. The first floor of the 1780s villa is fitted out as a single grand suite with large lofty bedroom, dressing room with extra bed and bathroom with bath boldly aligned on the window to admire the view. At the back, the old laundry is another surprise, faced throughout in white glazed tiles with rounded corners for easy cleaning. Currently it is a workshop.

The one blemish on this delightful place is that a link road to the M9 motorway to Stirling passes just a little too close. The upside is that Vellore is just thirty minutes' drive to both Edinburgh and Glasgow and fifteen minutes from the airport. Or you can commute in real style along the canal towpath all the way to Edinburgh – a bracing forty-five minutes by bicycle.

WEDDERBURN CASTLE · Duns

Built in castle-style in 1771–5 by Robert Adam for Patrick Home

ROBERT ADAM MADE HUNDREDS OF DRAWINGS of castle-style houses which were never built. Wedderburn, faced in warm smooth stone, shows just how handsome they all could have been. The main front with battlements and turrets is a welcoming sight with numerous large sash windows announcing a house that is light, airy and full of well-proportioned rooms.

I drove up in the early 1980s. Peering through the ground floor I saw dozens of iron bedsteads and mattresses. Moments later the new proprietor returned and explained he was starting a business running an old-people's home. For each resident he would receive a set sum and if several could be companionably accommodated in each room he stood to make a tidy profit. Whether the plumbing would be adequate for such a large influx seemed doubtful and the next I heard was that little had happened and the Home family, to whom the estate still belonged, was seriously concerned.

Happily the matter was brilliantly resolved and the castle is again a private house belonging to the Homes but available for fully serviced lets for weekends and holidays and celebrations. If you wish, there is a ballroom as well as drawing room, dining room and gallery. Twenty-two adults and up to six children can be accommodated in fourteen bedrooms. There is a billiard room, croquet, clay pigeon shooting and if you like, a full Highland Games will be held. Unusually, corkage is not charged on wine you have delivered or bring with you. The whole castle is back in first-class decorative order.

Wedderburn was built in 1770–76 for Patrick Home of Billie who, in a supreme gesture of self-confidence, set off on a prolonged Grand Tour, avoiding disturbance from builders.

Ranges of Georgian sash windows are capped by towers and battlements.

WALES

ALT-Y-BELA   Llangwm
Cruck-framed long house with tower added by Roger Edwards in 1599

The house was newly limewashed after the Spitalfields Trust rescued it from ruin.

ALT-Y-BELA IS LITTLE MORE THAN fifteen minutes from the Severn Bridge but as you ascend the long steep estate road a deep peace steals over you. I arrived in the summer of 2005 when restoration was complete and the house was about to go on the market. Strange as it seems, the rescue had been undertaken by the Spitalfields Trust, veteran saviours of more than fifty early 18th-century houses in London's Spitalfields. As the trust began to run out of London houses to take on, its members began to look further afield.

Alt-y-Bela had been newly limewashed and was almost dazzlingly white in the sun. The house stood along the edge of a cobbled farmyard with a tower at one end. The original medieval house was a typical Cruck-framed long house, with family and animals all under one roof.

In 1599 Roger Edwards, newly returned from extensive travels, built one of the first Renaissance towers in Monmouthshire, consisting of three storeys over a cellar, with parlour, bedroom and storage loft on the floors above. The tower is served by a handsome oak newel staircase which survives in remarkable condition.

The Spitalfields Trust began by restoring the least important building, a piggery, as a secure dry workshop for the carpenters – elsewhere water was pouring in through the roofs. Electricity had to be brought in from half a mile away, while water was sourced from a borehole and a sewage system installed.

Much of the beauty of the finished house lies in the quality of materials, polished floorboards, diamond glass in leaded cames for the wooden-mullioned windows, and slate and stone roof slabs.

Alt-y-Bela was bought by the landscape gardener Arne Maynard. His philosophy is that a successful garden is one with 'a perfect harmony between house, garden, history, owners and the surrounding landscape'. He could hardly have come to a better place.

BETTISFIELD PARK   Hanmer
Designed with a domed rotunda and an 1830s Italianate tower

CORNELIA BAYLEY, I WROTE IN *The Times* in March 1992, 'is a damsel in distress. Seemingly, against impossible odds, she has rescued Bettisfield Park, the vast crumbling seat of the Hanmers in Flintshire, near Wrexham, only to find the whole project endangered by a quarrel over the coping stones on a wall.'

Cornelia, who is also the saviour of Jacobean Plas Teg, bought Bettisfield in 1989. The house had been empty and decaying for years and Sir John Hanmer had sought permission to demolish, only to be refused after a public inquiry. In 1988 the council had resolved to serve a repairs order and shortly after Sir John agreed to sell to Mrs Bayley. There was one condition – a new wall, matching existing estate walls, had to be built between the house and the stables, where Sir John's son lived.

Mrs Bayley decided to demolish the derelict Victorian additions, restoring the house as a single family home. The house of the 1790s (built for Sir Thomas Hanmer, Bt) was very much in the style of the Wyatts, with a projecting rotunda that was capped by a shallow dome. Inside an abundance of fine plasterwork of the period survived. The architect and landscape gardener John Davenport was working here then.

A small army of builders went to work, many of them volunteers. The hall glowed in a pale Pavlosk pink. There was only one problem: when you turned the light switch, nothing happened. Bettisfield was landlocked by Hanmer property and Sir John had refused Manweb, the local electricity company, the necessary permission to lay cables across the land as, he asserted, the coping stones on the dividing wall had not been laid level. It was not until August 1992 that the issue was resolved and Cornelia was able to switch on the electricity and sell the house.

Before Cornelia Bailey embarked on its rescue, the house stood forlorn.

BODYSGALLEN — Llandudno

17th-century manor that began as a tower house serving nearby Conwy Castle

BODYSGALLEN IS SURROUNDED BY 200 acres of grounds, complete with woodland walk. Around the house you find a formal rose garden, a rockery and cascade, a walled garden, lily-pad ponds, a wild garden and several follies.

The house is a wonderful example of Welsh vernacular, without flamboyant features but solidly and beautifully built of local stone. The name means either 'house among thistles' or 'the abode of Cadwallon', a 6th-century chieftain. The oldest part of the hall is a five-storey tower, probably dating from the late 13th century, and possibly built as a watchtower for Conwy Castle.

Bodysgallen has been in the Mostyn family since the 16th century. Margaret Mostyn married Hugh Wynn, and it is their son, Robert Wynn, whose initials, with those of his wife Katherine, appear on the south gable with the date 1620. The early 17th-century range contains the large entrance hall, and an equally large drawing room above with coats of arms of the Mostyns, Wynns and Vaughans.

The harmony of the house today is largely due to a sensitive restoration by Lady Augusta Mostyn in around 1900 for her second son, Colonel Henry Mostyn. Brick chimneys and Georgian sashes disappeared and Bodysgallen assumed the mantle of a house that has grown from the rock on which it stands.

Following the death of Colonel Henry's widow in 1949, Bodysgallen entered a decline, becoming a guest house in 1969. Richard Broyd's company Historic House Hotels began restoration in 1980, opening the hotel three years later, and Bodysgallen has been immaculately maintained ever since in the best country-house tradition.

The box-edged parterres are planted on the pattern of the knot gardens laid out here in the 17th century.

6 PALACE STREET — Caernarfon
Late-medieval hall house saved from the bulldozer

ON DECEMBER 23, 1994 THE DISTRICT SURVEYOR of Caernarfon Council said to me testily, 'I am going to put this phone down now and you can be absolutely sure that demolition will begin on January 2.' SAVE was involved in a last-ditch attempt to avert demolition of 6 Palace Street, held to be the second oldest building in the town after Edward I's great castle. The Council had initially placed a compulsory purchase order on the building to save it from demolition but had changed its view and issued a dangerous structures notice instead. The local newspaper, *The Daily Post,* chimed in, saying, 'Shoppers in Caernarfon will have an extra cause for celebration in the New Year when a dilapidated building in Palace Street is finally demolished.'

Our only recourse was to secure an injunction from the High Court. Over the Christmas holiday I prepared an affidavit with the help of a solicitor friend, David Roberts, and on New Year's Eve Emma Phillips, SAVE's secretary, appeared at the High Court. Ours was the last case to be heard. We had tried every possible means to notify the council of the action but their offices were firmly closed. To meet their concerns about security (prompted by a particular local drunk who was prone to try to break into empty buildings) we offered to place a 24-hour watch on the building. To our relief, the judge granted an injunction without a time limit, leaving it to the council to return with a challenge.

The restored three-storey Caernarfon bay window is on the left of the house.

We promptly rang a security firm who, to our horror, quoted us £500 a day. Emma found a man who would mount the watch for £500 a week from an empty shop opposite. The next task was to find a builder. I rang the National Trust, who are active in North Wales, and they gave me a name. When he visited the property a week later, he rang to say 'Mr Binney – in my view the house should be demolished'.

We now learnt that the only builders we could employ had to be on the council's approved list. It looked like a classic *Catch 22* situation. But Huw

The first-floor hall has massive timber trusses that
have been repaired and restored.

Thomas, our architect, ascertained that one builder, Henry Jones Ltd, would do the job. Hope was revived. SAVE established a building preservation trust, Ymddiriedolaeth Treftadaeth Caernarfon (Caernarfon Heritage Trust) to take on the property but we had to take the risk of beginning work before we owned it as the compulsory purchase was not complete.

To many local people the building was simply an eyesore shored up by scaffolding. But Huw Thomas pointed out that the huge gash in the facade had been filled with a typical three-storey Caernarfon bay window.

Inside, concealed above later ceiling boards we were thrilled to find a trio of substantial roof trusses made of massive timbers. Therse appeared 15th-century in date and transpired to be part of a solar wing of a substantial house built on one of the original burgage plots that were set out when the town was founded by Edward I. The town was made up of three streest running north-south to the castle, with Palace Street in the centre. There were fifty-nine burgage plots in 1298 and sixty-three in 1309. 6 Palace Street was a substantial timber-frame house with gable to the street. Trading premises would have been on the ground floor with the living accomodation above. Some of the original wattle and daub infill of the timber box frame survived as well as fireplaces, and these helped to date the building to between 1400 and 1450.

With the help of grants from CADW and the Heritage Lottery Fund we repaired the building, which had an atmospheric cobbled yard at the back. The stone stack of the brick chimney proved to have no foundations and had to be quickly dismantled.

The Prince of Wales paid us a visit when it was nearly complete. When we put it on the market we had an offer from a firm of architects in Manchester, but after a year passed without a sale we were becoming desperate as interest was rolling up and our building preservation trust was in danger of becoming insolvent. At that moment the lady who ran the town's principal teashop appeared and bought the house. This was the perfect use, as the building would be open to the public and accessible to all. Restoration helped spark a new interest in Caernarfon's old walled town which, with the castle, is designated a World Heritage Site.

EDWINSFORD

Llansawel

The ancient seat of the Williams baronets dating back to the 16th century

IN THIS BOOK THERE ARE MANY HOUSES brought back from the brink. Edwinsford has been sitting begging to be restored for over half a century. Now many consider it to be beyond rescue. 'Ruined, and disastrously so, given its history and architectural interest' says *The Buildings of Wales*. Tom Lloyd, in SAVE's *The Lost Houses of Wales*, wrote 'In its slow demise, one of the saddest sights in South Wales today'. It was occupied during the Second World War by Polish refugees who, always resourceful provenders, grew mushrooms under the floorboards.

Edwinsford was the ancient seat of the Williams baronets. The oldest part of the house was square with a steep pyramid roof rising almost as high again as the walls and capped by paired square chimney stacks. This dated from *c*.1635. Beside it stood a 1670s block built for Sir Rice Williams. Here were two fine plaster ceilings and a massive oak staircase which is now at LLwynybrain, Llandovery. There were handsome lead statues on the roof as well as others in the gardens – of a gamekeeper, milkmaid and wild boar. There were two sets of Victorian additions, a dining room and service block added in 1842 for Sir James Hamlyn Williams, probably by Edward Haycock, and a taller block by the river dating from 1862.

Edwinsford is approached across a graceful arched bridge built in 1793 by David Edwards, which is a gentle echo of the great single-arch bridge his father William built over the River Taff at Pont-y-Prydd with a 140-ft span that would prevent it being washed away, like its predecessor, by the floods.

The Williams family of Edwinsford claimed descent through Ellen, wife of Llewelyn ap Phylip, from Henry I of England. In 1873 Sir James Hamlyn Williams-Drummond of Edwinsford owned 9,282 acres in Carmarthenshire. The family contributed eight high sheriffs, two lord lieutenants, three MPs and numerous JPs to local life.

The chimneys are set on the top of the gables of the garden front.

GWERCLAS HALL
Corwen
Dated 1767 and evidently built by a local builder using a pattern book

A MORE DELICIOUSLY QUIRKY GEORGIAN HOUSE than Gwerclas Hall in Denbighshire is hard to imagine. With its tea-caddy centre and matching gabled wings, it is an errant version of a Palladian villa, with no fewer than four handsome Venetian windows as well as a pair of Diocletian lunettes (although these are actually false) beneath the eaves.

Thomas Lloyd, the author of *The Lost Houses of Wales*, says: 'I use Gwerclas in my lectures to show the difference between an architect-designed house and one run up by a local builder using a pattern book.' Even the front door does not quite seem to fit the columned doorcase, although the slightly strange proportions of the top floor are explained by the cast-iron gutter that replaced the original cornice.

No matter – the effect is enchanting and the Hughes family who built it proudly set their coat of arms above the front door, with the date 1767 and initials 'HHLM' for Hugh Hughes Lloyd and his wife Margaret. On the shield are rampant lions and wild boars as well as the heads of three Englishmen said to have lost their lives at the battle of Oswestry. In the Middle Ages, according to the *Journal of the Merioneth Historical and Record Society*, the owners of the estate were barons of Edeyrnion, 'lords of royal blood', whose story shows 'the decline of the ancient house of Powys from kings and princes to small squires and gentlemen farmers'.

That said, the life of a gentleman farmer in mid-Georgian Wales appears to have been extremely agreeable. Gwerclas may look as if it is a small rectory, but inside it is a mini stately home with fine panelling and woodwork and a wonderfully preserved

Windows vary from floor to floor, creating an enchantingly quirky design.

Left: Panelled shutters fold back inside a Venetian window.
Right: An earlier stone-mullioned window still remains at the back.

world behind the green baize door. Virtually no alterations were carried out after 1824, when the house became a tenanted farm on the adjoining Newborough estate.

Steven West, who bought the house in the late 1980s with his partner, Tina Shaw, pointed to the unusual ridges in the plum-coloured brickwork. 'These ridges are the marks left by the drying racks on which the bricks were placed when they came out of the kiln.' Usually Georgian buildings are 'fair-faced', with the smooth side of the brick placed on the outside. Here the bricks are turned the other way round, creating an intriguing pattern, the more appealing as the handsome brickwork has never been repointed and glows a gloriously warm red as soon as the sun comes out.

Both Steven and Tina went to art school, are good with their hands and so were able to tackle much of the repair work themselves. He explained: 'We had been here six weeks before we discovered the gazebo at the back of the garden shrouded in ivy that had grown as tall as a tree.' Although ruinous, it transpired to be three storeys high with an arched seat below, a schoolroom on the first floor (nine children attended in 1841) and clock tower at the top.

At the back of the house soil had banked up against the lower walls, concealing mullioned windows that light the cellar. Here the house is built of stone, not brick, and all the windows, including the tall ladder window lighting the stairs, are rectangular leaded lights, not sashes. Tina renewed more than eighty windows, keeping the old glass wherever possible. 'I spent a day learning to stretch lead. It comes in 'H' sections and can be cut with a knife. You lay it out dry like a jigsaw, then reassemble it using a soldering iron.' The results are what you would expect from an accomplished artist – perfectly crisp and completely waterproof.

The front door opens into a handsome entrance hall, with stone paving laid in a diamond pattern. At the back a shallow baroque arch flanked by pilasters frames the view of the stair. Part of the charm is that the doorcases vary from one side of the room to the other. Above them are shadows left by vanished pediment tops. The paved corridor to the kitchen has a distinct dip. Here there is a wealth of early detail: a circular hole in the kitchen ceiling ('through it hung a rope for rocking the cradle above'), an early spit mechanism, hooks for curing hams, an ancient slate basin, a dairy and bread oven, a salting room and drying yard.

Gwerclas is laid out like a town house on four storeys. There is a sizeable vaulted cellar with freshly painted plaster. On the three main floors the rooms have snug early-Georgian proportions. The exception is the long first-floor great room, now the main bedroom, lit by two handsome Venetian windows.

The joinery is of a very high standard throughout. Shutter boxes are lined in oak and there is a whole hierarchy of doors. The grandest, to the great room, have raised and fielded panels on both sides as well as carved mouldings. Most rooms have handsome fireplaces with good grates. There is one baroque chimney piece with a keystone, a handsome Adamesque mantel in the drawing room and regency chimney pieces with circular stops at the corners.

The glorious oak staircase rises to the attic with two corkscrew balusters to a tread, swept-up handrails and matching dados. On the east side two bedrooms have steeply coved ceilings. Steven takes pride in the impressive timbers in the attic. 'There was woodworm, but the heartwood is so tough they could never touch it.'

Gwerclas has just over 6 acres and stands in glorious country with fine views across a stretch of former parkland to rolling hills. The approach from Corwen village crosses the River Dee over a long stone bridge that is still medieval in character. The flood plain below the house is unlikely to be built on, and further protection is afforded by the surrounding Newborough estate. Just up the road is Plas Uchaf, the 1400 predecessor of Gwerclas that was rescued from ruin by the Landmark Trust.

GWRYCH CASTLE   Abergele
Begun by Lloyd Hesketh Bamford-Hesketh in 1819 largely to his own designs

GWRYCH CASTLE IS AN OVERPOWERINGLY theatrical composition of embattled walls and towers climbing up a wooded hillside, more like a fortified town than a house. If it had been in its present abandoned state in the 1920s Randolph Hearst would have shipped it stone by stone to America. In fact building work only halted with the outbreak of war in 1914.

The castle was begun in 1819 by Lloyd Hesketh Bamford-Hesketh, who was largely his own architect, though he employed professionals to help him, notably Thomas Rickman, a pioneer of cast-iron tracery for gothic buildings. G.E. Street, architect of the Royal Courts in the Strand, added the marble staircase, rising over fifty steps in one straight ascent.

The Hesketh heiress, Winifred, Countess of Dundonald, lived here in full Edwardian splendour, bequeathing the castle on her death in 1924 to the royal family. Instead it was given to the Order of St John and then bought back by the Earl, who had to sell the contents to cover the cost. During the Second World War, Gwyrch was requisitioned by the Government, and played home to over two hundred Jewish refugees. In 1946 the 13th Earl sold Gwrych to Robert Rennie, who in turn sold to a

Leslie Salts. He opened the castle to the public for twenty years, attracting nearly ten million visitors, and earning the soubriquet of 'the showplace of Wales'.

Between 1968 and 1989 the castle had a series of owners, and underwent a variety of changes of function. It finally closed to the public in 1985. Serious decline set in after 1989 when Gwrych was sold to a property developer in California, Nick Tavaglione, who planned to turn it into a five-star hotel and opera house. Legal problems prevented this and during years of absentee ownership the roofs collapsed, bringing down ceilings and floors. The vandalism and theft were appalling yet Gwrych remained a majestic sight. So solid are the masonry walls that they could survive for centuries.

The battle to save the castle has been led by Mark Baker, who began his campaign when he was 11 years old. He has written a book on the castle and set up an excellent website (www.gwrychtrust.co.uk). With Michael Tree, who rescued nearby Trevor Hall, he formed a building preservation trust that offered to take over the house if Conwy County Council issued compulsory purchase proceedings. Their plan was to carry out structural repairs, give the main house a roof and replace windows so the building is weather-tight and can be offered for sale. A similar operation saved Soane's Pell Wall Hall.

In April 2007 came the sudden and exciting news that Gwrych Castle had been acquired by a Yorkshire company, Clayton Hotels. The price was £850,000 and the company is planning a £6 million restoration of the castle as a ninety-bedroom hotel, catering for weddings, conferences, parties and events. It is expected that the hotel will open in 2010.

Gwrych is dramatically built into a steep hillside and extended by castellated walls and towers.

GYRN CASTLE Mostyn
Regency castle built by a local cotton manufacturer, John Douglas

NO ONE EVER HAD A BETTER WAY of arriving at Gyrn Castle than Sir Edward Bates, 1st Baronet, who would sail from Liverpool in his own paddle steamer, docking at nearby Mostyn pier on the Flintshire coast. He would then enjoy a grand view of the Second Port of the Empire, a full 35 miles away, across his own rolling parkland, and the estuaries of the Dee and the Mersey with the Wirral peninsula between.

This magical place was on sale in 2006 for a fifth of the price that it would fetch in southern England or nearby Cheshire: at £2.5 million for the castle and 100 acres, or £3.5 million for the full 367 acres. Although the North Wales Expressway is only five minutes' drive away, you are in deep seclusion with nothing but pretty estate villages on the perimeter of your domain. To the south of the house, ancient woods hide a glorious long lake with trees coming down to the water – it brings in £20,000 a year in fishing fees. There is a battlemented gateway and lodge at the bottom of a long drive and numerous outbuildings.

The estate was bought in 1817 by John Douglas, a partner in a firm of cotton manufacturers at nearby Holywell. He built the present castle, a typical Georgian sham with sash windows and cardboard-looking walls but given a romantic flourish by tall, thin towers with more than a hint of San Gimignano.

Gyrn is picturesquely composed, in contrast to the perfect symmetry of many Georgian castle-style houses.

In 1856 the estate was bought by Sir Edward Bates, a ship owner and politician. He had started in the Halifax wool-finishing business begun by his father, and spent fifteen years in Calcutta and Bombay developing exports of the family woollen cloth and importing silk, skins and indigo. Returning to England, he chartered ships for the Bombay trade, doing so well that in three years he bought his first cutter, the *Jamsetjee Cursetjee*, which he named after his Parsee partner. It was a close and brilliant association which raised more than a few eyebrows in Victorian England.

By 1860 he had built a fleet of twenty-six vessels, rising to 130 to serve the Australian gold rush and returning via South America.

After his death in 1896 his three sons inherited, but when the elder two died the third, Percy, took over, emerging as one of the giants of the shipping industry.

His niche in history is secured by his role as chairman of Cunard in conceiving and building the two great transatlantic liners, *Queen Mary* and *Queen Elizabeth*, which did heroic service in the Second World War as fast troop carriers. In 1922 he had sold Gyrn to his brother Fredrick, a keen birdwatcher and photographer. On his death the estate, massively depleted by duties, passed to his nephew Sir Geoffrey, the 5th Baronet. A dashing tank commander in the Western Desert, he won both the MC and the DSO. Soldiers competed for a place in his tank until Geoffrey, an incorrigible fidget, was waiting behind German lines and mistakenly knocked a switch that turned his headlights on, thus revealing his position.

Inheriting Gyrn in 1957, he developed farming, fishing and shooting on the estate and served as High Sheriff. On his death in February last year the estate was left to a grandson who lives in Canada, and in July Christie's held a house sale of the contents. The interiors, still splendidly furnished in these photographs, are now bare, but this has not deterred purchasers from Sussex and beyond coming to dream of refurnishing this place as a home.

The front door opens into a darkly polished panelled hall with a grand coat of arms over the fireplace. The zigzag pattern in the panels is exotically oriental, complete with little brackets for porcelain ornaments. On either side of the fireplace is a wealth of weird Jacobean woodwork of the kind the exiled Victor Hugo used to embellish his extraordinary home in Guernsey.

The dining room, with its opulent plasterwork, is on the right, while to the left rooms at different levels suggest the incorporation of an early house. The grand set piece is the picture gallery, with a splendid top-lit roof supported on flying ribs. Here a portrait of the 1st Baronet still hangs with a plaque announcing that it was 'presented by thousands of the working classes' of his late Plymouth constituency as a mark of their respect and esteem.

A Georgian stair with a trio of column balusters to each step rises the height of the house, leading to bedrooms on first and second floors and offering glorious views over park and woods to the south and to the estuary to the north. Apart from stout metal windows that replaced some of the sashes, all is immensely old-fashioned and in parts more than a little decrepit. For lovers of country-house backstairs there are prize items such as twin wooden sinks and a forest of ham hooks hanging from the ceiling of the kitchen passage.

PARK COTTAGE   Leighton
1850s gingerbread cottage built on the estate of Liverpool banker John Naylor

IMAGINE THE PERFECT STAFFORDSHIRE pottery cottage: steep roofs, gables, dormer windows and a tiny walled garden in front. This is Park Cottage, as covetable a piece of gingerbread as you are likely to find. It is one of a large number of delightful (and sometimes dotty) estate buildings erected by the Liverpool banker John Naylor on the Leighton estate near Welshpool, which he was given as a wedding present in 1845, followed two years later by a handy £100,000 (about £10 million in today's money).

Naylor set about the mechanisation of his farms on a gigantic scale with the same enthusiasm as the Prince Consort displayed on his model farm at Windsor. The story goes that Naylor harboured ambitions for his daughter to marry the heir of Powys Castle across the valley but when his hopes were dashed he set about planting out the view of the castle with a grove of fast-growing redwoods.

'One of those trees is in the Guinness Book of Records as the tallest tree in Wales,' I was told by Andrew Petch, the teacher who was selling Park Cottage. The cottage overlooks Naylor's large farm buildings and engine house (today a leisure centre), with Shrewsbury just twenty minutes away by car.

Immediately behind Park Cottage is an enchanting folly (nine-sided rather than eight) which housed the wheel of a cable hoist that brought up slurry in palettes from the farm to be mixed with water and piped down to fields in the valley.

Next door to Park Cottage is the Cable House which powered a long-vanished two-track funicular railway of the 1870s, which was in working order until the whole

The house has a trio of gables with spiky cresting along the roof-houses.

4,000-acre estate was sold up in 1931. The family ascended the hill by train to take lunch in the black and white summer house (still surviving). Today you have to ascend on foot but have the pleasant surprise of walking along the ridge of Offa's Dyke – which runs adjacent to the cottage – when you reach the top.

The turbine in the Cable House was fed by a reservoir higher up the hill and all the way up the ravine beside the house the stream is stepped into a series of cascades. 'The sound of gentle splashing is very pleasant as you sit out with a glass of wine on a summer evening,' Andrew Petch says.

Just across from Park Cottage is what must be – in relation to the tiny arch at the bottom – the most massively over-engineered bridge in Britain. The stream feeds a long pond opposite Park Cottage, which is bordered by a serpentine stone wall that allows ducks and moorhens to breed undisturbed by dogs. Thanks to some recent deft work by a neighbour with puddling clay, the water level is now so healthy that it looks more like a full-blown canal than a simple millpond.

As originally built in the 1850s, Park Cottage has three, almost square rooms on the ground floor and three bedrooms above, all lit by dormer windows. The

The cottage stands opposite a large millpond.

previous owner discreetly extended the house at the back, providing a sitting room opening onto the garden, and a fourth bedroom. In doing this he introduced a trio of arches at the back of the hall opening onto the staircase. More recently, Petch had built a small utility room to one side, carefully matching the original brick and stone, which he was pleased to find described in the official listing document as 'a new wing added most sympathetically' – all 10 by 10 ft of it.

The original doors retain big X braces with Victorian chamfers. Newer, but nonetheless in keeping, is a series of doors inset with 19th-century coloured and etched glass – as well as one made specially for the Petches 'sandblasted with Victorian doyly patterns by the local headstone maker'.

The ceilings are unusually high for a cottage and the windows are not the little diamond panes you might expect, but well-proportioned late-Georgian sashes with glazing bars as slender as those on a Sheraton bookcase.

LLANGOED HALL Llyswen
Largely built in 1913–14 to the designs of Sir Clough Williams-Ellis

THE VENERABLE ARCHITECT OF PORT MEIRION, Clough Williams-Ellis, had just celebrated his ninetieth birthday when he arrived in tweeds and bow tie at the *Country Life* offices in high dudgeon that one of his best and most splendid country houses, Llangoed Hall in Breconshire, was under threat of demolition. Some architects hold that it is part of the natural order of things that buildings come and go. Not Clough. He felt passionately about his house. He was proud of its good looks and all the fine detailing, materials and craftsmanship that had gone into it when he converted it to a country house. The house had been begun in 1913 for Archibald Christy and was built of a brownish local stone with a lighter stone from Flintshire for the trim. The oldest part of the building dates back to 1632 and original features include the Jacobean chimneys and an oak door that leads from the library to the porch.

The owner, Gerard Chichester, wanted to replace Clough's house, retaining only the three-storey entrance porch. I wrote in Clough's support in *Country Life*. His house had been built on generous lines, with two long galleries, twenty bedrooms and power house, laundry, game larders and bothies. There was a public inquiry in 1975 and permission to demolish was refused. Various suitors appeared but none succeeded in buying it and decay continued. Finally Sir Bernard Ashley, husband of Laura, saw its potential, bought the property in 1987 and restored it as a stylish country-house hotel, which opened three years later.

Unexpected features include working steam engines in the pool room, bedrooms decorated by designers such as Tom Parr, as well as vintage touches such as cast-iron baths and Roberts radios. The first-floor bedrooms open off a 95-ft long gallery approached by a splendid carved oak staircase. Portraits by Whistler, Sickert and Augustus John adorn the walls.

The hall is designed in a Cotswold style with steep roofs, stone-mullioned windows and dormers.

PENCOED CASTLE
Llanmartin

Enlarged medieval castle bought for restoration in 1914 but left empty after a fire

Pencoed Castle is an extraordinary place to visit. Here is a very grand and substantial Tudor mansion, with solid walls and fine mullioned windows but not a pane of glass remaining. Thirty or forty years ago you might have thought that it was an ancient monument in the care of the Ministry of Works.

Sir Richard de la More had a house here in 1270 but by the late 15th century the estate had passed to a branch of the Morgan family of Tredegar. The present house is likely to have been built by Sir Thomas Morgan, who was knighted in 1544, was elected sheriff in both 1548 and 1549 and died in 1565. It is a distinctly outward looking house, proclaiming the peace and stability brought by the Tudors to Wales.

The last descendants of the Morgans sold the castle in 1701, and thereafter Pencoed appears to have become a farmhouse, falling steadily into decay. In 1914 the estate was bought by Lord Rhondda, who set about restoring the main part of the house, employing G.H. Kitchin as his architect. Following Lord Rhondda's death in 1918, his widow employed the architect Eric Francis in 1922–3 to build a new house nearby which she sold in 1931. The castle entered a new decline and in about 1960 a bungalow was built much too close. These new neighbours undoubtedly intrude but when I visited Pencoed it still stood in pleasant seclusion surrounded by pasture. Alarm bells rang loudly when a developer proposed a theme park in the grounds but in 2003 the castle was bought by another Morgan, Peter Morgan, who said that respect for the intregrity of the castle and its environs will govern all decisions that are made concerning its future.

Smooth stone walls and mullioned windows survive in remarkable condition.

PENHOW CASTLE   Newport

Well-preserved small fortified manor dating from the 12th century

PENHOW IS BACK IN THE HANDS OF THE FAMILY whose emblem of paired wings is carved above the castle entrance. Sir Roger de St Maur came from St Maur on the Loire and was at Penhow in 1129, when he witnessed the charter that founded the priory of Monmouth.

At the time, Penhow was one of a ring of castles that surrounded the great Norman castle at Chepstow. Built of local limestone, it is a castle in miniature, perched on a knoll, with the ground falling away steeply on three sides. The earliest part of the fabric is the rectangular tower on the west, probably dating from the 12th century. In the 13th century the tower was encircled by a battlemented wall and moat, and the lofty great hall was added in the 14th century but took its present form in the 15th century.

The hall range is two storeys high – the hood moulds of the upper chamber are carved with the emblems of Sir Thomas Bowles, who was knighted in 1482, and his wife. The impressive chimney breast served hearths on both levels of the castle and the importance of the upper chamber is emphasised by the spacious staircase housed in a gabled tower.

By 1714 the castle had become a tenanted farmhouse, ensuring that any changes were few, though this also meant that neglect inevitably began to set in.

Handsome stone gate piers frame the approach.

In 1973 Penhow was acquired by the young Stephen Weeks who, as a teenager, had led a spirited campaign in his home town to save the remains of Old Gosport in Hampshire. He recreated the upper chamber as a great hall with a new screen and new steeply pitched open roof. Others hold that this was originally a great chamber with a ground-floor hall below.

Much salvaged material was used in the restoration and the broad planks of the hall floor are the former sides of a barn near Reading. A lot of the wood used in the roof was elm, salvaged in the early 20th century when Dutch elm disease was first ravaging Britain. For the reconstructed timber screen in the great hall, Weeks obtained planks of oak from an estate in Cumbria. These were as tall and broad as medieval planks.

The carved angels along the walls were exotically copied in Kashmir from an original by the Edwardian church architect Sir Ninian Comper. The panelling in the two Charles II rooms was painted by Laura Stevens, a Newport decorator, with walnut graining in tiger-skin colours in the dining room, and pink and grey marbling in the Old Parlour. To avoid placing radiators against the panelling, one was ingeniously sunk in a pit in the floor and covered it with a florid Victorian iron floor grating.

In 2003 Penhow was bought by descendants of Roger de St Maur, ensuring the best form of continuity in what is often held as the oldest inhabited castle in Wales.

PIERCEFIELD — Chepstow
Designed by Sir John Soane in 1785 with wings added by Joseph Bonomi in 1797

JUST AS APSLEY HOUSE, the Duke of Wellington's home on Hyde Park Corner, rejoices in the title of No 1 London, so the new owner of Piercefield, if he or she succeeds in the Herculean task ahead of them, may christen their house No 1 Wales.

This is not just because Piercefield is the first great country house across the Severn Bridge. Even more so, it is thanks to Piercefield's stupendous position with a commanding view across the Wye and Severn rivers with the great suspension bridge standing majestically in the middle ground. It is the closest Britain has to offer to Olana, the home of the American landscape painter Frederick Owen Church, which commands 100 miles of the Hudson River.

To enjoy it you must first undertake one of the most challenging restorations of the 21st century. Piercefield is the work of Sir John Soane, to many England's greatest and most original architect. But today it is no more than a shell in the most parlous condition. Keystones slip from lintels, arches sag. There are no floors, ceilings or roof, no stairs, no windows. Most of the internal plaster has flaked away, leaving oak lath and bare brick. It is in a state of abandon as extreme as deserted plantation houses in the Caribbean.

Piercefield has been descending into this state for half a century, protected from vandalism thanks to its almost secret location, tucked away behind Chepstow racecourse. In the 1970s the owners of the racecourse obtained permission to turn it into an hotel, swamping it with a massive 200-bedroom extension. This was ironically the solution so ardently argued for mighty Toddington Hall in Gloucestershire by the chief executive of English Heritage, until Damian Hirst rode to its rescue in 2005.

Fortunately the hotel plans for Piercefield never proceeded. All thanks are now due to Northern Racing who took over the course in 2003 and are now addressing the problem vigorously and responsibly. Steve Clare, the development director, says, 'Our late chairman, Sir Stanley Clarke, was a real enthusiast for old buildings. We agonised over what to do and decided the best solution was to get permission to rebuild it as close to the original design as possible as a house.' To ascertain whether this was feasible, they commissioned structural engineers, quantity surveyors and the conservation architect Michael Davies and Partners to assess the building.

The cost of reconstruction and fitting out is estimated at £10 million – high, but likely to be a realistic sum. The carrot comes in the form of the 70 acres of rolling landscape in front of the house. Piercefield, as they liked to say in the 18th century, is 'embossomed' by woods, thickly planted ranges of glorious oaks with not a building in sight. In front of the house is a great sweep of steeply rolling parkland with the pale straw-coloured grass that is the mark of ancient pasture. The park trees are also mature oaks with the characteristic line that comes from cattle eating away lower branches, though here the park has been grazed for so long by sheep that newer boughs have now descended to the ground.

Piercefield is an early work of Soane, built for George Smith in 1785–93. Here Soane moved towards an ultra-sophisticated stripped-down Classicism with only the shallowest relief. Smith ran into financial difficulties and had to sell the house before it was finished. The new owner, Sir Mark Wood, Bt, possibly found Soane's design just a trifle too austere and promptly added a pair of delightful wings like Classical

Soane's fine masonry survives, awaiting reconstruction as a spectacular house.

The house surveys a magnificent stretch of rolling parkland with views down to the River Severn.

temple fronts enriched with Grecian white marble reliefs. One of them is still pristine in its carving, the other has been half eaten away by rain, which has washed down the facade. These wings were designed by Joseph Bonomi, who came to England to work for the Adam brothers and is alluded to as a fashionable architect in Jane Austen's *Sense and Sensibility*.

The park at Piercefield was landscaped by Colonel Valentine Morris, the son of a sugar planter in Antigua, who bought the estate in 1740. He laid out walks through the woodland including a grotto, druid's temple and giant's cave and opened up viewpoints on a clifftop walk along the River Wye.

Now that a mass of laurels and sycamores has been cleared from the immediate surroundings of the house, it is obvious that its history is more exciting still. Contained within the Soane shell is the substantial core of an earlier baroque house. Part of this is visible as a free-standing wing at the back with giant Ionic pilasters and arched windows. More is revealed inside Soane's shell, where wall plaster has fallen away to reveal baroque quoins, windows and niches.

As the archaeologist Warwick Rodwell showed when he undertook the melancholy task of dismantling Soane's work at Colomberie House in Jersey, Soane was a stickler for the very best construction. Here, the brick walls are a full 2 ft thick with a timber strut every eight courses. The house is faced in ashlar, crisply cut blocks of smooth squared stone. Everywhere fascinating details are exposed, such as the curved timbers in door arches, the notches for joists, the fireplaces, the flues and the still-perfect stone chimney stacks.

Rightly, the local council have stipulated a full archeological survey and part of the thrill for a buyer with a serious love of old buildings will lie in all the patient detective work that takes place even before restoration begins.

With the house comes the opportunity to make a new drive – the original Lion Gate now serves as an entrance to the racecourse stables. Behind Piercefield, a large walled garden and derelict stable range also await restoration by its new owner.

PLAS TEG   Hope
Jacobean house of 1610 for Sir John Trevor rescued by Cornelia Bayley

TWICE PLAS TEG HAS BEEN BROUGHT BACK from the very brink of collapse and break-up. This is an intensely romantic house, an example of the most sophisticated Renaissance and courtly taste in remote North Wales. It was built in about 1610 for Sir John Trevor to a perfectly symmetrical design with four towers at the corners – a plan advocated by the Italian architect Serlio in his much-used pattern book.

When Plas Teg stood empty and in danger of demolition after the Second World War, it was bought back by a member of the family, the eye surgeon Patrick Trevor Roper, who carried out basic repairs and let the house to ensure it was occupied. Eventually he found a young couple who were keen to take on the house as a long-term repair project and sold it to them for a modest sum. Within months it was back on the market for twice the price and Mr Trevor Roper had to buy it back again. This time the house was sold to Cornelia Bayley, who dedicated her energies and resources to restoring the house over the next ten years. But she overextended herself and the house was once again threatened as the building society obtained a possession order.

Among those who rallied to her cause was the Marquess of Anglesey, who had served for thirty-nine years on the Historic Buildings Council for Wales. He wrote that Cornelia 'was a lady of exceptional vigour, good taste and above all dedication to the saving of the house … the result is that the building is now in as perfect a structural condition as any in the Principality … Mrs Bayley is the Lord Curzon, the Ernest Cook of Wales, drawing friendless houses back from the brink.'

To forestall eviction I proposed that a charitable trust should take over, allowing Cornelia to remain as curator. But she extracted herself and remains in residence with her parrots, open on Sundays and other days by appointment.

Plas Teg has an intensely romantic silhouette of spiky gables, cupolas and finials.

RUPERRA CASTLE
Llanfedw
Emblematic castle dated 1626, built for Sir Thomas Morgan

THE RENAISSANCE RUPERRA CASTLE, in Rudry, near Caerphilly, has been a shell since it was set alight by Italian prisoners of war in 1941. In 1998 the castle, which then had ash trees growing in its great hall, was acquired by Ashraf Barakat, a Kuwaiti property developer.

Plans were submitted to Caerphilly Council for rebuilding the castle internally, converting its stables, and building fifteen new executive houses in the grounds. The houses were to approach within 20 yards of the castle and stand opposite its outbuildings, which are all listed.

Jan Teagle, who had lived in the laundry for nearly twenty years, told me: 'Ruperra is a magical place, quite unspoilt. This development is intrusive and alien and would ruin everything. It would be much better for Ruperra to be left a ruin.'

Ruperra was built in the 1620s for Sir Thomas Morgan, an MP and steward to the Earl of Pembroke. He was knighted by James I in 1623. Charles I came to stay in 1645.

Mark Girouard, an authority on Tudor and Stuart country houses, says: 'This is one of an important group of houses built by leading servants of the Crown. The carving on the porch is especially delicate.'

Since one of Ruperra's four corner towers has collapsed, costs of restoration have increased substantially. But the battle against unsuitable enabling development is being continued by The Friends of Ruperra Castle. The plan of the castle is well suited to create one or two apartments on each of its four floors, all of which would have fine views. Other Welsh houses in grave distress have been rescued. Ruperra is no less important.

With its circular towers, battlements and distinctive windows, Ruperra awaits its champion.

SKER HOUSE
Pyle
Mainly late 16th-century house with large first-floor hall, built for the Turbevilles

SKER HOUSE IN SOUTH GLAMORGAN STANDS ALONE among the sand dunes, a field away from the sea. But beneath is a foundation of solid rock which has enabled the house, which is of monastic origin, to survive while the nearby town of Kenfig was buried long ago beneath the sand.

At the Dissolution of the Monasteries, the abbey was sold to the Turbeville family, who added a great hall with a frieze of bird-headed men firing arrows at little Welsh dragons. The Turbevilles were Roman Catholics, and in the 16th and early 17th centuries several of the family were fined and imprisoned for recusancy. One family member confessed to involvement in Titus Oates's Popish Plot of 1678, and a Jesuit priest was found hiding in the house two years later.

The Turbevilles were forced to sell and the new owners left tenant farmers to run the place from the great hall. In 1766, John Curre simply bequeathed the vast impractical pile to his manservant. In 1977 came the final indignity. Sker, by now a blackened wreck, was declared unsafe, and tenant farmers moved to a house nearby. A pig-breeding unit was built less than 100 yards away.

In 1990 the Buildings at Risk Trust, aided by the local council, began a battle to acquire Sker. Meanwhile, the owner placed the house, with just 3 ft of land around it, into a £100 property company to avoid paying for repairs. Seven years later, the council finally activated a compulsory purchase order, enabling the BaR Trust to acquire the freehold of the house and 6 acres. The lottery fund gave £413,000 towards repairs, in addition to £250,000 promised by Cadw (the Welsh equivalent of English Heritage) for removal and reconstruction of the farm buildings, including the piggeries.

Sker has a happy ending. On completion of structural repairs, the house was bought by a leading columnist for the *Sunday Telegraph*, who has continued the restoration and laid out a garden.

Handsomely restored after years of extreme decay, the house stands a field away from the sea.

TRAWSGOED   Llanafan

The property of the Vaughans since 1200 with colourful Victorian interiors

TRAWSGOED IS A VAST PILE WITH NEARLY a hundred rooms set in 1,200 acres of park and woodlands in Ystwyth Valley, some 6 miles inland from Aberystwyth. There has been a house here since Roman times, when a large fortified encampment was established nearby. Trawsgoed, which translates as 'Crosswood' in English, came to the Vaughans in the year 1200. The house was sacked by Cromwellian forces and substantially rebuilt in the 17th century with a centre and matching wings by Sir John Vaughan, an eminent lawyer and Chief Justice of the Common Pleas. Through a series of purchases and marriages, the Vaughans steadily built up their landholdings. In the 18th century, the house was remodelled to give a Georgian north facade with a sandstone portico as well as a south-facing library, filling the space between the earlier wings.

The Vaughans were created Earls of Lisburne (an Irish peerage) in 1776. A vast chateau-like extension was added in the 1890s by the 6th Earl, whose revenues from the 42,000-acre estate were multiplied by royalties from nearby lead and zinc mines.

In 1945, the 7th Earl sold the best farms on generous terms to the tenants and the Ministry of Agriculture bought the house and 1,200-acre home farm, relieving the family of the burden of upkeep. The house became the headquarters for MAFF in Wales and eventually for the Welsh Office Agriculture Department. The farm became an Experimental Husbandry Farm.

After half a century in Government ownership the house was offered back to the Vaughan family at the District Valuer's price. At £500,000 it might have sounded a bargain in 1996 but Trawsgoed needed significant funds to restore it to a private house, so a development partner was brought in. Cottages and outlying properties were sold off and the Victorian wing converted into five apartments, but little restoration has been done to the interiors and facades of the oldest and most architecturally important parts of the house. The best solution would be to have people living in the house who will value its glorious setting and opulent architecture. But first the principal elements of the house need to be repaired and adapted. So far Trawsgoed's time has not yet come.

The parapet is carried over the refaced 17th-century wings of the stuccoed early-Victorian front.

TREVOR HALL   Llangollen

Brick front added to earlier house that survives with mullioned windows at the back

TREVOR HOUSE STANDS IN A GLORIOUS POSITION, looking south across the lush green Dee Valley. The house is named after its first owners, the Trevor family. In 1742 Thomas Lloyd added the fine brick facade. His mason was John Roberts, to whom we owe the handsome stone trim – keystones over the windows, quoins emphasising the corners and bands of stone defining the storeys.

The house was saved by the enterprising Michael Tree who bought it from the local farmer in 1987 with just 3 acres . He recalls: 'The whole top floor and roof had burnt out. Many of the upper rooms were without floors. The ground floor was used for rearing calves and lambing ewes. All the fixtures had gone and just one fireplace was left.' Ingeniously a fine set of new fireplaces was provided by Kevin Cannon, who had trained in Italy as a mason and had just stripped out the marble interior of a wet-fish shop.

The restoration involved taking out and repairing seventy-three windows. The tall Regency sashes on the left of the grand front retain the original glass. All the chimney stacks had to be rebuilt and some of the new oak for the floors came from the Powys Castle estate. Traditional lime mortar was used on the bare brick and stone walls but where partitions had to be reinstated on the top floor plasterboard was used. 'I backed it with plywood to avoid that awful drumming you get,' laughs Tree.

A house such as Trevor needs land to protect it and though Michael Tree was able to buy neighbouring woodland, he was unable to acquire either the park or the adjacent stables. His successors have achieved this and Trevor, which sleeps fourteen, can now be rented for house parties through Stately Home Holidays.

The grand brick front was added by the mason John Roberts in 1742 and restored in the late 1980s.

TROY HOUSE   Monmouth
Nobly austere house built for the Dukes of Beaufort in 1675–1700

TROY HOUSE'S TIME HAS BEEN a long time in coming. It was unoccupied when SAVE included it in *Tomorrow's Ruins* in 1978 and still awaits a solution today. Though the long facade is plain, it is handsomely proportioned with a run of large sash windows along the *piano nobile* and more old-fashioned mullioned and transom windows above and below.

The house takes its unusual name from the River Trothy, which runs just below. Its grand proportions are explained by the fact that it was built in 1681–4 for the 1st Duke of Beaufort who, a decade earlier, had built Great Castle House in the centre of Monmouth. Troy was built for his son and heir, the Marquess of Worcester, on his marriage. The shell cost the Duke £3,000 but the Marquess paid for 'finishing the house to his mind' according to a memorandum preserved at Badminton.

The house incorporates a late 16th-century long house and a substantial early 17th century cross wing with Jacobean ornamental plaster ceilings. There is also a grand stair rising round an open well, with sturdy corkscrew balusters, as well as later 18th- and 19th-century additions.

In 1900 much of the panelling was moved to the Beaufort seat at Badminton and the house sold to nuns, who ran it as a girls' school. One critical decision is whether the ugly additions made by the nuns can be removed and buildings of equivalent volume set elsewhere on the site, opening the way to explore and recreate an historic garden layout. Graham Freckhall Architects of Monmouth are now drawing up a scheme and, following the evolution of the building, four very handsome houses could be created with new housing for local people nearby.

West of the house is a large walled garden entered through a Jacobean doorway that formerly bore the date 1611.

Two types of early window remain, some with wooden mullions and transoms and twelve-pane sashes.

IRELAND

CARTON HOUSE   Maynooth
Grand Palladian palace fit for a Duke

CARTON HOUSE, IN THE FLAT LANDS OF Co. Kildare near Dublin, is one of the great palatial houses of Ireland. The land on which it stands was owned for 800 years by the Norman FitzGerald family, from 1315 the Earls of Kildare. In 1739 Robert, the 19th Earl, made Carton his principal seat. He chose the Franco-Dutch Richard Castle to obliterate and enlarge the old 17th-century house in an unusual baroque Palladian style, creating one of the great country houses of Georgian Ireland.

It was completed by 1747, the same year that the 20th Earl (in 1766 Duke of Leinster) married Emily, the beautiful, spirited 16-year-old daughter of the Duke of Richmond. They maintained a ducal lifestyle. A contemporary visitor noted '… French horns playing at every meal; and such a quantity of plate etc that one would imagine oneself in a palace. And there are servants without end…'

Emily fell in love with 'dear sweet Carton' and she and her husband spent much of their lives decorating and improving the house, where she produced a tribe of children, including Lord Edward FitzGerald, later one of the leaders of the 1798 rebellion.

The glories of the interior include a Chinese room (the wallpaper cut up in the manner of a print room) and one of the most breathtaking rooms in the whole of Ireland, a double-height saloon with sumptuous baroque plasterwork by the Swiss Lafrancini brothers. Further extensive alterations were made after 1815 by the 3rd Duke with money generated by the sale of Leinster House, now the Irish parliament building. Carton was now sufficiently grand that in 1849 Victoria and Albert came to stay. Gambling debts ensured the house passed out of the family in the 1920s but it has recently been extensively restored and is now a golf resort and hotel.

The original entrance front now looks out over the garden.

SHELL HOUSE AT CARTON   Maynooth
Bijou cottage transformed by the first Duchess of Leinster

ONE OF THE FINEST EXAMPLES OF THE 18TH-CENTURY PASSION for shellwork is found in the grounds of Carton House. The 17th century had seen a vogue for tulips for those with the money to indulge. The early 18th century, to a more rarified degree, witnessed a preoccupation with shells and the creation of shell houses. Sea captains were importuned to bring back specimen seeds and exotic shells from foreign shores and domestic beaches were denuded. Generally, but not always, the chatelaine of the house was gripped.

In the case of Carton it was Lady Emily, the first Duchess of Leinster, whose passion it was. Starting in the late 1740s as a new bride, and as the great house her husband was building was nearing completion, she transformed the interior of an existing thatched cottage with the aid of shells, stones, twigs and glass. Formal geometric patterns contain almost pyrotechnic displays and the deeply recessed gothic windows are picked out with radiating lines of different shell types.

The Shell House, used to entertain guests to tea, was one of the earliest structures in what was to become one of the finest landscapes of 18th century Ireland. The Duke had offered a premium to Capability Brown to come to Ireland, to no avail. Nonetheless he and his wife created a huge enclosed demesne of rolling parkland that by 1760 amounted to 1,100 acres surrounded by a 5-mile wall. The Rye Water was dammed and widened and a lake created, and a bridge built in 1763 by Thomas Ivory. The Duchess also had an ornamental dairy built as she was rather enamoured of her herd of black and white cows.

The original shell house was much enlarged in the 19th century.

CASTLEBORO HOUSE — Enniscorthy
A Classical ruin of an imposing scale burnt in 'the Troubles'

THE VAST SHELL OF CASTLEBORO HOUSE, set against the backdrop of the Blackstairs Mountains, has been described as the most imposing ruin in all Ireland. The Carew family built Castleboro House beside the Forestalstown river in 1770, across the river from their old house, on land they had owned for a century.

The Carews were of Welsh extraction and as a planter family were granted lands in Co. Waterford in 1668. Robert Carew was elevated to the Irish peerage in 1834 and in the 1840's the 'modern house of Castleboro' was destroyed by fire, apart from the west wing. This was incorporated in new plans devised by the Scottish architect, Daniel Robertson.

Robertson's reputation has been dogged by allegations of dubious behaviour, first in speculative building projects, which seems to have created financial difficulties for Robert Adam in whose office he had been a principal draftsman, and subsequently in Oxford, from where he left to settle in Ireland. There are stories of him, overweight and inebriated, being wheeled in a wheelbarrow around the gardens at Powerscourt in Co. Wicklow, where he was working on the magnificent Italian terraces.

Certainly Castleboro was built to very high standards with great attention to detail. A highly ornamental stone entablature carved with rosettes and scrolls runs along the entire building, supported by Corinthian columns with richly carved capitals and pilasters of the same order. Much in the manner of Powerscourt, stepped terraces descended to an artificial lake with a magnificent fountain. The house was burnt by the IRA in 1923.

The full length of the north front with its array of advancing and retreating pillars and pilasters.

CROM CASTLE
Newtownbutler

A baronial castle at the centre of a romantic – and historic – landscape

CROM CASTLE OVERLOOKS UPPER LOUGH ERNE, a 300-square-mile romantic wilderness of waterways studded with wooded islands and inlets, in its heyday the scene of fiercely competitive yacht races between the families whose country houses were built along its shores. The present castle was built in the 1830s for the 3rd Earl of Erne by the English architect Edward Blore in a suitably baronial manner with a varied, asymmetrical array of Tudor-inspired turrets, crenellated towers and corbelled oriel windows.

It is its setting, in a parkland of some 1,900 acres, that is the chief glory of Crom. The romance of this setting was heavily influenced by the painter and garden-designer William Gilpin, who worked closely with Blore. The original castle, close to the lake shore, has been turned into a picturesque ruin.

Built in 1611 by a Scottish planter, in 1644 it was acquired by the Crichtons, ancestors of the Earls of Erne. It withstood two Jacobite sieges in 1689 (2,500 men were reputed to have died here in July 1689 – five hundred drowned in the lake and two thousand put to the sword, the first major defeat of the Jacobite army) but was destroyed by fire in 1764. As the new house was being built, the ruins were transformed into a folly with the addition of 'ruined' walls and towers.

To the south of the old castle are traces of a late 17th-century formal garden and bowling green enclosed by a battlemented ha-ha. A famous pair of 400-year-old yews stand at the entrance to the old garden. Another folly was built on Gad Island in the lake as a famine-relief project in 1848 and used as an observatory. A magnificent two-storey boathouse was built on the lakeside and was home to the original Lough Erne Yacht Club when Crom and its neighbours were the epicentre of Fermanagh high society.

The crenellated and turreted front of Crom looks out over Upper Lough Erne.

DROMORE CASTLE · Pallaskenry

An outstanding medieval revival castle, authentic in every way – including damp

DROMORE, A MEDIEVAL CASTLE WITH PINNACLES and battlements, soaring roofs and tall round tower, all correct to the last detail and clearly designed with defence in mind, was built only in the late 1860s. It is a breathtaking creation designed by the Bristol architect E.W. Godwin for the 3rd Earl of Limerick. The Earl had a house in Bristol and shared a love of the antique with Godwin. When Limerick inherited his title and several thousand acres of Co. Limerick in 1866, he turned to Godwin to build a house befitting his status.

Godwin's intimate knowledge of Irish medieval castles, and the violence then a feature of Irish land reform, made a castle an attractive proposition. It also allowed Godwin full rein to his interest 'to bring before us those old times, to make history a reality'. But this was no sham castle, 'the entrances are well guarded, so that in the event of the country being disturbed the inmates of Dromore … might feel secure'.

All the major rooms face into the courtyard with few windows on the ground floor piercing the thick outside walls. Above there is a riot of stepped battlements, tall chimneys, corbelling and steeply pitched roofs, in profile a stouter version of that romantic agglomeration of buildings on the Rock of Cashel.

Godwin was a romantic medievalist, an aesthete who took part in period costume drama, but he was also immensely knowledgeable and at Dromore his exact understanding of medieval form and function allowed him to break out of the straightjacket of the Gothic Revival and build something of quality, full of art and originality. Alas, as perhaps authentic medieval castles should, the building suffered from damp and Godwin fell out with his patron.

An ancient round tower, a monk's cell and a corbelled bartizan proclaim the castle's antiquity.

EMO COURT   Emo
A restored palace in the Irish midlands full of rich and grand interiors

EMO COURT WAS BEGUN BY JAMES GANDON, one of the great European architects of the 18th century, for Lord Carlow in the early 1790s. Gandon had been persuaded to come to Ireland to design a new custom house in Dublin for an optimistic and expanding city. He went on to build three other iconic and palatial buildings in Dublin: the Four Courts, the King's Inns and extensive additions to the Houses of Parliament. These magnificent buildings, together with the Custom House, have a collective personality that defines so much of Dublin's visual character even today.

Emo Court was conceived on an equally palatial scale and has pleasing references for the cognoscenti to a wide range of contemporary Classical buildings in Britain and Ireland, as well as what has been described as a kind of 'Gallic grandeur'. It is also notable for prompting a later rash of full-height free standing domestic temple fronts. So grand was its execution that it was later in the 19th century a contender for the Irish residence of the Prince of Wales, later Edward VII. Lord Carlow, by now the Earl of Portarlington, died when off campaigning during the 1798 rebellion; his son, short of money, did not restart work on the building for another forty years, by a variety of other hands, and it was not until the 1860s that the great rotunda was complete.

For forty years of the last century it was a Jesuit Seminary until bought by a sympathetic and knowledgeable owner who realised many of the originally intended interior schemes with great brio. The restored rotunda, with its high, coffered dome top-lit by a lantern, is more like a magnificent public space than a domestic hall. Vast Corinthian capitals of Siena marble topped with gilded capitals soar to a double-height entablature. It is now owned by the state.

The entrance front masks the great dome, which is on the other side of the house.

FOTA   Carrigtuohill
A Regency house with spectacular interiors on a balmy island in Co. Cork

THE CHIEF DELIGHT OF FOTA IS ITS interiors, created by father-and-son team Richard and William Vitruvius Morrison for the Smith-Barry family in the 1820s. They transformed a plain, small house on an island with a benign climate into a Grecian tour de force. A severe Grecian front porch was added to the old house leading into the centre of the hall, which runs the width of the entrance front. Light flooding in from the windows reflects from the yellow, polished scagliola columns that march in pairs the length of the hall.

Eight yellow scagliola columns stand in the hall, which takes up the whole width of the old house.

Beyond, a cantilevered staircase with a brass handrail curves upwards to meet yet another pair of columns that support a richly stuccoed, domed ceiling. Motifs in high relief catch the eye at every turn. The interior makeover was matched in style and extravagance outside: huntsmen and hounds were given purpose-made buildings, a formal garden was laid out with a temple and orangery, and in the middle of the 19th century an arboretum was begun that is now world-famous.

The reign of the Smith-Barry family ended with the death of the daughter of the last Lord Barrymore and the magnificent collection of paintings and books was dispersed. Since then the house has undergone a lengthy and award-winning restoration.

The plain old house nestles amongst later additions.

GLIN CASTLE

Glin

A direct descendant of a real castle overlooking the Shannon Estuary

GLIN CASTLE IS THE SEAT OF the Knights of Glin, together with the White Knight and the Knight of Kerry the titular heads of the three branches of the FitzGerald house of Desmond. The Norman FitzGeralds settled in Ireland in the last quarter of the 12th century and today the 29th Knight of Glin in direct succession lives at Glin, a few miles from the old family castle at Shanid, the keep of which still partially stands. The plain 18th-century house at Glin was battlemented and coated in what is described by the present owner as 'uniquely Irish pastry-like rough cast' and given the title 'castle' in the early 19th century.

Inside the shell of the old house, built in the 1780s, is a memorable series of decorated rooms, neither large nor ostentatious, but beautifully proportioned, delicate and detailed. From the rigorously symmetrical front hall with its screen of fluted Corinthian columns, fanlighted doorcases lead to the twin ramps of the flying staircase beyond, light flooding from a Palladian window on the half landing. The hall ceiling, an elaborate affair in the Adam manner, is alive with naive plasterwork in high relief, neoclassical motifs jostling with flowers, foliage, Irish harps and armorial bearings. It is unique in that it preserves its original colouring of terracotta and apple green, although now somewhat faded and discoloured but redolent of the centuries to which it has borne witness. Part of the house's charm is that Glin was spared the worst excesses of 19th-century modernisation. When the money ran out work stopped, so abruptly that many of the third storey rooms were only recently completed.

The interiors are full of exquisite pieces of Irish furniture, many of which have been collected by the present owner, Desmond Fitzgerald, an authority on Irish art and architecture and president of the Irish Georgian Society.

The battlemented and rough-cast exterior gives no hint of the rich interiors.

HEADFORT HOUSE   Kells
Severely plain house with interiors of extraordinary quality

HEADFORT HOUSE WAS DESCRIBED BY an 18th-century observer as 'more like a college or an infirmary' but behind the forbidding facade is a scheme of interior decoration by Robert Adam of breathtaking quality. The Taylor (later Taylour) family, originally of Sussex, purchased the land around Kells in Co. Meath in 1660 and it was the fourth generation that instigated the building of the present house to a plain design largely by George Semple over ten years from 1760 to 1770. The next year Robert Adam, the undisputed master of polychrome low-relief decoration in the Roman manner, was commissioned to create the interiors of the principal rooms of the gaunt and undecorated house, his only considerable decorative work in Ireland and the only work to survive in its entirety. The climax of his scheme is a two-storey high double-cube ballroom or 'eating parlour' as it was originally known.

Members of the Taylour family were successively ennobled and the 2nd Earl was created Marquis of Headfort as a reward for voting for the dissolution of the Irish parliament in 1800. The family lived quietly and without particular distinction on their 1,000-acre estate until in 1946 the 5th Marquis leased the greater part of the house to a preparatory school which still flourishes there. The 6th Marquis resented the school and would repeatedly dive-bomb the house in his light aircraft during lessons. Later he was escorted from the Scilly Isles having attempted to procure the shooting of Prime Minister Harold Wilson, a charge he always denied.

The estate boasts many spectacular specimen trees planted in the 19th century and a model farmyard with an extensive semicircular range of buildings now converted into homes. The house looks out over formal gardens to the meandering River Blackwater, a tributary of the Boyne.

The entrance front of Headfort overlooks a complex topiary garden.

HILTON PARK   Clones
A house redolent of history – steel-shuttered against the troubles of the past

THERE HAS BEEN A HOUSE AT HILTON Park since the early 1600s when the local family of O'Toole sold their holdings to an 'incomer'. The Maddens, the present owners, had returned to Ireland with the Earl of Strafford in the 17th century. In 1734 Rev. Samuel Madden purchased the estate and built a house incorporating the original building. He took his duties seriously and in 1738 wrote a book with the portentous title: *Reflections and Resolutions Proper for the Gentlemen of Ireland, as to their Conduct for the Service of their Country, as Landlords, as Masters of Families, as Protestants, as Descended from British Ancestors, as Country Gentlemen and Farmers, as Justices of the*

The porte-cochère *was added to the entrance front in the late 19th-century rebuilding.*

Peace, as Merchants, as Members of Parliament. Samuel Madden was a philanthropist of such legendary generosity that he was known as 'Premium' Madden. He was also a co-founder of the Royal Dublin Society. His house was largely burnt down in 1803 and was rebuilt over the following years in an austere style – as usual for many Irish landlords, money was tight.

A Victorian Madden, feeling the house insufficient to reflect his status, approached various architects of the day to transform it into an Italian palazzo. In 1874 a young Dublin architect, William Hague, was appointed. He had the bright idea of giving the two-storey house added grandeur by digging out the basement. This allowed him to create a new suite of reception rooms in the new ground floor and a hall, inner hall, arcaded staircase (which meets the original Georgian staircase on the first floor) and gallery, as well as a ballroom, were added. The new entrance was reached via a grandiose portico topped with balustrades and urns and with a multitude of Ionic columns. The outside was encased in Dungannon sandstone with some added decoration to relieve the austerity.

The interior is a rich medley of styles from different periods. The dining room has a 'nautical' ceiling of ropes and oak leaves – a Madden ancestor had been Admiral of the Red in Nelson's fleet at Trafalgar. The hall is an essay in Victoriana, gleaming with brass and enamelled tiles (a foretaste of Hague's later career as a church architect), and the staircase is lit by stained glass. An unusual feature was the installation of heavy steel shutters – the front door too is unusually massive – in deference to the increasing violence of the land wars.

Hague's larger scheme, including domes and extra bays, was never built and the present house sits in beautiful grounds laid out in the 1870s.

LARCH HILL
Coole
Landscape studded with ten eccentric follies

AT LARCH HILL, ON THE BORDERS OF CO. MEATH AND CO. Kildare, it is not so much the 'plain and pleasant' house that is the attraction but the rare survival of an 18th-century *ferme ornée*, a gothic farmyard with stables, pigsties and dovecotes and its attendant landscaped parkland dotted with ornamental buildings, statuary, water features and picturesque walks. The landscape was a product of the Romantic Movement which swept away the formality of the 17th century and replaced it with an informal 'Arcadian' vision of nature.

A series of lakes and islands, replete with forts and follies, are overlooked by two gazebos and by all accounts the complex was intended as a cruder, simpler version of the pleasure grounds at Versailles where mock naval battles could be fought, observed from the rustic gazebos sited on higher ground. Eight acres of low-lying pasture were flooded, creating an expanse of water and a smaller lake connected by a narrow canal. A map of 1836 shows an island named 'Gibraltar', which contains a battlemented fort, complete with towers and turrets, housing a rooftop battery sporting gun-hole openings – on the battlements of the folly fort at Tyrella House in Co. Down, small cannon still survive. Another small island is connected to the shore by a causeway, possibly to embark the miniature men-of-war that might have plied the lake.

A fox-hunting theme gives some of the follies their raison d'etre. The squire of Larch Hill in the latter part of the 18th century was Robert Watson, master of the local foxhounds and the creator of the landscape. On a small island in the larger lake he built a circular temple with a large stone statue of Nimrod, the hunter, in

Fort Gibraltar – the miniature fort before restoration.

the centre. Convinced he would be reincarnated as a fox, so the story goes, he constructed a mausoleum for himself in the manner of a fox's earth. A simple vaulted space built into an artificial circular burial mound contains a vaulted chamber with two small square openings in the side walls at ground level – just large enough to accommodate a fox.

Other follies include a three-storey battlemented tower – the 'Cockle Tower' – with fine shellwork ceilings, a barrel-vaulted boathouse and a simple dairy with arched stained-glass windows and tiles from the early 1800s decorated with naval and military scenes. Following its purchase in 1994, the landscape has been subject to a six-year award-winning restoration. The lake was excavated, the ten follies rebuilt, and the estate is now open to the public.

LISMORE CASTLE   Lismore
Castle of the 17th and 19th centuries with medieval origin

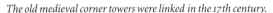

THE BATTLEMENTS OF LISMORE CASTLE RISE sheer above the River Blackwater in Co. Waterford, a dramatic view that richly complements its historic origins. What the visitor sees today, a romantic skyline of turrets and towers in profusion, dates largely from the 17th and 19th centuries but incorporates much older structures. The first was a monastery and seat of learning founded by St Carthage in AD 636 which, by the 9th century, was famous throughout Europe.

The first castle was built by Prince John in 1185, incorporating the monastic buildings. When he inherited the crown the castle became the seat of the local

The old medieval corner towers were linked in the 17th century.

Stone used in the 19th-century rebuilding was shipped from Derbyshire.

bishops. In 1589 the episcopal palace was leased to Sir Walter Raleigh. In 1602 he sold his lands to another Elizabethan adventurer, the 1st Earl of Cork, who shortly afterwards began rebuilding the castle. A gatehouse, incorporating an archway from the old monastery, and an outer gatehouse still survive.

Sacked in 1645, the castle was later rebuilt by the 2nd Earl, who entertained King James II there in 1689. In the next century it fell into ruin as the Earls of Cork, also Earls of Burlington, preferred to live in England. The castle passed by marriage to the Cavendishes, Dukes of Devonshire, in 1748, and it was the 6th Duke, the 'Bachelor Duke', who began the next phase of building and restoration in 1811, aided by the architect William Atkinson, and again in the 1850s, this time with the help of his good friend Sir Joseph Paxton, designer of the Crystal Place.

The Jacobean gabled ranges erected by the Earl of Cork between the corner towers of the old castle were given battlements, and the ruinous bishops' chapel was recreated as a medieval banqueting hall with stencilled interiors by Crace and Pugin in a welter of blue, red and gold.

Still in the ownership of the Dukes of Devonshire, parts of this vast and romantic building have survived for more than a thousand years.

THE CASINO AT MARINO   Clontarf
Celebrated Classical composition of the first rank

HEMMED IN BY HOUSES IN NORTH CO. DUBLIN is one of Europe's most exquisite buildings. It was designed to be a summer house as part of a Classical landscape, complete with hermitage, gothic room, rustic cottage and a 'cane house constructed after the eastern model', all now long gone apart from The Casino. Its apparently miniature scale and perfect proportions deceive the eye – it is much bigger than it looks. From the outside it appears a single-roomed structure, but actually contains sixteen different rooms. Three storeys and a flat-roofed viewing platform, once provided with a temporary canopy, provided every convenience for entertaining. Not only highly ornamental, it is also alive with symbolism, ready to be decoded by the initiated.

The Casino was designed by the young William Chambers, later to be one of the grandest architects of the 18th century, and built over more than twenty years from 1759 for the 1st Earl of Charlemont, regarded by his contemporaries as one of the most cultivated men of his day. Charlemont followed Italian precedent and built no walls around his estate, allowing open access to the public.

The Casino is a temple to good taste, its apparent simplicity from a distance masking the extensive use of extravagant Roman decorative detail carved to standards previously unseen in Ireland. Four different columned fronts, each unique, provide close up a dramatic sense of scale. Ingenuity is everywhere apparent: the columns are hollow to take rainwater from the roofs; the Classical urns are chimneys. The drama is enhanced by entering through an *Alice in Wonderland*-sized opening cut into the monumental door. Inside, the full splendour of the decorative scheme is revealed: coffered and panelled ceilings, friezes, garlands and trophies of Classical motifs abound and the floors are a riot of geometric inlays in rare woods.

Perfect proportions disguise the scale of The Casino.

MOUNT CONGREVE · Kilmeadan
One of the world's great gardens, full of rare plants

IN 2000, THE WORLD'S LEADING GARDENERS had risen in unison at a threat to one of the great gardens of the 20th century: a bypass proposal that would bring traffic roaring past the gates, raised on an elevated highway, and blasting through ancient shelter belts that protected rare Asiatic trees and shrubs from south-west gales.

The 100-acre gardens of Mount Congreve, near Waterford, are the creation of over seventy-five years of 93-year-old Ambrose Congreve. Some twenty years earlier he had placed the gardens in a trust which, twenty-one years after his death, will become the property of the Irish state. It is an astonishing gift. The gardens of Mount Congreve are in flower every month of the year, and for the city of Waterford, this is an opportunity to stretch the tourist season from March to early November.

Spring-flowering shrubs and trees are one of the wonders of nature and gardeners will often travel miles to see just one or two of the great magnolias in bloom. At Mount Congreve, all the great magnolias and dozens of recent hybrid cultivars are planted in such profusion that anyone arriving from mid March to late April is effectively guaranteed a spectacular display of white, pink and red blooms.

The pavillions of the garden front were remodelled in the mid 20th century.

The original 18th-century greenhouses still stand in the walled garden.

With them go wide rivers of daffodils, and a collection of over five hundred types of camellia. These give way towards the end of April to an even greater profusion of azaleas and rhododendrons continuing through to the end of June. July sees the start of a mile-long hydrangea walk with a staggering range of blooms.

The main body of the garden is laid out on rising ground along the banks of the River Suir but in the previous four years large new peninsulas had shot out along the inside of the park wall, creating huge areas of additional planting.

Congreve's main principle is to plant in large groups that astonish and delight at each turn. 'What you see here you won't see again for another hundred yards, except with tender varieties which can react very differently according to their position,' he said.

The bulk of the shrubs and flowering trees have grown up under a protective canopy of tall, widely spaced oaks and conifers. Particularly at the western end of the grounds, dozens of these trees are embowered with climbing roses and clematis.

The centrepiece is a splendid Georgian hothouse, filled with a dazzling display of large pink- and white-striped lilies, regal pelargoniums, cascading fuchsias, plumbago, perpetual flowering carnations, hibiscus, pink, blue, lavender and white streptocarpus and numerous rare orchids.

Not surprisingly, when Congreve learnt of the officially favoured route for the bypass, his thought was to leave Mount Congreve, abandoning its gardens to nature, for the state to reclaim after his death. To their credit the county councillors recognised the problem and drew up an alternative route which will take the bypass outside the shelter belt and be set back further from the gates on a lower embankment. They might even find that the road approaching Waterford has as fine a display of spring and autumn colour as any parkway in North America.

MYRTLE GROVE — Youghal
Unfortified Tudor manor house surviving beneath later additions

MYRTLE GROVE TODAY IS AN INTRIGUING HOUSE, a Tudor manor lying not far beneath a Georgian overlay, but its origins are far older. In 1464 a college was founded in Youghal, Ireland's first post-Norman monastic university, and the original house was occupied by the Warden of the College. After the Dissolution of the Monasteries a small unfortified manor house was built on the site, safe within the old town walls, parts of which still exist in the garden, and it is this house that forms the core of the present building (during restoration work, two books from the 15th century were found behind panelling).

In a countryside continually wracked by rebellion few unfortified Elizabethan or Jacobean houses were built in Ireland and Myrtle Grove is the only one to have survived in something like its original state. Sir Walter Raleigh, who came to Ireland to help put down the Desmond rebellion of 1579, was granted the house and

other forfeited land. The Desmond dynasty was crushed by 1583 and the plantation of Munster with English settlers began. Initially appointed a temporary administrator of Munster, Raleigh lived there, more off than on, for seventeen years. He spoke of ' ... my oriel window at Youghal' – two can still be seen – and it is in one of them, 'the deep embrasured window', that Raleigh and Spencer are thought to have read the manuscript of *The Fairie Queen*. Outside the front door is an ancient yew tree, under which, legend has it, Raleigh was smoking when a servant, thinking he was on fire, doused him with a bucket of water. Raleigh was mayor of Youghal in 1588 and sold his estates in 1602 to another Elizabethan adventurer, Richard Boyle, 1st Earl of Cork.

Although Myrtle Grove was altered in the 18th and 19th centuries, it is still unmistakably a Tudor manor house, and a great chamber, panelled in dark oak and with an elaborately carved chimney piece survives. Later in the 19th century it was owned by Sir John Pope Hennessy, on whom Trollope based the eponymous character in *Phineas Finn*.

One of the original oriel windows was reglazed in the 18th century.

NEWBRIDGE

Donabate

A rare example of a house with period decoration and furniture still intact

NEWBRIDGE WAS BUILT BETWEEN 1749 and 1750 for Charles Cobbe, Archbishop of Dublin from 1743, on land acquired more than a decade earlier. Cobbe had first come to Ireland as a young man in 1717 as chaplain to his cousin the Duke of Bolton, who had been appointed Lord Lieutenant. The higher ranks of clergy were then as much a part of society as the aristocracy, from whose numbers many were drawn, and an archbishop would need his own scaled-down version of a 'trophy' house. He employed the Dublin architect George Semple – fresh from a commission for the executors of Jonathan Swift, Dean of Dublin's St Patrick's Cathedral and author of *Gulliver's Travels*, who had died in 1745 – to create his rather stern house, faced in pink ashlar. The Cobbe family

The entrance front of Newbridge, its facade of pink ashlar stone glowing in the sunlight.

lived in the house until 1985, and it retains its spectacular interiors with original furnishings and decoration preserved intact thanks to an agreement with Dublin City Council, who have been restoring the house and its demesne.

The archbishop died in 1765 and Newbridge passed to his son, who had married a sister of the first Marquis of Waterford. Unlike the sober archbishop they were a sociable couple and soon after his death built a wing at the back of the house to accommodate new rooms for entertaining. A richly ornamented and pedimented doorcase frames the door to the drawing-room, a vast room measuring 42.9 ft by 25.6 ft. Above is an exuberant and elaborate rococo ceiling with a deep, coved cornice by Richard William, a pupil of one of the great stuccodores of 18th-century Ireland, Robert West. The room was redecorated in the Regency style by Thomas's grandson in the early 19th century and little has been changed since. Beyond, a picture gallery of even larger proportions was created to house a growing collection of works of art – a scout was constantly on the look-out for suitable pictures and statuary. Housed on crimson damask wallpaper, some forty-five paintings still survive. The Greek key pattern of the wall panels in the dining room echo the Irish Chippendale sideboards made especially for the room. Everywhere the Cobbe family crest is proudly in evidence. Of particular interest, as it is an unusual survival of the 18th-century passion for collecting, is 'Mr Cobbe's Museum', a curio room then much in vogue, also known as a 'Cabinet of Curiosities'. It contains souvenirs and trophies collected by the family on their travels.

JERSEY

MILLIONS WERE SPENT ON THIS PROPERTY over the 1990s. The garden is laid out in the grand manner and though just six years old when the house was on sale in 2000, it was already impressively mature and lush. It has the feel of one of the great Riviera gardens created early in the 20th century, with *parterres* commanding a glorious panorama over the vivid blue waters of south-facing St Aubin's Bay.

The magnificent *parterre*, with clipped sentinel cypresses and box-edged rose beds, stuns the eye in a single glance, and has a succession of no less than six fountain basins with sixteen floodlit fountains. To the sides there are cleverly framed views of the Elizabethan and Hanoverian castles, as well as the old fishermen's village of St Aubin. By contrast, the ugliness of modern St Helier is largely shielded. On a good day you can see as far as the remarkable archipelago of rocks that form Les Minquiers reef.

The surprise is to discover, beyond the last terrace, a huge expanse of valley garden created from a wilderness so thick that a handsome stone bridge dated 1918 was revealed as the brambles were cut back. On the descent, Jersey granite has been ingeniously laid to look like drystone walling.

At the bottom is a spectacular avenue of sixteen substantial *Magnolia grandiflora* surrounded by beds edged with lavender, and immediately above it a large Japanese

garden was still in the making, with stands of bamboo, huge boulders, slate chippings and sweeps of clear water bubbling down over gravel. This is overlooked by an extensive Chinese garden complete with statues and moon gate. The valley gardens ascend along a string of a dozen sizeable rock pools, stocked with salmon, trout and carp, with water tumbling from one to the other down an impressive series of rock steps. Thanks to a well-equipped pump house, the flow is better than virtually any of the island's natural streams.

The kernel of it is a house of the 1840s built for the Abraham de Gruchy family who, thirty years earlier, had started a small draper's shop which went on to become Jersey's largest department store.

The interior provides an intriguing insight as to how the rich want to live. The main rooms have an abundance of gilt plasterwork. You can dine in the large formal dining room, the private dining room, the conservatory or the kitchen or sit in the panelled library with a tray watching TV. Or retreat to the soundproofed basement with billiard room, bar and mini cinema, not to mention 'smoking room with air circulation system'. There is a private leisure complex with indoor pool, gymnasium with mirrored walls, exercise bar and music system and garaging for ten cars.

Bedroom accommodation in the house has actually been reduced (the attic reverting exclusively to storage) and there are just four bedroom suites in the main house. For visitors there are five guest cottages – within a single building but with their own entrances, sitting room, kitchen and one or two bedrooms; four further staff cottages are provided, each self-contained and with its own front door. A recluse need never encounter his guests at all.

The new formal gardens are set on a terrace looking out across the bay.

LES LUMIÈRES · St Brelade
Begun in 1932 and the masterpiece of the architect Arthur Grayson

JERSEY BOASTS A REMARKABLE GROUP of fine 1930s buildings in the International Style designed by the talented architect Arthur Grayson, who settled on the island. Les Lumières, set above the beautiful bay of St Brelade, survived in almost untouched condition, slowly decaying but barely altered, but when the owner moved to a nursing home the future looked bleak. The white walls were streaked with damp and potential purchasers wanted to radically alter the house, if not demolish it.

Les Lumières was commissioned by the builders' merchant Ernest 'Tony' Huelin in 1932 and was expected to cost £2,500, though delays pushed the price to £10,000. Like many 1930s houses, it is a stylishly asymmetrical composition dominated on the entrance side by a staircase bow with ladder window. The garden front has a corresponding three-storey bay window on an even more pronounced curve with wrap-around windows providing views over the cliffs. Streamlined balconies add a strong horizontal note and Grayson designed the garden around an equally bold axis in the form of an arrow path pointing out to sea.

Disaster was avoided when Save Jersey's Heritage helped achieve designation as a site of special interest, the equivalent of a Grade I listing. Further support came from the 20th Century Society and a painstaking restoration has now been completed. The house is once again a strong Mediterranean white and the single gate pier – considered very avant garde at the time – has been repaired, with the name of the house in Jazz-Age lettering.

The interiors were remarkable for the amount of fitted furniture that survived. All these were sent for restoration to the firm of Shaw and Riley near Harrogate and the new owners commissioned over twenty new pieces from the same firm. All the chromework, including the stair rail and the huge ceiling light in the lounge, was sent to a specialist firm near Leeds.

The stylish garden front looking out over St Brelade's Bay, before restoration began.

ST OUEN'S MANOR St Ouen

A fortified late-medieval house extended in the 17th century and remodelled in 1888–1910

MORE FRIENDLY WORDS CAN RARELY have been written by an English king to one of his subjects than these, added by Charles II to a letter to the Seigneur of St Ouen's Manor in Jersey: 'Carteret, I will add this to you under my owne hand that I can never forget the good services you have done to my father and to me, and if god bless me, you shall find I doe remember them to the advantage of you and yours: and for this you have the word of Your very loving friend, Charles R.'

The granite bastion walls were rebuilt with buttresses and balconies in the 19th century.

The date, significantly, was May 5, 1649, three months after Charles I had walked out onto the scaffold at Whitehall. At the Restoration Charles II more than made good his word, giving Sir George Carteret manors in Cornwall and Devon and the lands between the Hudson and Delaware rivers that Carteret named New Jersey.

At first sight, St Ouen's Manor might be taken for a grand baronial seat of late-Victorian date, with towers, turrets, gables, patterned roof tiles and bay windows. This impression is heightened by the large, deep-arched entrance porch projecting at an angle between two long wings, and on the right a rather awkward skylight suggesting a billiard room – a feature of 1900 date, which the present seigneur, Philip Malet de Carteret, endearingly refers to as 'great grandfather's mistakes'.

In 1483, Philippe de Carteret obtained Jersey's only known licence to crenellate from the Governor of Jersey, Richard Harliston, whose daughter Margaret was his wife. This allowed him to enclose his property so that he and his tenants could take refuge within defensive walls. This was some twenty years after the French occupation of the island in the 1460s, and before the growing strength of the Tudor Navy helped bring more permanent security to the islands.

By this time the T-shaped core of the present house was complete, consisting of a rectangular hall (the present hall) and two towers. Towards the end of the 15th century the massive east terrace had been formed. During the 18th century the Jersey manor went to sleep. A steward was installed and in 1795 the house was leased as a barracks.

In 1859 Edward Charles Malet assumed the name of Malet de Carteret and with his wife's money embarked on major building works. The architect, Edmund

The roofs step up to a central pyramid-roofed tower.

Berteau, built a handsome granite gate lodge and largely rebuilt the retaining walls east of the house, a virtuoso exercise in masonry, with buttresses, battered walls, projecting balconies and broad cushion capping to the tops of the walls. The architect Adolphus Curry remodelled the house, creating a new entrance court, heightening the towers and adding the new entrance porch. Inside, Carteret created a splendid great hall with wainscoting inset with numerous carved oak panels taken from Breton chests and cupboards.

The manor was taken over as a barracks during the German occupation of Jersey and on March 6, 1941, a fire broke out in the south-east wing, probably sparked by red-hot cinders falling out of the round iron stoves introduced by the Germans.

Though the estate had been in the family for over eight hundred years, the present seigneur, Philip Malet de Carteret, only secured it after a struggle. He had become a Catholic, and his father Guy, unwilling to see the family pew in St Ouen's Church lie empty, had left St Ouen's to his younger son, Rex.

In Philip's own words, 'my brother Rex had got into financial trouble and gone bankrupt. Much to my rage I heard he was going to sell the manor and live off the farms. So I mortgaged myself to the hilt, obtained the keys to the manor in 1978 and paid off the loans eight years later.' Today the future of St Ouen's is secure and a fresh order and elegance is being gently brought to the manor by a new chatelaine, Adele, whom the seigneur married in 1999 following the death of his first wife.

PETIT HIBEAUX — St Lawrence
16th-century granite farmhouse rescued from extreme decay

FOR YEARS THIS DELIGHTFUL FARMHOUSE was left to slowly decay until even whole sections of the roof collapsed as the beams inside rotted away. Carol-Anne Mawdsley, who finally bought the house in 2004 says, 'The interior was a wreck. Elders were growing inside the kitchen, trying to find their way out of the chimney. Windows and doors were all rotten. There was no electricity, no plumbing, not even running water.'

Restoration began swiftly. The house has been handsomely thatched in the Norman French style (without the decorative work common in East Anglia) using Turkish reed – the only source. Inside, floors have been laid in wide English oak planks – in Jersey, reclaimed timber is not allowed as it might prompt the dismantling of other historic buildings. Where beams with rotten ends had survived in the house, they were used in rooms with shorter spans. Windows and doors were remade using the rare survivors as templates. The whole interior was lime-rendered, giving the house an instant patina. There are five comfortable living rooms and six bedrooms, each with its own bath- or shower-room – essential as each bedroom is approached by a separate staircase.

The farmhouse had belonged to the Remon family for three hundred years. A 16th-century outdoor staircase leads up to a living room built over the cow byre. At right angles is a 19th-century wing faced in dressed granite. Though it looked little more than a cottage, Petit Hibeaux now makes a spacious and comfortable house with a private lair for each member of the family.

In Jersey, sash windows and sash boxes are traditionally painted in two colours.

SEAFIELD HOUSE   St Lawrence

Elegant Regency villa attributed to the English architect Robert Lugar

'HE BROUGHT HIS CHILDREN UP in fear of God and in horror of customs men.' So wrote the Baron de Frénilly of the Sieur Giffard, builder of Jersey's most remarkable Regency house. Frénilly, a strong Bourbon supporter, had come to Jersey in 1815 after Napoleon escaped from Elba. In his diary, he described Giffard as 'the leading banker, merchant and smuggler of Jersey, gallant presbyterian, pious, loyal, austere, sober … he has a very pretty house with an elegance that is completely English'.

Giffard had chosen one of the prime sites on the island's south coast looking out over the large and well-sheltered bay of St Aubin's, less than 200 yards from the vast sandy beach. Originally the garden stretched down to the dunes, but in 1870 it was cut off by the construction of the Jersey railway.

Below: The entrance front has a pretty loggia.
Bottom: The garden front has a columned rotunda and dome.

The entrance front faces north and is a pretty three-part composition with an elegant Ionic portico approached by a flight of Portland stone steps – quite a rarity in an island of granite. Pretty iron railings enclose a partly recessed loggia. On either side are handsome tripartite sash windows with matching Ionic columns. This entablature continues round the house like a belt until it reaches a splendid domed rotunda on the garden front.

Richard Miles, the present owner of Seafield, has found two engravings of a design for a house at Tor Worley near Birmingham that are almost identical to Seafield. They are the work of Robert Lugar, who was associated with the famous John Nash in Wales in the mid 1790s. Lugar designed pretty *cottages ornées* and castellated mansions, many of which are illustrated in a series of pattern books.

It is likely, therefore, that Lugar provided the designs for Seafield even if he himself never came to Jersey. The one significant difference is that the Tor Worley design lacks the second floor of the entrance front and the top stage of the dome, but it appears likely that those at Seafield were added later anyway.

The extensive gardens are planted informally in picturesque style.

Seafield was completed by 1809 when the island's official property register mentions '*une maison appellée Beau-Mur, que les dits seigneurs Dolbel et Giffard ont fait bâtir*'. Dolbel, part owner of the land, later sold back his share to Giffard.

Like many handsome Regency houses in the island, Seafield was let at times to army officers from England on half-pay, who came to Jersey where prices and taxes were low. Frénilly wrote of Jersey: 'It is the best country in the world and one lives for nothing. Our complete establishment, well-furnished, well-heated, with servants, scrubbed, polished, provided with everything in fact excepting food and drink only cost us ten shillings a week.'

Quite when *Beau-Mur* became Seafield is not clear but in September 1887 the house was let for a month to Princess Stephanie of Austria, the bride of Archduke Rudolph, the Crown Prince who was found dead with his mistress at Mayerling two years later. The house at this time belonged to the Le Gros family; they sold it in 1922 to Maxwell Vandeleur Blacker Douglas, who had spotted Seafield across a wall and gone straight to advocates in St Helier to make an offer.

During the Second World War his widow stayed in Jersey and a letter requisitioning Seafield survives in the house. Some months later, on June 12, 1943, the *Deutsche Zeitung* published a picture of the house under the headline '*Unser Soldatenheim*' [Our Service Club]. When the property was handed back at the end of the war, there were German signs over the doors and a huge map of the island marking all the German gun emplacements.

Seafield's large and pretty garden is now planted in best Regency gardenesque style with islands of shrubs and trees creating clever vistas.

STEEPHILL
St Saviour

Informal freestyle house by the architect Ernest Newton

STEEPHILL'S BUILDER, CHARLES JANVRIN ROBIN, descended from an ancient Jersey family that can be traced back to the 13th century. Following the fall of Quebec in 1759, Jersey merchants had moved in to take over the prosperous cod fisheries on the Gulf of St Lawrence and Newfoundland from the French. The Robin family played a leading role in the trade, building fishing stations all along the coast and selling dried cod to the West Indies and South America as well as to Portugal and the Mediterranean.

Charles Janvrin Robin was practising as a barrister in London and Steephill was intended as the family's summer home. He chose as his architect Ernest Newton, who had made a speciality of what was termed in Edwardian times 'the Smaller Country House'. Newton's son, W.G. Newton, explained his father's approach: 'Convenience, sunshine, weathertightness, a sense of home.' His father's designs, he said, 'grew out of simple workable shapes of windows, doors, chimneys, roofs'. On seeing one of his father's houses, a visitor was less likely to say 'This is a Newton house' than 'This is the house for the position'.

The entrance front has a domed porch embossed with scallop shells.

Left: The first-floor landing has distinctive cross-pattern balustrades.
Right: Newton's square pillars are carefully detailed.

The house is appropriately named as it stands on the brow of a hill above St Helier, next to the residence of the island's lieutenant-governor. The drive branches off through inconspicuous gates into large luxuriant grounds. On the right the land falls into a punchbowl, providing a glimpse of the heads of palm trees. A flash of white in the distance announces the house, then the flagpole of Government House comes into view followed by a glimpse of the pretty Regency villa where the Governor lives.

Steephill is seen across a rising sweep of lawn beneath the bows of two stately Turkey oaks. The house has a comfortable Edwardian air. The style is neo-Georgian with sash windows and louvred shutters. There is a subtle asymmetry, with a counter point between a tall oval-bodied chimney stack and a shallow canted bay, brought forward just enough to give movement to the facade. The portico, in the form of a *tempietto*, is half swallowed up in the facade. Its granite columns are each hewn from a single block of stone and the cast-lead gutter around the dome is prettily embossed with scallop shells, beads and diamonds. The garden front is enlivened by a pretty gently curving balcony with iron lattice balustrade.

Inside, the hall has the cigar-box look, fashionable in 1900 when the house was completed. Oak is used throughout, with panelling rising to the level of the trio of arches framing the view of the stairs. The panels are the small ones found in Elizabethan houses and fitted together with wooden pegs rather than nails. The black and white marble floor, laid in a diamond pattern, is inset with larger diamonds of a *verde-antico* green. This theme is picked up in the diamond pattern of the stair balustrade and the X-pattern panelling on the half landing. Newton took great care with detail such as the inlaid notches on the corners of the pillars supporting the arcade and the clusters of diamonds at the tops of the pillars.

'Let no view, however lovely, blind you to the fact that the sun must get into your rooms,' Newton wrote. He ensured there could be no dark corners in the library or drawing room by setting pairs of windows close together at the angles. The library

Louvred shutters add a French note to a very English Edwardian house.

has the same shoulder-height panelling as the hall, with built-in bookcases on three sides. The cupboards below the bookcases are swept forward to create a shallow shelf for ornaments or for opening books. The cupboard doors are completely flush, without handles. Originally the library had rich plasterwork including a deep floral frieze but this has disappeared. *The Builder* in 1901 recorded that the plaster ceilings were the work of a Mr Bankart, while the building work and joinery were contracted for by Mr Crill, and a Jersey architect, Reginald Lloyd, supervised the building work.

Behind the dining room, Newton designed an extensive servants' domain, consisting of pantry, butler's room, servants' hall, kitchen, scullery and larder. His son explained that in his father's work 'care is taken to see that a door left carelessly open shall not unmask the back passages. Bathrooms and lavatories have discreet approaches. Chairs round the fire can be out of the draught. Passages have no dark corners.' His plans manifest an aversion to rectangular rooms. He liked L-shaped spaces and rooms with bows and off-centre fireplaces.

Newton incorporated the conservatory and cellars of the existing house. Behind the conservatory is a delightful fernery, which has been restored under the direction of Frances Le Sueur, author of the definitive volume *Flora of Jersey*. It probably dates from the mid 19th century. The rockwork is a form of conglomerate, originally embedded with ormer shells. On the walls are dozens of little supports like the brackets for blue and white pots on Dutch chimney pieces, intended for small pots of ferns.

TRINITY MANOR — Trinity

15th century manor grandly remodelled by Sir Reginald Blomfield

As I leafed through the early pages of the visitors' book at Trinity Manor one entry stood out: April 2–6, 1920, Count I Youssoupoff. What brought a Russian aristocrat to a distant Channel Island manor house just three years after the Russian Revolution? The answer, of course, lay with his host, Athelstan Riley, whose interests in politics and travels made him seem like a character from Buchan's *Greenmantle*. 'I know every country in Europe' ran his address to the Electors of Oxford University in 1919. 'I am familiar with the Caucasus, with Armenia and the problems which centre round the Balkans and Constantinople, and if I had been in Parliament in March 1917 one warning voice would have been heard amidst the foolish rejoicings over the Russian Revolution.'

Athelstan Riley was deeply involved in Church affairs and fired with a desire to bring the Greek, Russian and Armenian Orthodox churches together. With this went a passion for travel and a preoccupation with chivalry. These strands came together vividly in a *curriculum vitae* compiled about 1919 for the Archbishop of Trebizond: 'AR, Seigneur de la Trinité (an ancient feudal property on the Island of Jersey); Commander of the Order of King George of Greece; Order of St Sava of Serbia … visited the Holy Mountain of Athos as a young man in 1883 and wrote an account of the monasteries.' Then comes the clue to Youssoupoff's visit to Trinity:

Blomfield's entrance front has a steep Normandy-style roof.

A.R. had 'recently made himself responsible for the religious necessities of the Russian refugees' and arranged for a large Anglican church in London to be placed at their disposal.

Aged 25 and still a bachelor, Athelstan Riley commissioned an ambitious Arts and Crafts house, No 2 Kensington Court, from the architect Sir T.G. Jackson in 1883–4. Fifteen years later his attention was focused on the acquisition of an ancient feudal seat. His first thoughts were of Cyprus, then of Sark, which would have made him a grand seigneur. But Sark was not available and in 1909 he purchased Trinity 'with all the dignities, rights and privileges attaching thereto as a francfief'.

One of the conditions he attached was that the Crown formally approved the sale and recognised him as Seigneur. His concern was that the previous owner had bought the property without Crown licence and as a result there was doubt whether he would be admitted to the Assize d'Héritage, held twice yearly in Jersey's Royal Court, to swear allegiance as Seigneur of Trinity. The Seigneur of Trinity was bound to present the king with a pair of mallard ducks when he visited the Island, a service of grand serjeanty that Riley was able to perform on July 21, 1921.

The house Riley had purchased was a 15th- and 16th-century manor built of pink Jersey granite with a characteristic arched front door on the south front. His

A stone bridge crosses over Blomfield's canal below a pretty garden room that is enclosed by clipped hornbeam trees.

thoughts turned to a suitable architect to work on the house and garden. A letter from Richard Norman Shaw offered advice. 'If I wanted to lay out a fine garden I should put it in the hands of Reginald Blomfield – he knows far more about it than any of us do – and what is so important he is one of the few men nowadays to have any appreciation of the grand manner.' Blomfield's first scheme suggested dressing the old manor house with shaped gables. Following a trip by Blomfield and Riley to St Malo and the Cotentin Peninsula, they decided to place a lofty roof in the French style over the old building. 'The ornamental finials were copied from one of the old houses overlooking the quay at St Malo,' said Riley. The *oeil de boeuf* and the casement windows that replaced the sashes are French.

The carving of the dining room chimneypiece shows that the seigneur was a haut justicier.

Blomfield created a new north entrance and formal *cour d'honneur* with a neatly cambered driving circle paved with large smooth beach pebbles. He also built two circular bastions on the south side of the house in 1929, using stone from an ancient staircase rescued from another old manor, L'Ancienneté, divided between the two bastions. Blomfield also designed a neat garden room made of clipped hornbeam.

Blomfield's porch opens into a combined hall and staircase divided by a screen of columns. The wrought-iron stair rail is similar to that at Moundsmere in Hampshire, built to Blomfield's designs in 1908–9. Beside the fireplace was a rope for pulling the bell on the roof to summon the family for meals. Nearby, Riley placed an intriguing olive-wood door that he had commissioned from Gregory, son of Demetrios, on his visit to Mount Athos in 1883 to stand between the dining room and chapel in his London house.

The hall opens into a large drawing room, or Grande Salle as Riley called it. The oak panelling, as in many other rooms of this date, was copied from a room that had been recently rescued from the Old Palace at Bromley-by-Bow and installed in the V&A Museum. The Seigneur designed it himself, and the work was done by his carpenter, John Parsons of St Teath, Cornwall.

After the death of Major Riley, Trinity Manor was sold to the millionaire housebuilder Steve Morgan. Following Mr Morgan's dramatic departure on the eve on his silver wedding anniversary ball, his wife, now Mrs Pam Bell, has succeeded as Seigneur. She has carried out a full restoration of the gardens and now keeps a prize-winning herd of Jersey cows.

4 Cumberland Place, Regent's Park, London 713-15
4 Maids of Honour Row, Richmond 726-7
4 The Crescent, Wisbech 61-2
6 Palace Street, Caernarfon 799-800
8 The Circus, Bath 460-1
10 College Yard, Worcester 676-7
48 Storey's Way, Cambridge 60
50 Oxford Gardens, Ladbroke Grove 728-9
72 Brook Street, Mayfair see Holland House
78 Derngate, Northampton 374-5

A

A La Ronde, Exmouth 111-12
The Abbey, Charlton Adam 467-8
Abbey Houses, Bury St Edmunds 520
Achnacarry, Spean Bridge 734
Adderbury House, Adderbury 404-5
Albury Park, Albury 550
Aldhams, Manningtree 177-8
Allerton Park, Allerton Mauleverer 678-9
The Almshouses, Preston-on-the-Weald Moors 446-7
Alt-y-Bela, Llangwm 796
Anderson Manor, Bere Regis 148
Apethorpe Hall, Oundle 354-5
Apley Park, Bridgnorth 428-30
Archerfield, Dirleton 735
Arisaig House, Mallaig 736
Ascot Place, Windlesham 26
Asgill House, Richmond-on-Thames 551
Ashbury Manor, Ashbury 406-7
Ashman's Hall, Beccles 518
Ashton Court, Bristol 454
Astley Pool House, Stourport 667
Auchinleck, Ochiltree 737
Axwell Park, Blaydon 166
Aynho, Aynho 356
Ayot Mountfitchet, Ayot St Peter 256-8
Ayshford Court, Sampford Peverell 113

B

Balbirnie, Fife 738
Balcombe Place, Balcombe 596-7
Ballencrieff Castle, Aberlady 739-40
Bank Hall, Bretherton 294
Barford House, Bridgwater 455-6
Barge House, Ross-on-Wye 249-50
Barkisland Hall, Barkisland 680-1
Barlaston Hall, Barlaston 499-501
Barrow Court, Barrow Gurney 457
8 The Circus, Bath 460-1
Bassett House, Bath 458-9
Bathealton Court, Bathealton 462
Beaurepaire, Basingstoke 224-6
Beenham Hatch, Bucklebury 27-8
Belcombe Court, Bradford-on-Avon 634
Belford Hall, Belford 382
Belhaven Hill House, Belhaven 741
Belsay Hall, Morpeth 383
Old Manor House, Beneden 264-7
Benham Park, Speen 29
Bentley Hall, Bentley 519
Bettisfield Park, Hamner 797
Bibury Court, Bibury 197-8
Biddulph Grange, Biddulph 502-3
Bishop's House, Bristol 463-4
Bispham Hall, Billinge 295
Blackburn Hall, Grinton 682
Blackland Park, Calne 635-6

Blanerne House, Duns 742
Blencowe Hall, Penrith 95-8
Bletchley Manor, Market Drayton 431
Boconnoc, Lostwithiel 84
Bodysgallen, Llandudno 798
Boringdon, Plymouth 114
Botleys, Chertsey 552
Bowden, Pangbourne 30-1
Bower House, Romford 179
Bowling Green, Milborne Port 149
Bradgate Stables, Leicester 303
Bradninch Manor, Bradninch 115-16
Bramcote Hall, Polesworth 618
Bramshill, Winchfield 227
Brancepeth Castle, Brancepeth 167
Brantwoode, Helensburgh 743-4
Braybrooke House, Salisbury 637-8
Breckles Hall, Breckles 328
Brereton Hall, Sandbach 67-9
Bretby Hall, Bretby 102-3
Bride Hall, Ayot St Lawrence 258-9
Bridge Place, Bridge 268-9
Fife House, Brighton 197-600
Brizlincote Hall, Bretby 103
The Broad House, Wroxham 329
The Great House, Brockamin 668
Brockhall Manor, Brockhall 357-8
Brockhurst Hall, Birkenhead 70
Brodsworth Hall, Doncaster 683-5
Brogyntyn, Oswestry 432-3
Brook Place, West End 553-4
Brook Street (no 72), Mayfair see Holland House
Brough Hall, Richmond (Yorkshire) 685-6
Brympton d'Evercy, Yeovil 465-6
The Manor House, Buckland 32-3
Bunny Hall, Bunny 392-3
Buntingsdale Hall, Market Drayton 434
Burles Lodge, Farnham 555-7
Burley-on-the-Hill, Oakham 304-5
Abbey Houses, Bury St Edmunds 520
Buxted Park, Buxted 600-1
Buxton Crescent, Buxton 104-5
Bylaugh Hall, Foulsham 330
Bywell Hall, Bywell 384

C

6 Palace Street, Caernarfon 799-800
Calke Abbey, Ashby-de-la-Zouch 106-7
Callaly Castle, Rothbury 385-6
48 Storey's Way, Cambridge 60
Canonteign Manor, Christow 119-20
Caroline Park, Edinburgh 747
Carton House, Maynooth 822
Shell House at Carton, Maynooth 822
The Casino at Marino, Clontarf 835
Castle Ashby, Denton 358-9
Castle Bromwich Hall, Castle Bromwich 619-20
Castle of Park, Cornhill 745-6
Castleboro House, Enniscorthy 824
Catchfrench Manor, Liskeard 85
Caverswall Castle, Stoke-on-Trent 504-6
Caythorpe Hall, Caythorpe 315-17
Cedar Cottage, Chobham 557-9
The Abbey, Charlton Adam, 467-8
Charleston Manor, Lewes 602-3
Chawton House, Chawton 228-9
Cheddington Court, Beaminster 150-1
Chicheley, Newport Pagnell 42-3
Chicksands Priory, Ampthill 18-19
Chillingham Castle, Chillingham 387

Chilworth Manor, Chilworth 560-1
Jacob's Ladder, Chinnor 408
Church House, Bibury 199-201
Churche's Mansion, Nantwich 71-2
Chute Lodge, Ludgershall 640
The Circus (no 8), Bath 460-1
Clegg Hall, Rochdale 296
Clifton Castle, Hambleton 687
Clifton Hall, Nottingham 393-5
Cockfield Hall, Yoxford 521-3
Colebrook House, Winchester 230-1
College Yard (no 10), Worcester 676-7
Colwick Hall, Nottingham 396
Compton Verney, Kineton 621-2
Constable Burton, Leyburn 688-9
Cooke's House, West Burton 603-5
Coombe Abbey, Coventry 623
Copped Hall, Epping 180-1
Corinthian Villa, Regent's Park 730
Cote House, Bampton 409-10
Coton Hall, Bridgnorth 435-6
Cound Hall, Shrewsbury 437
The Court House, Martock 481-2
Cragside, Rothbury 388-9
Craigengillan, Dalmellington 748
Cranborne Manor, Cranborne 152-4
Cransley Hall, Kettering 360-1
Crawford Manor, Crawford 297
The Crescent, Buxton 104-5
The Crescent (no 4), Wisbech 61-2
Crom Castle, Newtownbutler 825
Croome Court, Croome D'Abitot 669-71
Crowcombe Court, Crowcombe 469
Culham Court, Henley 34-6
Cullen House, Cullen 749-50
Cumberland Place (no 4), Regent's Park, London 713-15

D

Danson House, Bexleyheath 270-1
Derngate (no 78), Northampton 374-5
Dingley Hall, Market Harborough 362-3
Dixton Manor, Winchcombe 202-3
Doddington Hall, Nantwich 73-4
Dodington Park, Chipping Sodbury 204-6
Donington Hall, Castle Donington 306
Dowdeswell Court, Cheltenham 206-8
Downe Hall, Bridport 155
Dromore Castle, Pallaskenry 826
Duddingston House, Edinburgh 751
Duff House, Banff 752
Dumfries House, Cumnock 753
Dunham Lodge, Little Dunham 331-2
Dunmore Park, Dunmore 754
Durford Court, Petersfield 232-3

E

Eagle House, Mitcham 716
Eardisley, Eardisley 251-2
Earl Soham Lodge, Woodbridge 524-6
Eastwood Farm, Herstmonceux 606
Ebberston Hall, Pickering 690
Ecton Hall, Northampton 363-4
Edgcote House, Chipping Warden 365
Ednaston Manor, Ashbourne 108-9
Edwinsford, Llansawel 801
Eggesford House, Eggesford 121-2
Ellys Manor House, Ellys 318-19
Elsing Hall, Dereham 333-5
Emo Court, Emo 827
Encombe, Kingston 156-7
Endsleigh, Tavistock 123-6

Erskine House, Bishopton 755
Eydon Hall, Eydon 366-8

F

Fasque Castle, Fettercairn 756-7
Fawley House, Henley-on-Thames 411-13
Fife House, Brighton 597-600
Finedon Hall, Finedon 368-9
Flichity House, Flichity 758
Flintham Hall, Newark 397-8
Floors Castle, Kelso 759-61
Miller's Tower, Formakin 762-3
Formby Hall, Formby 298
Fort Horne, Thornton Seward 691
Fota, Carrigtuohill 828
Friar Park, Henley-on-Thames 414
Frognal House, Sidcup 272
Fulford Hall, Great Fulford 127
Fulvens House, Shere 562
Fyvie Castle, Turriff 764-5

G

Gibside, Rowlands Gill 168-9
Gillingham Hall, Beccles 336-7
Glin Castle, Glin 829
Goddards, Abinger Common 563
Gosfield Hall, Halstead 184-5
Governor's House, Berwick-upon-Tweed 390
Grace Dieu Manor, Ashby-de-la-Zouch 307
The Grange, Ramsgate 279
The Grange, Alresford *see* Grange Park
The Grange, Broadhembury 117-18
Grange Park, Alresford 234-5
Gray, House of, Dundee 766-7
Great Barr Hall, Great Barr 507
The Great House, Brockamin 668
The Manor House, Great Snoring 338
Great Treverran, Fowey 86-7
Green Lane Farm, Shamley Green 564
Greywalls, Gullane 768
Greyfriars, Wanborough 565-7
Gribloch, Stirling 769-70
Grimshaw Hall, Knowle 624-6
The Grove, St Lawrence 840-1
Grovelands, Southgate 717
Gunton Hall, Hanworth 339-43
Gwerclas Hall, Corwen 802-4
Gwrych Castle, Abergele 804-5
Gyrn Castle, Mostyn 806-7

H

The Ruin, Hackfall, Ripon 692-3
Hadspen, Castle Cary 470
Halswell, Goathurst 471-3
Hamsterley Hall, Rowlands Gill 170-1
Hanger Hill Garden Estate, Acton 718-19
Hapsford House, Frome 473-5
Harleyford Manor, Marlow 44-5
Harrington, Spilsby 320-2
The Hasells, Sandy 20-1
Haslington Hall, Crewe 75-6
Hatfield Priory, Chelmsford 186-7
Hayton Hall, Brampton 99-100
Headfort House, Kells 830
Heath House, Lower Tean 508-9
Hedenham Hall, Bungay 344
Hellaby Hall, Hellaby 694
Hengrave Hall, Bury St Edmunds 527-8
Heveningham Hall, Halesworth 529-30
Heythrop Park, Chipping Norton 415
High Head Castle, Ivegill 101
Highcliffe Castle, Christchurch 158-9
Hill, Christow 128

Hill Hall, Epping 188
The Hill, Hampstead 720
Hilton Park, Clones 831
Himley Hall, Himley 510
Hinwick House, Harrold 22-3
Holland House, Mayfair 721-3
Holliday Hall, Bredgar 273-4
Holly Mount, Beaconsfield 46-7
Holmdale, Holmbury St Mary 568-9
Holystreet Manor, Chagford 130-2
Home House, Portman Square, London 723-5
Homewood, Esher 570-1
Horham Hall, Thaxted 189-90
Horn of Plenty, Gulworthy 129
Horsley Towers, East Horsley 572
The Menagerie, Horton 370-1
House of Gray, Dundee 766-7
Howick Hall, Alnwick 391
Huf House, Weybridge 573-5
Hurst House, Woodford 190-1
Hylands House, Chelmsford 192-3

I, J

Ingestre Pavilion, Ingestre 511
Ingress Abbey, Greenhithe 275
Inverlochy Castle, Fort William 771
Ionic Villa, Regent's Park 730
Isfield Place, Uckfield 607-9
Islay Walton Manor, Castle Donington 308
The Ivy, Chippenham 639
Jacob's Ladder, Chinnor 408

K

Keith Hall, Inverurie 772-3
Kelly House, Launceston 132-3
Kildwick Hall, Skipton 695-7
King's Weston, Bristol 209
Kingston Lisle, Wantage 37-8
Kingston Maurward, Dorchester 160
Kingston Russell, Kingston Russell 161
Kirtlington Park, Kirtlington 416
Knightstone Manor, Crediton 134-5

L

Lambton Castle, Chester-le-Street 172
Lanhill House, Yatton Keynell 641
Larch Hill, Coole 832-3
Latimer Manor, West Kington 642-3
Lawton Hall, Alsager 77
Ledstone Hall, Pontefract 698
Leigh Court, Abbots Leigh 476-7
Park Cottage, Leighton 808-9
Les Lumières, St Brelade 842
Leyburn Hall, Leyburn 699
Lilford Castle, Lilford 372
Lismore Castle, Lismore 833-4
Little Bardfield Hall, Great Bardfield 194-5
Little Hautbois, Little Hautbois 345
Little Thakeham, Thakeham 610-11
Llangoed Hall, Llyswen 810
Lochton House, Abernyte 773-4
Longford Hall, Ashbourne 110
Lucas Almshouses, Woking 39-40
The Reader's House, Ludlow 438-9
Lupton House, Brixham 136
Luton Hoo, Luton 24-5

M

Mackerye End, Wheathampstead 260-1
Maids of Honour Row (no 4), Richmond-on-Thames 726-7
Manderston House, Duns 774-5
Old Manor House, Beneden 264-7

The Manor House, Buckland 32-3
The Manor House, Great Snoring 338
The Manor House, Milton Lilbourne 644
The Manor House, Ogbourne St George 647-50
The Manor House, Sutton Courtenay 421-2
Manor Lodge, Worksop 403
Maperton, Maperton 478-80
The Casino at Marino, Clontarf 835
Maristow House, Plymouth 137-9
The Court House, Martock 481-2
Mavisbank House, Loanhead 776
Maxstoke Castle, Coleshill 627-9
Maynards, Tenterden 276-7
Mears Ashby Hall, Mears Ashby 373
Melton Constable Hall, Melton Constable 346-7
Melville Castle, Lasswade 777
The Menagerie, Horton 370-1
Mentmore Towers, Leighton Buzzard 48-50
Middleton Park, Middleton Stoney 417
Milford House, Milford 576
Miller's Tower, Formakin 762-3
The Manor House, Milton Lilbourne 644
Minsterley Hall, Minsterley 440-1
Monkton House, West Dean 612-13
Morley Old Hall, Morley St Peter 348
Moundsmere Manor, Preston Candover 236-7
Mount Congreve, Kilmeadan 836-7
Munstead Grange, Godalming 577-9
Myrtle Grove, Youghal 838

N

Nansidwell, Falmouth 88-9
Narborough Hall, Narborough 349
Nether Swell Manor, Stow-on-the-Wold 210-11
Nethergate House, Clare 531-2
Netley Hall, Shrewsbury 442
Newbridge, Donabate 839
Newhailes, Musselburgh 778-9
Newport House, Newport Almeley 252-3
North Breache Manor, Ewhurst 579-81
North Luffenham Hall, Oakham 309-10
78 Derngate, Northampton 374-5
Norton Place, Market Rasen 322-4
Nun Monkton Hall, Nun Monkton 700-1
Nunton House, Nunton 645-6
Nutley Manor, Preston Candover 238-9

O

Oak Hill, Accrington 299
The Manor House, Ogbourne St George 647-50
Old Grammar School, Dedham 182-3
Old Manor House, Benenden 264-7
The Old Rectory, Yardley Hastings 380-1
Olden Manor, Higham 533-4
Orchardleigh, Frome 483-4
Orchards, Godalming 582
St Ouen's Manor, St Ouen 843-4
Oulton Hall, Leeds 702
Owlpen, Dursley 212
Oxford Gardens (no 50), Ladbroke Grove 728-9

P

Palace Street (no 6), Caernarfon 799-800
Paper Hall, Bradford 703
Parish's House, Timsbury 484-6
Park, Castle of, Cornhill 745-6
Park Close, Englefield Green 583-5
Park Cottage, Leighton 808-9

Patshull Hall, Burnhill Green 512-13
Paxhill, Haywards Heath 613-15
Peckforton Castle, Tarporley 78-9
Pellicane House, Sandwich 278
Pencoed Castle, Llanmartin 811
Penhow Castle, Newport 812-13
Petit Hibeaux, St Lawrence 845
Philipps House, Dinton 651-2
Piercefield, Chepstow 813-15
Piers Court, Stinchcombe 213
Pimlico House, Hemel Hempstead 262-3
Pitchford Hall, Pitchford 442-4
Pitmain Lodge, Kingussie 780
Plaish Hall, Church Stretton 445
Plas Teg, Hope 816
Poltimore, Poltimore 140
Port Eliot, St Germans 90
Poston House, Vowchurch 254-5
Poulton House, Marlborough 653-4
Poulton Manor, Poulton 214-15
The Almshouses, Preston-on-the-Weald
    Moors 446-7
Puttenham Priory, Puttenham 586-7

R

Ramsay Garden, Edinburgh 781
The Grange, Ramsgate 279
Rashleigh Barton, Chulmleigh 141-2
The Reader's House, Ludlow 438-9
Redlynch House, Redlynch 487
Regent's Park Villas, Regent's Park,
    London 730
Revesby Abbey, Horncastle 325-6
Ridgemead, Englefield Green 588-9
Rous Lench Court, Rous Lench 672-3
Rousdon House, Axminster 143
Rowden Manor, Chippenham 655-6
Rowton Castle, Rowton 448
The Ruin, Hackfall, Ripon 692-3
Ruperra Castle, Llanfedw 817
Rushton, Kettering 376

S

Saddlewood Manor, Leighterton 215-17
St Joseph's Abbey, Storrington 617
St Ouen's Manor, St Ouen 843-4
The Salutation, Sandwich 280-1
Sarsden House, Chipping Norton 418
Sawston Hall, Sawston 56
Scout Hall, Halifax 704
Seafield House, St Lawrence 846-7
Seaham Hall, Seaham 173
Sharpham House, Ashprington 144-5
Shaw House, Newbury 41
Shawford Park, Winchester 240-3
Shell House at Carton, Maynooth 823
Shillinglee Park, Haslemere 616
Shirburn Castle, Watlington 419-20
Shireoaks, Worksop 399
Shrubland Park, Ipswich 535-7
Shurland Hall, Isle of Sheppey 282
Sinai Park, Burton-on-Trent 514
Sker House, Pyle 818
Snowdenham Hall, Bramley 590
The Soke, Winchester 244-5
South Wraxhall Manor, Bradford-on-
    Avon 488-9
Stanford Hall, Stanford-upon-Soare 400
Stanton House, Highworth 657
Staunton Harold Hall, Ashby-de-la-
    Zouch 311-13
Stayley Hall, Staleybridge 300
Steephill, St Saviour 848-50
St Giles House, Wimborne St Giles 163-4
Stibbington Hall, Peterborough 57-9

Stinsford House, Dorchester 162
Stocken Hall, Stretton 313-14
Stocketts Manor, Oxted 591-3
Stockton, Heytersbury 658-9
Stoke Park, Stoke Bruerne 377
Stokesay Court, Stokesay 449-50
Stoneleigh Abbey, Kenilworth 630-1
Storey's Way (no 48), Cambridge 60
Sturford Mead, Warminster 660-1
Styche Hall, Market Drayton 451
Sundridge Park, Bromley 283-6
The Manor House, Sutton Courtenay
    421-2
Swinfen Hall, Lichfield 515
Swinsty Hall, Little Timble 705

T

Tabley Hall, Knutsford 80-1
Taymouth Castle, Aberfeldy 784
Thame Park, Thame 51-2
The Abbey, Charlton Adam 467-8
The Almshouses, Preston-on-the-Weald
    Moors 446-7
The Broad House, Wroxham 329
The Casino at Marino, Clontarf 835
The Circus (no 8), Bath 460-1
The Court House, Martock 481-2
The Crescent, Buxton 104-5
The Crescent (no 4), Wisbech 61-2
The Grange, Alresford *see* Grange Park
The Grange, Broadhembury 117-18
The Grange, Ramsgate 279
The Great House, Brockamin 668
The Grove, St Lawrence 840-1
The Hasells, Sandy 20-1
The Hill, Hampstead 720
The Ivy, Chippenham 639
The Manor House, Buckland 32-3
The Manor House, Milton Lilbourne 644
The Manor House, Ogbourne St George
    647-50
The Manor House, Sutton Courtenay
    421-2
The Menagerie, Horton 370-1
The Old Rectory, Yardley Hastings 380-1
The Reader's House, Ludlow 438-9
The Ruin, Hackfall, Ripon 692-3
The Salutation, Sandwich 280-1
The Soke, Winchester 244-5
The Vineyards, Beaulieu 248
Thirlestane Castle, Lauder 785-6
Thoresby Hall, Ollerton 401-2
Thorndon Hall, Brentwood 196
Thorpe Hall, Norwich 350-1
Thorpe Salvin Hall, Worksop 706
Thorpe Tilney Hall, Thorpe Tilney 327
Thurston End Hall, Hawkedon 538-9
Toddington Manor, Winchcombe 218-19
Tong Hall, Bradford 707
Tottenham Park, Marlborough 662-4
Towie Barclay, Turriff 787
Trafalgar House, Salisbury 664-5
Traigh House, Arisaig 788
Trawsgoed, Llanafan 819
Trehane, Truro 91-3
Trevor Hall, Langollen 820
Trewarthenick, Tregony 94
Trinity Manor, Trinity 851-3
Troy House, Monmouth 821
Tusmore House, Bicester 423-4
Twyford Moors House, Twyford Moors
    246-7
Tyninghame House, East Linton 789-91
Tyntesfield, Wraxall 490-2
Tyringham Hall, Newport Pagnell 53-4
Tysoe Manor, Upper Tysoe 632-3

U, V

Upton House, Tetbury 220-1
Vale Royal Abbey, Northwich 81-2
Valentine's, Ilford 731
Vellore House, Linlithgow 792-4
Ven House, Milborne Port 492-4
The Vineyards, Beaulieu 248

W

Wakefield Lodge, Potterspury 378-80
Waldershare, Eythorne 287
Wallington Hall, Downham Market 352-3
Walmoor House, Chester 83
Walpole House, Chiswick 732-3
Walworth Castle, Darlington 174
Wardour Castle, Tisbury 666
Weacombe, West Quantoxhead 495-7
Wedderburn Castle, Duns 795
Wentworth Woodhouse, Wentworth
    708-10
Westgate House, Long Melford 540-1
Weston Hall, Weston 516
White Gables, Gerrards Cross 55
Wilsley, Cranbrook 288-9
Wingfield Castle, Wingfield 542-3
Wingfield College, Wingfield 543-5
4 The Crescent, Wisbech 61-2
Wolverton Hall, Pershore 674-5
Womersley Hall, Womersley 711-12
Woodcroft Castle, Peterborough 63-5
Woodfold Park, Blackburn 301
Woodside House, Bath 498
Woolstaplers' Hall, Chipping Camden
    222-3
Woolton Hall, Liverpool 302
10 College Yard, Worcester 676-7
Manor Lodge, Worksop 403
Worlingham Hall, Beccles 546-7
Wothorpe Grandstand, Stamford 66
Wotton House, Dorking 594-5
Wraxhall House, Maiden Newton 165
Wrottesley Hall, Tettenhall 517
Wyfold Court, Henley-on-Thames 425-7
Wynyard Park, Stockton-on-Tees 175-6

Y

Yaldham Manor, Wrotham 290-1
Yardhurst, Ashford 292-3
The Old Rectory, Yardley Hastings 380-1
Yeaton Pevery, Shrewsbury 452-3
Yew Tree House, Earl Stonham 548-9
Youlston Park, Barnstaple 146-7

MAIN INDEX

Where several people share the same surname, the order in which their names appear in the index is normally determined by their first names or initials, ignoring any titles (such as Sir, Lady, Dr, etc) that come before the first name. An asterisk (*) after a first name indicates two or more relatives with identical names discussed at the same page references.

A colon (:) separates a place name or location from the name of the house. The place names and locations indexed are those given in the headings to the house articles.

Features usually discussed in house articles (eg doors, porches, entrance halls, fireplaces, gardens, etc) have not been separately indexed. Less common features (eg collections, friezes, gargoyles, etc) are indexed. Uses for houses (eg defence use, educational use, residential conversions, etc) may refer to past or present use, or to proposed, projected or rejected use.

1 Lewes Crescent *see* Fife House
2 Kensington Court 852
4 Cumberland Place 713-15
4 Maids of Honour Row 726-7
4 The Crescent (Wisbech) 61 -2
6 Palace Street 799-800
8 The Circus (Bath) 460-1, 634
10 College Yard 676-7
48 Storey's Way 60
50 Oxford Gardens 728-9
72 Brook Street *see* Holland House
78 Derngate 374-5

A

A La Ronde 111 -12
A.B. Fleming & Co 747
The Abbey (Charlton Adam) 467-8
Abbey Houses (Bury St Edmunds) 520
abbeys *see* monastic origins
Abbot's Hill 263
Abbots Leigh: Leigh Court 476-7, 738
Abbotsford House 746
Abbott, John 659
Abercorn, 8th Earl of 751
Aberfeldy: Taymouth Castle 784
Abergele: Gwrych Castle 79, 804-5
Aberlady: Ballencrieff Castle 739-40
Abernethy: Lochton House 773-4
Abingdon, Abbot of 421
Abinger, 3rd Baron 771
Abinger Common: Goddards 563
Abraham, Esmond 193
Accrington: Oak Hill 299
Achnacarry 734
Acton, Humphrey & Alice 674
Acton, Margaret 674
Acton, Thomas 674
Acton, William* 674
Acton: Hanger Hill Garden Estate 718-19
Ada, Countess of Lovelace 572
Adam brothers (Robert, James & John)
  associations with 206, 515, 738, 815, 824
  Bathealton Court ceiling

(attributed) 462
  comparisons to & 'Adamesque' 38, 155, 167, 213, 322, 332, 437, 529, 536, 722, 733, 752, 761, 774, 829
  Dumfries House (Robert & John) 753
  see also Adam, Robert (1728-1792)
Adam, Robert (1728-1792) 693
  Archerfield 735
  Compton Verney 621 -2
  Croome Court 669, 671
  Headfort House 830
  Home House 723-5
  Kedleston Hall 50, 535, 774, 775
  Luton Hoo 24
  Mellerstain House 789
  Seton House 782-3
  Wedderburn Castle 795
  Woolton Hall 302
  see also Adam brothers
Adam, Robert (b. 1948) 606
Adam, William
  Duff House 752
  Floors Castle 760
  Keith Hall 773
  Mavisbank House 776
Adderbury: Adderbury House 16, 161, 404-5
Adderbury House 16, 161, 404-5
Addyman & Kay 737
Admiralty Arch 178, 452, 569, 579
aedicule windows 220
Aesthetic Movement houses 743-4
Agace, Daniel 26
Agecroft Hall 72
Ahknaton, Sheikh Ahknaton, Crown Prince of Abu Dhabi 601
Ailesbury estate 654
Ailesbury, Marquesses of
  1 st Marquess & Marchioness 662, 663, 664
  2nd Marquess 664
  8th Marquess 663
air force use *see* defence use
Airlie, 6th Earl of (David Ogilvy) 746
airship, R-34 758
Aislabie, John 692
Aislabie, William 692
Aitkens, Philip 533
Al-Ghazzi, Abdul Amir 530
Alan of Brittany, Earl 524
Alanbrooke, Field Marshal Viscount 579
Albert, Prince (Prince Consort) 430, 517, 535, 631, 808, 822
Albury: Albury Park 550, 561
Albury Park 550, 561
Aldhams 177-8
Aldi (builders) 721
Aldridge, Conrad 767
Alexander II, King of Scotland 745
Alexander, Colonel Boyd 288
Alexander, Camilla 289
Alexander, Herbert & Edith 288-9
Alexander, Ianthe 288
Alexander, James 743
Alexandra, Queen 386
Ali, Hyder Ali, Sultan of Mysore 792
Ali, Mehmet 542
Allcroft, John Derby 449, 450
Allen, Ralph 480
Allendale, Barons & Viscounts 384
Allerton Mauleverer: Allerton Park 15, 678-9
Allerton Park 15, 678-9
Alliss, Peter 664
Almondell House 792
The Almshouses (Preston-on-the-Weald Moors) 446-7
Almshouses, Royal Grammar School, Worcester 580
Alnwick: Howick Hall 391
Alresford: Grange Park 234-5, 383, 536, 738
Alsager: Lawton Hall 16-17, 77, 330
Alston, Leigh 533

Alt-y-Bela 15, 282, 796
Althorp Park 561
Alwin 560
Amalgamated Engineering Union 601
Amcotts, Charles 322
Amcotts, Vincent 321
American bond/garden bond brickwork 650, 700
American Museum in Britain 459
Amir Al-Ghazzi, Abdul 530
Ampthill: Chicksands Priory 18-19, 21
Amurrio, Marques de 120
Ancaster, Earl of 310
Anderson, J.MacVicar Inverlochy Castle 771
  Patshull Hall 512
Anderson, Richard & Patricia 469
Anderson Manor 14, 148, 165
Andreae, Mark 237
Andreae, Sophie 499, 500
Anglesey, 7th Marquess of 816
Anglesey Abbey 584
animals & birds
  aquarium, Stibbington Hall 59
  aviaries, Lilford Castle 372
  bear story, Brereton Hall 68
  big game trophies, Callaly Castle 386
  birds, Lilford Castle 372
  cheetahs (Sir Frank Bowden's) 52
  ferme ornée, Larch Hill 832
  fishtank, Monkton House 612
  Jeddah (Major Larnach's Derby winner) 405
  mallard presentation, Trinity Manor 852
  The Menagerie 371
  sea lions, Stanford Hall 16, 400
  Sinai Park 514
  see also cattle herds; deer; dovecotes & pigeon houses; pigs
Anne of Bohemia, Queen (wife of Richard II) 542
Anne of Cleves 236, 259
Anne, Countess of Rosse 711, 712
Anne, Princess Royal & Princess of Orange 107
Annesley, Rev Francis 366
Annesley House 368
Anson family 371
Anspach, Margrave of 29
Anthony, Evelyn 160
ap Phylip, Llewelyn & Ellen 801
apartment conversions *see* residential conversions & enabling development
Apethorpe Hall 354-5
Apley Park 428-30, 453
Appleton Hall 350
Apsley House 813
aquarium, Stibbington Hall 59
Arbury Hall 19
Archer, Thomas
  Aynho 356
  Chicheley (attributed) 43
  Heythrop Park 415
Archerfield 735
Archibald, Rev 232
The Architect articles
  G.E. Street's obituary 568
  Munstead Grange 577
architectural models 208, 304
Ardern, Henry de 628
Ardizzone, Edward 34
Argyll, Dukes of 784
  2nd Duke 405, 747
  3rd Duke 751
Arisaig: Traigh House 788
Arisaig House 736
Arlington Court 121
Armistead, Colonel R.B. 701
Armstrong, Barons
  1 st Baron 388
  3rd Baron & Lady 389
Armstrong, Barons 388, 389
Armstrong-Jones, Antony (Lord Snowdon) 711
army use *see* defence use
Arnold, William

Cranborne Manor 153, 658
  Stockton 658-9
Arran, 8th & 9th Earls of 262, 263
Arran, Fiona, Countess of Arran 262-3
Arroll, Andrew 444
art collections & exhibitions
  Barber Institute of Fine Art 36
  Belsay Hall 383
  Calke Abbey 107
  Compton Verney 622
  Donington Hall 306
  Duff House 752
  Fyvie Castle 765
  Great Treverren 87
  Mentmore Towers 48-50
  Narborough Hall 349
  Newbridge 839
  Royal Academy 234, 283
  Seaham Hall 173
  Sharpham House 145
  Stokesay Court 449
  Tabley Hall 80-1
  Toddington Manor 17, 219
  Werner Collection 24, 25
  Wyfold Court 426
  see also sculpture
Art Deco
  Barkisland Hall bathroom 681
  Bibury Court library 197, 198
  Brantwoode bathroom 744
  Ridgemead bathroom 589
  Savoy Theatre 601
  Stanford Hall cinema-theatre 16, 400
  Woodside House 498
Art Fund 420
Art Nouveau
  Holmdale west wing 569
  Park Close 583-5
Artisan Mannerist 10-11
  Brook Place 11, 553-4
  Chilworth Manor 561
  Fulvens House 11, 562
  Harrington 321
  Mackerye End 260-1
  Nun Monkton Hall 700-1
  Yaldham Manor 291
  see also Commonwealth houses
Arts & Crafts 57, 195, 212, 351, 719
  2 Kensington Court 852
  48 Storey's Way 60
  Arisaig House 736
  Brantwoode 743-4
  Burles Lodge 555-7
  Cedar Cottage 555-7
  Downe Hall 155
  Durford Court 232-3
  Greyfriars 565-7
  Grimshaw Hall 624-6
  Holly Mount 46-7
  Munstead Grange 577-9
  North Breache Manor 579-81
  Ramsay Garden 781
  Snowdenham Hall 590
  Woolstaplers Hall 222-3
  Yeaton Pevery 452-3
  see also Edwardian
Arts & Crafts Movement in Surrey 57
arts centre use, Staunton Harold stables 312
Arundell, 8th Baron 666
Ascot Place 15, 26
Asgill, Sir Charles 551
Asgill House 15, 511, 551, 730
Ash family 349
Ash, G. Baron 542
Ash, Maurice & Ruth 145
Ashbee, C.R. & Jane 222-3
Ashbourne:
  Ednaston Manor 108-9
  Longford Hall 110
Ashbury: Ashbury Manor 406-7
Ashbury Manor 406-7
Ashby-de-la-Zouch:
  Calke Abbey 50, 106-7, 450, 757
  Grace Dieu Manor 307
  Staunton Harold Hall 13, 311 -13
Ashdown Park Hotel 25

Ashford: Yardhurst 292-3
Ashfordby-Trenchard, Rev John 657
Ashley family/Ashley Cooper family (Earls of Shaftesbury) 163-4, 641
Ashley, Sir Bernard & Laura 810
Ashley, Martin 623
Ashman's Hall 518
Ashprington: Sharpham House 6, 144-5
Ashton Court 454
Aslet, Clive 612
Assheton, Theophilus 296
Astley, Sir Jacob 346
Astley, Sir John 512
Astley Pool House 667
Aston, Mike 207-8
Aston Hall 67
Astor, David 421
Astor, Nancy Astor, 2nd Viscountess Astor (Lady Astor) 366
Astor, William Waldorf 764
astragals 13
astylar villas, description 551, 640
Athelhampton House 457
Athenaeum, Bury St Edmunds 518, 546
Athenaeum Club 493
Atherton, Dr Peter 54
Atkins, W.S. 569
Atkinson, Dale 173
Atkinson, Rev J.C. 699
Atkinson, Thomas 686
Atkinson, William
  Himley Hall 510
  Hylands House greenhouses 193
  Lismore Castle 834
Atkyns, Abraham* 37
Attlee, Clement 714
Attwood, John 193
Aubrey, John 488, 656
Auchinleck, 8th Laird (Lord Auchinleck) 737
Auchinleck 737
Audley End House 761, 764
Aulaf, King of Northumbria 790
Austen, Cassandra* 229
Austen, Edward 228-9
Austen, Rev George & Mrs Cassandra 228-9
Austen, Jane 229, 593, 631, 815
Austin, Brian 66
Auxiliaries, Wolverton Hall 674-5
Avery, Neil 429
aviaries, Lilford Castle 372
Axminster: Rousdon House 143
Axwell Park 166, 384
Ayers, Charles Roberts 120
Aylesford, Earl of 785
Aylmer, General Arthur 174
Aynho 16, 356
Aynho: Aynho 16, 356
Ayot Mountfitchet 256-8
Ayot St Lawrence: Bride Hall 258-9
Ayot St Peter: Ayot Mountfitchet 256-8
Ayshford Court 113
Ayton, John 525

B

Bachelor Duke *see* Devonshire, 6th Duke of
Bacon, Sir Edmund 337
Bacon, Francis 219
Bacon, Rev John 535
Bacon, Sir Nathaniel 336
Bacon, Nicholas 535
Badminton House 215, 821
Bagri, Lord (life peer) 730
Baguley Hall 75
Baillie, A.M. 346
Baillie Scott, M.H. 30, 743
  48 Storey's Way 60
Baker (butler to 6th Duke of Devonshire) 600
Baker, Sir Herbert 610
  Eydon Hall 368
  Greyfriars additions 566, 567
  Howick Hall 391
Baker, Mark 805

Balbirnie 738
Balcombe: Balcombe Place 596-7
Balcombe Place 596-7
Baldwin, Thomas 485
Balfour, Arthur 286
Balfour, General Robert 738
Ballencrieff Castle 739-40
Ballentine family 758
ballrooms
  Callaly Castle 386
  Fife House 599
  Gosfield Hall 184, 185
  Headfort House 830
  St Joseph's Abbey 617
  Shawford Park 240, 241
  Tottenham Park 321
  Wedderburn Castle 795
baluster modifications, Regent's Park Villas 730
Bamburgh Castle 388, 389
Bamford-Hesketh, Lloyd Hesketh 804
Bamford-Hesketh, Winifred 804
Bampton: Cote House 409-10
Banff: Duff House 752
Bank of England 368, 536
Bank Hall 294
Bankart, Mr 850
Banks, Sir Joseph 326
Banks, R.R. 330
Bannenberg, John 661
Bannerman, Julian 639
Banqueting House
  Gibside 168, 169
  The Ruin (Mowbray Point), Hackfall 692-3
Bansley, Jane 252
Barakat, Ashraf 817
Barber Institute of Fine Art 36
Barclay family 787
Barclay, Brigadier Peter 331
Barclay de Tolly, Prince Michael 787
Bardewell, Thomas 344
Barford Hall 7
Barford House 455-6
Barge House 17, 249-50
Baring, Charles Baring, 2nd Baron Howick 391
Baring, Rosa 322
Barkisland: Barkisland Hall 680-1
Barkisland Hall 680-1
Barlaston: Barlaston Hall 45, 499-501, 510
Barlaston Hall 45, 499-501, 510
barley-sugar chimney stacks 290, 291, 334, 528
Barnato family 588, 589
Barnato, Captain Woolf 588
Barnes, Philip 103
barns
  Ashbury Manor 407
  Bride Hall 258, 259
  Brook Place 554
  Charleston Manor 603
  Cockfield Hall 523
  Cooke's House 605
  Court House, Bentley Hall 519
  Fulvens House 562
  Green Lane Farm 564
  Isfield Place 609
  Saddlewood Manor 217
  Stocketts Manor 591, 593
  Thurston End Hall 539
  Tysoe Manor 633
  Wolverton Hall 674
Barnsley, William & Jane 251-2
Barnsley Park 52
Barnstaple: Youlston Park 146-7
baronial & Scottish baronial
  Blanerne House 742
  Crom Castle 825
  Cullen House 749-50
  Flichity House 758
  Floors Castle 759-61
  Fyvie Castle 764-5
  Ramsay Garden 781
  Thirlestane Castle 785-6
  Tyninghame House 789-91
Baroque
  Adderbury House 404-5
  Biddulph Grange 502-3
  Bramcote Hall 618

Brizlincote Hall 103
Bunny Hall 392-3
Buntingsdale Hall 434
Burley-on-the-Hill 304-5
Calke Abbey 106-7
Carton House 822
Chicheley 14, 42-3
Cound Hall 437
Crowcombe Court 469
Governor's House (Berwick-upon-Tweed) 390
The Great House (Brockamin) 668
Great Treverren 86-7
Halswell 471-2
Harrington 321
Hellaby Hall 694
Heythrop Park 415
Himley Hall 510
Hinwick House 22-3
Holland House 721-3
Holliday Hall 273-4
Hurst House 190-1
Hylands House 192-3
Iver Grove 11
The Ivy 639
Kingston Lisle 37-8
Kingston Maurward 160
Kingston Russell 161
Mentmore Towers 48-50
Milford House 576
Moundsmere Manor 12, 236-7, 853
Nunton House 645-6
Old Grammar School 182-3
Piercefield 815
Shireoaks water garden 399
Tyringham Hall 53-4, 404
Upton House 220-1
Ven House 12, 492-4
Wentworth Woodhouse 708-10
Barratt family 441
Barron, William 103
Barrow Court 457
Barrow Gurney: Barrow Court 457
Barry, Sir Charles
  association with & comparisons to 397, 425, 568, 678, 761
  Horsley Towers 572
  Shrubland Park 13, 535, 536, 537
Barry Jr., Charles 330
Barwell, Keith & Maggie 374
Basingstoke: Beaurepaire 224-6
Baspole, William 345
Bassett House 458-9
Bassett-Lowke, W.J. 374, 375
Bastard, Lieutenant Edmund 145
Bastard, John & William 493
Bateman, James 502
Bates, Alan 346
Bates, Sir Edward 806, 807
Bates, Fredrick 807
Bates, Sir Geoffrey 807
Bates, Sir Percy 807
Bath, Marquesses of
  4th Marquess 440, 661
  6th Marquess & Marchioness (Daphne) 660
Bath:
  8 The Circus 460-1, 634
  Bassett House 458-9
  Woodside House 17, 498
Bathealton: Bathealton Court 462
Bathealton Court 462
bathrooms
  8 The Circus (Bath) 461
  78 Derngate 375
  Ayot Mountfitchet 257, 258
Barkisland Hall 681
Beenham Hatch 28
Brantwoode 744
Culham Court 36
Dixton Manor 203
Dowdeswell Court 208
Fawley House 413
Fife House 599
Gillingham Hall 337
Holland House 722
Monkton House 613
Moundsmere Manor 237
Nethergate House 532
Ridgemead House 589

Rous Lench Court 673
Saddlewood Manor 217
Shawford Park 242
Sturford Mead 661
Tottenham Park 663
Ven House 494
Yew Tree House 549
  see also loos
Bathurst family 197
Batoni, Pompeo 765
Battersea Polytechnic 577
Bayley, Cornelia
Bettisfield Park 797
Plas Teg 816
Baynes, John 179
Beaconsfield: Holly Mount 46-7
Beaminster: Cheddington Court 150-1
bear emblem, Brereton family 68
Beardmore, Sir William Beardmore, 1st Baron Invernairn 758
Beatty, 1st Earl 363
Beatty, Admiral Lord 42
Beauchamp, Rose & Payn de 19
Beauchamp, William 554
Beaudesert 170
Beaufort, Dukes of
  1st Duke 215, 821
  4th Duke 294
Beaufort, Lady Margaret 481, 629
Beaulieu: The Vineyards 248
Beaumont family 384
Beaumont, Thomas Richard 384
Beaumont, Thomas Wentworth 384
Beaurepaire 224-6
Beaven, Christopher 636
Beaverbrook, 1st Baron (Lord Beaverbrook) 660
Beccles:
  Ashman's Hall 518
  Gillingham Hall 336-7
  Worlingham Hall 546-7
Beckford, William 19, 459, 723
Beckwith, T. 687
Bective, 2nd Earl of (later 1st Marquess of Headfort) 830
bed & breakfast see hotel & related use
Bedford, Dukes of
  6th Duke & Duchess (Georgiana) 123, 126
  8th Duke 129
  11th Duke 161
  12th Duke 126
Bedford, Earls of 161
  1st Earl 123
  2nd Earl 84
Bedford Square 155
beds
  78 Derngate guest room 375
  Calke Abbey state bed 107
  Edward James's at Monkton House 613
Beechwood House 483
Beenham Hatch 27-8
bees, mortar 645, 653
Behrens, Felicity & Michael 34
Behrens, Peter 375
Belcombe Court 634
Belford: Belford Hall 382, 384
Belford Hall 382, 384
Belhaven: Belhaven Hill House 741
Belhaven Hill House 741
Bell family 353
Bell, Currer see Bronte, Charlotte
Bell, Henry 353
Bell, Pam 853
Bell, Philip 353
Bellairs, Mrs 65
Belle Epoque style, Luton Hoo 24-5
Belsay 383, 476, 536, 738
Belton Hall 50, 321, 363, 492
belvederes
  Fisher's Hall, Hackfall 692
  Rousdon House 143
  Shrubland Park 535, 536-7
  Thoresby Hall 402
  Waldershare 287
  Wothorpe Grandstand 66
  Wyfold Court 427

Benenden family 264
Benenden: Old Manor House 264-7
Benenden School 265
Benham Park 29
Bennet family 480
Bennet, Christopher 637
Bennet, Jane 480
Bennet, Philip 480
Bennett, John (builder) 729
Bennett, John (MP) 659
Benson, Constantine & Morvyth 240-1
Benson, Jeremy 733
Bentley, J.F. 590
Bentley, W.O. 588
Bentley: Bentley Hall 519
Bentley Hall 519
Benton Jones, Sir Peter 59
Bere Regis: Anderson Manor 14, 148
Bergonzoli, Giulio 24
Berkeley, 4th Earl of 371
Berkeley family 205
Bernasconi, Francesco 19
Berteau, Edmund 843-4
Bertram, William 255
Berwick-upon-Tweed: Governor's House 390
Bess of Hardwick 399
Bethel Hospital, Norwich 347
Bethell, Mr 617
Betjeman, Sir John 520, 635, 654, 719
Bettisfield Park 797
Beverley market cross 707
Beville, Sir Robert 59
Bewela, Wanis 354-5
Bexleyheath: Danson House 6, 45, 270-1, 640
Bibury:
  Bibury Court 197-8
  Church House 199-201
Bibury Court 197-8
Bicester: Tusmore House 423-4
Bicknell, Julian 424
Bicton Park 636
Biddulph: Biddulph Grange 502-3
Biddulph Grange 502-3
big game trophies, Callaly Castle 386
Biggs, Harry 658-9
Biggs, Henry 658
Bigod, Hugh Bigod, 1st Earl of Norfolk 524
billiard rooms
  Bowden 31
  Cransley Hall 360, 361
  Doddington Hall 73
  Flichity House 758
  Nansidwell 88
  Nether Swell Manor 210
  Stocketts Manor 593
  Tyntesfield 492
  Wolverton Hall 675
Billinge: Bispham Hall 11, 295
Bilton, Anton 669
  Adderbury House 16, 404, 405
  Tyringham Hall 16, 54, 404
Bilton, Laurence, Croome Court 16, 669-71
Binney, George 189
Binney, Marcus
  Belhaven Hill House meeting 741
  early campaigns & journalism 7-9
  Highcliffe Castle campaign 7, 159
  Horham Hall residence 189-90
  house period preferences 9-14
  Sir Robert Taylor studies 6-7, 499, 640
Binning, Lords see Haddington, Earls of
Binns, Henry W. 657
Bird, Adrian 232
Bird, Colonel Tom 225, 226
birdcage room, Grovelands 717
birds see animals & birds
Birk, Lady (life peer) 685-6
Birkenhead: Brockhurst Hall 70
Birley, Sir Oswald & Lady

Rhoda 602-3
Birmingham Cathedral 625
Birr Castle 711
Bishopp, E.F. 523
Bishop's House (Bristol) 463-4
Bishopstrow House 661
Bishopton: Erskine House 755
Bispham Hall 11, 295
Black, James (architect) 773
Black, James (plasterer) 740
Black, Rodney 167
black & white houses
  of Cheshire 11, 71, 75-6
  of Shropshire 11, 438-44, 452-3
  of Suffolk 531-4, 538-9
Black Prince, Edward the 224, 542, 543
Blackburn family 682
Blackburn, Ernest 610-11
Blackburn: Woodfold Park 17, 301
Blackburn Hall 682
Blacker Douglas, Maxwell Vandeleur 847
Blackfriars Bridge 423
Blackland Park 12, 635-6
Blackwell 60
Blaise Hamlet 112
Blakiston, Thomas 350
Blakiston, William 169
Blane, Douglas 446
Blanerne House 742
Blantyre, 11th Lord 755
Blaydon: Axwell Park 166, 384
Blayds, John* 702
Blencowe, Adam de 95
Blencowe, Grace 96
Blencowe, Henry 95, 96
Blencowe, Henry Prescot 97
Blencowe Hall 95-8
Blenheim Palace 43, 156, 209, 404, 561, 639, 664, 711
Bletchley Manor 431
Blickling Hall 698, 761
blinds mechanism, Brodsworth Hall 684
Blois family 521
Blois, Sir Ralph 523
Blomfield, Sir Arthur 568
Blomfield, Sir Reginald 457
  Apethorpe Hall 354-5
  Hill Hall 188
  Moundsmere Manor 12, 236-7, 853
  Trinity Manor 851-3
  Waldershare 287
Blore, Edward
  Crom Castle 825
  Goodrich Court 554
  Vale Royal Abbey 81
Blow, Detmar 328
Blunt, Sir Anthony 725
Blunt, John 312
Boconnoc 84
Bodiam Castle 12, 419, 420, 504
Bodysgallen 798
Boleyn, Anne 282, 521, 642
Bolsover Castle 399, 505
Bolton, 2nd Duke of 839
Bolton, John 554
bomb damage, Cockfield Hall 523
bond types see brickwork
Bonnie Prince Charlie see Stewart, Charles Edward
Bonomi, Ignatius 172
Bonomi, Joseph
  Lambton Castle 172
  Piercefield wings 813, 815
'Boofy' Gore, 8th Earl of Arran 262, 263
bookcases
  Bishop's House (Bristol) 464
  Coton Hall 436
  Dowdeswell Court 207
  Ednaston Manor 108-9
  Eydon Hall 368
  The Grange (Ramsgate) 279
  Orchardleigh 483
  Pellicane House 278
  Ridgemead House 589
  Rous Lench Court 673
  Saddlewood Manor 217
  Walworth Castle 174
  see also libraries
books, false
  Danson House 271

Hatfield Priory 187
boomerang plan *see* Y-plan
Boord family 613, 615
Boord, Ninian 613
boot scrapers, Fife House 598
Booth family 307
Boringdon 114, 268
Borwick, Leonard 605
Boswell, Alexander Boswell,
  8th Laird of Auchinleck 737
Boswell, James 94, 737
Boteler, Sir Philip* 259
Botleys 552
bottle wells, Poulton House
  654
Boughton, Sir Edward 255
Boulanger, Marcel 210
Boulton, Matthew 507
Bourbon, Antoine de 158
Bourneville Estate 625
Boutwood, Jim 548
Bowden, Sir Frank 52
Bowden 30-1
Bower, John 502
Bower House 179
Bowes, George 169
Bowles, Sir Thomas 812
Bowling Green 149
Bowood House 190, 191
Bowyers Company/London
  Guild of Bowyers 308
Boy Scouts Association,
  Bispham Hall 295
Boyd, Sir John 270, 640
Boyle, Richard Boyle, 1st Earl
  of Cork 834, 838
Boyle, Richard Boyle, 3rd Earl
  of Burlington (Lord
  Burlington) 164, 372, 394,
  484, 662, 709
Boyne, 7th & 9th Viscounts
  167
Bracebridge family 67
Bracebridge Hall *see* Brereton
  Hall
Bracewell, Thomas 294
Bracka, Ivor 343
Braco, 1st Baron (William
  Duff) 752
Bradford, 1st Earl of 446
Bradford, Ida, Countess of
  Bradford (wife of 4th Earl)
  619
Bradford:
  Paper Hall 703
  Tong Hall 707
Bradford-on-Avon:
  Belcombe Court 634
  South Wraxhall Manor
  488-9
Bradgate House 303
Bradgate Stables 303
Bradley, James 419
Bradninch: Bradninch Manor
  10, 12, 115-16
Bradninch Manor 10, 12, 115-
  16
Bradshaw, Joan & Robert 660,
  661
Braemes, Sir Arnold 268
Bramcote Hall 618
Bramley, Robin 336
Bramley: Snowdenham Hall
  15, 590
Brampton: Hayton Hall 99-
  100
Bramshill 227
Brancepeth: Brancepeth
  Castle 167
Brancepeth Castle 167
Brand, Phyllis & Robert
  Henry (1st Baron Brand)
  366, 368
Brand, Virginia 367
Brando, Marlon 601
Brandon, Charles Brandon,
  1st Duke of Suffolk (2nd
  creation) 544
Brantwoode 743-4
brasses, Sir Hugh Hastings in
  Elsing church 333
Brassey, Alfred 415
Brassey, Leonard Brassey, 1st
  Baron Brassey 354
Brassey, Thomas 354
Bray, William 554
Braybrooke, William de 637
Braybrooke House 637-8
breach of promise, 6th
  Marquess of Northampton

633
Breadalbane, Earls &
  Marquesses of
  2nd Marquess 784
  4th Earl & 1st Marquess 784
Breckles: Breckles Hall 10, 14,
  328
Breckles Hall 10, 14, 328
Brecon, Lois & Bill 746
Breda Room, Goodrich Court
  & Brook Place 554
Bredgar: Holliday Hall 11 , 273-
  4
Bremo, Virigina, USA 366
Brenchley, Sir William 264
Brentwood: Thorndon Hall
  13, 196
Brereton, Sir William* &
  Brereton family 67-9
Brereton Hall 67-9
bressumer beams
  Bentley Hall 519
  Olden Manor 533
Bretby:
  Bretby Hall 102-3
  Brizlincote Hall 103
Bretby Hall 102-3
Bretherton: Bank Hall 294
Brettingham, Matthew 342
Bretton Hall 384
brew house, Nunton House
  646
brickwork
  burnt headers 653
  chequer pattern 251, 381
  Cossey brick 426
  diapers 308, 320, 353, 393,
  608
  drying racks 803
  English baroque 274
  English bond 67, 539, 593,
  608, 650
  Essex brick 186
  fair-faced 803
  Flemish bond 562, 608
  galleting 290, 561
  garden bond/American
  bond 650, 700
  halfpenny pointing 187
  header bond 645
  mortar bees 645, 653
  Norfolk redbrick manor
  houses 338, 344, 345, 348,
  352-3
  penny-struck pointing 187,
  561, 645
  rubbed brick 182, 184, 287,
  726
  Tudor 190, 538
Bride Hall 258-9
Bridge: Bridge Place 268-9
Bridge Place 268-9
Bridgeman, Sir John 619
Bridges, John 65
bridges
  8 The Circus (Bath) 461
  Anderson Manor 148
  Blackfriars Bridge 423
  Carton House 823
  Caverswall Castle 504
  Compton Verney 622
  Copped Hall 181
  Dumfries House 753
  Earl Soham Lodge 524
  Edwinsford 801
  Gwerclas Hall 804
  The Hill 720
  Jacob's Ladder 408
  Norton Place 324
  Park Cottage 809
  Pont-y-Prydd 801
  Puttenham Priory 586
  Trinity Manor 852
  Westminster Bridge 380
  Wotton House 595
Bridgman, C. 179
Bridgnorth:
  Apley Park 428-30, 453
  Coton Hall 435-6
Bridgwater: Barford House
  455-6
Bridport: Downe Hall 155
Briggs, R.A. 248
Brighton: Fife House 597-600
Brighton Museum 271
Bristol, 4th Earl of 518
Bristol:
  Ashton Court 454
  Bishop's House 463-4
  King's Weston 17, 209

Bristow, Ian 725
Brite, James 227
British Journal, on Maids of
  Honour Row 726-7
British Museum 24, 99, 755
Brittain, Baron 21
Britten, Robert 21
Brixham: Lupton House 136
Brizlincote Hall 103
The Broad House 329
Broadhembury: The Grange
  117-18
Broadlands 486
Brocas family 224
Brocas, Sir Bernard 224
Brockamin: The Great House
  668
Brocket, 2nd Baron (Lord
  Brocket) 227
Brocket Hall 260, 535
Brockhall: Brockhall Manor
  357-8
Brockhall Hall 357
Brockhall Manor 357-8
Brockhurst Hall 70
Brocklehurst, Ralph 427
Brodie, Francis 753
Brodie, James 357, 358
Brodsworth Hall 683-5
Brogyntyn, Owain 432
Brogyntyn 432-3
Broke, 12th & 19th Barons
  Willoughby de Broke 621
Bromley: Sundridge Park 283-
  6, 775
Bronte, Duke of *see* Nelson
Bronte, Charlotte 695
Bronte, Emily 695
Brook Place 11 , 553-4
Brook Street (no 72) *see*
  Holland House
Brooke, Robert 521
Brooke, Robert Greville
  Brooke, 2nd Baron Brooke
  (Lord Brooke) 629
Brooking, Charles 238
Brough Hall 685-6, 699
Brougham, Henry Richmond
  101
Brougham, John 101
Broughton, Henry
  Broughton, 2nd Baron
  Fairhaven 584, 585
Broughton, Rev Sir Thomas
  73
Broughton, Urban Hanlon &
  Cara (Lady Fairhaven) 584-5
Broughton, Urban Huttleston
  Broughton, 1st Baron
  Fairhaven 584-5
Broughty Castle 767
Brown, Andrew 82
Brown, Capability
  associations with &
  comparisons to 14, 144,
  146, 156, 430, 504, 579, 823
  Benham Park 29
  Compton Verney 621
  Croome Court 16, 622, 669-
  71
  Dodington Park 204
  Heveningham Hall 12, 529
  Patshull Hall 512, 513
  Thorndon Hall 196
  Tottenham Park 662, 664
Brown, Henry 636
Brown, James 737
Brown, John 740
Brown, William & Mary 792
Browne family 334
Browne, Major & Mrs
  Alexander 385, 386
Browne, Major A.S.C. 385, 386
Browne, George Washington
  741
Browne, Samuel 313
Browning, John 255
Broyd, Richard 798
Bruce, Sir William 785
Brunei, Sultan of 730
Brunel, Isambard Kingdom 90
Bryce, David 402, 764, 773, 786
  Cullen House 750
Bryce, John 764, 821-2
Brympton d'Evercy 465-6
Buccleuch, Dukes of 747
Buchan, John 88, 851
Buck, Samuel 700
Buck, Squire 543
Buckingham, Dukes of (first

creation)
  1st Duke (Humphrey
  Stafford) 628
  3rd Duke 628, 633
Buckingham, Dukes of
  (second creation), 1st Duke
  (George Villiers) 354
Buckingham, Marquesses of
  1st Marquess 185
  2nd Marquess 185
Buckingham House 22
Buckingham Palace 178, 283,
  452, 579, 585
Buckland: The Manor House
  32-3
Buckland Hall 32
Buckleburry: Beenham Hatch
  27-8
Buckley, Wilfred 236
Budget, Hubert 416
The Builder articles
  Mackenzie, William
  Macdonald 773-4
  Steephill 850
  Yeaton Pevery 453
Building News articles
  Little Thakeham 611
  North Breache Manor 580
Buildings At Risk Trust 140,
  818
Buildings of England articles
  see Pevsner, Nikolaus &
  Pevsner Architectural Guides
  articles
Buildings of Scotland articles
  see Pevsner, Nikolaus &
  Pevsner Architectural Guides
  articles
Buildings of Wales articles *see*
  Pevsner, Nikolaus & *Pevsner
  Architectural Guides* articles
Bullen, Michael 232
bull's eye windows (*oeil-de-
  boeuf*), description 46, 220
Bulmer, Edward 725
bungalow eating 606
Bungay: Hedenham Hall 344
Bunny: Bunny Hall 16, 103,
  392-3
Bunny Hall 16, 103, 392-3
Buntingsdale Hall 434
burbage plots, Caernarfon 800
Burdon, V. 689
Burges, William 246, 743
Burghley, Barons
  1st Baron (William
  Cecil/Lord Burghley) 153,
  361
  2nd Baron (Thomas Cecil,
  1st Earl of Exeter) 361
Burghley House 66, 153, 403
Burgundy, Philip III, Duke of
  Burgundy 759
Burke, C.T. 46
Burke, Henry 351
Burles Lodge 555-7
Burley-in-the-Hill 304-5, 313
Burlington, Earls of 834
  3rd Earl (Richard
  Boyle/Lord Burlington) 164,
  372, 394, 484, 662, 709
Burlington Harry *see* Flitcroft,
  Henry
Burn, William 508
  Achnacarry 734
  Blanerne House 742
  Patshull Hall terraces 512
  Revesby Abbey 325-6
  Stoneleigh Abbey 630
  Thirlestane Castle 786
  Tyninghame House 789-91
Burnett-Hitchcock, Charles
  143
Burnhill Green: Patshull Hall
  17, 429, 512-13
Burrell Company 781
Burton, Andrew 173
Burton, Decimus 493, 494
Burton, Jean 326
Burton-on-Trent:
  Sinai Park 514
Burton Park 604
Bury St Edmunds:
  Abbey Houses 520
  Hengrave Hall 527-8
Bute, Earls & Marquesses of
  753
  3rd Earl 24, 616
  3rd Marquess 753
  7th Marquess 753

Butler, Tiggy 721
Butten, Ernest 286
Butterfield, William 246
Buxted: Buxted Park 600-1
Buxted Park 600-1
Buxton, Christopher
  Barlaston Hall inquiry 499
  Compton Verney 622
  Kirtlington Park 416, 616,
  622
  Shillinglee Park 15, 616
Buxton: The Crescent 104-5
Buzzard, Sir Edward Farquhar
  578
Bylaugh Hall 330
Byron, George Gordon, Lord
  Byron 173, 572
Bywell: Bywell Hall 384
Bywell Hall 384

C

Cabal Ministry 164
Cable House, Leighton estate
  808-9
Cadbury family 625
Cade, Jack 628
Cadell, Robert 792
Cadw 800, 818
Cadwallon (chieftain) 798
Caernarfon: 6 Palace Street
  799-800
Caernarfon Castle 63, 799
Caernarfon Heritage Trust
  799
Cahn, Sir Julian & Lady 400
Caine, Percy 191
Cairndhu 744
Calais Staple 10, 318
Calcutt, Sir David 230
California Mission style,
  Ridgemead 588-9
Calke Abbey 50, 106-7, 450,
  757
Callaly Castle 385-6
Calne: Blackland Park 12,
  635-6
Cals, Robert 222
Calverley, John 702
Cambridge: 48 Storey's Way
  60
Cambridge University &
  colleges 22, 39, 101 , 158, 354,
  481, 648, 754
Camerons of Lochiel &
  Donald Cameron 734
Campbell family 784
Campbell, Colen & *Vitruvius
  Britannicus* 377, 552
  Ebberston Hall 690
canals *see* lakes, pools & canals
candle-snuffer turrets 790, 791
Cannon, Kevin 820
Cannon Street, London,
  Herbert Huntly-Gordon's
  buildings 556
Canons Ashby 450
Canonteign Manor 119-20
Canova, Antonio 126
cantilevered staircases,
  descriptions 14, 324, 379
Cantlie, Hugh 382
Capitalrise 104
Capper, S. Henbest 781
Cardiff Castle 753
Cardigan, Earl of 663
care homes *see* hospital &
  related use; retirement
  home use
Carew family 824
Carew, Robert 824
Carew, Thomas 469
Cargill, David & Shirley 335
Carlow, 2nd Viscount (Lord
  Carlow) 827
Carlton Club 204
Carlton House 476
Carlton House Terrace 112, 175
Carmody, Vincent 722
Carnarvon, Earls of 103
Carnegie, Andrew 764
Carnwath, Robert 234, 364
Carolean & Caroline
  Bridge House 268-9
  Coombe Abbey 623
  Cranborne Manor 152-4
  Dingley Hall 362
  Grange Park 235
  Lucas Almshouses 39-40
  Melton Constable Hall
  346-7

860

Ramsbury Manor 281, 346
Shawford Park 240-3
Walpole House 732-3
Caroline, Countess of
Dalkeith 747
Caroline, Queen 107, 726
Carpenter, Margeret 661
Carr of York, John 712
Clifton Hall 394, 395
Colwick Hall 396
Constable Burton 7, 687,
688-9
The Crescent, Buxton 104-5
Norton Place 7, 322-4
Tabley Hall 80-1
Carrigtuohill: Fota 828
Carrisbrook Castle 154
Carshalton House 561
Carter, Howard 490
Carter, John 384
Carter, L.T. 426
Carter, Tony & Sue 238, 239
Carteret, Edward Charles
Malet de 843, 844
Carteret, Sir George 843
Carteret, Guy Malet de 844
Carteret, Philip & Adele Malet
de 843, 844
Carteret, Philippe & Margeret
de 843
Carteret, Rex Malet de 844
Cartland, Barbara 364
Carton House 822, 823
Cartwright family 215, 356
Cartwright, Francis 161
Carven estate (Ashbury
Manor) 407
carvings
Aldhams 177
Apethorpe Hall 354
Blackburn Hall 682
Blencowe Hall 95-6
Brereton Hall 68
Bunny Hall 392
Castle Bromwich Hall 619
Castleboro House 824
Caverswall Castle 506
Cockfield Hall 523
The Crescent, Buxton 104
Hinwick House 22
Miller's Tower 763
Moundsmere Manor 236,
237
Nun Monkton Hall 701
Olden Manor 534
Park Close 583
Penhow Castle 813
The Reader's House 439
Revesby Abbey 326
Ridgemead 589
Shrubland Park 536
Stibbington Hall 59
Stockton 659
Thurston End Hall 538
Toddington Manor 218
Tong Hall 707
Trinity Manor 853
Twyford Moors House 247
Tyntesfield 491
Westgate House 540
Wingfield College 544
Woolstaplers Hall 223
Wyfold Court 426
see also inscriptions & tags;
monuments & tombstones
casement windows,
description 363, 600, 645
Casentini, Chevalier Giovanni
683, 684
The Casino at Marino 835
Casson, Tom 681
Casson Conder Partnership
100
Castle, Barbara 681
Castle, Richard 822
Castle Ashby 358-9, 380
Castle Bromwich: Castle
Bromwich Hall 619-20
Castle Bromwich Hall 619-20
Castle Cary: Hadspen 470
Castle Donington:
Donington Hall 306
Islay Walton Manor 308
Castle Drogo 131
Castle Howard 43, 209, 639,
708
Castle Huntly 767
Castle of Park 745-7
Castleboro House 824

Castlereagh, Viscount (Lord
Castlereagh) 176
castles, slighted 96
Catchfrench Manor 85
cathedrals
Birmingham Cathedral 625
Coventry Cathedral 769
St Paul's Cathedral 577
Salisbury Cathedral & Close
157, 520, 637-8, 651, 791
Westminster Cathedral 590
Winchester Cathedral 230,
244
Worcester Cathedral 676
see also churches
Catherine of Braganza, Queen
716
Catherine the Great 366
cattle herds
Carton House 823
Castle of Park 746
Chillingham 132, 386
Holystreet Manor 132
Knightstone Manor 135
Catto, Thomas Catto, 1st
Baron Catto (Lord Catto)
569
Caus Castle 440, 441
Cautley, H. Munro 531 - 2
Cavendish, William
Cavendish, 6th Duke of
Devonshire (Bachelor
Duke) 597, 599, 600, 728, 834
Caverswall Castle 12, 504-6
caves
Friar Park 414
see also grottos
Cayley, Sir Kenelm 690
Caythorpe: Caythorpe Hall
315-17
Caythorpe Hall 315-17
Cayzer, Major Bernard 486
Cecil, Henry Cecil, 1st
Marquess of Exeter 66
Cecil, Robert Cecil, 1st Earl of
Salisbury 153
Cecil, Sir Thomas Cecil, 2nd
Baron Burghley & 1st Earl of
Exeter 361
Cecil, William Cecil, 1st Baron
Burghley (Lord Burghley)
153, 361
Cecil House 153
Cedar Cottage 557-9
cedar shingles 557, 558
Centre Point 281
Chadwick, James 731
Chafy, Rev W.K.W. 673
Chagford: Holystreet Manor
130-2
chaise percee, Culham Court
36
Chambers, Sir William 405
The Casino at Marino 835
Culham Court 34-5
Duddingston House 751
Poston House 254-5
Styche Hall 451
Champernowne family 137
Champneys, Basil 569
Chance, Ian & Hilary 543, 544,
545
Chance, William & Julia 582
chandelier mechanism,
Cheddington Court 151
Chandos, 1st Duke of 41, 456
Chantrey, Sir Francis 547
chapels
The Abbey (Charlton
Adam) 467
The Almshouses (Preston-
on-the-Weald Moors) 447
Ashbury Manor 407
Ayshford Court 113
Beenham Hatch 28
Callaly Castle 386
Churche's Mansion 72
Coton Hall 435, 436
Dodington Park 205
Donington Hall 306
Elsing Hall 333
Gibside 168
Gillingham Hall 337
Grace Dieu Manor 307
Hayton Hall 100
Hengrave Hall 527, 528
Henry VII chapel,
Westminster Abbey 476,
527
Holystreet Manor 131

Knightstone Manor 134
Ledstone Hall 698
Leyburn Hall 699
Lucas Almshouses 40
Maristow House 137
Ridgemead 589
St Joseph's Abbey 617
Sawston Hall 56
Stoneleigh Abbey 631
Thorpe Hall 350
Towie Barclay 787
Tyntesfield 490, 492
Tyringham Hall 54
Walmoor House 83
Wardour Castle 666
Woodcroft Castle 65
Wynyard Park 176
see also churches
Chaplin, Reginald 549
Chapman, Jane 480
Chapman, Scarborough 480
Charlemont, 1st Earl of 835
Charles I, King 52, 63, 65, 114,
377, 378, 740, 817, 843
Charles II, King 114, 164, 268,
378, 422, 631, 716, 732, 772,
843
Charles V, Holy Roman
Emperor 521
Charles X, King of France 306
Charles, Prince of Wales 217,
255, 800
Charles Mellier & Co 775
Charleston Manor 602-3
Charlie, Bonnie Prince see
Stewart, Charles Edward
Charlotte, Queen 138
Charlton Adam: The Abbey
467-8
Charlton House 257
Chartist movement riots,
Colwick Hall 396
Chastleton House 444
Chatham, 1st Earl of (William
Pitt the Elder) 156, 460
Chatsworth House 287, 492,
554, 599
Chatwin, J.A. 625
Chawton: Chawton House
228-9
Chawton House 228-9
Cheddington Court 150-1
cheetahs, Sir Frank Bowden's
52
Chelmsford:
Hatfield Priory 186-7
Hylands House 7, 192-3
Chelsea House 153
Cheltenham: Dowdeswell
Court 16, 185, 206-8, 356
chemical weapon detector 602
Chepstow: Piercefield 813-15
Chepstow Castle 812
Chepstow racecourse 813, 814
chequer pattern brickwork
251, 381
Cherrill, Virginia, USA 417
Chertsey: Botleys 552
Cheshire, Group Captain
Leonard 312, 313
Cheshire Homes
Staunton Harold Hall 311 -13
Wardour Castle 666
Chester, Sir John 42, 43
Chester, Sir William 43
Chester: Walmoor House 83
Chester Terrace 713
Chester-le-Street, Lambton
Castle 172
Chesterfield, Earls of
1st Earl 102
2nd Earl 103
3rd Earl 103
5th Earl 103
Chesterfield, Lady 103
Chetwynd, 2nd Viscount 511
Chevening House 268
Cheyne, Sir Thomas 282
Chicheley 14, 42-3
Chichester family 146
Chichester, Gerard 810
Chicksands Priory 18-19, 21
children's home use
Formby Hall 298
Horham Hall 189
House of Gray 767
Walpole House 733
see also educational use

Chillingham Castle 385, 387
Chillingham cattle herd 132,
386, 387
Chilworth: Chilworth Manor
560-1
Chilworth Manor 560-1
chimney stacks
Albury Park 550
Aldhams 177
barley-sugar 290, 291, 334, 528
Blanerne House 742
Brook Place 553
Craigengillan 748
Elsing Hall 334
Great Snoring Manor 338
Greywalls 768
Hedenham Hall 344
Hengrave Hall 528
Holystreet Manor 130
King's Weston 209
Lilford Castle 372
Little Hautbois 345
Longford Hall 110
Mackerye End 261
Mears Ashby Hall 373
Minsterley Hall 441
Nethergate House 532
North Luffenham Hall 309
Nun Monkton Hall 700
Old Manor House
(Benenden) 265-6
Orchards 582
Plaish Hall 445
Poulton Manor 214, 215
Revesby Abbey 325
The Salutation 280
The Soke 244, 245
Stocketts Manor 591
Thurston End Hall 539
Wotton House 594
Wraxhall House 165
Wyfold Court 426
Yaldham Manor 290, 291
Yeaton Pevery 453
Chinese Garden, Biddulph
Grange 502
Chinese Room, Youlston Park
147
Chinnor: Jacob's Ladder 14,
408
Chippendale, Thomas 753
Chippenham:
Rowden Manor 655-6
The Ivy 639
Chippenham town hall &
Neeld Hall 641
Chipping Camden:
Woolstaplers Hall 222-3
Chipping Norton:
Heythrop Park 415
Sarsden House 418
Chipping Sodbury:
Dodington Park 13, 59, 74,
204-6
Chipping Warden: Edgcote
House 365
Chiswick: Walpole House
732-3
Chiswick House 484, 662
Chobham: Cedar Cottage
557-9
Cholmeley, Sir Montague 324
Cholmondeley family 81
Cholmondeley, Lord George
59
Christchurch: Highcliffe
Castle 7, 158-9
Christie, Agatha 76
Christie, Julie 346
Christow:
Canonteign Manor 119-20
Hill 128
Christy, Archibald 810
Chrystal, Sir George 601
Chulmleigh: Rashleigh Barton
141-2
Church, Frederick Owen 813
Church House (Bibury) 199-
201
Church House (Bristol) see
Bishop's House (Bristol)
Church Stretton: Plaish Hall
445
Churche, Rychard & Margerye
71
Churche's Mansion 11, 13,
71-2
churches
Bibury 199
Biggs family pew 659

Blackburn (St John's) 301
Blackland Park 635
Brough Hall (St Paulinus)
686
Buckland 33
Buxted Park 600
Caverswall 504
Charlton Adam 467
Chesil Church 244, 245
Dinton 651
Edgcote 365
Elsing 333
Great Ponton 318, 319
Hengrave Hall 528
Isfield Place 607
Kildwick 696
Little Hautbois 345
Maristow House 138
Mildenhall 654
Ogbourne St George 648,
650
Podington 22
Ramsgate (St Augustine's)
279
St George's, Hanover Square
664
St Paul's, Covent Garden 551
Seton Collegiate Church 783
St-Martin-in-the-Fields 446
Staunton Harold 312
Stinsford 162
Tyninghame House 790
Wardour Castle 666
see also cathedrals; chapels
Churchill, Sir Winston 176,
191, 560, 579, 674
see also Special Operations
Executive use
Chute, John 298
Chute Lodge 640
cinemas see theatres &
cinemas
Cipriani, G.B. 665
The Circus, Bath (No 8) 460-
1, 634
Civil War see English Civil War
Clare, John 65
Clare, Steve 814
Clare: Nethergate House 531 -
2
Clarence, Duke of (later
William IV) 698
Clarendon Building 404
Claridges Hotel, London 138,
601
Clark, Sir Kenneth 221
Clarke family 197, 198, 199
Clarke, George Somers 425,
426
Clarke, Sir Orme & Elfrida
197-8
Clarke, Sir Stanley 814
Clarke, Sir Tobias 199
Clavering family 385
Clavering, Sir John 385
Clavering, John & Anne 385
Clavering, Ralph 386
Clavering, Robert 385
Clavering, Sir Thomas 166
Claverton Manor 459
Clayton, Sir Robert 44
Clayton, Sir William 44
Clease, Thomas 71
Clegg Hall 11, 268, 296
Clements, Adam 564
Clenden, Thomas 373
Clerk, Sir John 776
Cleveland, Barbara Villiers,
Duchess of Cleveland 378,
732
Clifford, Laura May 307
Clifford, T. Dalton 154
Clifford, Sir Timothy 791
Clifton family 393, 394
Clifton, Gervase* 394, 395
Clifton, Colonel Percy Robert
393
Clifton, Sir Robert 394-5
Clifton Castle 687
Clifton Hall 16, 393-5
Clifton Hill House 463
Clifton-Taylor, Alec 439
clinics see hospital & related
use
Clinton, John de 627, 628
Clinton, William de Clinton,
1st Earl of Huntingdon 627
Clive, Robert Clive, 1st Baron
Clive (Clive of India) 451
Clive-Ponsonby-Fane,

Charles 466
Cliveden 664
clocks
  Monkton House 612
  Park Close 585
  Thoresby Hall 402
Clones: Hilton Park 831
Clontarf: The Casino at
  Marino 835
close studding 276, 289, 292,
  538
Clotworthy, John & Mary 141
Clough, Robert 440
clubs *see* country club & night
  club use; golf courses &
  clubs
Clumber Park 601
Clutton, Henry 596
Clutton House 214
coal sheds, Hanger Hill
  Garden Estate 719
Coates, John 695
Coates, Wells 570
Cobbe family 839
Cobbe, Charles 839
Cobbett, William 560, 561
Cockayne, Charles Cockayne,
  1st Viscount Cullen 376
Cockayne, Sir William 376
Cockerell, C.R. 38
  Grange Park orangery 235
Cockerell, S.P. 432
Cockfield Hall 521-3
Cockle Tower, Larch Hill 833
Codrington family 204, 205-6
Codrington, Christopher* 206
Codrington, Sir William 206
coffin drop, Churche's
  Mansion 11, 72
Cogan, Alma 194
Cohen, Benjamin 551
Cohen, Robert 603
Coke, Clement 110
Coke, Sir Edward (Lord Chief
  Justice) 110
Coke, Thomas Coke, 1st Earl
  of Leicester 110, 688
Cole, Martin 21
Colebrook, 'Bill' Avray 183
Colebrook House 230-1
Coleridge, J.D. 554
Coleridge, John 305
Coleshill: Maxstoke Castle
  504, 627-9
Coleshill House 163
college use *see* educational use;
  police colleges
College Yard (no 10) 676-7
Collier, Jim 198
Colomberie House 815
colonnades
  Archerfield 735
  Bassett House 458, 459
  Brereton Hall 69
  Burley-on-the-Hill 304, 305
  Clifton Hall 394, 395
  Compton Verney 622
  Dodington Park 204, 205
  Eastwood Farm 606
  Gunton Hall 339, 340-1, 343
  The Hill 720
  Leigh Court 476
  Sarsden House 418
  Stoke Park 377
coloured glass *see* stained,
  coloured & engraved glass
Colquhoun, Fiona (Countess
  of Arran) 262-3
Colquhoun, Iain 262
Colquhoun, Sir Iain 262
Colt, Harry 196
Colt, H.S. 167
Colt houses 558
Colthurst, Oliver & Caroline
  442, 444
Colville, 4th Viscount 547
Colville, John & Helen 769,
  770
Colvin, Sir Auckland 525
Colvin, Brenda 646
Colvin, Sir Howard 107
Colvin, Hugh 645
Colwick Hall 16, 396
Commonwealth houses
  Staunton Harold church 312
  Wimborne House 163-4
  see also Artisan Mannerist
Comper, Sir Ninian 813
Compton family 358-9, 633
  Henry Compton, 1st Baron

Compton 359
Spencer Compton, 7th
  Marquess of
  Northampton 358, 380
William Compton, 1st Earl
  of Northampton 359
William Compton, 6th
  Marquess of
  Northampton 633
Compton Verney 621-2
Compton Wynyates 633
Comyns, Sir John 193
conference centres *see* hotel &
  related use
Congreve, Ambrose 632, 836-7
Congreve, John 758
Coningsby, William 353
Connell, John 92-3
conservation areas, Hanger
  Hill Garden Estate 718-19
conservatories, glasshouses &
  orangeries
  Astley Pool House 667
  Bicton Park 636
  Blackland Park 636
  Brereton Hall 69
  Bylaugh Hall 330
  Carlton House 476
  Cheddington Court 151
  Dowdeswell Court 208
  Fawley House 411
  Fife House 599
  Flintham 11, 398
  Frampton Oranagery 220
  Gibside 168, 169
  Grange Park 235
  Heath House 508
  Hylands House 193
  Maperton 478, 480
  Mount Congreve 837
  Nansidwell 89
  Nutley Manor 239
  Sarsden House 418
  Shirburn Castle 420
  Steephill 850
  Stoneleigh Abbey 630
  Thame Park 52
  Tottenham Park 662
  Ven House 493, 494
'conserve as found' question
  685, 706, 778-9
Constable Burton 7, 688-9
Constable, John 182, 183, 193
contents & contents sales
  Allerton Park 678-9
  Barkisland Hall 681
  Brodsworth Hall 683, 684
  Bunny Hall 393
  Calke Abbey 106-7, 757
  Cragside 389
  Cranborne Manor 154
  Croome Court 669
  Dumfries House 753
  Fasque Castle 757
  Fota 828
  Fyvie Castle 765
  Griblech 770
  Gwrych Castle 804
  Gyrn Castle 807
  Halswell 471
  Heveningham Hall 529, 530
  Les Lumières 842
  Mentmore Towers 48-50
  Monkton House 612-13
  Newbridge 839
  Orchardleigh 483-4
  Philipps House 652
  Pitchford Hall 442, 444
  Stokesay Court 449, 450
  Tyninghame House 789
  Tyntesfield 490-2
  Ven House 493
  Wingfield Castle 543
convalescent homes *see*
  hospital & related use
convents, seminaries &
  religious retreats
  Caverswall Castle 505-6
  Emo Court 827
  Hengrave Hall 527
  Highcliffe Castle 159
  Nun Monkton Hall 701
  St Joseph's Abbey 617
  Troy House 821
  Wardour Castle 666
  Woolton Hall 302
  see also monastic origins
conversions *see* hotel & related
  use; office conversions &
  use; residential conversions

& enabling development
Conwy Castle 798
Conyers, John 180
Conyers, Julia 517
Cook, Ernest 816
Cook, Captain James 326
Cooke, Edward William 483
Cooke, John 640
Cooke's House 603-5
Cooksey, Alice 674
Cooksey, William 674
Coole: Larch Hill 832-3
Coombe Abbey 363, 623
Cooper, David 499
Cooper, Mr 718
Cooper, Nicholas 76, 296
Cooper, Colonel Reggie 134
Cooper, Thomas Sidney 449
Cooper, Todd 598
Coote, Sir Eyre 792
Cope family 227
Copledyke, John 321
Copped Hall 180-1, 517
Corbusier, Le 570
Cordeux, Dr R.H. 393
Corinthian Villa, Regent's
  Park 730
Cork, Earls of
  1st Earl (Richard Boyle) 834,
    838
  2nd Earl 834
Cornell, Anthony 348
Cornforth, John 686
Cornhill: Castle of Park 745-7
Cornish, Samuel* 587
Corpse Way 682
Corry, Herbert William 291
Corsham Court 283
Corsley Manor 661
Cory-Wright family 260
Corydnon, Nick 217
Cote Baptist Chapel 409
Cote House 409-10
Cothay Manor 134
Coton Hall 435-6
cottage conversions *see*
  residential conversions &
  enabling development
'Cottentots' 425
council ownership *see* local
  government properties
Cound Hall 437
country baroque *see* Baroque
country club & night club use
  Bank Hall 294
  Bridge Place 268
  Heythrop Park 415
  Little Bardfield Hall 194
Country Houses Association
  16, 185, 356, 550
Country Life articles &
  publications
  A La Ronde 111, 112
  Apley Park 429
  Aynho 356
  Barlaston Hall 499, 501
  Barrow Court 457
  Bibury Court 197
  Biddulph Grange 502
  Binney, Marcus, early work
    7, 9
  Bowling Green 149
  Brodsworth Hall 684
  Brough Hall 685, 686
  Brympton d'Evercy 465
  Buxted Park 101
  Bywell Hall 384
  Calke Abbey state bed 107
  Caroline Park 747
  Caverswall Castle 505, 506
  Clegg Hall 296
  Constable Burton 7, 689
  Cooke's House 604
  Cound Hall 437
  Cragside 388-9
  Doddington Hall 73-4
  Ellys Manor House 318
  Finedon Hall 369
  The Grange
    (Broadhembury) 118
  Harleyford Manor 44
  Harrington Hall 320
  Heath House 508
  High Head Castle 101
  The Ivy 639
  Kildwick Hall 697
  Lambton Castle 172
  Llangoed Hall 7, 810
  The Manor House
    (Buckland) 32, 33

The Manor House
  (Ogbourne St George)
  647, 649
Manor House (Sutton
  Courtenay) 422
Maperton 9
Nether Swell Manor 210
Newhailes 778
North Breache Manor 580
North Luffenham Hall 310
Oulton Hall 702
Paine, James 384
Ridgemead 589
Rous Lench Court 672
The Salutation 280
Sarsden House 418
Shillinglee Park 616
Stanton House 657
Stibbington Hall 59
Trafalgar House 664
Tyringham Hall 54
Upton House 220-1
Ven House 493
Countryman advertisement,
  Cedar Cottage 558
county council ownership *see*
  local government properties
Courage family 590
Court House, Bentley Hall 519
The Court House (Martock)
  481-2
Courtauld, Jeanne 604, 605
Courtauld, Major & Mrs J.S.
  603, 604
Courtauld, Samuel 185
Courtauld, Sir Stephen &
  Lady Virginia 198
Courtauld Institute of Art 725
Courtenay, Catherine 92
Courtenay, Reginald 421
Couse, Kenton 552
Coventry, Earls of 669
Coventry: Coombe Abbey
  363, 623
Coventry Cathedral 769
Cowdray Park 282
Cowell, Mr & Mrs 186, 187
Coxwell-Rogers, Geoffrey &
  Aileen 208
Coxwell-Rogers, Richard 208
Crace, John Dibblee 441, 599,
  834
cradle-rocking mechanism,
  Gwerclas Hall 804
Cradock, Matthew 505
Cragside 388-9
Craigengillan 748
Cranborne Manor 152-4, 615,
  658
Cranborne: Cranborne
  Manor 152-4, 615, 658
Cranbrook: Wilsley 288-9
Crane, Sir Francis 377
Cransley Hall 12, 360-1
Craven, 1st Earl of 421
Craven, 6th Baron (Lord
  Craven) 29
Craven family & estate 407,
  623
Crawford, Alan 222
Crawford: Crawford Manor
  297
Crawford Manor 297
Crawfurd, Gibbs 615
Crediton: Knightstone Manor
  10, 134-5
crenellating *see* licence to
  crenellate
The Crescent, Buxton 104-5
The Crescent, Wisbech (No 4)
  61-2
Cressett, Edward 437
Cresswell, Estcourt 197
Cressy, Thomas 392
Creswell, Alexander 235
Crewe: Haslington Hall 75-6
Crewe House 722
Crichton family 825
Crichton, Richard 738
Crill, Mr 850
Cripps, Henry 221
Cripps, Nathaniel* 221
Crisp, Sir Frank 368, 414
Critchley-Salmonson, Dennis
  132
Crocker, George 227
Croft-Murray, Edward 726,
  727
Croker Mansion 227

Crom Castle 825
Cromwell, Oliver 96, 553, 673,
  706
Cromwellian houses *see*
  Artisan Mannerist;
  Commonwealth houses
Croome Court 16, 622, 669-71
Croome D'Abitot: Croome
  Court 16, 622, 669-71
Crosby Hall 170
Crosland, Anthony 685-6
Crosse, Francis & Elizabeth
  532
Crossley, Mr 265
crow-stepped gables 344, 348
Crowcombe: Crowcombe
  Court 7, 17, 456, 469
Crowcombe Court 7, 17, 456,
  469
Crowen: Gwerclas Hall 17,
  802-4
Crowfield Hall 535
Crown Commissioners 140,
  714, 730
Crowther of Syon Lodge 198
cruck-framed long house, Alt-
  y-Bela 796
Cruickshank, Dan 251
Crystal Palace 11, 48, 398
Cubitt, Major Frank Astley 350
Culham Court 9, 34-6
Cullen, 1st Viscount (Charles
  Cockayne) 376
Cullen House 15, 749-50, 772
Cullen: Cullen House 15, 749-
  50, 772
Culliford family 156
Culzean Castle 782
Cumberland, Duke of 26
Cumberland Place (no 4) 713-
  15
Cumberland Terrace 713, 714
Cummock: Dumfries House
  753
Cundy, Thomas (the Older &
  the Younger) 662, 663
Cunningham, Betty 364
cupolas *see* domes, cupolas &
  rotundas
curio room, Newbridge 839
Curre, John 818
Currer family 695
Currer, Henry 696
Currey, Henry 728-9
Currie, William 572
Curry, Adolphus 844
Cursell, Roger de 495
Curston, Lord 136
Curzon, 1st Marquess (Lord
  Curzon) 816
Curzon family 774
Curzon, Eveline 774
Curzon, George 774
Custom House, King's Lynn
  347, 353
Cutt, Sir John 189
Cynewulf, King of the West
  Saxons 421

D

Daily Post article, on Edward
  Shepherd 721
Dain, M.J. 303
Dale, Anthony 599
Dalgleish, Lin 739
Dali, Salvador 612
Dalkeith, Caroline, Countess
  of Dalkeith 747
Dalmellington: Craigengillan
  748
Dalmeny House 754
Dalrymple family 778
Dalrymple, Sir David 778
Dalrymple, William 572
Dalton, Charles & Sylvia
  Grant 684
Dalton, John 439
Daly, Nigel 431
Dann, Peter 499
Danson House 6, 45, 270-1,
  640
Darlington: Walworth Castle
  174
Dartmouth, 4th Earl of 512
Darwin, Erasmus 507
Dashwood, Charles Vere 400
Dashwood, Sir James 416
Daunt, Thomas & Margery
  212
Davenport, John 797
David, Elizabeth 183

Davidson family 176
Davies, Michael 814
Davis, Arthur (Mewes & Davis) 24, 25, 53, 774
Davy family 119
Davy, Henry 546, 547
Dawber, (Sir Edward) Guy
Bowling Green 149
Nether Swell Manor 210-11
Dawkins, Henry 664-5, 665
Dawkins, James 665
day houses 473
de Amurrio, Marques 120
de Arden, Henry 628
de Beauchamp, Rose & Payn 19
de Blencowe, Adam 95
de Bourbon, Antoine 158
de Braybrooke, William 697
de Broke, 12th & 19th Barons
Willoughby de Broke 621
de Carteret, Edward Charles Malet 843, 844
de Carteret, Guy Malet 844
de Carteret, Philip & Adele Malet 843, 844
de Carteret, Philippe & Margeret 843
de Carteret, Rex Malet 844
de Chappell family 176
de Clinton, John 627
de Clinton, William de Clinton, 1 st Earl of Huntingdon 627
de Copledyke family 321
de Cursell, Roger 495
de Figueiredo, Peter 75
de Frénilly, Baron 846, 847
de Gruchy, Abraham 841
de Harrington, John 321
de la More, Sir Richard 811
de la Pole family
Edmund, 6th Earl & 3rd Duke of Suffolk 543
John, 5th Earl & 2nd Duke of Suffolk 543
Sir Michael, 1 st Earl of Suffolk 542-3
Michael, 2nd Earl of Suffolk 543
William, 4th Earl & 1 st Duke of Suffolk 543
de la Rue, Thomas 21
De La Warr family 607
de Langton family 176
de Lisle family 176
de Lisle, Alice 37
de Lumisden, Adam 742
de Lumisden, Gilbert 742
de Olias, Marquesa 120
de Rothesay, Lord Stuart 158-9
de Rothschild, Hannah (Countess of Rosebery) 49
de Rothschild, James 61
de Rothschild, Baron Meyer Amschel 48-9
de St Germain, Comte 726
de St Maur, Sir Roger 812, 813
de Saumarez, 6th & 7th Barons 537
de Sousa, Jacques 448
de Stafford family 628, 632
de Staveley family 300
de Tabley, 1 st Baron (Sir John Fleming Leicester) 80
de Tolly, Prince Michael Barclay 787
de Verdun, Roesia 307
de Vere, Robert de Vere, Duke of Ireland 627
De Vere Hotels 702
de Vesci, Lady 213
de Wend Fenton, Major 690
de Wingfield, Sir John 542, 543
Deakin, Anthony 91, 92
Dean, Marcus 792
Dean, Ptolemy 54
Dedham: Old Grammar School 182-3
Dee, Rowland 350
deer
Gunton Hall 343
Shrubland Park 537
Swinfen Hall 515
Tyringham Hall 16, 53
Deering, J.P. Gandy 535, 536
defence
Achnacarry 734
Arisaig House 736

Balcombe Place 597
Buntingsdale Hall 434
chemical weapon detector 661
Chicksands Priory 18, 19
Compton Verney 621-2
Doddington Hall 74
Donington Hall 306
Dowdeswell Court 206
Ecton Hall 364
Greywalls 768
The Hasells 18
as hospital see hospital & related use
Inverlochy Castle 771
Lilford Castle 372
The Manor House (Ogbourne St George) 647
Philipps House 652
Pitchford Hall 443
Rushton 376
Sawston Hall 56
Shurland Hall 282
Staunton Harold Hall 312
Stocken Hall 313-14
Stockton 659
Stokesay Court 449
Tottenham Park 662
Wallington Hall 353
Walworth Castle 174
Wolverton Hall 674
Womersley Hall 711
Wraxhall Hall 16
see also Auxiliaries; German Occupation of Jersey; Special Operations Executive use
Defoe, Daniel 304, 481, 552
Delamere, 1 st Lord 81
Delvaux, Laurent 187
Delves-Broughton family 76
Demetrios (father of Gregory) 853
Deneux, Jean 595
Denis, Peter 727
Denman, Lady Gertrude (Trudie) 597
Denton: Castle Ashby 358-9, 380
Depp, Johnny 404
Derby, 17th Earl of (Lord Derby) 768
Dereham: Elsing Hall 69, 333-5
Derngate (No 78) 374-5
Derngate Trust 374, 375
design models 208, 304
Desmond, house of 829, 838
Despenser, Henry 350
Destruction of the Country House exhibition 7-8, 112, 272, 502, 776
Devereux, Sir Edward 619
Devereux, Robert Devereux, 2nd Earl of Essex 353
Devey, George 602
Pitchford Hall remodelling 444
Devlin, George 120
Devonshire, Dukes of 834
5th Duke 354
6th Duke (Bachelor Duke) 597, 599, 600, 728, 834
Dey, Richard 345
diamonds
Pitt diamon 84
Wolverton Hall 674
diaper brickwork 308, 320, 353, 393, 608
Dickens, Charles 197, 252
Dickenson family 263
Diestelkamp, Edward 570
Digby, Kenelm 310
Digby, Simon* 310
Dilke, William 629
Dill, Field Marshal Sir John 579
dingles, Hackfall 692
Dingley Hall 339, 362-3
Dinton: Philipps House 651-2
Dinton House see Philipps House
Diocletian, villa, description 66, 327, 332, 689
Dirleton: Archerfield 735
Disraeli, Benjamin 44
Dissolution of the Monasteries & English Reformation
The Abbey (Charlton

Adam) 467
Ashbury Manor 407
Barrow Court 457
Chicksands Priory 19
Coombe Abbey 623
Encombe 156
Endsleigh 123
The Hasells 21
Maristow House 137
Moundsmere Manor 236
Myrtle Grove 838
Nun Monkton Hall 701
Poulton Manor 215
Sinai Park 514
Sker House 818
Stockton 658
Stoneleigh Abbey 630
Thame Park 51
Thorpe Hall 350
Vale Royal Abbey 81
Dixon, D.P. 386
Dixon, Jeremy (Dixon Jones architects) 424
Dixton Manor 202-3
Dobson, John
Belford Hall 382
Lambton Castle 172
Dodd, Alan 146
Doddington Hall 73-4
Dodington Park 13, 59, 74, 204-6
dog kennels, Brockhall Manor 357
dog-gates & hound-gates
Halswell 472
Rashleigh Barton 142
Dolan, Michael 643
Dolbel, Sieur 847
Dolben, Sir John English 368
Dolliffe, James & Mary 716
Dolman, Thomas 41
domes, cupolas & rotundas
Ashman's 518
Belcombe Court 634
Bettisfield Park 797
Brogyntyn 433
Clifton 395
Cockfield Hall 522, 523
Craigengillan 748
Croome Court 671
Eagle House 716
Eastwood Farm 606
Ebberston Hall 690
Elsing Hall 69, 333
Emo Court 827
Fasque Castle 756
Gillingham Hall 336, 337
Halswell 471
Hamsterley Hall 170
The Hill 720
Home House 724, 725
Lochton House 773
Lucas Almshouses 39
North Breache Manor 581
Norton Place 323, 324
Old Bailey 577
Oulton Hall 702
Parish's House 485
Poston House 254, 255
Ranelagh Gardens, Chelsea 365
The Ruin, Hackfall 692, 693
St Paul's Cathedral 577
The Salutation 281
Seafield House 846, 847
Sharpham House 145
Shrubland Park 536, 537
Sundridge Park 283, 284, 286
Thoresby Hall 402
Tusmore House 424
Tyringham Hall 53
White Gables 55
Worlingham Hall 547
Domesday listings
Boconnoc 84
Chilworth Manor 560
Cransley Hall 361
Dixton Manor 202
Earl Soham Lodge 524
Harrington Hall 321
Nun Monkton Hall 701
Nutley Manor 238, 239
Wallington Hall 352
Weacombe 495
Dominique (interior designer) 198
Donabate: Newbridge 839
Donald Insall Associates 252, 717

Donaldson's Hospital 761
Doncaster: Brodsworth Hall 683-5
Donington Hall 306
Donthorne, W.J. 158
door bells, Fife House 598
Dorchester, Bishop of 51
Dorchester:
Kingston Maurward 160
Stinsford House 162
Dorking: Wotton House 594-5
Dormer, Henry 304
double-pile plan, The Manor House (Milton Lilbourne) 644
double Wealden houses 264
Douglas, John (architect)
Archerfield 735
Vale Royal Abbey 81
Walmoor House 83
Douglas, John (cotton manufacturer) 801
Douglas, Dame Mary 750
Douglas, Maxwell Vandeleur Blacker 847
Douglas Smith & Barley 718
dovecotes & pigeon houses
Belcombe Court 634
Blackland Park 635
Bridge Place 268
Brockhall Manor 357
Charleston Manor 602
Church House (Bibury) 199
Clifton 393
Cockfield Hall 523
Grimshaw Hall 626
Stanton House 657
Wilsley 289
Dowdeswell Court 16, 185, 206-8, 356
dower houses
Bretby Hall 103
Dumfries House 753
Earl Soham Lodge 524
House of Gray 767
Park Close 585
Thorpe Tilney Hall 327
Weston Hall 516
Downe, 8th Viscount 363
Downe, Captain William 155
Downe Hall 155
Downes, Kerry 273
Downes St Quintin, Matthew Chitty 729
Downham Market:
Wallington Hall 352-3
Drake, Sir Bernard 134
Drake, Sir Francis 76, 114, 134, 501, 560
Drake, Margaret 134
Drapers' Company 39, 40
Drayson, Jennifer 265
Drewe, Edward 117
Drewe, Sir Thomas 117
Drogheda family 583
Dromore Castle 826
Drummond, Henry 550, 561
Drummuir Castle 746
Drury, Alfred 457
Drury, Rev Dr Joseph 134
Drury, Martin 571
Dryden, John 405
Ducas, Robert 657
Ducie family 257
Duckworth family 483
Duckworth, William 483
Duddingston House 751
Dudley, 2nd Earl of 240
Dudley, 4th Viscount 240
Dudley, Lord Guildford 96
Dudley, John, 1 st Duke of Northumberland 56
Duff, Alexander Duff, 1 st Duke of Fife 752
Duff, William Duff, 1 st Baron Braco & 1 st Earl of Fife 752
Duff Gordon, Lachlan 746
Duff House 752
Dukeries, Thoresby Hall 401-2
Dumfries, 4th Earl of 753
Dumfries, Johnny 753
Dumfries House 753
Dunbar, John 762
Dunbar-Nasmith, Sir James 150-1
Duncan, James 745, 746
Duncan, Major 792
Duncan, Perry 769
Dundas, Henry Dundas, 1 st

Viscount Melville 777
Dundee: House of Gray 766-7
Dundonald, Earls of
12th Earl & Countess (Winifred Bamford-Hesketh) 804
13th Earl 804
Dunfermline, 1 st Earl of (Alexander Seton) 764
Dunham Lodge 331-2
Dunmore, 5th Earl of 754
Dunmore Park 754
Dunmore: Dunmore Park 754
Dunn-Yarker, Mr 699
Dunottar Castle 772
Duns:
Blanerne House 742
Manderston House 774-5
Wedderburn Castle 795
Dunster Castle 495
Durford Court 232-3
Durham, Earls of 172
Durham, 'Wizard of Durham' (Thomas Wright) 370-1, 636
Dursley: Owlpen 212
dust door, Westgate House 540
Dyall, Valentine 76
Dye, Heather Martin 564
Dyke, David 100
Dyke, Tina 100
Dyrham Park 389
Dysart, Elizabeth, Countess of Dysart 785
Dyson, James 13, 59, 74, 204, 206

E

E-plan
Bibury Court 197-8
Breckles Hall 328
Brereton Hall 67-9
Canonteign Manor 119-20
Gillingham Hall 336-7
Grimshaw Hall 626
Latimer Manor 642-3
Paxhill 613-15
The Soke 244-5
Stibbington Hall 57-9
Thurston End Hall 538-9
Eagle House 716
Eardisley 251-2
Earl Soham Lodge 524-6
Earl Stonham: Yew Tree House 548-9
earthquake damage
Cound Hall 437
High Head Castle 101
San Francisco 580
East Horsley: Horsley Towers 572
East Linton: Tyninghame House 15, 32, 735, 789-91
Eastawe, John 527
Eastbury House 161
Easton Neston 208
Eastwood Farm 606
Eaton Hall 424
Ebberston Hall 7, 690
Eboral, George 631
Ecclleshall Castle 504
Economist Building 470
Ecton: Ecton Hall 363-4
Ecton Hall 363-4
Ede, Robin Moore 35
Eden, Admiral 322
Edeyrnion, Barons of 802
Edgar, Roberta 676, 677
Edgcote House 365
Edinburgh:
Caroline Park 747
Duddingston House 751
Ramsay Garden 781
Ednaston Manor 108-9
Edred, King 156, 406
Edric, Count 406
educational use
78 Derngate 375
Apley Park 429
Axwell Park 166, 384
Balcombe Place 596
Bassett House 458
Belhaven Hill House 741
Blanerne House 742
Bowden 31
Bower House 179
Braybrooke House 637
Brereton Hall 67
Brympton d'Evercy 466
Bunny Hall 393
Churche's Mansion 71

Chute Lodge 640
Clifton Hall 16, 393
The Court House (Martock) 481-2
Croome Court 669
Doddington Hall 74
Eagle House 716
Emo Court 827
Grace Dieu Manor 307
Grittleton House 641
Hatfield Priory 186, 187
Hayton Hall 99-100
Headfort House 830
Hengrave Hall 527
Heythrop Park 415
Himley Hall 510
Hurst House 191
Ingress Abbey 275
King's Weston 209
Kingston Maurward 160
Lawton Hall 77
Lupton House 136
The Manor House (Buckland) 33
Maristow House 138
Milton Abbey 202
Myrtle Grove 838
Nether Swell Manor 210
Nethergate House 531
Old Grammar School 182-3
Ramsay Garden 781
Redlynch House 487
Rousdon House 143
Rowton Castle 448
Rushton 376
Sawston Hall 56
Shaw House 41
Stinsford House 162
Tabley Hall 52
Taymouth Castle 784
Toddington Manor 218
Tottenham Park 662
Troy House 81
Walmoor House 83
Walpole House 733
Walworth Castle 174
Wardour Castle 666
Wentworth Woodhouse 8, 708, 709
Wotton House 594
Yeaton Pevery 452
see also children's home use
educational use, Apethorpe Hall 354
Edward the Confessor, King 520, 560
Edward I, King 63, 81, 742, 799, 800
Edward III, King 224, 275, 333, 627, 759
Edward IV, King 543
Edward VI, King 259, 350, 521, 688, 740
Edward VII, King 283, 386, 583, 597, 663, 827
Edward VIII, King (later Duke of Windsor) 176, 510
Edward the Black Prince 224, 542, 543
Edwardes, Thomas Henry Hope 442
Edwardian
 Barrow Court gardens 457
 Belhaven Hill House 741
 Bowden 30-1
 Catchfrench Manor 85
 Flichity House 758
 Luton Hoo 24-5
 Manderston House 774-5
 Melton Constable Hall extensions 346
 Miller's Tower 762-3
 Moundsmere Manor 12, 236-7, 853
 Nansidwell 88-9
 Nether Swell Manor 210
 Steephill 848-50
 see also Arts & Crafts
Edwards, David 801
Edwards, Peter & Joan 59
Edwards, Roger 796
Edwards, William 801
Edwinsford 801
Eggesford: Eggesford House 121-2
Eggesford House 121-2
'Egyptians' 787
Eisenhower, Dwight D. 74
Eldon, Earls of
 1st Earl 156

3rd Earl 157
Elephant Cage 18
Elgar, Sir Edward 676
Elgin, 7th Earl of (Lord Elgin) 158, 535, 735
Elibank, 1st Lord 739, 740
Elite Hotels 25
Elizabeth I, Queen 127, 153, 227, 244, 362, 432, 624, 682
 visits to houses 114, 184, 189, 202, 224, 359, 689
Elizabeth II, Queen 176, 659
Elizabeth the Queen Mother, Queen 132, 206
Elizabeth of Bohemia (Winter Queen) 421
Elizabeth of York 543
Elizabeth, Countess of Dysart 785
Elizabeth, Countess of Home 723, 725
Elizabethan & Tudor
 The Abbey (Charlton Adam) 467-8
 Apethorpe Hall 354-5
 Ashbury Manor 406-7
 Ayshford Court 113
 Beaurepaire 224-6
 Bentley Hall 519
 Bibury Court 197-8
 Bispham Hall 295
 Blackburn Hall 682
 Bletchley Manor 431
 Boringdon 114
 Bradninch Manor 10, 115-16
 Breckles Hall 10, 328
 Brereton Hall 67-9
 Bride Hall 258-9
 Brough Hall 685-6
 Brympton d'Evercy 465-6
 Canonteign Manor 119-20
 Castle Ashby 358-9
 Castle Bromwich Hall 619-20
 Catchfrench Manor 85
 Chawton House 228-9
 Churche's Mansion 11, 13, 71-2
 Cockfield Hall 521-3
 Colebrook House 230-1
 Constable Burton 688
 Cooke's House 603-5
 Dingley Hall 362-3
 Dixton Manor 202-3
 Ellys Manor House 10, 318-19
 Formby Hall 298
 Fulford 127
 Gillingham Hall 336-7
 Gosfield Hall 184-5
 Great Snoring Manor 338
 Grimshaw Hall 624-6
 Halswell 472, 473
 Harrington Hall 320-2
 Haslington Hall 75-6
 Hedenham Hall 344
 Hengrave Hall 527-8
 Hill Hall 188
 Holystreet Manor 130-2
 Horham Hall 189-90
 Isfield Place 607-9
 Knightstone Manor 10, 134-5
 Latimer Manor 642
 Little Bardfield Hall 194-5
 Little Hautbois 10, 345
 The Manor House (Buckland) 32-3
 The Manor House (Lindfield) 14
 Manor House (Sutton Courtenay) 421-2
 Manor Lodge (Worksop) 403
 Maynards 17, 276-7
 Minsterley Hall 440-1
 Morley Old Hall 348
 Myrtle Grove 838
 Narborough Hall 349
 Nethergate House 531-2
 Norfolk redbrick manor houses 338, 344, 345, 348, 352-3
 Olden Manor 14, 533-4
 Paxhill 613-15
 Pencoed Castle 811
 Pitchford Hall 442-4
 Plaish Hall 445
 Poltimore 140

The Reader's House 438-9
Rous Lench Court 672-3
Rowden Manor 655-6
Rushton 376
Sawston Hall 56
Shaw House 41
Shireoaks 399
Shurland Hall 282
Sinai Park 514
The Soke 244-5
 staircase styles 14
Stayley Hall 300
Swinsty Hall 705
Thorpe Hall 350-1
Thorpe Salvin Hall 706
Thurston End Hall 538-9
Trinity Manor 851-3
Wallington Hall 352-3
Walpole House 732-3
Womersley Hall 712
Ellard, Harry 621
Ellen (wife of Llewelyn ap Phylip) 801
Ellington, Marc 787
Elliot, Archibald 784
Elliot, James (architect) 784
Elliot, James (conservation officer) 461
Ellis, Mary 130, 132
Ellys, Anthony 318
Ellys Manor House 10, 318-19
Ellys, Thomas 318
Ellys: Ellys Manor House 10, 318-19
elopements 145
Elsing Hall 69, 333-5
Eltham Palace 198
Ely, Bishops of 61
Emery, William 333, 504, 543
Emo: Emo Court 827
Emo Court 827
enabling development see residential conversions & enabling development
Encombe 12, 14, 156-7
Endsleigh 123-6
Engels, Frederick 680
England family 271
Englefield Green:
 Park Close 583-5
 Ridgemead 9, 588-9
English, Alan 595
English bond brickwork 67, 539, 593, 608, 650
English Civil War
 Blencowe Hall 96-7
 Boringdon 114
 Braemes, Sir Arnold 268
 Caus Castle 440
 Cranborne Manor 154
 Cullen House 750
 Fulford 127
 Kildwick Hall 695
 Maxstoke Castle 629
 Rous Lench Court 673
 Shirburn Castle 420
 Trawsgoed 819
 Wimborne Houses 163-4
 Woodcott Castle 63-5
 see also Artisan Mannerist; Commonwealth houses
English Heritage 5:
 Apethorpe Hall 355
 Baguley Hall 75
 Barlaston Hall 500-1
 Belford Hall 382
 Belsay Hall 383
 Berwick-upon-Tweed barracks 390
 Bramcote Hall 618
 Brodsworth Hall 683-5
 Buntingsdale Hall 434
 The Crescent, Buxton 105
 Danson House 270-1
 Downe Hall 155
 Great Treverren 87
 Hackfall 692
 Heath House conservatory 508
 Highcliffe Castle 159
 Hill Hall 188
 Kelly House 133
 Kentish houses volumes 264, 265
 Melton Constable Hall 347
 Paper Hall 703
 Pitchford Hall 442, 444
 Revesby Abbey 326
 Shurland Hall 282
 Stokesay Court 449, 450

Thorpe Salvin Hall 706
Toddington Manor 218, 219, 814
Tottenham Park, on risk register 662
Wimborne Houses grotto 164
Wothorpe Grandstand 66
English Reformation see Dissolution of the Monasteries & English Reformation
engraved glass see stained, coloured & engraved glass
Enniscorthy: Castleboro House 824
entails 100
Enthoven, Angela 473, 474, 475
Epping:
 Copped Hall 180-1, 517
 Hill Hall 188
Erddig 757
Erdeswick, Sampson 504
Erith, Raymond 34
Erne, 3rd Earl of 825
Ernest George & Yeates 138, 143
Erskine, Alastair 723
Erskine House 755
Esher: Homewood 570-1
Eshton Hall 294
Essex, 2nd Earl of (Robert Devereux) 353
Essex, Sir William 407
Eton College 282
Etruscan Room, Home House 725
European Regional Development Fund 631
Euston, Earl of (Henry Fitzroy, 1st Duke of Grafton) 378
Evelyn family 594
Evelyn, Rev Edmund Boscawen 291
Evelyn, George 594
Evelyn, John 44
 Albury Park gardens 550
 Wotton House gardens 594, 595
Everard, Ambrose & Martha 539
Everard, Captin John Guy Courtnay 455
Evered, John & Anne 455
Evered, Robert Guy 455
'evergreen marchioness' (Maria Tollemache) 663
evolution, Huxley-Wilberforce debate 517
Ewhurst: North Breache Manor 579-81
Exeter, 1st Earl of (Thomas Cecil) 361, 403
Exeter, 1st Marquess of (Henry Cecil) 66
exhibitions
 Destruction of the Country House 7-8, 112, 272, 502
 The Garden 160, 502
 Treasure Houses of Britain 370
 see also art collections & exhibitions
Exmouth, Viscounts
 1st Viscount (Sir Edward Pellew) 119-20, 145
 9th Viscount 120
Exmouth: A La Ronde 111-12
explosives damage
 Cockfield Hall 523
 Tottenham Park 662
exported rooms
 Agecroft Hall 72
 dining room, Kirtlington Park 416
 Jacobean room, The Grange (Broadhembury) 117-18
 tapestry room, Croome Court 669
 see also salvaged materials
Eydon: Eydon Hall 9, 14, 366-8
Eydon Hall 9, 14, 366-8
Eythorne: Waldershare 287
Eyton, Tom & Dorothy 293

F

fair-faced brickwork 803
Fairfax family 712
Fairhaven, Barons

1st Baron (Urban Huttleston Broughton) 584-5
2nd Baron (Henry Broughton) 584, 585
Fairhaven, Lady Fairhaven (Cara Broughton) 584-5
Fairyland Trust 349
Falkner, Harold 555-7
Falmouth: Nansidwell 88-9
false books
 Danson House 271
 Hatfield Priory 187
Fane family 466
Fane, Sir Francis Fane, 1st Earl of Westmorland 354
Fane, John Fane, 7th Earl of Westmorland 354
Farington, Joseph 688
farm use
 Aldhams 178
 Archerfield 735
 Ashbury Manor 406, 407
 Beenham Hatch 27
 Blencowe Hall 97-8
 Boringdon 114
 Bride Hall 259
 Brizlincote Hall 103
 Brockhall Manor 357
 Clegg Hall 296
 Crawford Manor 297
 Ebberston Hall 690
 Fulvens House 562
 Green Lane Farm 564
 Gwerclas Hall 803
 Holliday Hall 273
 Lanhill House 641
 Larch Hill ferme ornÈe 832
 Little Hautbois 345
 Nutley Manor 238
 Park Cottage 808
 Pencoed Castle 811
 Penhow Castle 812
 Petit Hibeaux 845
 Poulton House 654
 Redlynch House 487
 Shurland Hall 282
 Sker House 818
 Stocken Hall 313-14
 Trawsgoed 819
 Trevor Hall 820
 Tysoe Manor 633
 Vellore House 792
 Wingfield Castle 542
 see also cattle herds; pigs
Farnham: Burles Lodge 555-7
Farr, Michael 678
Farr: Flichity House 758
Farrer brothers 280, 281
Fasque Castle 756-7
Fawkes, Guy 244
Fawley House 411-13, 741
Feathers Inn, Ludlow 438
Felling Hall 380
Fellowes, Newton 121
Fels, Joseph 223
Fenton, Major de Wend 690
Fenton, Joseph 296
Fenton, Richard 593
Fenwick, Guy & Elsie 310
Fenwick, James 384
Fenwick, William 384
ferme ornÈe, Larch Hill 832
fernery, Steephill 850
Ferrers Arts & Crafts Centre 312
Ferrey, Benjamin
 Brogyntyn service ranges 432
 Stockton 659
Fesche, Cardinal 271
Fetherston-Dilke family 629
Fettercairn: Fasque Castle 756-7
Field of the Cloth of Gold 488, 521
Field, Mr 405
Fife, 1st Duke & Duchess of 597
Fife, 1st Earl of (William Duff) 752
Fife: Balbirnie 738
Fife House 597-600
50 Oxford Gardens 728-9
Figueiredo, Peter de 75
film use see television & film use
financial information
 A La Ronde 111-12
 The Abbey (Charlton

Adam) 468
Albury Park 550
Apethorpe Hall 355
Apley Park 428
Barge House 249
Belford Hall 382
Brereton Hall 67
Brodsworth Hall 683, 684
Bunny Hall 392
Burley-on-the-Hill 304
Calke Abbey 106
Castle Bromwich Hall 620
Chilworth Manor 561
Constable Burton 688
Cragside 389
The Crescent, Buxton 104, 105
Croome Court 669, 670
Crowcombe Court 469
Doddington Hall 73
Eagle House 716
Edgcote House 365
Eggesford House 121
Erskine House 755
Fyvie Castle 764
Grace Dieu Manor 307
Gunton Hall 342
Gwrych Castle 804, 805
Gyrn Castle 806
Hackfall 692
Hanger Hill Garden Estate 719
The Hasells 21
Hayton Hall 100
Hengrave Hall 527
Heveningham Hall 529
High Head Castle 101
Hill Hall 188
Hinwick House 23
Huf Haus 575
Keith Hall 772
Kelly House 132
Kirtlington Park 416
Lanhill House 641
Les Lumières 842
Lucas Almshouses 39
Manderston House 775
Maristow House 137, 138
Maxstoke Castle 629
Melville Castle 777
Mentmore Towers 50
Miller's Tower 762
Orchardleigh 483
Oulton Hall 702
Park Cottage 808
Philipps House 651
Piercefield 814
Pitchford Hall 442, 444
Poltimore 140
Ridgemead 588
St Ouen's Manor 844
Sarsden House 418
Shaw House 41
Shirburn Castle 419, 420
Shrubland Park 535
Sker House 818
Stocken Hall 314
Stokesay Court 449
Tabley Hall 80-1
Thirlestane Castle 786
Thorpe Salvin Hall 706
Toddington Manor 218
Tong Hall 707
Trawsgoed 819
Trehane 93
Troy House 517
Tyntesfield 490
Tysoe Manor 633
Ven House 493
Wardour Castle 666
Wentworth Woodhouse 708, 710
Weston Hall 516
Worlingham Hall 546
see also exported rooms; specific funding bodies (eg Heritage Lottery Fund)
Finch, Daniel Finch, 2nd Earl of Nottingham 304
Finch, Wilfred 305
Findlater, Earls of
1st Earl of (James Ogilvy) 750
3rd Earl 750
4th Earl 750
Finedon: Finedon Hall 368-9
Finedon Hall 368-9
Finn, Paul 707
fire damage
The Abbey (Charlton Adam) 468

Achnacarry 734
Albury Park 550
Allerton Park 679
Arisaig House 736
Ballencrieff Castle 739, 740
Beaurepaire 224
Bispham Hall 295
Blackland Park 635
Blanerne House 742
Boringdon 114
Botleys 552
Burley-on-the-Hill 304-5
Buxted Park 601
Castleboro House 824
Colwick Hall 396
Copped Hall 180, 181
Crom Castle 825
Crowcombe Court 7, 469
Culham Court 34
Cullen House 750
Eardisley 251-2
Great Barr Hall 507
Gunton Hall 342
Halswell 472
Harrington Hall 320
Heveningham Hall 530
Heythrop Park 415
Hill Hall 188
Hilton Park 831
Howick Hall 391
Hurst House 191
Lochton Castle 773
Longford Hall 110
Lupton House 136
Maristow House 137, 138
Milford House 576
Nantwich 71
Oulton Hall 702
Pencoed Castle 811
Redlynch House 487
Ruperra Castle 817
St Ouen's Manor 844
Sarsden House 418
Shawford Park 241
Shillinglee Park 616
Shireoaks 399
Stoke Park 377
Thorndon Hall 196
Thorpe Hall 350
Thorpe Tilney Hall 327
Trehane 91-3
Trevor Hall 820
Waldershare 287
Worksop Manor 403
Wrottesley Hall 517
fire escapes, Puttenham Priory 586
fire hydrants, Halswell 472
fire insurance plaques, Thurston End Hall 538
Firth, James 678
Fisher's Hall, Hackfall 692
fishing holidays see shoots & sporting estates
fishtank, Monkton House 612
Fitzgerald family 822, 823, 829
Edward (Lord Edward FitzGerald) 822
Emily, 1st Duchess of Leinster 822, 823
James, 20th Earl of Kildare & 1st Duke of Leinster 822, 823
Robert, 19th Earl of Kildare 822
Fitzgerald, Desmond 829
Fitzgerald, Colonel Thomas 480
Fitzhamon, Robert 153
Fitzroy, Charles Fitzroy, 2nd Duke of Grafton 378, 380
Fitzroy, Henry Fitzroy, Earl of Euston & 1st Duke of Grafton 378
Fitzwilliam, Earls 708
Fitzwilliam family 63
Fitzwilliam, Peter 708
flats conversions see residential conversions & enabling development
Fleet Street, London, Herbert Huntly-Gordon's buildings 585
Fleetwood-Hesketh, Peter & Roger 313
Fleming, A.B. 747
Fleming, Ian 674
Fleming, Captain Peter 674
Fleming, Sir Thomas 244-5
Flemish bond brickwork 562,

608
Fletcher, Sir Banister 307
Fletcher, James Douglas 780
Fletcher, Thomas 249
Fletcher, W.H. 400
Fletcher, WPC Yvonne 354
Flichity House 758
Flick, Mick 26
Flight & Robson organs 476
Flintham 11, 397-8
Flitcroft, Henry (Burlington Harry)
Bower House 179
Lilford Castle 372
Redlynch House 487
Wimborne Houses 164
Floors Castle 759-61
Foley, 1st Baron (Lord Foley) 253
Foley, Paul 253
Folley family 45
follies, obelisks & temples
Auchinleck 737
Belcombe Court 634
Boconnoc 84
Burles Lodge 556
Chicksands Priory 19
Crom Castle 825
Croome Court 671
Dunham Lodge 332
Eastwood Farm 606
Fort Horne 691
Gibside 168
Gwerclas Hall gazebo 803
Hackfall 692-3
Hadspen 470
Halswell 471, 472, 473
Isfield Place gazebo 607, 609
Kingston Maurward 160
Larch Hill 832-3
The Menagerie 370-1
Park Cottage 808
Piercefield 815
Piers Court 213
The Pineapple, Dunmore 754
South Wraxhall Manor gazebo 489
Wentworth Woodhouse 710
Youlston Park 147
Folly Farm 13, 14, 16
Fonthill Abbey 19, 784
Fonthill House 240
Forbes, Margaret 764
Forbes-Leith, Alexander
Forbes-Leith, Baron Leith of Fyvie 764, 765
Forbes-Leith, Sir Andrew 765
Ford, Sir Edward & Lady Virginia 367
Ford, John 319
Foreign Office Architects 470
Forestry Commission 343
Formakin: Miller's Tower 762-3
Formby family 298
Formby, John* 298
Formby, William 298
Formby: Formby Hall 298
Formby Hall 298
Forrest, Douglas 750
Fort, Thomas 487
Fort Gibralter, Larch Hill 832
Fort Horne 691
Fort William: Inverlochy Castle 771
Forte, Sir Rocco 126
Fortescue family 84
48 Storey's Way 60
Foss, John 687
Foster, Norman 208
Foster, William Orme 428-9
Foster & Worth 480
Fota 828
Fotheringay Castle 59
Foulsham: Bylaugh Hall 330
Fountains Abbey 692
Fowey: Great Treverren 86-7
Fowler, Charles 138
Fowler, Sir James Kingston 248
Fowler, John 203, 712
Fox, George 221
Fox, Sir Stephen 487
Foxbury Manor 286
Foxholm 15
Frampton Orangery 220
Frances, Lady Londonderry (3rd Marchioness) 173, 175, 176

Francis, Eric 811
Fraser, Stuart 210
Freckhall, Graham 821
Frederick, Major-General Edward 240
Free style, Yeaton Pevery 452-3
Freeman, Jennifer 66, 518
Freeman, John 640
Freeman, Roger 18
Freeman, William 640
French Gothic
Friar Park 414
Wyfold Court 15, 425-7
Frènilly, Baron de 846, 847
Frere, Philip 59
frescoes see murals & wall paintings
Fretwell, Ralph 694
Friar Park 368, 414
Friend family 489
friezes
8 The Circus (Bath) 460
48 Storey's Way 60
78 Derngate 374
Ashbury Manor 407
Bowden 30
Brereton Hall 68
Caythorpe Hall 317
Cooke's House 605
Ebberston Hall 690
Fasque Castle 757
Great Snoring Manor 338
Harrington Hall 321
Kildwick Hall 697
Knightstone Manor 134
North Breache Manor 580
Nun Monkton Hall 701
Paxhill 615
Philipps House 652
Rowden Manor 655
Scout Hall 704
Sker House 818
Stockton 659
Stoneleigh Abbey 631
Thame Park 52
Tusmore House 424
Tyringham Hall 54
Wentworth Woodhouse 709
Yeaton Pevery 453
Frognal House 272
Frome:
Hapsford House 473-5
Orchardleigh 483-4
Frost, Mr & Mrs Oliver 647
Frost, Tim 647, 648
Fulford, Francis & Fulford family 127, 132
Fulford 127
Fuller, Ray 516
Fulvens House 11, 562
funicular railway, Leighton estate 808-9
Furnese, Sir Henry 287
Furnese, Sir Robert 287
Fussell, Henry Austin & Margaret 661
Fyvie Castle 50, 764-5

G
Gabcik, Jozef 788
Gabriel, C.B. 557-8
Gabriel, Ralph 558
Gage family 528
Gainsborough, Thomas 765
Gallagher, Paul 173
galleries
A La Ronde Shell Gallery 112
Apethorpe Hall long gallery 354
Ashton Court Long Gallery 454
Breckles Hall attics 328
Brereton Hall 68
Canonteign Manor long gallery gym 119, 120
Cockfield Hall 522, 523
Croome Court long gallery 670
Fawley House orangery gallery 411
Gosfield Hall Secret Gallery 185
Gyrn Castle picture gallery 807
Llangoed Hall 810
Mentmore Towers 50
Newbridge picture gallery 839
Sawston Hall Long Gallery 56
Swinsty Hall 705

Wingfield College 545
Wyfold Court picture gallery 426, 427
Wynyard Park Sculpture Gallery 175-6
see also minstrels' galleries
galleting 290, 561
Galsworthy, John 565
Galton, Samuel 507
Gamble, Sir David 215
Gandon, James 827
Gandy Deering, J.P. 535, 536
Garbett, Alfred 49
garden bond/American bond brickwork 650, 700
garden creators & designers
Alexander, Herbert (Wilsley) 289
Anne, Countess of Rosse (Womersley Hall) 711
Barry, Sir Charles (Shrubland Park) 537
Bateman, James (Biddulph Grange) 502
Blackburn, Ernest (Little Thakeham) 610
Caine, Percy (Hurst House) 191
Cargill, David & Shirley (Elsing Hall) 335
Chance, Hilary (Wingfield College) 545
Chester, Sir John (Chicheley) 43
Colvin, Brenda (Nunton House) 646
Congreve, Ambrose (Mount Congreve) 632, 836-7
Cooper, Colonel Reggie (Knightstone Manor) 134
Cory-Wright family (Mackerye End) 260
Courtauld, Jeanne (Cooke's House) 604, 605
Cowell, Mrs (Hatfield Priory) 186, 187
Crisp, Sir Frank (Friar Park) 414
Evelyn, John 550, 594, 595
Fenwick, Guy & Elsie (North Luffenham Hall) 310
Gilpin, William 825
Giubelli, Luciano (Saddlewood Manor) 217
Godfrey, Walter (Charleston Manor) 602-3
Goode, Cary (Newport House) 253
Greswell, John & Marian (Weacombe) 495
Grey, Lord & Lady (Howick Hall) 391
Gruffyed, John St Bodfan (Cote House) 409
Haddington, Dowager Lady (Tyninghame House) 789
Hambro, Sir Charles (Dixton Manor) 202
Heald, Lady (Chilworth Manor) 560, 561
Hobhouse, Penelope 470, 475
Holland, Wilfrid (Cooke's House) 605
Howick, Lord & Lady (Howick Hall) 391
Kirby, Ian (The Menagerie) 371
Le Sueur, Frances (Steephill fernery) 850
Leverhulme, 1st Viscount (The Hill) 720
London, George 43
Lord & Lady Fairhaven (Park Close & Anglesey Abbey) 584
Loudon, John Claudius 26, 337
McKenzie, Laura (Greywalls) 768
Maitland, Lady (Harrington Hall) 320
Makins, Dwight (Beaurepaire) 225
Mander, Sir Nicholas & Lady (Owlpen) 12
Mawson, Thomas (The Hill) 720
Maynard, Arne (Alt-y-Bela) 796

Monck, Sir Charles (Belsay Hall) 383
Morris, Captain Valentine (Piercefield) 815
Nesfield, W.A. (Newport House) 253
Page, Russell (Sturford Mead) 660
Pickering, Lionel (Ednaston Manor) 109
Pinwill, Captain William (Trehane) 91
Pope, Nori & Sandra (Hadspen) 470
Roper, Lanning (Church House, Bibury) 199
Salisbury, Dowager Lady (Cranborne Manor) 152
Scott, John (Great Barr Hall) 507
Smithers, Sir Peter (Colebrook House) 230-1
Street, G.E. (Holmdale) 568
Thomas, Francis Inigo (Barrow Court) 457
Trehane, David (Trehane) 92
Triggs, H. Inigo (Durford Court) 232
Verey, Rosemary 199, 475
Wield, Adrian (Tysor Manor) 632
Wise, Henry 43
Woods, Richard (Hatfield Priory) 186
see also Brown, Capability; Jekyll, Gertrude; Lutyens, Sir Edwin; Repton, Humphry
The Garden exhibition 160, 502
Garden History Society 218
The Gardener's Magazine 26
garderobes
    Ashbury Manor 407
    Ballncrieff Castle 740
gargoyles, Floors Castle 761
Garnier, Richard 268
Garramor House 788
Garrett, Daniel 416
    Gibside Banqueting House & stables 168, 169
Garth, Edward Turnour Garth, 1st Earl of Winterton 616
Gaunt, John of 542
Gaussen, Bernard 539
Gavigan, Patricia 554
Gawdy, Sir Francis 353
Gawn, Roger 347
gazebos
    Gwerclas Hall 803
    Isfield Place 607, 609
    Larch Hill 832
    South Wraxhall Manor 489
Geddes, Sir Patrick 781
Gentle, Sir Gervase the Gentle 394
'Gentle Lochiel' 734
Gentleman's Magazine 529
George I, King 378
George II, King 378, 726
George III, King 36, 138, 160, 451, 550
George IV, King 123, 283, 420, 459, 476, 651, 662, 698, 755, 777
George V, King 578, 708
George VI, King 578, 613, 659
George, Prince George, Duke of Kent 510
George family 652
George, Sir Ernest 138, 143
George, George 473, 474
George Inn, Glastonbury 542
Georgian
    4 The Crescent (Wisbech) 61-2
    4 Maids of Honour Row 726-7
    Abbey Houses (Bury St Edmunds) 520
    The Almshouses (Preston-on-the-Weald Moors) 446-7
    Barford Hall 7
    Barford House 455-6
    Bathealton Court 462
    Belhaven Hill House 741
    Blackland Park 635-6

Boconnoc 84
Bradninch Manor 115-16
Bretby Hall 102-3
Brogyntyn 432-3
Carton House 822, 823
Catchfrench Manor 85
Chicheley 14, 42-3
Colebrook House 230-1
Colwick Hall 396
Constable Burton 688-9
Copped Hall 180-1, 517
The Crescent, Buxton 104-5
Crowcombe Court 469
Culham Court 9, 34-6
Dodington Park 204-6
Dunham Lodge 331-2
Gibside 168-9
Gosfield Hall 184-5
Gwerclas Hall 17, 802-4
Hamsterley Hall 170-1
The Hasells 20-1
Howick Hall 391
Ingestre Pavilion 511
Kelly House 132-3
Lawton Hall 16-17, 77
Luton Hoo 24-5
The Manor House (Buckland) 32-3
The Manor House (Lindfield) 14
Milford House 15
Narborough Hall 349
Newport House 252-3
Paxhill great hall 614
Poltimore 140
Rowton Castle 448
Shillinglee Park 616
Stanford Hall 400
Staunton Harold Hall 311-13
Stocken Hall 313
Thame Park 51-2
Thorpe Tilney Hall 327
Trafalgar House 664-5
Trawsgoed 819
Trewarthenick 94
Valentine's 731
Weacombe 495-7
Womersley Hall 711-12
Youlston Park 146-7
Georgian Group 164, 218, 714
Georgiana, Duchess of Bedford 123
German Occupation of Jersey St Ouen's Manor 844
Seafield House 847
Gerrard, Mollie 554
Gerrards Cross: White Gables 55
Getty Museum 187
Ghazzi, Abdul Amir Al- 530
ghost hunting & haunting
    Chillingham Castle 387
    Morley Old Hall 348
    Rous Lench Court 673
Gibbons, Grinling 147, 237, 536, 589, 619
Gibbs, George Gibbs, 2nd Baron Wraxall (Lord Wraxall) 490
Gibbs, H.M. 457
Gibbs, James
    associations with & comparisons to 101, 405, 411
    Book of Architecture 699
    Compton Verney stables 621
    Gibbs windows 446, 495, 497
    Kirtlington Park designs 416
    Patshull Hall 17, 429, 512-13
Gibbs, William 490
Gibside 168-9
Gibson, Lord (life peer) 106
Gibson, Mark 748
Gidleigh Park Hotel 131
Giffard, Sieur 846, 847
Gilbert of Sempringham & Gilbertine Order 19
Gilbert Scott, Sir George 78, 246, 507, 568
Gillies, Peter 739-40
Gilling Castle 699
Gillingham Hall 336-7
'Gillingham Sir Edmund' (Sir Edmund Bacon) 337
Gillot, Joseph 625
Gilpin, William 692, 825
Gimbrett, John 728
Girdlestone, Edward Steed 59

Girouard, Mark
    on Brodsworth Hall 684
    on Caverswall Castle 505
    on Peckforton Castle 78
    on Ruperra Castle 817
    on South Wraxhall Manor 488, 489
    on Tyntesfield 490
    on Worksop Manor 403
Gist family 203
Giubelli, Luciano 217
Gladstone, Peter 757
Gladstone, Sir William 757
Gladstone, William Ewart 49, 757
glass, stained *see* stained, coloured & engraved glass
glasshouses *see* conservatories, glasshouses & orangeries
Gledhill, John & Sarah 681
Gleeson Homes 17, 77
Glenapp Castle 52
Glin, Knights of 829
Glin: Glin Castle 829
Glin Castle 829
gloriette, King's Weston 209
Glyndebourne Festival Opera 235
Goathurst: Halswell 471-3
Godalming:
    Munstead Grange 577-9
    Orchards 563
Goddards 563
Godfrey family 191
Godfrey, Walter 602-3
Godlewski, Leo 399
Godwin, E.W. 743, 826
Goelet, May 761
Golders Green Park 720
Goldney House 463
Goldsmith, Alan 194
Goldsworthy, Major-General Walter Tuckfield 291
golf courses & clubs
    Archerfield 735
    Balbirnie 738
    Brancepeth Castle 167
    Carton House 822
    Duddingston House 751
    Heythrop Park 415
    Orchardleigh 484
    Oulton Hall 702
    Patshull Hall 513
    Sundridge Park 283, 286
    Taymouth Castle 784
    Thorndon Hall 196
    Tottenham Park 663, 664
    Vale Royal Abbey 82
    Wallington Hall 352
Gomme, Andor 11, 515
Goode, Cary 253
Goode, Richard 252-3
Goodrich Court 554
Goodridge, Henry Edmund 459
Gordon, 4th Duke & Duchess of 123, 780
Gordon family (Gordons of Fyvie) 764, 765
Gordon family (Gordons of Park) 746
Gordon, Lady Georgiana (Georgiana, Duchess of Bedford) 123
Gordon, Captain John 746
Gordon, Lachlan Duff 746
Gordon, Sir William 746
Gordon, General William 764, 765
Gordon-Duff family 746
Gore, 'Boofy' Gore, 8th Earl of Arran 262, 263
Gore, William 432
Gore-Brown family 248
Gorell Committee 714
Gorhambury House 260
Gort, 5th, 6th & 7th Viscounts 170
Gosfield Hall 184-5
Gosford, 2nd Earl of (Lord Gosford) 547
Gosforth House 384
Gosnall, John* 519
Gothic Revival
    Allerton Park 15, 678-9
    Apley Park 428-30
    Dromore Castle 826
    Elsing Hall 332-5
    Erskine House 755
    Grace Dieu Manor 307
    Fulford 127

The Grange (Ramsgate) 279
Great Barr Hall 507
Heath House 12, 14, 508-9
Highcliffe Castle 158-9
Holmdale 568-9
Ingress Abbey 188, 275
North Breache Manor 579-81
Toddington Manor 17, 218-19
Twyford Moors House 246-7
Tyntesfield 490-2
Wyfold Court 15, 188, 275, 425-7
see also French Gothic; Tudor Gothic
Gothick Revival *see* Regency/18th century Gothic; Strawberry Hill Gothick
Gotts, John 539
Goudge, Edward 619
Governor's House (Berwick-upon-Tweed) 390
Gow, Ian 778
Grace Dieu Manor 307
graffiti *see* inscriptions & tags
Grafton, Dukes of
    1st Duke (Henry Fitzroy, Earl of Euston) 378
    2nd Duke (Charles Fitzroy) 378, 380
Graham, Eric 100
Graham, James Gillespie 734
Graham, Thomas Henry 100
Graham Freckhard Architects 821
Grahame, Kenneth 44
Grainge, William 705
grandstands, Wothorpe Grandstand 66
The Grange (Alresford) *see* Grange Park
The Grange (Broadhembury) 117-18
The Grange (Ramsgate) 279
Grange Park 234-5, 383, 536, 738
Grange Park Opera 235
Grant, Cary 417
Grant Dalton, Charles & Sylvia 684
Grant Duff, Sir Mountstuart & Lady 529
Gratrix, Mrs Gordon 148
gravel workings 303, 382
Gray, 1st, 2nd, 3rd & 12th Lords 767
Gray family 767
Gray, Sir Andrew Gray, 1st Lord Gray 767
Gray, Johnny 460
Gray, Thomas 648
Gray, Walker 717
Gray, House of 766-7
Grayson, Arthur 842
Great Bardfield: Little Bardfield Hall 194-5
Great Barr: Great Barr Hall 507
Great Barr Hall 507
Great Castle House 821
Great Fulford: Fulford 127
great halls & chambers
    The Abbey (Charlton Adam) 468
    Allerton Park 678
    The Almshouses (Preston-on-the-Weald Moors) 447
    Ashbury Manor 406
    Ayot Mountfitchet 257
    Ayshford Court 113
    Ballncrieff Castle 740
    Bentley Hall 519
    Bletchley Manor 431
    Borigdon 114
    Bradninch Manor 115-16
    Breckles Hall 328
    Canonteign Manor 120
    Cheddington Court 150-1
    Clifton Hall 395
    Cockfield Hall 522, 523
    The Court House (Martock) 482
    Earl Soham Lodge 525
    Ednaston Manor 108
    Elsing Hall 333, 334, 335
    Erskine House 755
    Fulford 127

Gwerclas Hall 804
Harrington Hall 321
Haslington Hall 76
Hengrave Hall 527, 528
Hill 128
Horham Hall 189
Kildwick Hall 695, 696-7
Knightstone Manor 10
Latimer Manor 643
Manor House (Sutton Courtenay) 422
Manor Lodge (Worksop) 403
Maxstoke Castle 629
Maynards 276
Mentmore Towers 50
Morley Old Hall 348
Myrtle Grove 838
Old Manor House (Benenden) 264, 265, 266
Olden Manor 533, 534
Owlpen 21
Paxhill 614
Penhow Castle 812, 813
Plaish Hall 445
Rashleigh Barton 141, 142
Sawston Hall 56
Sker House 818
Snowdenham Hall 590
South Wraxhall Manor 488, 489
Stayley Hall 300
Stocketts Manor 592, 593
Stockton 659
Thurston End Hall 539
Towie Barclay 787
Trafalgar House 665
Tysoe Manor 633
Upton House 221
Vale Royal Abbey 82
Wakefield Lodge 380
Walpole House 733
Wealden houses 264, 266
Wilsley 289
Wingfield College 543, 545
Woolstaplers Hall 223
Yaldham Manor 290, 291
Yardhurst 292, 293
Youlston Park 146
The Great House (Brockamin) 668
Great House Court 131
Great Snoring: The Manor House 338
Great Treverren 86-7
Greek Cross plan, Brook Place 553-4
Greek Revival
    Balbirnie 738
    Bassett House 458-9
    Belsay Hall 383, 476, 536, 738
    Brogyntyn 432-3
    Fota 828
    Grange Park 234-5, 383, 536, 738
    Leigh Court 476-7, 738
    Maperton 479
    Regency Villa, Regent's Park 730
    Shrubland Park 535-7
    Trafalgar House portico 665
Green, Mr 121
Green Lane Farm 564
Greenhill, Anthony 498
Greenhithe: Ingress Abbey 188, 275
greenhouses *see* conservatories, glasshouses & orangeries
Greenway, Thomas 639
Greenwood, Mrs P.A. 596
Gregor, Francis 94
Gregor, Sarah & Gordon 94
Gregory XVI, Pope 686
Gregory (son of Demetrios) 853
Grenville, George (1712-1770) 616
Grenville, George Grenville (1753-1813), 1st Marquess of Buckingham 185
Greswell, John & Marian 495
Greswell, W.T. 495
Greville, Robert Greville, 2nd Baron Brooke (Lord Brooke) 629
Grey, 2nd Earl (Charles Grey) 391
Grey, 5th Earl & Lady Grey (Charles & Mabel Grey) 391

Grey, George Harry Grey, 7th Earl of Stamford 303
Grey, Henry Grey, 1st Duke of Kent 249
Grey, Lady Jane 56, 96, 521
Grey, Lady Katherine 521
Greyfriars 565-7
Greystoke Castle 97
Greywalls 768
Gribble, Sir Edward* 362
Gribloch 9, 769-70
Griffin, Sir Edward* 362
Grillet 102
Grimm, S.H. 613
Grimshaw family 625
Grimshaw Hall 624-6
Grimsthorpe Castle 322
Grimwood, Rev Thomas 182
Grinton: Blackburn Hall 682
Grittleton House 641
Grosvenor, Robert Grosvenor, 2nd Earl Grosvenor (Lord Grosvenor) 432
Grosvenor Estate 346, 721
Grosvenor House 662
grottos
  Ascot Place 13, 26
  Bassett House 459
  Belcombe Court 634
  Encombe 157
  The Menagerie 371
  Piercefield 815
  Wimborne Houses 164
  see also caves; shell grottos & galleries
The Grove 840-1
Grovelands 717
Gruchy, Abraham de 841
Gruffyed, John St Bodfan 409
Guidi, Paolo 273, 274
Guild of Handicrafts 222-3
Guildford, Earls of 287
Guildford: Chilworth Manor 560-1
Guildhall, Kingston upon Thames 178
Gullane: Greywalls 768
Gulworthy: Horn of Plenty 129
Gummer, John 606
Gummow, Benjamin 432
gunpowder mills, Chilworth Manor 560, 561
Gunton Hall 339-43, 346
Guthrie, Alexander 758
Guy, Andrew 455
Guy, Anne 455
Gwerclas Hall 17, 802-4
Gwrych Castle 79, 804-5
Gwynne, Patrick 570-1
Gyrn Castle 806-7

H
H-plan
  The Abbey (Charlton Adam) 467-8
  Bradninch Manor 115-16
  Churche's Mansion 71-2
  Constable Burton (Elizabethan house) 688
  Green Lane Farm 564
  Knightstone Manor 134-5
  Little Thakeham 610-11
  Olden Manor 533-4
  Paper Hall 703
  Plaish Hall 445
  Rashleigh Barton 141-2
ha-has
  Crom Castle 825
  Croome Court 671
  Encombe 157
  Eydon Hall 367
  Fawley House 413
  Moundsmere Manor 236
  Sharpham House 144
  Stanton House 657
  Tysoe Manor 633
Hackcock, Edward 442
Hackfall 692-3
Haddington, Dowager Lady 789
Haddington, Earls of
  1st Earl (Sir Thomas Hamilton) 790
  2nd Earl 772
  6th Earl 790-1
  12th Earl 789
  13th Earl 789
Hadham Hall 194
Hadspen 470

Hague, William 831
Haigh, Diane 60
Halesworth: Heveningham Hall 12, 13, 529-30
Halfpenny, William 220
halfpenny pointing 187
Halifax, 2nd Earl of 370
Halifax: Scout Hall 704
Hall, Sir Benjamin 253
Hall, James & Carol 501
Hall, Sir John 176
Hall, Marshall 636
Hall, Mr & Mrs M.W. 563
hall houses
  6 Palace Street 799-800
  Ayot Mountfitchet 256-8
  Bentley Hall 519
  Charleston Manor 602-3
  Haslington Hall 75-6
  Olden Manor 533-4
  Rashleigh Barton 141-2
  Stocketts Manor 591-3
  Wealden houses 264-7, 292-3
  Yew Tree House 548-9
hall-parlours 578
hall stoves, Caythorpe Hall 317
Hallamshire Historic Buildings Society 706
Halstead: Gosfield Hall 184-5
Halswell 471-3
Halswell Park Trust 471
Ham House 785
Hambleden, 4th Viscount 34
Hambleton: Clifton Castle 687
Hambro, Sir Charles 202
Hambro, Charles (Lord Hambro, life peer) 203
Hambro, Cherry (Lady Hambro) 203
Hambro, Rose (Lady Hambro) 203
Hamilton, 14th Duke of 735
Hamilton, Craig 221
Hamilton, I.B.M. 136
Hamilton, Margaret 772
Hamilton, Stella 183
Hamilton, Sir Thomas
  Hamilton, 1st Earl of Haddington 790
Hamilton, Violet 318
hammer-beam roofs
  Allerton Park 678
  Donington St John 406
  Horsley Towers 572
  Plaish Hall 445
Hampstead: The Hill 720
Hampton Court Palace 9, 43, 236, 268, 492, 568, 594, 678
Hamsterley Hall 170-1
Hanbury, Christine 193
Hanbury, Colonel James 305
Hanbury, Jos 305
Hanbury-Tracy, Charles
  Hanbury-Tracy, 1st Baron Sudeley 218
Handel, George Frideric 273, 274
Hands, Julia 601
Hangar, Peter 59
Hanger, Rev John & Joan 59
Hanger Hill Garden Estate 718-19
Hankey, J.A. 596
Hanmer family 797
Hanmer, Sir John 797
Hanmer, Sir Thomas 735
Hanmer: Bettisfield Park 797
Hansford Johnson, Pamela 532
Hanworth: Gunton Hall 339-43, 346
Hapsford House 473-5
Harboard, Felix 43
Harbord, Doris 339
Harbord, Edward Harbord, 3rd Baron Suffield 342
Harbord, Sir William 342
Harbord-Harbord, Edward 343
Harcourt, Dowager Viscountess 587
Hardwick, Bess of 399
Hardwick, P.C. 164
Hardwick Hall 399, 680
Hardy, Thomas 162
Hare, Augustus 615

Hare Krishna community, Croome Court 669
harem, Buxted Park 601
Hargreaves, Thomas 299
Harlech, 1st Baron (J.R. Ormsby-Gore) 432
Harlech Castle 63
Harleyford Manor 6, 35, 44-5
Harliston, Margeret 843
Harliston, Richard 843
Harlow, Katherina 273
Harmer, James 275
Harold, King 607
Harpur-Crewe, Sir Henry 107
Harpur-Crewe, Mr Henry 106
Harrington Hall 320-2
Harrington, James 310
Harrington, John de 321
Harris, Hugh 740
Harris, John 7, 48, 117, 287, 313, 499, 554, 725, 751, 776
Harris, Kate 441
Harris, Thomas 449
Harrison family 495
Harrison, Catherine 324
Harrison, Henry 94
Harrison, John* 324
Harrold, Geoffrey 346, 347
Harrold: Hinwick House 22-3
Harrowby, Lord 500
Hartley, L.P. 331
Harvey, Frances 712
Harvey, John 520
Harvey, Tobias 712
Harvey, W. Alexander 625
Harvey-Hawke, Cassandra 712
Harvey-Hawke, Frances 712
The Hasells 20-1
Haslemere: Shillinglee Park 15, 616
Haslington Hall 75-6
Hastings, 22nd Baron (Lord Hastings) 346
Hastings, Marquesses of
  1st Marquess (Francis Rawdon Hastings) 306
  4th Marquess 306, 308
Hastings, Sir Hugh 333
Hastings, John 248
Hastings, John & Anne 333
Hastings, Laurence Hastings, 1st Earl of Pembroke 333
Hatchlands Park 569
Hatfield House 115, 153, 260, 395
Hatfield Priory 186-7
Hauptfuhrer, Fred 15, 551
Havelock, General Sir Henry 275
Havelock, William 275
Hawke, 3rd Baron 712
Hawkedon: Thurston End Hall 538-9
Hawksmoor, Nicholas 208, 390, 404
Haworth Parsonage 695
Hay Trust 777
Haycock, Edward 801
Haydon-Baillie, Wensley 710
Hayne, Charles 136
Hayton Hall 99-100
Haywards Heath: Paxhill 613-15
header bond brickwork 645
Headcort, 1st, 5th & 6th Marquesses of 830
Headfort House 830
Heald, Sir Lionel & Lady 560, 561
Healey Hall 296
Hearst, Randolph 804
Hearsum, John 375
heart motifs, Voysey's 566, 567
Heath, Cuthbert 'C.E.' 580
Heath, Edward 234
Heath House 12, 14, 508-9
Heathcote family 313
Heathcote, Pat 746
heating
  10 College Yard 677
  Barge House 250
  Castle of Park 745, 746
  Caythorpe Hall 317
  Coton Hall 436
  Craigengillan 748
  Croome Court 670
  Holystreet Manor 130, 131
  Penhow Castle 813
  Philipps House 652
  Puttenham Priory 586

Shawford Park 242
Tyntesfield 491
Wingfield College 544-5
Hedenham Hall 344
Heidegger, John James 726, 727
Heinz, Drew & Jack 26
Helena, Duchess of Manchester 773
Helensburgh: Brantwoode 743-4
Hellaby: Hellaby Hall 694
Hellaby Hall 694
Hemel Hempstead: Pimlico House 262-3
Henderson, Mr & Mrs John 792-4
Henderson, William 400
Hengrave Hall 527-8
Henley-on-Thames:
  Culham Court 9, 34-6
  Fawley House 411-13, 741
  Friar Park 414
  Wyfold Court 15, 188, 275, 425-7
Hennessy, Sir John Pope 838
Henri IV, King 158
Henry I, King 801
Henry II, King 259, 378, 421
Henry III, King 378, 409
Henry IV, King 628
Henry V, King 205
Henry VI, King 628, 648
Henry VII, King 406, 481, 543, 607, 629, 727
  tomb & memorial chapel 187, 476, 527
Henry VIII, King 114, 187, 205, 236, 259, 282, 318, 350, 488, 504, 521, 543, 607, 740
Henry of Grosmont, Earl of Lancaster 333
Henry the Treasurer 238
Henry Jones Ltd 799
Henry Lucas Hospital 39-40
Herbert, Lady Catherine 446
Herbert, Sir William Herbert, 1st Earl of Pembroke 658
Hereward the Wake 746
Heriot's Hospital 761
Heritage Link 359
Heritage Lottery Fund 41, 126, 159, 454, 620, 779, 800, 818
Hermon, Edward 425-6
Hermon, Frances Caroline 426-7
Heronden 6
Herstmonceux: Eastwood Farm 606
Herstmonceux Castle 606
Hertford House 210
Heseltine, Michael 20, 235, 299, 313, 515, 529-30
Hesketh, 3rd Baron (Lord Hesketh) 208
Hesketh, Robert 771
Heton, Sir Thomas 387
Heveningham Hall 12, 13, 529-30
Hever Castle 764
Hewett, Henry 399
Hewett, Sir Thomas 420
Hewlings, Richard 404
Heydrich, Reinhard 788
Heytersbury: Stockton 658-9
Heythrop Park 415
Heywood family 137-8
Heywood, James 138
Heywood, James Modyford 138
Heywood, Peter 138
H.H. Martyn Ltd 26
Hicks, David 43
Hiddleton, Tommy 748
Higford family 203
Higford, Sir John 202, 203
High Head Castle 101
Higham: Olden Manor 14, 533-4
Highclere Castle 103
Highcliffe Castle 7, 158-9
Highgrove House 217, 255
Highworth: Stanton House 657
Hilditch, George 551
Hilditch, James Bracebridge 551
Hildyard family 397
Hildyard, Myles 397, 398
Hildyard, Robert 398

Hill 128
The Hill 720
Hill, John 770
Hill, Robin 687
Hill, Sir Roland 409
Hill Hall 188
Hill House 743
Hillsborough, Nicholas 687
Hilton, Paul 250
Hilton Park 831
Himley: Himley Hall 510
Himley Hall 428, 510
Hindle, John Fowden 301
Hine, T.C. 397-8
Hinton, Bruce 526
Hinwick House 22-3
Hirst, Damien 17, 218, 219, 814
Historic Buildings Council 133, 446, 684
Historic Buildings Council for Wales 816
Historic House Hotels 798
Historic Houses Association 127
Historic Scotland 752, 767, 783
Hitler, Adolf 647
Hoare family 751
Hobbs, Christopher 370-1
Hobhouse family 470
Hobhouse, Henry (architect) 29
Hobhouse, Niall 470
Hobhouse, Penelope Hadspen 470
  Hapsford House gardens 475
Hodge, Robert & Frances Caroline 426-7
Hodges family 467
Hodges, John 464
Hogarth, William 727
Holaday (Holliday), Edward 273, 274
Holcroft, Thomas 81
Holford, George 391
Holiday, Henry 13
holiday lets *see* hotel & related use
Holkham Hall 110
Holland, Henry (architect) 29
Holland, Sir Henry (physician) 721
Holland, John 399, 403
Holland, Wilfrid 604, 605
Holland House 721-3
Holliday, Edward 273, 274
Holliday Hall 1, 273-4
Holloway, Benjamin 456
Holly Mount 46-7
Holmbury St Mary: Holmdale 568-9
Holmdale 568-9
Holme Lacy 218
Holmes, John Augustus 762
Holystreet Manor 130-2
Home, 8th Earl & Countess of (Elizabeth, Countess of Home) 723, 725
Home family 795
Home, Patrick (Patrick Home of Billie) 795
Home House 723-5
Homes, Mr 506
Homewood 570-1
Honington Hall 733
Hope, William Williams 376
Hope: Plas Teg 797, 816
Hope-Edwardes, Thomas Henry 442
Hopedene 569
Hopper, Thomas 476
Hopton, Sir Arthur 521
Hopton, Sir Owen 521
Horde, Alan 409
Horde, Sir Thomas* 410
Horham Hall 189-90
Horn, Simon 239
Horn of Plenty 129
Horncastle: Revesby Abbey 325-6
Horne, Captain 691
horse racing
  Adderbury House 405
  Colwick Hall 396
  Middleton Park 417
  Wothorpe Grandstand 66
Horsley, J.C. 288
Horsley Towers 572
Horton: The Menagerie 370-1
Horton House 370
Hoskyns, Alicia 637
hospital & related use

8 The Circus (Bath) 460
Apley Park 429
Biddulph Grange 502
Botleys 552
Brancepeth Castle 167
Bretby Hall 102-3
Burley-on-the-Hill 305
Dowdeswell Court 206
Erskine House 755
Goddards 563
Grovelands 717
The Hasells 20
The Hill 720
Himley Hall 510
King's Weston 209
Leigh Court 476
Lilford Castle 372
Nansidwell 89
Newport House 252
Patshull Hall 512
Paxhill 613
Pitmain Lodge 780
Poltimore 140
Puttenham Priory 587
Ridgemead 588
Shawford Park 241
Staunton Harold Hall 311-13
Stibbington Hall 59
Tabley Hall 81
Taymouth Castle 784
Tottenham Park 662
Trewarthenick 94
Tyringham Hall 53-4
Wyfold Court 425
hotel & related use
Archerfield 735
Arisaig House 736
Ashdown Park Hotel 25
Balbirnie 738
Bibury Court 198
Bodysgallen 798
Boringdon 114
The Broad House 329
Buxted Park 600-1
Bylaugh Hall 330
Carton House 822
Castle of Park 745-6
Caverswall Castle 506
Cheddington Court 151
Churche's Mansion 72
Claridges Hotel, London
  138, 601
Colwick Hall 16, 396
Coombe Abbey 623
The Crescent, Buxton 104,
  105
Duddingston House 751
Endsleigh 126
Erskine House 755
Gidleigh Park Hotel 131
Goddards 563
Great Snoring Manor 338
Great Treverren 87
Greywalls 768
Gwrych Castle 805
Hayton Hall 99-100
Hellaby Hall 694
Heythrop Park 415
Home House 725
Horn of Plenty 129
Horsley Towers 572
House of Gray 767
Inverlochy Castle 771
Kildwick Hall 695
King's Weston 17
Little Bardfield Hall 194
Little Thakeham 611
Llangoed Hall 810
Luton Hoo 25
Manderston House 775
Melville Castle 777
Mentmore Towers 50
Milford House 576
Nansidwell 89
Netley Hall 442
Old Grammar School 183
Orchardleigh 484
Oulton Hall 702
Patshull Hall 17
Peckforton Castle 17, 78-9
Philipps House 652
Piercefield 813-14
Ritz Hotel, London 24, 54,
  236, 238, 774
Rowton Castle 448
Rushton 376
Savoy Hotel, London 601
Sawston Hall 56
Seaham Hall 173
Stanton House 657

Sundridge Park 286
Swinfen Hall 515
Taymouth Castle 784
Thoresby Hall 401 - 2
Toddington Manor 218-19,
  814
Tottenham Park 662, 663
Tresanton 126
Trevor Hall 820
Wallington Hall 352
Walworth Castle 174
Wedderburn Castle 795
Weston Hall 17, 516
Woolton Hall 302
Wotton House 595
Hotel des Andelys 158, 159
Hotham family 690
Houghton, Lord (life peer)
  681
Houghton Hall 187
Houldditch, Richard 561
hound-gates see dog-gates &
  hound-gates
House of Gray 766-7
House of Nairne 767
Houseman, John 676
houses & cottages conversions
  see residential conversions &
  enabling development
Houses of Parliament 218, 425,
  572, 678, 679, 761
Housman, A.E. 288
Housman, Laurence 288
Howard, Lady Catherine 236
Howard, Charles Howard,
  11th Duke of Norfolk 97
Howard, Henry Howard, 6th
  Duke of Norfolk 550
Howard, Henry Howard, Earl
  of Surrey 524
Howard, John 67, 68, 69
Howard, Robert 290
Howard, Thomas Howard,
  3rd Duke of Norfolk 350
Howe, 5th Earl (Lord Howe)
  306
Howell, Edward 121, 122
Howell, Peter 425
Howgill Castle 96
Howick, Charles Baring, 2nd
  Baron Howick 391
Howick, Lady Mary 391
Howick Hall 391
Huddleston, Sir Edmond 56
Huddleston, Sir John 56
Hudson, Dr Michael 63-5
Hudson, Sir Robert & Lady
  188
Huelin, Ernest 'Tony' 842
Huf, Peter & Huf family 573-5
Huf Haus 573-5
Huggeford, Johannes (Sir
  John Higford) 202, 203
Hughes family 802
Hughes, Helen 271
Hughes Lloyd, Hugh &
  Margaret 802
Hugo, Victor 158, 504, 506, 807
Hulton, Edward 587
Hungerford family 363
Hungerford, Sir Edward 656
Hunsden, Thomas 261
Hunt, John 22
Hunter, Charles 188
hunting lodges
  The Abbey (Charlton
    Adam) 467-8
  Bradgate Stables 303
  Caverswall Castle 504-6
  Cranborne Manor 152, 153
  Earl Soham Lodge 524
  Pitmain Lodge 780
  Sinai Park 514
  Traigh House 788
  Wakefield Lodge 378-80
  see also shoots & sporting
    estates
Huntingdon, 1st Earl of
  (William de Clinton) 627
Huntly-Gordon, Herbert 583,
  585
Hurst House 190-1
Hurstbourne Park 121
Hussey family 315
Hussey, Christopher
  on A La Ronde 111
  Avray Tipping cartoon 9
  on Brympton d'Evercy 465
  on Ednaston Manor 108
  on Endsleigh 126

on Manor House (Sutton
    Courtenay) 422
Hutton, Elizabeth 682
Hutton, Timothy 687
Huxley, T.H. 517
Hyams, Harry 281
Hyde, John 37
Hyde, William 37
Hyder Ali, Sultan of Mysore
  792
hydro-electric plant,
  Holystreet Manor 130
Hylands House 7, 192-3

I

icehouses
  Auchinleck 737
  Puttenham Priory 586
  Upton House 221
Ickworth House 518, 546
Ideal Home article, 78
  Derngate 374
Ihne, Ernst Eberhard von 53
Ilchester, 1st, 5th & 6th Earls of
  487
Ilford: Valentine's 731
imperial staircases,
  description 205, 430, 509
industrial diamonds,
  Wolverton Hall 674
Ingestre: Ingestre Pavilion 511
Ingestre Hall 511, 516
Ingestre Pavilion 511
Ingham family 265
Ingham, Benjamin 698
Ingilby, Sir John & Lady 322
inglenook windows 581
Ingress Abbey 188, 275
Innes, Mike 139
Innes, Robert 762-3
Insall, Donald 252, 717
inscriptions & tags
  Blencowe Hall 95-6
  Bower House 179
  Brantwoode 744
  Brereton Hall 69
  Brizlincote Hall 103
  Caroline Park 747
  Castle Ashby 359
  Churche's Mansion 71, 72
  The Court House (Martock)
    481
  Dingley Hall 362
  Finedon Hall 368
  Fyvie Castle 765
  Great Ponton church 318
  Hengrave Hall 528
  Minsterley Hall 441
  Orchards 582
  Park Close 585
  Rous Lench Court 672
  Swinsty Hall 705
  Tong Hall 707
  Yeaton Pevery 453
  see also carvings;
    monuments &
    tombstones
insurance payments see
  financial information
insurance plaques, Thurston
  End Hall 538
International Style, Les
  Lumières 14, 17, 842
Inveraray Castle 784
Inverlochy Castle 771
Invernairn, 1st Baron (Sir
  William Beardmore) 758
Inverurie, Lord 773
Inverurie: Keith Hall 772
Ionic Villa, Regent's Park 730
Ionides, Basil 601
Ipswich: Shrubland Park 13,
  535-7
Ipswich windows 422
Ireland, Duke of (Robert de
  Vere) 627
Ireson, Nathaniel 11
  Barford House 456
  Crowcombe Court 456, 469
  Redlynch House 487
  Ven House 492-4
Ironside, Field Marshall the
  1st Lord Ironside 348
Irving, Washington 67
Isfield Place 607-9
Isham, Sir Justinian 361
Islay Walton Manor 308
Isle of Sheppey: Shurland Hall
  15, 282
Ison, Walter 189-90

Italianate
  50 Oxford Gardens 728-9
  Bassett House 458, 458-9
  Bettisfield Park tower 797
  Brodsworth Hall 683-5
  Coton Hall tower 435
  development by Sir Charles
    Barry 397, 536, 537
  Flintham 397-8
  Oulton Hall 702
  Shrubland Park 535
Ivan, Michael 183
Ivegill: High Head Castle 101
Iver Grove 11
Ivory, Thomas 823
The Ivy 639

J

Jackson, Sir T.G. 853
Jackson-Stops, Gervase 107,
  370-1, 450, 639
Jackson-Stops, Tim 446
Jacksons (plasterers) 263
Jacob's Ladder 14, 408
Jacobean
  Anderson Manor 14, 148
  Apethorpe Hall 354-5
  Bank Hall 294
  Bramshill 227
  Bridge Place 268-9
  Castle Ashby 358-9
  Castle Bromwich Hall
    interiors 619-20
  Caverswall Castle 504-6
  Clegg Hall 296
  Cockfield Hall 521 -3
  Cranborne Manor 152-4
  Gibside 618-9
  The Grange
    (Broadhembury) 117-18
  Lilford Castle 372
  Llangoed Hall 810
  Mears Ashby Hall 373
  Newton Surmaville 8
  Plas Teg 816
  Rashleigh Barton 141 -2
  Ruperra Castle 817
  Stibbington Hall 57-9
  Stibbngton Hall 57-9
  Stockton 658-9
  Troy House 821
  Wraxhall House 165
  Jacobean room, The Grange
    (Broadhembury) 117-18
Jacobethan
  Bradgate Stables 303
  Bylaugh Hall 330
  Heath House 12, 14, 508-9
  Revesby Abbey 325-6
  Stokesay Court 449-50
Jacobite risings 699, 726, 734,
  746, 780
Jacob's Ladder 14, 408
James I, King (James VI of
  Scotland) 82, 96, 117, 153,
  227, 354, 378, 421, 521, 689,
  759, 785, 817
James II, King of Great Britain
  164, 362, 410, 834
James II, King of Scotland 758
James IV, King of Scotland 759
James, Edward 612-13
James, Henry 478
James, John (antiquary) 703
James, John (architect) 160,
  664
James, William 768
James Powell & Sons 33
Jane Austen's House museum
  229
January, Louise 764
Janvrin Robin, Charles 848
Jardine, William 349
Jeanes, James 455
Jebb, Philip 423
  Beenham Hatch 27-8
  Ingestre Pavilion 511
  Jebb jib door 255, 511
  Poston House 254-5
Jeckell, Thomas see Jekyll,
  Thomas
Jeddah (Major Larnach's
  Derby winner) 405
Jefferies, Miss 531 -2
Jefferson, L.W. 97
Jefferson, Thomas 459
Jekyll, Gertrude
  comparisons to 768
  Goddards garden 563
  misattributions 605, 610

Munstead Grange garden
  577-8, 579
Munstead Wood 577, 582,
  605
Puttenham Priory garden
  plans 587
Jekyll, Thomas (Thomas
  Jeckell)
  Elsing Hall 333, 334-5
  Little Hautbois church 345
Jellicoe, Sir Geoffrey 212
Jenkins, Simon 544
Jennison, Thomas 174
Jersey, 9th Earl of 417
Jersey, Occupation of see
  German Occupation of
  Jersey
Jervis, Simon 49
Jervoise, George Purefoy 238
Jessop, Major Thomas 322
jettied upper stories,
  description 293, 533
Jewell, Herbert 240
Jewson, Norman 212
jib door, Jebb 255, 511
Job room & fireplace,
  Bradninch Manor 10, 115-16
Joel, Betty 770
John, King 152, 153, 259, 585,
  833
John, Augustus 810
John of Gaunt 542
John Gilmour's Marriage
  Settlement 618
John McAslan & Partners 286,
  374
John Smith & Co 314
Johnson, Andrew 198
Johnson, Francis 327
Johnson, Pamela Hansford
  532
Johnson, Dr Samuel 24, 737,
  778
Johnson, Sarah Jane 270
Johnson, Thomas 508
Johnson-Marshall, Percy 751
Joldwynds 569
Joli, Antonio 726, 727
Jones, Bridget 173
Jones, Chester 35
Jones, Edward (Dixon Jones
  architects) 424
Jones, Henry 799
Jones, Inigo
  associations with &
    comparisons to 104, 154,
    380, 430, 454, 466, 551, 695
  Stoke Park 377
Jones, Sir Peter Benton 59
Jones, William (architect) 365
Jones, William
  (mathematician) 419
Joseph, King of Naples 539
Jowell, Tessa 355
Joyce, William & Elizabeth 519
Joynes, Henry 561
Joynt, Mr & Mrs Harry 645,
  646
Julian's 134
Juniper, William 185

K

Kagan, Lord (life peer) 680,
  681
Kale, Elaine 791
Kaner, Jake 374
Kani, Wasfi 235
Kauffman, Angelica 191, 283
Kay, Thomas 439
Kedleston Hall 50, 535, 774,
  775
Keene, James Whitshed 551
Keith, John Keith, 1st Earl of
  Kintore 772
Keith Hall 772-3
Kekewyche, George 85
Kells: Headfort House 830
Kelly, Warin & Kelly family
  132, 133
Kelly House 132-3
Kelmscott Manor 197
Kelso: Floors Castle 759-61
Kemp, Thomas 598
Kenilworth: Stoneleigh Abbey
  630-1
Kenilworth Castle 628
Kennedy, George 198
Kensington Court (no 2) 852
Kensington Palace 304
Kent, Dukes of

1st Duke (Henry Grey) 249, 721
TRH Duke & Duchess of Kent (Prince George & Princess Marina) 510
Kent, William
  comparisons to 161, 208
  Wakefield Lodge 14, 378-80
Kenulf, King of the West Saxons 421
Kenyon, Edward 337
Ker family 759
Ker, Robert Ker, 1st Earl of Roxburghe 759
Kesteven, Lady 256, 257
Kettering:
  Cransley Hall 12, 360-1
  Rushton 376
Kettleburgh 524
Key, Robert 104
Keynes, John Maynard 648
Kildare, Earls of 822
  19th Earl (Robert FitzGerald) 822
  20th Earl & 1st Duke of Leinster (James Fitzgerald) 822, 823
Kildwick Hall 695-7
Kilmeadan: Mount Congreve 632, 836-7
Kilowatt House see Woodside
Kineton: Compton Verney 621-2
Kinfauns Castle 767
King, Benjamin 631
King, Cecil 36
King, Henry 608
king posts
  Cheddington Court 151
  Old Manor House (Benenden) 266
  Paper Hall 703
  Stocketts Manor 592
  Wilsley 289
King's Room, Sundridge Park 283, 286
King's Weston 17, 209
Kingsley, Elizabeth 21
Kingsley, Heylock 21
Kingston: Encombe 12, 14, 156-7
Kingston Lacey 163
Kingston Lisle 37-8
Kingston Maurward 160
Kingston Russell: Kingston Russell 161
Kingston Russell 161
Kingussie: Pitmain Lodge 780
Kinnear family 773
Kinross, John 774
Kintore, Earls of
  1st Earl (John Keith) & Countess (Margaret Hamilton) 772-3
  10th Earl & Countess 773
  12th Earl 772, 773
Kip, Johannes 688
Kirby, Ian 371
Kirby, Richard 188
Kirkduncan, Archdeacon 534
Kirkham, Andrea 549
Kirtlington: Kirtlington Park 416, 616, 622
Kirtlington Park 416, 616, 622
Kitchin, G.H. 811
Kite, Maggie 501
Knight family 228
Knight, Edward Austen 228-9
Knight, Joan 59
Knight, John 185
Knight, Thomas & Catherine 228
Knights of Glin 829
Knightstone Manor 10, 134-5
Knole 197, 268
Knowle: Grimshaw Hall 624-6
Knutsford: Tabley Hall 80-1
König, F.A. 53
Kortright, Cornelius 193
Kubale, Christopher 210
Kulikowski, Florian 53
Kyle, Tommy 12, 493-4
Kytson, Sir John 527

L

la More, Sir Richard de 811
la Zouche, Edward la Zouche, 11th Baron Zouche 227
Labouchere, Pierre Caesar 193
Ladbroke Grove, London: 50

Oxford Gardens 728-9
Lade, Edward 290
Lafrancini brothers 822
Laing, David 260, 261
Laing, Sir Maurice 53
Laing, Samuel 133
lakes, pools & canals
  Ascot Place 13, 26
  Astley Pool House 667
  Bassett House 459
  Belcombe Court 634
  Biddulph Grange 503
  Blackland Park 12, 635, 636
  Bradninch Manor 12, 116
  Carton House 823
  Cedar Cottage 559
  Cheddington Court 150, 151
  Chicheley 43
  Chilworth Manor 561
  Colebrook House 230-1
  Craigengillan 748
  Cransley Hall 12, 360
  Croome Court 671
  Dodington Park 13, 204
  Ebberston Hall 690
  Encombe 156, 157
  Friar Park 414
  Gillingham Hall 336
  Gunton Hall 339
  Gyrn Castle 806
  Hackfall 692
  Halswell 471
  Heveningham Hall 12, 13, 529
  Inverlochy Castle 771
  Kingston Maurward 160
  Larch Hill 832-3
  Latimer Manor 643
  Little Thakeham 610
  Moundsmere Manor 236
  Narborough Hall 349
  Park Cottage 809
  Patshull Hall 512, 513
  Philipps House 651
  Ridgemead 589
  Shawford Park 240
  Shireoaks 399
  Stanford Hall 16, 400
  Stanton House 657
  Stocketts Manor 591, 592, 593
  Stoke Park 377
  Sturford Mead 2-3, 660
  Styche Hall 451
  Trinity Manor 852
  Tyringham Hall 13, 54
  Ven House 494
  Wakefield Lodge 378
  Wallington Hall 352
  Weacombe 495, 496, 497
  Wingfield College 545
Lamb, Charles 260
Lambert, General 97
Lambton family
  Antony, Viscount Lambton 172
  J.G., 1st Earl of Durham 172
  Lucy (Lady Lucinda) 172
  Ned, 7th Earl of Durham 172
  W.H. 172
Lambton Castle 172
Lancaster, Earl of (Henry of Grosmont) 332
Lancaster, Nancy 366
Lancaster, Osbert 232, 272, 448, 588
Land Army 597
Landmark Trust 255, 282, 287, 704
Auchinleck 737
Banqueting House, Gibside 168, 169
Goddards 563
The Grange (Ramsgate) 279
Ingestre Pavilion 511
Lansdown Tower 459
The Pineapple, Dunmore 754
Plas Uchaf 804
Robin Hood's Hut, Halswell Park 471, 473
The Ruin, Hackfall 692-3
Landseer, Sir Edwin 123, 597
Lane, Joseph & Josiah 26
Lang, Ian 776
Lang, Mr 749
Langley, Batty 667
Langleys 701
Langston, James 418

Lanhill House 641
Lanscroon, Gerard 305
Lansdown Tower 459
Larch Hill 832-3
Larnach, Major James 405
Larsen, Henning 622
LASSCO 767
Lasswade: Melville Castle 777
Latimer, Hugh 642
Latimer Manor 642-3
Latin tags see inscriptions & tags
Latymer, Barons 701
Laud, Archbishop 269
Lauder: Thirlestane Castle 785-6, 789
Lauderdale, 1st Duke & Duchess 785, 786
Lauderdale, 9th Earl of 786
Launceston: Kelly House 132-3
laundries
  Acton 718
  Miller's Tower 762, 763
  Park Close 585
  Ruperra Castle 817
  Vellore House 794
Laurie, Northall 615
Laurino, Duchess of 265
lavatories see loos
Lawdy, John 259
Lawrence, Thomas 765
Lawrence, William* 165
Lawson family 685, 686
Lawson, Sir William 686
Lawton, Charles 77
Lawton, Robert 77
Lawton Hall 16-17, 77, 330
Le Corbusier 570
Le Gros family 847
Le Sueur, Frances 850
Learmont, David 778
Lecky, Effie 12, 493, 494
Ledstone Hall 13, 698
Lee, Anne 325, 326
Lee, Harry Lancelot 435
Lee, General Robert E. 435
Lee, Thomas 121, 435
Leeds: Oulton Hall 702
Leeds Castle 504
Lees Court 700
Lees-Milne, James 107, 622, 651
legal cases
  6 Palace Street 799
  Barlaston Hall 45, 499-500, 510
  Barnsley family 252
  breach of promise, 6th Marquess of Northampton 633
  Brodsworth Hall 683
  Downe Hall 155
  Gwrych Castle 809
  Shirburn Castle 419, 420
  Tyntesfield 490
Leicester, 1st Earl of (Thomas Coke) 110
Leicester, Sir John Fleming 80
Leicester: Bradgate Stables 567
Leicester-Warren, Colonel John 80
Leifnorris Castle 753
Leigh family 630, 631
Leigh, Mr & Mrs Gerald 367, 368
Leigh, John 24
Leigh, Sir Thomas 630
Leigh, Rev Thomas 631
Leigh Court 476-7, 738
Leigh-Wood, Oliver 548, 549
Leighterton: Saddlewood Manor 14, 215-17
Leighton, Frederick, Baron 568
Leighton, William 445
Leighton: Park Cottage 808-9
Leighton Buzzard: Mentmore Towers 48-51
Leinster, Dukes of
  1st Duke & Duchess (James & Emily FitzGerald) 822, 823
  3rd Duke 822
Leinster House 822
Leiper, William 743-4
Leith, 1st Baron Leith (Alexander Leith/Lord Leith) 764, 765

Leland, John 205, 318, 504, 687
Lennox, 2nd Duke of 750
Lennoxlove House 785
Leoni, Giacomo 196
Lerner, Sandy 228, 229
Les Lumières 14, 17, 842
Letts, George 194
Levens Hall 672
Leverhulme, 1st Viscount (Lord Leverhulme) 720
Leverton, Thomas 155
Levy, Judith 727
Lewes: Charleston Manor 602-3
Lewes Crescent (No 1) see Fife House
Lewis, James 366-8
Lewis, Sir John 698
Lewis, Pam 475
Lewis, Paul & GenèviÈve 482
Leyburn:
  Constable Burton 7, 688-9
  Leyburn Hall 699
Leyburn Hall 699
libraries
  Albury Park 550
  Allerton Park 679
  Barlaston Hall 500, 501
  Beenham Hatch 28
  Bibury Court 197, 198
  Chawton House 228, 229
  Chicheley 43
  Chicksands Priory 19
  Coton Hall 436
  Cullen House 15, 750
  Danson House 271
  Eggesford House 122
  Flintham 398
  The Grange (Ramsgate) 279
  Gribloch 769
  Halswell 472
  Harleyford Manor 44
  Hatfield Priory 187
  Holmdale 569
  Mackerye End 261
  Maperton 480
  Newhailes 778
  Philipps House 652
  Pitmain Lodge 780
  Saddlewood Manor 217
  The Salutation 281
  Shawford Park 241
  Shirburn Castle 419, 420
  Shrubland Park 536
  Steephill 849-50
  Sturford Mead 661
  Trawsgoed 819
  Tyringham Hall 54
  Vellore House 793
  see also bookcases
licence to crenellate
  Apley Park 428
  Caverswall Castle 504
  Chillingham Castle 387
  High Head Castle 101
  Maxstoke Castle 627
  St Ouen's Manor 843
  Shirburn Castle 420
  Wingfield Castle 542
Lichfield: Swinfen Hall 8, 515
Liddiard, William 654
lighting
  Callaly Castle 386
  Cragside 388
  Earl Soham Lodge 526
  Leigh Court gasoliers 476
  Wyfold Court 426
lightning damage, Thorpe Tilney Hall 327
Lilford, 1st, 4th & 7th Barons 372
Lilford family 294
Lilford: Lilford Castle 372
Lilford Castle 372
Lilford Hall 294
Limerick, 3rd Earl of 826
Lindsay, Colonel & Mrs 422
Lindsay, Ian 734
Linlithgow: Vellore House 792-4
Linnell, John 765
Lisburne, 6th & 7th Earls of 819
Lisle, Alice de 37
Lismore: Lismore Castle 833-4
Lismore Castle 833-4
Lister, Ross 447
Little family 221
Little, Charlotte 221
Little, Major Cosmo 221

Little Bardfield Hall 194-5
Little Boarhunt 232
Little Dunham: Dunham Lodge 331-2
Little Hautbois 10, 345
Little Hautbois: Little Hautbois 10, 345
Little Moreton Hall 442
Little Roydon 413
Little Thakeham 610-11
Little Timble: Swinsty Hall 705
Littlebury, William 182
Littlecote House 218
Littlewood, Joan 183, 595
Livadia (steam yacht) 744
Liverpool, Earls of
  2nd Earl (Lord Liverpool, Prime Minister) 80
  3rd Earl 601
Liverpool: Woolton Hall 302
Llanafan: Trawsgoed 819
Llandudno: Bodysgallen 798
Llanfedw: Ruperra Castle 174, 817
Llangoed Hall 7, 810
Llangollen: Trevor Hall 805, 820
Llangym: Alt-y-Bela 15, 282, 796
Llanmartin: Pencoed Castle 811
Llansawel: Edwinsford 801
Lloyd, David 438, 439
Lloyd, Hugh Hughes & Margaret 802
Lloyd, Reginald 850
Lloyd, Thomas (author) 801, 802
Lloyd, Thomas (Trevor Hall) 820
Llwynybrain 801
Llyswen: Llangoed Hall 7, 810
Loanhead: Mavisbank House 776
local government properties
  Abbey Houses (Bury St Edmunds) 520
  Ashton Court 454
  Balbirnie 738
  Bassett House 458
  Botleys 552
  Coombe Abbey 623
  The Crescent, Buxton 104-5
  Danson House 270-1
  Duff House 752
  Eagle House 716
  Gosfield Hall 185
  Grovelands 717
  Highcliffe Castle 158-9
  The Hill 720
  Himley Hall 510
  Hylands House 192-3
  Ingress Abbey 275
  Maristow House 138
  Nether Swell Manor 210
  Newbridge 819
  Newport House 252
  Oak Hill 299
  Oulton Hall 702
  Shaw House 41
  Swinsty Hall 705
  Valentine's 731
  Walworth Castle 174
  Wentworth Woodhouse 708
  Westgate House 540
Lochiel, Camerons of 734
lochs see lakes, pools & canals
Lochton Castle 773
Lochton House 773-4
Lockyer, Sir Thomas 480
Lomas family 103
Lombe, Sir John 330
London, George 43
Londonderry, Marchionesses of
  Frances, Lady Londonderry (3rd Marchioness) 173, 175
  Theresa, Lady Londonderry (6th Marchioness) 176
Londonderry, Marquesses of
  1st Marquess 176
  2nd Marquess (Lord Castlereagh) 176
  3rd Marquess (Charles William Stewart) 175, 176
  6th Marquess 176
  7th Marquess 176
  8th Marquess 176
  9th Marquess 176

Long family 488
Long, Edwin 426
Long, Sir Henry 488
Long, Robert 488
long houses
Alt-y-Bela 796
Troy House 821
Long Melford: Westgate House 540-1
Longford, Sir Nicholas 110
Longford Hall 110
Longleat 440, 441, 659, 660, 661
Longspee, Nicholas 637
loos
Ashbury Manor garderobe 407
Ayot Mountfitchet thunderbox 258
Ballencrieff Castle garderobes 740
Bletchley Manor fireplace loo 431
Caythorpe Hall thunderbox 317
Culham Court chaise percee 36
Eydon Hall early water closet 368
Fife House Edward VII lavatory 598
Shawford Park 'his & hers' loos 242
Lopes family 137, 138
Lopes, Sir Massey Lopes, 1 st Baron Roborough 138
Lopes, Sir Massey Manasseh 138
Lord, Rupert 176
Lords, House of see Houses of Parliament
Lorimer, Sir Robert Greywalls 768
Miller's Tower 762-3
Lostwithiel: Boconnoc 84
Lothian Buildings Preservation Trust 776
Loudon, John Claudius 26, 337
Loudon Castle 784
Louis XV, King of France 726
Louis XVIII, King of France 184
Louise, Princess Royal & Duchess of Fife 597
The Love of Angels (statue) 24
Lovelace
1 st Earl 572
Ada, Countess of Lovelace 572
Lowder, John 112
Lowe, Louise 185
Lower Tean: Heath House 12, 14, 508-9
Lowry, Bernard 674
Lucas, Henry 39
Lucas Almshouses 39-40
Luddington family 352
Luddington, Andrew 352
Luddington, James 353
Ludgershall: Chute Lodge 640
Ludlow; The Reader's House 438-9
Ludlow Castle 439
Lugar, Robert 846
Lulworth Castle 174
Lumisden, Adam de 742
Lumisden, Gilbert de 742
Lumley, John 304
Lumsdaine family 742
Lumsden family 742
Lunar Society meetings 507
Lupton House 136
Luton: Luton Hoo 24-5, 260, 774
Luton Hoo 24-5, 260, 774
Lutyens, Sir Edwin
associations with & comparisons to 9, 12, 30, 131, 143, 195, 232, 240, 244, 411, 577, 743, 762
Breckles Hall alterations & gardens 328
Cedar Cottage 557-9
Chicheley opinion 43
Ednaston Manor 108-9
Folly Farm 13, 14, 16
Goddards 563
Greywalls 768
Little Thakeham 610-11

Middleton Park 417
Monkton House 612-13
Orchards 582
Redlynch House wings 487
The Salutation 280-1
Tyringham Hall pavilions 13, 53, 54
Lutyens, Robert
Middleton Park 417
Ridgemead 9, 588-9
Lutyens Trust 563
Lycett Green, Candida & Rupert 635-6
Lyle family 232
Lypp Powys, Mrs Philip 36
Lyson, Daniel & Samuel, & Magna Britannia 138
Lyster, Henry & Lady Charlotte 448
Lyster, Colonel Richard 448
Lytes Cary Manor 468
Lyttelton, Alfred 768
Lyttelton, Sir Richard 84

M
McAdam, John* 748
McAlpine, Alistair (Lord McAlpine, life peer) 411
McAlpine, David 413
McAslan, John 286, 374
Macbeth, Robert John (Ross & Macbeth) 758
Macclesfield, Earls of
1 st, 2nd, 3rd & 7th Earls 419
9th Earl 419, 420
Macclesfield Psalter 420
McComb, Mike & Sharon 298
McCorquodale, Alexander 354
McCorquodale, Marjorie 354
McCorquodale, Raine (Countess Spencer) 364
MacDermott, Beatrice 400
MacDiarmid, Major Niall Campbell 59
Macdonald, Major Simon 788
Macdonell, Aeneas Ranald 788
McFadyen, Tom 737
MacFarlane, Neil 106
Macfarlanes of Glasgow 729
McGill, Alexander 767
MacGregor, Caroline 769
MacGregor, James 769, 770
Machin, Francis 446-7, 667
Mackenzie, Alexander 782, 783
McKenzie, Laura 768
Mackenzie, William Macdonald 773
Mackerye End 260-1
Mackintosh, Charles Rennie 78 Derngate 374-5
Hill House 743
McKreth, Donald 66
Mackworth, Bulkeley 434
Mackworth, Richard 434
Mackworth-Dolben, William & Frances 368-9
McLaughlin, Niall 408
McMahon, Rodney 232
Macmillan, Harold 176
McNive, Peter 301
McNiven, Charles 301
MacQueen, Thomas Potter 19
Madden family 831
Madden, Rev Samuel 'Premium' 831
MAFF headquarters, Trawsgoed 819
magazine articles see specific magazines (eg Country Life)
Magna Britannia 138
Maharishi Mahesh Yogi 50
Maiden Newton: Wraxhall House 165
Maids of Honour Row (no 4) 726-7
Maison Jansen 748
Maitland, Sir John (Chancellor of Scotland) 785
Maitland, Sir John (MP) & Lady 320
Maitland-Carew, Captain Gerald 786
Makins, Dwight 225
Makins, Sir Roger (Baron Sherfield) & Lady 224-5
Malet, Edward Charles 843
Malet de Carteret, Edward Charles 843, 844
Malet de Carteret, Guy 844

Malet de Carteret, Philip & Adele 843, 844
Malet de Carteret, Rex 844
Malkin, Oliver 269
Malkin, Peter 268
Mallaig: Arisaig House 736
Maloney, John 693
Maltyward family 539
The Man Who Never Was 647, 650
Manchester, Helena, Duchess of Manchester (wife of 9th Duke) 773
Mander, Sir Nicholas & Lady 212
Manderston House 774-5
Manifold Trust 500
Mann family 525
Mann, Major William Edgar 525, 526
Manningtree: Aldhams 177-8
The Manor House (Buckland) 32-3
Manor House (Chipperfield) 263
The Manor House (Lindfield) 14
The Manor House (Milton Lilbourne) 644
The Manor House (Ogbourne St George) 647-50
Manor House (Sutton Courtenay) 421-2
Manor Kingdom group 754
Manor Lodge (Worksop) 403
Manton of Compton Verney, 1 st Baron 621
Manvers, 3rd Earl 402
Mapledurham House 614
Mapperton House 478
Mar Hall see Erskine House
March-Phillips, Ambrose Lisle & Laura May 307
March-Phillips, Charles 307
March-Phillips, Gus 148
Margaret of Anjou, Queen (wife of Henry VI) 543
Margaret, Countess of Suffolk 487
Marie Antoinette, Queen of France 49, 123
Marie Josephine, Queen of France 184
Marina, Princess Marina, Duchess of Kent 510
Maristow House 137-9
Markcrow, Martin 447
Market Drayton:
Bletchley Manor 431
Buntingsdale Hall 434
Styche Hall 451
Market Harborough: Dingley Hall 339, 362-3
Market Rasen: Norton Place 7, 322-4
Markham, Daisy 633
Marlborough, Sarah, 1 st Duchess 561
Marlborough:
Poulton House 653-4
Tottenham Park 662-4
Marlow: Harleyford Manor 6, 35, 44-5
Marot, Daniel 707
Marsh Court 545
Marshall, Edward 356
Martin, David 276, 277
Martin, Jas 76
Martin, Joseph Critchley 349
Martin, Kit 15, 499
Archerfield 735
Burley-on-the-Hill 305, 313
Callaly Castle 385-6
Compton Verney 621
The Crescent, Buxton 104, 105
Cullen House 15, 749, 750, 772
Dingley Hall 339, 362-3
Ecton Hall 363-4
Gunton Hall 339-43, 346
The Hasells 18
Keith Hall 772-3
Maristow House 139
Melton Constable Hall 346

Miller's Tower 762-3
Revesby Abbey 325
Stocken Hall 313-14
Stokesay Court 449-50
Stoneleigh Abbey 631
Tyninghame House 15, 32, 735, 789-91
Wentworth Woodhouse 709
Martin, Sally 339
Martin, William 103
Martin-Atkins, Edward* 37
Martin Dye, Heather 567
Martock: The Court House 481-2
Martyn, H.H. 26
martyrdom, Ridley & Latimer 642
Mary I, Queen (Mary Tudor) 56, 521, 642
Mary II, Queen (William & Mary) 185
Mary, Queen (consort of George V) 486, 587
Mary, Queen of Scots 59, 353, 740
Mary Tudor (Queen Mary I) 56, 521, 642
Mary Tudor (sister of Henry VIII) 544
Masefield, John 222
Maskelyne, Maurice 221
Mason, Sean & Sarah 17, 249, 250
Massey, Cecil Aubrey 400
Mathews, Binny & Stuart 87
Mathie, William 753
Matilda, Queen 153
Matthews, Paul 17
Maud of Wallingford 648
Maudrell, Henry 636
Maudrell, Thomas 636
Maugham, Syrie 560
Maury, Commander Matthew Fontaine 517
mausoleums see monuments & tombstones
Mavisbank House 776
Mawbey, Sir Joseph 552
Mawson, Thomas 720
Maxstoke Castle 504, 627-9
May, Hugh 346, 619
May, Mr 49
Mayall, Lees 660
Mayerling Incident 847
Mayfair, London: Holland House 721-3
Maynard, Arne 796
Maynards 17, 276-7
Maynooth:
Carton House 822, 823
Shell House at Carton 823
Meadows, Sally 130, 131, 132
Mears Ashby: Mears Ashby Hall 373
Mears Ashby Hall 373
medieval origins
6 Palace Street 799-800
10 College Yard 676-7
The Abbey (Charlton Adam) 467-8
Alt-y-Bela 796
Apley Park 428-30
Ashbury Manor 406-7
Ayot Mountfitchet 256-8
Beaurepaire 224-6
Bentley Hall 519
Blackburn Hall 682
Bodysgallen 798
Brancepeth Castle 167
Bride Hall 258-9
Brogyntyn 432-3
Castle of Park 745-6
Caverswall Castle 504-6
Charleston Manor 602-3
Chicksands Priory 18-19, 21
Chillingham Castle 387
Chilworth Manor 560-1
Cooke's House 603-5
Coombe Abbey 623
The Court House (Martock) 481-2
Cullen House 749-50
Earl Soham Lodge 524-6
Elsing Hall 333-5
Grace Dieu Manor 307
Gwerclas Hall 802
Harrington Hall 320-2
Hill 128
Knightstone Manor 134-5
Ledstone Hall 698

Lismore Castle 833-4
The Manor House (Ogbourne St George) 647-50
Manor House (Sutton Courtenay) 421-2
Maxstoke Castle 627-9
Old Manor House (Benenden) 264-7
Owlpen 212
Pencoed Castle 811
Penhow Castle 812-13
Pitchford Hall 442-4
Port Eliot 90
Rashleigh Barton 141-2
Rous Lench Court 672-3
Shirburn Castle 419-20
The Soke 244-5
South Wraxall Manor 488-9
Stocketts Manor 591-3
Stoneleigh Abbey 630-1
Swinsty Hall 705
Thame Park 51-2
Thirlestane Castle 785, 785-6
Thorpe Hall 350-1
Towie Barclay 787
Trawsgoed 819
Tyninghame House 789-91
Tysoe Manor 632-3
Vale Royal Abbey 81-2
Wakefield Lodge 378-80
Wealden houses 264-7, 292-3
Wilsley 288-9
Wingfield Castle 542-3
Wingfield College 543-5
Woodcroft Castle 63-5
Woolstaplers Hall 222-3
Yaldham Manor 290-1
Yardhurst 292-3
Yew Tree House 548-9
Youlston Park 146-7
Medlycott, Rev Sir Hubert 493
Medlycott, James 492-3
Medworth, Joseph 61
Mehmet Ali 746
Melbury House 444
Mellerstain House 789
Mellier, Charles 775
Mellor, David 444
Mellor, Peter 704
Melton Constable: Melton Constable Hall 331, 339, 346-7
Melton Constable Hall 331, 339, 346-7
Melville, Viscounts
1 st Viscount (Henry Dundas) 777
9th Viscount 777
Melville, Rodney 622
Melville Castle 777
memorials see monuments & tombstones
The Menagerie 370-1
Mendes, Fernando 716
Mentmore Towers 48-9
menus
James I at Cranborne Manor 153-4
Nutley Manor tea 238
Merewether, John 636
Merivale Moore plc 576
Mervyn White, Prentice & Partners 55
Messel, Anne 711
Messel, Oliver 711
Metropolitan Museum of Art 187, 416, 669
Mewes & Davis (Charles Mewes & Arthur Davis) 24, 25, 53, 774
Meyrick, Sir Samuel Rush 554
Michael Barclay de Tolly, Prince 797
Michael Davies & Partners 814
Michel, David Robert 161
Michel, John 161
Michell, Louisa 36
Michell, Richard 34, 36
Michell family (Clegg Hall) 296
Middleton family (Shrubland Park) 535, 537
Middleton, Broke 537
Middleton, Henry 535
Middleton, Sir W.F. 535
Middleton, William 535
Middleton Hall 303

Middleton Park 417
Middleton Place, Charleston (USA) 535
Mies van der Rohe, Ludwig 408, 571
Milbanke, Anne Isabella 173
Milbanke, Sir Ralph 173
Milborne Port:
  Bowling Green 149
  Ven House 12, 404, 492-4
Mildmay family 240
Mildmay, Alfred 561
Mildmay, Henry 240
Mildmay, Sir Walter 354
Miles, Sir Philip 476
Miles, Philip John 209
Miles, Philip Napier 209
Miles, Richard 846
Milford: Milford House 576
Milford House 576
military use *see* defence use; German Occupation of Jersey
Millais, John Everett 765
Miller, Sir James 774, 775
Miller, Sanderson 33, 184
Miller's Tower 762-3
Millington, Sir Thomas 185
Mills, Canon 232
Mills, Peter 215
Mills, Thomas 500, 501
Milner, H.H. 453
Milton Abbey 202
Milton Lilbourne: The Manor House 644
mining
  Wentworth Woodhouse 708
  see also National Coal Board; subsidence
Minsterley: Minsterley Hall 440-1
Minsterley Hall 440-1
minstrels' galleries
  Ayot Mountfitchet 257
  Hengrave Hall 528
  Little Thakeham 610
  Manor House (Sutton Courtenay) 422
  Old Manor House (Benenden) 265, 267
  South Wraxhall Manor 488
  Stocketts Manor 593
Mirrielees, Mrs D. 563
Mirrielees, Sir Frederick 563
mirrors & pier glasses
  Allerton Park 679
  Danson House 271
  Dowdeswell Court 207, 208
  Fife House 598, 599
  Luton Hoo 25
Mitcham: Eagle House 716
Mitchell, A. 26
Mitchell, Arnold 30
Mitchell, John 704
Mitchell, Sidney 773
moats
  Beaurepaire 224, 225, 226
  Breckles Hall 328
  Caverswall Castle 12, 504
  Dunham Lodge 332
  Earl Soham Lodge 524, 526
  Elsing Hall 333, 335
  Isfield Place 609
  Maxstoke Castle 627
  Morley Old Hall 348
  Old Manor House (Benenden) 265
  Shirburn Castle 419, 420
  Thurston End Hall 539
  Tysoe Manor 633
  Wingfield Castle 542
  Woodcroft Castle 63, 64
models, architectural 208, 304
Modernism/Modern Movement
  78 Derngate 374-5
  Homewood 570-1
  Jacob's Ladder 14, 408
  Woodside House 17, 498
Moggeridge, Hal 623
Mohun, Sir William 84
Moira, 2nd Earl of (Francis Rawdon Hastings) 306
Molyneux, Richard 302
Mompesson House 637
monastic origins
  The Abbey (Charlton Adam) 467-8
  Ashbury Manor 406-7
  Barrow Court 457

Blackburn Hall 682
Boringdon 114
Bride Hall 258-9
Chicksands Priory 18-19, 21
Chilworth Manor 560
Coombe Abbey 623
Cullen House 749-50
Grace Dieu Manor 307
Hatfield Priory 186
Ledstone Hall 698
Lismore Castle 833-4
The Manor House (Ogbourne St George) 647-50
Manor House (Sutton Courtenay) 421
Moundsmere Manor 236
Myrtle Grove 838
Nun Monkton Hall 701
Port Eliot 90
Poulton Manor 215
Sinai Park 514
Sker House 818
Stoneleigh Abbey 630-1
Thame Park 51-2
Tyninghame House 790
Vale Royal Abbey 81-2
  see also convents, seminaries & religious retreats
Monck, Sir Charles 383
monkey carvings, Miller's Tower 763
Monkton House 612-13
Monmouth, 1st Duke of & Monmouth Rebellion 378, 410
Monmouth: Troy House 821
Monro, Jean 486
Montacute House 466
Montagu of Beaulieu, Barons
  2nd Baron 248
  3rd Baron (Lord Montagu) 613, 684
Montagu, Edwin 328
Montagu, George 380
Montgomery, Field Marshal Viscount (General Montgomery) 613
Monti, Raffaele 49, 190
Montmorency family 149
Monument Trust 382, 434
monuments & tombstones
  Barford House residents 455
  Boord family of Paxhill 615
  Broughton, Rev Sir Thomas 73
  Clifton, Colonel Percy Robert 393
  Copledyke, John 321
  Coxwell-Rogers, Richard 208
  Currer, Henry 696
  Dunham Lodge obelisk 332
  Godfrey family of Woodford 191
  Hastings, Sir Hugh 333
  Hengrave Hall church 528
  Henry VII 187
  Kildwick church 696
  Lee family of Coton Hall 435
  Liddiard, William 654
  Nelson, Admiral Lord 332
  Ogilvy, Alexander 750
  Orlebar, in Podinton church 22
  Parkyns, Sir Thomas 392
  Paylor, Nathaniel 701
  St Innocent's shrine & relics 686
  Seton Collegiate Church 783
  Shurley family of Isfield Place 607
  Sparrow family of Worlingham Hall 547
  Watson, John 833
  Wentworth Woodhouse 710
  Wright, John 186
  Wyndham family of Philipps House 651
  see also carvings; inscriptions & tags
Moor Park 662
Moore, Dudley 601
Moore, Keith 626
Moore Ede, Brian 35
Moores, Sir Peter 622
Moores Jr., John 298
Moppes brothers, van 674
Morant, Boyd & Morant

furniture 483
Mordaunt family 247
More, Lady 442
More, Sir Richard de la 811
Moreing, Charles 275
Morgan family 811
Morgan, Anne 560
Morgan, J. Pierpont 764
Morgan, Sir John 560
Morgan, Peter 811
Morgan, Steve 853
Morgan, Sir Thomas (knighted 1544) 811
Morgan, Sir Thomas (knighted 1623) 817
Morgan, William 560
Morish, Captain Henry 474
Morley, Anne 333
Morley Old Hall 348
Morley St Peter: Morley Old Hall 348
Morning Post article, on Archerfield 735
Morpeth: Belsay Hall 383, 476, 536, 738
Morris, Charles 371
Morris, David 441
Morris, Roger 405
Morris, Colonel Valentine 815
Morris, William 197, 245, 548, 590
Morris-Jones, Nigel & Jane 251, 252
Morrison, Alfred 240
Morrison, James 240
Morrison, Major J.S.F. 167
Morrison, Mabel 240
Morrison, Richard 828
Morrison, Sara 488
Morrison, William Vitruvius 828
mortar bees 645, 653
Mortimer, Roger 627
Morton, Brian 77, 251, 500
Morton, Neil 586
Mostyn family 798
Mostyn, Lady Augusta 798
Mostyn, Colonel Henry 798
Mostyn, Margaret 798
Mostyn: Gyrn Castle 806-7
motor racing
  Captain Woolf Barnato 588
  Donington Park 306
  Santa Pod raceway 23
Moundsmere Manor 12, 236-7, 853
Mount Congreve 632, 836-7
Mount Stuart 753, 767
Mount Temple, Lady 486
Mount Vernon, Virginia, USA 543
Mountain, Sir Brian & Lady 241
Mountbatten, Louis & Edwina, Earl & Countess Mountbatten of Burma 486
Mountfitchet Castle 194
Mountford, Edward 577-9
Mowbray Castle, Hackfall 692
Mowbray Point (The Ruin), Hackfall 692-3
Mowl, Tim 218
Moxham, Mr & Mrs 482
Moxley 569
Muilman, Peter 186
Mundy, Mr 342
Munstead Grange 577-9
Munstead Wood 577, 582, 605
murals & wall paintings
  4 Maids of Honour Row 726, 727
  Beaurepaire 225
  Bower House 179
  Breckles Hall 328
  Brodsworth Hall 684-5
  Burley-on-the-Hill 305
  Castle Bromwich Hall 620
  Clifton Hall 395
  Danson House 270
  Dixton Manor 203
  Ellys Manor House 319
  Elsing Hall 335
  Gosfield Hall 185
  Grovelands 717
  Hapsford House 474-5
  Knightstone Manor 134
  Maynards 277
  Nutley Manor 239
  Rowton Castle 448
  Snowdenham Hall 590

The Soke 245
South Wraxhall Manor 489
Stanford Hall 400
Stibbington Hall 58
Sturford Mead 661
Trafalgar House 665
The Vineyards 248
Wilsley 289
Wotton House 595
murder holes, Maxstoke Castle 628
Murray, Sir Gideon 740
Murray, James 740
Murray, John 740
Murray Rumsey, Commander Robert 636
museums
  1 Royal Crescent (Bath) 486
  American Museum in Britain 459
  Brighton Museum 271
  British Museum 24, 99, 755
  Getty Museum 187
  Jane Austen's House museum 229
  Metropolitan Museum of Art 187, 416, 669
  Natural History Museum 415
  Newbridge curio room 839
  The Reader's House 439
  Sir John Soane's museum 375, 725
  Speed Art Museum 117
  Stibbington Hall 59
  Tong Hall 707
  Wallace Collection 210
  see also Victoria & Albert Museum
music & recording studios
  Burles Lodge 557
  Woodside House 498
music events
  Charleston Manor 603
  Trafalgar House 665
  see also opera
Music Room, Home House 725
Musselburgh: Newhailes 778-9
Musters, John 396
Muthalagappan, Selva & Kumar 396
Muthesius, Hermann 578
Mutual Householders Associaton 185, 356, 550
Mylne, Robert
  King's Weston 209
  Thirlestane Castle 785
  Tusmore House 423
Myott, Irene 72
Myrtle Grove 838
Mysore, Hyder Ali, Sultan of Mysore 792

N
Nadir, Asil 305
Nairn, Ian 554
Nairne, House of 767
Naked Beauty (statue) 190, 191
Nansidwell 88-9
Nantwich:
  Churche's Mansion 11, 13, 71-2
  Doddington Hall 73-4
Napoleon Bonaparte 84, 271, 846
Napoleon III, Emperor 44
Narborough: Narborough Hall 349
Narborough Hall 349
Nares, Gordon 73
Nash, John 846
  4 Cumberland Place 713-15
  Grovelands 717
  Regent's Park terraces 283, 713-15, 730
  Shirburn Castle entrance hall 420
  Sundridge Park 283-6
Nathan, Ronnie 663, 664
National Coal Board 401, 499-500, 510, 684
National Galleries of Scotland 752, 761
National Gallery 306, 478, 754
National Heritage Memorial Fund 50, 104, 106, 112, 442, 444, 492, 500, 684, 762, 765, 789

National Land Fund 376, 389
National Lottery *see* Heritage Lottery Fund
National Trust
  A La Ronde 112
  advisers & staff 370, 450, 490, 570, 571, 799
  Anglesey Abbey 584
  Arlington Court 121
  Ashdown House 407, 450
  Biddulph Grange garden 502-3
  Calke Abbey 50, 106-7, 450, 757
  Chastleton House 444
  comparisons to 157, 238
  Cragside 388-9
  Croome Court 669, 671
  English School, Dedham 182
  Erddig 759
  Gibside 168-9
  Heveningham Hall 529
  Home House (considered) 725
  Homewood 570-1
  Kedleston Hall 774, 775
  land covenants & ownership 34, 88, 497
  Little Moreton Hall 442
  Lytes Cary 468
  Mompesson House 637
  Montacute 466
  Nymans Garden 711
  Peckover 61
  Philipps House 651-2
  Pitchford Hall 442, 444
  Runnymede 585
  Speke Hall 442
  Staunton Harold church 312
  Stokesay Court 449, 450
  Treasurer's House (Martock) 481
  Tyntesfield 246, 490-2
  Uppark 654
  The Vyne 226
National Trust for Scotland
  advisers & staff 734, 778, 783
  Culzean Castle 782
  Fyvie Castle 764-5
  Hill House 743
  Newhailes 778-9
  Tyninghame House (considered) 789
Natural History Museum 415
Naylor, Chris & Kate 79
Naylor, John 808
Naylor, Tony & Gina 79
Needle's Eye, Wentworth Woodhouse 710
Neeld, Sir Audley Dallas 641
Neeld, Lady Caroline 641
Neeld, John 641
Neeld, Joseph 641
Neker, Thomas 527
Nelson, 1st Viscount (Admiral Lord Nelson) 332, 664, 831
Nelson, Rev William Nelson, Earl Nelson of Trafalgar 664
neo-classical
  Duddingston House 751
  Heveningham Hall 529-30
  Lochton House 773-4
  Norton Place 322-4
  Woodfold Park 301
neo-Georgian, Steephill 848-50
Nesbit, William 735
Nesfield, W.A.
  Bylaugh 330
  Coombe Abbey 623
Nesfield, W. Eden 625
Ness Glen 748
Nether Swell Manor 210-11
Nethergate House 531-2
Netley Hall 442
Nevile, Christopher 320
Neville, Claude 468
New Vitruvius Britannicus 73
Newark: Flintham 11, 397-8
Newbold, Clifford 719
Newborough, Rev Page 439
Newbridge 839
Newbury:, Shaw House 41
Newcastle, Dukes of
  1st Duke 616
  4th Duke 725
Newdigate, Sir Roger 19, 180
Newell, Christopher 327
Newhailes 778-9

Newman, John 441
Newman, Cardinal John
  Henry 307
Newport: Penhow Castle 812-
  13
Newport Almeley: Newport
  House 252-3
Newport House 252-3
Newport Pagnell:
  Chicheley 14, 42-3
  Tyringham Hall 13, 16, 53-4,
  404
newspaper articles *see* specific
  newspapers (eg *The Times*)
Newton, Ernest 848-50
Newton, Sir Isaac 392, 419, 420
Newton, Kate 514
Newton, W.G. 848
Newton Surmaville 8
Newtownbutler: Crom Castle
  825
Nichols, Andrew 225
Nicoll, Patrick & Annabel 34,
  36
Nicolson, Harold 134
night club use *see* country club
  & night club use
Nightingale, Frederick 198
Nisbet, James 738
Norfolk, Earls & Dukes of 524
  1st Earl (Hugh Bigod) 524
  3rd Duke (Thomas
  Howard) 350
  6th Duke (Henry Howard)
  550
  11th Duke (Charles
  Howard) 97
Norman, Cranborne Manor
  152-4
Norman, Robert & Carrie
  61-2
Norman Shaw, Richard 853
  Cragside 388-9
  Old English style 568, 569,
  744
  Wilsley House 288
Norris, John & Elizabeth 639
North Breache Manor 579-81
North Luffenham Hall 309-10
North Norfolk Building
  Preservation Trust 347
Northampton, 1st Earl of
  (William Compton) 359
Northampton, Marquesses of
  6th Marquess (William
  Compton) 633
  7th Marquess (Spencer
  Compton) 358, 380
Northampton:
  78 Derngate 374-5
  Ecton Hall 363-4
Northern Heritage Trust 382
Northern Racing 814
Northumberland, Dukes of
  550, 561
  1st Duke (John Dudley) 56
Northwich: Vale Royal Abbey
  81-2
Norton Place 7, 322-4
Norwich, Bishops of 304
Norwich: Thorpe Hall 350-1
Nostell Priory 707
Nottingham, 2nd Earl of
  (Daniel Finch) 304
Nottingham:
  Clifton Hall 16, 393-5
  Colwick Hall 16, 396
Nottingham Castle 394, 627
Nugent, 1st Earl (Robert
  Nugent) 185
Nun Monkton: Nun Monkton
  Hall 700-1
Nun Monkton Hall 700-1
Nunton: Nunton House 645-6
Nunton House 645-6
nursing homes *see* hospital &
  related use; retirement
  home use
Nutley Manor 238-9
Nutting, Captain A.R.S. 579
Nutting, Lady 42
Nutting, Peter 579-81
Nymans Garden 711

O
Oak Hill 299
Oakes, Orbell Ray 539
Oakham:
  Burley-on-the-Hill 304-5,
  313

North Luffenham Hall 309-
  10
oast houses
  Isfield Place 609
  Stocketts Manor 591
Oates, Titus 818
Oatley, Sir George 464
obelisks *see* follies, obelisks &
  temples
observatories, Shirburn Castle
  419
The Observer 421
Occupation of Jersey *see*
  German Occupation of
  Jersey
Ochiltree: Auchinleck 737
Octagon Developments 714
Odo, Bishop of Bayeux 560
O'Donaghue family 65
office conversions & use
  Benham Park 29
  Botleys 552
  Caroline Park 747
  Castle Bromwich Hall 620
  Donington Hall 306
  Duddingston House 751
  Eagle House 716
  Leigh Court 476
  Paper Hall 703
  Puttenham Priory 586
  Tong Hall 707
  Trawsgoed 819
  Wotton House 594
Ogbourne St George: The
  Manor House 647-50
Ogilvy family 767
Ogilvy, Alexander 750
Ogilvy, David Ogilvy, 6th Earl
  of Airlie (Lord Ogilvy) 746
Ogilvy, James Ogilvy, 1st Earl
  of Findlater 750
Ogilvy, Sir Walter Ogilvy, 1st
  Lord Ogilvy of Deskford 750
Oglethorpe, General James
  586
Olana, New York State, USA
  813
Old Bailey 577
Old English
  Brantwoode 743-4
  Holmdale 568-9
  influence on Playfair 761
Old Grammar School 182-3
Old Lochton *see* Lochton
  House
The Old Manor Hall (Walton-
  on-Thames) 7
Old Manor House
  (Benenden) 264-7
Old Palace, Bromley-by-Bow
  614, 853
The Old Rectory (Yardley
  Hastings) 1, 380-1
Old Thorndon Hall 187
Oldcastle, Sir John 253
Olde Ende 130
Olden Manor 14, 53-4
Older, Mark 281
Olias, Marquesa de 120
Oliver, Basil 608
Ollepen, Margery 212
Ollerton: Thoresby Hall 218,
  401-2
Olney Jr., Samuel 207
O'Neil, E.S. 288
Opdahl, ÿrnulf 173
opera & opera companies
  Compton Verney 622
  Glyndebourne Festival
  Opera 235
  Grange Park Opera 235
  Pavilion Opera 327
  Thurston End Hall 539
Opie, John 765
Orange, Prince & Princess of
  107
orangeries *see* conservatories,
  glasshouses & orangeries
Orbell, Tim 539
Orchardleigh 483-4
Orchards 582
Order of St John of Jerusalem
  804
O'Reilly, Captain & Mrs Derek
  659
organs
  Danson House 271
  Leigh Court 476
oriel windows, description
  223

Orlebar family 22, 23
Orlebar, Richard & Diana 22
Ormerod, George 75
Ormsby, Mary Jane 432
Ormsby-Gore, J.R. Ormsby-
  Gore, 1st Baron Harlech 432
Ormsby-Gore, William &
  Mary Jane 432
Orphoot, Whiting & Lindsay
  736
Orpin, Sir William 288
Osbaldestone, George ('Squire
  of England') 690
Osborne, Sir John & Osborne
  family 19
Osborne, Michael 741
Osborne House 535
Osgodby, William 637
Osmond, Sam 567
Osterley Park 606
Oswald, Arthur
  Chicheley attribution 43
  Kingston Maurward
  attribution 160
  Shillinglee Park article 616
Oswestry: Brogyntyn 432-3
O'Toole family 831
Ottley, Thomas 443
Oulton Hall 702
Oundle: Apethorpe Hall 354-5
Owen, Sir John 432
Owen, William 432
Owlpen 212
Oxford Gardens (no 50) 728-9
Oxford University & colleges
  153, 218, 223, 354, 404, 424,
  457, 658
Oxted: Stocketts Manor 591-3

P
Pace, Richard 37
Packe, Colonel G.H. 315, 316
Page, Russell 660
Page, William & Bridget 59
Paget family 215
Paget, Sir William 514
Paine, James 712
  Axwell Park 166
  Belford Hall 382, 384
  Bywell Hall 384
  Shrubland Park 535-7
  Thorndon Hall 13, 196
  Wardour Castle 666
Painshill Park 169
Painted Hall, Greenwich 179
paintings & sketches
  of Astley Pool House 667
  of Bridge Place 268
  of Constable Burton 688
  of Cound Hall 437
  of Danson House 270
  of Dixton Manor 202
  of Elsing Hall 334
  of Fasque Castle 756
  of Gillingham Hall 336, 337
  of Greyfriars 566
  of Hedenham Hall 344
  of House of Gray 767
  of Minsterley Hall 441
  of Nun Monkton Hall 700-1
  of Paxhill 613
  of Tong Hall 707
  of Tor Worley 846
  see also art collections;
  murals & wall paintings;
  specific artists (eg Turner)
Pakington & Enthoven 650
Palace of Westminster *see*
  Houses of Parliament
Palace Street (no 6) 799-800
Paler, George 701
Palladian
  Apethorpe Hall 354-5
  Ascot Place 13, 26
  Asgill House 551
  Auchinleck 737
  Barlaston Hall 499-501
  Belcombe Court 634
  Blackland Park 635-6
  Botleys 552
  Bower House 179
  Brough Hall 685-6
  Buckland Hall 32
  Burles Lodge interiors 556
  Bywell Hall 384
  Carton House 822
  Chute Lodge 640
  Clifton Castle 687
  Colwick Hall 396
  Constable Burton 7, 688-9

Craigengillan stables 748
Culham Court 34-6
Duddingston House 751
Ebberston Hall 7, 690
Edgcote House 365
Eydon Hall 9, 14, 366-8
Gibside stable block 168
Gunton Hall 339-43
Gwerclas Hall 802-4
Harleyford Manor 6, 35,
  44-5
House of Gray 766-7
Ingestre Pavilion 511
Kelly House 132-3
Kingston Russell 161
Kirtlington Park 416
Leigh Court 476-7
Lochton House 773-4
Lupton House 136
Mavisbank House 776
Milford House 576
Newhailes 778-9
Norton Place 322-4
Parish's House 484-6
Puttenham Priory 587
Regent's Park Villas 730
Sharpham House 144-5
Shrubland Park 535-7
Tabley Hall 80-1
Thame Park 51-2
Thorndon Hall 196
Thorpe Tilney Hall 327
Trewarthenick 94
Tusmore House 423-4
Upton House 220-1
  villas 220
Wakefield Lodge 378-80
Waldershare belvedere 287
Wentworth Woodhouse
  708-10
Wimborne House 163-4
Wolverton Hall 674-5
Palladio, Andrea 551
Pallaskenry: Dromore Castle
  826
Palmer, 4th Baron (Lord
  Palmer) 775
Palmer, Elizabeth 551
Palmer, Lewis 391
Palmer, Mabel 391
Palmer-Astley, Francis
  Dukinfield 736
Palmer-Tomkinson family 238
Palmerston, 3rd Viscount
  (Lord Palmerston) 597
panelling
  4 Maids of Honour Row 727
  Ashbury Manor 407
  Auchinleck 737
  Ayot Mountfitchet 257
  Barkisland Hall 681
  Breda Room 554
  Bridge Place 268
  Brook Place 554
  Burles Lodge 556
  Canonteign Manor 120
  Caverswall Castle 506
  Cedar Cottage 558
  Charleston Manor 602
  Chawton House 228
  Churche's Mansion 72
  Colebrook House 231
  Cooke's House 603, 605
  The Court House (Martock)
  482
  Eagle House 716
  Elsing Hall 335
  Fawley House 413
  The Grange
  (Broadhembury) 117-18
  The Grange (Ramsgate) 279
  Great Treverren 82
  Gyrn Castle 807
  Harrington Hall 321
  Hatfield Priory 187
  Horham Hall 189-90
  House of Gray 767
  Kelly House 132, 133
  Kildwick Hall 697
  Kingston Russell 161
  The Manor House
  (Ogbourne St George) 650
  Manor House (Sutton
  Courtenay) 422
  Minsterley Hall 441
  Munstead Grange 578
  Nunton House 646
  Old Grammar School 183
  Old Palace, Bromley-by-
  Bow 851

Paxhill 614
Pellicane House 278
Penhow Castle 813
Penwho Castle 813
Rous Lench Court 673
Rowden Manor 655-6
St Ouen's Manor 844
Steephill 849, 850
Stibbington Hall 58
Stinsford House 162
Stockton 659
Stoneleigh Abbey 630, 631
Thame Park 52
Tong Hall 707
Trinity Manor 853
Troy House 821
Wallington Hall 353
Walpole House 732, 733
Wilsley 289
Wingfield College 544, 545
Yeaton Pevery 453
Youlston Park 146
Pangbourne: Bowden 30-1
Paper Hall 703
papier mache mouldings,
  Auchinleck 737
Pappet, Miss 727
Papworth, J.B. 193
pargetting
  Little Bardfield Hall 194
  Yew Tree House 548
Parish, Captain & Mrs John
  484-5, 486
Parish's House 484-6
Park, Castle of 745-6
Park Close 583-5
Park Cottage 808-9
Parker family 114
Parker, John (Boringdon) 114
Parker, John (carriage driver)
  545
Parker, Thomas (joiner) 469
Parker, Thomas (Puttenham
  Priory) 587
parks
  Apley Park 429, 430
  Ashton Court 454
  Axwell Park 166
  Balbirnie 738
  Barford House 455, 456
  Benham Park 29
  Blackland Park 635
  Bretby Hall 102-3
  Brogyntyn 433
  Brough Hall 685
  Buxted Park 601
  Calke Abbey 106
  Callaly Castle 385, 386
  Carton House 823
  Cockfield Hall 521, 523
  Constable Burton 688, 689
  Crom Castle 825
  Croome Court 669
  Doddington Hall 73
  Dodington Park 204
  Downe Hall 155
  Duddingston House 751
  Dumfries House 753
  Dunmore Park 754
  Eggesford House 121
  Eydon Hall 367
  Floors Castle 759
  Gibside 169
  Golders Green Park 720
  Grovelands 717
  Gunton Hall 339, 343
  Halswell 471
  Heath House 509
  Hengrave Hall 528
  Highcliffe Castle 7, 158
  Keith Hall 772, 773
  Kingston Lisle 37
  The Manor House
  (Buckland) 33
  Miller's Tower 763
  Narborough Hall 349
  Newhailes 779
  North Luffenham Hall 309
  Philipps House 651
  Piercefield 815
  Poston House 255
  Puttenham Priory 586
  Shillinglee Park 616
  Shireoaks 399
  Shrubland Park 537
  Staunton Harold Hall 311,
  312
  Swinfen Hall 515
  Thorndon Hall 196
  Tottenham Park 662
  Trawsgoed 819

Trevor Hall 820
Trewarthenick 94
Tyningham House 789
Tyringham Hall 53
Valentine's 731
Wakefield Lodge 378
Waldershare 287
Wentworth Woodhouse 708, 710
Wimborne Houses 164
Worlingham Hall 547
Youlston Park 146, 147
see also Brown, Capability; Repton, Humphry
Parkyns, Sir Thomas Parkyns, 1st Baron Rancliffe ('the wrestling baronet') 103, 392–3
Parliament *see* Houses of Parliament
Parminter, Jane & Mary 112
Parr, Tom 810
Parry, Edward 332
Parry, Sidney Gampier 310
Parsons, John 853
Parsons, Martin 711, 712
Parsons, William 315
Paston, Edward 350
Paston, Sir William 350
Paterson, John
    Brancepeth Castle 167
    Fasque Castle 756–7
    Keith Hall 773
Patshull Hall 17, 429, 512–13
pausilippe 550
Pavilion Opera 327
pavilions
    Auchinleck 737
    Barford House 455
    Belcombe Court 634
    Burles Lodge 555–7
    Copped Hall 181
    Culham Court 35
    Ebberston Hall 690
    Gunton Hall 340–1, 342
    Hampton Court Palace 9
    Holmdale 569
    Ingestre Pavilion 511
    Leyburn Hall 699
    The Menagerie 371
    Mount Congreve 836
    Nutley Manor 238, 239
    Paxhill 615
    The Pineapple, Dunmore 754
    Poston House 254, 255
    Puttenham Priory 587
    Stanford Hall 400
    Stoke Park 377
    Thorpe Tilney Hall 327
    Tyringham Hall 53, 54
    Vellore House 792
    Wrottesley Hall 517
Pavillon, Charles 270
Paxhill 613–15
Paxton, Sir Joseph 11, 48, 398, 597, 834
Paylor, George 701
Paylor, Nathaniel* 700, 701
Payne, Sir Ralph 640
Pearce, Jeremy 699
Pearson, J.L. 304
Peck, Gregory 601
Peckforton Castle 17, 78–9
Peckham, Arthur Nye 291
Peckham, James 290
Peckham, Reginald 290
Peckover family 61
Peek, Sir Henry 143
Peel, Edmund 83
pele towers
    Blencowe Hall 95–8
    Callaly Castle 385
    Hayton Hall 99
Pell Well Hall 805
Pellew, Sir Edward Pellew, 1st Viscount Exmouth 119–20, 145
Pellicane House 278
Pember, Devereux 253
Pember, Thomas 253
Pembroke, Earls of
    1st Earl, 4th creation (Laurence Hastings) 333
    1st Earl, 10th creation (William Herbert) 658
    3rd Earl, 10th creation 817
Pencoed Castle 811
Penhow Castle 812–13
Penistone, David 520

Pennine Heritage Trust, Clegg Hall 268, 296
penny-struck pointing 187, 561, 645
Penrith: Blencowe Hall 95–8
Percy family 701
Percy Johnson-Marshall & Partners 751
Period Living article, Puttenham Priory 586
Perkin & Backhouse 702
Perkins, Margaret Tudor 111–12
Perkins, Bryan 360, 361
Perkins, James
    Aynho 16, 356
    Dowdeswell Court 16, 185, 206, 207, 208, 356
    Gosfield Hall 185
Perkins, Margaret 674
Persaud, Ron & Kay 613, 614, 615
Pershore: Wolverton Hall 674–5
Pesaro Palace 730
Petch, Andrew 808, 809
Peter, Alexander 753
Peterborough, Abbots of 63
Peterborough, Earls of 247
Peterborough, Soke of 63, 244
Peterborough:
    Stibbington Hall 57–9
    Woodcroft Castle 63–5
Peters, Judge 640
Petersfield: Durford Court 232–3
Petit Hibeaux 845
Peto, Sir Henry 151
Petre, 8th & 9th Barons 196
Pevsner, Nikolaus & *Pevsner Architectural Guides*
    articles 223
    Brympton d'Evercy 465
    Canonteign Manor 119, 120
    Chawton House 228
    Durford Court 232
    Edwinsford 801
    Falkner, Harold 557
    Gribloch 769
    Hanger Hill Garden Estate 718
    Inverlochy Castle 771
    Minsterley Hall 441
    Netley Hall 442
    Peckforton Castle 78
    Saddlewood Manor 215
    Seton House 783
    Staunton Harold Hall 311
    Tyringham Hall 53
    Wakefield Lodge 380
    Woodcroft Castle 63
pews, Biggs family 659
Pewterers' Hall 472
Phelps, Mr 486
Philimore, Claud 423
Philip III, Duke of Burgundy 759
Philipps, Bertram 652
Philipps House 651–2
Philips family 509
Phillimore, Claud 424
Phillips, Emma 799
Phillips, Nicholas 25
Pickard, A.E. 762
Pickering, Lionel 109
Pickering: Ebberston Hall 7, 690
Pickford, Joseph 110
Pickstock, Roland 432
Picturesque
    The Abbey (Charlton Adam) 467–8
    Hackfall 692
    Heath House 12, 14, 508–9
    Lanhill House 641
    Stocketts Manor 591–3
    villas 458
pier glasses *see* mirrors & pier glasses
Pierce, Edward 619
Piercefield 813–15
Piers Court 213
pigeon houses *see* dovecotes & pigeon houses
Pigot, Sir George 512
pigs, piggeries & pigsties
    Alt-y-Bela 796
    Botleys 552
    Sker House 818
    Stocken Hall 314

Pilgrim family 89
pill box, Chilworth Manor 561
Pimlico House 262–3
Pinch, John 661
Pinder, Catherine 324
Pinder, Rev Robert 324
The Pineapple, Dunmore 754
pineapples 422
Pinfold family 213
Pinochet, General Augusto 717
Pinwill, Captain William 91
Pirie, Sarah 691
piscina, Woodcroft Castle 65
Pitchford: Pitchford Hall 442–4
Pitchford Hall 442–4
Pitmain Lodge 780
Pitt, George 160
Pitt, John 156–7, 160
Pitt, Thomas, 1st Earl Camelford 84
Pitt, Thomas iDiamondi 84
Pitt, William (Pitt the Elder/Earl of Chatham) 156, 460
Pitt, William Morton 160
P.J. Livesey Group
    Hill Hall 188
    Ingress Abbey 275
    Wyfold Court 15, 427
Plaish Hall 445
planters, Ridgemead 589
Plas Teg 797, 816
Plas Uchaf 804
plasterwork & stucco decoration
    48 Storey's Way 60
    Apethorpe Hall 355
    Ballencrieff Castle 740
    Barlaston Hall 501
    Bathealton Court 462
    Belcombe Court 634
    Belford Hall 382
    Bettisfield Park 797
    Bridge Place 269
    Brockhurst Hall 70
    Brough Hall 686
    Caroline Park 747
    Carton House 822
    Castle Bromwich Hall 619
    Clifton Hall 395
    Cooke's House 605
    Coton Hall 436
    Cransley Hall 361
    Croome Court 669
    Edwinsford 801
    Fasque Castle 756–7
    Fota 828
    Glin Castle 829
    The Grove 841
    Gyrn Castle 807
    Halswell 471, 472, 473
    Harleyford Manor 44
    Heath House 509
    Hilton Park 831
    Holland House 722
    Home House 724, 725
    Knightstone Manor 10
    Little Bardfield Hall 194
    Melton Constable Hall 346
    Munstead Grange 578
    Newbridge 839
    Olden Manor 534
    Oulton Hall 702
    Paxhill 614, 615
    Pimlico House 263
    Poulton House 654
    Ramsay Garden 781
    Rashleigh Barton 141, 142
    Shrubland Park 536
    Steephill 850
    Stockton 659
    Stoneleigh Abbey 630, 631
    Sundridge Park 283, 286
    Taymouth Castle 784
    Thirlestane Castle 785, 786
    Tottenham Park 662, 663
    Trafalgar House 665
    Troy House 821
    Upton House 221
    Wentworth Woodhouse 709
    Womersley Hall 712
    Youlston Park 146–7
    see also pargetting
plate racks, Hanger Hill Garden Estate 719
Platt, John 707

Player, W.G. 108, 109
Playfair, James 777
Playfair, William Henry 759, 761
Plowden & Smith 271
Plunket, 6th Baron (Lord Plunket) 659
Plymouth:
    Boringdon 114
    Maristow House 137–9
Pocock, J.C. 60
Pococke, Bishop 761
Podington church 22
Pogges family 409
pointing, penny-struck 187, 561, 645
Pole, de la *see* de la Pole family
Polesworth: Bramcote Hall 618
police colleges
    Bramshill 227
    King's Weston 209
Polizzi, Olga 126
Pollard, Richard 302
polo grounds, Kirtlington Park 416
Poltimore 140
ponds *see* lakes, pools & canals
Pont-y-Prydd bridge 801
Pontefract: Ledstone Hall 13, 698
Ponting, C.E. 468
Poole, Colin & Michele 442
pools *see* lakes, pools & canals
Pope, Nori & Sandra 470
Pope, Robin 664
Pope Hennessy, Sir John 838
Port Eliot 90
Portarlington, 1st Earl of 827
portego 403
portes cochÈre
    Apley Park 430
    Brodsworth Hall 683
    Dunmore Park 754
    Fasque Castle 756
    Flintham 397
    Heath House 508
    Hilton Park 831
    Inverlochy Castle 771
    Sarsden House 418
    Valentine's 731
    Woolton Hall 302
    Wynyard Park 175
porticoes
    Balbirnie 738
    Benham Park 184
    Brockhurst Hall 70
    Brogyntyn 432
    Buxted Park 601
    Calke Abbey 107
    Caythorpe Hall 315–16
    Constable Burton 688, 689
    Croome Court 670
    Dodington Park 13, 204
    Dowdeswell Court 206, 207
    Duddingston House 751
    Eastwood Farm 606
    Emo Court 827
    Eydon Hall 366, 367
    Grange Park 234, 235
    Grovelands 717
    The Hasells 21
    Hilton Park 831
    Himley Hall 510
    Howick Hall 391
    Kirtlington Park 416
    Leigh Court 476, 477
    Luton Hoo 24
    Manderston House 775
    Melton Constable Hall 346
    The Menagerie pavilions 371
    Philipps House 652
    Seafield House 846
    Seaham 173
    Steephill 849
    Tabley Hall 80, 81
    Thorndon Hall 13, 196
    Trafalgar House 665
    Trawsgoed 801
    Tusmore House 423, 424
    Wentworth Woodhouse 709
    Wynyard Park 175
portières, Brodsworth Hall 685
Portman Estate 725
Portman Square, London: Home House 723–5
Portsmouth, 6th Earl of 121
Portwood, George 313
Portyngton, Mr 403
Postins, David 256, 257

Poston House 254–5
Potterspury: Wakefield Lodge 14, 378–80
Poulteney, Thomas 304
Poulton: Poulton Manor 214–15
Poulton House 653–4
Poulton Manor 214–15
pouncing designs 501
Powell, Ken 296
Powell, Turner 130–1
power boat racing, Countess of Arran 263
power supply
    Callaly Castle 386
    Holystreet Manor 130
    Woodside House 498
Powerscourt 834
Powis, Lybbe 44
Powis Castle 808, 820
Pownall, Jane 145
Pownall, Captain Philemon 144, 145
Powys family (Barons Lilford) 372
Powys, Mrs Philip Lypp 36
Powys, Thomas 372
Praed, William 53
Pratt, Joseph 552
Pratt, Roger 346, 619
prefabrication, Huf Haus 573–5
Preston family 63
Preston Candover:
    Moundsmere Manor 12, 236–7, 853
    Nutley Manor 238–9
Preston-on-the-Weald Moors: The Almshouses 446–7
Prestonpans: Seton House 782–3
Price, Chancellor 676
Price, David 320
Price, Leo 499
priest holes
    Brook Place 554
    Sawston Hall 56
    Thorpe Hall 350
Priestley, Joseph 507
Prince, John 11
    Buntingsdale Hall Hall 434
    Cound Hall 437
Prince Regent *see* George IV
Prior, E.S. 155
Prior Park 480
priories *see* monastic origins
prison & related use
    Apethorpe Hall 355
    Axwell Park 166, 384
    Bassett House 458
    Donington Hall 306
    Hill Hall 188
    Staunton Harold Hall 312
    Stocken Hall 8, 313–14
    Swinfen Hall 8, 515
Pritchard, Thomas Farnolls 435, 443, 667
prize ships 144, 484, 587
Procter, Basil 562
prodigy houses
    Bramshill 227
    Brereton Hall 67–9
    Cockfield Hall 521–3
    Fyvie Castle 764–5
Prowse, Thomas 180
public inquiries
    Archerfield 735
    Barlaston Hall 499–500, 510
    Bettisfield Park 797
    Brympton d'Evercy 466
    Burley-on-the-Hill 305
    Governor's House (Berwick-upon-Tweed) 390
    The Hasells 20
    Hellaby Hall 694
    Hylands House 192
    Llangoed Hall 810
    Revesby Abbey 325
    Stocken Hall 313
pubs
    Colwich Hall 396
    Danson House stables 271
    Feathers Inn, Ludlow 438
    George Inn, Glastonbury 406
    Newport House clock house 253
    The Salutation site 280, 281
Pugin, A.W.N.

Albury Park 550
comparisons to 678
Grace Dieu Manor chapel 307
Lismore Castle 834
The Grange (Ramsgate) 279
wallpapers 279, 679
Pugin, Edward 279
Purslow, Martin 270
Puttenham: Puttenham Priory 586-7
Puttenham Priory 586-7
Pye, William 173
Pygott, Francis 21
Pyle: Sker House 818
Pym, Francis* 20, 21
Pym, William 21
Pythouse 659

Q

Quarenghi, Giacomo 366
Queen Anne
Aldhams 177-8
Braybrooke House 637
The Broad House 329
Cound Hall 437
Cransley Hall 12, 360-1
Eagle House 716
Eardisley 251 -2
Ednaston Manor 108-9
Fawley House 411-13
flush-set sash windows 13, 637
Great Treverren 86-7
Herondon 6
Isfield Place 607-9
The Manor House (Milton Lilbourne) 644
Milford House 576
North Luffenham Hall 309
Nunton House 645-6
The Old Rectory (Yardley Hastings) 380-1
Poulton House 853-4
Rowton Castle 448
Trehane 91-3
Wolverton Hall 674-5
Queen Elizabeth & *Queen Mary* (ships) 807
The Queen magazine, on Nethergate House 532
Queen Mother, Queen Elizabeth the Queen Mother 132, 206
Queen's House, Greenwich 380
Quiney, Anthony 293
Quinn, Margaret 719

R

R-34 airship 758
RAC building 24, 53
racecourse, Chepstow 813, 814
racing *see* specific types (eg motor racing)
radiators *see* heating
Radnor, Earls of 645
Raeburn, Henry 765
railings
50 Orchard Gardens 729
Fife House 597, 598
Railton, William 307
railways, Leighton estate funicular railway 808-9
Raine, Countess Spencer 364
rainwater gutter, The Manor House (Ogbourne St George) 650
rainwater heads
Adderbury House 404
Anderson Manor 148
Bibury Court 197
Brogyntyn 432
Chicheley 43
Colebrook House 231
Dunham Lodge 332
Eagle House 716
The Ivy 639
Leyburn Hall 699
Nethergate House 532
Park Close 583
Paxhill 615
Poulton House 653
Sawston Hall 5
Stibbington Hall 58, 59
Stocketts Manor 593
Stockton 659
Trehane 91, 92
Twyford Moors House 247
Valentine's 731

Wilsley 289
Raleigh, Sir Walter 114, 353, 716, 834, 838
Ralli, Sir Strati 224
Ramsay, Sir Alexander 756
Ramsay Garden 781
Ramsbury Manor 281, 346, 653
Ramsgate: The Grange 279
Rancliffe, Barons
1 st Baron (Sir Thomas Parkyns, the 'wrestling baronet') 103, 392-3
2nd Baron 393
Randyll family 560-1
Randyll, Morgan 561
Randyll, Vincent 561
Ranger's House, Greenwich 25
Rannie, Sir David 777
Rannie, Elizabeth 777
Rashleigh Barton 141-2
Ratcliffe, Tim 611
Ratcliffe family 400
Raven, Thomas 345
Rawnsley, Edward Preston 322
Ray, Martha 539
Raymond, Charles 731
Rayson, Thomas 410
The Reader's House 438-9
Ream, Lilian 61
rectory use
The Abbey (Charlton Adam) 467
Ellys Manor House 318-19
Fawley House 411-13
Great Snoring Manor 338
The Old Rectory (Yardley Hastings) 380-1
St Joseph's Abbey 617
Red Books *see* Repton, Humphry & Red Books
Redland Court House 464
Redlynch: Redlynch House 487
Redlynch House 487
Redmill, John 235
Reform Club 450, 536
Reformation *see* Dissolution of the Monasteries & English Reformation
refugee hostels
Donington Hall 306
Edwinsford 801
Gwrych Castle 804
Hayton Hall 100
Trehane 91
Tysoe Manor 633
Regency
4 The Crescent (Wisbech) 61 -2
4 Cumberland Place 713-15
A La Ronde 111-12
Achnacarry 734
Ashman's Hall 518
Balbirnie 738
Bassett House 458-9
Brereton Hall 67-9
Brockhurst Hall 70
Brogyntyn 432-3
Caythorpe Hall 315-17
Church House (Bibury) 199-201
Clifton Castle 687
Coton Hall 435-6
Dowdeswell Court 206-8
Endsleigh 123-6
Fasque Castle 756-7
Fota 828
Grange Park 234-5, 383, 536, 738
Gunton Hall 339-43
Gyrn Castle 806-7
Hapsford House 473-5
Hayton Hall 99-100
Himley Hall 510
Hylands House 192-3
Kingston Lisle 37-8
Lambton Castle 172
Lochton House 773-4
Maperton 9, 14, 478-80
Nutley Manor 238-9
Oak Hill 299
Parish's House 484-6
Poltimore 140
Sarsden House 418
Seafield House 846-7
Sturford Mead 660-1
Tottenham Park 662-4
Westgate House 540-1

Worlingham Hall 546-7
Regency/18th century Gothic
Apley Park 428-30
Brereton Hall 67-9
Chicksands Priory 18-19
Erskine House 755
Gibside Banqueting House 168, 169
see also Strawberry Hill Gothick
Regency Villa, Regent's Park 730
Regent's Park, London:
4 Cumberland Place 713-15
Nash terraces 283, 713-15, 730
Regent's Park Villas 730
Regent's Park Villas 730
Reilly Developments 17, 301
religious retreats *see* convents, seminaries & religious retreats
Remon family 845
Rendel, Stuart, 1st Baron Rendel (Lord Rendel) 569
Rendlesham, 5th Baron (Lord Rendlesham) 683
Rennie, John 275
Rennie Mackintosh, Charles 78 Derngate 374-5
Hill House 743
Rennie, Robert 804
Repton, George Stanley 418
Repton, Humphry & Red Books 508
Endsleigh 123, 126
Grovelands 717
Hill Hall 188
Hylands House 193
Oulton Hall 702
Sarsden House 418
Sundridge Park 283
The Hasells 20, 21
Trewarthenick 94
residential conversions & enabling development
Adderbury House 405
The Almshouses (Preston-on-the-Weald Moors) 446-7
Apethorpe Hall 355
Apley Park 429
Archerfield 735
Axwell Park 166
Belford Hall 382
Biddulph Grange 502-3
Brancepeth Castle 167
Bretby Hall 102-3
Brockhurst Hall 70
Brough Hall 686
Brympton d'Evercy 466
Buntingsdale Hall 434
Burley-on-the-Hill 304, 305
Callaly Castle 385, 386
Caroline Park 747
Chute Lodge 640
Cragside 388
Crawford Manor 297
Croome Court 671
Crowcombe Court 469
Dingley Hall 362-3
Downe Hall 155
Duddingston House 751
Dunmore Park 754
Ecton Hall 363-4
Finedon Hall 369
Governor's House (Berwick-upon-Tweed) 390
Grimshaw Hall 626
Grovelands 717
Gunton Hall 339-43, 346
The Hasells 20-1
Hayton Hall 100
Heath House 509
High Head Castle 101
Hill Hall 188
Ingress Abbey 275
The Ivy 639
Keith Hall 772-3
Kirtlington Hall 416
Lawton Hall 16-17, 17
Ledstone Hall 698
Maristow House 139
Melton Constable Hall 346-7
Melville Castle 777
Middleton Park 417
Milford House 576
Miller's Tower 762-3

Nether Swell Manor 210-11
Nethergate House 532
Orchards 532
Oulton Hall 702
Ramsay Garden 781
Redlynch House 487
Revesby Abbey 325-6
Rousdon House 143
Ruperra Castle 817
St Joseph's Abbey 15, 617
Shillinglee Park 15, 616
Snowdenham Hall 15, 590
Stayley Hall 300
Stinsford House 162
Stocken Hall 313-14
Stokesay Court 450
Stoneleigh Abbey 631
Styche Hall 451
Sundridge Park 286
Thorndon Hall 196
Trawsgoed 819
Troy House 821
Tyninghame House 15, 32, 735, 789-91
Valentine's 731
Waldershare 287
Walmoor House 83
Wardour Castle 666
Wentworth Woodhouse 709
Weston Hall 516
Woodfold Park 17, 301
Wrottesley Hall 517
Wyfold Court 425-7
Yeaton Pevery 453
restaurant use *see* hotel & related use
retirement home use
Adderbury House 404, 405
Albury Park 550
Aynho 356
Balcombe Place 597
Crowcombe Court 469
Frognal House 272
Goddards 563
Gosfield Hall 185
Maristow House 138
Oak Hill 299
Wedderburn Castle 795
Revesby Abbey 325-6
Revett, Nicholas 665
Reynolds, Fiona 490
Reynolds, Joshua 765
Reynolds, Paul 516
Rhodes, David & Joan 681
Rhondda, 1 st Viscount & Viscountess (Lord & Lady Rhondda) 811
Ricardo, Halsey 582
Richard II, King 542, 627
Richard III, King 543
Richards, Patricia Kenneth 417
Richardson, Sir Albert 380-1
Richardson, Caroline 265
Richardson, Pamplin 539
Richardson, Mr & Mrs Peter 381
Richardson, Thomas 338
Richelieu, Cardinal 96
Richmond, 2nd Duke of 822
Richmond, John 344
Richmond (Yorkshire):
Brough Hall 685-6, 699
Richmond-on-Thames:
4 Maids of Honour Row 726-7
Asgill House 15, 511, 551, 730
Rickman, Thomas 804
Ridding, George 230
Ridgemead 9, 588-9
Ridley family 480
Ridley, Nicholas 642
Riley, Athelstan 851-3
Ripley Castle 322
Ripon: Hackfall 692-3
Ritz, Cèsar & Marie Louise 588, 677
Ritz Hotel, London 24, 54, 236, 238, 774
River Teign 130, 131, 132
Roake, Quentin 17, 276, 277
Robarts, Elsie 310
Roberts, David 799
Roberts, Edward 656
Roberts, John 820
Roberts, Owen & Anne 523
Roberts, Wenham 110
Robertson, Daniel 824
Robertson, James & Felicity (Nansidwell) 89
Robertson, James

(Duddingston House park) 751
Robin, Charles Janvrin 848
Robin Hood's Hut, Halswell Park 471, 473
Robinson family 361, 705
Robinson, Geoffrey 582
Robinson, Henry 361
Robinson, John* 361
Robinson, John Martin 34, 49
Robinson, Sir Thomas 709
Roborough, 1st Baron (Sir Henry Lopes) 138
Robson, Michael 348
Rochdale: Clegg Hall 11, 268, 296
Roche, Brian & Elizabeth 259
Rochester, 2nd Earl of (John Wilmot) 404-5
Rock of Cashel 826
rockeries, Culham Court 36
Rockingham, Marquesses of
1 st Marquess 708, 709
2nd Marquess 708, 710
Rodney, Admiral George 587
Rodney Melville & Partners 622
Rodwell, Kirsty 501
Rodwell, Warwick 623, 815
Rogers family 208
Rogers, Cara 584-5
Rogers, Ginger 769
Rogers, Hester 206, 208
Rolph, Dr Gerald 15, 678, 679
Romanov, Anastasia 24, 25
Romford: Bower House 179
Romney, George 765
Rooke, Susan 639
Rookes, William 703
rooms sold *see* exported rooms
Roosevelt, Alfred 197
Roosevelt, Elfrida 197
Roosevelt, Theodore 197
Rootes, Lord 281
Roper, Lanning 199
Roper, Patrick Trevor 816
Rosebery, Earls of
4th Earl 754
5th Earl (Lord Rosebery) & Countess (Hannah de Rothschild) 49-50
Ross, Alexander (Ross & Macbeth) 758
Ross-on-Wye: Barge House 17, 249-50
Rosse, Earls of
4th Earl & Countess 712
6th Earl & Countess (Michael & Anne) 711, 712
Rosser, Mike 17
Rossi, Anthony 351
Roston, Paul 129
Rothbury:
Callaly Castle 385-6
Cragside 388-9
Rothermere, Viscounts (Lord Rothermere) 262, 265
Rothery, Mr 327
Rothesay, Lord Stuart de 158-9
Rothschild, Hannah de (Countess of Rosebery) 49
Rothschild, James de 61
Rothschild, Baron Meyer Amschel de 48-9
rotundas *see* domes, cupolas & rotundas
'rough wooing' 740
Rous, Sir Thomas 673
Rous Lench: Rous Lench Court 672
Rous Lench Court 672
Rousdon House 143
Rouse, Clive 319
Rouse-Broughton, Sir Henry 673
Rowan, Alistair 782
Rowden Manor 655-6
Rowland, Paul 206
Rowlands, Dr M.J. 580
Rowlands Gill:
Gibside 168-9
Hamsterley Hall 170-1
Rowlatt, Sir Sidney 88-9
Rowntree, Nick & Louise 558
Rowton: Rowton Castle 448
Rowton Castle 448
Roxburgh Castle 759
Roxburghe, Dukes & Earls of

1st Earl (Robert Ker) 759
5th Earl & 1st Duke 759, 761
6th Duke & Duchess 761
10th Duke & Duchess 761
Royal Academy 234, 283
Royal Automobile Club
building 24, 53
Royal Commission on
Historical Monuments 76,
249
Royal Courts of Justice 568,
804
*Royal Horticultural Society
Journal* 91
Rudd, Thomas 176
Rudolph, Archduke Rudolph,
Crown Prince of Austria 847
Rue, Thomas de la 21
The Ruin (Mowbray Point),
Hackfall 692-3
Rumsey, Commander Robert
Murray 636
Rundell, Philip 641
Rundle, Abraham 132-3
Runeckles family 548
Runeckles, Arthur 548
Runnymede 585
Ruperra Castle 174, 817
Rupert, Prince 268
Rushton 376
Ruskin, John 743
Russell, Emma 167
Russell, Matthew 167
Russell, William 167
Ryan, Sim Van Der 552
Ryder, Captain Richard 154
Rysbrack, John Michael 464

S

Sackville, Barbara 197
Sackville, Elizabeth 197
Sackville, Henry 197
Sackville, Sir Thomas 197
Sackville-West, Vita 176, 335
The Sacrifice of Diana (statue)
187
saddlestones 591
Saddleworth Manor 14, 215-17
Said, Wafic 424
Sainsbury family 238
Sainsbury, Simon 382
St Albyn family 495
St Andrews, Bishops of 790
St Aubyn, (James)Piers 138
St Baldred 790
St Brelade: Les Lumières 14, 17,
842
St Carthage 833
St Clair, Major-General G.P. &
Charlotte 221
St Dunstan 406
St George's, Hanover Square
664
St Germain, Comte de 726
St Germans, 9th & 10th Earls
of 90
St Germans:
Catchfrench Manor 85
Port Eliot 90
St Innocent's shrine & relics
686
St James's Palace 217, 282
St John Hope, Lady (Miss
Jefferies) 531 -2
St Joseph's Abbey 15, 617
St Lawrence:
The Grove 840-1
Petit Hibeaux 845
Seafield House 846-7
St Martin-in-the-Fields 446
St Maur, Sir Roger de 812, 813
St Ouen: St Ouen's Manor
843-4
St Ouen's Manor 843-4
St Paulinus Church, Brough
Hall 686
St Paul's Cathedral 577
St Paul's Church, Covent
Garden 551
St Quintin family 728
St Quintin, Matthew Chitty
Downes 729
St Saviour: Steephill 848-50
St Thomas's Hospital 728
Sainthill, Peter 115
Salamonic columns 539, 620
Salder, Rev Ottiwell 495
Salisbury, Dowager Lady 152
Salisbury, Earls of
1st Earl (Robert Cecil) 153

2nd Earl 153 -4
Salisbury, Marquesses of
2nd Marquess 154
3rd Marquess (Lord
Salisbury, Prime Minister)
154
4th Marquess 154
5th Marquess 154
Salisbury:
Braybrooke House 637-8
Trafalgar House 664-5
Salisbury Cathedral & Close
157, 520, 637-8, 651, 726
Salisbury House 153
salmon-fishing record 759
Salt II, Titus 449
Saltoun, Lords 745
Saltram House 114
Salts, Leslie 805
The Salutation 280-1
salvaged materials
Barge House 250
Breda Room panelling,
Goodrich Court & Brook
Place 554
Burles Lodge 555-7
Buxted Park 601
The Court House (Martock)
482
Green Lane Farm 564
Hamsterley Hall 170
Hatfield Priory 1867
Highcliffe Castle 158-9
Horham Hall Georgian
room 189
House of Gray 767
Hurst House Painted room
190, 191
Jersey restrictions 845
Old Palace, Bromley-by-
Bow rooms 614, 853
Penhow Castle 813
see also exported rooms
Salvin, Anthony
Brancepeth Castle 167
Mears Ashby Hall 373
Peckforton Castle 17, 78
Thoresby Hall 401 -2
Sambrook, Pamela 646
Sampford Peverell: Ayshford
Court 113
Sandbach: Brereton Hall 67-9
Sandby, Thomas 26
Sandelson, Robert 349
Sanderson, John
Copped Hall 180-1
Kirtlington Park 416
Sandford, Grace 96
Sandford, Henry 706
Sandford, John 443
Sandford, Sir Richard 96
Sandringham House 430
Sandwich:
Pellicane House 278
The Salutation 280-1
Sandy: The Hasells 20-1
Sandys, Francis
Ashman's Hall 518
Worlingham Hall 546-7
Sanford, Anthony 215
Sarah, 1st Duchess of
Marlborough 561
Sargent, Sir Malcolm 209
Sargent, Ron & Yvonne 506
Sarsden House 418
Saumarez, de *see* de Saumarez
Savage, Sir John 67-8
SAVE campaigns &
publications 8, 14
6 Palace Street 799-800
Apethorpe Hall 355
Ashman's Hall 518
Auchinleck 737
Balcombe Place 596
Barlaston Hall 45, 499-501,
510
Belsay Hall 383
Billingsgate Fish Market 382
Brockhurst Hall 70
Brough Hall 685-6
Calke Abbey 106-7
Clegg Hall 296
Compton Verney 621
Crawford Manor 297
Danson House 45
Ecton Hall 363-4
Edwinsford 801
Grange Park 234-5, 383
Grovelands 717
Harleyford Manor 44

Hellaby Hall 694
Lawton Hall 77
Ledstone Hall 698
Mavisbank House 776
Maynards 276, 277
Mentmore Towers 48-50
Monkton House 612
Revesby Abbey 325-6
Sinai Park 514
Stayley Hall 8, 300
Stocken Hall 8, 313-14
Swinfen Hall 8, 515
Tabley Hall 81
Thorpe Salvin Hall 706
Toddington Manor 218
Troy House 821
Tyntesfield 490
Woolton Hall 302
Yeaton Pevery 452-3
Save Jersey's Heritage 842
Savoy Hotel, London 601
Savoy Theatre 601
Sawston: Sawston Hall 56
Sawston Hall 56
Sayer, C.E. 445
Sayer, Edward 445
Schellinks, Willem 268
Schimmelman, Count 427
Schomberg Scott, Walter 734
school use *see* educational use
Schroder family 583
Schueller, Arnold 554
Schultz, Robert Weir 753
Scott, Sir Claude 283
Scott, David 93
Scott, Sir Francis 507
Scott, Sir George Gilbert 78,
246, 507, 568
Scott, John 507
Scott, Sir John Murray 210
Scott, Joseph 507
Scott, Mrs Michael 659
Scott, Sir Samuel (6th
Baronet) 286
Scott, Sandy & Linda 215, 217
Scott, Sir Walter 746, 759, 792
Scott, Walter Montagu 210
Scott, Walter Schomberg 734
Scottish baronial *see* baronial
& Scottish baronial
Scottish Historic Buildings
Trust 737
Scout Association, Bispham
Hall 295
Scout Hall 704
sculpture
Aynho casts collection 16,
356
Barlaston Hall portrait
heads 501
Barrow Court garden 457
Bergonzoli's *The Love of
Angels* 24
Canova's *The Three Graces*
126
Chantrey's Sparrow family
monument 547
Delvaux's *The Sacrifice of
Diana* 187
Dowdeswell Coourt casts
collection 16, 206, 208,
356
Edwinsford lead statues 801
Monti's *Naked Beauty* 190,
191
Rysbrack's bust of John
Strahan 464
Torrigiani's portrait busts
187
Wentworth Woodhouse
709, 710
Winston Churchill statue
191
Wynyard Park Sculpture
Gallery 175-6
see also art collections
sea lions, Stanford Hall 16, 400
Seafield, Earls of
1st Earl 750
7th Earl 750
13th Earl 749
Seafield House 846-7
Seaham: Seaham Hall 173
Seaham Hall 173
Seaham Harbour 175
Searle, Catherine 155
Seaton Delaval Hall 404
secret room, Wolverton Hall
674, 675
Selwood, Abbot John 406

semi-fortified manor houses
127
seminaries *see* convents,
seminaries & religious
retreats
Semple, George
Headfort House 830
Newbridge 839
Serlio, Sebastiano 69, 816
Seton, Alexander Seton, 1st
Earl of Dunfermline 764
Seton House 782-3
settees *see* sofas & settees
72 Brook Street *see* Holland
House
78 Derngate 374-5
Sewell, General Horace 633
Seymour, Edward Seymour,
1st Duke of Somerset
(Protector Somerset) 188
Seynthill, Peter 115
Sezincote 733
Shackleton, Ernest 758
Shadrach room, Stockton 659
Shaftesbury, Abbess of 156
Shaftesbury, Earls of
1st, 3rd, 4th, 5th & 7th Earls
163-4
6th Earl 641
Shamley Green: Green Lane
Farm 564
Sharpham House 6, 144-5
Shaw, George Bernard 375
Shaw, John 508
Shaw, Richard Norman *see*
Norman Shaw, Richard
Shaw, Tina 17, 803
Shaw House 41
Shawford Park 4-5, 240-3
Sheafe family 289
Sheafe, Edmond 289
Sheafe, Harmon 289
Shelborne, Lord 197
Shelburne, Earls of 197
shell grottos, galleries &
houses
Blackland Park 636
Cockle Tower at Larch Hill
833
Goldney House 463
The Menagerie 371
Shell Gallery, A La Ronde 112
Shell House at Carton 823
Wimborne Houses 164
Shell House at Carton 823
Shelton, Sir John 338
Shelton, Theophilus 707
Shepherd, Edward 721 -2
Sheppey, Isle of: Shurland Hall
15, 282
Shere: Fulvens House 11, 562
Sherfield, Baron (Sir Roger
Makins) 224-5
Sherfield Lodge 224
Sherman, John & Margaret 134
Sherman, William 134
Shields, John Gillies 306, 308
Shiercliff, Edward 464
Shillinglee Park 15, 616
shingles, cedar 557, 558
Shinwell, Manny (Emanuel)
708
Shipley, Conrad Mordaunt
246, 247
Shipman, Kenneth 601
ships
Livadia (steam yacht) 744
prize captures 144, 484, 587
*Queen Elizabeth & Queen
Mary* 807
shipyards, Sir William
Beardmore's 758
Shirburn Castle 419-20
Shireoaks 399
Shirley, Thomas 430
shoes in roof beams, Great
Treverren 87
shooting box, Poston House
254-5
shoots & sporting estates
Bank Hall 294
Blanerne House 742
Fasque Castle 757
Floors Castle 759
Gribloch 93
Gyrn Castle 806, 807
Netley Hall 442
Nutley Manor 238
Pitmain Lodge 780

Traigh House 788
see also hunting lodges
Shopley Hall 342
Shovelstrode Manor 130
Shrewsbury, Earls of 511, 516
7th Earl 403
12th Earl & 1st Duke 415
16th Earl 307
Shrewsbury, Elizabeth,
Countess of Shrewsbury
(Bess of Hardwick) 399
Shrewsbury:
Cound Hall 437
Netley Hall 442
Yeaton Pevery 452-3
Shrewsbury Abbey 441
Shropshire Homes 447
Shrubland Park 13, 535-7
Shugborough Estate169 371
Shurland Hall 15, 282
Shurley family 607, 608
Shurley, Edward 607
Shurley, John* 607
shutters
Bishop's House (Bristol) 464
Brockhall Manor 358
Caythorpe Hall 316
Cedar Cottage 557
Coton Hall 436
Gwerclas Hall 803, 804
Harleyford Manor 44
Hilton Park 831
Mackerye End 261
Maxstoke Castle 628
Middleton Park 417
Peckforton Castle 78
The Soke 245
Staunton Harold Hall 313
Tysoe Manor 633
Vellore House 794
Westgate House 540
Wolverton Hall 675
Wothorpe Grandstand 66
Siberichts, Jan 268
Sickert, Walter 810
Sidcup: Frognal House 272
Sidley family 348
sieges
Crom Castle 825
Shirburn Castle 420
Siege of Vellore 792
Sillars family 282
Silver Staircase, Manderston
House 775
Simpson, James 767
Simpson & Brown's 737
Sinai Park 514
Sinclair, Fiona 762
single pile houses
Braybrooke House 638
Fife House 599
Great Treverren 86-7
Little Hautbois 545
Mackerye End 260-1
The Manor House
(Ogbourne St George)
647-50
Nethercote House 531 -2
The Old Rectory (Yardley
Hastings) 380-1
Sir John Burnet Tait Powell
694
Sir John Soane's museum 375,
725
Sir Richard Sutton Settled
Estates 29
Sironi, Giuseppe 598
6 Palace Street 799-800
Skeffington Smyth, Violet 659
Sker House 818
Skibo Castle 764
Skipton: Kildwick Hall 695-7
Slanning, John 137
slate
Collyweston stone slates 310
Cotswold stone slates 409
Delabole 88, 94
graded roof slates 46, 47,
142, 361, 372
Horsham 591
Westmoreland 46, 47
slighted castles 96, 706
Slingsby Castle 505
Slydell, Nigel 460, 461
Small, John 791
Smedley family 767
Smirke, Sir Robert
Erskine House 755
Hayton Hall 99, 100
Kinfauns Castle 767

Luton Hoo 24
Oulton Hall 702
Smirke, Sydney
  Hayton Hall 99, 100
  Lambton Castle 172
Smith, Charles Samuel 630
Smith, Douglas 718
Smith, Sir Edward 188
Smith, Francis (Smith of
  Warwick) 11, 365, 434, 493,
  510, 515
  The Almshouses (Preston-
    on-the-Weald Moors)
    446-7
  Brogyntyn 432-3
  Chicheley 43
  Compton Verney 621 -2
  Heythrop Park 415
  Patshull Hall 512
  Stoneleigh Abbey 630-1
  Thame Park 51
  Wrottesley Hall 517
Smith, George 814
Smith, Hatchard 611
Smith, James 778
Smith, John (architect) 773
Smith, Sir John (Landmark
  Trust) 500-1, 704
Smith, Sir Thomas (Hill Hall)
  188
Smith, Thomas (Milford
  House) 576
Smith, W.H. 34
Smith, William
  Edgcote House stables 365
  Kirtlington Park 416
Smith-Barry family 828
Smither, Mr 736
Smithers, Sir Peter 230, 231
smoke hoods, Yew Tree House
  548, 549
Smyth family 454
Smythson, John 399
  Caverswall Castle 504, 505
  Clifton Hall great chamber
    395
Smythson, Peter 470
Smythson, Robert 395, 505,
  706
  Manor Lodge (Worksop)
    403
  Shireoaks 399
Snook, Violet 155
Snow, C.P. 532
Snowdenham Hall 15, 590
Snowdon, 1st Earl of (Lord
  Snowdon/Antony
  Armstrong-Jones) 711
soakaway, Blackland Park 636
Soane, Sir John
  Albury Park 550
  associations with &
    comparisons to 16, 435,
    536, 777
  Aynho 356
  Colombeire House 815
  Pell Well Hall 805
  Piercefield 813-15
  Port Eliot 90
  Sir John Soane's museum
    375, 725
  Tyringham Hall 53-4, 604
  Worlingham Hall plans 546
Society for the Protection of
  Ancient Buildings 93, 128,
  520, 548, 659
SOE use *see* Special
  Operations Executive use
sofas & settees
  Dali (Mae West lips) 612-13
  Mackintosh 374
The Soke 244-5
Soke of Peterborough 63, 244
Somers Clarke, George 425,
  426
Somersby Hall 322
Somerset, 1st Duke of
  (Protector Somerset) 188
Somerset House 35
sonnets, introduction to
  England 524
Sortwell, Peter 194
Sotheby, Colonel & Mrs 364
Sousa, Jacques de 448
South Audley Street houses,
  Shepherd's 722
South Sea Bubble 37, 561, 692,
  731
South Wraxhall Manor 488-9
Southampton, 1st Earl of 114

Southgate: Grovelands 717
Southgate Grove *see*
  Grovelands
Southwell, Edward 209
Southwood, Thomas 480
Sparke, John 527
Sparrow, John 422
Sparrow, Mary 547
Sparrow, Robert 546, 547
Spean Bridge: Achnacarry 734
Special Operations Executive
  use:
  Anderson Manor 148
  Arisaig House 736
  Belhaven Hill House 741
  Bride Hall 258
  Lupton House 136
  Middleton Park resident 417
  Traigh House 788
  The Vineyards 248
  Wraxhall House 165
Speed Art Museum 117
Speen: Benham Park 29
Speke Hall 442
Spelman family 349
Spence, Sir Basil 9, 215, 769,
  770
Spence, James 407
Spence, Robert 407
Spencer, 2nd Earl 561
Spencer, Raine, Countess
  Spencer 364
Spenser, Edmund 838
Spilsby: Harrington Hall
  320-2
Spitalfields Trust 446
  Alt-y-Bela 15, 282, 796
  Shurland Hall 15, 282
sporting estates *see* hunting
  lodges; shoots & sporting
  estates
Springfield, Dusty 194
squarsons
  Annesley, Rev Francis 366
  Ashfordby-Trenchard, Rev
    John 657
  Bacon, Rev John 535
  Yarker, Luke* 699
'Squire of England' (George
  Osbaldestone) 690
stables
  Ashman's Hall 518
  Bettisfield Park 797
  Bradgate Stables 303
  Brogyntyn 433
  Callaly Castle 386
  Chawton House 228
  Compton Verney 621
  Craigengillan 748
  Crowcombe Court 469
  Danson House 271
  Dodington Park 205
  Dunham Lodge 332
  Edgcote House 365
  Elsing Hall 335
  Eydon Hall 368
  Gibside 168, 169
  Green Lane Farm 564
  Gunton Hall 339, 342
  Home House 725
  Keith Hall 773
  The Manor House
    (Buckland) 33
  Newport House 253
  North Luffenham Hall 310
  Redlynch House 487
  Rowden Manor origins 656
  Shrubland Park 537
  Staunton Harold Hall 312-13
  Stockton 658-9
  Stoneleigh Abbey 630, 631
  Styche Hall 451
  Thorpe Tilney Hall 327
  Weacombe 497
  Youlston Park 147
Stackhouse family 92
Stackhouse, Emily 92
Stafford family 628, 632
Stafford, Humphrey Stafford,
  1st Duke of Buckingham 628
stained, coloured & engraved
  glass
  Buckland church 33
  Churche's Mansion 72
  Dixton Manor 203
  Hengrave Hall 527
  Highcliffe Castle 159
  Hilton Park 831
  Larch Hill follies 833
  Netley Hall 442

Seaham Hall 173
Snowdenham Hall 590
Stocketts Manor 593
Tong Hall 707
Weacombe 497
Womersley Hall 712
Woodside House 498
Wyfold Court 426
Yaldham Manor 291
Yew Tree House 549
staircase styles, descriptions
  13 -14
  cantilevered 14, 324, 379
  double staircase 365
  Elizabethan 14
  imperial 205, 430, 509
  sword steps 319
  turnpike stairs 740
Staley Hall *see* Stayley Hall
Stamford, 7th Earl of (George
  Harry Grey) 303
Stamford: Wothorpe
  Grandstand 66
Stamp, Gavin 613
Stancomb, Michael 456
Standlynch House *see*
  Trafalgar House
Stanford, Adam 219
Stanford Hall 16, 400
Stanford-upon-Soare,
  Stanford Hall 16, 400
Stanhope, James Banks 325,
  326
Stanhope, Philip 103
Stanhope, Philip Dormer 103
Stanhope, Richard 326
Stansted Mountfitchet Castle
  194
Stanton House 657
state bed, Calke Abbey 107
statues *see* art collections;
  sculpture
Staunton Harold Hall 13, 311 -
  13
Stayley Hall 8, 11, 300
Stayleybridge: Stayley Hall 8,
  11, 300
Stead, Jason 296
Steel, Thomas 616
Steephill 848-50
Stephanie, Crown Princess of
  Austria 847
Stevens, Jocelyn 105, 155, 188,
  442, 444, 618
Stevens, Laura 813
Stevenson, Archie 776
Stewart, Charles Edward
  (Bonnie Prince Charlie)
  699, 726, 734, 746
Stewart, Charles William
  Stewart, 3rd Marquess of
  Londonderry 175, 176
Stibbington Hall 57-9
Sticky Wicket gardens 475
Stiffkey Old Hall 336
Stinchcombe: Piers Court 213
Stinsford House 162
Stirling: Gribloch 9, 769-70
Stobo Castle 784
'stockbroker Tudor' 12, 232
Stockdale family 373
Stockdale, Freddie
  Eastwood Farm 606
  Pavilion Opera 327
Stocken Hall 8, 313 -14
Stocketts Manor 591 -3
Stockton 658-9
Stockton-on-Tees: Wynyard
  Park 175-6
Stoke Bruerne: Stoke Park 377,
  487
Stoke-on-Trent: Caverswall
  Castle 12, 504-6
Stoke Park 377, 487
Stokes, Leonard 88
Stokesay: Stokesay Court 449-
  50
Stokesay Court 449-50
stone balls on gate piers,
  meaning 310, 603
stoneblocking, Sturford Mead
  661
Stoneleigh Abbey 510, 630-1
Storey's Way (No 48) 60
Storrington: St Joseph's Abbey
  15, 617
Stoughton family 212
Stourhead 634, 751
Stourport: Astley Pool House
  667

Stourton, 19th Baron (Lord
  Stourton) 678
Stourton Castle 428
Stout's Hill 220
Stow-on-the-Wold, Nether
  Swell Manor 210-11
Stowe Landscape Gardens 662
Strachey, Sir Henry 474
Strachey, Julia 582
Strafford, 1st Earl of (Sir
  Thomas Wentworth) 698,
  831
Strahan, John 463, 464, 495
Strang, James 792
Stratfield Saye House 160, 175
Stratford Hall, Virginia, USA
  435
Stratton Hall 383
Strawberry Hill Gothick
  Ashton Court dining room
    454
  Astley Pool House 667
  Beenham Hatch 28
  Catchfrench Manor 85
  Chicksands Priory 18-19
  Ecton Hall 363-4
  Formby Hall 298
  The Grange
    (Broadhembury) 118
  Great Barr Hall 507
  The Great House
    (Brockamin) 668
  The Manor House
    (Buckland) 32-3
  The Menagerie pavilion 371
  Sturford Mead library 661
  see also Regency/18th
    century Gothic
Streatlam Castle 380
Street, Arthur 569
Street, G.E.
  Gwrych Castle staircase 804
  Holmdale 568-9
Street, Maraquita 568
Stretton: Stocken Hall 8, 313 -
  14
Strode, William 481
Strong, Sir Roy 7, 219
strong room, Wolverton Hall
  674, 675
Stuart, James 665
Stubbs, George 709
stucco decoration *see*
  plasterwork & stucco
  decoration
Studley Royal 692
Sturdy, William 615
Sturford Mead 2-3, 660-1
Sturgis, Julian 565, 567
Styche Hall 451
subsidence
  Barlaston Hall 499-500
  Brodsworth Hall 684
  Lambton Castle 172
  Mackerye End 260
  Mavisbank House 776
  Old Manor House
    (Benenden) 267
  Shawford Park 242
  Thoresby Hall 691
Sudbury town hall 540
Sudeley, Barons
  1st Baron (Charles
    Hanbury-Tracy) 218
  4th Baron 218
  7th Baron 219
Sudeley Castle 202
Sudell, Henry 301
Sue Ryder Homes, Staunton
  Harold Hall 311 -13
Sueur, Frances Le 850
Suffield, 1st & 3rd Barons 342
Suffolk, Dukes & Earls of (1st
  creation)
  Edmund de la Pole, 6th Earl
    & 3rd Duke 543
  John de la Pole, 5th Earl &
    2nd Duke 543
  Sir Michael de la Pole, 1st
    Earl 542-3
  Michael de la Pole, 2nd Earl
    543
  William de la Pole, 4th Earl
    & 1st Duke 543
Suffolk, Dukes of (2nd
  creation), 1st Duke (Charles
  Brandon) 544
Suffolk, Margaret, Countess of
  Suffolk 45
Sullivan, Sir Arthur 567

Sultan of Brunei 730
Sultan of Mysore (Hyder Ali)
  792
Summerson, Sir John 521
Sumner, Richard 587
Sunday Telegraph
  Sker House purchaser 818
  Wimborne House article
    163
The Sunday Times, Grange
  Park 234
sundials
  Barrow Court 457
  Bunny Hall 393
  Callaly Castle 385
  Cooke's House 603
  Great Treverren 86
  Harrington Hall 321
  Hedenham Hall 344
  Lanhill House 641
  Rashleigh Barton 142
  Tong Hall 707
Sundridge Park 283 -6, 775
Surman, Robert 731
Surrealism, Monkton House
  612-13
Surrey, Earl of (Henry
  Howard) 524
Surtees, Anthony 170
Surtees, Bessie 170
Surtees, R.S. 170
Sutcliffe, John 335
Sutherland, Robert 441
Sutro, Alfred 593
Sutro, Edward 593
Sutton Courtenay: Manor
  House 421 -2
Sutton, Peter 139
Sutton, Thomas 500
Sutton Place 338
swagger baroque
  Bramcote Hall 618
  Hinwick House 22-3
  Holliday Hall 273-4
  The Ivy 639
  Ven House 492-4
Swan, Abraham 365
Swan, Rachel & Chris 174
Swannell, Major D.W.A. 381
Swanton Farmhouse *see*
  Holliday Hall
Swift, Jonathan 839
Swinburne, R.H. 170
Swinfen Hall 8, 515
Swinsty Hall 705
Swiss Cottages
  Biddulph Grange 502
  Brogyntyn 433
  Endsleigh 123
  Shrubland Park 535, 537
sword steps 319
Swynfen, Samuel 515
Syles, Henry 707
Syndale Court 700
Syon Park 38, 529, 530
Sysonby, Dowager Lady 486

T

T-plan, St Ouen's Manor 843
Tabley, 1st Baron de (Sir John
  Fleming Leicester) 80
Tabley Hall 80-1
Talman, William 287
Tamar View (Horn of Plenty)
  129
Tanfield, Sir Lawrence 410
Tanner, John 540-1
taps, Brereton Hall 69
Tarbat, Viscount &
  Viscountess (George &
  Anne) 747
Tarporley: Peckforton Castle
  17, 78-9
Tatlin, Vladimir 545
Tavaglione, Nick 805
Tavistock: Endsleigh 123-6
Taylor family 705
Taylor (Taylour) family 830
Taylor, Caspar 654
Taylor, Clive 318, 319
Taylor, Guy 320
Taylor, John 268
Taylor, Sir John 640
Taylor, Michael Angelo 698
Taylor, Mollie 498
Taylor, Sir Robert
  Asgill House 511, 551
  associations with 283, 698
  Barlaston Hall 499-501
  Chute Lodge 640

Culham Court 9, 35
Danson House 6, 45, 270-1, 640
Godfrey family memorial 191
Grafton Street houses 640
Harleyford Manor 6, 35, 44-5
Heveningham Hall 529
Sharpham House 6, 144-5
Taylor, William 471-2
Taylour family 830
Taymouth Castle 784
Teagle, Jan 817
teashop, 6 Palace Street 799-800
Teddington Hall 623
Teign, River 130, 131, 132
television & film use
4 The Crescent (Wisbech) 61
Chillingham Castle 387
Little Bardfield Hall 195
Luton Hoo 24
Manderston House 775
Melton Constable Hall 331, 346
Morley Old Hall 348
Thame Park 17, 51
Tempest, Sir George 707
Tempest, John* 176
Temple, Shirley 370
temples *see* follies, obelisks & temples
Templeton's Carpet Factory 743
Tempsford Aerodrome 20
Tennyson, Alfred, Lord Tennyson 12, 322
Tenterden: Maynards 17, 276-7
terracotta ornament, Great Snoring Manor 338
Terry, Christopher 101
Terry, Quinlan 424
Eydon Hall stables 368
Fawley House 411-13
Regent's Park Villas 730
Tetbury: Upton House 220-1
Tettenhall: Wrottesley Hall 517
Thackeray, William Makepeace 597, 733
Thakeham: Little Thakeham 610-11
Thame: Thame Park 17, 51-2
Thame Park 17, 51-2
thatched roofs
Petit Hibeaux 845
Yew Tree House 548-9
Thaxted:
Horham Hall 189-90
Little Bardfield Hall 194-5
The Abbey (Charlton Adam) 467-8
The Almshouses (Preston-on-the-Weald Moors) 446-7
The Broad House 329
The Casino at Marino 835
The Circus, Bath (No 8) 460-1, 634
The Court House (Martock) 481-2
The Crescent, Buxton 104-5
The Crescent, Wisbech (No, 4) 61-2
The Grange (Alresford) *see* Grange Park
The Grange (Broadhembury) 117-18
The Grange (Ramsgate) 279
The Great House (Brockamin) 668
The Grove 840-1
The Hasells 20-1
The Hill 720
The Ivy 639
The Man Who Never Was 647, 650
The Manor House (Buckland) 32-3
The Manor House (Great Snoring) 338
The Manor House (Lindfield) 14
The Manor House (Milton Lilbourne) 644
The Manor House (Ogbourne St George) 647-50
The Menagerie 370-1
The Old Manor Hall (Walton-on-Thames) 7

The Old Rectory (Yardley Hastings) 1, 380-1
The Pineapple, Dunmore 754
The Reader's House 438-9
The Salutation 280-1
The Soke 244-5
The Vineyards 248
The Vyne 526
theatres & cinemas
Charleston Manor 603
Cheddington Court 151
Culham Court 34
Grange Park 235
Nutley Manor 239
Savoy Theatre 601
Stanford Hall 16, 400
Tusmore House 424
Wilsley 289
theft, from Crowcombe Court 469
Thelusson, Charles Sabine 683
Thelusson, Isaac 683
Thelusson, Peter 683
Theobalds 153
Theresa, Lady Londonderry (6th Marchioness) 176
Thirlestane Castle 785-6, 789
Thockmorton family 32
Thomas, James 641
Thomas, Francis Inigo 457
Thomas, Huw 799, 800
Thompson, James 641
Thompson, William 690
Thoresby Hall 218, 401-2
Thornbury Castle 633
Thorndon Hall 13, 196
Thorne, Howard 447
Thornhill, Clara 376
Thornhill, Sir James
Bower House 179
Gosfield Hall 185
Thornton family 357
Thornton Seward: Fort Horne 691
Thornycroft, Sir John 733
Thorold, Sir Guy 59
Thorpe, John 362
Thorpe Hall (Norwich) 350-1
Thorpe Hall (Peterborough) 163
Thorpe Salvin Hall 706
Thorpe Tilney: Thorpe Tilney Hall 327
Thorpe Tilney Hall 327
Thorvaldsen, Bertel 193
'three acres & a cow' 78
The Three Graces (statue) 126
Thresher, Elizabeth 639
Thurburn, Major A.H. 361
Thurely, Simon 355
Thurfleda 259
Thursby, Mrs 437
Thurston End Hall 538-9
Thwaites family 301
Thynne family 440-1
Sir Henry Frederick Thynne 440
Thomas Thynne, 1 st Viscount Weymouth 440
see also Bath, Marquesses of
Tilden, Philip 161, 180-2
tiles
50 Oxford Gardens 728, 729
Barkisland Hall bathroom 681
Blencowe Hall 98
Bowden 30
Brantwoode 744
Brodsworth Hall 684
Caverswall Castle 506
cedar shingles 557, 558
Flichity House 758
The Grange (Ramsgate) 279
Holly Mount 46, 47
Kentish tile-hanging 267, 276
Larch Hill follies 833
Monkton House 612
Old Manor House (Benenden) 267
Orchards 542
Park Close laundry 585
Port Eliot 90
Vellore House laundry 794
Tillard, Andrew & Sarah-Jane 608, 609
Tillotson, John & Elizabeth 731
timber-framed houses
Cheshire 11, 71-2, 75-6

close studding 289, 292, 538
Huf Haus 573-5
Shropshire 11, 438-44, 452-3
Suffolk 10, 531-4, 538-9
Wealden houses 10, 264-7, 292-3
see also relevant periods (eg medieval origins)
Timbercombe (White Gables) 55
The Times
Bassett House advertisement 459
Bettisfield Park article 797
Binney, Marcus, as Architecture Correspondent 8-9, 14
Brereton Hall advertisements 67
Brough Hall article 685
Calke Abbey correspondence 106-7
Coombe Abbey article 623
Duddingston House article 751
Edgcote House article 365
Hellaby Hall article 694
Hylands House article 193
Little Bardfield Hall article 194
Melville Castle article 777
Milford House article 576
Newhailes article 779
Pitchford Hall article 442
Stinsford House article 162
Vale Royal Abbey article 81
Yaldham Manor advertisement 291
Timsbury: Parish's House 484-6
Tinkler family 561
Tipping, Avray 9, 437, 492
Tisbury: Wardour Castle 666
Titmarsh, Jean 61
Toddington Manor 17, 218-19, 814
Tollemache, Elizabeth 519
Tollemache, John* (of Bentley Hall) 519
Tollemache, John (Lord Tollemache, of Peckforton Castle) 78, 79
Tollemache, Lyonell* 519
Tollemache, Maria (later Marchioness of Ailesbury) 663
Tolly, Prince Michael Barclay de 787
tombstones *see* monuments & tombstones
Tong Hall 707
topiary
48 Storey's Way 60
Anderson Manor 148
Bowling Green 149
Cooke's House 603, 604, 605
Cote House 409, 410
The Grove 840
Isfield Place 609
Levens Hall 672
Mackerye End 261
North Luffenham Hall 309, 310
Owlpen 212
Park Close 583
Rous Lench Court 672, 673
Rushton 376
Shawford Park 242-3
South Wraxall Manor 489
Ven House 493, 494
Wilsley 289
Wingfield College 545
Yaldham Manor 291
Topp, Edward 658
Topp, John* 658, 659
Topp, Mary 659
Tor Worley 846
Torrigiani, Pietro 187
Torrington, Lord 21
Tottenham Park 662-4
tower houses
Ballencrieff Castle 739-40
Bodysgallen 798
Keith Hall 772-3
Miller's Tower 762-3
staircase styles 13-14
Towie Barclay 787
towers
Alt-y-Bela 796
Bank Hall 294

Beaurepaire 225, 226
Bettisfield Park 797
Bodysgallen 798
Boringdon 114
Bradgate Stables 303
Bunny Hall 392
Castle Bromwich Hall 619
Castle of Park 745, 746
Caverswall Castle 504, 506
Cote House 409
Coton Hall 435
Crom Castle 825
Croome Court 670
Cullen House 749, 750
Dromore Castle 826
Flichity House 758
Flintham 397
Fyvie Castle 764, 765
Gillingham Hall 336, 337
Grace Dieu Manor 307
Great Ponton church 318
Gunton Tower 343
Gwrych Castle 804, 805
Gyrn Castle 806
Holmdale 568
Horsley Towers 572
House of Gray 766
Lanhill House 641
Lismore Castle 833, 834
Maxstoke Castle 627, 628, 629
Mears Ashby Hall 373
Mentmore Towers 48, 49
Nether Swell Manor 211
Park Close 583, 585
Penhow Castle 812
Plas Teg 816
Rousdon House 143
Rowton Castle 448
Ruperra Castle 817
St Ouen's Manor 843, 844
Seton House 782
Shirburn Castle 419, 420
Shrubland Park 535, 537
Shurland Hall 282
Taymouth Castle 784
Thirlestane Castle 785
Thorpe Salvin Hall 706
Twyford Moors House 246
Tyninghame House 790
Vellore House 792
Walworth Castle 519
Wedderburn Castle 795
White Gables 55
Woodcroft Castle 63
Wyfold Court 425, 427
see also pele towers; tower houses; turrets
Towie Barclay 787
Townesend, William 404, 405
Trafalgar, Earl Nelson of 664
Trafalgar, Battle of 831
Trafalgar House 664-5
Trafford family 329
Traigh House 788
Tranter, Nigel 739
Travellers' Club 536
Trawsgoed 819
Treasure Houses of Britain exhibition 370
Treasurer's House (Martock) 481
Treasures of Ludlow 255
Trebizond, Archbishop of 851
Tree, Michael 730, 805, 820
treehouse, Pitchford Hall 443, 444
tree-ring dating, Yaldham Manor 290
Tregonwell, John 148
Tregony: Trewarthenick 94
Trehane, David 92
Trehane, Jeremy 92
Trehane 91-3
Tresanton (hotel) 126
Tresham family 376
Trevor family 820
Trevor, Sir John 816
Trevor Hall 805, 820
Trevor Roper, Patrick 816
Trewarthenick 94
Triggs, H. Inigo 232
Trinity: Trehane Manor 851-3
Trinity Manor 851-3
Tripe & Wakeham 664
triple hung sashes 459
Trippe, Simon 231
Tritton, Sir Geoffrey 657
Trollope, Anthony 838

Trollope, Robert 385
Troy House 821
Trubshaw, Charles 511
Trubshaw, Thomas 508
Truro: Trehane 91-3
trust properties
1 Royal Crescent (Bath) 486
6 Palace Street 799-800
78 Derngate 375
Allerton Park 15, 678-9
Alt-y-Bela 15, 282, 796
Asgill House 15, 511, 551, 730
Belford 382
Chawton House 228-9
Clegg Hall 268, 296
Copped Hall 180-1
Croome Court 671
Doddington Hall 73-4
Goddards 563
Gwrych Castle 804-5
Hackfall 692-3
Halswell follies & temples 471
Howick Hall gardens 391
Mavisbank House 776
Melville Castle 777
Miller's Tower 762
Mount Congreve 836-7
Mount Stuart 753
Poltimore 140
Sharpham House 144-5
Shurland Hall 15, 282
Tabley Hall 81
Thirlestane Castle 785-6, 789
Wardour Castle chapel 666
Wentworth Woodhouse park & follies 710
see also Landmark Trust; National Trust; National Trust for Scotland
Tudor *see* Elizabethan & Tudor; stockbroker Tudor
Tudor Gothic
Albury Park 550
Donington Hall 306
Dunmore Park 754
Eggesford House 121-2
Grace Dieu Manor 307
Hayton Hall 99-100
Horsley Towers 572
Park Close 583, 585
Toddington Manor 17, 218-19
see also Gothic Revival
Tudor-Craig, Pamela 682
Tudor Perkins, Margaret 111-12
Tuersley, Nigel 666
Tufnell, Samuel 701
tunnels
Encombe 157
The Manor House (Ogbourne St George) 650
Wolverton Hall 674
Turbeville family 818
Turnbull & Scott 26
Turner family 87
Turner, J.M.W. 129, 205, 692
Turnour, Edward* 616
turnpike stairs 740
turrets
Brereton Hall 67-8
candle-snuffer 790, 791
Cranborne Manor 152
Crom Castle 825
Croome Court 670
Cullen House 749, 750
Dixton Manor 203
Donington Hall 306
Fasque Castle 756
Flichity House 758
Floors Castle 759, 760, 761
Fyvie Castle 764, 765
Grace Dieu Manor 307
Great Snoring Manor 338
Hengrave Hall 527
Horsley Towers 572
Lismore Castle 833, 834
The Manor House (Buckland) 33
Melville Castle 777
Ramsay Garden 781
Seton House 782
Thirlestane Castle 785
Tyninghame House 790, 791
Vellore House 793
Walmoor House 83
Wedderburn Castle 795
Wotton House 594
Turriff:

Fyvie Castle 50, 764-5
Towie Barclay 787
Tuscan Villa, Regent's Park 730
Tusmore House 423-4
Twyford Moors: Twyford Moors House 246-7
Twyford Moors House 246-7
Tyninghame House 15, 32, 735, 789-91
Tynte, Sir Halswell 472
Tyntesfield 246, 490-2
Tyrella House 832
Tyringham Hall 13, 16, 53-4, 404
Tysoe Manor 632-3
Tyssen family 349
Tyttenhanger House 260

U
U-plan, Redlynch House 487
Uckfield: Isfield Place 607-9
Umfreyville, Samuel Charles & Emma 275
Underley Hall 294
Underwood, Thomas 582
universities
Bath 209
Bristol 463, 464
Cambridge University & colleges 22, 39, 101, 158, 354, 481, 648, 754
Essex 192
Manchester 81
Nottingham Trent 393
Oxford University & colleges 153, 218, 223, 354, 404, 424, 457, 658
Ramsay Garden 781
Sheffield 709
Youghal 838
Unsworth, Gerald 232
Unsworth, William Frederick 232
Uppark 654
Upper Tysoe: Tysoe Manor 632-3
Upton House 220-1
Urquhart family 792

V
V&A see Victoria & Albert Museum
Vaizey, Lord 107
Vale Royal Abbey 81-2
Valentine's 731
Van Der Ryan, Sim 552
van Moppes brothers 674
Vanbrugh, Sir John
associations with & comparisons to 156, 161, 237, 322, 404, 415, 561, 621, 723
Governor's House, Berwick-upon-Tweed (attributed) 390
King's Weston 17, 209
Vandeput, Sir John 664
Vane-Tempest, Lady Frances (Frances, Lady Londonderry) 173, 175, 176
Vane-Tempest, Sir Henry 176
Vanneck, Andrew 529
Vanneck, Gerard 529
Vaughan family (Bodysgallen) 798
Vaughan family (Trawsgoed) 819
Vaughan, Sir John 819
Vellore, Siege of 792
Vellore House 792-4
Ven House 12, 404, 492-4
Venetian windows, description 263, 458, 803
verandas
78 Derngate 375
Bassett House 459
Endsleigh 124, 126
Hapsford House 473
Traigh House 788
Verdun, Roesia de 307
Vere, Robert de Vere, Duke of Ireland 627
Vereker, Standish Robert Vereker, 7th Viscount Gort 170
Verey, David 199
Verey, Rosemary 199, 475
Vernon, George 76
Vernon, Muriel 76
Vernon, Ralph (or Richard) 76

Vernon, Admiral Richard 76
Vernon, Tony & Jane 76
Vernons of Sudbury 76
Vertue, George 621
Verulam, Dione 261
Vesci, Lady de 213
Vestey, Mr & Mrs William 161
Veysey, William 259
Victoria, Queen 248, 275, 426, 430, 631, 733, 746, 771, 777, 822
Victoria & Albert Museum 178, 187, 374, 452
Destruction of the Country House exhibition 7-8, 112, 272, 502, 776
The Garden exhibition 160, 502
rooms from Old Palace, Bromley-by-Bow 614, 853
Victoria County Histories 429
Victorian
50 Oxford Gardens 728-9
Abbey Houses (Bury St Edmunds) 520
Allerton Park 15, 678-9
Balcombe Place 596-7
Blackland Park 635-6
Cheddington Court 150
Finedon Hall 368-9
Flintham 11, 397-8
Foxholm 15
Heath House 12, 14, 508-9
Hilton Park 831
Horham Hall 189-90
Horn of Plenty 129
Lambton Castle 172
Mears Ashby Hall 373
Mentmore Towers 48-50
Netley Hall 442
Orchardleigh 483-4
Peckforton Castle 17, 78-9
Poulton House 654
Rous Lench Court 672-3
Rousdon House 143
Stokesay Court 449-50
Thoresby Hall 218, 401-2
Trawsgoed 819
Tyntesfield 246, 490-2
Walmoor House 83
Wyfold Court 15, 188, 275, 425-7
see also Arts & Crafts; Gothic Revival; Jacobethan
Victorian Society 66, 279, 425
Villa Lante 487
Villa Savoie 570
villa styles
astylar 551, 640
James Lewis' comments 366-7
Palladian 220
Picturesque 458
Villiers, Barbara Villiers, Duchess of Cleveland 378, 732
Villiers, George Villiers, 1st Duke of Buckingham 354
Vince, Stephen 330
The Vineyards 248
Vipan, John Alexander Maylin 59
Vipan, John Maylin 59
Vitruvius Britannicus
Colen Campbell 377, 552
New Vitruvius Britannicus (Richardson) 73
Vivian, George 459
Vogue article, Isfield Place 608
von Ihne, Ernst Eberhard 53
Vowchurch: Poston House 254-5
Vowles, Brian 431
Voysey, Charles
associations with & comparisons to 30, 57, 577, 578, 583, 743
Greyfriars 565-7
Holly Mount 46-7
Vulliamy, Lewis
Norton Place porch 324
Seaham 173
The Vyne 226

W
Waddington, Mary Ann 691
Wade, Michael 665
Wakefield, Sir Humphrey 387
Wakefield, Norris 612, 613
Wakefield Lodge 14, 378-80

Wakehurst Place 615
Wakeman, Sir Offley 452
Waldershare 287
Wales, Princes & Princesses of see by name (eg Charles) or by name as king (eg Edward VII) or queen (eg Caroline)
Walker-Munro, Thomas I.M. 409
wall-building dispute, Bettisfield Park 797
wall paintings see murals & wall paintings
Wallace, Sir Richard & Lady 210
Wallace Collection 210
Wallington, John 213
Wallington: Shirburn Castle 419-20
Wallington Hall 352-3
wallpaper
Allerton Park 678
Brodsworth Hall 684
Carton House 822
'En Avant' paper (Pugin) 279
The Grange (Ramsgate) 279
Halswell 472
lyncrusta 65
Monkton House 612
Pugin papers 279, 679
Youlston Park 147
Wallroth, Commander 248
Walmoor House 83
Walpole, Horace 19, 33, 298, 371, 380, 443, 507, 552, 692, 726, 732
see also Strawberry Hill Gothick
Walpole, Sir Robert 187, 732
Walpole, Thomas 732
Walpole House 732-3
Walsingham, Sir Francis 432
Walton, Todd (Walton, Oriel Farnell) 480
Walworth Castle 174
Wanborough: Greyfriars 565-7
Wantage: Kingston Lisle 37-8
Ward-Thomas, Michael 190
Wardour Castle 424, 666
Ware, Isaac 19
Ware, Peter 501
Warhol, Andy 219
Warminster: Sturford Mead 2-3, 660-1
Warnes, Rev. Edward 345
Warningleigh 615
Warren, Essie 128
Warwick, Dione 194
Washington, George 236, 543
water gardens
Shireoaks 399
South Wraxhall Manor 489
Studley Royal 692
Sturford Mead 2-3, 660
water supply
Brereton Hall 69
Cable House, Leighton estate 69
Eydon Hall 368
Waterford, 1st Marquess of 839
Waterhouse, Alfred 246
Heythrop Park 415
Waterhouse, Edwin 569
Waterworth, Thomas 104
Watkins-Wynn, Sir William 432
Watson, Joseph Watson, 1st Baron Manton of Compton Verney 621
Watson, Robert 832-3
Watt, James 253, 507
Watt, James Watt Gibbs 253
wattle & daub, Yew Tree House 548-9
Watts, Colonel Humphrey 76
Waugh, Auberon 213
Waugh, Evelyn 146, 213, 660
Wayne, John & Jennifer 174
Weacombe 495-7
Wealden houses 264-7, 292-3
Weaver, Giles & Roz 768
Weaver, Colonel John 768
Weaver, Lawrence 747
Webb, Sir Aston 177-8, 585
Holmdale west wing 569
North Breache Manor 579-81
Yeaton Pevery 452-3

Webb, Henry Barlow 569
Webb, John 430
Webb, Maurice 177-8
Webb, Philip 569
Arisaig House 736
Webbe, Alexander 562
Webster, George 294
Wedderburn Castle 795
Wedgwood, Josiah 507
Wedgwood company 499
Weeks family 466
Weeks, Stephen 813
Weighton, Bob 499
Weiland, Tim & Caroline 504
Weir Schultz, Robert 753
Wellesley, Arthur Wellesley, 1st Duke of Wellington 175, 813
Wellesley, Gerald Wellesley, 7th Duke of Wellington 486
Wellington, Dukes of
1st Duke (Arthur Wellesley) 175, 813
7th Duke (Gerald Wellesley) 486
Wells, H.T. 568
wells, Poulton House 654
Wenceslas, King of Bohemia 542
Wenham family 51, 52
Wentworth, Sir John 184
Wentworth, Sir Thomas Wentworth, 1st Earl of Strafford 698, 831
Wentworth: Wentworth Woodhouse 8, 708-10
Wentworth Woodhouse 8, 708-10
Werner, Harold & Anastasia 24, 25
Werner, Sir Julius 24
Werner art collection 24, 25
West, Danny 474-5
West, Mae 612
West, Robert 839
West, Steven 17, 803
West, William 33
West Burton: Cooke's House 603-5
West Dean: Monkton House 612-13
West End: Brook Place 11, 553-4
West Kington: Latimer Manor 642-3
West Quantoxhead: Weacombe 495-7
West Riding gable windows 703, 705
Westgate House 540-1
Westminster, Dukes of
1st Duke 83
6th Duke 72
Westminster, Palace of see Houses of Parliament
Westminster Abbey 157, 187, 476, 527, 568
Westminster Bridge 380
Westminster Cathedral 590
Westmorland, Earls of
1st Earl (Francis Fane) 354
7th Earl (John Fane) 354
Weston, John 289
Weston: Weston Hall 516
Weston Hall 516
Westonbirt Arboretum 391
Westwood, Robert 197
Westwood, William 197
Wetherell, Peter 721
Weybridge: Huf Haus 573-5
Weymouth, Viscounts
1st Viscount (Thomas Thynne) 440
see also Bath, Marquesses of
Whalley family 550
W.H.Colt (builders) 558
Wheathampstead: Mackerye End 260-1
Wheeler, Sir Mortimer 520
Whichcotes family 327
whispering doors & chambers 482, 659, 673
Whistler, James McNeill 810
Whistler, Rex 328, 371, 660
Whitaker, John 26
White, Mervyn 55
White, Thomas 738
White, William 332, 336
White Gables 55
Whitelaw, William 313
Whitfield, Sir William 423-4

Whitingham, Selby 80
Whitmore, Thomas 428
Whitmore, Sir William 428
Whitworth, Captain C. 701
Whitworth, Caroline 683, 684
Whyte, Chek
Bunny Hall 16, 393
Clifton Hall 16, 395
Colwick Hall 16, 396
Stanford Hall 16, 400
Widcombe Manor 480
Widerberg, Nicolaus 173
Wield, Adrian & Benedicta 632, 633
Wigham-Richardson, Caroline & Jennifer 265
Wigham-Richardson, Sir George 265, 266
Wightwick, George 136
Wilberforce, Bishop Samuel 517
Wilkie, David 765
Wilkins, William
Donington Hall 306
Dunmore Park 754
National Gallery 306, 754
Wilks, Mick 674
Willement, Thomas 138
William & Mary
fireplace positioning 245
Gosfield Hall 184-5
The Old Rectory (Yardley Hastings) 380-1
Saddlewood Manor 14, 215-17
William I, King (William the Conqueror) 61, 153, 426, 560, 632
William II, King (William Rufus) 153
William III, King (William & Mary) 9, 185, 215, 304
William IV, King 52, 698
William IV, Prince of Orange 107
William of Wykeham 224
William, Richard 839
William Paca House 390
Williams family (baronets) 801
Williams, Captain & Mrs Basil 539
Williams, Sir James Hamlyn 801
Williams, John 91-2
Williams, Pamela 684
Williams, Sir Rice 801
Williams, Stanton 622
Williams, Tony 482
Williams-Drummond, Sir James Hamlyn 801
Williams-Ellis, Sir Clough 7, 810
Williamson, Lady Eve 681
Willoughby de Broke, 12th & 19th Barons 621
Wills Tower 464
Wilmot, John Wilmot, 2nd Earl of Rochester 404-5
Wilsley 288-9
Wilslow House 288
Wilson, Harold 36, 680-1, 830
Wilson, James 459
Wilson, Michael
mill conversion 680
St Joseph's Abbey 15, 617
Snowdenham Hall 15, 590
Wilton House 154
Wimborne House 163-4
Wimborne St Giles:
Wimborne House 163-4
Winchcombe:
Dixton Manor 202-3
Toddington Manor 17, 218-19, 814
Winchester:
Colebrook House 230-1
Shawford Park 4-5, 240-3
The Soke 244-5
Winchester Cathedral 230, 244
Winchester College 224, 230, 236
Winchfield: Bramshill 227
wind vanes
Lanhill House 641
Ridgemead 589
Winde, Captain William 363
Castle Bromwich Hall 619-20
Coombe Abbey 623
Windlesham: Ascot Place 13, 26

window styles, descriptions 13
aedicule windows 220
astragals 13
bull's eye windows (oeil-de-boeuf) 46, 220
casements 363, 600, 645
Diocletian windows 66, 327, 332, 689
flush-set sash windows 13, 637
Gibbs windows 446, 495
inglenook window 581
Ipswich windows 422
Jebb jib door 255, 511
Jersey painting traditions 845
leads shapes 357
oriel windows 223
Scottish sash windows 763, 793
sliding sash windows 13, 321, 698
triple hung sashes 459
Venetian windows 263, 458, 803
West Riding gable 703, 705
wrap-around windows 498, 559
Windsor, Duke of (formerly Edward VIII) 176, 510
Windsor Castle 123, 252, 459, 651
Wingfield, Sir John 542, 543
Wingfield:
  Wingfield Castle 542-3
  Wingfield College 543-5
Wingfield Castle 542-3
Wingfield College 543-5
Wingfield-Digby, Mrs Margery 636
Winifred, Countess of Dundonald (wife of 12th Earl) 804
Winslow Hall 10, 14
Winter Queen (Elizabeth of Bohemia) 421
Winterton, 1st & 6th Earls of 616
Wisbech: 4 The Crescent 61-2
Wisbech Castle 61
Wise, Henry 43
Wiseman, John 539
Wiser, Helen & Victor 515

Witney, John & Sue 569
'Wizard of Durham' (Thomas Wright) 370-1, 636
Woburn Abbey 123, 126
Wodehouse, Francis 328
Wodehouse, P.G. 428
Woking: Lucas Almshouses 39-40
Wollaton Hall 49, 764
Wolsey, Cardinal Thomas 259, 568
Wolverton Hall 365, 674-5
Wolvesey Palace 231
Women's Land Army 597
Womersley: Womersley Hall 711
Womersley Hall 711
Wood family 705
Wood, Anthony 65
Wood, Sir John 528
Wood, John (Wood the Elder)
  8 The Circus 460, 634
  Belcombe Court 634
Wood, John (Wood the Younger) 32, 104
  8 The Circus 460-1
Wood, Sir Mark 814
Wood, Robert 665
Wood House 181
Woodbridge: Earl Soham Lodge 524-6
Woodcroft family 63
Woodcroft Castle 63-5
wooden houses
  Cedar Cottage 557-9
  see also timber-framed houses
Woodfold Park 17, 301
Woodford: Hurst House 190-1
Woodland Trust 692
Woods, James 308
Woods, Richard 186
Woodside House 17, 498
Woodward, Christopher 459
Woodward, Shaun 418
woodwork treatment 678
Woodyer, Henry
Twyford Moors House 246-7
Tyntesfield 246
Woolstaplers Hall 222-3

Woolston, Sir Guy 354
Woolton Hall 302
Worcester, 5th Earl of 255
Worcester, Bishops of 197
Worcester, Marquess of 821
Worcester: 10 College Yard 676-7
Worcester Cathedral 676
Worksop:
  Manor Lodge 403
  Shireoaks 399
  Thorpe Salvin Hall 706
Worksop Manor 403
Worlingham Hall 518, 546-7
Worrall family 464
Worrall, Samuel 464
Worsley, Giles 377
Worth Abbey 615
Wothorpe Grandstand 66
Wothorpe Lodge 403
Wotton House 594-5
Wragg, J.D. 103
Wraxall, 2nd Baron (George Gibbs/Lord Wraxall) 490
Wraxall, Sir Nathaniel 552
Wraxall: Tyntesfield 490-2
Wraxall House 165
Wren, Sir Christopher 43, 236, 304, 411, 471, 577, 723
  Winslow Hall 10, 14
'wrestling baronet' (Sir Thomas Parkyns/1st Baron Rancliffe) 103, 392-3
Wright, Benjamin 631
Wright, Bridget* 59
Wright, Frank Lloyd 408
Wright, John 186, 187
Wright, Thomas ('Wizard of Durham')
  Blackland Park shell house (attributed) 636
  The Menagerie 370-1
Wright, William 59
Wriothesley, Thomas Wriothesley, 1st Earl of Southampton 114
Wrotham: Yaldham Manor 290-1
Wrotham Park 19
Wrottesley, General George 517

Wrottesley, Sir John (1st Baron Wrottesley) 517
Wrottesley, John (2nd Baron Wrottesley) 517
Wrottesley, Sir Walter 517
Wrottesley Hall 517
Wroxham: The Broad House 329
W.S. Atkins 569
Wyatt, Benjamin (1709-1772) 515
Wyatt, Benjamin Dean (1775-1852) 175
Wyatt, George 448
Wyatt, James 73, 515, 735
  Bretby Hall 103
  Chicksands Priory 19
  Copped Hall 180
  Dodington Park 74, 204-6
  Gunton Hall 342
  Heveningham Hall 529-30
Wyatt, Jeffery 103
Wyatt, Lewis 197
Wyatt, Philip 175
Wyatt, Samuel 515
  Doddington Hall 73-4
  Sundridge Park 283, 286
Wyatt, Thomas Henry 483
Wyatville, Sir Jeffry 158, 459, 630
  Endsleigh 123-6
  Philipps House 651-2
  Stockton staircase 658
Wyfold Court 15, 188, 275, 425-7
Wykeham, William of 224
Wykeham-Musgrave, W.A. 52
Wyndham family 651-2
Wyndham, George 651-2
Wyndham, William & Laetitia 651, 652
Wynn family 798
Wynn, Hugh & Margaret 798
Wynn, Robert & Katherine 798
Wynnstay Hall 432
Wynyard Park 175-6
Wythes, Ernest 180-1
Wythes, George 180
Wyvill family 688, 689
Wyvill, Charles 689
Wyvill, Sir Marmaduke* 688

Y
Y-plan
  Gribloch 769
  White Gables 75
Yaldham Manor 290-1
Yarde-Buller, Sir John 136
Yardhurst 292-3
Yardley Hastings: The Old Rectory 1, 380-1
Yarker, Alice & John 699
Yarker, Luke* 699
Yates family 32
Yatton Keynell: Lanhill House 641
Yeates, Alfred 138
Yeatman-Biggs, Major 659
Yeaton Pevery 452-3
Yeovil: Brympton d'Evercy 465-6
Yerbury, Francis 634
Yew Tree House 548-9
Ymddiriedolaeth Treftadaeth Caernarfon 799
York, Duke & Duchess of see Elizabeth the Queen Mother; George VI
Youghal: Myrtle Grove 838
Youlston Park 146-7
Young, Arthur 324, 692
Young, Robert & Sophia 193
Youssoupoff, Count I. 851
Yoxford: Cockfield Hall 521-3
YWCA hostel, Philipps House 652

Z
Z-plan
  Castle of Park 745-6
  Keith Hall 772
Zimmerman, Helena 773
Zouche, 11th Baron (Edward la Zouche) 227

AUTHOR'S ACKNOWLEDGMENTS

My first thanks are to colleagues at *The Times*, to Anne Ashworth, Editor of *Bricks & Mortar* and before her, Anne Spackman, for giving me the opportunity week by week to seek out beautiful and fascinating houses – and to other colleagues, notably Andrew Riley, Judith Heywood and John Blandy, who have edited my articles, to Jenny Hodges and Margaret Clark who have coordinated photography, and before them to Bridget Callaghan and Jane Owen. Thanks also to Ian Brunskill of the *Times Register*.

At SAVE Britain's Heritage I owe a debt to Adam Wilkinson and David Plaisant and, before them, successive SAVE secretaries beginning with Sarah Seymour, followed by Matthew Saunders, Sophie Andreae, Ken Powell, Marianne Watson-Smyth, Emma Phillips and Richard Pollard; to Save assistants including Katherine Griffiths, Sara Alleyn, Emma Milne, Anthony Peers, Deborah Churchill and Ela Palmer. Special thanks to Margaret Richardson, Oliver Leigh-Wood, Colin Amery

Among owners and restorers of houses I have had help from Kit and Sally Martin, James and Carol Hall, Maldwin and Gilly Drummond, Diane and John Nutting, Jennifer Freeman, Francis Fulford, Warin Kelly, Sir Toby Clark, Sir Humphrey Wakefield, Binny and Stuart Mathews, Olga Polizzi, Anton Bilton, James Perkins Christopher Buxton, Edward Howell, Christopher Terry, Richard Broyd, Mark Ellington and Mark Gibson.

John Harris has been a mentor from the very beginning, Sir Howard Colvin helped with many of my initial researches – Alastair Laing, Simon Jervis, the late Clive Wainwright, the late Gervase Jackson-Stops, the late Giles Worsley, John Hardy, Mark Girouard, Lucinda Lambton, John Martin Robinson, the late Walter Ison, Richard Haslam, Anthony Emery, Tim Mowl, Tim Knox, Peter de Figueiredo, Richard Garnier, Alec Cobbe, Alan Powers, Charles Brooking, Edward Bulmer, Douglas Blain and Christopher Gibbs have all given generously of their time and knowledge. My special thanks are due to Sir Roy Strong, who by asking me to help organise the exhibition *The Destruction of the Country House* at the V&A in 1974, fuelled the search for endangered houses in need of rescue.

In Scotland, I have drawn deeply on the knowledge of David Walker and his son, David and also of Ian Gow, Peter Burman, James Simpson and Kitty Cruft. In Wales, Tom Lloyd has been a constant source of information on the history – and plight – of fine houses as has Michael Tree. In Ireland, my abundant thanks to the Knight of Glin, Desmond Guinness, John Redmill, Alistair Rowan and Maurice Craig.

At *Country Life* over forty years, numerous colleagues have guided, helped and enthused me, beginning with the late John Cornforth and followed by Clive Aslet, Michael Hall, Jeremy Musson and Mary Miers and and the present editor Mark Hedges, as well as Caroline Heslop, Susan Moore, Deidre Chappell, Camilla Costello. To Alex Starkey, *Country Life*'s ace photographer over many years, I owe many of the very best photographs taken for my

PICTURE CREDITS

Weidenfeld & Nicolson would like to thank all those who have kindly lent us photographs for use in the book. We have made our best effort to acknowledge the correct copyright holder for all of the pictures but will, if notified, correct any errors in future editions.

Allerton Park: 678 (both), 679; Richard J. Anderson: 469; Apex News and Picture: 117, 118; Richard Bryant/Arcaid.co.uk: 374, 375; Balbirnie House: 738; Bellevue Marketing/Hand Picked Hotels: 600, 601 (both); By kind permission of Mr and Mrs Anton Bilton: 53, 54; Marcus Binney: 4-5, 13, 18, 19, 21 (both), 26, 32, 41, 42, 43, 44, 45, 52, 57, 58, 62, 64, 66, 72, 73, 74 (both), 77, 78, 79, 80, 86, 101, 103, 105, 107, 124-5, 126, 136, 139, 143 (both), 148, 155 (both), 156, 157, 158, 159, 160, 162, 168, 169, 177, 179, 180, 181 (both), 189, 192, 196, 208, 219, 227, 234, 235, 248, 251, 256, 259, 261, 272, 282, 287, 292, 294, 296, 298, 304, 305, 311, 312, 314, 325, 326, 327, 330, 334, 354, 355, 359, 360, 361, 362, 364, 368, 370, 371, 372, 376, 377, 382, 383, 385, 386, 387, 388, 390, 391, 392, 394, 395, 396, 397, 398, 399, 400, 401, 402, 406, 416, 419, 420, 425, 426, 427, 434, 437, 443, 444, 446, 447, 449, 450, 456, 458, 460, 461, 465, 466, 467, 479, 481, 487, 490, 491, 493, 494, 499, 500, 501, 502, 503, 508, 509, 511, 516, 517, 527, 528, 538, 552, 553, 560, 564, 572, 573, 574, 590, 594, 595, 596, 597, 598, 599, 612 (all), 614, 615, 616, 618, 621, 622, 624-5, 626, 630, 631 (both), 640, 657, 662, 663, 665, 666, 669, 670, 671, 672, 675, 690, 691, 696, 702, 708, 709, 710, 716, 720 (both), 730, 732, 733, 735, 736, 741, 749, 751, 752, 754, 755, 756, 762, 763 (both), 766, 767, 772, 777, 781, 782, 785, 786, 788, 789, 790, 791, 794, 796, 798, 801, 802, 803 (both), 805, 811, 814, 815, 816, 820, 826, 831, 832, 833, 834, 836, 837, 842, 845, 880, 828 (top); The Bluecoat Press: 302; Boconnoc Enterprises: 84; Boringdon Hall Hotel: 114; Edward Bulmer Ltd: 724; Carrick Howell & Lawrence Architects: 121, 122; Carter Jonas/Knight Frank: 695; Noel Channon: 90; Charles Church: 211; Chawton House: 228; /Newbury Smith Photography: 229; Clifton Castle: 687; Cluttons: 23, 264, 265 (both), 266-267, 278; Alec Cobbe: 839; Cook Arkwright: 818; Coombe Abbey Hotel: 623; Country Life Picture Library: 161, 582, 610, 611; /Clive Bournsnell: 843, 844; /J.Cockayne: 339, 340-341, 342, 343; /Mark Fiennes: 20, 848, 849 (both), 850; /J. Gibson: 38, 152, 153, 214, 215, 220, 221, 320, 321, 322, 323, 378, 379, 542, 548, 602, 658, 659, 699, 700, 701, 757, 759, 760, 761, 765, 846 (both), 847; /Simon Jauncey: 734; /A. Starkey: 37, 106, 144, 154, 384, 455, 520, 546, 547 (both), 627, 628, 629, 685, 686, 688, 689, 851, 852; DARE Restoration: 166; Jago Dean: 403; Gary Doak: 792, 793 (all); Alban Donohue: 549; Dyson Limited: 204 F. Eastwood: 606; Nils Erin: 81, 82 (both); English Heritage: 297; /Boris Baggs: 270, 271 (both); English Heritage Photographic Library: 731; /John Critchley: 683; www.elitehotels.co.uk: 24, 25(a); Eric Ellington: 787; Bryan Evans: 718, 719; Paul Finn: 707; Sam Frost: 647, 648-9, 650 (both); GA Town & Country: 745; The Georgian Group: 11; J. Mark Gibson: 748; Glin Castle: 829; Alan Goldsmith: 194; Grace Dieu School: 307; Andrew Grant: 667, 668, 676; Hamptons International: 7, 55, 565, 566, 567; F. Hauptfuhrer: 551; Headfort/Michael Bolton: 830; Heythrop Park: 415; Home House: 723, 725; The Horn of Plenty Country House and Hotel: 129; Justin Hunt: 721; The Interior Archive/Christopher Simon Sykes: 825; Inverlochy Castle: 771; The Irish Picture Library: 838; Jackson Stops & Staff: 1, 75, 109, 113, 128, 230, 231, 331, 350, 351, 381, 524, 525, 526, 562, 682; Kings Weston House: 209; Knight Frank: 2-3, 9, 16, 27, 35, 36, 46, 47, 51, 68-69, 88, 89, 98, 102, 116, 119, 120, 130, 131, 135, 141, 142, 149, 150, 151, 198, 200-201, 222, 239, 249, 253, 254, 288, 308, 328, 344, 348, 366, 367, 373, 404, 405, 418, 421, 432, 433, 488, 489, 486, 497 (both), 498, 519, 533, 534, 535, 536, 537, 580-581, 588, 589, 607, 608-609, 619, 620, 641, 645, 646, 651, 660, 661, 726, 727, 742, 840-841; Lady Williamson: 680; The Landmark Trust: 279, 563, 693; /Keith Hunter: 737; Lane Fox: 14, 31, 71; Will Layzell: 477; Leigh Court: 476, 477; Lillicrap Chilcott: 85; Llangoed Hall: 810; Miles Macinnes: 95; 96-7 Sir Nicholas Mander: 212; Manderston: 775; Kit Martin: 137; Robin Matthews: 576; James Morris: 470; Dr Timothy Mowl: 454, 457, 471, 472, 473, 483, 484, 634 (both), 817; Margot Mulcahy: 828 (bottom); The National Trust for Scotland: 778, 779; Newsteam International: 808, 809; Nock Deighton: 438, 439; NTPL: 111; /Dennis Gilbert: 570, 571; James Perkins: 356; Octagon: 713, 714; PJ Livesey: 275; Friends of Poltimore: 140; Priory Healthcare: 717; RCAHMS: 747, 784; John Redmill: 822, 823, 824, 827, 835; Edward Rokita: 110 Rowton Castle Hotel: 448; Dae Sasitorn/lastrefuge.co.uk: 172; SAVE: 29, 48, 49, 50, 70, 174, 188, 193, 280, 295, 299, 300, 301, 303, 306, 369, 389, 417, 445, 452, 453, 507, 510, 514, 515, 518, 639, 694, 698, 703, 704, 706 (both), 768, 776, 797, 799, 800, 821; Savills: 8, 10, 12, 15, 25 (b and c), 39, 40, 56, 91, 92-3, 94, 123, 127, 146-7, 175, 176, 182, 184 (both), 185, 191 (all), 207, 213, 216, 217 (both), 225, 226, 233, 240, 241 (both), 242-3, 244, 246, 247, 284-5, 286 (both), 318, 319, 329, 333, 335, 336, 337, 338, 345, 349, 352, 353, 357, 358, 408, 410, 411, 412, 413, 423, 424, 428, 429, 430, 431, 435, 436, 440, 441 (both), 451, 462, 463, 474, 475 (both), 478, 485, 486, 504, 506 (both), 512, 513, 521, 522, 529, 530, 531, 541, 544, 545 (both), 555, 556 (all), 568, 569, 577, 578 (both), 583, 584, 585, 587, 603, 604, 605, 635, 636, 642, 643, 644, 711, 712 (both), 722 (both), 728, 729 (both), 743, 753, 780, 819; /Castle Studios: 276; Carole Savin: 557, 559 Seaham Hall Hotel: 173; Sharpham Hall: 145; Adrian Sherratt: 365; Simon Gidman: 167; South West News Service: 205; Strutt & Parker: 6, 83, 269, 273, 274, 290, 291, 309, 315, 316, 317 (both), 591, 592, 593, 637, 653, 705, 774, 806; /Adrian Wield: 632, 633; N. Whalley: 550 (both) Mike Wilkinson: 769; Michael Wilson Restorations: 617; Woolley & Wallis: 655, 656;

articles; other beautiful photographs have been take for me by Jonathan Gibson, the late Mark Fiennes and Malcolm Crowthers.

At English Heritage I extend warm thanks to Lord Montagu and Jocelyn Stevens, Simon Thurley, Philip Davies, Richard Hewlings and numerous colleagues, including especially Beth McHattie, Debra Isaac and Anya Matthews in the Press Office.

At the National Trust I have had help over many years from many of those involved with the care of historic houses, notably Martin Drury and Merlin Waterson, Jonathan Marsden and Jeffrey Howarth and the current Director-General Fiona Reynolds. Valuable help has come at different times from the staff of the SPAB, the Georgian Group, Victorian Society and the Ancient Monuments Society as well as from the Landmark Trust and its director Peter Pearce. Dame Jennifer Jenkins and the late Sir John Smith were both formidable allies in the rescue of Barlaston Hall and many other battles, as was Simon Jenkins who blazed the trail with his remarkable book on houses open to the public, *England's Thousand Best Houses*.

Fascinating information on country houses used by SOE during the Second World War has come from M.R.D. Foot, Duncan Stuart and Valerie Collins. In Jersey help and encouragement has come from Tim and Mary Clode, David Roberts and Carol-Anne Mawdsley, Alastair, Anne and Will Layzell, Sue Lea, Jane Jones and Philip Hewat-Jaboor.

On my travels I have stayed with many friends, Crispin and Anita Hasler, Adrian Fort, James and Jose Brett, Michael and Lucy Archer, Will Palin, Alexander and Mary Creswell, Peter and Rosemary Andreae, Tom and Carrie Cocke, Charles and Carolyn de Salis, and Edward Rooth

This book could not have been completed without enormous and most generous help from the estate agents for many of the houses in this book: at Knight Frank, Olivia Smith, Davina Macdonald-Lockhart and Camilla Lindsay; At Savills, above all John Vaughan, but also Juliet Walker, Louis de Soissons, Nick Sweeney, Martin Lamb, Tony Morris-Eyton and Richard Gaynor; at Jackson-Stops & Staff, Tim, Mark and Quintin Jackson-Stops and Dawn Carritt; at MCPR; Rosie Gimlette, Belinda Fowler and Ilana Cargill; at Strutt & Parker, Joy Moon and before her David Taylor, who provided the first house of the week in *The Times*, and Sam Gibson; Andrew Grant; Jo Ashby and Kate Oliver at Hamptons; Lucy Gaynor at Jago Dean; Lucy Gaynor at Hamptons.

At Weidenfeld, Michael Dover invited me to write the book, giving help and encouragement beyond what any author could expect, Robin Douglas-Withers, my editor, has been unsurpassed for her patience, stamina, good nature, and exemplary organisation. Thanks also to designer Austin Taylor for his constant resourcefulness under pressure, Justin Hunt for a very lively cover and Sue Bosanko, the indexer, for her knowledgeable attention to detail and for her astute and brilliant cross-checking. Belinda Harley, my literary agent, played a crucial role in the conception of the book, while without the (much-tested) forbearance of my wife Anne and sons Francis and Christopher it could never have been completed.

Marcus Binney

First published in Great Britain in 2007
by Weidenfeld & Nicolson
10 9 8 7 6 5 4 3 2 1

Text copyright © Marcus Binney 2007
Design and layout © Weidenfeld & Nicolson 2007

A CIP catalogue record for this book is available from
the British Library.

ISBN: 978-0-297-84455-6

EDITOR: Robin Douglas-Withers
DESIGNER: Austin Taylor
JACKET DESIGN: Justin Hunt
INDEX: Susan Bosanko

Colour reproduction by DL Interactive UK
Printed and bound in Spain by Cayfosa Quebecor

Weidenfeld & Nicolson
The Orion Publishing Group Ltd
Orion House
5 Upper St Martin's Lane
London WC2H 9EA

An Hachette Livre UK Company

The Orion Publishing Group's policy is to use papers that are natural, renewable and
recyclable products and made from wood grown in sustainable forests. The logging and
manufacturing processes are expected to conform to the environmental regulations of the
country of origin.

CAPTIONS
Page 1: *The Old Rectory, Yardley
Hastings Northamptonshire, is
built of corruscatingly pretty
pale pink brick and dated 1701.*

Pages 2–3: *Sturford Mead,
Wiltshire, is a Regency gem
reflected in still waters.*

Page 4–5: *Shawford Park in
Hampshire is ravishing Charles
II house seen across a formally-
planted sunken garden.*

Above: *A detail from Stokesay
Court, Shropshire.*

**Weidenfeld & Nicolson would like to point out that the great majority of the houses in this
book are in private ownership and not open to visitors. The book is not intended to be and
should not be used in any way as a guide book to houses open to the public. Those few
houses open to visitors will have a website clearly stating opening times and entry prices.**